CHILTON BOOK COMPANY

REPAIR MANUAL

FORD MERCURY LINCOLN 1968-88

All U.S. and Canadian models of FORD Country Sedan, Country Squire, Crown Victoria, Custom, Custom 500, Galaxie 500, LTD (through 1982), Ranch Wagon, XL ● MERCURY Colony Park, Commuter, Marquis (through 1982). Gran Marquis, Monterey, Park Lane ● LINCOLN Continental (through 1981), Town car

Vice President and General Manager JOHN P. KUSHNERICK
Editor-in-Chief KERRY A. FREEMAN, S.A.E.
Managing Editor DEAN F. MORGANTINI, S.A.E.
Senior Editor RICHARD J. RIVELE, S.A.E.
Senior Editor W. CALVIN SETTLE, JR., S.A.E.

CHILTON BOOK COMPANY
Radnor, Pennsylvania
19089

CONTENTS

GENERAL INFORMATION and MAINTENANCE

1 How to use this book
2 Tools and Equipment
9 Routine Maintenance

ENGINE PERFORMANCE and TUNE-UP

69 Tune-Up Procedures
75 Tune-Up Specifications

ENGINE and ENGINE OVERHAUL

111 Engine Electrical System
129 Engine Mechanical
131 Engine Troubleshooting
140 Engine Specifications

EMISSION CONTROLS

217 Emission Controls System and Service

FUEL SYSTEM

291 Fuel System Service

CHASSIS ELECTRICAL

358 Heating and Air Conditioning
383 Accessory Service
389 Instruments and Switches
391 Lights, Fuses and Flashers
393 Trailer Wiring

DRIVE TRAIN

402 Manual Transmission
412 Clutch
416 Automatic Transmission
435 Driveline
440 Rear Axle

SUSPENSION and STEERING

447 Front Suspension
455 Rear Suspension
467 Steering

BRAKES

507 Front Drum Brakes
512 Front Disc Brakes
524 Rear Drum Brakes
541 Specifications

BODY

542 Exterior
594 Interior

MECHANIC'S DATA

618 Mechanic's Data
620 Glossary
626 Abbreviations
628 Index

**316 Chilton's Fuel Economy
and Tune-Up Tips**

**604 Chilton's Body Repair
Tips**

SAFETY NOTICE

Proper service and repair procedures are vital to the safe, reliable operation of all motor vehicles, as well as the personal safety of those performing repairs. This book outlines procedures for servicing and repairing vehicles using safe, effective methods. The procedures contain many NOTES, CAUTIONS and WARNINGS which should be followed along with standard safety procedures to eliminate the possibility of personal injury or improper service which could damage the vehicle or compromise its safety.

It is important to note that repair procedures and techniques, tools and parts for servicing motor vehicles, as well as the skill and experience of the individual performing the work vary widely. It is not possible to anticipate all of the conceivable ways or conditions under which vehicles may be serviced, or to provide cautions as to all of the possible hazards that may result. Standard and accepted safety precautions and equipment should be used during cutting, grinding, chiseling, prying, or any other process that can cause material removal or projectiles.

Some procedures require the use of tools specially designed for a specific purpose. Before substituting another tool or procedure, you must be completely satisfied that neither your personal safety, nor the performance of the vehicle will be endangered.

Although the information in this guide is based on industry sources and is as complete as possible at the time of publication, the possibility exists that the manufacturer made later changes which could not be included here. While striving for total accuracy, Chilton Book Company cannot assume responsibility for any errors, changes, or omissions that may occur in the compilation of this data.

PART NUMBERS

Part numbers listed in this reference are not recommendations by Chilton for any product by brand name. They are references that can be used with interchange manuals and aftermarket supplier catalogs to locate each brand supplier's discrete part number.

SPECIAL TOOLS

Special tools are recommended by the vehicle manufacturer to perform their specific job. Use has been kept to a minimum, but where absolutely necessary, they are referred to in the text by the part number of the tool manufacturer. These tools can be purchased, under the appropriate part number, from Owatonna Tool Company, Owatonna, MN 55060 or an equivalent tool can be purchased locally from a tool supplier or parts outlet. Before substituting any tool for the one recommended, read the SAFETY NOTICE at the top of this page.

ACKNOWLEDGMENTS

Chilton Book Company expresses its appreciation to the Ford Motor Company, Dearborn, Michigan, for their generous assistance.

Chilton's Repair Manual: Ford/Mercury/Lincoln 1968–88
ISBN 0-8019-7846-7 pbk.
Library of Congress Catalog Card No. 87-47929

General Information and Maintenance

HOW TO USE THIS BOOK

Chilton's Repair & Tune-Up Guide for the Ford, Mercury and Lincoln cars is intended to teach you about the inner workings of your car and save you money on its upkeep.

The first two chapters will be the most used, since they contain maintenance and tune-up information and procedures. Studies have shown that a properly tuned and maintained car can get at least 10% better gas mileage (which translates into lower operating costs) and periodic maintenance will catch minor problems before they turn into major repair bills. The other chapters deal with the more complex systems of your car. Operating systems from engine through brakes are covered to the extent that the average do-it-yourselfer becomes mechanically involved. This book will not explain such things as rebuilding the differential for the simple reason that the expertise required and the investment in special tools make this task impractical and uneconomical. It will give you the detailed instructions to help you change your own brake pads and shoes, tune-up the engine, replace spark plugs and filters, and do many more jobs that will save you money, give you personal satisfaction and help you avoid expensive problems.

A secondary purpose of this book is a reference guide for owners who want to understand their car and/or their mechanics better. In this case, no tools at all are required. Knowing just what a particular repair job requires in parts and labor time will allow you to evaluate whether or not you're getting a fair price quote and help decipher itemized bills from a repair shop.

Before attempting any repairs or service on your car, read through the entire procedure outlined in the appropriate chapter. This will give you the overall view of what tools and supplies will be required. There is nothing more frustrating than having to walk to the bus stop on Monday morning because you were short one gasket on Sunday afternoon. So read ahead and plan ahead. Each operation should be approached logically and all procedures thoroughly understood before attempting any work. Some special tools that may be required can often be rented from local automotive jobbers or places specializing in renting tools and equipment. Check the yellow pages of your phone book.

All chapters contain adjustments, maintenance, removal and installation procedures, and overhaul procedures. When overhaul is not considered practical, we tell you how to remove the failed part and then how to install the new or rebuilt replacement. In this way, you at least save the labor costs. Backyard overhaul of some components (such as the alternator or water pump) is just not practical, but the removal and installation procedure is often simple and well within the capabilities of the average car owner.

Two basic mechanic's rules should be mentioned here. First, whenever the LEFT side of the car or engine is referred to, it is meant to specify the DRIVER'S side of the car. Conversely, the RIGHT side of the car means the PASSENGER'S side. Second, all screws and bolts are removed by turning counterclockwise, and tightened by turning clockwise.

Safety is always the most important rule. Constantly be aware of the dangers involved in working on or around an automobile and take proper precautions to avoid the risk of personal injury or damage to the vehicle. See the section in this chapter, Servicing Your Vehicle Safely, and the SAFETY NOTICE on the acknowledgment page before attempting any service procedures and pay attention to the instructions provided. There are 3 common mistakes in mechanical work:

1. Incorrect order of assembly, disassembly or adjustment. When taking something apart or

putting it together, doing things in the wrong order usually just costs you extra time; however it CAN break something. Read the entire procedure before beginning disassembly. Do everything in the order in which the instructions say you should do it, even if you can't immediately see a reason for it. When you're taking apart something that is very intricate (for example a carburetor), you might want to draw a picture of how it looks when assembled at one point in order to make sure you get everything back in its proper position. We will supply exploded views whenever possible, but sometimes the job requires more attention to detail than an illustration provides. When making adjustments (especially tune-up adjustments), do them in order. One adjustment often affects another and you cannot expect satisfactory results unless each adjustment is made only when it cannot be changed by any other.

2. Overtorquing (or undertorquing) nuts and bolts. While it is more common for overtorquing to cause damage, undertorquing can cause a fastener to vibrate loose and cause serious damage, especially when dealing with aluminum parts. Pay attention to torque specifications and utilize a torque wrench in assembly. If a torque figure is not available remember that, if you are using the right tool to do the job, you will probably not have to strain yourself to get a fastener tight enough. The pitch of most threads is so slight that the tension you put on the wrench will be multiplied many times in actual force on what you are tightening. A good example of how critical torque is can be seen in the case of spark plug installation, especially where you are putting the plug into an aluminum cylinder head. Too little torque can fail to crush the gasket, causing leakage of combustion gases and consequent overheating of the plug and engine parts. Too much torque can damage the threads or distort the plug, which changes the spark gap at the electrode. Since more and more manufacturers are using aluminum in their engine and chassis parts to save weight, a torque wrench should be in any serious do-it-yourselfer's tool box.

There are many commercial chemical products available for ensuring that fasteners won't come loose, even if they are not torqued just right (a very common brand is Loctite®). If you're worried about getting something together tight enough to hold, but loose enough to avoid mechanical damage during assembly, one of these products might offer substantial insurance. Read the label on the package and make sure the product is compatible with the materials, fluids, etc. involved before choosing one.

3. Crossthreading. This occurs when a part such as a bolt is screwed into a nut or casting at the wrong angle and forced, causing the threads to become damaged. Crossthreading is more likely to occur if access is difficult. It helps to clean and lubricate fasteners, and to start threading with the part to be installed going straight in, using your fingers. If you encounter resistance, unscrew the part and start over again at a different angle until it can be inserted and turned several times without much effort. Keep in mind that many parts, especially spark plugs, use tapered threads so that gentle turning will automatically bring the part you're threading to the proper angle if you don't force it or resist a change in angle. Don't put a wrench on the part until it's been turned in a couple of times by hand. If you suddenly encounter resistance and the part has not seated fully, don't force it. Pull it back out and make sure it's clean and threading properly.

Always take your time and be patient; once you have some experience, working on your car will become an enjoyable hobby.

TOOLS AND EQUIPMENT

Naturally, without the proper tools and equipment it is impossible to properly service your vehicle. It would be impossible to catalog each tool that you would need to perform each or every operation in this book. It would also be unwise for the amateur to rush out and buy an expensive set of tools an the theory that he may need one or more of them at sometime.

The best approach is to proceed slowly, gathering together a good quality set of those tools that are used most frequently. Don't be misled by the low cost of bargain tools. It is far better to spend a little more for better quality. Forged wrenches, 6 or 12 point sockets and fine tooth ratchets are by far preferable to their less expensive counterparts. As any good mechanic can tell you, there are few worse experiences than trying to work on a car with bad tools. Your monetary savings will be far outweighed by frustration and mangled knuckles.

Certain tools, plus a basic ability to handle tools, are required to get started. A basic mechanics tool set, a torque wrench, and, for 1976 and later models, a Torx® bits set. Torx® bits are hexlobular drivers which fit both inside and outside on special Torx® head fasteners used in various places on some cars.

Begin accumulating those tools that are used most frequently; those associated with routine maintenance and tune-up.

In addition to the normal assortment of screwdrivers and pliers you should have the following tools for routine maintenance jobs (your

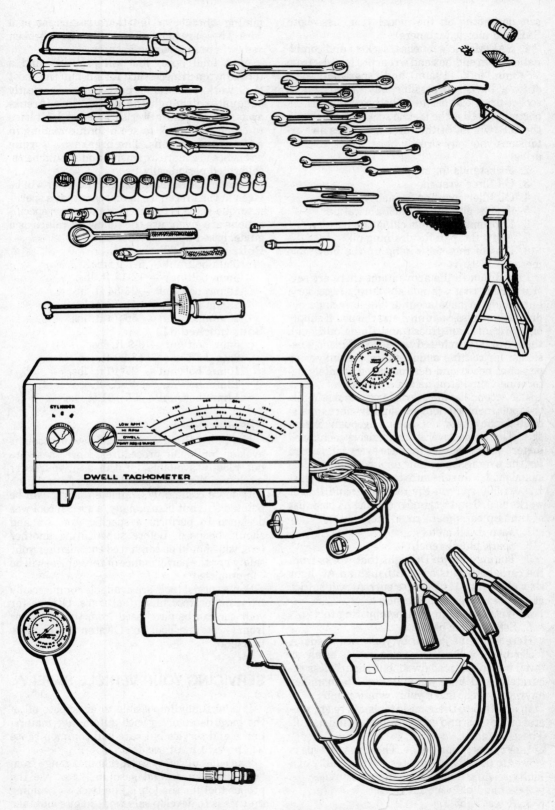

The tools and equipment shown here will handle the majority of the maintenance on a car

car, depending on the model year, uses both SAE and metric fasteners):

1. SAE/Metric wrenches, sockets and combination open end/box end wrenches in sizes from ⅛″ (3mm) to ¾″ (19mm), and a spark plug socket (¹³⁄₁₆″ or ⅝″). If possible, buy various length socket drive extensions. One break in this department is that the metric sockets available in the U.S. will all fit the ratchet handles and extensions you may already have (¼, ⅜, and ½″ drive).

2. Jackstands for support.
3. Oil filter wrench.
4. Oil filler spout or funnel.
5. Grease gun for chassis lubrication.
6. Hydrometer for checking the battery.
7. A low flat pan for draining oil.
8. Lots of rags for wiping up the inevitable mess.

In addition to the above items there are several others that are not absolutely necessary, but handy to have around. These include oil-dry, a transmission funnel and the usual supply of lubricants, antifreeze and fluids, although these can be purchased as needed. This is a basic list for routine maintenance, but only your personal needs and desires can accurately determine your list of necessary tools.

The second list of tools is for tune-ups. While the tools involved here are slightly more sophisticated, they need not be outrageously expensive. There are several inexpensive tach/dwell meters on the market that are every bit as good for the average mechanic as a $100.00 professional model. Just be sure that it goes to at least 1,200-1,500 rpm on the tach scale and that it works on 4, 6 and 8 cylinder engines. A basic list of tune-up equipment could include:

1. Tach-dwell meter
2. Spark plug wrench
3. Timing light (a DC light that works from the car's battery is best, although an AC light that plugs into 110V house current will suffice at some sacrifice in brightness)
4. Wire spark plug gauge/adjusting tools
5. Set of feeler blades.

Here again, be guided by your own needs. A feeler blade will set the point gap as easily as dwell meter will read dwell, but slightly less accurately. And since you will need a tachometer anyway ... well, make your own decision.

In addition to these basic tools, there are several other tools and gauges you may find useful. These include:

1. A compression gauge. The screw-in type is slower to use, but eliminates the possibility of a faulty reading due to escaping pressure
2. A manifold vacuum gauge
3. A test light
4. An induction meter. This is used for determining whether or not there is current in a wire. These are handy for use if a wire is broken somewhere in a wiring harness.

As a final note, you will probably find a torque wrench necessary for all but the most basic work. The beam type models are perfectly adequate, although the newer click (breakaway) type are more precise, and you don't have to crane your neck to see a torque reading in awkward situations. The breakaway torque wrenches are more expensive and should be recalibrated periodically.

Torque specification for each fastener will be given in the procedure in any case that a specific torque value is required. If no torque specifications are given, use the following values as a guide, based upon fastener size:

Bolts marked 6T
>6mm bolt/nut — 5-7 ft. lbs.
>8mm bolt/nut — 12-17 ft. lbs.
>10mm bolt/nut — 23-34 ft. lbs.
>12mm bolt/nut — 41-59 ft. lbs.
>14mm bolt/nut — 56-76 ft. lbs.

Bolts marked 8T
>6mm bolt/nut — 6-9 ft. lbs.
>8mm bolt/nut — 13-20 ft. lbs.
>10mm bolt/nut — 27-40 ft. lbs.
>12mm bolt/nut — 46-69 ft. lbs.
>14mm bolt/nut — 75-101 ft. lbs.

Special Tools

Normally, the use of special factory tools is avoided for repair procedures, since these are not readily available for the do-it-yourselfer mechanic. When it is possible to perform the job with more commonly available tools, it will be pointed out, but occasionally, a special tool was designed to perform a specific function and should be used. Before substituting another tool, you should be convinced that neither your safety nor the performance of the vehicle will be compromised.

Some special tools are available commercially from major tool manufacturers. Others for your car can be purchased from you dealer or from Owatonna Tool Co., Owatonna, Minnesota 55060.

SERVICING YOUR VEHICLE SAFELY

It is virtually impossible to anticipate all of the hazards involved with automotive maintenance and service but care and common sense will prevent most accidents.

The rules of safety for mechanics range from "don't smoke around gasoline," to "use the proper tool for the job." The trick to avoiding injuries is to develop safe work habits and take every possible precaution.

Do's

● Do keep a fire extinguisher and first aid kit within easy reach.

● Do wear safety glasses or goggles when cutting, drilling, grinding or prying. If you wear glasses for the sake of vision, then they should be made of hardened glass that can serve also as safety glasses, or wear safety goggles over your regular glasses.

● Do shield your eyes whenever you work around the battery. Batteries contain sulfuric acid. In case of contact with the eyes or skin, flush the area with water or a mixture of water and baking soda and get medical attention immediately.

● Do use safety stands for any under-car service. Jacks are for raising vehicles; safety stands are for making sure the vehicle stays raised until you want it to come down. Whenever the vehicle is raised, block the wheels remaining on the ground and set the parking brake.

● Do use adequate ventilation when working with any chemicals. Asbestos dust resulting from brake lining wear cause cancer.

● Do disconnect the negative battery cable when working on the electrical system.

● Do follow manufacturer's directions whenever working with potentially hazardous materials. Both brake fluid and antifreeze are poisonous if taken internally.

● Do properly maintain your tools. Loose hammerheads, mushroomed punches and chisels, frayed or poorly grounded electrical cords, excessively worn screwdrivers, spread wrenches (open end), cracked sockets, slipping ratchets, or faulty droplight sockets can cause accidents.

● Do use the proper size and type of tool for the job being done.

● Do when possible, pull on a wrench handle rather than push on it, and adjust you stance to prevent a fall.

● Do be sure that adjustable wrenches are tightly adjusted on the nut or bolt and pulled so that the face is on the side of the fixed jaw.

● Do select a wrench or socket that fits the nut or bolt. The wrench or socket should sit straight, not cocked.

● Do strike squarely with a hammer. avoid glancing blows.

● Do set the parking brake and block the wheels if the work requires that the engine be running.

Don't's

● Don't run an engine in a garage or anywhere else without proper ventilation—EVER! Carbon monoxide is poisonous. It is absorbed by the body 400 times faster than oxygen. It takes a long time to leave the human body and you can build up a deadly supply of it in your system by simply breathing in a little every day. You may not realize you are slowly poisoning yourself. Always use power vents, windows, fans or open the garage doors.

● Don't work around moving parts while wearing a necktie or other loose clothing. Short sleeves are much safer than long, loose sleeves. Hard-toed shoes with neoprene soles protect your toes and give a better grip on slippery surfaces. Jewelry such as watches, fancy belt buckles, beads, or body adornment of any kind is not safe while working around a car. Long hair should be hidden under a hat or cap.

● Don't use pockets for toolboxes. A fall or bump can drive a screwdriver deep into you body. Even a wiping cloth hanging from the back pocket can wrap around a spinning shaft or fan.

● Don't smoke when working around gasoline, cleaning solvent or other flammable material.

● Don't smoke when working around the battery. When the battery is being charged, it gives off explosive hydrogen gas.

● Don't use gasoline to wash your hands. There are excellent soaps available. Gasoline may contain lead, and lead can enter the body through a cut, accumulating in the body until you are very ill. Gasoline also removes all the natural oils from the skin so that bone dry hands will suck up oil and grease.

● Don't service the air conditioning system unless you are equipped with the necessary tools and training. The refrigerant, R-12, is extremely cold and when exposed to the air, will instantly freeze any surface it comes in contact with, including your eyes. Although the refrigerant is normally non-toxic, R-12 becomes a deadly poisonous gas in the presence of an open flame. One good whiff of the vapors from burning refrigerant can be fatal.

SERIAL NUMBER IDENTIFICATION

Vehicle Identification Number

1968-80

The official vehicle identification number for title and registration purposes is tamped on a metal tag, which is fastened to the top of the instrument panel. The tag is located on the driver's side, visible through the windshield. The first digit in the vehicle identification number is the model year of the car (0-1970, 4-1974, etc.). The second digit is the assembly plant code for the plant in which the vehicle was built. the

Engine Application Chart

No. of Cylinders and Cu. In. Displacement	Actual Displacement			Type	Built by	Engine Code	Years
	Cu. In.	CC	Liters				
6-240	239.7	3,929.1	3.9	OHV	Ford	V	1968–72
8-255	255.3	4,183.1	4.2	OHV	Ford	D	1981–82
8-302	301.5	4,942.2	5.0	OHV	Ford	G	1968–79
						F	1980–85
						N	1986–88
8-351W	351.9	5,765.9	5.8	OHV	Ford	H	1970–74
						G	1978–84
						H	1985–88
8-351C	351.9	5,765.9	5.8	OHV	Ford		1972–74
8-351M	351.9	5,765.9	5.8	OHV	Ford	H	1975–78
8-390	389.9	6,390.5	6.4	OHV	Ford	Y	1968–71
						X	1968 280 HP
						Z	1968 315 HP
8-400	402.1	6,589.6	6.6	OHV	Ford	Z	1971–78
8-428	426.9	6,996.8	6.9	OHV	Ford	Q	1968–70
						P	1968–70 PI
8-429	428.8	7,026.6	7.0	OHV	Ford	N	1968–73
						P	1971–72 PI
						K	1969–71 320 HP
						N	1968–71 360 HP
6-460	459.8	7,535.5	7.5	OHV	Ford	A	1972–78
						C	1972–78 PI
8-462	461.7	7,565.3	7.6	OHV	Ford	G	1968

Manual Transmission Application Chart

Transmission Types	Years	Models
Ford 3.03 3-speed	1968–71	Ford
Ford 4-speed	1968–69	Ford

Automatic Transmission Application Chart

Transmission	Years	Models
Ford C4 3-speed	1966–74	All models
	1978–80	All models
Ford C6 3-speed	1968–80	All models
Ford FMX 3-speed	1968–80	All models
Ford CW 3-speed	1974–75	Ford
Ford AOI 4-speed	1980–88	All models

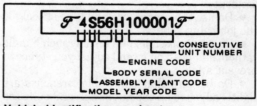

Vehicle identification number tag

third and fourth digits are the body serial code designations (2-dr sedan, 4-dr sedan). The fifth digit is the engine code which identifies the type of engine originally installed in the vehicle (see the Engine Codes chart). The last six digits are the consecutive unit numbers which start at 100,001 for the first car of a model year built at each assembly plant.

From 1981

Beginning in 1981, the serial number contains seventeen or more digits or letters. The

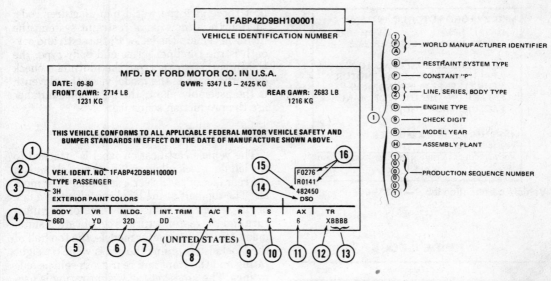

	1FABP42D9BH100001
	VEHICLE IDENTIFICATION NUMBER

- ① ⓕ Ⓐ — WORLD MANUFACTURER IDENTIFIER
- Ⓑ — RESTRAINT SYSTEM TYPE
- Ⓟ — CONSTANT "P"
- ④ ② — LINE, SERIES, BODY TYPE
- Ⓓ — ENGINE TYPE
- ⑨ — CHECK DIGIT
- Ⓑ — MODEL YEAR
- Ⓗ — ASSEMBLY PLANT
- ① ⓞ ⓞ ⓞ ⓞ ① — PRODUCTION SEQUENCE NUMBER

MFD. BY FORD MOTOR CO. IN U.S.A.

DATE: 09-80   GVWR: 5347 LB – 2425 KG
FRONT GAWR: 2714 LB   REAR GAWR: 2683 LB
           1231 KG   1216 KG

THIS VEHICLE CONFORMS TO ALL APPLICABLE FEDERAL MOTOR VEHICLE SAFETY AND
BUMPER STANDARDS IN EFFECT ON THE DATE OF MANUFACTURE SHOWN ABOVE.

VEH. IDENT. NO. 1FABP42D9BH100001
TYPE PASSENGER
3H
EXTERIOR PAINT COLORS

F0276
R0141
482450
DSO

BODY	VR	MLDG.	INT. TRIM	A/C	R	S	AX	TR
66D	YD	32D	DD	A	2	C	6	XBBBB

(UNITED STATES)

2. Vehicle type
3. Paint
4. Body type code
5. Vinyl roof
6. Body side moulding
7. Trim code—(First code letter = fabric and seat type. Second code = color)
8. Air conditioning
9. Radio

10. Sun/moon roof
11. Axle ratio
12. Transmission
13. Springs—Front l. and r., rear l. and r. (4 codes)
14. District sales office
15. PTO/SPL order number
16. Accessory reserve load

Vehicle identification—from 1981

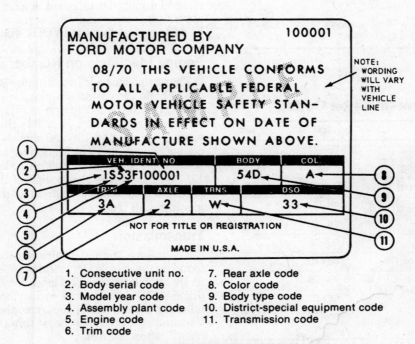

MANUFACTURED BY FORD MOTOR COMPANY   100001

08/70 THIS VEHICLE CONFORMS TO ALL APPLICABLE FEDERAL MOTOR VEHICLE SAFETY STANDARDS IN EFFECT ON DATE OF MANUFACTURE SHOWN ABOVE.

NOTE: WORDING WILL VARY WITH VEHICLE LINE

VEH. IDENT. NO.	BODY	COL.
1S53F100001	54D	A

TRIM	AXLE	TRNS	DSO
3A	2	W	33

NOT FOR TITLE OR REGISTRATION

MADE IN U.S.A.

1. Consecutive unit no.
2. Body serial code
3. Model year code
4. Assembly plant code
5. Engine code
6. Trim code
7. Rear axle code
8. Color code
9. Body type code
10. District-special equipment code
11. Transmission code

Vehicle certification label—1970–72

```
┌─────────────────────────────────────────┐
│ MFD. BY FORD MOTOR CO. IN U.S.A.         │
│   DATE:  9/73              GVWR 5892      │
│   GAWR: FRONT 2964, REAR 2928            │
│                                           │
│   THIS VEHICLE CONFORMS TO ALL           │
│   APPLICABLE FEDERAL MOTOR               │
│   VEHICLE SAFETY STANDARDS IN            │
│   EFFECT ON THE DATE OF MANU-            │
│   FACTURE SHOWN ABOVE.                    │
│                                           │
│ 4S56H100001      PASSENGER               │
│ VEH. IDENT. NO. │      TYPE              │
│ BODY │ COLOR │ TRIM │ TRANS. │ AXLE │ DSO │
│ 57F  │  1C   │  KA  │   X    │  2   │ 48  │
└─────────────────────────────────────────┘
```
Vehicle certification label—1973–80

Engine Codes

Code	Engine	Years
V	6-240	68–72
D	8-255	81–82
F	8-302	68–85
H	8-351	70–79
G	8-351	80–85
Y	8-390	68–71
X (280 hp)	8-390	68
Z (315 hp)	8-390	68
S	8-400	71–79
Q	8-428	68
P	8-428 PI	68–70
N	8-429	72–73
P	8-429 PI	71–72
K (320 hp)	8-429	69–71
N (360 hp)	8-429	68–71
P (370 hp)	8-428 PI	70
A	8-460	69–78
C	8-460 PI	72–78
G	8-462	68

Transmission Codes

Type	Year	Code
3 speed manual	68–71	1
4 speed manual	68	5
4 speed manual	69	6
C4 automatic	68–74	W
C4 automatic	78–80	W
AOD*	80–83	T
FMX automatic	68–80	X
CW automatic	74–75	Y
C6 automatic	68–80	U
C6 automatic (towing)	68–79	Z

* Automatic Overdrive

first three give the world manufacturer code; the fourth is the type of restraint system; the fifth will remain the letter **P**; the sixth and seventh is the car line, series and body type; the eighth is the engine type; the ninth is a check digit; the tenth is the model year; the eleventh is the assembly plant; the remaining number are the production sequence.

Vehicle Certification Label

The vehicle certification label is attached to the left door lock pillar on 2-door models and on the rear face of the driver's door on 4-door models. The top half of the label contains the name of the vehicle manufacturer, date of manufacture and the manufacturer's certification statement. On 1973 and later models, the top half of the label also contains the gross vehicle weight rating and the front and rear gross vehicle axle ratings. The gross vehicle weight rating is useful in determining the lead carrying capacity of your car. merely subtract the curb weight from the posted gross weight and what is left over is how much you can haul around. The bottom half of the vehicle certification label contains the vehicle identification number (as previously described), the body type code, the exterior pant color code, the interior trim color and material code, the rear axle code (see Rear Axle Codes chart), the transmission code (see Transmission Codes chart) and the district and special order codes.

The vehicle certification label is constructed of special material to guard against its alteration. If it is tampered with or removed, it will be destroyed or the word **VOID** will appear.

Engine Identifictaion Number

The engine identification number is found on the vehicle identification plate which is attached to the top left (driver's) side of the instrument panel, which is visible through the windshield. On the 1968-80 models the fifth digit of the vehicle identification number represents the engine identification code. On the 1981-88 models the eighth digit of the vehicle identification number represents the engine identification code.

Transmission

The transmission identification code can be found on the vehicle identification number, and on the vehicle certification label (located on the driver's side door) on the earlier models. The following list is a list for the transmission identification code digit location, within the vehicle identification number:

1. 1968-76: The 11th digit in the vehicle cer-

tification label will usually be the transmission code.

2. 1977-78: The 10th digit in the vehicle identification number will be the transmission code.

3. 1979: The 13th digit in the vehicle identification number will be the transmission code.

4. 1980: The 15th digit in the vehicle identification number will be the transmission code.

5. 1981-88: The 12th digit in the vehicle identification number will be the transmission code.

Drive Axle Identification

A metal tag stamped with the model designation and gear ratio is usually secured to one of the rear cover to housing bolts. The axle identification code number can also be found on the vehicle identification number or the vehicle certification label, depending on the year and model. The following list is a list for the transmission identification code digit location, within the vehicle identification number:

1. 1968-77: The 11th digit in the vehicle identification number will usually be the rear axle code. On some of the earlier models, the number may be located on the vehicle certification label.

2. 1977-78: The 11th digit in the vehicle identification number will be the rear axle code.

3. 1979: The 12th digit in the vehicle identification number will be the rear axle code.

4. 1980: The 14th digit in the vehicle identification number will be the rear axle code.

5. 1981-88: The 11th digit in the vehicle identification number will be the rear axle code.

ROUTINE MAINTENANCE

Air Filter Replacement

All engines are equipped with a dry type, replaceable air filter element. The element should be replaced the the recommended intervals shown on the Maintenance Chart in this Chapter. If your vehicle is operated under severely dusty conditions or severe operating conditions, more frequent changes are necessary. Inspect the element at least twice a year. Early spring and at the beginning of fall are good times for the inspection. Remove the element and check for holes in the filter. Check the cleaner housing for signs of dirt or dust that has leaked through the filter element. Place a light on the inside of the element and look through the filter at the light. If no glow of light can be seen through the element material, replace the fil-

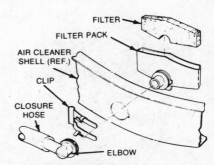

Crankcase ventilation filter

ter. If holes in the filter are apparent or signs of dirt leakage through the filter are noticed, replace the filter.

REMOVAL AND INSTALLATION

Air Cleaner Assembly

1. Disconnect all hoses, ducts and vacuum tubes from the air cleaner assembly.

2. Remove the top cover wing nut and grommet (if equipped). Remove any side bracket mount retaining bolts (if equipped). Remove the air cleaner assembly from the top of the carburetor or intake assembly.

3. Remove the cover and the element, wipe clean all inside surfaces of the air cleaner housing and cover. Check the condition of the mounting gasket (cleaner base to carburetor). Replace the mounting gasket if it is worn or broken.

4. Reposition the cleaner assembly, element and cover on the carburetor or intake assembly.

5. Reconnect all hoses, duct and vacuum hoses removed. Tighten the wing nut finger tight.

Element

The element can, in most cases, be replaced by removing the wing nut and cleaner assembly cover. If the inside of the housing is dirty, however, remove the assembly for cleaning to prevent dirt from entering the carburetor.

Crankcase Ventilation Filter

Replace or inspect cleaner mounted crankcase ventilation filter (on models equipped) at the same time the air cleaner filter element is serviced. To replace the filter, simply remove the air cleaner top cover and pull the filter from its housing. Push a new filter into the housing and install the air cleaner cover. If the filter and plastic holder need replacement, remove the clip mounting the feed tube to the air cleaner housing (hose already removed) and remove the assembly from the air cleaner. Installation is the reverse of removal.

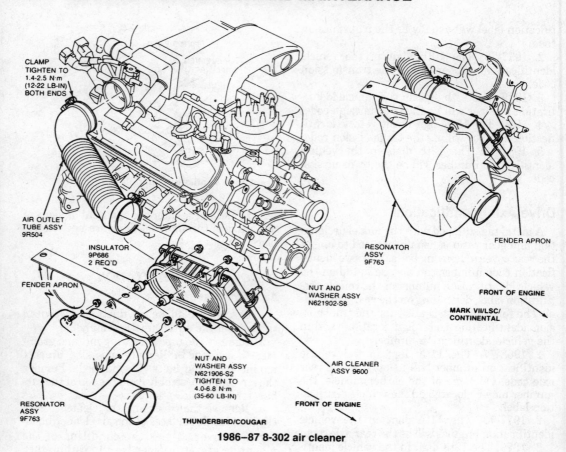

CLAMP TIGHTEN TO 1.4-2.5 N·m (12-22 LB-IN) BOTH ENDS

AIR OUTLET TUBE ASSY 9R504

INSULATOR 9P686 2 REQ'D

FENDER APRON

NUT AND WASHER ASSY N621902-S8

NUT AND WASHER ASSY N621906-S2 TIGHTEN TO 4.0-6.8 N·m (35-60 LB-IN)

AIR CLEANER ASSY 9600

RESONATOR ASSY 9F763

FRONT OF ENGINE

THUNDERBIRD/COUGAR

1986–87 8-302 air cleaner

RESONATOR ASSY 9F763

FENDER APRON

FRONT OF ENGINE

MARK VII/LSC/ CONTINENTAL

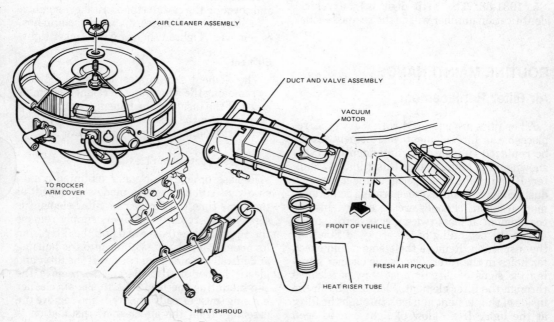

AIR CLEANER ASSEMBLY

DUCT AND VALVE ASSEMBLY

VACUUM MOTOR

TO ROCKER ARM COVER

FRONT OF VEHICLE

FRESH AIR PICKUP

HEAT RISER TUBE

HEAT SHROUD

Typical 1980–83 V8 air cleaner

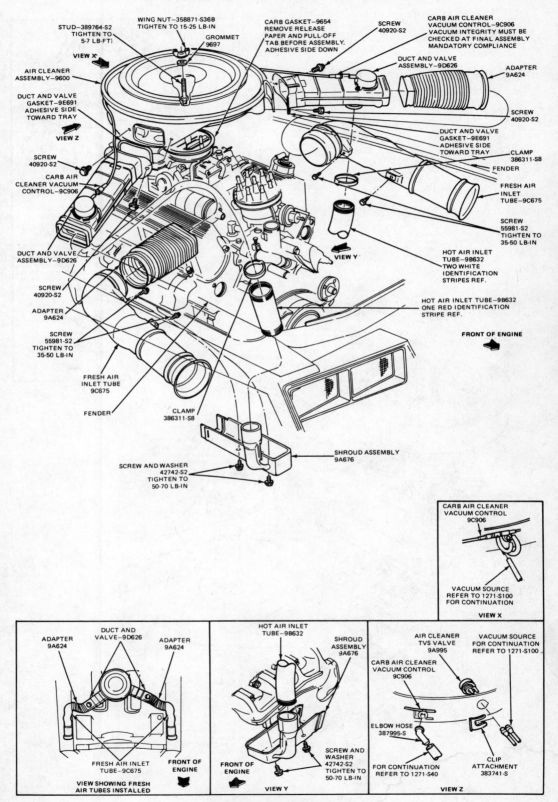

STUD—389764-S2
TIGHTEN TO
5-7 LB-FT)

VIEW X

WING NUT—358871-S36B
TIGHTEN TO 15-25 LB-IN

GROMMET
9697

CARB GASKET—9654
REMOVE RELEASE
PAPER AND PULL-OFF
TAB BEFORE ASSEMBLY.
ADHESIVE SIDE DOWN

SCREW
40920-S2

CARB AIR CLEANER
VACUUM CONTROL—9C906
VACUUM INTEGRITY MUST BE
CHECKED AT FINAL ASSEMBLY
MANDATORY COMPLIANCE

AIR CLEANER
ASSEMBLY—9600

DUCT AND VALVE
GASKET—9E691
ADHESIVE SIDE
TOWARD TRAY

VIEW Z

SCREW
40920-S2

CARB AIR
CLEANER VACUUM
CONTROL—9C906

DUCT AND VALVE
ASSEMBLY—9D626

SCREW
40920-S2

ADAPTER
9A624

SCREW
55981-S2
TIGHTEN TO
35-50 LB-IN

FRESH AIR
INLET TUBE
9C675

FENDER

CLAMP
386311-S8

SCREW AND WASHER
42742-S2
TIGHTEN TO
50-70 LB-IN

DUCT AND VALVE
ASSEMBLY—9D626

ADAPTER
9A624

SCREW
40920-S2

DUCT AND VALVE
GASKET—9E691
ADHESIVE SIDE
TOWARD TRAY

CLAMP
386311-S8

FENDER

FRESH AIR
INLET—9C675

SCREW
55981-S2
TIGHTEN TO
35-50 LB-IN

VIEW Y

HOT AIR INLET
TUBE—9B632
TWO WHITE
IDENTIFICATION
STRIPES REF.

HOT AIR INLET TUBE—9B632
ONE RED IDENTIFICATION
STRIPE REF.

FRONT OF ENGINE

SHROUD ASSEMBLY
9A676

CARB AIR CLEANER
VACUUM CONTROL
9C906

VACUUM SOURCE
REFER TO 1271-S100
FOR CONTINUATION

VIEW X

ADAPTER
9A624

DUCT AND
VALVE—9D626

ADAPTER
9A624

FRESH AIR INLET
TUBE—9C675

**FRONT OF
ENGINE**

VIEW SHOWING FRESH
AIR TUBES INSTALLED

HOT AIR INLET
TUBE—9B632

SHROUD
ASSEMBLY
9A676

**FRONT OF
ENGINE**

SCREW AND
WASHER
42742-S2
TIGHTEN TO
50-70 LB-IN

VIEW Y

AIR CLEANER
TVS VALVE
9A995

VACUUM SOURCE
FOR CONTINUATION
REFER TO 1271-S100

CARB AIR CLEANER
VACUUM CONTROL
9C906

ELBOW HOSE
387995-S

FOR CONTINUATION
REFER TO 1271-S40

CLIP
ATTACHMENT
383741-S

VIEW Z

1983–85 8-302HO air cleaner

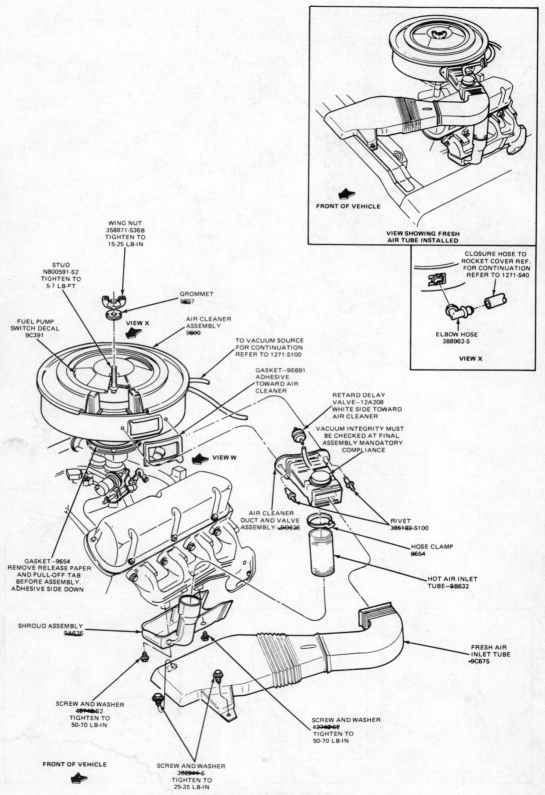

FRONT OF VEHICLE

VIEW SHOWING FRESH
AIR TUBE INSTALLED

CLOSURE HOSE TO
ROCKET COVER REF.
FOR CONTINUATION
REFER TO 1271-S40

ELBOW HOSE
388962-S

VIEW X

WING NUT
358871-S36B
TIGHTEN TO
15-25 LB-IN

STUD
N800591-S2
TIGHTEN TO
5-7 LB-FT

GROMMET
9697

VIEW X

FUEL PUMP
SWITCH DECAL
9C391

AIR CLEANER
ASSEMBLY
9600

TO VACUUM SOURCE
FOR CONTINUATION
REFER TO 1271-S100

GASKET—9E691
ADHESIVE
TOWARD AIR
CLEANER

RETARD DELAY
VALVE—12A208
WHITE SIDE TOWARD
AIR CLEANER

VACUUM INTEGRITY MUST
BE CHECKED AT FINAL
ASSEMBLY MANDATORY
COMPLIANCE

VIEW W

AIR CLEANER
DUCT AND VALVE
ASSEMBLY—9D626

RIVET
385189-S100

HOSE CLAMP
9654

GASKET—9654
REMOVE RELEASE PAPER
AND PULL-OFF TAB
BEFORE ASSEMBLY.
ADHESIVE SIDE DOWN

HOT AIR INLET
TUBE—9B632

SHROUD ASSEMBLY
9A676

FRESH AIR
INLET TUBE
—9C675

SCREW AND WASHER
42740-62
TIGHTEN TO
50-70 LB-IN

SCREW AND WASHER
42740-62
TIGHTEN TO
50-70 LB-IN

FRONT OF VEHICLE

SCREW AND WASHER
382944-S
TIGHTEN TO
25-35 LB-IN

1984—85 8-302 air cleaner

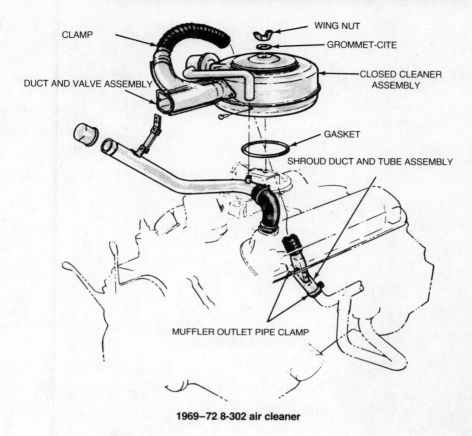

CLAMP

WING NUT

GROMMET-CITE

DUCT AND VALVE ASSEMBLY

CLOSED CLEANER
ASSEMBLY

GASKET

SHROUD DUCT AND TUBE ASSEMBLY

MUFFLER OUTLET PIPE CLAMP

1969–72 8-302 air cleaner

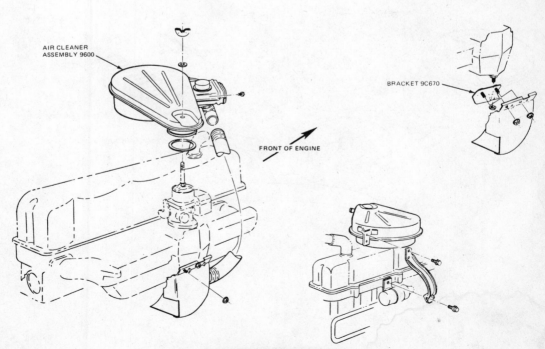

AIR CLEANER
ASSEMBLY 9600

BRACKET 9C670

FRONT OF ENGINE

1969–74 6-240, 6-300 air cleaner

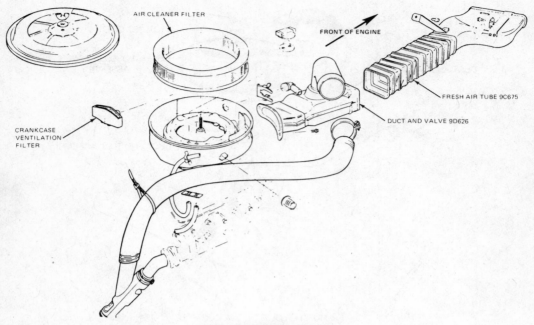

1973–74 8-302 air cleaner

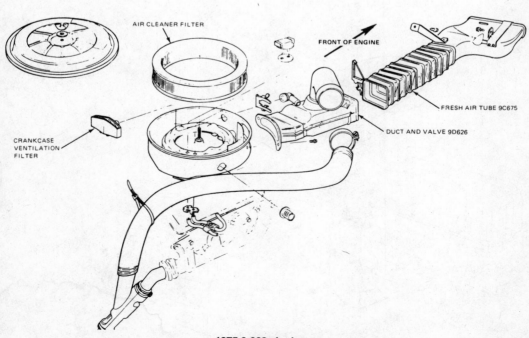

1975 8-302 air cleaner

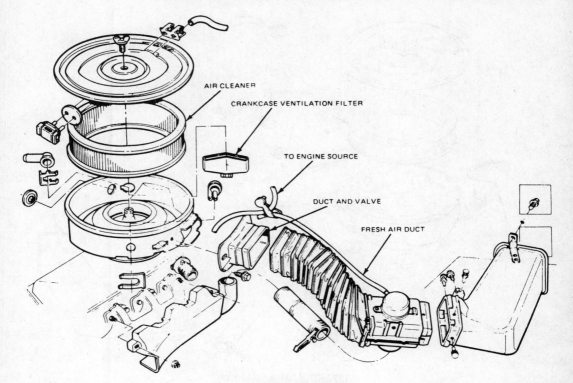

AIR CLEANER

CRANKCASE VENTILATION FILTER

TO ENGINE SOURCE

DUCT AND VALVE

FRESH AIR DUCT

1975 8-460 air cleaner

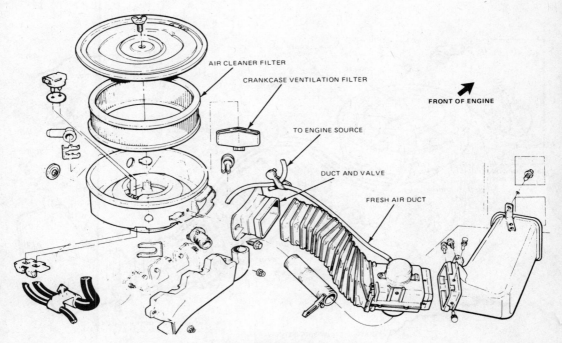

AIR CLEANER FILTER

CRANKCASE VENTILATION FILTER

FRONT OF ENGINE

TO ENGINE SOURCE

DUCT AND VALVE

FRESH AIR DUCT

1976–77 8-460 air cleaner

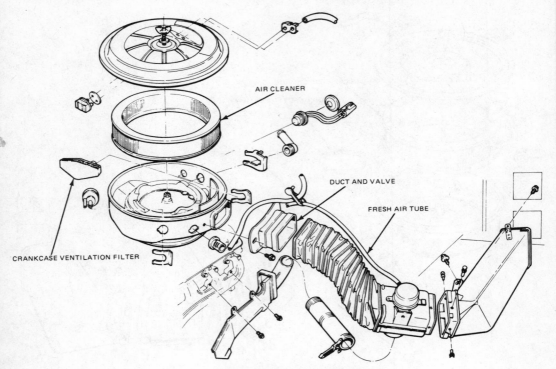

AIR CLEANER

DUCT AND VALVE

FRESH AIR TUBE

CRANKCASE VENTILATION FILTER

1975–77 8-351 air cleaner

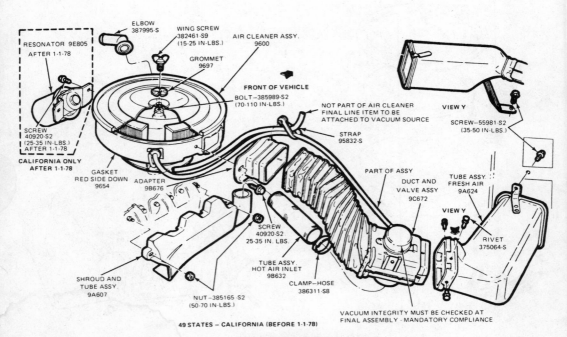

ELBOW
387995-S

WING SCREW
382461-S9
(15-25 IN·LBS.)

AIR CLEANER ASSY.
9600

RESONATOR 9E805
AFTER 1-1-78

GROMMET
9697

FRONT OF VEHICLE

BOLT–385989-S2
(70-110 IN·LBS.)

NOT PART OF AIR CLEANER
FINAL LINE ITEM TO BE
ATTACHED TO VACUUM SOURCE

VIEW Y

SCREW–55981-S2
(35-50 IN·LBS.)

SCREW
40920-S2
(25-35 IN·LBS.)
AFTER 1-1-78

STRAP
95832-S

CALIFORNIA ONLY
AFTER 1-1-78

GASKET
RED SIDE DOWN
9654

ADAPTER
9B676

PART OF ASSY.

DUCT AND
VALVE ASSY.
9C672

TUBE ASSY.
FRESH AIR
9A624

VIEW Y

RIVET
375064-S

SCREW
40920-S2
25-35 IN. LBS.

SHROUD AND
TUBE ASSY.
9A607

NUT–385165-S2
(50-70 IN·LBS.)

TUBE ASSY.
HOT AIR INLET
9B632

CLAMP–HOSE
386311-S8

VACUUM INTEGRITY MUST BE CHECKED AT
FINAL ASSEMBLY · MANDATORY COMPLIANCE

49 STATES – CALIFORNIA (BEFORE 1-1-78)

1978 8-460 air cleaner

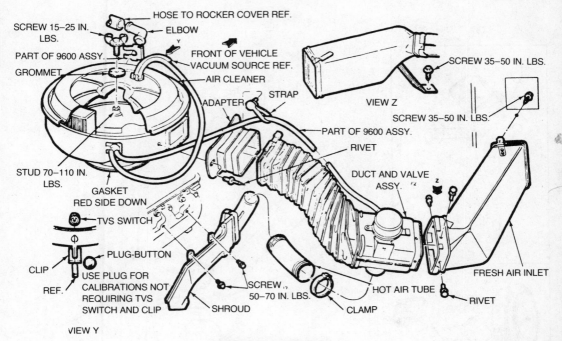

1978 8-351 air cleaner

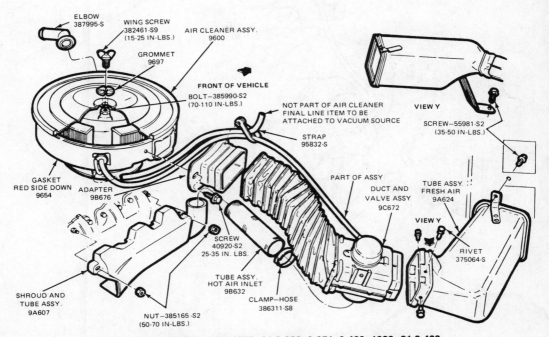

Air cleaner used on the 1979–81 8-302, 8-351, 8-460; 1980–81 8-400

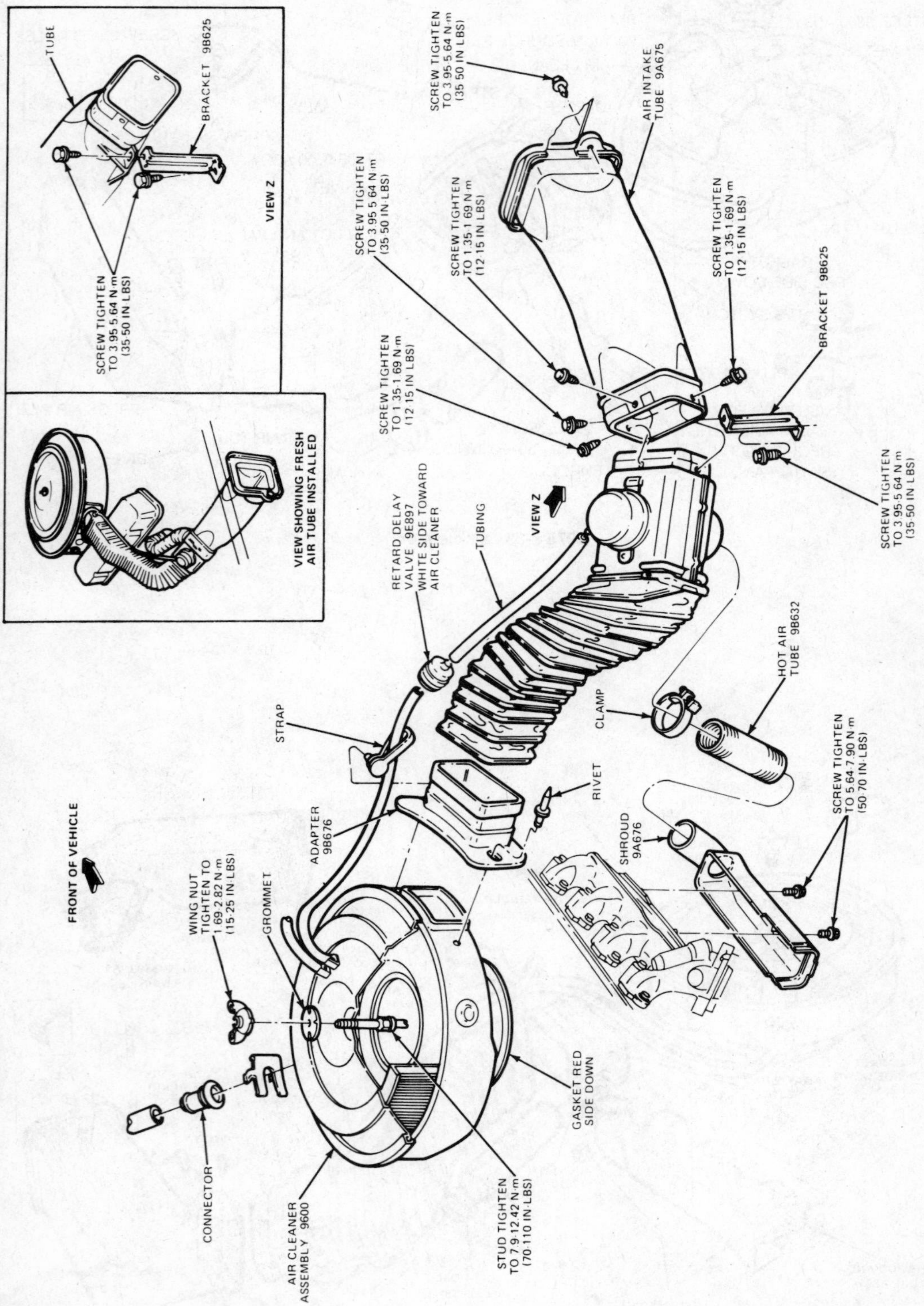

1982–85 8-302 air cleaner

FRONT OF VEHICLE

VIEW Z

VIEW SHOWING FRESH AIR TUBE INSTALLED

TUBE

BRACKET 9B625

SCREW TIGHTEN TO 3.95 5.64 N·m (35 50 IN LBS)

SCREW TIGHTEN TO 3.95 5.64 N·m (35 50 IN LBS)

AIR INTAKE TUBE 9A675

SCREW TIGHTEN TO 3.95 5.64 N·m (35 50 IN LBS)

SCREW TIGHTEN TO 1.35 1.69 N·m (12 15 IN LBS)

SCREW TIGHTEN TO 1.35 1.69 N·m (12 15 IN LBS)

SCREW TIGHTEN TO 1.35 1.69 N·m (12 15 IN LBS)

BRACKET 9B625

SCREW TIGHTEN TO 3.95 5.64 N·m (35 50 IN LBS)

RETARD DELAY VALVE 9E897 WHITE SIDE TOWARD AIR CLEANER

TUBING

HOT AIR TUBE 9B632

CLAMP

SCREW TIGHTEN TO 5.64 7.90 N·m (50 70 IN LBS)

STRAP

ADAPTER 9B676

RIVET

SHROUD 9A676

WING NUT TIGHTEN TO 1.69 2.82 N·m (15 25 IN LBS)

GROMMET

CONNECTOR

AIR CLEANER ASSEMBLY 9600

STUD TIGHTEN TO 7.9 12.42 N·m (70 110 IN LBS)

GASKET RED SIDE DOWN

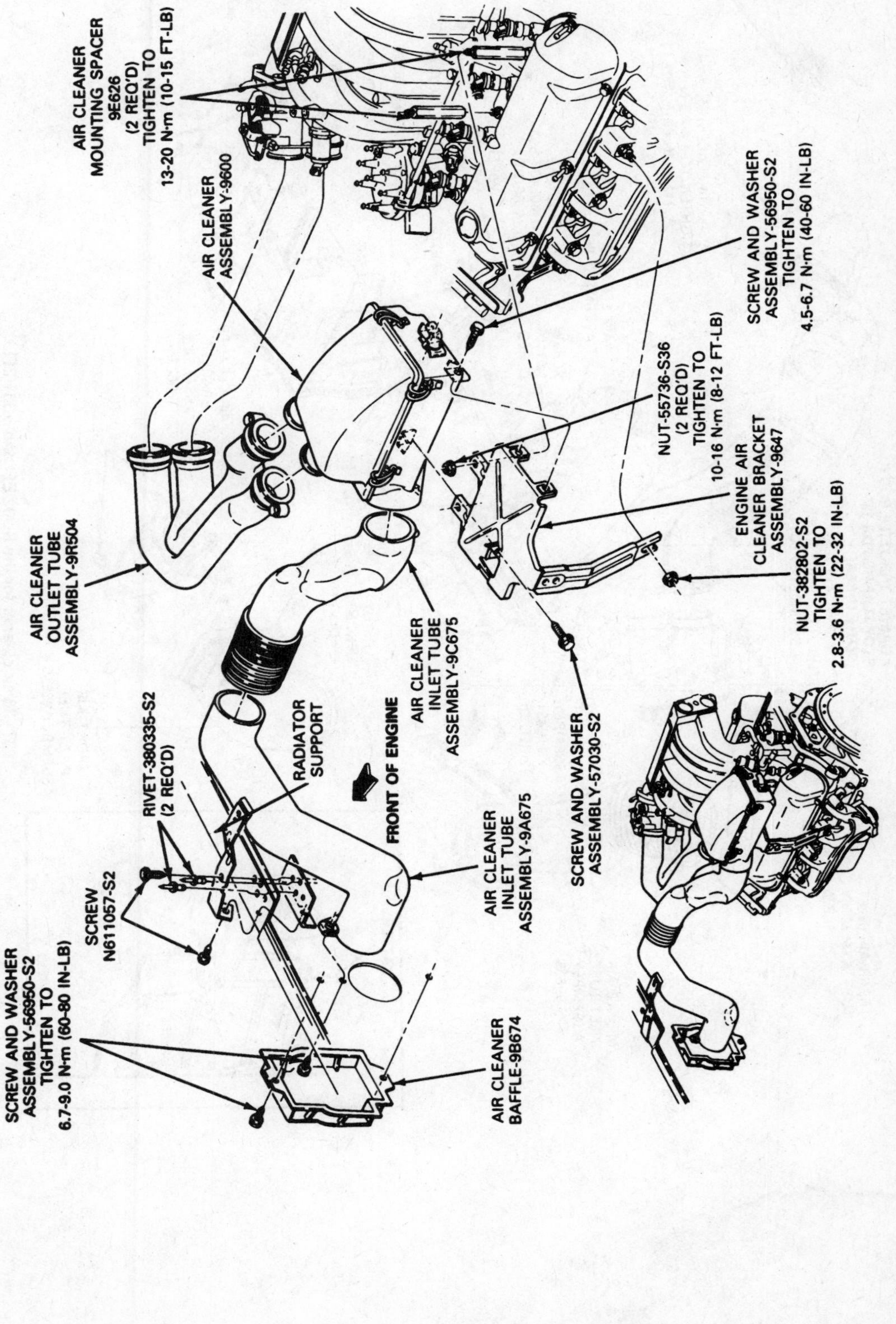

AIR CLEANER
MOUNTING SPACER
9E626
(2 REQ'D)
TIGHTEN TO
13-20 N·m (10-15 FT-LB)

AIR CLEANER
ASSEMBLY-9600

SCREW AND WASHER
ASSEMBLY-56950-S2
TIGHTEN TO
4.5-6.7 N·m (40-60 IN-LB)

AIR CLEANER
OUTLET TUBE
ASSEMBLY-9R504

NUT-55736-S36
(2 REQ'D)
TIGHTEN TO
10-16 N·m (8-12 FT-LB)

ENGINE AIR
CLEANER BRACKET
ASSEMBLY-9647

NUT-382802-S2
TIGHTEN TO
2.8-3.6 N·m (22-32 IN-LB)

AIR CLEANER
INLET TUBE
ASSEMBLY-9C675

RADIATOR
SUPPORT

FRONT OF ENGINE

RIVET-380335-S2
(2 REQ'D)

SCREW
N611057-S2

AIR CLEANER
INLET TUBE
ASSEMBLY-9A675

SCREW AND WASHER
ASSEMBLY-57030-S2

SCREW AND WASHER
ASSEMBLY-56950-S2
TIGHTEN TO
6.7-9.0 N·m (60-80 IN-LB)

AIR CLEANER
BAFFLE-9B674

1986 8-302 air cleaner

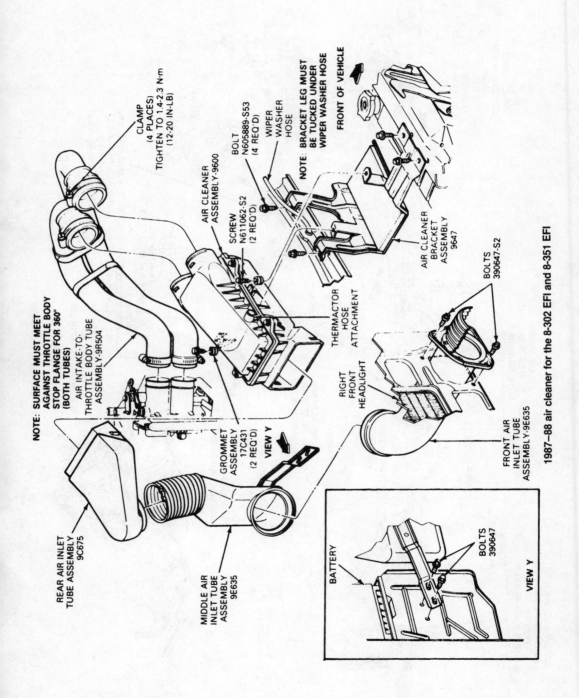

NOTE: SURFACE MUST MEET AGAINST THROTTLE BODY STOP FLANGE FOR 360° (BOTH TUBES)

AIR INTAKE-TO-THROTTLE BODY TUBE ASSEMBLY-9R504

CLAMP (4 PLACES) TIGHTEN TO 1.4-2.3 N·m (12-20 IN-LB)

AIR CLEANER ASSEMBLY-9600

SCREW N611062-S2 (2 REQ'D)

BOLT N605889-S53 (4 REQ'D)

WIPER WASHER HOSE

NOTE: BRACKET LEG MUST BE TUCKED UNDER WIPER WASHER HOSE

FRONT OF VEHICLE

AIR CLEANER BRACKET ASSEMBLY 9647

BOLTS 390647-S2

THERMACTOR HOSE ATTACHMENT

RIGHT FRONT HEADLIGHT

FRONT AIR INLET TUBE ASSEMBLY-9E635

1987-88 air cleaner for the 8-302 EFI and 8-351 EFI

GROMMET ASSEMBLY 17C431 (2 REQ'D)

VIEW Y

REAR AIR INLET TUBE ASSEMBLY 9C675

MIDDLE AIR INLET TUBE ASSEMBLY 9E635

BATTERY

BOLTS 390647

VIEW Y

Fuel Filter

REPLACEMENT

CAUTION: *NEVER SMOKE WHEN WORKING AROUND OR NEAR GASOLINE! MAKE SURE THAT THERE IS NO IGNITION SOURCE NEAR YOU WORK AREA!*

REMOVAL AND INSTALLATION

Carbureted Engines with Inline Hose Connected Filters

1. Remove the air cleaner assembly.
2. Loosen the hose clamps or compress with a pair of pliers and slide the clamps down the hose away from the carburetor and filter.
3. Unscrew the filter from the carburetor.
4. Disconnect the filter from the hose and discard the filter, hose and clamps. Replacement filters usually come with a length of hose and new clamps, always use the new hose and clamps when replacing the filter.
5. Reverse the removal procedure to install the fuel filter. After installation, start the engine and check for fuel leaks.

Carbureted Engines with Inverted Nut (Steel Line) Connected Filters

1. Remove the air cleaner assembly.
2. Position an $^{11}/_{16}$" (or appropriate) size wrench on the filter hex nut to hold the filter in position and remove the steel line from the filter using a suitable wrench.
3. Unscrew the filter from the carburetor.
4. Install the new filter in the reverse order of removal. Start the engine and check for fuel leaks.

VV Carburetors

Model 2700VV and 7200VV carburetors use a replaceable filter located behind the carburetor inlet fitting. To replace these filters:
1. Wait until the engine is cold.
2. Remove the air cleaner assembly.
3. Place some absorbant rags under the inlet fitting.
4. Using a back-up wrench on the inlet fitting, unscrew the fuel line from the inlet fitting.
CAUTION: *It is possible for gasoline to spray*

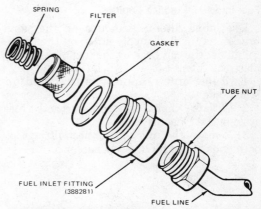

In-carburetor type filter used on the 2700VV and 7200VV

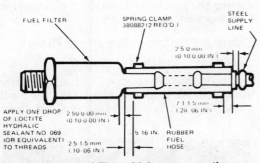

Screw-in type fuel filter with hose connection

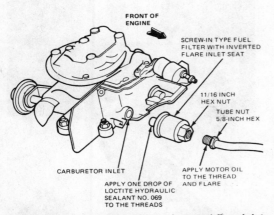

Screw-in type fuel filter with an inverted flare inlet seat

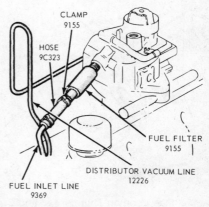

1966–67 inline fuel filter

in all directions when unscrewing the line! This rarely happens, but it is possible, so protect your eyes!

5. Move the fuel line out of the way and unscrew the inlet fiting from the carburetor.

6. Pull out the filter. The spring behind the filter may come with it.

7. Install the new filter. Some new filters come with a new spring. Use it.

8. Coat the threads of the inlet fitting with non-hardening, gasoline-proof sealer and screw it into place by hand. Tighten it snugly with the wrench.

WARNING: *Do not overtighten the inlet fitting! The threads in the carburetor bowl are soft metal and are easily stripped! You don't want to damage these threads!!*

9. Using the back-up wrench on the inlet fitting, screw the fuel line into the fitting and tighten it snugly. Do not overtighten the fuel line!

10. Remove the fuel-soaked rags, wipe up any spilled fuel and start the engine. Check the connections for leaks.

Fuel Injected Gasoline Engines

The inline filter is mounted on the same bracket as the fuel supply pump on the frame rail under the car, back by the fuel tank. To replace the filter:

1. Raise and support the rear end on jackstands.

2. With the engine off, depressurize the fuel system. See Chapter 5.

3. Remove the quick-disconnect fittings at both ends of the filter. See Chapter 5.

4. Remove the filter and retainer from the bracket.

5. Remove the rubber insulator ring from the filter.

6. Remove the filter from the retainer.

7. Install the new filter into the retainer, noting the direction of the flow arrow.

8. Install a new rubber insulator ring.

9. Install the retainer and filter on the bracket and tighten the screws to 60 in. lbs.

10. Install the fuel lines using new retainer clips.

11. Start the engine and check for leaks.

PCV Valve

All models use a closed ventilation system with a sealed breather cap connected to the air cleaner by a rubber hose. The PCV valve is usually mounted in the valve cover and connected to the intake manifold by a rubber hose. Its task is to regulate the amount of crankcase (blow-by) gases which are recycled.

Since the PCV valve works under severe load it is very important that it be replaced at the interval specified in the maintenance chart. Replacement involves removing the valve from the grommet in the rocker arm cover disconnecting the hose(s) and installing a new valve. Do not attempt to clean a used valve.

Exhaust Control Valve (Heat Riser)
1968-71

Some models are equipped with exhaust control (heat riser) valves located near the head pipe connection in the exhaust manifold. these

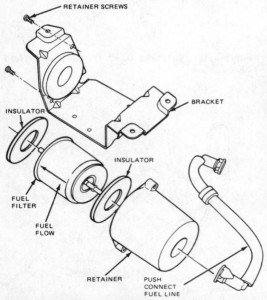

In-line fuel filter used on Thunderbird and Cougar with fuel injection

Six cylinder heat riser

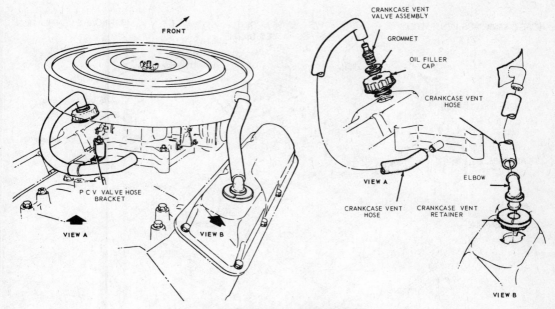

PCV valve installation—302 V8

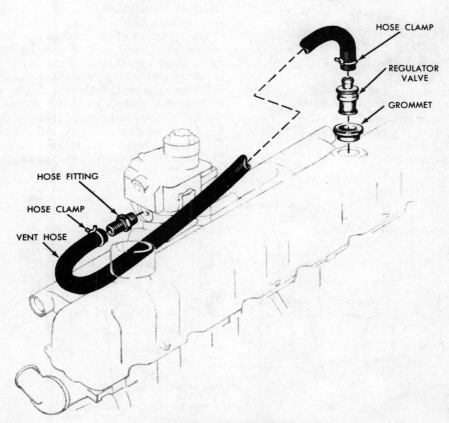

Early inline 6-cylinder PCV system

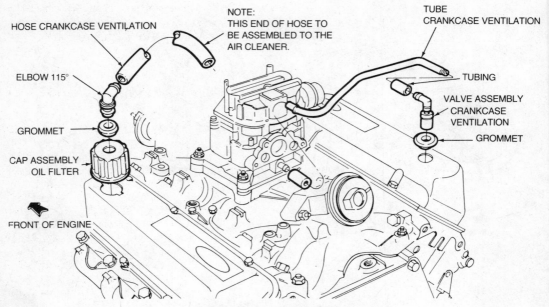

HOSE CRANKCASE VENTILATION

NOTE:
THIS END OF HOSE TO
BE ASSEMBLED TO THE
AIR CLEANER.

TUBE
CRANKCASE VENTILATION

ELBOW 115°

TUBING

VALVE ASSEMBLY
CRANKCASE
VENTILATION

GROMMET

GROMMET

CAP ASSEMBLY
OIL FILTER

FRONT OF ENGINE

1975 and later PCV system

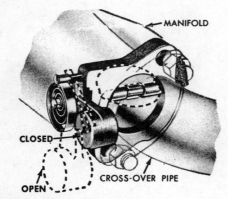

MANIFOLD

CLOSED

OPEN

CROSS-OVER PIPE

Eight cylinder heat riser

valves aid initial warmup in cold weather by restricting exhaust gas flow slightly. The heat generated by this restriction is transferred to the intake manifold where it result in improved fuel vaporization.

The operation of the exhaust control valve should be checked every 6 months or 6,000 miles. Make sure that the thermostatic spring is hooked on the stop pin and that the tension holds the valve shut. Rotate the counter weight by hand and make sure that it moves freely through about 90 degrees of rotation. A valve which is operating properly will open when light finger pressure is applied (cold engine). Lubricate the shaft bushings with a mixture of

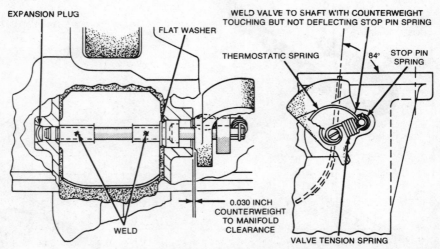

EXPANSION PLUG

FLAT WASHER

WELD VALVE TO SHAFT WITH COUNTERWEIGHT
TOUCHING BUT NOT DEFLECTING STOP PIN SPRING

THERMOSTATIC SPRING

84°

STOP PIN
SPRING

0.030 INCH
COUNTERWEIGHT
TO MANIFOLD
CLEARANCE

WELD

VALVE TENSION SPRING

Heat riser valve plate position and counterweight clearance

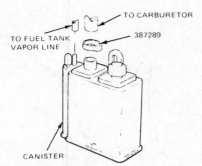

Typical carbon canister

penetrating oil and graphite. Operate the valve manually a few times to work in the lubricant.

Evaporative Emissions Canister

The canister functions to cycle the fuel vapor from the fuel tank and carburetor float chamber into the intake manifold and eventually into the cylinders for combustion. The activated charcoal element within the canister acts as a storage device for the fuel vapor at times when the engine operating condition will not permit fuel vapor to burn efficiently.

The only required service for the evaporative emissions canister is inspection at the interval specified in the maintenance chart. If the charcoal element is gummed up the entire canister should be replaced. Disconnect the canister purge hose(s), loosen the canister retaining bracket, lift out the canister. Installation is the reverse of removal.

Crankcase Filler Cap Cleaning

At the recommended intervals in the maintenance chart, the oil filler cap must be cleaned. Disconnect the positive crankcase ventilation hose from the cap and lift the cap from the rocker cover. soak the cap in kerosene or mineral

spirits to clean the internal element of sludge and blow-by material. After agitating the cap in the solution, shake the cap dry. Reinstall the cap and connect the hose.

Battery

FLUID LEVEL (EXCEPT MAINTENANCE FREE BATTERIES)

Check the battery electrolyte level at least once a month, or more often in hot weather or during periods of extended car operation. The level can be checked through the case on translucent polypropylene batteries; the cell caps must be removed on other models. The electrolyte level in each cell should be kept filled to the split ring inside, or the line marked on the outside of the case.

If the level is low, add only distilled water, or colorless, odorless drinking water, through the opening until the level is correct. Each cell is completely separate from the others, so each must be checked and filled individually.

If water is added in freezing weather, the car should be driven several miles to allow the water to mix with the electrolyte. Otherwise, the battery could freeze.

SPECIFIC GRAVITY (EXCEPT MAINTENANCE FREE BATTERIES)

At least once a year, check the specific gravity of the battery. It should be between 1.20 in.Hg and 1.26 in.Hg at room temperature.

The specific gravity can be check with the use of an hydrometer, an inexpensive instrument available from many sources, including auto parts stores. The hydrometer has a squeeze bulb at one end and a nozzle at the other. Battery electrolyte is sucked into the hydrometer until the float is lifted from its seat. The specific gravity is then read by noting the position of the float. Generally, if after charging, the specific gravity between any two cells varies more

SPECIFIC GRAVITY (@ 80°F.) AND CHARGE	
Specific Gravity Reading	
(use the minimum figure for testing)	
Minimum	Battery Charge
1.260	100% Charged
1.230	75% Charged
1.200	50% Charged
1.170	25% Charged
1.140	Very Little Power Left
1.110	Completely Discharged

Battery specific gravity. Some testers have colored balls which correspond to the numerical values in the left column

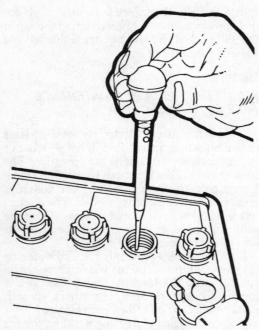

Checking the battery with a battery hydometer

Clean battery cable clamps with a wire brush

than 50 points (0.50), the battery is bad and should be replaced.

It is not possible to check the specific gravity in this manner on sealed (maintenance free) batteries. Instead, the indicator built into the top of the case must be relied on to display any signs of battery deterioration. If the indicator is dark, the battery can be assumed to be OK. If the indicator is light, the specific gravity is low, and the battery should be charged or replaced.

CABLES AND CLAMPS

Once a year, the battery terminals and the cable clamps should be cleaned. Loosen the

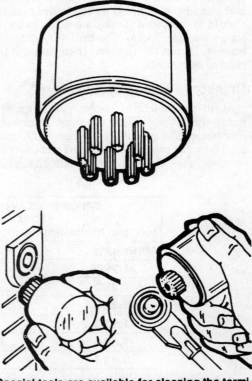

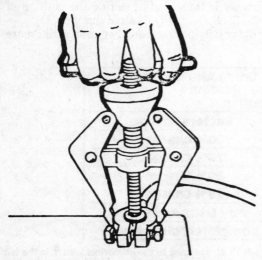

Use a puller to remove the battery cable

Special tools are available for cleaning the terminals and cable clamps on side terminal batteries

clamps and remove the cables, negative cable first. On batteries with posts on top, the use of a puller specially made for the purpose is recommended. These are inexpensive, and available in auto parts stores. Side terminal battery cables are secured with a bolt.

Clean the cable lamps and the battery terminal with a wire brush, until all corrosion, grease, etc., is removed and the metal is shiny. It is especially important to clean the inside of the clamp thoroughly, since a small deposit of foreign material or oxidation there will prevent a sound electrical connection and inhibit either starting or charging. Special tools are available for cleaning these parts, one type for conventional batteries and another type for side terminal batteries.

Before installing the cables, loosen the battery holddown clamp or strap, remove the battery and check the battery tray. Clear it of any debris, and check it for soundness. Rust should be wire brushed away, and the metal given a coat of anti-rust paint. Replace the battery and tighten the holddown clamp or strap securely, but be careful not to overtighten, which will crack the battery case.

After the clamps and terminals are clean, reinstall the cables, negative cable last; do not hammer on the clamps to install. Tighten the clamps securely, but do not distort them. Give the clamps and terminals a thin external coat of grease after installation, to retard corrosion.

Check the cables at the same time that the terminals are cleaned. If the cable insulation is cracked or broken, or if the ends are frayed, the cable should be replaced with a new cable of the same length and gauge.

CAUTION: *Keep flame or sparks away from the battery; it gives off explosive hydrogen gas. Battery electrolyte contains sulphuric acid. If you should splash any on your skin or in your eyes, flush the affected area with plenty of clear water. If it lands in your eyes, get medical help immediately.*

Windshield Wipers

For maximum effectiveness and longest element lift, the windshield and wiper blades should be kept clean. Dirt, tree sap, road tar and so on will cause streaking, smearing and blade deterioration if left on the glass. It is advisable to wash the windshield carefully with a commercial glass cleaner at least once a month. Wipe off the rubber blades with the wet rag afterwards. Do not attempt to move the wipers by hand; damage to the motor and drive mechanism will result.

If the blades are found to be cracked, broken or torn, they should be replaced immediately.

Replacement intervals will vary with usage, although ozone deterioration usually limits blade lift to about one year. If the wiper pattern is smeared or streaked, or if the blade chatters across the glass, the elements should be replaced. It is easiest and most sensible to replace the elements in pairs.

There are basically three different types of refills, which differ in their method of replacement. One type has two release buttons, approximately 1/3 of the way up from the ends of the blade frame. Pushing the buttons down releases a lock and allows the rubber filler to be removed from the frame. The new filler slides back into the frame and locks in place.

The second type of refill has two metal tabs which are unlocked by squeezing them together. The rubber filler can then be withdrawn from the frame jaws. A new refill is installed by inserting the refill into the front frame jaws and sliding it rear ward to engage the remaining frame jaws. There are usually four jaws. Be certain when installing that the refill is engaged in all of them. At the end of its travel, the tabs will lock into place on the front jaws of the wiper blade frame.

The third type is a refill made from polycarbonate. The refill has a simple locking device at one end which flexes downward out of the groove into which the jaws of the holder fit, allowing easy release. By sliding the new refill through all the jaws and pushing through the slight resistance when it reaches the end of its travel, the refill will lock into position.

Regardless of the type of refill used, make sure that all of the frame jaws are engaged as the refill is pushed into place and locked. The metal blade holder and frame will scratch the glass if allowed to touch it.

ARM AND BLADE REPLACEMENT

A detailed description and procedures for replacing the wiper arm and blade is found in Chapter 6.

Belts

Once a year or at 12,000 mile intervals, the tension (and condition) of the alternator, power steering (if so equipped), air conditioning (if so equipped), and Thermactor air pump drive belts should be checked, and, if necessary, adjusted. Loose accessory drive belts can lead to poor engine cooling and diminish alternator, power steering pump, air conditioning compressor or Thermactor air pump output. A belt that is too tight places a severe strain on the water pump, alternator, power steering pump, compressor or air pump bearings.

Replace any belts that is so glazed, worn or

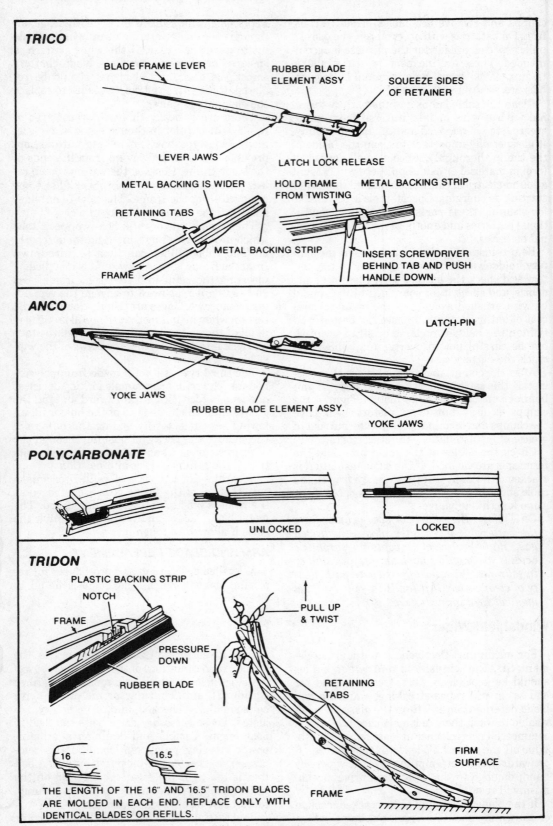

TRICO

BLADE FRAME LEVER

RUBBER BLADE
ELEMENT ASSY

SQUEEZE SIDES
OF RETAINER

LEVER JAWS

LATCH LOCK RELEASE

METAL BACKING IS WIDER

HOLD FRAME
FROM TWISTING

METAL BACKING STRIP

RETAINING TABS

METAL BACKING STRIP

FRAME

INSERT SCREWDRIVER
BEHIND TAB AND PUSH
HANDLE DOWN.

ANCO

LATCH-PIN

YOKE JAWS

RUBBER BLADE ELEMENT ASSY.

YOKE JAWS

POLYCARBONATE

UNLOCKED

LOCKED

TRIDON

PLASTIC BACKING STRIP

NOTCH

FRAME

PULL UP
& TWIST

PRESSURE
DOWN

RUBBER BLADE

RETAINING
TABS

FIRM
SURFACE

16

16.5

THE LENGTH OF THE 16" AND 16.5" TRIDON BLADES
ARE MOLDED IN EACH END. REPLACE ONLY WITH
IDENTICAL BLADES OR REFILLS.

FRAME

Wiper insert replacement

HOW TO SPOT WORN V-BELTS

V-Belts are vital to efficient engine operation—they drive the fan, water pump and other accessories. They require little maintenance (occasional tightening) but they will not last forever. Slipping or failure of the V-belt will lead to overheating. If your V-belt looks like any of these, it should be replaced.

This belt has deep cracks, which cause it to flex. Too much flexing leads to heat build-up and premature failure. These cracks can be caused by using the belt on a pulley that is too small. Notched belts are available for small diameter pulleys.

Cracking or weathering

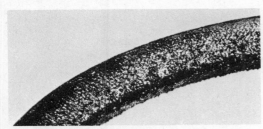

Oil and grease on a belt can cause the belt's rubber compounds to soften and separate from the reinforcing cords that hold the belt together. The belt will first slip, then finally fail altogether.

Softening (grease and oil)

Glazing is caused by a belt that is slipping. A slipping belt can cause a run-down battery, erratic power steering, overheating or poor accessory performance. The more the belt slips, the more glazing will be built up on the surface of the belt. The more the belt is glazed, the more it will slip. If the glazing is light, tighten the belt.

Glazing

The cover of this belt is worn off and is peeling away. The reinforcing cords will begin to wear and the belt will shortly break. When the belt cover wears in spots or has a rough jagged appearance, check the pulley grooves for roughness.

Worn cover

This belt is on the verge of breaking and leaving you stranded. The layers of the belt are separating and the reinforcing cords are exposed. It's just a matter of time before it breaks completely.

Separation

stretched that it cannot be tightened sufficiently.

NOTE: *The material used in late model drive belts is such that the belts do not show wear. Replace belts at least every three years.*

On vehicles with matched belts, replace both belts. New belts are to be adjusted to a tension of 140 lbs. (½″, ⅜″, and ¹⁵⁄₃₂″ wide belts) or 80 lbs (¼″ wide belts) measured on a belt tension gauge. Any belt that has been operating for a minimum of 10 minutes is considered a used belt. In the first 10 minutes, the belt should stretch to its maximum extent. After 10 minutes, stop the engine and recheck the belt tension. Belt tension for a used belt should be maintained at 110 lbs (all except ¼″ wide belts) or 60 lbs (¼″ wide belts). If a belt tension gauge is not available, the following procedures may be used.

ADJUSTMENTS FOR ALL EXCEPT THE SERPENTINE (SINGLE) BELT

CAUTION: *On models equipped with an electric cooling fan, disconnect the negative battery cable or fan motor wiring harness connector before replacing or adjusting drive belts. The fan may come on, under certain circumstances, even though the ignition is off.*

Alternator (Fan Drive) Belt

1. Position a ruler perpendicular to the drive belt at its longest run. Test the tightness of the belt by pressing it firmly with your thumb. The deflection should not exceed ¼″.

2. If the deflection exceeds ¼″, loosen the alternator mounting and adjusting arm bolts.

3a. On 1968-72 V8 and 6 cylinder models, use a pry bar or broom handle to move the alternator toward or away from the engine until the proper tension is reached.

WARNING: *Apply tension to the front of the alternator only. Positioning the pry bar against the rear end housing will damage the alternator.*

3b. On 1973 and later V8 models, place a 1″

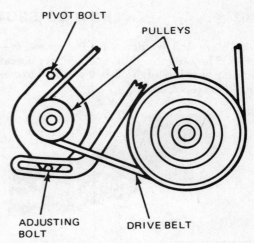

Alternator belt adjustment

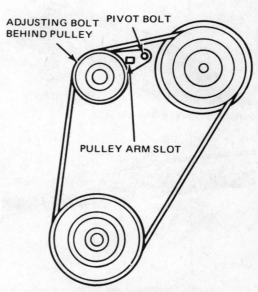

Air conditioning belt adjustment

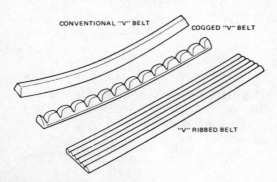

Drive belt types

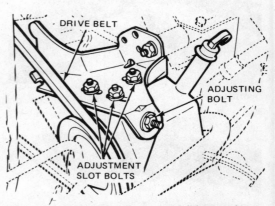

Power steering belt adjustment (slider type)

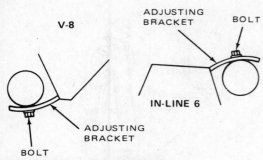

Air pump adjustment points

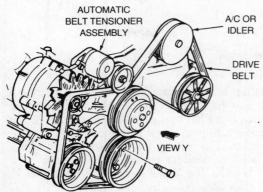

INSTALLATION WITH THERMACTER AIR PUMP

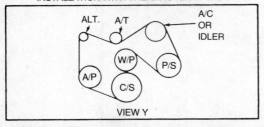

8-302, 8-351 EFI engine accessory drive belts

open-end or adjustable wrench on the adjusting arm bolt and pull on the wrench until the proper tension is achieved.

4. Holding the alternator in place to maintain tension, tighten the adjusting arm bolt. Recheck the belt tension. When the belt is properly tensioned, tighten the alternator mounting bolt.

Power Steering Drive Belt

ALL 6-CYLINDER AND 1971-72 V8 MODELS

1. Holding a ruler perpendicular to the drive belt at its longest run, test the tightness of the belt by pressing it firmly with your thumb. The deflection should not exceed ¼".

2. To adjust the belt tension, loosen the adjusting and mounting bolts on the front face of the steering pump cover plate (hub side).

3. Using a pry bar or broom handle on the pump hub as shown, move the power steering

pump toward or away from the engine until the proper tension is reached. Do not pry against the reservoir as it is relatively soft and easily deformed.

4. Hold the pump in place, tighten the adjusting arm bolt and then recheck the belt tension. When the belt is properly tensioned tighten the mounting bolts.

1973 AND LATER V8 MODELS (EXCEPT SINGLE DRIVE BELT)

1. Position a ruler perpendicular to the drive belt at its longest run. Test the tightness of the belt by pressing it firmly with your thumb. The deflection should be about ¼".

2. To adjust the belt tension, loosen the three bolts in the three elongated adjusting slots at the power steering pump attaching bracket.

3. Turn the steering pump drive belt adjusting nut as required until the proper deflection is obtained. Turning the adjusting nut clockwise will increase tension and decrease deflection; counterclockwise will decrease tension and increase deflection.

4. Without disturbing the pump, tighten the three attaching bolts.

Air Conditioning Compressor Drive Belt

1. Position a ruler perpendicular to the drive belt at its longest run. Test the tightness of the belt by pressing it firmly with your thumb. The deflection should not exceed ¼".

2. If the engine is equipped with an idler pulley, loosen the idler pulley adjusting boot, insert a pry bar between the pulley and the engine (or in the idler pulley adjusting slot), and adjust the tension accordingly. If the engine is not equipped with an idler pulley, the alternator must be moved to accomplish this adjustment, as outlined under Alternator (Fan Drive) Belt.

3. When the proper tension is reached, tighten the idler pulley adjusting bolt (if so equipped) or the alternator adjusting and mounting bolts.

Thermactor Air Pump Drive Belt

1. Position a ruler perpendicular to the drive belt at its longest run. Test the tightness of the belt by pressing it firmly with your thumb. The deflection should be about ¼".

2. To adjust the belt tension, loosen the adjusting arm bolt slightly. If necessary, also loosen the mounting belt slightly.

3. Using a pry bar or broom handle, pry against the pump rear cover to move the pump toward or away from the engine as necessary.

WARNING: *Do not pry against the pump housing itself, as damage to the housing may result.*

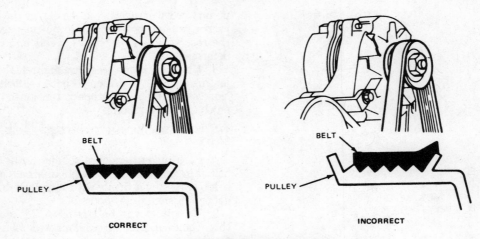

Ribbed belt installation

4. Holding the pump in place, tighten the adjusting arm bolt and recheck the tension. When the belt is properly tensioned, tighten the mounting bolt.

Single (Serpentine) Drive Belt

Some late models (starting in 1979) feature a single, wide, ribbed V-belt that drives the water pump, alternator and power steering. To install a new belt, simply retract the belt tensioner with a pry bar and slide the old belt off of the pulleys. Slip on a new belt and release the tensioner. The spring powered tensioner eliminates the need for periodic adjustments.

WARNING: *Check to make sure that the V-ribbed belt is located properly in all drive pulleys before applying tensioner pressure.*

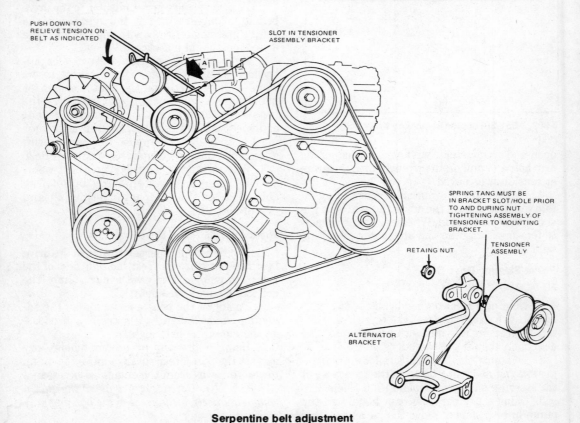

Serpentine belt adjustment

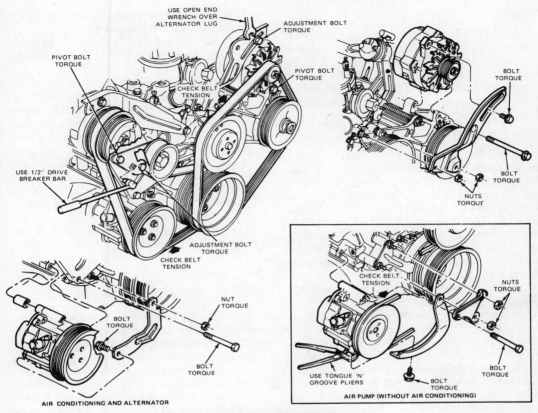

USE OPEN END WRENCH OVER ALTERNATOR LUG

ADJUSTMENT BOLT TORQUE

PIVOT BOLT TORQUE

CHECK BELT TENSION

PIVOT BOLT TORQUE

BOLT TORQUE

USE 1/2" DRIVE BREAKER BAR

BOLT TORQUE

NUTS TORQUE

ADJUSTMENT BOLT TORQUE

CHECK BELT TENSION

NUT TORQUE

BOLT TORQUE

BOLT TORQUE

CHECK BELT TENSION

NUTS TORQUE

BOLT TORQUE

USE TONGUE 'N' GROOVE PLIERS

BOLT TORQUE

BOLT TORQUE

AIR CONDITIONING AND ALTERNATOR

AIR PUMP (WITHOUT AIR CONDITIONING)

Late model belt tension adjustments

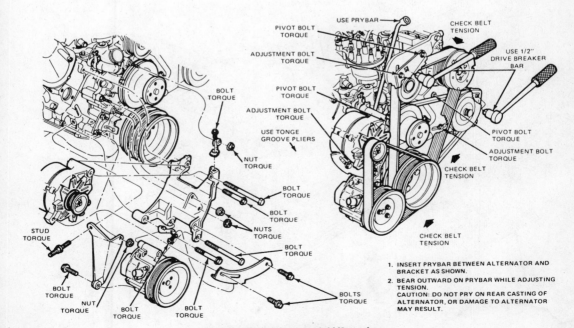

USE PRYBAR

CHECK BELT TENSION

PIVOT BOLT TORQUE

ADJUSTMENT BOLT TORQUE

PIVOT BOLT TORQUE

ADJUSTMENT BOLT TORQUE

USE TONGE GROOVE PLIERS

USE 1/2" DRIVE BREAKER BAR

PIVOT BOLT TORQUE

ADJUSTMENT BOLT TORQUE

CHECK BELT TENSION

CHECK BELT TENSION

BOLT TORQUE

NUT TORQUE

BOLT TORQUE

BOLT TORQUE

NUTS TORQUE

BOLT TORQUE

STUD TORQUE

BOLT TORQUE

NUT TORQUE

BOLT TORQUE

BOLT TORQUE

BOLTS TORQUE

1. INSERT PRYBAR BETWEEN ALTERNATOR AND BRACKET AS SHOWN.

2. BEAR OUTWARD ON PRYBAR WHILE ADJUSTING TENSION.
   CAUTION: DO NOT PRY ON REAR CASTING OF ALTERNATOR, OR DAMAGE TO ALTERNATOR MAY RESULT.

Belt installation late model V8 engines

Hoses

CAUTION: *On models equipped with an electric cooling fan, disconnect the negative battery cable, or fan motor wiring harness connector before replacing any radiator/heater hose. The fan may come on, under certain circumstances, even though the ignition is Off.*

REPLACEMENT

Inspect the condition of the radiator and heater hoses periodically. Early spring and at the beginning of the fall or winter, when you are performing other maintenance, are good times. Make sure the engine and cooling system are cold. Visually inspect for cracking, rotting or collapsed hoses, replace as necessary. Run your hand along the length of the hose. If a weak or swollen spot is noted when squeezing the hose wall, replace the hose.

1. Drain the cooling system into a suitable container (if the coolant is to be reused).

CAUTION: *When draining the coolant, keep in mind that cats and dogs are attracted by the ethylene glycol antifreeze, and are quite likely to drink any that is left in an uncovered container or in puddles on the ground. This will prove fatal in sufficient quantity. Always drain the coolant into a sealable container. Coolant should be reused unless it is contaminated or several years old.*

2. Loosen the hose clamps at each end of the hose that requires replacement.

3. Twist, pull and slide the hose off the radiator, water pump, thermostat or heater connection.

4. Clean the hose mounting connections. Position the hose clamps on the new hose.

5. Coat the connection surfaces with a water resistant sealer and slide the hose into position. Make sure the hose clamps are located beyond the raised bead of the connector (if equipped) and centered in the clamping area of the connection.

6. Tighten the clamps to 20-30 in. lbs. Do not overtighten.

7. Fill the cooling system.

8. Start the engine and allow it to reach normal operating temperature. Check for leaks.

Air Conditioning
GENERAL SERVICING PROCEDURES

The most important aspect of air conditioning service is the maintenance of pure and adequate charge of refrigerant in the system. A refrigeration system cannot function properly if a significant percentage of the charge is lost. Leaks are common because the severe vibration encountered in an automobile can easily cause a sufficient cracking or loosening of the air conditioning fittings. As a result, the extreme operat-

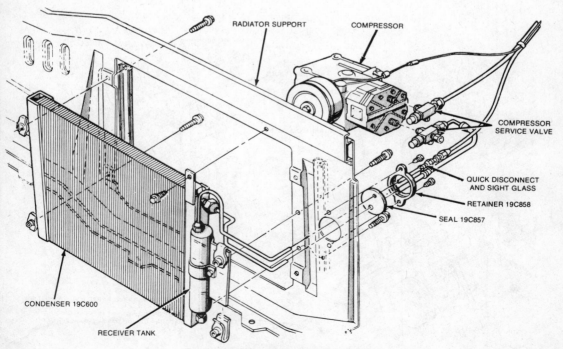

Typical air conditioning installation

HOW TO SPOT BAD HOSES

Both the upper and lower radiator hoses are called upon to perform difficult jobs in an inhospitable environment. They are subject to nearly 18 psi at under hood temperatures often over 280°F., and must circulate nearly 7500 gallons of coolant an hour—3 good reasons to have good hoses.

A good test for any hose is to feel it for soft or spongy spots. Frequently these will appear as swollen areas of the hose. The most likely cause is oil soaking. This hose could burst at any time, when hot or under pressure.

Swollen hose

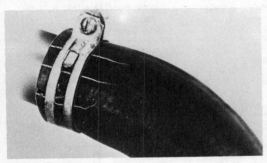

Cracked hoses can usually be seen but feel the hoses to be sure they have not hardened; a prime cause of cracking. This hose has cracked down to the reinforcing cords and could split at any of the cracks.

Cracked hose

Weakened clamps frequently are the cause of hose and cooling system failure. The connection between the pipe and hose has deteriorated enough to allow coolant to escape when the engine is hot.

Frayed hose end (due to weak clamp)

Debris, rust and scale in the cooling system can cause the inside of a hose to weaken. This can usually be felt on the outside of the hose as soft or thinner areas.

Debris in cooling system

Troubleshooting Basic Air Conditioning Problems

Problem	Cause	Solution
There's little or no air coming from the vents (and you're sure it's on)	• The A/C fuse is blown • Broken or loose wires or connections • The on/off switch is defective	• Check and/or replace fuse • Check and/or repair connections • Replace switch
The air coming from the vents is not cool enough	• Windows and air vent wings open • The compressor belt is slipping • Heater is on • Condenser is clogged with debris • Refrigerant has escaped through a leak in the system • Receiver/drier is plugged	• Close windows and vent wings • Tighten or replace compressor belt • Shut heater off • Clean the condenser • Check system • Service system
The air has an odor	• Vacuum system is disrupted • Odor producing substances on the evaporator case • Condensation has collected in the bottom of the evaporator housing	• Have the system checked/repaired • Clean the evaporator case • Clean the evaporator housing drains
System is noisy or vibrating	• Compressor belt or mountings loose • Air in the system	• Tighten or replace belt; tighten mounting bolts • Have the system serviced

Sight glass condition
  Constant bubbles, foam or oil streaks
  Clear sight glass, but no cold air
  Clear sight glass, but air is cold
  Clouded with milky fluid
	
	• Undercharged system
	
	• No refrigerant at all
	• System is OK
	• Receiver drier is leaking dessicant
		
		• Charge the system
		
		• Check and charge the system
		
		• Have system checked

Large difference in temperature of lines	• System undercharged	• Charge and leak test the system
Compressor noise	• Broken valves • Overcharged • Incorrect oil level • Piston slap • Broken rings • Drive belt pulley bolts are loose	• Replace the valve plate • Discharge, evacuate and install the correct charge • Isolate the compressor and check the oil level. Correct as necessary. • Replace the compressor • Replace the compressor • Tighten with the correct torque specification
Excessive vibration	• Incorrect belt tension • Clutch loose • Overcharged • Pulley is misaligned	• Adjust the belt tension • Tighten the clutch • Discharge, evacuate and install the correct charge • Align the pulley
Condensation dripping in the passenger compartment	• Drain hose plugged or improperly positioned • Insulation removed or improperly installed	• Clean the drain hose and check for proper installation • Replace the insulation on the expansion valve and hoses
Frozen evaporator coil	• Faulty thermostat • Thermostat capillary tube improperly installed • Thermostat not adjusted properly	• Replace the thermostat • Install the capillary tube correctly • Adjust the thermostat
Low side low—high side low	• System refrigerant is low • Expansion valve is restricted	• Evacuate, leak test and charge the system • Replace the expansion valve
Low side high—high side low	• Internal leak in the compressor—worn	• Remove the compressor cylinder head and inspect the compressor. Replace the valve plate assembly if necessary. If the compressor pistons, rings or

Troubleshooting Basic Air Conditioning Problems (cont.)

Problem	Cause	Solution
Low side high—high side low (cont.)		cylinders are excessively worn or scored replace the compressor
	• Cylinder head gasket is leaking	• Install a replacement cylinder head gasket
	• Expansion valve is defective	• Replace the expansion valve
	• Drive belt slipping	• Adjust the belt tension
Low side high—high side high	• Condenser fins obstructed	• Clean the condenser fins
	• Air in the system	• Evacuate, leak test and charge the system
	• Expansion valve is defective	• Replace the expansion valve
	• Loose or worn fan belts	• Adjust or replace the belts as necessary
Low side low—high side high	• Expansion valve is defective	• Replace the expansion valve
	• Restriction in the refrigerant hose	• Check the hose for kinks—replace if necessary
	• Restriction in the receiver/drier	• Replace the receiver/drier
	• Restriction in the condenser	• Replace the condenser
Low side and high side normal (inadequate cooling)	• Air in the system	• Evacuate, leak test and charge the system
	• Moisture in the system	• Evacuate, leak test and charge the system

ing pressures of the system force refrigerant out.

The problem can be understood by considering what happens to the system as it is operated with a continuous leak. Because the expansion valve regulates the flow of refrigerant to the evaporator, the level of refrigerant there is fairly constant. The receiver/drier stores any excess of refrigerant, and so a loss will first appear there as a reduction in the level of liquid. As this level nears the bottom of the vessel, some refrigerant vapor bubbles will begin to appear in the stream of liquid supplied to the expansion valve. This vapor decreases the capacity of the expansion valve very little as the valve opens to compensate for its presence. As the quantity of liquid in the condenser decreases, the operating pressure will drop there and throughout the high side of the system. As the R-12 continues to be expelled, the pressure available to force the liquid through the expansion valve will continue to decrease, and, eventually, the valve's orifice will prove to be too much of a restriction for adequate flow even with the needle fully withdrawn.

At this point, low side pressure will start to drop, and severe reduction in cooling capacity, marked by freeze-up of the evaporator coil, will result. Eventually, the operating pressure of the evaporator will be lower than the pressure of the atmosphere surrounding it, and air will be drawn into the system wherever there are leaks in the low side.

Because all atmospheric air contains at least some moisture, water will enter the system and mix with the R-12 and the oil. Trace amounts of moisture will cause sludging of the oil, and corrosion of the system. Saturation and clogging of the filter-drier, and freezing of the expansion valve orifice will eventually result. As air fills the system to a greater and greater extend, it will interfere more and more with the normal flows of refrigerant and heat.

A list of general precautions that should be observed while doing this follows:

1. Keep all tools as clean and dry as possible.

2. Thoroughly purge the service gauges and hoses of air and moisture before connecting them to the system. Keep them capped when not in use.

3. Thoroughly clean any refrigerant fitting before disconnecting it, in order to minimize the entrance of dirt into the system.

4. Plan any operation that requires opening the system beforehand in order to minimize the length of time it will be exposed to open air. Cap or seal the open ends to minimize the entrance of foreign material.

5. When adding oil, pour it through an extremely clean and dry tube or funnel. Keep the oil capped whenever possible. Do not use oil that has not been kept tightly sealed.

6. Use only refrigerant 12. Purchase refrigerant intended for use in only automotive air conditioning system. Avoid the use of refrigerant 12 that may be packaged for another use, such as cleaning, or powering a horn, as it is impure.

7. Completely evacuate any system that has been opened to replace a component, other than when isolating the compressor, or that has leaked sufficiently to draw in moisture and air. This requires evacuating air and moisture with a good vacuum pump for at least one hour.

If a system has been open for a considerable length of time it may be advisable to evacuate the system for up to 12 hours (overnight).

8. Use a wrench on both halves of a fitting that is to be disconnected, so as to avoid placing torque on any of the refrigerant lines.

ADDITIONAL PREVENTIVE MAINTENANCE CHECKS

Antifreeze

In order to prevent heater core freeze-up during air conditioner operation, it is necessary to maintain permanent type antifreeze protection of + 15°F (− 9°C) or lower. A reading of − 15°F (− 26°C) is ideal since this protection also supplies sufficient corrosion inhibitors for the protection of the engine cooling system.

WARNING: *Do not use antifreeze longer than specified by the manufacturer.*

Radiator Cap

For efficient operation of an air conditioned car's cooling system, the radiator cap should have a holding pressure which meets manufacturer's specifications. A cap which fails to hold these pressure should be replaced.

Condenser

Any obstruction of or damage to the condenser configuration will restrict the air flow which is essential to its efficient operation. It is therefore, a good rule to keep this unit clean and in proper physical shape.

NOTE: *Bug screens are regarded as obstructions.*

Condensation Drain Tube

This single molded drain tube expels the condensation, which accumulates on the bottom of the evaporator housing, into the engine compartment.

If this tube is obstructed, the air conditioning performance can be restricted and condensation buildup can spill over onto the vehicle's floor.

SAFETY PRECAUTIONS

Because of the importance of the necessary safety precautions that must be exercised when working with air conditioning systems and R-12 refrigerant, a recap of the safety precautions are outlined.

1. Avoid contact with a charged refrigeration system, even when working on another part of the air conditioning system or vehicle. If a heavy tool comes into contact with a section of copper tubing or a heat exchanger, it can easily cause the relatively soft material to rupture.

2. When it is necessary to apply force to a fitting which contains refrigerant, as when checking that all system couplings are securely tightened, use a wrench on both parts of the fitting involved, if possible. This will avoid putting torque on the refrigerant tubing. (It is advisable, when possible, to use tube or line wrenches when tightening these flare nut fittings.)

3. Do not attempt to discharge the system by merely loosening a fitting, or removing the service valve caps and cracking these valves. Precise control is possibly only when using the service gauges. Place a rag under the open end of the center charging hose while discharging the system to catch any drops of liquid that might escape. Wear protective gloves when connecting or disconnecting service gauge hoses.

4. Discharge the system only in a well ventilated area, as high concentrations of the gas can exclude oxygen and act as an anesthetic. When leak testing or soldering this is particularly important, as toxic gas is formed when R-12 contacts any flame.

5. Never start a system without first verifying that both service valves are backseated, if equipped, and that all fittings are throughout the system are snugly connected.

6. Avoid applying heat to any refrigerant line or storage vessel. Charging may be aided by using water heated to less than 125°F (52°C) to warm the refrigerant container. Never allow a refrigerant storage container to sit out in the sun, or near any other source of heat, such as a radiator.

7. Always wear goggles when working on a system to protect the eyes. If refrigerant contacts the eye, it is advisable in all cases to see a physician as soon as possible.

8. Frostbite from liquid refrigerant should be treated by first gradually warming the area with cool water, and then gently applying petroleum jelly. A physician should be consulted.

9. Always keep refrigerant can fittings capped when not in use. Avoid sudden shock to the can which might occur from dropping it, or from banging a heavy tool against it. Never carry a refrigerant can in the passenger compartment of a car.

10. Always completely discharge the system before painting the vehicle (if the paint is to be baked on), or before welding anywhere near the refrigerant lines.

TEST GAUGES

Most of the service work performed in air conditioning requires the use of a set of two

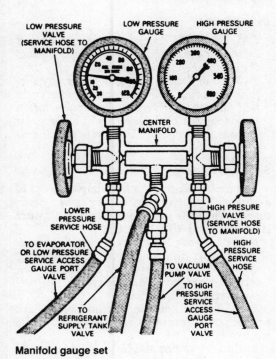

Manifold gauge set

HOSE CONNECTION

SCHRADER VALVE

VALVE CORE DEPRESSOR

TEST HOSE

COMPRESSOR

SERVICE GAGE PORT

Schrader valve

gauges, one for the high (head) pressure side of the system, the other for the low (suction) side.

The low side gauge records both pressure and vacuum. Vacuum readings are calibrated from 0 to 30 inches Hg and the pressure graduations read from 0 to no less than 60 psi.

The high side gauge measures pressure from 0 to at last 600 psi.

Both gauges are threaded into a manifold that contains two hand shut-off valves. Proper manipulation of these valves and the use of the attached test hoses allow the user to perform the following services:

1. Test high and low side pressures.

2. Remove air, moisture, and contaminated refrigerant.

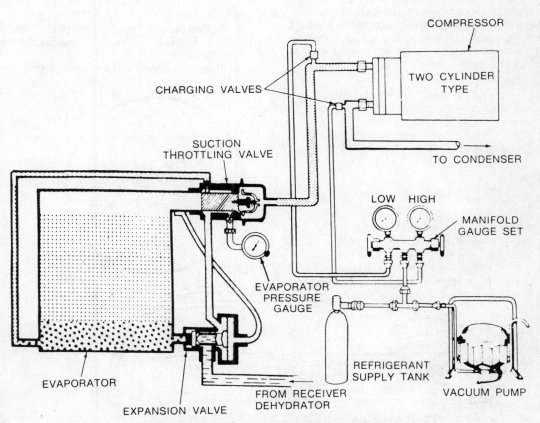

Gauge connections on the Tecumseh compressor

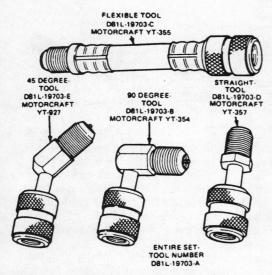

FLEXIBLE TOOL
D81L-19703-C
MOTORCRAFT YT-355

45 DEGREE·
TOOL
D81L-19703-E
MOTORCRAFT
YT-927

90 DEGREE·
TOOL
D81L-19703-B
MOTORCRAFT YT-354

STRAIGHT·
TOOL
D81L-19703-D
MOTORCRAFT
YT-357

ENTIRE SET·
TOOL NUMBER
D81L-19703-A

High pressure service valve and adapter

3. Purge the system (of refrigerant).
4. Charge the system (with refrigerant).

The manifold valves are designed so that they have no direct effect on gauge readings, but serve only to provide for, or cut off, flow of refrigerant through the manifold. During all testing and hook-up operations, the valves are kept in a close position to avoid disturbing the refrigeration system. The valves are opened only to purge the system or refrigerant or to charge it.

INSPECTION

CAUTION: *The compressed refrigerant used in the air conditioning system expands into the atmosphere at a temperature of* $-22°F$ *(* $-30°C$ *) or lower. This will freeze any surface, including your eyes, that it contacts. In addition, the refrigerant decomposes into a poisonous gas in the presence of a flame. Do not open or disconnect any part of the air conditioning system.*

Sight Glass Check

You can safely make a few simple checks to determine if your air conditioning system needs service. The tests work best if the temperature is warm (about 70°F [21.1°C]).

NOTE: *If your vehicle is equipped with an aftermarket air conditioner, the following system check may not apply. You should contact the manufacturer of the unit for instructions on systems checks.*

1. Place the automatic transmission in Park or the manual transmission in Neutral. Set the parking brake.
2. Run the engine at a fast idle (about 1,500 rpm) either with the help of a friend or by temporarily readjusting the idle speed screw.
3. Set the controls for maximum cold with the blower on High.
4. Locate the sight glass in one of the system lines. Usually it is on the left alongside the top of the radiator.
5. If you see bubbles, the system must be re-

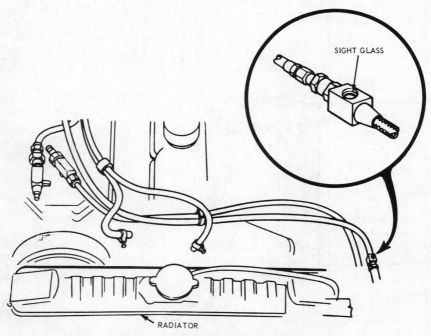

SIGHT GLASS

RADIATOR

Typical air conditioning sight glass location

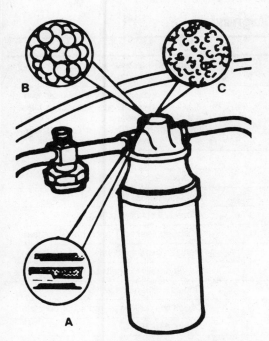

Oil streaks (A), constant bubbles (B) or foam (C) indicate there is not enough refrigerant in the system. Occasional bubbles during initial operation is normal. A clear sight glass indicates a proper charge of refrigerant or no refrigerant at all, which can be determined by the presence of cold air at the outlets in the car. If the glass is clouded with a milky white substance, have the receiver/drier checked professionally

charged. Very likely there is a leak at some point.

6. If there are no bubbles, there is either no refrigerant at all or the system is fully charged. Feel the two hoses going to the belt-driven com-

pressor. If they are both at the same temperature, the system is empty and must be recharged.

7. If one hose (high pressure) is warm and the other (low pressure) is cold, the system may be all right. However, you are probably making these tests because you think there is something wrong, so proceed to the next step.

8. Have an assistant in the car turn the fan control on and off to operate the compressor clutch. Watch the sight glass.

9. If bubbles appear when the clutch is disengaged and disappear when it is engaged, the system is properly charged.

10. If the refrigerant takes more than 45 seconds to bubble when the clutch is disengaged, the system is overcharged. This usually causes poor cooling at low speeds.

CAUTION: *If it is determined that the system has a leak, it should be corrected as soon as possible. Leaks may allow moisture to enter and cause a very expensive rust problem.*

NOTE: *Exercise the air conditioner for a few minutes, every two weeks or so, during the cold months. This avoids the possibility of the compressor seals drying out from lack of lubrication.*

TESTING THE SYSTEM

1. Connect a gauge set.
2. Close (clockwise) both gauge set valves.
4. Park the car in the shade, at least 5 feet from any walls. Start the engine, set the parking brake, place the transmission in NEUTRAL and establish an idle of 1,100-1,300 rpm.
5. Run the air conditioning system for full cooling, in the MAX or COLD mode.
6. The low pressure gauge should read 5-20

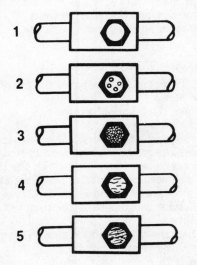

1 Clear sight glass — system correctly charged or over-charged

2 Occasional bubbles — refrigerant charge slightly low

3 Oil streaks on sight glass — total lack of refrigerant

4 Heavy stream of bubbles — serious shortage of refrigerant

5 Dark or clouded sight glass — contaminent present

Sight glass inspection

Pressure Diagnosis

Condition	Possible Cause	Correction
Low side low—High side low	System refrigerant low	Evacuate, leak test, and charge system
Low side high—High side low	Internal leak in compressor—worn	Remove compressor cylinder head and inspect compressor. Replace valve plate assembly if necessary. If compressor pistons, rings, or cylinders are excessively worn or scored, replace compressor.
	Head gasket leaking	Install new cylinder head gasket
	Expansion valve	Replace expansion valve
	Drive belt slipping	Set belt tension
Low side high—High side high	Clogged condenser fins	Clean out condenser fins
	Air in system	Evacuate, leak test, and charge system
	Expansion valve	Replace expansion valve
	Loose or worn fan belts	Adjust or replace belts as necessary
Low side low—High side high	Expansion valve	Replace expansion valve
	Restriction in liquid line	Check line for kinks—replace if necessary
	Restriction in receiver	Replace receiver
	Restriction in condenser	Replace condenser
Low side and high side normal (inadequate cooling)	Air in system	Evacuate, leak test, and charge system
	Moisture in system	Evacuate, leak test, and charge system.

psi; the high pressure gauge should indicate 120-180 psi.

WARNING: *These pressures are the norm for an ambient temperature of 70-80°F (21-27°C). Higher air temperatures along with high humidity will cause higher syustem pressures. At idle speed and an ambient temperature of 110°F (43°F), the high pressure reading can exceed 300 psi.*

Under these extreme conditions, you can keep the pressures down by directing a large electric floor fan through the condenser.

DISCHARGING THE SYSTEM

1. Remove the caps from the high and low pressure charging valves in the high and low pressure lines.

2. Turn both manifold gauge set hand valves to the fully closed (clockwise) position.

3. Connect the manifold gauge set.

4. If the gauge set hoses do not have the gauge port actuating pins, install fitting adapters T71P-19703-S and R on the manifold gauge set hoses. If the car does not have a service access gauge port valve, connect the gauge set low pressure hose to the evaporator service access gauge port valve. A special adapter, T77L-19703-A, is required to attach the manifold gauge set to the high pressure service access gauge port valve.

5. Place the end of the center hose away from you and the car.

6. Open the low pressure gauge valve slightly and allow the system pressure to bleed off.

7. Whe the system is just about empty, open the high pressure valve very slowly to avoid losing an excessive amount of refrigerant oil. Allow any remaining refrigerant to escape.

EVACUATING THE SYSTEM

NOTE: *This procedure requires the use of a vacuum pump.*

1. Connect the manifold gauge set.

2. Discharge the system.

3. On 1983 and later models, make sure that the low pressure gauge set hose is connected to the low pressure service gauge port on the top center of the accumulator/drier assembly and the high pressure hose connected to the high pressure service gauge port on the compressor discharge line.

4. Connect the center service hose to the inlet fitting of the vacuum pump.

5. Turn both gauge set valves to the wide open position.

6. Start the pump and note the low side gauge reading.

7. Operate the pump until the low pressure gauge reads 25-30 in.Hg. Continue running the vacuum pump for 10 minutes more. If you've replaced some component in the system, run the pump for an additional 20-30 minutes.

8. Leak test the system. Close both gauge set valves. Turn off the pump. The needle should remain stationary at the point at which the pump was turned off. If the needle drops to zero rapidly, there is a leak in the system which must be repaired.

LEAK TESTING

Some leak tests can be performed with a soapy water solution. There must be at least a ½ lb. charge in the system for a leak to be detected. The most extensive leak tests are performed with either a Halide flame type leak tester or the more preferable electronic leak tester.

In either case, the equipment is expensive, and, the use of a Halide detector can be **extremely** hazardous!

CHARGING THE SYSTEM

CAUTION: *NEVER OPEN THE HIGH PRESSURE SIDE WITH A CAN OF REFRIGERANT CONNECTED TO THE SYSTEM! OPENING THE HIGH PRESSURE SIDE WILL OVERPRESSURIZE THE CAN, CAUSING IT TO EXPLODE!*

1968-82

1. Connect the gauge set.
2. Close (clockwise) both gauge set valves.
3. Connect the center hose to the refrigerant can opener valve.

CAUTION: *KEEP THE CAN IN AN UPRIGHT POSITION!*

4. Make sure the can opener valve is closed, that is, the needle is raised, and connect the valve to the can. Open the valve, puncturing the can with the needle.

5. Loosen the center hose fitting at the pressure gauge, allowing refrigerant to purge the hose of air.

6. Open the low side gauge set valve and the can valve.

7. Start the engine and turn the air conditioner to the maximum cooling mode. Run the engine at about 1,500 rpm. The compressor will operate and pull refrigerant gas into the system.

NOTE: *To help speed the process, the can may be placed, upright, in a pan of warm water, not exceeding 125°F (52°C).*

8. If more than one can of refrigerant is needed, close the can valve and gauge set low

side valve when the can is empty and connect a new can to the opener. Repeat the charging process until the sight glass indicates a full charge. The frost line on the outside of the can will indicate what portion of the can has been used.

CAUTION: *NEVER ALLOW THE HIGH PRESSURE SIDE READING TO EXCEED 240 psi.*

9. When the charging process has been completed, close the gauge set valve and can valve. Run the system for at least five minutes to allow it to normalize. Low pressure side reading should be 4-25 psi; high pressure reading should be 120-210 psi at an ambient temperature of 70-90°F (21-32°C).

10. Loosen both service hoses at the gauges to allow any refrigerant to escape. Remove the gauge set and install the dust caps on the service valves.

NOTE: *Multi-can dispensers are available which allow a simultaneous hook-up of up to four 1 lb. cans of R-12.*

CAUTION: *Never exceed the recommended maximum charge for the system.*

The maximum charge for systems is:

1968-79: 4¼ lbs.
1980-81: 3½ lbs.
1982: 2½ lbs.

1983-88

1. Connect the gauge set.
2. Close (clockwise) both gauge set valves.
3. Connect the center hose to the refrigerant can opener valve.
4. Make sure the can opener valve is closed, that is, the needle is raised, and connect the valve to the can. Open the valve, puncturing the can with the needle.
5. Loosen the center hose fitting at the pressure gauge, allowing refrigerant to purge the hose of air. When the air is bled, tighten the fitting.

CAUTION: *IF THE LOW PRESSURE GAUGE SET HOSE IS NOT CONNECTED TO THE ACCUMULATOR/DRIER, KEEP THE CAN IN AN UPRIGHT POSITION!*

6. Disconnect the wire harness snap-lock connector from the clutch cycling pressure switch and install a jumper wire across the two terminals of the connector.

7. Open the low side gauge set valve and can valve.

8. Allow refrigerant to be drawn into the system.

9. When no more refrigerant is drawn into the system, start the engine and run it at about 1,500 rpm. Turn on the system and operate it at the full high position. The compressor will operate and pull refrigerant gas into the system.

NOTE: *To help speed the process, the can*

may be placed, upright, in a pan of warm water, not exceeding 125°F (52°C).

10. If more than one can of refrigerant is needed, close the can valve and gauge set low side valve when the can is empty and connect a new can to the opener. Repeat the charging process until the sight glass indicates a full charge. The frost line on the outside of the can will indicate what portion of the can has been used.

CAUTION: *NEVER ALLOW THE HIGH PRESSURE SIDE READING TO EXCEED 240 psi.*

11. When the charging process has been completed, close the gauge set valve and can valve. Remove the jumper wire and reconnect the cycling clutch wire. Run the system for at least five minutes to allow it to normalize. Low pressure side reading should be 4-25 psi; high pressure reading should be 120-210 psi at an ambient temperature of 70-90°F (21-32°C).

12. Loosen both service hoses at the gauges to allow any refrigerant to escape. Remove the gauge set and install the dust caps on the service valves.

NOTE: *Multi-can dispensers are available which allow a simultaneous hook-up of up to four 1 lb. cans of R-12.*

CAUTION: *Never exceed the recommended maximum charge for the system.*

The maximum charge for systems is 2½ lb.

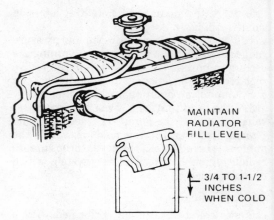

MAINTAIN RADIATOR FILL LEVEL

3/4 TO 1-1/2 INCHES WHEN COLD

Vertical flow radiator

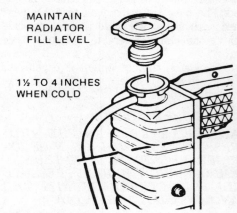

MAINTAIN RADIATOR FILL LEVEL

1½ TO 4 INCHES WHEN COLD

Crossflow radiator

Cooling System

FLUID RECOMMENDATIONS

When additional coolant is required to maintain the proper level, always add a 50/50 mixture of antifreeze/coolant and water.

LEVEL CHECK

Exercise extreme care when removing the cap from a hot radiator. Wait a few minutes until the engine has time to cool somewhat, then wrap a thick towel around the radiator cap and slowly turn it counterclockwise to the first stop. Step back and allow the pressure to release from the cooling system. Then, when the steam has stopped venting, press down on the cap, turn it one more stop counterclockwise and remove the cap.

The coolant level in the radiator should be checked on a monthly basis, preferably when the engine is cold. On a cold engine, the coolant level should be maintained at one inch below the filler neck on vertical flow radiators, and 2½" below the filler neck at the **COLD FILL** mark on crossflow radiators. On cars equipped with the Coolant Recovery System, the level is maintained at the **COLD LEVEL** mark in the translucent plastic expansion bottle. Top up as

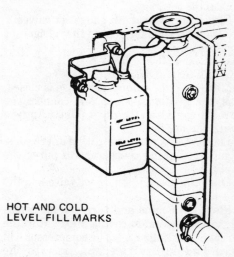

HOT AND COLD LEVEL FILL MARKS

Coolant recovery system

necessary with a mixture of 50% water and 50% ethylene glycol antifreeze, to ensure proper rust, freezing and boiling protection. If you have to add coolant more often than once a month or if you have to add more than one quart at a time, check the cooling system for leads. Also check for water in the crankcase oil, indicating a blown cylinder head gasket.

DRAIN AND REFILL

CAUTION: *When draining the coolant, keep in mind that cats and dogs are attracted by the ethylene glycol antifreeze, and are quite likely to drink any that is left in an uncovered container or in puddles on the ground. This will prove fatal in sufficient quantity. Always drain the coolant into a sealable container. Coolant should be reused unless it is contaminated or several years old.*

Completely draining and refilling the cooling system every two years at least will remove accumulated rust, scale and other deposits.

NOTE: *Use a good quality antifreeze with water pump lubricants, rust inhibitors and other corrosion inhibitors along with acid neutralizers. Use a permanent type coolant that meets specification ESE-M97B44A or the equivalent.*

1. Drain the existing antifreeze and coolant. Open the radiator and engine drain petcocks (models equipped), or disconnect the bottom radiator hose, at the radiator outlet. Set the heater temperature controls to the full HOT position.

NOTE: *Before opening the radiator petcock, spray it with some penetrating lubricant.*

2. Close the petcock or reconnect the lower hose and fill the system with water.
3. Add a can of quality radiator flush.
4. Idle the engine until the upper radiator hose gets hot.
5. Drain the system again.
6. Repeat this process until the drained water is clear and free of scale.
7. Close all petcocks and connect all the hoses.
8. If equipped with a coolant recovery system, flush the reservoir with water and leave empty.
9. Determine the capacity of your cooling system (see capacities specifications). Add a 50/50 mix of quality antifreeze (ethylene glycol) and water to provide the desired protection.

SYSTEM INSPECTION

Most permanent antifreeze/coolant have a colored dye added which makes the solution an excellent leak detector. When servicing the cooling system, check for leakage at:
- All hoses and hose connections
- Radiator seams, radiator core, and radiator draincock
- All engine block and cylinder head freeze (core) plugs, and drain plugs
- Edges of all cooling system gaskets (head gaskets, thermostat gasket)
- Transmission fluid cooler
- Heating system components, water pump
- Check the engine oil dipstick for signs of coolant in the engine oil
- Check the coolant in the radiator for signs of oil in the coolant

Investigate and correct any indication of coolant leakage.

Check the Radiator Cap

While you are checking the coolant level, check the radiator cap for a worn or cracked gasket. If the cap doesn't seal properly, fluid will be lost and the engine will overheat.

A worn cap should be replaced with a new one.

Clean Radiator of Debris

Periodically clean any debris such as leaves, paper, insects, etc., from the radiator fins. Pick the large pieces off by hand. The smaller pieces can be washed away with water pressure from a hose.

Carefully straighten any bent radiator fins with a pair of needle nose pliers. Be careful, the

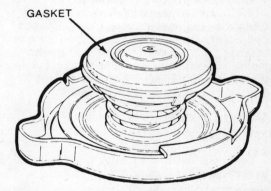

GASKET

Check the radiator cap gasket for cuts or cracks

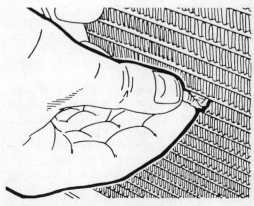

Clean the radiator fins of debris

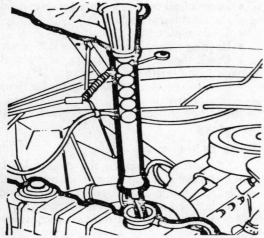

Testing coolant protection with an antifreeze tester

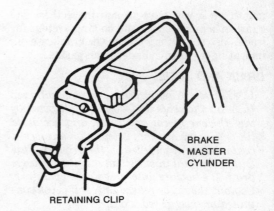

Master cylinder cover retaining clip

fins are very soft. Don't wiggle the fins back and forth too much. Straighten them once and try not to move them again.

CHECKING SYSTEM PROTECTION

A 50/50 mix of coolant concentrate and water will usually provide protection to $-35°F$ ($-37°C$). Freeze protection may be checked by using a cooling system hydrometer. Inexpensive hydrometers (floating ball types) may be obtained from a local department store (automotive section) or an auto supply store. Follow the directions packaged with the coolant hydrometer when checking protection.

Master Cylinder
LEVEL CHECK

The brake fluid in the master cylinder should be checked every 6 months/6,000 miles.

Cast Iron Reservoir

1. Park the vehicle on a level surface and open the hood.
2. Pry the retaining spring bar holding the cover onto the master cylinder to one side.
3. Clean any dirt from the sides and top of the cover before removal. Remove the master cylinder cover and gasket.
4. Add fluid, if necessary, to within 3/8" of the top of the reservoir, or to the full level indicator (on models equipped).
5. Push the gasket bellows back into the cover. Reinstall the gasket and cover and position the retainer spring bar.

Plastic Reservoir

Check the fluid level on the side of the reservoir. If fluid is required, remove the screw on

the and remove the filler cap and gasket from the master cylinder. Fill the reservoir to the full line in the reservoir. Install the filler cap, making sure the gasket is properly seated in the cap.

FLUID RECOMMENDATION

Use only Heavy Duty Brake Fluid meeting DOT3 specifications.

Power Steering
LEVEL CHECK

Check the power steering fluid level every 6 months/6,000 miles.
1. Park the vehicle on a level surface. Run the engine until normal operating temperature is reached.
2. Turn the steering all the way to the left and then all the way to the right several times. Center the steering wheel and shut off the engine.
3. Open the hood and check the power steering reservoir fluid level.

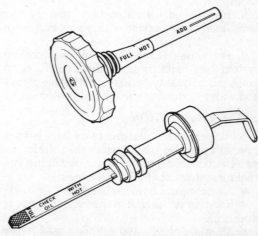

Typical power steering pump reservoir dipsticks

4. Remove the filler cap and wipe the dipstick attached clean.

5. Re-insert the dipstick and tighten the cap. Remove the dipstick and note the fluid level indicated on the dipstick.

6. The level should be at any point below the Full mark, but not below the Add mark.

7. Add fluid as necessary. Do not overfill.

FLUID RECOMMENDATION

Add power steering fluid; do not overfill the reservoir.

Steering Gear Lubricant

If there is binding in the steering gear or if the wheels do not return to a straight-ahead position after a turn, the lubricant level of the steering gear should be checked. Remove the filler plug using a $^{11}/_{16}''$ open-end wrench and remove the lower cover bolt using a $^9/_{16}''$ wrench, to expose both holes. Slowly turn the steering wheel to the left until it stops. At this point, lubricant should be rising in the lower cover bolt hole. Then slowly turn the steering wheel to the right until it stops. At this point, lubricant should be rising in the filler plug hole. If the lubricant does not rise when the wheel is turned, add a small amount of SAE 90 steering gear lubricant until it does. Replace the cover bolt and the filler plug when finished.

FLUIDS AND LUBRICANTS

Fuel Recommendations

It is important to use fuel of the proper octane rating in your car. Octane rating is based on the quantity of anti-knock compounds added to the fuel and it determines the speed at which the gas will burn. The lower the octane rating, the faster it burns. The higher the octane, the slower the fuel will burn and a greater percentage of compounds in the fuel prevent spark ping (knock), detonation and preignition (dieseling).

As the temperature of the engine increases, the air/fuel mixture exhibits a tendency to ignite before the spark plug is fired. If fuel of an octane rating too low for the engine is used, this will allow combustion to occur before the piston has completed its compression stroke, thereby creating a very high pressure very rapidly.

Fuel of the proper octane rating, for the compression ratio and ignition timing of your car, will slow the combustion process sufficiently to allow the spark plug enough time to ignite the mixture completely and smoothly. Many non-catalyst models are designed to run on regular fuel. The use of some super-premium fuel is no substitution for a properly tuned and maintained engine. Chances are that if your engine exhibits any signs of spark ping, detonation or pre-ignition when using regular fuel, the ignition timing should be checked against specifications or the cylinder head should be removed for decarbonizing.

Vehicles equipped with catalytic converters must use UNLEADED GASOLINE ONLY. Use of unleaded fuel shortened the life of spark plugs, exhaust systems and EGR valves and can damage the catalytic converter. Most converter equipped models are designed to operate using unleaded gasoline with a minimum rating of 87 octane. Use of unleaded gas with octane ratings lower than 87 can cause persistent spark knock which could lead to engine damage.

Light spark knock may be noticed when accelerating or driving up hills. The slight knocking may be considered normal (with 87 octane) because the maximum fuel economy is obtained under condition of occasional light spark knock. Gasoline with an octane rating higher than 87 may be used, but it is not necessary (in most cases) for proper operation.

If spark knock is constant, when using 87 octane, at cruising speeds on level ground, ignition timing adjustment may be required.

Engine
OIL RECOMMENDATION

When adding the oil to the crankcase or changing the oil or filter, it is important that oil of an equal quality to original be used in your car. The use of inferior oils may void your warranty. Generally speaking, oil that has been rated **SF** by the American Petroleum Institute will prove satisfactory.

Oil of the SF variety performs a multitude of functions in addition to its basic job of reducing friction of the engine's moving parts. Through a balanced formula of polymeric dispersants and metallic detergents, the oil prevents high temperature and low temperature deposits and also keeps sludge and dirt particles in suspension. Acids, particularly sulphuric acid, as well as other products of combustion of sulphur fuels, are neutralized by the oil. These acids, if permitted to concentrate, may cause corrosion and rapid wear of the internal parts of the engine.

It is important to choose an oil of the proper viscosity for climatic and operational conditions. Viscosity in an index of the oil's thickness at different temperatures. A thicker oil (higher numerical rating) is needed for high temperature operation, whereas thinner oil (lower numerical rating) is required for cold weather operation. Due to the need for an oil that embodies both these characteristics in parts of the country where there is wide temperature varia-

Oil Viscosity— Temperature Chart

When Outside Temperature Is Consistently	Use SAE Viscosity Number
SINGLE GRADE OILS	
−10°F to 32°F	10W
10°F to 60°F	20W-20
32°F to 90°F	30
Above 60°F	40
MULTIGRADE OILS	
Below 32°F	5W-30*
−10°F to 90°F	10W-30
Above −10°F	10W-40
Above 10°F	20W-40

*When sustained high-speed operation is anticipated, use the next higher grade.

tion within a small period of time, multigrade oils have been developed. Basically a multigrade oil is thinner at low temperatures and thicker at high temperatures. For example, a 10W-40 oil exhibits the characteristics of a 10 weight oil when the car is first started and the oil is cold. Its lighter weight allows it to travel to the lubricating surfaces quicker and offer less resistance to starter motor cranking then, let's say, a straight 30 weight oil. But after the engine reaches operating temperature, the 10W-40 oil begins acting like a straight 40 weight oil, its heavier weight providing greater lubricating protection and less susceptibility to foaming than a straight 30 weight oil. Whatever your driving needs, the oil viscosity/temperature chart should prove useful in selecting the proper grade. The SAE viscosity rating is printed or stamped on the top of every oil container.

OIL LEVEL CHECK

The engine oil level should be checked frequently. For instance, at each refueling stop. Be sure that the vehicle is parked on a level surface with the engine off. Also, allow a few minutes after turning off the engine for the oil to drain into the pan or an inaccurate reading will result.

1. Open the hood and remove the engine oil dipstick.
2. Wipe the dipstick with a clean, lint-free rag and reinsert it. Be sure to insert it all the way.
3. Pull out the dipstick and note the oil level. It should be between the SAFE (MAX) mark and the ADD (MIN) mark.
4. If the level is below the lower mark, replace the dipstick and add fresh oil to bring the level within the proper range. Do not overfill.
5. Recheck the oil level and close the hood.

NOTE: *Use a multi-grade oil with API classification SF.*

OIL CHANGE

NOTE: *The engine oil and oil filter should be changed at the same time, at the recommended intervals on the maintenance schedule chart.*

1. Run the engine to normal operating temperature.
2. After the engine has reached operating temperature, shut it off, firmly apply the parking brake, and block the wheels.
3. Raise and support the front end on jackstands.
4. Place a drip pan beneath the oil pan and remove the drain plug.

CAUTION: *The oil could be very hot! Protect yourself by using rubber gloves if necessary.*

5. Allow the engine to drain thoroughly.

WARNING: *On some V8 engines a dual sump oil pan was used. When changing the oil, both drain plugs (front and side) must be removed. Failure to remove both plugs can lead to an incorrect oil level reading.*

6. While the oil is draining, replace the filter as described below.
7. When the oil has completely drained, clean the threads of the plug and coat them with non-hardening sealer or Teflon® tape and install the plug. Tighten it snugly.

WARNING: *The threads in the oil pan are easily stripped! Don not overtighten the plug!*

8. Fill the crankcase with the proper amount of oil shown in the Capacities Chart in this chapter.
9. Start the engine and check for leaks.

REPLACING THE OIL FILTER

1. Place the drip pan beneath the oil filter.
2. Using an oil filter wrench, turn the filter counterclockwise to remove it.

CAUTION: *The oil could be very hot! Protect yourself by using rubber gloves if necessary.*

3. Wipe the contact surface of the new filter clean and coat the rubber gasket with clean engine oil.

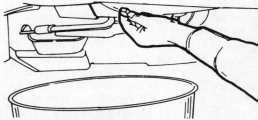

By keeping inward pressure on the plug as you unscrew it, oil won't escape past the threads

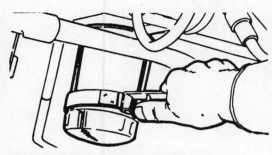

Remove the oil filter with a strap wrench

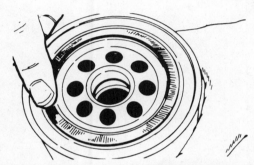

Lubricate the gasket on the new filter with clean engine oil. A dry gasket may not make a good seal and will allow the filter to leak

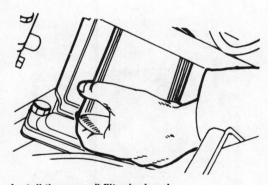

Install the new oil filter by hand

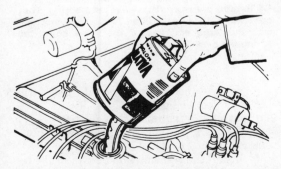

Add oil through the capped opening in the cylinder head cover

4. Clean the mating surface of the adapter on the block.

5. Screw the new filter into position on the block using hand pressure only. Do not use a strap wrench to install the filter! Then hand-turn the filter ½-¾ additional turn.

Transmission

FLUID RECOMMENDATIONS

Manual Transmissions:
All units use SAE 85W/90

Automatic Transmissions:
- 1968-79 C4 — Type F
- 1980-81 C4 — Dexron®II
- 1968-78 C6 — Dexron®II
- 1968-80 FMX — Type F
- 1974-75 CW — Type F
- 1980-88 AOD — Dexron®II

LEVEL CHECK

Automatic Transmissions

It is very important to maintain the proper fluid level in an automatic transmission. If the level is either too high or too low, poor shifting operation and internal damage are likely to occur. For this reason a regular check of the fluid level is essential.

1. Drive the vehicle for 15-20 minutes to allow the transmission to reach operating temperature.

2. Park the car on a level surface, apply the parking brake and leave the engine idling. Shift the transmission and engage each gear, then place the gear selector in P (PARK).

3. Wipe away any dirt in the areas of the transmission dipstick to prevent it from falling into the filler tube. Withdraw the dipstick, wipe it with a clean, lint-free rag and reinsert it until it seats.

4. Withdraw the dipstick and note the fluid level. It should be between the upper (FULL) mark and the lower (ADD) mark.

5. If the level is below the lower mark, use a funnel and add fluid in small quantities through the dipstick filler neck. Keep the en-

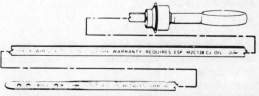

Typical automatic transmission dipstick

C-6 automatic transmission dipstick (note the special fluid designation)

FILL AND FLUID SPECIFICATIONS (DIPSTICK INFORMATION)

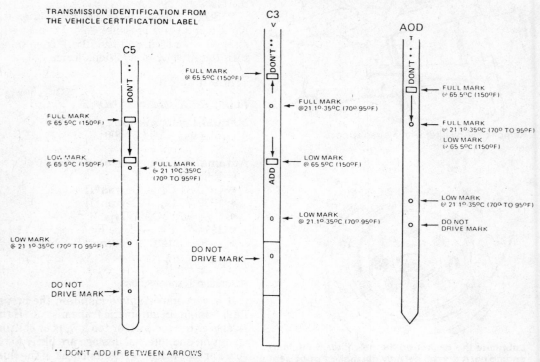

** DON'T ADD IF BETWEEN ARROWS

Automatic transmission dipstick markings for late models

gine running while adding fluid and check the level after each small amount. Do not overfill.

Manual Transmission

The fluid level should be checked every 6 months/6,000 miles, whichever comes first.

1. Park the car on a level surface, turn off the engine, apply the parking brake and block the wheels.

2. Remove the filler plug from the side of the transmission case with a proper size wrench. The fluid level should be even with the bottom of the filler hole.

3. If additional fluid is necessary, add it through the filler hole using a siphon pump or squeeze bottle.

4. Replace the filler plug; do not overtighten.

DRAIN AND REFILL

Automatic Transmission

C4

1. Raise the vehicle, so that the transmission oil pan is readily accessible. Safely support on jackstands.

2. Disconnect the fluid filler tube from the pan and allow the fluid to drain into an appropriate container.

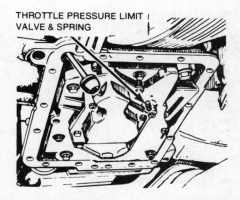

C4 throttle pressure limit valve and spring. They are held in place by the filter. The valve is installed with the large end toward the valve body; the spring fits over the valve stem

3. Remove the transmission oil pan attaching bolts, pan and gasket.

To install the transmission oil pan:

4. Clean the transmission oil pan and transmission mating surfaces.

5. Install the transmission oil pan in the reverse order of removal, torquing the attaching bolts to 10-16 ft. lbs. and using a new gasket.

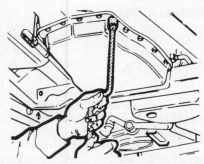

Many late model vehicles have no drain plug. Loosen the pan bolts and allow one corner of the pan to hang, so that the fluid will drain out

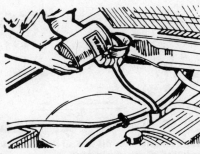

Fill the transmission with the required amount of fluid. Do not overfill. Start the engine and run the selector through all the shift points. Check the fluid and add as necessary

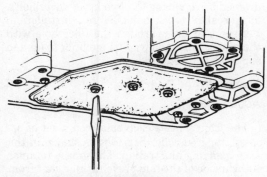

Removing automatic transmission filter

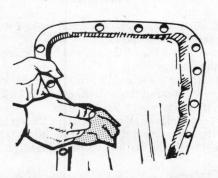

Clean the pan thoroughly with a safe solvent and allow it to air dry

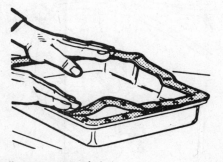

Install a new pan gasket

Fill the transmission with 3 qts. of the correct type fluid.

6. Lower the vehicle. Start the engine and move the gear selector through shift pattern. Allow the engine to reach normal operating temperature.

7. Check the transmission fluid. Add fluid, if necessary, to maintain correct level.

C6, FMX, AOD

1. Raise the car and support on jackstands.
2. Place a drain pan under the transmission.
3. Loosen the pan attaching bolts and drain the fluid from the transmission.
4. When the fluid has drained to the level of the pan flange, remove the remaining pan bolts working from the rear and both sides of the pan to allow it to drop and drain slowly.
5. When all of the fluid has drained, remove the pan and clean it thoroughly. Discard the pan gasket.
6. Place a new gasket on the pan, and install the pan on the transmission. Tighten the attaching bolts to 12-16 ft. lbs.
7. Add three 3 quarts of fluid to the transmission through the filler tube.
8. Lower the vehicle. Start the engine and move the gear selector through shift pattern. Allow the engine to reach normal operating temperature.
9. Check the transmission fluid. Add fluid, if necessary, to maintain correct level.

Manual Transmission

1. Place a suitable drain pan under the transmission.
2. Remove the drain plug and allow the gear lube to drain out.
3. Replace the drain plug, remove the filler plug and fill the transmission to the proper level with the required fluid.
4. Reinstall the filler plug.

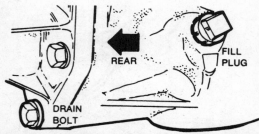

Manual transmission fill and drain plugs, using a tailshaft bolt as the drain plug

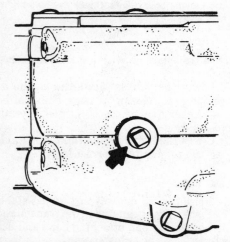

Manual transmission fill and drain plugs with the drain plug at the bottom center

Rear Axle (Differential)
FLUID LEVEL CHECK

Like the manual transmission, the rear axle fluid should be checked every six months/6,000 miles. A filler plug is provided near the center of the rear cover or on the upper (driveshaft) side of the gear case. Remove the plug and check to ensure that the fluid level is even with the bottom of the filler hole. Add SAE 85W/90/95 gear lube as required. If the vehicle is equipped with a limited slip rear axle, add the required special fluid. Install the filler plug but do not overtighten.

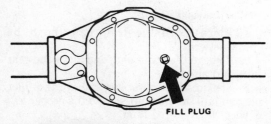

Dana/Spicer axle fill plug location

DRAIN AND REFILL

Normal maintenance does not require changing the rear axle fluid. However, to do so, remove the rear drain plug (models equipped), the lower two cover bolts, or the cover. Catch the drained fluid in a suitable container. If the rear cover was removed, clean the mounting surfaces of the cover and rear housing. Install a new gasket (early models) or (on late models) apply a continuous bead of Silicone Rubber Sealant (D6AZ-19562-A/B or the equivalent) around the rear housing face inside the circle of bolt holes. Install the cover and tighten the bolts. Parts must be assembled within a half hour after the sealant is applied. If the fluid was drained by removing the two lower cover bolts, apply sealant to the bolts before reinstallation. Fill the rear axle through the filler hole with the proper lube. Add friction modifier to limited slip models if required.

Front Wheel Bearings
ADJUSTMENT

The front wheels each rotate on a set of opposed, tapered roller bearings as shown in the accompanying illustration. The grease retainer at the inside of the hub prevents lubricant from leaking into the brake drum.

1. Raise and support the front end on jackstands.
2. Remove the grease cap and remove excess grease from the end of the spindle.
3. Remove the cotter pin and nut lock shown in the illustration.
4. Rotate the wheel, hub and drum assembly while tightening the adjusting nut to 17-25 ft. lbs. in order to seat the bearings.
5. Back off the adjusting nut ½, then retighten the adjusting nut to 10-15 in. lbs.
6. Locate the nut lock on the adjusting nut so

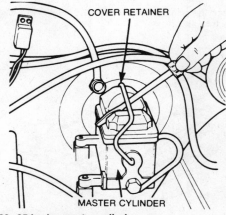

1969–85 brake master cylinder

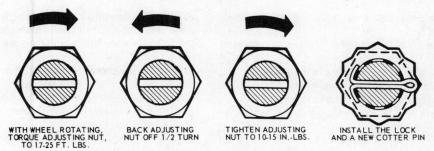

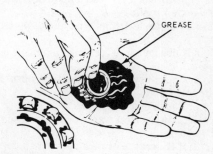

WITH WHEEL ROTATING, TORQUE ADJUSTING NUT, TO 17-25 FT. LBS.

BACK ADJUSTING NUT OFF 1/2 TURN

TIGHTEN ADJUSTING NUT TO 10-15 IN.-LBS.

INSTALL THE LOCK AND A NEW COTTER PIN

Front wheel bearing adjusting sequence

that the castellations on the lock are lined up with the cotter pin hole in the spindle.

7. Install the new cotter pin, bending the ends of the cotter pin around the castellated flange of the nut lock.

8. Check the wheel for proper rotation, then install the grease cap. If the wheel still does not rotate properly, inspect and clean or replace the wheel bearings and cups.

REMOVAL, REPACKING, AND INSTALLATION

Before handling the bearings, there are a few things that you should remember to do and not to do.

Remember to DO the following:

• Remove all outside dirt from the housing before exposing the bearing.

• Treat a used bearing as gently as you would a new one.

Packing bearings

• Work with clean tools in clean surroundings.

• Use clean, dry canvas gloves, or at least clean, dry hands.

• Clean solvents and flushing fluids are a must.

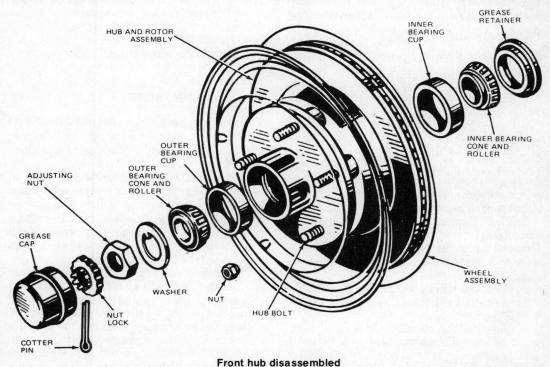

HUB AND ROTOR ASSEMBLY

INNER BEARING CUP

GREASE RETAINER

INNER BEARING CONE AND ROLLER

OUTER BEARING CUP

OUTER BEARING CONE AND ROLLER

ADJUSTING NUT

GREASE CAP

WASHER

NUT

NUT LOCK

HUB BOLT

COTTER PIN

WHEEL ASSEMBLY

Front hub disassembled

• Use clean paper when laying out the bearings to dry.

• Protect disassembled bearings from rust and dirt. Cover them up.

• Use clean rags to wipe bearings.

• Keep the bearings in oil-proof paper when they are to be stored or are not in use.

• Clean the inside of the housing before replacing the bearing.

Do NOT do the following:

• Don't work in dirty surroundings.

• Don't use dirty, chipped or damaged tools.

• Try not to work on wooden work benches or use wooden mallets.

• Don't handle bearings with dirty or moist hands.

• Do not use gasoline for cleaning; use a safe solvent.

• Do not spin-dry bearings with compressed air. They will be damaged.

• Do not spin dirty bearings.

• Avoid using cotton waste or dirty cloths to wipe bearings.

• Try not to scratch or nick bearing surfaces.

• Do not allow the bearing to come in contact with dirt or rust at any time.

1. Raise and support the front end on jackstands.

2. Remove the wheel cover. Remove the wheel.

3. Remove the caliper from the disc and wire it to the underbody to prevent damage to the brake hose. For floating caliper brakes, follow Steps 3, 4, 5, and 6 under Caliper Assembly Service.

4. Remove the grease cap from the hub. Then, remove the cotter pin, nut lock, adjusting nut and flat washer from the spindle. Remove the outer bearing assembly from the hub.

5. Pull the hub and disc assembly off the wheel spindle.

6. Remove and discard the old grease retainer. Remove the inner bearing cone and roller assembly from the hub.

7. Clean all grease from the inner and outer bearing cups with solvent. Inspect the cups for pits, scratches, or excessive wear. If the cups are damaged, remove them with a drift.

8. Clean the inner and outer cone and roller assemblies with solvent and shake them dry. If the cone and roller assemblies show excessive wear or damage, replace them with the bearing cups as a unit.

9. Clean the spindle and the inside of the hub with solvent to thoroughly remove all old grease.

10. Covering the spindle with a clean cloth, brush all loose dirt and dust from the brake assembly. Remove the cloth carefully so as to not get dirt on the spindle.

11. If the inner and/or outer bearing cups were removed, install the replacement cups on the hub. Be sure that the cups seat properly in the hub.

12. It is imperative that all old grease be removed from the bearings and surrounding surfaces before repacking. The new lithium-based grease is not compatible with the sodium base grease used in the past.

13. Install the hub and disc on the wheel spindle. To prevent damage to the grease retainer and spindle threads, keep the hub centered on the spindle.

14. Install the outer bearing cone and roller assembly and the flat washer on the spindle. Install the adjusting nut.

15. Adjust the wheel bearings by torquing the adjusting nut to 17-25 ft. lbs. with the wheel rotating to seat the bearing. Then back off the adjusting nut ½ turn. Retighten the adjusting nut to 10-15 in. lbs. Install the locknut so that the castellations are aligned with the cotter pin hole. Install the cotter pin. Bend the ends of the cotter pin around the castellations of the locknut to prevent interference with the radio static collector in the grease cap. Install the grease cap.

WARNING: *New bolts must be used when servicing floating caliper units. The upper bolt must be tightened first. For floating caliper units, follow Steps 19, 20, and 21 under Caliper Assembly Service in Chapter 8. For sliding caliper units, follow Steps 12-19 under Shoe and Lining Replacement in Chapter 9.*

16. Install the wheels.

17. Install the wheel cover.

Tires

INFLATION PRESSURE

Tire inflation is the most ignored item of auto maintenance. Gasoline mileage can drop as much as .8% for every 1 pound per square inch (psi) of under inflation.

Two items should be a permanent fixture in every glove compartment; a tire pressure gauge and a tread depth gauge. Check the tire air pressure (including the spare) regularly with a pocket type gauge. Kicking the tires won't tell you a thing, and the gauge on the service station air hose is notoriously inaccurate.

The tire pressures recommended for your car are usually found on the left floor or in the owner's manual. Ideally, inflation pressure should be checked when the tires are cool. When the air becomes heated it expands and the pressure increases. Every 10 degree rise (or drop) in temperature means a difference in 1 psi, which also explains why the tire appears to lose air on a very cold night. when it is impossible to check the tires cold, allow for pressure build-up due to heat. If the hot pressure exceeds the cold pressure by more than 15 psi, reduce your speed, load or both. Otherwise internal heat is created in the tire. When the heat approaches the temperature at which the tire was cured, during manufacture, the tread can separate from the body.

CAUTION: *Never counteract excessive pressure build-up by bleeding off air pressure (let-ting some air out). This will only further raise the tire operating temperature.*

Before starting a long trip with lots of luggage, you can add about 2-4 psi to the tires to make them run cooler, but never exceed the maximum inflation pressure on the side of the tire.

TREAD DEPTH

All tires made since 1968, have 8 built-in tread wear indicator bars that show up as ½″

Troubleshooting Basic Wheel Problems

Problem	Cause	Solution
The car's front end vibrates at high speed	• The wheels are out of balance • Wheels are out of alignment	• Have wheels balanced • Have wheel alignment checked/adjusted
Car pulls to either side	• Wheels are out of alignment • Unequal tire pressure • Different size tires or wheels	• Have wheel alignment checked/adjusted • Check/adjust tire pressure • Change tires or wheels to same size
The car's wheel(s) wobbles	• Loose wheel lug nuts • Wheels out of balance • Damaged wheel • Wheels are out of alignment • Worn or damaged ball joint • Excessive play in the steering linkage (usually due to worn parts) • Defective shock absorber	• Tighten wheel lug nuts • Have tires balanced • Raise car and spin the wheel. If the wheel is bent, it should be replaced • Have wheel alignment checked/adjusted • Check ball joints • Check steering linkage • Check shock absorbers
Tires wear unevenly or prematurely	• Incorrect wheel size • Wheels are out of balance • Wheels are out of alignment	• Check if wheel and tire size are compatible • Have wheels balanced • Have wheel alignment checked/adjusted

Troubleshooting Basic Tire Problems

Problem	Cause	Solution
The car's front end vibrates at high speeds and the steering wheel shakes	• Wheels out of balance • Front end needs aligning	• Have wheels balanced • Have front end alignment checked
The car pulls to one side while cruising	• Unequal tire pressure (car will usually pull to the low side) • Mismatched tires • Front end needs aligning	• Check/adjust tire pressure • Be sure tires are of the same type and size • Have front end alignment checked
Abnormal, excessive or uneven tire wear See "How to Read Tire Wear"	• Infrequent tire rotation • Improper tire pressure • Sudden stops/starts or high speed on curves	• Rotate tires more frequently to equalize wear • Check/adjust pressure • Correct driving habits
Tire squeals	• Improper tire pressure • Front end needs aligning	• Check/adjust tire pressure • Have front end alignment checked

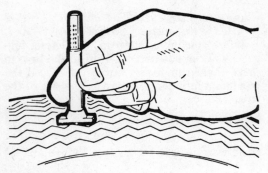

Tire tread depth gauge

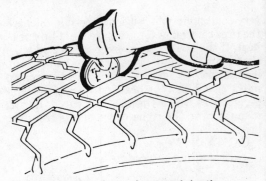

A penny used to determine tread depth

wide smooth bands across the tire when $\frac{1}{16}''$ of tread remains. The appearance of tread wear indicators means that the tires should be replaced. In fact, many states have laws prohibiting the use of tires with less than $\frac{1}{16}''$ tread.

You can check your own tread depth with inexpensive gauge or by using a Lincoln head penny. Slip the Lincoln penny into several tread grooves. If you can see the top of Lincoln's head in 2 adjacent grooves, the tires have less than

Tire Size Comparison Chart

"Letter" sizes			Inch Sizes	Metric-inch Sizes		
"60 Series"	"70 Series"	"78 Series"	1965–77	"60 Series"	"70 Series"	"80 Series"
			5.50-12, 5.60-12	165/60-12	165/70-12	155-12
		Y78-12	6.00-12			
		W78-13	5.20-13	165/60-13	145/70-13	135-13
		Y78-13	5.60-13	175/60-13	155/70-13	145-13
			6.15-13	185/60-13	165/70-13	155-13, P155/80-13
A60-13	A70-13	A78-13	6.40-13	195/60-13	175/70-13	165-13
B60-13	B70-13	B78-13	6.70-13	205/60-13	185/70-13	175-13
			6.90-13			
C60-13	C70-13	C78-13	7.00-13	215/60-13	195/70-13	185-13
D60-13	D70-13	D78-13	7.25-13			
E60-13	E70-13	E78-13	7.75-13			195-13
			5.20-14	165/60-14	145/70-14	135-14
			5.60-14	175/60-14	155/70-14	145-14
			5.90-14			
A60-14	A70-14	A78-14	6.15-14	185/60-14	165/70-14	155-14
	B70-14	B78-14	6.45-14	195/60-14	175/70-14	165-14
	C70-14	C78-14	6.95-14	205/60-14	185/70-14	175-14
D60-14	D70-14	D78-14				
E60-14	E70-14	E78-14	7.35-14	215/60-14	195/70-14	185-14
F60-14	F70-14	F78-14, F83-14	7.75-14	225/60-14	200/70-14	195-14
G60-14	G70-14	G77-14, G78-14	8.25-14	235/60-14	205/70-14	205-14
H60-14	H70-14	H78-14	8.55-14	245/60-14	215/70-14	215-14
J60-14	J70-14	J78-14	8.85-14	255/60-14	225/70-14	225-14
L60-14	L70-14		9.15-14	265/60-14	235/70-14	
	A70-15	A78-15	5.60-15	185/60-15	165/70-15	155-15
B60-15	B70-15	B78-15	6.35-15	195/60-15	175/70-15	165-15
C60-15	C70-15	C78-15	6.85-15	205/60-15	185/70-15	175-15
	D70-15	D78-15				
E60-15	E70-15	E78-15	7.35-15	215/60-15	195/70-15	185-15
F60-15	F70-15	F78-15	7.75-15	225/60-15	205/70-15	195-15
G60-15	G70-15	G78-15	8.15-15/8.25-15	235/60-15	215/70-15	205-15
H60-15	H70-15	H78-15	8.45-15/8.55-15	245/60-15	225/70-15	215-15
J60-15	J70-15	J78-15	8.85-15/8.90-15	255/60-15	235/70-15	225-15
	K70-15		9.00-15	265/60-15	245/70-15	230-15
L60-15	L70-15	L78-15, L84-15	9.15-15			235-15
	M70-15	M78-15				255-15
		N78-15				

Note: Every size tire is not listed and many size comparisons are approximate, based on load ratings. Wider tires than those supplied new with the vehicle, should always be checked for clearance.

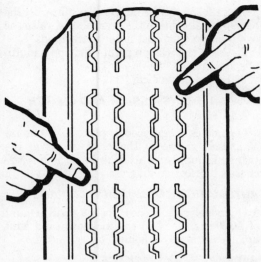

Replace a tire that shows the built-in "bump strip"

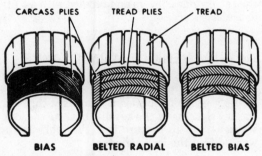

CARCASS PLIES   TREAD PLIES   TREAD

BIAS   BELTED RADIAL   BELTED BIAS

Types of tire construction

$\frac{1}{16}$" tread left and should be replaced. You can measure snow tires in the same manner by using the tails side of the Lincoln penny. If you can see the top of the Lincoln memorial, it's time to replace the snow tires.

TIRE ROTATION

Tire rotation is recommended every 6000 miles or so, to obtain maximum tire wear. The pattern you use depends on whether or not your car has a usable spare. Radial tires should not be cross-switched (from one side of the car to the other); they last longer if their direction of rotation is not changed. Snow tires sometimes have directional arrows molded into the side of the carcass; the arrow shows the direction of rotation. They will wear very rapidly if the rotation is reversed. Studded tires will lose their studs if their rotational direction is reversed.

NOTE: *Mark the wheel position or direction of rotation on radial tires or studded snow tires before removing them.*

CAUTION: *Never use a space-saver spare for tire rotation or as a regular tire.*

STORAGE

Store the tires at the proper inflation pressure if they are mounted on wheels. Keep them in a cool dry place, laid on their sides. If the tires are stored in the garage or basement, do not let them stand on a concrete floor; set them on stripe of wood.

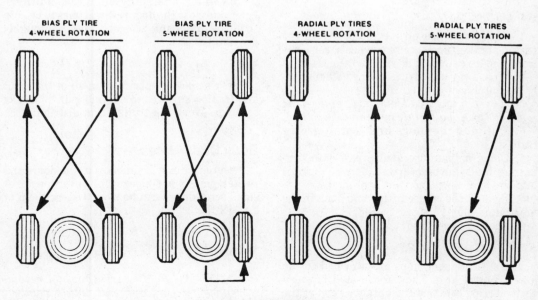

| BIAS PLY TIRE 4-WHEEL ROTATION | BIAS PLY TIRE 5-WHEEL ROTATION | RADIAL PLY TIRES 4-WHEEL ROTATION | RADIAL PLY TIRES 5-WHEEL ROTATION |

Tire rotation patterns

BUYING NEW TIRES

When buying new tires, give some thought to the following points, especially is you are considering a switch to larger tires or a different profile series:

1. All four tires must be of the same construction type. This rule cannot be violated. Radial, bias, and bias-belted tires must not be mixed.

2. The wheels should be the correct width for the tire. Tire dealers have charts of tire and rim compatibility. A mismatch will cause sloppy handling and rapid tire wear. the tread width should match the rim width (inside bead to inside bead) within an inch. For radial tires, the rim width should be 80% or less of the tire (not tread) width.

3. The height (mounted diameter) of the new tires can change speedometer accuracy, engine speed at a given road speed, duel mileage, acceleration, and ground clearance. Tire manufacturers furnish full measurement specifications.

4. The spare tire should be usable, at least for short distance and low speed operation, with the new tires.

5. There shouldn't be any body interference when loaded, on bumps, or in turns.

Chassis Greasing

NOTE: *Depending on the year and model, vehicles may have plugs or grease fittings in all steering/suspension linkage or pivot points. Follow the instructions under Ball Joints if equipped with these plugs. Newer models have sealed points and lubrication is not necessary.*

BALL JOINTS

1. Park the vehicle on a level surface, set the parking brake, block the rear wheels, raise the front end and support it with jackstands.

2. Wipe away any dirt from the ball joint lubrication plugs.

NOTE: *The upper ball joint has a plug on the top; the lower ball joint has one on the bottom.*

3. Pull out the plugs and install grease fittings.

4. Using a hand-operated grease gun containing multi-purpose grease, force lubricant into the joint until the joint boot swells.

5. Remove the grease fitting and push in the lubrication plug.

6. Lower the vehicle.

STEERING ARM STOPS

The steering arm stops are attached to the lower control arm. They are located between each steering arm and the upturned end of the front suspension strut.

1. Park the vehicle on a level surface, set the parking brake, block the rear wheels, raise the front end and support it with jackstands.

2. Clean the friction points and apply multi-purpose grease.

3. Lower the vehicle.

MANUAL TRANSMISSION AND CLUTCH LINKAGE

On models so equipped, apply a small amount of chassis grease to the pivot points of the transmission and clutch linkage as per the chassis lubrication diagram.

AUTOMATIC TRANSMISSION LINKAGE

On models so equipped, apply a small amount of 10W engine oil to the kickdown and shift linkage at the pivot points.

PARKING BRAKE LINKAGE

At yearly intervals or whenever binding is noticeable in the parking brake linkage, lubricate the cable guides, levers and linkage with a suitable chassis grease.

OUTSIDE VEHICLE MAINTENANCE

Lock Cylinders

Apply graphite lubricant sparingly through the key slot. Insert the key and operate the lock several times to be sure that the lubricant is worked into the lock cylinder.

Door Hinges and Hinge Checks

Spray a silicone lubricant on the hinge pivot points to eliminate any binding conditions. Open and close the door several times to be sure that the lubricant is evenly and thoroughly distributed.

Trunk Lid

Spray a silicone lubricant on all of the pivot and friction surfaces to eliminate any squeaks or binds. Work the trunk lid to distribute the lubricant

Body Drain Holes

Be sure that the drain holes in the doors and rocker panels are cleared of obstruction. A small screwdriver can be used to clear them of any debris.

PUSHING AND TOWING

WARNING: *Push-starting is not recommended for cars equipped with a catalytic converter. Raw gas collecting in the converter may cause damage. Jump starting is recommended.*

To push-start your manual transmission equipped car (automatic transmission models cannot be push started), make sure of bumper alignment. If the bumper of the car pushing does not match with your car's bumper, it would be wise to tie an old tire either on the back of your car, or on the front of the pushing car. Switch the ignition to **ON** and depress the clutch pedal. Shift the transmission to third gear and hold the accelerator pedal about halfway down. signal the push car to proceed, when the car speed reaches about 10 mph, gradually

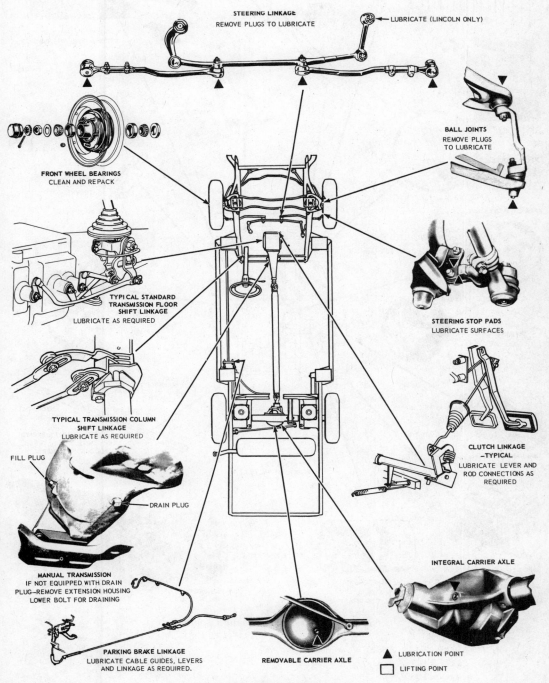

STEERING LINKAGE
REMOVE PLUGS TO LUBRICATE

← LUBRICATE (LINCOLN ONLY)

BALL JOINTS
REMOVE PLUGS
TO LUBRICATE

FRONT WHEEL BEARINGS
CLEAN AND REPACK

TYPICAL STANDARD
TRANSMISSION FLOOR
SHIFT LINKAGE
LUBRICATE AS REQUIRED

STEERING STOP PADS
LUBRICATE SURFACES

TYPICAL TRANSMISSION COLUMN
SHIFT LINKAGE
LUBRICATE AS REQUIRED

CLUTCH LINKAGE
–TYPICAL
LUBRICATE LEVER AND
ROD CONNECTIONS AS
REQUIRED

FILL PLUG

DRAIN PLUG

MANUAL TRANSMISSION
IF NOT EQUIPPED WITH DRAIN
PLUG–REMOVE EXTENSION HOUSING
LOWER BOLT FOR DRAINING

INTEGRAL CARRIER AXLE

PARKING BRAKE LINKAGE
LUBRICATE CABLE GUIDES, LEVERS
AND LINKAGE AS REQUIRED.

REMOVABLE CARRIER AXLE

▲ LUBRICATION POINT
▢ LIFTING POINT

Chassis lubrication points

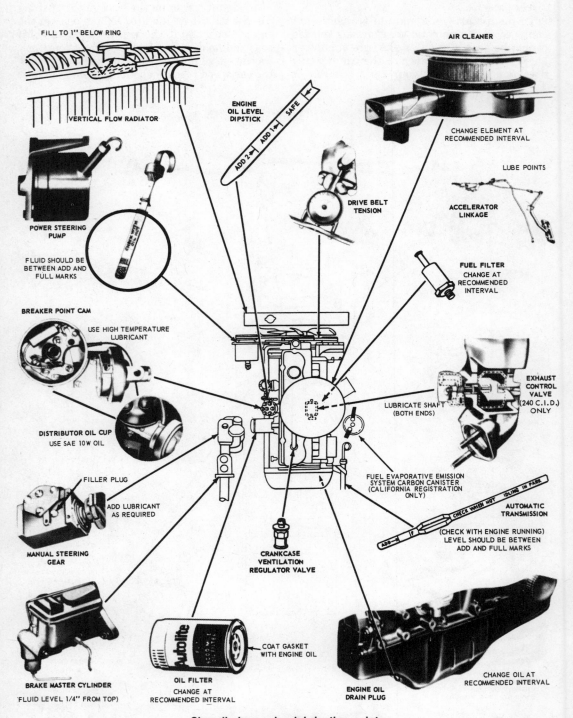

FILL TO 1" BELOW RING

VERTICAL FLOW RADIATOR

ENGINE OIL LEVEL DIPSTICK

ADD 2 — ADD 1 — SAFE

AIR CLEANER

CHANGE ELEMENT AT RECOMMENDED INTERVAL

LUBE POINTS

POWER STEERING PUMP

FLUID SHOULD BE BETWEEN ADD AND FULL MARKS

DRIVE BELT TENSION

ACCELERATOR LINKAGE

FUEL FILTER
CHANGE AT RECOMMENDED INTERVAL

BREAKER POINT CAM

USE HIGH TEMPERATURE LUBRICANT

EXHAUST CONTROL VALVE (240 C.I.D.) ONLY

DISTRIBUTOR OIL CUP
USE SAE 10W OIL

LUBRICATE SHAFT (BOTH ENDS)

FILLER PLUG

ADD LUBRICANT AS REQUIRED

FUEL EVAPORATIVE EMISSION SYSTEM CARBON CANISTER (CALIFORNIA REGISTRATION ONLY)

AUTOMATIC TRANSMISSION

CHECK WHEN HOT IDLING IN PARK

ADD — F

(CHECK WITH ENGINE RUNNING) LEVEL SHOULD BE BETWEEN ADD AND FULL MARKS

MANUAL STEERING GEAR

CRANKCASE VENTILATION REGULATOR VALVE

BRAKE MASTER CYLINDER
(FLUID LEVEL 1/4" FROM TOP)

OIL FILTER
CHANGE AT RECOMMENDED INTERVAL

COAT GASKET WITH ENGINE OIL

ENGINE OIL DRAIN PLUG

CHANGE OIL AT RECOMMENDED INTERVAL

Six-cylinder engine lubrication points

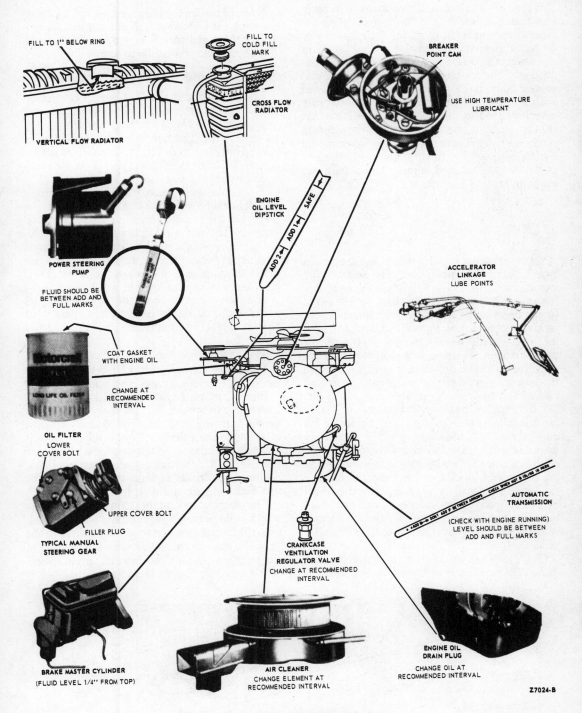

FILL TO 1" BELOW RING

VERTICAL FLOW RADIATOR

FILL TO COLD FILL MARK

CROSS FLOW RADIATOR

BREAKER POINT CAM

USE HIGH TEMPERATURE LUBRICANT

POWER STEERING PUMP

FLUID SHOULD BE BETWEEN ADD AND FULL MARKS

ENGINE OIL LEVEL DIPSTICK

SAFE
ADD 1
ADD 2

ACCELERATOR LINKAGE LUBE POINTS

COAT GASKET WITH ENGINE OIL

CHANGE AT RECOMMENDED INTERVAL

OIL FILTER

LOWER COVER BOLT

UPPER COVER BOLT

FILLER PLUG

TYPICAL MANUAL STEERING GEAR

CRANKCASE VENTILATION REGULATOR VALVE
CHANGE AT RECOMMENDED INTERVAL

AUTOMATIC TRANSMISSION

(CHECK WITH ENGINE RUNNING) LEVEL SHOULD BE BETWEEN ADD AND FULL MARKS

BRAKE MASTER CYLINDER
(FLUID LEVEL 1/4" FROM TOP)

AIR CLEANER
CHANGE ELEMENT AT RECOMMENDED INTERVAL

ENGINE OIL DRAIN PLUG
CHANGE OIL AT RECOMMENDED INTERVAL

Z7024-B

V8 engine lubrication points

release the clutch pedal. The car engine should start, if not have the car towed.

If the transmission and rear axle are in proper working order, the car can be towed with the rear wheels on the ground for distances under 15 miles at speeds no greater then 30 mph. If the transmission or rear is known to be damaged or if the car has to be towed over 15 miles or over 30 mph the car must be dollied or towed with the rear wheels raised and the steering wheel secured so that the front wheels remain in the straight-ahead position. The steering wheel must be clamped with a special clamping device designed for towing service. If the key controlled lock is used damage to the lock and steering column may occur.

JACKING

Your car is equipped with either a scissors type jack, or a bumper jack. The scissor-type jack is placed under the side of the car so that it fits into the notch in the vertical rocker panel flange nearest the wheel to be changed. These jacking notches are located approximately 8 inches from the wheel opening on the rocker panel flanges. Bumper jack slots or flats are provided on the front and rear bumper. Be sure the jack is inserted firmly and is straight before raising the vehicle.

When raising the car with a scissors or bumper jack follow these precautions: Park the car on level spot, put the selector in P (PARK) with an automatic transmission or in reverse if your car has a manual transmission, apply the parking brake and block the front and the back of the wheel that is diagonally opposite the wheel being changed. These jacks are fine for changing a tire, but never crawl under the car when it is supported only by the scissors or bumper jack.

CAUTION: *If you're going to work beneath the vehicle, always support it on jackstands.*

TRAILER TOWING

Factory trailer towing packages are available on most cars. However, if you are installing a trailer hitch and wiring on your car, there are a few thing that you ought to know.

Trailer Weight

Trailer weight is the first, and most important, factor in determining whether or not your vehicle is suitable for towing the trailer you have in mind. The horsepower-to-weight ratio should be calculated. The basic standard is a ratio of 35:1. That is, 35 pounds of GVW for every horsepower.

To calculate this ratio, multiply you engine's rated horsepower by 35, then subtract the weight of the vehicle, including passengers and luggage. The resulting figure is the ideal maximum trailer weight that you can tow. One point to consider: a numerically higher axle ratio can offset what appears to be a low trailer weight. If the weight of the trailer that you have in mind is somewhat higher than the weight you just calculated, you might consider changing your rear axle ratio to compensate.

Hitch Weight

There are three kinds of hitches: bumper mounted, frame mounted, and load equalizing.

Bumper mounted hitches are those which attach solely to the vehicle's bumper. Many states prohibit towing with this type of hitch, when it attaches to the vehicle's stock bumper, since it subjects the bumper to stresses for which it was not designed. Aftermarket rear step bumpers, designed for trailer towing, are acceptable for use with bumper mounted hitches.

Frame mounted hitches can be of the type which bolts to two or more points on the frame, plus the bumper, or just to several points on the frame. Frame mounted hitches can also be of the tongue type, for Class I towing, or, of the receiver type, for classes II and III.

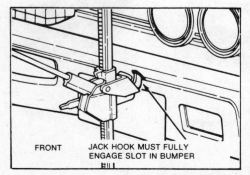

FRONT   JACK HOOK MUST FULLY ENGAGE SLOT IN BUMPER

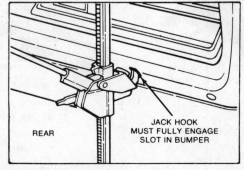

REAR   JACK HOOK MUST FULLY ENGAGE SLOT IN BUMPER

Bumper jack installation—1971–77 models

JUMP STARTING A DEAD BATTERY

The chemical reaction in a battery produces explosive hydrogen gas. This is the safe way to jump start a dead battery, reducing the chances of an accidental spark that could cause an explosion.

Jump Starting Precautions

1. Be sure both batteries are of the same voltage.
2. Be sure both batteries are of the same polarity (have the same grounded terminal).
3. Be sure the vehicles are not touching.
4. Be sure the vent cap holes are not obstructed.
5. Do not smoke or allow sparks around the battery.
6. In cold weather, check for frozen electrolyte in the battery. Do not jump start a frozen battery.
7. Do not allow electrolyte on your skin or clothing.
8. Be sure the electrolyte is not frozen.
CAUTION: *Make certain that the ignition key, in the vehicle with the dead battery, is in the OFF position. Connecting cables to vehicles with on-board computers will result in computer destruction if the key is not in the OFF position.*

Jump Starting Procedure

1. Determine voltages of the two batteries; they must be the same.
2. Bring the starting vehicle close (they must not touch) so that the batteries can be reached easily.
3. Turn off all accessories and both engines. Put both cars in Neutral or Park and set the handbrake.
4. Cover the cell caps with a rag—do not cover terminals.
5. If the terminals on the run-down battery are heavily corroded, clean them.
6. Identify the positive and negative posts on both batteries and connect the cables in the order shown.
7. Start the engine of the starting vehicle and run it at fast idle. Try to start the car with the dead battery. Crank it for no more than 10 seconds at a time and let it cool off for 20 seconds in between tries.
8. If it doesn't start in 3 tries, there is something else wrong.
9. Disconnect the cables in the reverse order.
10. Replace the cell covers and dispose of the rags.

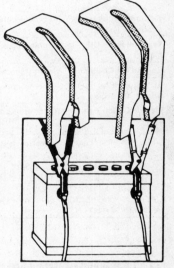

Side terminal batteries occasionally pose a problem when connecting jumper cables. There frequently isn't enough room to clamp the cables without touching sheet metal. Side terminal adaptors are available to alleviate this problem and should be removed after use.

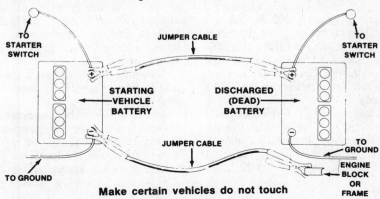

TO STARTER SWITCH   JUMPER CABLE   TO STARTER SWITCH

STARTING VEHICLE BATTERY   DISCHARGED (DEAD) BATTERY

JUMPER CABLE

TO GROUND

ENGINE BLOCK OR FRAME

TO GROUND

Make certain vehicles do not touch

This hook-up for negative ground cars only.

Recommended Equipment Checklist

Equipment	Class I Trailers Under 2,000 pounds	Class II Trailers 2,000-3,500 pounds	Class III Trailers 3,500-6,000 pounds	Class IV Trailers 6,000 pounds and up
Hitch	Frame or Equalizing	Equalizing	Equalizing	Fifth wheel Pick-up truck only
Tongue Load Limit**	Up to 200 pounds	200-350 pounds	350-600 pounds	600 pounds and up
Trailer Brakes	Not Required	Required	Required	Required
Safety Chain	3/16" diameter links	1/4" diameter links	5/16" diameter links	—
Fender Mounted Mirrors	Useful, but not necessary	Recommended	Recommended	Recommended
Turn Signal Flasher	Standard	Constant Rate or heavy duty	Constant Rate or heavy duty	Constant Rate or heavy duty
Coolant Recovery System	Recommended	Required	Required	Required
Transmission Oil Cooler	Recommended	Recommended	Recommended	Recommended
Engine Oil Cooler	Recommended	Recommended	Recommended	Recommended
Air Adjustable Shock Absorbers	Recommended	Recommended	Recommended	Recommended
Flex or Clutch Fan	Recommended	Recommended	Recommended	Recommended
Tires	***	***	***	***

NOTE: The information in this chart is a guide. Check the manufacturer's recommendations for your car if in doubt.

*Local laws may require specific equipment such as trailer brakes or fender mounted mirrors. Check your local laws. Hitch weight is usually 10-15% of trailer gross weight and should be measured with trailer loaded.

**Most manufacturer's do not recommend towing trailers of over 1,000 pounds with compacts. Some intermediates cannot tow Class III trailers.

***Check manufacturer's recommendations for your specific car trailer combination.

—Does not apply

Load equalizing hitches are usually used for large trailers. Most equalizing hitches are welded in place and use equalizing bars and chains to level the vehicle after the trailer is hooked up.

The bolt-on hitches are the most common, since they are relatively easy to install.

Check the gross weight rating of your trailer. Tongue weight is usually figured as 10% of gross trailer weight. Therefore, a trailer with a maximum gross weight of 2,000 lb. will have a maximum tongue weight of 200 lb. Class I tarilers fall into this category. Class II trailers are those with a gross weight rating of 2,000-3,500 lb., while Class III trailers fall into the 3,500-6,000 lb. category. Class IV trailers are those over 6,000 lb. and are for use with fifth wheel trucks, only.

When you've determined the hitch that you'll need, follow the manufacturer's installation instructions, exactly, especially when it comes to fastener torques. The hitch will subjected to a lot of stress and good hitches come with hard-ened bolts. Never substitute an inferior bolt for a hardened bolt.

Wiring

Wiring the car for towing is fairly easy. There are a number of good wiring kits available and these should be used, rather than trying to design your own. All trailers will need brake lights and turn signals as well as tail lights and side marker lights. Most states require extra marker lights for overly wide trailers. Also, most states have recently required back-up lights for trailers, and most trailer manufacturers have been building trailers with back-up lights for several years.

Additionally, some Class I, most Class II and just about all Class III trailers will have electric brakes.

Add to this number an accessories wire, to operate trailer internal equipment or to charge the trailer's battery, and you can have as many as seven wires in the harness.

Determine the equipment on your trailer and

Capacities

Year	Engine No. Cyl Displacement (Cu in.)	Engine Crankcase Add 1 Qt For New Filter	Transmission Pts To Refill After Draining			Drive Axle (pts)	Gasoline Tank (gals) ■	Cooling System (qts)	
			Manual		Automatic			With Heater	With A/C
			3-Speed	4-Speed					
1968	6-240	4	3.5	—	See	5	25	13	13
	8-302	4	3.5	—	chart	5	25	13.7	13.7
	8-390	4	3.5	4.0	below	5	25	20.2	20.2
	8-427	5	—	4.0		5	25	20.6	20.6
	8-428	4	—	4.0		5	25	19.4	19.4
1969	6-240	4	3.5	—		5	24.5	14.3	14.3
	8-302	4	3.5	—		4.5	24.5	15.4	15.6
	8-390	4	3.5	—		4.5	24.5	20.1	20.5
	8-428P	4	—	—		4.5	24.5	19.7	19.7
	8-429	4	—	4.0		4.5	24.5	20.5	21.5
1970	6-240	4	3.5	—		5	24.5	14.4	14.4
	8-302	4	3.5	—		4.5	24.5	15.4	15.6
	8-351	4	3.5	—		4.5	24.5	16.5	16.9
	8-390	4	3.5	—		4.5	24.5	20.1	20.5
	8-428P	4	—	—		4.5	24.5	19.7	19.7
	8-429	4	—	—	See	4.5	24.5	18.6	19.0
1971	6-240	4	3.5	—	chart	5	22.5	14.1	14.1
	8-302	4	3.5	—	below	4.5	22.5	15.2	15.6
	8-351	4	3.5	—		4.5	22.5	16.3	16.7
	8-390	4	—	—		4.5	22.5	20.3	26.3
	8-400	4	—	—		4.5	22.5	17.6	17.6
	8-429	4	—	—		4.5	22.5	18.8	18.8
1972	6-240	4	—	—		4	22	14.2	14.2
	8-302	4	—	—		4.5	22	15.2	15.2
	8-351	4	—	—		4.5	22	16.3	16.3
	8-400	4	—	—		5	22	17.7	18.3
	8-429	4	—	—		5	22	18.8	19.5
1973	8-351	4	—	—		4.5	22	16.3	16.3
	8-400	4	—	—		5	22	17.7	18.3
	8-429	4	—	—		5	22	18.8	19.5
1974–77	8-351	4	—	—		4.5	22 ③④	16.3	①
	8-400	4	—	—	See	5	22 ③④	18.0	18.0
	8-460	4 ②	—	—	chart	5	22 ③④	19.4	19.4
1978	8-302	4	—	—	below	5	24.2	16.9	16.9
	8-351	4	—	—		5	24.2	16.9	16.9
	8-400	4	—	—		5	24.2	16.9	16.9
	8-460	4	—	—		5	24.2	18.6	19.0
1979	8-302	4	—	—		3.5	19.0	13.3	13.4
	8-351	4	—	—		4.0	19.0	13.3	13.4

Capacities (cont.)

Year	Engine No. Cyl Displacement (Cu In.)	Engine Crankcase Add 1 Qt For New Filter	Transmission Pts To Refill After Draining			Drive Axle (pts)	Gasoline Tank (gals) ■	Cooling System (qts)	
			Manual		Automatic			With Heater	With A/C
			3-Speed	4-Speed					
1980	8-302	4 ⑤	—	—		3.5 ⑥	19	13.0	13.3
	8-351	4 ⑤	—	—	See	3.5 ⑥	19	13.9	14.0
1981–82	8-255	4 ⑤	—	—	chart	3.5 ⑥	20	14.8	15.2
	8-302	4 ⑤	—	—	below	3.5 ⑥	20 ⑦	13.0	13.4
	8-351	4 ⑤	—	—		3.5 ⑥	20	13.8 ⑧	13.8 ⑧
1983–88	8-302	4 ⑤	—	—		3.5 ⑥	20 ⑦	13.3 ⑧	13.4 ⑧
	8-351	4 ⑤	—	—		3.5 ⑥	20	13.8 ⑧	13.8 ⑧

① 351W—17.1 qts; 351C—16.3 qts; 351M—16.3 qts
② 460 Police Interceptor—7½ qts with filter and oil cooler
③ 1975–77 Sedans—24.2 gals
④ Sedan with auxiliary tank—32.3 gals
  Wagon with auxiliary tank—29.0 gals
⑤ Two drain plugs are used on the oil pan
⑥ 4 pts with 8.5 in ring gear
⑦ 18.0 gal with CFI—18.5 gal wagons with CFI
⑧ Trailer towing H.D. system—15.0 qts
  16.4 police
  14.4—1985

■ Station Wagons:
  '68–'70—20 gals
  '71—22 gals
  '72–'78—21 gals
  '79–'81—20 gals
P Police
—Not applicable

Automatic Transmission Dry Refill Capacities (Pts) ①

Year	Code	Capacities
1968–69	U, Z	26
1968–79	W	20.5
1968–76	X, Y	22
1970–79	U, Z	25.5
1980	W	20
	X	22
	T	24
	U	23.6
1981 and later	T	24

① Converter and transmission completely dry. If the converter is not drained, add 8 pts, run engine and check, add as necessary.

buy the wiring kit necessary. The kit will contain all the wires needed, plus a plug adapter set which included the female plug, mounted on the bumper or hitch, and the male plug, wired into, or plugged into the trailer harness.

When installing the kit, follow the manufacturer's instructions. The color coding of the wires is standard throughout the industry.

One point to note, some domestic vehicles, and most imported vehicles, have separate turn signals. On most domestic vehicles, the brake lights and rear turn signals operate with the same bulb. For those vehicles with separate turn signals, you can purchase an isolation unit so that the brake lights won't blink whenever the turn signals are operated, or, you can go to your local electronics supply house and buy four diodes to wire in series with the brake and turn signal bulbs. Diodes will isolate the brake and turn signals. The choice is yours. The isolation units are simple and quick to install, but far more expensive than the diodes. The diodes, however, require more work to install properly, since they require the cutting of each bulb's wire and soldering in place of the diode.

One final point, the best kits are those with a spring loaded cover on the vehicle mounted socket. This cover prevents dirt and moisture from corroding the terminals. Never let the vehicle socket hang loosely. Always mount it securely to the bumper or hitch.

Cooling
ENGINE

One of the most common, if not THE most common, problem associated with trailer towing is engine overheating.

With factory installed trailer towing packages, a heavy duty cooling system is usually in-

Maintenance Interval Chart

Operation	'68–'70	'71	'72	'73	'74	'75	'76	'77–'79	'80–'83	'84–'85
ENGINE										
Air cleaner replacement—6 cyl	12	12	12	—	—	—	—	—	—	—
Air cleaner replacement—V8	24	24	12	12	24	20	20	30	30	30
Air intake temperature control system check	12	12	12	12	12	15	15	20	22.5	22.5
Carburetor idle speed and mixture, fast idle, throttle solenoid adj	12	12	12	12	24	15	15	22.5	30	30
Cooling system check	12	12	12	12	12	15	15	12	12	12
Coolant replacement; system draining and flushing	24	24	24	24	24	40	40	45	52.5	52.5
Crankcase breather cap cleaning	6	6	6	12	12	20	20	30	52.5	52.5
Crankcase breather filter replacement (in air cleaner)	24	6	6	8	24	20	20	30	52.5	52.5
Distributor breaker points inspection	12	12	12	12	6	—	—	—	—	—
Distributor breaker points replacement	12	12	12	24	24	—	—	—	—	—
Distributor cap and rotor inspection	12	12	12	24	①	15	15	22.5	22.5	22.5
Drive belts adjustment	12	12	12	12	12	15	15	22.5	30	30
Evaporative control system check; inspect carbon canister	—	12	12	12	24	20	20	30	52.5	52.5
Exhaust control valve (heat riser) lubrication and inspection	6	6	6	8	6	15	15	15	15	15
Exhaust gas recirculation system (EGR) check	—	—	—	12	12	15	15	15	15	15
Fuel filter replacement	12	12	12	12	6	15	10	10	12	12
Ignition timing adjustment	12	12	12	12	②	⑥	⑥	⑥	⑥	⑥
Intake manifold bolt torque check (V8 only)	12	12	12	24	12	15	15	15	15	15
Oil change	6	6	6	4	6	5	5	7.5	7.5	7.5
Oil filter replacement	6	6	6	8	12	10	10	15	15	15
PCV system valve replacement, system cleaning	12	12	12	12	24	20	20	22.5	52.5	52.5
Spark plug replacement; plug wire check	12	12	12	12	③	15	15	22.5	30	30
Thermactor air injection system check	12	—	—	—	24	15	15	22.5	22.5	22.5
CHASSIS										
Automatic transmission band adjustment	④⑤	⑤	⑤	⑤	⑤	⑤	⑤	⑤	⑤	⑤
Automatic transmission fluid level check	6	6	6	8	12	15	15	15	15	15
Brake system inspection, lining replacement	30	30	30	24	24	25	30	30	30	30
Brake master cylinder reservoir fluid level check	6	6	6	8	12	15	30	30	30	30
Clutch pedal free-play adjustment	6	6	—	—	—	—	—	—	—	—
Front suspension ball joints and steering linkage lubrication	36	36	36	36	36	30	30	30	30	30

Maintenance Interval Chart (cont.)

Operation	'68–'70	'71	'72	'73	'74	'75	'76	'77–'79	'80–'83	'84–'85
CHASSIS										
Front wheel bearings cleaning, adjusting and repacking	30	30	30	24	24	25	30	30	30	30
Manual transmission fluid level check	6	6	—	—	—	—	—	—	—	—
Power steering pump reservoir fluid level check	6	6	6	4	6	15	15	15	15	15
Rear axle fluid level check	6	6	6	8	12	15	15	15	15	15
Steering arm stop lubrication; steering linkage inspection	6	12	12	12	12	15	15	15	15	15

① Conventional ignition—24; electronic ignition—18
② Conventional ignition—12; electronic ignition—18
③ Conventional ignition—12; electronic ignition—18
④ Normal service—36,000 mi. only; severe (fleet) service—6,000/18,000/36,000 mi. intervals—1968 only
⑤ Normal service—12,000 mi. only; severe (fleet) service—6,000/18,000/30,000 mi. intervals
⑥ Periodic adjustment unnecessary

cluded. Heavy duty cooling systems are available as optional equipment on most cars, with or without a trailer package. If you have one of these extra-capacity systems, you shouldn't have any overheating problems.

If you have a standard cooling system, without an expansion tank, you'll definitely need to get an aftermarket expansion tank kit, preferably one with at least a 2 quart capacity. These kits are easily installed on the radiator's overflow hose, and come with a pressure cap designed for expansion tanks.

Another helpful accessory is a Flex Fan. These fan are large diameter units are designed to provide more airflow at low speeds, with blades that have deeply cupped surfaces. The blades then flex, or flatten out, at high speed, when less cooling air is needed. These fans are far lighter in weight than stock fans, requiring less horsepower to drive them. Also, they are far quieter than stock fans.

If you do decide to replace your stock fan with a flex fan, note that if your car has a fan clutch, a spacer between the flex fan and water pump hub will be needed.

Aftermarket engine oil coolers are helpful for prolonging engine oil life and reducing overall engine temperatures. Both of these factors increase engine life.

While not absolutely necessary in towing Class I and some Class II trailers, they are recommended for heavier Class II and all Class III towing.

Engine oil cooler systems consist of an adapter, screwed on in place of the oil filter, a remote filter mounting and a multi-tube, finned heat exchanger, which is mounted in front of the radiator or air conditioning condenser.

TRANSMISSION

An automatic transmission is usually recommended for trailer towing. Modern automatics have proven reliable and, of course, easy to operate, in trailer towing.

The increased load of a trailer, however, causes an increase in the temperature of the automatic transmission fluid. Heat is the worst enemy of an automatic transmission. As the temperature of the fluid increases, the life of the fluid decreases.

It is essential, therefore, that you install an automatic transmission cooler.

The cooler, which consists of a multi-tube, finned heat exchanger, is usually installed in front of the radiator or air conditioning compressor, and hooked inline with the transmission cooler tank inlet line. Follow the cooler manufacturer's installation instructions.

Select a cooler of at least adequate capacity, based upon the combined gross weights of the car and trailer.

Cooler manufacturers recommend that you use an aftermarket cooler in addition to, and not instead of, the present cooling tank in your car radiator. If you do want to use it in place of the radiator cooling tank, get a cooler at least two sizes larger than normally necessary.

NOTE: *A transmission cooler can, sometimes, cause slow or harsh shifting in the transmission during cold weather, until the fluid has a chance to come up to normal operating temperature. Some coolers can be purchased with or retrofitted with a temperature bypass valve which will allow fluid flow through the cooler only when the fluid has reached operating temperature, or above.*

Engine Performance and Tune-Up

2

TUNE-UP PROCEDURES

In order to extract the full measure of performance and economy from your engine it is essential that it be properly tuned at regular intervals. A regular tune-up will keep your vehicle's engine running smoothly and will prevent the annoying minor breakdowns and poor performance associated with an untuned engine.

A complete tune-up should be performed every 12,000 miles or twelve months, whichever comes first. This interval should be halved if the vehicle is operated under severe conditions, such as trailer towing, prolonged idling, continual stop and start driving, or if starting or running problems are noticed. It is assumed that the routine maintenance described in Chapter 1 has been kept up, as this will have a decided effect on the results of a tune-up. All of the applicable steps of a tune-up should be followed in order, as the result is a cumulative one.

If the specifications on the tune-up sticker in the engine compartment disagree with the Tune-Up Specifications chart in this chapter, the figures on the sticker must be used. The sticker often reflects changes made during the production run.

Spark Plugs

A typical spark plug consists of a metal shell surrounding a ceramic insulator. A metal electrode extends downward through the center of the insulator and protrudes a small distance. Located at the end of the plug and attached to the side of the outer metal shell is the side electrode. The side electrode bends in at a 90° angle so that its tip is even with, and parallel to, the tip of the center electrode. The distance between these two electrodes (measured in thousandths of an inch) is called the spark plug gap. The spark plug in no way produces a spark but merely provides a gap across which the current can arc. The coil produces anywhere from

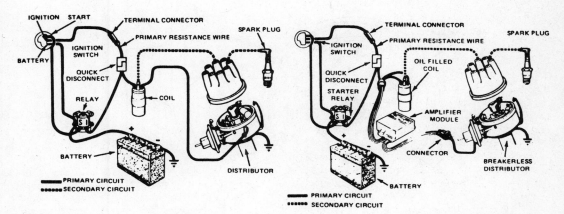

CONVENTIONAL   BREAKERLESS

Typical ignition systems

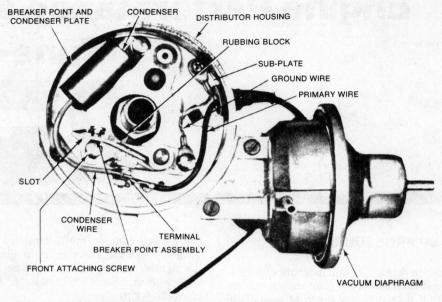

Typical breaker point distributor—cap and rotor removed

20,000 to 40,000 volts which travels to the distributor where it is distributed through the spark plug wires to the spark plugs. The current passes along the center electrode and jumps the gap to the side electrode, and, in do doing, ignites the air/fuel mixture in the combustion chamber.

SPARK PLUG HEAT RANGE

Spark plug heat range is the ability of the plug to dissipate heat. The longer the insulator (or the farther it extends into the engine), the hotter the plug will operate; the shorter the insulator the cooler it will operate. A plug that absorbs little heat and remains too cool will quickly accumulate deposits of oil and carbon since it is not hot enough to burn them off. This leads to plug fouling and consequently to misfiring. A plug that absorbs too much heat will have no deposits, but, due to the excessive heat, the electrodes will burn away quickly and in some instances, preignition may result. Preignition takes place when plug tips get so hot that they glow sufficiently to ignite the fuel/air mixture

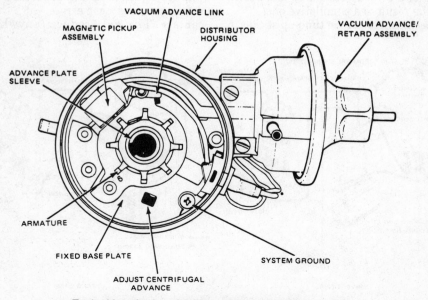

Typical breakerless ignition—cap and rotor removed

Troubleshooting Engine Performance

Problem	Cause	Solution
Hard starting (engine cranks normally)	• Binding linkage, choke valve or choke piston	• Repair as necessary
	• Restricted choke vacuum diaphragm	• Clean passages
	• Improper fuel level	• Adjust float level
	• Dirty, worn or faulty needle valve and seat	• Repair as necessary
	• Float sticking	• Repair as necessary
	• Faulty fuel pump	• Replace fuel pump
	• Incorrect choke cover adjustment	• Adjust choke cover
	• Inadequate choke unloader adjustment	• Adjust choke unloader
	• Faulty ignition coil	• Test and replace as necessary
	• Improper spark plug gap	• Adjust gap
	• Incorrect ignition timing	• Adjust timing
	• Incorrect valve timing	• Check valve timing; repair as necessary
Rough idle or stalling	• Incorrect curb or fast idle speed	• Adjust curb or fast idle speed
	• Incorrect ignition timing	• Adjust timing to specification
	• Improper feedback system operation	• Refer to Chapter 4
	• Improper fast idle cam adjustment	• Adjust fast idle cam
	• Faulty EGR valve operation	• Test EGR system and replace as necessary
	• Faulty PCV valve air flow	• Test PCV valve and replace as necessary
	• Choke binding	• Locate and eliminate binding condition
	• Faulty TAC vacuum motor or valve	• Repair as necessary
	• Air leak into manifold vacuum	• Inspect manifold vacuum connections and repair as necessary
	• Improper fuel level	• Adjust fuel level
	• Faulty distributor rotor or cap	• Replace rotor or cap
	• Improperly seated valves	• Test cylinder compression, repair as necessary
	• Incorrect ignition wiring	• Inspect wiring and correct as necessary
	• Faulty ignition coil	• Test coil and replace as necessary
	• Restricted air vent or idle passages	• Clean passages
	• Restricted air cleaner	• Clean or replace air cleaner filler element
	• Faulty choke vacuum diaphragm	• Repair as necessary
Faulty low-speed operation	• Restricted idle transfer slots	• Clean transfer slots
	• Restricted idle air vents and passages	• Clean air vents and passages
	• Restricted air cleaner	• Clean or replace air cleaner filter element
	• Improper fuel level	• Adjust fuel level
	• Faulty spark plugs	• Clean or replace spark plugs
	• Dirty, corroded, or loose ignition secondary circuit wire connections	• Clean or tighten secondary circuit wire connections
	• Improper feedback system operation	• Refer to Chapter 4
	• Faulty ignition coil high voltage wire	• Replace ignition coil high voltage wire
	• Faulty distributor cap	• Replace cap
Faulty acceleration	• Improper accelerator pump stroke	• Adjust accelerator pump stroke
	• Incorrect ignition timing	• Adjust timing
	• Inoperative pump discharge check ball or needle	• Clean or replace as necessary
	• Worn or damaged pump diaphragm or piston	• Replace diaphragm or piston

Troubleshooting Engine Performance (cont.)

Problem	Cause	Solution
Faulty acceleration (cont.)	· Leaking carburetor main body cover gasket	· Replace gasket
	· Engine cold and choke set too lean	· Adjust choke cover
	· Improper metering rod adjustment (BBD Model carburetor)	· Adjust metering rod
	· Faulty spark plug(s)	· Clean or replace spark plug(s)
	· Improperly seated valves	· Test cylinder compression, repair as necessary
	· Faulty ignition coil	· Test coil and replace as necessary
	· Improper feedback system operation	· Refer to Chapter 4
Faulty high speed operation	· Incorrect ignition timing	· Adjust timing
	· Faulty distributor centrifugal advance mechanism	· Check centrifugal advance mechanism and repair as necessary
	· Faulty distributor vacuum advance mechanism	· Check vacuum advance mechanism and repair as necessary
	· Low fuel pump volume	· Replace fuel pump
	· Wrong spark plug air gap or wrong plug	· Adjust air gap or install correct plug
	· Faulty choke operation	· Adjust choke cover
	· Partially restricted exhaust manifold, exhaust pipe, catalytic converter, muffler, or tailpipe	· Eliminate restriction
	· Restricted vacuum passages	· Clean passages
	· Improper size or restricted main jet	· Clean or replace as necessary
	· Restricted air cleaner	· Clean or replace filter element as necessary
	· Faulty distributor rotor or cap	· Replace rotor or cap
	· Faulty ignition coil	· Test coil and replace as necessary
	· Improperly seated valve(s)	· Test cylinder compression, repair as necessary
	· Faulty valve spring(s)	· Inspect and test valve spring tension, replace as necessary
	· Incorrect valve timing	· Check valve timing and repair as necessary
	· Intake manifold restricted	· Remove restriction or replace manifold
	· Worn distributor shaft	· Replace shaft
	· Improper feedback system operation	· Refer to Chapter 4
Misfire at all speeds	· Faulty spark plug(s)	· Clean or replace spark plug(s)
	· Faulty spark plug wire(s)	· Replace as necessary
	· Faulty distributor cap or rotor	· Replace cap or rotor
	· Faulty ignition coil	· Test coil and replace as necessary
	· Primary ignition circuit shorted or open intermittently	· Troubleshoot primary circuit and repair as necessary
	· Improperly seated valve(s)	· Test cylinder compression, repair as necessary
	· Faulty hydraulic tappet(s)	· Clean or replace tappet(s)
	· Improper feedback system operation	· Refer to Chapter 4
	· Faulty valve spring(s)	· Inspect and test valve spring tension, repair as necessary
	· Worn camshaft lobes	· Replace camshaft
	· Air leak into manifold	· Check manifold vacuum and repair as necessary
	· Improper carburetor adjustment	· Adjust carburetor
	· Fuel pump volume or pressure low	· Replace fuel pump
	· Blown cylinder head gasket	· Replace gasket
	· Intake or exhaust manifold passage(s) restricted	· Pass chain through passage(s) and repair as necessary
	· Incorrect trigger wheel installed in distributor	· Install correct trigger wheel

Troubleshooting Engine Performance (cont.)

Problem	Cause	Solution
Power not up to normal	• Incorrect ignition timing	• Adjust timing
	• Faulty distributor rotor	• Replace rotor
	• Trigger wheel loose on shaft	• Reposition or replace trigger wheel
	• Incorrect spark plug gap	• Adjust gap
	• Faulty fuel pump	• Replace fuel pump
	• Incorrect valve timing	• Check valve timing and repair as necessary
	• Faulty ignition coil	• Test coil and replace as necessary
	• Faulty ignition wires	• Test wires and replace as necessary
	• Improperly seated valves	• Test cylinder compression and repair as necessary
	• Blown cylinder head gasket	• Replace gasket
	• Leaking piston rings	• Test compression and repair as necessary
	• Worn distributor shaft	• Replace shaft
	• Improper feedback system operation	• Refer to Chapter 4
Intake backfire	• Improper ignition timing	• Adjust timing
	• Faulty accelerator pump discharge	• Repair as necessary
	• Defective EGR CTO valve	• Replace EGR CTO valve
	• Defective TAC vacuum motor or valve	• Repair as necessary
	• Lean air/fuel mixture	• Check float level or manifold vacuum for air leak. Remove sediment from bowl
Exhaust backfire	• Air leak into manifold vacuum	• Check manifold vacuum and repair as necessary
	• Faulty air injection diverter valve	• Test diverter valve and replace as necessary
	• Exhaust leak	• Locate and eliminate leak
Ping or spark knock	• Incorrect ignition timing	• Adjust timing
	• Distributor centrifugal or vacuum advance malfunction	• Inspect advance mechanism and repair as necessary
	• Excessive combustion chamber deposits	• Remove with combustion chamber cleaner
	• Air leak into manifold vacuum	• Check manifold vacuum and repair as necessary
	• Excessively high compression	• Test compression and repair as necessary
	• Fuel octane rating excessively low	• Try alternate fuel source
	• Sharp edges in combustion chamber	• Grind smooth
	• EGR valve not functioning properly	• Test EGR system and replace as necessary
Surging (at cruising to top speeds)	• Low carburetor fuel level	• Adjust fuel level
	• Low fuel pump pressure or volume	• Replace fuel pump
	• Metering rod(s) not adjusted properly (BBD Model Carburetor)	• Adjust metering rod
	• Improper PCV valve air flow	• Test PCV valve and replace as necessary
	• Air leak into manifold vacuum	• Check manifold vacuum and repair as necessary
	• Incorrect spark advance	• Test and replace as necessary
	• Restricted main jet(s)	• Clean main jet(s)
	• Undersize main jet(s)	• Replace main jet(s)
	• Restricted air vents	• Clean air vents
	• Restricted fuel filter	• Replace fuel filter
	• Restricted air cleaner	• Clean or replace air cleaner filter element
	• EGR valve not functioning properly	• Test EGR system and replace as necessary
	• Improper feedback system operation	• Refer to Chapter 4

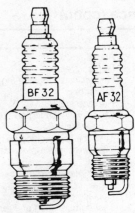

Typical spark plugs—left is $^{13}/_{16}$ in. (18 mm); right is $^5/_8$ in. (14 mm)

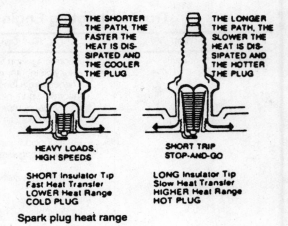

THE SHORTER THE PATH, THE FASTER THE HEAT IS DISSIPATED AND THE COOLER THE PLUG

THE LONGER THE PATH, THE SLOWER THE HEAT IS DISSIPATED AND THE HOTTER THE PLUG

HEAVY LOADS, HIGH SPEEDS

SHORT TRIP STOP-AND-GO

SHORT Insulator Tip
Fast Heat Transfer
LOWER Heat Range
COLD PLUG

LONG Insulator Tip
Slow Heat Transfer
HIGHER Heat Range
HOT PLUG

Spark plug heat range

before the actual spark occurs. This early ignition will usually cause a pinging during low speeds and heavy loads.

The general rule of thumb for choosing the correct heat range when picking a spark plug is: if most of your driving is long distance, high speed travel, use a colder plug; if most of your driving is stop and go, use a hotter plug. Original equipment plugs are compromise plugs, but most people never have occasion to change their plugs from the factory recommended heat range.

REPLACING SPARK PLUGS

A set of spark plugs usually requires replacement after about 20,000 to 30,000 miles, depending on your style of driving. In normal operation, plug gap increases about 0.001" for every 1,000-2,500 miles. As the gap increases, the plug's voltage requirement also increases. It re-

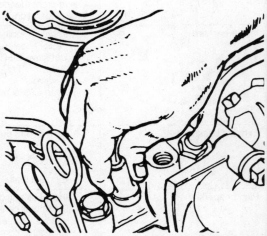

Twist and pull on the rubber boot to remove the spark plug wires; never pull on the wire itself

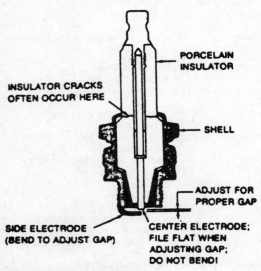

PORCELAIN INSULATOR

INSULATOR CRACKS OFTEN OCCUR HERE

SHELL

ADJUST FOR PROPER GAP

SIDE ELECTRODE (BEND TO ADJUST GAP)

CENTER ELECTRODE; FILE FLAT WHEN ADJUSTING GAP; DO NOT BEND!

Cross section of a spark plug

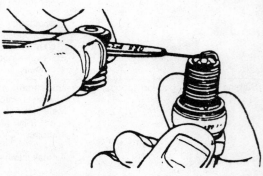

Always use a wire gauge to check the electrode gap

quires a greater voltage to jump the wider gap and about two to three times as much voltage to fire a plug at high speeds than at idle.

When you're removing spark plugs, you should work on one at a time. Don't start by removing the plug wires all at once, because un-

Tune-Up Specifications

When analyzing compression test results, look for uniformity among cylinders rather than specific pressures.

Year	Engine No. Cyl Displacement (cu in.)	Spark Plugs Type	Spark Plugs Gap (in.)	Distributor Point Dwell (deg)	Distributor Point Gap (in.)	Ignition Timing (deg) ▲ Man Trans	Ignition Timing (deg) ▲ Auto Trans	Valves Intake Opens ▪(deg)●	Fuel Pump Pressure (psi)	Idle Speed (rpm) ▲ Man Trans*	Idle Speed (rpm) ▲ Auto Trans ▲
1968	6-240	BF-42	.034	35–40	.027	6B	6B	12	4–6	600	500
	8-302	BF-32	.034	24–29	.021	6B	6B	16	4–6	625	550②
	8-390	BF-32	.034	24–29③	.021③	6B	6B	13	4½–6½	625	550
	8-390	BF-32	.034	24–29③	.021③	6B	6B	16	4½–6½	625	550
	8-428	BF-32	.034	24–29③	.021③	6B	6B	16	4½–6½	625	550
	8-428PI	BF-32	.034	26–31	.017	—	6B	18	4½–6½	—	600
	8-462	BF42	.034	24–29	.021	—	6B	20	5–6	—	550
1969	6-240	BF-42	.034	35–40	.027	6B	6B	12	4–6	775/550	550
	8-302	BF-42	.034	24–29③	.021③	6B	6B	16	4½–6½	650	550②
	8-390	BF-42	.034	24–29③	.021③	6B	6B	13	4½–6½	650	550
	8-428PI	BF-32	.034	24–29③	.021③	—	6B	18	4½–6½	—	600
	8-429	BF-42	.034	26–31	.017	—	6B	16	4½–6½	—	550
	8-429	BF-42	.034	24–29③	.021③	6B	6B	16	4½–6½	650	550
1970	6-240	BF-42	.034	35–40	.027	6B	6B	12	4–6	800/500	500
	8-302	BF-42	.034	24–29	.021	6B	6B	16	4–6	575 [800/500]	575 [600/500]
	8-351W	BF-42	.034	24–29	.021	10B	10B	11	5–7	575 [700/500]	575 [600/500]
	8-390	BF-42	.034	24–29③	.021③	6B	6B	13	5–7	570/500	600/500
	8-428PI	BF-32	.034	24–29	.021	—	6B	18	4½–6½	—	600/500
	8-429	BRF-42	.034	24–29③	.021③	6B	6B	16	5–7	—	600/500
	8-429	BRF-42	.034	24–29③	.021③	6B	6B	16	5–7	700/500	600/500
1971	6-240	BRF-42	.034	33–38	.027	6B	6B	18	4–6	800/500	600/500
	8-302	BRF-42	.034	24–29	.021	6B	6B	16	4–6	575 [800/500]	575 [650/500]

Tune-Up Specifications (cont.)

When analyzing compression test results, look for uniformity among cylinders rather than specific pressures.

Year	Engine No. Cyl Displacement (cu in.)	Spark Plugs Type	Gap (in.)	Distributor Point Dwell (deg)	Point Gap (in.)	Ignition Timing (deg) ▲ Man Trans	Auto Trans	Valves Intake Opens ▪(deg)●	Fuel Pump Pressure (psi)	Idle Speed (rpm) ▲ Man Trans*	Auto Trans
1971	8-351W	BRF-42	.034	24–29	.021	6B	6B	11	5–7	575 [775/500]	575 [600/500]
	8-351C	ARF-42	.034	24–29	.021	—	6B	12	5–7	—	625/550
	8-390	BRF-42	.034	24–29	.021	—	6B	13	5–7	—	600/475
	8-400	ARF-42	.034	26–31	.017	—	10B(6B)	17	5–7	—	625/500
	8-429PI	ARF-42	.034	27½–29½	.020	—	10B	32	5–7	—	650/500
	8-429	BRF-42	.034	24–29③	.021③	—	4B	16	5–7	—	600
	8-429	BRF-42	.034	24–29③	.021③	4B	4B	16	5–7	700	600
1972	6-240	BRF-42	.034	35–39	.027	—	6B	18	4–6	—	500
	8-302	BRF-42	.034	26–30	.017	—	6B	16	5–7	—	575 [600/500]
	8-351W	BRF-42	.034	26–30	.017	—	6B	11	5–7	—	575 [600/500]
	8-351C	ARF-42	.034	26–30	.017	—	6B	12	5–7	—	600/500
	8-400	ARF-42	.034	26–30	.017	—	6B	17	5–7	—	625/500
	8-429	BRF-42	.034	26–30	.017	—	10B	8	5–7	—	600/500
	8-429PI	ARF-42	.034	26–30	.017	—	10B	32	Electric	—	650/500
1973	8-351W	BRF-42	.034	26–30	.017	—	6B	11	5–7	—	575 [600/500]
	8-351C	ARF-42	.034	26–30	.017	—	6B	12	5–7	—	600/500
	8-400	ARF-42	.034	26–30	.017	—	6B	17	5–7	—	625/500
	8-429	BRF-42	.034	26–30	.017	—	10B	8	5–7	—	600/500
	8-429PI	ARF-42	.034	26–30	.017	—	10B	32	Electric	—	650/500

Year	Engine	Plug	Gap								Idle
1974	8-351W	BRF-42	.034④	26–30	.014–.020	—	6B	15	4–6	—	600/500
	8-351C	ARF-42	.044	26–30	.014–.020	—	14B	19½	5½–6½	—	700/500
	8-400	ARF-42	.044⑧	⑥	⑥	—	12B	17	5½–6½	—	625/500
	8-460	ARF-52	.054⑦	⑥	⑥	—	14B	8	5½–6½	—	650/500⑤
	8-460PI	ARF-52	.054	⑥	⑥	—	10B	18	Electric	—	700/500
1975	8-351M	ARF-42	.044	⑥	⑥	—	8B	19½	5½–6½	—	700/500
	8-400	ARF-42	.044	⑥	⑥	—	6B	17	5½–6½	—	625/500
	8-460	ARF-52	.044	⑥	⑥	—	14B	8	6.2–7.2	—	650/500
	8-460PI	ARF-52	.044	⑥	⑥	—	14B	18	Electric	—	650/500
1976	8-351M	ARF-52	.044	Electronic	Electronic	—	12B⑨	19½	6½–7½	—	650/500
	8-400	ARF-52	.044	Electronic	Electronic	—	10B	17	6½–7½	—	650/500
	8-460	ARF-52	.044	Electronic	Electronic	—	8B⑩	8	7.2–8.2	—	650/500
	8-460PI	ARF-52	.044	Electronic	Electronic	—	8B⑩	8	Electric	—	650/500
1977	8-351M	ARF-52	.050	Electronic	Electronic	—	8B	19½	6½–7½	—	650/500
	8-400	ARF-52	.050	Electronic	Electronic	—	8B	17	6½–7½	—	650/500
	8-460	ARF-52-6	.060	Electronic	Electronic	—	16B	8	7–8	—	650/500
1978	8-302	ARF-52 (ARF-52-6)	.050 (.060)	Electronic	Electronic	—	14B	16	5½–6½	—	650
	8-351W	ARF-52 (ARF-52-6)	.050 (.060)	Electronic	Electronic	—	4B	23	4–6	—	650
	8-351M	ARF-52 (ARF-52-6)	.050 (.060)	Electronic	Electronic	—	12B(16B)	19½	6½–7½	—	650
	8-400	ARF-52 (ARF-52-6)	.050 (.060)	Electronic	Electronic	—	13B(16B)	17	6½–7½	—	650
	8-460	ARF-52 (ARF-52-6)	.050 (.060)	Electronic	Electronic	—	10B	8	7¼–8¼	—	580
	8-460	ARF-52-6	.060	Electronic	Electronic	—	16B	18	7¼–7¼	—	580
1979	8-302	ASF-52⑫	.050⑫	Electronic	Electronic	—	14B	16	5½–6½	—	550
	8-351W	ASF-52	.050	Electronic	Electronic	—	4B (EECII)⑪	23	6½–8	—	550

Tune-Up Specifications (cont.)

When analyzing compression test results, look for uniformity among cylinders rather than specific pressures.

Year	Engine No. Cyl Displacement (cu in.)	Spark Plugs Type	Gap (in.)	Distributor Point Dwell (deg)	Point Gap (in.)	Ignition Timing (deg) ▲ Man Trans	Ignition Timing (deg) ▲ Auto Trans	Valves Intake Opens ■(deg)●	Fuel Pump Pressure (psi)	Idle Speed (rpm) ▲ Man Trans*	Idle Speed (rpm) ▲ Auto Trans
1980	8-302	ASF-52 ⑫	.050 ⑫	Electronic		—	6B ⑫	16	5½–6½	—	550 ⑭
	8-351W	ASF-52	.050	Electronic		—	10B	23	6½–8	—	550 ⑭
1981–82	8-255	ASF-52	.050	Electronic		—	⑮	16	6–8	—	500 ⑭
	8-302	ASF-52	.050	Electronic		—	⑮	17	39½ ⑬	—	550 ⑭
	8-351	ASF-52	.050	Electronic		—	⑮	23	6½–8	—	550 ⑭
1983–88	8-302	ASF-52	.050	Electronic		—	⑮	N/A	6½–8	—	600
	8-302	ASF-52	.050	Electronic		—	⑮	N/A	39½ ⑬	—	550
	8-351	ASF-52 ⑯	.050	Electronic		—	⑮	N/A	6½–8	—	600

NOTE: The underhood sticker reflects production changes and calibrations, always use the "underhood specs" if they differ from the ones on this chart.

▲ See text for procedure

● Figures in parentheses indicate California engine

■ All figures Before Top Dead Center

* Figures in brackets are for solenoid equipped vehicles only. In all cases where two figures are separated by a slash, the first is for idle speed with solenoid energized and the automatic transmission in Drive, while the second is for idle speed with solenoid disconnected and automatic transmission in Neutral.

① Adjust mechanical lifters, intake and exhaust, to .025 inch with engine hot

② A/C off

③ For engines equipped with single diaphragm distributors, adjust point dwell to 26–31 degrees and point gap to .017 inch

④ .044 on California models

⑤ 675/500 for California engines

⑥ Solid State (breakerless) ignition

⑦ .044 on California models

⑧ .054 on California models

⑨ 8BTDC @ 650 rpm in California

⑩ 14BTDC @ 650 rpm in California

⑪ California engines have variable EEC II timing; see the text for a description.

⑫ ASF-52-6 Calif; .060 gap; 10B;

⑬ CFI—Central Fuel Injection.

⑭ In Drive

⑮ See underhood sticker

⑯ ASF42—see underhood sticker.

B Before Top Dead Center

C Cleveland

NA Not available

PI Police Interceptor

TDC Top Dead Center

W Windsor

— Not applicable

M Modified Cleveland design

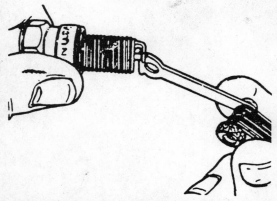

Adjust the electrode gap by bending the side electrode

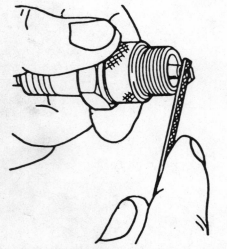

Plugs that are in good condition can be filed and re-used

less you number them, they may become mixed up. Take a minute before you begin and number the wires with tape. The best location for numbering is near where the wires come out of the cap.

NOTE: *On models equipped with electronic ignition, apply a small amount of silicone dielectric compound (D7AZ-19A331-A or the equivalent) to the inside of the terminal boots whenever an ignition wire is disconnected from the plug, or coil/distributor cap connection.*

1. Twist the spark plug boot and remove the boot and wire from the plug. Do not pull on the wire itself as this will ruin the wire.

2. If possible, use a brush or gag to clean the area around the spark plug. Make sure that all the dirt is removed so that none will enter the cylinder after the plug is removed.

3. Remove the spark plug using the proper size socket. Truck models use either a ⅝" or ¹³⁄₁₆" size socket depending on the engine. Turn the socket counterclockwise to remove the plug. Be sure to hold the socket straight on the plug to avoid breaking the plug, or rounding off the hex on the plug.

4. Once the plug is out, check it against the plugs shown in the Color section to determine engine condition. This is crucial since plug readings are vital signs of engine condition.

5. Use a round wire feeler gauge to check the plug gap. The correct size gauge should pass through the electrode gap with a slight drag. If you're in doubt, try one size smaller and one larger. The smaller gauge should go through easily while the larger one shouldn't go through at all. If the gap is incorrect, use the electrode bending tool on the end of the gauge to adjust the gap. When adjusting the gap, always bend the side electrode. The center electrode is non-adjustable.

6. Squirt a drop of penetrating oil on the threads of the new plug and install it. Don't oil the threads too heavily. Turn the plug in clockwise by hand until it is snug.

7. When the plug is finger tight, tighten it with a wrench. If you don't have a torque wrench, tighten the plug as shown.

8. Install the plug boot firmly over the plug. Proceed to the next plug.

CHECKING AND REPLACING SPARK PLUG CABLES

Visually inspect the spark plug cables for burns, cuts, or breaks in the insulation. Check the spark plug boots and the nipples on the distributor cap and coil. Replace any damaged wiring. If no physical damage is obvious, the wires can be checked with an ohmmeter for excessive resistance. (See the tune-up and troubleshooting section).

When installing a new set of spark plug cables, replace the cables on at a time so there will be no mixup. Start by replacing the longest cable first. Install the boot firmly over the spark plug. Route the wire exactly the same as the original. Insert the nipple firmly into the tower on the distributor cap. Repeat the process for each cable.

DURASPARK PLUG WIRES

The spark plug wires used with the DURA SPARK system are 8mm to contain the higher output voltage. There are two types of wires used in the system and some engines will have both types. It is important to properly identify the type of wire used for each cylinder before replacements are made.

Both types are blue in color and have silicone jacketing. The insulation material underneath the jacketing may be EPDM or another silicone layer separated by glass braid. the cable incorporating EPDM is used where engine temperatures are cooler and are identified with the letter **SE** with black printing. The silicone jacket silicone insulation type is used where high engine temperatures are present and is identified with the letters **SS** with white printing.

The cables are also marked with the cylinder number, model year and date of cable manufacture (quarter and year). Service replacement wires will not have cylinder numbers, or manufacture date.

NOTE: *On any vehicle equipped with a catalytic converter, never allow the engine to run for more than 30 seconds with a spark plug wire disconnected. Use a oscilloscope for testing and diagnosis. Do not puncture wires or use adapters that can cause misfiring. Unburned fuel in the cylinders will ignite in the converter as it is exhausted and damage the converter.*

Removal

When removing spark plug wires, use great care. Grasp and twist the insulator back and forth on the spark plug to free the insulator. Do not pull on the wire directly as it may become separated from the connector inside the insulator.

Installation

1. Install each wire in or on the proper terminal of the distributor cap. Be sure the terminal connector inside the insulator is fully seated. The No. 1 terminal is identified on the cap.

2. On 8-cylinder engines, remove the brackets from the old spark plug wire set and install them on the new set in the same relative position. Install the wires in the brackets on the valve rocker arm covers. Connect the wires to the proper spark plugs. Install the coil high tension lead.

The wires in the left bank bracket must be positioned in the bracket in a special order to avoid cylinder cross-fire. Be sure to position the wire in the bracket in the order from front to rear.

Whenever a DURA SPARK high tension wire is removed for any reason from a spark plug, coil, or distributor terminal housing, silicone grease must be applied to the boot before it is reconnected. Using a small clean tool, coat the entire interior surface of the boot with Ford Silicone grease (D7AZ 19A331-A or equivalent).

NOTE: *Should you become mixed up as to wire location, refer to the firing order illustrations.*

FIRING ORDERS

To avoid confusion, replace spark plug wires one at a time.

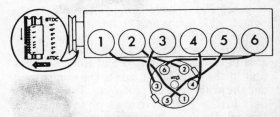

6 cylinder engine - 1,5,3,6,2,4

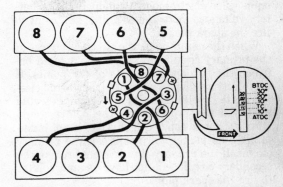

V8 engine, except H.O.302, 351, 400—1,5,4,2,6,3,7,8

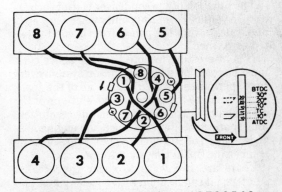

H.O.302, 351 and 400 V8 engines—1,3,7,2,6,5,4,8

POINT TYPE IGNITION

All 1968-73 and some 1974 Fords use breaker point type ignition systems.

Breaker Points

The points function as a circuit breaker for the primary circuit of the ignition system. The ignition coil must boost the 12 volts of electrical pressure supplied by the battery to as much as

25,000 volts in order to fire the plugs. To do this, the coil depends on the points and the condenser to make a clean break in the primary circuit.

The coil has both primary and secondary circuits. When the ignition is turned on, the battery supplies voltage through the coil to the points. The points are connected to ground, completing the primary circuit. As the current passes through the coil, a magnetic field is created in the iron center core of the oil. As the cam in the distributor turns, the points open and the primary circuit collapses. The magnetic field in the primary circuit of the coil cuts through the secondary circuit winding around the iron core. Because of the scientific phenomenon called electromagnetic induction, the battery voltage is increased to a level sufficient to fire the spark plugs.

When the points open, the electrical charge in the primary circuit jumps the gap created between the two open contacts of the points. If this electrical charge were not transferred elsewhere, the metal contacts of the points would melt and the gap between the points would start to change rapidly. If this gap is not maintained, the points will not break the primary circuit. If the primary circuit is not broken, the secondary circuit will not have enough voltage to fire the spark plugs.

Condenser

The function of the condenser is to absorb excessive voltage from the points when they open and thus prevent the points from becoming pitted or burned.

It is interesting to note that the above cycle must be completed by the ignition system every time spark fires. In a V8 engine, all of the spark plugs fire once for every two revolutions of the crankshaft. That means that in one revolution, four spark plugs fire. So when the engine is at an idle speed of 800 rpm, the points are opening and closing 3,200 times a minute.

There are two ways to check the breaker point gap: it can be done with a feeler gauge or a dwell meter. Either way you set the points, you are basically adjusting the amount of time that the points remain open. The time is measured in degrees of distributor rotation. When you measure the gap between the breaker points with a feeler gauge, you are setting the maximum amount the points will open when the rubbing block on the points is on a high point of the distributor cam. When you adjust the points with a dwell mete, you are adjusting the number of degrees that the points will remain closed before they start to open as a high point of the distributor cam approaches the rubbing block of the points.

When you replace a set of points, always replace the condenser at the same time.

When you change the point gap or dwell, you will also have the ignition timing. So, if the point gap or dwell is changed, the ignition timing must be adjusted also.

INSPECTION OF THE POINTS

1. Disconnect the high tension wire from the top of the distributor and the coil.
2. Remove the distributor cap by prying off the spring clips on the sides of the cap.
3. Remove the rotor from the distributor shaft by pulling it straight up. Examine the condition of the rotor. If it is cracked or the metal tip is excessively worn or burned it should be replaced.
4. Pry open the contacts of the points with a screwdriver and check the condition of the con-

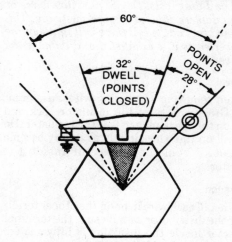

Typical breaker point dwell

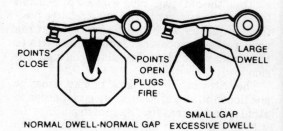

NORMAL DWELL-NORMAL GAP   SMALL GAP EXCESSIVE DWELL

WIDE GAP
INSUFFICIENT DWELL

Dwell angle functions

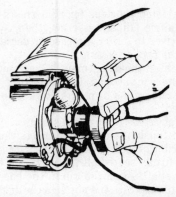

Removing the rotor on the point-type distributor

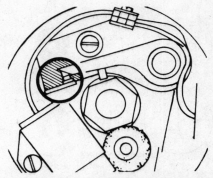

Once the points are installed, make certain that the contact surfaces are properly aligned. If there is misalignment, correct it by bending the STATIONARY arm, NOT THE MOVING ARM! Use a pair of needle-nosed pliers to bend the arm.

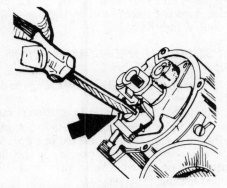

Removing the point holddown screws

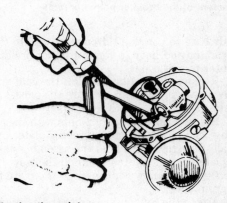

Adjusting the points

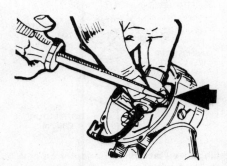

Removing the condenser

tacts. If they are excessively worn, burned or pitted, they should be replaced.

5. If the points are in good condition, adjust them, and replace the rotor and the distributor cap. If the points need to be replaced, follow the replacement procedure given below.

REPLACEMENT OF THE BREAKER POINTS AND CONDENSER

1. Remove the coil high tension wire from the top of the distributor cap. Remove the distributor cap from the distributor and place it out of the way. Remove the rotor from the distributor shaft.

2. Loosen the screw that holds the condenser lead to the body of the breaker points and remove the condenser lead from the points.

3. Remove the screw that holds and grounds the condenser to the distributor body. Remove the condenser from the distributor and discard it.

4. Remove the points assembly attaching screws and adjustment lockscrews. A screwdriver with a holding mechanism will come in

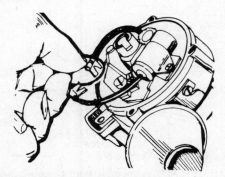

Removing the wires from the points

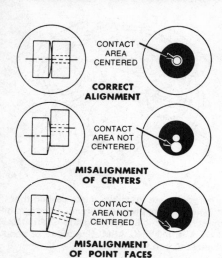

Alignment of the breaker point contacts

handy here so you don't drop a screw into the distributor and have to remove the entire distributor to retrieve it.

5. Remove the points. Wipe off the cam and apply new cam lubricant. Discard the old set of points.

6. Position the new set of points with the locating peg in the hole on the breaker plate, and install the screws that hold the assembly onto the plate. Do not tighten them all the way.

7. Attach the new condenser to the plate to the ground screw.

8. Attach the condenser lead to the points at the proper place.

9. Apply a small amount of cam lubricant to the shaft where the rubbing block of the points touches.

Dwell Angle

ADJUSTMENT OF THE BREAKER POINTS WITH A FEELER GAUGE

1. If the contact points of the assembly are not parallel, bent the stationary contact so they make contact across across the entire surface of the contacts. Bend only the stationary bracket part of the point assembly, not the movable contact.

2. Turn the engine until the rubbing block of the points is on one of the high points of the distributor cam. You can do this by either turning the ignition switch to the start position and releasing it quickly (bumping the engine) or by using a wrench on the bolt that holds the crankshaft pulley to the crankshaft. Be sure to remove the wrench before starting the engine!

3. Place the correct size feeler gauge between the contacts. Make sure it is parallel with the contact surfaces.

4. With your free hand, insert a screw driver

into the notch provided for adjustment or into the eccentric adjusting screw, then twist the screw driver to either increase or decrease the gap to the proper setting.

5. Tighten the adjustment lockscrew and recheck the contact gap to make sure that it didn't change when the lockscrew was tightened.

6. Replace the rotor and distributor cap, and the high tension wire that connects the top of the distributor and the coil. Make sure that the rotor is firmly seated all the way onto the distributor shaft. Align the tab in the base of the distributor cap with the notch in the distributor body. Make sure that the cap is firmly seated on the distributor and that the retainer springs are in place. Make sure that the end of the high tension wire is firmly placed in the top of the distributor and the coil.

ADJUSTMENT OF THE BREAKER POINTS WITH A DWELL METER

1. Adjust the points with a feeler gauge as described above.

2. Connect the dwell meter to ignition circuit according to the manufacturer's instructions. One lead of the meter is connected to a ground an the other lead is to be connected to the distributor post on the coil. An adapter is usually provided for this purpose.

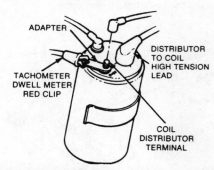

Installing dwell/tachometer adapter on coil (1974 and earlier models)

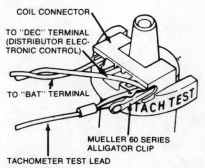

Attaching dwell/tachometer lead to coil connector (1975 and later models)

3. If the dwell meter has a set line on it, adjust the meter to zero the indicator.

4. Start the engine.

NOTE: *Be careful when working on any vehicle while the engine is running. Make sure that the transmission is in Neutral and that the parking brake is applied. Keep hands, clothing, tools, and the wires of the test instruments clear of the rotating fan blades.*

5. Observe the reading on the dwell meter. If the reading is within the specified range, turn off the engine and remove the dwell meter.

6. If the reading is above the specified range, the breaker point gap is too small. If the reading gets below the specified range, the gap is too large. In either case, the engine must be stopped and the gap adjusted in the manner previously covered. After making the adjustment, start the engine and check the reading on the dwell meter. When the correct reading is obtained, disconnect the dwell meter.

7. Check the adjustment of the ignition timing.

ELECTRONIC IGNITION SYSTEMS

Basically, four electronic ignition systems have been used in Ford Motor Company vehicles from 1974-88:

1. DuraSpark I
2. DuraSpark II
3. DuraSpark III
4. Universal Distributor-TFI (EEC-IV)

In 1974, Ford began the use of breakerless ignition systems. The original system was named simply, Breakerless Ignition System. Later, in 1977, this system was named DuraSpark. DuraSpark I and DuraSpark II systems are nearly identical in operation, and virtually identical in appearance. The DuraSpark I uses a special control module which senses current flow through the ignition coil and adjusts the coil on-time for maximum spark intensity. If the DuraSpark I module senses that the ignition is ON, but the distributor shaft is not turning, the current to the coil is turned OFF by the module. The DuraSpark II system does not have this feature. The coil is energized for the full amount of time that the ignition switch is ON. Keep this in mind when servicing the DuraSpark II system, as the ignition system could inadvertently fire while performing ignition system services (such as distributor cap removal) while the ignition is ON. All DuraSpark II systems are easily identified by having a two-piece, flat topped distributor cap.

DuraSpark I was discontinued after the 1981 model year.

In 1980, the new DuraSpark III system was introduced. This version is based on the previous systems, but the input signal is controlled by the EEC system, rather than as function of engine timing and distributor armature posi-

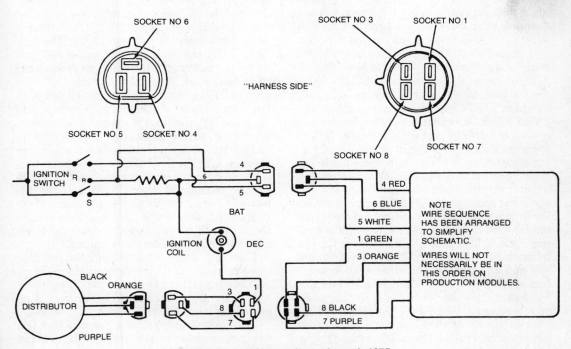

Solid state ignition testing—through 1975

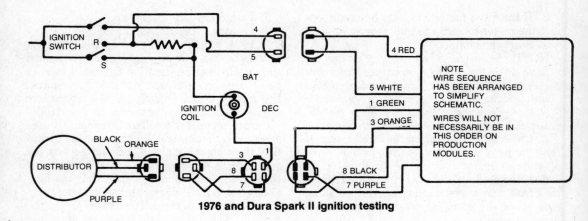

1976 and Dura Spark II ignition testing

tion. The distributor, rotor, cap, and control module are unique to this system; the spark plugs and plug wires are the same as those used with the DuraSpark II system. Although the DuraSpark II and III control modules are similar in appearance, they cannot be interchanged between systems.

Some 1978 and later engines use a special DuraSpark Dual Mode ignition control module. The module is equipped with an altitude sensor, and an economy modulator. This module, when combined with the additional switches and sensor, varies the base engine timing according to altitude and engine load conditions. DuraSpark Dual Mode ignition control modules have three wiring harness from the module.

Some 1981 and later DuraSpark II systems used with some 8-302 cu.in. engines are quipped with a Universal Ignition Module (UIM) which includes a run/retard function. The operation of the module is basically the same as the DuraSpark Dual Mode module.

The Universal Distributor (EEC-IV) has a diecast base which incorporates an externally mounted TFI-IV ignition module, and contains a Hall Effect vane switch stator assembly and provision for fixed octane adjustment. No distributor calibration is required and initial timing adjustment is normally not required. The primary function of the EEC-IV Universal Distributor system is to direct high secondary voltage to the spark plugs. In addition, the distributor supplies crankshaft position and frequency information to a computer using a profile Ignition Pickup. The Hall Effect switch in the distributor consists of a Hall Effect device on one side and a magnet on the other side. A rotary cup which has windows and tabs rotates and passes through the space between the device and the magnet. When a window is between the sides of the switch the magnetic path is not completed and the switch is Off, sending no signal. When a tab passes between the switch the

magnetic path is completed and the Hall Effect Device is turned On and a signal is sent. The voltage pulse (signal) is used by is EEC-IV system for sensing crankshaft position and computing the desired spark advance based on engine demand and calibration.

DuraSpark I
OPERATION

With the ignition switch **ON**, the primary circuit is on and the ignition coil is energized. When the armature spokes approach the magnetic pickup coil assembly, they induce the voltage which tells the amplifier to turn the coil primary current off. A timing circuit in the amplifier module will turn the current on again after the coil field has collapsed. When the current is on, it flows from the battery through the ignition switch, the primary windings of the ignition coil, and through the amplifier module circuits to ground. When the current is off, the magnetic field built up in the ignition coil is allowed to collapse, inducing a high voltage into the secondary windings of the coil. High voltage is produced each time the field is built up and collapsed. When DuraSpark is used in conjunction with the EEC, the EEC computer tells the DuraSpark module when to turn the coil primary current off or on. In this case, the armature position is only a reference signal of engine timing, used by the EEC computer in combination with other reference signals to determine optimum ignition spark timing.

The high voltage flows through the coil high tension lead to the distributor cap where the rotor distributes it to one of the spark plug terminals in the distributor cap. This process is repeated for every power stroke of the engine.

Ignition system troubles are caused by a failure in the primary and/or the secondary circuit; incorrect ignition timing; or incorrect distribu-

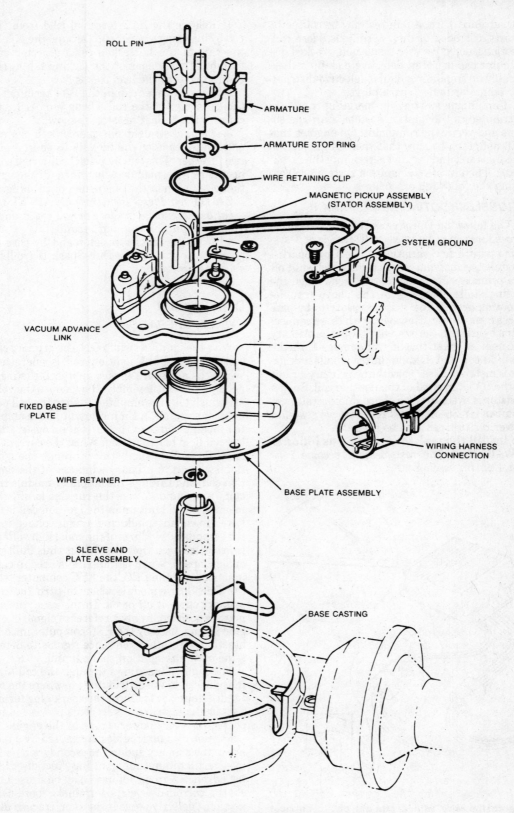

ROLL PIN

ARMATURE

ARMATURE STOP RING

WIRE RETAINING CLIP

MAGNETIC PICKUP ASSEMBLY
(STATOR ASSEMBLY)

SYSTEM GROUND

VACUUM ADVANCE
LINK

FIXED BASE
PLATE

WIRING HARNESS
CONNECTION

WIRE RETAINER

BASE PLATE ASSEMBLY

SLEEVE AND
PLATE ASSEMBLY

BASE CASTING

Breakerless V8 distributor disassembled

tor advance. Circuit failures may be caused by shorts, corroded or dirty terminals, loose connections, defective wire insulation, cracked distributor cap or rotor, defective pick-up coil assembly or amplifier module, defective distributor points or fouled spark plugs.

If an engine starting or operating trouble is attributed to the ignition system, start the engine and verify the complaint. On engines that will not start, be sure that there is gasoline in the fuel tank and the fuel is reaching the carburetor. Then locate the ignition system problem using the following procedures.

TROUBLESHOOTING DURASPARK I

The following DuraSpark II troubleshooting procedures may be used on DuraSpark I systems with a few variations. The DuraSpark I module has internal connections which shut off the primary circuit in the run mode when the engine stalls. To perform the above troubleshooting procedures, it is necessary to by-pass these connections. However, with these connections by-passed, the current flow in the primary becomes so great that it will damage both the ignition coil and module unless a ballast resistor is installed in series with the primary circuit at the BAT terminal of the ignition coil. Such a resistor is available from Ford (Motorcraft part number DY-36). A 1.3Ω, 100 watt wire-wound power resistor can also be used.

To install the resistor, proceed as follows.
WARNING: *The resistor will become very hot during testing.*

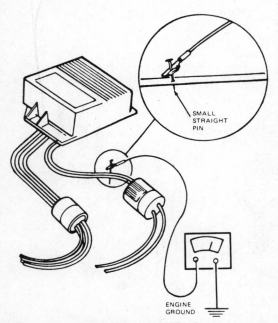

Pierce the wire with a straight pin to connect tester

1. Release the BAT terminal lead from the coil by inserting a paper cup through the hole in the rear of the horseshoe coil connector and manipulating it against the locking tab in the connector until the lead comes free.
2. Insert a paper clip in the BAT terminal of the connector of the coil. Using jumper leads, connect the ballast resistor as shown.
3. Using a straight pin, pierce both the red and white leads of the module to short these two together. This will by-pass the internal connections of the module which turn off the ignition circuit when the engine is not running.
CAUTION: *Pierce the wires only AFTER the ballast resistor is in place or you could damage the ignition coil and module.*
4. With the ballast resistor and by-pass in place, proceed with the DuraSpark II troubleshooting procedures.

Dura Spark II
SYSTEM OPERATION

With the ignition switch **ON**, the primary circuit is on and the ignition coil is energized. When the armature spokes approach the magnetic pickup coil assembly, they induce the voltage which tells the amplifier to turn the coil primary current off. A timing circuit in the amplifier module will turn the current on again after the coil field has collapsed. When the current is on, it flows from the battery through the ignition switch, the primary windings of the ignition coil, and through the amplifier module circuits to ground. When the current is off, the magnetic field built up in the ignition coil is allowed to collapse, inducing a high voltage into the secondary windings of the coil. High voltage is produced each time the field is thus built up and collapsed. When DuraSpark is used in conjunction with the EEC, the EEC computer tells the DuraSpark module when to turn the coil primary current off or on. In this case, the armature position is only a reference signal of engine timing, used by the EEC computer in combination with other reference signals to determine optimum ignition spark timing.

The high voltage flows through the coil high tension lead to the distributor cap where the rotor distributes it to one of the spark plug terminals in the distributor cap. This process is repeated for every power stroke of the engine.

Ignition system troubles are caused by a failure in the primary and/or the secondary circuit; incorrect ignition timing; or incorrect distributor advance. Circuit failures may be caused by shorts, corroded or dirty terminals, loose connections, defective wire insulation, cracked distributor cap or rotor, defective pick-up coil assembly or amplifier module, defective distributor points or fouled spark plugs.

If an engine starting or operating trouble is attributed to the ignition system, start the engine and verify the complaint. On engines that will not start, be sure that there is gasoline in the fuel tank and the fuel is reaching the carburetor. Then locate the ignition system problem using the following procedures.

TROUBLESHOOTING DURASPARK II

The following procedures can be used to determine whether the ignition system is working or not. If these procedures fail to correct the problem, a full troubleshooting procedure should be performed.

Preliminary Checks

1. Check the battery's state of charge and connections.
2. Inspect all wires and connections for breaks, cuts, abrasions, or burn spots. Repair as necessary.
3. Unplug all connectors one at a time and inspect for corroded or burned contacts. Repair and plug connectors back together. DO NOT remove the dielectric compound in the connectors.

4. Check for loose or damaged spark plug or coil wires. A wire resistance check is given at the end of this section. If the boots or nipples are removed on 8mm ignition wires, reline the inside of each with new silicone dielectric compound (Motorcraft WA-10).

Special Tools

To perform the following tests, two special tools are needed; the ignition test jumper shown in the illustration and a modified spark plug. Use the illustration to assembly the ignition test jumper. The test jumper must be used when performing the following tests. The modified spark plug is basically a spark plug with the side electrode removed. Ford makes a special tool called a Spark Tester for this purpose, which besides not having a side electrode is equipped with a spring clip so that it can be grounded to engine metal. It is recommended that the Spark Tester be used as there is less change of being shocked.

Run Mode Spark Test

NOTE: *The wire colors given here are the main colors of the wires, not the dots or hashmarks.*

Test Sequence

	Test Voltage Between	Should Be	If Not, Conduct
1980–82			
Key On	Socket #4 and Engine Ground	Battery Voltage ±0.1 Volt	Module Bias Test
	Socket #1 and Engine Ground	Battery Voltage ±0.1 Volt	Battery Source Test
Cranking	Socket #5 and Engine Ground	8 to 12 volts	Cranking Test
	Jumper #1 to #8—Read Coil "Bat" Term & Engine Ground	more than 6 volts	Starting Circuit Test
	Sockets #7 and #3	½ volt minimum wiggle	Distributor Hardware Test
Key Off	Sockets #7 and #3 Socket #8 and Engine Ground Socket #7 and Engine Ground Socket #3 and Engine Ground	400 to 800 ohms 0 ohms more than 70,000 ohms more than 70,000 ohms	Magnetic Pick-up (Stator) Test
	Socket #4 and Coil Tower	7000 to 13,000 ohms	Coil Test
	Socket #1 and Coil "Bat" Term	1.0 to 2.0 ohms Breakerless & Dura Spark II	
		0.5 to 1.5 ohms Dura-Spark I	
	Socket #1 and Engine Ground	more than 4.0 ohms	Short Test
	Socket #4 and Coil "Bat" Term (Except Dura-Spark I)	1.0 to 2.0 ohms Breakerless	Resistance Wire Test
		0.7 to 1.7 ohms Dura Spark II	

IGNITION SYSTEM
II. Primary (Low Voltage) Portion—A. Dura Spark II

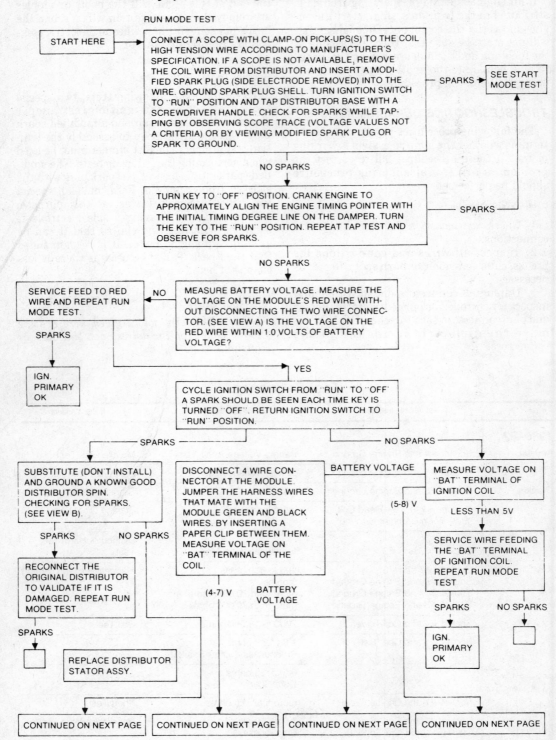

RUN MODE TEST

START HERE → CONNECT A SCOPE WITH CLAMP-ON PICK-UPS(S) TO THE COIL HIGH TENSION WIRE ACCORDING TO MANUFACTURER'S SPECIFICATION. IF A SCOPE IS NOT AVAILABLE, REMOVE THE COIL WIRE FROM DISTRIBUTOR AND INSERT A MODIFIED SPARK PLUG (SIDE ELECTRODE REMOVED) INTO THE WIRE. GROUND SPARK PLUG SHELL. TURN IGNITION SWITCH TO "RUN" POSITION AND TAP DISTRIBUTOR BASE WITH A SCREWDRIVER HANDLE. CHECK FOR SPARKS WHILE TAPPING BY OBSERVING SCOPE TRACE (VOLTAGE VALUES NOT A CRITERIA) OR BY VIEWING MODIFIED SPARK PLUG OR SPARK TO GROUND. — SPARKS → SEE START MODE TEST

NO SPARKS ↓

TURN KEY TO "OFF" POSITION. CRANK ENGINE TO APPROXIMATELY ALIGN THE ENGINE TIMING POINTER WITH THE INITIAL TIMING DEGREE LINE ON THE DAMPER. TURN THE KEY TO THE "RUN" POSITION. REPEAT TAP TEST AND OBSERVE FOR SPARKS. — SPARKS

NO SPARKS ↓

SERVICE FEED TO RED WIRE AND REPEAT RUN MODE TEST. ← NO — MEASURE BATTERY VOLTAGE. MEASURE THE VOLTAGE ON THE MODULE'S RED WIRE WITHOUT DISCONNECTING THE TWO WIRE CONNECTOR. (SEE VIEW A) IS THE VOLTAGE ON THE RED WIRE WITHIN 1.0 VOLTS OF BATTERY VOLTAGE?

SPARKS ↓

IGN. PRIMARY OK

YES →

CYCLE IGNITION SWITCH FROM "RUN" TO "OFF" A SPARK SHOULD BE SEEN EACH TIME KEY IS TURNED "OFF". RETURN IGNITION SWITCH TO "RUN" POSITION.

— SPARKS —   — NO SPARKS —

SUBSTITUTE (DON'T INSTALL) AND GROUND A KNOWN GOOD DISTRIBUTOR SPIN. CHECKING FOR SPARKS. (SEE VIEW B).

DISCONNECT 4 WIRE CONNECTOR AT THE MODULE. JUMPER THE HARNESS WIRES THAT MATE WITH THE MODULE GREEN AND BLACK WIRES. BY INSERTING A PAPER CLIP BETWEEN THEM. MEASURE VOLTAGE ON "BAT" TERMINAL OF THE COIL. — BATTERY VOLTAGE → MEASURE VOLTAGE ON "BAT" TERMINAL OF IGNITION COIL

(5-8) V

LESS THAN 5V ↓

SPARKS ↓   NO SPARKS ↓

RECONNECT THE ORIGINAL DISTRIBUTOR TO VALIDATE IF IT IS DAMAGED. REPEAT RUN MODE TEST.

SERVICE WIRE FEEDING THE "BAT" TERMINAL OF IGNITION COIL. REPEAT RUN MODE TEST.

SPARKS ↓

REPLACE DISTRIBUTOR STATOR ASSY.

(4-7) V   BATTERY VOLTAGE

SPARKS ↓   NO SPARKS ↓

IGN. PRIMARY OK

| CONTINUED ON NEXT PAGE | CONTINUED ON NEXT PAGE | CONTINUED ON NEXT PAGE | CONTINUED ON NEXT PAGE |

IGNITION SYSTEM (CONTINUED)
II. Primary (Low Voltage) Portion (continued)
A. Dura Spark II (continued)

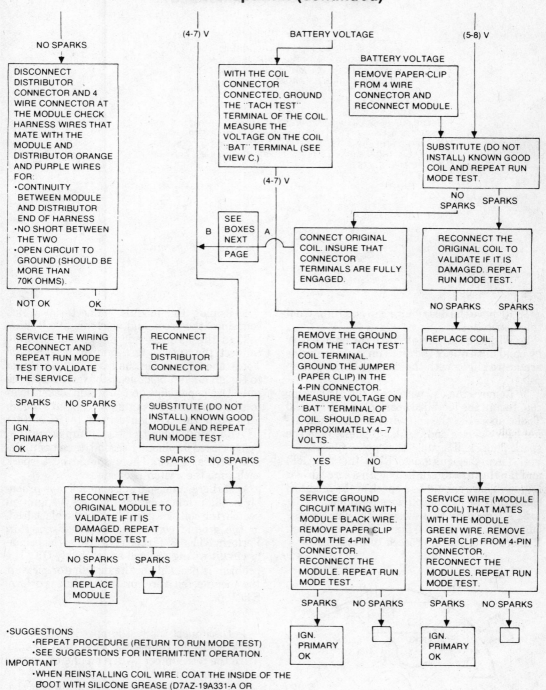

NO SPARKS

DISCONNECT DISTRIBUTOR CONNECTOR AND 4 WIRE CONNECTOR AT THE MODULE CHECK HARNESS WIRES THAT MATE WITH THE MODULE AND DISTRIBUTOR ORANGE AND PURPLE WIRES FOR:
• CONTINUITY BETWEEN MODULE AND DISTRIBUTOR END OF HARNESS
• NO SHORT BETWEEN THE TWO
• OPEN CIRCUIT TO GROUND (SHOULD BE MORE THAN 70K OHMS).

NOT OK — OK

SERVICE THE WIRING RECONNECT AND REPEAT RUN MODE TEST TO VALIDATE THE SERVICE.

SPARKS   NO SPARKS

IGN. PRIMARY OK

RECONNECT THE DISTRIBUTOR CONNECTOR.

SUBSTITUTE (DO NOT INSTALL) KNOWN GOOD MODULE AND REPEAT RUN MODE TEST.

SPARKS   NO SPARKS

RECONNECT THE ORIGINAL MODULE TO VALIDATE IF IT IS DAMAGED. REPEAT RUN MODE TEST.

NO SPARKS   SPARKS

REPLACE MODULE

(4-7) V   BATTERY VOLTAGE   (5-8) V

BATTERY VOLTAGE

WITH THE COIL CONNECTOR CONNECTED, GROUND THE "TACH TEST" TERMINAL OF THE COIL. MEASURE THE VOLTAGE ON THE COIL "BAT" TERMINAL (SEE VIEW C.)

(4-7) V

B   SEE BOXES NEXT PAGE   A

CONNECT ORIGINAL COIL. INSURE THAT CONNECTOR TERMINALS ARE FULLY ENGAGED.

REMOVE THE GROUND FROM THE "TACH TEST" COIL TERMINAL. GROUND THE JUMPER (PAPER CLIP) IN THE 4-PIN CONNECTOR. MEASURE VOLTAGE ON "BAT" TERMINAL OF COIL. SHOULD READ APPROXIMATELY 4-7 VOLTS.

YES   NO

SERVICE GROUND CIRCUIT MATING WITH MODULE BLACK WIRE. REMOVE PAPER CLIP FROM THE 4-PIN CONNECTOR. RECONNECT THE MODULE. REPEAT RUN MODE TEST.

SPARKS   NO SPARKS

IGN. PRIMARY OK

REMOVE PAPER CLIP FROM 4 WIRE CONNECTOR AND RECONNECT MODULE.

SUBSTITUTE (DO NOT INSTALL) KNOWN GOOD COIL AND REPEAT RUN MODE TEST.

NO SPARKS   SPARKS

RECONNECT THE ORIGINAL COIL TO VALIDATE IF IT IS DAMAGED. REPEAT RUN MODE TEST.

NO SPARKS   SPARKS

REPLACE COIL.

SERVICE WIRE (MODULE TO COIL) THAT MATES WITH THE MODULE GREEN WIRE. REMOVE PAPER CLIP FROM 4-PIN CONNECTOR. RECONNECT THE MODULES. REPEAT RUN MODE TEST.

SPARKS   NO SPARKS

IGN. PRIMARY OK

• SUGGESTIONS
    • REPEAT PROCEDURE (RETURN TO RUN MODE TEST)
    • SEE SUGGESTIONS FOR INTERMITTENT OPERATION.
IMPORTANT
    • WHEN REINSTALLING COIL WIRE. COAT THE INSIDE OF THE BOOT WITH SILICONE GREASE (D7AZ-19A331-A OR EQUIVALENT) USING SMALL, CLEAN SCREWDRIVER BLADE.

IGNITION SYSTEM (CONTINUED)
II. Primary (Low Voltage) Portion (Continued)
A. Dura Spark II (continued)

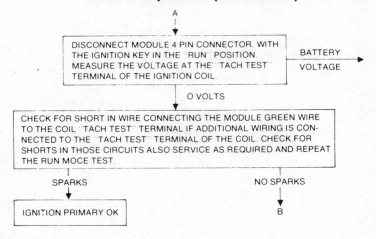

STEP 1

1. Remove the distributor cap and rotor from the distributor.

2. With the ignition off, turn the engine over by hand until one of the teeth on the distributor armature aligns with the magnet in the pickup coil.

3. Remove the coil wire from the distributor cap. Install the modified spark plug (see Special Tools, above) in the coil wire terminal and using heavy gloves and insulated pliers, hold the spark plug shell against the engine block.

4. Turn the ignition to RUN (not START) and tap the distributor body with a screwdriver handle. There should be a spark at the modified spark plug or at the coil wire terminal.

5. If a good spark is evident, the primary circuit is OK: perform the Start Mode Spark Test. If there is no spark, proceed to STEP 2.

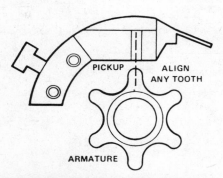

Align the armature tooth with the pickup

STEP 2

1. Unplug the module connector(s) which contain(s) the green and black module leads.

2. In the harness side of the connector(s), connect the special test jumper (see Special Tools, above) between the leads which connect to the green and black leads of the module pig tails. Use paper clips on connector socket holes to make contact. Do not allow clips to ground.

3. Turn the ignition switch to RUN (not START) and close the test jumper switch. Leave closed for about 1 second, then open. Repeat several times. There should be a spark each time the switch is opened.

4. If there is no spark, the problem is probably in the primary circuit through the ignition switch, the coil, the green lead or the black lead, or the ground connection in the distributor; Perform STEP 3. If there is a spark, the primary circuit wiring and coil are probably OK. The problem is probably in the distributor pick-up, the module red wire, or the module: perform STEP 6.

STEP 3

1. Disconnect the test jumper lead from the black lead and connect it to a good ground. Turn the test jumper switch on and off several times as in STEP 2.

2. If there is no spark, the problem is probably in the green lead, the coil, or the coil feed circuit: perform STEP 5.

3. If there is spark, the problem is probably in the black lead or the distributor ground connection: perform STEP 4.

IGNITION SYSTEM (CONTINUED)
II. Primary (Low Voltage) Portion (continued)
A. Dura Spark II (continued)

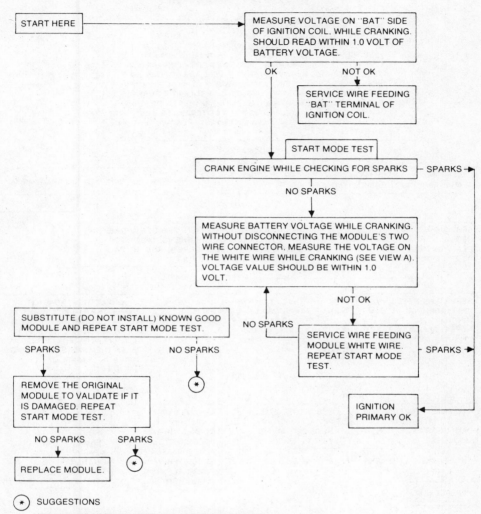

(*) SUGGESTIONS
> •REPEAT PROCEDURE (RETURN TO RUN MODE TEST)
> •SEE SUGGESTIONS FOR INTERMITTENT OPERATION.

IMPORTANT
> •WHEN REINSTALLING COIL WIRE, COAT THE INSIDE OF THE BOOT WITH SILICONE GREASE (D7AZ-19A331-A OR EQUIVALENT DOW 111 OR GE-G627) USING A SMALL, CLEAN SCREWDRIVER BLADE.

STEP 4

1. Connect an ohmmeter between the black lead and ground. With the meter on its lowest scale, there should be no measurable resistance in the circuit. If there is resistance, check the distributor ground connection and the black lead from the module. Repair as necessary, remove the ohmmeter, plug in all connections and repeat STEP 1.

2. If there is no resistance, the primary ground wiring is OK: perform STEP 6.

STEP 5

1. Disconnect the test jumper from the green lead and ground and connect it between the TACH-TEST terminal of the coil and a good ground to the engine.

2. With the ignition switch in the RUN position, turn the jumper switch on. Hold it on for about 1 second then turn it off as in Step 2. Repeat several times. There should be a spark each time the switch in turned off. If there is no spark, the problem is probably in the primary

RUN MODE TEST

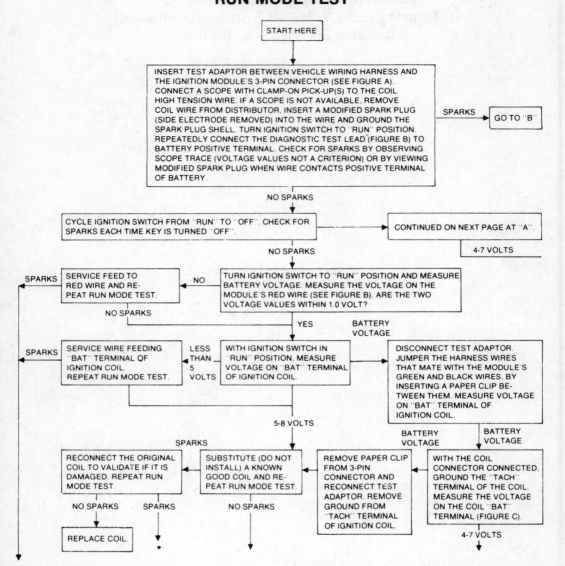

START HERE

INSERT TEST ADAPTOR BETWEEN VEHICLE WIRING HARNESS AND THE IGNITION MODULE'S 3-PIN CONNECTOR (SEE FIGURE A). CONNECT A SCOPE WITH CLAMP-ON PICK-UP(S) TO THE COIL HIGH TENSION WIRE. IF A SCOPE IS NOT AVAILABLE, REMOVE COIL WIRE FROM DISTRIBUTOR, INSERT A MODIFIED SPARK PLUG (SIDE ELECTRODE REMOVED) INTO THE WIRE AND GROUND THE SPARK PLUG SHELL. TURN IGNITION SWITCH TO "RUN" POSITION. REPEATEDLY CONNECT THE DIAGNOSTIC TEST LEAD (FIGURE B) TO BATTERY POSITIVE TERMINAL. CHECK FOR SPARKS BY OBSERVING SCOPE TRACE (VOLTAGE VALUES NOT A CRITERION) OR BY VIEWING MODIFIED SPARK PLUG WHEN WIRE CONTACTS POSITIVE TERMINAL OF BATTERY.

SPARKS → GO TO "B"

NO SPARKS

CYCLE IGNITION SWITCH FROM "RUN" TO "OFF". CHECK FOR SPARKS EACH TIME KEY IS TURNED "OFF".

CONTINUED ON NEXT PAGE AT "A".

4-7 VOLTS

NO SPARKS

SPARKS ← SERVICE FEED TO RED WIRE AND RE-PEAT RUN MODE TEST. ← NO ← TURN IGNITION SWITCH TO "RUN" POSITION AND MEASURE BATTERY VOLTAGE. MEASURE THE VOLTAGE ON THE MODULE'S RED WIRE (SEE FIGURE B). ARE THE TWO VOLTAGE VALUES WITHIN 1.0 VOLT?

NO SPARKS

YES

BATTERY VOLTAGE

SPARKS ← SERVICE WIRE FEEDING "BAT" TERMINAL OF IGNITION COIL. REPEAT RUN MODE TEST. ← LESS THAN 5 VOLTS ← WITH IGNITION SWITCH IN "RUN" POSITION, MEASURE VOLTAGE ON "BAT" TERMINAL OF IGNITION COIL.

DISCONNECT TEST ADAPTOR. JUMPER THE HARNESS WIRES THAT MATE WITH THE MODULE'S GREEN AND BLACK WIRES, BY INSERTING A PAPER CLIP BE-TWEEN THEM. MEASURE VOLTAGE ON "BAT" TERMINAL OF IGNITION COIL.

5-8 VOLTS

BATTERY VOLTAGE

BATTERY VOLTAGE

SPARKS

RECONNECT THE ORIGINAL COIL TO VALIDATE IF IT IS DAMAGED. REPEAT RUN MODE TEST.

SUBSTITUTE (DO NOT INSTALL) A KNOWN GOOD COIL AND RE-PEAT RUN MODE TEST.

REMOVE PAPER CLIP FROM 3-PIN CONNECTOR AND RECONNECT TEST ADAPTOR. REMOVE GROUND FROM "TACH" TERMINAL OF IGNITION COIL.

WITH THE COIL CONNECTOR CONNECTED, GROUND THE "TACH" TERMINAL OF THE COIL. MEASURE THE VOLTAGE ON THE COIL "BAT" TERMINAL (FIGURE C).

NO SPARKS   SPARKS

NO SPARKS

4-7 VOLTS

REPLACE COIL.

*

*SUGGESTIONS:

•REPEAT PROCEDURE (START AT RUN MODE TEST)

•SEE SUGGESTIONS FOR INTERMITTENT OPERATION

circuit running through the ignition switch to the coil BAT terminal, or in the coil itself. Check coil resistance (test given later in this section), and check the coil for internal shorts or opens. Check the coil feed circuit for opens, shorts, or high resistance. Repair as necessary, reconnect all connectors and repeat STEP 1. If there is spark, the coil and its feed circuit are OK. The problem could be in the green lead be-tween the coil and the module. Check for an open or short, repair as necessary, reconnect all connectors and repeat STEP 1.

STEP 6

To perform this step, a voltmeter which is not combined with a dwell meter is needed. The slight needle oscillations (½v) you'll be looking for may not be detectable on the combined voltmeter/dwell meter unit.

1. Connect a voltmeter between the orange and purple leads on the harness side of the module connectors.

CAUTION: *On catalytic converter equipped cars, disconnect the air supply line between*

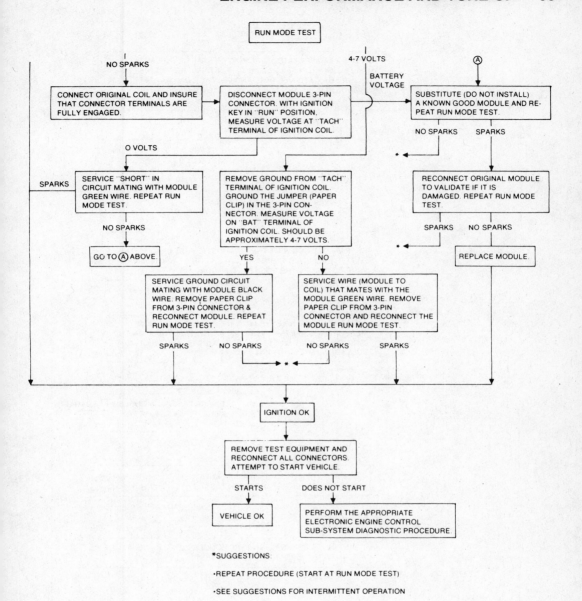

RUN MODE TEST

CONNECT ORIGINAL COIL AND INSURE THAT CONNECTOR TERMINALS ARE FULLY ENGAGED.

DISCONNECT MODULE 3-PIN CONNECTOR. WITH IGNITION KEY IN "RUN" POSITION, MEASURE VOLTAGE AT "TACH" TERMINAL OF IGNITION COIL.

SUBSTITUTE (DO NOT INSTALL) A KNOWN GOOD MODULE AND RE-PEAT RUN MODE TEST.

SERVICE "SHORT" IN CIRCUIT MATING WITH MODULE GREEN WIRE. REPEAT RUN MODE TEST.

REMOVE GROUND FROM "TACH" TERMINAL OF IGNITION COIL. GROUND THE JUMPER (PAPER CLIP) IN THE 3-PIN CON-NECTOR. MEASURE VOLTAGE ON "BAT" TERMINAL OF IGNITION COIL. SHOULD BE APPROXIMATELY 4-7 VOLTS.

RECONNECT ORIGINAL MODULE TO VALIDATE IF IT IS DAMAGED. REPEAT RUN MODE TEST.

GO TO (A) ABOVE.

REPLACE MODULE.

SERVICE GROUND CIRCUIT MATING WITH MODULE BLACK WIRE. REMOVE PAPER CLIP FROM 3-PIN CONNECTOR & RECONNECT MODULE. REPEAT RUN MODE TEST.

SERVICE WIRE (MODULE TO COIL) THAT MATES WITH THE MODULE GREEN WIRE. REMOVE PAPER CLIP FROM 3-PIN CONNECTOR AND RECONNECT THE MODULE RUN MODE TEST.

IGNITION OK

REMOVE TEST EQUIPMENT AND RECONNECT ALL CONNECTORS. ATTEMPT TO START VEHICLE.

VEHICLE OK

PERFORM THE APPROPRIATE ELECTRONIC ENGINE CONTROL SUB-SYSTEM DIAGNOSTIC PROCEDURE.

*SUGGESTIONS:

•REPEAT PROCEDURE (START AT RUN MODE TEST)

•SEE SUGGESTIONS FOR INTERMITTENT OPERATION

the Thermactor by-pass valve and the manifold before cranking the engine with the ignition off. This will prevent damage to the catalytic converter. After testing, run the engine for at least 3 minutes before reconnecting the by-pass valve, to clear excess fuel from the exhaust system.

2. Set the voltmeter on its lowest scale and crank the engine. The meter needle should oscillate slightly (about ½v). If the meter does not oscillate, check the circuit through the magnetic pick-up in the distributor for open, shorts, shorts to ground and resistance. Resistance between the orange and purple leads should be 400-1,000Ω, and between each lead and ground should be more than 70,000Ω. Repair as necessary, reconnect all connectors and repeat STEP 1.

If the meter oscillates, the problem is probably in the power feed to the module (red wire) or in the module itself: proceed to STEP 7.

STEP 7

1. Remove all meters and jumpers and plug in all connectors.

2. Turn the ignition switch to the RUN position and measure voltage between the battery positive terminal and engine ground. It should be 12 volts.

3. Next, measure voltage between the red

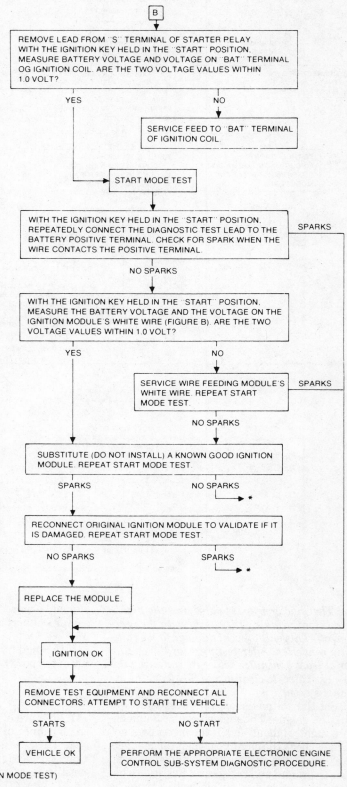

B

REMOVE LEAD FROM "S" TERMINAL OF STARTER PELAY.
WITH THE IGNITION KEY HELD IN THE "START" POSITION,
MEASURE BATTERY VOLTAGE AND VOLTAGE ON "BAT" TERMINAL
OG IGNITION COIL. ARE THE TWO VOLTAGE VALUES WITHIN
1.0 VOLT?

YES   NO

SERVICE FEED TO "BAT" TERMINAL
OF IGNITION COIL.

START MODE TEST

WITH THE IGNITION KEY HELD IN THE "START" POSITION,
REPEATEDLY CONNECT THE DIAGNOSTIC TEST LEAD TO THE
BATTERY POSITIVE TERMINAL. CHECK FOR SPARK WHEN THE
WIRE CONTACTS THE POSITIVE TERMINAL.   SPARKS

NO SPARKS

WITH THE IGNITION KEY HELD IN THE "START" POSITION,
MEASURE THE BATTERY VOLTAGE AND THE VOLTAGE ON THE
IGNITION MODULE'S WHITE WIRE (FIGURE B). ARE THE TWO
VOLTAGE VALUES WITHIN 1.0 VOLT?

YES   NO

SERVICE WIRE FEEDING MODULE'S   SPARKS
WHITE WIRE. REPEAT START
MODE TEST.

NO SPARKS

SUBSTITUTE (DO NOT INSTALL) A KNOWN GOOD IGNITION
MODULE. REPEAT START MODE TEST.

SPARKS   NO SPARKS
                                    ➞ *

RECONNECT ORIGINAL IGNITION MODULE TO VALIDATE IF IT
IS DAMAGED. REPEAT START MODE TEST.

NO SPARKS   SPARKS
                                ➞ *

REPLACE THE MODULE.

IGNITION OK

REMOVE TEST EQUIPMENT AND RECONNECT ALL
CONNECTORS. ATTEMPT TO START THE VEHICLE.

STARTS   NO START

VEHICLE OK   PERFORM THE APPROPRIATE ELECTRONIC ENGINE
CONTROL SUB-SYSTEM DIAGNOSTIC PROCEDURE.

*SUGGESTIONS:

•REPEAT PROCEDURE (START AT RUN MODE TEST)

•SEE SUGGESTIONS FOR INTERMITTENT OPERATION

lead of the module and engine ground. To mark this measurement, it will be necessary to pierce the red wire with a straight pin and connect the voltmeter to the straight pin and to ground. DO NOT ALLOW THE STRAIGHT PIN TO GROUND ITSELF!

4. The two readings should be within one volt of each other. If not within one volt, the problem is in the power feed to the red lead. Check for shorts, open, or high resistance and correct as necessary. After repairs, repeat Step 1.

If the readings are within one volt, the problem is probably in the module. Replace it with a good module and repeat STEP 1. If this corrects the problem, reconnect the old module and repeat STEP 1. If the problem returns, permanently install the new module.

Start Mode Spark Test

NOTE: *The wire colors given here are the main colors of the wires, not the dots or hashmarks.*

1. Remove the coil wire from the distributor cap. Install the modified spark plug mentioned under Special Tools, above, in the coil wire and ground it to engine metal either by its spring clip (Spark Tester) or by holding the spark plug shell against the engine block with insulated pliers.

NOTE: *See CAUTION under STEP 6 of Run Mode Spark Test, above.*

2. Have an assistant crank the engine using the ignition switch and check for spark. If there is good spark, the problem is probably in distributor cap, rotor, ignition cables or spark plugs. If there is no spark, proceed to Step 3.

3. Measure the battery voltage. Next, measure the voltage at the white wire of the module while cranking the engine. To mark this measurement, it will be necessary to pierce the white wire with a straight pin and connect the voltmeter to the straight pin and to ground. DO NOT ALLOW THE STRAIGHT PIN TO GROUND ITSELF. The battery voltage and the voltage at the white wire should be within 1 volt of each other. If the readings are not within 1 volt of each other, check and repair the feed through the ignition switch to the white wire. Recheck for spark (Step 1). If the readings are within 1 volt of each other, or if there is still no spark after the power feed to white wire is repaired, proceed to Step 4.

4. Measure the coil BAT terminal voltage while cranking the engine. The reading should be within 1 volt of battery voltage. If the readings are not within 1 volt of each other, check and repair the feed through the ignition switch to the coil. If the readings are within 1 volt of each other, the problem is probably in the igni-

tion module. Substitute another module and repeat the test for spark (Step 1).

TFI-IV System
SYSTEM OPERATION

The TFI-IV ignition system features a universal distributor using no centrifugal or vacuum advance. The distributor has a die cast base which incorporates an integrally mounted TFI (Thick Film Integrated) ignition module, a Hall Effect vane switch stator assembly and provision for fixed octane adjustment. The TFI system uses an E-Core ignition coil in lieu of the DuraSpark coil. No distributor calibration is required and initial timing is not a normal adjustment, since advance etc. is controlled by the EEC-IV system.

GENERAL TESTING

Ignition Coil Test

The ignition coil must be diagnosed separately from the rest of the ignition system.

1. Primary resistance is measured between the two primary (low voltage) coil terminals, with the coil connector disconnected and the ignition switch off. Primary resistance should be 0.3-1.0Ω.

2. On DuraSpark ignitions, the secondary resistance is measured between the BATT and high voltage (secondary) terminals of the ignition coil with the ignition off, and the wiring from the coil disconnected. Secondary resistance must be $8,000$-$11,500\Omega$.

3. If resistance tests are okay, but the coil is still suspected, test the coil on a coil tester by following the test equipment manufacturer's instructions for a standard coil. If the reading differs from the original test, check for a defective harness.

Spark Plug Wire Resistance

Resistance on these wires must not exceed $5,000\Omega$ per foot. To properly measure this, remove the wires from the plugs, and remove the distributor cap. Measure the resistance through the distributor cap at that end. Do not pierce any ignition wire for any reason. Measure only from the two ends.

NOTE: *Silicone grease must be re-applied to the spark plug wires whenever they are removed. When removing the wires from the spark plugs, a special tool should be used. do not pull on the wires. Grasp and twist the boot to remove the wire. Whenever the high tension wires are removed from the plugs, coil, or distributor, silicone grease must be applied to the boot before reconnection. Use a clean small screwdriver blase to coat the entire inte-*

1976 Test Sequence

	Test Voltage Between	Should Be	If Not, Conduct
Key On	Socket #4 and Engine Ground	Battery Voltage ± 0.1 Volt	Battery Source Test
	Socket #1 and Engine Ground	Battery Voltage ± 0.1 Volt	Battery Source Test
Cranking	Socket #5 and Engine Ground	8 to 12 volts	Check Supply Circuit (starting) through Ignition Switch
	Jumper #1 to #8 Read #6	more than 6 volts	Starting Circuit Test
	Pin #3 and Pin #8	½ volt minimum AC or any DC volt wiggle	Distributor Hardware Test
Key Off	Socket #8 and #3 Socket #7 and Engine Ground Socket #8 and Engine Ground Socket #3 and Engine Ground	400 to 800 ohms 0 ohms more than 70,000 ohms more than 70,000 ohms	Magnetic Pick-up (Stator) Test
	Socket #4 and Coil Tower	7,000 to 13,000 ohms	Coil Test
	Socket #1 and Engine Ground	more than 4.0 ohms	Short Test

rior surface with Ford silicone grease D7AZ-19A331-A, Dow Corning #111, or General Electric G-627.

Adjustments

The air gap between the armature and magnetic pick-up coil in the distributor is not adjustable, nor are there any adjustment for the amplifier module. Inoperative components are simply replaced. Any attempt to connect components outside the vehicle may result in component failure.

TROUBLESHOOTING THE TFI-IV SYSTEM

NOTE: *After performing any test which requires piercing a wire with a straight pin, remove the straight pin and seal the holes in the wire with silicone sealer.*

Ignition Coil Secondary Voltage

1. Disconnect the secondary (high voltage) coil wire from the distributor cap and install a spark tester between the coil wire and ground.
2. Crank the engine. A good, strong spark should be noted at the spark tester. If spark is noted, but the engine will not start, check the spark plugs, spark plug wiring, and fuel system. If there is no spark at the tester: Check the ignition coil secondary wire resistance; it should be no more than 5,000Ω per foot. Inspect the ignition coil for damage and/or carbon tracking. With the distributor cap removed, verify that the distributor shaft turns with the engine; if it does not, repair the engine as required. If the fault was not found proceed to the next test.

Ignition Coil Primary Circuit Switching

1. Insert a small straight pin in the wire which runs from the coil negative (−) terminal

to the TFI module, about 1″ from the module. WARNING: *The pin must not touch ground!*
2. Connect a 12 VDC test lamp between the straight pin and an engine ground.
3. Crank the engine, noting the operation of the test lamp. If the test lamp flashes, proceed to the next test. If the test lamp lights but does not flash, proceed to the Wiring Harness test. If the test lamp does not light at all, proceed to the Primary Circuit Continuity test.

Ignition Coil Resistance

Refer to the General Testing for an explanation of the resistance tests. Replace the ignition coil if the resistance is out of the specification range.

Wiring Harness

1. Disconnect the wiring harness connector from the TFI module; the connector tabs must be PUSHED to disengage the connector. Inspect the connector for damage, dirt, and corrosion.
2. Attach the negative lead of a voltmeter to the base of the distributor. Attach the other voltmeter lead to a small straight pin. With the ignition switch in the RUN position, insert the straight pin into the No. 1 terminal of the TFI module connector. Note the voltage reading. With the ignition switch in the RUN position, move the straight pin to the No. 2 connector terminal. Again, note the voltage reading. Move the straight pin to the No. 3 connector terminal, then turn the ignition switch to the START position. Note the voltage reading then turn the ignition OFF.
3. The voltage readings should all be at least 90% of the available battery voltage. If the readings are okay, proceed to the Stator Assembly

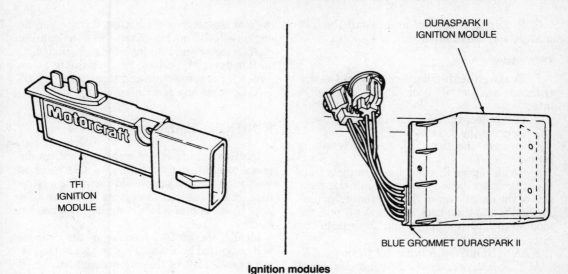

Ignition modules

and Module test. If any reading is less than 90% of the battery voltage, inspect the wiring, connectors, and/or ignition switch for defects. if the voltage is low only at the No. 1 terminal, proceed to the ignition coil primary voltage test.

Stator Assembly and Module

1. Remove the distributor from the engine.
2. Remove the TFI module from the distributor.

3. Inspect the distributor terminals, ground screw, and stator wiring for damage. Repair as necessary.
4. Measure the resistance of the stator assembly, using an ohmmeter. If the ohmmeter reading is 800-975Ω, the stator is okay, but the TFI module must be replaced. If the ohmmeter reading is less than 800Ω or more than 975Ω; the TFI module is okay, but the stator module must be replaced.

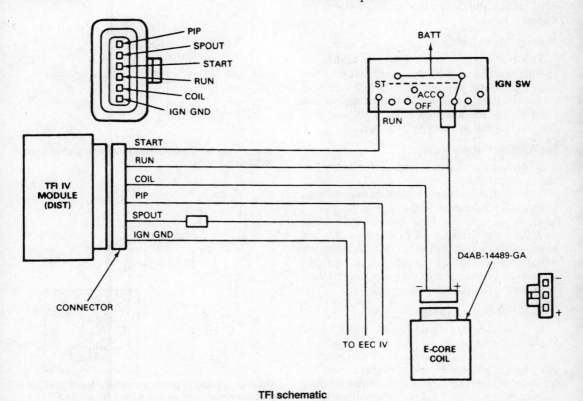

TFI schematic

5. Repair as necessary and install the TFI module and the distributor.

TFI Module

1. Remove the distributor cap from the distributor, and set it aside (spark plug wires intact).

2. Disconnect the TFI harness connector.

3. Remove the distributor.

4. Remove the two TFI module retaining screws.

5. To disengage the modules terminals from the distributor base connector, pull the right side of the module down the distributor mounting flange and then back up. Carefully pull the module toward the flange and away from the distributor.

WARNING: *Step 5 must be followed EX-ACTLY; failure to do so will result in damage to the distributor module connector pins.*

6. Coat the TFI module baseplate with a thin layer of silicone grease (FD7AZ-19A331-A or its equivalent).

7. Place the TFI module on the distributor base mounting flange. Position the module assembly toward the distributor bowl and carefully engage the distributor connector pins. Install and torque the two TFI module retaining screws to 9-16 in. lbs.

8. Install the distributor assembly.

9. Install the distributor cap and check the engine timing.

Primary Circuit Continuity

This test is performed in the same manner as the previous Wiring Harness test, but only the No. 1 terminal conductor is tested (ignition switch in Run position). If the voltage is less than 90% of the available battery voltage, proceed to the coil primary voltage test.

Ignition Coil Primary Voltage

1. Attach the negative lead of a voltmeter to the distributor base.

2. Turn the ignition switch ON and connect the positive voltmeter lead to the negative (−) ignition coil terminal. Note the voltage reading and turn the ignition OFF. If the voltmeter reading is less than 90% of the available battery voltage, inspect the wiring between the ignition module and the negative (−) coil terminal, then proceed to the last test, which follows.

Ignition Coil Supply Voltage

1. Attach the negative lead of a voltmeter to the distributor base.

2. Turn the ignition switch ON and connect the positive voltmeter lead to the positive (+) ignition coil terminal. Note the voltage reading then turn the ignition OFF. If the voltage read-

ing is at least 90% of the battery voltage, yet the engine will still not run; first, check the ignition coil connector and terminals for corrosion, dirt, and/or damage; second, replace the ignition switch if the connectors and terminal are okay.

3. Connect any remaining wiring.

IGNITION TIMING

Ignition timing is the measurement, in degrees of crankshaft rotation, of the point at which the spark plugs fire in each of the cylinders. It is measured in degrees before or after Top Dead Center (TDC) of the compression stroke.

Ideally, the air/fuel mixture in the cylinder will be ignited by the spark plug just as the piston passes TDC of the compression stroke. If this happens, the piston will be beginning the power stroke just as the compressed and ignited air/fuel mixture starts to expand. The expansion of the air/fuel mixture then forces the piston down on the power stroke and turns the crankshaft.

Because it takes a fraction of a second for the spark plug to ignite the mixture in the cylinder, the spark plug must fire a little before the piston reaches TDC. Otherwise, the mixture will not be completely ignited as the piston passes

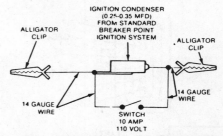

Test jumper wire switch used for testing Dura Spark ignition systems

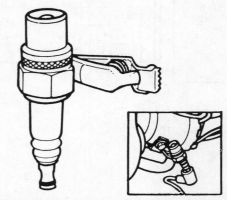

Spark plug tester; actually a modified spark plug (side electrode removed) with a spring for ground

reaches TDC. This only holds true, however, when the engine is at idle speed.

As the engine speed increases, the piston go faster. The spark plugs have to ignite the fuel even sooner if it is to be completely ignited when the piston reaches TDC.

With the both the Point Type and DuraSpark

TDC and the full power of the explosion will not be used by the engine.

The timing measurement is given in degrees of crankshaft rotation before the piston reaches TDC (BTDC, or Before Top Dead Center). If the setting for the ignition timing is 5°BTDC, each spark plug must fire 5° before each piston

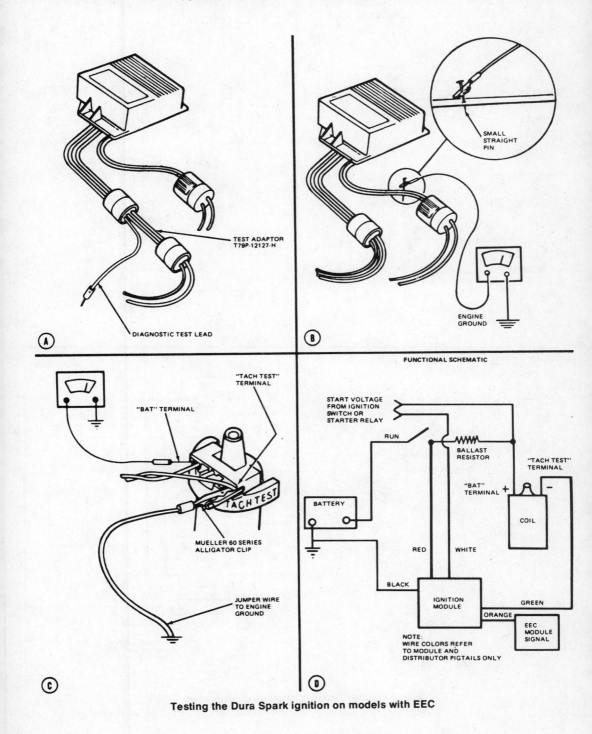

Testing the Dura Spark ignition on models with EEC

systems, the distributor has a means to advance the timing of the spark as the engine speed increases. This is accomplished by centrifugal weights within the distributor and a vacuum diaphragm mounted on the side of the distributor. It is necessary to disconnect the vacuum lines from the diaphragm when the ignition timing is being set.

With the TFI-IV system, ignition timing is calculated at all phases of vehicle operation by the TFI module.

If the ignition is set too far advanced (BTDC),

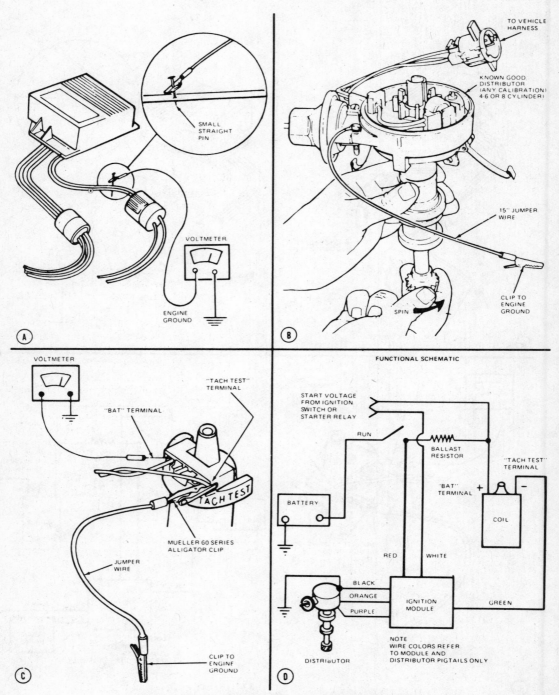

Testing the Dura Spark ignition on models without EEC

the ignition and expansion of the fuel in the cylinder will occur too soon and tend to force the piston down while it is still traveling up. This causes engine ping. If the ignition spark is set too far retarded after TDC (ATDC), the piston will have already passed TDC and started on its way down when the fuel is ignited. This will cause the piston to be forced down for only a portion of its travel. This will result in poor engine performance and lack of power.

The timing is best checked with a timing light. This device is connected in series with the No. 1 spark plug. The current that fires the spark plug also causes the timing light to flash.

There is a notch on the crankshaft pulley on all 6-cylinder engines. A scale of degrees of crankshaft rotation is attached to the engine block in such a position that the notch will pass close by the scale. On the V8 engines, the scale is located on the crankshaft pulley and a pointer is attached to the engine block so that the scale will pass close by. When the engine is running, the timing light is aimed at the mark on the crankshaft pulley and the scale.

IGNITION TIMING ADJUSTMENT

With the DuraSpark system, only an initial timing adjustment is possible. Ignition timing is not considered to be a part of tune-up or routine maintenance.

With the TFI-IV system no ignition timing adjustment is possible and none should be attempted.

Point Type Systems

1. Locate the timing marks on the crankshaft pulley and the front of the engine.
2. Clean off the timing marks so that you can see them.
3. Mark the timing marks with a piece of chalk or white paint. Color the mark on the scale that will indicate the correct timing when it is aligned with the mark on the pulley or the pointer. It is also helpful to mark the notch in the pulley or the tip of the pointer with a small dab of color.
4. Attach a dwell meter/tachometer to the engine.
5. Attach a timing light according to the manufacturer's instructions.
6. Disconnect the distributor vacuum line at the distributor and plug the vacuum line. A small bolt, center punch or similar object is satisfactory for a plug.
7. Check to make sure that all of the wires clear the fan and then start the engine.
8. Adjust the idle to the correct setting.

9. Aim the timing light at the timing marks. If the marks that you put on the pulley and the engine are aligned when the light flashes, the timing is correct. Turn off the engine and remove the tachometer and the timing light. If the marks are not in alignment, proceed with the following steps.
10. Loosen the distributor lockbolt just enough so that the distributor can be turned with a little effort.
11. With the timing light aimed at the pulley and the marks on the engine, turn the distributor in the direction of rotor rotation to regard the spark, and in the opposite direction of rotor rotation to the advance spark. Align the marks on the pulley and the engine with the flashes of the timing light.
12. When the marks are aligned, tighten the distributor lockbolt and recheck the timing with the timing light to make sure that the distributor did not move when you tightened the lockbolt.
13. Turn off the engine and remove the timing light.

DuraSpark Systems

1. Locate the timing marks on the crankshaft pulley and the front of the engine.
2. Clean the timing marks so that you can see them.
3. Mark the timing marks with a piece of chalk or with paint. Color the mark on the scale that will indicate the correct timing when it is aligned with the mark on the pulley or the pointer. It is also helpful to mark the notch in the pulley or the tip of the pointer with a small dab of color.
4. Attach a tachometer to the engine.
5. Attach a timing light according to the manufacturer's instructions. If the timing light has three wires, one is attached to the No. 1 spark plug with an adapter. The other wires are connected to the battery. The red wire goes to the positive side of the battery and the black wire is connected to the negative terminal of the battery.
6. Disconnect the vacuum line to the distributor at the distributor and plug the vacuum line. A golf tee does a fine job.
7. Check to make sure that all of the wires clear the fan and then start the engine.
8. Adjust the idle to the correct setting.
9. Aim the timing light at the timing marks. if the marks that you put on the flywheel or pulley and the engine are aligned with the light flashes, the timing is correct. Turn off the engine and remove the tachometer and the timing light. If the mark are not in alignment, replace the ignition module.

VALVE LASH

All engines used in full sized Ford products, from 1968 to the present, are equipped with hydraulic valve lifters. Valve systems with hydraulic valve lifters operate with zero clearance in the valve train, and because of this the rocker arms are nonadjustable. The only means by which valve system clearance can be altered is by installing 0.060" over-or-undersize pushrods; but, because of the hydraulic lifter's natural ability to compensate for slack in the valve train, all components of the valve system should be checked for wear if there is excessive play in the system.

When a valve in the engine is in the closed position, the valve lifter is resting on the base circle of the camshaft lobe and the pushrod is in its lowest position. To remove this additional clearance from the valve train, the valve lifter expands to maintain zero clearance in the valve system. When a rocker arm is loosened or removed from the engine, the lifter expands to its fullest travel. When the rocker arm is reinstalled on the engine, the proper valve setting is obtained by tightening the rocker arm to a specified limit. But with the lifter fully expanded, if the camshaft lobe is on a high point it will require excessive torque to compress the lifter and obtain the proper setting. Because of this, when any component of the valve system has been removed, a preliminary valve adjustment procedure must be followed to ensure that when the rocker arm is reinstalled on the engine and tightened, the camshaft lobe for that cylinder is in the low position. For preliminary valve adjustment procedure refer to Chapter 3.

ADJUSTMENT

6-240

1. Crank the engine until the TDC mark on the crankshaft damper is aligned with timing pointer on the cylinder front cover.
2. Scribe a mark on the damper at this point.
3. Scribe two more marks on the damper, each equally spaced from the first mark (see illustration).
4. With the engine on TDC of the compression stroke, (mark A aligned with the pointer) back off the rocker arm adjusting nut until there is end-play in the pushrod. Tighten the adjusting nut until all clearance is removed, then tighten the adjusting nut one additional turn. To determine when all clearance is removed from the rocker arm, turn the pushrod with the fingers. When the pushrod can no longer be turned, all clearance has been removed.
5. Repeat this procedure for each valve,

turning the crankshaft ⅓ turn to the next mark each time and following the engine firing order of 1-5-3-6-2-4.

1969 8-302

Some early models are equipped with adjustable rockers whereas the later models are equipped with positive stop type rocker mounting studs. Positive stop equipped rockers are adjusted by turning the adjusting nut down until it stops. You can identify a positive stop mounting stud by determining whether or not the shank portion of the stud that is exposed just above the cylinder head is the same diameter as the threaded portion at the top of the stud, to which the rocker arm retaining nut attaches. If the shank portion is larger than the threaded area, it is a positive stop mounting stud. Use the procedure given below for adjusting the valve lash on positive stop type mounting stud equipped vehicles.

There are two different procedures for adjusting the valves on the V8 engines. One is a preferred procedure and one is an alternate procedure. The preferred procedure is recommended, but the alternate procedure may be used.

NOTE: *These procedures are not tune-up procedures, but rebuild procedures to be performed only after valve train reassembly.*

PREFERRED PROCEDURE THROUGH 1969

1. Position the piston(s) on TDC of the compression stroke, using the timing mark on the crankshaft pulley as a reference for starting with the No. 1 cylinder. You can tell if a piston is coming up on its compression stroke by removing the spark plug of the cylinder you are working on and placing your thumb over the hole while the engine is cranked over. Air will try to force its way past you thumb when the piston comes upon the compression stroke. Make sure that the high tension coil wire leading to the distributor is removed before cranking the engine. Remove the valve covers.
2. Starting with No. 1 cylinder, and the piston in the position as mentioned above, apply pressure to slowly bleed down the valve lifter until the plunger is completely bottomed.
3. While holding the valve lifter in the fully collapsed position, check the available clearance between the rocker arm and the valve stem tip. Use a feeler gauge.
4. If the clearance is not within the specified amount, rotate the rocker arm stud nut clockwise to decrease the clearance and counterclockwise to increase the clearance. Normally, one turn of the rocker arm stud nut will vary the clearance by 0.066". Check the breakaway torque of each stud nut with a torque wrench,

turning it counterclockwise. It should be any-where from 4.5 to 15 ft. lbs. Replace the nut and/or the stud as necessary.

5. When both valves for the No.1 cylinder have been adjusted, proceed on to the other valves, following the firing order sequence 1-5-4-2-6-3-7-8.

6. Replace the valve covers and gaskets.

ALTERNATE PROCEDURE THROUGH 1969

Follow Step 1 of the preferred procedure given above, but instead of collapsing the lifter as in Step 2, loosen the rocker retaining nut until there is endplay present in the pushrod; then tighten the nut to remove all pushrod-to-rocker arm clearance has been eliminated, tighten the stud nut an additional ¾ turn to place the lifter plunger in the desired operating range.

Repeat this procedure for all of the cylinders, using the firing order sequence as a guide. It takes ¼ turn of the crankshaft to bring the next piston in the firing order sequence up to TDC at the end of its compression stroke.

Collapsed Tappet Gap Clearance:
Allowable: 0.071-0.193″
Desired: 0.096-0.165″

1970 and Later 8-302
8-351
8-460

1. Crank the engine until the No. 1 cylinder is at TDC of the compression stroke and the timing pointer is aligned with the mark on the crankshaft damper.

2. Scribe a mark on the damper at this point.

3. Scribe two additional marks on the damper (see illustration).

4. With the timing pointer aligned with mark 1 on the damper, tighten the following valves on the specified torque:
- 8-302 and 8-460: Nos. 1, 7 and 8 Intake; Nos. 1, 5 and 4 Exhaust
- 8-351: Nos. 1, 4 and 8 Intake; Nos. 1,3 and 7 Exhaust

5. Rotate the crankshaft 180° to point 2 and tighten the following valves:
- 8-302 and 8-460: Nos. 5 and 4 Intake; Nos. 2 and 6 Exhaust
- 8-351: Nos. 3 and 7 Intake; Nos. 6 and 6 Exhaust

6. Rotate the crankshaft 270° to point 3 and tighten the following valves:
- 8-302 and 8-460: Nos. 2, 3 and 6 Intake; Nos. 7, 3 and 8 Exhaust
- 8-351: Nos. 2, 5 and 6 Intake; Nos. 4, 5 and 8 Exhaust

7. Rocker arm tightening specifications are:
- 8-302 and 8-351: tighten the nut until it contacts the rocker shoulder, then torque to 18-20 ft. lbs.

- 8-460: tighten the nut until it contacts the rocker shoulder, then torque to 18-22 ft. lbs.

CARBURETOR ADJUSTMENTS

This section contains only carburetor adjustments as they normally apply to engine tune-up. Descriptions of the carburetor and complete adjustment procedures can be found in Chapter 5.

When the engine in your car is running, air/fuel mixture from the carburetor is being drawn into the engine by a partial vacuum which is created by the downward movement of the pistons on the intake stroke of the 4-stroke cycle of the engine. The amount of air/fuel mixture which enters the engine is controlled by throttle plate(s) in the bottom of the carburetor. When the engine is not running the throttle plate(s) is (are) closed completely blocking off the bottom of the carburetor from the inside of the engine. The throttle plates are connected, through the throttle linkage, to the accelerator in the passenger compartment of the car. After you start the engine and put the transmission in gear, you depress the accelerator to start the car moving. What you actually are doing when you depress the accelerator is opening the throttle plate(s) in the carburetor to admit more of the air/fuel mixture to the engine. The farther you open the throttle plates in the carburetor, the higher the engine speed becomes.

As previously stated, when the engine is not running, the throttle plates in the carburetor are closed. When the engine is idling, it is necessary to open the throttle plate slightly. To prevent having to keep your foot on the accelerator when the engine is idling, an idle speed adjusting screw was added to the carburetor. This screw has the same effect as keeping your foot slightly depressed on the accelerator. The idle speed adjusting screw contacts a lever (the throttle lever) on the outside of the carburetor. When the screw is turning in, it opens the throttle plate on the carburetor, raising the idle speed of the engine. This screw is called the curb idle adjusting screw, and the procedures in this section will tell you how to adjust it.

In addition to the curb idle adjusting screw, most engines have a throttle solenoid positioner. Ford has found it necessary to raise the idle speed on the these engines to obtain a smooth engine idle. When the key is turned **off**, the current to the spark plugs is cut off and the engine normally stops running. However, if an engine has a high operating temperature and a high idle speed, it is possible for the temperature of the cylinder, instead of the spark plug, to ignite the air/fuel mixture. Then this happens, the engine continues to run after the key is turned off. To solve this problem, a throttle solenoid was added to the carburetor. The solenoid is a cylinder with an adjustable plunger and an electrical lead. When the ignition key is turned to **on**, the solenoid plunger extends to contact the carburetor throttle lever and raise the idle speed of the engine. when the ignition key is turned **off**, the solenoid is de-energized and the solenoid plunger falls back from the throttle lever. this allows the throttle lever to fall back and rest on the curb idle adjusting screw. this closes the throttle plates far enough so that the engine will not run on.

Since it is difficult for the engine to draw the air/fuel mixture from the carburetor with the small amount of throttle plate opening that is present when the engine is idling, an idle mixture passage is provided in the carburetor. This passage delivers air/fuel mixture to the engine from a hole which is located in the bottom of the carburetor below the throttle plates. This idle mixture passage contains an adjustment screw which restricts the amount of air/fuel mixture which enters the engine at idle. The procedures given in this section will tell how to set the idle mixture adjusting screw(s).

NOTE: *With the electric solenoid disengaged, the carburetor idle speed adjusting screw must make contact with the throttle lever to prevent the throttle plates from jamming in the throttle bore when the engine is turned Speed and Mixture*

1968-73

1. With the engine off, turn the idle fuel mixture screw and limiter cap to the full counterclockwise position.
2. Turn the idle speed adjusting screw(s) out until the throttle plate(s) seats in the throttle bore(s).
3. Make certain that the solenoid plunger is not interfering with the throttle lever.
4. Turn the idle speed adjusting screw in until it just contacts the stop on the throttle shaft and lever assembly, then turn the screw inward 1½ turns.
5. Start the engine and warm it up.
6. Check, and if necessary, adjust the ignition timing.
7. Put the transmission in neutral (manual) or drive (automatic). Set the parking brake. Block the wheels.
8. Check that the choke plate is in the full open position; turn the headlights on high beam.
9. Install a tachometer according to the manufacturer's instructions.
10. If possible leave the air cleaner on while making adjustments.

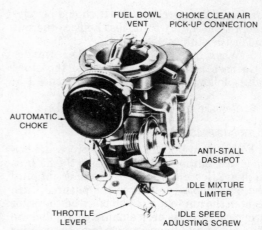
Carburetor adjustment—1969–71 Carter YF

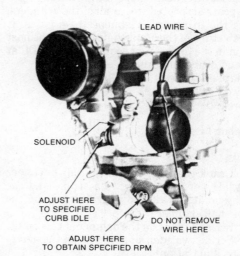
Carter YF with throttle solenoid positioner

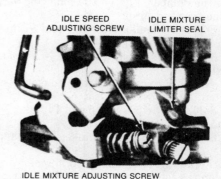
Carburetor adjustments—1968 Carter YF

11. Loosen the solenoid locknut and turn the solenoid in or out to obtain the specified idle speed.
12. Disconnect the solenoid lead wire and place the automatic transmission in neutral.

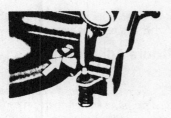

MODEL 1101 1-V

.MODELS
2100 2-V AND 4100 4-V

MODEL 4300 4-V

Idle speed screw locations

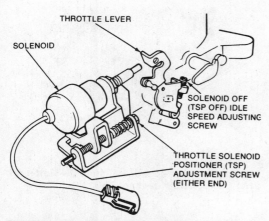

Throttle solenoid positioner adjustment—Motorcraft 2100, 2150, 4300, 4350

13. Adjust the carburetor throttle stop screw to obtain 500 rpm.

14. Connect the lead wire and open the throttle slightly by hand.

15. Turn the mixture adjusting screw(s) inward to obtain the smoothest possible idle with the air cleaner installed.

Idle Speed Adjustment

1974-76

1. Remove the air cleaner and plug the vacuum lines.

2. Set the parking brake and block the wheels.

Idle mixture limiters installed—Motorcraft 4300 shown

3. Connect a tachometer according to the manufacturer's instructions.

4. Run the engine to normalize underhood temperatures.

5. Check, and if necessary, reset the ignition timing.

6. Make certain that the choke plate is fully open.

7. Place the manual transmission in neutral; the automatic in Drive. Block the wheels.

8. Turn the solenoid adjusting screw in or out to obtain the specified idle speed. The idle

speed is the higher of the two rpm figures on the underhood specification sticker.

9. Disconnect the solenoid lead wire. Place the automatic transmission in neutral.

10. Turn the solenoid off adjusting screw to obtain the solenoid off rpm. This is the lower of the two rpm figures on the underhood specifications sticker.

11. Connect the solenoid lead wire and open the throttle slightly to allow the solenoid plunger to extend.

12. Stop the engine, replace the air cleaner and connect the vacuum lines. Check the idle speed. Readjust if necessary with the air cleaner installed.

1977-88

1. Remove the air cleaner and disconnect and plug the vacuum lines.

2. Block the wheels, apply the parking brake, turn off all accessories, start the engine and run it to normalize underhood temperatures.

3. Check that the choke plate is fully open and connect a tachometer according to the manufacturer's instructions.

4. Check the throttle stop positioner (TSP)-off speed as follows:

   a. Collapse the plunger by forcing the throttle lever against it.

   b. Place the transmission in neutral and check the engine speed. If necessary, adjust to specified TSP-Off speed with the throttle adjusting screw. See the underhood sticker.

5. Place the manual transmission in neutral; the automatic in Drive and make certain the TSP plunger is extended.

6. Turn the TSP until the specified idle speed is obtained.

7. Install the air cleaner and connect the vac-uum lines. Check the idle speed. Adjust, if necessary, with the air cleaner on.

Idle Mixture Adjustment

1974-87

NOTE: *For this procedure, Ford recommends a propane enrichment procedure. This requires special equipment not available to the general public. In lieu of this equipment the following procedure may be followed to obtain satisfactory idle mixture.*

1. Block the wheels, set the parking brake and run the engine to bring it to normal operating temperature.

2. Disconnect the hose between the emission canister and the air cleaner.

3. On engines equipped with the Thermactor® air injection system, the routing of the vacuum lines connected to the dump valve will have to be temporarily changed. Mark them for reconnection before switching them.

4. For valves with one or two vacuum lines at the side, disconnect and plug the lines.

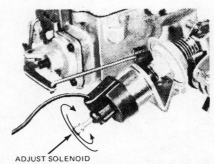

ADJUST SOLENOID

Location of idle speed adjustment—Motorcraft 2150 with solenoid dashpot TSP

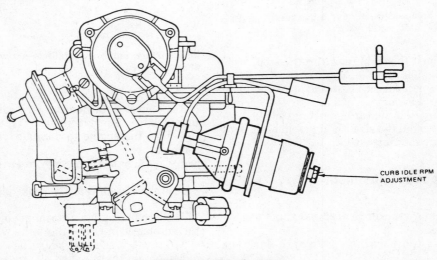

CURB IDLE RPM ADJUSTMENT

VOTM curb idle adjustment

5. For valves with one vacuum line at the top, check the line to see if it is connected to the intake manifold or an intake manifold source such as the carburetor or distributor vacuum line. If not, remove and plug the line at the dump valve and connect a temporary length of vacuum hose from the dump valve fitting to a source of intake manifold vacuum.

6. Remove the limiter caps from the mixture screws by CAREFULLY cutting them with a sharp knife.

7. Place the transmission in neutral and run the engine at 2,500 rpm for 15 seconds.

8. Place the automatic transmission in Drive; the manual in neutral.

9. Adjust the idle speed to the higher of the two figures given on the underhood sticker.

10. Turn the idle mixture screws to obtain the highest possible rpm, leaving the screws in the leanest position that will maintain this rpm.

11. Repeat steps 7 thru 10 until further adjustment of the mixture screws does not increase the rpm.

12. Turn the screws in until the lower of the two idle speed figures is reached. Turn the screws in ¼ turn increments each to insure a balance.

13. Turn the engine off and remove the tachometer. Reinstall all equipment.

NOTE: *Rough idle, that cannot be corrected by normal service procedures on 1977 and later models, may be cause by leakage between the EGR valve body and diaphragm. To determine if this is the cause:*

1. Tighten the EGR bolts to 15 ft. lbs. Connect a vacuum gauge to the intake manifold.

2. Lift to exert a sideways pressure on the diaphragm housing. If the idle changes or the reading on the vacuum gauge varies, replace the EGR valve.

GASOLINE FUEL INJECTION ADJUSTMENTS

These engines have idle speed controlled by the TFI-IV/EEC-IV system and no adjustment is possible.

CATALYTIC CONVERTER PRECAUTIONS

Since 1974, most Fords and Mercurys have been equipped with catalytic converters to clean up exhaust emissions after they leave the engine. Naturally, lead-free fuel must be used in order to avoid contaminating the converter and rendering it useless. However, there are

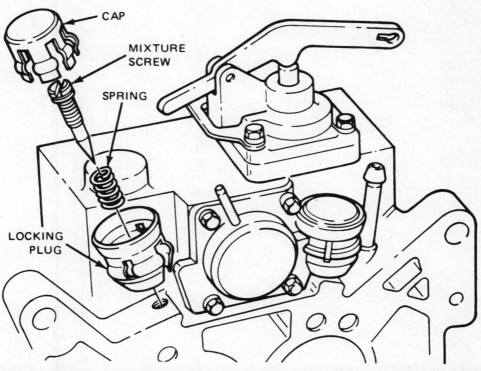

CAP

MIXTURE SCREW

SPRING

LOCKING PLUG

Some 1980 and later 2150 models have 2-piece metal plugs and caps in place of plastic limiter caps on the idle mixture adjusting screws. They should be carefully removed before attempting any adjustments.

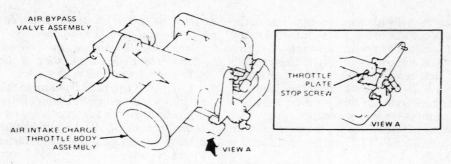

EFI adjustment

other precautions which should be taken to prevent a large amount of unburned hydrocarbon from reaching the converter. Should a sufficient amount of HC reach the converter, the unit could overheat, possibly damaging the converter or nearby mechanical components. There is even the possibility that a fire could be started. Therefore, when working on your car, the following conditions should be avoided:

1. The use of fuel system cleaning agents and additives.

2. Operating the car with a closed choke or a submerged carburetor float.

3. Extended periods of engine run-on (dieseling).

4. Turning off the ignition with the car in motion.

5. Ignition or charging system failure.

6. Misfiring of one or more spark plugs.

7. Disconnecting a spark plug wire while testing for a bad wire or plug, or poor compression in one cylinder.

8. Pushing or tow-starting the car, especially when hot.

9. Pumping the gas pedal when attempting to start a hot engine.

ENGINE ELECTRICAL

Understanding the Engine Electrical System

The engine electrical system can be broken down into three separate and distinct systems:

1. The starting system.
2. The charging system.
3. The ignition system.

BATTERY AND STARTING SYSTEM

Basic Operating Principles

The battery is the first link in the chain of mechanisms which work together to provide cranking of the automobile engine. In most modern cars, the battery is a lead/acid electrochemical device consisting of six 2v subsections connected in series so the unit is capable of producing approximately 12v of electrical pressure. Each subsection, or cell, consists of a series of positive and negative plates held a short distance apart in a solution of sulfuric acid and water. The two types of plates are of dissimilar metals. This causes a chemical reaction to be set up, and it is this reaction which produces current flow from the battery when its positive and negative terminals are connected to an electrical appliance such as a lamp or motor. The continued transfer of electrons would eventually convert the sulfuric acid in the electrolyte to water, and make the two plates identical in chemical composition. As electrical energy is removed from the battery, its voltage output tends to drop. Thus, measuring battery voltage and battery electrolyte composition are two ways of checking the ability of the unit to supply power. During the starting of the engine, electrical energy is removed from the battery. However, if the charging circuit is in good condition and the operating conditions are normal, the power removed from the battery will be replaced by the generator (or alternator) which will force electrons back through the battery, reversing the normal flow, and restoring the battery to its original chemical state.

The battery and starting motor are linked by very heavy electrical cables designed to minimize resistance to the flow of current. Generally, the major power supply cable that leaves the battery goes directly to the starter, while other electrical system needs are supplied by a smaller cable. During starter operation, power flows from the battery to the starter and is grounded through the car's frame and the battery's negative ground strap.

The starting motor is a specially designed, direct current electric motor capable of producing a very great amount of power for its size. One thing that allows the motor to produce a great deal of power is its tremendous rotating speed. It drives the engine through a tiny pinion gear (attached to the starter's armature), which drives the very large flywheel ring gear at a greatly reduced speed. Another factor allowing it to produce so much power is that only intermittent operation is required of it. This, little allowance for air circulation is required, and the windings can be built into a very small space.

The starter solenoid is a magnetic device which employs the small current supplied by the starting switch circuit of the ignition switch. This magnetic action moves a plunger which mechanically engages the starter and electrically closes the heavy switch which connects it to the battery. The starting switch circuit consists of the starting switch contained within the ignition switch, a transmission neutral safety switch or clutch pedal switch, and the wiring necessary to connect these in series with the starter solenoid or relay.

A pinion, which is a small gear, is mounted to a one-way drive clutch. This clutch is splined to the starter armature shaft. When the ignition switch is moved to the **start** position, the solenoid plunger slides the pinion toward the fly-wheel ring gear via a collar and spring. If the teeth on the pinion and flywheel match proper-ly, the pinion will engage the flywheel immedi-ately. If the gear teeth butt one another, the spring will be compressed and will force the gears to mesh as soon as the starter turns far enough to allow them to do so. As the solenoid plunger reaches the end of its travel, it closes the contacts that connect the battery and start-er and then the engine is cranked.

As soon as the engine starts, the flywheel ring gear begins turning fast enough to drive the pinion at an extremely high rate of speed. At this point, the one-way clutch begins allow-ing the pinion to spin faster than the starter shaft so that the starter will not operate at ex-cessive speed. When the ignition switch is re-leased from the starter position, the solenoid is de-energized, and a spring contained within the solenoid assembly pulls the gear out of mesh and interrupts the current flow to the starter.

Some starter employ a separate relay, mount-ed away from the starter, to switch the motor and solenoid current on and off. The relay thus replaces the solenoid electrical switch, buy does not eliminate the need for a solenoid mounted on the starter used to mechanically engage the starter drive gears. The relay is used to reduce the amount of current the starting switch must carry.

THE CHARGING SYSTEM

Basic Operating Principles

The automobile charging system provides electrical power for operation of the vehicle's ig-nition and starting systems and all the electri-cal accessories. The battery services as an elec-trical surge or storage tank, storing (in chemi-cal form) the energy originally produced by the engine driven generator. The system also pro-vides a means of regulating generator output to protect the battery from being overcharged and to avoid excessive voltage to the accessories.

The storage battery is a chemical device in-corporating parallel lead plates in a tank con-taining a sulfuric acid/water solution. Adjacent plates are slightly dissimilar, and the chemical reaction of the two dissimilar plates produces electrical energy when the battery is connected to a load such as the starter motor. The chemi-cal reaction is reversible, so that when the gen-erator is producing a voltage (electrical pres-sure) greater than that produced by the bat-tery, electricity is forced into the battery, and the battery is returned to its fully charged state.

The vehicle's generator is driven mechanical-ly, through V-belts, by the engine crankshaft. It consists of two coils of fine wire, one stationary (the stator), and one movable (the rotor). The rotor may also be known as the armature, and consists of fine wire wrapped around an iron core which is mounted on a shaft. The electric-ity which flows through the two coils of wire (provided initially by the battery in some cases) creates an intense magnetic field around both rotor and stator, and the interaction between the two fields creates voltage, allowing the gen-erator to power the accessories and charge the battery.

There are two types of generators: the earlier is the direct current (DC) type. The current produced by the DC generator is generated in the armature and carried off the spinning ar-mature by stationary brushes contacting the commutator. The commutator is a series of smooth metal contact plates on the end of the armature. The commutator is a series of smooth metal contact plates on the end of the armature. The commutator plates, which are separated from one another by a very short gap, are connected to the armature circuits so that current will flow in one directions only in the wires carrying the generator output. The gen-erator stator consists of two stationary coils of wire which draw some of the output current of the generator to form a powerful magnetic field and create the interaction of fields which gener-ates the voltage. The generator field is wired in series with the regulator.

Newer automobiles use alternating current generators or alternators, because they are more efficient, can be rotated at higher speeds, and have fewer brush problems. In an alterna-tor, the field rotates while all the current pro-duced passes only through the stator winding. The brushes bear against continuous slip rings rather than a commutator. This causes the cur-rent produced to periodically reverse the direc-tion of its flow. Diodes (electrical one-way switches) block the flow of current from travel-ing in the wrong direction. A series of diodes is wired together to permit the alternating flow of the stator to be converted to a pulsating, but unidirectional flow at the alternator output. The alternator's field is wired in series with the voltage regulator.

The regulator consists of several circuits. Each circuit has a core, or magnetic coil of wire, which operates a switch. Each switch is con-nected to ground through one or more resis-tors. The coil of wire responds directly to sys-tem voltage. When the voltage reaches the re-quired level, the magnetic field created by the winding of wire closes the switch and inserts a resistance into the generator field circuit, thus reducing the output. The contacts of the switch cycle open and close many times each second to precisely control voltage.

While alternators are self-limiting as far as maximum current is concerned, DC generators employ a current regulating circuit which responds directly to the total amount of current flowing through the generator circuit rather than to the output voltage. The current regulator is similar to the voltage regulator except that all system current must flow through the energizing coil on its way to the various accessories.

Ignition Coil

REMOVAL AND INSTALLATION

1. Disconnect the battery ground.
2. Disconnect the two small and one large wire from the coil.
3. Disconnect the condenser connector from the coil, if equipped.
4. Unbolt and remove the coil.
5. Installation is the reverse of removal.

Ignition Module

REMOVAL AND INSTALLATION

Removing the module, on all models, is a matter of simply removing the fasteners that attach it to the fender or firewall and pulling apart the connectors. When unplugging the connectors, pull them apart with a firm, straight pull. NEVER PRY THEM APART! To pry them will cause damage. When reconnecting them, coat the mating ends with silicone dielectric grease to waterproof the connection. Press the connectors together firmly to overcome any vacuum lock caused by the grease.

NOTE: *If the locking tabs weaken or break, don't replace the unit. Just secure the connection with electrical tape or tie straps.*

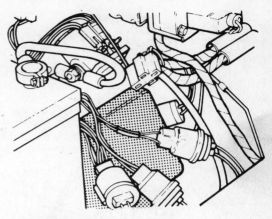

Typical control module

Distributor

REMOVAL AND INSTALLATION

1. Remove the air cleaner on V8 engines. On 6-cylinder engines, removal of a Thermactor® (air) pump mounting bolt and drive belt will allow the pump to be moved to the side and permit access to the distributor. If necessary, disconnect the Thermactor® air filter and lines as well.
2. Remove the distributor cap and position the cap and ignition wires to the side.
3. Disconnect the wire harness plug from the distributor connector. Disconnect and plug the vacuum hoses from the vacuum diaphragm assembly. (DuraSpark®III systems are not equipped with a vacuum diaphragm).
4. Rotate the engine (in normal direction of rotation) until No. 1 piston is on TDC (Top Dead Center) of the compression stroke. The TDC mark on the crankshaft pulley and the pointer should align. Rotor tip pointing at No. 1 position on distributor cap.
5. On DuraSpark®I or II, turn the engine a slight bit more (if required) to align the stator

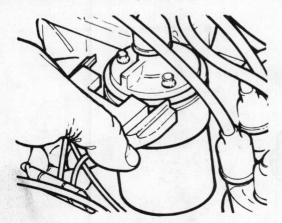

Typical coil connector removal

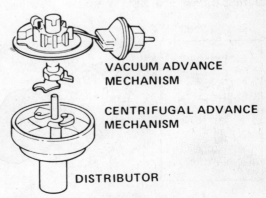

VACUUM ADVANCE MECHANISM

CENTRIFUGAL ADVANCE MECHANISM

DISTRIBUTOR

Dual advance distributor (typical)

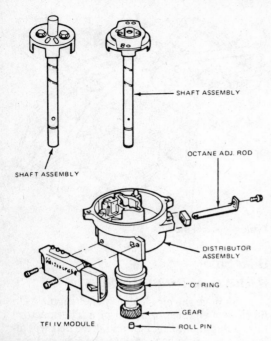

SHAFT ASSEMBLY

SHAFT ASSEMBLY

OCTANE ADJ. ROD

DISTRIBUTOR ASSEMBLY

"O" RING

GEAR

TFI IV MODULE

ROLL PIN

Universal TFI distributor

(pick-up coil) assembly pole with an (closest) armature pole. On DuraSpark®III, the distributor sleeve groove (when looking down from the top) and the cap adaptor alignment slot should align. On models equipped with EEC-IV (1984 and later), remove the rotor (2 screws) and note the position of the polarizing square and shaft plate for reinstallation reference.

6. Scribe a mark on the distributor body and engine black to indicate the position of the rotor tip and position of the distributor in the engine. DuraSpark®III and some EEC-IV system distributors are equipped with a notched base and will only locate at one position on the engine.

7. Remove the holddown bolt and clamp located at the base of the distributor. (Some DuraSpark®III and EEC-IV system distribu-

tors are equipped with a special holddown bolt that requires a Torx® Head Wrench for removal). Remove the distributor from the engine. Pay attention to the direction the rotor tip points when the drive gear disengages. For reinstallation purposes, the rotor should be at this position to insure proper gear mesh and timing.

8. Avoid turning the engine, if possible, while the distributor is removed. If the engine is turned from TDC position, TDC timing marks will have to be reset before the distributor is installed; Steps 4 and 5.

9. Position the distributor in the engine with the rotor aligned to the marks made on the distributor, or to the place the rotor pointed when the distributor was removed. The stator and armature or polarizing square and shaft plate should also be aligned. Engage the oil pump intermediate shaft and insert the distributor until fully seated on the engine, if the distributor does not fully seat, turn the engine slightly to fully engage the intermediate shaft.

10. Follow the above procedures on models equipped with an indexed distributor base. Make sure when positioning the distributor that the slot in the distributor base will engage the block tab and the sleeve/adaptor slots are aligned.

11. After the distributor has been fully seated on the block install the holddown bracket and bolt. On models equipped with an indexed base, tighten the mounting bolt. On other models, snug the mounting bolt so the distributor can be turned for ignition timing purposes.

12. The rest of the installation is in the reverse order of removal. Check and reset the ignition timing on applicable models.

NOTE: *A silicone compound is used on rotor tips, distributor cap contacts and on the inside of the connectors on the spark plugs cable and module couplers. Always apply silicone dielectric compound after servicing any component of the ignition system. Various models*

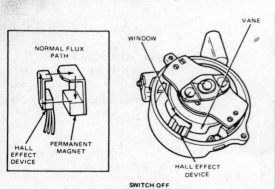

NORMAL FLUX PATH

WINDOW

VANE

HALL EFFECT DEVICE

PERMANENT MAGNET

HALL EFFECT DEVICE

SWITCH OFF (WINDOW AT SWITCH)

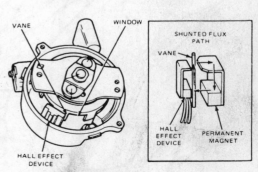

VANE

WINDOW

SHUNTED FLUX PATH

VANE

HALL EFFECT DEVICE

HALL EFFECT DEVICE

PERMANENT MAGNET

SWITCH ON (VANE AT SWITCH)

Hall Effect-On/Off switching

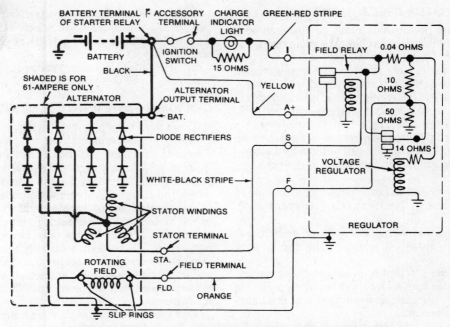

Alternator charging circuit w/indicator light—rear terminal type

use a multi-point rotor which do not require the application of dielectric compound.

Alternator

The alternator charging system consists of the alternator, voltage regulator, warning light, battery, and fuse link wire.

A failure of any component of the charging system can cause the entire system to stop functioning. Because of this, the charging sys-

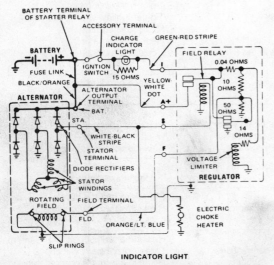

Alternator charging circuit w/indicator light—side terminal type

tem can be very difficult to troubleshoot when problems occur.

When the ignition key is turned on, current flows from the battery, through the charging system indicator light on the instrument panel, to the voltage regulator, and to the alternator. Since the alternator is not producing any current, the alternator warning light comes on. When the engine is started, the alternator begins to produce current and turns the alternator light off. As the alternator turns and produces current, the current is divided in two ways: part to the battery to charge the battery and power the electrical components of the vehicle, and part is returned to the alternator to enable it to increase its output. In this situation, the alternator is receiving current from the battery and from itself. A voltage regulator is wired into the current supply to the alternator to prevent it from receiving too much current which would cause it to put out too much current. Conversely, if the voltage regulator does not allow the alternator to receive enough current, the battery will not be fully charged and will eventually go dead.

The battery is connected to the alternator at all times, whether the ignition key is turned on or not. If the battery were shorted to ground, the alternator would also be shorted. This would damage the alternator. To prevent this, a fuse link is installed in the wiring between the battery and the alternator on all 1970 and later models. If the battery is shorted, the fuse link is melted, protecting the alternator.

ALTERNATOR PRECAUTIONS

Several precautions must be observed with alternator equipped vehicles to avoid damaging the unit. They are as follows:

1. If the battery is removed for any reason, make sure that it is reconnected with the correct polarity. Reversing the battery connections may result in damage to the one-way rectifiers.

2. When utilizing a booster battery as a starting aid, always connect it as follows: positive to positive, and negative (booster battery) to a good ground on the engine of the car being started.

3. Never use a fast charger as a booster to start cars with alternating current (AC) circuits.

4. When servicing the battery with a fast charger, always disconnect the car battery cables.

5. Never attempt to polarize an alternator.

6. Avoid long soldering times when replacing diodes or transistors. Prolonged heat is damaging to alternators.

7. Do not use test lamps of more than 12 volts (V) for checking diode continuity.

8. Do not short across or ground any of the terminals on the alternator.

9. The polarity of the battery, alternator, and regulator must be matched and considered before making any electrical connections within the system.

10. Never separate the alternator on an open circuit. Make sure that all connections within the circuit are clean and tight.

11. Disconnect the battery terminals when performing any service on the electrical system. This will eliminate the possibility of accidental reversal of polarity.

12. Disconnect the battery ground cable if arc welding is to be done on any part of the car.

CHARGING SYSTEM TROUBLESHOOTING

There are many possible ways in which the charging system can malfunction. Often the source of a problem is difficult to diagnose, requiring special equipment and a good deal of experience. This is usually not the case, however, where the charging system fails completely and causes the dash board warning light to come on or the battery to become dead. To troubleshoot a complete system failure only two pieces of equipment are needed: a test light, to determine that current is reaching a certain point; and a current indicator (ammeter), to determine the direction of the current flow and its measurement in amps.

This test works under three assumptions:

1. The battery is known to be good and fully charged.

2. The alternator belt is in good condition and adjusted to the proper tension.

3. All connections in the system are clean and tight.

NOTE: *In order for the current indicator to give a valid reading, the car must be equipped with battery cables which are of the same gauge size and quality as original equipment battery cables.*

Troubleshooting Basic Charging System Problems

Problem	Cause	Solution
Noisy alternator	· Loose mountings · Loose drive pulley · Worn bearings · Brush noise · Internal circuits shorted (High pitched whine)	· Tighten mounting bolts · Tighten pulley · Replace alternator · Replace alternator · Replace alternator
Squeal when starting engine or accelerating	· Glazed or loose belt	· Replace or adjust belt
Indicator light remains on or ammeter indicates discharge (engine running)	· Broken fan belt · Broken or disconnected wires · Internal alternator problems · Defective voltage regulator	· Install belt · Repair or connect wiring · Replace alternator · Replace voltage regulator
Car light bulbs continually burn out— battery needs water continually	· Alternator/regulator overcharging	· Replace voltage regulator/alternator
Car lights flare on acceleration	· Battery low · Internal alternator/regulator problems	· Charge or replace battery · Replace alternator/regulator
Low voltage output (alternator light flickers continually or ammeter needle wanders)	· Loose or worn belt · Dirty or corroded connections · Internal alternator/regulator problems	· Replace or adjust belt · Clean or replace connections · Replace alternator or regulator

1. Turn off all electrical components on the car. Make sure the doors of the car are closed. If the car is equipped with a clock, disconnect the clock by removing the lead wire from the rear of the clock. Disconnect the positive battery cable from the battery and connect the ground wire on a test light to the disconnected positive battery cable. Touch the probe end of the test light to the positive battery post. The test light should not light. If the test light does light, there is a short or open circuit on the car.

2. Disconnect the voltage regulator wiring harness connector at the voltage regulator. Turn on the ignition key. Connect the wire on a test light to a good ground (engine bolt). Touch the probe end of a test light to the ignition wire connector into the voltage regulator wiring connector. This wire corresponds to the **I** terminal on the regulator. If the test light goes on, the charging system warning light circuit is complete. If the test light does not come on and the warning light on the instrument panel is on, either the resistor wire, which is parallel with the warning light, or the wiring to the voltage regulator, is defective. If the test light does not come on and the warning light is not on, either the bulb is defective or the power supply wire form the battery through the ignition switch to the bulb has an open circuit. Connect the wiring harness to the regulator.

3. Examine the fuse link wire in the wiring harness from the starter relay to the alternator. If the insulation on the wire is cracked or split, the fuse link may be melted. Connect a test light to the fuse link by attaching the ground wire on the test light to an engine bolt and touching the probe end of the light to the bottom of the fuse link wire where it splices into the alternator output wire. If the bulb in the test light does not light, the fuse link is melted.

4. Start the engine and place a current indicator on the positive battery cable. Turn off all electrical accessories and make sure the doors are closed. If the charging system is working properly, the gauge will show a draw of less than 5 amps. If the system is not working properly, the gauge will show a draw of more than 5 amps. A charge moves the needle toward the battery, a draw moves the needle away from the battery. Turn the engine off.

5. Disconnect the wiring harness from the voltage regulator at the regulator at the regulator connector. Connect a male spade terminal (solderless connector) to each end of a jumper wire. Insert one end of the wire into the wiring harness connector which corresponds to the **A** terminal on the regulator. Insert the other end of the wire into the wiring harness connector which corresponds to the **F** terminal on the regulator. Position the connector with the jumper wire installed so that it cannot contact any metal surface under the hood. Position a current indicator gauge on the positive battery cable. Have an assistant start the engine. Observe the reading on the current indicator. Have your assistant slowly raise the speed of the engine to about 2,000 rpm or until the current indicator needle stops moving, whichever comes first. Do not run the engine for more than a short period of time in this condition. If the wiring harness connector or jumper wire becomes excessively hot during this test, turn off the engine and check for a grounded wire in the regulator wiring harness. If the current indicator shows a charge of about three amps less than the output of the alternator, the alternator is working properly. If the previous tests showed a draw, the voltage regulator is defective. If the gauge does not show the proper charging rate, the alternator is defective.

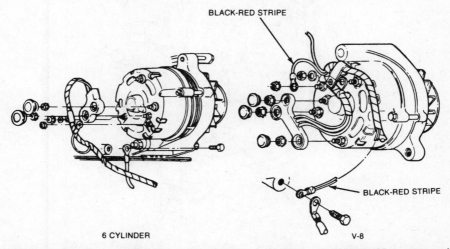

BLACK-RED STRIPE

BLACK-RED STRIPE

6 CYLINDER

V-8

1968–72 alternator wiring harness connections—typical Autolite except 65 ampere unit

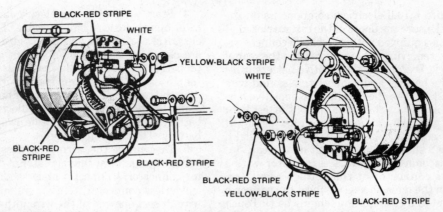

1968–72 alternator wiring harness connections—Leece-Neville 65 ampere unit

REMOVAL AND INSTALLATION

1. Disconnect the negative battery cable from the battery.

2. Disconnect the wires from the alternator.

3. Loosen the alternator mounting bolts and remove the drive belt.

NOTE: *Some 1981 and later cars are equipped with a ribbed, K-section belt and automatic tensioner. A special tool must be made to remove the tension from the tensioner arm. Loosen the idler pulley pivot and adjuster bolts before using the tool. See the accompanying illustration for tool details.*

4. Remove the alternator mounting bolts and spacer (if equipped), and remove the alternator.

5. To install, position the alternator on its brackets and install the attaching bolts and spacer (if so equipped).

6. Connect the wires to the alternator.

7. Position the drive belt on the alternator pulley. Adjust the belt tension as outlined in Chapter 1.

8. Connect the negative battery cable.

Voltage Regulator

Voltage regulators used through 1978 were either electromechanical or transistorized. The electromechanical regulator is not adjustable, and has to be replaced as a unit when faulty. The transistorized regulator is adjustable by

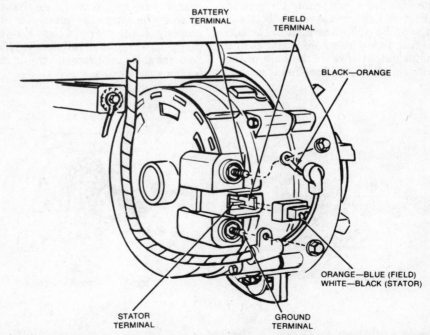

1972 and later alternator wiring harness connections—Autolite (Motorcraft) side terminal unit

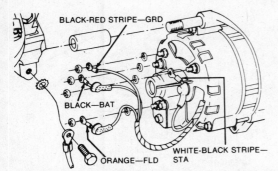

BLACK-RED STRIPE—GRD

BLACK—BAT

ORANGE—FLD

WHITE-BLACK STRIPE—STA

1968–72 alternator wiring harness connections —Autolite 65 ampere unit

CHARGE INDICATOR LIGHT TERMINAL

FIELD COIL TERMINAL

FIELD RELAY TERMINAL

BATTERY TERMINAL FOR FIELD SUPPLY VOLTAGE

Motorcraft electro-mechanical regulator connections

means of a screw located in the transistor circuit board. The cover of the electromechanical regulator is held in place by non-removable rivets, while the transistorized regulator cover is held on by Phillips screws.

Beginning in 1979, only solid state regulators were used. One type is used only on vehicles with an ammeter. The other type is used on warning light equipped vehicles. The solid state regulators are preset at the factory and it is not possible to adjust them.

REMOVAL AND INSTALLATION

1. Remove the battery ground cable. On models with the regulator mounted behind the battery, it is necessary to remove the battery holddown, and to move the battery.

2. Remove the regulator mounting screws.

3. Disconnect the regulator from the wiring harness.

4. Mount the regulator to the regulator mounting plate. The radio suppression condenser mounts under one mounting screw; the ground lead under the other mounting screw. Tighten the mounting screws.

5. If the battery was moved to gain access to the regulator, position the battery and install the holddown. Connect the battery ground cable, and test the system for proper voltage regulation.

TESTING

Motorcraft

Any electro-mechanical regulator which does not perform to specifications must be replaced. A transistorized regulator may be adjusted if not up to specifications as per the test. The accompanying illustration shows the voltage limiter adjustment screw location beneath the regulator cover.

Before proceeding with the test, make sure that the alternator drive belt tension is properly adjusted, the battery has a good charge (specific gravity of 1.250 or better), and that all charging system electrical connections are clean and tight. A voltmeter is needed for this test. The test is as follows:

1. Connect a voltmeter to the battery, with the positive lead to the battery positive terminal and the negative lead to the battery negative terminal. Turn off all electrical equipment. Check and record the voltmeter reading with the engine stopped.

2. Connect a tachometer to the engine, with the red (positive) lead to the distributor terminal on the ignition coil and the black (negative)

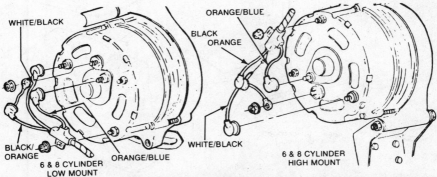

WHITE/BLACK

ORANGE/BLUE

BLACK ORANGE

BLACK/ORANGE

ORANGE/BLUE

6 & 8 CYLINDER LOW MOUNT

WHITE/BLACK

6 & 8 CYLINDER HIGH MOUNT

1973 and later Motorcraft alternator wiring harness connections—rear terminal units

lead to a good ground, such as an engine bolt.

3. Place the transmission in Neutral or Park and start the engine. Increase the engine speed to 1,800-2,200 rpm for 2-3 minutes to bring the engine and regulator to operating temperature. Check and record the voltmeter reading. It should now be 1 to 2 volts higher than the first reading. This is the regulated voltage reading. If the reading is less than 1 volt or greater than 2½ volts, the regulator must be replaced or adjusted.

4. If the reading is between 1 and 2 volts, turn on the headlights and heater blower to load the alternator. The voltage should not decrease more than ½ volt from the regulated voltage reading in Step 3. If the voltage drop is greater than ½ volt, the regulator should be replaced.

Leece-Neville Electro-Mechanical Unit

1. Connect a voltmeter to the battery post terminals.

2. Start the engine. Disconnect the regulator field (F) lead and connect it to the battery terminal of the regulator.

CAUTION: *Do not run the engine with the regulator wiring in this position any longer than necessary as excessive voltage could damage the alternator.*

3. Stop the engine. Disconnect the field (F) lead from the battery terminal and reconnect it to the field terminal on the regulator. If the voltmeter reads 15-20 volts or greater, the regulator is defective and must be replaced.

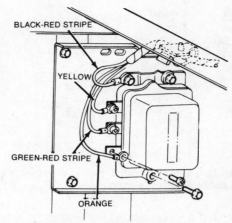

Leece-Neville regulator connections

Field Relay Test

NOTE: *Make sure that the battery has a good charge (specific gravity of 1.250) for this test. Connect the voltmeter as in the "Regulator Test.lick is heard, check for battery voltage at the IGN terminal of the regulator with the ignition switch in the IGN position. With battery voltage at the IGN terminal and if no clicking is heard while operating the ignition switch, the field relay is defective necessitating replacement of the voltage regulator unit.*

VOLTAGE ADJUSTMENT

Leece-Neville Electro-Mechanical Unit

1. Run the engine for 10-15 minutes to allow the regulator to reach operating temperature.

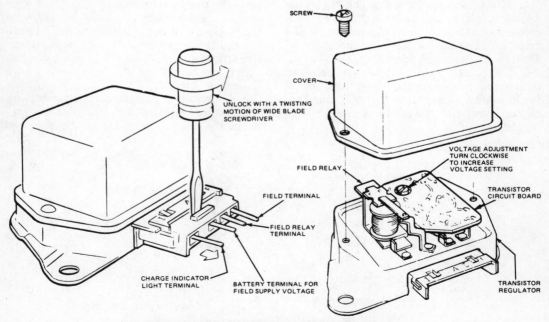

Motorcraft transistorized regulator adjustment

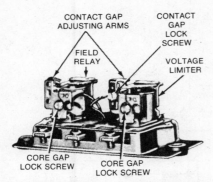

Leece-Neville regulator gap adjustments

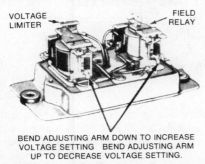

BEND ADJUSTING ARM DOWN TO INCREASE
VOLTAGE SETTING   BEND ADJUSTING ARM
UP TO DECREASE VOLTAGE SETTING.

Leece-Neville regulator voltage adjustments

Connect a voltmeter across the battery posts. Turn off all electrical equipment. Check the voltage at the battery. It should be 13.9-14.1 volts.

2. The voltage control adjustment (voltage limiter) is adjusted at the component closest to the F terminal. Remove the regulator cover. Voltage may be increased by raising the spring tension and decreased by lowering the spring tension. To adjust the spring tension, move the lower spring mounting tab.

NOTE: *Voltage will drop about ½ volt when the regulator cover is installed and should be compensated for in the adjustment.*

3. After making the adjustment, cycle the regulator by stopping and starting the engine. This will indicate if the adjustment is stable. If the voltage reading has changed, follow Steps 1 and 2 until the correct voltage is obtained.

VOLTAGE LIMITER ADJUSTMENT

Transistorized Regulator Only

NOTE: *The only reason for making this adjustment is if the alternator field current voltage is too high or too low. The test to determine this information should be performed at a garage with professional testing equipment.*

1. Run the engine to normal operating temperature and then shut it off.

2. Remove the regulator cover.

3. Using a plastic strip as a screwdriver, turn the adjusting screw clockwise to increase the voltage setting, counterclockwise to decrease the setting.

4. Install the regulator cover.

Starting System

The battery is the first link in the chain of mechanisms which work together to provide cranking of the automobile engine. In most modern cars, the battery is a lead-acid electrochemical device consisting of six 2-voltsubsections connected in series so the unit is capable of producing approximately 12 V of electrical pressure. Each subsection, or cell, consists of a series of positive and negative plates held a short distance apart in a solution of sulfuric acid and water. The two types of plates are of dissimilar metals. this causes a chemical reaction to be set up, and it is this reaction which produces current flow from the battery when its positive and negative terminals are connected to an electrical appliance such as a lamp or motor. the continued transfer of electrons would eventually convert the sulfuric acid in the electrolyte to water, and make the two plates identical in chemical composition. As electrical energy is removed from the battery, its voltage output tends to drop. Thus, measuring battery voltage and battery electrolyte composition are two ways of checking the

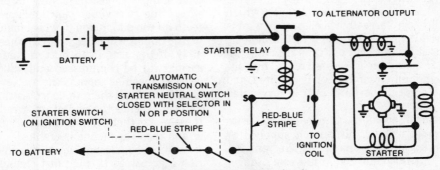

Positive engagement starter circuit

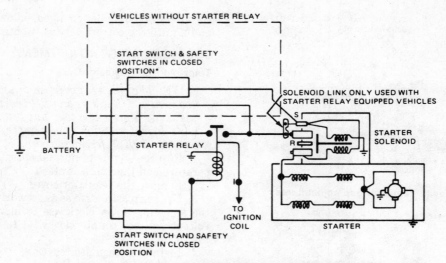

Solenoid actuated starter circuit—with and without starter relay

ability of the unit to supply power. During the starting of the engine, electrical energy is removed from the battery. However, if the charging circuit is in good condition and the operating conditions are normal, the power removed from the battery will be replaced by the alternator which will force electrons back through the battery, reversing the normal flow, and restoring the battery to its original chemical state.

The battery and starting motor are linked by very heavy electrical cables designed to minimize resistance to the flow of current. Generally, the major power supply cable that leaves the battery goes directly to the starter, while the other electrical system needs are supplied by a smaller cable. During starter operation, power flows from the battery to the starer and is grounded through the car's frame and the battery's negative ground strap.

The starting motor is a specially designed, direct current electric motor capable of producing a very great amount of power for its size. One thing that allows the motor to produce a great deal of power is its tremendous rotating speed. It drives the engine through a tiny pinion gear (attached to the starter's armature), which drives the very large flywheel ring gear at a greatly reduced speed. Another factor allowing it to procedure so much power is that only intermittent operation is required of it. Thus, little allowance for air circulation is required, and the windings can be built into a very small space.

The starter solenoid is a magnetic device which employs the small current supplied by the starting switch circuit of the ignition switch. This magnetic action moves a plunger which mechanically engages the starter.

Positive engagement Ford starters, except those used with 429 and 460 V8 engines, employ a separate relay, mounted away from the starter, to switch the motor and solenoid current on and off, from the battery. The relay thus replaces the solenoid electrical switch, but does not eliminate the need to mechanically engage the starter drive gears. The relay is used to reduce the amount of current the starting switch must carry. On solenoid actuated starter installed in 429 and 460 V8 engines, the contacts in the solenoid take the place of the relay.

The starting switch circuit consists of the starting switch contained within the ignition switch, a transmission neutral safety switch or clutch pedal switch which prevents the car from being started in any gear but Neutral or Park (automatic only), and the wiring necessary to connect these in series with the starter solenoid or relay.

A pinion, which is a small gear, is mounted to a one-way drive clutch. this clutch is splined to the starter armature shaft. When the ignition switch is moved to the "start" position, the solenoid plunger slides the pinion toward the flywheel ring gear via a collar and spring. If the teeth on the pinion and flywheel match properly, the pinion will engage the flywheel immediately. If the gear teeth butt one another, the spring will be compressed and will force the gears to mash as soon as the starter turns far enough to allow them to do so. As the solenoid plunger reaches the end of its travel, it closes the contacts that connect the battery and starter and then the engine is cranked.

As soon as the engine starts, the flywheel ring gear beings turning fast enough to drive the pinion at an extremely high rate of speed.

At this point, the one-way clutch begins allowing the pinion to spring faster than the starter shaft so that the starter will not operate at excessive speed. When the ignition switch is released from the starter position, the solenoid is de-energized, and a spring contained within the solenoid assembly pulls the gear out of the mesh and interrupts the current flow to the starter.

Starter

All 6-cylinder models, and V8 models except the 429 and 460 V8 engines, use the positive engagement starter. This medium duty unit uses a remote starter relay to open and close the circuit to the battery.

The starter installed in 429 and 460 V8 models is the solenoid actuated starter. this heavy duty unit uses an outboard solenoid mounted atop the starter which has an internal electrical switch to open and close the circuit to the battery.

If, for some reason (such as an engine swap), a solenoid actuated starter is installed in a car originally equipped with a starter relay (any car not originally equipped with a 429 or 460 V8), a special connector link must be installed on the starter solenoid. This link connects the battery terminal with the solenoid operating windings. Therefore, when the key is turned to the Start position, the starter solenoid is actuated, sending battery current to the solenoid. the solenoid than operates the starter through the solenoid internal contacts. See the accompanying illustration for the proper installation of the connector link.

Troubleshooting Basic Starting System Problems

Problem	Cause	Solution
Starter motor rotates engine slowly	• Battery charge low or battery defective	• Charge or replace battery
	• Defective circuit between battery and starter motor	• Clean and tighten, or replace cables
	• Low load current	• Bench-test starter motor. Inspect for worn brushes and weak brush springs.
	• High load current	• Bench-test starter motor. Check engine for friction, drag or coolant in cylinders. Check ring gear-to-pinion gear clearance.
Starter motor will not rotate engine	• Battery charge low or battery defective	• Charge or replace battery
	• Faulty solenoid	• Check solenoid ground. Repair or replace as necessary.
	• Damage drive pinion gear or ring gear	• Replace damaged gear(s)
	• Starter motor engagement weak	• Bench-test starter motor
	• Starter motor rotates slowly with high load current	• Inspect drive yoke pull-down and point gap, check for worn end bushings, check ring gear clearance
	• Engine seized	• Repair engine
Starter motor drive will not engage (solenoid known to be good)	• Defective contact point assembly	• Repair or replace contact point assembly
	• Inadequate contact point assembly ground	• Repair connection at ground screw
	• Defective hold-in coil	• Replace field winding assembly
Starter motor drive will not disengage	• Starter motor loose on flywheel housing	• Tighten mounting bolts
	• Worn drive end busing	• Replace bushing
	• Damaged ring gear teeth	• Replace ring gear or driveplate
	• Drive yoke return spring broken or missing	• Replace spring
Starter motor drive disengages prematurely	• Weak drive assembly thrust spring	• Replace drive mechanism
	• Hold-in coil defective	• Replace field winding assembly
Low load current	• Worn brushes	• Replace brushes
	• Weak brush springs	• Replace springs

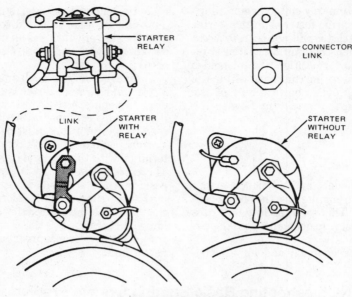

Solenoid connector link

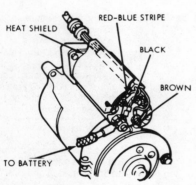

Solenoid actuated starter connections

REMOVAL AND INSTALLATION

1. Disconnect the negative battery cable.

2. Raise the front of the car and install jackstands beneath the frame. Firmly apply the parking brake and place blocks in back of the rear wheels.

3. Disconnect the heavy starter cable at the starter. On solenoid actuated starters (429 and 460 V8 only) label and disconnect the wires from the solenoid.

4. Turn the front wheels fully to the right. On many models, it will be necessary to remove the two bolts retaining the steering idler arm to the frame to gain access to the starter, and/or remove the shake braces if in the way.

5. Remove the starter mounting bolts and remove the starter.

6. Reverse the above procedure to install.

Torque the mounting bolts to 15-20 ft. lbs. and the idler arm retaining bolts to 28-35 ft. lbs. (if removed). Make sure that the nut securing the heavy cable to the starter is snugged down tightly.

OVERHAUL

Solenoid Actuated Starter

DISASSEMBLY

1. Disconnect the copper strap from the starter terminal on the solenoid, remove the retaining screws and remove the solenoid from the drive housing.

2. Loosen the retaining screw and slide the brush cover band back on the starter frame for access to the brushes.

3. Remove the commutator brushes from their holders. Hold each spring away from the brush with a hook, while sliding the brush out of the holder.

4. Remove the through-bolts and separate the drive-end housing, starter frame and brush end plate assemblies.

5. Remove the solenoid plunger and shift fork assembly. If either the plunger or fork is to be replaced, they can be separated by removing the roll pin.

6. Remove the armature and drive assembly from the frame. Remove the drive stop ring and slide the drive assembly off the armature shaft.

7. Remove the drive stop ring retainer from the drive housing.

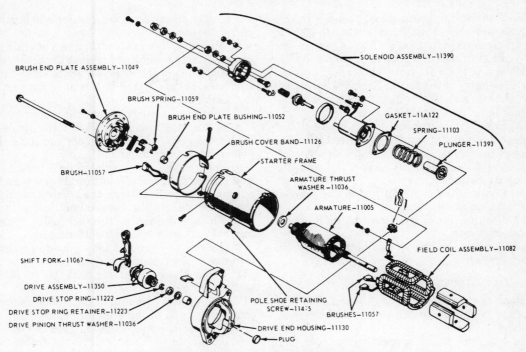

Solenoid actuated starter disassembled

(Labels in figure:)

SOLENOID ASSEMBLY–11390

BRUSH END PLATE ASSEMBLY–11049

BRUSH SPRING–11059

BRUSH END PLATE BUSHING–11052

GASKET–11A122

SPRING–11103

PLUNGER–11393

BRUSH COVER BAND–11126

STARTER FRAME

BRUSH–11057

ARMATURE THRUST WASHER–11036

ARMATURE–11005

FIELD COIL ASSEMBLY–11082

SHIFT FORK–11067

DRIVE ASSEMBLY–11350

DRIVE STOP RING–11222

DRIVE STOP RING RETAINER–11223

DRIVE PINION THRUST WASHER–11036

POLE SHOE RETAINING SCREW–114:5

BRUSHES–11057

DRIVE END HOUSING–11130

PLUG

CLEANING AND INSPECTION

1. Do not wash the drive because the solvent will wash out the lubricant, causing the drive to slip. Use a brush or compressed air to clean the drive, field coils, armature, commutator, armature shaft front end plate, and rear end housing. Wash all other parts in solvent and dry the parts.

2. Inspect the armature windings for broken or burned insulation and unsoldered connections.

3. Check the armature for open circuits and grounds.

4. Check the commutator for run-out. Inspect the armature shaft and the two bearings for scoring and excessive wear. On a starter with needle bearings, apply a small amount of grease to the needles. If the commutator is rough, or more than 0.005″ out-of-round, turn it down.

5. Check the brush holders for broken springs and the insulated brush holders for shorts to ground. Tighten any rivets that may be loose. Replace the brushes if worn to ¼″ in length.

6. Check the brush spring tension. Replace the spring is the tension is not within specified limits (80 ounces minimum).

7. Inspect the field coils for burned or broken insulation and continuity. Check the field brush connections and lead insulation. A brush kit is available. All other assemblies are to be replaced rather than repaired.

8. Examine the wear pattern on the starter drive teeth. The pinion teeth must penetrate to a depth greater than ½ the ring gear tooth depth, to eliminate premature ring gear and starter drive failure.

9. Replace starter drives and ring gears with milled, pitted or broken teeth or evidence of inadequate engagement.

ASSEMBLY

1. Install a small amount of Lubriplate on the armature shaft splines. Install the drive assembly on the armature shaft and install a new stop ring.

2. Apply a small amount of Lubriplate on the shift lever pivot pin. Position the solenoid plunger and shaft lever assembly in the drive housing.

3. Place a new retainer in the drive housing. Apply a small amount of Lubriplate to the drive end of the armature shaft. Place the armature and drive assembly into the drive housing. Be sure that the shift lever tangs properly engage the drive assembly.

4. Apply a small amount of Lubriplate on the commutator end of the armature shaft.

5. Position the frame and field assembly to the drive housing. Be sure that the frame is properly indexed to the drive housing assembly.

6. Position the brush plate assembly to the frame assembly. Be sure that the brush plate is properly indexed to the drive housing assembly.

7. Place the brushes in their holders. Pull each spring away from the holder with a hook to allow entry of the brush. Press the insulated brush leads away from all other interior components to prevent possible shorts.

8. Position the rubber gasket between the solenoid mounting and the upper outside surface of the frame. Position the starter solenoid with the metal gasket (if used), and install the solenoid mounting screws.

9. Connect the copper strap to the starter terminal on the solenoid.

10. Position the cover band and tighten the retaining screw.

11. Connect the starter to a battery to check its operation.

BRUSH REPLACEMENT

Replace the starter brushes when they are worn to ¼″. Always install a complete set of new brushes.

1. Disconnect the copper strap from the starter terminal on the solenoid.

2. Loosen the retaining screw and slide the brush cover band back on the starter frame for access to the brushes.

3. Remove the commutator brushes from their holders. Hold each spring away from the brush with a hook, while sliding the brush out of the holder.

4. Remove the through-bolts and separate the drive end housing, starter frame and brush end plate assemblies.

5. Remove the ground brush retaining screws from the frame and remove the brushes.

6. Cut the insulated brush leads from the field coils, as close to the field connection point as possible.

7. Clean and inspect the starter motor.

8. Replace the brush end plate, if the insulator between the field brush holder and the end plate is cracked or broken.

9. Position the new insulated field brushes' lead on the field coil connection. Position and crimp the clip provided with the brushes to hold the brush lead to the connection. Solder the lead, clip, and connection together, using rosin core solder. Use a 300-watt soldering iron.

10. Install the ground brush leads to the frame with the retaining screws.

11. Clean the commutator with 00 or 000 sandpaper.

12. Apply a small amount of Lubriplate on the commutator end of the armature shaft.

13. Position the rubber gasket over the solenoid plunger lever, then position the frame to the end housing so that the wide slot in the frame clear the plunger lever and the end housing dowel is indexed with its frame slot.

14. Position the brush assembly to the frame assembly. Be sure that the brush plate is properly indexed to the frame. Install the through-bolts, making certain that the insulated brush lead is not between the through-bolt and the frame, and tighten to 45 to 85 in. lbs.

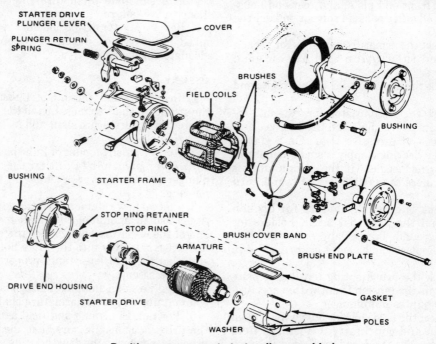

Positive engagement starter disassembled

15. Place the brushes in their holders. Pull each spring away from the holder with a hook to allow entry of the brush. Press the insulated brush leads away from all the other interior components to prevent possible shorts.

16. Slide the cover band into position and tighten the retaining screw.

17. Connect the copper strap to the starter terminal on the solenoid.

18. Connect the starter to a battery to check its operation.

STARTER DRIVE REPLACEMENT

All Except 429 and 460 V8 (Positive Engagement Type)

1. Remove the starter from the engine.
2. Remove the brush cover band.
3. Remove the starter drive plunger lever cover.
4. Loosen the through-bolts just enough to allow removal of the drive end housing and the starter drive plunger lever return spring.
5. Remove the pivot pin which attaches the starter drive plunger lever to the starter frame and remove the lever.
6. Remove the stop-ring retainer and stop-ring from the armature shaft.
7. Remove the starter drive from the armature shaft.
8. Inspect the teeth on the starter drive. If they are excessively worn, inspect the teeth on the ring gear of the flywheel. If the teeth on the flywheel are excessively worn, the flywheel ring gear should be replaced.

9. Apply a thin coat of white grease to the armature shaft, in the area in which the starter drive operates.

10. Install the starter drive on the armature shaft and install a new stop-ring.

11. Position the starter drive plunger lever on the starter frame and install the pivot pin. Make sure the plunger lever is properly engaged with the starter drive.

12. Install a new stop-ring retainer on the armature shaft.

13. Fill the drive end housing bearing fore ¼ full with grease.

14. Position the starter drive plunger lever return spring and the drive end housing to the starter frame.

15. Tighten the starter through-bolts to 55-75 in. lbs.

16. Install the starter drive plunger lever cover and the brush cover band on the starter.

17. Install the starter.

OVERHAUL

Positive Engagement Starter

1. Disconnect the field coil connection from the solenoid motor terminal.

2. Remove the solenoid attaching screws, solenoid and plunger return spring. Rotate the solenoid 90° to remove it.

3. Remove the through-bolts and brush end plate.

4. Rempove the brush springs and brushes from the plastic brush holder and remove the brush holder. Keep track of the location of the

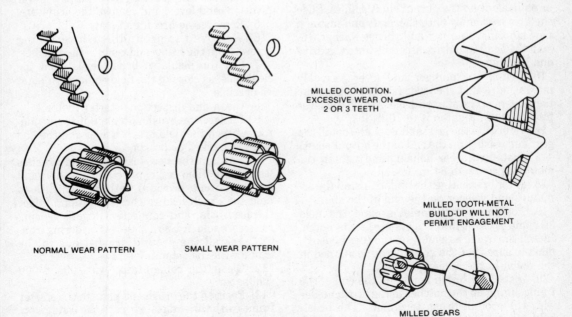

NORMAL WEAR PATTERN   SMALL WEAR PATTERN

MILLED CONDITION. EXCESSIVE WEAR ON 2 OR 3 TEETH

MILLED TOOTH-METAL BUILD-UP WILL NOT PERMIT ENGAGEMENT

MILLED GEARS

Starter drive ring and pinion wear patterns

brush holder with regard to the brush terminals.

5. Remove the frame assembly.

6. Remove the armature assembly.

7. Remove the screw from the gear housing and remove the gear housing.

8. Remove the plunger and lever pivot screw and remove the plunger and lever.

9. Remove the gear, output shaft and drive assembly.

10. Remove the thrust washer, retainer, drive stop ring and slide the drive assembly off of the output shaft.

WARNING: *Don't wash the drive because the solvent will wash out the lubricant, causing the drive to slip. Use a brush or compressed air to clean the drive, field coils, armature, gear and housing.*

11. Inspect the armature windings for broken or burned insulation, and open connections at the commutator. Check for any signs of grounding.

12. Check the commutator for excessive runout. If the commutator is rough or more than 0.127mm out-of-round, replace it or correct the problem as necessary.

13. Check the plastic brush holder for cracks or broken pads. Replace the brushes if worn to a length less than ¼″ (6mm) in length. Inspect the field coils and plastic bobbins for burned or damaged areas. Check the continuity of the coil and brush connections. A brush replacement kit is available. Any other worn or damaged parts should be replaced.

14. Apply a thin coating of Lubriplate 777®, or equivalent on the output shaft splines. Slide the drive assembly onto the shaft and install a new stopring, retainer and thrust washer. Install the shaft and drive assembly into the drive end housing.

15. Install the plunger and lever assembly making sure that the lever notches engage the flange ears of the starter drive. Attach the lever pin screw and tighten it to 10 ft. lbs.

16. Lubricate the gear and washer. Install the gear and washer on the end of the output shaft.

17. Install the gear housing and tighten the mounting screw to 84 in. lbs.

18. After lubricating the pinion, install the armature and washer on the end of the shaft.

19. Position the grommet around the field lead and press it into the starter frame notch. Install the frame assembly on the gear housing, making sure that the grommet is positioned in the notch in the housing.

20. Install the brush holder on the end of the frame, lining up the notches in the brush holder with the ground brush terminals. The brush holder is symmetrical and can be installed with either notch and brush terminal.

21. Install the brush springs and brushes. The positive brush leads must be placed in their respective slots to prevent grounding.

22. Install the brush endplate, making sure that the insulator is properly positioned. Install and tighten the through-bolts to 84 in. lbs.

NOTE: *The brush endplate has a threaded hole in the protruding ear which must be oriented properly so the starter-to-vacuum pump support bracket can be installed.*

23. Install the return spring on the solenoid plunger and install the solenoid. Attach the 2 solenoid attaching screws and tighten them to 84 in. lbs. Apply a sealing compound to the junction of the solenoid case flange, gear and drive end housings.

24. Attach the motor field terminal to the **M** terminal of the solenoid, and tighten the fasteners to 30 in. lbs.

25. Check the starter no-load current draw. Maximum draw should be 190 amps.

BRUSH REPLACEMENT

Replace the starter brushes when they are worn to ¼″. Always install a complete set of new brushes.

1. Loosen and remove the brush cover band, gasket, and starter drive plunger lever cover. Remove the brushes from their holders.

2. Remove the two through-bolts from the starter frame.

3. Remove the drive end housing and the plunger lever return spring.

4. Remove the starter drive plunger lever pivot pin and lever, and remove the armature.

5. Remove the brush end plate.

6. Remove the ground brush retaining screws from the frame and remove the brushes.

7. Cut the insulated brush leads from the field coils, as close to the field connection point as possible.

8. Clean and inspect the starter motor.

9. Replace the brush end plate if the insulator between the field brush holder and the end plate is cracked or broken.

10. Position the new insulated field brushes lead on the filed coil connection. Position and cramp the clip provided with the brushes to hold the brush lead to the connection. Solder the lead, clip, and connection together using rosin core solder. Use a 300-watt soldering iron.

11. Install the ground brush leads to the frame with the retaining screws.

12. Clean the commutator with 00 or 000 sandpaper.

13. Position the brush end plate to the starter frame, with the end plate boss in the frame slot.

14. Install the armature in the starter frame.

15. Install the starter drive gear plunger lever

to the frame and starter drive assembly, and install the pivot pin.

16. Partially fill the drive end housing bearing bore with grease (approximately ¼ full). Position the return spring on the plunger lever, and the drive end housing to the starter frame. Install the through-bolts and tighten to specified torque (55 to 75 in. lbs.). Be sure that the stop ring retainer is seated properly in the drive end housing.

17. Install the commutator brushes in the brush holder. Center the brush springs on the brushes.

18. Position the plunger lever cover and brush cover band, with its gasket, on the starter. Tighten the bank retainer screw.

19. Connect the starter to a battery to check its operation.

Starter Relay

REMOVAL AND INSTALLATION

1. Disconnect the positive battery cable from the battery terminal. With dual batteries, disconnect the connecting cable at both ends.

2. Remove the nut securing the positive battery cable to the relay.

3. Remove the positive cable and any other wiring under that cable.

4. Tag and remove the push-on wires from the front of the relay.

5. Remove the nut and disconnect the cable from the starter side of the relay.

6. Remove the relay attaching bolts and remove the relay.

7. Installation is the reverse of removal.

Battery

REMOVAL AND INSTALLATION

1. Remove the holddown screws from the battery box. Loosen the nuts that secure the cable ends to the battery terminals. Lift the battery cables from the terminals with a twisting motion.

2. If there is a battery cable puller available, make use of it. Lift the battery from the vehicle.

3. Before installing the battery in the vehicle, make sure that the battery terminals are clean and free from corrosion. Use a battery terminal cleaner on the terminals and on the inside of the battery cable ends. If a cleaner is not available, use a heavy sandpaper to remove the corrosion. A mixture of baking soda and water will neutralize any acid. Place the battery in the vehicle. Install the cables on the terminals. Tighten the nuts on the cable ends. Smear a light coating of grease on the cable ends and the tops of the terminals. This will prevent buildup of oxidized acid on the terminals and the cable

ends. Install and tighten the nuts of the battery box.

ENGINE MECHANICAL

Design

A number of different engines have been used from 1968. All of the engines use conventional cast iron, water cooled blocks. The cylinder heads are of the overhead valve design and the valves are actuated by pushrods and hydraulic valve lifters. The engines fall into five basic families.

A 240 cubic inch, inline 6-cylinder engine is used in some models between 1968 and 1972. Unlike some of the smaller 6-cylinder engines used in other Ford products, this six has a detachable intake manifold.

The second family is a remarkable series of small and medium sized V8 engines. They are; the 255, 302 and 351 Windsor engines. the 302 was the standard engine from 1968 through 1972 and then again from 1978 through 1980. The 351W medium sized V8 was installed in various models from 1969. In 1981 the 255 cubic inch V8 became the standard engine, installed in the Ford and Mercury, replacing the 302. the "new" engine is derived from the 302. the 255 Features weight reduction by about sixty pounds (from the 302) and has been designed to be adaptable to a variety of fuel metering systems. In 1981, the 302 and 351 (and a high output version of the 351, for police and towing) were offered as options. The 255 cu. in. engine has been dropped for the 1983 model year. 302 and 351 cu. in. engines are the only ones available. The 351 cu. in. is available in a standard or high output version.

The third engine family includes the 351 Cleveland, 351 Modified, and the 400 V8s. the 351C is used on 1972-74 models. the 351M, which is a modified Cleveland design, is used starting in 1975. The 400 V8 is installed in 1971-78 models. This family of engines is based on the smaller 302-351W series, but enjoys a higher volumetric efficiency quotient due to its larger valves and better breathing semi-hemispherical combustion chambers.

The fourth engine family includes the 390, 428 and 462 cubic inch V8s. The 390 V8 may be found in 1968-71 models. The 428 V8 is used in 1968-71 models. the 462 V8 is used in the 1968 Lincoln. These engines are the last examples of the Y-block design, first introduced in the mid-fifties. Identifying features of these engines are the shaft mounted rocker arms, and an intake manifold that extends beneath the valve cover.

The last group of engines includes the 429

and 460 V8s. the 429 V8 is installed in 1969-73 models. the 460 V8 may be found in full size Fords starting in 1974. It was last used in 1978. this family of engines was introduced to replace the old Y-block series, and is also based on the smaller 302-351W design. Identifying features of these powerplants are their great bulk and the tunnelport shaped configuration of the intake manifold.

Engine Overhaul Tips

Most engine overhaul procedures are fairly standard. In addition to specific parts replacement procedures and complete specifications for your individual engine, this chapter also is a guide to accept rebuilding procedures. Examples of standard rebuilding practice are shown and should be used along with specific details concerning your particular engine.

Competent and accurate machine shop services will ensure maximum performance, reliability and engine life.

In most instances it is more profitable for the do-it-yourself mechanic to remove, clean and inspect the component, buy the necessary parts and deliver these to a shop for actual machine work.

On the other hand, much of the rebuilding work (crankshaft, block, bearings, piston rods, and other components) is well within the scope of the do-it-yourself mechanic.

TOOLS

The tools required for an engine overhaul or parts replacement will depend on the depth of your involvement. With a few exceptions, they will be the tools found in a mechanic's tool kit (see Chapter 1). More in-depth work will require any or all of the following:

- a dial indicator (reading in thousandths) mounted on a universal base
- micrometers and telescope gauges
- jaw and screw-type pullers
- scraper
- valve spring compressor
- ring groove cleaner
- piston ring expander and compressor

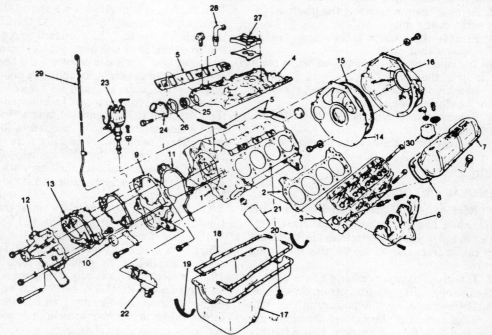

1. Cylinder block	11. Front cover gasket	21. Oil filter
2. Cylinder head gasket	12. Water pump	22. Fuel pump
3. Cylinder head	13. Water pump gasket	23. Distributor
4. Intake manifold	14. Rear cover plate	24. Thermostat housing
5. Intake manifold gasket	15. Flywheel	25. Thermostat
6. Exhaust manifold	16. Flywheel housing	26. Thermostat gasket
7. Valve cover	17. Oil pan	27. Carburetor spacer
8. Valve cover gasket	18. Oil pan gasket	28. Heater hose fitting
9. Front cover	19. Front main seal	29. Dipstick
10. Front cover seal	20. Rear main seal	30. Filler cap

Exploded view of stationary engine components—255, 302 and 351V

Troubleshooting Engine Mechanical Problems

Problem	Cause	Solution
External oil leaks	• Fuel pump gasket broken or improperly seated	• Replace gasket
	• Cylinder head cover RTV sealant broken or improperly seated	• Replace sealant; inspect cylinder head cover sealant flange and cylinder head sealant surface for distortion and cracks
	• Oil filler cap leaking or missing	• Replace cap
	• Oil filter gasket broken or improperly seated	• Replace oil filter
	• Oil pan side gasket broken, improperly seated or opening in RTV sealant	• Replace gasket or repair opening in sealant; inspect oil pan gasket flange for distortion
	• Oil pan front oil seal broken or improperly seated	• Replace seal; inspect timing case cover and oil pan seal flange for distortion
	• Oil pan rear oil seal broken or improperly seated	• Replace seal; inspect oil pan rear oil seal flange; inspect rear main bearing cap for cracks, plugged oil return channels, or distortion in seal groove
	• Timing case cover oil seal broken or improperly seated	• Replace seal
	• Excess oil pressure because of restricted PCV valve	• Replace PCV valve
	• Oil pan drain plug loose or has stripped threads	• Repair as necessary and tighten
	• Rear oil gallery plug loose	• Use appropriate sealant on gallery plug and tighten
	• Rear camshaft plug loose or improperly seated	• Seat camshaft plug or replace and seal, as necessary
	• Distributor base gasket damaged	• Replace gasket
Excessive oil consumption	• Oil level too high	• Drain oil to specified level
	• Oil with wrong viscosity being used	• Replace with specified oil
	• PCV valve stuck closed	• Replace PCV valve
	• Valve stem oil deflectors (or seals) are damaged, missing, or incorrect type	• Replace valve stem oil deflectors
	• Valve stems or valve guides worn	• Measure stem-to-guide clearance and repair as necessary
	• Poorly fitted or missing valve cover baffles	• Replace valve cover
	• Piston rings broken or missing	• Replace broken or missing rings
	• Scuffed piston	• Replace piston
	• Incorrect piston ring gap	• Measure ring gap, repair as necessary
	• Piston rings sticking or excessively loose in grooves	• Measure ring side clearance, repair as necessary
	• Compression rings installed upside down	• Repair as necessary
	• Cylinder walls worn, scored, or glazed	• Repair as necessary
	• Piston ring gaps not properly staggered	• Repair as necessary
	• Excessive main or connecting rod bearing clearance	• Measure bearing clearance, repair as necessary
No oil pressure	• Low oil level	• Add oil to correct level
	• Oil pressure gauge, warning lamp or sending unit inaccurate	• Replace oil pressure gauge or warning lamp
	• Oil pump malfunction	• Replace oil pump
	• Oil pressure relief valve sticking	• Remove and inspect oil pressure relief valve assembly
	• Oil passages on pressure side of pump obstructed	• Inspect oil passages for obstruction

Troubleshooting Engine Mechanical Problems (cont.)

Problem	Cause	Solution
No oil pressure (cont.)	• Oil pickup screen or tube obstructed • Loose oil inlet tube	• Inspect oil pickup for obstruction • Tighten or seal inlet tube
Low oil pressure	• Low oil level • Inaccurate gauge, warning lamp or sending unit • Oil excessively thin because of dilution, poor quality, or improper grade • Excessive oil temperature • Oil pressure relief spring weak or sticking • Oil inlet tube and screen assembly has restriction or air leak • Excessive oil pump clearance • Excessive main, rod, or camshaft bearing clearance	• Add oil to correct level • Replace oil pressure gauge or warning lamp • Drain and refill crankcase with recommended oil • Correct cause of overheating engine • Remove and inspect oil pressure relief valve assembly • Remove and inspect oil inlet tube and screen assembly. (Fill inlet tube with lacquer thinner to locate leaks.) • Measure clearances • Measure bearing clearances, repair as necessary
High oil pressure	• Improper oil viscosity • Oil pressure gauge or sending unit inaccurate • Oil pressure relief valve sticking closed	• Drain and refill crankcase with correct viscosity oil • Replace oil pressure gauge • Remove and inspect oil pressure relief valve assembly
Main bearing noise	• Insufficient oil supply • Main bearing clearance excessive • Bearing insert missing • Crankshaft end play excessive • Improperly tightened main bearing cap bolts • Loose flywheel or drive plate • Loose or damaged vibration damper	• Inspect for low oil level and low oil pressure • Measure main bearing clearance, repair as necessary • Replace missing insert • Measure end play, repair as necessary • Tighten bolts with specified torque • Tighten flywheel or drive plate attaching bolts • Repair as necessary
Connecting rod bearing noise	• Insufficient oil supply • Carbon build-up on piston • Bearing clearance excessive or bearing missing • Crankshaft connecting rod journal out-of-round • Misaligned connecting rod or cap • Connecting rod bolts tightened improperly	• Inspect for low oil level and low oil pressure • Remove carbon from piston crown • Measure clearance, repair as necessary • Measure journal dimensions, repair or replace as necessary • Repair as necessary • Tighten bolts with specified torque
Piston noise	• Piston-to-cylinder wall clearance excessive (scuffed piston) • Cylinder walls excessively tapered or out-of-round • Piston ring broken • Loose or seized piston pin • Connecting rods misaligned • Piston ring side clearance excessively loose or tight • Carbon build-up on piston is excessive	• Measure clearance and examine piston • Measure cylinder wall dimensions, rebore cylinder • Replace all rings on piston • Measure piston-to-pin clearance, repair as necessary • Measure rod alignment, straighten or replace • Measure ring side clearance, repair as necessary • Remove carbon from piston

Troubleshooting Engine Mechanical Problems (cont.)

Problem	Cause	Solution
Valve actuating component noise	• Insufficient oil supply	• Check for: (a) Low oil level (b) Low oil pressure (c) Plugged push rods (d) Wrong hydraulic tappets (e) Restricted oil gallery (f) Excessive tappet to bore clearance
	• Push rods worn or bent	• Replace worn or bent push rods
	• Rocker arms or pivots worn	• Replace worn rocker arms or pivots
	• Foreign objects or chips in hydraulic tappets	• Clean tappets
	• Excessive tappet leak-down	• Replace valve tappet
	• Tappet face worn	• Replace tappet; inspect corresponding cam lobe for wear
	• Broken or cocked valve springs	• Properly seat cocked springs; replace broken springs
	• Stem-to-guide clearance excessive	• Measure stem-to-guide clearance, repair as required
	• Valve bent	• Replace valve
	• Loose rocker arms	• Tighten bolts with specified torque
	• Valve seat runout excessive	• Regrind valve seat/valves
	• Missing valve lock	• Install valve lock
	• Push rod rubbing or contacting cylinder head	• Remove cylinder head and remove obstruction in head
	• Excessive engine oil (four-cylinder engine)	• Correct oil level

- ridge reamer
- cylinder hone or glaze breaker
- Plastigage®
- engine stand

The use of most of these tools is illustrated in this chapter. Many can be rented for a one-time use from a local parts jobber or tool supply house specializing in automotive work.

Occasionally, the use of special tools is called for. See the information on Special Tools and Safety Notice in the front of this book before substituting another tool.

INSPECTION TECHNIQUES

Procedures and specifications are given in this chapter for inspecting, cleaning and assessing the wear limits of most major components. Other procedures such as Magnaflux® and Zyglo® can be used to locate material flaws and stress cracks. Magnaflux® is a magnetic process applicable only to ferrous materials. The Zyglo® process coats the material with a fluorescent dye penetrant and can be used on any material Check for suspected surface cracks can be more readily made using spot check dye. The dye is sprayed onto the suspected area, wiped off and the area sprayed with a developer. Cracks will show up brightly.

OVERHAUL TIPS

Aluminum has become extremely popular for use in engines, due to its low weight. Observe the following precautions when handling aluminum parts:

- Never hot tank aluminum parts (the caustic hot tank solution will eat the aluminum.
- Remove all aluminum parts (identification tag, etc.) from engine parts prior to the tanking.
- Always coat threads lightly with engine oil or anti-seize compounds before installation, to prevent seizure.
- Never overtorque bolts or spark plugs especially in aluminum threads.

Stripped threads in any component can be repaired using any of several commercial repair kits (Heli-Coil®, Microdot®, Keenserts®, etc.).

When assembling the engine, any parts that will be frictional contact must be prelubed to provide lubrication at initial start-up. Any product specifically formulated for this purpose can be used, but engine oil is not recommended as a prelube.

When semi-permanent (locked, but removable) installation of bolts or nuts is desired, threads should be cleaned and coated with Loctite® or other similar, commercial non-hardening sealant.

Troubleshooting the Cooling System

Problem	Cause	Solution
High temperature gauge indication—overheating	• Coolant level low	• Replenish coolant
	• Fan belt loose	• Adjust fan belt tension
	• Radiator hose(s) collapsed	• Replace hose(s)
	• Radiator airflow blocked	• Remove restriction (bug screen, fog lamps, etc.)
	• Faulty radiator cap	• Replace radiator cap
	• Ignition timing incorrect	• Adjust ignition timing
	• Idle speed low	• Adjust idle speed
	• Air trapped in cooling system	• Purge air
	• Heavy traffic driving	• Operate at fast idle in neutral intermittently to cool engine
	• Incorrect cooling system component(s) installed	• Install proper component(s)
	• Faulty thermostat	• Replace thermostat
	• Water pump shaft broken or impeller loose	• Replace water pump
	• Radiator tubes clogged	• Flush radiator
	• Cooling system clogged	• Flush system
	• Casting flash in cooling passages	• Repair or replace as necessary. Flash may be visible by removing cooling system components or removing core plugs.
	• Brakes dragging	• Repair brakes
	• Excessive engine friction	• Repair engine
	• Antifreeze concentration over 68%	• Lower antifreeze concentration percentage
	• Missing air seals	• Replace air seals
	• Faulty gauge or sending unit	• Repair or replace faulty component
	• Loss of coolant flow caused by leakage or foaming	• Repair or replace leaking component, replace coolant
	• Viscous fan drive failed	• Replace unit
Low temperature indication—undercooling	• Thermostat stuck open	• Replace thermostat
	• Faulty gauge or sending unit	• Repair or replace faulty component
Coolant loss—boilover	• Overfilled cooling system	• Reduce coolant level to proper specification
	• Quick shutdown after hard (hot) run	• Allow engine to run at fast idle prior to shutdown
	• Air in system resulting in occasional "burping" of coolant	• Purge system
	• Insufficient antifreeze allowing coolant boiling point to be too low	• Add antifreeze to raise boiling point
	• Antifreeze deteriorated because of age or contamination	• Replace coolant
	• Leaks due to loose hose clamps, loose nuts, bolts, drain plugs, faulty hoses, or defective radiator	• Pressure test system to locate source of leak(s) then repair as necessary
	• Faulty head gasket	• Replace head gasket
	• Cracked head, manifold, or block	• Replace as necessary
	• Faulty radiator cap	• Replace cap
Coolant entry into crankcase or cylinder(s)	• Faulty head gasket	• Replace head gasket
	• Crack in head, manifold or block	• Replace as necessary
Coolant recovery system inoperative	• Coolant level low	• Replenish coolant to FULL mark
	• Leak in system	• Pressure test to isolate leak and repair as necessary
	• Pressure cap not tight or seal missing, or leaking	• Repair as necessary
	• Pressure cap defective	• Replace cap
	• Overflow tube clogged or leaking	• Repair as necessary
	• Recovery bottle vent restricted	• Remove restriction

Troubleshooting the Cooling System (cont.)

Problem	Cause	Solution
Noise	• Fan contacting shroud	• Reposition shroud and inspect engine mounts
	• Loose water pump impeller	• Replace pump
	• Glazed fan belt	• Apply silicone or replace belt
	• Loose fan belt	• Adjust fan belt tension
	• Rough surface on drive pulley	• Replace pulley
	• Water pump bearing worn	• Remove belt to isolate. Replace pump.
	• Belt alignment	• Check pulley alignment. Repair as necessary.
No coolant flow through heater core	• Restricted return inlet in water pump	• Remove restriction
	• Heater hose collapsed or restricted	• Remove restriction or replace hose
	• Restricted heater core	• Remove restriction or replace core
	• Restricted outlet in thermostat housing	• Remove flash or restriction
	• Intake manifold bypass hole in cylinder head restricted	• Remove restriction
	• Faulty heater control valve	• Replace valve
	• Intake manifold coolant passage restricted	• Remove restriction or replace intake manifold

NOTE: *Immediately after shutdown, the engine enters a condition known as heat soak. This is caused by the cooling system being inoperative while engine temperature is still high. If coolant temperature rises above boiling point, expansion and pressure may push some coolant out of the radiator overflow tube. If this does not occur frequently it is considered normal.*

Troubleshooting the Serpentine Drive Belt

Problem	Cause	Solution
Tension sheeting fabric failure (woven fabric on outside circumference of belt has cracked or separated from body of belt)	• Grooved or backside idler pulley diameters are less than minimum recommended	• Replace pulley(s) not conforming to specification
	• Tension sheeting contacting (rubbing) stationary object	• Correct rubbing condition
	• Excessive heat causing woven fabric to age	• Replace belt
	• Tension sheeting splice has fractured	• Replace belt
Noise (objectional squeal, squeak, or rumble is heard or felt while drive belt is in operation)	• Belt slippage	• Adjust belt
	• Bearing noise	• Locate and repair
	• Belt misalignment	• Align belt/pulley(s)
	• Belt-to-pulley mismatch	• Install correct belt
	• Driven component inducing vibration	• Locate defective driven component and repair
	• System resonant frequency inducing vibration	• Vary belt tension within specifications. Replace belt.
Rib chunking (one or more ribs has separated from belt body)	• Foreign objects imbedded in pulley grooves	• Remove foreign objects from pulley grooves
	• Installation damage	• Replace belt
	• Drive loads in excess of design specifications	• Adjust belt tension
	• Insufficient internal belt adhesion	• Replace belt
Rib or belt wear (belt ribs contact bottom of pulley grooves)	• Pulley(s) misaligned	• Align pulley(s)
	• Mismatch of belt and pulley groove widths	• Replace belt
	• Abrasive environment	• Replace belt
	• Rusted pulley(s)	• Clean rust from pulley(s)
	• Sharp or jagged pulley groove tips	• Replace pulley
	• Rubber deteriorated	• Replace belt

Troubleshooting the Serpentine Drive Belt (cont.)

Problem	Cause	Solution
Longitudinal belt cracking (cracks between two ribs)	• Belt has mistracked from pulley groove • Pulley groove tip has worn away rubber-to-tensile member	• Replace belt • Replace belt
Belt slips	• Belt slipping because of insufficient tension • Belt or pulley subjected to substance (belt dressing, oil, ethylene glycol) that has reduced friction • Driven component bearing failure • Belt glazed and hardened from heat and excessive slippage	• Adjust tension • Replace belt and clean pulleys • Replace faulty component bearing • Replace belt
"Groove jumping" (belt does not maintain correct position on pulley, or turns over and/or runs off pulleys)	• Insufficient belt tension • Pulley(s) not within design tolerance • Foreign object(s) in grooves • Excessive belt speed • Pulley misalignment • Belt-to-pulley profile mismatched • Belt cordline is distorted	• Adjust belt tension • Replace pulley(s) • Remove foreign objects from grooves • Avoid excessive engine acceleration • Align pulley(s) • Install correct belt • Replace belt
Belt broken (Note: identify and correct problem before replacement belt is installed)	• Excessive tension • Tensile members damaged during belt installation • Belt turnover • Severe pulley misalignment • Bracket, pulley, or bearing failure	• Replace belt and adjust tension to specification • Replace belt • Replace belt • Align pulley(s) • Replace defective component and belt
Cord edge failure (tensile member exposed at edges of belt or separated from belt body)	• Excessive tension • Drive pulley misalignment • Belt contacting stationary object • Pulley irregularities • Improper pulley construction • Insufficient adhesion between tensile member and rubber matrix	• Adjust belt tension • Align pulley • Correct as necessary • Replace pulley • Replace pulley • Replace belt and adjust tension to specifications
Sporadic rib cracking (multiple cracks in belt ribs at random intervals)	• Ribbed pulley(s) diameter less than minimum specification • Backside bend flat pulley(s) diameter less than minimum • Excessive heat condition causing rubber to harden • Excessive belt thickness • Belt overcured • Excessive tension	• Replace pulley(s) • Replace pulley(s) • Correct heat condition as necessary • Replace belt • Replace belt • Adjust belt tension

REPAIRING DAMAGED THREADS

Several methods of repairing damaged threads are available. Heli-Coil® (shown here), Keenserts® and Microdot® are among the most widely used. All involve basically the same principle – drilling out stripped threads, tapping the hole and installing a prewound insert – making welding, plugging and oversize fasteners unnecessary.

Two types of thread repair inserts are usually supplied: a standard type for most Inch Coarse, Inch Fine, Metric Course and Metric Fine thread sizes and a spark lug type to fit most spark plug port sizes. Consult the individual manufacturer's catalog to determine exact applications. Typical thread repair kits will contain a selection of prewound threaded inserts, a tap (corresponding to the outside diameter threads of the insert) and an installation tool. Spark plug inserts usually differ because they require a tap equipped with pilot threads and a combined reamer/tap section. Most manufacturers also supply blister-packed thread repair inserts separately in addition to a master kit containing a variety of taps and inserts plus installation tools.

Before effecting a repair to a threaded hole, remove any snapped, broken or damaged bolts or studs. Penetrating oil can be used to free frozen threads. The offending item can be removed with locking pliers or with a screw or stud extractor. After the hole is clear, the thread can be repaired, as shown in the series of accompanying illustrations.

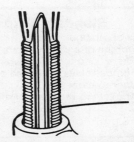

With the tap supplied, tap the hole to receive the thread insert. Keep the tap well oiled and back it out frequently to avoid clogging the threads

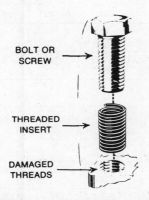

BOLT OR SCREW

THREADED INSERT

DAMAGED THREADS

Damaged bolt holes can be repaired with thread repair inserts

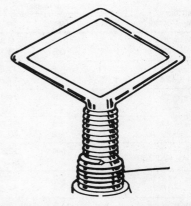

Screw the threaded insert onto the installation tool until the tang engages the slot. Screw the insert into the tapped hole until it is ¼–½ turn below the top surface. After installation break off the tang with a hammer and punch

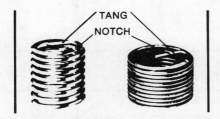

TANG

NOTCH

Standard thread repair insert (left) and spark plug thread insert (right)

Drill out the damaged threads with specified drill. Drill completely through the hole or to the bottom of a blind hole

Checking Engine Compression

A noticeable lack of engine power, excessive oil consumption and/or poor fuel mileage measured over an extended period are all indicators of internal engine war. Worn piston rings, scored or worn cylinder bores, blown head gaskets, sticking or burnt valves and worn valve seats are all possible culprits here. A check of each cylinder's compression will help you locate the problems.

As mentioned in the Tools and Equipment section of Chapter 1, a screw-in type compression gauge is more accurate that the type you simply hold against the spark plug hole, although it takes slightly longer to use. It's worth it to obtain a more accurate reading. Follow the procedures below.

1. Warm up the engine to normal operating temperature.

2. Remove all the spark plugs.

3. Disconnect the high tension lead from the ignition coil.

Standard Torque Specifications and Fastener Markings

In the absence of specific torques, the following chart can be used as a guide to the maximum safe torque of a particular size/grade of fastener.

- There is no torque difference for fine or coarse threads.
- Torque values are based on clean, dry threads. Reduce the value by 10% if threads are oiled prior to assembly.
- The torque required for aluminum components or fasteners is considerably less.

U.S. Bolts

SAE Grade Number	1 or 2			5			6 or 7		
Number of lines always 2 less than the grade number.									
Bolt Size (Inches)—(Thread)	Maximum Torque			Maximum Torque			Maximum Torque		
	Ft./Lbs.	Kgm	Nm	Ft./Lbs.	Kgm	Nm	Ft./Lbs.	Kgm	Nm
¼—20	5	0.7	6.8	8	1.1	10.8	10	1.4	13.5
—28	6	0.8	8.1	10	1.4	13.6			
⁵⁄₁₆—18	11	1.5	14.9	17	2.3	23.0	19	2.6	25.8
—24	13	1.8	17.6	19	2.6	25.7			
⅜—16	18	2.5	24.4	31	4.3	42.0	34	4.7	46.0
—24	20	2.75	27.1	35	4.8	47.5			
⁷⁄₁₆—14	28	3.8	37.0	49	6.8	66.4	55	7.6	74.5
—20	30	4.2	40.7	55	7.6	74.5			
½—13	39	5.4	52.8	75	10.4	101.7	85	11.75	115.2
—20	41	5.7	55.6	85	11.7	115.2			
⁹⁄₁₆—12	51	7.0	69.2	110	15.2	149.1	120	16.6	162.7
—18	55	7.6	74.5	120	16.6	162.7			
⅝—11	83	11.5	112.5	150	20.7	203.3	167	23.0	226.5
—18	95	13.1	128.8	170	23.5	230.5			
¾—10	105	14.5	142.3	270	37.3	366.0	280	38.7	379.6
—16	115	15.9	155.9	295	40.8	400.0			
⅞— 9	160	22.1	216.9	395	54.6	535.5	440	60.9	596.5
—14	175	24.2	237.2	435	60.1	589.7			
1— 8	236	32.5	318.6	590	81.6	799.9	660	91.3	894.8
—14	250	34.6	338.9	660	91.3	849.8			

Metric Bolts

Relative Strength Marking	4.6, 4.8			8.8		
Bolt Markings						
Bolt Size Thread Size x Pitch (mm)	Maximum Torque			Maximum Torque		
	Ft./Lbs.	Kgm	Nm	Ft./Lbs.	Kgm	Nm
6 x 1.0	2–3	.2–.4	3–4	3–6	.4–.8	5–8
8 x 1.25	6–8	.8–1	8–12	9–14	1.2–1.9	13–19
10 x 1.25	12–17	1.5–2.3	16–23	20–29	2.7–4.0	27–39
12 x 1.25	21–32	2.9–4.4	29–43	35–53	4.8–7.3	47–72
14 x 1.5	35–52	4.8–7.1	48–70	57–85	7.8–11.7	77–110
16 x 1.5	51–77	7.0–10.6	67–100	90–120	12.4–16.5	130–160
18 x 1.5	74–110	10.2–15.1	100–150	130–170	17.9–23.4	180–230
20 x 1.5	110–140	15.1–19.3	150–190	190–240	26.2–46.9	160–320
22 x 1.5	150–190	22.0–26.2	200–260	250–320	34.5–44.1	340–430
24 x 1.5	190–240	26.2–46.9	260–320	310–410	42.7–56.5	420–550

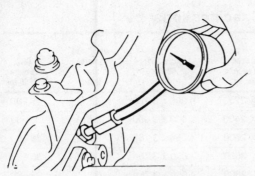

The screw-in type compression gauge is more accurate

4. On fully open the throttle either by operating the carburetor throttle linkage by hand or by having an assistant floor the accelerator pedal.

5. Screw the compression gauge into the no.1 spark plug hole until the fitting is snug.

WARNING: *Be careful not to crossthread the plug hole. On aluminum cylinder heads use extra care, as the threads in these heads are easily ruined.*

6. Ask an assistant to depress the accelerator pedal fully on both carbureted and fuel injected vehicles. Then, while you read the compression gauge, ask the assistant to crank the engine two or three times in short bursts using the ignition switch.

7. Read the compression gauge at the end of each series of cranks, and record the highest of these readings. Repeat this procedure for each of the engine's cylinders. Compare the highest reading of each cylinder to the compression pressure specification in the Tune-Up Specifications chart in Chapter 2. The specs in this chart are maximum values.

A cylinder's compression pressure is usually acceptable if it is not less than 80% of maximum. The difference between any two cylinders should be no more than 12-14 pounds.

8. If a cylinder is unusually low, pour a tablespoon of clean engine oil into the cylinder through the spark plug hole and repeat the compression test. If the compression comes up after adding the oil, it appears that the cylinder's piston rings or bore are damaged or worn. If the pressure remains low, the valves may not be seating properly (a valve job is needed), or the head gasket may be blown near that cylinder. If compression in any two adjacent cylinders is low, and if the addition of oil doesn't help the compression, there is leakage past the head gasket. Oil and coolant water in the combustion chamber can result from this problem. There may be evidence of water droplets on the engine dipstick when a head gasket has blown.

Engine

Before starting to tear out your engine, and trying up both yourself and your car for a length of time, there are a few preliminary steps that should be taken. Jot down those engine and transmission numbers (see Chapter 1) and make a trip to your parts dealer to order all those gaskets, hoses, belts, filter, etc. which are in need of replacement. This will help avoid last minute or weekend parts dashes that can tie up a car even longer. Also, have enough oil, antifreeze, transmission fluid, etc. on hand for the job.

If the car is still running, have the engine, engine compartment, and underbody steam cleaned, or at least hosed off at one of those coin-operated, do-it-yourself car washes. The less dirt, the better. Have all of the necessary tools together. These should include a sturdy hydraulic jack and a pair of jackstands of sufficient capacity, a chain/pulley engine hoist of sufficient test strength, a wooden block and a small jack to support the oil pan or transmission, a can of penetrating fluid to help loosen rust nuts and bolts, a few jars or plastic containers to store and identify used engine hardware, and a punch or bottle of brush paint to matchmark adjacent parts to aid reassembly. Once you have all of your parts, tools, and fluids together, proceed with the task.

REMOVAL

1. Scribe the hood hinge outline on the underhood, disconnect the hood and remove.

2. Drain the entire cooling system and crankcase.

CAUTION: *When draining the coolant, keep in mind that cats and dogs are attracted by the ethylene glycol antifreeze, and are quite likely to drink any that is left in an uncovered container or in puddles on the ground. This will prove fatal in sufficient quantity. Always drain the coolant into a sealable container. Coolant should be reused unless it is contaminated or several years old.*

3. Remove the air cleaner, disconnect the battery at the cylinder head. On automatic transmission equipped cars, disconnect the fluid cooler lines at the radiator.

4. Remove the upper and lower radiator hoses and remove the radiator. If equipped with air conditioning, unbolt the compressor and position compressor out of way with refrigerant lines intact. Unbolt and lay the refrigerant condenser forward without disconnecting the refrigerant lines.

NOTE: *If there is not enough slack in the refrigerant lines to position the compressor out*

General Engine Specifications

Year	Engine No. Cyl Displacement (cu in.)	Carburetor Type	Advertised Horsepower @ rpm ▪	Advertised Torque @ rpm (ft. lbs.) ▪	Bore and Stroke (in.)	Advertised Compression Ratio	Oil Pressure @ 2050 rpm
1968	6-240	1 bbl	150 @ 4000	234 @ 2200	4.000 x 3.180	9.2 : 1	35 – 60
	8-302	2 bbl	210 @ 4400	295 @ 2400	4.000 x 3.000	9.5 : 1	35 – 60
	8-390	2 bbl	270 @ 4400	390 @ 2600	4.050 x 3.784	9.5 : 1	35 – 60
	8-390	2 bbl	280 @ 4400	403 @ 2600	4.050 x 3.784	10.5 : 1	35 – 60
	8-390	4 bbl	315 @ 4600	427 @ 2800	4.050 x 3.784	10.5 : 1	35 – 60
	8-428	4 bbl	345 @ 4600	462 @ 2800	4.130 x 3.984	10.5 : 1	35 – 60
	8-428PI	4 bbl	360 @ 5400	459 @ 3200	4.130 x 3.984	10.5 : 1	35 – 60
	8-429	4 bbl	360 @ 4600	480 @ 2800	4.360 x 3.590	10.5 : 1	35 – 60
	8-462	4 bbl	340 @ 4600	485 @ 2800	4.380 x 3.380	10.25 : 1	45 – 60
1969	6-240	1 bbl	150 @ 4000	234 @ 2200	4.000 x 3.180	9.2 : 1	35 – 60
	8-302	2 bbl	210 @ 4400	295 @ 2400	4.000 x 3.000	9.5 : 1	35 – 60
	8-390	2 bbl	270 @ 4400	390 @ 2600	4.050 x 3.784	9.5 : 1	35 – 60
	8-390	2 bbl	280 @ 4400	430 @ 2600	4.050 x 3.784	10.5 : 1	35 – 60
	8-428PI	4 bbl	360 @ 5400	459 @ 3200	4.130 x 3.984	10.5 : 1	35 – 60
	8-429	2 bbl	320 @ 4400	460 @ 2200	4.360 x 3.590	10.5 : 1	35 – 60
	8-429	4 bbl	360 @ 4600	476 @ 2800	4.360 x 3.590	11.0 : 1	35 – 60
1970	6-240	1 bbl	150 @ 4000	234 @ 2200	4.000 x 3.180	9.2 : 1	35 – 60
	8-302	2 bbl	210 @ 4400	295 @ 2400	4.000 x 3.000	9.5 : 1	35 – 60
	8-351 W	2 bbl	250 @ 4600	355 @ 2600	4.000 x 3.500	9.5 : 1	35 – 60
	8-390	2 bbl	270 @ 4400	390 @ 2600	4.050 x 3.784	9.5 : 1	35 – 60
	8-428 PI	4 bbl	360 @ 5400	459 @ 3200	4.130 x 3.984	10.5 : 1	35 – 60
	8-429	2 bbl	320 @ 4400	460 @ 2200	4.360 x 3.590	10.5 : 1	35 – 60
	8-429	4 bbl	360 @ 4600	476 @ 2800	4.360 x 3.590	11.0 : 1	35 – 60
1971	6-240	1 bbl	140 @ 4000	230 @ 2200	4.000 x 3.180	8.9 : 1	35 – 60
	8-302	2 bbl	210 @ 4600	296 @ 2600	4.000 x 3.000	9.0 : 1	35 – 60
	8-351 W	2 bbl	240 @ 4600	350 @ 2600	4.000 x 3.500	8.9 : 1	35 – 60
	8-390	2 bbl	255 @ 4400	376 @ 2600	4.050 x 3.784	9.5 : 1	35 – 60
	8-400	2 bbl	260 @ 4400	400 @ 2200	4.000 x 4.000	9.0 : 1	50 – 70
	8-429	2 bbl	320 @ 4400	460 @ 2200	4.360 x 3.590	10.5 : 1	35 – 75
	8-429	4 bbl	360 @ 4600	480 @ 2800	4.360 x 3.590	10.5 : 1	35 – 75
	8-429 PI	4 bbl	370 @ 5400	450 @ 3400	4.360 x 3.590	11.0 : 1	35 – 75
1972	6-240	1 bbl	103 @ 3800	170 @ 2200	4.000 x 3.180	8.5 : 1	35 – 60
	8-302	2 bbl	140 @ 4000	239 @ 2000	4.000 x 3.000	8.5 : 1	35 – 60
	8-351 W	2 bbl	153 @ 3800	266 @ 2000	4.000 x 3.500	8.3 : 1	35 – 60
	8-351 C	2 bbl	163 @ 3800	277 @ 2000	4.000 x 3.500	8.6 : 1	35 – 60
	8-400	2 bbl	172 @ 4000	298 @ 2200	4.000 x 4.000	8.4 : 1	50 – 70
	8-429	4 bbl	208 @ 4400	322 @ 2800	4.362 x 3.590	8.5 : 1	35 – 75
	8-429	4 bbl	212 @ 4400	327 @ 2600	4.362 x 3.590	8.5 : 1	35 – 75
	8-460	4 bbl	200 @ 4400	326 @ 2800	4.362 x 3.850	8.5 : 1	35 – 75
	8-460	4 bbl	212 @ 4400	342 @ 2800	4.362 x 3.850	8.5 : 1	35 – 75

General Engine Specifications (cont.)

Year	Engine No. Cyl Displacement (cu In.)	Carburetor Type	Advertised Horsepower @ rpm ■	Advertised Torque @ rpm (ft. lbs.) ■	Bore and Stroke (in.)	Advertised Compression Ratio	Oil Pressure @ 2050 rpm
1973	8-351 W	2 bbl	153 @ 3800	266 @ 2000	4.000 x 3.500	8.3 : 1	35–60
	8-351 C	2 bbl	163 @ 3800	277 @ 2000	4.000 x 3.500	8.6 : 1	35–60
	8-400	2 bbl	172 @ 4000	298 @ 2200	4.000 x 4.000	8.4 : 1	50–70
	8-429	4 bbl	208 @ 4400	322 @ 2800	4.362 x 3.590	8.5 : 1	35–75
	8-429	4 bbl	212 @ 4400	327 @ 2600	4.362 x 3.590	8.5 : 1	35–75
	8-460	4 bbl	200 @ 4400	326 @ 2800	4.362 x 3.850	8.5 : 1	35–75
	8-460	4 bbl	212 @ 4400	342 @ 2800	4.362 x 3.850	8.5 : 1	35–75
1974	8-351 W	2 bbl	162 @ 4000	275 @ 2200	4.000 x 3.500	8.2 : 1	45–65
	8-351 C	2 bbl	163 @ 4200	278 @ 2000	4.000 x 3.500	8.0 : 1	45–75
	8-400	2 bbl	170 @ 3400	330 @ 2000	4.000 x 4.000	8.0 : 1	45–75
	8-460	4 bbl	195 @ 3800	335 @ 2600	4.362 x 3.850	8.0 : 1	35–65
	8-460 PI	4 bbl	275 @ 4400	395 @ 2800	4.362 x 3.850	8.8 : 1	25–65
1975	8-351 M	2 bbl	148 @ 3800 ①	243 @ 2400 ②	4.000 x 3.500	8.0 : 1	45–75
	8-400	2 bbl	158 @ 3800 ③	276 @ 2000 ④	4.000 x 4.000	8.0 : 1	45–75
	8-460	4 bbl	218 @ 4000	369 @ 2600 ⑤	4.362 x 3.850	8.0 : 1	35–65
	8-460 PI	4 bbl	226 @ 4000	374 @ 2600	4.362 x 3.850	8.0 : 1	35–65
1976–77	8-351 M	2 bbl	152 @ 3800	274 @ 1600	4.000 x 3.500	8.0 : 1	45–75
	8-400 ⑥	2 bbl	180 @ 3800	336 @ 1800	4.000 x 4.000	8.0 : 1	45–75
	8-460	4 bbl	202 @ 3800	352 @ 1600	4.362 x 3.850	8.0 : 1	35–65
	8-460 PI	4 bbl	202 @ 3800	352 @ 1600	4.362 x 3.850	8.0 : 1	35–65
1978	8-302	2 bbl	134 @ 3400	248 @ 1600	4.000 x 3.000	8.4 : 1	40–60
	8-351 W	2 bbl	144 @ 3200	277 @ 1600	4.000 x 3.500	8.3 : 1	40–60
	8-351 M	2 bbl	145 @ 3400	273 @ 1800	4.000 x 3.500	8.0 : 1	50–75
	8-400	2 bbl	160 @ 3800	314 @ 1800	4.000 x 4.000	8.0 : 1	50–75
	8-460	4 bbl	202 @ 4000	348 @ 2000	4.362 x 3.850	8.0 : 1	35–65
	8-460 PI	4 bbl	202 @ 3800	352 @ 1600	4.362 x 3.850	8.0 : 1	35–65
1979	8-302	VV	134 @ 3400	248 @ 1600	4.000 x 3.000	8.4 : 1	40–60
	8-351 W	2 bbl	144 @ 3200	277 @ 1600	4.000 x 3.500	8.3 : 1	40–60
	8-351 W Calif.	VV	139 @ 3200	270 @ 1600	4.000 x 3.500	8.3 : 1	40–60
1980–81	8-255	VV	119 @ 3800	194 @ 2200	3.680 x 3.000	8.8 : 1	40–60
	8-302	VV	130 @ 3600	230 @ 1600	4.000 x 3.000	8.4 : 1	40–60
	8-351 W	VV	140 @ 3400	265 @ 2000	4.000 x 3.500	8.3 : 1	40–60
1982	8-255	VV	119 @ 3800	194 @ 2200	3.680 x 3.000	8.8 : 1	40–60
	8-302	VV	130 @ 3600	230 @ 1600	4.000 x 3.000	8.4 : 1	40–60
	8-302	EFI	130 @ 3400	230 @ 2200	4.000 x 3.000	8.4 : 1	40–60
	8-351	VV	140 @ 3400	265 @ 2000	4.000 x 3.500	8.3 : 1	40–60

General Engine Specifications (cont.)

Year	Engine No. Cyl Displacement (cu in.)	Carburetor Type	Advertised Horsepower @ rpm ■	Advertised Torque @ rpm (ft. lbs.) ■	Bore and Stroke (in.)	Advertised Compression Ratio	Oil Pressure @ 2050 rpm
1983–88	8-302	W	130 @ 3600	230 @ 1600	4.000 x 3.000	8.4:1	40–60
	8-302	CFI	140 @ 3200	250 @ 1600	4.000 x 3.000	8.4:1	40–60
	8-351	VV	140 @ 3400 ⑦	265 @ 2000 ⑦	4.000 x 3.500	8.4:1	40–60

■ Beginning 1972, horsepower and torque are SAE net figures. They are measured at the rear of the transmission with all accessories installed and operating. Since the figures vary when a given engine is installed in different models, some are representative rather than exact.

W Windsor Design
C Cleveland Design
CFI Central Fuel Injection
M Modified Cleveland Design
PI Police Intercepter
VV Variable Venturi
① California cars—150 @ 3800 rpm

② California cars—244 @ 2800 rpm
③ California cars—144 @ 3600 rpm
④ California cars—255 @ 2200 rpm
⑤ California cars—367 @ 2600 rpm
⑥ California only—400 cu in. engine equipped with 4 bbl carburetor
⑦ H.O. 180 @ 3600 285 @ 2400

Valve Specifications

Year	Engine No. Cyl Displacement (cu in.)	Seat Angle (deg)	Face Angle (deg)	Spring Test Pressure (lbs @ in.)	Spring Installed (lbs @ in.)	Stem to Guide Clearance (in.) Intake	Exhaust	Stem Diameter (in.) Intake	Exhaust
1968	6-240	45	44	197 @ 1.30	1¹¹⁄₁₆	.0010–.0027	.0010–.0027	.3420	.3420
	8-302	45	44	180 @ 1.23	1²¹⁄₃₂	.0010–.0027	.0015–.0032	.3420	.3415
	8-390	45	44	220 @ 1.38	1¹³⁄₁₆	.0010–.0024	.0015–.0032	.3715	.3710
	8-427	①	②	268 @ 1.31	1¹³⁄₁₆	.0010–.0024	.0020–.0034	.3715	.3705
	8-428	45	44	220 @ 1.38	1¹³⁄₁₆	.0010–.0024	.0015–.0032	.3715	.3710
	8-429	45	44	253 @ 1.33	1¹³⁄₁₆	.0010–.0027	.0010–.0027	.3420	.3420
	8-462	45	44	220 @ 1.39	1²¹⁄₃₂	.0008–.0025	.0010–.0027	.3715	.3710
1969	6-240	45	44	197 @ 1.30	1¹¹⁄₁₆	.0010–.0027	.0010–.0027	.3420	.3420
	8-302	45	44	180 @ 1.23	1²¹⁄₃₂	.0010–.0027	.0015–.0032	.3420	.3415
	8-390	45	44	220 @ 1.38	1¹³⁄₁₆	.0010–.0027	.0015–.0032	.3715	.3710
	8-429	45	44	251 @ 1.33	1¹³⁄₁₆	.0010–.0027	.0010–.0027	.3420	.3420
1970	6-240	45	44	197 @ 1.30	1¹¹⁄₁₆	.0010–.0027	.0010–.0027	.3420	.3420
	8-302	45	44	180 @ 1.23	1²¹⁄₃₂	.0010–.0027	.0015–.0032	.3420	.3415
	8-351	45	44	215 @ 1.34	1²⁵⁄₃₂	.0010–.0027	.0010–.0027	.3420	.3415
	8-390	①	44	220 @ 1.38	1¹³⁄₁₆	.0010–.0027	.0015–.0032	.3715	.3710
	8-429	45	44	253 @ 1.33	1¹³⁄₁₆	.0010–.0027	.0010–.0027	.3420	.3420
1971	6-240	45	44	197 @ 1.30	1¹¹⁄₁₆	.0010–.0027	.0010–.0027	.3420	.3420
	8-302	45	44	180 @ 1.23	1²¹⁄₃₂	.0010–.0027	.0015–.0032	.3420	.3415
	8-351 ③	45	44	215 @ 1.34	1²⁵⁄₃₂	.0010–.0027	.0015–.0032	.3420	.3415
	8-351 ④	45	44	210 @ 1.42	1¹³⁄₁₆	.0010–.0027	.0015–.0032	.3420	.3415
	8-390	①	44	220 @ 1.38	1¹³⁄₁₆	.0010–.0027	.0015–.0032	.3715	.3710
	8-400	45	44	226 @ 1.39	1¹³⁄₁₆	.0010–.0027	.0015–.0032	.3420	.3415
	8-429	45	45	253 @ 1.33	1¹³⁄₁₆	.0010–.0027	.0015–.0032	.3420	.3415
1972	6-240	45	44	197 @ 1.30	1¹¹⁄₁₆	.0010–.0027	.0010–.0027	.3420	.3420
	8-302	45	44	200 @ 1.31	1¹¹⁄₁₆	.0010–.0027	.0015–.0032	.3420	.3415

Valve Specifications (cont.)

Year	Engine No. Cyl Displacement (cu in.)	Seat Angle (deg)	Face Angle (deg)	Spring Test Pressure (lbs @ in.)	Spring Installed (lbs @ in.)	Stem to Guide Clearance (in.)		Stem Diameter (in.)	
						Intake	Exhaust	Intake	Exhaust
1972	8-351 ③	45	44	215 @ 1.34	1²⁵/₃₂	.0010–.0027	.0015–.0032	.3420	.3415
	8-351 ④	45	44	210 @ 1.42	1¹³/₁₆	.0010–.0027	.0015–.0032	.3420	.3415
	8-400	45	44	226 @ 1.39	1¹³/₁₆	.0010–.0027	.0015–.0032	.3420	.3415
	8-429	45	45	229 @ 1.33	1¹³/₁₆	.0010–.0027	.0010–.0027	.3420	.3420
	8-460	45	45	229 @ 1.33	1¹³/₁₆	.0010–.0027	.0010–.0027	.3420	.3420
1973–74	8-351 ③	45	44	200 @ 1.34	1²⁵/₃₂	.0010–.0027	.0015–.0032	.3420	.3415
	8-351 ④	45	44	210 @ 1.42 ⑤	1¹³/₁₆	.0010–.0027	.0015–.0032	.3420	.3415
	8-400	45	44	226 @ 1.39	1¹³/₁₆	.0010–.0027	.0015–.0032	.3420	.3415
	8-429	45	45	229 @ 1.33	1¹³/₁₆	.0010–.0027	.0010–.0027	.3420	.3420
	8-460	45	45	229 @ 1.33	1¹³/₁₆	.0010–.0027	.0010–.0027	.3420	.3420
1975–77	8-351 ⑥	45	44	226 @ 1.39	1¹³/₁₆	.0010–.0027	.0015–.0032	.3420	.3415
	8-400	45	44	226 @ 1.39	1¹³/₁₆	.0010–.0027	.0015–.0032	.3420	.3415
	8-460	45	45	253 @ 1.33	1¹³/₁₆	.0010–.0027	.0010–.0027	.3420	.3420
1978–81	8-255 8-302	45	44	⑦	1¹¹/₁₆ ⑪	.0010–.0027	.0015–.0032	.3420	.3415
	8-351 W	45	44	⑩	1¹³/₁₆ ⑪	.0010–.0027	.0015–.0032	.3420	.3415
	8-351 M	44¹/₂–45	45¹/₂–45³/₄	226 @ 1.39	1¹³/₁₆	.0010–.0027	.0015–.0032	.3420	.3415
	8-400	44¹/₂–45	45¹/₂–45³/₄	226 @ 1.39	1¹³/₁₆	.0010–.0027	.0015–.0032	.3420	.3415
	8-460	44¹/₂–45	45¹/₂–45³/₄	⑧	1¹³/₁₆	.0010–.0027	.0010–.0027	.3420	.3420
	8-460 PI	44¹/₂–45	45¹/₂–45³/₄	⑨	1¹³/₁₆	.0010–.0027	.0010–.0027	.3420	.3420
1982–88	8-255 ⑯	44¹/₂–45	45¹/₂–45³/₄	192 @ 1.40 ⑫	1⁴³/₆₄ ⑮	.0010–.0027	.0015–.0032	.3416–.3423	.3411–.3418
	8-302	45	45	204 @ 1.36 ⑬	1⁴³/₆₄ ⑮	.0010–.0027	.0015–.0032	.3416–.3423	.3411–.3418
	8-351	45	45	204 @ 1.33 ⑭	1⁴⁹/₆₄ ⑮	.0010–.0027	.0015–.0032	.3416–.3423	.3411–.3418

① Intake valve seat angle 30°
  Exhaust valve seat angle 45°
② Intake valve face angle 29°
  Exhaust valve face angle 44°
③ Windsor heads
④ Cleveland heads
⑤ 1974 models—226 @ 1.39
⑥ Modified Cleveland heads
⑦ 1977–78: Intake 200 @ 1.31; Exhaust: 200 @ 1.20
  1979–81: Intake 190–212 @ 1.36; Exhaust: 190–210 @ 1.20

⑧ Intake: 240 @ 1.33, Exhaust: 253 @ 1.33
⑨ Intake: 315 @ 1.32, Exhaust: 315 @ 1.33
⑩ Intake: 200 @ 1.34, Exhaust: 200 @ 1.20
⑪ Exhaust: 1⁵/₈
⑫ Exhaust: 191 @ 1.23
⑬ Exhaust: 200 @ 1.20
⑭ Exhaust: 205 @ 1.15
⑮ Exhaust: 1³⁷/₆₄
⑯ Discontinued in 1983

of the way, the refrigerant in the system must be evacuated (using proper safety precautions) before the lines can be disconnected from the compressor.

5. Remove the fan, fan belt and upper pulley. On models equipped with an electric cooling fan, disconnect the power lead and remove the fan and shroud as an assembly.

6. Disconnect the heater hoses from the engine.

7. Disconnect the alternator wires at the alternator, the starter cable at the starter, the accelerator rod at the carburetor.

8. Disconnect and plug the fuel tank line at the fuel pump on models equipped with fuel injection, depressurize the fuel system.

Torque Specifications
All readings in ft. lbs.

Year	Engine No. Cyl Displacement (cu in.)	Cylinder Head Bolts	Rod Bearing Bolts	Main Bearing Bolts	Crankshaft Pulley Bolt	Flywheel to Crankshaft Bolts	Manifold Intake	Manifold Exhaust
1968	6-240	70–75	40–45	60–70	130–145	75–85	25	25
	8-302	65–70	19–24	60–70	70–90	75–85	21	15½
	8-390, 428, 429	80–90	40–45	95–105	70–90	75–85	33½	15½
	8-462	125–135	40–45	95–105	75–90	75–85	23–28	15–21
1969	6-240	70–75	40–45	60–70	130–150	75–85	25	25
	8-302	65–72	19–24	60–70	70–90	75–85	24	14
	8-390, 428	80–90	40–45	95–105	70–90	75–85	33½	21
	8-429	130–140	40–45	95–105	70–90	75–85	27½	30½
1970	6-240	70–75	40–45	60–70	130–150	75–85	25	25
	8-302	65–72	19–24	60–70	70–90	75–85	24	14
	8-351	95–100	40–45	95–105	70–90	75–85	23–25	18–24
	8-390	80–90	①	95–105	70–90	75–85	32–35	18–24
	8-429	130–140	40–45	95–105	70–90	75–85	27½	30½
1971	6-240	70–75	40–45	60–70	130–150	75–85	25	25
	8-302	65–72	19–24	60–70	70–90	75–85	24	14
	8-351	95–100	40–45	95–105	70–90	75–85	23–25	18–24 ②
	8-390	80–90	40–45	95–105	70–90	75–85	32–35	18–24
	8-400	95–105	40–45	95–105	70–90	75–85	27–33	12–16
	8-429	130–140	40–45	95–105	70–90	75–85	27½	30½
1972	6-240	70–75	40–45	60–70	130–150	75–85	23–28	23–28
	8-302	65–72	19–24	60–70	70–90	75–85	23–25	12–16
	8-351 W	105–112	40–45	95–105	100–130	75–85	23–25	18–24
	8-351C, 400	95–105 ③	40–45 ④	⑤	70–90	75–85	⑥	12–16
	8-429, 460	130–140	40–45	95–105	70–90	75–85	25–30	28–33
1973–88	8-351 W	105–112	40–45	95–105	100–130	75–85	23–25	18–24
	8-351C, 351M, 400	95–105	40–45	⑤	70–90	75–85	⑥	12–16
	8-429, 460	130–140	40–45	95–105	70–90	75–85	25–30	28–33
	8-255, 302	65–72	19–24	60–70	70–90	75–85	23–25	18–24

NOTE: Tighten cylinder head bolts in 3 steps; the first 20 ft. lbs. less than maximum torque, the second 10 ft. lbs. less than maximum torque, and the third maximum torque

① 390—40–45; 428—53–58
② 351C engine—12–16
③ 351 HO—120
④ 351 HO—40–45
⑤ ½ x 13 in. bolt—95–105
 ⅜ x 16 in. bolt—35–45
⑥ ⁵⁄₁₆ in. bolt—21–25
 ⅜ in. bolt—27–23
 ¼ in. bolt—6–9

9. Disconnect the coil primary wire at the coil. Disconnect the wires at the oil pressure and water temperature sending units. Disconnect the brake booster vacuum line, if so equipped.

10. Remove the starter and dust seal.

11. On cars with manual transmission, remove the clutch retracting spring. Disconnect the clutch equalizer shaft and arm bracket at the underbody rail and remove the arm bracket and equalizer shaft.

12. Raise the car and safely support on

Piston and Ring Specification—All Engines

	Top Compression	Bottom Compression	Oil Control	Piston to Bore Clearance
Ring gap	.010–.020	.010–.020	.015–.055 ①	—
Side clearance	.002–.004	.002–.004	Snug	—
Piston clearance	—	—	—	.0014–.0022 ②

① 1972–74; 351 and 400 is .015–.069   ② 255, 302 and 351W is .0018–.0026

jackstands. Remove the flywheel or converter housing upper retaining bolts.

13. Disconnect the exhaust pipe or pipes at the exhaust manifold. Disconnect the right and left motor mount at the underbody bracket. Remove the flywheel or converter housing cover. On models so equipped, disconnect the engine roll damper on the left front of the engine from the frame.

14. On cars with manual transmission, remove the lower wheel housing bolts.

15. On models with automatic transmission, disconnect the throttle valve vacuum line at the intake manifold and disconnect the converter from the flywheel. Remove the converter housing lower retaining bolts. On models with power steering, disconnect the power steering pump from the cylinder head. Remove the drive belt and wire steering pump out of the way. Do not disconnect the hoses.

16. Lower the car. Support the transmission and flywheel or converter housing with a jack.

17. Attach an engine lifting hook. Lift the en-

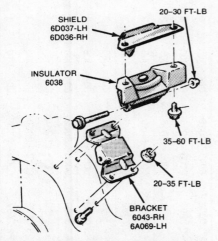

302, 351V front engine supports (255 similar)

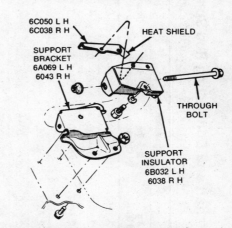

1969–71 429 V8 front engine supports

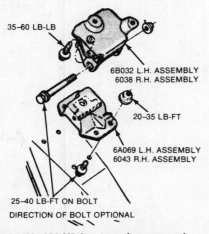

351C, 351M, 400 V8 front engine supports

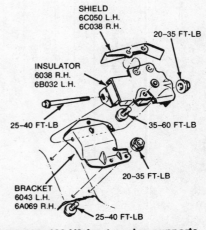

1973–78 429, 460 V8 front engine supports

Crankshaft and Connecting Rod Specifications

All measurements are given in inches

Year	Engine No. Cyl Displacement (cu in.)	Crankshaft					Connecting Rod		
		Main Brg Journal Dia	Main Brg Oil Clearance	Shaft End-Play	Thrust on No.	Journal Diameter	Oil Clearance	Side Clearance
1968	6-240	2.3986–2.3990	.0008–.0024	.004–.008	5	2.1232–2.1246	.0007–.0028	.014–.020
	8-302	2.2486–2.2490	.0005–.0024	.004–.008	3	2.1232–2.1246	.0007–.0028	.014–.020
	8-390, 427, 428, 429	2.7488–2.7492	.0008–.0012	.004–.008	3	2.4384–2.4388	.0007–.0028	.014–.020
	8-462	2.8994–2.9002	.0016	.006	3	2.5992–2.6000	.0016	.006
1969	6-240	2.3982–2.3990	.0005–.0015	.004–.008	5	2.1228–2.1236	.0008–.0015	.006–.013
	8-302	2.2482–2.2490	.0005–.0015	.004–.008	3	2.1228–2.1236	.0008–.0015	.010–.020
	8-390	2.7484–2.7492	.0013–.0025	.004–.010	3	2.4380–2.4388	.0008–.0015	.010–.020
	8-428	2.7484–2.7492	.0010–.0020	.004–.010	3	2.4380–2.4388	.0020–.0030	.010–.020
	8-429	2.9994–3.0002	.0005–.0015	.004–.008	3	2.4992–2.5000	.0008–.0015	.010–.020
1970	6-240	2.3982–2.3990	.0005–.0015	.004–.008	5	2.1228–2.1236	.0008–.0026	.006–.013
	8-302	2.2482–2.2490	.0005–.0015	.004–.008	3	2.1228–2.1236	.0008–.0026	.010–.020
	8-351	2.9994–2.3002	.0013–.0025	.004–.008	3	2.3103–2.3111	.0008–.0026	.010–.020
	8-390	2.7484–2.7492	.0005–.0025	.004–.008	3	2.4380–2.4388	.0008–.0026	.010–.020
	8-428	2.7484–2.7492	.0008–.0020	.004–.008	3	2.4380–2.4388	.0008–.0026	.010–.020
	8-429	2.9994–3.0002	.0005–.0025	.004–.008	3	2.4992–2.5000	.0008–.0026	.010–.020
1971	6-240	2.3982–2.3990	.0005–.0022	.004–.008	5	2.1228–2.1236	.0008–.0026	.006–.013
	8-302	2.2482–2.2490	.0005–.0024①	.004–.008	3	2.1228–2.1236	.0008–.0026	.010–.020
	8-351W	2.9994–3.0002	.0013–.0030	.004–.008	3	2.3103–2.3111	.0008–.0026	.010–.020
	8-351C	2.7484–2.7492	.0009–.0026	.004–.010	3	2.3103–2.3111	.0008–.0026	.010–.020
	8-390	2.7484–2.7492	.0008–.0020	.004–.008	3	2.4380–2.4388	.0010–.0030	.010–.020

Year	Engine							
	8-400	2.9994–3.0002	.0009–.0026	.004–.010	3	2.3103–2.3111	.0008–.0026	.010–.020
	8-429	2.9994–3.0002	.0005–.0025	.004–.008	3	2.4992–2.5000	.0008–.0028	.010–.020
1972	6-240	2.3982–2.3990	.0005–.0022	.004–.008	5	2.1228–2.1236	.0008–.0026	.006–.013
	8-302	2.2482–2.2490	.0005–.0024 ①	.004–.008	3	2.1228–2.1236	.0008–.0026	.010–.020
	8-351W	2.9994–3.0002	.0008–.0026	.004–.008	3	2.3103–2.3111	.0008–.0026	.010–.020
	8-351C	2.7484–2.7492	.0011–.0028	.004–.010	3	2.3103–2.3111	.0011–.0026	.010–.020
	8-400	2.9994–3.0002	.0011–.0028	.004–.010	3	2.3103–2.3111	.0011–.0026	.010–.020
	8-429	2.9994–3.0002	.0010–.0020 ②	.004–.008	3	2.4992–2.5000	.0008–.0028	.010–.020
	8-460	2.9994–3.0002	.0010–.0020 ②	.004–.008	3	2.4992–2.5000	.0008–.0026	.010–.020
1973–74	8-351W	2.9994–3.0002	.0008–.0026	.004–.008	3	2.3103–2.3111	.0008–.0026	.010–.020
	8-351C	2.7484–2.7492	.0011–.0028	.004–.010	3	2.3103–2.3111	.0011–.0026	.010–.020
	8-400	2.9994–3.0002	.0011–.0028	.004–.010	3	2.3103–2.3111	.0011–.0026	.010–.020
	8-429	2.9994–3.0002	.0010–.0020 ②	.004–.008	3	2.4992–2.5000	.0008–.0026	.010–.020
	8-460	2.9994–3.0002	.0010–.0020 ②	.004–.008	3	2.4992–2.5000	.0008–.0026	.010–.020
1975–77	8-351M	2.9994–3.0002	.0009–.0026	.004–.008	3	2.3103–2.3111	.0008–.0026	.010–.020
	8-400	2.9994–3.0002	.0009–.0026	.004–.008	3	2.3103–2.3111	.0008–.0026	.010–.020
	8-460	2.9994–3.0002	.0009–.0027 ③	.004–.008	3	2.4992–2.5000	.0008–.0028	.010–.020
1978–88	8-255, 302	2.2482–2.2490	.0005–.0015 ④	.004–.008	3	2.1228–2.1236	.0008–.0015	.010–.020
	8-351W	2.9994–3.0002	.0008–.0015	.004–.008	3	2.3103–2.3111	.0008–.0015	.010–.020
	8-351M, 400	2.9994–3.0002	.0008–.0015	.004–.008	3	2.3103–2.3111	.0008–.0015	.010–.020
	8-460	2.9994–3.0002	.0008–.0015	.004–.008	3	2.4992–2.5000	.0008–.0015	.010–.020

① #1—.0001–.0018
② #1—.010–.015
③ #1 bearing—.0004–.0022 in.
④ #1 bearing—.0001–.0015

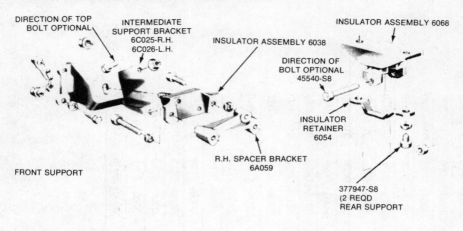

DIRECTION OF TOP
BOLT OPTIONAL

INTERMEDIATE
SUPPORT BRACKET
6C025-R.H.
6C026-L.H.

INSULATOR ASSEMBLY 6038

INSULATOR ASSEMBLY 6068

DIRECTION OF
BOLT OPTIONAL
45540-S8

INSULATOR
RETAINER
6054

R.H. SPACER BRACKET
6A059

FRONT SUPPORT

377947-S8
(2 REQD
REAR SUPPORT

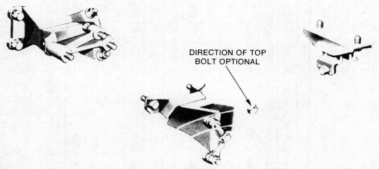

DIRECTION OF TOP
BOLT OPTIONAL

Six-cylinder engine front and rear supports

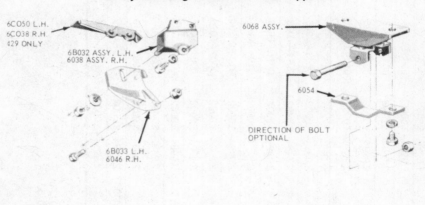

6C050 L.H.
6C038 R.H.
429 ONLY

6B032 ASSY. L.H.
6038 ASSY. R.H.

6B033 L.H.
6046 R.H.

6068 ASSY.

6054

DIRECTION OF BOLT
OPTIONAL

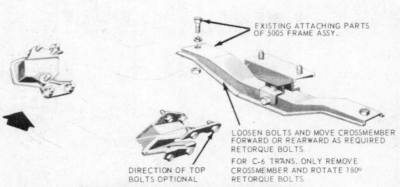

EXISTING ATTACHING PARTS
OF 5005 FRAME ASSY.

LOOSEN BOLTS AND MOVE CROSSMEMBER
FORWARD OR REARWARD AS REQUIRED
RETORQUE BOLTS.

FOR C-6 TRANS. ONLY REMOVE
CROSSMEMBER AND ROTATE 180°
RETORQUE BOLTS.

DIRECTION OF TOP
BOLTS OPTIONAL

390, 428 V8 engine front and rear supports

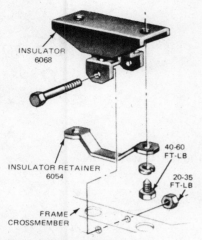

INSULATOR
6068

40-60
FT-LB

INSULATOR RETAINER
6054

20-35
FT-LB

FRAME
CROSSMEMBER

Rear engine support—All V8

gine up and out of the compartment and onto a workstand.

18. Place a new gasket on the exhaust pipe flange.

19. Attach an engine sling and lifting device. Lift the engine from the workstand.

20. Lower the engine into the engine compartment. Be sure the exhaust manifold(s) is in proper alignment with the muffler inlet pipe(s), and the dowels in the block engage the holes in the flywheel housing.

On cars with automatic transmission, start the converter pilot into the crankshaft, making sure that the converter studs align with the flexplate holes.

On cars with manual transmission, start the transmission main drive gear into the clutch disc. If the engine hangs up after the shaft enters, rotate the crankshaft slowly (with transmission in gear) until the shaft and clutch disc splines mesh.

21. Install the flywheel or converter housing upper bolts.

22. Install the engine support insulator to bracket retaining nuts. Disconnect the engine lifting sling and remove the lifting brackets.

23. Raise the front of the car. Connect the exhaust line(s) and tighten the attachments.

24. Install the starter.

25. On cars with manual transmission, install the remaining flywheel housing-to-engine bolts. Connect the clutch release rod. Position the clutch equalizer bar and bracket, and install the retaining bolts. Install the clutch pedal retracting spring.

26. On cars with automatic transmission, remove the retainer holding the converter in the housing. Attach the converter to the flywheel. Install the converter housing inspection cover and the remaining converter housing retaining bolts.

27. Remove the support from the transmission and lower the car.

28. Connect the engine ground strap and coil primary wire.

29. Connect the water temperature gauge wire and the heater hose at the coolant outlet housing. Connect the accelerator rod at the bellcrank.

30. On cars with automatic transmission, connect the transmission filler tube bracket. Connect the throttle valve vacuum line.

31. On cars with power steering, install the drive belt and power steering pump bracket. Install the bracket retaining bolts. Adjust the drive belt to proper tension.

32. Remove the plug from the fuel tank line. Connect the flexible fuel line and the oil pressure sending unit wire.

33. Install the pulley, belt, spacer, and fan. Adjust the belt tension.

34. Tighten the alternator adjusting bolts. Connect the wires and the battery ground cable.

35. Install the radiator. Connect the radiator hoses. On air conditioned cars, install the compressor and condenser.

36. On cars with automatic transmission, connect the fluid cooler lines. On cars with power brakes, connect the brake booster line.

37. Install the oil filter.

38. Bring the crankcase to the full level with the correct grade of oil. Run the engine at fast idle and check for leaks. Install the air cleaner and make the final engine adjustments.

39. Install and adjust the hood.

Valve Cover

REMOVAL AND INSTALLATION

6-240

1. Remove the air cleaner and heat chamber air inlet hose, if so equipped.

2. Remove the automatic choke tube, if so equipped, and the fresh air tube from the valve cover.

3. Remove the thermactor bypass valve and air supply hoses, as needed.

4. Disconnect the spark plug wires. Remove the wire bracket if necessary.

5. Remove any other necessary parts, then remove the valve cover.

6. Installation is the reverse of removal.

NOTE: *Always use new gaskets when installing the valve covers.*

V8 Engines

NOTE: *When disconnecting wires and vacuum lines, label them for reinstallation identification.*

1. Remove the air cleaner assembly.
2. On the right side:
   a. Disconnect the automatic choke heat chamber hose from the inlet tube near the right valve cover if equipped.
   b. Remove the automatic choke heat tube if equipped and remove the PCV valve and hose from the valve cover. Disconnect the EGR valve hoses.
   c. Remove the Thermactor® bypass valve and air supply hoses as necessary to gain clearance.
   d. Disconnect the spark plug wires from the plugs with a twisting pulling motion; twist and pull on the boots only, never on the wire; position the wires and mounting bracket out of the way.
   e. Remove the valve cover mounting bolts; remove the valve cover.
3. On the left side:
   a. Remove the spark plug wires and bracket.
   b. Remove the wiring harness and any vacuum hose from the bracket.
   c. Remove the valve cover mounting bolts and valve cover.
4. Clean all old gasket material from the valve cover and cylinder head mounting surfaces.
5. Installation is the reverse of removal. Use oil resistant sealing compound and a new valve cover gasket. When installing the valve cover gasket, make sure all the gasket tangs are engaged into the cover notches provided.

Rocker Arm Shaft/Rocker Arms
REMOVAL AND INSTALLATION

V8 Engines

1. On the right side, remove:
   a. Disconnect the automatic choke heat chamber air inlet hose.
   b. Remove the air cleaner and duct.
   c. Remove the automatic choke heat tube.
   d. Remove the PCV fresh air tube from the rocker cover, and disconnect the EGR vacuum amplifier hoses.
2. Remove the Thermactor® by-pass valve and air supply hoses.
3. Disconnect the spark plug wires.
4. On the left side, remove:
   a. Remove the wiring harness from the clips.
   b. Remove the rocker arm cover.
5. Remove the rocker arm stud nut or bolt, fulcrum seat and rocker arm.
6. Lubricate all parts with heavy SF oil before installation. When installing, rotate the crankshaft until the lifter is on the base of the cam circle (all the way down) and assemble the

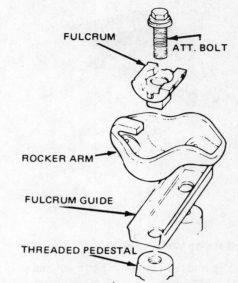

1980–82 255, 302 rocker arm assembly

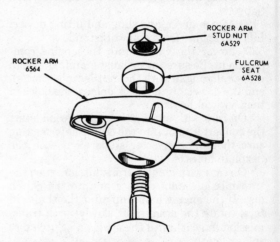

6-240,300 valve rocker arm assembly

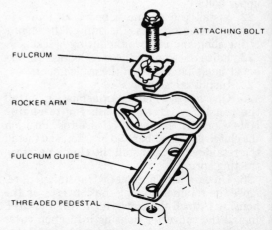

Valve rocker arm assembly for the 8-302,351W 1979 and later

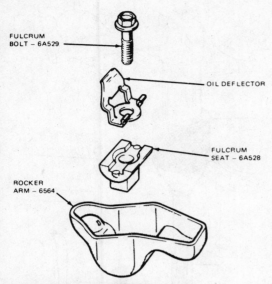

FULCRUM
BOLT – 6A529

OIL DEFLECTOR

FULCRUM
SEAT – 6A528

ROCKER
ARM – 6564

8-400,460 valve rocker arm assembly

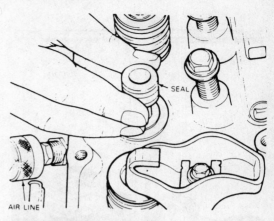

SEAL

AIR LINE

Replacing the valve stem seal

rocker arm. Torque the nut or bolt to 17-23 ft. lbs.

NOTE: *Some later engines use RTV sealant instead of valve cover gaskets.*

Rocker Arms

8-390, 8-428 and 8-462 engines utilize shaft-mounted rocker arm assemblies. Removal and Installation procedures for these rocker arm assemblies are included under the Cylinder Head Removal and Installation procedure. Remem-ber that the oil holes must always face down-ward and that the large rocker shaft retaining bolt is always the second from the front of the engine. In all cases, the torque sequence for the rocker shaft retaining bolts is from the front to the rear of the engine, two turns at a time. Torque the retaining bolt to 40-45 ft. lbs.

The 6-240 and all other V8 engines are equipped with individual stud-mounted or ped-estal bolt and fulcrum mounted rocker arms. Use the following procedure to remove the rocker arms:

1. Disconnect the choke heat chamber air hose, the air cleaner and inlet duct assembly, the choke heat tube, PCV valve and hose and the EGR hoses (if so equipped).

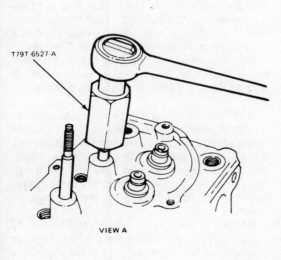

T79T-6527-A

VIEW A

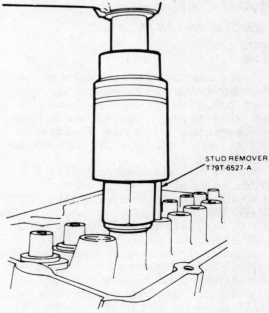

STUD REMOVER
T79T-6527-A

VIEW B

Removing the rocker arm stud on the 6-240,300

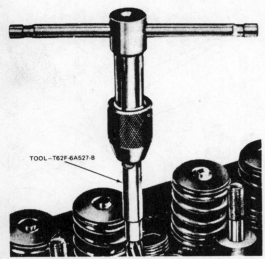

Reaming the rocker arm stud hole on the 6-240,300

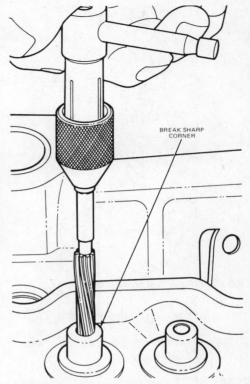

BREAK SHARP CORNER

Reaming the valve guides—typical

2. On models so equipped, disconnect the Thermactor by-pass valve and air supply hoses.

3. Label and disconnect the spark plug wires at the plugs. Remove the plug wires from the looms.

4. Remove the valve cover attaching bolts and remove the cover(s).

5. Remove the valve rocker arm stud nut, fulcrum seat, and then the rocker arm.

6. Reverse the above procedure to install, taking care to adjust the valve lash as outlined under Preliminary Valve Adjustment.

Rocker Studs

REMOVAL AND INSTALLATION

6-240
8-302

Rocker arm studs which are broken or have damaged threads may be replaced with standard studs. Studs which are loose in the cylinder head must be replaced with oversize studs which are available for service. The amount of oversize and diameter of the studs are as follows:

- 0.006″ (0.152mm) oversize: 0.3774-0.3781″ (9.586-9.604mm)
- 0.010″ (0.254mm) oversize: 0.3814-0.3821″ (9.688-9.705mm)
- 0.015″ (0.381mm) oversize: 0.3864-0.3871″ (9.815-9.832mm)

A tool kit for replacing the rocker studs is available and contains a stud remover and two oversize reamers: one for 0.006″ (0.152mm) and one for 0.015″ (0.381mm) oversize studs. For 0.010″ (0.254mm) oversize studs, use reamer tool T66P-6A527-B. to press the replacement studs into the cylinder head, use the stud re-

placer tool T69P-6049-D. Use the smaller reamer tool first when boring the hole for oversize studs.

1. Remove the valve rocker cover(s) by moving all hoses aside and unbolting the cover(s). Position the sleeve of the rocker arm stud remover over the stud with the bearing end down. When working on a 302 V8, cut the threaded part of the stud off with a hacksaw. Thread the puller into the sleeve and over the stud until it is fully bottomed. Hold the sleeve with a wrench and rotate the puller clockwise to remove the stud.

An alternate method of removing the rocker studs without the special tool is to put spacers over the stud until just enough threads are left showing at the top so a nut can be screwed onto the top of the rocker arm stud and get a full bite. Turn the nut clockwise until the stud is removed, adding spacers under the nut as necessary.

NOTE: *If the rocker stud was broken off flush with the stud boss, use a screw extractor to remove the broken off part of the stud from the cylinder head.*

2. If a loose rocker arm stud is being replaced, ream the stud bore for the selected oversize stud.

NOTE: *Keep all metal particles away from the valves.*

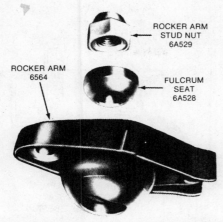

Valve rocker arm and related parts—240 six, 302 V8, 351W V8

3. Coat the end of the stud with Lubriplate®. Align the stud and installer with the stud bore and top the sliding driver until it bottoms. When the installer contacts the stud boss, the stud is installed to its correct height.

Thermostat

REMOVAL AND INSTALLATION

CAUTION: *When draining the coolant, keep in mind that cats and dogs are attracted by the ethylene glycol antifreeze, and are quite likely to drink any that is left in an uncovered container or in puddles on the ground. This will prove fatal in sufficient quantity. Always drain the coolant into a sealable container. Coolant should be reused unless it is contaminated or several years old.*

1. Open the drain cock and drain the radiator so the coolant level is below the coolant outlet elbow which houses the thermostat.

NOTE: *On some models it will be necessary*

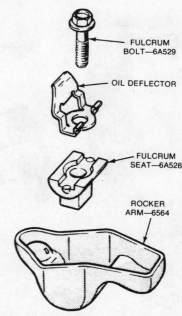

Valve rocker arm and related parts—fulcrum mounted

to remove the distributor cap, rotor and vacuum diaphragm in order to gain access to the thermostat housing mounting bolts.

2. Remove the outlet elbow retaining bolts and position the elbow sufficiently clear of the intake manifold or cylinder head to provide access to the thermostat.

3. Remove the thermostat and the gasket.

4. Clean the mating surfaces of the outlet elbow and the engine to remove all old gasket material and sealer. Coat the new gasket with water resistant sealer. Install the thermostat in the block on 8-351W and 8-400, then install the gasket. On all other engines, position the gasket on the engine, and install the thermostat in the

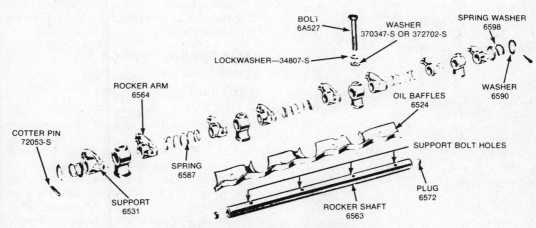

390, 428, 462 valve rocker arm shaft assembly

Installing thermostat

RECESS

BRIDGE

FLATS

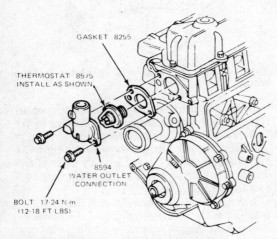

GASKET 8255

THERMOSTAT 8575
INSTALL AS SHOWN

8594
WATER OUTLET
CONNECTION

BOLT 17-24 N·m
(12-18 FT LBS)

Inline 6-cylinder thermostat installation

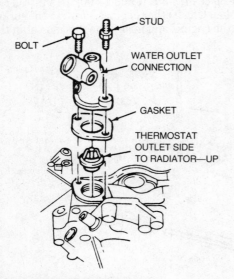

STUD

BOLT

WATER OUTLET
CONNECTION

GASKET

THERMOSTAT
OUTLET SIDE
TO RADIATOR—UP

Thermostat installation for the V8

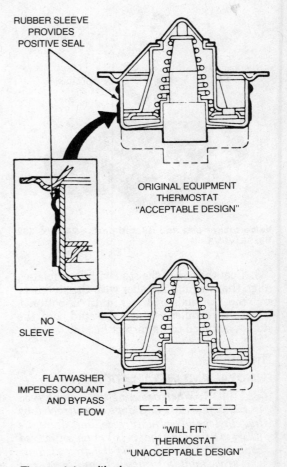

RUBBER SLEEVE
PROVIDES
POSITIVE SEAL

ORIGINAL EQUIPMENT
THERMOSTAT
"ACCEPTABLE DESIGN"

NO
SLEEVE

FLATWASHER
IMPEDES COOLANT
AND BYPASS
FLOW

"WILL FIT"
THERMOSTAT
"UNACCEPTABLE DESIGN"

Thermostat positioning

coolant elbow. The thermostat must be rotated clockwise to lock it in position on all 8-255, 8-302 and 8-351W engines.

5. Install the outlet elbow and retaining bolts on the engine. Torque the bolts to 12-15 ft. lbs.

6. Refill the radiator. Run the engine at operating temperature and check for leaks. Recheck the coolant level.

Intake Manifold

REMOVAL AND INSTALLATION

V8 Except 460 and Fuel Injection

1. Drain the cooling system and disconnect the negative battery cable. Remove the air cleaner assembly.

CAUTION: *When draining the coolant, keep in mind that cats and dogs are attracted by the ethylene glycol antifreeze, and are quite likely to drink any that is left in an uncovered container or in puddles on the ground. This will prove fatal in sufficient quantity. Always drain the coolant into a sealable container.*

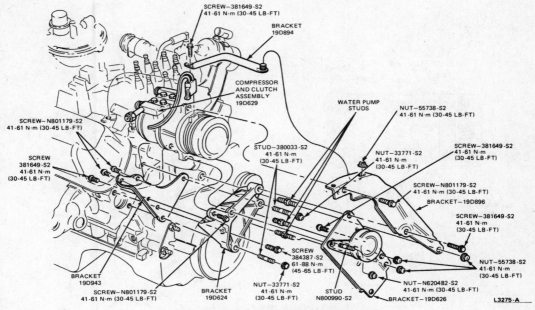

1982 8-255 and 8-302 compressor installation

Coolant should be reused unless it is contaminated or several years old.

2. Disconnect the upper radiator hose and water pump by-pass hose from the thermostat housing and/or intake manifold. Disconnect the temperature sending unit wire connector. Remove the heater hose from the choke housing bracket and disconnect the hose from the intake manifold.

3. Disconnect the automatic choke heat

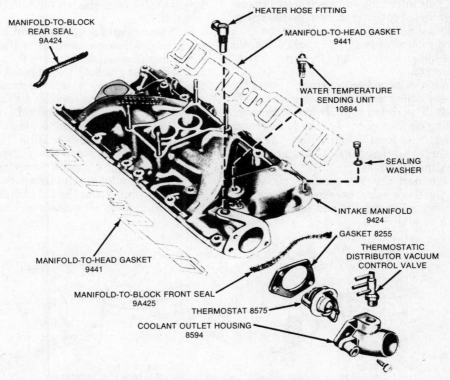

302, 351W intake manifold assembly—255, 428, 429 and 460 similar

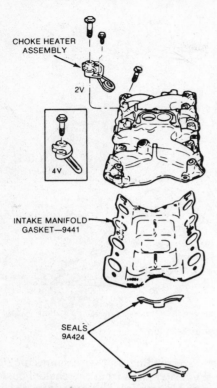

CHOKE HEATER ASSEMBLY

2V

4V

INTAKE MANIFOLD GASKET—9441

SEALS 9A424

351C, 351M, 400 V8 intake manifold assembly

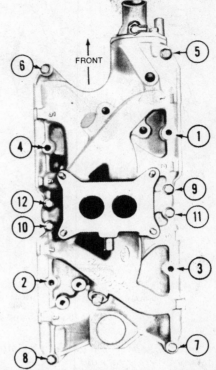

FRONT

Intake manifold torque sequence—255 and 302 V8

chamber air inlet tube and electric wiring connector from the carburetor. Remove the crankcase ventilation hose, vacuum hoses and EGR hose and coolant lines (if equipped). Label the various hoses and wiring for reinstallation identification.

4. On 390, 428 and 462 engines, remove the valve covers, the rocker arm assemblies and the pushrods. The rocker arm should be removed by backing off each of the four bolts two turns at a time, from front to back. Keep the pushrods in order so that they can be installed in their original positions.

5. Disconnect the Thermactor® air supply hose at the check valve. Loosen the hose clamp at the check valve bracket and remove the air

by-pass valve from the bracket and position to one side.

6. Remove all carburetor and automatic transmission linkage attached to the carburetor or intake manifold. Remove the speed control servo and bracket, if equipped. Disconnect the fuel line and any remaining vacuum hoses or wiring from the carburetor, CFI unit, solenoids, sensors, or intake manifold.

7. On V8 engines, disconnect the distributor vacuum hoses from the distributor. Remove the distributor cap and mark the relative position of the rotor on the distributor housing. Disconnect the spark plug wires at the spark plugs and the wiring connector at the distributor. Remove the distributor holddown bolt and remove the

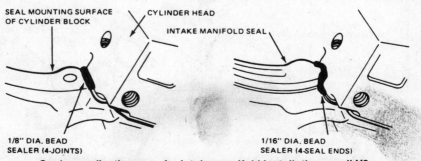

SEAL MOUNTING SURFACE OF CYLINDER BLOCK

CYLINDER HEAD

INTAKE MANIFOLD SEAL

1/8" DIA. BEAD SEALER (4-JOINTS)

1/16" DIA. BEAD SEALER (4-SEAL ENDS)

Sealer application area for intake manifold installation on all V8s

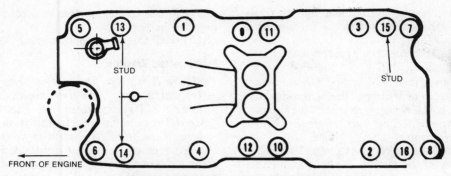

Intake manifold torque sequence—351W V8

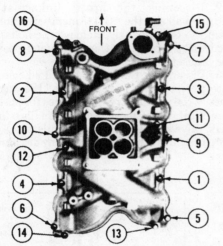

Intake manifold torque sequence—429, 460 V8

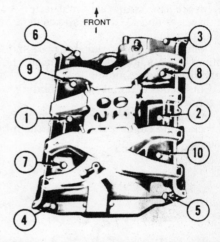

Intake manifold torque sequence—390, 428 V8

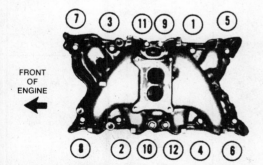

Intake manifold torque sequence—351C, 351M, 400 V8

distributor. (See Distributor Removal and Installation).

8. If your car is equipped with air conditioning and the compressor or mounting brackets interfere with manifold removal, remove the brackets and compressor and position them out of the way. Do not disconnect any compressor lines.

9. Remove the intake manifold mounting bolts. Lift off the intake manifold and carburetor.

10. Clean all gasket mounting surfaces.

11. Apply a 1/8" (3mm) bead of RTV sealant at each end of the engine where the intake manifold seats. Install the intake gaskets and the manifold.

12. On V8 engines, make sure the intake gaskets interlock with the end seals. Use silicone rubber sealer (RTV) on the end seals.

13. After installing the intake manifold, run a finger along the manifold ends to spread the RTV sealer and to make sure the end seals have not slipped out of place.

14. Torque the manifold mounting bolts to the required specifications in the proper sequence. Recheck the torque after the engine has reached normal operating temperature.

15. Install the brackets and compressor.

16. On V8 engines, connect the distributor vacuum hoses to the distributor.

17. Install the distributor cap.

18. Connect the spark plug wires at the spark plugs and the wiring connectors at the distributor.

19. Install the distributor. (See Distributor Removal and Installation).

20. install all carburetor and automatic transmission linkage attached to the carburetor or intake manifold.

21. Install the speed control servo and bracket, if equipped.

22. Connect the fuel line and any remaining vacuum hoses or wiring at the carburetor, CFI unit, solenoids, sensors, or intake manifold.

23. Connect the Thermactor® air supply hose at the check valve.

24. Install the air by-pass valve on its bracket.

25. Connect the automatic choke heat chamber air inlet tube and electric wiring connector at the carburetor.

26. Install the crankcase ventilation hose, vacuum hoses and EGR hose and coolant lines (if equipped).

27. Connect the upper radiator hose and water pump by-pass hose at the thermostat housing and/or intake manifold.

28. Connect the temperature sending unit wire connector.

29. Install the heater hose on the choke housing bracket and connect the hose at the intake manifold.

30. Fill the cooling system and connect the negative battery cable.

31. Install the air cleaner assembly.

Fuel Injected Engines

NOTE: *Discharge fuel system pressure before starting any work that involves disconnecting fuel system lines. See Fuel Supply Manifold removal and installation procedures (Gasoline Fuel System section).*

1. To remove the upper manifold: Remove the air cleaner. Disconnect the electrical connectors at the air bypass valve, throttle position sensor and EGR position sensor.

2. Disconnect the throttle linkage at the throttle ball and the AOD transmission linkage from the throttle body. Remove the bolts that secure the bracket to the intake and position the bracket and cables out of the way.

3. Disconnect the upper manifold vacuum fitting connections by removing all the vacuum lines at the vacuum tree (label lines for position identification). Remove the vacuum lines to the EGR valve and fuel pressure regulator.

4. Disconnect the PCV system by disconnect-

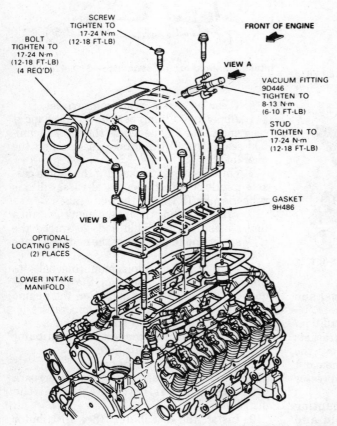
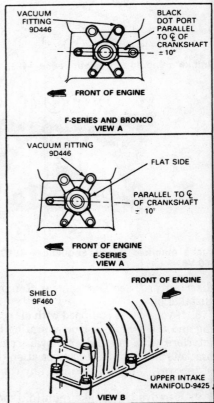

8-302 EFI/8-351 EFI upper intake manifold installation

ing the hose from the fitting at the rear of the upper manifold.

5. Remove the two canister purge lines from the fittings at the throttle body.

6. Disconnect the EGR tube from the EGR valve by loosening the flange nut.

7. Remove the bolt from the upper intake support bracket to upper manifold. Remove the upper manifold retaining bolts and remove the upper intake manifold and throttle body as an assembly.

8. Clean and inspect all mounting surfaces of the upper and lower intake manifolds.

9. Position a new mounting gasket on the lower intake manifold and install the upper manifold in the reverse order of removal. Mounting bolts are torqued to 12-18 ft. lbs.

10. To remove the lower intake manifold: Upper manifold and throttle body must be removed first.

11. Drain the cooling system.

CAUTION: *When draining the coolant, keep in mind that cats and dogs are attracted by the ethylene glycol antifreeze, and are quite likely to drink any that is left in an uncovered container or in puddles on the ground. This will prove fatal in sufficient quantity. Always drain the coolant into a sealable container. Coolant should be reused unless it is contaminated or several years old.*

12. Remove the distributor assembly, cap and wires.

13. Disconnect the electrical connectors at the engine, coolant temperature sensor and sending unit, at the air charge temperature sensor and at the knock sensor.

14. Disconnect the injector wiring harness from the main harness assembly. Remove the ground wire from the intake manifold stud. The ground wire must be installed at the same position it was removed from.

15. Disconnect the fuel supply and return lines from the fuel rails.

16. Remove the upper radiator hose from the

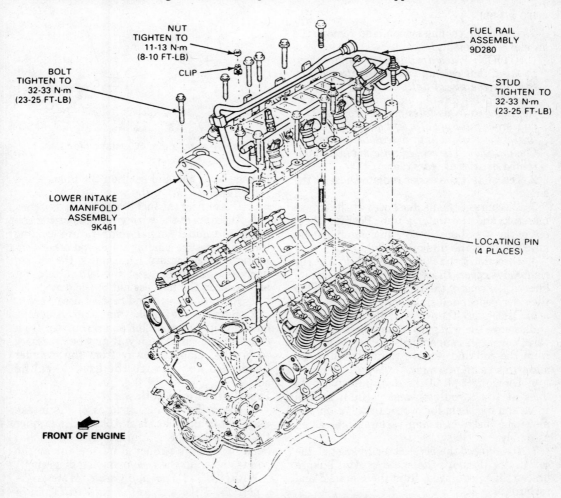

8-302 EFI/8-351 EFI lower intake manifold installation

thermostat housing. Remove the bypass hose. Remove the heater outlet hose at the intake manifold.

17. Remove the air cleaner mounting bracket. Remove the intake manifold mounting bolts and studs. Pay attention to the location of the bolts and studs for reinstallation. Remove the lower intake manifold assembly.

18. Clean and inspect the mounting surfaces of the heads and manifold.

19. Apply a $\frac{1}{16}''$ (1.6mm) bead of RTV sealer to the ends of the manifold seal (the junction point of the seals and gaskets). Install the end seals and intake gaskets on the cylinder heads. The gaskets must interlock with the seal tabs.

20. Install locator bolts at opposite ends of each head and carefully lower the intake manifold into position. Install and tighten the mounting bolts and studs to 23-25 ft. lbs. Install the remaining components in the reverse order of removal.

8-460 w/4-bbl

1. Drain the cooling system and remove the air cleaner assembly.

CAUTION: *When draining the coolant, keep in mind that cats and dogs are attracted by the ethylene glycol antifreeze, and are quite likely to drink any that is left in an uncovered container or in puddles on the ground. This will prove fatal in sufficient quantity. Always drain the coolant into a sealable container. Coolant should be reused unless it is contaminated or several years old.*

2. Disconnect the upper radiator hose at the engine.

3. Disconnect the heater hoses at the intake manifold and the water pump. Position them out of the way. Loosen the water pump by-pass hose clamp at the intake manifold.

4. Disconnect the PCV valve and hose at the right valve cover. Disconnect all of the vacuum lines at the rear of the intake manifold and tag them for proper reinstallation.

5. Disconnect the wires at the spark plugs, and remove the wires from the brackets on the valve cover. Disconnect the high tension wire from the coil and remove the distributor cap and wires as an assembly.

6. Disconnect all of the distributor vacuum lines at the carburetor and vacuum control valve and tag them for proper installation. Remove the distributor and vacuum lines as an assembly.

7. Disconnect the accelerator linkage at the carburetor. Remove the speed control linkage bracket, if so equipped, from the manifold and carburetor.

8. Remove the bolts holding the accelerator

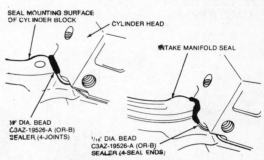

1/8" DIA. BEAD C3AZ-19528-A (OR-B) SEALER (4-JOINTS)

INTAKE MANIFOLD GASKET

CYLINDER HEAD

INTAKE MANIFOLD SEAL

1/16" DIA. BEAD C3AZ-19526-A (OR-B) SEALER (4-SEAL ENDS)

SEAL MOUNTING SURFACE OF CYLINDER BLOCK

RTV sealer installation, 302, 351W, 460 intake manifold

SEAL MOUNTING SURFACE OF CYLINDER BLOCK

CYLINDER HEAD

INTAKE MANIFOLD SEAL

1/8" DIA. BEAD C3AZ-19526-A (OR-B) SEALER (4-JOINTS)

1/16" DIA. BEAD C3AZ-19526-A (OR-B) SEALER (4-SEAL ENDS)

RTV sealer installation, 400 intake manifold

linkage bellcrank and position the linkage and return springs out of the way.

9. Disconnect the fuel line at the carburetor.

10. Disconnect the wiring harness at the coil battery terminal, engine temperature sending unit, oil pressure sending until, and other connections as necessary. Disconnect the wiring harness from the clips at the left valve cover and position the harness out of the way.

11. Remove the coil and bracket assembly.

12. Remove the intake manifold attaching bolts and lift the manifold and carburetor from the engine as an assembly. It may be necessary to pry the manifold away from the cylinder heads. Do not damage the gasket sealing surfaces.

Installation is as follows:

1. Clean the mating surfaces of the intake manifold, cylinder heads and block with lacquer thinner or similar solvent. Apply a $\frac{1}{8}''$ (3mm) bead of silicone/rubber RTV sealant at the points shown in the accompanying diagram.

WARNING: *Do not apply sealer to the waffle portions of the seals as the sealer will rupture the end seal material.*

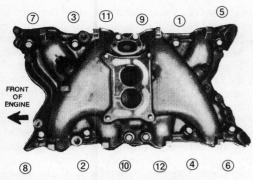

400 V8 intake manifold torque sequence

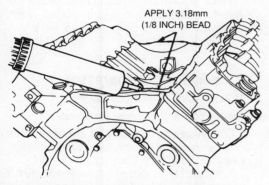

APPLY 3.18mm
(1/8 INCH) BEAD

Applying RTV sealer to the intake manifold

2. Position the new seals on the block and press the seal locating extensions into the holes in the mating surfaces.

3. Apply a $\frac{1}{16}''$ (1.6mm) bead of sealer to the outer end of each manifold seal for the full length of the seal (4 places). As before, do not apply sealer to the waffle portion of the end seals.

NOTE: *This sealer sets in about 15 minutes, depending on brand, so work quickly but carefully. DO NOT DROP ANY SEALER*

INTO THE MANIFOLD CAVITY. IT WILL FORM AND SET AND PLUG THE OIL GALLERY.

4. Position the manifold gasket onto the block and heads with the alignment notches under the dowels in the heads. Be sure gasket holes align with head holes.

5. Install the manifold and related equipment in reverse order of removal.

Combination Manifold

REMOVAL AND INSTALLATION

6-240

1. Remove the air cleaner. Remove the carburetor linkage and kick down linkage from the engine.

2. Disconnect the fuel line from the carburetor and all vacuum lines from the manifolds.

3. Remove the negative battery cable, then remove the alternator mounting bolts and remove the alternator from the engine with the wires attached.

4. Disconnect the muffler inlet pipe from the engine.

5. Remove the manifold attaching parts from the engine, and remove the two manifolds as an assembly.

6. To separate the manifolds, remove the carburetor and then remove the nuts which secure the manifolds together.

7. Clean all gasket areas and reverse above procedure to install; using all new gaskets. Torque to specifications listed in the "Torque Specifications" chart.

Exhaust Manifold

NOTE: *Although, in most cases, the engine does not have exhaust manifold gasket installed by the factory, aftermarket gaskets are available from parts stores.*

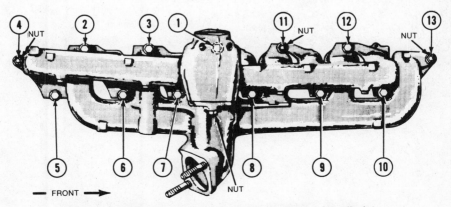

Intake and exhaust manifold torque sequence—six cylinder

REMOVAL AND INSTALLATION

V8 Engines

1. If removing the right side exhaust manifold, remove the air cleaner and related parts and the heat stove, if so equipped.

2. On 8-351M and 8-400 engines: if the left exhaust manifold is being removed, first drain the engine oil and remove the oil filter. On 8-255, 8-302 and 8-351W engines, dipstick and tube removal may be required. Remove any speed control brackets that interfere.

CAUTION: *The EPA warns that prolonged contact with used engine oil may cause a number of skin disorders, including cancer! You should make every effort to minimize your exposure to used engine oil. Protective gloves should be worn when changing the oil. Wash your hands and any other exposed skin areas as soon as possible after exposure to used engine oil. Soap and water, or waterless hand cleaner should be used.*

3. Disconnect the exhaust manifold(s) from the muffler (or converter) inlet pipe(s).

NOTE: *On certain vehicles with automatic transmission and column shift it may be necessary to disconnect the selector lever crossshaft for clearance.*

4. Disconnect the spark plug wires and remove the spark plugs and heat shields. Disconnect the EGR sensor (models so equipped), and heat control valve vacuum line (models so equipped).

NOTE: *On some engines the spark plug wire heat shields are removed with the manifold. Transmission dipstick tube and Thermactor® air tube removal may be required on certain models. Air tube removal is possible by cutting the tube clamp at the converter.*

5. Remove the exhaust manifold attaching bolts and washers, and remove the manifold(s).

6. Inspect the manifold(s) for damaged gasket surfaces, cracks, or other defects.

7. Clean the mating surfaces of the manifold(s), cylinder head and muffler inlet pipe(s).

8. Install the manifold(s) in reverse order of removal. Torque the mounting bolts to the value listed in the Torque Specifications chart. Start with the centermost bolt and work outward in both directions.

Air Conditioning Compressor

REMOVAL AND INSTALLATION

2-Cylinder York or Tecumseh Compressor

1. Discharge the system and disconnect the two hoses from the compressor. Cap the openings immediately! See Chapter 1.

2. Energize the clutch and remove the clutch mounting bolt.

3. Install a ⅝-11 bolt in the clutch driveshaft

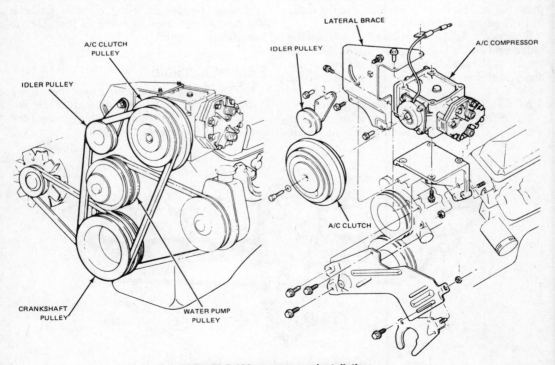

1974–79 8-460 compressor installation

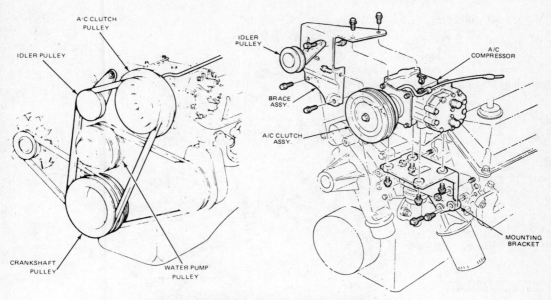

1980–81 8-400/8-460 compressor installation

hole. With the cltuch still energized, tighten the bolt to remove the clutch from the shaft.

4. Disconnect the clutch wire at the connector.

5. Loosen the idler pulley or alternator and remove the drive belt and clutch, then remove the mounting bolts and compressor.

6. Installation is the reverse of removal. Prior to installation, if a new compressor is being installed, drain the oil from the old compressor into a calibrated container, then drain the oil from the new compressor into a clean container and refill the new compressor with the same amount of oil that was in the old one. Install the clutch and bolt finger-tight, install the compressor on the mounting bracket and install those bolts finger-tight. Connect the clutch wire and energize the clutch. Tighten the clutch bolt to 23 ft. lbs. Tighten the compressor mounting bolts to 30 ft. lbs. Make all other con-

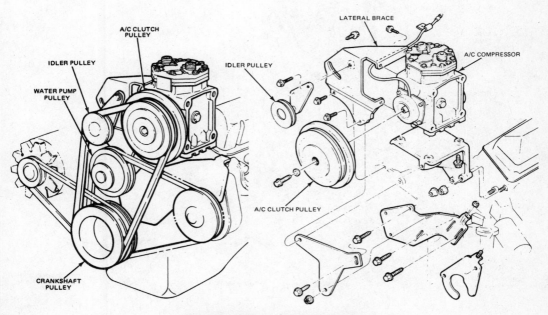

1974–80 8-351 compressor installation

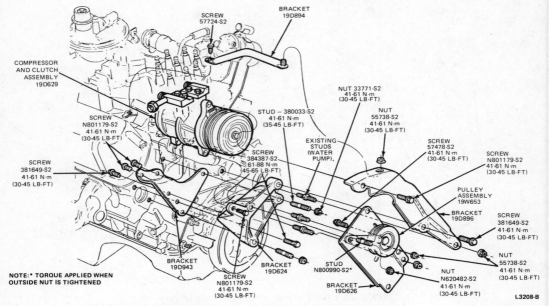

8-351 compressor installation through 1979

nections and evacuate, charge and leak test the system. See Chapter 1.

FS-6 6-Cylinder Axial Compressor

1982 8-255 ENGINE
1982-88 8-302 ENGINE

1. Discharge the refrigerant system. See Chapter 1.

2. Disconnect the two refrigerant lines from the compressor. Cap the openings immediately!

3. Remove tension from the drive belt. Remove the belt

4. Disconnect the clutch wire at the connector.

5. Remove the two nuts from the rear support bracket. Remove the three bolts from the

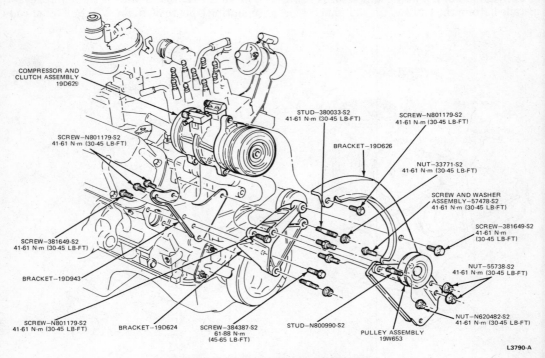

8-302 compressor installation through 1979

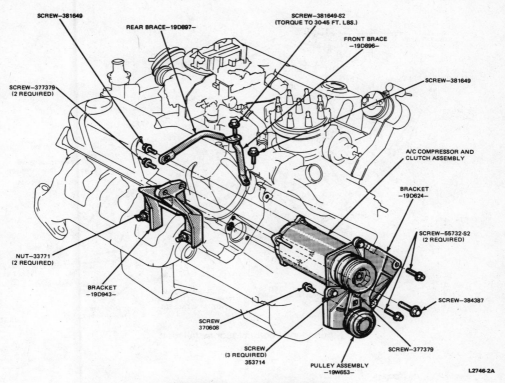

SCREW–381649

REAR BRACE –19D897–

SCREW–381649-S2
(TORQUE TO 30-45 FT. LBS.)

FRONT BRACE
–19D896–

SCREW–381649

SCREW–377379
(2 REQUIRED)

A/C COMPRESSOR AND
CLUTCH ASSEMBLY

BRACKET
–19D624–

SCREW–55732-S2
(2 REQUIRED)

NUT–33771
(2 REQUIRED)

BRACKET
–19D943–

SCREW–384387

SCREW
370608

SCREW–377379

SCREW
(3 REQUIRED)
353714

PULLEY ASSEMBLY
–19W653–

L2746-2A

1980 8-302 compressor installation

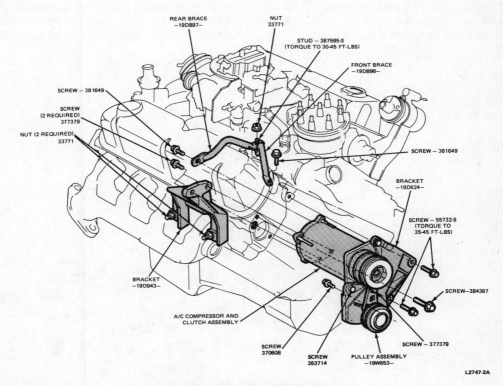

REAR BRACE
–19D897–

NUT
33771

STUD – 387595-S
(TORQUE TO 30-45 FT-LBS)

FRONT BRACE
–19D896–

SCREW – 381649

SCREW
(2 REQUIRED)
377379

NUT (2 REQUIRED)
33771

SCREW – 381649

BRACKET
–19D624–

SCREW – 55732-S
(TORQUE TO
35-45 FT-LBS)

BRACKET
–19D943–

SCREW–384387

A/C COMPRESSOR AND
CLUTCH ASSEMBLY

SCREW
370608

SCREW
353714

SCREW – 377379

PULLEY ASSEMBLY
–19W653–

L2747-2A

1980 8-351 compressor installation

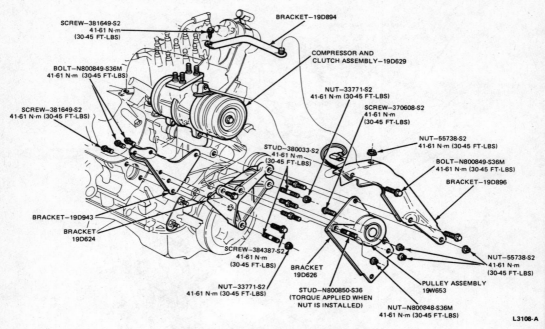

Nippondenso compressor installation

front bosses on the bracket. On 1985-86 models, remove one bolt from the front of the tubular brace and remove the tubular brace.

6. Rotate the compressor towards the left side of the engine compartment until the compressor upper boss clears the support.

7. Remove the compressor and rear support as an assembly.

8. Installation is the reverse of removal. Use new O-rings coated with clean refrigerant oil at all fittings. New, replacement compressors contain 10 oz. of refrigerant oil. Prior to installa-

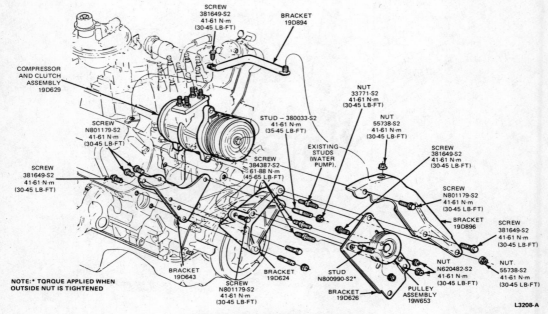

1981 8-302 compressor installation

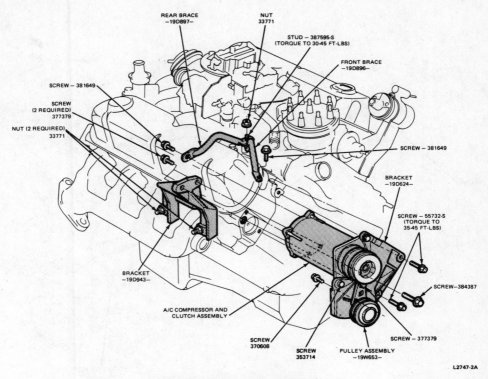

1981 8-351 compressor installation

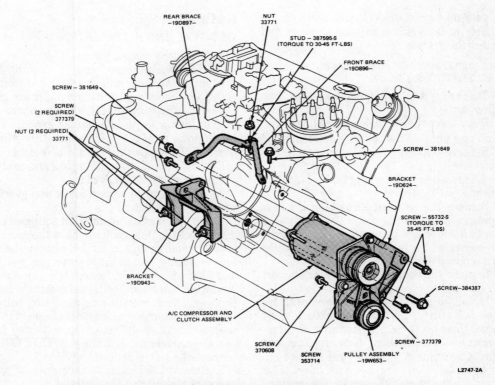

1981 8-351 compressor installation with automatic temperature control

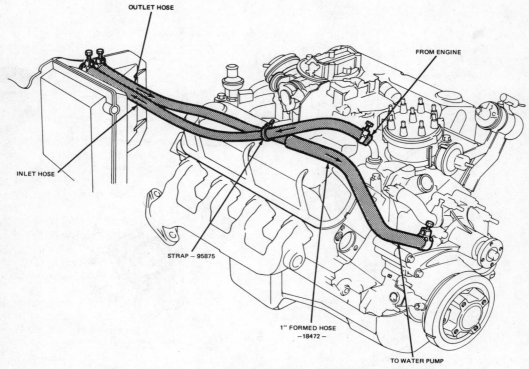

OUTLET HOSE

FROM ENGINE

INLET HOSE

STRAP – 95875

1" FORMED HOSE
– 18472 –

TO WATER PUMP

1981 8-302 compressor installation with automatic temperature control

tion, pour off 4 oz. of oil. This will maintain the oil charge in the system. Evacuate, charge and leak test the system.

1986-88 MODELS WITH AUTOMATIC TEMPERATURE CONTROL AND THE 8-302 ENGINE

1. Discharge the refrigerant system. See Chapter 1.
2. Disconnect the two refrigerant lines from the compressor. Cap the openings immediately!
3. Remove tension from the drive belt. Remove the belt
4. Disconnect the clutch wire at the connector.
5. Remove the two bolts attaching the rear compressor brace to the power steering pump support. Remove the three bolts attaching the front bosses of the compressor to the power steering pump and the compressor brace.
6. Remove the compressor and rear support as an assembly.
7. Installation is the reverse of removal. Install all bolts finger-tight before tightening any of them. Use new O-rings coated with clean refrigerant oil at all fittings. New, replacement compressors contain 10 oz. of refrigerant oil. Prior to installation, pour off 4 oz. of oil. This will maintain the oil charge in the system. Evacuate, charge and leak test the system.

Radiator
REMOVAL AND INSTALLATION

1. Drain the cooling system.
CAUTION: *When draining the coolant, keep in mind that cats and dogs are attracted by the ethylene glycol antifreeze, and are quite likely to drink any that is left in an uncovered container or in puddles on the ground. This will prove fatal in sufficient quantity. Always drain the coolant into a sealable container. Coolant should be reused unless it is contaminated or several years old.*
2. Disconnect the upper, lower and overflow hoses at the radiator.
3. On automatic transmission equipped cars, disconnect the fluid cooler lines at the radiator.
4. Depending on the model, remove the two top mounting bolts and remove the radiator and shroud assembly, or remove the shroud mounting bolts and position the shroud out of the way, or remove the side mounting bolts. If the air conditioner condenser is attached to the radiator, remove the retaining bolts and position the condenser out of the way. DO NOT disconnect the refrigerant lines.
5. Remove the radiator attaching bolts or top brackets and lift out the radiator.
6. If a new radiator is to be installed, transfer

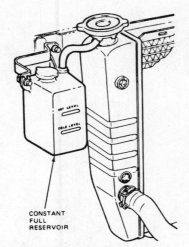

Constant-full cooling system

the petcock from the old radiator to the new one. On cars equipped with automatic transmissions, transfer the fluid cooler line fittings from the old radiator.

7. Position the radiator and install, but do not tighten, the radiator support bolts. On cars equipped with automatic transmissions, connect the fluid cooler lines. Then, tighten the radiator support bolts or shroud and mounting bolts.

8. Connect the radiator hoses. Close the radiator petcock. Fill and bleed the cooling system.

9. Start the engine and bring it to operating temperature. Check for leaks.

10. On cars equipped with automatic transmissions, check the cooler lines for leaks and interference. Check the transmission fluid level.

Electro-Drive Cooling Fan
REMOVAL AND INSTALLATION

Various models, are equipped with a bracket-mounted electric cooling fan that replaces the conventional water pump mounted fan.

Operation of the fan motor is dependent on engine coolant temperature and air conditioner compressor clutch engagement. The fan will run only when the coolant temperature is approximately 180° or higher, or when the compressor clutch is engaged. The fan, motor and mount can be removed as an assembly after disconnecting the wiring harnesses and mounting bolts.

CAUTION: *The cooling fan is automatic and may come on at any time without warning even if the ignition is switched OFF. To avoid possible injury, always disconnect the negative battery cable when working near the electric cooling fan.*

1. Disconnect the battery ground.

2. Remove the fan wiring harness from the clip.

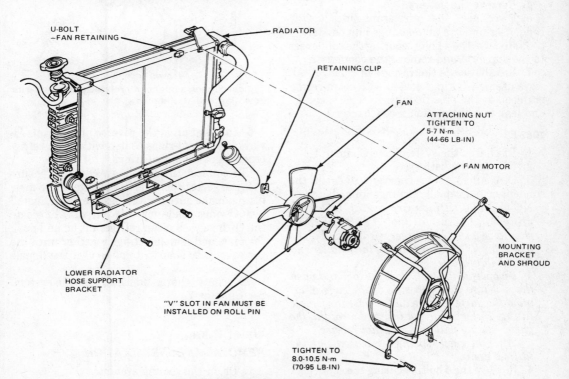

Gasoline engine electric cooling fan

3. Unplug the harness at the fan motor connector.

4. Remove the 4 mounting bracket attaching screws and remove the fan assembly from the car.

5. Remove the retaining clip from the end of the motor shaft and remove the fan.

6. Installation is the reverse of removal.

Air Conditioning Condenser

REMOVAL AND INSTALLATION

1968-78

1. Discharge the system. See Chapter 1.
2. Disconnect the refrigerant lines at the condenser and cap all openings immediately!
3. Remove the upper radiator mounts and tilt the radiator rearward.
4. Remove the four condenser mounting screws and lift out the condenser.
5. Installation is the reverse of removal. Always use new O-rings coated with clean refrigerant oil at the pipe fittings. Evacuate, charge and leak test the system. See Chapter 1.

1979-81

1. Discharge the system. See Chapter 1.
2. Remove the 6 attaching screws and remove the grille.
3. Move the ambient cutoff switch away from the front of the radiator and condenser.
4. Remove the battery.
5. Disconnect the refrigerant lines at the condenser and cap all openings immediately!
6. Remove the 4 bolts securing the condenser to the supports and remove the condenser.
7. Installation is the reverse of removal. Always use new O-rings coated with clean refrigerant oil at the pipe fittings. Evacuate, charge and leak test the system. See Chapter 1.

1982-88

1. Discharge the system. See Chapter 1.
2. Remove the battery.
3. Disconnect the refrigerant lines at the condenser and cap all openings immediately!
NOTE: *The fittings are spring-lock couplings and a special tool, T81P-19623-G, should be used. The larger opening end of the tool is for ½" discharge lines; the smaller end for ⅜" liquid lines.*

To operate the tool, close the tool and push the tool into the open side of the cage to expand the garter spring and release the female fitting. If the tool is not inserted straight, the garter spring will cock and not release.

After the garter spring is released, pull the fittings apart.

4. Remove the 4 bolts securing the condenser to the supports and remove the condenser.

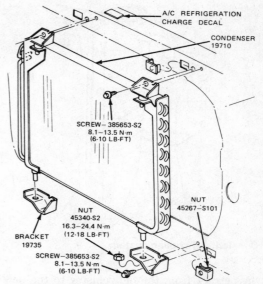

1982–87 air conditioning condenser installation

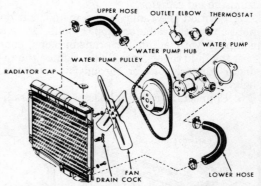

Typical cooling system and related parts—V8 with downflow radiator shown

5. Installation is the reverse of removal. Always use new O-rings coated with clean refrigerant oil at the pipe fittings.

To connect the couplings, check to ensure that the garter spring is in the cage of the male fitting, make sure the fittings are clean, install new O-rings made for this purpose, lubricate the O-rings with clean refrigerant oil and push the male and female fittings together until the garter springs snaps into place over the female fitting.

Evacuate, charge and leak test the system. See Chapter 1.

Water Pump

REMOVAL AND INSTALLATION

1. Drain the cooling system.
CAUTION: *When draining the coolant, keep*

in mind that cats and dogs are attracted by the ethylene glycol antifreeze, and are quite likely to drink any that is left in an uncovered container or in puddles on the ground. This will prove fatal in sufficient quantity. Always drain the coolant into a sealable container. Coolant should be reused unless it is contaminated or several years old.

2. Disconnect the negative battery cable.

3. On cars with power steering, remove the drive belt.

4. If the vehicle is equipped with air conditioning, remove the idler pulley bracket and air conditioner drive belt.

5. On engines with a Thermactor®, remove the belt.

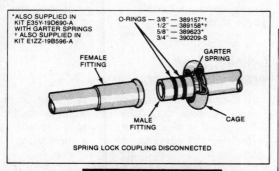

*ALSO SUPPLIED IN KIT E35Y-19D690-A WITH GARTER SPRINGS
† ALSO SUPPLIED IN KIT E1ZZ-19B596-A

O-RINGS — 3/8" — 389157*†
1/2" — 389158*†
5/8" — 389623*
3/4" — 390209-S

FEMALE FITTING

GARTER SPRING

MALE FITTING   CAGE

SPRING LOCK COUPLING DISCONNECTED

TO DISCONNECT COUPLING

CAUTION — DISCHARGE SYSTEM BEFORE DISCONNECTING COUPLING

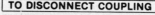
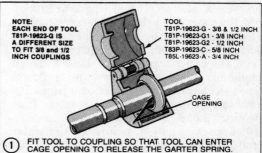

NOTE:
EACH END OF TOOL T81P-19623-G IS A DIFFERENT SIZE TO FIT 3/8 and 1/2 INCH COUPLINGS

TOOL
T81P-19623-G - 3/8 & 1/2 INCH
T81P-19623-G1 - 3/8 INCH
T81P-19623-G2 - 1/2 INCH
T83P-19623-C - 5/8 INCH
T85L-19623-A - 3/4 INCH

CAGE OPENING

① FIT TOOL TO COUPLING SO THAT TOOL CAN ENTER CAGE OPENING TO RELEASE THE GARTER SPRING.

TO CONNECT COUPLING

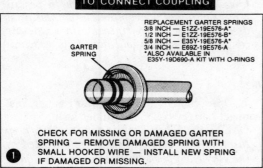

GARTER SPRING

REPLACEMENT GARTER SPRINGS
3/8 INCH — E1ZZ-19E576-A*
1/2 INCH — E1ZZ-19E576-B*
5/8 INCH — E35Y-19E576-A*
3/4 INCH — E69Z-19E576-A
*ALSO AVAILABLE IN E35Y-19D690-A KIT WITH O-RINGS

① CHECK FOR MISSING OR DAMAGED GARTER SPRING — REMOVE DAMAGED SPRING WITH SMALL HOOKED WIRE — INSTALL NEW SPRING IF DAMAGED OR MISSING.

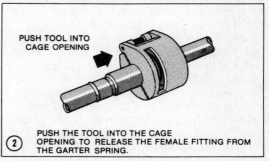

PUSH TOOL INTO CAGE OPENING

② PUSH THE TOOL INTO THE CAGE OPENING TO RELEASE THE FEMALE FITTING FROM THE GARTER SPRING.

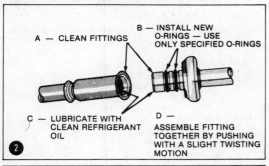

A — CLEAN FITTINGS

B — INSTALL NEW O-RINGS — USE ONLY SPECIFIED O-RINGS

C — LUBRICATE WITH CLEAN REFRIGERANT OIL

D — ASSEMBLE FITTING TOGETHER BY PUSHING WITH A SLIGHT TWISTING MOTION

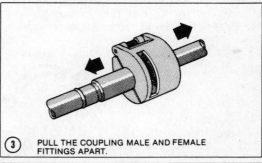

③ PULL THE COUPLING MALE AND FEMALE FITTINGS APART.

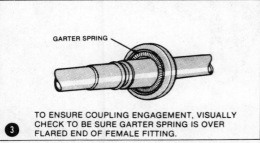

GARTER SPRING

③ TO ENSURE COUPLING ENGAGEMENT, VISUALLY CHECK TO BE SURE GARTER SPRING IS OVER FLARED END OF FEMALE FITTING.

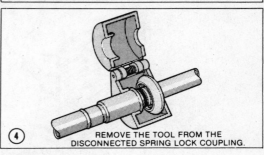

④ REMOVE THE TOOL FROM THE DISCONNECTED SPRING LOCK COUPLING.

Quick-connect coupling procedure

6. Disconnect the lower radiator hose and heater hose from the water pump.

7. On cars equipped with a fan shroud, remove the retaining screws and position the shroud rearward.

8. Remove the fan, fan clutch and spacer from the engine, and if the car is equipped with an electric motor driven fan, remove the fan as an assembly for working clearance.

9. On cars equipped with a water pump mounted alternator, loosen the alternator mounting bolts, remove the alternator belt and remove the alternator adjusting arm bracket from the water pump. If interference is encountered, remove the air pump pulley and pivot bolts. Remove the air pump adjusting bracket. Swing the upper bracket aside. Detach the air conditioner compressor and lay it aside. Do not disconnect any of the air conditioning lines. Remove any accessory mounting brackets from the water pump.

10. Loosen the by-pass hose at the water pump, if so equipped.

11. Remove the water pump retaining screws and remove the pump from the engine.

NOTE: *The 6-240 originally has a one-piece gasket for the cylinder front cover and the water pump. Trim away the old gasket at the edge of the cylinder cover and replace with a service gasket.*

12. Clean any gasket material from the pump mounting surface. On engines equipped with a water pump backing plate, remove the plate, clean the gasket surfaces, install a new gasket and plate on the water pump.

13. Remove the heater hose fitting from the old pump and install it on the new pump.

14. Coat both sides of the new gasket with a water resistant sealer, then install the pump reversing the procedure. Tighten the attaching bolts diagonally, in rotation, to 12-15 ft. lbs. (8-255, 8-302, 8-351, 8-400 V8), 15-20 ft. lbs. (6-240, 8-429, 8-460, V8) or 20-25 ft. lbs. (8-390, 8-428, 8-462 V8).

15. Connect the lower radiator hose, heater hose, and water pump by-pass hose at the water pump.

16. Install all accessory brackets attaching to the water pump. Install the pump pulley on the pump shaft.

Cylinder Head
REMOVAL AND INSTALLATION

NOTE: *On cars with air conditioning, remove the mounting bolts and the drive belt, and position the compressor out of the way. Remove the compressor upper mounting bracket from the cylinder head.*

CAUTION: *If the compressor refrigerant lines do not have enough slack to permit repositioning of the compressor without first disconnecting the refrigerant lines, the air conditioning system will have to be evacuated. See Chapter 1.*

6-240

1. Drain coolant and remove air cleaner. Disconnect battery cable at cylinder head.

CAUTION: *When draining the coolant, keep in mind that cats and dogs are attracted by the ethylene glycol antifreeze, and are quite likely to drink any that is left in an uncovered container or in puddles on the ground. This will prove fatal in sufficient quantity. Always*

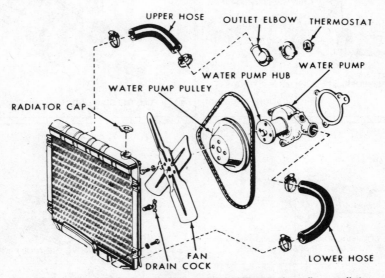

Cooling system and related parts—typical V8 with downflow radiator

drain the coolant into a sealable container. Coolant should be reused unless it is contaminated or several years old.

2. Disconnect exhaust pipe at manifold.

3. Disconnect accelerator retracting spring, choke control cable and accelerator rod at carburetor.

4. Disconnect fuel line and distributor control vacuum line at the carburetor.

5. Disconnect coolant tubes from carburetor spacer. Disconnect coolant and heater hoses.

6. Disconnect distributor control vacuum line at distributor and fuel inlet line at the filter. Remove lines as an assembly.

7. On an engine equipped with positive crankcase ventilation, disconnect the emission exhaust tube.

8. Disconnect spark plug wires at the plugs and the small wire from the temperature sending unit. On an engine equipped with a Thermactor exhaust emission control system, disconnect the air pump hose at the air manifold assembly. Unscrew the tube nuts and remove the air manifold. Disconnect the anti-backfire valve air and vacuum lines at the intake manifold. On a car equipped with power brakes, disconnect the brake vacuum line at the intake manifold.

9. Remove the rocker arm cover.

10. Loosen the rocker arm stud nut so that the rocker arm can be rotated to one side. Remove valve pushrods and keep them in sequence.

11. Remove one cylinder head bolt from each end and install two $\frac{7}{16}$"-14 guide studs.

12. Remove remaining cylinder head bolts, then remove cylinder head.

13. Prior to installation, clean head and block surfaces.

14. Apply sealer to both sides of head gasket. Position gasket over guide studs or dowel pins.

NOTE: *Apply gasket sealer only to steel shim head gaskets. Steel/asbestos composite head gaskets are to be installed without any sealer.*

15. Install new gasket on the exhaust pipe flange.

16. Lift the cylinder head over the guide studs and slide it carefully into place while guiding the exhaust manifold studs into the exhaust pipe flange.

17. Coat cylinder head attaching bolts with water resistant sealer and install (but do not tighten), the head bolts.

18. Torque the head, in proper sequence, and in three progressive steps to 75 ft. lbs.

19. Lubricate both ends of the pushrods and insert them in their original bores and sockets.

20. Lubricate valve stem tips and rocker arm pads.

21. Position the rocker arms and tighten the

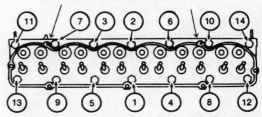

Cylinder head bolt torque sequence, 6-240,300

stud nuts enough to hold the pushrods in position.

22. Do a preliminary, cold valve lash adjustment.

23. Install exhaust pipe-to-manifold nuts and lockwashers. Torque to 17-22 ft. lbs.

24. Connect radiator and heater hoses. Connect coolant tubes at the carburetor spacer.

25. Connect distributor vacuum line and the carburetor fuel line. Connect battery cable to cylinder head.

26. On engines equipped with positive crankcase ventilation, clean components thoroughly and install.

NOTE: *On engines equipped with a Thermactor exhaust emission control system, install the air manifold assembly on the cylinder head. Connect the air pump outlet hose to the air manifold. Connect the anti-backfire valve, air and vacuum lines to the intake manifold.*

27. Connect accelerator rod pull-back spring. Connect choke control cable and the accelerator rod at the carburetor.

28. Connect distributor control vacuum line at distributor. Connect carburetor fuel line at fuel filter.

29. Connect temperature sending unit wire at sending unit. Connect spark plug wires.

30. Completely fill and bleed the cooling system.

31. Run engine for a minimum of 30 minutes at 1,200 rpm to stabilize engine temperature. Then, check for coolant and oil leaks.

32. Adjust engine idle mixture speed. check valve lash and adjust, if necessary.

33. Install valve rocker arm cover, then the air cleaner.

All V8

1. Drain the cooling system.

CAUTION: *When draining the coolant, keep in mind that cats and dogs are attracted by the ethylene glycol antifreeze, and are quite likely to drink any that is left in an uncovered container or in puddles on the ground. This will prove fatal in sufficient quantity. Always drain the coolant into a sealable container.*

Coolant should be reused unless it is contaminated or several years old.

2. Remove the intake manifold and the carburetor or CFI unit as an assembly.

3. Disconnect the spark plug wires, marking them as to placement. Position them out of the way of the cylinder head. Remove the spark plugs.

4. Disconnect the resonator or muffler inlet pipe(s) at the exhaust manifold(s).

NOTE: *On some 8-351 and 8-400 engines, it may be necessary to remove the exhaust manifolds from the cylinder heads to gain access to the lower head bolts.*

5. Disconnect the battery ground cable at the cylinder head (if applicable).

6. On cars with air conditioning, remove the mounting bolts and the drive belt, and position the compressor out of the way of the cylinder head. Remove the compressor upper mounting bracket from the cylinder head.

7. In order to remove the left cylinder head, on cars equipped with power steering, it may be necessary to remove the steering pump and bracket, remove the drive belt, and wire or tie the pump out of the way, but in such a way as to prevent the loss of its fluid.

8. In order to remove the right head it may be necessary to remove the alternator mounting bracket bolt and spacer, the ignition coil, and the air cleaner inlet duct from the right cylinder head.

9. In order to remove the left cylinder head on a car equipped with Thermactor exhaust emission control system, disconnect the hose from the air manifold on the left cylinder head.

10. If the right cylinder head is to be removed on a car equipped with a Thermactor exhaust emission control system, remove the Thermactor air pump and its mounting bracket. Disconnect the hose from the air manifold on the right cylinder head.

11. On 8-390, 8-428, and 8-462 engines, unbolt the rocker arm shafts from front to back, two turns at a time, and remove the rocker shaft and arm assembly. On all other V8 engines, loosen the rocker arm stud nuts or mounting bolts enough to rotate the rocker arms to one side in order to facilitate the removal of the pushrods. On all V8 engines, remove the pushrods in sequence, so that they may be installed in their original positions. On all V8 engines except the 8-390 and 8-428, remove the exhaust valve stem caps.

NOTE: *After rotating the rocker arms from the valve stems, remove the exhaust valve caps from the stems of the exhaust valves. They are small and easy to lose. Remember to reinstall them.*

12. Remove the cylinder head attaching bolts,

noting their positions. Lift the cylinder head off the block. Remove and discard the old cylinder head gasket.

13. Prior to installation, clean all surfaces where gaskets are to be installed. These include the cylinder head, intake manifold, rocker arm (valve) cover, and the cylinder block contact surfaces.

14. Position the new cylinder head gasket over the cylinder dowels on the block. Coat the head bolts with water resistant sealer. Position new gaskets on the muffler inlet pipes at the exhaust manifold flange.

15. Position the cylinder head to the block, and install the head bolts, each in its original position. On all engines on which the exhaust manifold has been removed from the head to facilitate removal, it is necessary to properly guide the exhaust manifold studs into the muffler inlet pipe flange when installing the head.

16. Following the cylinder head torque sequence diagrams, step-torque the cylinder head bolts in three stages. First, torque the bolts to 20 ft. lbs. less than the maximum figure listed in the Torque Specifications chart. Second, torque the bolts to 10 ft. lbs. less than the maximum figure. Finally, torque the bolts to the maximum figure in the chart. At this point, tighten the exhaust manifold-to-cylinder head attaching bolts to specifications.

17. Tighten the nuts on the exhaust manifold studs at the muffler inlet flanges to 18 ft. lbs.

18. Clean and inspect the pushrods one at a time. clean the oil passage within each pushrod with a suitable solvent and blow the passage out with compressed air. Check the ends of the pushrods for nicks, grooves, roughness, or excessive wear. Visually inspect the pushrods for straightness, and replace any bent ones. Do not attempt to straighten pushrods.

19. Install the pushrods in their original positions. Apply Lubriplate or a similar product to the valve stem tips and to the pushrod guides in the cylinder head. Install the exhaust valve stem caps.

20. On 390 and 428 V8 engines, the intake manifold and rocker arm and shaft assemblies must now be installed. When tightening down

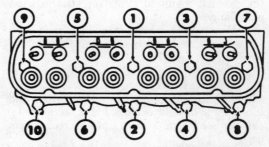

Cylinder head bolt torque sequence, all gasoline V8's

the rocker arm shaft assembly, make sure that the oil holes face downward, the identification notch faces downward and toward the front (right bank) or toward the rear (left bank), and that the crankshaft damper has the "XX" mark aligned with the pointer. The rocker arms bolts are tightened front to rear, two turns at a time, to avoid bending pushrods.

21. On all V8 engines except the 390 and 428, apply white grease to the fulcrum seats and sockets. Turn the rocker arms to their proper positions and tighten the stud nuts or mounting bolts enough to hold the rocker arms in position. Make sure that the lower ends of the pushrods have remained properly seated in the valve lifters.

22. On all V8 engines except the 390, 428 and 462, perform a preliminary valve adjustment.

23. Apply a coat of oil-resistant sealer to the upper side of the new valve cover gasket. Position the gasket on the valve cover with the cemented side of the gasket facing the valve cover. Install the valve covers and tighten the bolts to 3–5 ft. lbs.

24. Install the intake manifold and carburetor or CFI unit.

25. Refer to Steps 7-11 (inclusive) of the Removal procedure and reverse the procedures if applicable to your car.

26. Adjust all drive belts which were removed.

27. Refill the cooling system.

28. Connect the battery ground cable at the cylinder head (if applicable).

29. Install the spark plugs and connect the spark plug wires.

30. Start the engine and check for leaks.

31. With the engine running, check and adjust the carburetor idle speed and mixture.

32. With the engine running, listen for abnormal valve noises or irregular idle and correct them.

CYLINDER HEAD OVERHAUL

1. Remove the cylinder head(s) from the car engine (see Cylinder Head Removal and Installation). Place the head(s) on a workbench and remove any manifolds that are still connected. Remove all rocker arm retaining parts and the rocker arms, if still installed.

2. Turn the cylinder head over so that the mounting surface is facing up and support it evenly on wood blocks.

3. Use a scraper and remove all of the gasket material stuck to the head mounting surface. Mount a wire carbon removal brush in an electric drill and clean away the carbon on the valves and head combustion chambers.

CAUTION: *When scraping or decarbonizing the cylinder head, take care not to damage or nick the gasket mounting surface.*

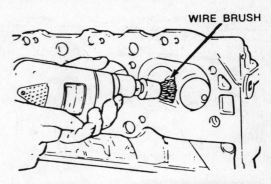

Removing the carbon from the cylinder head with a wire brush and electric drill

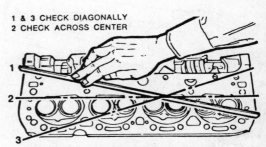

Checking the cylinder head for warpage

4. Number the valve heads with a permanent felt-tip marker for cylinder location.

CLEANING AND INSPECTING

Chip carbon away from the valve heads, combustion chambers, and ports, using a chisel made of hardwood. Remove the remaining deposits with a stiff wire brush.

NOTE: *Be sure that the deposits are actually removed, rather than burnished.*

Clean the remaining cylinder head parts with cleaning solvent. Do not remove the protective coating from the springs. Check for cracks and/or damage. Repair as needed.

RESURFACING

NOTE: *Resurfacing should only be performed by a reputable machine shop. The following you can do to determine if resurfacing is necessary.*

Place a straightedge across the gasket surface of the cylinder head. Using feeler gauges, determine the clearance at the center of the straightedge. If warpage exceeds 0.003" in a 6" span, or 0.006" over the total length, the cylinder head must be resurfaced.

NOTE: *If warpage exceeds the manufacturer's maximum tolerance for material removal, the cylinder head must be replaced.*

When milling the cylinder heads of V-type engines, the intake manifold mounting position is

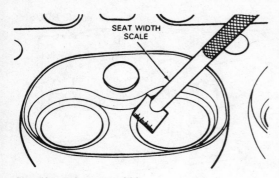

Checking valve seat width

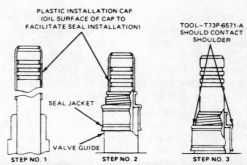

STEP NO. 1– WITH VALVES IN HEAD PLACE PLASTIC INSTALLATION CAP OVER END OF VALVE STEM.
STEP NO. 2– START VALVE STEM SEAL CAREFULLY OVER CAP. PUSH SEAL DOWN UNTIL JACKET TOUCHES TOP OF GUIDE.
STEP NO. 3– REMOVE PLASTIC INSTALLATION CAP. USE INSTALLATION TOOL–T73P-6571-A OR SCREWDRIVERS TO BOTTOM SEAL ON VALVE GUIDE.

Valve stem seal installation

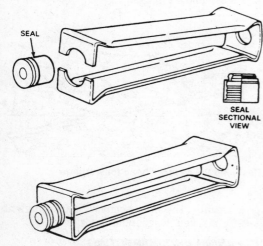

Valve stem seal installation tool for the 8-460

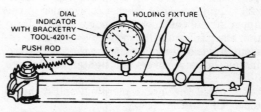

Checking pushrod runout

STEP 1 - SET NO. 1 PISTON ON T.D.C. AT END OF COMPRESSION STROKE ADJUST NO. 1 INTAKE AND EXHAUST
STEP 4 - CHECK NO. 6 INTAKE AND EXHAUST

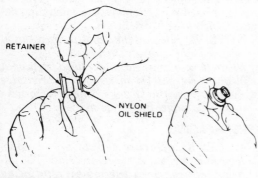

Installing the nylon oil shield

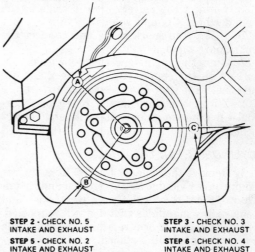

STEP 2 - CHECK NO. 5 INTAKE AND EXHAUST
STEP 5 - CHECK NO. 2 INTAKE AND EXHAUST

STEP 3 - CHECK NO. 3 INTAKE AND EXHAUST
STEP 6 - CHECK NO. 4 INTAKE AND EXHAUST

6-300 valve clearance checking

altered, and must be corrected by milling the manifold flange a proportionate amount.

WARNING: *Do not plane or grind more than 0.010" from the original cylinder head gasket surface.*

PRELIMINARY VALVE ADJUSTMENT

All engines used in full-size Ford products, from 1968 to the present are equipped with hydraulic valve lifters. Valve systems with hydraulic valve lifters operate with zero clearance in the valve train, and because of this the rocker arms are nonadjustable. The only means by which valve system clearances can be altered is by installing 0.060" over or undersize pushrods; but, because of the hydraulic lifter's natural ability to compensate for slack in the valve train, all components of the valve system

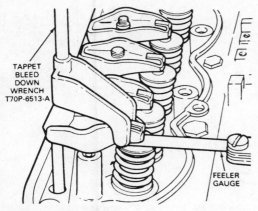

Valve clearance check

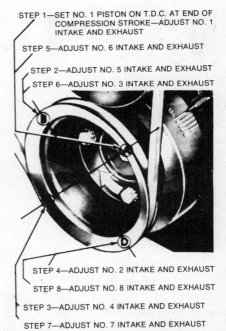

STEP 1—SET NO. 1 PISTON ON T.D.C. AT END OF
  COMPRESSION STROKE ADJUST NO. 1
  INTAKE AND EXHAUST
STEP 4—ADJUST NO. 6 INTAKE AND EXHAUST

STEP 2—
ADJUST NO. 5
INTAKE AND
EXHAUST

STEP 3—
ADJUST NO. 3
INTAKE AND
EXHAUST

STEP 5—
ADJUST NO. 2
INTAKE AND
EXHAUST

STEP 6—
ADJUST NO. 4
INTAKE AND
EXHAUST

Position of crankshaft for preliminary valve adjustment—six-cylinder

STEP 1—SET NO. 1 PISTON ON T.D.C. AT END OF
  COMPRESSION STROKE—ADJUST NO. 1
  INTAKE AND EXHAUST

STEP 5—ADJUST NO. 6 INTAKE AND EXHAUST

STEP 2—ADJUST NO. 5 INTAKE AND EXHAUST

STEP 6—ADJUST NO. 3 INTAKE AND EXHAUST

STEP 4—ADJUST NO. 2 INTAKE AND EXHAUST

STEP 8—ADJUST NO. 8 INTAKE AND EXHAUST

STEP 3—ADJUST NO. 4 INTAKE AND EXHAUST

STEP 7—ADJUST NO. 7 INTAKE AND EXHAUST

Position of crankshaft for preliminary valve adjustment—1968–69 302 V8 without positive stop rocker arm stud

should be checked for wear if there is excessive play in the system.

When a valve in the engine is in the closed position, the valve lifter is resting on the base circle of the camshaft lobe and the pushrod is in its lowest position. To remove this additional clearance from the valve train, the valve lifter expands to maintain zero clearance in the valve system. When a rocker arm is loosened or removed from the engine, the lifter expands to its fullest travel. When the rocker arm is reinstalled on the engine, the proper valve setting is obtained by tightening the rocker arm to a specified limit. But with the lifter fully expanded, if the camshaft lobe is on a high point it will require excessive torque to compress the lifter and obtain the proper setting. Because of this, when any component of the valve system has been removed, a preliminary valve adjustment procedure must be followed to ensure that when the rocker arm is reinstalled on the engine and tightened, the camshaft lobe for that cylinder is in the low position.

6-240

1. Crank the engine until the TDC mark on the crankshaft damper is aligned with timing pointer on the cylinder front cover.

2. Scribe a mark on the damper at this point.

3. Scribe two more marks on the damper, each equally spaced from the first mark (see illustration).

4. With the engine on TDC of the compression stroke, (mark A aligned with the pointer) back off the rocker arm adjusting nut until there is end-play in the pushrod. Tighten the adjusting nut until all clearance is removed, then tighten the adjusting nut one additional turn on 1969 and later models and ¾ of a turn on all 1968 models. To determine when all clearance is removed from the rocker arm, turn the pushrod with the fingers. When the push-

rod can no longer be turned, all clearance has been removed.

5. Repeat this procedure for each valve, turning the crankshaft ⅓ turn to the next mark each time and following the engine firing order of 1-5-3-6-2-4.

With No. 1 at TDC at end of compression stroke make a chalk mark at points B and C approximately 90 degrees apart.

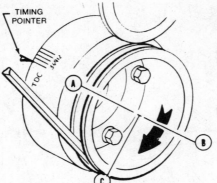

TIMING POINTER

POSITION A – No. 1 at TDC at end of compression stroke.
POSITION B – Rotate the crankshaft 180 degrees (one half revolution) clockwise from POSITION A.
POSITION C – Rotate the crankshaft 270 degrees (three quarter revolution) clockwise from POSITION B.

Position of crankshaft for preliminary valve adjustment—302, 351, 400, 429 and 460 V8

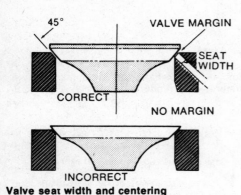

Valve seat width and centering

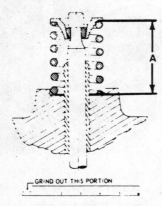

Measure the valve spring installed height (A) with a modified steel rule

1968-69 302 V8

NOTE: *This procedure for the early 302 V8 engine is designed for engines in which the rocker arm mounting studs do not incorporate a positive stop shoulder on the mounting stud. these engines were originally equipped with this kind of stud. However, due to pro-*

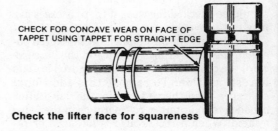

CHECK FOR CONCAVE WEAR ON FACE OF TAPPET USING TAPPET FOR STRAIGHT EDGE

Check the lifter face for squareness

duction differences, it is possible some early 8-302 engines may be encountered that are equipped with positive stop rocker arm mounting studs. Before following this procedure, verify that the rocker arm mounting studs do not incorporate a positive stop shoulder. On studs without a positive stop, the shank portion of the stud that is exposed just above the cylinder head is the same diameter as the threaded portion, at the top of the stud, to which the rocker arm retaining nut attaches. If the shank portion of the stud is of greater diameter than the threaded portion, this identifies it as a positive stop rocker arm stud and the procedure for the 8-351 engine should be followed.

1. Crank the engine until the No. 1 cylinder is at TDC of the compression stroke and the timing pointer is aligned with the mark on the crankshaft damper.

2. Scribe a mark on the damper at this point.

3. Scribe three more marks on the damper, dividing the damper into quarters (see illustration).

4. With mark **A** aligned with the timing pointer, adjust the valves on the No. 1 cylinder by backing off the adjusting nut until the pushrod has free play in it. Then, tighten the nut until there is no free play in the rocker arm. this can be determined by turning the pushrod while tightening the nut; when the pushrod can no longer be turned, all clearance has been re-

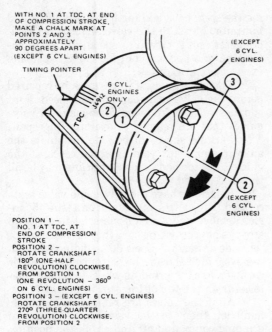

WITH NO. 1 AT TDC, AT END
OF COMPRESSION STROKE,
MAKE A CHALK MARK AT
POINTS 2 AND 3
APPROXIMATELY
90 DEGREES APART
(EXCEPT 6 CYL. ENGINES)

TIMING POINTER

(EXCEPT
6 CYL.
ENGINES)

6 CYL.
ENGINES
ONLY

TDC

(EXCEPT
6 CYL.
ENGINES)

POSITION 1 –
NO. 1 AT TDC, AT
END OF COMPRESSION
STROKE
POSITION 2 –
ROTATE CRANKSHAFT
180° (ONE-HALF
REVOLUTION) CLOCKWISE,
FROM POSITION 1
(ONE REVOLUTION – 360°
ON 6 CYL. ENGINES)
POSITION 3 – (EXCEPT 6 CYL. ENGINES)
ROTATE CRANKSHAFT
270° (THREE-QUARTER
REVOLUTION) CLOCKWISE,
FROM POSITION 2

Crankshaft pulley marking for preliminary valve adjustment

moved. After the clearance has been removed, tighten the nut an additional ¾ of a turn.

5. Repeat this procedure for each valve, turning the crankshaft ¼ turn to the next mark each time and following the engine firing order of 1-5-4-2-6-3-7-8.

All Other V8 Engines

1. Crank the engine until the No. 1 cylinder is at TDC of the compression stroke and the timing pointer is aligned with the mark on the crankshaft damper.

2. Scribe a mark on the damper at this point.

3. Scribe two additional marks on the damper (see illustration).

4. With the timing pointer aligned with mark A on the damper, tighten the following valves to the specified torque:

- 255, 302, 429, and 460 No. 1, 7 and 8 Intake; No. 1, 5, and 4 exhaust.
- 351 and 400 No. 1, 4, and 8 intake; No. 1, 3, and 7 exhaust.

5. Rotate the crankshaft 180° to point **B** and tighten the following valves:

- 255, 302, 429 and 460 No. 5 and 4 intake; No. 2 and 6 exhaust
- 351 and 400 No. 3 and 7 intake; No. 2 and 6 exhaust

6. Rotate the crankshaft 270° to point **C** and tighten the following valves:

- 255, 302, 429 and 460 No. 2, 3, and 6 intake; No. 7, 3 and 8 exhaust.

- 351 and 400 No. 2, 5, and 6 intake; No. 4, 5, and 8 exhaust.

7. Rocker arm tightening specifications are: 255, 302 and 351W tighten nut until it contacts the rocker shoulder, then torque to 18-20 ft. lbs.; 351C and 400 tighten bolt to 18-25 ft. lbs.; 428 and 460 tighten nut until it contacts rocker shoulder, then torque to 18-22 ft. lbs.

Valves and Springs

REMOVAL AND INSTALLATION

1. Block the head on its side, or install a pair of head-holding brackets made especially for valve removal.

2. Use a socket slightly larger than the valve stem and keepers, place the socket over the valve stem and gently hit the socket with a plastic hammer to break loose any varnish buildup.

3. Remove the valve keepers, retainer, spring shield and valve spring using a valve spring compressor (the locking C-clamp type is the easiest kind to use).

4. Put the parts in a separate container numbered for the cylinder being worked on; do not mix them with other parts removed.

5. Remove and discard the valve stem oil seals. A new seal will be used at assembly time.

6. Remove the valves from the cylinder head and place them, in order, through numbered holes punched in a stiff piece of cardboard or wood valve holding stick.

NOTE: *The exhaust valve stems, on some en-*

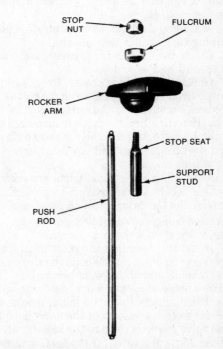

STOP
NUT

FULCRUM

ROCKER
ARM

STOP SEAT

SUPPORT
STUD

PUSH
ROD

Positive stop rocker arm stud and nut

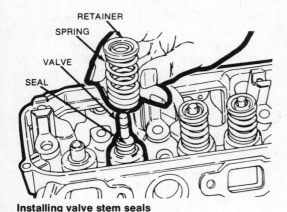

RETAINER
SPRING
VALVE
SEAL

Installing valve stem seals

gines, are equipped with small metal caps. Take care not to lose the caps. Make sure to re-install them at assembly time. Replace any caps that are worn.

7. Use an electric drill and rotary wire brush to clean the intake and exhaust valve ports, combustion chamber and valve seats. In some cases, the carbon will need to be chipped away. Use a blunt pointed drift for carbon chipping. Be careful around the valve seat areas.

8. Use a wire valve guide cleaning brush and safe solvent to clean the valve guides.

9. Clean the valves with a revolving wires brush. Heavy carbon deposits may be removed with the blunt drift.

NOTE: *When using a wire brush to clean carbon on the valve ports, valves etc., be sure that the deposits are actually removed, rather than burnished.*

10. Wash and clean all valve springs, keepers, retaining caps etc., in safe solvent.

11. Clean the head with a brush and some safe solvent and wipe dry.

12. Check the head for cracks. Cracks in the cylinder head usually start around an exhaust valve seat because it is the hottest part of the combustion chamber. If a crack is suspected but cannot be detected visually have the area checked with dye penetrant or other method by the machine shop.

13. After all cylinder head parts are reasonably clean, check the valve stem-to-guide clearance. If a dial indicator is not on hand, a visual inspection can give you a fairly good idea if the guide, valve stem or both are worn.

14. Insert the valve into the guide until slight away from the valve seat. Wiggle the valve sideways. A small amount of wobble is normal, excessive wobble means a worn guide or valve stem. If a dial indicator is on hand, mount the indicator so that the stem of the valve is at 90° to the valve stem, as close to the valve guide as possible. Move the valve off the seat, and measure the valve guide-to-stem clearance by rock-

ing the stem back and forth to actuate the dial indicator. Measure the valve stem using a micrometer and compare to specifications to determine whether stem or guide wear is causing excessive clearance.

15. The valve guide, if worn, must be repaired before the valve seats can be resurfaced. Ford supplies valves with oversize stems to fit valve guides that are reamed to oversize for repair. The machine shop will be able to handle the guide reaming for you. In some cases, if the guide is not too badly worn, knurling may be all that is required.

16. Reface, or have the valves and valve seats refaced. The valve seats should be a true 45° angle. Remove only enough material to clean up any pits or grooves. Be sure the valve seat is not too wide or narrow. Use a 60° grinding wheel to remove material from the bottom of the seat for raising and a 30° grinding wheel to remove material from the top of the seat to narrow.

17. After the valves are refaced by machine, hand lap them to the valve seat. Clean the grinding compound off and check the position of face-to-seat contact. Contact should be close to the center of the valve face. If contact is close to the top edge of the valve, narrow the seat; if too close to the bottom edge, raise the seat.

18. Valves should be refaced to a true angle of 44°. Remove only enough metal to clean up the valve face or to correct runout. If the edge of a valve head, after machining, is $\frac{1}{32}$" (0.8mm) or less replace the valve. The tip of the valve stem should also be dressed on the valve grinding machine, however, do not remove more than 0.010" (0.254mm).

19. After all valve and valve seats have been machined, check the remaining valve train parts (springs, retainers, keepers, etc.) for wear. Check the valve springs for straightness and tension.

20. Install the valves in the cylinder head and metal caps.

21. Install new valve stem oil seals.

22. Install the valve keepers, retainer, spring shield and valve spring using a valve spring compressor (the locking C-clamp type is the easiest kind to use).

23. Check the valve spring installed height, shim or replace as necessary.

CHECKING VALVE SPRINGS

Place the valve spring on a flat surface next to a carpenter's square. Measure the height of the spring, and rotate the spring against the edge of the square to measure distortion. If the spring height varies (by comparison) by more than $\frac{1}{16}$" (1.6mm) or if the distortion exceeds $\frac{1}{16}$" (1.6mm), replace the spring.

Have the valve springs tested for spring pres-

Check the valve springs:

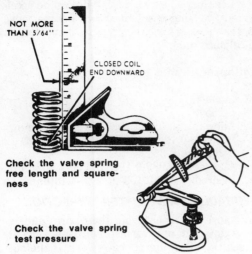

Check the valve spring free length and square-ness

Check the valve spring test pressure

Checking the valve springs

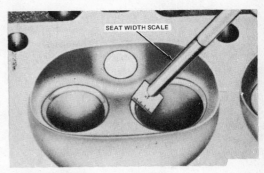

Checking the valve seat width

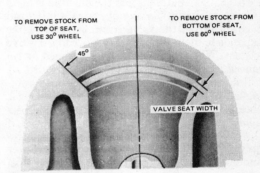

Facing the valve seat

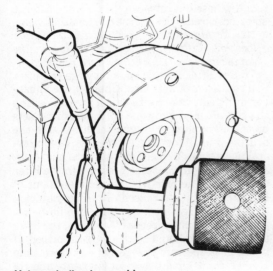

Valve grinding by machine

sure at the installed and compressed (installed height minus valve lift) height using a valve spring tester. Springs should be within one pound, plus or minus each other. Replace springs as necessary.

VALVE SPRING INSTALLED HEIGHT

After installing the valve spring, measure the distance between the spring mounting pad and the lower edge of the spring retainer. Compare the measurement to specifications. If the installed height is incorrect, add shim washers between the spring mounting pad and the spring. Use only washers designed for valve springs, available at most parts houses.

VALVE STEM OIL SEALS

When installing valve stem oil seals, ensure that a small amount of oil is able to pass the seal to lubricate the valve stems and guide walls, otherwise, excessive wear will occur.

VALVE SEATS

If the valve seat is damaged or burnt and cannot be serviced by refacing, it may be possible to have the seat machined and an insert installed. Consult an automotive machine shop for their advice.

VALVE GUIDES

Worn valve guides can, in most cases, be reamed to accept a valve with an oversized stem. Valve guides that are not excessively worn or distorted may, in some cases, be knurled rather than reamed. However, if the valve stem is worn reaming for an oversized valve stem is the answer since a new valve would be required.

Knurling is a process in which metal is displaced and raised, thereby reducing clearance. Knurling also produces excellent oil control. The possibility of knurling instead of reaming the valve guides should be discussed with a machinist.

HYDRAULIC VALVE CLEARANCE

Hydraulic valve lifters operate with zero clearance in the valve train, and because of this the rocker arms are nonadjustable. The only means by which valve system clearances can be altered is by installing over or undersize pushrods; but, because of the hydraulic lifter's natural ability to compensate for slack in the valve train, all components of all the valve system should be checked for wear if there is excessive play in the system.

When a valve in the engine is in the closed position, the valve lifter is resting on the base circle of the camshaft lobe and the pushrod is in its lowest position. To remove this additional clearance from the valve train, the valve lifter expands to maintain zero clearance in the valve system. When a rocker arm is loosened or removed from the engine, the lifter expands to it fullest travel. When the rocker arm is reinstalled on the engine, the proper valve setting is obtained by tightening the rocker arm to a specified limit. But with the lifter fully expanded, if the camshaft lobe is on a high point it will require excessive torque to compress the lifter and obtain the proper setting. Because of this, when any component of the valve system has been removed, a preliminary valve adjustment procedure must be followed to ensure that when the rocker arm is reinstalled on the engine and tightened, the camshaft lobe for that cylinder is in the low position.

To determine whether a shorter or loner push rod is necessary, make the following check:

Mark the crankshaft pulley as described under Preliminary Valve Adjustment procedure. Follow each step in the procedure. As each valve is positioned, mount a suitable hydraulic lifter compressor tool on the rocker arm. Slowly apply pressure to bleed down the lifter until the plunger is completely bottomed. Take care to avoid excessive pressure that might bend the pushrod. Hold the lifter in bottom position and check the available clearance between the rocker arm and the valve stem tip with a feeler gauge. If the clearance is less than specified, install an undersized pushrod. If the clearance is greater than specified, install an oversized pushrod. When compressing the valve spring to remove the pushrods, be sure the piston in the individual cylinder is below TDC to avoid contact between the valve and the piston. To replace a pushrod, it will be necessary to remove the valve rocker arm shaft assembly on inline engines. Upon replacement of a valve pushrod, valve rocker arm shaft assembly or hydraulic valve lifter, the engine should not be cranked or rotated until the hydraulic lifters have had an opportunity to leak down to their normal operation position. The leak down rate can be accelerated by using the tool shown on the valve rocker arm and applying pressure in a direction to collapse the lifter.

Collapsed tappet gap

V8 Engines
- 8-255
  Allowable: 0.098-0.198″ (2.489-5.029mm)
  Desired: 0.123-0.173″ (3.124-4.394mm)
- 8-302 and 8-351
  Allowable: 0.089-0.193″ (2.260-4.902mm)
  Desired: 0.096-0.163″ (2.438-4.140mm)

HYDRAULIC VALVE LIFTER INSPECTION

Remove the lifters from their bores and remove any gum and varnish with safe solvent. Check the lifters for concave wear. If the bottom of the lifter is worn concave or flat, replace the lifter. Lifters are built with a convex bottom, flatness indicates wear. If a worn lifter is detected, carefully check the camshaft for wear.

NOTE: *Mark lifters for cylinder and position location. Lifters must be reinstalled in the same bore from which they were removed.*

To test lifter leak down, submerge the lifter in a container of kerosene. Chuck a used pushrod or its equivalent into a drill press. Position the container of kerosene so the pushrod acts on the lifter plunger. Pump the lifter with the drill press until resistance increases. Pump several more times to bleed any air from the lifter. Apply very firm, constant pressure to the lifter and observe the rate which fluid bleeds out of the lifter. If the lifter bleeds down very quickly (less than 15 seconds), the lifter should be replaced. If the time exceeds 60 seconds, the lifter is sticking and should be cleaned or replaced. If the lifter is operating properly (leak down time 15-60 seconds) and not worn, lubricate and reinstall it in the engine.

Oil Pan

REMOVAL AND INSTALLATION

6-240

1. Drain the crankcase and also drain the cooling system.

CAUTION: *When draining the coolant, keep in mind that cats and dogs are attracted by the ethylene glycol antifreeze, and are quite likely to drink any that is left in an uncovered container or in puddles on the ground. This will prove fatal in sufficient quantity. Always drain the coolant into a sealable container. Coolant should be reused unless it is contaminated or several years old.*

2. Remove the radiator.

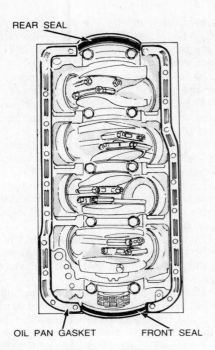

REAR SEAL

OIL PAN GASKET   FRONT SEAL

Typical oil pan gasket and seal installation

3. Raise the vehicle on a hoist.

4. Remove the engine front support insulator to support bracket nuts and washers on both supports. Raise the front of the engine with a transmission jack and wood block and place 1″ (25mm) thick wood blocks between the front support insulators and support brackets. Lower the engine and remove the transmission jack.

5. Remove the oil pan attaching bolts and lower the pan to the crossmember. Remove the 2 oil pump inlet tube and screw assembly bolts and drop the assembly in the pan. Remove the oil pan. Remove the oil pump inlet tube attaching bolts. Remove the inlet tube and screen assembly from the oil pump and leave it in the bottom of the oil pan. Remove the oil pan gaskets. Remove the inlet tube and screen from the oil pan.

6. Clean the gasket surfaces of the oil pump, oil pan and cylinder block. Remove the rear main bearing cap to oil pan seal and cylinder front cover to oil pan seal. Clean the seal grooves.

7. Apply oil resistant sealer in the cavities between the bearing cap and cylinder block. Install a new seal in the rear main bearing cap and apply a bead of oil resistant sealer to the tapered ends of the seal.

8. Install new side gaskets on the oil pan with oil resistant sealer. Position a new oil pan to cylinder front cover seal on the oil pan.

9. Clean the inlet tube and screen assembly and place it in the oil pan.

10. Position the oil pan under the engine. Install the inlet tube and screen assembly on the oil pump with a new gasket. Tighten the screws to 5-7 ft. lbs. Position the oil pan against the cylinder block and install the attaching bolts. Tighten the bolts in sequence to 10-12 ft. lbs.

11. Raise the engine with a transmission jack and remove the wood blocks from the engine front supports. Lower the engine until the front support insulators are positioned on the support brackets. Install the washers and nuts on the insulator studs and tighten the nuts.

12. Install the starter and connect the starter cable.

13. Lower the vehicle. Install the radiator.

14. Fill the crankcase and cooling system.

15. Start the engine and check for coolant and oil leaks.

1968-69 8-302, 8-351W

1. Remove oil level dipstick. Drain oil pan. CAUTION: *The EPA warns that prolonged contact with used engine oil may cause a number of skin disorders, including cancer! You should make every effort to minimize your exposure to used engine oil. Protective gloves should be worn when changing the oil. Wash your hands and any other exposed skin areas as soon as possible after exposure to used engine oil. Soap and water, or waterless hand cleaner should be used.*

2. Disconnect stabilizer bar from lower control arms, and pull ends down.

3. Remove oil pan attaching bolts and position pan on front crossmember.

4. Remove one oil inlet tube bolt and loosen the other to position tube out of way to remove pan.

5. Turn crankshaft as required for clearance to remove pan.

6. Install in reverse of above.

1970-78 8-302, 8-351W

1. Remove the oil dipstick (on pan entry models only).

2. Remove the bolts attaching the fan shroud to the radiator and position the shroud over the fan.

3. Remove the nuts and lockwashers attaching the engine support insulators to the chassis bracket.

4. If equipped with an automatic transmission, disconnect the oil cooler line at the left side of the radiator.

5. Raise the engine and place wood blocks under the engine supports.

6. Drain the crankcase.

CAUTION: *The EPA warns that prolonged*

contact with used engine oil may cause a number of skin disorders, including cancer! You should make every effort to minimize your exposure to used engine oil. Protective gloves should be worn when changing the oil. Wash your hands and any other exposed skin areas as soon as possible after exposure to used engine oil. Soap and water, or waterless hand cleaner should be used.

7. Remove the oil pan attaching bolts and lower the oil pan onto the crossmember.

8. Remove the two bolts attaching the oil pump pickup tube to the oil pump. Remove nut attaching oil pump pickup tube to the number 3 main bearing cap stud. Lower the pick-up tube and screen into the oil pan.

9. Remove the oil pan from the vehicle.

10. Clean oil pan, inlet tube and gasket surfaces. Inspect the gasket sealing surface for damages and distortion due to overtightening of the bolts. Repair and straighten as required.

11. Position a new oil pan gasket and seal to the cylinder block.

12. Position the oil pick-up tube and screen to the oil pump, and install the lower attaching bolt and gasket loosely. Install nut attaching to number 3 main bearing cap stud.

13. Place the oil pan on the crossmember. Install the upper pick-up tube bolt. Tighten the pick-up tube bolts.

14. Position the oil pan to the cylinder block and install the attaching bolts. Tighten to 10-12 ft. lbs.

All Other V8 Engines Through 1978

1. Remove the shroud from the radiator and position it rearward over the fan. Disconnect the battery negative cable.

2. Raise and support the car on jackstands. Drain the oil. Position the transmission cooler lines out of the way, if necessary. Remove the sway bar attaching bolts and move the sway bar forward on the struts.

CAUTION: *The EPA warns that prolonged contact with used engine oil may cause a number of skin disorders, including cancer! You should make every effort to minimize your exposure to used engine oil. Protective gloves should be worn when changing the oil. Wash your hands and any other exposed skin areas as soon as possible after exposure to used engine oil. Soap and water, or waterless hand cleaner should be used.*

3. Remove nuts and lockwashers from the engine front support insulator-to-intermediate support bracket.

4. Install a block of wood on a jack and position a jack under the leading edge of the pan.

5. Raise the engine approximately 1¼" and insert a 1" block between the insulator and

crossmember. Remove the floor jack. On 8-351C, 8-351M, 8-400 and 8-460 V8s, remove the starter. On 8-460 V8s through 1977, remove the oil filter.

6. Remove the oil pan attaching screws and lower the pan to the frame crossmember.

7. Turn the crankshaft to obtain clearance between the crankshaft counterweight and the rear of the pan.

8. Remove the oil pump attaching bolts.

9. Position the tube and the screen out of the way and remove the pan.

10. To install, clean the gasket mounting surfaces thoroughly. Coat the surfaces on the block and pan with sealer. Position the pan side gaskets on the engine block.

11. Install the front cover oil seal on the cover, with the tabs over the pan side gaskets. Install the rear main cap seal with the tabs over the pan side gaskets.

12. Install the pan mounting bolts, tightening them on each side from the center outwards to 9-11 ft. lbs. for $5/16$" bolts, 7-9 ft. lbs. of ¼" bolts. Complete the installation by reversing Steps 1-5.

1979-85 Without EGR Cooler

1. Remove the air cleaner and disconnect the accelerator and kickdown rods at the carburetor.

2. Remove the accelerator mounting bracket bolts and remove the bracket.

3. Remove the fan shroud attaching bolts and position the shroud up and over the fan.

4. Disconnect the windshield wiper motor wiring from the harness and remove the wiper motor.

5. Disconnect the windshield washer hose.

6. Remove the wiper motor mounting cover.

7. Remove the dipstick and remove the dipstick retaining bolt from the exhaust manifold.

CAUTION: *The EPA warns that prolonged contact with used engine oil may cause a number of skin disorders, including cancer! You should make every effort to minimize your exposure to used engine oil. Protective gloves should be worn when changing the oil. Wash your hands and any other exposed skin areas as soon as possible after exposure to used engine oil. Soap and water, or waterless hand cleaner should be used.*

8. Raise the car and support on jackstands. Drain the crankcase.

NOTE: *Engines with dual pump must be drained by removing both drain plugs.*

9. Disconnect the fuel line at the fuel pump.

10. Disconnect the inlet pipes from the exhaust manifold.

11. Remove the dipstick tube from the oil pan.

12. Loosen the rear engine mount attaching

nuts. Remove the engine mount through bolts.

13. Remove the shift selector crossover bolts and remove the crossover.

14. Disconnect the transmission kickdown rod.

15. Remove the torque converter cover.

16. Remove the brake line retainer from the front crossmember.

17. Place a jack under the engine and raise it as far as it will go.

18. Place a small block of wood between each engine mount and the chassis brackets to support the engine. Remove the jack.

19. Remove the oil pan attaching bolts and lower the oil pan.

20. Remove the three oil pump attaching bolts from the cylinder block and allow the pump to fall into the pan.

21. Remove the oil pan from the car.

22. Inspect the oil pan for damage. Thoroughly clean the oil pump pick-up tube and screen assembly.

23. Install the front cover oil seal on the cover, with the tabs over the pan side gaskets. Install the rear main cap seal with the tabs over the pan side gaskets.

24. Position the pan under the car and install the pump.

25. Install the pan mounting bolts, tightening them on each side from the center outwards to 9-11 ft. lbs. for $^5/_{16}"$ bolts, 7-9 ft. lbs. of $^1/_4"$ bolts. Complete the installation by reversing Steps 1-5.

26. Connect the engine mounts. Install the jack.

27. Install the brake line retainer at the front crossmember.

28. Install the torque converter cover.

29. Connect the transmission kickdown rod.

30. Install the shift selector crossover bolts and install the crossover.

31. Install the engine mount through bolts. Tighten the rear engine mount attaching nuts.

32. Install the dipstick tube.

33. Connect the inlet pipes at the exhaust manifold.

34. Connect the fuel line at the fuel pump.

35. Lower the car.

36. Fill the crankcase.

37. Install the dipstick and install the dipstick retaining bolt from the exhaust manifold.

38. Install the wiper motor mounting cover.

39. Connect the windshield washer hose.

40. Install the wiper motor. Connect the windshield wiper motor wiring at the harness.

41. Install the fan shroud.

42. Install the accelerator mounting bracket.

43. Connect the accelerator and kickdown rods at the carburetor.

44. Install the air cleaner.

1979-85 with EGR Cooler, EEC, or MCU

1. Refer to Steps 1-7 of the above procedure.

2. Remove the Thermactor air pump tube retaining clamp. Remove the air cross-over tube from the rear of the engine.

3. Raise the car and drain the crankcase.

CAUTION: *The EPA warns that prolonged contact with used engine oil may cause a number of skin disorders, including cancer! You should make every effort to minimize your exposure to used engine oil. Protective gloves should be worn when changing the oil. Wash your hands and any other exposed skin areas as soon as possible after exposure to used engine oil. Soap and water, or waterless hand cleaner should be used.*

4. Remove the filler tube from the oil pan and drain the transmission.

5. Remove the starter motor.

6. Remove the fuel line from the fuel pump.

7. Disconnect the inlet pipes from the exhaust manifold.

8. Remove the exhaust gas oxygen sensor from the exhaust manifold.

9. Disconnect the air tube attaching clamps from the torque converter.

10. Remove the torque converter inspection cover.

11. Disconnect the exhaust pipes at the catalytic converter outlet.

12. Remove the catalytic converter secondary air tube. Remove the inlet pipes at the exhaust manifold.

13. Refer to Steps 11-23 of the 1978 procedure.

1986-88 V8 Engines

WARNING: *On vehicles equipped with a dual sump oil pan, both drain plugs must be removed to thoroughly drain the crankcase.*

When raising the engine for oil pan removal clearance, drain the cooling system, disconnect the hoses, check the fan-to-radiator clearance when jacking. Remove the radiator if clearance is inadequate.

CAUTION: *When draining the coolant, keep in mind that cats and dogs are attracted by the ethylene glycol antifreeze, and are quite likely to drink any that is left in an uncovered container or in puddles on the ground. This will prove fatal in sufficient quantity. Always drain the coolant into a sealable container. Coolant should be reused unless it is contaminated or several years old.*

1. Remove the fan shroud attaching bolts, positioning the fan shroud back over the fan. Remove the dipstick and tube assembly. Disconnect the negative battery cable.

2. Drain the crankcase.

CAUTION: *The EPA warns that prolonged contact with used engine oil may cause a number of skin disorders, including cancer! You should make every effort to minimize your exposure to used engine oil. Protective gloves should be worn when changing the oil. Wash your hands and any other exposed skin areas as soon as possible after exposure to used engine oil. Soap and water, or waterless hand cleaner should be used.*

3. On rack and pinion models disconnect the steering flex coupling. Remove the two bolts attaching the steering gear to the main crossmember and let the steering gear rest on the frame away from the oil pan. Disconnect the power steering hose retaining clamp from the frame.

4. Remove the starter motor.

5. Remove the idler arm bracket retaining bolts (models equipped) and pull the linkage down and out of the way.

6. Disconnect and plug the fuel line from the gas tank at the fuel pump. Disconnect and lower the exhaust pipe/converter assemblies if they will interfere with pan removal/installation. Raise the engine and place two wood blocks between the engine mounts and the vehicle frame. Remove the converter inspection cover.

WARNING: *On fuel injected models, depressurize the system prior to line disconnection.*

7. Remove the rear K-brace (four bolts).

8. Remove the oil pan attaching bolts and lower the oil pan on the frame.

9. Remove the oil pump attaching bolts and the inset tube attaching nut from the No.3 main bearing cap stud and lower the oil pump into the oil pan.

10. Remove the oil pan, rotating the crankshaft as necessary to clear the counterweights.

11. Clean the gasket mounting surfaces thoroughly. Coat the surfaces on the block and pan with sealer. Position the pan side gaskets on the engine block. Install the front cover oil seal on the cover, with the tabs over the pan side gaskets. Install the rear main cap seal with the tabs over the pan side gaskets.

12. Position the oil pump and inlet tube into the oil pan. Slide the oil pan into position under the engine. With the oil pump intermediate shaft in position in the oil pump, position the oil pump on the cylinder block, and the inlet tube on the stud on the No. 3 main bearing cap attaching bolt. Install the attaching bolts and nut and tighten to specification.

Position the oil pan on the engine and install the attaching bolts. Tighten the bolts (working from the center toward the ends) 9-11 ft. lbs. for $5/16$" bolts and 7-9 ft. lbs. for $1/4$" bolts.

13. Position the steering gear on the main crossmember. Install the two attaching bolts and tighten them to specification. Connect the steering flex coupling.

14. Position the rear K-braces and install the four attaching bolts.

15. Raise the engine and remove the wood blocks.

16. Lower the engine and install the engine mount attaching bolts. Tighten them to specification. Install the converter inspection cover.

17. Install the oil dipstick and tube assembly, and fill crankcase with the specified engine oil. Install the idler arm.

18. Connect the transmission oil cooler lines. Connect the battery cable.

19. Position the shroud on the radiator and install the two attaching bolts. Start the engine and check for leaks.

Oil Pump

REMOVAL AND INSTALLATION

1. Remove the oil pan as outlined under the previous applicable Oil Pan Removal and Installation procedure.

2. On 8-255, 8-302 and 8-351W applications, remove the oil pump inlet tube and screen assembly.

3. Remove the oil pump attaching bolts. Lower the oil pump, gasket, and intermediate driveshaft from the crankcase. If not already removed, remove and clean the inlet tube and screen assembly.

4. To install, prime the oil pump by filling either the inlet or outlet port with engine oil. Rotate the pump shaft to distribute the oil within the pump body.

5. Position the intermediate driveshaft into

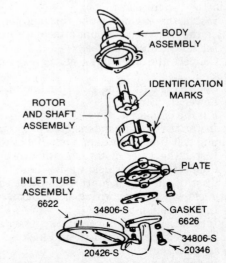

Oil pump used on 6 and 8 cylinder engines

NOTE: INNER TO OUTER ROTOR
TIP CLEARANCE MUST
NOT EXCEED .012 WITH
FEELER GAUGE INSERTED
1/2" MINIMUM AND ROTORS
REMOVED FROM PUMP
HOUSING.

Checking inner rotor tip clearance

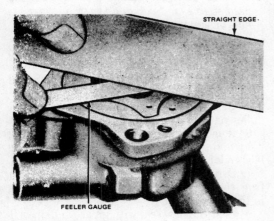

STRAIGHT EDGE

FEELER GAUGE

Checking rotor end play

the distributor socket. With the shaft firmly seated in the socket, the stop on the shaft should contact the roof of the crankcase. Remove the shaft and position the stop as necessary.

6. Insert the intermediate driveshaft into the oil pump. Using a new gasket, install the pump and shaft as an assembly. Do not attempt to force the pump into position if it will not seat readily. If necessary, rotate the intermediate driveshaft hex into a new position so that it will mesh with the distributor shaft.

7. Torque the oil pump attaching bolts to 12-15 ft. lbs. on the 6-240 engines, 22-32 ft. lbs. on the 8-255, 8-302 and 8-351W, 25-35 ft. lbs. on the 8-351C, 8-351M and 8-400, and 20-25 ft. lbs. on the 8-390, 8-428, 8-429, 8-460, 8-462.

8. Clean and install the inlet tube and screen assembly.

9. Install the oil pan as previously outlined under Oil Pan Removal and Installation.

OVERHAUL

1. Wash all parts in solvent and dry them thoroughly with compressed air. Use a brush to clean the inside of the pump housing and the pressure relief valve chamber. Be sure all dirt and metal particles are removed.

2. Check the inside of the pump housing and the outer race and rotor for damage or excessive wear or scoring.

3. Check the mating surface of the pump cover for wear. If the cover mating surface is worn, scored, or grooved, replace the pump.

4. Measure the inner rotor tip clearance.

5. With the rotor assembly installed in the housing, place a straight edge over the rotor assembly and the housing. Measure the clearance (rotor end play) between the straight edge and the rotor and the outer race.

6. Check the drive shaft to housing bearing clearance by measuring the OD of the shaft and the ID of the housing bearing.

7. Components of the oil pump are not serviced. If any part of the pump requires replacement, replace the complete pump assembly.

8. Inspect the relief valve spring to see if it is collapsed or worn.

9. Check the relief valve piston for scores and free operation in the bore.

Crankshaft Pulley (Vibration Damper)

REMOVAL AND INSTALLATION

1. Remove the fan shroud, as required. If necessary, drain the cooling system and remove the radiator. Remove drive belts from pulley.

CAUTION: *When draining the coolant, keep in mind that cats and dogs are attracted by the ethylene glycol antifreeze, and are quite likely to drink any that is left in an uncovered container or in puddles on the ground. This will prove fatal in sufficient quantity. Always drain the coolant into a sealable container.*

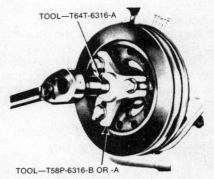

TOOL—T64T-6316-A

TOOL—T58P-6316-B OR -A

Removing crankshaft damper—six-cylinder and 390, 428 V8

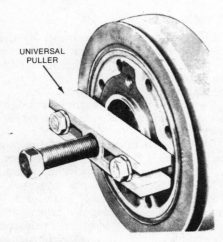

Removing crankshaft damper—V8 except 390, 428, 462 V8

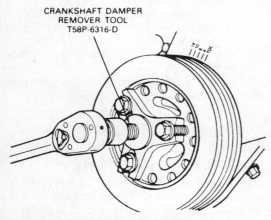

Removing the 6-300 crankshaft damper

Coolant should be reused unless it is contaminated or several years old.

2. On those engines with a separate pulley, remove the retaining bolts and separate the pulley from the vibration damper.

3. Remove the vibration damper/pulley retaining bolt from the crankshaft end.

4. Using a puller, remove the damper/pulley from the crankshaft.

5. Upon installation, align the key slot of the pulley hub to the crankshaft key. Complete the assembly in the reverse order of removal. Torque the retaining bolts to specifications.

Timing Gear Cover and Oil Seal
REMOVAL AND INSTALLATION

6-240

1. Drain the cooling system and disconnect the radiator upper hose at the coolant outlet el-

bow and remove the two upper radiator retaining bolts.

CAUTION: *When draining the coolant, keep in mind that cats and dogs are attracted by the ethylene glycol antifreeze, and are quite likely to drink any that is left in an uncovered container or in puddles on the ground. This will prove fatal in sufficient quantity. Always drain the coolant into a sealable container. Coolant should be reused unless it is contaminated or several years old.*

2. Raise the vehicle and drain the crankcase.

CAUTION: *The EPA warns that prolonged contact with used engine oil may cause a number of skin disorders, including cancer! You should make every effort to minimize your exposure to used engine oil. Protective gloves should be worn when changing the oil. Wash your hands and any other exposed skin areas as soon as possible after exposure to used engine oil. Soap and water, or waterless hand cleaner should be used.*

3. Remove the splash shield and the automatic transmission oil cooling lines, if so equipped, then remove the radiator.

4. Loosen and remove the fan belt, fan and pulley.

5. Use a gear puller to remove the crankshaft pulley damper.

6. Remove the cylinder front cover retaining bolts and gently pry the cover away from the block. Remove the gasket.

7. Drive out the old seal with a pin punch from the rear of the cover. Clean out the recess in the cover.

8. Coat the new seal with grease and drive it into the cover until it is fully seated. Check the seal to make sure that the spring around the seal is in the proper position.

9. Clean the cylinder front cover and the gasket surface of the cylinder block. Apply an oil resistant sealer to the new front cover gasket and install the gasket onto the cover.

10. Position the front cover assembly over the end of the crankshaft and against the cylinder block. Start, but do not tighten, the cover and pan attaching screws. Slide a front cover alignment tool (Ford part no. T68P-6019-A or equivalent) over the crank stub and into the seal bore of the cover. Tighten all front cover and oil pan attaching screws to 12-18 ft. lbs. front cover; 10-15 ft. lbs. oil pan, tightening the oil pan screws first.

NOTE: *Trim away the exposed portion of the old oil pan gasket flush with the front of the engine block. Cut and position the required portion of a new gasket to the oil pan and apply sealer to both sides.*

11. Lubricate the hub of the crankshaft damper pulley with Lubriplate® to prevent

damage to the seal during installation or on initial starting of the engine.

12. Install and assemble the remaining components in the reverse order of removal, starting from Step 4. Start the engine and check for leaks.

Timing Cover and Chain

REMOVAL AND INSTALLATION

V8 Engines, Except the 8-460

1. Drain the cooling system, remove the air cleaner and disconnect the battery.

CAUTION: *When draining the coolant, keep in mind that cats and dogs are attracted by the ethylene glycol antifreeze, and are quite likely to drink any that is left in an uncovered container or in puddles on the ground. This will prove fatal in sufficient quantity. Always drain the coolant into a sealable container. Coolant should be reused unless it is contaminated or several years old.*

2. Disconnect the transmission cooler lines and radiator hoses and remove the radiator.

3. Disconnect the heater hose at water pump. Slide the water pump by-pass hose clamp toward the pump.

4. Loosen the alternator mounting bolts at the alternator. Remove the alternator support bolt at the water pump. Remove the Thermactor® pump on all engines so equipped. If equipped with power steering or air conditioning, unbolt the component, remove the belt,

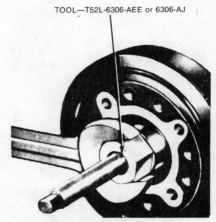

TOOL—T52L-6306-AEE or 6306-AJ

Installing crankshaft damper—all engines

FUEL PUMP ECCENTRIC   DOWEL

CRANKSHAFT FRONT OIL SLINGER

Fuel pump eccentric and front oil slinger installed—V8 except 390, 428, 462

TIMING MARKS

Aligning timing marks—all V8s

and lay the pump or compressor aside with the lines attached.

5. Remove the fan, spacer, pulley, and drive belt.

6. Drain the crankcase.

CAUTION: *The EPA warns that prolonged contact with used engine oil may cause a number of skin disorders, including cancer! You should make every effort to minimize your exposure to used engine oil. Protective gloves should be worn when changing the oil. Wash your hands and any other exposed skin areas as soon as possible after exposure to*

REFERENCE POINT

Measuring timing chain deflection—typical

used engine oil. *Soap and water, or waterless hand cleaner should be used.*

7. Remove the pulley from the crankshaft pulley adapter. Remove the capscrew and washer from the front end of the crankshaft. Remove the crankshaft pulley adapter with a puller.

8. On 390 and 428 V8, use a suitable tool to pull the crankshaft sleeve away from the cylinder front cover. Remove the sleeve from the engine.

9. Disconnect the fuel pump outlet line at the pump. Remove the fuel pump retaining bolts and lay the pump to the side. Remove the engine oil dipstick.

10. Remove the front cover attaching bolts.

11. Remove the crankshaft oil slinger if so equipped.

12. Check timing chain deflection.

13. Rotate the engine until the sprocket timing marks are aligned as shown in the valve timing illustration.

14. Remove the crankshaft sprocket capscrew, washers, and fuel pump eccentric. Slide both sprockets and chain forward and off as an assembly.

15. Position the sprockets and chain on the camshaft and crankshaft with both timing marks dot-to-dot on a centerline. Install the fuel pump eccentric, washers and sprocket attaching bolt. Torque the sprocket attaching bolt to 40-45 ft. lbs.

16. Install the crankshaft front oil slinger.

17. Clean the front cover and mating surfaces of old gasket material. Install a new oil seal in the cover. Use a seal driver tool, if available.

18. Coat a new cover gasket with sealer and position it on the block.

NOTE: *Trim away the exposed portion of the oil pan gasket flush with the cylinder block. Cut and position the required portion of a*

new gasket to the oil pan, applying sealer to both sides of it.

19. Install the front cover, using a crankshaft-to-cover alignment tool. Coat the threads of the attaching bolts with sealer. Torque the attaching bolt to 12-15 ft. lbs.

20. Install the fuel pump and connect the fuel pump outlet tube.

21. Install the crankshaft pulley adapter and torque the attaching bolt. Install the crankshaft pulley.

22. Install the water pump pulley, drive belt, spacer and fan.

23. Install the alternator support bolt at the water pump. Tighten the alternator mounting bolts. Adjust the drive belt tension. Install the Thermactor® pump if so equipped.

24. Install the radiator and connect all coolant and heater hoses. Connect the battery cables.

25. Refill the cooling system and the crankcase. Install the dipstick.

26. Start the engine and operate it at fast idle.

27. Check for leaks, install the air cleaner. Adjust the ignition timing and make all final adjustments.

8-460

1. Drain the cooling system and crankcase. CAUTION: *When draining the coolant, keep in mind that cats and dogs are attracted by the ethylene glycol antifreeze, and are quite likely to drink any that is left in an uncovered container or in puddles on the ground. This will prove fatal in sufficient quantity. Always drain the coolant into a sealable container. Coolant should be reused unless it is contaminated or several years old.*

2. Remove the radiator shroud and fan.

3. Disconnect the upper and lower radiator hoses, and the automatic transmission oil cooler lines from the radiator.

4. Remove the radiator upper support and remove the radiator.

5. Loosen the alternator attaching bolts and air conditioning compressor idler pulley and remove the drive belts with the water pump pulley. Remove the bolts attaching the compressor support to the water pump and remove the bracket (support), if so equipped.

6. Remove the crankshaft pulley from the vibration damper. Remove the bolt and washer attaching the crankshaft damper and remove the damper with a puller. Remove the woodruff key from the crankshaft.

7. Loosen the by-pass hose at the water pump, and disconnect the heater return tube at the water pump.

8. Disconnect and plug the fuel inlet and out-

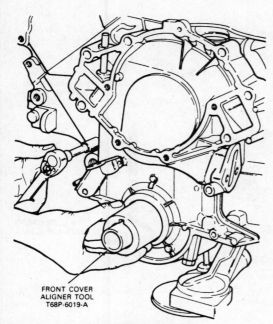

FRONT COVER
ALIGNER TOOL
T68P-6019-A

Aligning the front cover on the 8-460

let lines at the fuel pump, and remove the fuel pump.

9. Remove the bolts attaching the front cover to the cylinder block. Cut the oil pan seal flush with the cylinder block face with a thin knife blade prior to separating the cover from the cylinder block. Remove the cover and water pump as an assembly. Discard the front cover gasket and oil pan seal.

10. Transfer the water pump if a new cover is going to be installed. Clean all of the gasket sealing surfaces on both the front cover and the cylinder block.

11. Coat the gasket surface of the oil pan with sealer. Cut and position the required sections of a new seal on the oil pan. Apply sealer to the corners.

12. Drive out the old front cover oil seal with a pin punch. Clean out the seal recess in the cover. coat a new seal with Lubriplate® or equivalent grease. Install the seal, making sure the seal spring remains in the proper position. A front cover seal tool, Ford part no. T72J-117 or equivalent, makes installation easier.

13. Coat the gasket surfaces of the cylinder block and cover with sealer and position the new gasket on the block.

14. Position the front cover on the cylinder block. Use care not to damage the seal and gasket or mislocate them.

15. Coat the front cover attaching screws with sealer and install them.

NOTE: *It may be necessary to force the front cover downward to compress the oil pan seal*

in order to install the front cover attaching bolts. Use a screwdriver or drift to engage the cover screw holes through the cover and pry downward.

16. Assemble and install the remaining components in the reverse order of removal. Tighten the front cover bolts to 15-20 ft. lbs., the water pump attaching screws to 12-15 ft. lbs., the crankshaft damper to 70-90 ft. lbs., the crankshaft pulley to 35-50 ft. lbs., fuel pump to 19-27 ft. lbs., the oil pan bolts to 9-11 ft. lbs. for the $\frac{5}{16}$" screws and to 7-9 ft. lbs. for the $\frac{1}{4}$" screws, and the alternator pivot bolt to 45-57 ft. lbs.

CHECKING TIMING CHAIN DEFLECTION

To measure timing chain deflection, rotate the crankshaft clockwise to take up slack on the

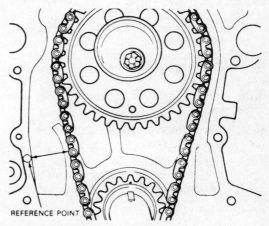

REFERENCE POINT

Checking V8 timing chain deflection

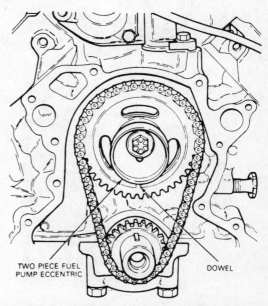

TWO PIECE FUEL
PUMP ECCENTRIC

DOWEL

Fuel pump eccentric installed on the 8-302 and 8-351

left side of chain. Choose a reference point and measure the distance from this point and the chain. Rotate the crankshaft in the opposite direction to take up slack on the right side of the chain. Force the left (slack) side of the chain out and measure the distance to the reference point chosen earlier. The difference between the two measurements is the deflection.

The timing chain should be replaced if the deflection measurement exceeded the specified limit. The deflection measurement should not exceed ½" (13mm).

CAMSHAFT ENDPLAY MEASUREMENT

The camshaft gears used on some engines are easily damaged if pried upon while the valve train load is on the camshaft. Loosen the rocker arm nuts or rocker arm shaft support bolts before checking the camshaft endplay.

Push the camshaft toward the rear of engine, install and zero a dial indicator, then pry between the camshaft gear and the block to pull the camshaft forward. If the endplay is excessive, check for correct installation of the spacer. If the spacer is installed correctly, replace the thrust plate.

MEASURING TIMING GEAR BACKLASH

Use a dial indicator installed on block to measure timing gear backlash. Hold the gear firmly against the block while making the measurement. If excessive backlash exists, replace both gears.

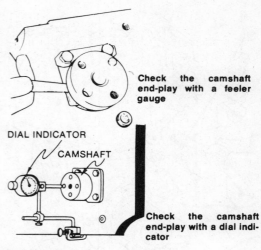

Check the camshaft end-play with a feeler gauge

DIAL INDICATOR

CAMSHAFT

Check the camshaft end-play with a dial indicator

Checking crankshaft end-play

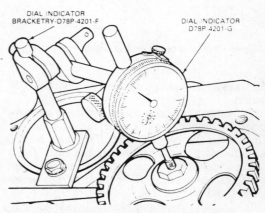

DIAL INDICATOR BRACKETRY-D78P-4201-F

DIAL INDICATOR D78P-4201-G

Checking camshaft endplay on gasoline V8s

Timing Chain

REMOVAL AND INSTALLATION

V8

1. Remove the front cover.
2. Rotate the crankshaft counterclockwise to take up the slack on the left side of the chain.
3. Establish a reference point on the cylinder block and measure from this point to the chain.
4. Rotate the crankshaft in the opposite direction to take up the slack on the right side of the chain.
5. Force the left side of the chain out with your fingers and measure the distance between the reference point and the chain. The timing chain deflection is the difference between the two measurements. If the deflection exceeds ½" (13mm), replace the timing chain and sprockets.

To replace the timing chain and sprockets:

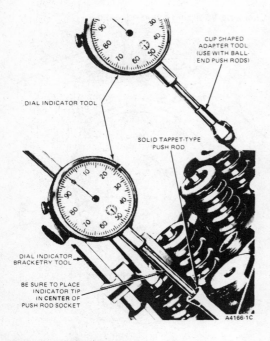

90

CUP SHAPED ADAPTER TOOL (USE WITH BALL-END PUSH RODS)

DIAL INDICATOR TOOL

SOLID TAPPET-TYPE PUSH ROD

DIAL INDICATOR BRACKETRY TOOL

BE SURE TO PLACE INDICATOR TIP IN CENTER OF PUSH ROD SOCKET

A4166-1C

Checking camshaft lobe lift

6. Turn the crankshaft until the timing marks on the sprockets are aligned vertically.

7. Remove the camshaft sprocket retaining screw and remove the fuel pump eccentric and washers.

8. Alternately slide both of the sprockets and timing chain off the crankshaft and camshaft until free of the engine.

9. Position the timing chain on the sprockets so that the timing marks on the sprockets are aligned vertically. Alternately slide the sprockets and chain onto the crankshaft and camshaft sprockets.

10. Install the fuel pump eccentric washers and attaching bolt on the camshaft sprocket. Tighten to 40-45 ft. lbs.

11. Install the front cover.

Timing Gears

REMOVAL AND INSTALLATION

6-240

1. Drain the cooling system and remove the front cover.

CAUTION: *When draining the coolant, keep in mind that cats and dogs are attracted by the ethylene glycol antifreeze, and are quite likely to drink any that is left in an uncovered container or in puddles on the ground. This*

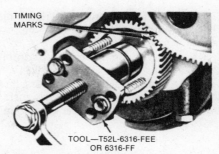
TOOL—T52L-6316-FEE
OR 6316-FF
Removing crankshaft timing gear

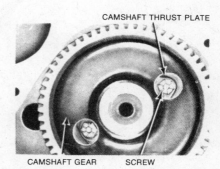
CAMSHAFT THRUST PLATE
CAMSHAFT GEAR   SCREW
Camshaft thrust plate screw locations—six-cylinder

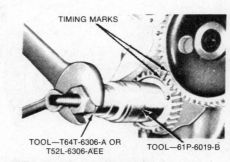
TIMING MARKS
TOOL—T64T-6306-A OR
T52L-6306-AEE   TOOL—61P-6019-B
Installing crankshaft timing gear

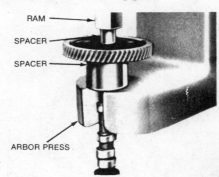
RAM
SPACER
SPACER
ARBOR PRESS
Removing the camshaft gear using a press

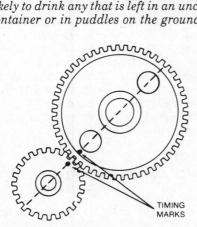
TIMING MARKS
Aligning timing marks—six-cylinder

TOOL—T64T-6306-A
TOOL—T65L-6306-A
Installing camshaft timing gear

will prove fatal in sufficient quantity. Always drain the coolant into a sealable container. Coolant should be reused unless it is contaminated or several years old.

2. Crank the engine until the timing marks on the camshaft and crankshaft gears are aligned.

3. Use a gear puller to removal both of the timing gears.

4. Before installing the timing gears, be sure that the key and spacer are properly installed. Align the gear key way with the key and install

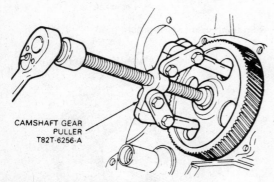

Removing the 6-300 camshaft gear

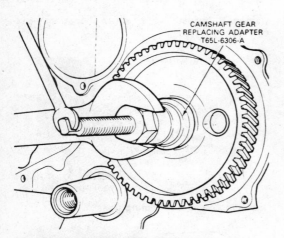

Installing the camshaft gear on the 6-300

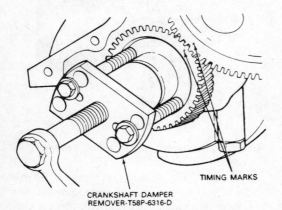

Removing the crankshaft gear from the 6-300

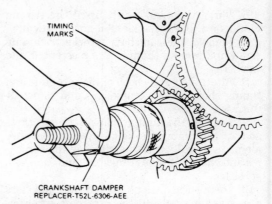

Installing the crankshaft gear on the 6-300

the gear on the camshaft. Be sure that the timing marks line up on the camshaft and the crankshaft gears and install the crankshaft gear.

5. Install the front cover, and assemble the rest of the engine in the reverse order of disassembly. Fill the cooling system.

Front Cover Oil Seal

REMOVAL AND INSTALLATION

It is recommended to replace the cover seal any time the front cover is removed.

1. With the cover removed from the car, drive the old seal from the rear of cover with a pinpunch. Clean out the recess in the cover.

2. Coat the new seal with grease and drive it into the cover until it is fully seated. Check the seal after installation to be sure the spring is properly positioned in the seal.

Camshaft

REMOVAL AND INSTALLATION

6-240

1. Remove the grille, radiator, and timing cover.

2. Remove the distributor, fuel pump, oil pan and oil pump.

3. Align the timing marks. Unbolt the camshaft thrust plate, working through the holes in the camshaft gear.

4. Loosen the rocker arms, remove the pushrods, take off the side cover and remove the valve lifter with a magnet.

5. Remove the camshaft very carefully to prevent nicking the bearings.

6. Oil the camshaft bearing journals and use Lubriplate® or something similar on the lobes. Install the camshaft, gear, and thrust plate, aligning the gear marks. Tighten down the thrust plate. Make sure that the camshaft endplay is not excessive.

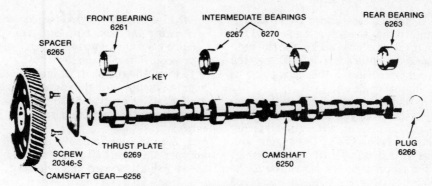

Six-cylinder camshaft and related parts

7. The last item to be replaced is the distributor. The rotor should be at the firing position for no. 1 cylinder, with the timing gear marks aligned.

V8

1. Remove the intake manifold and valley pan, if so equipped.

2. Remove the rocker covers, and either remove the rocker arm shafts or loosen the rockers on their pivots and remove the pushrods. On 390 and 428 engines it is necessary to remove the rocker arm shafts to remove the intake manifold. The pushrods must be reinstalled in their original positions.

3. Remove the valve lifters in sequence with a magnet. They must be replaced in their original positions.

4. Remove the timing gear cover and timing chain and sprockets.

5. In addition to the radiator and air conditioning condenser, if so equipped, it may be necessary to remove the front grille assembly and the hook lock assembly to gain the necessary

clearance to code the camshaft out of the front of the engine.

6. Coat the camshaft with engine oil liberally before installing it. Slide the camshaft into the engine very carefully so as not to scratch the bearing bores with the camshaft lobes. Install the camshaft thrust plate and tighten the attaching screws to 9-12 ft. lbs. Measure the camshaft end-play. If the end-play is more than 0.009″ (0.228mm), replace the thrust plate. Assemble the remaining components in the reverse order of removal.

CHECKING CAMSHAFT

Camshaft Lobe Lift

Check the lift of each lobe in consecutive order and make a note of the reading.

1. Remove the fresh air inlet tube and the air cleaner. Remove the heater hose and crankcase ventilation hoses. Remove valve rocker arm cover(s).

2. Remove the rocker arm stud nut or fulcrum bolts, fulcrum seat and rocker arm.

3. Make sure the pushrod is in the valve tap-

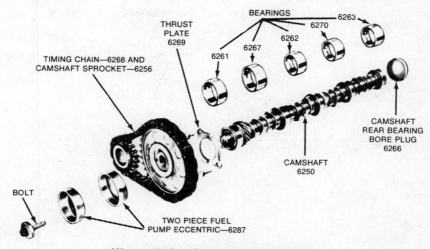

V8 camshaft and related parts—typical

pet socket. Install a dial indicator D78P-4201-B or equivalent. so that the actuating point of the indicator is in the push rod socket (or the indicator ball socket adaptor tool 6565-AB is on the end of the push rod) and in the same plane as the push rod movement.

4. Disconnect the I terminal and the S terminal at the starter relay. Install an auxiliary starter switch between the battery and S terminals of the start relay. Crank the engine with the ignition switch off. Turn the crankshaft over until the tappet is on the base circle of the camshaft lobe. At this position, the push rod will be in its lowest position.

5. Zero the dial indicator. Continue to rotate the crankshaft slowly until the push rod is in the fully raised position.

6. Compare the total lift recorded on the dial indicator with the specification shown on the Camshaft Specification chart.

To check the accuracy of the original indicator reading, continue to rotate the crankshaft until the indicator reads zero. If the left on any lobe is below specified wear limits listed, the camshaft and the valve tappet operating on the worn lobe(s) must be replaced.

7. Install the dial indicator and auxiliary starter switch.

8. Install the rocker arm, fulcrum seat and stud nut or fulcrum bolts. Check the valve clearance. Adjust if required (refer to procedure in this chapter).

9. Install the valve rocker arm cover(s) and the air cleaner.

Camshaft End Play

NOTE: *On all V8 engines, prying against the aluminum/nylon camshaft sprocket, with the valve train load on the camshaft, can break or damage the sprocket. Therefore, the rocker arm adjusting nuts must be backed off, or the rocker arm and shaft assembly must be loos-*

ened sufficiently to free the camshaft. After checking the camshaft end play, check the valve clearance. Adjust if required (refer to procedure in this chapter).

1. Push the camshaft toward the rear of the engine. Install a dial indicator (Tool D78P-4201-F, -G or equivalent so that the indicator point is on the camshaft sprocket attaching screw.

2. Zero the dial indicator. Position a prybar between the camshaft gear and the block. Pull the camshaft forward and release it. Compare the dial indicator reading with the specifications.

3. If the end play is excessive, check the spacer for correct installation before it is removed. If the spacer is correctly installed, replace the thrust plate.

4. Remove the dial indicator.

CAMSHAFT BEARING REPLACEMENT

1. Remove the engine following the procedures in this chapter and install it on a work stand.

2. Remove the camshaft, flywheel and crankshaft, following the appropriate procedures. Push the pistons to the top of the cylinder.

3. Remove the camshaft rear bearing bore plug. Remove the camshaft bearings with Tool T65L-6250-A or equivalent.

4. Select the proper size expanding collet and

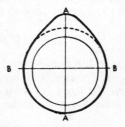

Camshaft lobe measurement

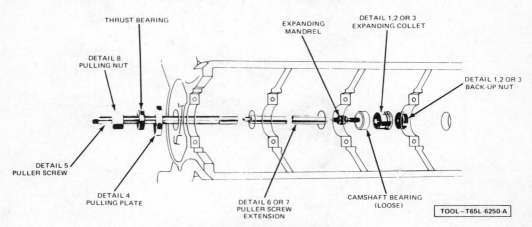

Camshaft bearing replacement

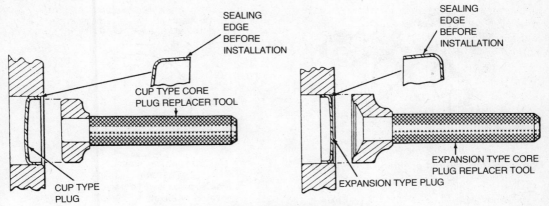

Core plugs and installation tools

back-up nut and assemble on the mandrel. With the expanding collet collapsed, install the collet assembly in the camshaft bearing and tighten the back-up nut on the expanding mandrel until the collet fits the camshaft bearing.

5. Assemble the puller screw and extension (if necessary) and install on the expanding mandrel. Wrap a cloth around the threads of the puller screw to protect the front bearing or journal. Tighten the pulling nut against the thrust bearing and pulling plate to remove the camshaft bearing. Be sure to hold a wrench on the end of the puller screw to prevent it from turning.

6. To remove the front bearing, install the puller from the rear of the cylinder block.

7. Position the new bearings at the bearing bores, and press them in place with tool T65L-6250-A or equivalent. Be sure to center the pulling plate and puller screw to avoid damage to the bearing. Failure to use the correct expanding collet can cause severe bearing damage. Align the oil holes in the bearings with the oil holes in the cylinder block before pressing bearings into place.

NOTE: *Be sure the front bearing is installed 0.020-0.035" (0.508-0.889mm) for the inline six cylinder engines, 0.005-0.020" (0.127-0.508mm) for the V8.*

8. Install the camshaft rear bearing bore plug.

9. Install the camshaft, crankshaft, flywheel and related parts, following the appropriate procedures.

10. Install the engine in the car, following procedures described earlier in this chapter.

Pistons and Connecting Rods
REMOVAL AND INSTALLATION

6-240

1. Drain the cooling system and the crankcase.

CAUTION: *When draining the coolant, keep in mind that cats and dogs are attracted by the ethylene glycol antifreeze, and are quite likely to drink any that is left in an uncovered container or in puddles on the ground. This will prove fatal in sufficient quantity. Always drain the coolant into a sealable container. Coolant should be reused unless it is contaminated or several years old.*

2. Remove the cylinder head.

3. Remove the oil pan, the oil pump inlet tube and the oil pump.

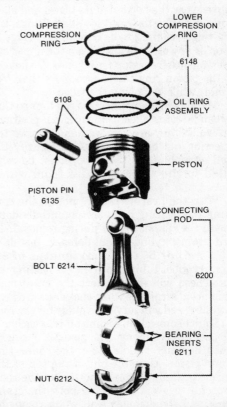

Typical piston, connecting rod and related parts

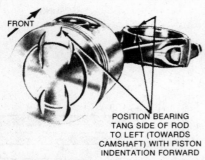

POSITION BEARING
TANG SIDE OF ROD
TO LEFT (TOWARDS
CAMSHAFT) WITH PISTON
INDENTATION FORWARD

FRONT

Correct piston and rod position—six-cylinder

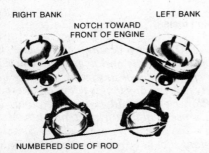

RIGHT BANK   LEFT BANK
NOTCH TOWARD
FRONT OF ENGINE

NUMBERED SIDE OF ROD

Correct piston and rod position—255, 302, 351V, 429 and 460 V8

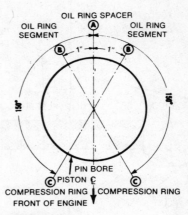

OIL RING SPACER
OIL RING
SEGMENT   A   OIL RING
SEGMENT
B   1"   1"   B
150°   190°
PIN BORE
C   PISTON   C
COMPRESSION RING   COMPRESSION RING
FRONT OF ENGINE

Piston ring spacing

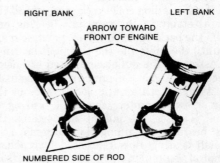

RIGHT BANK   LEFT BANK
ARROW TOWARD
FRONT OF ENGINE

NUMBERED SIDE OF ROD

Correct piston and rod position—351C, 351M, 400 V8

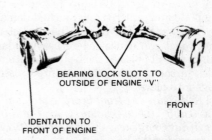

LEFT BANK   RIGHT BANK

BEARING LOCK SLOTS TO
OUTSIDE OF ENGINE "V"

FRONT

IDENTATION TO
FRONT OF ENGINE

Correct piston and rod position—390, 428 V8

4. Turn the crankshaft until the piston to be removed is at the bottom of its travel and place a cloth on the piston head to collect filings. Using a ridge reaming tool, remove any ridge of carbon or any other deposit from the upper cylinder walls where piston travel ends. Do not cut into the piston ring travel area more than $\frac{1}{32}$" (0.8mm) while removing the ridge.

5. Mark all of the connecting rod caps so that they can be reinstalled in the original positions from which they are removed and remove the connecting rod bearing cap. Also identify the piston assemblies as they, too, must be reinstalled in the same cylinder from which removed.

6. With the bearing caps removed, the connecting rod bearing bolts are potentially damaging to the cylinder walls during removal. To guard against cylinder wall damage, install 4" (101.6mm) or 5" (127mm) lengths of $\frac{3}{8}$" (9.5mm) rubber tubing onto the connecting rod bolts. These will also protect the crankshaft journal from scratches when the connecting rod is installed, and will serve as a guide for the rod.

7. Squirt some clean engine oil into each cylinder before removing the pistons. Using a wooden hammer handle, push the connecting rod and piston assembly out of the top of the cylinder (pushing from the bottom of the rod). Be careful to avoid damaging both the crank journal and the cylinder wall when removing the rod and piston assembly.

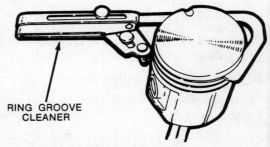

RING GROOVE
CLEANER

Cleaning the piston ring grooves

8. Before installing the piston/connecting rod assembly, be sure to clean all gasket mating surfaces, oil the pistons, piston rings and the cylinder walls with light engine oil.

9. Be sure to install the pistons in the cylinders from which they were removed. The connecting rod and bearing caps are numbered from 1 to 6 beginning at the front of the engine. The numbers on the connecting rod and bearing cap must be on the same side when installed in the cylinder bore. If a connecting rod is ever transposed from one engine or cylinder to another, new bearings should be fitted and the connecting rod should be numbered to correspond with the new cylinder number. The notch on the piston head goes toward the front of the engine.

10. Make sure the ring gaps are properly spaced around the circumference of the piston. Make sure rubber hose lengths are fitted to the rod bolts. Fit a piston ring compressor around the piston and slide the piston and connecting rod assembly down into the cylinder bore, pushing it in with the wooden hammer handle. Push the piston down until it is only slightly below the top of the cylinder bore. Guide the connecting rods onto the crankshaft bearing journals carefully, using the rubber hose lengths, to avoid damaging the crankshaft.

11. Check the bearing clearance of all the rod bearings, fitting them to the crankshaft bearing journals.

12. After the bearings have been fitted, apply a light coating of engine oil to the journals and bearings.

13. Turn the crankshaft until the appropriate bearing journal is at the bottom of its stroke, then push the piston assembly all the way down until the connecting rod bearing seats on the crankshaft journal. Be careful not to allow the bearing cap screws to strike the crankshaft bearing journals and damage them.

14. After the piston and connecting rod assemblies have been installed, check the connecting rod side clearance on each crankshaft journal.

15. Prime and install the oil pump and the oil pump intake tube, then install the oil pan.

16. Reassemble the rest of the engine in the reverse order of disassembly.

V8 Engines

1. Drain the cooling system and the crankcase.

CAUTION: *When draining the coolant, keep in mind that cats and dogs are attracted by the ethylene glycol antifreeze, and are quite likely to drink any that is left in an uncovered container or in puddles on the ground. This will prove fatal in sufficient quantity. Always*

drain the coolant into a sealable container. Coolant should be reused unless it is contaminated or several years old.

2. Remove the intake manifold.

3. Remove the cylinder heads.

4. Remove the oil pan.

5. Remove the oil pump.

6. Turn the crankshaft until the piston to be removed is at the bottom of its travel, then place a cloth on the piston head to collect filings.

7. Remove any ridge of deposits at the end of the piston travel from the upper cylinder bore, using a ridge reaming tool. Do not cut into the piston ring travel area more than $\frac{1}{32}$" (0.8mm) when removing the ridge.

8. Make sure that all of the connecting rod bearing caps can be identified, so they will be reinstalled in their original positions.

9. Turn the crankshaft until the connecting rod that is to be removed is at the bottom of its stroke and remove the connecting rod nuts and bearing cap.

10. With the bearing caps removed, the connecting rod bearing bolts are potentially damaging to the cylinder walls during removal. To guard against cylinder wall damage, install four or five inch lengths of $\frac{3}{8}$" (0.8mm) rubber tubing onto the connecting rod bolts. These will also protect the crankshaft journal from scratches when the connecting rod is installed, and will serve as a guide for the rod.

11. Squirt some clean engine oil into each cylinder before removing the piston assemblies. Using a wooden hammer handle, push the connecting rod and piston assembly out of the top of the cylinder (pushing from the bottom of the rod). Be careful to avoid damaging both the crank journal and the cylinder wall when removing the rod and piston assembly.

12. Remove the bearing inserts from the connecting rod and cap if the bearings are to be replace, and place the cap onto the piston/rod assembly from which it was removed.

13. Install the piston/rod assemblies in the same manner as that for the 6-240 engines. See the procedure given for 6-240 engines.

NOTE: *The connecting rod and bearing caps are numbered from 1 to 4 in the right bank and from 5 to 8 in in the left bank, beginning at the front of the engine. The numbers on the rod and cap must be on the same side when they are installed in the cylinder bore. Also, the largest chamfer at the bearing end of the rod should be positioned toward the crank pin thrust face of the crankshaft and the notch in the head of the piston faces toward the front of the engine.*

14. See the appropriate component procedures to assemble the engine.

Piston Ring and Wrist Pin

REMOVAL

All of the Ford engines covered in this guide utilize pressed-in wrist pins, which can only be removed by an arbor press. The piston/connecting rod assemblies should be taken to an engine specialist or qualified machinist for piston removal and installation.

A piston ring expander is necessary for removing the piston rings without damaging them; any other method (screwdriver blades, pliers, etc.) usually results in the rings being bent, scratched or distorted, or the piston itself being damaged. When the rings are removed, clean the ring grooves using an appropriate ring groove cleaning tool, using care not to cut too deeply. Thoroughly clean all carbon and varnish from the piston with solvent.

WARNING: *Do not use a wire brush or caustic solvent (acids, etc.) on pistons.*

Inspect the pistons for scuffing, scoring, cracks, pitting, or excessive ring groove wear. If these are evident, the piston must be replaced.

The piston should also be checked in relation to the cylinder diameter. Using a telescoping gauge and micrometer, or a dial gauge, measure the cylinder bore diameter perpendicular (90%) to the piston pin, 2½" (64mm) below the cylinder block deck (surface where the block mates with the heads). Then, with the micrometer, measure the piston, perpendicular to its wrist pin on the skirt. the difference between the two measurements is the piston clearance. If the clearance is within specifications or slightly below (after the cylinders have been bored or hones), finish honing is all that is necessary. If the clearance is excessive, try to obtain a slightly larger piston to bring clearance to within specifications. If this is not possible, obtain the first oversize piston and hone (or if necessary, bore) the cylinder to size. Generally, if the cylinder bore is tapered 0.005" (0.127mm) or more or is out-of-round 0.003" (0.076mm) or more, it is advisable to rebore for the smallest possible oversize piston and rings.

After measuring, mark pistons with a felt tip pen for reference and for assembly.

NOTE: *Cylinder honing and/or boring should be performed by a reputable, professional mechanic with the proper equipment. In some cases, clean-up honing can be done with the cylinder block in the car, but most excessive honing and all cylinder boring must be done with the block stripped and removed from the car.*

MEASURING THE OLD PISTONS

Check used piston-to-cylinder bore clearance as follows:

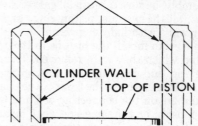

RIDGE CAUSED BY CYLINDER WEAR

CYLINDER WALL

TOP OF PISTON

Cylinder bore ridge

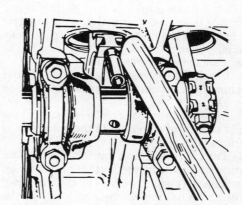

Match the connecting rod and cap with scribe marks

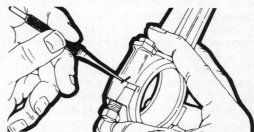

Push the piston out with a hammer handle

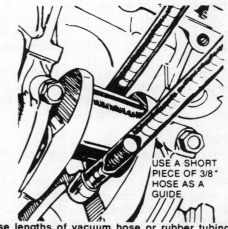

USE A SHORT PIECE OF 3/8" HOSE AS A GUIDE

Use lengths of vacuum hose or rubber tubing to protect the crankshaft journals and cylinder walls during installation

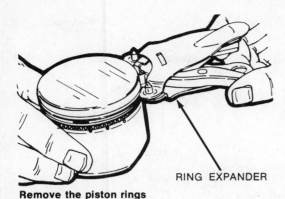

RING EXPANDER

Remove the piston rings

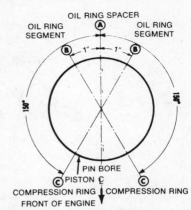

OIL RING SPACER

OIL RING SEGMENT

OIL RING SEGMENT

1" — 1"

150°

150°

PIN BORE

PISTON C

COMPRESSION RING | COMPRESSION RING

FRONT OF ENGINE

Piston ring spacing (all engines)

1. Measure the cylinder bore diameter with a telescope gauge.

2. Measure the piston diameter. When measuring the pistons for size or taper, measurements must be made with the piston pin removed.

3. Subtract the piston diameter from the cylinder bore diameter to determine piston-to-bore clearance.

4. Compare the piston-to-bore clearances obtained with those clearances recommended. Determine if the piston-to-bore clearance is in the acceptable range.

5. When measuring taper, the largest reading must be at the bottom of the skirt.

SELECTING NEW PISTONS

1. If the used piston is not acceptable, check the service piston size and determine if a new piston can be selected. (Service pistons are available in standard, high limit and standard oversize.

2. If the cylinder bore must be reconditioned, measure the new piston diameter, then hone the cylinder bore to obtain the preferred clearance.

3. Select a new piston and mark the piston to identify the cylinder for which it was fitted. (On some vehicles, oversize pistons may be found.

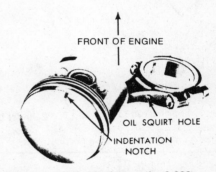

FRONT OF ENGINE

OIL SQUIRT HOLE

INDENTATION NOTCH

Piston and rod positioning on the 6-200

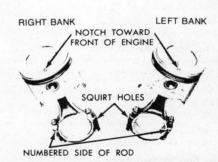

RIGHT BANK   LEFT BANK

NOTCH TOWARD FRONT OF ENGINE

SQUIRT HOLES

NUMBERED SIDE OF ROD

Piston and rod positioning on the V6-232, V8-255, 302

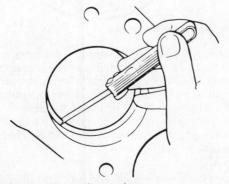

Check the piston ring end gap

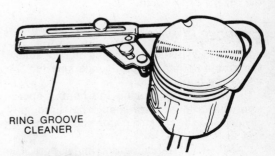

RING GROOVE CLEANER

Clean the piston ring grooves

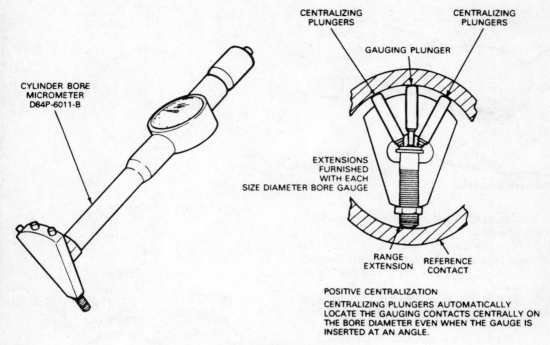

Cylinder bore micrometer

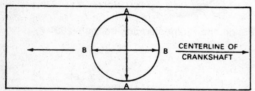

A - At Right angle to center line of engine
B - Parallel to center line of engine

Top Measurement: Make 12.70mm (1/2 inch) below top of block deck

Bottom Measurement: Make within 12.70mm (1/2 inch) above top of piston - when piston is at its lowest travel (B.D.C)

Bore Service Limit: Equals the average of "A" and "B" when measured at the center of the piston travel.

Taper: Equals difference between "A" top and "A" bottom.

Out-of-Round: Equals difference between "A" and "B" when measured at the center of piston travel.

Refer to Specification tables at end of each engine section.

Cylinder bore measurement

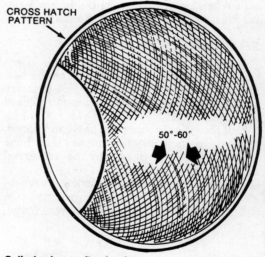

Cylinder bore after honing

These pistons will be 0.254mm [0.010"] oversize).

CYLINDER HONING

1. When cylinders are being honed, follow the manufacturer's recommendations for the use of the hone.

2. Occasionally, during the honing operation, the cylinder bore should be thoroughly cleaned and the selected piston checked for correct fit.

3. When finish-honing a cylinder bore, the hone should be moved up and down at a suffi-

cient speed to obtain a very fine uniform surface finish in a cross-hatch pattern of approximately 45-65° included angle. The finish marks should be clean but not sharp, free from imbedded particles and torn or folded metal.

4. Permanently mark the piston for the cylinder to which it has been fitted and proceed to hone the remaining cylinders.

WARNING: *Handle the pistons with care. Do not attempt to force the pistons through the cylinders until the cylinders have been honed to the correct size. Pistons can be distorted through careless handling.*

5. Thoroughly clean the bores with hot water and detergent. Scrub well with a stiff bristle brush and rinse thoroughly with hot water. It is extremely essential that a good cleaning operation be performed. If any of the abrasive material is allowed to remain in the cylinder bores, it will rapidly wear the new rings and cylinder bores. The bores should be swabbed several times with light engine oil and a clean cloth and then wiped with a clean dry cloth. CYLINDERS SHOULD NOT BE CLEANED WITH KEROSENE OR GASOLINE! Clean the remainder of the cylinder block to remove the excess material spread during the honing operation.

PISTON RING END GAP

Piston ring end gap should be checked while the rings are removed from the pistons. Incorrect end gap indicates that the wrong size rings are being used; ring breakage could occur.

Compress the piston rings to be used in a cylinder, one at a time, into that cylinder. Squirt clean oil into the cylinder, so that the rings and the top 2″ (51mm) of cylinder wall are coated. Using an inverted piston, press the rings approximately 1″ (25mm) below the deck of the block. Measure the ring end gap with the feeler gauge, and compare to the Ring Gap chart in this chapter. Carefully pull the ring out of the cylinder and file the ends squarely with a fine file to obtain the proper clearance.

PISTON RING SIDE CLEARANCE CHECK AND INSTALLATION

Check the pistons to see that the ring grooves and oil return holes have been properly cleaned. Slide a piston ring into its groove, and check the side clearance with a feeler gauge. On gasoline engines, make sure you insert the gauge between the ring and its lower land (lower edge of the groove), because any wear that occurs forms a step at the inner portion of the lower land. If the piston grooves have worn to the extend that relatively high steps exist on the lower land, the piston grooves have worn to the extent that relatively high steps exist on the lower land, the piston should be replaced, because these will interfere with the operation of the new rings and ring clearance will be excessive. Piston rings are not furnished in oversize widths to compensate for ring groove wear.

Install the rings on the piston, lowest ring first, using a piston ring expander. There is a high risk of breaking or distorting the rings, or scratching the piston, if the rings are installed by hand or other means.

Position the rings on the piston as illustrated; spacing of the various piston ring gaps is

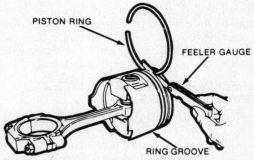

Check the piston ring side clearance

Install the piston using a ring compressor

crucial to proper oil retention and even cylinder wear. When installing new rings, refer to the installation diagram furnished with the new parts.

Connecting Rod Bearings
INSPECTION

Connecting rod bearings for the engines covered in this guide consist of two halves or shells which are interchangeable in the rod and cap. when the shells are placed in position, the ends extend slightly beyond the rod and cap surfaces so that when the rod bolts are torqued the shells will be clamped tightly in place to insure positive seating and to prevent turning. A tang holds the shells in place.

NOTE: *The ends of the bearing shells must never be filed flush with the mating surfaces of the rod and cap.*

If a rod bearing becomes noisy or is worn so that its clearance on the crank journal is sloppy, a new bearing of the correct undersize must be selected and installed since there is a provision for adjustment.

WARNING: *Under no circumstances should the rod end or cap be filed to adjust the bearing clearance, nor should shims of any kind be used.*

Inspect the rod bearings while the rod assemblies are out of the engine. If the shells are scored or show flaking, they should be replaced.

If they are in good shape, check for proper clearance on the crank journal (see below). Any scoring or ridges on the crank journal means the crankshaft must be reground and fitted with undersized bearings, or replaced.

CHECKING BEARING CLEARANCE AND REPLACING BEARINGS

NOTE: *Make sure connecting rods and their caps are kept together, and that the caps are installed in the proper direction.*

Replacement bearings are available in standard size, and in undersizes for reground crankshaft. Connecting rod-to-crankshaft bearing clearance is checked using Plastigage® at either the top or bottom of each crank journal. the Plastigage® has a range of 0 to 0.003″ (0.076mm).

1. Remove the rod cap with the bearing shell. Completely clean the bearing shell and the crank journal, and blow any oil from the oil hole in the crankshaft.

NOTE: *The journal surfaces and bearing shells must be completely free of oil, because Plastigage® is soluble in oil.*

2. Place a strip of Plastigage® lengthwise along the bottom center of the lower bearing shell, then install the cap with shell and torque the bolt or nuts to specification. DO NOT TURN the crankshaft with the Plastigage® installed in the bearing.

3. Remove the bearing cap with the shell. The flattened Plastigage® will be found sticking to either the bearing shell or crank journal. Do not remove it yet.

4. Use the printed scale on the Plastigage® envelope to measure the flattened material at its widest point. The number within the scale which most closely corresponds to the width of the Plastigage® indicated bearing clearance in thousandths of an inch.

5. Check the specifications chart in this chapter for the desired clearance. It is advisable to install a new bearing if clearance exceeds 0.003″ (0.076mm); however, if the bearing is in good condition and is not being checked because of bearing noise, bearing replacement is not necessary.

6. If you are installing new bearings, try a standard size, then each undersize in order until one is found that is within the specified limits when checked for clearance with Plastigage®. Each under size has its size stamped on it.

7. When the proper size shell is found, clean off the Plastigage® material from the shell, oil the bearing thoroughly, reinstall the cap with its shell and torque the rod bolt nuts to specification.

NOTE: *With the proper bearing selected and the nuts torqued, it should be possible to move the connecting rod back and forth freely on the crank journal as allowed by the specified connecting rod end clearance. If the rod cannot be moved, either the rod bearing is too far undersize or the rod is misaligned.*

Piston and Connecting Rod
ASSEMBLY AND INSTALLATION

Install the connecting rod to the piston making sure piston installation notches and any marks on the rod are in proper relation to one another. Lubricate the wrist pin with clean engine oil and install the pin into the rod and piston assembly by using an arbor press as required. Install the wrist pin snaprings if equipped, and rotate them in their grooves to make sure they are seated. To install the piston and rod assemblies:

1. Make sure the connecting rod big bearings (including end cap) are of the correct size and properly installed.

2. Fit rubber hoses over the connecting rod bolt to protect the crankshaft journals, as in the Piston Removal procedure. Coat the rod bearings with clean oil.

3. Using the proper ring compressor, insert the piston assembly into the cylinder so that the notch in the top of the piston faces the front of the engine (this assumes that the dimple(s) or other markings on the connecting rods are in correct relation to the piston notch(s)).

4. From beneath the engine, coat each crank journal with clean oil. Pull the connecting rod, with the bearing shell in place, into position against the crank journal.

5. Remove the rubber hoses. Install the bearing cap and cap nuts and torque to specification.

NOTE: *When more than one rod and piston assembly is being installed, the connecting rod cap attaching nuts should only be tightened enough to keep each rod in position until all have been installed. This will ease the installation of the remaining piston assemblies.*

6. Check the clearance between the sides of the connecting rods and the crankshaft using a feeler gauge. Spread the rods slightly with a screwdriver to insert the gauge. If clearance is below the minimum tolerance, the rod may be machined to provide adequate clearance. If clearance is excessive, substitute an unworn rod, and recheck. If clearance is still outside specifications, the crankshaft must be welded and reground, or replaced.

7. Replace the oil pump if removed, and the oil pan.

8. Install the cylinder head(s) and intake manifold.

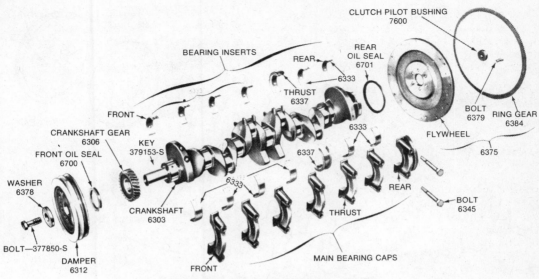

Crankshaft and related parts—six-cylinder

Crankshaft and Main Bearings.

REMOVAL AND INSTALLATION

Engine Removed

1. With the engine removed from the vehicle and placed in a work stand, disconnect the spark plug wires from the spark plugs and remove the wires and bracket assembly from the attaching stud on the valve rocker arm cover(s) if so equipped. Disconnect the coil to distributor high tension lead at the coil. Remove the distributor cap and spark plug wires as an assembly. Remove the spark plugs to allow easy rotation of the crankshaft.

2. Remove the fuel pump and oil filter. Slide the water pump by-pass hose clamp (if so

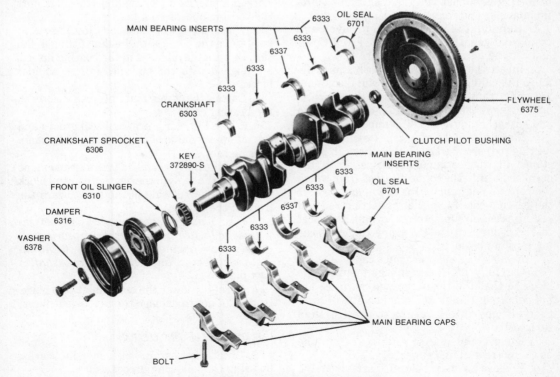

Crankshaft and related parts—typical V8

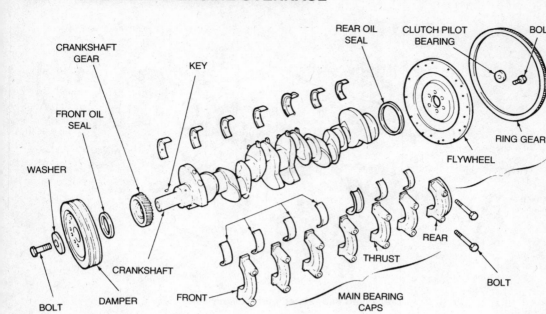

6-300 crankshaft and bearings

equipped) toward the water pump. Remove the alternator and mounting brackets.

3. Remove the crankshaft pulley from the crankshaft vibration damper. Remove the capscrew and washer from the end of the crankshaft. Install a universal puller, Tool T58P-6316-D or equivalent on the crankshaft vibration damper and remove the damper.

4. Remove the cylinder front cover and crankshaft gear, refer to Cylinder Front Cover and Timing Chain in this chapter.

5. Invert the engine on the work stand. Remove the clutch pressure plate and disc (manual shift transmission). Remove the flywheel and engine rear cover plate. Remove the oil pan and gasket. Remove the oil pump.

6. Make sure all bearing caps (main and connecting rod) are marked so that they can be installed in their original locations. Turn the crankshaft until the connecting rod from which the cap is being removed is down, and remove the bearing cap. Push the connecting rod and piston assembly up into the cylinder. Repeat this procedure until all the connecting rod bearing caps are removed.

7. Remove the main bearings caps.

8. Carefully lift the crankshaft out of the block so that the thrust bearing surfaces are not damaged. Handle the crankshaft with care to avoid possible fracture to the finished surfaces.

9. Remove the rear journal seal from the block and rear main bearing cap.

10. Remove the main bearing inserts from the block and bearing caps.

11. Remove the connecting rod bearing inserts from the connecting rods and caps.

12. If the crankshaft main bearing journals have been refinished to a definite undersize, install the correct undersize bearings. Be sure the bearing inserts and bearing bores are clean. Foreign material under the inserts will distort the bearing and cause a failure.

13. Place the upper main bearing inserts in position in the bores with the tang fitting in the slot. Be sure the oil holes in the bearing inserts are aligned with the oil holes in the cylinder block.

14. Install the lower main bearing inserts in the bearing caps.

15. Clean the rear journal oil seal groove and the mating surfaces of the block and rear main bearing cap.

16. Dip the lip-type seal halves in clean engine oil. Install the seals in the bearing cap and block with the undercut side of the seal toward the front of the engine.

NOTE: *This procedure applies only to engines with two piece rear main bearing oil seals. those having one piece seals (6-240 engines) will be installed after the crankshaft is in place.*

17. Carefully lower the crankshaft into place. Be careful not to damage the bearing surfaces.

CHECKING MAIN BEARING CLEARANCES

18. Check the clearance of each main bearing by using the following procedure:

a. Place a piece of Plastigage® or its equiv-

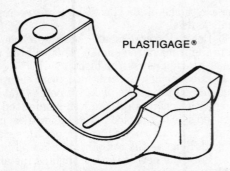

PLASTIGAGE®

Plastigauge installed on the lower bearing shell—typical

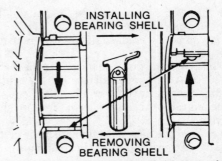

INSTALLING BEARING SHELL

REMOVING BEARING SHELL

Remove or install the upper bearing insert using a roll-out pin

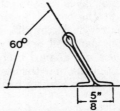

60°

$\frac{5''}{8}$

Home-made bearing roll-out pin

alent, on bearing surface across full width of bearing cap and about ¼″ (6mm) off center.

b. Install cap and tighten bolts to specifications. Do not turn crankshaft while Plastigage® is in place.

c. Remove the cap. Using Plastigage® scale, check width of Plastigage® at widest point to get the minimum clearance. Check at narrowest point to get maximum clearance. Difference between readings is taper of journal.

d. If clearance exceeds specified limits, try a 0.001″ (0.0254mm) or 0.002″ (0.051mm) undersize bearing in combination with the standard bearing. Bearing clearance must be within specified limits. If standard and 0.002″ (0.051mm) undersize bearing does not bring clearance within desired limits, refinish crankshaft journal, then install undersize bearings.

NOTE: *Refer to Rear Main Oil Seal removal and installation, for special instructions in applying RTV sealer to rear main bearing cup.*

19. Install all the bearing caps except the thrust bearing cap (no. 3 bearing on all except the 6-240 which use the no. 5 as the thrust bearing). BE sure the main bearing caps are installed in their original locations. Tighten the bearing cap bolts to specifications.

21. install the thrust bearing cap with the bolts finger tight.

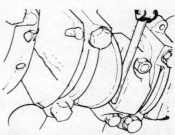

Check the connecting rod side clearance with a feeler gauge

22. Pry the crankshaft forward against the thrust surface of the upper half of the bearing.

23. hold the crankshaft forward and pry the thrust bearing cap to the rear. This will align the thrust surfaces of both halves of the bearing.

24. Retain the forward pressure on the crankshaft. Tighten the cap bolts to specifications.

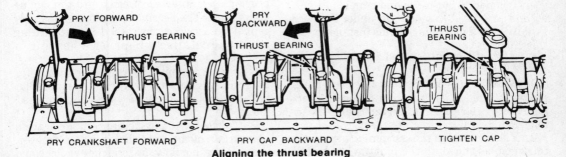

PRY FORWARD

THRUST BEARING

PRY CRANKSHAFT FORWARD

PRY BACKWARD

THRUST BEARING

PRY CAP BACKWARD

THRUST BEARING

TIGHTEN CAP

Aligning the thrust bearing

25. Check the crankshaft end play using the following procedures:

a. Force the crankshaft toward the rear of the engine.

b. Install a dial indicator (tools D78P-4201-F, -G or equivalent) so that the contact point rests against the crankshaft flange and the indicator axis is parallel to the crankshaft axis.

c. Zero the dial indicator. Push the crankshaft forward and note the reading on the dial.

d. If the end play exceeds the wear limit listed in the Crankshaft and Connecting Rod Specifications chart, replace the thrust bearing. If the end play is less than the minimum limit, inspect the thrust bearing faces for scratches, burrs, nicks, or dirt. If the thrust faces are not damaged or dirty, then they probably were not aligned properly. Lubricate and install the new thrust bearing and align the faces following procedures 21 through 24.

26. On 6-240 engines with one piece rear main bearing oil seal, coat a new crankshaft rear oil seal with oil and install using Tool T65P-6701-A or equivalent. Inspect the seal to be sure it was not damaged during installation.

27. Install new bearing inserts in the connecting rods and caps. Check the clearance of each bearing, following the procedure (18a through 18d).

28. After the connecting rod bearings have been fitted, apply a light coat of engine oil to the journals and bearings.

29. Turn the crankshaft throw to the bottom of its stroke. Push the piston all the way down until the rod bearing seats on the crankshaft journal.

30. Install the connecting rod cap. Tighten the nuts to specification.

31. After the piston and connecting rod assemblies have been installed, check the side clearance with a feeler gauge between the connecting rods on each connecting rod crankshaft journal. Refer to Crankshaft and Connecting Rod specifications chart in this chapter.

32. Install the timing chain and sprockets or gears, cylinder front cover and crankshaft pulley and adapter, following steps under Cylinder Front Cover and Timing Chain Installation in this chapter.

Engine in the Car

1. With the oil pan, oil pump and spark plugs removed, remove the cap from the main bearing needing replacement and remove the bearing from the cap.

2. Make a bearing roll-out pin, using a bent cotter pin as shown in the illustration. Install the end of the pin in the oil hole in the crankshaft journal.

3. Rotate the crankshaft clockwise as viewed from the front of the engine. This will roll the upper bearing out of the block.

4. Lube the new upper bearing with clean engine oil and insert the plain (unnotch) end between the crankshaft and the indented or notched side of the block. Roll the bearing into place, making sure that the oil holes are aligned. Remove the roll pin from the oil hole.

5. Lube the new lower bearing and install it in the main bearing cap. Install the main bearing cap onto the block, making sure it is positioned in proper direction with the matchmarks in alignment.

6. Torque the main bearing cap to specification.

NOTE: *See Crankshaft Installation for thrust bearing alignment.*

CRANKSHAFT CLEANING AND INSPECTION

NOTE: *handle the crankshaft carefully to avoid damage to the finish surfaces.*

1. Clean the crankshaft with solvent, and blow out all oil passages with compressed air. On the 6-240 engine, clean the oil seal contact surface at the rear of the crankshaft with solvent to remove any corrosion, sludge or varnish deposits.

2. Use crocus cloth to remove any sharp edges, burrs or other imperfections which might damage the oil seal during installation or cause premature seal wear.

NOTE: *Do not use crocus cloth to polish the seal surfaces. A finely polished surface may produce poor sealing or cause premature seal wear.*

3. Inspect the main and connecting rod journals for cracks, scratches, grooves or scores.

4. Measure the diameter of each journal at least four places to determine out-of-round, taper or undersize condition.

5. On an engine with a manual transmission, check the fit of the clutch pilot bearing in the bore of the crankshaft. A needle roller bearing and adapter assembly is used as a clutch pilot bearing. It is inserted directly into the engine crank shaft. The bearing and adapter assembly cannot be serviced separately. A new bearing must be installed whenever a bearing is removed.

6. Inspect the pilot bearing, when used, for roughness, evidence of overheating or loss of lubricant. Replace if any of these conditions are found.

7. On the 6-240 engine, inspect the rear oil seal surface of the crankshaft for deep grooves, nicks, burrs, porosity, or scratches which could

damage the oil seal lip during installation. Remove all nicks and burrs with crocus cloth.

Main Bearings

1. Clean the bearing inserts and caps thoroughly in solvent, and dry them with compressed air.

NOTE: *Do not scrape varnish or gum deposits from the bearing shells.*

2. Inspect each bearing carefully. Bearings that have a scored, chipped, or worn surface should be replaced.

3. The copper-lead bearing base may be visible through the bearing overlay in small localized areas. This may not mean that the bearing is excessively worn. It is not necessary to replace the bearing if the bearing clearance is within recommended specifications.

4. Check the clearance of bearings that appear to be satisfactory with Plastigage® or its equivalent. Fit the new bearings following the procedure Crankshaft and Main Bearings removal and installation, they should be reground to size for the next undersize bearing.

5. Regrind the journals to give the proper clearance with the next undersize bearing. If the journal will not clean up to maximum undersize bearing available, replace the crankshaft.

6. Always reproduce the same journal shoulder radius that existed originally. Too small a radius will result in fatigue failure of the crankshaft. Too large a radius will result in bearing failure due to radius ride of the bearing.

7. After regrinding the journals, chamfer the oil holes, then polish the journals with a #320 grit polishing cloth and engine oil. Crocus cloth may also be used as a polishing agent.

COMPLETING THE REBUILDING PROCESS

Fill the oil pump with oil, to prevent cavitating (sucking air) on initial engine start up. Install the oil pump and the pickup tube on the engine. Coat the oil pan gasket as necessary, and install the gasket and the oil pan. Mount the flywheel and the crankshaft vibration damper or pulley on the crankshaft.

NOTE: *Always use new bolts when installing the flywheel. Inspect the clutch shaft pilot bushing in the crankshaft. If the bushing is excessively worn, remove it with an expanding puller and a slide hammer, and tap a new bushing into place.*

Position the engine, cylinder head side up. Lubricate the lifters, and install them into their bores. Install the cylinder head, and torque it as specified. Insert the pushrods (where applicable), and install the rocker shaft(s) (if so equipped) or position the rocker.

Install the intake and exhaust manifolds, the carburetor(s), the distributor and spark plugs. Mount all accessories and install the engine in the car. Fill the radiator with coolant, and the crankcase with high quality engine oil.

BREAK-IN PROCEDURE

Start the engine, and allow it to run at low speed for a few minutes, while checking for leaks. Stop the engine, check the oil level, and fill as necessary. Restart the engine, and fill the cooling system to capacity. Check and adjust the ignition timing. Run the engine at low to medium speed (800–2,500 rpm) for approximately ½ hour, and retorque the cylinder head bolts. Road test the car, and check again for leaks.

NOTE: *Some gasket manufacturers recommend not retorquing the cylinder head(s) due to the composition of the head gasket. Follow the directions in the gasket set.*

Flywheel/Flex Plate and Ring Gear

NOTE: *Flex plate is the term for a flywheel mated with an automatic transmission.*

REMOVAL AND INSTALLATION

All Engines

NOTE: *The ring gear is replaceable only on engines mated with a manual transmission. Engines with automatic transmissions have ring gears which are welded to the flex plate.*

1. Remove the transmission and transfer case.

2. Remove the clutch, if equipped, or torque converter from the flywheel. The flywheel bolts should be loosened a little at a time in a cross pattern to avoid warping the flywheel. On cars with manual transmissions, replace the pilot bearing in the end of the crankshaft if removing the flywheel.

3. The flywheel should be checked for cracks and glazing. It can be resurfaced by a machine shop.

4. If the ring gear is to be replaced, drill a hole in the gear between two teeth, being careful not to contact the flywheel surface. Using a cold chisel at this point, crack the ring gear and remove it.

6. Polish the inner surface of the new ring gear and heat it in an oven to about 600°F (316°C). Quickly place the ring gear on the flywheel and tap it into place, making sure that it is fully seated.

WARNING: *Never heat the ring gear past 800°F (426°C), or the tempering will be destroyed.*

7. Position the flywheel on the end of the crankshaft. Torque the bolts a little at a time,

Checking flywheel face runout

in a cross pattern, to the torque figure shown in the Torque Specifications Chart.

8. Install the clutch or torque converter.

9. Install the transmission and transfer case.

Rear Main Bearing Oil Seal
REPLACEMENT
1968-69 302, 351W V8

NOTE: *The rear oil seal originally installed in these engines is a rope (fabric) type seal. However, all service replacements are of the rubber type. To remove the rope type seal and install the rubber type, the following procedure is used.*

1. Drain the crankcase and remove the oil pan. (See oil pan removal).

CAUTION: *The EPA warns that prolonged contact with used engine oil may cause a number of skin disorders, including cancer! You should make every effort to minimize your exposure to used engine oil. Protective gloves should be worn when changing the oil. Wash your hands and any other exposed skin areas as soon as possible after exposure to used engine oil. Soap and water, or waterless hand cleaner should be used.*

2. Remove the lower half of the rear main bearing cap and, after removing the old seal from the cap, drive out the pin in the bottom of the seal groove with a punch.

3. Loosen all main bearings caps and allow the crankshaft to lower slightly.

NOTE: *The crankshaft should not be allowed to drop more than $1/32$".*

4. With a 6" length of $3/16$" brazing rod, drive up on either exposed end of the top half of the oil seal. When the opposite end of the seal starts to protrude, have a helper grasp it with pliers and gently pull while the driver end is being tapped.

5. After removing both halves of the rope seal and the retaining pin from the lower half of the bearing cap, follow Steps 4 through 10 of the following procedure for 1970 and later engines to install the rubber seal.

1970 and Later V8

NOTE: *Refer to the "build" dates listed below to determine if the engine is equipped with a split-type or one piece rear main oil seal. Engines after the date indicated have a one-piece*

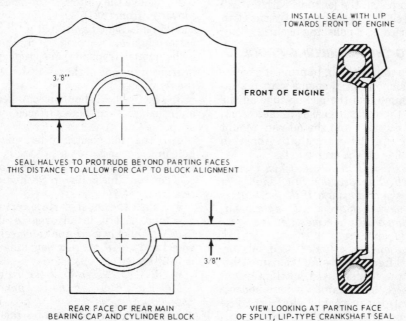

SEAL HALVES TO PROTRUDE BEYOND PARTING FACES
THIS DISTANCE TO ALLOW FOR CAP TO BLOCK ALIGNMENT

3/8''

REAR FACE OF REAR MAIN
BEARING CAP AND CYLINDER BLOCK

3/8''

FRONT OF ENGINE

INSTALL SEAL WITH LIP
TOWARDS FRONT OF ENGINE

VIEW LOOKING AT PARTING FACE
OF SPLIT, LIP-TYPE CRANKSHAFT SEAL

Installing split-type rubber rear oil seal

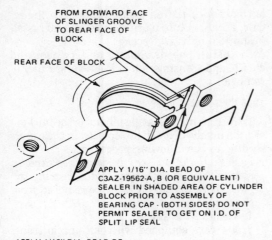

FROM FORWARD FACE
OF SLINGER GROOVE
TO REAR FACE OF
BLOCK

REAR FACE OF BLOCK

APPLY 1/16" DIA. BEAD OF
C3AZ-19562-A, B (OR EQUIVALENT)
SEALER IN SHADED AREA OF CYLINDER
BLOCK PRIOR TO ASSEMBLY OF
BEARING CAP - (BOTH SIDES) DO NOT
PERMIT SEALER TO GET ON I.D. OF
SPLIT LIP SEAL

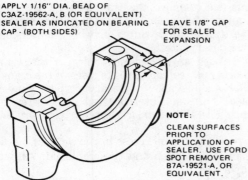

APPLY 1/16" DIA. BEAD OF
C3AZ-19562-A, B (OR EQUIVALENT)
SEALER AS INDICATED ON BEARING
CAP - (BOTH SIDES)

LEAVE 1/8" GAP
FOR SEALER
EXPANSION

NOTE:
CLEAN SURFACES
PRIOR TO
APPLICATION OF
SEALER. USE FORD
SPOT REMOVER.
B7A-19521-A, OR
EQUIVALENT.

Applying silicone sealer to rear main bearing cap and block

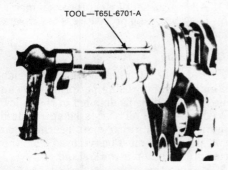

TOOL—T65L-6701-A

Installing crankshaft rear oil seal—1968–69 six-cylinder

seal. 302 V8: after 12/1/82; 351W V8: after 7/11/83.

SPLIT-TYPE SEAL

1. Remove the oil pan and the oil pump (if required).

2. Loosen all the main bearing cap bolts, thereby lowering the crankshaft slightly but not to exceed $\frac{1}{32}''$ (0.8mm).

3. Remove the rear main bearing cap, and remove the oil seal from the bearing cap and cylinder block. On the block half of the seal use a

OIL PUMP

OIL PUMP SCREEN

INLET
TUBE

Typical oil pump and inlet tube installed—390, 428 V8 shown

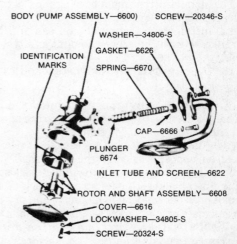

BODY (PUMP ASSEMBLY—6600)   SCREW—20346-S

WASHER—34806-S

IDENTIFICATION
MARKS

GASKET—6626

SPRING—6670

CAP—6666

PLUNGER
6674

INLET TUBE AND SCREEN—6622

ROTOR AND SHAFT ASSEMBLY—6608

COVER—6616

LOCKWASHER—34805-S

SCREW—20324-S

Typical oil pump disassembled—six-cylinder shown

seal removal tool, or install a small metal screw in one end of the seal, and pull on the screw to remove the seal. Exercise caution to prevent scratching or damaging the crankshaft seal surfaces.

4. Remove the oil seal retaining pin from the bearing cap if so equipped. The pin is not used with the split-lip seal.

5. Carefully clean the seal groove in the cap and block with a brush and solvent such as lacquer thinner, spot remover, or equivalent, or trichlorethylene. Also, clean the area thoroughly, so that no solvent touches the seal.

6. Dip the split lip-type seal halves in clean engine oil.

7. Carefully install the upper seal (cylinder block) into its groove with undercut side of the seal toward the FRONT of the engine, by rotat-

ing it on the seal journal of the crankshaft until approximately ⅜″ (9.5mm) protrudes below the parting surface.

Be sure no rubber has been shaved from the outside diameter of the seal by the bottom edge of the groove. Do not allow oil to get on the sealer area.

8. Tighten the remaining bearing cap bolts to the specifications listed in the Torque chart at the beginning of this chapter.

9. Install the lower seal in the rear main bearing cap under undercut side of seal toward the FRONT of the engine, allow the seal to protrude approximately ⅜″ (9.5mm) above the parting surface to mate with the upper seal when the cap is installed.

10. Apply an even ¹⁄₁₆″ (1.6mm) bead of RTV silicone rubber sealer, to the areas shown, following the procedure given in the illustration.

NOTE: *This sealer sets up in 15 minutes.*

11. Install the rear main bearing cap. Tighten the cap bolts to specifications.

12. Install the oil pump and oil pan. Fill the crankcase with the proper amount and type of oil.

13. Operate the engine and check for oil leaks.

ONE PIECE SEAL

1. Remove the transmission, clutch and flywheel or driveplate after referring to the appropriate section for instructions.

2. Punch two holes in the crankshaft rear oil seal on opposite sides of the crankshaft just above the bearing cap to the cylinder block split line. Install a sheet metal screw in each of the holes or use a small slide hammer, and pry the crankshaft rear main oil seal from the block.

WARNING: *Use extreme caution not to scratch the crankshaft oil seal surface.*

3. Clean the oil seal recess in the cylinder block and main bearing cap.

4. Coat the seal and all of the seal mounting

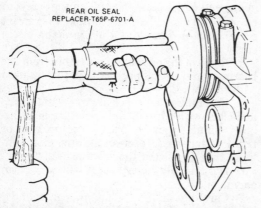

REAR OIL SEAL
REPLACER-T65P-6701-A

Installing the 1-piece rear main seal on gasoline engines

surfaces with oil and install the seal in the recess, driving it into place with an oil seal installation tool or a large socket.

5. Install the driveplate or flywheel and clutch, and transmission in the reverse order of removal.

1968-69 6-240

If the rear main bearing oil seal is the only operation involved, it can be replaced in the car according to the following procedure.

NOTE: *If the oil seal is being replaced in conjunction with a rear main bearing replacement, the engine must be removed from the car.*

1. Remove the starter.

2. On cars equipped with automatic transmissions, remove the transmission. On cars equipped with manual transmissions, remove the transmission, clutch, flywheel and engine rear cover plate.

3. With an awl, punch holes in the main bearing oil seal, on opposite sides of the crankshaft and just above the bearing cap to cylinder block split line. Insert a sheet metal screw in each hole. With two large screwdrivers, pry the oil seal out.

4. Clean the oil recess in the cylinder block, main bearing cap and the crankshaft sealing surface.

5. Lubricate the entire oil seal. Then, install and drive the seal into its seal 0.005″ below the face of the cylinder block with Ford tool T-65L-6701-A, or a socket of the proper diameter.

6. The remaining procedure is the reverse of removal.

1970-72 6-240

If the crankshaft rear oil seal replacement is the only operation being performed, it can be done in the vehicle as detailed in the following procedure. If the oil seal is being replaced in conjunction with a rear main bearing replacement, the engine must be removed from the vehicle and install on a work stand.

1. Remove the starter.

2. Remove the transmission from the vehicle, following procedures in Chapter 6.

3. On manual shift transmission, remove the pressure plate and cover assembly and the clutch disc following the procedure in Chapter 7.

4. Remove the flywheel attaching bolts and remove the flywheel and engine rear cover plate.

5. Use an awl to punch two holes in the crankshaft rear oil seal. Punch the holes on opposite sides of the crankshaft and just above the bearing cap to cylinder block split line. Install a sheet metal screw in each hole. Use two large

screwdrivers or small pry bars and pry against both screws at the same time to remove the crankshaft rear oil seal. It may be necessary to place small blocks of wood against the cylinder block to provide a fulcrum point for the pry bars. Use caution throughout this procedure to avoid scratching or otherwise damaging the crankshaft oil seal surface.

6. Clean the oil seal recess in the cylinder block and main bearing cap.

7. Clean, inspect and polish the rear oil seal rubbing surface on the crankshaft. Coat the new oil seal and the crankshaft with a light film of engine oil. Start the seal in the recess with the seal lip facing forward and install it with a seal driver. Keep the tool straight with the centerline of the crankshaft and install the seal until the tool contacts the cylinder block surface. Remove the tool and inspect the seal to be sure it was not damaged during installation.

8. Install the engine rear cover plate. Position the flywheel on the crankshaft flange. Coat the threads of the flywheel attaching bolts with oil-resistant sealer and install the bolts. Tighten the bolts in sequence across from each other to the specifications listed in the Torque chart at the beginning of this Chapter.

9. On a manual shift transmission, install the clutch disc and the pressure plate assembly following the procedure in Chapter 7.

10. Install the transmission, following the procedure in Chapter 7.

EXHAUST SYSTEM

Safety Precautions

For a number of reasons, exhaust system work can be the most dangerous type of work you can do on your car. Always observe the following precautions:

• Support the car extra securely. Not only will you often be working directly under it, but you'll frequently be using a lot of force, say, heavy hammer blows, to dislodge rusted parts. This can cause a car that's improperly supported to shift and possibly fall.

• Wear goggles. Exhaust system parts are always rusty. Metal chips can be dislodged, even when you're only turning rusted bolts. Attempting to pry pipes apart with a chisel makes the chips fly even more frequently.

• If you're using a cutting torch, keep it a great distance from either the fuel tank or lines. Stop what you're doing and feel the temperature of the fuel bearing pipes on the tank frequently. Even slight heat can expand and/or vaporize fuel, resulting in accumulated vapor, or even a liquid leak, near your torch.

• Watch where your hammer blows fall and make sure you hit squarely. You could easily tap a brake or fuel line when you hit an exhaust system part with a glancing blow. Inspect all lines and hoses in the area where you've been working.

CAUTION: *Be very careful when working on or near the catalytic converter. External temperatures can reach 1,500°F (816°C) and more, causing severe burns. Removal or installation should be performed only on a cold exhaust system.*

Special Tools

A number of special exhaust system tools can be rented from auto supply houses or local stores that rent special equipment. A common one is a tail pipe expander, designed to enable you to join pipes of identical diameter.

It may also be quite helpful to use solvents designed to loosen rusted bolts or flanges. Soaking rusted parts the night before you do the job can speed the work of freeing rusted parts considerably. Remember that these solvents are often flammable. Apply only to parts after they are cool!

CAUTION: *When working on exhaust systems, ALWAYS wear protective goggles! Avoid working on a hot exhaust system!*

Muffler

REMOVAL AND INSTALLATION

NOTE: *The following applies to exhaust systems using clamped joints. Some models, use welded joints at the muffler. These joints will, of course, have to be cut.*

1968-79

1. Raise and support the rear end on jackstands placed under the frame, allowing the rear axle to lower to the full length of its travel.

2. Remove the U-bolt clamping the inlet pipe to the muffler.

3. Unbolt the rear suppoprt bracket from the muffler.

4. Unbolt the intermediate support bracket from the muffler.

5. Remove the muffler outlet clamp and remove the muffler.

6. Installation is the reverse of removal. Always use new clamps. Always install all parts loosely until they are aligned and all clearances are satisfied. Torque the support bracket bolts to 14 ft. lbs.; the flange nuts to 30 ft. lbs.

V8 System with a Single Converter

1. Raise and support the car on jackstands placed under the frame, to allow the rear axle to lower to the full limit of its travel.

2. Unbolt the muffler inlet flange from the converter outlet flange.

3. Remove the tailpipe support bracket.

4. Slide the muffler rearward and off of the converter flange.

5. Installation is the reverse of removal. Always use new clamps. Always install all parts loosely until they are aligned and all clearances are satisfied. Torque the support bracket bolts to 14 ft. lbs.; the flange nuts to 30 ft. lbs.

V8 System with a Double Converter

1. Raise and support the car on jackstands placed under the frame, to allow the rear axle to lower to the full limit of its travel.

2. Unbolt the muffler inlet flange from the Y-pipe.

3. Remove the tailpipe support bracket.

4. Separate the muffler from the Y-pipe.

5. Installation is the reverse of removal. Always use new clamps. Always install all parts loosely until they are aligned and all clearances are satisfied. Torque the support bracket bolts to 14 ft. lbs.; the clamp nuts to 35 ft. lbs.

1982 Cars with the V8 Engines

1. Raise and support the car on jackstands placed under the frame, to allow the rear axle to lower to the full limit of its travel.

2. Unbolt the muffler inlet flange from the converter outlet flange.

3. Remove the tailpipe support bracket.

4. Remove the muffler support bracket attaching screws.

5. Separate the muffler from the converter.

6. Installation is the reverse of removal. Always use new clamps. Always install all parts loosely until they are aligned and all clearances are satisfied. Torque the support bracket bolts to 14 ft. lbs.; the clamp nuts to 35 ft. lbs.

1983-88 Cars with the V8 Engines

1. Disconnect both rear shock absorber lower mounting bolts.

2. Raise and support the car on jackstands placed under the frame, to allow the rear axle to lower to the full limit of its travel, WITHOUT STRETCHING THE BRAKE HOSE.

3. Unbolt the muffler inlet flange from the converter outlet flange.

4. Remove the tailpipe support bracket.

5. Remove the muffler support bracket attaching screws.

6. Separate the muffler from the converter.

7. Installation is the reverse of removal. Always use new clamps. Always install all parts loosely until they are aligned and all clearances are satisfied. Torque the support bracket bolts to 14 ft. lbs.; the clamp nuts to 35 ft. lbs.

Front Exhaust Pipe

REMOVAL AND INSTALLATION

1968-79

1. Raise and support the front end on jackstands.

2. On cars equipped with and exhaust shield, remove the shield(s).

3. Support the muffler.

4. Remove the muffler inlet clamp.

5. Unbolt the front pipe from the catalytic converter.

6. Remove the heat shield brackets.

7. Separate the front pipe from the muffler slip joint connection. It may be necessary to remove the rear hanger connections for clearance purposes.

8. Unbolt the pipe ends from the exhaust manifolds.

9. Installation is the reverse of removal. Always use new clamps. Always relpace the pipe ends-to-manifold packings. Always install all parts loosely and align the system so that clearances between the system components and surrounding parts are adequate. Torque the support bracket bolts to 14 ft. lbs.; the clamp nuts to 35 ft. lbs.; the flange nuts to 30 ft. lbs.

V8 System with a Single Converter

1. Raise and support the front end on jackstands.

2. Support the muffler with wire.

3. Unbolt the converter inlet pipe from the Y-pipe.

4. Unbolt the Y-pipe from the exhaust manifold and remove the pipe.

5. Installation is the reverse of removal. Always use new clamps. Always replace the pipe ends-to-manifold packings. Always install all parts loosely and align the system, making sure the clearances between system components and surrounding parts are adequate. Torque the clamp nuts to 35 ft. lbs.; the flange nuts to 30 ft. lbs.

V8 System with a Double Converter

1. Raise and support the front end on jackstands.

2. Remove the clamp attaching the Y-pipe to the muffler inlet pipe.

3. Remove the heat shields.

4. Unbolt the Y-pipe flanges from the converters.

5. Lower the Y-pipe until the inlet flanges clear the converters. It may be necessary to remove the muffler support bracket for clearance purposes.

6. Support the muffler and remove the Y-pipe.

7. Installation is the reverse of removal. Al-

ways use new clamps. Always replace the pipe ends-to-manifold packings. Always install all parts loosely and align the system, making sure that all clearances between the system parts and surrounding components are adequate. Torque the clamp nuts to 35 ft. lbs.; the flange nuts to 30 ft. lbs.

1982-88 Models with the V8 Engine

1. Raise and support the front end on jackstands.
2. Remove the clamp attaching the Y-pipe to the converter inlet pipe.
3. Unbolt the Y-pipe flanges from the exhaust manifolds.
4. Remove the Y-pipe.
5. Installation is the reverse of removal. Always use new clamps. Always replace the pipe ends-to-manifold packings. Always install all parts loosely and align the system, making sure that all clearances between the system parts and surrounding components are adequate. Torque the clamp nuts to 35 ft. lbs.; the flange nuts to 30 ft. lbs.

Catalytic Converter
REMOVAL AND INSTALLATION
1968-79

1. Raise and support the car on jackstands.
2. Remove the heat shield(s).
3. Support the inlet pipe with a length of wire at the #3 crossmember.
4. Remove thd discard the inlet pipe-to-converter flange bolts.
5. Remove the heat shield brackets.
6. Remove the converter-to-manifold flage nuts.
7. Slide the inlet pipes rearward until the converter can be removed.
8. Installation is the reverse of removal. Always use new clamps. Always replace the pipe ends-to-manifold packings. Always install all parts loosely and align the system, making sure that all clearances between the system parts and surrounding components are adequate. Torque the flange nuts to 30 ft. lbs.; the manifold nuts to 35 ft. lbs.

V8 System with a Single Converter

1. Raise and support the car on jackstands.
2. Remove the heat shield.
3. Unbolt the Y-pipe from the converter flange.
4. Unbolt the muffler at the converter flange.
5. Separate the flanges and remove the converter.
6. Installation is the reverse of removal. Always use new clamps. Always replace the pipe

ends-to-manifold packings. Always install all parts loosely and align the system, making sure that all clearances between the system parts and surrounding components are adequate. Torque the flange nuts to 30 ft. lbs.; the manifold nuts to 35 ft. lbs.

V8 System with a Double Converter

1. Raise and support the car on jackstands.
2. Remove the heat shields.
3. Support the Y-pipe with a wire.
4. Unbolt the Y-pipe flanges from the converter flanges.
5. Unbolt the converter flange at the manifolds.
6. Slide the inlet pipe rearward until the converters can be removed. Separate the flanges and remove the converters.
7. Installation is the reverse of removal. Always use new clamps. Always replace the pipe ends-to-manifold packings. Always install all parts loosely and align the system, making sure that all clearances between the system parts and surrounding components are adequate. Torque the flange nuts to 30 ft. lbs.; the manifold nuts to 35 ft. lbs.

1982-83 Cars with the V8 Engine

1. Raise and support the car on jackstands.
2. If the converters are the air-injected, dual type, disconnect the air injection tube from the cover.
3. Unbolt the Y-pipe flanges from the converter flanges.
4. Unbolt the converter flange at the manifolds.
5. Slide the inlet pipe rearward until the converters can be removed. Separate the flanges and remove the converters.
6. Installation is the reverse of removal. Always use new clamps. Always replace the pipe ends-to-manifold packings. Always install all parts loosely and align the system, making sure that all clearances between the system parts and surrounding components are adequate. Torque the flange nuts to 30 ft. lbs.; the manifold nuts to 35 ft. lbs.

1986-88 V8 Except the 8-302 HO

1. Raise and support the front end on jackstands.
2. Remove the bolts attaching the Y-pipe to the converter inlet flange.
3. Remove the nuts attaching the muffler inlet pipe to the converter outlet flange.
4. Separate the catalytic converter inlet and outlet flange connections.
5. Remove the converter.

6. Installation is the reverse of removal. Always use new clamps. Always replace the pipe ends-to-manifold packings. Always install all parts loosely and align the system, making sure that all clearances between the system parts and surrounding components are adequate. Torque the flange nuts to 30 ft. lbs.; the manifold nuts to 35 ft. lbs.

1984-85 V8
1986-88 with the 8-302 HO

1. Raise and support the car on jackstands.
2. Disconnect the air injection tube from the cover.

3. Unbolt the Y-pipe flanges from the converter flanges.
4. Unbolt the converter flange at the muffler.
5. Slide the inlet pipe rearward until the converters can be removed. Separate the flanges and remove the converters.
6. Installation is the reverse of removal. Always use new clamps. Always replace the pipe ends-to-manifold packings. Always install all parts loosely and align the system, making sure that all clearances between the system parts and surrounding components are adequate. Torque the flange nuts to 30 ft. lbs.; the manifold nuts to 35 ft. lbs.

Emission Controls

EMISSION CONTROLS

There are three basic sources of automotive pollution in the modern internal combustion engine. They are the crankcase with its accompanying blow-by vapors, the fuel system with its evaporation of unburned gasoline, and the combustion chambers with their resulting exhaust emissions. Pollution arising from the incomplete combustion of fuel generally falls into three categories: hydrocarbons (HC), carbon monoxide (CO), and oxides of nitrogen (NOx).

Emission Control Equipment

1968 through 1973

Emission controls between 1968 and 1973 are fairly simple compared to later systems. Below are listed the emission controls common to, but not necessarily on, all models: Air pump, Closed positive crankcase ventilation (PCV), Calibrated carburetor and distributor, Dual vacuum advance on the distributor, Deceleration valve (6 cylinder), Heated air cleaner, Vapor control system canister storage, Fresh air intake tube to the air cleaners, Electronic distributor modulator, various Vacuum check valves and EGR (exhaust gas recirculation).

1974

Late 1973 and 1974 models use an Exhaust GAs Recirculation System (EGR) to control oxides of nitrogen. On V8 engines, exhaust gases travel through the exhaust gas crossover passage in the intake manifold. A portion of these gases is diverted into a spacer which is mounted under the carburetor. The EGR control valve, which is attached to the rear of the spacer, consists of a vacuum diaphragm with an attached plunger which normally blocks off exhaust gases from entering the intake manifold. The EGR valve is controlled by a vacuum line from the carburetor which passes through a ported vacu-um switch. The EGR ported vacuum switch provides vacuum to the EGR valve at coolant temperatures above 125°F. The vacuum diaphragm then opens the EGR valve permitting exhaust gases to flow through the carburetor spacer and enter the intake manifold where they combine with the fuel mixture and enter the combustion chambers. The exhaust gases are relatively oxygen-free and ten to dilute the combustion charge. This lowers peak combustion temperature thereby reducing oxides of nitrogen.

All models with a 351C, 400, or 460 V8 use the new Delay Vacuum By-pass (DVB) park control system. This system provides two paths by which carburetor vacuum can reach the distributor vacuum advance. the system consists of a spark delay valve, a check valve, a solenoid vacuum valve, and an ambient temperature switch. When the ambient temperature is below 49°F, the temperature switch contacts are open and the vacuum solenoid is open (de-energized). Under these conditions, vacuum will flow from the carburetor, through the open solenoid, and to the distributor. Since the spark delay valve resists the flow of carburetor vacuum, the vacuum will always flow through the vacuum solenoid when it is open, since this is the path of least resistance. When the ambient temperature rises above 60°F, the contacts in the temperature switch (which is located in the door post) close. This passes ignition switch current to the solenoid, energizing the solenoid. This blocks one of the two vacuum paths. All distributor vacuum must now flow through the spark delay valve. When carburetor vacuum rises above a certain level on acceleration, a rubber valve in the spark delay valve blocks vacuum from passing through the valve from from 5 to 30 seconds.

After this time delay has elapsed, normal vacuum is supplied to the distributor. when the vacuum solenoid is closed, (temperature above

60°F), the vacuum line from the solenoid to the distributor is vented to the atmosphere. To prevent the vacuum that is passing through the spark delay valve from escaping through the solenoid into the atmosphere, a one-way check valve is installed in the vacuum line from the solenoid to the distributor.

In order to meet 1974 California emission control standards, all 1974 Ford cars sold in that state are equipped with a Thermactor (air injection) system to control hydrocarbons and carbon monoxide. The EGR system is retained to control oxides of nitrogen.

1975

All full size Ford Motor Co. cars are equipped with catalytic converters. California models are equipped with two converters, while models sold in the 49 states have only one unit.

Catalytic converters convert noxious emission of hydrocarbons (HC) and carbon monoxide (CO) into harmless carbon dioxide and water. The units are installed in the exhaust system ahead of the mufflers and are designed, if the engine is properly tuned, to last 50,000 miles before replacement.

In addition to the converters, most 1975 Ford, Mercury and Lincoln cars are equipped with the Thermactor air pump (air injection system) previously mentioned. the air injection system, which afterburns the uncombusted fuel mixture in the exhaust ports, is needed with the converters to prevent an overly rich mixture from reaching the converter, and to help supply oxygen to aid in converter reaction.

Other emission control equipment for 1975 includes a carryover of the Positive Crankcase Ventilation (PCV) System, the Fuel Evaporative Control System, and exhaust gas recirculation.

Emission control related improvements for 1975 include standard Solid State (breakerless) Ignition, induction hardened exhaust valve seats, exhaust manifold redesign, vacuum operated heat riser valves, and improved carburetors with ore precise fuel metering control and a mechanical high speed bleed system.

All cars equipped with the 429 V8 engine use a Cold Start Spark Advance (CSSA) System in 1975 to aid in cold start driveability. Basically, the system will allow full vacuum advance to the distributor until the coolant temperature reaches 125°F.

1976

For 1976, the complexity of emission control equipment has been reduced on Ford products. The average number of emission control components has been reduced from 25 to 11 on most cars. All 1976 models have catalytic con-

verters. In addition, a new proportional exhaust gas recirculation system has been introduced. Exhaust backpressure regulates the EGR valve spark port vacuum signal to modulate the recirculation of gases, matching EGR flow to engine load.

1977-79

Most emission controls are carryover from 1976. One exception, however, is the EEC-II (Electronic Engine Control) system. It is installed on all Mercurys with the optional 351W V8, and on LTDs sold in California with that engine.

The system is based on EEC-I (EEC systems are described later in this chapter), but certain components have been changed to improve performance and reliability, and to reduce complexity and cost. EEC-II controls spark timing, EGR, and air/fuel ratio (mixture). A solid state module incorporating a digital microprocessor and other integrated circuits interprets information sent by seven sensors, calculates spark advance, EGR flow rate and fuel flow trim, and sends electrical signals to control the ignition module, EGR valve actuator, and an electric stepper motor in the carburetor. EEC-II also controls purging of vapors in the storage canister to prevent overly rich mixtures, high altitude fuel mixture adjustments, Thermactor (air pump) air flow, and cold engine (fast idle) functions. Because the throttle idle position, ignition timing and mixture are controlled electronically, these functions cannot be adjusted in the conventional manner.

1980

The major change in the emission control system for 1980 is in the EEC. The new system, EEC-III, performs the same function as EEC-II but uses a new electronic control module. The EEC system computes information and makes any necessary changes about 30 times a second, controlling the fuel/air mixture, EGR, ignition timing and the air flow to the exhaust emission system.

1981-86

The application of EEC-III is continued and EEC-IV and TFI-IV are introduced. Components include an oxygen sensor, a variable mixture carburetor, a three-way oxidation/reduction catalytic converter, an air pump, and a computer module.

Briefly, the three-way catalyst, which oxidizes HC and CO into H_2O and CO_2, and reduces NOx into N_2 and O_2, is only able to operate efficiently within a narrow range of exhaust gas content. An ideal air/fuel ratio (14.7:1, which is called stoichiometry) is needed for the converter to work properly. The oxygen sensor, installed in the exhaust manifold, monitors the exhaust mixture and sends a signal to the module. The module then determines whether the air/fuel mixture is correct; if not, it sends a signal to the mixture control solenoid vacuum valve, altering the mixture slightly to bring it back within the narrow band required by the converter.

The Thermactor (air pump) system provides the converter with oxygen for the oxidation reaction.

8-302
8-351 w/Fuel Injection:
Positive Crankcase Ventilation system (PCV)
Evaporative Emission system (canister)
Three-way Catalyst (TWC)
Conventional Oxidation Catalyst (COC)
Electronic Fuel Injection Fuel System (EFI)
Electronic Engine Control IV system (EEC-IV)
Electronic (Sonic) Exhaust Gas Recirculation (EEGR)
Managed Thermactor Air system (MTA)
Air Management 1 system (AM1)
Air Management 2 system (AM2)
Thick Film Ignition system (TFI-IV)
Bypass Air idle speed control (BPA)

8-351 w/4-bbl Carburetor:
Positive Crankcase Ventilation system (PCV)
Evaporative Emission system (canister)
Three-way Catalyst (TWC)
Conventional Oxidation Catalyst (COC)
Holley 4180C 4-bbl carburetor
Integral backpressure EGR valve (IBP)
Managed Thermactor Air System (MTA)
Dura Spark II Ignition System (DS-II)

Ford Electronic Engine Control System

NOTE: *Because of the complicated nature of the EEC systems, special tools and procedures are necessary for testing and troubleshooting. The EEC systems should be serviced by qualified mechanics using the required equipment.*

EEC-I

Ford's EEC-I system was introduced in 1978, on the Lincoln Versailles. Designed to precisely control ignition timing, EGR and Thermactor (air pump) flow, the system consists of an Electronic Control Assembly (ECA), seven monitoring sensors, a DuraSpark II ignition module and coil, a special distributor assembly, and EGR system designed to operate on air pressure.

The ECA is a solid state micro computer, consisting of a processor assembly and a calibra-

tion assembly. the processor continuously receives inputs from the seven sensors, which it converts to usable information for the calculating section of the computer. It also performs ignition timing, Thermactor and EGR flow calculations, processes the information and sends out signals to the ignition module and control solenoids to adjust the timing and flow of the systems accordingly. The calibration assembly contains the memory and programming for the processor.

Processor inputs come from sensors monitoring manifold pressure, barometric pressure, engine coolant temperature, inlet air temperature, crankshaft position, throttle position, and EGR valve position.

The manifold absolute pressure sensor determines changes in intake manifold pressure (barometric pressure minus manifold vacuum) which result from changes in engine load and speed, or in atmospheric pressure. Its signal is used by the ECA to set part throttle spark advance and EGR flow rate.

Barometric pressure is monitored by a sensor mounted on the firewall. Measurements taken are converted into usable electrical signal. The ECA uses this reference for altitude dependent EGR flow requirements.

Engine coolant temperature is measured at the rear of the intake manifold by a sensor consisting of a brass housing containing a thermistor (resistance decreases as temperature rises). When reference voltage (about 9 volts, supplied by the processor to all sensors(is applied to the sensor, the resistance can be measured by the resulting voltage drop. Resistance is then interpreted as coolant temperature by the ECA. This sensor replaces both the PVS and EGR PVS in conventional systems. EGR flow is cut off by the ECA when a predetermined temperature value is reached. The ECA will also advance initial ignition timing to increase idle speed if the coolant overheats due to prolonged idle. A faster idle speed increases coolant and radiator air flow.

Inlet air temperature is measured by a sensor mounted in the air cleaner. It functions in the same way as the coolant sensor. the ECA uses it signal for proper spark advance and Thermactor flow. At high inlet temperatures (above 90°F) the ECA modifies timing advance to prevent spark knock.

The crankshaft is fitted with a four-lobed powdered metal pulse ring, positioned 10° BTDC. Its position is constantly monitored by the crankshaft position sensor. Signals are sent to the ECA describing both the position of the crankshaft at any given moment, and the frequency of the pulses (engine rpm). These signals are used to determine optimum ignition

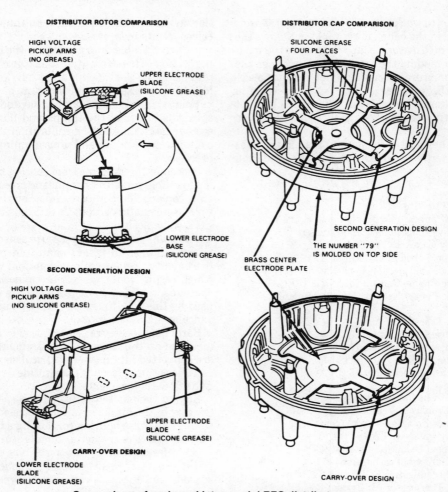

DISTRIBUTOR ROTOR COMPARISON

HIGH VOLTAGE
PICKUP ARMS
(NO GREASE)

UPPER ELECTRODE
BLADE
(SILICONE GREASE)

LOWER ELECTRODE
BASE
(SILICONE GREASE)

SECOND GENERATION DESIGN

HIGH VOLTAGE
PICKUP ARMS
(NO SILICONE GREASE)

UPPER ELECTRODE
BLADE
(SILICONE GREASE)

CARRY-OVER DESIGN

LOWER ELECTRODE
BLADE
(SILICONE GREASE)

DISTRIBUTOR CAP COMPARISON

SILICONE GREASE
FOUR PLACES

SECOND GENERATION DESIGN

THE NUMBER "79"
IS MOLDED ON TOP SIDE

BRASS CENTER
ELECTRODE PLATE

CARRY-OVER DESIGN

Comparison of early and later model EEC distributor caps

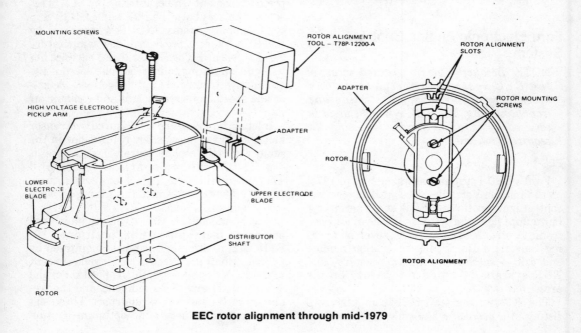

MOUNTING SCREWS

ROTOR ALIGNMENT
TOOL — T78P-12200-A

ROTOR ALIGNMENT
SLOTS

ADAPTER

ROTOR MOUNTING
SCREWS

HIGH VOLTAGE ELECTRODE
PICKUP ARM

ADAPTER

ROTOR

LOWER
ELECTRODE
BLADE

UPPER ELECTRODE
BLADE

DISTRIBUTOR
SHAFT

ROTOR

ROTOR ALIGNMENT

EEC rotor alignment through mid-1979

timing advance. If either the sensor or wiring is broken, the ECA will not receive a signal, and thus be unable to send any signal to the ignition module. This will prevent the engine from starting.

The throttle position sensor is a rheostat connected to the throttle plate shaft. Changes in throttle plate angle change the resistance value of the reference voltage supplied by the processor. Signals are interpreted in one of three ways by the ECA.

- Closed throttle (idle or deceleration).
- Part throttle (cruise)
- Full throttle (maximum acceleration)

A position sensor is built into the EGR valve. The ECA uses its signal to determine EGR valve position. The valve and position sensor are replaced as a unit, should with fail.

CAUTION: *Because of the complicated nature of this system, special diagnostic tools are necessary for troubleshooting. Any troubleshooting without these tools must be limited to mechanical checks of connectors and wiring.*

The distributor is locked in place during engine manufacture; no rotational adjustment is possible for initial ignition timing, since all timing is controlled by the ECA. There are no mechanical advance mechanisms or adjustments under the rotor, thus there is no need to remove it except for replacement.

EEC-II

The second generation EEC II system was introduced in 1979 on full size Fords and Mercurys. It is based on the EEC I system used on the Versailles, but some changes have been made to reduce complexity and cost, increase the number of controlled functions, and improve reliability and performance.

In general, the EEC-II system operates in the same manner as EEC-I. An Electronic Control Assembly (ECA) monitors reports from six sensors, and adjust the EGR flow, ignition timing, Thermactor (air pump) air flow, and carburetor air/fuel mixture in response to the incoming signals. Although there are only six sensors, seven conditions are monitored. The sensors are:

1. Engine Coolant Temperature.
2. Throttle position.
3. Crankshaft Position.
4. Exhaust Gas Oxygen.
5. Barometric and Manifold Absolute Pressure.
6. EGR Valve Position.

These sensors function in the same manner as the EEC-I sensors, and are described in the EEC-I section. Note that inlet air temperature is not monitored in the EEC-II system, and that the barometric and manifold pressure sensors have been combined into one unit. One more change from the previous system is in the location of the crankshaft sensor: it is mounted on the front of the engine, behind the vibration damper and crankshaft pulley.

The biggest difference between EEC-I and EEC-II is that the newer system is capable of continually monitoring and adjusting the carburetor air/fuel ratio. Monitoring is performed by the oxygen sensor installed in the right exhaust manifold; adjustment is made via an electric stepper motor installed on the model 7200 VV carburetor.

The stepper motor has four separate armature windings, which can be sequentially energized by the ECA. As the motor varies the position of the carburetor metering valve, the amount of control vacuum exposed to the fuel bowl is correspondingly altered. Increased vacuum reduces pressure in the fuel bowl, causing a leaner air/fuel mixture, and vice versa. During engine starting and immediately after, the ECA sets the motor at a point dependent on its initial position. Thereafter, the motor position is changed in response to the ECA calculations of the six input signals.

EEC-II is also capable of controlling purging of vapors from the evaporative emission control storage canister. A canister purge solenoid, a combination solenoid and valve, is located in the line between the intake manifold purge fitting and the carbon canister. It controls the flow of vapors from the canister to the intake manifold, opening and closing in response to signals from the ECA.

WARNING: *As is the case with EEC I, diagnosis and repair of the system requires special tools and equipment.*

The distributor is locked in place during engine manufacture; no rotational adjustment is possible for initial ignition timing, since all timing is controlled by the ECA. There are no mechanical advance mechanisms or adjustments under the ignition rotor, and thus there is no need to remove it except for replacement.

Air/fuel mixture is entirely controlled by the ECA; no adjustments are possible.

EEC-III

EEC-III was introduced in 1980. It is a third generation system developed entirely from EEC-II. The only real differences between EEC-II and III are contained within the Electronic Control Assembly (ECA) and the DuraSpark ignition module. The EEC-III system uses a separate program module which plugs into the main ECA module. This change allows various programming calibrations for specific applications to be made to the program module, while allowing the main ECA module to be standardized. Additionally, EEC-III uses a DuraSpark III ignition module, which contains fewer electronic functions than the DuraSpark II module; the functions have been incorporated into the main ECA module. there is no interchangeability between the DuraSpark II and III modules.

NOTE: *Since late 1979 emission controls and air/fuel mixtures have been controlled by various electronic methods. An electronically controlled feedback carburetor is used to precisely calibrate fuel metering, many vacuum check valves, solenoids and regulators have been added and the electronic control boxes (ECU and MCU) can be calibrated and programmed in order to be used by different engines and under different conditions.*

EEC-IV

Most 1984 and later US models are equipped with the EEC-IV system. The heart of the EEC-IV system is a microprocessor called an electronic control assembly (ECA). The ECA receives data from a number of sensors and other electronic components (switches, relays, etc.). Based on information received and information programmed in the ECA's memory, it generates output signals to control various relays, solenoids and other actuators. The ECA in the EEC-IV system has calibration modules located inside the assembly that contain calibration specifications for optimizing emissions, fuel economy and driveability. The calibration module is called a PROM.

A potentiometer senses the position of an airflow meter in the engine's air induction system and generates a voltage signal that varies with the amount of air drawn into the engine. A sensor is the area of the airflow meter measures the temperature of the incoming air and transmits a corresponding electrical signal. Another temperature sensor inserted in the engine coolant tells if the engine is cold or warmed up. and a switch that senses throttle plate position produces electrical signals that tell the control unit when the throttle is closed or wide open.

A special probe (oxygen sensor) in the exhaust manifold measures the amount of oxygen in the exhaust gas, which is a indication of combustion efficiency, and sends a signal to the control unit. The sixth signal, Crankshaft position information, is transmitted by a sensor integral with the new design distributor.

The EEC-IV microcomputer circuit process the input signals and produces output control signals to the fuel injectors to regulate fuel discharge to the injectors. The EEC-IV distributor incorporates a Hall Effect vane switch stator assembly and an integrally mounted thickfilm module. When the Hall Effect device is tuned on and a pulse is produced, the EEC-IV electronics computes crankshaft position and engine demand to calibrate spark advance.

TFI-IV System

The TFI-IV ignition system features a universal distributor using no centrifugal or vacuum advance. The distributor has a die cast base which incorporates an integrally mounted TFI (Thick Film Integrated) ignition module, a Hall Effect vane switch stator assembly and provision for fixed octane adjustment. The TFI system uses an E-Core ignition coil in lieu of the DuraSpark coil. No distributor calibration is required and initial timing is not a normal adjustment, since advance etc. is controlled by the EEC-IV system.

The Universal Distributor (EEC-IV) has a diecast base which incorporates an externally mounted TFI-IV ignition module, and contains a Hall Effect vane switch stator assembly and provision for fixed octane adjustment. No distributor calibration is required and initial timing adjustment is normally not required. The primary function of the EEC-IV Universal Distributor system is to direct high secondary voltage to the spark plugs. In addition, the distributor supplies crankshaft position and frequency information to a computer using a profile Ignition Pickup. The Hall Effect switch in the distributor consists of a Hall Effect device on one side and a magnet on the other side. A rotary cup which has windows and tabs rotates and passes through the space between the device and the magnet. When a window is between the sides of the switch the magnetic path is not completed and the switch is Off, sending no signal. When a tab passes between the switch the magnetic path is completed and the Hall Effect Device is turned On and a signal is sent. The voltage pulse (signal) is used by is EEC-IV system for sensing crankshaft position and computing the desired spark advance based on engine demand and calibration.

The heart of the EEC-IV system is a microprocessor called the Electronic Control Assembly (ECA). The ECA receives data from a number of sensors, switches and relays. The ECA contains a specific calibration for peak fuel economy, drivability and emissions control. Based on information stored in its memory, the ECA generates siganls to control the various engine functions.

The ECA calibraction module is located inside the ECA assembly. On all cars, the ECA is located on the left of the firewall, behind the kick panel.

EMISSION COMPONENTS

NOTE: *The following emission control devices described can be tested and maintained, any not mentioned should be serviced by qualified mechanics using the required equipment.*

Positive Crankcase Ventilation System

All 1968 and later models are equipped with a positive crankcase ventilation (PCV) system to control crankcase blow-by vapors. The system consists of a PCV valve and oil separator mounted on top of the valve cover, a nonventilated oil filter cap, and a pair of hoses supplying filtered intake air to the valve cover and delivering the crankcase vapors from the valve cover to the intake manifold (6-cylinder) or carburetor (V8). The system functions as follows:

When the engine is running, a small portion of the gases which are formed in the combustion chamber leak by the piston rings and enter the crankcase. Since these gases are under pressure, they tend to escape from the crankcase and enter the atmosphere. If these cases are allowed to remain in the crankcase for any period of time, they contaminate the engine oil and cause sludge to build up in the crankcase. If the gases are allowed to escape into the atmosphere, they pollute the air, with unburned hydrocarbons.

The job of the crankcase emission control equipment is to recycle these gases back into the engine combustion chamber where they are reburned.

The crankcase (blow-by) gases are recycled in the following way: as the engine is running, clean, filtered air is drawn through the air filter and into the crankcase. As the air passes through the crankcase, it picks up the combustion gases and carries them out of the crank-

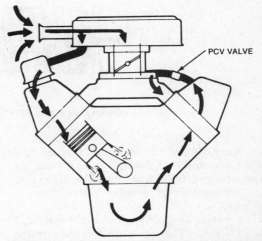

PCV VALVE

Positive crankcase ventilation system operation —V8

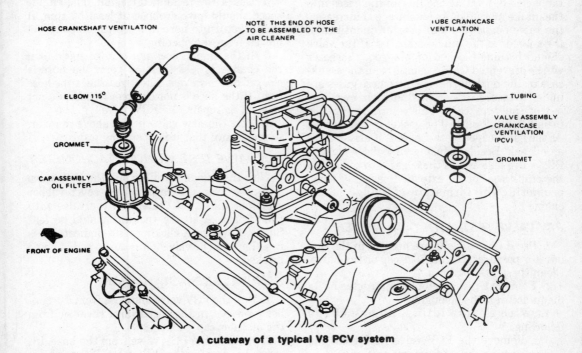

HOSE CRANKSHAFT VENTILATION

NOTE THIS END OF HOSE TO BE ASSEMBLED TO THE AIR CLEANER

TUBE CRANKCASE VENTILATION

ELBOW 115°

TUBING

VALVE ASSEMBLY CRANKCASE VENTILATION (PCV)

GROMMET

GROMMET

CAP ASSEMBLY OIL FILTER

FRONT OF ENGINE

A cutaway of a typical V8 PCV system

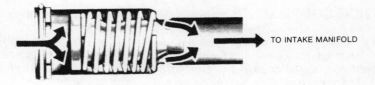

LOW SPEED OPERATION—HIGH MANIFOLD VACUUM

HIGH SPEED OPERATION—LOW MANIFOLD VACUUM

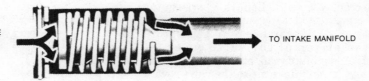

A cutaway view of a PCV valve showing its operation

case, through the oil separator, through the PCV valve, and into the induction system. As they enter the intake manifold, they are drawn into the combustion chamber where they are reburned.

The most critical component in the system is the PCV valve. This valve controls the amount of gases which are recycled into the combustion chamber. At low engine speeds, the valve is partially closed, limiting the flow of the gases into the intake manifold. As engine speed increases, the valve opens to admit greater quantities of the gases into the intake manifold. If the valve should become blocked or plugged, the gases will be prevented from escaping from the crankcase by the normal route. Since these gases are under pressure, they will find their own way out of the crankcase. This alternate route is usually a weak oil seal or gasket in the engine. As the gas escapes by the gasket, it also creates an oil leak. Besides causing oil leaks, a clogged PCV valve also allows these gases to remain in the crankcase for an extended period of time, promoting the formation of sludge in the engine.

PCV VALVE TEST, WITH TACHOMETER

1. See if any deposits are present in the carburetor passages, the oil filler cap or the hoses. Clean these are required.

2. Connect a tachometer, as instructed by its manufacturer, to the engine.

3. With engine idling, do one of the following:

    a. Remove the PCV valve hose from the crankcase or the oil filter connections.

    b. On cars with the PCV valve located in a grommet on the valve cover, remove both the valve and the grommet.

NOTE: *If the valve and the hoses are not clogged up, a hissing sound should be present.*

4. Check the tachometer reading. Place a finger over the valve or hose opening (a suction should be felt).

5. Check the tachometer again. The engine speed should have dropped at least 50 rpm. It should return to normal when the finger is removed from the opening.

6. If the engine does not change speed or if the change is less than 50 rpm, the hose is clogged or the valve is defective. Check the hose first. If the hose is not clogged, replace, do not attempt to repair, the PCV valve.

7. Test the new valve in the above manner, to make sure that it is operating properly.

PCV VALVE TEST, WITHOUT TACHOMETER

With the engine running, pull the PCV valve and hose from the valve rocker cover rubber grommet. Block off the end of the valve with your finger. A strong vacuum should be felt. Shake the valve; a clicking noise indicates it is free. Replace the valve if it is suspected of being blocked.

REMOVAL AND INSTALLATION

1. Pull the PCV valve and hose from the rubber grommet in the rocker arm cover or from the oil filler cap.

2. Remove the PCV valve from the hose. Inspect the inside of the PCV valve. If the valve is

gummy it can be cleaned in a suitable, safe solvent. However, replacing a clogged, gummed up PCV valve with a new one is suggested.

3. Soak the rubber ventilation hose(s) in a low volatility petroleum base solvent to loosen the deposits. Pass a suitable cleaning brush through them and blow out with compressed air or let air-dry.

4. Thoroughly wash the crankcase breather cap (if equipped) in solvent and shake dry. Do not dry with compressed air; damage to the filtering material may result.

5. Replace any hard or cracked hoses or ones that are clogged and cannot be cleaned.

6. The installation of the hoses and PCV valve is in the reverse order of removal.

Fuel Evaporative Control System

1970 models manufactured for sale in California, and all 1971 and later models nationwide are equipped with a fuel evaporative control system to prevent the evaporation of unburned gasoline. The 1970 system consists of a sealed fuel tank filler cap, an expansion area at the top of the gas tank, a combination vapor separator and expansion tank assembly, a 3-way vapor control valve, a carbon canister located in the engine compartment which stores these vapors, and the hoses which connect this equipment. the 1971 and later system consists of a special vacuum/pressure relief filler cap, and expansion area at the top of the fuel tank, a foam-filled vapor separator mounted on top of the fuel tank, a carbon canister which stores fuel vapors and hoses which connect this equipment. On both systems, the carburetor fuel

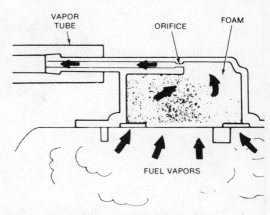

Fuel vapors entering vapor separator

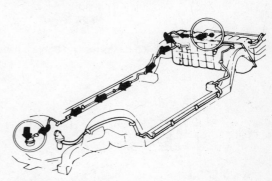

Routing of fuel tank vapors

bowl vapors are retained within the fuel bowl until the engine is started, at which point they are internally vented into the engine for burning. The system functions as follows:

Changes in atmospheric temperature cause

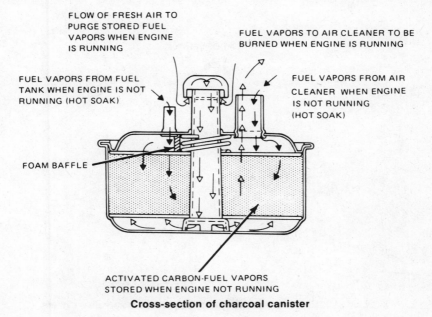

Cross-section of charcoal canister

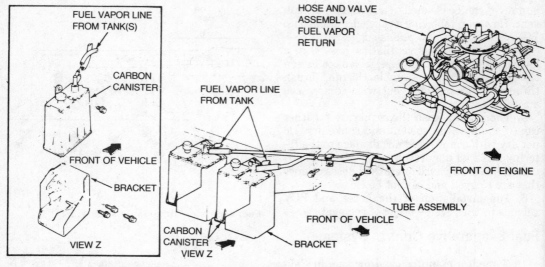

1987 8-460 California and Canada heavy duty carbureted evaporative system

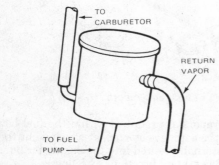

Vapor separator

the gasoline in fuel tanks to expand or contract. If this expansion and consequent vaporization take place in a conventional fuel tank, the fuel vapors escape through the filler cap or vent hose and pollute the atmosphere. The fuel evaporative emission control system prevents this by routing the gasoline vapors to the engine where they are burned.

As the gasoline in the fuel tank of a parked car begins to expand due to heat, the vapor that forms moves to the top of the fuel tank. The fuel tanks on all 1970 and later cars are enlarged so that there exists an area representing

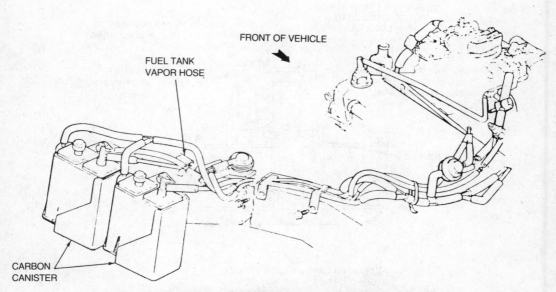

8-351 49 States and Canada heavy duty carbureted evaporative system

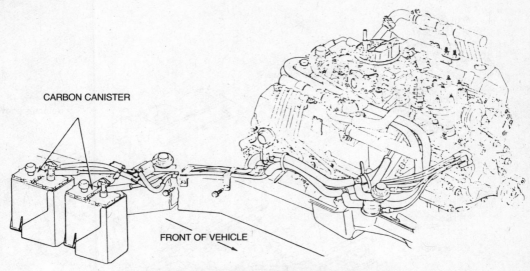

CARBON CANISTER

FRONT OF VEHICLE

8-460 49 States heavy duty carbureted evaporative system

10-20% of the total fuel tank volume above the level of the fuel tank filler tube where these gases may collect. The vapors then travel upward into the vapor separator which prevents liquid gasoline from escaping from the fuel tank. The fuel vapor is then drawn through the vapor separator outlet hose, through the 3-way vapor control valve (1970 only), then to the charcoal canister in the engine compartment. The vapor enters the canister, passes through a charcoal filter, and then exist through the canister's grated bottom. As the vapor passes through the charcoal, it is cleansed by hydrocarbons, so that the air that passes out of the bottom of the canister is free of pollutants.

When the engine is started, Vacuum from the carburetor draws fresh air into the canister. As the entering air passes through the charcoal in the canister, it picks up the hydrocarbons that were deposited there by the fuel vapors. this mixture of hydrocarbons and fresh air is then carried through a hose in the air cleaner. In the carburetor, it combines with the incoming air/fuel mixture and enters the combustion chambers of the engine where it is burned.

On both systems, there still remains the problem of allowing air into the tank to replace the gasoline Displaced during normal use and the problem of Relieving excess pressure from the fuel tank should it reach a dangerous level.

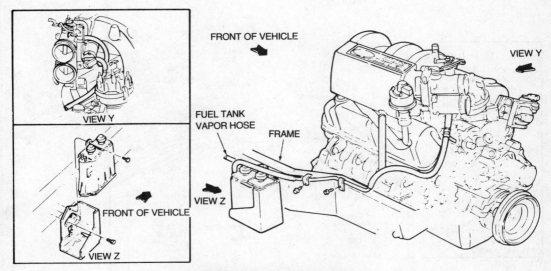

VIEW Y

FRONT OF VEHICLE

VIEW Y

FUEL TANK VAPOR HOSE

FRAME

VIEW Z

FRONT OF VEHICLE

VIEW Z

8-302 EFI Canada evaporative system

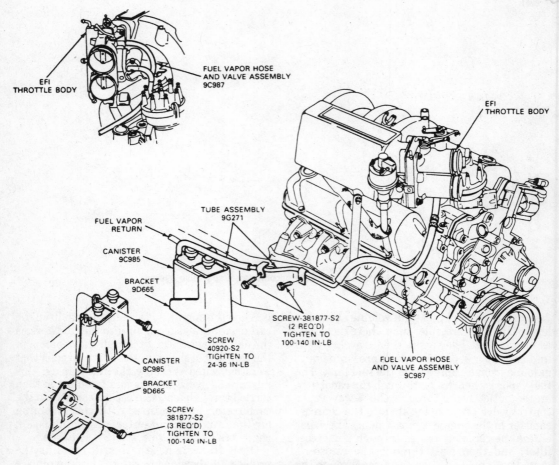

1987-88 8-302 EFI evaporative system

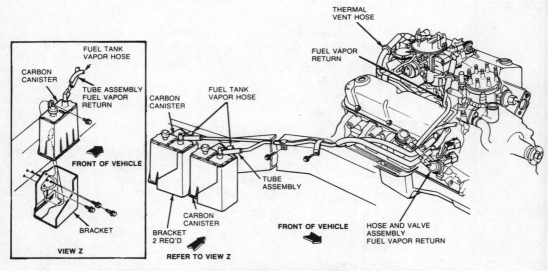

8-351 4-bbl 49 States and High Altitude light duty carbureted evaporative system

On 1970 systems, the 3-way control valve accomplishes this. On 1971 and later systems, the special filler cap Performs this task. Under normal circumstances, the filler cap functions as a check valve, allowing air to enter the tank to replace the fuel consumed. At the same time it prevents vapors from escaping from the cap. In case of severe pressure within the tank, the filler cap valve opens, venting the pollutants to the atmosphere.

DIAGNOSIS AND TESTING

Canister Purge Regulator Valve

1. Disconnect the hoses at the purge regulator valve. Disconnect the electrical lead.
2. Connect a vacuum pump to the vacuum source port.
3. Apply 5 in.Hg to the port. The valve should hold the vacuum. If not, replace it.

Canister Purge Valve

1. Apply vacuum to port **A**. The valve should hold vacuum. If not, replace it.
2. Apply vacuum to port **B**. Valves E5VE-AA, E4VE-AA and E77E-AA should show a slight vacuum leak-down. All other valves should hold vacuum. If the valve doesn't operate properly, replace it.
3. Apply 16 in.Hg to port **A** and apply vacuum to port **B**. Air should pass. On valves E5VE-AA, E4VE-AA and E77E-AA, the flow should be greater than that noted in Step 2.
NOTE: *Never apply vacuum to port C. Doing so will damage the valve.*
4. If the valve fails to perform properly in any of these tests, replace it.

VENT VALVE REPLACEMENT

Except for 1970 models manufactured for sale in California, the only service performed on the evaporative control system is the replacement of the charcoal (carbon) canister at the intervals listed in the maintenance schedule in Chapter 1. The above mentioned California registered 1970 models require replacement of the 3-way vent valve once a year or every 12,000 miles. The procedure is as follows.
1. Working under the vehicle, disconnect two hoses from the control valve. Remove the vent valve cover.
2. Remove two attaching bolts and remove the valve from the crossmember of the rear of the gas tank.
3. To install, position the valve to the crossmember and install two attaching bolts.
4. Connect the two hoses to the valve assembly. Install the cover.

CANISTER REMOVAL AND INSTALLATION

Loosen and remove the canister mounting bolts from the mounting bracket. Disconnect the purge hose from the air cleaner and the feed hose from the fuel tank. Discard the old canister and install a new unit. Make sure that the hoses are connected properly.

Thermactor System

The Thermactor emission control system makes use of a belt driven air pump to inject fresh air into the hot exhaust stream through the engine exhaust ports. The result is the extending burning of those fumes which were not completely ignited in the combustion chamber, and the subsequent reduction of some of the hydrocarbon and carbon monoxide content of the exhaust emissions into harmless carbon dioxide and water.

The Thermactor system is composed of the following components:
1. Air supply pump (belt driven)
2. Air by-pass valve
3. Check valves
4. Air manifold (internal or external)
5. Air supply tubes (on external manifold only).

Air for the Thermactor system is cleaned by means of a centrifugal filter fan mounted on the air pump driveshaft. the air filter does not require a replaceable element.

To prevent excessive pressure, the air pump is equipped with a pressure relief valve which uses a replaceable plastic plug to control the pressure setting.

The Thermactor air pump has sealed bearings which are lubricated for the life of the unit, and preset rotor vane and bearing clearances, which do not require an periodic adjustments.

The air supply from the pump is controlled by the air by-pass valve, sometimes called a dump valve. During deceleration, the air by-pass valve opens, momentarily diverting the air supply through a silencer and into the atmosphere, thus preventing backfires within the exhaust system.

A check valve is incorporated in the air inlet side of the air manifolds. Its purpose is to prevent exhaust gases from backing up into the Thermactor system. This valve is especially important in the event of drive belt failure, and during deceleration, when the air by-pass valve is dumping the air supply.

The air manifolds and air supply tubes channel the air from the Thermactor air pump into the exhaust ports of each cylinder, thus completing the cycle of the Thermactor system.

THERMACTOR SYSTEM CHECKS

Before performing an extensive diagnosis of the emission control systems, verify that all specifications on the Certification Label are met, because the following systems or components may cause symptoms that appear to be emission related.

    a. Improper vacuum connections
    b. Vacuum leaks.
    c. Ignition timing
    d. Plugs, wires, cap and rotor
    e. Carburetor float level
    f. Carburetor main metering jets.
    g. Choke operation

Fabricating a Test Gauge Adapter

In order to test the three major components of a Thermactor system (air pump, check valve and bypass valve), a pressure gauge and adapter are required. The adapter can be fabricated as follows:

1. Obtain these items:
    a. ½″ pipe tee
    b. ½″ pipe, 2 inches long and threaded at one end
    c. ½″ pipe plug
    d. ½″ reducer bushing or other suitable gauge adapter.
2. Apply sealer to threaded ends of pipe, plug and bushing. Assemble as shown in the illustration.
3. Drill an $^{11}/_{32}″$ diameter hole through center of pipe plug. Clean out chips after drilling.

4. Attach pressure gauge with ¼ psi increments to bushing or adapter.

Air Pump Tests

WARNING: *Do not hammer on, pry or bend the pump housing while tightening the drive belt or testing the pump.*

BELT TENSION AND AIR LEAKS

1. Before proceeding with the tests, check the pump drive belt tension to see if it is within specifications.
2. Turn the pump by hand. If it has seized, the belt will slip, producing noise. disregard any chirping, squealing, or rolling sounds from inside the pump; these are normal when it is turned by hand.
3. Check the hoses and connections for leaks. Hissing or a blast of air is indicative of a leak. Soapy water, applied lightly around the areas in question, is a good method of detecting leaks.

AIR OUTPUT TEST

1. Disconnect the air supply hose at the antibackfire valve.
2. Connect a vacuum gauge, using a suitable adaptor, to the air supply hose.
NOTE: *If there are two hoses plug the second one.*
3. With the engine at normal operating temperature, increase the idle speed and watch the vacuum gauge.
4. The air flow from the pump should be

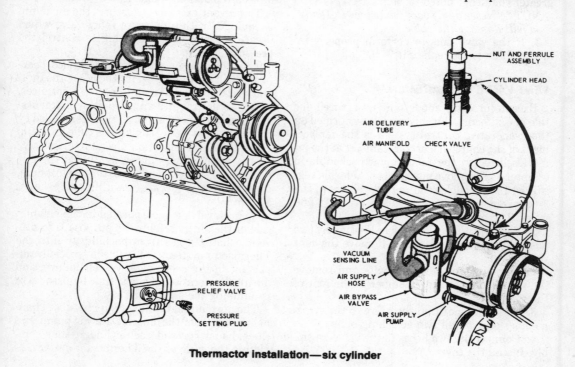

Thermactor installation—six cylinder

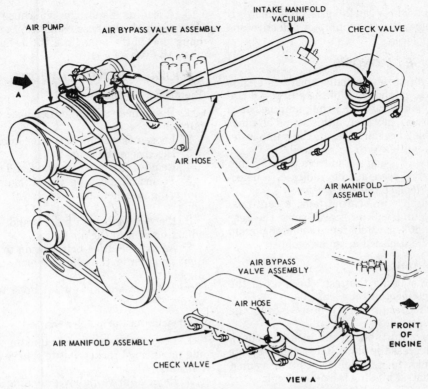

Typical thermactor installation—V8 except 390 and 428

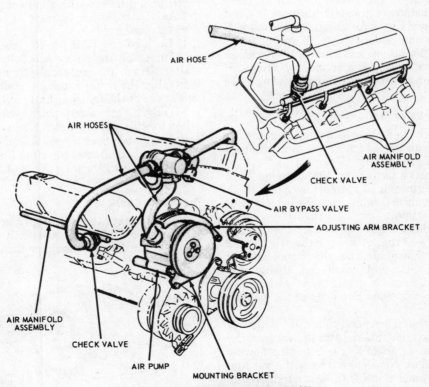

Thermactor installation—390, 428 V8

steady and fall between 2-6 psi. If it is unsteady or falls below this, the pump is defective and must be replaced.

PUMP NOISE DIAGNOSIS

The air pump is normally noisy; as engine speed increases, the noise of the pump will rise in pitch. The rolling sound the pump bearings make is normal; however, if this sound becomes objectionable at certain speeds, the pump is defective and will have to be replaced.

A continual hissing sound from the air pump pressure relief valve at idle, indicates a defective valve. Replace the relief valve.

If the pump rear bearing fails, a continual knocking sound will be heard. since the rear bearing is not separately replaceable, the pump will the to be replaced as an assembly.

Check Valve Test

1. Before starting the test, check all of the hoses and connections for leaks.

2. Detach the air supply hose(s) from the check valve.

3. Insert a suitable probe into the check valve and depress the plate. Release it; the plate should return to its original position against the valve seat. If binding is evident, replace the valve.

4. Repeat step 3 if two valves are used.

5. With the engine running at normal operating temperature, gradually increase it speed to 1,500 rpm. Check for exhaust gas leakage. If any is present, replace the valve assembly.

NOTE: *Vibration and flutter of the check valve at idle speed is a normal condition and does not mean that the valve should be replaced.*

Air Bypass Valve Test

1. Detach the hose, which runs from the bypass valve to the check valve, at the bypass valve hose connection.

2. Connect a tachometer to the engine. With the engine running at normal idle speed, check to see that air is flowing from the bypass valve hose connection.

3. Speed the engine up, so that it is running at 1,500-2,000 rpm. Allow the throttle to snap shut. The flow of air from the bypass valve at the check valve hose connection should stop momentarily and air should then flow from the exhaust port on the valve body or the silencer assembly.

4. repeat step 3 several times. If the flow of air is not diverted into the atmosphere from the valve exhaust port of if it fails to stop flowing from the hose connection, check the vacuum lines and connections. If these are tighten, the valve is defective and requires replacement.

5. A leaking diaphragm will cause the air to flow out both the hose connection and the exhaust port at the same time. If this happens, replace the valve.

REMOVAL AND INSTALLATION

Thermactor Air Pump

1. Disconnect the air outlet hose at the air pump.

2. Loosen the pump belt tension adjuster.

3. Disengage the drive belt.

4. Remove the mounting bolt and air pump.

5. To install, position the air pump on the mounting bracket and install the mounting bolts.

6. Place drive belt in pulleys and attach the adjusting arm to the air pump.

7. Adjust the drive belt tension to specifications and tighten the adjusting arm and mounting bolts.

8. connect the air outlet hose to the air pump.

Thermactor Air Pump Filter Fan

1. Loosen the air pump adjusting arm bolt and mounting bracket bolt to relieve drive belt tension.

2. Remove drive pulley attaching bolts and pull drive pulley off the air pump shaft.

3. Pry the outer disc loose; then, pull off the centrifugal filter fan with slip-joint pliers.

WARNING: *Do not attempt to remove the metal drive hub!*

4. Install a new filter fan by drawing it into position, using the pulley and bolts as an installer. Draw the fan evenly by alternately tightening the bolts, making certain that the outer edge of the fan slips into the housing.

NOTE: *A slight interference with the housing bore is normal. After a new fan is installed, it may squeal upon initial operation, until its outer diameter sealing lip has worn in, which may require 20 to 30 miles of operation.*

Thermactor Check Valve

1. Disconnect the air supply hose at the valve. (Use a 1¼" crowfoot wrench, the valve has a standard, right hand pipe thread).

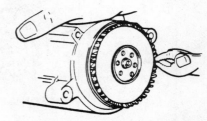

Thermactor air pump filter fan removal

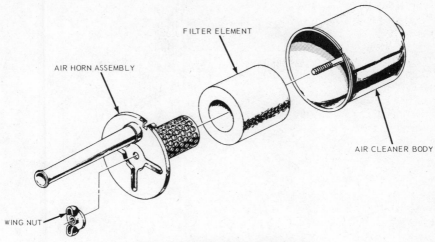

Early model Thermactor air cleaner

2. Clean the threads on the air manifold adaptor or air supply tube with a wire brush. do not blow compressed air through the check valve in either direction.

3. Install the check valve and tighten.

4. Connect the air supply hose.

Thermactor Air By-pass Valve

1. Disconnect the air and vacuum hoses at the air by-pass valve body.

2. Position the air by-pass valve, and connect the respective hoses.

Managed Thermactor Air System

The MTA system is used to inject fresh air into the exhaust manifolds or catalytic conveters via an air control valve. Under some operating conditions, the air can be dumped back into the atmosphere via an air bypass valve. On some applications the two valves are combined into one unit. The air bypass valve

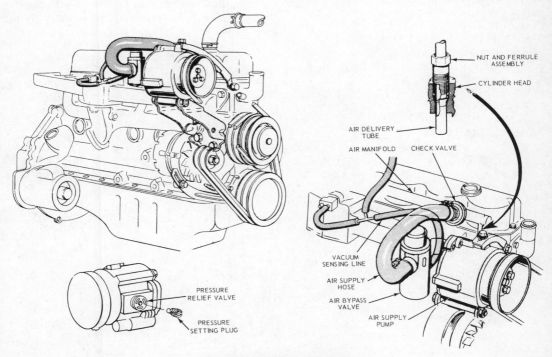

1969 6-240 Thermactor system

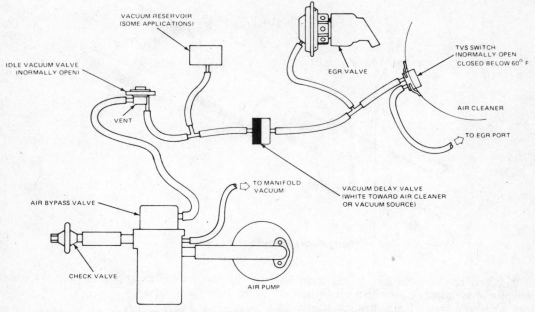

1978 Thermactor idle valve with vacuum delay valve

can be either the normally closed type, when the valves are separate, or the normally open type, when the valves are combined.

Normally Closed Air Bypass Valve Functional Test

1. Disconnect the air supply hose at the valve.

2. Run the engine to normal operating temperature.

3. Disconnect the vacuum line and make sure vacuum is present. If no vacuum is present, remove or bypass any restrictors or delay valves in the vacuum line.

4. Run the engine at 1,500 rpm with the vacuum line connected. Air pump supply air

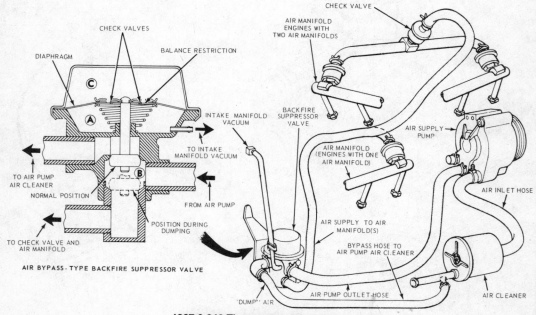

1967 6-240 Thermactor vacuum components

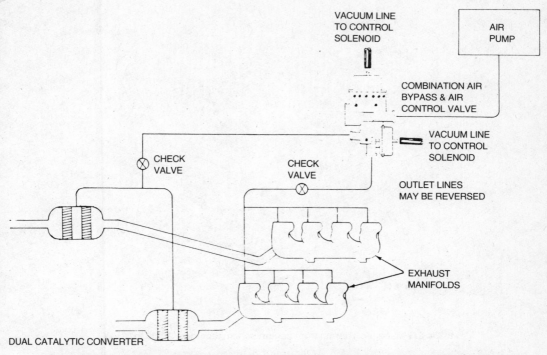

Managed Thermactor system with combined bypass/control valve—electronically controlled

should be heard and felt at the valve outlet.

5. With the engine still at 1,500 rpm, disconnect the vacuum line. Air at the outlet should shut off or dramatically decrease. Air pump supply air should now be felt or heard at the silencer ports.

6. If the valve doesn't pass each of these tests, replace it.

Normally Open Air Bypass Valve Functional Test

1. Disconnect the air supply hose at the valve.

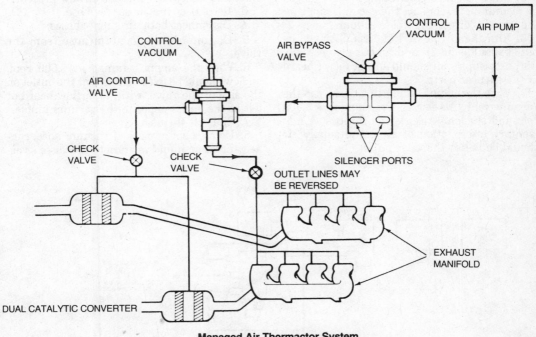

Managed Air Thermactor System

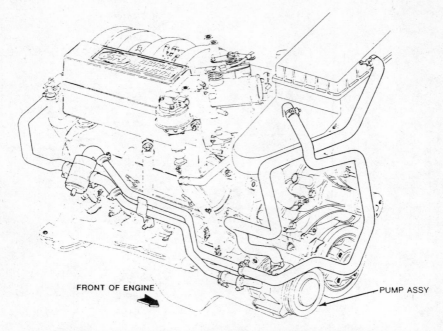

8-351 EFI Managed Thermactor vacuum schematic under 8,500 lb. GVW

2. Run the engine to normal operating temperature.

3. Disconnect the vacuum lines from the valve.

4. Run the engine at 1,500 rpm with the vacuum lines disconnected. Air pump supply air should be heard and felt at the valve outlet.

5. Shut off the engine. Using a spare length of vacuum hose, connect the vacuum nipple of the valve to direct manifold vacuum.

6. Run the engine at 1,500 rpm. Air at the outlet should shut off or dramatically decrease. Air pump supply air should now be felt or heard at the silencer ports.

7. With the engine still in this mode, cap the vacuum vent. Accelerate the engine to 2,000 rpm and suddenly release the throttle. A momentary interruption of air pump supply air should be felt at the valve outlet.

8. If the valve doesn't pass each of these tests, replace it. Reconnect all lines.

Air Control Valve Functional Test

1. Run the engine to normal operating temperature, then increase the speed to 1,500 rpm.

2. Disconnect the air supply hose at the valve inlet and verify that there is airflow present.

3. Reconnect the air supply hose.

4. Disconnect both air supply hoses.

5. Disconnect the vacuum hose from the valve.

6. With the engine running at 1,500 rpm, airflow should be felt and heard at the outlet on the side of the valve, with no airflow heard or felt at the outlet opposite the vacuum nipple.

7. Shut off the engine.

8. Using a spare piece of vacuum hose, connect direct manifold vacuum to the valve's vac-

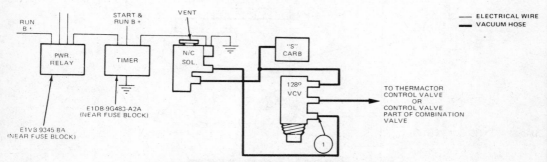

Thermactor air timer system vacuum schematic

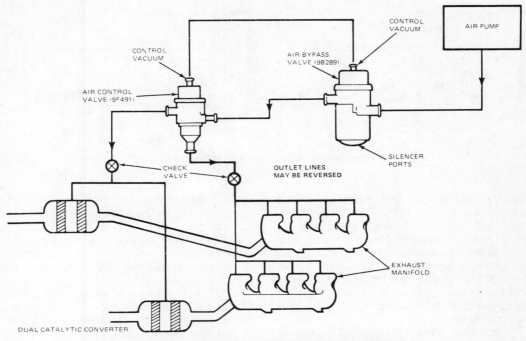

General vacuum schematic for the Managed Thermactor system

uum fitting. Airflow should be heard and felt at the outlet opposite the vacuum nipple, and no airflow should be present at the other outlet.

9. If the valve is not functioning properly, replace it.

Air Supply Pump Functional Check

1. Check and, if necessary, adjust the belt tension. Press at the mid-point of the belt's longest straight run. You should be able to depress the belt about ½" at most.

2. Run the engine to normal operating temperature and let it idle.

3. Disconnect the air supply hose from the bypass control valve. If the pump is operating properly, airflow should be felt at the pump outlet. The flow should increase as you increase the engine speed. The pump is not servicable and should be replaced if it is not functioning properly.

Improved Combustion System

All 1968 models equipped with automatic transmission, all 1969 models except the 428 Police Interceptor engine, and all 1970 and later models (regardless of other exhaust emission control equipment) are equipped with the Improved Combustion (IMCO) System. The IMCO System controls emissions arising from the incomplete combustion of the air/fuel mixture in the cylinders. the IMCO system incorporates a number of modifications to the distribu-

tor spark control system, the fuel system, and the internal design of the engine.

Internal engine modifications include the following: elimination of surface irregularities and crevices as well as a low surface area-to-volume ratio in the combustion chambers, a high velocity intake manifold combined with short exhaust ports, selective valve timing and a higher temperature and capacity cooling system.

Modifications to the fuel system include the following: recalibrated carburetors to achieve a leaner air/fuel mixture, more precise calibration of the choke mechanism, the installation of idle mixture limiter caps and a heated air intake system.

Modifications to the distributor spark control system include the following: a modified centrifugal advance curve, the use of dual diaphragm distributors in most applications, a ported vacuum switch, a deceleration valve and a spark delay valve.

Heated Air Intake System

The heated air intake portion of the air cleaner consists of a thermostat or bimetal switch and vacuum motor and a spring loaded temperature control door in the snorkel of the air cleaner. The temperature control door is located between the end of the air cleaner snorkel which draws in air from the engine compartment and the duct that carries heated air up

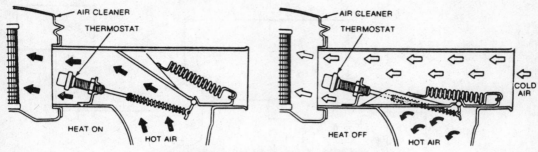

Temperature-operated duct and valve assembly

from the exhaust manifold. when underhood temperature is below 90°F, the temperature control door blocks off underhood air from entering the air cleaner and allows only heated air from the exhaust manifold to be drawn into the air cleaner. When underhood temperature rises above 130°F, the temperature control door blocks off heated air from the exhaust manifold and allows only underhood air to be drawn into the air cleaner.

By controlling the temperature of the engine intake air this way, exhaust emissions are lowered and fuel economy is improved. In addition, throttle plate icing is reduced, and cold weather driveability is improved from the necessary leaner mixtures.

DUCT AND VALVE ASSEMBLY TEST

1. Either start with a cold engine or remove the air cleaner from the engine for at least half an hour. While cooling the air cleaner, leave the engine compartment hood open.
2. Tape a thermometer, of known accuracy, to the inside of the air cleaner so that it is near the temperature sensor unit. Install the air cleaner on the engine but do not fasten its securing nut.
3. Start the engine. With the engine cold and

the outside temperature less than 90°F, the door should be in the **heat on** position (closed to outside air).

4. Operate the throttle lever rapidly to ½ to ¾ of its opening and release it. The air door should open to allow outside air to enter and then close again.
5. Allow the engine to warm up to normal temperature. Watch the door. when it opens to the outside air, remove the cover from the air cleaner. the temperature should be over 90°F and no more than 130°F; 105°F is about normal. If the door noes not work within these temperature ranges, or fails to work at all, check for linkage or door binding.

If binding is not present and the air door is not working, proceed with the vacuum tests given below. if these indicate no faults in the vacuum motor and the door is not working, the temperature sensor is defective and must be replaced.

VACUUM MOTOR TEST

Be sure that the vacuum hose that runs between the temperature switch and the vacuum motor is not pinched by the retaining clip under the air cleaner. This could prevent the air door from closing.

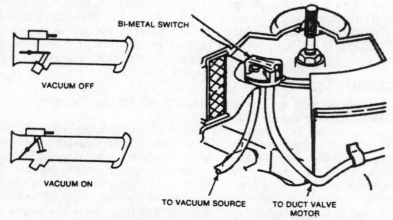

Vacuum-operated duct and valve assembly

1. Check all vacuum lines and fittings for leaks. Correct any leaks. If none are found, proceed with the test.

2. Remove the hose which runs from the sensor to the vacuum motor. Run a hose directly from the manifold vacuum source to the vacuum motor.

3. If the motor closes the air door, it is functioning properly and the temperature sensor is defective.

4. If the motor does not close the door and no binding is present in its operation, the vacuum motor is defective and must be replaced.

NOTE: *If an alternate vacuum source is applied to the motor, insert a vacuum gauge in the line by using a T-fitting. Apply at least 9 in. Hg of vacuum in order to operate the motor.*

REMOVAL AND INSTALLATION

Temperature Operated Duct and Valve Assembly

1. Remove the hex-head cap screws which secure the air intake duct and valve assembly to the air cleaner.

2. Remove the air intake duct and valve assembly from the engine.

3. If the duct and valve assembly was removed because of a suspected temperature malfunction, check the operation of the thermostat and valve plate assembly. Refer to the Air Intake Duct test for the proper procedure.

4. If inspection reveals that the valve plate is sticking or the thermostat is malfunctioning, remove the thermostat and valve plates as follows:

    a. Detach the valve plate tension spring from the valve plate using long-nosed pliers.

    b. Loosen the thermostat locknut and unscrew the thermostat from the mounting bracket.

    c. Grasp the valve plate and withdraw it from the duct.

5. Install the air intake duct and valve assembly on the shroud tube.

6. Connect the air intake duct and valve assembly to the air cleaner and tighten the hexhead retaining cap screws.

7. If it was necessary to disassemble the thermostat and air duct and valve, assemble the unit as follows:

    a. Install the valve plate. Install the locknut on the thermostat, and screw the thermostat into the mounting bracket. Install the valve plate tension spring on the valve plate and duct.

    b. Check the operation of the thermostat and air duct assembly. Refer to the Air Intake Duct Test for the proper procedure. Tighten the locknut.

8. Install the vacuum override motor (if applicable) and check for proper operation.

Vacuum Operated Duct and Valve Assembly

1. Disconnect the vacuum hose at the vacuum motor.

2. Remove the hex head cap screws which secure the air intake duct and valve assembly to the air cleaner.

3. Remove the duct and valve assembly from the engine.

4. Position the duct and valve assembly to the air cleaner and heat stove tube. Install the attaching cap screws.

5. Connect the vacuum line at the vacuum motor.

Dual Diaphragm Distributors

Dual diaphragm distributors are installed in most 1968 and later models and appear in many different engine/transmission/equipment combinations.

The dual distributor diaphragm is a two-chambered housing which is mounted on the side of the distributor. The outer side of the housing is a distributor vacuum advance mechanism, connected to the carburetor by a vacuum hose. the purpose of the vacuum advance is to advance ignition timing according to the conditions under which the engine is operating. This device has been used on automobiles for many years not and its chief advantage is economical engine operation. The second side of the dual diaphragm is the side that has been added to help control engine exhaust emissions at idle and during deceleration.

The inner side of the dual diaphragm is connected by a vacuum hose to the intake manifold. When the engine is idling or decelerating, intake manifold vacuum is high and carburetor vacuum is low. Under these conditions, intake manifold vacuum, applied to the inner side of the dual diaphragm, retards ignition timing to promote more complete combustion of the air fuel mixture in the engine combustion chambers.

DUAL DIAPHRAGM TEST

1. Connect a timing light to the engine. Check the ignition timing.

NOTE: *Before proceeding with the tests, disconnect any spark control devices, distributor vacuum valves, etc. If these are left connected, inaccurate result may be obtained.*

2. Remove the retard hose from the distributor and plug it. Increase the engine speed. The timing should advance. If it fails to do so, then the vacuum unit is faulty and must be replaced.

3. Check the timing with the engine at normal idle speed. Unplug the retard hose and con-

nect it to the vacuum unit. The timing should instantly be retarded. If this does not occur, the retard diaphragm has a leak and the vacuum unit must be replaced.

REMOVAL AND INSTALLATION

1. Remove the distributor cap and rotor.
2. Disconnect the vacuum lines.
3. Remove the clip that secure the diaphragm arm to the distributor advance plate.
4. Remove the screws that attach the diaphragm to the distributor (outside of the distributor).
5. Carefully remove the unit by tilting it downward to disengage the diaphragm arm from the plate.
6. Installation is the reverse of removal. Consult the instructions that come with the new diaphragm as to the calibration of the unit.

Ported Vacuum Switch (Distributor Vacuum Control Valve)

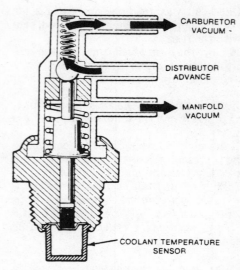

Ported vacuum switch operation

The distributor vacuum control valve is a temperature sensitive valve which screws into the water jacket of the engine. Three vacuum lines are attached to the vacuum control valve: one which runs from the carburetor to the control valve, one which runs from the control valve to the distributor vacuum advance (outer) chamber, and one which runs from the intake manifold to the distributor vacuum control valve.

During normal engine operation, vacuum from the carburetor passes through the top nipple on the distributor control valve, through the valve to the second nipple on the valve, and out the second nipple on the valve to the distributor vacuum advance chamber. when the engine however, carburetor vacuum is very low, so that there is little, if any, vacuum in the passageways described above.

If the engine should begin to overheat while idling, a check ball inside the distributor vacuum control which normally blocks off the third nipple of the valve (intake manifold vacuum) moves upward to block off the first nipple (carburetor vacuum). This applies intake manifold vacuum (third nipple) to the distributor vacuum advance chamber (second nipple). Since intake manifold vacuum is very high while the engine is idling, ignition timing is advanced by the

3-PORT PVS OPERATION

- **EGR/CSC** – switches EGR vacuum from EGR system to distributor advance with cold engine.
- **Cold Start Spark Advance (CSSA)** – supplies manifold vacuum to distributor below 125° F. coolant temperature.
- **Coolant Spark Control (CSC)** – cuts off distributor advance below hot engine temperature.
- **Cooling PVS** – switches advance vacuum from spark port to manifold vacuum if engine overheats.

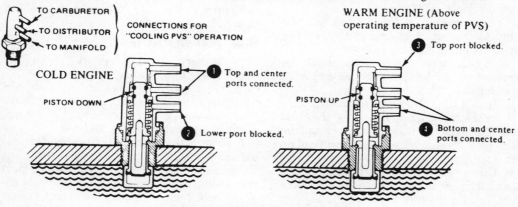

Ported vacuum switch (PVS) operation

application of intake manifold vacuum to the distributor vacuum advance chamber. This raises the engine idle speed and helps to cool the engine.

PORTED VACUUM SWITCH (DISTRIBUTOR VACUUM CONTROL VALVE) TEST

1. Check the routing and connection of all vacuum hoses.

2. Attach a tachometer to the engine.

3. Bring the engine up to the normal operating temperature. The engine must not be overheated.

4. Note the engine rpm, with the transmission in neutral, and the throttle in the curb idle position.

5. Disconnect the vacuum hose from the intake manifold at the temperature sensing valve. Plug or clamp the hose.

6. Note the idle rpm with the hose disconnected. If there is no change in rpm, the valve is good. If there is a drop of 100 or more rpm, the valve should be replaced. Replace the vacuum line.

7. check to make sure that the all season cooling mixture meets specifications, and that the correct radiator cap is in place and functioning.

8. Block the radiator air flow to induce a higher-than-normal temperature condition.

9. Continue to operate until the engine temperature or heat indicator shows above normal.

If the engine speed by this time has increased 100 or more rpm, the temperature sensing valve is satisfactory. If not, it should be replaced.

Deceleration Valve

Some IMCO equipped 1968-72 engines are equipped with a distributor vacuum advance control valve (deceleration valve) which is used with dual-diaphragm distributors to further aid in controlling ignition timing. The deceleration valve is in the vacuum line which runs from the outer (advance) diaphragm to the carburetor; the normal vacuum supply for the distributor. During deceleration, the intake manifold vacuum rises causing the deceleration valve to close off the carburetor vacuum source and connect the intake manifold vacuum source to the distributor advance diaphragm. The increase in vacuum provides maximum ignition timing advance, thus providing more complete fuel combustion, and decreasing exhaust system backfiring.

DECELERATION VALVE TEST

1. Connect the tachometer to the engine and bring the engine to the normal operating temperature.

2. Check the idle speed and set it to specifications with the headlights on high beam, as necessary.

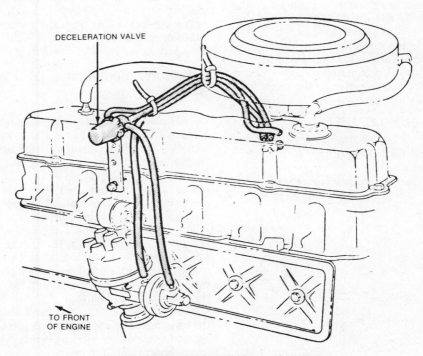

DECELERATION VALVE

TO FRONT
OF ENGINE

Deceleration valve installation—six cylinder

3. Turn off the headlights and note the idle rpm.

4. Remove the plastic cover from the valve. Slowly turn the adjusting screw counterclockwise without pressing in. After 5, and no more than 6 turns, the idle speed should suddenly increase to about 1000 rpm. if the speed does not increase after six turns, push inward on the valve spring retainer and release. Speed should now increase.

5. Slowly turn the adjusting screw clockwise until the idle speed drops to the speed noted in Step 3. Make one more turn clockwise.

6. Increase the engine speed to 2000 rpm, hold for 5 seconds, and release the throttle. The engine speed should return idle speed within 4 seconds. If idle is not resumed in 4 seconds, back off the dashpot adjustment and repeat the check. if the idle is not resumed in 3 seconds with the dashpot back off, turn the deceleration valve adjustment screw an addition quarter turn clockwise and repeat the check. Repeat the quarter turn adjustment and idle return checks until the engine returns to idle within the required time.

7. If it takes more than one complete turn from Step 5 to meet the idle return time specifications, replace the valve.

Spark Delay Valve

he spark delay valve is a plastic, spring-loaded, color coded valve which is installed in the vacuum line to the distributor advance diaphragm on many 1971 and later models. Under heavy throttle applications, the valve will close, blocking normal carburetor vacuum to the distributor. After the designated period of closed time, the valve opens, restoring the carburetor vacuum to the distributor.

SPARK DELAY VALVE TEST

NOTE: *If the distributor vacuum line contains a cut-off solenoid, it must be open during this test.*

1. Detach the vacuum line from the distribu-

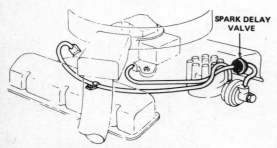

Spark delay valve installation

tor at the spark delay valve end. connect a vacuum gauge to the valve, in its place.

2. Connect a tachometer to the engine. Start the engine and rapidly increase its speed to 2,000 rpm with the transmission in neutral.

3. As soon as the engine speed is increased, the vacuum gauge reading should drop to zero.

4. Hold the engine speed at a steady 2,000 rpm. It should take longer than two seconds for the gauge to register 6 in.Hg. If it takes less than two seconds, the valve is defective and must be replaced.

5. If it takes longer than the number of seconds specified for the gauge to reach 6 in.Hg, disconnect the vacuum gauge from the spark delay valve. Disconnect the hose which runs from the spark delay valve to the carburetor at the valve end. Connect the vacuum gauge to this hose.

6. Start the engine and increase its speed to 2,000 rpm. The gauge should indicate 10-16 in.Hg. If it does not, there is a blockage in the carburetor vacuum port or else the hose itself is plugged or broken. If the gauge reading is within specification, the valve is defective.

7. Reconnect all vacuum lines and remove the tachometer, once testing is completed.

REMOVAL AND INSTALLATION

1. Locate the spark delay valve in the distributor vacuum line and disconnect it from the line.

2. Install a new spark delay valve in the line, making sure that the black end of the valve is connected to the line from the carburetor and the color coded end is connected to the line from the spark delay valve to the distributor.

Distributor Modulator (Dist-O-Vac) System

1970 models equipped with automatic transmission and the 240, 302, or 390 2 bbl engines, and 1971 models equipped with automatic transmission and the 240, 390 2 bbl, or 429 4 bbl engines are equipped with a Dist-O-Vac spark control system. this system is used in conjunction with all of the IMCO system equipment except the deceleration valve.

The three components of the Dist-O-Vac system are the speed sensor, the thermal switch, and the electronic control module. the electronic control module consists of two sub assemblies: the electronic control amplifier and the three-way solenoid valve.

The speed sensor, a small unit mounted in the speedometer cable, contains a rotating magnet and a stationary winding which is insulated from the ground. The magnet, which rotates with the speedometer cable, generates a small

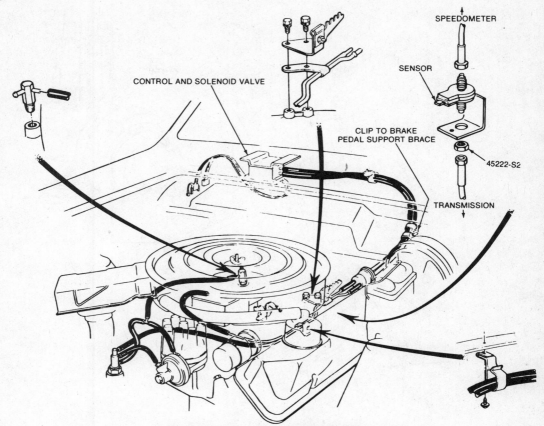

CONTROL AND SOLENOID VALVE

SPEEDOMETER

SENSOR

CLIP TO BRAKE
PEDAL SUPPORT BRACE

45222-S2

TRANSMISSION

Early Typical Dist-O-Vac system installation

voltage which increases directly with speed. This voltage is directed to the electronic control amplifier.

The thermal switch consists of a bimetallic element switch which is mounted in the right door pillar and senses the temperature, of the air. The switch is closed at 58°F or lower, and open at temperatures about 58°F. This switch is also connected to the electronic control amplifier.

Within the electronic control module case, there is a printed circuit board and an electronic amplifier. The speed sensor and thermal switch are connected to this assembly. The thermal switch is the dominant circuit. When the temperature of the outside air is 58°F or lower, the circuit is closed, so that regardless of speed, the electronic control amplifier will not trigger the three-way solenoid valve. At temperatures above 58°F, however, the thermal switch circuit is open, allowing the circuit from the speed sensor to take over and control the action of the solenoid valve.

The three-way solenoid valve is located within the electronic control module and below the printed circuit board of the amplifier. It is vent-

ed to the atmosphere at the top, and connect at the bottom of the carburetor spark port (small hose) and the primary (advance) side of the dual-diaphragm distributor (large hose). the large hose is also channeled through the temperature sensing valve. the small hose is equipped with an air bleed to provide a positive airflow in the direction of the carburetor. the air bleed purges the hose of vacuum, thus assuring that raw gasoline will not be drawn through the hose and into the distributor diaphragm.

When the thermal switch is closed (air temperature 58°F or lower), or when it is open and the speed sensor is not sending out a strong enough voltage signal (speeds below approximately 35 mph), the amplifier will not activate the solenoid valve and the valve is in the closed position, blocking the passage of air from the small tube through the large tube. With the valve in this position, the larger hose is vented to the atmosphere through the top opening in the three-way valve assembly. Consequently, no vacuum is being supplied to the primary diaphragm on the distributor, and, therefore, no vacuum advance.

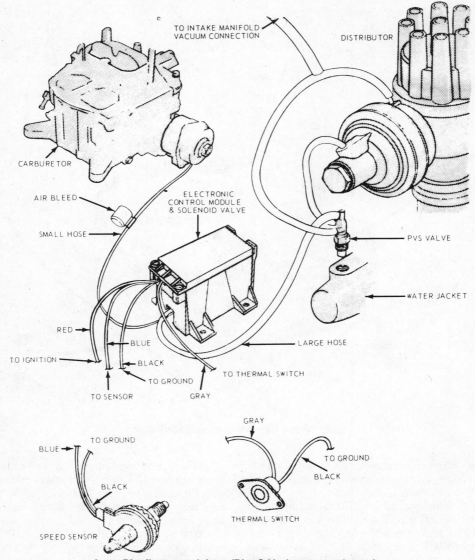

TO INTAKE MANIFOLD
VACUUM CONNECTION

DISTRIBUTOR

CARBURETOR

AIR BLEED

SMALL HOSE

ELECTRONIC
CONTROL MODULE
& SOLENOID VALVE

PVS VALVE

WATER JACKET

RED

BLUE

LARGE HOSE

TO IGNITION

BLACK

TO GROUND

TO THERMAL SWITCH

TO SENSOR

GRAY

GRAY

TO GROUND

BLUE

BLACK

TO GROUND

BLACK

SPEED SENSOR

THERMAL SWITCH

Later Distributor modulator (Dist-O-Vac) system schematic

When the air temperature is above 58°F and/or the speed of the car is sufficient to generate the required voltage (35 mph or faster), the valve opens, blocking the vent to the atmosphere while opening the vacuum line from the carburetor spark port to the primary diaphragm of the distributor.

Electronic Spark Control

1972 Fords manufactured for sale in California equipped with a 351C or 400 V8, and all 1972 Fords equipped with the 429 Police Interceptor engine, use the electronic spark control system.

Electronic Spark Control is a system which

blocks off carburetor vacuum to the distributor vacuum advance mechanism under certain temperature and speed conditions. the Electronic Spark Control System consists of four components: a temperature sensor, a speed sensor, an amplifier, and a distributor modulator vacuum valve. The system services to prevent ignition timing advance (by blocking off carburetor vacuum from the distributor vacuum advance mechanism) until the car reaches a speed of 35 mph when the ambient temperature is over 65°F.

The temperature sensor, which is mounted on the front face of the left door pillar, monitors the outside air temperature and relays this information to the amplifier. The amplifier,

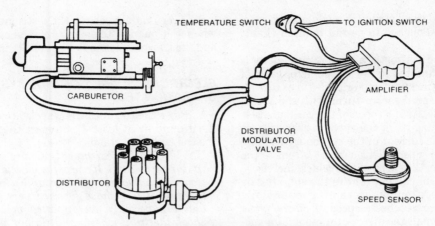

Early Electronic spark control system schematic

which is located under the instrument panel, controls the distributor modulator vacuum valve. The modulator valve, which is attache to the ignition coil mounting bracket, is connected into the carburetor vacuum line to the distributor, and is normally open. If the temperature of the outside air is below 48°F, the contacts in the temperature sensor are open and no signal is sent to the amplifier. since no signal is sent to the amplifier, the amplifier does not send a signal to the distributor modulator valve, and the vacuum passage from the carburetor to the dis-

tributor vacuum advance remains open. When the outside temperature rises to 65°F or above, the contacts in the temperature sensor close, and a signal is sent to the amplifier. The amplifier relays the message to the distributor modulator, which closes to block the vacuum passage to the distributor, preventing ignition timing advance.

When the ambient temperature is 65°F or above, ignition timing advance is prevented until the amplifier receives a signal from the speed sensor that the speed of the vehicle has reached

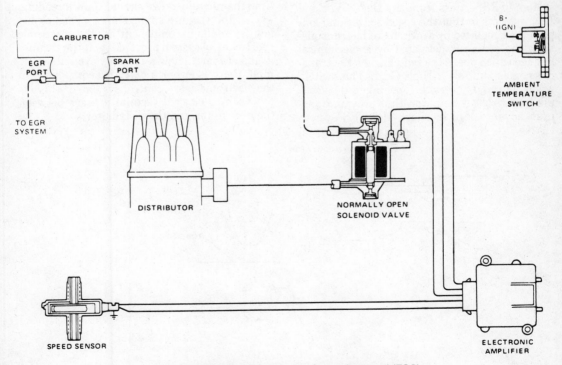

Later Schematic of the electronic spark control (ESC)

35 mph, and the distributor modulator vacuum valve can be opened to permit ignition timing advance.

The speed sensor is a miniature generator which is connected to the speedometer cable of the car. As the speedometer cable turns, the inside of the speed sensor turns with the speedometer cable. As the speed of the car increases, a rotating magnet in the speed sensor induces an electronic current in the stationary winding in the speed sensor. This current is sent to the amplifier. As the speed of the vehicle increases, the amount of current sent to the amplifier by the speed sensor increases proportionately. When the car reaches a speed of 35 mph, the amplifier signals the distributor modulator vacuum valve to open, allowing carburetor vacuum to be sent to the distributor vacuum advance chamber. This permits the ignition timing to advance.

It should be noted that this system operates only when the ambient temperature is 65°F or above, and then only when the speed of the car is below 35 mph.

Transmission Regulated Spark System

1972 models equipped with the 240 Six or the 351 W V8 and automatic transmission use a transmission regulated spark control system.

The transmission regulated spark control system (TRS) differs from the Dist-O-Vac and ESC systems in that the speed sensor and amplifier are replaced by a switch on the transmission. the switch is activated by a mechanical linkage which opens the switch when the transmission is shifted in High Gear. The switch, when opened, triggers the opening of the vacuum lines to the distributor, thus providing vacuum advance. So, in short, the TRS system

blocks vacuum advance to the distributor only when the outside temperature is above 65°F and the transmission is in First or Second gear.

ELECTRONIC SPARK CONTROL SYSTEM OPERATION TEST

1. Raise the car until the wheels are clear of the ground by at least 4". Support the rear of the car with jack stands.

CAUTION: *The car must be firmly supported during this test. If one of the wheels should come in contact with the ground while it is turning, it will move forward very rapidly and unexpectedly. As an extra precaution, chock the front wheels and do not stand in front of the vehicle while the wheels are turning!*

2. Disconnect the vacuum hose from the distributor vacuum advance chamber. This is the outer hose on vans with dual diaphragm vacuum advance units.
3. Connect the hose to a vacuum gauge.
4. Pour hot water on the temperature sensing switch to make sure that it is above 65°F.
5. Start the engine and apply the foot brake. Depress the clutch and shift the transmission into High gear. Release the hand brake and slowly engage the clutch.
6. Have an assistant observe the vacuum gauge while you raise the speed of the engine until the speedometer reads 35 mph, at which time the vacuum gauge should show a reading.
7. If the vacuum gauge shows a reading below 35 mph, a component in the electronic spark control system is defective. If the vacuum gauge does not show a reading, even above 35 mph, there is either a defective component in the electronic spark control system, or there is a broken or clogged vacuum passage between the carburetor and the distributor.

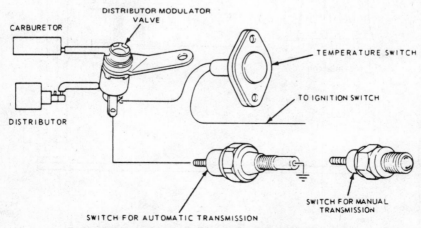

Transmission regulated spark control system schematic

REMOVAL AND INSTALLATION

Dist-O-Vac and ESC Temperature Sensor

1. Open the right door and remove the two screws which attach the temperature sensor to the right door pillar.
2. Disconnect the lead wires from the temperature sensor.
3. Connect the lead wires to the new sensor.
4. Position the sensor on the door pillar and install the attaching screws.

Dist-O-Vac and ESC Speed Sensor

1. Disconnect the lead wires from the sensor.
2. Disconnect the speed sensor from the speedometer cable.
3. Position the O-rings on both ends of the new speed sensor.
4. connect both ends of the speedometer cable to the speed sensor.
5. Connect the lead wires to the speed sensor.

ESC Amplifier

1. Locate the amplifier under the instrument panel, near the glove compartment.
2. Disconnect the wiring harness from the amplifier.
3. Remove the two amplifier attaching screws and remove the amplifier.
4. Position a new amplifier under the instrument panel and connect the wiring harness to it.
5. Install the two amplifier attaching screws.

ESC Distributor Vacuum Modulator Valve

1. Tag the hoses that attach to the modulator and disconnect them from the amplifier.

2. Disconnect the lead wires from the modulator.
3. Remove the No. 2 left front valve cover bolt (6-cylinder) or the inboard left front valve cover bolt and remove the modulator.
4. Position the new modulator on the valve cover and install the attaching bolt.
5. Connect the wires and hoses to the modulator.

Exhaust Gas Recirculation System

EEGR

The Electronic EGR system (EEGR) is found in all systems in which EGR flow is controlled according to computer commands by means of an EGR valve position sensor (EVP) attached to the valve.

The EEGR valve is operated by a vacuum signal from the dual EGR Solenoid Valves, or the elctronic vacuum regulator which actuates the valve diaphragm.

As supply vacuum overcomes the spring load, the diaphragm is actuated lifting the pintle off of its seat allowing the exhaust gas to flow. The amount of flow is directly proportional to the pintle position. The EVP sensor sends an electrical signal notify the EEC of its position.

The EEGR valve is not servicable. The EVP sensor must be serviced separately.

IBP EGR

The Integral Backpressure (IBP) EGR system combines inputs of EGR port vacuum and backpressure into one unit. The valve requires both inputs for proper operation. The valve won't operate on vacuum alone.

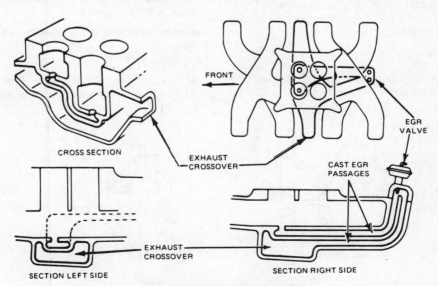

CROSS SECTION

FRONT

EXHAUST CROSSOVER

EGR VALVE

CAST EGR PASSAGES

SECTION LEFT SIDE

EXHAUST CROSSOVER

SECTION RIGHT SIDE

Floor entry EGR valve operation

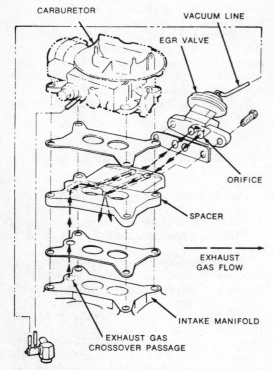

CARBURETOR
VACUUM LINE
EGR VALVE
ORIFICE
SPACER
EXHAUST GAS FLOW
INTAKE MANIFOLD
EXHAUST GAS CROSSOVER PASSAGE

Spacer entry EGR valve operation

There are two types of backpressure valves: the poppet type and the tapered pintle type.

Ported EGR

The ported EGR valve is operated by engine vacuum alone. A vacuum siganl from the carburetor activates the EGR valve diaphragm. As the vacuum signal increase it gradually opens the valve pintle allowing exhaust gases to flow. The amount of flow is directly proportional to the pintle position.

SYSTEM TEST

1. Allow the engine to warm up, so that the coolant temperature has reached at least 125°F.

2. Disconnect the vacuum hose which runs from the temperature cut-in valve to the EGR valve at the EGR valve end. Connect a vacuum gauge to this hose with a T-fitting.

3. Increase engine speed. Do not exceed half throttle or 3,000 rpm. The gauge should indicate a vacuum. If no vacuum is present, check the following:

   a. The carburetor: look for a clogged vacuum port.

   b. The vacuum hoses: including the vacuum hoses to the transmission modulator.

   c. The temperature cut-in valve: if no vacuum is present at its outlet with the engine temperature above 125°F and vacuum available from the carburetor, the valve is defective.

4. If all the above test are positive, check the EGR valve itself.

5. Connect an outside vacuum source and a vacuum gauge to the valve.

6. Apply vacuum to the EGR valve. The valve should open at 3-10 in.Hg, the engine idle speed should slow down and the idle quality should become more rough.

7. If this does not happen, i.e., the EGR valve remains closed, the EGR valve is defective and must be replaced.

8. If the valve stem moves but the idle remains the same, the valve orifice is clogged and must be cleaned.

NOTE: *If an outside vacuum source is not available, disconnect the hose which runs between the EGR valve and the temperature cut-in valve and plug the hose connections on the cut-in valve. Connect the EGR valve hose to a source of intake manifold vacuum and watch the idle. The results should be the same as in steps 6-7, above.*

Temperature Cut-In Valve EGR Ported Vacuum Switch

VALVE BENCH TEST

1. Remove the valve from the engine.

2. Connect an outside source of vacuum to

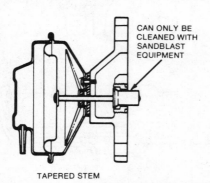

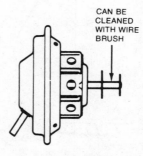

CAN ONLY BE CLEANED WITH SANDBLAST EQUIPMENT

CAN BE CLEANED WITH WIRE BRUSH

TAPERED STEM

EXPOSED STEM

EGR valve comparison

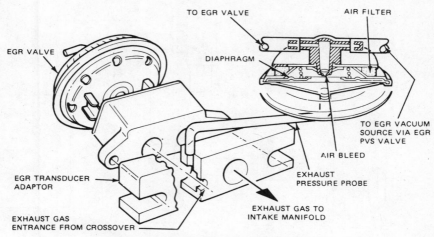

TO EGR VALVE

AIR FILTER

EGR VALVE

DIAPHRAGM

TO EGR VACUUM
SOURCE VIA EGR
PVS VALVE

AIR BLEED

EGR TRANSDUCER
ADAPTOR

EXHAUST
PRESSURE PROBE

EXHAUST GAS TO
INTAKE MANIFOLD

EXHAUST GAS
ENTRANCE FROM CROSSOVER

EGR valve exhaust backpressure tranducer

the top port on the valve. Leave the bottom port vented to the atmosphere.

3. Use ice or an aerosol spray to cool the valve below 60°F.

4. Apply 20 in.Hg vacuum to the valve. the valve should hold a minimum of 19 in.Hg vacuum for 5 minutes without leaking down.

5. Leave the vacuum source connected to the valve and place it, along with a high temperature thermometer, into a nonmetallic, heat resistance container full of water.

6. Heat the water. The vacuum in the valve should drop to zero once the temperature of the water reaches about 125°F.

7. Replace the valve if it fails either of the tests.

EGR Valve Cleaning

Remove the EGR valve for cleaning. Do not strike or pry on the valve diaphragm housing or supports, as this may damage the valve operating mechanism and/or change the valve calibration. Check orifice hole in the EGR valve body for deposits. A small hand drill of no more than 0.060″ diameter may be used to clean the hole if plugged. Extreme care must be taken to avoid enlarging the hole or damaging the surface of the orifice plate.

VALVES WHICH CANNOT BE DISASSEMBLED

Valves which are riveted or otherwise permanently assembled should be replaced if highly contaminated; they cannot be cleaned.

VALVE WHICH CAN BE DISASSEMBLED

Separate the diaphragm section from the main mounting body. Clean the valve plates, stem, and the mounting plate, using a small power-driven rotary type wire brush. Take care

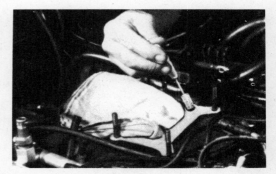

Cleaning EGR exhaust gas entry port in intake manifold

Cleaning EGR spacer exhaust passages

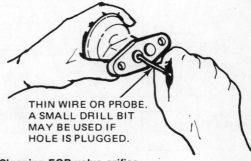

THIN WIRE OR PROBE. A SMALL DRILL BIT MAY BE USED IF HOLE IS PLUGGED.

Cleaning EGR valve orifice

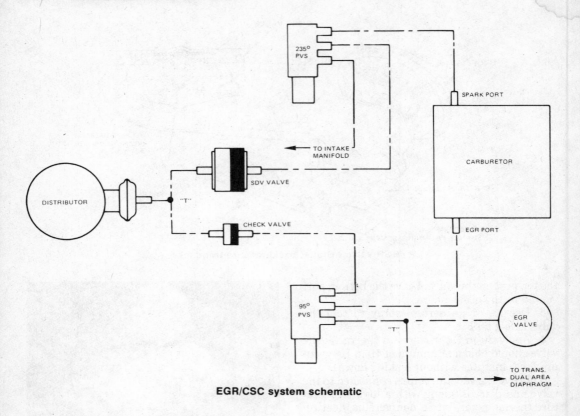

EGR/CSC system schematic

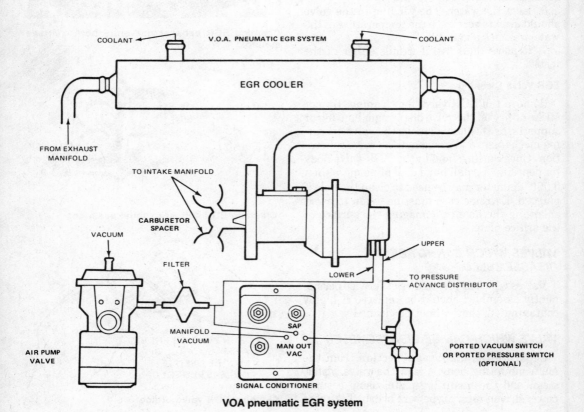

VOA pneumatic EGR system

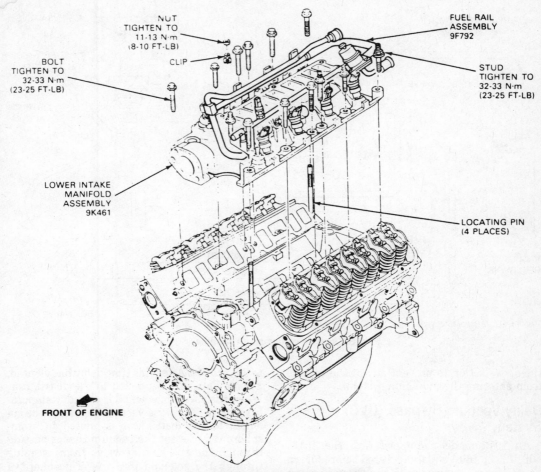

NUT
TIGHTEN TO
11-13 N·m
(8-10 FT-LB)

CLIP

BOLT
TIGHTEN TO
32-33 N·m
(23-25 FT-LB)

FUEL RAIL
ASSEMBLY
9F792

STUD
TIGHTEN TO
32-33 N·m
(23-25 FT-LB)

LOWER INTAKE
MANIFOLD
ASSEMBLY
9K461

LOCATING PIN
(4 PLACES)

FRONT OF ENGINE

8-302, 351 EFI fuel charging assembly

not to damage the parts. Remove deposits between stem and valve disc by using a steel blade or shim approximately 0.028″ thick in a sawing motion around the stem shoulder at both sides of the disc.

The poppet must wobble and move axially before reassembly.

Clean the cavity and passages in the main body of the valve with a power-driven rotary wire brush. If the orifice plate has a hole less than 0.450″ it must be removed from cleaning. Remove all loosened debris using compressed iar. Reassemble the diaphragm section on the main body using a new gasket between them. Torque the attaching screws to specification. Clean the orifice plate and the counterbore in the valve body. Reinstall the orifice plate using a small amount of contact cement to retain the plate in place during assembly of the valve to the carburetor spacer. Apply cement to only outer edges of the orifice plate to avoid restriction of the orifice.

EGR Supply Passages and Carburetor Space Cleaning

Remove the carburetor and carburetor spacer on engines so equipped. Clean the supply tube with a small power-driven rotary type wire brush or blast cleaning equipment. Clean the exhaust gas passages in the spacer using a suitable wire brush and/or scraper. The machined holes in the spacer can be cleaned by using a suitable round wire brush. Hard encrusted material should be probed loose first, then brushed out.

EGR Exhaust Gas Channel Cleaning

Clean the exhaust gas channel, where applicable, in the intake manifold, using a suitable carbon scraper. Clean the exhaust gas entry port in the intake manifold by hand passing a suitable drill bit thru the holes to auger out the deposits. Do not use a wire brush. The manifold riser bore(s) should be suitably plugged during

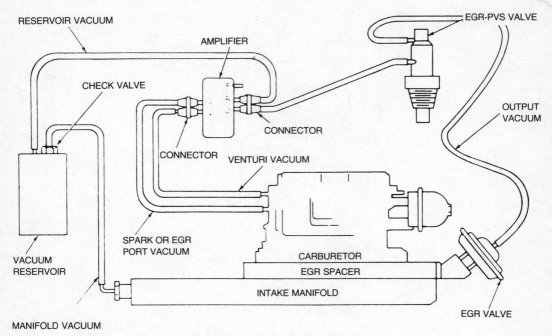

EGR system with vaccum amplifier

the above action to prevent any of the residue from entering the induction system.

Delay Vacuum By-pass (DVB) System

All 1973 models equipped with the 351C, 400, 429 or 460 V8 manufactured before March 15, 1973 are equipped with the Delay Vacuum Bypass spark control system. This system provides two paths by which carburetor vacuum can reach the distributor vacuum advance. The system consists of a spark delay valve, a check valve, a solenoid vacuum valve, and an ambient temperature switch. When the ambient temperature is below 49°F, the temperature switch contacts are open and the vacuum solenoid is open (deenergized). Under these condition, vacuum will flow from the carburetor, through the open solenoid, and to the distributor. Since the spark delay valve resists the flow of carburetor vacuum, the vacuum will always flow thorugh the vacuum solenoid when it is open, since this is the path of least resistance. When the ambient temperature rises above 60°F, the contacts in the temperature switch (which is located in the door post) close. this passes ignition switch currecnt to the solenoid, energizing the solenoid. This blocks one of the two vacuum paths. All distributor vacuum must now flow thorugh the spark delay valve. when carburetor vacuum rises above a certain level on acceleration, a rubber valve in the spark delay valve blocks vacuum from passing thorugh the valve for from 5

to 30 seconds. After this time delay has elapsed, normal vacuum is supplied to the distributor. When the vacuum solenoid is closed, (temperature above 60°F), the vacuum line from the solenoid to the distributor is vented to atmosphere. To prevent the vacuum that is passing through the spark delay valve from escaping through the solenoid into the atmosphere, a one-way check valve is installed in the vacuum line from the solenoid to the distributor.

Cold Temperature Actuated Vacuum (CTAV) System

This system is installed on aome 1973 models manufactured after March 15, 1973 and many

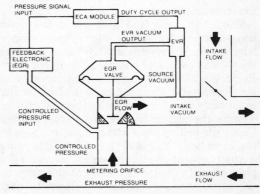

Pressure feedback electronic EGR system vacuum schematic

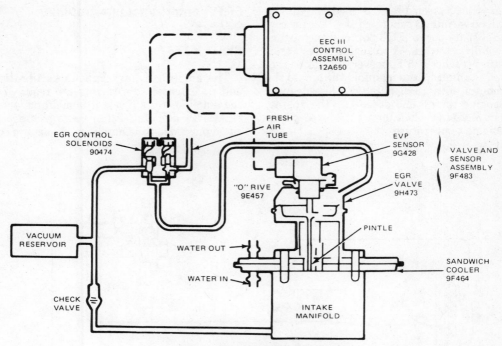

EEC-III EGR vacuum schematic

1974 models to control distributor spark advance. It is basically a refinement of the DVB or TAV spark control systems with the temperature switch relocated in the air cleaner and latching relay added to maintain a strong vacuum signal to the distributor, whether it be EGR port or spark port carburetor vacuum, and to keep the system from intermittently switching vacuum signals when the intake air is between 49 and 60°F. When the temperature switch closes at 60°F, the latching relay (normally off) is energized and stays on until the ignition switch is turned off. The latching relay then overrides the temperature switch and forces the solenoid valve to keep the spark port vacuum system closed and open the EGR port vacuum system. This prevents full vacuum advance, once the engine is warmed-up, thereby lowering emissions.

EGR/Coolant Spark Control (CSC) System

The EGR/CSC system is used on most 1974 and later models. It regulates both distributor spark advance and the EGR valve operation according to coolant temperature by sequentially switching vacuum signals.

The major EGR/CSC system components are:
1. 95°F EGR/PVS valve;
2. Spark Delay Valve (SDV);
3. Vacuum check valve.

When the engine coolant temperature is below 82°F, the EGR/PVS valve admits carburetor EGR port vacuum (occurring at about 2,500 rpm) directly to the distributor advance diaphragm, through the one-way check valve.

At the same time, the EGR/PVS valve shuts off carburetor EGR vacuum to the EGR valve and transmission diaphragm.

When engine coolant temperature is 95°F and above, the EGR/PVS valve is actuated and directs carburetor EGR vacuum to the EGR valve and transmission instead of the distributor. At temperatures between 82-95°F, the EGR-PVS valve may be open, closed, or in mid-position.

The SDV valve delay carburetor spark vacuum to the distributor advance diaphragm by restricting the vacuum signal through the SDV valve from a predetermined time. During normal acceleration, little or no vacuum is admitted to the distributor advance diaphragm until acceleration is completed, because of (1) the time delay of the SDV valve and (2) the re-routing of EGR port vacuum if the engine coolant temperature is 95°F or higher.

The check valve blocks off vacuum signal from the SDV to the EGR/PVS so that carburetor spark vacuum will not dissipated when the EGR/PVS is actuated above 95°F.

The 235°F PVS is not part of the EGR/PVS system, but is connected to the distributor vacuum advance to prevent engine overheating while idling (as on previous models). At idle speed, no vacuum is generated at either the carburetor spark port or EGR port and engine timing is fully retarded. When engine coolant temperature reaches 235°F, hoever, the valve is actuated to admit intake manifold vacuum to the distributor advance diaphragm. This advances the engine timing and speeds up the engine. The increase in coolant flow and fan speed lowers engine temperature.

EGR Venturi Vacuum Amplifier System

SYSTEM TEST

The amplifiers have built-in carlibrations and no external adjustments are required. If the amplifier tests reveal it is malfunctioning, replace the amplifier. All connections are located on one side of the amplifier. A vacuum con-

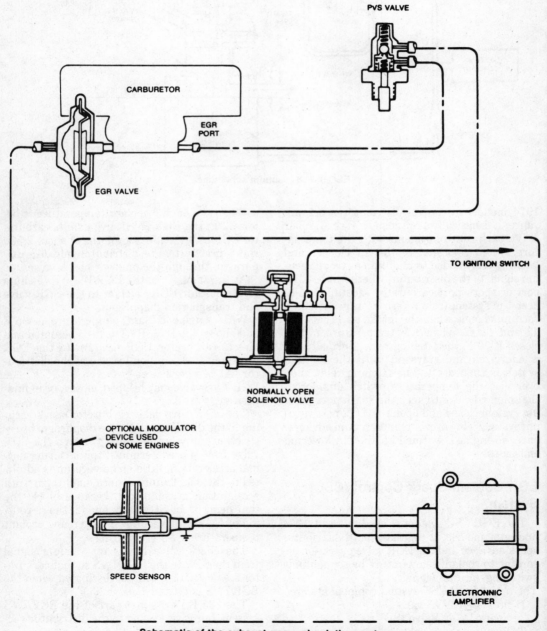

Schematic of the exhaust gas recirculation system

nector and hose assembly is used to assure that proper connections are made at the amplifier. The amplifier is retained with a sheetmetal screw.

1. Operate the engine until normal operating temperatures are reached.

2. Before the vacuum amplifier is checked, inspect all other basic components of the EGR System (EGR valve, EGR/PVS valve, hoses, routing, etc).

3. Check vacuum amplifier connecitons for proper routing and installation. If necessary, refer to the typical vacuum amplifier schematic.

4. Remove hose at EGR valve.

5. Connect vacuum gauge to EGR hose. Gauge must read in increments of at least 1 in.Hg graduation.

6. Remove hose at carburetor venturi (leave off).

7. With engine at curb idle speed, vacuum gauge reading should be within ± 0.3 in.Hg of specified bias valve as shown in amplifier specifications for other than zero bias. Zero bias may read from 0 to 0.5 in.Hg. If out of specification, replace amplifier.

8. Depress accelerator and release after engine has reached 1500 to 2000 rpm. After engine has returned to idle, the vacuum must return to bias noted in step 7. If bias has changed, replace amplifier. Also, if vacuum shows a marked increase (greater than 1 in.Hg) during acceleration period, the amplifier should be replaced.

9. Hook up venturi hose at carburetor with engine at curb idle rpm. If a sizeable increase in output vacuum is observed, (more than 0.5 in.Hg above step 7), check idle speed. High idle speed could increase output vacuum due to venturi vacuum increase. See engine decal for correct idle specifications.

10. Check amplifier reservoir and connections as follows: Disconnect external reservoir hose to amplifier and AP or plug. Depress accelerator rapidly to 1500 to 2000 rpm. The vacuum

should increase to 4 in.Hg or more. If out of specifications, replace amplifier.

Cold Start Spark Advance (CSSA) System

All 1975-78 models using the 460 V8 are equipped with the CSSA System. It is a modification of the existing spark control system to aid in cold start driveability. The system uses a coolant temperature sensing vacuum switch located on the thermostat housing. When the engine is cold (below 125°F), it permits full manifold vacuum to the distributor advance diaphragm. After the engine warms up, normal spark control (retard) resumes.

Vacuum Operated Heat Control Valve (VOHV)

To further air cold start driveability during engine warmup, most 1975 and later engines use a VOHV located between the exhaust manifold and the exhaust inlet (header) pipe.

When the engine is first started, the valve is closed, blocking exhaust gases from exiting from one bank of cylinders. These gases are then diverted back through the intake manifold crossover passage under the carburetor. The result is quick heat to the carburetor and choke.

The VOHV is controlled by a ported vacuum switch which uses manifold vacuum to keep the vacuum motor on the valve closed until the coolant reaches a predetermined warm-up valve. When the engine is warmed-up, the PVS shuts off vacuum to the VOHV, and a strong return spring opens the VOHV butterfly.

TESTING THE VACUUM OPERATED HEAT RISER

Testing the vacuum operated heat riser valve is a matter of making sure it opens and closes freely. You can move it by hand to see if it works, on a warm engine. On a cold engine, the

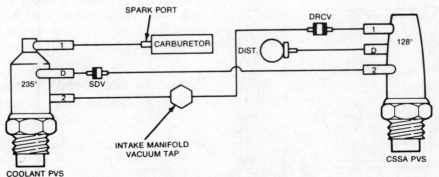

CSSA system schematic

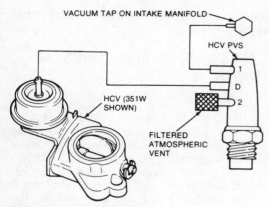

VOHV system schematic

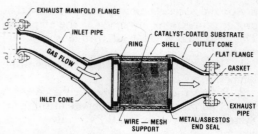

Sectional view of catalytic converter

valve should be closed, and disconnecting the hose should allow it to open (engine idling). On a cold engine, there should be vacuum at the vacuum actuator. On a warm engine the vacuum should be shut off.

Dual Signal Spark Advance (DSSA) System

The DSSA system is used on many engines. It incorporates a spark delay valve (SDV) and a one-way check valve to provide improved spark and EGR function during mild acceleration.

The check valve prevents spark port vacuum from reaching the EGR valve and causing excessive EGR valve flow. It also prevents EGR port vacuum, which could result in improper spark advance due to weakened signal. The SDV permits application of full EGR vacuum to the distributor vacuum advance diaphragm during mild acceleration. During steady speed or cruise conditions, EGR port vacuum is applied to the EGR valve and spark port vacuum is applied to the distributor vacuum advance diaphragm.

Catalytic Converter System

Starting in 1975 most models have a catalytic converter(s) located in the exhaust system. the converter works as a gas reactor, and its catalytic function is to speed up the heat producing chemical reaction between the exhaust gas components in order to reduce the air pollutants in the engine exhaust.

The catalyst material is contained in a sealed, honeycombed chamber. It is the surface of the catalyst material that plays a major role in the heat-producing chemical reaction. There are basically three types of catalytic converters:

1. The conventional oxidation catalyst (COC); used to oxidize hydrocarbons (HC) and carbon monoxide (CO).

2. The three-way catalyst (TWC); not only works on HC and CO but also reduces nitrogen oxides (NOx).

3. The light off catalyst (LOC); arranged in series with the main catalytic converter, is designed to handle the exhaust emissions during engine warmup when the main converter has not reached the proper temperature for maximum efficiency.

In order to provide oxygen necessary to obtain the converter's maximum efficiency a secondary air source is provided by the air pump (thermactor). The system is protected by several devices that block out the secondary air when the engine is laboring under any abnormal hot or cold operating situation.

The catalytic converter is expect to function without service for at least 50,000 miles. Use of leaded fuel would quickly cause catalyst failure and an expensive repair bill.

Bypass Air Idle Speed Control

The air bypass solenoid is used to control the engine idle speed and is operated by the EEC module.

The valve allows air to pass around the throttle plates to control:

- Cold engine fast idle
- Cold starting
- Dashpot operation

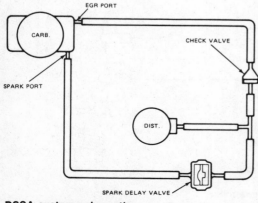

DSSA system schematic

- Over-temperature idle boost
- Engine load correction

The valve is not servicable and correction is by replacement only.

Emissions Maintenance Warning Light (EMW)

DESCRIPTION

All gasoline engined cars built for sale outside of California employ this device.

The EMW consists of an instrument panel mounted amber light imprinted with the word EGR, EMISS, or EMISSIONS. The light is connected to a sensor module located under the instrument panel. The purpose is the warn the driver that the 60,000 mile emission system maintenance is required on the vehicle. Specific emission system maintenance requirements are listed in the truck's owner's manual maintenance schedule.

RESETTING THE LIGHT

1. Turn the key to the OFF position.
2. Lightly push a phillips screwdriver through the 0.2″ diameter hole labeled RESET, and lightly press down and hold it.
3. While maintaining pressure with the screwdriver, turn the key to the RUN position. The EMW lamp will light and stay lit as long as you keep pressure on the screwdriver. Hold the screwdriver down for about 5 seconds.
4. Remove the screwdriver. The lamp should go out with 2-5 seconds. If not, repeat steps 1-3.
5. Turn the key OFF.
6. Turn the key to the RUN position. The lamp will light for 2-5 seconds and then go out. If not, repeat the rest procedure.

NOTE: *If the light comes on between 15,000*

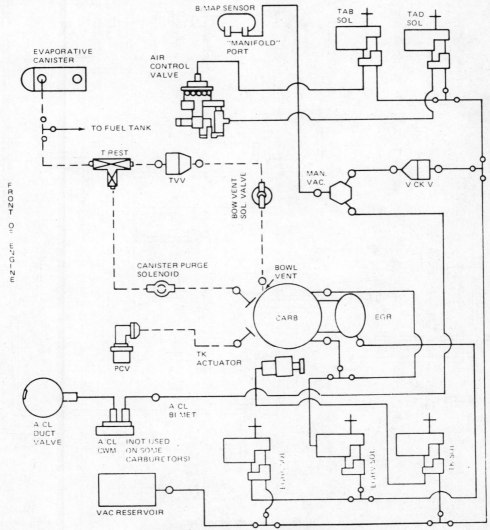

EEC-III, FBC vacuum schematic for the 8-351

and 45,000 miles or between 75,000 and 105,000 miles, you'll have to replace the 1,000 hour pre-timed module.

Oxygen Sensor

REMOVAL AND INSTALLATION

The oxygen sensor is located in the exhaust headpipe. To replace it, unplug the connector and unscrew the sensor.

Replacement senors will be packaged with anti-sieze compound for the threads. If not, or if you are reinstalling the old unit, the threads MUST be coated with anti-sieze compound! Torque the sensor to 12 ft. lbs.

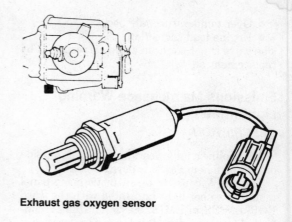

Exhaust gas oxygen sensor

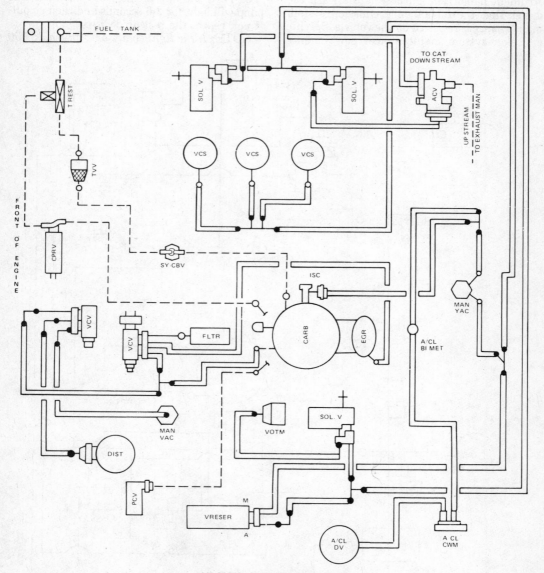

V8 MCU vacuum schematic

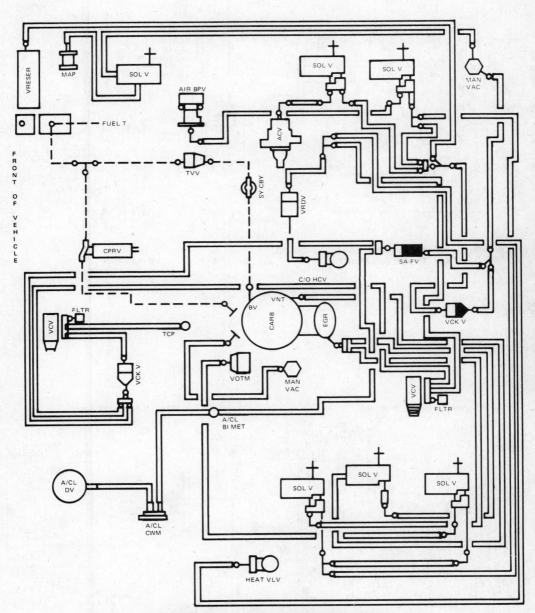

EEC-III, FBC vacuum schematic for the 8-302

CALIF. ONLY A/C & NON A/C

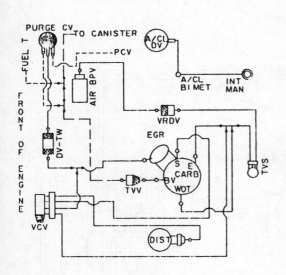

CALIBRATION: 0—52S—RO   DATE: 5—24—79
4.9L TRUCK CALIF. A/T

49S   A/C & NON A/C

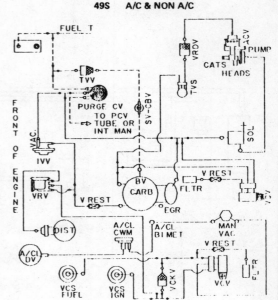

CALIBRATION: 0—13A—RIO   DATE: 10—11—79
5.0L FORD/MERC SWNG 49S A/T

49S   A/C & NON A/C

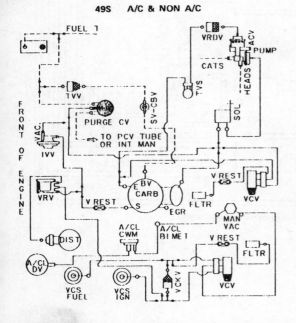

CALIBRATION: 0—13A—RO   DATE: 7—18—79
5.0L 49S FORD—MERC SED A/T

49S   A/C & NON A/C

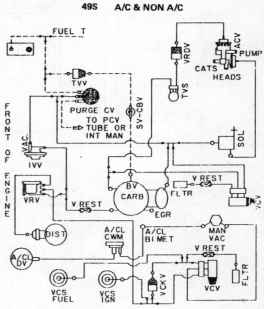

CALIBRATION: 0—13A—RII   DATE: 10—23—79
5.0L FORD/MERC SDN 49S A/T

49S A/C & NON A/C

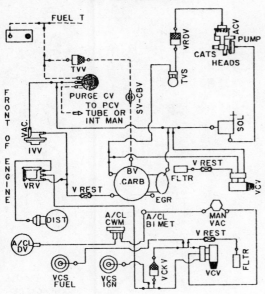

CALIBRATION: 0–13A–R14 DATE: 2–25–80
5.0L FORD/MERC SDN 49S A/T

49S A/C & NON A/C

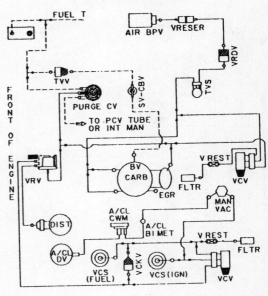

CALIBRATION: 0–13D–R11 DATE: 3–4–80
5.0L FORD & MERC SDN 49S

49S A/C & NON A/C

CALIBRATION: 0–13F–RO DATE: 7–18–79
5.0L 49S FORD–MERC S/W A/T

49S A/C & NON A/C

CALIBRATION: 0–13F–RII DATE: 10–23–79
5.0L FORD/MERC SDN 49S A/T

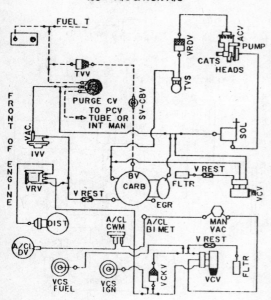

CALIBRATION: 0–13F–R12   DATE: 2–25–80
5.0L FORD & MERC S.W. 49S A/T

CALIBRATION: 0–14N–RO   DATE: 7–23–79
5.0L CALIF LINC/MARK FORD/MERC F10D

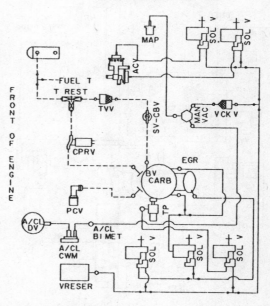

CALIBRATION: 0–12A–RO   DATE: 8–7–79
5.8L(W) 49S FORD/MERC/LINC/MARK F10D

CALIBRATION: 0–12A–R5   DATE: 10–19–79
5.8L(W) FORD/MERC 49S

49S A/C & NON A/C

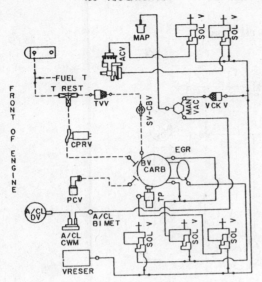

49S A/C & NON A/C

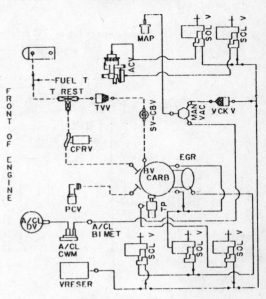

CALIBRATION: 0—12B—RO   DATE: 8—7—79
5.8L(W) 49S FORD/MERC/LINC/MARK F10D

CALIBRATION: 0—12C—R5   DATE: 10—24—79
5.8L (W) FORD/MERC SW/SDN 49S

CANADA A/C & NON A/C

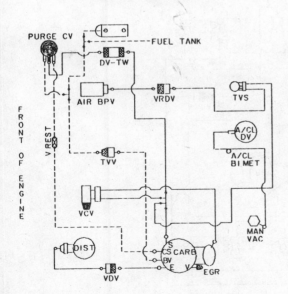

A/C & NON A/C

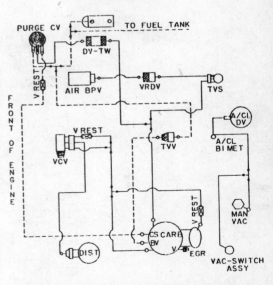

CALIBRATION: 0—12G—R0   DATE: 08—23—79
5.8L (W) LINCOLN/MARK CANADA

CALIBRATION: 0—12H—R10 DATE: 10—09—79
5.8L (W) FORD/FORD S.W./MERC/MERC
S.W.

CANADA   A/C & NON A/C

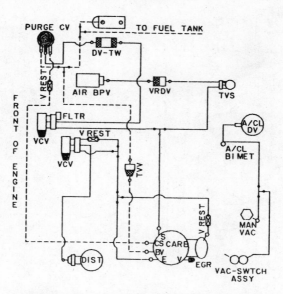

CALIBRATION: 0—12H—ROO DATE: 08—29—79
5.8L(W) FORD/FORD SWGN/MERC/
MERC SWGN

A/C & NON A/C

CALIBRATION: 0—12I—RIO   DATE: 01—17—80
5.8L FORD/MERC H.O.

1981—255 CID (4.2L) engines

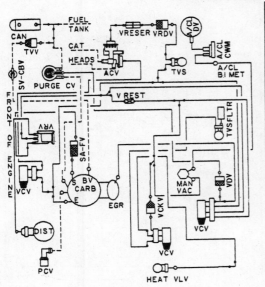

CALIBRATION: 1—18F—R1   DATE: 7-23-80

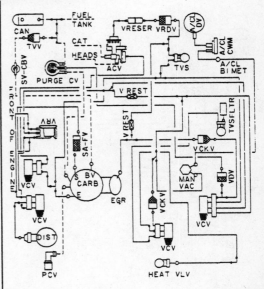

CALIBRATION: 1—18H—R12   DATE: 10-1-80

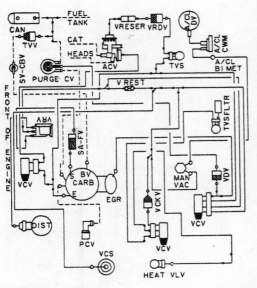

CALIBRATION: 1—18K—R2   DATE: 9-6-80

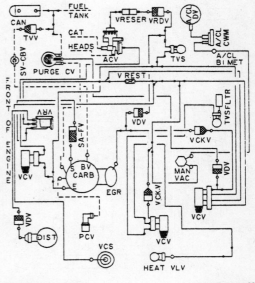

CALIBRATION: 1—18K—R12   DATE: 11-11-80

1981—255 CID (4.2L) engines

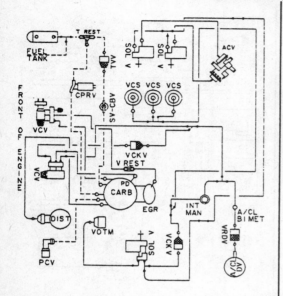

CALIBRATION: 1—18M—R1

DATE: 8-22-80

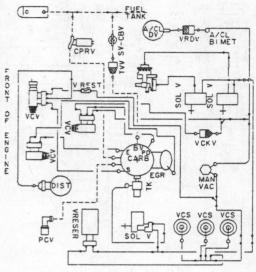

CALIBRATION: 1—18N—R0

DATE: 7-10-80

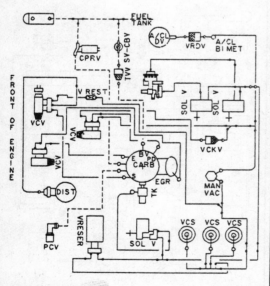

CALIBRATION: 1—18R—R0

DATE: 7-10-80

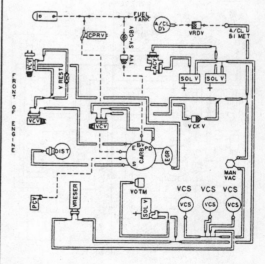

CALIBRATION: 1—18T—R0

DATE: 11-17-80

1981—255 CID (4.2L) engines

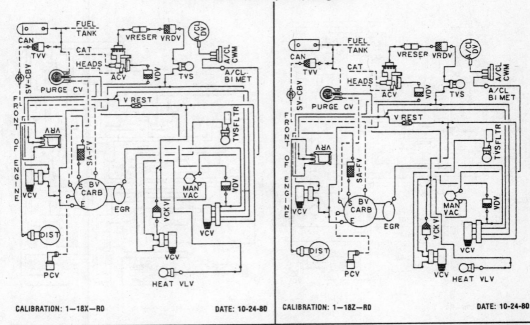

CALIBRATION: 1—18X—R0   DATE: 10-24-80

CALIBRATION: 1—18Z—R0   DATE: 10-24-80

1981—302 CID (5.0L) engines

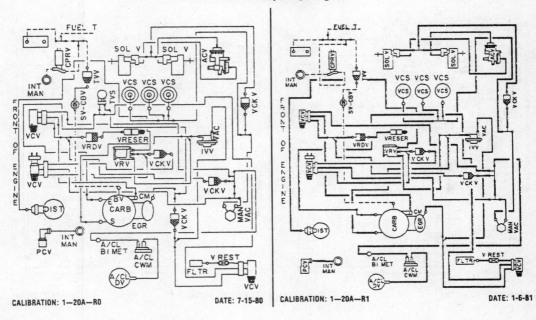

CALIBRATION: 1—20A—R0   DATE: 7-15-80

CALIBRATION: 1—20A—R1   DATE: 1-6-81

1981—302 CID (5.0L) engines

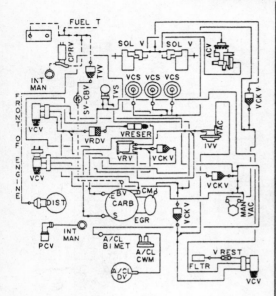

CALIBRATION: 1—20N—R0   DATE: 9-5-80

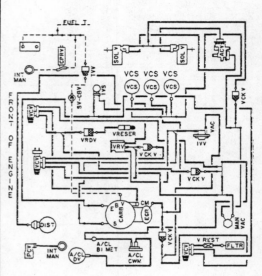

CALIBRATION: 1—20N—R10   DATE: 1-13-81

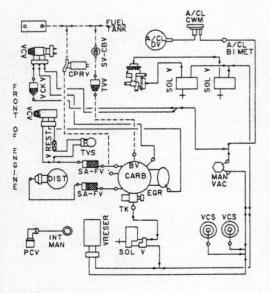

CALIBRATION: 1—20T—R0   DATE: 6-30-80

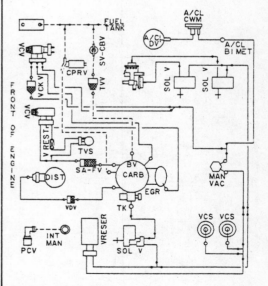

CALIBRATION: 1—20T—R11   DATE: 1-27-81

1981—351 CID (5.8L) engines

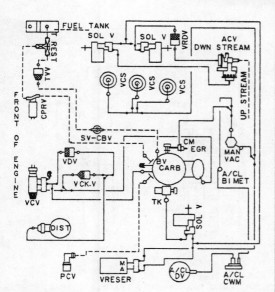

CALIBRATION: 1—24P—RO

CANADIAN

DATE: 8-8-80

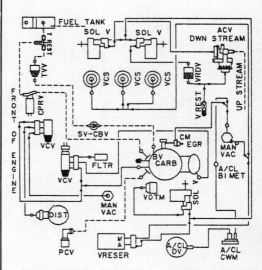

CALIBRATION: 1—24P—R21

DATE: 11-11-80

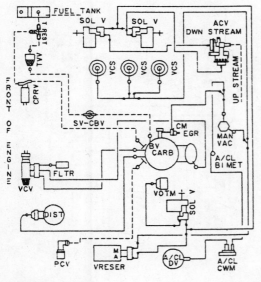

CALIBRATION: 1-24P-R22

CANADIAN

DATE: 11-26-80

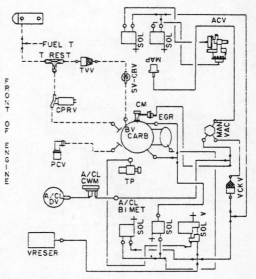

CALIBRATION: 1—24R—RO

DATE: 7-30-80

1982—4.2L (255 CID) V8 engines

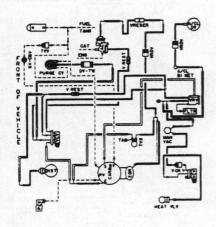

CALIBRATION: 2-18B-R0—AUTO. TRANS.—EXC. HIGH ALT.

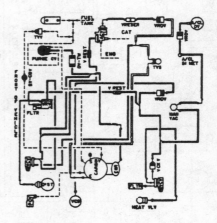

CALIBRATION: 2-18C-R04—AUTO. TRANS.—FEDERAL
CALIBRATION: 2-18C-R05—AUTO. TRANS. WO/AC—FEDERAL

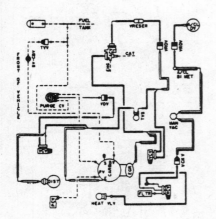

CALIBRATION: 2-18B-R13—AUTO. TRANS.—EXC. HIGH ALT.

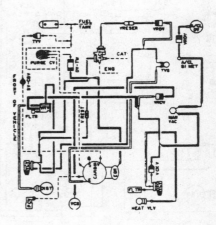

CALIBRATION: 2-18C-R11—AUTO. TRANS.—FEDERAL

1982—4.2L (255 CID) V8 engines

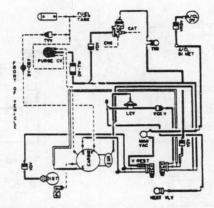

CALIBRATION: 2-18X-R0—AUTO. TRANS.—HIGH ALT.

1982—5.0L (302 CID) V8 engines (Carb.)

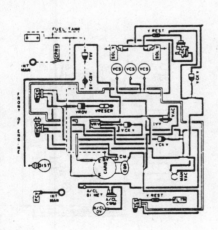

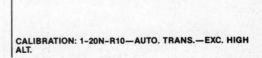

CALIBRATION: 1-20B-R1—AUTO. TRANS.—EXC. HIGH ALT.

CALIBRATION: 1-20N-R10—AUTO. TRANS.—EXC. HIGH ALT.

1982—5.0L (302 CID) V8 engines (Carb.)

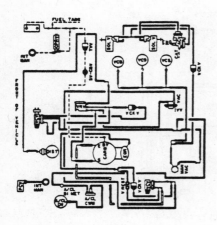

CALIBRATION: 2-20B-R0—AUTO. TRANS.—FEDERAL

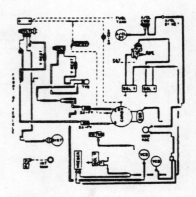

CALIBRATION: 2-20R-R2—AUTO. TRANS.—EXC. HIGH ALT.

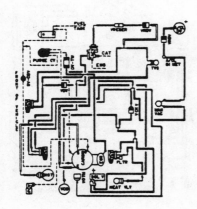

CALIBRATION: 2-20D-R1—AUTO. TRANS.—EXC. HIGH ALT.

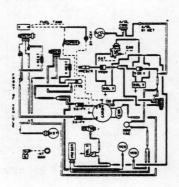

CALIBRATION: 2-20R-R16—AUTO. TRANS.—EXC. HIGH ALT.

1982—5.0L (302 CID) V8 engines (Carb.)

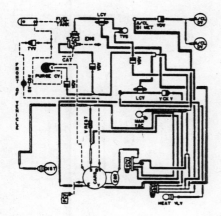

1982—5.0L (302 CID) V8 engines (CFI)

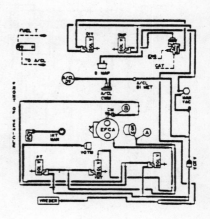

CALIBRATION: 2-21Y-R10—MANUAL TRANS.—HIGH ALT.

CALIBRATION: 2-22A-R0—AUTO. TRANS.—FEDERAL

1982—5.0L (302 CID) V8 engines (CFI)

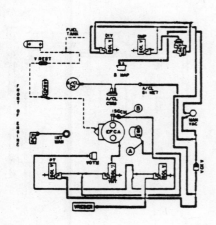

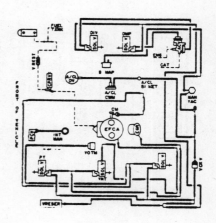

CALIBRATION: 1-22B-R0—AUTO. TRANS.—HIGH ALT.
CALIBRATION: 1-22P-R0—AUTO. TRANS.—CALIFORNIA

CALIBRATION: 2-22Y-R11—AUTO. TRANS.—EXC.
CALIFORNIA

1983—5.0L (302 CID) V8 Engines

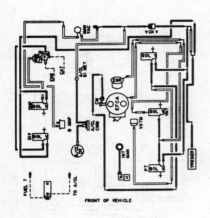

CALIBRATION: 2-22A-R00—AUTO. TRANS.—EXC. HIGH ALT.

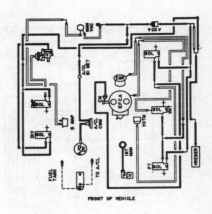

CALIBRATION: 2-22A-R17—AUTO. TRANS.—CALIFORNIA

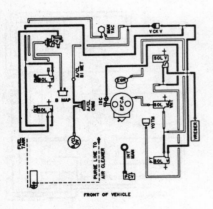

CALIBRATION: 2-22A-R15—AUTO. TRANS.—CALIFORNIA

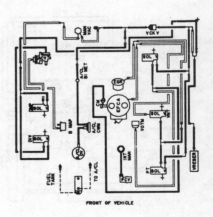

CALIBRATION: 2-22A-R19—AUTO. TRANS.—CALIFORNIA

1983—5.0L (302 CID) V8 Engines

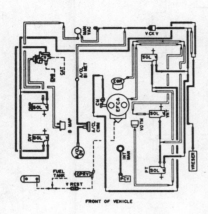

CALIBRATION: 2-22Y-R11—AUTO. TRANS.—EXC. CALIFORNIA

CALIBRATION: 3-21A-R03 (2 PC ACV) MANUAL TRANS.— ALL

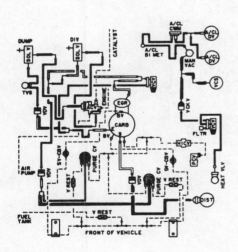

CALIBRATION: 3-21A-R03 (1 PC ACV) MANUAL TRANS.— ALL

CALIBRATION: 3-21A-R11 (1 PC ACV) MANUAL TRANS.— ALL

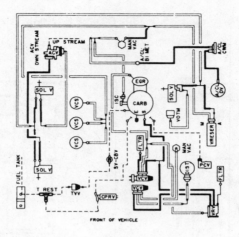

CALIBRATION: 2-24P-R10—AUTO. TRANS.—ALL

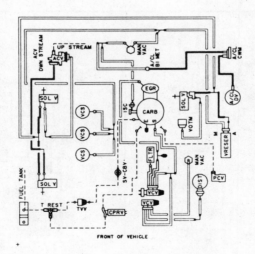

CALIBRATION: 2-24P-R11—AUTO. TRANS.—CANADA

1983—5.8L (351 CID) V8 Engines

1984—5.0L (302 CID) V8 engines

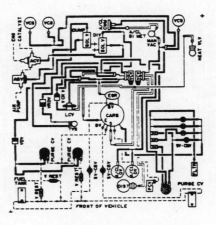

CALIBRATION: 4-21A-R15—MANUAL TRANS.—FEDERAL

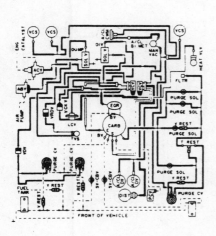

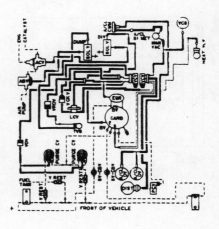

CALIBRATION: 4-21A-R02—MANUAL TRANS.—EXC. CALIFORNIA

CALIBRATION: 4-21P-R12—MANUAL TRANS.—CALIF. AND CANADA

1984—5.0L (302 CID) V8 engines

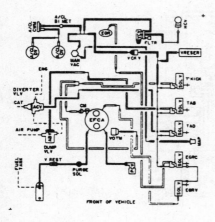

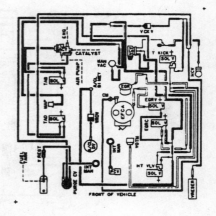

CALIBRATION: 4-22A-R13—AUTO. TRANS.—ALL

CALIBRATION: 4-22C-R00—AUTO. TRANS.—ALL

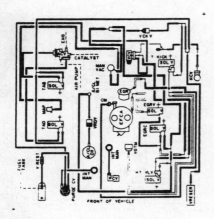

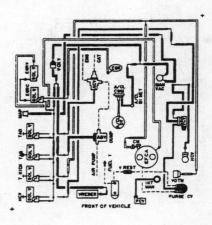

CALIBRATION: 4-22B-R00—AUTO. TRANS.—ALL

CALIBRATION: 4-22D-R00—AUTO. TRANS.—CALIFORNIA

1984—5.0L (302 CID) V8 engines

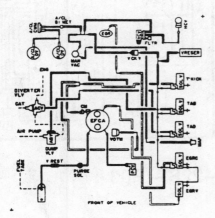

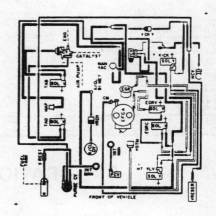

CALIBRATION: 4-22P-R12—AUTO. TRANS.—CALIFORNIA

CALIBRATION: 4-22Q-R00—AUTO. TRANS.—CALIFORNIA

1984—5.8L (351 CID) V8 engines

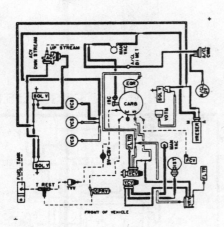

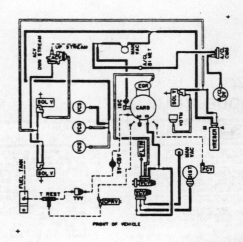

CALIBRATION: 4-24P-R00—AUTO. TRANS.—ALL

CALIBRATION: 4-24P-R11—AUTO. TRANS.—CANADA

MODEL YEAR: 1985

ENGINE: 5.0L

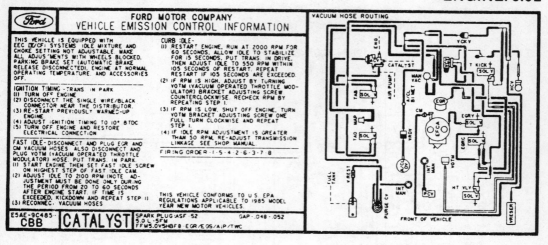

CALIBRATION: 4—22B—R00

MODEL YEAR: 1985

ENGINE: 5.0L

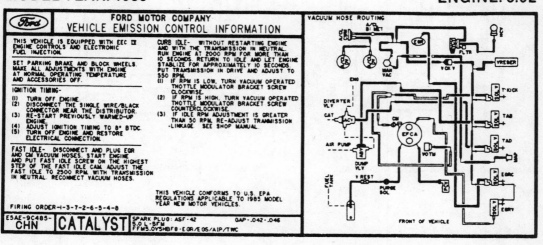

CALIBRATION: 4—22A—R13

MODEL YEAR: 1985   **ENGINE: 5.0L**

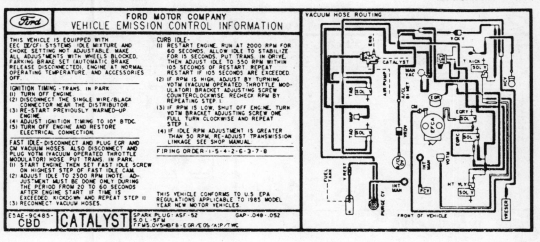

CALIBRATION: 4—22H—R00

MODEL YEAR: 1985   **ENGINE: 5.0L**

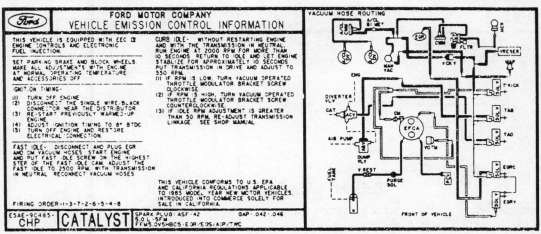

CALIBRATION: 4—22P—R12

MODEL YEAR: 1985   **ENGINE: 5.0L**

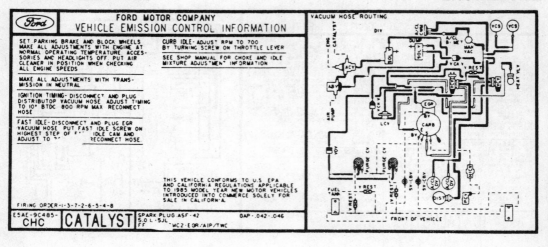

CALIBRATION: 5—21P—R00

MODEL YEAR: 1985   **ENGINE: 5.0L**

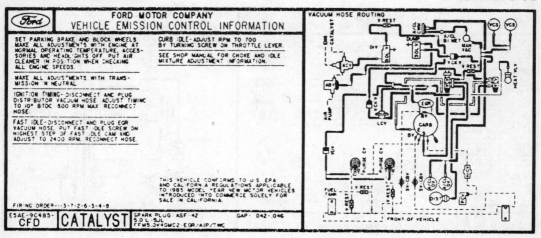

CALIBRATION: 5—21Q—R00

MODEL YEAR: 1985   **ENGINE: 5.0L**

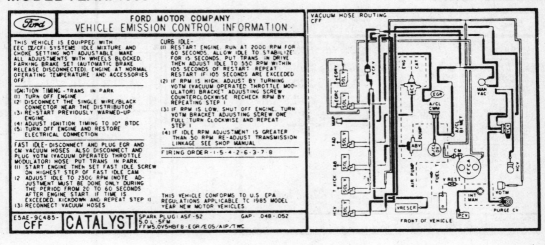

CALIBRATION: 5—22D—R00

MODEL YEAR: 1985   **ENGINE: 5.0L**

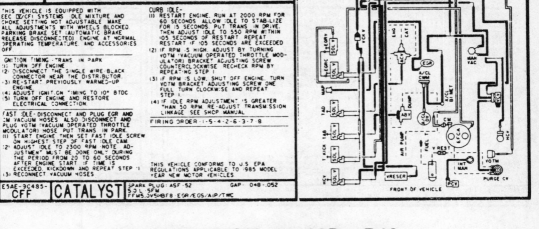

CALIBRATION: 5—22D—R10

MODEL YEAR: 1985 **ENGINE: 5.0L**

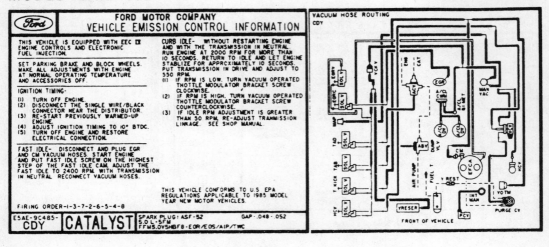

FORD MOTOR COMPANY
VEHICLE EMISSION CONTROL INFORMATION

THIS VEHICLE IS EQUIPPED WITH EEC IV ENGINE CONTROLS AND ELECTRONIC FUEL INJECTION.

SET PARKING BRAKE AND BLOCK WHEELS. MAKE ALL ADJUSTMENTS WITH ENGINE AT NORMAL OPERATING TEMPERATURE AND ACCESSORIES OFF.

IGNITION TIMING:
(1) TURN OFF ENGINE.
(2) DISCONNECT THE SINGLE WIRE/BLACK CONNECTOR NEAR THE DISTRIBUTOR.
(3) RE-START PREVIOUSLY WARMED-UP ENGINE.
(4) ADJUST IGNITION TIMING TO 10° BTDC.
(5) TURN OFF ENGINE AND RESTORE ELECTRICAL CONNECTION.

FAST IDLE- DISCONNECT AND PLUG EGR AND CM VACUUM HOSES. START ENGINE AND PUT FAST IDLE SCREW ON THE HIGHEST STEP OF THE FAST IDLE CAM. ADJUST THE FAST IDLE TO 2400 RPM WITH TRANSMISSION IN NEUTRAL. RECONNECT VACUUM HOSES.

CURB IDLE- WITHOUT RESTARTING ENGINE AND WITH THE TRANSMISSION IN NEUTRAL, RUN ENGINE AT 2000 RPM FOR MORE THAN 10 SECONDS. RETURN TO IDLE AND LET ENGINE STABILIZE FOR APPROXIMATELY 10 SECONDS. PUT TRANSMISSION IN DRIVE AND ADJUST TO 550 RPM.
(1) IF RPM IS LOW, TURN VACUUM OPERATED THROTTLE MODULATOR BRACKET SCREW CLOCKWISE.
(2) IF RPM IS HIGH, TURN VACUUM OPERATED THROTTLE MODULATOR BRACKET SCREW COUNTERCLOCKWISE.
(3) IF IDLE RPM ADJUSTMENT IS GREATER THAN 50 RPM RE-ADJUST TRANSMISSION LINKAGE. SEE SHOP MANUAL.

THIS VEHICLE CONFORMS TO U.S EPA REGULATIONS APPLICABLE TO 1985 MODEL YEAR NEW MOTOR VEHICLES.

FIRING ORDER-1-3-7-2-6-5-4-8

E5AE-9C485-CDY **CATALYST**
SPARK PLUG: ASF-52   GAP .048-.052
5.0 L-5FM
FFM5.0V5HBF8-EGR/EOS/AIP/TWC

CALIBRATION: 5—22L—R00

MODEL YEAR: 1985 **ENGINE: 5.0L**

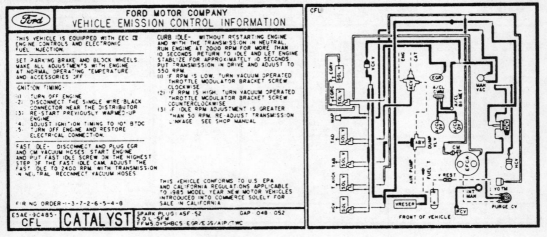

FORD MOTOR COMPANY
VEHICLE EMISSION CONTROL INFORMATION

THIS VEHICLE IS EQUIPPED WITH EEC IV ENGINE CONTROLS AND ELECTRONIC FUEL INJECTION.

SET PARKING BRAKE AND BLOCK WHEELS. MAKE ALL ADJUSTMENTS WITH ENGINE AT NORMAL OPERATING TEMPERATURE AND ACCESSORIES OFF.

IGNITION TIMING:
(1) TURN OFF ENGINE.
(2) DISCONNECT THE SINGLE WIRE/BLACK CONNECTOR NEAR THE DISTRIBUTOR.
(3) RE-START PREVIOUSLY WARMED-UP ENGINE.
(4) ADJUST IGNITION TIMING TO 10° BTDC.
(5) TURN OFF ENGINE AND RESTORE ELECTRICAL CONNECTION.

FAST IDLE- DISCONNECT AND PLUG EGR AND CM VACUUM HOSES. START ENGINE AND PUT FAST IDLE SCREW ON THE HIGHEST STEP OF THE FAST IDLE CAM. ADJUST THE FAST IDLE TO 2400 RPM WITH TRANSMISSION IN NEUTRAL. RECONNECT VACUUM HOSES.

CURB IDLE- WITHOUT RESTARTING ENGINE AND WITH THE TRANSMISSION IN NEUTRAL, RUN ENGINE AT 2000 RPM FOR MORE THAN 10 SECONDS. RETURN TO IDLE AND LET ENGINE STABILIZE FOR APPROXIMATELY 10 SECONDS. PUT TRANSMISSION IN DRIVE AND ADJUST TO 550 RPM.
(1) IF RPM IS LOW, TURN VACUUM OPERATED THROTTLE MODULATOR BRACKET SCREW CLOCKWISE.
(2) IF RPM IS HIGH, TURN VACUUM OPERATED THROTTLE MODULATOR BRACKET SCREW COUNTERCLOCKWISE.
(3) IF IDLE RPM ADJUSTMENT IS GREATER THAN 50 RPM. RE-ADJUST TRANSMISSION LINKAGE. SEE SHOP MANUAL.

THIS VEHICLE CONFORMS TO U.S. EPA AND CALIFORNIA REGULATIONS APPLICABLE TO 1985 MODEL YEAR NEW MOTOR VEHICLES INTRODUCED INTO COMMERCE SOLELY FOR SALE IN CALIFORNIA.

FIRING ORDER-1-3-7-2-6-5-4-8

E5AE-9C485-CFL **CATALYST**
SPARK PLUG: ASF-52   GAP .048-.052
5.0 L-5FM
FFM5.0V5HBC5-EGR/EOS/AIP/TWC

CALIBRATION: 5—22M—R01

MODEL YEAR: 1985   **ENGINE: 5.0L**

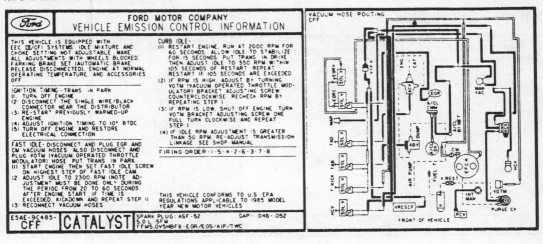

CALIBRATION: 5—22R—R00

MODEL YEAR: 1985   **ENGINE: 5.0L**

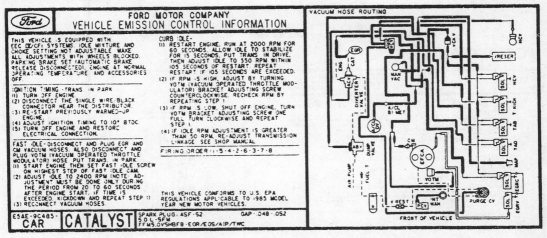

CALIBRATION: 5—22T—R00

CALIBRATION: 6—21A—R00

MODEL YEAR: 1986

ENGINE: 5.0L

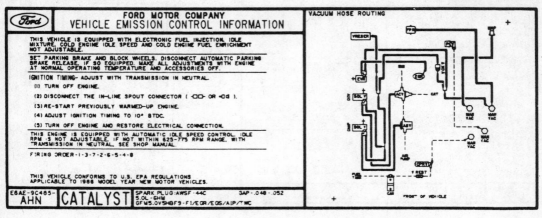

CALIBRATION: 6—21B—R00

MODEL YEAR: 1986

ENGINE: 5.0L

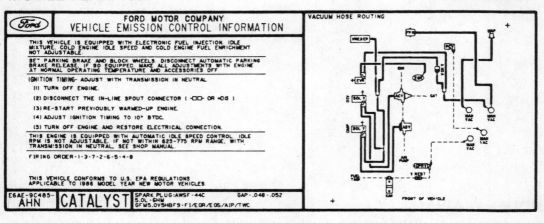

CALIBRATION: 6—22B—R00

MODEL YEAR: 1986

ENGINE: 5.0L

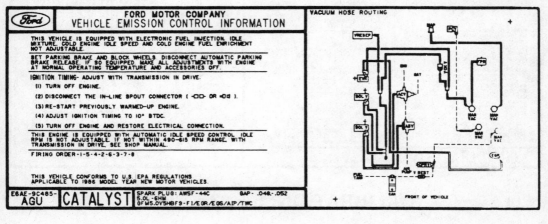

CALIBRATION: 6—22A—R00

MODEL YEAR: 1986   **ENGINE: 5.0L**

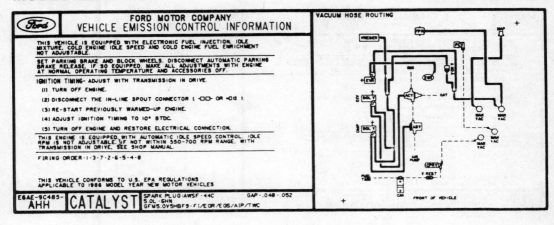

CALIBRATION: 6—22E—R00

MODEL YEAR: 1986   **ENGINE: 5.0L**

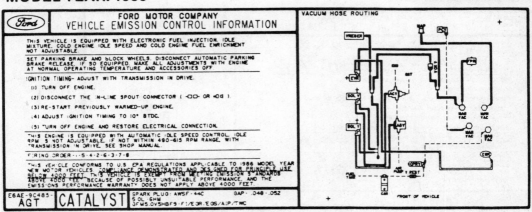

CALIBRATION: 6—22F—R00

MODEL YEAR: 1986   **ENGINE: 5.0L**

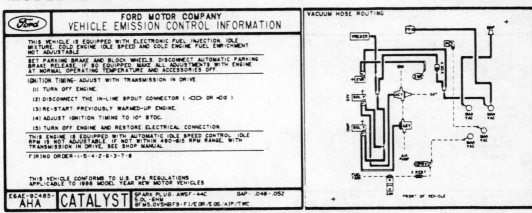

CALIBRATION: 6—22G—R00

MODEL YEAR: 1986   **ENGINE: 5.0L**

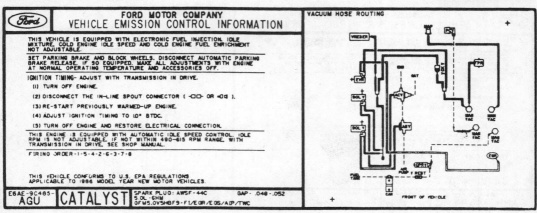

CALIBRATION: 6—22H—R00

MODEL YEAR: 1986   **ENGINE: 5.0L**

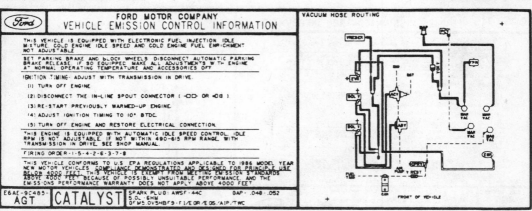

CALIBRATION: 6—22L—R00

MODEL YEAR: 1986   **ENGINE: 5.0L**

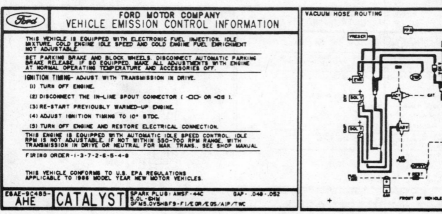

CALIBRATION: 6—22K—R00

MODEL YEAR: 1986   **ENGINE: 5.0L**

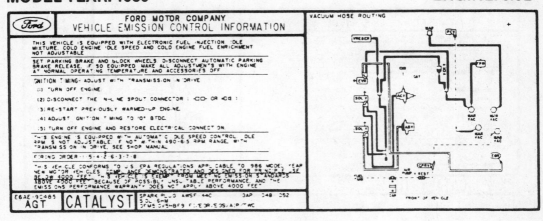

CALIBRATION: 6—22R—R00

MODEL YEAR: 1986   **ENGINE: 5.0L**

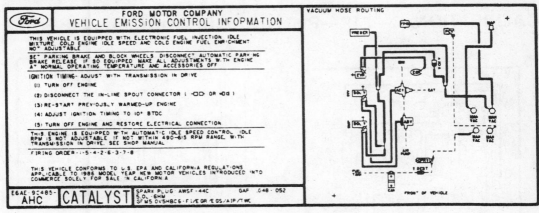

CALIBRATION: 6—22Q—R00

MODEL YEAR: 1986   **ENGINE: 5.0L**

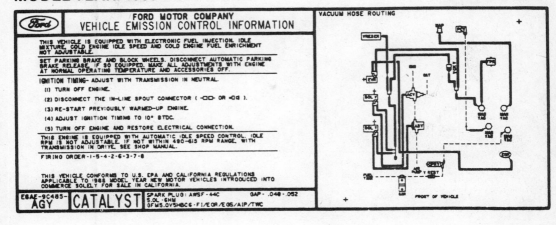

CALIBRATION: 6—23A—R00

MODEL YEAR: 1986 **ENGINE: 5.0L**

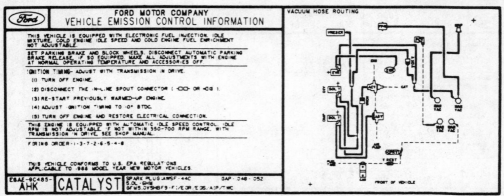

ENGINE: 5.8L

CALIBRATION: 4—24P—R00 # CALIBRATION: 4—24P—R11

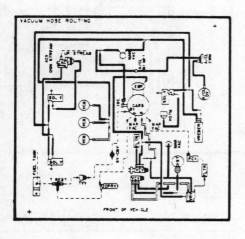 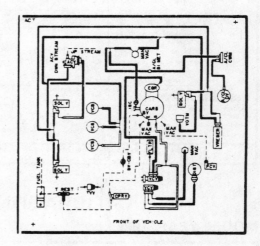

Fuel System

5

GENERAL FUEL SYSTEM COMPONENTS

Mechanical Fuel Pump

A single action mechanical fuel pump, driven by the camshaft, is used on all carbureted models except some 429 and 460 engines.

Some Police Interceptor 429 and 460 engines use an electric fuel pump locted in the gas tank. The gas tank must be removed to service the electric fuel pump.

The mechanical fuel pump is located at the lower left side of the engine block on 6-240 engines, and at the lower left side of the cylinder front cover on V8 models.

TESTING AND ADJUSTMENT

No adjustments may be made to the fuel pump. Before removing and replacing the old fuel pump, the following test may be made while the pump is still installed on the engine. CAUTION: *To avoid accidental ignition of fuel during the test, first remove the coil high tension wire from the distributor and the coil.* Incorrect fuel pump pressure and low volume

Troubleshooting Basic Fuel System Problems

Problem	Cause	Solution
Engine cranks, but won't start (or is hard to start) when cold	• Empty fuel tank • Incorrect starting procedure • Defective fuel pump • No fuel in carburetor • Clogged fuel filter • Engine flooded • Defective choke	• Check for fuel in tank • Follow correct procedure • Check pump output • Check for fuel in the carburetor • Replace fuel filter • Wait 15 minutes; try again • Check choke plate
Engine cranks, but is hard to start (or does not start) when hot— (presence of fuel is assumed)	• Defective choke	• Check choke plate
Rough idle or engine runs rough	• Dirt or moisture in fuel • Clogged air filter • Faulty fuel pump	• Replace fuel filter • Replace air filter • Check fuel pump output
Engine stalls or hesitates on acceleration	• Dirt or moisture in the fuel • Dirty carburetor • Defective fuel pump • Incorrect float level, defective accelerator pump	• Replace fuel filter • Clean the carburetor • Check fuel pump output • Check carburetor
Poor gas mileage	• Clogged air filter • Dirty carburetor • Defective choke, faulty carburetor adjustment	• Replace air filter • Clean carburetor • Check carburetor
Engine is flooded (won't start accompanied by smell of raw fuel)	• Improperly adjusted choke or carburetor	• Wait 15 minutes and try again, without pumping gas pedal • If it won't start, check carburetor

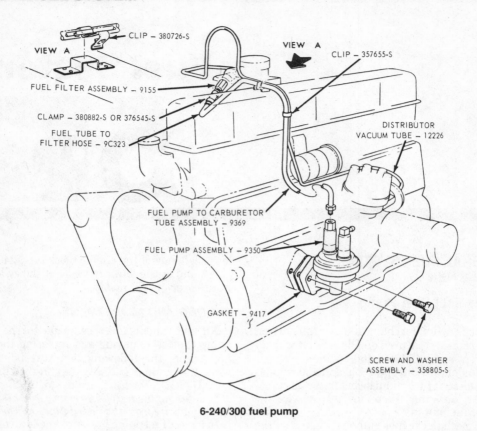

6-240/300 fuel pump

(flow rate) are the two most likely fuel pump troubles that will affect engine performance. Low pressure will cause a lean mixture and fuel starvation at high speeds and excessive pressure will cause high fuel consumption and carburetor flooding.

To determine that the fuel pump is in satisfactory operating condition, tests for both fuel pump pressure and volume should be performed.

The test are performed with the fuel pump installed on the engine and the engine at normal operating temperature and at idle speed.

Before the test, make sure that the replaceable fuel filter has been changed at the proper mileage interval. If in doubt, install a new filter.

Pressure Test

1. Remove the air cleaner assembly. Disconnect the fuel inlet line of the fuel filter at the carburetor. Use care to prevent fire, due to fuel spillage. Place an absorbent cloth under the connection before removing the line to catch any fuel that might flow out of the line.

2. Connect a pressure gauge, a restrictor and a flexible hose between the fuel filter and the carburetor.

3. Position the flexible hose and the

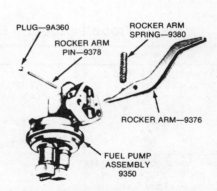

Carter permanently-sealed fuel pump—V8

restrictor so that the fuel can be discharged into a suitable, graduated container.

4. Before taking a pressure reading, operate the engine at the specified idle rpm and vent the system into the container by opening the hose restrictor momentarily.

5. Close the hose restrictor, allow the pressure to stabilize and note the reading. The pressure should be 5 psi.

If the pump pressure is not within 4-6 psi and the fuel lines and filter are in satisfactory condition, the pump is defective and should be replaced.

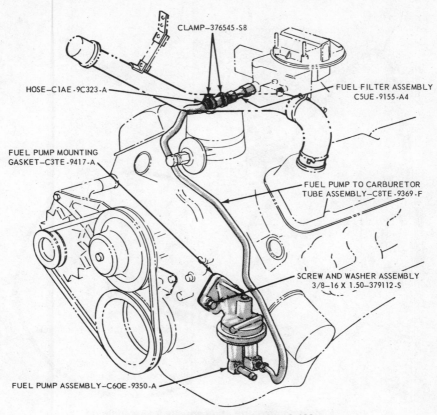

CLAMP—376545-S8

HOSE—C1AE-9C323-A

FUEL FILTER ASSEMBLY
C5UE-9155-A4

FUEL PUMP MOUNTING
GASKET—C3TE-9417-A

FUEL PUMP TO CARBURETOR
TUBE ASSEMBLY—C8TE-9369-F

SCREW AND WASHER ASSEMBLY
3/8—16 X 1.50—379112-S

FUEL PUMP ASSEMBLY—C6OE-9350-A

Carbureted V8 fuel pump, except 8-460

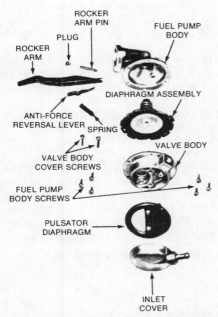

ROCKER
ARM PIN

FUEL PUMP
BODY

PLUG

ROCKER
ARM

DIAPHRAGM ASSEMBLY

ANTI-FORCE
REVERSAL LEVER
SPRING

VALVE BODY

VALVE BODY
COVER SCREWS

FUEL PUMP
BODY SCREWS

PULSATOR
DIAPHRAGM

INLET
COVER

Carter Police Interceptor fuel pump disassembled

If the pump pressure is within the proper range, perform the test for fuel volume.

Volume Test

1. Operate the engine at the specified idle rpm.

2. Open the hose restrictor and catch the fuel in the container while observing the time it takes to pump 1 pint. 1 pint should be pumped in 20 seconds. If the pump does not pump to specifications, check for proper fuel tank venting or a restriction in the fuel line leading from the fuel tank to the carburetor before replacing the fuel pump.

REMOVAL AND INSTALLATION

1. Disconnect the plug and inlet and outlet lines from the fuel pump.

2. Remove the fuel pump retaining bolts and carefully pull the pump and old gasket away from the block.

3. Discard the old gasket. Clean the mating surfaces on the block and position a new gasket on the block, using oil resistant sealer.

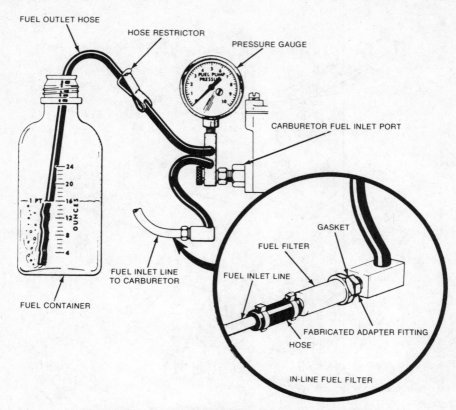

Typical fuel pump pressure and capacity test equipment

4. Mount the fuel pump and gasket to the engine block, being careful to insert the pump lever (rocker arm) in the engine block, aligning it correctly above the camshaft lobe.

NOTE: *If resistance is felt while positioning the fuel pump on the block, the camshaft lobe is probably on the high position. To ease installation, connect a remote engine starter switch to the engine adn tap the switch until resistance fades.*

5. While holding the pump securely against the block, install the retaining bolts. On 6-240 engines, torque the bolts to 12-15 ft. lbs.; 20-24 ft. lbs. on the 8-302; 14-20 on the 8-351; 19-27 ft. lbs. on all other engines.

6. Unplug and connect the fuel lines at the pump.

7. Start the engine and check for fuel leaks. Also check for oil leaks where the fuel pump attaches to the block.

Electric Fuel Pump
REMOVAL AND INSTALLATION

Two electric pumps are used on fuel injected models; a low pressure boost pump mounted in

the fuel tank and a high pressure pump mounted on the vehicle frame. Models equipped with the 8-429 and 8-460 carbureted engines use a single low pressure pump mounted in the fuel tank.

On injected models the low pressure pump is used to provide pressurized fuel to the inlet of the high pressure pump and helps prevent noise and heating problems. The externally mounted high pressure pump is capable of supplying 15.9 gallons of fuel an hour. System pressure is controlled by a pressure regulator mounted on the engine.

On internal fuel tank mounted pumps tank removal is required. Frame mounted models can be accessed from under the vehicle. Prior to servicing release system pressure (see Fuel Supply Manifold details). Disconnect the negative battery cable prior to pump removal.

Low Pressure In-Tank Pump through 1984

1. Disconnect the negative battery cable.
2. Depressurize the system and drain as much gas from the tank by pumping out through the filler neck.
3. Raise and support the rear end on jackstands.

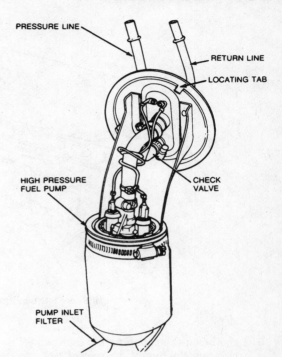

High pressure in-tank electric fuel pump

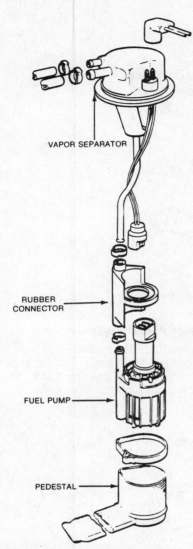

Electric fuel pump and related parts

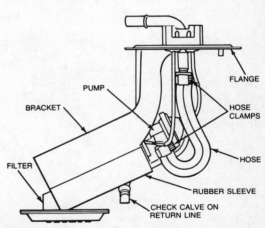

Low pressure in-tank electric fuel pump used with the 6-232 and 8-302 engines

4. Disconnect the fuel supply, return and vent lines at the right and left side of the frame.

5. Disconnect the wiring to the fuel pump.

6. Support the gas tank, loosen and remove the mounting straps. Remove the gas tank.

7. Disconnect the lines and harness at the pump flange.

8. Clean the outside of the mounting flange and retaining ring. Turn the fuel pump lock ring counterclockwise and remove.

9. Remove the fuel pump.

10. Clean the mounting surfaces. Put a light coat of grease on the mounting surfaces and on the new sealing ring. Install the new fuel pump.

11. Installation is in the reverse order of removal. If you have a single high pressure pump system, fill the tank with at least 10 gals. of gas. Turn the ignition key ON for three seconds. Re-

peat 6 or 7 times until the fuel system is pressurized. Check for any fitting leaks. Start the engine and check for leaks.

High Pressure External Pump through 1984

1. Disconnect the negative battery cable.

2. Depressurize the fuel system.

3. Raise and support the rear of the vehicle on jackstands.

4. Disconnect the inlet and outlet fuel lines.

5. Disconnect the electrical harness connection.

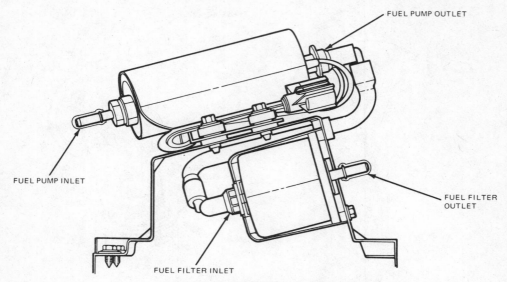

FUEL PUMP OUTLET

FUEL PUMP INLET

FUEL FILTER OUTLET

FUEL FILTER INLET

High pressure in-line electric fuel pump

6. Bend down the retaining tab and remove the pump from the mounting bracket ring.

7. Install in reverse order, make sure the pump is indexed correctly in the mounting bracket insulator.

1985-88 High Pressure In-Tank Pump

1. Depressurize the system.
2. Disconnect the negative battery cable.
3. Drain as much gas from the tank by pumping out through the filler neck.

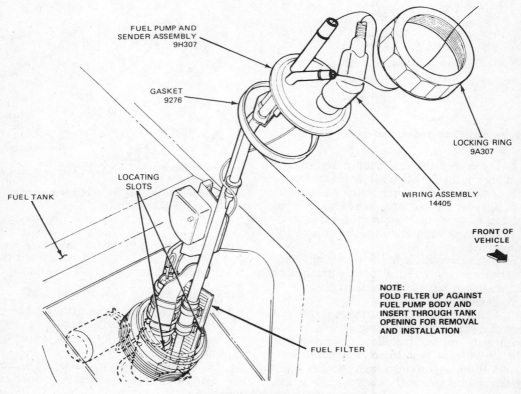

FUEL PUMP AND SENDER ASSEMBLY 9H307

GASKET 9276

LOCATING SLOTS

FUEL TANK

LOCKING RING 9A307

WIRING ASSEMBLY 14405

FRONT OF VEHICLE

NOTE: FOLD FILTER UP AGAINST FUEL PUMP BODY AND INSERT THROUGH TANK OPENING FOR REMOVAL AND INSTALLATION

FUEL FILTER

In-tank electric fuel pump

4. Raise and support the rear end on jackstands.

5. Disconnect the filler hose, fuel supply, return and vent lines at the right and left side of the frame.

6. Disconnect the wiring to the fuel pump.

7. Support the gas tank, loosen and remove the mounting straps. Remove the gas tank.

8. Disconnect the lines and harness at the pump flange.

9. Clean the outside of the mounting flange and retaining ring. Turn the fuel pump lock ring counterclockwise and remove.

10. Remove the fuel pump.

11. Clean the mounting surfaces. Put a light coat of grease on the mounting surfaces and on the new sealing ring. Install the new fuel pump.

12. Installation is in the reverse order of removal. If you have a single high pressure pump system, fill the tank with at least 10 gals. of gas. Turn the ignition key ON for three seconds. Repeat 6 or 7 times until the fuel system is pressurized. Check for any fitting leaks. Start the engine and check for leaks.

Quick-Connect Line Fittings
REMOVAL AND INSTALLATION

NOTE: *Quick-Connect (push) type fittings must be disconnected using proper procedures or the fitting may be damaged. Two types of retainers are used on the push connect fittings. Line sizes of ³⁄₈" and ⁵⁄₁₆" use a hairpin clip retainer. ¼" line connectors use a Duck bill clip retainer.*

Hairpin Clip

1. Clean all dirt and/or grease from the fittings. Spread the two clip legs about an ⅛" each to disengage from the fitting and pull the clip outward from the fitting. Use finger pressure only, do not use any tools.

2. Grasp the fittings and hose assembly and pull away from the steel line. Twist the fitting and hose assembly slightly while pulling, if necessary, when a sticking condition exists.

3. Inspect the hairpin clip for damage, replace the clip if necessary. Reinstall the clip in position on the fitting.

4. Inspect the fitting and inside of the connector to insure freedom Of dirt or obstruction. Install fitting into the connector and push together. A click will be heard when the hairpin snaps into proper connection. Pull on the line to insure full engagement.

Duck Bill Clip

1. A special tool is available for Ford for removing the retaining clip (Ford Tool No. T82L-9500-AH). If the tool is not on hand see Step 2.

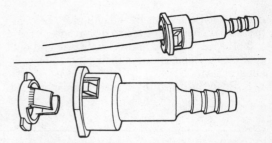

Push-connect type fitting with a duck-bill clip

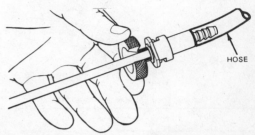

Connector removal using a push-connect disconnection tool

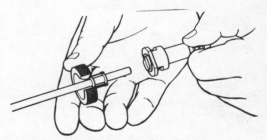

Pulling off the push-connect fitting

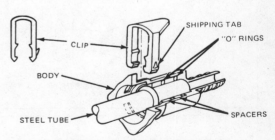

Push-connect type fitting with a hairpin clip

Align the slot on the push connector disconnect tool with either tab on the retaining clip. Pull the line from the connector.

2. If the special clip tool is not available, use a pair of narrow 6" locking pliers with a jaw width of 0.2" or less. Align the jaws of the pliers with the openings of the fitting case and compress the part of the retaining clip that engages the case. Compressing the retaining clip will release the fitting which may be pulled from the

connector. Both sides of the clip must be compressed at the same time to disengage.

3. Inspect the retaining clip, fitting end and connector. Replace the clip if any damage is apparent.

4. Push the line into the steel connector until a click is heard, indicating the clip is in place. Pull on the line to check engagement.

Fuel Tank

CAUTION: *NEVER SMOKE AROUND OR NEAR GASOLINE! GASOLINE VAPORS*

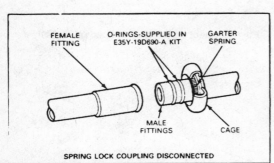

SPRING LOCK COUPLING DISCONNECTED

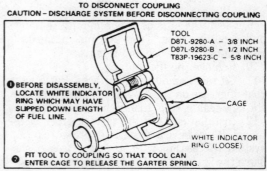

TO DISCONNECT COUPLING
CAUTION – DISCHARGE SYSTEM BEFORE DISCONNECTING COUPLING

TOOL
D87L-9280-A – 3/8 INCH
D87L-9280-B – 1/2 INCH
T83P-19623-C – 5/8 INCH

❶ BEFORE DISASSEMBLY, LOCATE WHITE INDICATOR RING WHICH MAY HAVE SLIPPED DOWN LENGTH OF FUEL LINE.

❷ FIT TOOL TO COUPLING SO THAT TOOL CAN ENTER CAGE TO RELEASE THE GARTER SPRING.

TO CONNECT COUPLING

REPLACEMENT GARTER SPRINGS
3/8 INCH – E1ZZ-19E576-A
1/2 INCH – E1ZZ-19E576-B
5/8 INCH – E35Y-19E576-A
ALSO AVAILABLE IN
E35Y-19D690-A KIT

❶ CHECK FOR MISSING OR DAMAGED GARTER SPRING – REMOVE DAMAGED SPRING WITH SMALL HOOKED WIRE – INSTALL NEW SPRING IF DAMAGED OR MISSING.

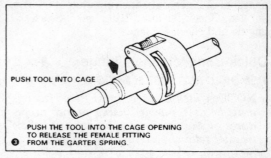

❸ PUSH THE TOOL INTO THE CAGE OPENING TO RELEASE THE FEMALE FITTING FROM THE GARTER SPRING.

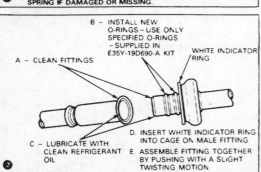

B – INSTALL NEW O-RINGS – USE ONLY SPECIFIED O-RINGS – SUPPLIED IN E35Y-19D690-A KIT

A – CLEAN FITTINGS

C – LUBRICATE WITH CLEAN REFRIGERANT OIL

D. INSERT WHITE INDICATOR RING INTO CAGE ON MALE FITTING

E. ASSEMBLE FITTING TOGETHER BY PUSHING WITH A SLIGHT TWISTING MOTION

❷

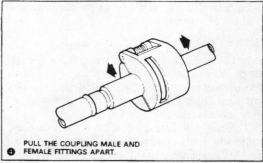

❹ PULL THE COUPLING MALE AND FEMALE FITTINGS APART.

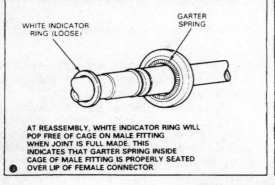

❸ AT REASSEMBLY, WHITE INDICATOR RING WILL POP FREE OF CAGE ON MALE FITTING WHEN JOINT IS FULL MADE. THIS INDICATES THAT GARTER SPRING INSIDE CAGE OF MALE FITTING IS PROPERLY SEATED OVER LIP OF FEMALE CONNECTOR.

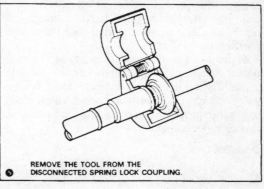

❺ REMOVE THE TOOL FROM THE DISCONNECTED SPRING LOCK COUPLING.

Metal spring-lock connectors

ARE EXTREMELY FLAMMABLE! EVEN THE PROXIMITY OF LIGHTED SMOKING MATERIAL CAN CAUSE AN EXPLOSION AND FIRE!

REMOVAL AND INSTALLATION

NOTE: *On engines with fuel injection, before disconnecting any fuel line, relieve the pressure from the fuel system. On engines with CFI, relieve the system pressure at the pressure relief valve mounted on the throttle body. Special tool T80L-9974-A, or its equivalent, is needed for this procedure.*

On the 8-302 with EFI, the valve is located in the metal engine fuel line at the left front corner of the engine.

Before opening the fuel system on EFI engines:

1. Remove the fuel tank cap.

2. Disconnect the vacuum hose from the fuel pressure regulator located on the engine fuel rail.

3. Using a hand vacuum pump, apply about 25 in.Hg to the pressure regulator. Fuel pressure will be released into the fuel tank through the fuel return hose.

1. Raise and support the rear end on jackstands.

2. Disconnect the battery ground cable.

3. Siphon off as much gasoline as possible into an approved container.

NOTE: *On cars with fuel injection, the fuel tank has small reservoirs inside to maintain the fuel level at or near the fuel pick-up. These reservoirs are difficult to drain in as much as they may block the siphoning hose. You'll have to try different angle and repeated attempts with the siphoning hose. Be patient.*

4. Place a pan under the fuel fill hose and disconnect the fuel filler hose at the tank. Pour any drained fuel into an approved container.

5. Place a floor jack, cushioned with a length of wood, under the fuel tank.

6. Remove the fuel tank strap nuts and lower the fuel tank just enough to disconnect the fuel liquid and vapor lines, and the fuel sending unit wire.

On cars so equipped, remove the air deflector from the tank retaining straps. The deflector is retained with pop rivets.

On cars cars equipped with a metal retainer which fastens the filler pipe to the tank, remove the screw attaching the retainer to the fuel tank flange.

7. Continue lowering the tank once all lines are disconnected, and remove it from the car.

8. Installation is the reverse of removal. The fuel vapor line should be retaped in position in the ribbed channel atop the tank.

CARBURETED FUEL SYSTEM

Electric Choke

Starting in 1973, all models use an electrically-assisted choke to reduce exhaust emissions of carbon monoxide during warmup. The system consists of a choke cap, a thermostatic spring, a bimetal sensing disc (switch) and a ceramic positive temperature coefficient (PTC) heater.

The choke is powered from the center tap of the alternator, so that current is constantly applied to the temperature sensing disc. The system is grounded through the carburetor body. At temperatures below approximately 60 degrees F, the switch is open and no current is supplied to the ceramic heater, thereby resulting in normal unassisted thermostatic spring choking action. When the temperature rises above about 60 degrees F, the temperature sensing disc closes and current is supplied to the heater, which in turn, acts on the thermostatic spring. Once the heater starts, it causes the thermostatic spring to pull the choke plate(s) open within 1½ minutes, which is sooner than it would open if nonassisted.

ELECTRIC CHOKE OPERATIONAL TEST

1. Detach the electrical lead from the choke cap.

2. Use a jumper lead to connect the terminal

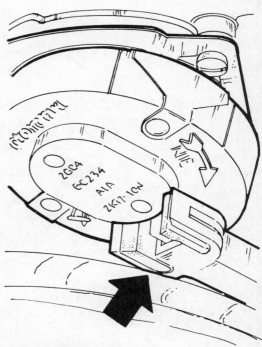

Electric choke hookup

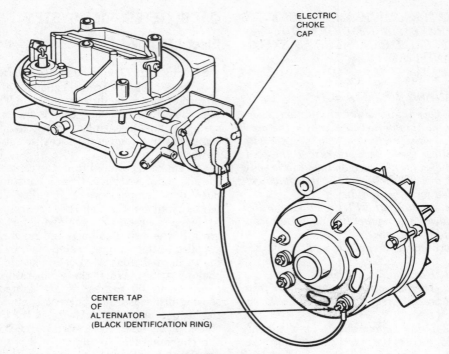

ELECTRIC
CHOKE
CAP

CENTER TAP
OF
ALTERNATOR
(BLACK IDENTIFICATION RING)

Electric choke wiring

on the choke cap and the wire terminal, so that the electrical circuit is still completed.

3. Start the engine.

4. Hook up a test light between the connector on the choke lead and ground.

5. The test light should glow. If it does not, current is not being supplied to the electrically assisted choke.

6. Connect the test light between the terminal on the alternator and the terminal on the

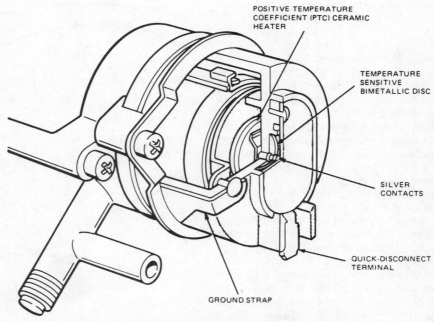

POSITIVE TEMPERATURE
COEFFICIENT (PTC) CERAMIC
HEATER

TEMPERATURE
SENSITIVE
BIMETALLIC DISC

SILVER
CONTACTS

QUICK-DISCONNECT
TERMINAL

GROUND STRAP

Electric choke components

choke cap. If the light now glows, replace the lead, since it is not passing current to the choke assist.

CAUTION: *Do not ground the terminal on the alternator while performing Step 6.*

7. If the light still does not glow, the fault lies somewhere in the electrical system. Check the system out.

If the electrically assisted choke receives power but still does not appear to be functioning properly, reconnect the choke lead and proceed with the rest of the test.

8. Tape the bulb end of the thermometer to the metallic portion of the choke housing.

9. If the electrically assisted choke operates below 55°F (13°C), it is defective and must be replaced.

10. Allow the engine to warm up to 80-100°F (27-38°C); at these temperatures the choke should operate for about 1½ minutes.

11. If it does not operate for this length of time, check the bimetallic spring to see if it is connected to the tang on the choke lever.

12. If the spring is connected and the choke is not operating properly, replace the cap assembly.

Carburetors

In accordance with Federal emissions regulations, all carburetors are equipped with idle mixture screw limiter caps. These caps are installed to prevent tampering with the carburetor fuel mixture screws so that the engine cannot be adjusted to a richer idle mixture.

Most models are equipped with a throttle solenoid positioner. The purpose of a throttle solenoid to to prevent the engine from running on (dieseling) after the ignition is turned off. Dieseling is a common occurrence with many cars using emission control systems that require a leaner fuel mixture, a higher operating temperature, and a higher curb idle speed. The throttle solenoid prevents running-on and dieseling by closing the throttle plate(s) after the key is turned off, thereby shutting off the air and gas to the overheated combustion chamber.

THROTTLE SOLENOID (ANTIDIESELING SOLENOID) TEST

1. Turn the ignition key on and open the throttle. The solenoid plunger should extend (solenoid energize).

2. Turn the ignition off. The plunger should retract, allowing the throttle to close.

WARNING: *With the anti-dieseling de-energized, the carburetor idle speed adjusting screw must make contact with the throttle shaft to prevent the throttle plates from jam-* *ming in the throttle bore when the engine is turned off.*

3. If the solenoid is functioning properly and the engine is still dieseling, check for one of the following:

    a. High idle or engine shut off speed.

    b. Engine timing not set to specification.

    c. Binding throttle linkage.

    d. Too low an octane fuel being used.

Correct any of these problems as necessary.

4. If the solenoid fails to function as outlined in Steps 1-2, disconnect the solenoid leads; the solenoid should de-energize. If it does not, it is jammed and must be replaced.

5. Connect the solenoid to a 12 V power source and to ground. Open the throttle so that the plunger can extend. If it does not, the solenoid is defective.

6. If the solenoid is functioning correctly and no other source of trouble can be found, the fault probably lies in the wiring between the solenoid and the ignition switch or in the ignition switch itself. Remember to reconnect the solenoid when finished testing.

NOTE: *On some 1970-71 models, dieseling may occur when the engine is turned off because of feedback through the alternator warning light circuit. A diode kit is available from Ford to cure this problem. A failure of this diode may also lead to a similar problem.*

REMOVAL AND INSTALLATION

1. Remove the air cleaner.

2. Disconnect the throttle cable or rod at the throttle lever. Disconnect the distributor vacuum line, exhaust gas recirculation line (1973 and later models), inline fuel filter, choke heat tube and the positive crankcase ventilation hose at the carburetor.

3. Disconnect the throttle solenoid (if so equipped) and electric choke assist (1973 and later models) at their connectors. Remove the wires to the carburetor on the 7200 VV.

4. Remove the carburetor retaining nuts. Lift off the carburetor carefully, taking care not to spill any fuel. Remove the carburetor mounting gasket and discard it. Remove the carburetor mounting spacer, if so equipped, from the intake manifold.

5. Prior to installation, clean the gasket mounting surfaces of the intake manifold, spacer, (if so equipped), and carburetor. when using a spacer, use two new gaskets, sandwiching the spacer between the gaskets. If a spacer is not used, only one new carburetor mounting gasket is required.

6. Place the new gasket(s) and spacer (if so equipped) on the carburetor mounting studs. Position the carburetor on top of the gasket and hand tighten the retaining nuts. Then tighten

Carburetor Specifications

Year	Fuel Level (in.) Dry	Float Adj (in.) Wet	Fast Idle Cam Index Setting (in.)	Anti-Stall Dashpot Adj (in.)	Accelerator Pump Operating Rod Position (in overtravel lever)	Dechoke Clearance Adjustment (in.)	Automatic Choke Thermostatic Spring Housing Adj	Choke Plate Pull-Down Clearance Adj (in.)
Autolite 1101								
1968–69	13/32		—	0.080	—	15/16	3 Lean	0.200
Carter YF								
1968	7/32		0.0035	0.100	—	0.250	Index	0.280
1969	7/32		0.0035	None	—	0.250	Index	0.280
1970	3/8		Man. 0.029 Auto. 0.035	Auto 7/64	—	0.250	Man.—Index Auto.—1 lean	0.225
1971	3/8		Man. 0.190 Auto. 0.200	Auto. 0.100	—	0.250	Index	Man. 0.200 Auto. 0.230
1972	3/8		0.220	0.100	—	0.250	1 Lean	0.230
Autolite (Motorcraft) 2100								
1968	302—3/8, 351, 390—31/64	3/4 7/8	302 MT—0.110 302 AT—0.120 390 MT—0.170 390 AT—0.100	1/8	302—2 390—3	0.060	302 MT—Index 302 AT—1 Lean 390 All—Index	302 MT—0.120 302 AT—0.140 390 MT—0.210 390 AT—0.100
1969	302—3/8, 351, 390,—31/64 429	3/4 7/8	302 All—0.110 351, 390, 429 AT— 0.100 390 MT—0.170	1/8	302 MT—3 302 AT—2 351, 390,—3 429	0.060	302 MT—2 Rich 302 AT—Index 351, 429—2 Rich 390 MT—1 Rich 390 AT—2 Rich	302 MT—0.130 302, 351 AT— 0.120 390 MT—0.210 390, 429 AT— 0.130

Year								
1970	7/16	13/16	302 All—0.130 / 351 MT—0.190 / 351 AT—0.170 / 390 MT—0.170 / 390, 429 AT—0.160	AT—1/8	302, 351 MT—3 / 302 AT—2 / 351 AT—4 / 390, 429—3	0.060	302 All—1 Rich / 351 All—2 Lean / 390 MT—1 Rich / 390 AT—2 Rich / 429 All—2 Rich	302 All—0.150 / 351 MT—0.230 / 390 MT—0.210 / 351, 390 AT—0.200 / 429 All—0.200
1971	7/16	13/16	302 MT—0.150 / 351 MT—0.190 / 302, 351 AT—0.130 / 390, 400,—0.160 / 429	351 AT, 400 AT—1/8 / 429 AT	302 MT—3 / 302 AT—2 / 351, / 390, / 400, / 429,—3	0.060	302, 351 MT—1 Rich / 302, 351 AT—Index / 390 AT—Index / 400, 429 AT—1 Rich	302 MT—0.170 / 302 AT—0.150 / 351 MT—0.220 / 351, 400 AT—0.190 / 390, 429 AT—0.200
1972	7/16	13/16	302, 351W—0.130 / 351C—0.160 / 400—0.150	302, 351W—1/8	302 All—2 / 351 All—3 / 400 (49 states)—4 / 400 (Calif.)—3	302, 400—0.060 / 351C, 351W—0.030	302, 351C—1 Rich / 351W, 400—Index	302 All—0.150 / 351 W All—0.140 / 351C All—0.190 / 400 (49 states)—0.180 / 400 (Calif.)—0.170
1973	7/16	See procedure	None		All—3	—	351W—2 Rich / 351C, 400—3 Rich	0.160 ①
1974	7/16	See procedure	None		351W, 351C—2 / 400—3	—	351W—2 Rich / 351C, 400—3 Rich	0.160 ①

Motorcraft 2150

Year								
1975	7/16	See procedure	None		②	—	3 Rich	0.125
1976–77	7/16	See procedure	None		#2	—	③	0.160
1978–79	7/16	See procedure	None		#2	—	③	0.160

Carburetor Specifications (cont.)

Year	Fuel Level (In.) Dry	Float Adj (In.) Wet	Fast Idle Cam Index Setting (In.)	Anti-Stall Dashpot Adj (In.)	Accelerator Pump Operating Rod Position (In overtravel lever)	Dechoke Clearance Adjustment (In.)	Automatic Choke Thermostatic Spring Housing Adj	Choke Plate Pull-Down Clearance Adj (In.)
Autolite 4100								
1968–69	Primary 17/32 Secondary 11/16	20/32 11/16	0.120	3/32–1/8	#3	0.060	2 Rich	0.140
Autolite (Motorcraft) 4300								
1968	25/32		0.100	3/32	#3	0.300	MT—1 Rich AT—2 Rich	MT—0.120 AT—0.140
1969	25/32		MT—0.220 AT—0.160	MT—3/32	#2	0.300	MT—Index AT—1 Rich	MT—0.270 AT—0.230
1970	428 PI—1.0 429—25/32		428 PI—0.120 429 MT—0.220	428 PI—0.080 429—0.070	428 PI—#3 429—#2	0.300	428 PI—2 Rich 429—Index	428 PI—0.160 429 MT—0.250 429 AT—0.220
1971	49/64		0.170	1/16	#2	0.300	Index	0.220
1972	49/64		429 AT—0.200 429 PI—0.190	None	#1	0.300	429 AT—2 Rich 429 PI—Index	429 AT—0.220 429 PI—0.215
1973	429, 460 AT —.76 460 PI—.88		429 AT—0.200 460 AT—0.190 460 PI—0.200	None	#1	0.300	Index	429, 460 AT— 0.210 460 PI—0.200
1974	3/4		0.200	None	#1	0.300	Index	460 PI—0.200 460 PI—0.230

Motorcraft 4350

1975	460-4V—15/16 460 PI—31/32	0.160	None	#1	0.300	2 Rich	Initial—0.160 Delayed—0.190
1976–78	460-4V—1.0 460-PI—0.96	460 4V—0.140 460-PI—0.160	None	#2	0.300	2 Rich	Initial—0.140 Delayed— 0.190④

Carter Thermo-Quad®

1974	11/16	0.099	None	Inner	0.130	Index	0.250

① Overrich choke setting—increase in steps of 0.020 in.
Lean choke setting—decrease clearance in steps of 0.020 in.
② D50E-BA, CA—3
  D5AE-AA, EA—3
  D50E-GA; D5ME-BA, FA—2
③ D6WE-AA—3 Rich
  D6AE-HA, D6ME-AA—3 Rich
  D6WE-BA—2 Rich
④ 460 PI—Initial—0.160
  Delayed—0.210

the nuts in a criss-cross pattern to 10-15 ft. lbs.

7. Connect the throttle linkage, the distributor vacuum line, exhaust gas recirculation line (1973 and later models), inline fuel filter, choke heat tube, positive crankcase ventilation hose, throttle solenoid (if so equipped) and electric-choke assist (1973 and later models).

8. Adjust the curb idle speed, the idle fuel mixture and the accelerator pump stroke

(Autolite-Motorcraft 2 and 4 barrel carburetors only).

OVERHAUL

All Types Except 2700 VV and 7200 VV

WARNING: *The 2700 VV and 7200 VV are part of the extremely sophisticated EEC system. Do not attempt to overhaul these units. Efficient carburetion depends greatly on*

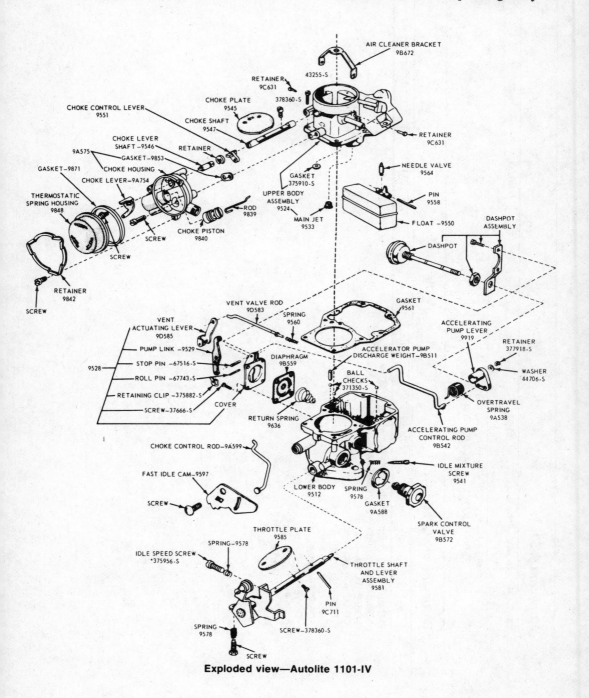

Exploded view—Autolite 1101-IV

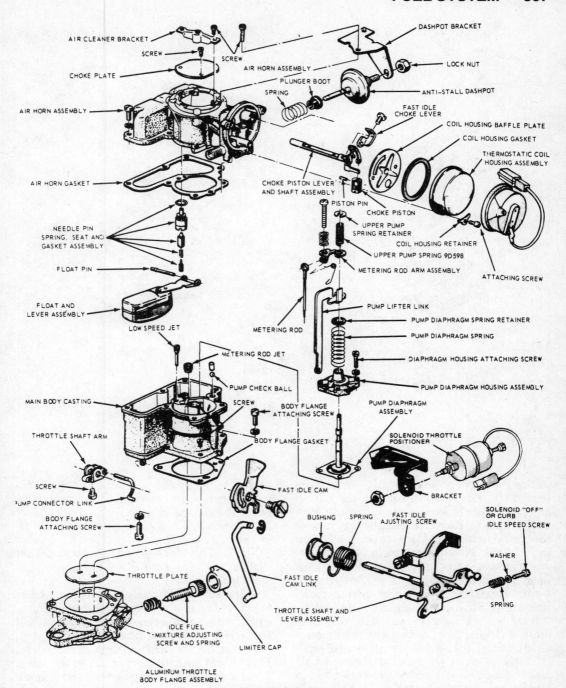

Exploded view—Carter YF-IV

careful cleaning and inspection during overhaul, since dirt, gum, water, or varnish in or on the carburetor parts are often responsible for poor performance.

Overhaul your carburetor in a clean, dust free area. Carefully disassemble the carburetor, referring often to the exploded views. Keep all similar and look-alike parts segregated during the disassembly and cleaning to avoid accidental interchange during assembly. Make a note of all jet sizes.

When the carburetor is disassembled, wash all parts (except diaphragms, electric choke units, pump plunger, and any other plastic,

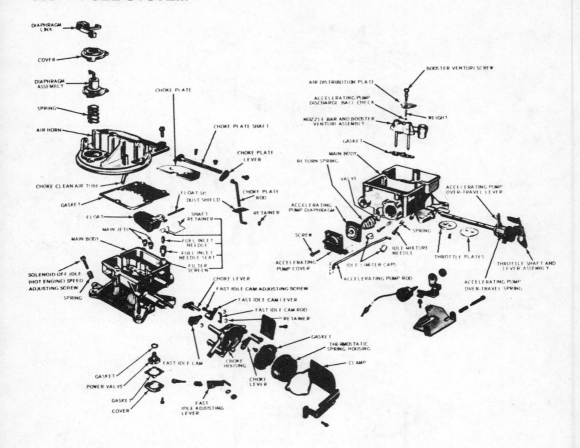

leather, fiber, or rubber parts) in clean carburetor solvent. Do not leave parts in the solvent any longer than is necessary to sufficiently loosen the deposits. Excessive cleaning may remove the special finish from the float bowl and choke valve bodies, leaving these parts unfit for service. Rinse all parts in clean solvent and blow them dry with compressed air or allow them to air dry. Wipe clean all cork, plastic, leather, and fiber parts with a clean, lint-free cloth.

Blow out all passages and jets with compressed air and be sure that there are no restrictions or blockages. never use wire of similar tools to clean jets, fuel passages, or air bleeds. Clean all jets and valves separately to avoid accidental interchange.

Check all parts for wear or damage. If wear or damage is found, replace the defective parts. Especially check the following:

1. Check the float needle and seat for wear. If wear is found, replace the complete assembly.

2. Check the float hinge pin for wear and the float(s) for dents or distortion. Replace the float if fuel has leaked into it.

3. Check the throttle and choke shaft bores for wear or an out-of-round condition. Damage or wear to the throttle arm, shaft, or shaft bore will often require replacement of the throttle body. These parts require a close tolerance of fit; wear may allow air linkage, which could affect starting and idling.

NOTE: *Throttle shafts and bushings are not included in overhaul kits. They can be purchased separately.*

4. Inspect the idle mixture adjusting needles for burrs for grooves. Any such condition requires replacement of the needle, since you will not be able to obtain a satisfactory idle.

5. Test the accelerator pump check valves. They should pass air one way but on the other. Test for proper seating by blowing and sucking on the valve. Replace the valve is necessary. If the valve is satisfactory, wash the valve again to remove breath moisture.

6. Check the bowl cover for warped surfaces with a straightedge.

7. Closely inspect the valves and seats for wear and damage, replacing as necessary.

8. After the carburetor is assembled, check the choke valve for freedom of operation.

Carburetor overhaul kits are recommended for each overhaul. These kits contain all gas-

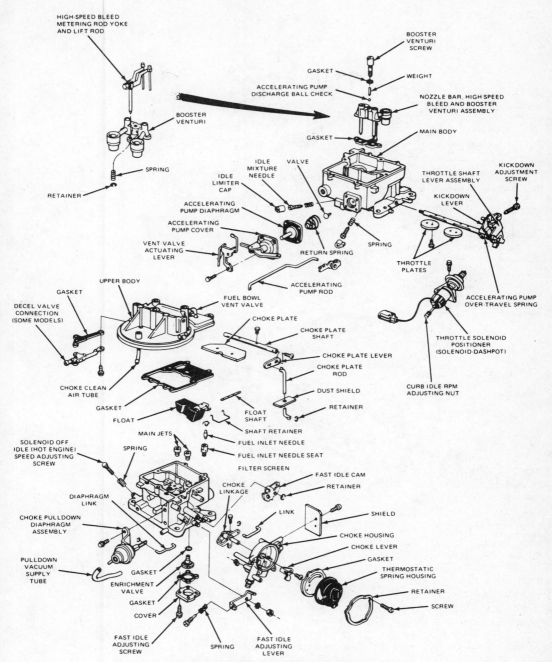

Exploded view—Motorcraft 2150-2V

kets and new parts to replace those which deteriorate most rapidly. Failure to replace all parts supplied with the kit (especially gaskets) can result in poor performance later.

Some carburetor manufacturers supply overhaul kits of three basic types: minor repair; major repair; and gasket kits. Basically, they contain the following:

Minor Repair Kits:
- All gasket
- Float needle valve
- Volume control screw
- All diaphragms
- Spring for the pump diaphragm

Major Repair Kits:
- All jets and gaskets

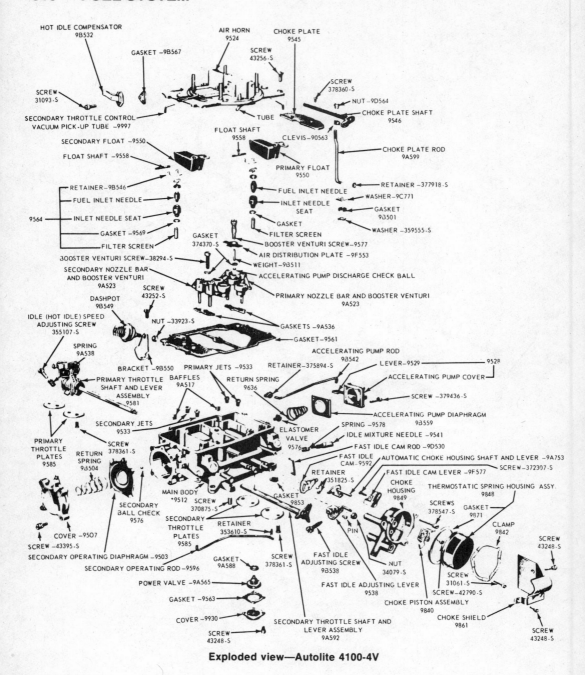

Exploded view—Autolite 4100-4V

- All diaphragms
- Float needle valve
- Volume control screw
- Pump ball valve
- Float
- Complete intermediate rod
- Intermediate pump lever
- Some cover holddown screws and washers

Gasket Kits:
- All gaskets

After cleaning and checking all components, reassemble the carburetor, using new parts and referring to he exploded view. When reassembling, make sure that all screws and jets are tight in their seats, but do not overtighten as the tops will be distorted. Tighten all screws gradually, in rotation. Do not tighten needle valves into their seats; uneven jetting will result. Always use new gaskets. Be sure to adjust the float level when reassembling.

Adjustments

NOTE: *Adjustments for the 2700VV and 7200VV, are covered following adjustments for all other carburetors.*

AUTOMATIC CHOKE HOUSING ADJUSTMENT

All Carburetors

By rotating the spring housing of the automatic choke, the reaction of the choke to engine temperature can be controlled. To adjust, remove the air cleaner assembly, loosen the thermostatic spring housing retaining screws and set the spring housing to the specified index mark. The marks are shown in the accompanying illustration. After adjusting the setting, tighten the retaining screws and replace the air cleaner assembly to the carburetor.

CHOKE PLATE PULL-DOWN CLEARANCE ADJUSTMENT

Autolite 1101

1. Remove the air cleaner assembly.
2. Remove the choke cover and thermostatic coil assembly. Block the throttle valve half open so that the fast idle screw does not contact the fast idle cam.

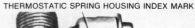

THERMOSTATIC SPRING HOUSING INDEX MARK

CHOKE HOUSING INDEX MARK

Automatic choke housing adjustment

3. Bend a 0.036″ wire gauge at a 90 degree angle about ⅛″ from the end. Insert the bent end between the lower edge of the choke piston slot and the upper edge of the right hand slot in the choke housing (see the illustration).
4. Move the piston lever counterclockwise until the gauge fits snugly in the slot. Hold the gauge in place by exerting light pressure on the lever.

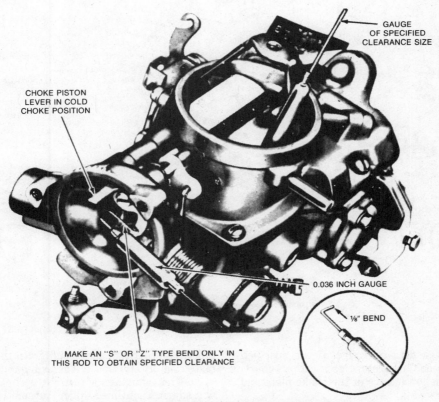

GAUGE OF SPECIFIED CLEARANCE SIZE

CHOKE PISTON LEVER IN COLD CHOKE POSITION

0.036 INCH GAUGE

⅛″ BEND

MAKE AN "S" OR "Z" TYPE BEND ONLY IN THIS ROD TO OBTAIN SPECIFIED CLEARANCE

Adjusting choke plate pull-down—Autolite 1101

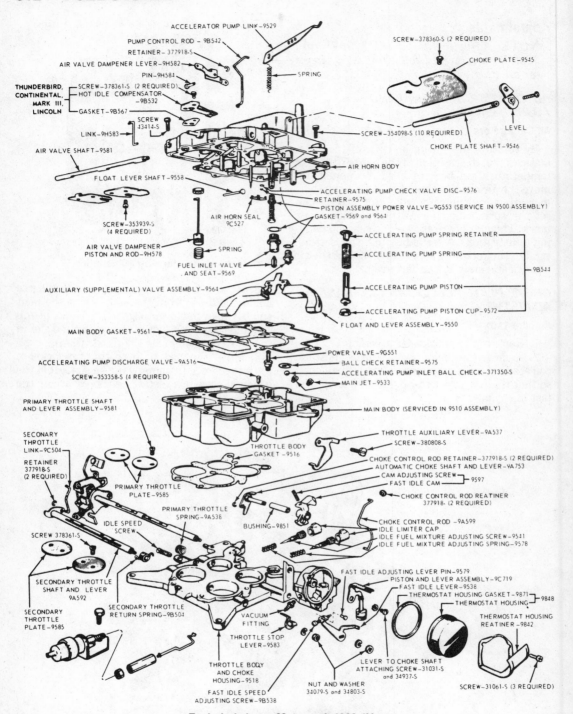

ACCELERATOR PUMP LINK–9529
PUMP CONTROL ROD – 9B542
RETAINER– 377918-S
AIR VALVE DAMPENER LEVER–9H582
PIN–9H584
SCREW–378361-S (2 REQUIRED)
HOT IDLE COMPENSATOR –9B532
GASKET–9B567
SCREW 43414-S
LINK–9H583
AIR VALVE SHAFT–9581
FLOAT LEVER SHAFT–9558
SCREW–353939-S (4 REQUIRED)
AIR VALVE DAMPENER PISTON AND ROD–9H578
SPRING
FUEL INLET VALVE AND SEAT–9569
AUXILIARY (SUPPLEMENTAL) VALVE ASSEMBLY–9564
MAIN BODY GASKET–9561
ACCELERATING PUMP DISCHARGE VALVE–9A516
SCREW–353358-S (4 REQUIRED)
PRIMARY THROTTLE SHAFT AND LEVER ASSEMBLY–9581
SECONARY THROTTLE LINK–9C504
RETAINER 377918-S (2 REQUIRED)
PRIMARY THROTTLE PLATE–9585
SCREW 378361-S
IDLE SPEED SCREW
SECONDARY THROTTLE SHAFT AND LEVER 9A592
SECONDARY THROTTLE PLATE–9585
SECONDARY THROTTLE RETURN SPRING–9B504
PRIMARY THROTTLE SPRING–9A538
BUSHING–9851
VACUUM FITTING
THROTTLE STOP LEVER–9583
FAST IDLE SPEED ADJUSTING SCREW–9B538
THROTTLE BODY AND CHOKE HOUSING–9518
NUT AND WASHER 34079-S and 34803-S

THUNDERBIRD, CONTINENTAL, MARK III, LINCOLN

SCREW–378360-S (2 REQUIRED)
CHOKE PLATE–9545
SCREW–354098-S (10 REQUIRED)
LEVEL
CHOKE PLATE SHAFT–9546
AIR HORN BODY
ACCELERATING PUMP CHECK VALVE DISC–9576
RETAINER–9575
PISTON ASSEMBLY POWER VALVE–9G553 (SERVICE IN 9500 ASSEMBLY)
GASKET–9569 and 9564
AIR HORN SEAL 9C527
ACCELERATING PUMP SPRING RETAINER
ACCELERATING PUMP SPRING
ACCELERATING PUMP PISTON
ACCELERATING PUMP PISTON CUP–9572
9B544
FLOAT AND LEVER ASSEMBLY–9550
POWER VALVE–9G551
BALL CHECK RETAINER–9575
ACCELERATING PUMP INLET BALL CHECK–371350-S
MAIN JET–9533
MAIN BODY (SERVICED IN 9510 ASSEMBLY)
THROTTLE AUXILIARY LEVER–9A537
SCREW–380808-S
CHOKE CONTROL ROD RETAINER–377918-S (2 REQUIRED)
AUTOMATIC CHOKE SHAFT AND LEVER–9A753
CAM ADJUSTING SCREW
FAST IDLE CAM   9597
CHOKE CONTROL ROD REATINER 377918- (2 REQUIRED)
CHOKE CONTROL ROD –9A599
IDLE LIMITER CAP
IDLE FUEL MIXTURE ADJUSTING SCREW–9541
IDLE FUEL MIXTURE ADJUSTING SPRING–9578
FAST IDLE ADJUSTING LEVER PIN–9579
PISTON AND LEVER ASSEMBLY–9C719
FAST IDLE LEVER–9538
THERMOSTAT HOUSING GASKET–9871
THERMOSTAT HOUSING   9848
THERMOSTAT HOUSING REATINER–9842
LEVER TO CHOKE SHAFT ATTACHING SCREW–31031-S and 34937-S
SCREW–31061-S (3 REQUIRED)
THROTTLE BODY GASKET–9516

Exploded view—Motorcraft 4300-4V

5. Insert a drill or gauge of the specified thickness (see Carburetor Specifications chart) between the lower edge of the choke plate and the air horn wall.

6. To adjust, carefully bend the choke piston link (in an S or Z-shaped bend) until the choke plate clearance is that of the drill gauge.

7. After adjustment, install the choke cover and adjust as outlined under Automatic Choke Housing Adjustment. Install the air cleaner.

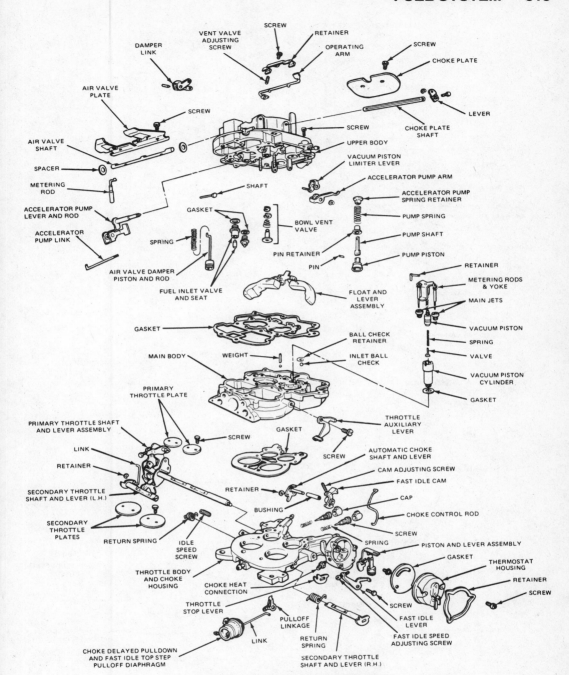

DAMPER LINK

VENT VALVE ADJUSTING SCREW

SCREW

RETAINER

OPERATING ARM

SCREW

CHOKE PLATE

AIR VALVE PLATE

SCREW

LEVER

AIR VALVE SHAFT

SCREW

CHOKE PLATE SHAFT

SPACER

UPPER BODY

METERING ROD

SHAFT

VACUUM PISTON LIMITER LEVER

ACCELERATOR PUMP ARM

ACCELERATOR PUMP LEVER AND ROD

GASKET

ACCELERATOR PUMP SPRING RETAINER

ACCELERATOR PUMP LINK

SPRING

BOWL VENT VALVE

PUMP SPRING

PUMP SHAFT

PIN RETAINER

PUMP PISTON

PIN

AIR VALVE DAMPER PISTON AND ROD

RETAINER

FUEL INLET VALVE AND SEAT

FLOAT AND LEVER ASSEMBLY

METERING RODS & YOKE

MAIN JETS

GASKET

VACUUM PISTON

BALL CHECK RETAINER

SPRING

MAIN BODY

WEIGHT

INLET BALL CHECK

VALVE

PRIMARY THROTTLE PLATE

VACUUM PISTON CYLINDER

GASKET

PRIMARY THROTTLE SHAFT AND LEVER ASSEMBLY

SCREW

GASKET

THROTTLE AUXILIARY LEVER

LINK

AUTOMATIC CHOKE SHAFT AND LEVER

RETAINER

SCREW

CAM ADJUSTING SCREW

FAST IDLE CAM

SECONDARY THROTTLE SHAFT AND LEVER (L.H.)

RETAINER

CAP

SECONDARY THROTTLE PLATES

BUSHING

CHOKE CONTROL ROD

RETURN SPRING

IDLE SPEED SCREW

SCREW

SPRING

PISTON AND LEVER ASSEMBLY

GASKET

THROTTLE BODY AND CHOKE HOUSING

THERMOSTAT HOUSING

RETAINER

CHOKE HEAT CONNECTION

SCREW

THROTTLE STOP LEVER

PULLOFF LINKAGE

RETURN SPRING

SCREW

FAST IDLE LEVER

FAST IDLE SPEED ADJUSTING SCREW

CHOKE DELAYED PULLDOWN AND FAST IDLE TOP STEP PULLOFF DIAPHRAGM

LINK

SECONDARY THROTTLE SHAFT AND LEVER (R.H.)

Exploded view—Motorcraft 4350-4V

Carter YF

1. Remove the carburetor air cleaner, and remove the choke thermostatic spring housing.

2. Bend a section of 0.026″ diameter wire at a 90 degree angle approximately ⅛″ from one end.

3. Insert the bent end of the wire gauge between the choke piston slot and the righthand slot in the choke housing. Rotate the choke pis-

ton lever counterclockwise until the gauge is snug in the piston slot.

4. Exert light pressure upon the choke piston lever to hold the gauge in position. check the specified clearance with a drill of the correct diameter between the lower edge of the choke plate and the carburetor bore.

5. Choke plate pull-down clearance may be adjusted by bending the choke piston lever as

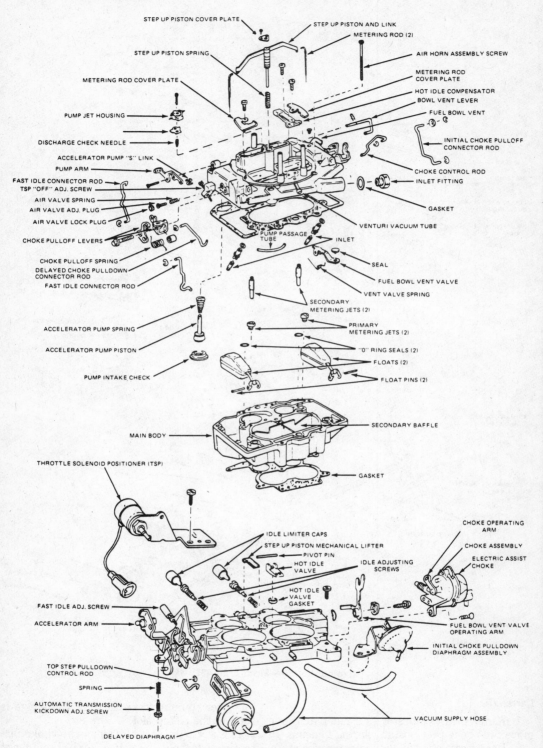

Exploded view—Carter Thermo-Quad®

Adjusting choke plate pull-down—Carter YF

required to obtain the desired clearance. It is recommended that the choke piston lever be removed prior to bending, in order to prevent distorting the piston link.

6. Install the choke thermostatic spring housing and gasket, and set the housing to the proper specification.

Autolite 2100, 4100

1968-69

1. Follow Steps 1-5 Autolite 1101.
2. Turn the adjusting nut (see the illustration) as required until the choke plate clearance is that of the drill gauge.
3. After adjustment, install the choke cover and adjust as outlined under Automatic Choke Housing Adjustment.

Motorcraft 2100

1970-74

1. Remove the air cleaner.
2. With the engine at its normal operating temperature, loosen the choke thermostatic spring housing retaining screws, and set the housing 90 degrees in rich direction.
3. Disconnect and remove teh choke heat tube from the choke housing.
4. Turn the fast idle adjusting screw outward one full turn.
5. Start the engine. Use a drill of the specified diameter to check the clearance between

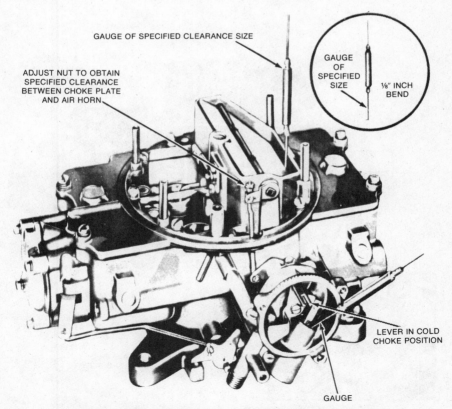

Adjusting choke plate pull-down—Autolite 2100, 4100—1968—69

the lower edge of the choke plate and the air horn wall.

6. To adjust the clearance, turn the diaphragm stopscrew (located on the underside of the choke diaphragm housing). Turning clockwise will decrease the clearance; counterclockwise will increase it.

7. Connect the choke heat tube, and set the choke thermostatic spring housing to the proper specification. Adjust the fast idle speed to specifications.

Motorcraft 2150

1. Remove the air cleaner assembly.

2. Set the throttle on the top step of the fast idle cam.

3. Noting the position of the choke housing cap, loosen the retaining screws and rotate the cap 90 degrees in the rich (closing) direction.

4. Activate the pull-down motor by manually forcing the pull-down control diaphragm link in the direction of applied vacuum or by applying vacuum to the external vacuum tube.

5. Using a drill gauge of the specified diameter, measure the clearance between the choke plate and the center of the air horn wall nearest the fuel bowl.

6. To adjust, reset the diaphragm stop on the end of the choke pull-down diaphragm.

7. After adjusting, reset the choke housing cap to the specified notch. check and reset fast idle speed, if necessary. Install the air cleaner.

Autolite (Motorcraft) 4300, 4350

1. Follow Steps 1-5 under Autolite 1101.

2. To adjust loosen the hex head screw (left hand thread) on the choke plate shaft and pry the link away from the tapered shaft. Using a drill gauge 0.010″ thinner than the specified clearance (to allow for tolerances in the linkage), insert the gauge between the lower edge of the choke plate and the air horn wall. Hold the choke plate against the gauge and maintain a light pressure in a counterclockwise direction on the choke lever. The, with the choke piston snug against the 0.036″ wire gauge and the choke plate against the 0.010″ smaller drill gauge, tighten the hex head screw (left hand thread) on the choke plate shaft. After tightening the hex head screw, make a final check using a drill gauge of the specified clearance between the choke plate and air horn.

3. After adjustment, install the choke cover

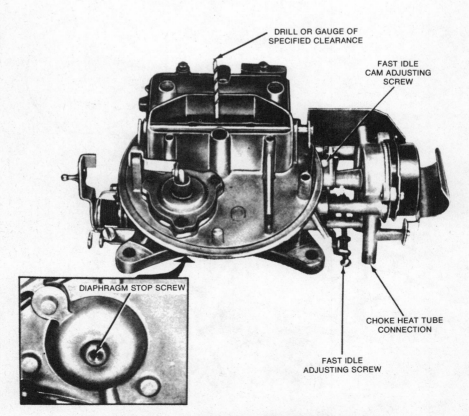

Adjusting choke plate pull-down—Motorcraft 2100 (1970–74)

DRILL OR GAUGE OF
SPECIFIED CLEARANCE

FAST IDLE
CAM ADJUSTING
SCREW

DIAPHRAGM STOP SCREW

CHOKE HEAT TUBE
CONNECTION

FAST IDLE
ADJUSTING SCREW

CHILTON'S
FUEL ECONOMY
& TUNE-UP TIPS

Tune-up • Spark Plug Diagnosis • Emission Controls

Fuel System • Cooling System • Tires and Wheels

General Maintenance

CHILTON'S FUEL ECONOMY & TUNE-UP TIPS

Fuel economy is important to everyone, no matter what kind of vehicle you drive. The maintenance-minded motorist can save both money and fuel using these tips and the periodic maintenance and tune-up procedures in this Repair and Tune-Up Guide.

There are more than 130,000,000 cars and trucks registered for private use in the United States. Each travels an average of 10-12,000 miles per year, and, and in total they consume close to 70 billion gallons of fuel each year. This represents nearly ⅔ of the oil imported by the United States each year. The Federal government's goal is to reduce consumption 10% by 1985. A variety of methods are either already in use or under serious consideration, and they all affect you driving and the cars you will drive. In addition to "down-sizing", the auto industry is using or investigating the use of electronic fuel delivery, electronic engine controls and alternative engines for use in smaller and lighter vehicles, among other alternatives to meet the federally mandated Corporate Average Fuel Economy (CAFE) of 27.5 mpg by 1985. The government, for its part, is considering rationing, mandatory driving curtailments and tax increases on motor vehicle fuel in an effort to reduce consumption. The government's goal of a 10% reduction could be realized — and further government regulation avoided — if every private vehicle could use just 1 less gallon of fuel per week.

How Much Can You Save?

Tests have proven that almost anyone can make at least a 10% reduction in fuel consumption through regular maintenance and tune-ups. When a major manufacturer of spark plugs sur-

TUNE-UP

1. Check the cylinder compression to be sure the engine will really benefit from a tune-up and that it is capable of producing good fuel economy. A tune-up will be wasted on an engine in poor mechanical condition.

2. Replace spark plugs regularly. New spark plugs alone can increase fuel economy 3%.

3. Be sure the spark plugs are the correct type (heat range) for your vehicle. See the Tune-Up Specifications.

Heat range refers to the spark plug's ability to conduct heat away from the firing end. It must conduct the heat away in an even pattern to avoid becoming a source of pre-ignition, yet it must also operate hot enough to burn off conductive deposits that could cause misfiring.

The heat range is usually indicated by a number on the spark plug, part of the manufacturer's designation for each individual spark plug. The numbers in bold-face indicate the heat range in each manufacturer's identification system.

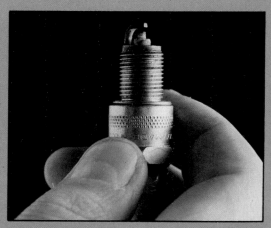

Periodically, check the spark plugs to be sure they are firing efficiently. They are excellent indicators of the internal condition of your engine.

Manufacturer	Typical Designation
AC	R **45** TS
Bosch (old)	WA **145** T30
Bosch (new)	HR **8** Y
Champion	RBL **15** Y
Fram/Autolite	41**5**
Mopar	P-**62** PR
Motorcraft	BRF-**42**
NGK	BP **5** ES-15
Nippondenso	W **16** EP
Prestolite	14GR **5** 2A

On AC, Bosch (new), Champion, Fram/Autolite, Mopar, Motorcraft and Prestolite, a higher number indicates a hotter plug. On Bosch (old), NGK and Nippondenso, a higher number indicates a colder plug.

4. Make sure the spark plugs are properly gapped. See the Tune-Up Specifications in this book.

5. Be sure the spark plugs are firing efficiently. The illustrations on the next 2 pages show you how to "read" the firing end of the spark plug.

6. Check the ignition timing and set it to specifications. Tests show that almost all cars have incorrect ignition timing by more than 2°.

veyed over 6,000 cars nationwide, they found that a tune-up, on cars that needed one, increased fuel economy over 11%. Replacing worn plugs alone, accounted for a 3% increase. The same test also revealed that 8 out of every 10 vehicles will have some maintenance deficiency that will directly affect fuel economy, emissions or performance. Most of this mileage-robbing neglect could be prevented with regular maintenance.

Modern engines require that all of the functioning systems operate properly for maximum efficiency. A malfunction anywhere wastes fuel. You can keep your vehicle running as efficiently and economically as possible, by being aware of your vehicle's operating and performance characteristics. If your vehicle suddenly develops performance or fuel economy problems it could be due to one or more of the following:

PROBLEM	POSSIBLE CAUSE
Engine Idles Rough	Ignition timing, idle mixture, vacuum leak or something amiss in the emission control system.
Hesitates on Acceleration	Dirty carburetor or fuel filter, improper accelerator pump setting, ignition timing or fouled spark plugs.
Starts Hard or Fails to Start	Worn spark plugs, improperly set automatic choke, ice (or water) in fuel system.
Stalls Frequently	Automatic choke improperly adjusted and possible dirty air filter or fuel filter.
Performs Sluggishly	Worn spark plugs, dirty fuel or air filter, ignition timing or automatic choke out of adjustment.

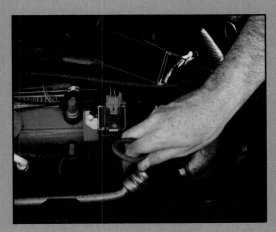

Check spark plug wires on conventional point type ignition for cracks by bending them in a loop around your finger.

Be sure that spark plug wires leading to adjacent cylinders do not run too close together. (Photo courtesy Champion Spark Plug Co.)

7. If your vehicle does not have electronic ignition, check the points, rotor and cap as specified.

8. Check the spark plug wires (used with conventional point-type ignitions) for cracks and burned or broken insulation by bending them in a loop around your finger. Cracked wires decrease fuel efficiency by failing to deliver full voltage to the spark plugs. One misfiring spark plug can cost you as much as 2 mpg.

9. Check the routing of the plug wires. Misfiring can be the result of spark plug leads to adjacent cylinders running parallel to each other and too close together. One wire tends to pick up voltage from the other causing it to fire "out of time".

10. Check all electrical and ignition circuits for voltage drop and resistance.

11. Check the distributor mechanical and/or vacuum advance mechanisms for proper functioning. The vacuum advance can be checked by twisting the distributor plate in the opposite direction of rotation. It should spring back when released.

12. Check and adjust the valve clearance on engines with mechanical lifters. The clearance should be slightly loose rather than too tight.

SPARK PLUG DIAGNOSIS

Normal

APPEARANCE: This plug is typical of one operating normally. The insulator nose varies from a light tan to grayish color with slight electrode wear. The presence of slight deposits is normal on used plugs and will have no adverse effect on engine performance. The spark plug heat range is correct for the engine and the engine is running normally.

CAUSE: Properly running engine.

RECOMMENDATION: Before reinstalling this plug, the electrodes should be cleaned and filed square. Set the gap to specifications. If the plug has been in service for more than 10-12,000 miles, the entire set should probably be replaced with a fresh set of the same heat range.

Oil Deposits

APPEARANCE: The firing end of the plug is covered with a wet, oily coating.

CAUSE: The problem is poor oil control. On high mileage engines, oil is leaking past the rings or valve guides into the combustion chamber. A common cause is also a plugged PCV valve, and a ruptured fuel pump diaphragm can also cause this condition. Oil fouled plugs such as these are often found in new or recently overhauled engines, before normal oil control is achieved, and can be cleaned and reinstalled.

RECOMMENDATION: A hotter spark plug may temporarily relieve the problem, but the engine is probably in need of work.

Incorrect Heat Range

APPEARANCE: The effects of high temperature on a spark plug are indicated by clean white, often blistered insulator. This can also be accompanied by excessive wear of the electrode, and the absence of deposits.

CAUSE: Check for the correct spark plug heat range. A plug which is too hot for the engine can result in overheating. A car operated mostly at high speeds can require a colder plug. Also check ignition timing, cooling system level, fuel mixture and leaking intake manifold.

RECOMMENDATION: If all ignition and engine adjustments are known to be correct, and no other malfunction exists, install spark plugs one heat range colder.

Photos Courtesy Fram Corporation

Carbon Deposits

APPEARANCE: Carbon fouling is easily identified by the presence of dry, soft, black, sooty deposits.

CAUSE: Changing the heat range can often lead to carbon fouling, as can prolonged slow, stop-and-start driving. If the heat range is correct, carbon fouling can be attributed to a rich fuel mixture, sticking choke, clogged air cleaner, worn breaker points, retarded timing or low compression. If only one or two plugs are carbon fouled, check for corroded or cracked wires on the affected plugs. Also look for cracks in the distributor cap between the towers of affected cylinders.

RECOMMENDATION: After the problem is corrected, these plugs can be cleaned and reinstalled if not worn severely.

MMT Fouled

APPEARANCE: Spark plugs fouled by MMT (Methycyclopentadienyl Maganese Tricarbonyl) have reddish, rusty appearance on the insulator and side electrode.

CAUSE: MMT is an anti-knock additive in gasoline used to replace lead. During the combustion process, the MMT leaves a reddish deposit on the insulator and side electrode.

RECOMMENDATION: No engine malfunction is indicated and the deposits will not affect plug performance any more than lead deposits (see Ash Deposits). MMT fouled plugs can be cleaned, regapped and reinstalled.

High Speed Glazing

APPEARANCE: Glazing appears as shiny coating on the plug, either yellow or tan in color.

CAUSE: During hard, fast acceleration, plug temperatures rise suddenly. Deposits from normal combustion have no chance to fluff-off; instead, they melt on the insulator forming an electrically conductive coating which causes misfiring.

RECOMMENDATION: Glazed plugs are not easily cleaned. They should be replaced with a fresh set of plugs of the correct heat range. If the condition recurs, using plugs with a heat range one step colder may cure the problem.

Ash (Lead) Deposits

APPEARANCE: Ash deposits are characterized by light brown or white colored deposits crusted on the side or center electrodes. In some cases it may give the plug a rusty appearance.

CAUSE: Ash deposits are normally derived from oil or fuel additives burned during normal combustion. Normally they are harmless, though excessive amounts can cause misfiring. If deposits are excessive in short mileage, the valve guides may be worn.

RECOMMENDATION: Ash-fouled plugs can be cleaned, gapped and reinstalled.

Detonation

APPEARANCE: Detonation is usually characterized by a broken plug insulator.

CAUSE: A portion of the fuel charge will begin to burn spontaneously, from the increased heat following ignition. The explosion that results applies extreme pressure to engine components, frequently damaging spark plugs and pistons.

Detonation can result by over-advanced ignition timing, inferior gasoline (low octane) lean air/fuel mixture, poor carburetion, engine lugging or an increase in compression ratio due to combustion chamber deposits or engine modification.

RECOMMENDATION: Replace the plugs after correcting the problem.

Photos Courtesy Champion Spark Plug Co.

EMISSION CONTROLS

13. Be aware of the general condition of the emission control system. It contributes to reduced pollution and should be serviced regularly to maintain efficient engine operation.

14. Check all vacuum lines for dried, cracked or brittle conditions. Something as simple as a leaking vacuum hose can cause poor performance and loss of economy.

15. Avoid tampering with the emission control system. Attempting to improve fuel econ-

FUEL SYSTEM

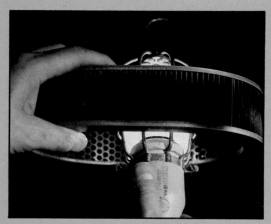

Check the air filter with a light behind it. If you can see light through the filter it can be reused.

Extremely clogged filters should be discarded and replaced with a new one.

18. Replace the air filter regularly. A dirty air filter richens the air/fuel mixture and can increase fuel consumption as much as 10%. Tests show that ⅓ of all vehicles have air filters in need of replacement.

19. Replace the fuel filter at least as often as recommended.

20. Set the idle speed and carburetor mixture to specifications.

21. Check the automatic choke. A sticking or malfunctioning choke wastes gas.

22. During the summer months, adjust the automatic choke for a leaner mixture which will produce faster engine warm-ups.

COOLING SYSTEM

29. Be sure all accessory drive belts are in good condition. Check for cracks or wear.

30. Adjust all accessory drive belts to proper tension.

31. Check all hoses for swollen areas, worn spots, or loose clamps.

32. Check coolant level in the radiator or expansion tank.

33. Be sure the thermostat is operating properly. A stuck thermostat delays engine warm-up and a cold engine uses nearly twice as much fuel as a warm engine.

34. Drain and replace the engine coolant at least as often as recommended. Rust and scale

TIRES & WHEELS

38. Check the tire pressure often with a pencil type gauge. Tests by a major tire manufacturer show that 90% of all vehicles have at least 1 tire improperly inflated. Better mileage can be achieved by over-inflating tires, but never exceed the maximum inflation pressure on the side of the tire.

39. If possible, install radial tires. Radial tires deliver as much as ½ mpg more than bias belted tires.

40. Avoid installing super-wide tires. They only create extra rolling resistance and decrease fuel mileage. Stick to the manufacturer's recommendations.

41. Have the wheels properly balanced.

omy by tampering with emission controls is more likely to worsen fuel economy than improve it. Emission control changes on modern engines are not readily reversible.

16. Clean (or replace) the EGR valve and lines as recommended.

17. Be sure that all vacuum lines and hoses are reconnected properly after working under the hood. An unconnected or misrouted vacuum line can wreak havoc with engine performance.

23. Check for fuel leaks at the carburetor, fuel pump, fuel lines and fuel tank. Be sure all lines and connections are tight.

24. Periodically check the tightness of the carburetor and intake manifold attaching nuts and bolts. These are a common place for vacuum leaks to occur.

25. Clean the carburetor periodically and lubricate the linkage.

26. The condition of the tailpipe can be an excellent indicator of proper engine combustion. After a long drive at highway speeds, the inside of the tailpipe should be a light grey in color. Black or soot on the insides indicates an overly rich mixture.

27. Check the fuel pump pressure. The fuel pump may be supplying more fuel than the engine needs.

28. Use the proper grade of gasoline for your engine. Don't try to compensate for knocking or "pinging" by advancing the ignition timing. This practice will only increase plug temperature and the chances of detonation or pre-ignition with relatively little performance gain.

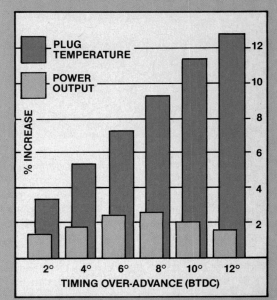

Increasing ignition timing past the specified setting results in a drastic increase in spark plug temperature with increased chance of detonation or preignition. Performance increase is considerably less. (Photo courtesy Champion Spark Plug Co.)

that form in the engine should be flushed out to allow the engine to operate at peak efficiency.

35. Clean the radiator of debris that can decrease cooling efficiency.

36. Install a flex-type or electric cooling fan, if you don't have a clutch type fan. Flex fans use curved plastic blades to push more air at low speeds when more cooling is needed; at high speeds the blades flatten out for less resistance. Electric fans only run when the engine temperature reaches a predetermined level.

37. Check the radiator cap for a worn or cracked gasket. If the cap does not seal properly, the cooling system will not function properly.

42. Be sure the front end is correctly aligned. A misaligned front end actually has wheels going in differed directions. The increased drag can reduce fuel economy by .3 mpg.

43. Correctly adjust the wheel bearings. Wheel bearings that are adjusted too tight increase rolling resistance.

Check tire pressures regularly with a reliable pocket type gauge. Be sure to check the pressure on a cold tire.

GENERAL MAINTENANCE

Check the fluid levels (particularly engine oil) on a regular basis. Be sure to check the oil for grit, water or other contamination.

A vacuum gauge is another excellent indicator of internal engine condition and can also be installed in the dash as a mileage indicator.

44. Periodically check the fluid levels in the engine, power steering pump, master cylinder, automatic transmission and drive axle.

45. Change the oil at the recommended interval and change the filter at every oil change. Dirty oil is thick and causes extra friction between moving parts, cutting efficiency and increasing wear. A worn engine requires more frequent tune-ups and gets progressively worse fuel economy. In general, use the lightest viscosity oil for the driving conditions you will encounter.

46. Use the recommended viscosity fluids in the transmission and axle.

47. Be sure the battery is fully charged for fast starts. A slow starting engine wastes fuel.

48. Be sure battery terminals are clean and tight.

49. Check the battery electrolyte level and add distilled water if necessary.

50. Check the exhaust system for crushed pipes, blockages and leaks.

51. Adjust the brakes. Dragging brakes or brakes that are not releasing create increased drag on the engine.

52. Install a vacuum gauge or miles-per-gallon gauge. These gauges visually indicate engine vacuum in the intake manifold. High vacuum = good mileage and low vacuum = poorer mileage. The gauge can also be an excellent indicator of internal engine conditions.

53. Be sure the clutch is properly adjusted. A slipping clutch wastes fuel.

54. Check and periodically lubricate the heat control valve in the exhaust manifold. A sticking or inoperative valve prevents engine warm-up and wastes gas.

55. Keep accurate records to check fuel economy over a period of time. A sudden drop in fuel economy may signal a need for tune-up or other maintenance.

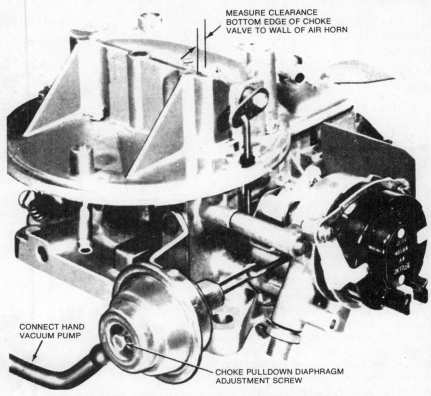

MEASURE CLEARANCE
BOTTOM EDGE OF CHOKE
VALVE TO WALL OF AIR HORN

CONNECT HAND
VACUUM PUMP

CHOKE PULLDOWN DIAPHRAGM
ADJUSTMENT SCREW

Adjusting choke plate pull-down—Motorcraft 2150

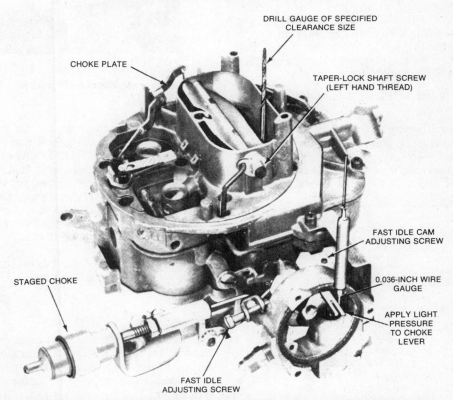

DRILL GAUGE OF SPECIFIED
CLEARANCE SIZE

CHOKE PLATE

TAPER-LOCK SHAFT SCREW
(LEFT HAND THREAD)

FAST IDLE CAM
ADJUSTING SCREW

0.036-INCH WIRE
GAUGE

STAGED CHOKE

APPLY LIGHT
PRESSURE
TO CHOKE
LEVER

FAST IDLE
ADJUSTING
SCREW

Choke plate pull-down and fast idle cam adjustment—Motorcraft 4300 (4350 similar)

and adjust as outlined under Automatic Choke Housing Adjustment.

4. Install the air cleaner.

FLOAT LEVEL ADJUSTMENT

Autolite 1101

1. Remove the carburetor air horn and gasket from the carburetor.

2. Measure the distance from the gasket surface of the air horn to the top of the float. If the measurement is not within the specified tolerance, bend the float arm tab as necessary to obtain the specified dimension. Be careful not to exert any pressure on the fuel inlet needle, as this will damage it and result in an improper fuel level within the float bowl.

3. Install the carburetor air horn to the main body of the carburetor, using a new gasket.

Carter YF

The float level is adjusted dry in the following manner: Remove the carburetor air horn and gasket from the carburetor. Using a gauge made to the proper dimension, invert a air horn assembly and check the clearance between the top of the float and the bottom of the air horn. When checking the float level, the air horn should be held at eye level adn the float lever arm should be resting on the pin of the needle valve. The float lever arm may be bent in order to adjust the float clearance. However, do not bend the tab at the end of the float arm, as this will prevent the float from bottoming in the fuel bowl when the bowl is empty. Using a new gasket, install the carburetor air horn.

Autolite (Motorcraft) 2100, 21500, 4100

DRY ADJUSTMENT

This preliminary setting of the float level adjustment must be done with the carburetor removed from the engine.

1. Remove the air horn and see that the float is raised and the fuel inlet needle is seated.

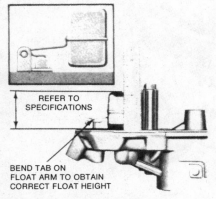

Float level adjustment—Autolite 1101

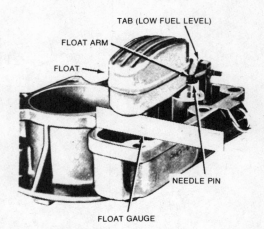

Float level adjustment—Carter YF

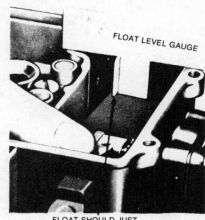

FLOAT SHOULD JUST TOUCH AT THIS POINT

Dry float level adjustment--Motorcraft 2100, 2150, 4100

Check the distance between the top surface of the main body (with the gasket removed) and the top surface of the float. Depress the float tab to seat the fuel inlet needle. Take a measurement near the center of the float, at a point ⅛" from the free end. If you are using a prefabricated float gauge, place the gauge in the corner of the enlarged end section of the fuel bowl. The gauge should touch the float near the end, but not on the end radius.

2. If necessary, bend the tab on the end of the float to bring the setting within the specified limits.

WET ADJUSTMENT

1. Bring the engine to its normal operating temperature, park the car on as nearly level a surface as possible, and stop the engine.

2. Remove the air cleaner assembly from the carburetor.

3. Remove the air horn retaining screws and

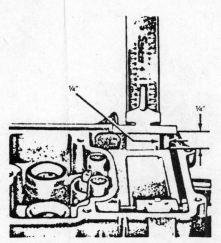

Wet float level adjustment—Motorcraft 2100, 2150, 4150

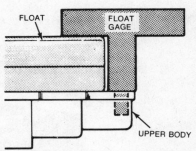

Float setting with rebuilding kit gauge—4300, 4350

the carburetor identification tag. Leave the air horn and gasket in position on the carburetor main body. Start the engine, let it idle for several minutes, rotate the air horn out of the way, and remove the gasket to provide access to the float assembly.

4. With the engine idling, use a standard depth scale to measure the vertical distance from the top machined surface of the carburetor main body to the level of the fuel in the fuel bowl. This measurement must be made at least ¼″ away from any vertical surface in order to assure an accurate reading.

5. Stop the engine before making any adjustment to the float level. Adjustment is accomplished by bending the float tab (with contacts the fuel inlet valve) up or down as required to raise or lower the fuel level. After making an adjustment, start the engine, and allow it to idle for several minutes before repeating the fuel level check. Repeat as necessary until the proper fuel level is attained.

6. Reinstall the air horn with a new gasket and secure it with the screw. Include the installation of the identification tag in its proper location.

7. Check the idle speed, fuel mixture, and dashpot adjustments. Install the air cleaner assembly.

Autolite (Motorcraft) 4300, 4350

1. Refer to the illustration for details of construction of a tool for checking the parallel setting of the dual pontoons.

2. Install the gauge on the carburetor and set it to the specified height.

3. Check the clearance and alignment of the pontoons to the gauge. Both pontoons should just barely touch the gauge for the proper set-

ting. Pontoons may be aligned if necessary by slightly twisting them.

4. To adjust the float level, bend the primary needle tab down to raise the float and up to lower it.

Carter Thermo-Quad

1. Taking note of their placement, disconnect all linkages and rods which connect the bowl cover to the carburetor body.

2. Remove the 10 screw retaining bowl cover the body.

3. Using legs to protect the throttle valves, remove the bowl cover. Invert the bowl cover, taking care not to lose any of the samll parts.

4. With the bowl cover inverted and the floats resting on the seated needle, measure the distance between the bowl cover (new gasket installed) to the bottom side of each float.

5. If not to specifications, bend the float lever to suit.

NOTE: *Never allow the lip of the float to be pressed against the needle when adjusting the float height.*

6. Reverse Step 1-3 to install. Make sure that the float pin does not protrude past the edge of the bowl cover.

DECHOKE CLEARANCE ADJUSTMENT

Carter YF

1. Remove the carburetor air cleaner.

2. Hold the throttle plate to the full open position while closing the choke plate as far as possible without forcing it. Use a drill of the proper diameter (see Carburetor Specifications chart) to check the clearance between the choke plate and air horn.

3. Adjust as necessary by bending the pawl on the fast idle speed lever. Bend forward to increase clearance and backward to decrease clearance.

Autolite (Motorcraft) 4300, 4350

1. Remove the air cleaner assembly.

2. Remove the automatic choke spring housing from the carburetor.

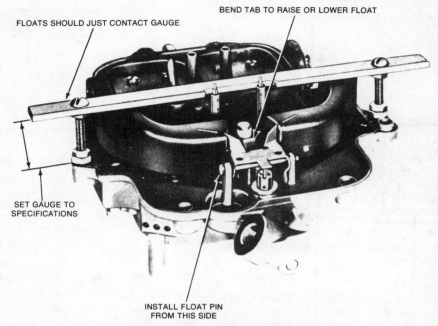

FLOATS SHOULD JUST CONTACT GAUGE

BEND TAB TO RAISE OR LOWER FLOAT

SET GAUGE TO
SPECIFICATIONS

INSTALL FLOAT PIN
FROM THIS SIDE

Float setting with fabricated gauge—4300, 4350

3. With the throttle plate wide open and the choke plate closed as far as possible without forcing it, insert a drill gauge of the specified diameter between the choke plate and air horn.

4. To adjust, bend the arm on the choke trip lever. Bend downward to increase clearance

and upward to decrease clearance. After adjusting, recheck the clearance.

5. Install the automatic choke housing, taking care to engage the thermostatic spring with the tang on the choke lever and shaft assembly.

6. Adjust the automatic choke setting. In-

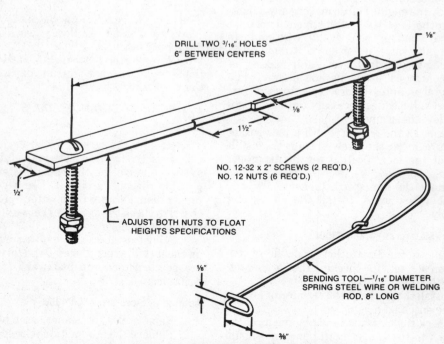

DRILL TWO ³/₁₆" HOLES
6" BETWEEN CENTERS

⅛"

⅛"

1½"

NO. 12-32 x 2" SCREWS (2 REQ'D.)
NO. 12 NUTS (6 REQ'D.)

½"

ADJUST BOTH NUTS TO FLOAT
HEIGHTS SPECIFICATIONS

⅛"

BENDING TOOL—¹/₁₆" DIAMETER
SPRING STEEL WIRE OR WELDING
ROD, 8" LONG

⅜"

Float gauge and bending tool details—4300, 4350

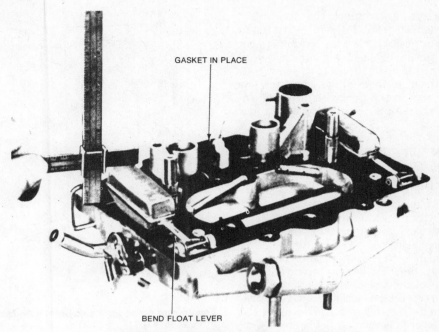

GASKET IN PLACE

BEND FLOAT LEVER

Checking float height—Carter Thermo-Quad®

stall the air cleaner. Adjust the idle speed and dashpot, if so equipped.

METERING ROD ADJUSTMENT

Carter YF

With the carburetor air horn and gasket removed from the carburetor, unscrew the idle speed adjusting screw until the throttle plate is tightly closed in the throttle bore. Press downward on the end of the diaphragm shaft until

DRILL OR GAUGE OF SPECIFIED SIZE

THROTTLE WIDE OPEN

Checking dechoke clearance—Motorcraft 4300, 4350

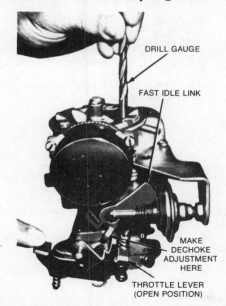

DRILL GAUGE

FAST IDLE LINK

MAKE DECHOKE ADJUSTMENT HERE

THROTTLE LEVER (OPEN POSITION)

Dechoke clearance adjustment—Carter YF

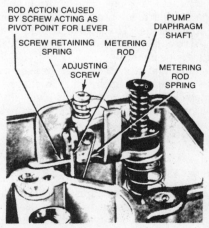

ROD ACTION CAUSED BY SCREW ACTING AS PIVOT POINT FOR LEVER

SCREW RETAINING SPRING

METERING ROD

PUMP DIAPHRAGM SHAFT

ADJUSTING SCREW

METERING ROD SPRING

Metering rod adjustment—Carter YF

the metering rod arm contacts the lifter link at the diaphragm stem. With the metering rod in the preceding position, turn the rod adjustment screw (see the accompanying illustration) until the metering rod just bottoms in the body casting. Turn the metering rod adjusting screw one additional turn in the clockwise direction. Install the carburetor air horn along with a new gasket.

ACCELERATOR PUMP STROKE ADJUSTMENT

Autolite (Motorcraft) 2100, 2150, 4100

In order to keep the exhaust emission level of the engine within specified limits, the accelerating pump stroke has been preset at the factory. The addition holes are provided for metering engine-transmission body application only. the primary throttle shaft lever (overtravel lever) has four holes and the accelerating pump link two holes to control the pump stroke. The accelerating pump operating rod should be in the overtravel lever hole number listed in the Carburetor Specification chart, and in the inboard hole (hole closest to the pump plunger) in the accelerating pump link. If the pump stroke has been changed from the specified settings, use the following procedure to correct the stroke.

1. Release the operating rod from the retaining clip by pressing the tab end of the clip toward the rod while pressing the rod away from the clip until it disengages.

2. Position the clip over the specified hole (see Carburetor Specification chart) in the overtravel lever. Press the ends of the clip together and insert the operating rod through the clip and the overtravel lever. Release the clip to engage the rod.

Autolite (Motorcraft) 4300

The pump stroke is preset at the factory to limit exhaust emissions. The addition holes in the operating arm are provided for different engine applications. The stroke should not be changed from the specified hole (see Carburetor Specifications chart).

The only adjustments possible are the pump stroke and pump stem height. To change the pump stroke, merely remove the pivot pin and reposition it in the specified hole. To adjust the pump stem height, bend the operating rod at the angles, taking care not to cause binds in the system.

Motorcraft 4350

The accelerator pump adjustment is preset at the factory for reduced exhaust emissions. Adjustment is provided only for different engine installations. The adjustment is internal, with

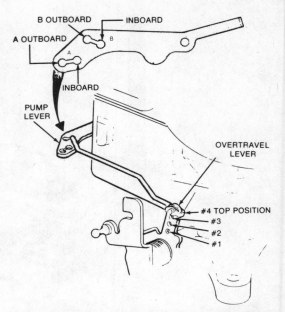

Accelerator pump stroke adjustment—Motorcraft 2100, 2150, 4100

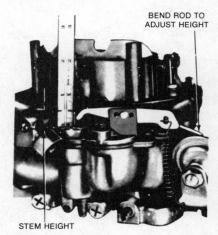

Accelerator pump stroke and piston stem height—Motorcraft 4300

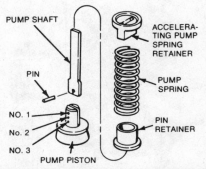

Accelerator pump stroke adjustment—Motorcraft 4350

three piston-to-shaft pin positions in the pump piston.

To check that the shaft pin is located in the specified piston hole, remove the carburetor air horn and invert it. Disconnect the accelerator pump from the operating arm by pressing downward on the spring and sliding the arm out of the pump shaft slot. Disassemble the spring and nylon keeper retaining the adjustment pin. If the pin is not in its specified hole, remove it, reposition the shaft to the correct hole in the piston assembly and reinstall the pin. The, slide the nylon retainer over the pin and position the spring on the shaft. Finally, compress the spring on the shaft and install the pump on the pump arm.

NOTE: *Under no circumstances should you adjust the stroke of the accelerator pump by turning the vacuum limiter lever adjusting nut. This adjustment is preset at the factory and modification could result in poor cold driveability.*

ANTI-STALL DASHPOT ADJUSTMENT

All Carburetors

Having made sure that the engine idle speed and mixture are correct and that the engine is at normal operating temperature, loosen the anti-stall dashpot locking nut (see accompanying illustration). With the throttle held closed, depress the plunger with a screwdriver blade and measure the clearance between the throttle

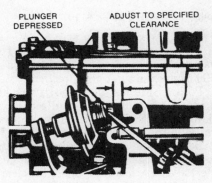

Typical anti-stall dashpot adjustment

lever and the plunger tip. If the clearance is not as specified in the Carburetor Specification charts, turn the dashpot until the proper clearance is obtained between the throttle lever and the plunger tip. After tightening the locking nut, recheck the adjustment.

FAST IDLE CAM INDEX SETTING

Carter YF

1. Position the fast idle screw on the kickdown step of the fast idle cam against the shoulder of the high step.

2. Adjust by bending the choke plate connecting rod to obtain the specified clearance between the lower edge of the choke plate and the carburetor bore.

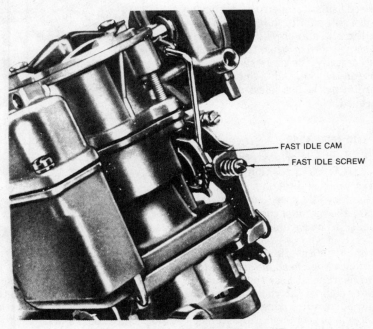

Fast idle cam index setting—Carter YF

Autolite (Motorcraft) 2100, 4100

1968-72

1. Loosen the choke thermostatic spring housing retaining screws and position the housing 90 degrees in the right direction.

2. Position the fast idle speed screw at the kick-down step of the fast idle cam. This kickdown step is identified by a small **V** stamped in the side of the casting.

3. Be sure that the fast idle cam is in the kick-down position while checking or adjusting the fast idle cam clearance. Check the clearance between the lower edge of the choke plate and the wall of the air horn by inserting a drill of the specified diameter between them. Adjustment may be accomplished by turning the fast idle cam adjusting screw clockwise to increase or counterclockwise to decrease the clearance.

4. Set the choke thermostatic spring housing to specifications, and adjust the antistall dashpot, idle speed, and fuel mixture.

Motorcraft 2100, 21500

1973 AND LATER

1. Loosen the choke thermostatic spring housing retaining screws and rotate the housing 90 degrees in the rich direction.

2. Position the fast idle speed screw or lever on the high step of the cam.

3. Depress the choke pull-down diaphragm against the diaphragm stop screw therby placing the choke in the pull-down position.

4. While holding the choke pull-down diaphragm depressed, slightly open the throttle and allow the fast idle cam to fall.

5. Close the throttle and check the position of the fast idle cam jor lever. When the fast idle cam is adjusted correctly, the screw should contact the **V** mark on the cam. Adjustment is accomplished by rotating the fast idle cam adjusting screw as needed.

Autolite (Motorcraft) 4300, 4350

1. Loosen the choke thermostatic spring housing retaining screw and position the housing 90 degrees in the rich direction.

2. Position the fast idle speed screw at the kick-down step of the fast idle cam. This kickdown step is identified by a small **V** stamped in the side of the casting.

3. Be sure that the fast idle cam is in the kick-down position while checking or adjustin the fast idle cam clearance. Check the clearance between the lower edge of the choke plate and the wall of the air horn by inserting a drill of the specified diameter between them. Adjustment may be accomplished by tuning the fast idle

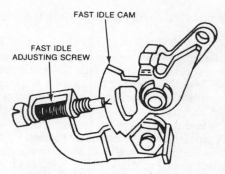

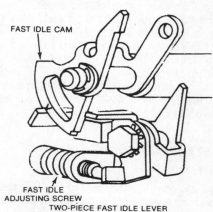

Fast idle cam index setting—Motorcraft 2100

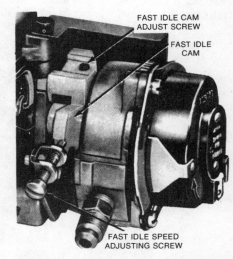

Fast idle cam index setting—Motorcraft 4300, 4350

cam adjusting screw clockwise to increase and counterclockwise to decrease the clearance.

4. Set the choke thermostatic spring housing to specifications, and adjust the antistall dashpot, idle speed, and fuel mixture.

Motorcraft 2700VV and 7200VV

DESIGN

Since the design of the 2700VV (variable venturi) carburetor differs considerably from the other carburetors in the Ford lineup, an explanation in the theory and operation is presented here.

In exterior appearance, the variable venturi carburetor is similar to conventional carburetor and, like a conventional carburetor, it uses a normal float and fuel bowl system. However, the similarity end there. In place of the normal choke plate and fixed area venturis, the 2700VV carburetor has a pair of small oblong castings in the top of the upper carburetor body where you would normally expect to see the choke plate. These castings slide back and forth across the top of the carburetor in response to fuel-air demands. Their movement is controlled by a spring-loaded diaphragm valve regulated by a vacuum signal taken below the venturis in the throttle bores. As the throttle is opened, the strength of the vacuum signal increases, opening the venturis and allowing more air to enter the carburetor.

Fuel is admitted into the venturi area by means of tapered metering rods that fit into the main jets. These rods are attached to the venturis, and, as the venturis open or close in response to air demand, the fuel needed to maintain the proper mixture increase or decreases as the metering rods slide in the jets. In comparison to a conventional carburetor with fixed venturis and a variable air supply, this system provides much more precise control of the fuel-air supply during all modes of operation. Because of the variable venturi principle, there are fewer fuel metering systems and fuel passages. The only auxiliary fuel metering systems required are an idle trim, accelerator pump (similar to a conventional carburetor), starting enrichment, and cold running enrichment.

NOTE: *Adjustment, assembly and disassembly of this carburetor require special tools for some of the operations. These tools are available (see the Tools and Equipment Section). Do not attempt any operations on this carburetor without first checking to see if you need the special tools for that particular operation. The adjustment and repair procedures given here mention when and if you will need the special tools.*

The Motorcraft model 7200 variable venturi (VV) carburetor shares most of its design features with the model 2700VV. The major difference between the two is that the 7200VV is designed to work with Ford's EEC (electronic engine control) feedback system. The feedback system precisely controls the air/fuel ration by varying signals to the feedback control monitor located on the carburetor, which opens or closes the metering valve in response. This expands or reduces the amount of control vacuum above the fuel bowl, leaning or richening the mixture accordingly.

FLOAT LEVEL ADJUSTMENT

1. Remove and invert the upper part of the carburetor, with the gasket in place.
2. Measure the vertical distance between the carburetor body, outside the gasket, and the bottom of the float.
3. To adjust, bend the float operating lever that contacts the needle valve. Make sure that the float remains parallel to the gasket surface.

FLOAT DROP ADJUSTMENT

1. Remove and hold upright the upper part of the carburetor.
2. Measure the vertical distance between the carburetor body, outside the gasket, and the bottom of the float.

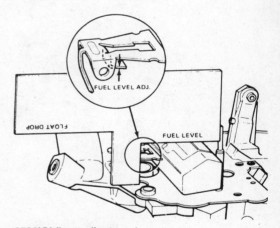

2700VV float adjustment

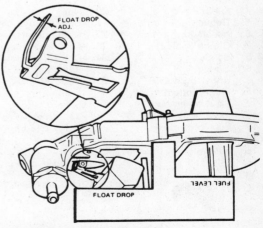

2700 VV float drop adjustment

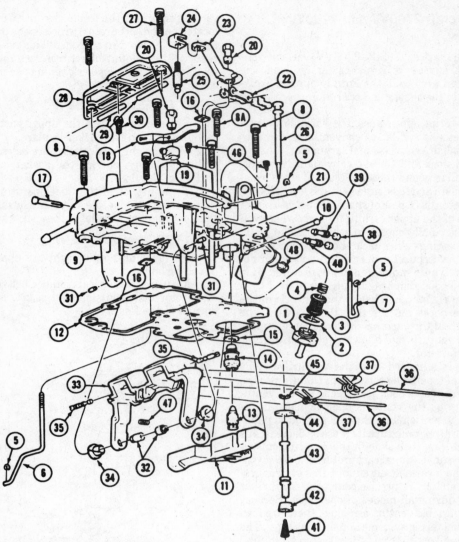

1.	Fuel inlet fitting	17.	Pin	33.	Venturi valve
2.	Fuel inlet fitting gasket	18.	Accelerator pump link	34.	Venturi valve pivot pin bushing
3.	Fuel filter	19.	Accelerator pump swivel	35.	Metering rod pivot pin
4.	Fuel filter spring	20.	Nut	36.	Metering rod
5.	Retaining E-ring	21.	Choke hinge pin	37.	Metering rod spring
6.	Accelerator pump rod	22.	Cold enrichment rod lever	38.	Cup plug
7.	Choke control rod	23.	Cold enrichment rod swivel	39.	Main metering jet assembly
8.	Screw	24.	Control vacuum regulator	40.	O-ring
8A.	Screw		adjusting nut	41.	Accelerator pump return spring
9.	Upper body	25.	Control vacuum regulator	42.	Accelerator pump cup
10.	Float hinge pin	26.	Cold enrichment rod	43.	Accelerator pump plunger
11.	Float assembly	27.	Screw	44.	Internal vent valve
12.	Float bowl gasket	28.	Venturi valve cover plate	45.	Retaining E-ring
13.	Fuel inlet valve	29.	Roller bearing	46.	Idle trim screw
14.	Fuel inlet seat	30.	Venturi air bypass screw	47.	Venturi valve limiter adjusting screw
15.	Fuel inlet seat gasket	31.	Venturi valve pivot plug	48.	Pipe plug
16.	Dust seal	32.	Venturi valve pivot pin		

Typical upper body—VV carburetor (2700VV shown)

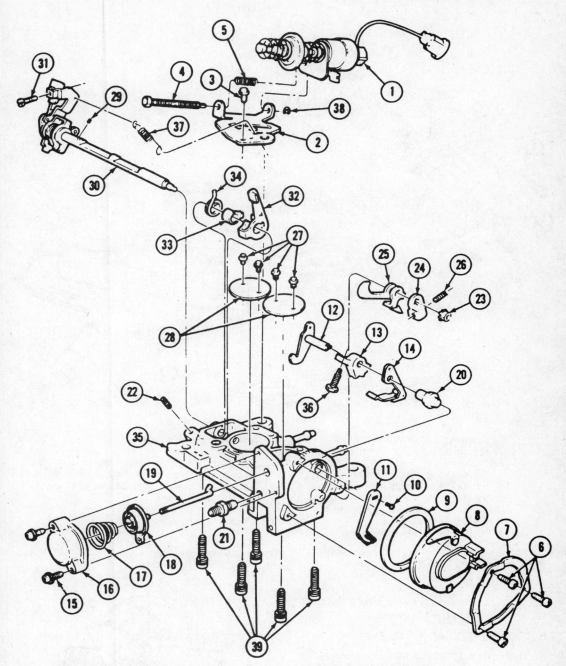

1. Throttle return control device
2. Throttle return control device bracket
3. Mounting screw
4. Adjusting screw
5. Adjusting screw spring
6. Screw
7. Choke thermostatic housing retainer
8. Choke thermostatic housing
9. Choke thermostatic housing gasket
10. Screw
11. Choke thermostatic lever
12. Choke lever and shaft assembly
13. Fast idle cam
14. High cam speed positioner assembly
15. Screw
16. High cam speed positioner diaphragm cover
17. High cam speed positioner diaphragm spring
18. High cam speed positioner diaphragm assembly
19. High cam speed positioner rod
20. Choke housing bushing

2700VV throttle body

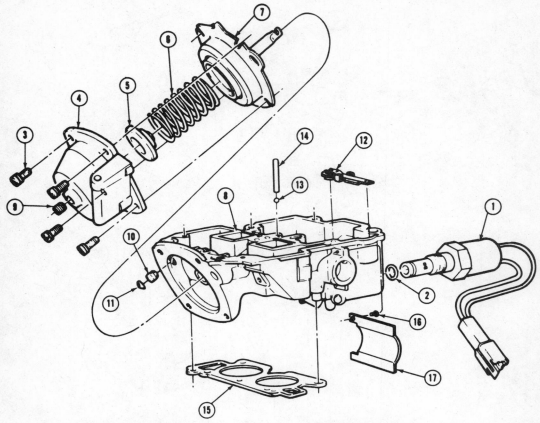

1. Cranking enrichment solenoid
2. O-ring seal
3. Screw
4. Venturi valve diaphragm cover
5. Venturi valve diaphragm spring guide
6. Venturi valve diaphragm spring
7. Venturi valve diaphragm assembly
8. Main body
9. Venturi valve adjusting screw
10. Wide open stop screw
11. Plug expansion
12. Cranking fuel control assembly
13. Accelerator pump check ball
14. Accelerator pump check ball weight
15. Throttle body gasket
16. Screw
17. Choke heat shield

Typical main body—VV carburetor (2700VV shown)

3. Adjust by bending the stop tab on the float lever that contacts the hinge pin.

FAST IDLE SPEED ADJUSTMENT

1. With the engine warmed up and idling, place the fast idle lever on the step of the fast idle cam specified on the engine compartment sticker or in the specifications chart. Disconnect and plug the EGR vacuum line.

2. Make sure the high speed cam positioner lever is disengaged.

3. Turn the fast idle speed screw to adjust to the specified speed.

FAST IDLE CAM ADJUSTMENT

You will need a special tool for this job: Ford calls it a stator cap (#T77L-9848-A). It fits over

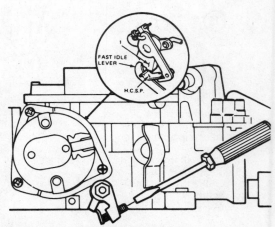

2700 VV fast idle speed adjustment

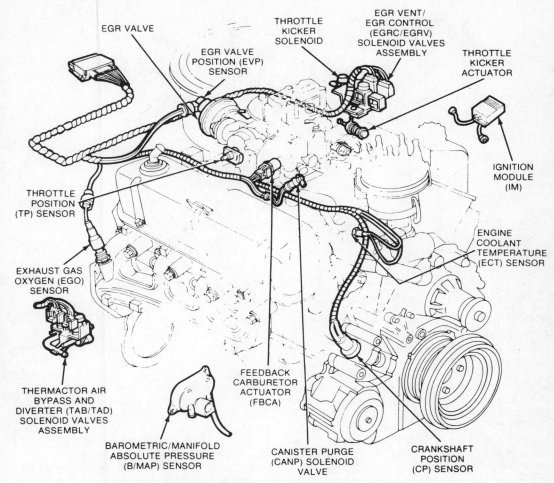

VV feedback carburetor wiring and vacuum diagram

the choke thermostatic lever when the choke cap is removed.

1. Remove the choke coil cap. On 1980 and later California models, the choke cap is riveted in place. The top rivets will have to be drilled out. The bottom rivet will have to be driven out from the rear. New rivets must be used upon installation.

2. Place the fast idle lever in the corner of the specified step of the fast idle cam (the highest step is first) with the high speed cam positioner retracted.

3. If the adjustment is being made with the carburetor removed, hold the throttle lightly close with a rubber band.

4. Turn the stator cap clockwise until the lever contacts the fast idle cam adjusting screw.

5. Turn the fast idle cam adjusting screw until the index mark on the cap lines up with the specified mark on the casting.

6. Remove the stator cap. Install the choke coil cap and set it to the specified housing mark.

COLD ENRICHMENT METERING ROD ADJUSTMENT

A dial indicator and the stator cap are required for this adjustment.

1. Remove the choke coil cap. See Step 1 of the Fast idle Cam Adjustment.

2. Attach a weight to the choke coil mechanism to seat the cold enrichment rod.

3. Install and zero a dial indicator with the tip of top of the enrichment rod. Raise and release the weight to verify zero on the dial indicator.

4. With the stator cap at the index position, the dial indicator should read the specified dimension. Turn the adjusting nut to correct it.

5. Install the choke cap at the correct setting.

CONTROL VACUUM ADJUSTMENT

1977 Only

1. Make sure the idle speed is correct.
2. Using a $5/32$" Allen wrench, turn the ventu-

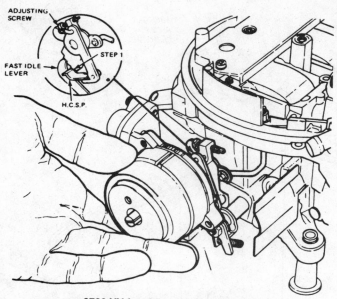

2700 VV fast idle cam adjustment

ri valve diaphragm adjusting screw clockwise until the valve is firmly closed.

3. Connect a vacuum gauge to the vacuum tap on the venturi valve cover.

4. Idle the engine and use a ⅛″ Allen wrench to turn the venturi by-pass adjusting screw to the specified vacuum setting. You may have to correct the idle speed.

5. Turn the venturi valve diaphragm adjusting screw counterclockwise until the vacuum drops to the specified setting. You will have to work the throttle to get the vacuum to drop.

6. Reset the idle speed.

1980-82

This adjustment is necessary only on non-feedback systems.

1. Remove the carburetor. Remove the venturi valve diaphragm plug with a center-punch.

2. If the carburetor has a venturi valve by-pass, remove it be removing the two cover retaining screw; invert and remove the by-pass screw plug from the cover with a drift. Install the cover.

3. Install the carburetor. Start the engine and allow it to reach normal operating tempera-

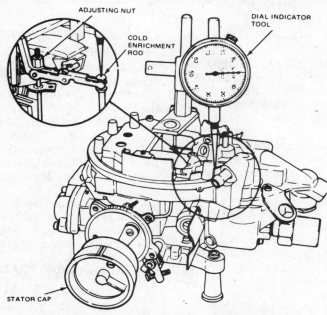

2700 VV cold enrichment metering rod adjustment

ture. Connect a vacuum gauge to the venturi valve cover. Set the idle speed to 500 rpm with the transmission in Drive.

4. Push and hold the venturi valve closed. Adjust the bypass screw to obtain a reading of 8 in. H_2O on the vacuum gauge. Make sure the idle speed remains constant. Open and close the throttle and check the idle speed.

5. With the engine idling, adjust the venturi valve diaphragm screw to obtain a reading of 6 in. H_2O. Set the curb idle to specification. Install new venturi valve bypass and diaphragm plugs.

INTERNAL VENT ADJUSTMENT

Through 1978 Only

This adjustment is required whenever the idle speed adjustment is changed.

1. Make sure the idle speed is correct.

2. Place a 0.010″ feeler gauge between the accelerator pump stem and the operating link.

3. Turn the nylon adjusting nut until there is a slight drag on the gauge.

VENTURI VALVE LIMITER ADJUSTMENT

1. Remove the carburetor. Take off the venturi valve cover and the two rollers.

2. Use a center punch to loosen the expansion plug at the rear of the carburetor main body on the throttle side. Remove it.

3. Use an Allen wrench to remove the venturi valve wide open stop screw.

4. Hold the throttle wide open.

5. Apply a light closing pressure on the venturi valve and check the gap between the valve and the air horn wall. To adjust, move the venturi valve to the wide open position and insert an Allen wrench into the stop screw hole. Turn clockwise to increase the gap. Remove the wrench and check the gap again.

6. Replace the wide open stop screw and turn it clockwise until it contact the valve.

7. Push the venturi valve wide open and check the gap. Turn the stop screw to bring the gap to specifications.

8. Reassemble the carburetor with a new expansion plug.

CONTROL VACUUM REGULATOR ADJUSTMENT

There are two systems used. The earlier system's C.V.R. rod threads directly through the arm. The revised system, introduced in late 1977, has a ⅜″ nylon hex adjusting nut on the C.V.R. rod and a flange on the rod.

Early System

1. Make sure that the cold enrichment metering rod adjustment is correct.

2. Rotate the choke coil cap half a turn clockwise from the index mark. Work the throttle to set the fast idle cam.

3. Press down lightly on the regulator rod. If there is no down travel, turn the adjusting screw counterclockwise until some travel is felt.

4. Turn the regulator rod clockwise with an Allen wrench until the adjusting nut just begins to rise.

5. Press lightly on the regulator rod. If there is any down travel, turn the adjusting screw clockwise in ¼ turn increments until it is eliminated.

6. Return the choke coil cap to the specified setting.

Revised System

The cold enrichment metering rod adjustment must be checked and set before making this adjustment.

1. After adjusting the cold enrichment metering rod, leave the dial indicator in place but remove the stator cap. Do not re-zero the dial indicator.

2. Press down on the C.V.R. rod until it bottoms on its seat. Measure this amount of travel with the dial indicator.

3. If the adjustment is incorrect, hold the ⅜″ C.V.R. adjusting nut with a box wrench to prevent it from turning. Use a ³⁄₃₂″ Allen wrench to turn the C.V.R. rod; turning counterclockwise will increase the travel, and vice-versa.

HIGH SPEED CAM POSITIONER ADJUSTMENT

Through 1979 Only

1. Place the high speed cam positioner in the corner of the specified cam step, counting the highest step as the first.

2. Place the fast idle lever in the corner of the positioner.

3. Hold the throttle firmly closed.

4. Remove the diaphragm cover. Adjust the diaphragm assembly clockwise until it lightly bottoms. Turn it counterclockwise ½-1½ turns until the vacuum port and diaphragm hole line up.

5. Replace the cover.

IDLE MIXTURE ADJUSTMENT

Through 1977 Only

The results of this adjustment should be checked with an emissions tester, to make sure that emission limits are not exceeded. Idle mixture (idle trim) is not adjustable 1978 and later models.

1. Remove the air cleaner only.

2. Use a $\frac{3}{32}''$ Allen wrench to adjust the mixture for each barrel by turning the air adjusting screw. Turn it clockwise to richen.

DISASSEMBLY

NOTE: *Special tools are required. If you have any doubts about your ability to successfully complete this procedure, leave it to a professional service person.*

Upper Body

1. Remove the fuel inlet fitting, fuel filter, gasket and spring.
2. Remove the screws retaining the upper body assembly and remove the upper body.
3. Remove the float hinge pin and float assembly.
4. Remove the fuel inlet valve, seat and gasket.
5. Remove the accelerator pump rod and the choke control rod.
6. Remove the accelerator pump link retaining pin and the link.
7. Remove the accelerator pump swivel and the retaining nut.
8. Remove the E-ring on the choke hinge pin and slide the pin out of the casting.
9. Remove the cold enrichment rod adjusting nut, lever and swivel; remove the control vacuum nut and regulator as an assembly.
10. Remove the cold enrichment rod.
11. Remove the venturi valve cover plate and roller bearings. Remove the venturi valve cover plate and roller bearings. Remove the venturi air bypass screw.
12. Using special tool T77P-9928-A, press the tapered plugs out of the venturi valve pivot pins.
13. Remove the venturi valve pivot pins, bushings and the venturi valve.
14. Remove the metering rod pivot pins, springs and metering rods. Be sure to mark the rods so that you know on which side they belong. Also, keep the venturi valve blocked open when working on the jets.
15. Using tool T77L-9533-B, remove the cup plugs.
16. Using tool T77L-9533-A, turn each main metering jet clockwise, counting the number of turns until they bottom in the casting. You will need to know the number of turns when you reassemble the carburetor. Remove the jets and mark them so that you know on which side they belong. Don't lose the O-rings.
17. Remove the accelerator pump plunger assembly.
18. Remove the idle trim screws. Remove the venturi valve limiter adjusting screw.
19. Assembly is the reverse of disassembly.

Main Body

1. Remove the cranking enrichment solenoid and the O-ring seal.
2. Remove the venturi valve cover, spring guide, and spring. Remove the venturi valve.
3. Remove the throttle body.
4. Remove the choke heat shield.
5. Assembly is in the reverse order.

CENTRAL FUEL INJECTION (CFI)

Description

Central Fuel Injection (CFI) is a throttle body injection system in which two fuel injectors are mounted in a common throttle body, spraying fuel down through the throttle valves at the bottom of the body and into the intake manifold.

Operation

Fuel is supplied from the fuel tank by a high pressure, in-tank fuel pump. The fuel passes through a filter and is sent to the throttle body where a regulator keeps the fuel delivery pressure at a constant 39 psi. The two fuel injectors are mounted vertically above the throttle plates and are connected in line with the fuel pressure regulator. Excess fuel supplied by the pump, but not needed by the engine, is returned to the fuel tank by a steel fuel return line.

The fuel injection system is linked with and controlled by the Electronic Engine Control (EEC) system.

Air and Fuel Control

The throttle body assembly is comprised of six individual components which perform the job of mixing the air and fuel to the ideal ratio for controlling exhaust emissions and providing performance and economy. The six components are: air control, fuel injector nozzles, fuel pressure regulator, fuel pressure diagnostic valve, cold engine speed control, and throttle position sensor.

Air Control

Air flow to the engine is controlled by two butterfly valves mounted in a two piece, die-cast aluminum housing called the throttle body. The butterfly valves, or throttle valves, are identical in design to the throttle plates of a conventional carburetor and are actuated by a similar linkage and pedal cable arrangement.

Fuel Injector Nozzles

The fuel injector nozzles are mounted in the throttle body and are electro-mechanical devices which meter and atomize the fuel delivered to the engine. The injector valve bodies consist of a solenoid actuated pintle and needle valve assembly. An electrical control signal from the EED electronic processor activates the solenoid causing the pintle to move inward off its seat and allowing fuel to flow. the fuel flow through the injector is controlled by the amount of time the injector solenoid holds the pintle off its seat.

Fuel Pressure Regulator

The fuel pressure regulator is mounted on the throttle body. The regulator smooths out fuel pressure drops from the fuel pump. It is not sensitive to back pressure in the return line to the tank.

A second function of the pressure regulator is to maintain fuel supply pressure upon engine and fuel pump shut down. The regulator acts as a check valve and traps fuel between itself and the fuel pump. This promotes rapid start ups and helps prevent fuel vapor formation in the lines, or vapor lock. The regulator makes sure that the pressure of the fuel at the injector nozzles stays at a constant 39 psi.

Fuel Pressure Diagnostic Valve

A Schrader-type diagnostic pressure valve is located at the top of the throttle body. This valve can be used by service personnel to monitor fuel pressure, bleed down the system pressure prior to maintenance and to bleed out air which may have been introduced during assembly or filter servicing. A special Ford Tool (T80L-9974-A) is used to accomplish these procedures.

CAUTION: *Under no circumstances should compressed air be forced into the fuel system using the diagnostic valve.*

Cold Engine Speed Control

The cold engine speed control serves the same purpose as the fast idle speed device on a carbureted engine, which is to raise engine speed during cold engine idle. A throttle stop cam positioner is used. the cam is positioned by a bimetal spring and an electric heating element. The cold engine speed control is attached to the throttle body. As the engine heats up, the fast idle cam on the cold engine speed control is gradually repositioned by the bimetal spring, heating element and EEC computer until normal idle speed is reached. The EEC computer automatically kicks down the fast idle cam to a lower step (lower engine speed) by supplying vacuum to the automatic kickdown motor which physically moves the high speed cam a predetermined time after the engine starts.

Throttle Position Sensor

This sensor is attached to the throttle body and is used to monitor changes in throttle plate position. the throttle position sensor sends this information to the computer, which uses it to select proper air/fuel mixture, spark timing and EGR control under different engine operating conditions.

Fuel System Inertia Switch

In the event of a collision, the electrical contacts in the inertia switch open and the fuel pump automatically shuts off. The fuel pump will shut off even if the engine does not stop running. The engine, however, will stop a few seconds after the fuel pump stops. It is not possible to restart the engine until the inertia switch is manually reset. The switch is located in the luggage compartment on the left hinge support on all models. To reset, depress both buttons on the switch at the same time.

CAUTION: *Do not reset the inertia switch until the complete fuel system has been inspected for leaks.*

FUEL CHARGING ASSEMBLY REMOVAL AND INSTALLATION

1. Remove the air cleaner.
2. Release the pressure from the fuel system at the diagnostic valve using Tool T80L-9974-A or its equivalent.
3. Disconnect the throttle cable and transmission throttle valve lever.
4. Disconnect the fuel, vacuum and electrical connections. Use care to prevent combustion of spilled fuel.
5. Remove the fuel charging assembly retaining nuts then remove the fuel charging assembly.
6. Remove the mounting gasket from the intake manifold.
7. Installation is the reverse of removal. Tighten the fuel charging assembly nuts to 120 in. lbs.

THROTTLE BODY DISASSEMBLY AND ASSEMBLY

1. Remove the air cleaner mounting stud in order to separate the upper body from the throttle body.
2. Turn the fuel charging assembly (throttle body) over and remove the four screws from the bottom of the throttle body.
3. Separate the throttle body (lower half) from the main body (upper half).
4. Remove the old gasket. If it is stuck and scraping is necessary, use only a plastic or wood scraper. Take care not to damage the gasket surfaces.

5. Remove the three pressure regulator mounting screws. Remove the pressure regulator.

6. Disconnect the electrical connectors at each injector by pulling outward on the connector and not on the wire. Loosen but do not re-

move the wiring harness retaining screw. Push in on the harness tabs to remove it from the upper body.

7. Remove the fuel injector retaining screw. Remove the injection retainer.

8. Pull the injectors, one at a time, from the

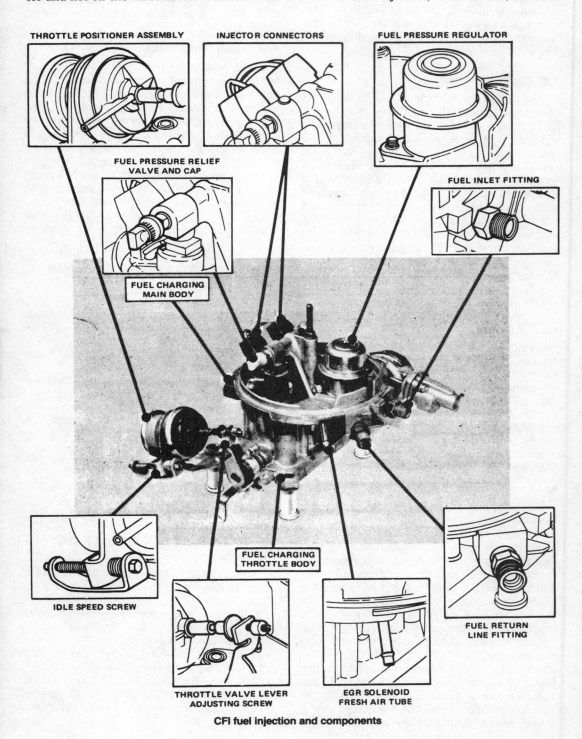

THROTTLE POSITIONER ASSEMBLY

INJECTOR CONNECTORS

FUEL PRESSURE REGULATOR

FUEL PRESSURE RELIEF
VALVE AND CAP

FUEL INLET FITTING

FUEL CHARGING
MAIN BODY

IDLE SPEED SCREW

FUEL CHARGING
THROTTLE BODY

FUEL RETURN
LINE FITTING

THROTTLE VALVE LEVER
ADJUSTING SCREW

EGR SOLENOID
FRESH AIR TUBE

CFI fuel injection and components

upper body. Mark the injectors for identification, they must be reinstalled in the same position (choke or throttle side). Each injector is equipped with a small O-ring. If the O-ring does not come out with the injector, carefully pick out of body.

9. Remove the fuel diagnostic valve assembly.

10. Remove the choke cover by drilling the retaining rivets. A ⅛″ or No. 30 drill is required. A choke mounting kit for installation is available from Ford.

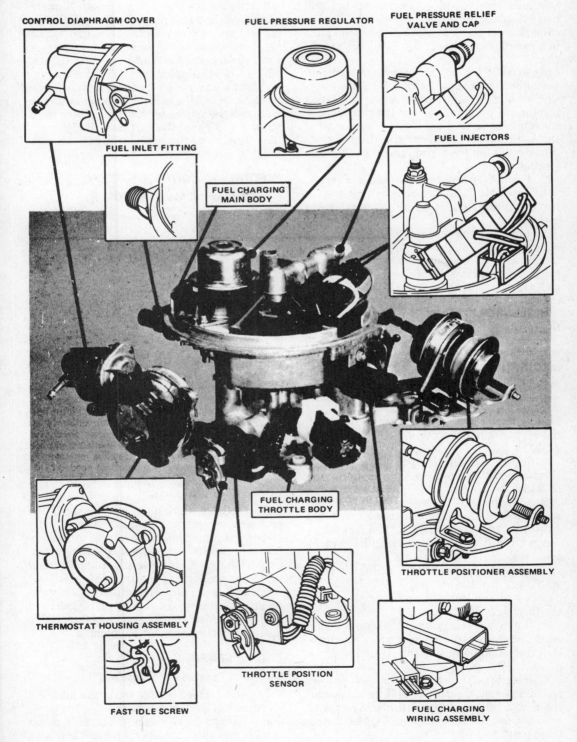

CONTROL DIAPHRAGM COVER

FUEL PRESSURE REGULATOR

FUEL PRESSURE RELIEF VALVE AND CAP

FUEL INLET FITTING

FUEL CHARGING MAIN BODY

FUEL INJECTORS

THERMOSTAT HOUSING ASSEMBLY

FUEL CHARGING THROTTLE BODY

THROTTLE POSITIONER ASSEMBLY

FAST IDLE SCREW

THROTTLE POSITION SENSOR

FUEL CHARGING WIRING ASSEMBLY

11. Remove the choke cap retaining ring, choke cap and gasket. Remove the thermostat lever screw and lever. Remove the fast idle cam assembly and control rod positioner.

12. Hold the control diaphragm cover in position and remove the two mounting screws. Carefully remove the cover, spring and pull down diaphragm.

13. Remove the fast idle retaining nut, fast idle cam adjuster lever, fast idle lever and E-clip.

14. Remove the potentiometer (sensor) connector bracket retaining screw. Mark the throttle body and throttle position sensor for correct installation position. Remove the throttle sensor retaining screws and slide the sensor off of the throttle shaft. Remove the throttle positioner retaining screw and remove the throttle positioner.

15. Perform any necessary cleaning or repair.

16. Assemble the upper body by first installing the fuel diagnostic fuel pressure valve assembly.

17. Lubricate the new injector O-rings with a light grade oil. Install the O-rings on each injector. Install the injectors in their appropriate choke or throttle side position. Use a light, twisting, pushing motion to install the injectors.

18. Install the injector retainer and tighten the retaining screw to 30-60 in. lbs.

19. Install the injector wiring harness and snap into position. Tighten the harness retaining screw to 8-10 in. lbs.

20. Snap the electrical connectors into position on the injectors. Lubricate the fuel pressure regulator O-ring with light oil. Install the O-ring and new gasket on the regulator, install the regulator and tighten retaining screws to 27-40 in. lbs.

21. Install the throttle positioner onto the throttle body. Tighten the retaining screw to 32-44 in. lbs.

22. hold the throttle sensor (potentiometer) with the location identification mark (see step 14) in the 12 o'clock position. The two rotary tangs should be at 3 o'clock and 9 o'clock positions.

23. Slide the sensor onto the throttle shaft with the identification mark still in the 12 o'clock position. Hold the sensor firmly against the throttle body.

24. Rotate the sensor until the identification marks on the sensor and body are aligned. Install the retaining screws and tighten to 13-18 in. lbs.

25. Install the sensor wiring harness bracket retaining screw, tighten to 18-22 in. lbs. Install the E-clip, fast idle lever, fast idle adjustment lever and fast idle retaining nut. Tighten the retaining nut to 16-20 in. lbs.

26. Install the pull down diaphragm, spring and cover. Hold the cover in position and tighten the retaining screws to 13-19 in. lbs.

27. Install the fast idle control rod positioner, fast idle cam and the thermostat lever. Tighten the retaining screw to 13-19 in. lbs.

28. Install the choke cap gasket, bi-metal spring, cap and retaining ring. Install new rivets and snug them with the rivet gun. do not break rivets, loosely install so choke cover can rotate. Index choke and break rivets to tighten.

29. Install the gasket between the main body and the throttle body. Place the throttle body in position. Install the four retaining screws loosely. Install the air cleaner stud and tighten to 70-95 in. lbs. Tighten the four retaining screws.

30. The rest of the assembly is in the reverse order of disassembly.

ELECTRONIC CONTROL SYSTEM
Electronic Control Assembly (ECA)

The Electronic Control Assembly (ECA) is a solid-state micro-computer consisting of a processor assembly and a calibration assembly. It is located under the instrument panel or passenger's seat and is usually covered by a kick panel. 1981-82 models use an EEC-III engine control system, while 1983 and later models use the EEC-IV. Although the two systems are similar in appearance and operation, the ECA units are not interchangeable. A multipin connector links the ECA with all system components. The processor assembly is housed in an aluminum case. It contains circuits designed to continuously sample input signals from the engine sensors. It then calculates and sends out proper control signals to adjust air/fuel ratio, spark timing and emission system operation. The processor also provides a continuous reference voltage to the B/MAP, EVP, and TPS sensors. EEC-III reference voltage is 8-10 volts, while EEC-IV systems use a 5 volt reference signal. The calibration assembly is contained in a black plastic housing which plugs into the top of the processor assembly. It contains the memory and programming information used by the processor to determine optimum operating conditions. different calibration information is used in different vehicle applications, such as California or Federal models. For this reason, careful identification of the engine, year, model and type of electronic control system is essential to insure correct component replacement.

ENGINE SENSORS
Air Charge Temperature Sensor (ACT)

The ACT is threaded into the intake manifold air runner. It is located directly below the accelerator linkage on V8 engines. The ACT monitors air/fuel charge temperature and sends an appropriate signal to the ECA. This information is used to correct fuel enrichment for variations in intake air density due to temperature changes.

Barometric & Manifold Absolute Pressure Sensors (B/MAP)

The B/MAP sensor on V8 engines is located on the right fender panel in the engine compartment. The barometric sensor signals the ECA of changes in atmospheric pressure and density to regulate calculated air flow into the engine. The MAP sensor monitors and signals the ECA of changes in intake manifold pressure which result from engine load, speed and atmospheric pressure changes.

Crankshaft Position (CP) Sensor

The purpose of the CP sensor is to provide the ECA with an accurate ignition timing reference (when the piston reaches 10°BTDC) and injector operation information (twice each crankshaft revolution). The crankshaft vibration damper is fitted with a 4 lobe pulse ring. As the crankshaft rotates, the pulse ring lobes interrupt the magnetic field at the tip of the CP sensor.

EGR Valve Position Sensor (EVP)

This sensor, mounted on EGR valve, signals the computer of EGR opening so that it may subtract EGR flow from total air flow into the manifold. In this way, EGR flow is excluded from air flow information used to determine mixture requirements.

Engine Coolant Temperature Sensor (ECT)

The ECT is threaded into the intake manifold water jacket directly above the water pump bypass hose. The ECT monitors coolant temperature and signals the ECA, which then uses these signals for mixture enrichment (during cool operation), ignition timing and EGR operation. The resistance value of the ECT increases with temperature, causing a voltage signal drop as the engine warms up.

Exhaust Gas Oxygen Sensor (EGO)

The EGO is mounted in the right side exhaust manifold on V8 engines. The EGO monitors oxygen content of exhaust gases and sends a constantly changing voltage signal to the ECA. The ECA analyzes this signal and adjusts the air/fuel mixture to obtain the optimum (stoichiometric) ratio.

Thick Film Integrated Module Sensor (TFI)

The TFI module sensor plugs into the distributor just below the distributor cap and replaces the CP sensor on some engines. Its function is to provide the ECA with ignition timing information, similar to what the CP sensor provides.

Throttle Position Sensor (TPS)

The TPS is mounted on the right side of the throttle body, directly connected to the throttle shaft. The TPS senses the throttle movement and position and transmits an appropriate electrical signal to the ECA. These signals are used by the ECA to adjust the air/fuel mixture, spark timing and EGR operation according to engine load at idle, part throttle, or full throttle. The TPS is nonadjustable.

ON-CAR SERVICE

NOTE: *Diagnostic and test procedures on the EEC-III and EEC-IV electronic control system require special test equipment. Have the testing done by a professional.*

Fuel Pressure Tests

The diagnostic pressure valve (Schrader type) is located at the top of the Fuel charging main body. This valve provides a convenient point for service personnel to monitor fuel pressure, bleed down the system pressure prior to maintenance, and to bleed out air which may become trapped in the system during filter replacement. A pressure gauge with a adapter is required to perform pressure tests.

CAUTION: *Under no circumstances should compressed air be forced into the fuel system using the diagnostic valve. Depressing the pin in the diagnostic valve will relieve system pressure by expelling fuel into the throttle body.*

System Pressure Test

Testing fuel pressure requires the use of a special pressure gauge (T80L-9974-A or equivalent) that attaches to the diagnostic pressure tap on the fuel charging assembly. Depressurize the fuel system before disconnecting any lines.

1. Disconnect the fuel return line at the throttle body (in-tank high pressure pump) and connect the hose to a 1 quart calibrated container. Connect a pressure gauge.

2. Disconnect the electrical connector at the fuel pump. The connector is located ahead of fuel tank (in-tank high pressure pump) or just forward of pump outlet (in-line high pressure pump). Connect an auxiliary wiring harness to the connector of the fuel pump. Energize the pump for 10 seconds by applying 12 volts to the auxiliary harness connector, allowing the fuel to drain into the calibrated container. Note the fuel volume and pressure gauge reading.

3. Correct fuel pressure should be 35-45 psi (241-310 kPa). Fuel volume should be 10 ozs. in 10 seconds (minimum) and fuel pressure

should maintain a minimum of 30 psi (206 kPa) immediately after pump cut-off.

If the pressure condition is met, but the fuel flow is not, check for blocked filter(s) and fuel supply lines. After correcting the problem, repeat the test procedure. If the fuel flow is still inadequate, replace the high pressure pump. If the flow specification is met but the pressure is not, check for a worn or damaged pressure regulator valve on the throttle body. If both the pressure and fuel flow specifications are met, but the pressure drops excessively after de-energizing, check for a leaking injector valve(s) and/or pressure regulator valve. If the injector valves and pressure regulator valve are okay, replace the high pressure pump. If no pressure or flow is seen in the fuel system, check for blocked filters and fuel lines. If no trouble is found, replace the inline fuel pump, in-tank fuel pump and the fuel filter inside the tank.

Fuel Injector Pressure Test

1. Connect pressure gauge T80L-9974-A, or equivalent, to the fuel pressure test fitting. Disconnect the coil connector from the coil. Disconnect the electrical lead from one injector and pressurize the fuel system. Disable the fuel pump by disconnecting the inertia switch or the fuel pump relay and observe the pressure gauge reading.

2. Crank the engine for 2 seconds. Turn the ignition OFF and wait 5 seconds, then observe the pressure drop. If the pressure drop is 2-16 psi (14-110 kPa), the injector is operating properly. Reconnect the injector, activate the fuel pump, then repeat the procedure for other injector.

3. If the pressure drop is less than 2 psi (14 kPa) or more than 16 psi (110 kPa), switch the electrical connectors on injectors and repeat the test. If the pressure drop is still incorrect, replace the disconnected injector with one of the same color code, then reconnect both injectors properly and repeat the test.

4. Disconnect and plug the vacuum hose at EGR valve. It may be necessary to disconnect the throttle kicker solenoid and use the throttle body stop screw to set the engine speed. Start and run the engine at 1,800 rpm (2,000 rpm on 1984 and later models). Disconnect the left injector electrical connector. Note the rpm after the engine stabilizes (around 1,200 rpm). Reconnect the injector and allow the engine to return to high idle.

5. Perform the same procedure for the right injector. Note the difference between the rpm readings of the left and right injectors. If the difference is 100 rpm or less, check the oxygen sensor. If the difference is more than 100 rpm, replace both injectors.

CFI COMPONENT TESTS

NOTE: *Complete CFT system diagnosis requires the use of special test equipment. Have the system tested professionally.*

Before beginning any component testing, always check the following:

• Check the ignition and fuel systems to ensure there is fuel and spark.

• Remove the air cleaner assembly and inspect all vacuum and pressure hoses for proper connection to fittings. Check for damaged or pinched hoses.

• Inspect all sub-system wiring harnesses for proper connections to the EGR solenoid valves, injectors, sensors, etc.

• Check for loose or detached connectors and broken or detached wires. Check that all terminals are seated firmly and are not corroded. Look for partially broken or frayed wires or any shorting between the wires.

• Inspect the sensors for physical damage. Inspect the vehicle electrical system. Check the battery for full charge and cable connections for tightness.

• Inspect the relay connector and make sure the ECA power relay is securely attached and making a good ground connection.

High Pressure In-Tank Pump

Disconnect the electrical connector just forward of the fuel tank. Connect a voltmeter to the body wiring harness connector. Turn the key ON while watching the voltmeter. Voltage should rise to battery voltage, then return to

CFI Resistance Specifications

Component	Resistance (Ohms)
Air Charge Temp (ACT)	
1981–83	1700–60,000
1984	1100–58,000
Coolant (ECT) Sensor	
1981–83	1100–8000
1984—Engine Off	1300–7700
1984—Engine On	1500–4500
Crank Position Sensor	100–640
FGB	30–70
EGR Vent Solenoid	30–70
Fuel Pump Relay	50–100
Throttle Kicker Solenoid	50–100
Throttle Position Sensor	
1981–83 Closed Throttle	3000–5000
1984 Closed Throttle	550–1100
Wide Open Throttle	More than 2100
TAB Solenoid	50–100
TAD Solenoid	50–100

zero after about 1 second. Momentarily turn the key to the **START** position. Voltage should rise to about 8 volts while cranking. If voltage is not specified, check electrical system.

High Pressure Inline & Low Pressure In-Tank Pumps

Disconnect the electrical connector at the fuel pumps. Connect a voltmeter to the body wiring harness connector. Turn the key **ON** while watching the voltmeter. The voltage should rise to battery voltage, then return to zero after about 1 second. If the voltage is not as specified, check the inertia switch and the electrical system. Connect an ohmmeter to the inline pump wiring harness connector. If no continuity is present, check the continuity directly at the inline pump terminals. If no continuity at the inline pump terminals, replace the inline pump. If continuity is present, service or replace the wiring harness.

Connect an ohmmeter across the body wiring harness connector. If continuity is present (about 5 ohms), the low pressure pump circuit is OK. If no continuity is present, remove the fuel tank and check for continuity at the in-tank pump flange terminals on top of the tank. If continuity is absent at the in-tank pump flange terminals, replace the assembly. If continuity is present at the in-tank pump but not in the harness connector, service or replace the wiring harness at the in-tank pump.

Solenoid and Sensor Resistance Tests

All CFI components must be disconnected from the circuit before testing the resistance with a suitable ohmmeter. Replace any component whose measured resistance does not agree with the specifications chart. Shorting the wiring harness across a solenoid valve can burn out the circuitry in the ECA that control the solenoid valve actuator. Exercise caution when testing the solenoid valves to avoid accidental damage to ECA.

ELECTRONIC MULTI-POINT FUEL INJECTION (EFI)

Description

The Electronic Fuel Injector System (EFI) is classified as a multi-point, pulse time, mass air flow fuel injection system. Fuel is metered into the intake air stream in accordance with engine demand through four injectors mounted on a

Ford Electronic Fuel Injection Troubleshooting

Symptom	Possible Problem Areas
Surging, backfire, misfire, runs rough	1. EEC distributor rotor registry ① 2. EGR solenoid(s) defective 3. Distributor, cap, body, rotor, ignition wires, plugs, coil defective 4. Pulse ring behind vibration damper misaligned or damaged 5. Spark plug fouling
Stalls on deceleration	1. EGR solenoid(s) or valve defective 2. EEC distributor rotor registry ①
Stalls at idle	1. Idle speed wrong 2. Throttle kicker not working
Hesitates on acceleration	1. Acceleration enrichment system defective 2. Fuel pump ballast bypass relay not working
Fuel pump noisy	1. Fuel pump ballast bypass relay not working
Engine won't start	1. Fuel pump power relay defective, no spark, EGR system defective, no or low fuel pressure 2. Crankshaft position sensor not seated, clearance wrong, defective 3. Pulse ring behind vibration damper misaligned, sensor tabs damaged 4. Power and ground wires open or shorted, poor electrical connections 5. Inertia switch tripped
Engine starts and stalls or runs rough	1. Fuel pump ballast wire defective 2. Manifold absolute pressure (MAP) sensor circuit not working 3. Low fuel pressure 4. EGR system problem 5. Microprocessor and calibration assembly faulty
Starts hard when cold	1. Cranking signal circuit faulty

tuned intake manifold. A blow-through turbocharger system is utilized to reduce fuel delivery time and increase power.

An on board vehicle electronic engine control (EEC) computer accepts inputs from various engine sensors to compute the required fuel flow rate necessary to maintain a prescribed air/fuel ration throughout the entire engine operational range. The computer then outputs a command to the fuel injectors to meter the approximate quantity of fuel.

Operation

The fuel delivery sub-system consists of a high pressure, chassis mounted, electric fuel pump delivering fuel from the fuel tank through a 20 micron fuel filter to a fuel charging manifold assembly.

The fuel charging manifold assembly incorporates electrically actuated fuel injectors directly above each of the engine's four intake ports. The injectors, when energized, spray a metered quantity of fuel into the intake air stream.

A constant fuel pressure drop is maintained across the injector nozzles by a pressure regulator. The regulator is connected in series with the fuel injectors and positioned down stream from them. Excess fuel supplied by the pump, but not required by the engine, passes through the regulator and returns to the fuel tank through a fuel return line.

All injectors are energized simultaneously, once every crankshaft revolution. The period of time that the injectors are energized (injector on-time or the pulse width) is controlled by the vehicles' Engine Electronic Control (EEC) computer. Air entering the engine is measured by a vane air flow meter located between the air cleaner and the fuel charging manifold assembly. This air flow information and input from various other engine sensors is used to compute the required fuel flow rate necessary to maintain a prescribed air/fuel ratio for the given en-

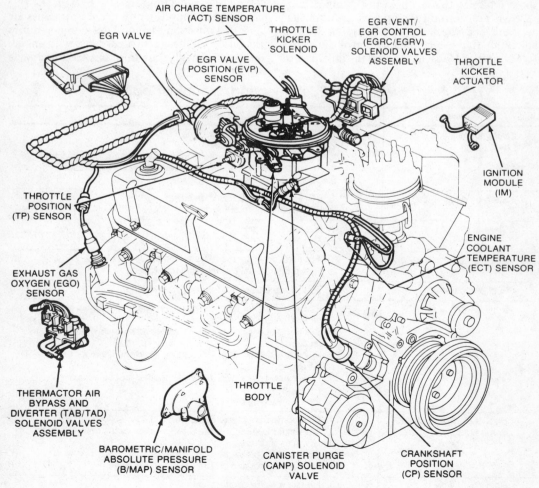

EFI wiring and vacuum diagram

gine operation. The computer determines the needed injector pulse width and outputs a commend to the injector to meter the exact quantity of fuel.

COMPONENT DESCRIPTION

Fuel Injectors

The fuel injector nozzles are electro-mechanical devices which both meter and atomize fuel delivered to the engine. The injectors are mounted in the lower intake manifold and are positioned so that their tips are directing fuel just ahead of the engine intake valves. The injector bodies consist of a solenoid actuated pintle and needle valve assembly. An electrical control signal from the Electronic Engine Control unit activates the injector solenoid causing the pintle to move inward off the seat, allowing fuel to flow. Since the injector flow orifice is fixed and the fuel pressure drop across the injector tip is constant, fuel flow to the engine is regulated by how long the solenoid is energized. Atomization is obtained by countouring the pintle at the point where the fuel separates.

Fuel Pressure Regulator

The fuel pressure regulator is attached to the fuel supply manifold assembly downstream of the fuel injectors. It regulates the fuel pressure supplied to the injectors. The regulator is a diaphragm operated relief valve in which one side of the diaphragm senses fuel pressure and the other side is subjected to intake manifold pressure. The nominal fuel pressure is established by a spring preload applied to the diaphragm. Balancing one side of the diaphragm with manifold pressure maintains a constant fuel pressure drop across the injectors. Fuel, in excess of that used by the engine, is bypassed through the regulator and returns to the fuel tank.

Air Vane Meter Assembly

The air vane meter assembly is located between the air cleaner and the throttle body and is mounted on a bracket near the LH shock tower. The vane air meter contains two sensors which furnish input to the Electronic Control Assembly; a vane airflow sensor and a vane air temperature. The air vane meter measures the mass of air flow to the engine. Air flow through the body moves a vane mounted on a pivot pin. This vane is connected to a variable resistor (potentiometer) which in turn is connected to a 5 volt reference voltage. The output of this potentiometer varies depending on the volume of air flowing through the sensor. The temperature sensor in the air vane meter measures the incoming air temperature. These two inputs, air volume and temperature, are used by the

Electronic Control Assembly to compute the mass air flow. This valve is then used to compute the fuel flow necessary for the optimum air/fuel ratio which is fed to the injectors.

Air Throttle Body Assembly

The throttle body assembly controls air flow to the engine through a single butterfly-type valve. The throttle position is controlled by conventional cable/cam throttle linkage. The body is a single piece die casting made of aluminum. It has a single bore with an air bypass channel around the throttle plate. This by-pass channel controls both cold and warm engine idle air flow control as regulated by an air bypass valve assembly mounted directly to the throttle body. The valve assembly is an electromechanical device controlled by the EEC computer. It incorporates a linear actuator which positions a variable area metering valve.

Other features of the air throttle body assembly include:

- An adjustment screw to set the throttle plate at a minimum idle airflow position.
- A preset stop to locate the WOT position.
- A throttle body mounted throttle position sensor.
- A PCV fresh air source located up-stream of the throttle plate.
- Individual ported vacuum taps (as required) for PCV and EVAP control signals.

Fuel Supply Manifold Assembly

The fuel supply manifold assembly is the component that delivers high pressure fuel from the vehicle fuel supply line to the four fuel injectors. The assembly consists of a single preformed tube or stamping with four injector connector, a mounting flange for the fuel pressure regulator, a pressure relief valve for diagnostic testing or field service fuel system pressure bleed down and mounting attachments which locate the fuel manifold assembly and provide fuel injector retention.

Air Intake Manifold

The air intake manifold is a two piece (upper and lower intake manifold) aluminum casting. Runner lengths are turned to optimize engine torque and power output. The manifold provides mounting flanges for the air throttle body assembly, fuel supply manifold and accelerator control bracket and the EGR valve and supply tube. Vacuum taps are provided to support various engine accessories. Pockets for the fuel injectors are machined to prevent both air and fuel leakage. The pockets, in which the injectors are mounted, are placed to direct the injector fuel spray immediately in front of each engine intake valve.

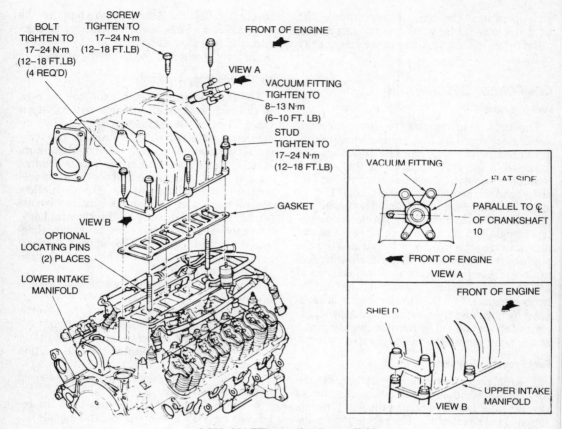

8-302, 351 EFI upper intake manifold

Relieving Fuel System Pressure

NOTE: *A special tool is necessary for this procedure.*

1. Make sure the ignition switch is in the OFF position.
2. Disconnect the battery ground.
3. Remove the fuel filler cap.
4. Using EFI Pressure Gauge T80L-9974-A, or equivalent, at the fuel pressure relief valve (located in the fuel line in the upper right corner of the engine compartment) relieve the fuel system pressure. A valve cap must first be removed to gain access to the pressure relief valve.

Air Bypass Valve

REMOVAL AND INSTALLATION

1. Disconnect the wiring at the valve.
2. Remove the 2 retaining screws and lift off the valve.
3. Discard the gasket and clean and inspect the mating surfaces.
4. Install the valve with a new gasket, tightening the screws to 102 in. lbs.
5. Connect the wiring.

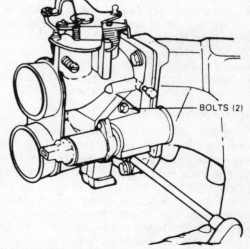

8-302, 351 EFI air bypass valve

Air Intake Throttle Body

REMOVAL AND INSTALLATION

1. Disconnect the air intake hose.
2. Disconnect the throttle position sensor and air by-pass valve connectors.

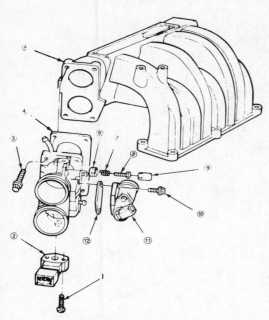

1. Screw and washer assembly—M4 × 22
2. Throttle position sensor
3. Bolt—5 16–18 × 1.25
4. Gasket—air intake charge throttle
5. Manifold—intake upper
6. Plug—throttle plate set screw locking
7. Spring—throttle plate set screw
8. Screw—10.32 × 1 50 hex head slotted
9. Cap—throttle plate set screw
10. Bolt—M6 × 20
11. Air bypass valve assembly
12. Gasket—air bypass

8-302, 351 throttle body removal

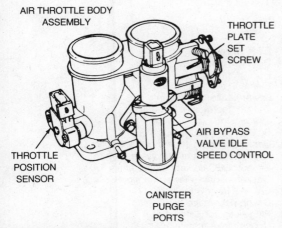

AIR THROTTLE BODY
ASSEMBLY

THROTTLE
PLATE
SET
SCREW

THROTTLE
POSITION
SENSOR

AIR BYPASS
VALVE IDLE
SPEED CONTROL

CANISTER
PURGE
PORTS

8-302, 351 air throttle body

3. Remove the four throttle body mounting nuts and carefully separate the air throttle body from the upper intake manifold.

4. Remove and discard the mounting gasket. Clean all mounting surfaces using care not to damage the gasket surfaces of the throttle body and manifold. Do not allow any material to drop into the intake manifold.

5. Install the throttle body in the reverse order of removal. The mounting nuts are tightened to 12-18 ft. lbs.

Fuel Charging Assembly

REMOVAL AND INSTALLATION

1. Relieve the fuel system pressure.

2. Disconnect the battery ground cable and drain the cooling system.

CAUTION: *When draining the coolant, keep in mind that cats and dogs are attracted by the ethylene glycol antifreeze, and are quite likely to drink any that is left in an uncovered container or in puddles on the ground. This will prove fatal in sufficient quantity. Always drain the coolant into a sealable container. Coolant should be reused unless it is contaminated or several years old.*

3. Label and disconnect the wiring at the:
● Throttle position sensor
● Air bypass valve
● EGR sensor

4. Label and disconnect the following vaccum connectors:
● EGR valve
● Fuel pressure regulator
● Upper intake manifold vacuum tree

5. Disconnect the PCV hose at the upper intake manifold.

6. Remove the throttle linkage at the throttle ball and AOD transmission linkage at the throttle body.

7. Unbolt the cable bracket from the manifold and position the cables and bracket away from the engine.

8. Disconnect the 2 canister purge lines at the throttle body.

9. Disconnect the water heater lines from the throttle body.

10. Remove the EGR tube.

11. Remove the screw and washer which retains the upper intake manifold support bracket to the upper intake manifold.

12. Remove the 6 bolts which retain the upper intake manifold.

13. Remove the upper intake manifold assembly from the lower intake manifold.

14. Remove the distributor. (See Chapter 3).

15. Disconnect the wiring at the:
● Engine coolant temperature sensor.
● Engine temperature sending unit.
● Air charge temperature sensor.
● Knock sensor.
● Electrical vacuum regulator.
● Thermactor solenoids.

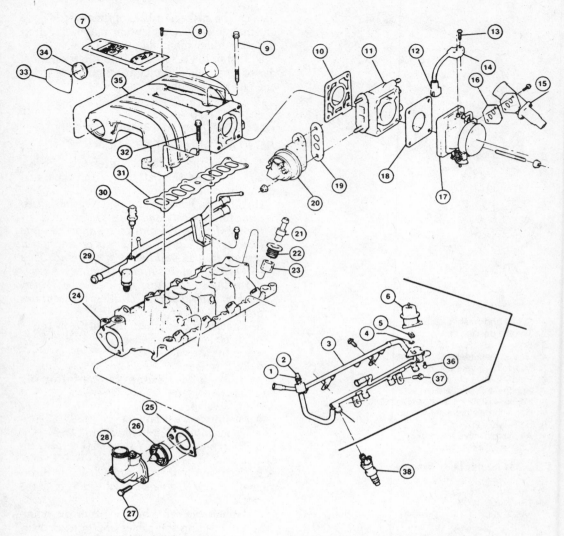

1. Schrader valve
2. Cap-Schrader valve
3. Fuel rail assy
4. Seal O-ring $\frac{5}{16}$-18 × 6.07 inch
5. Gasket, fuel pressure regulator
6. Fuel pressure regulator
7. Cover, upper manifold
8. Screw
9. Bolt $\frac{5}{16}$-18 × 6.07 inch
10. Gasket, EGR spacer
11. EGR spacer
12. Connector, tp sensor (pia tps)
13. Screw
14. Sensor, throttle position
15. Throttle air bypass valve
16. Gasket, throttle air bypass valve
17. Throttle body assy
18. Gasket, throttle body
19. Gasket, EGR valve
20. EGR valve assy
21. PCV valve assy
22. PCV grommet
23. Element, crankcase vent
24. Lower intake manifold
25. Gasket, thermostat housing
26. Thermostat
27. Bolt $\frac{5}{16}$-18 × 3.50 inch
28. Connector assy, engine coolant outlet
29. Tube, heater water supply and return
30. Sensor, EEC coolant temperature
31. Gasket, upper to lower manifold
32. Bolt $\frac{5}{16}$-18 × 1.62 inch
33. Cover, decorative end
34. Plug—cap 1.75 inch dia.
35. Upper intake manifold
36. Screw—socket head 5.0 × 0.8 × 1.0
37. Botl, att rail assy to lower manifold
38. Fuel injector

Fuel injection components used on the 1987 8-302

16. Disconnect the injector wiring harness at the main harness.

17. Remove the EGO ground wire at its intake manifold stud. Note the position of the stud and bround wire for installation.

18. Disconnect the fuel supply and return lines from the fuel rails using tool T81P-19623-G or G1.

19. Remove the upper radiator hose.

20. Remove the coolant bypass hose.

21. Disconnect the heater outlet hose at the manifold.

22. Remove the air cleaner bracket.

23. Remove the coil.

24. Noting the location of each bolt, remove the intkae manifold retaining bolts.

25. Remove the lower intake manifold from the head.

26. Clean and inspect all mating surfaces. All surfaces MUST be flat and free from debris or damage!

27. Clean and oil all fastener threads.

28. Place a $\frac{1}{16}$" bead of RTV silicone sealant to the end seals' junctions.

29. Position the end seals on the block.

30. Install 2 locator pins at opposite corners of the block.

31. Position the lower manifold on the head using new gaskets. Install the bolts and remove the locating pins.

32. Tighten the bolts to 25 ft. lbs. in sequence. Wait ten minutes and retorque the bolts in sequence.

33. Install the coil.

34. Connect the cooling system hoses.

35. Connect the fuel supply and return lines.

36. Connect the wiring at the:
- Engine coolant temperature sensor.
- Engine temperature sending unit.
- Air charge temperature sensor.
- Knock sensor.
- Electrical vacuum regulator.
- Thermactor solenoids.

37. Install the distributor.

38. Position the upper manifold and new gasket on the lower manifold. Install the fasteners finger tight.

39. Install the upper intake manifold support on the manifold and tighten the retaing screw to 30 ft. lbs.

40. Torque the upper-to-lower manifold fasteners to 18 ft. lbs.

41. Install the EGR tube. Torque the fittings to 35 ft. lbs.

42. Install the canister purge lines at the throttle body.

43. Connect the water heater lines at the throttle body.

44. Connect the PCV hose.

45. Install the accelerator cable and throttle linkages.

46. Connect the vacuum hoses.

47. Connect the electrical wiring.

48. Connect the air intake hose, air bypas hose and crankcase vent hose.

49. Connect the battery ground.

50. Refill the cooling system.

51. Install the fuel pressure relief cap. Turn the ignition switch from **OFF** to **ON** at least half a dozen times, **WITHOUT STARTING THE ENGINE**, leaving it in the ON position for about 5 seconds each time. This will build up fuel pressure in the system.

52. Start the engine and allow it to run at idle until normal operating temperature is reached. Check for leaks.

Fuel Injectors
REMOVAL AND INSTALLATION

1. Relieve the fuel system pressure.

2. Disconnect the battery ground.

3. Remove the upper intake manifold.

4. Disconnect the wiring at the injectors.

5. Pull upward on the injector body while gently rocking it from side-to-side.

6. Inspect the O-rings on the injector for any sign of leakage or damage. Replace any suspected O-rings.

7. Inspect the plastic cap at the top of each injector and replace it if any sign of deterioration is noticed.

8. Lubricate the O-rings with clean engine oil ONLY!

9. Install the injectors by pushing them in with a gentle rocking motion.

10. Install the fuel supply manifold.

11. Connect the electrical wiring.

12. Install the upper intake manifold.

Fuel Pressure Regulator
REMOVAL AND INSTALLATION

1. Relieve the fuel system pressure.

2. Disconnect the vacuum line at the regulator.

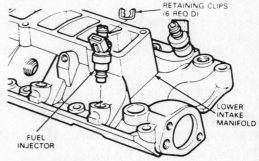

8-320, 351 EFI fuel injector

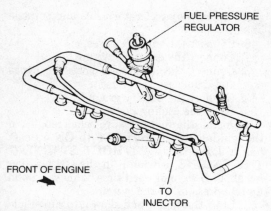

8-302, 351 fuel pressure regulator

3. Remove the 3 allen screws from the regulator housing.

4. Remove the regulator.

5. Inspect the regulator O-ring for signs of deterioration or damage. Discard the gasket.

6. Lubricate the O-ring with clean engine oil ONLY!

7. Make sure that the mounting surfaces are clean.

8. Using a new gasket, install the regulator. Tighten the retaining screws to 40 in. lbs.

9. Connect the vacuum line.

Fuel Supply Manifold

REMOVAL AND INSTALLATION

1. Relieve the fuel system pressure.

2. Remove the upper manifold.

3. Disconnect the chassis fuel inlet and outlet lines at the fuel supply manifold using tool T81P-19623-G or G1.

4. Disconnect the fuel supply and return lines at the fuel supply manifold.

5. Remove the 4 fuel supply manifold retaining bolts.

6. Carefully disengage the manifold from the injectors and lift it off.

7. Inspect all components for signs of damage. Make sure that the injector caps are clean.

8. Place the fuel supply manifold over the injectors and seat the injectors carefully in the manifold.

9. Install the 4 bolts and torque them to 20 ft. lbs.

10. Connect the fuel lines.

11. Install the upper manifold.

Lower Intake Manifold

REMOVAL AND INSTALLATION

1. Relieve the fuel system pressure.

2. Disconnect the battery ground cable and drain the cooling system.

CAUTION: *When draining the coolant, keep in mind that cats and dogs are attracted by the ethylene glycol antifreeze, and are quite likely to drink any that is left in an uncovered container or in puddles on the ground. This will prove fatal in sufficient quantity. Always drain the coolant into a sealable container. Coolant should be reused unless it is contaminated or several years old.*

3. Label and disconnect the wiring at the:
- Throttle position sensor
- Air bypass valve
- EGR sensor

4. Label and disconnect the following vacuum connectors:
- EGR valve
- Fuel pressure regulator
- Upper intake manifold vacuum tree

5. Disconnect the PCV hose at the upper intake manifold.

6. Remove the throttle linkage at the throttle ball and AOD transmission linkage at the throttle body.

7. Unbolt the cable bracket from the manifold and position the cables and bracket away from the engine.

8. Disconnect the 2 canister purge lines at the throttle body.

9. Disconnect the water heater lines from the throttle body.

10. Remove the EGR tube.

11. Remove the screw and washer which retains the upper intake manifold support bracket to the upper intake manifold.

12. Remove the 6 bolts which retain the upper intake manifold.

13. Remove the upper intake manifold assembly from the lower intake manifold.

14. Remove the distributor. (See Chapter 3).

15. Disconnect the wiring at the:
- Engine coolant temperature sensor.
- Engine temperature sending unit.
- Air charge temperature sensor.
- Knock sensor.
- Electrical vacuum regulator.
- Thermactor solenoids.

16. Disconnect the injector wiring harness at the main harness.

17. Remove the EGO ground wire at its intake manifold stud. Note the position of the stud and bround wire for installation.

18. Disconnect the fuel supply and return lines from the fuel rails using tool T81P-19623-G or G1.

19. Remove the upper radiator hose.

20. Remove the coolant bypass hose.

21. Disconnect the heater outlet hose at the manifold.

22. Remove the air cleaner bracket.

23. Remove the coil.

24. Noting the location of each bolt, remove the intkae manifold retaining bolts.

25. Remove the lower intake manifold from the head.

26. Clean and inspect all mating surfaces. All surfaces MUST be flat and free from debris or damage!

27. Clean and oil all fastener threads.

28. Place a $\frac{1}{16}$" bead of RTV silicone sealant to the end seals' junctions.

29. Position the end seals on the block.

30. Install 2 locator pins at opposite corners of the block.

31. Position the lower manifold on the head using new gaskets. Install the bolts and remove the locating pins.

32. Tighten the bolts to 25 ft. lbs. in sequence. Wait ten minutes and retorque the bolts in sequence.

33. Install the coil.

34. Connect the cooling system hoses.

35. Connect the fuel supply and return lines.

36. Connect the wiring at the:
- Engine coolant temperature sensor.
- Engine temperature sending unit.
- Air charge temperature sensor.
- Knock sensor.
- Electrical vacuum regulator.
- Thermactor solenoids.

37. Install the distributor.

38. Position the upper manifold and new gasket on the lower manifold. Install the fasteners finger tight.

39. Install the upper intake manifold support on the manifold and tighten the retaing screw to 30 ft. lbs.

40. Torque the upper-to-lower manifold fasteners to 18 ft. lbs.

41. Install the EGR tube. Torque the fittings to 35 ft. lbs.

42. Install the canister purge lines at the throttle body.

43. Connect the water heater lines at the throttle body.

44. Connect the PCV hose.

45. Install the accelerator cable and throttle linkages.

46. Connect the vacuum hoses.

47. Connect the electrical wiring.

48. Connect the air intake hose, air bypas hose and crankcase vent hose.

49. Connect the battery ground.

50. Refill the cooling system.

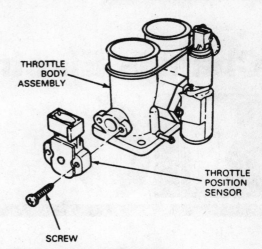

8-302, 351 throttle position sensor

51. Install the fuel pressure relief cap. Turn the ignition switch from **OFF** to **ON** at least half a dozen times, **WITHOUT STARTING THE ENGINE**, leaving it in the ON position for about 5 seconds each time. This will build up fuel pressure in the system.

52. Start the engine and allow it to run at idle until normal operating temperature is reached. Check for leaks.

Throttle Position Sensor

REMOVAL AND INSTALLATION

1. Disconnect the wiring harness from the TPS.

2. Matchmark the sensor and throttle body for installation reference.

3. Remove the 2 retaining screws and remove the TPS.

4. Install the TPS so that the wiring harness is parallel with the venturi bores, then, rotate the TPS clockwise to align the scribe marks.

CAUTION: *Slide the rotary tangs into position over the throttle shaft blade, then rotate the TPS CLOCKWISE ONLY to the installed position. FAILURE TO INSTALL THE TPS IN THIS MANNER WILL RESULT IN EXCESSIVE IDLE SPEEDS!*

5. Tighten the retaining screws to 16 in. lbs.

NOTE: *When correctly installed, the TPS wirning harness should be pointing directly at the air bypass valve.*

6. Connect the wiring.

Chassis Electrical

UNDERSTANDING AND TROUBLESHOOTING ELECTRICAL SYSTEMS

At the rate with which both import and domestic manufacturers are incorporating electronic control systems into their production lines, it won't be long before every new vehicle is equipped with one or more on-board computer. These electronic components (with no moving parts) should theoretically last the life of the vehicle, provided nothing external happens to damage the circuits or memory chips.

While it is true that electronic components should never wear out, in the real world malfunctions do occur. It is also true that any computer-based system is extremely sensitive to electrical voltages and cannot tolerate careless or haphazard testing or service procedures. An inexperienced individual can literally do major damage looking for a minor problem by using the wrong kind of test equipment or connecting test leads or connectors with the ignition switch ON. When selecting test equipment, make sure the manufacturers instructions state that the tester is compatible with whatever type of electronic control system is being serviced. Read all instructions carefully and double check all test points before installing probes or making any test connections.

The following section outlines basic diagnosis techniques for dealing with computerized automotive control systems. Along with a general explanation of the various types of test equipment available to aid in servicing modern electronic automotive systems, basic repair techniques for wiring harnesses and connectors is given. Read the basic information before attempting any repairs or testing on any computerized system, to provide the background of information necessary to avoid the most common and obvious mistakes that can cost both time and money. Although the replacement and testing procedures are simple in themselves, the systems are not, and unless one has a thorough understanding of all components and their function within a particular computerized control system, the logical test sequence these systems demand cannot be followed. Minor malfunctions can make a big difference, so it is important to know how each component affects the operation of the overall electronic system to find the ultimate cause of a problem without replacing good components unnecessarily. It is not enough to use the correct test equipment; the test equipment must be used correctly.

Safety Precautions

CAUTION: *Whenever working on or around any computer based microprocessor control system, always observe these general precautions to prevent the possibility of personal injury or damage to electronic components.*

• Never install or remove battery cables with the key ON or the engine running. Jumper cables should be connected with the key OFF to avoid power surges that can damage electronic control units. Engines equipped with computer controlled systems should avoid both giving and getting jump starts due to the possibility of serious damage to components from arcing in the engine compartment when connections are made with the ignition ON.

• Always remove the battery cables before charging the battery. Never use a high output charger on an installed battery or attempt to use any type of "hot shot" (24 volt) starting aid.

• Exercise care when inserting test probes into connectors to insure good connections without damaging the connector or spreading the pins. Always probe connectors from the rear (wire) side, NOT the pin side, to avoid accidental shorting of terminals during test procedures.

• Never remove or attach wiring harness connectors with the ignition switch ON, especially to an electronic control unit.

• Do not drop any components during service procedures and never apply 12 volts directly to any component (like a solenoid or relay) unless instructed specifically to do so. Some component electrical windings are designed to safely handle only 4 or 5 volts and can be destroyed in seconds if 12 volts are applied directly to the connector.

• Remove the electronic control unit if the vehicle is to be placed in an environment where temperatures exceed approximately 176°F (80°C), such as a paint spray booth or when arc or gas welding near the control unit location in the car.

ORGANIZED TROUBLESHOOTING

When diagnosing a specific problem, organized troubleshooting is a must. The complexity of a modern automobile demands that you approach any problem in a logical, organized manner. There are certain troubleshooting techniques that are standard:

1. Establish when the problem occurs. Does the problem appear only under certain conditions? Were there any noises, odors, or other unusual symptoms?

2. Isolate the problem area. To do this, make some simple tests and observations; then eliminate the systems that are working properly. Check for obvious problems such as broken wires, dirty connections or split or disconnected vacuum hoses. Always check the obvious before assuming something complicated is the cause.

3. Test for problems systematically to determine the cause once the problem area is isolated. Are all the components functioning properly? Is there power going to electrical switches and motors? Is there vacuum at vacuum switches and/or actuators? Is there a mechanical problem such as bent linkage or loose mounting screws? Doing careful, systematic checks will often turn up most causes on the first inspection without wasting time checking components that have little or no relationship to the problem.

4. Test all repairs after the work is done to make sure that the problem is fixed. Some causes can be traced to more than one component, so a careful verification of repair work is important to pick up additional malfunctions that may cause a problem to reappear or a different problem to arise. A blown fuse, for example, is a simple problem that may require more than another fuse to repair. If you don't look for a problem that caused a fuse to blow, for example, a shorted wire may go undetected.

Experience has shown that most problems tend to be the result of a fairly simple and obvious cause, such as loose or corroded connectors or air leaks in the intake system; making careful inspection of components during testing essential to quick and accurate troubleshooting. Special, hand held computerized testers designed specifically for diagnosing the EEC-IV system are available from a variety of aftermarket sources, as well as from the vehicle manufacturer, but care should be taken that any test equipment being used is designed to diagnose that particular computer controlled system accurately without damaging the control unit (ECU) or components being tested.

NOTE: *Pinpointing the exact cause of trouble in an electrical system can sometimes only be accomplished by the use of special test equipment. The following describes commonly used test equipment and explains how to put it to best use in diagnosis. In addition to the information covered below, the manufacturer's instructions booklet provided with the tester should be read and clearly understood before attempting any test procedures.*

TEST EQUIPMENT

Jumper Wires

Jumper wires are simple, yet extremely valuable, pieces of test equipment. Jumper wires are merely wires that are used to bypass sections of a circuit. The simplest type of jumper wire is merely a length of multistrand wire with an alligator clip at each end. Jumper wires are usually fabricated from lengths of standard automotive wire and whatever type of connector (alligator clip, spade connector or pin connector) that is required for the particular vehicle being tested. The well equipped tool box will have several different styles of jumper wires in several different lengths. Some jumper wires are made with three or more terminals coming from a common splice for special purpose testing. In cramped, hard-to-reach areas it is advisable to have insulated boots over the jumper wire terminals in order to prevent accidental grounding, sparks, and possible fire, especially when testing fuel system components.

Jumper wires are used primarily to locate open electrical circuits, on either the ground (-) side of the circuit or on the hot (+) side. If an electrical component fails to operate, connect the jumper wire between the component and a good ground. If the component operates only with the jumper installed, the ground circuit is open. If the ground circuit is good, but the component does not operate, the circuit between the power feed and component is open. You can sometimes connect the jumper wire directly from the battery to the hot terminal of the component, but first make sure the component uses 12 volts in operation. Some electrical components, such as fuel injectors, are designed to operate on about 4 volts and running 12 volts directly to the injector terminals can burn out the wiring. By inserting an inline fuseholder between a set of test leads, a fused jumper wire can be used for bypassing open circuits. Use a 5 amp fuse to provide protection against voltage spikes. When in doubt, use a voltmeter to check the voltage input to the component and measure how much voltage is being applied normally. By moving the jumper wire successively back from the lamp toward the power source, you can isolate the area of the circuit where the open is located. When the component stops functioning, or the power is cut off, the open is in the segment of wire between the jumper and the point previously tested.

CAUTION: *Never use jumpers made from wire that is of lighter gauge than used in the circuit under test. If the jumper wire is of too small gauge, it may overheat and possibly melt. Never use jumpers to bypass high resistance loads (such as motors) in a circuit. Bypassing resistances, in effect, creates a short circuit which may, in turn, cause damage and fire. Never use a jumper for anything other than temporary bypassing of components in a circuit.*

12 Volt Test Light

The 12 volt test light is used to check circuits and components while electrical current is flowing through them. It is used for voltage and ground tests. Twelve volt test lights come in different styles but all have three main parts; a ground clip, a probe, and a light. The most commonly used 12 volt test lights have pick-type probes. To use a 12 volt test light, connect the ground clip to a good ground and probe wherever necessary with the pick. The pick should be sharp so that it can penetrate wire insulation to make contact with the wire, without making a large hole in the insulation. The wrap-around light is handy in hard to reach areas or where it is difficult to support a wire to push a probe pick into it. To use the wrap around light, hook the wire to probed with the hook and pull the trigger. A small pick will be forced through the wire insulation into the wire core.

CAUTION: *Do not use a test light to probe electronic ignition spark plug or coil wires. Never use a pick-type test light to probe wiring on computer controlled systems unless specifically instructed to do so. Any wire insulation that is pierced by the test light probe should be taped and sealed with silicone after testing.*

Like the jumper wire, the 12 volt test light is

used to isolate opens in circuits. But, whereas the jumper wire is used to bypass the open to operate the load, the 12 volt test light is used to locate the presence of voltage in a circuit. If the test light glows, you know that there is power up to that point; if the 12 volt test light does not glow when its probe is inserted into the wire or connector, you know that there is an open circuit (no power). Move the test light in successive steps back toward the power source until the light in the handle does glow. When it does glow, the open is between the probe and point previously probed.

NOTE: *The test light does not detect that 12 volts (or any particular amount of voltage) is present; it only detects that some voltage is present. It is advisable before using the test light to touch its terminals across the battery posts to make sure the light is operating properly.*

Self-Powered Test Light

The self-powered test light usually contains a 1.5 volt penlight battery. One type of self-powered test light is similar in design to the 12 volt test light. This type has both the battery and the light in the handle and pick-type probe tip. The second type has the light toward the open tip, so that the light illuminates the contact point. The self-powered test light is dual purpose piece of test equipment. It can be used to test for either open or short circuits when power is isolated from the circuit (continuity test). A powered test light should not be used on any computer controlled system or component unless specifically instructed to do so. Many engine sensors can be destroyed by even this small amount of voltage applied directly to the terminals.

Open Circuit Testing

To use the self-powered test light to check for open circuits, first isolate the circuit from the vehicle's 12 volt power source by disconnecting the battery or wiring harness connector. Connect the test light ground clip to a good ground and probe sections of the circuit sequentially with the test light. (start from either end of the circuit). If the light is out, the open is between the probe and the circuit ground. If the light is on, the open is between the probe and end of the circuit toward the power source.

Short Circuit Testing

By isolating the circuit both from power and from ground, and using a self-powered test light, you can check for shorts to ground in the circuit. Isolate the circuit from power and ground. Connect the test light ground clip to a good ground and probe any easy-to-reach test point in the circuit. If the light comes on, there is a short somewhere in the circuit. To isolate the short, probe a test point at either end of the isolated circuit (the light should be on). Leave the test light probe connected and open connectors, switches, remove parts, etc., sequentially, until the light goes out. When the light goes out, the short is between the last circuit component opened and the previous circuit opened.

NOTE: *The 1.5 volt battery in the test light does not provide much current. A weak battery may not provide enough power to illuminate the test light even when a complete circuit is made (especially if there are high resistances in the circuit). Always make sure that the test battery is strong. To check the battery, briefly touch the ground clip to the probe; if the light glows brightly the battery is strong enough for testing. Never use a self-powered test light to perform checks for opens or shorts when power is applied to the electrical system under test. The 12 volt vehicle power will quickly burn out the 1.5 volt light bulb in the test light.*

Voltmeter

A voltmeter is used to measure voltage at any point in a circuit, or to measure the voltage drop across any part of a circuit. It can also be used to check continuity in a wire or circuit by indicating current flow from one end to the other. Voltmeters usually have various scales on the meter dial and a selector switch to allow the selection of different voltages. The voltmeter has a positive and a negative lead. To avoid damage to the meter, always connect the negative lead to the negative (-) side of circuit (to ground or nearest the ground side of the circuit) and connect the positive lead to the positive (+) side of the circuit (to the power source or the nearest power source). Note that the negative voltmeter lead will always be black and that the positive voltmeter will always be some color other than black (usually red). Depending on how the voltmeter is connected into the circuit, it has several uses.

A voltmeter can be connected either in parallel or in series with a circuit and it has a very high resistance to current flow. When connected in parallel, only a small amount of current will flow through the voltmeter current path; the rest will flow through the normal circuit current path and the circuit will work normally. When the voltmeter is connected in series with a circuit, only a small amount of current can flow through the circuit. The circuit will not work properly, but the voltmeter reading will show if the circuit is complete or not.

Available Voltage Measurement

Set the voltmeter selector switch to the 20V position and connect the meter negative lead to the negative post of the battery. Connect the positive meter lead to the positive post of the battery and turn the ignition switch ON to provide a load. Read the voltage on the meter or digital display. A well charged battery should register over 12 volts. If the meter reads below 11.5 volts, the battery power may be insufficient to operate the electrical system properly. This test determines voltage available from the battery and should be the first step in any electrical trouble diagnosis procedure. Many electrical problems, especially on computer controlled systems, can be caused by a low state of charge in the battery. Excessive corrosion at the battery cable terminals can cause a poor contact that will prevent proper charging and full battery current flow.

Normal battery voltage is 12 volts when fully charged. When the battery is supplying current to one or more circuits it is said to be "under load". When everything is off the electrical system is under a "no-load" condition. A fully charged battery may show about 12.5 volts at no load; will drop to 12 volts under medium load; and will drop even lower under heavy load. If the battery is partially discharged the voltage decrease under heavy load may be excessive, even though the battery shows 12 volts or more at no load. When allowed to discharge further, the battery's available voltage under load will decrease more severely. For this reason, it is important that the battery be fully charged during all testing procedures to avoid errors in diagnosis and incorrect test results.

Voltage Drop

When current flows through a resistance, the voltage beyond the resistance is reduced (the larger the current, the greater the reduction in voltage). When no current is flowing, there is no voltage drop because there is no current flow. All points in the circuit which are connected to the power source are at the same voltage as the power source. The total voltage drop always equals the total source voltage. In a long circuit with many connectors, a series of small, unwanted voltage drops due to corrosion at the connectors can add up to a total loss of voltage which impairs the operation of the normal loads in the circuit.

INDIRECT COMPUTATION OF VOLTAGE DROPS

1. Set the voltmeter selector switch to the 20 volt position.

2. Connect the meter negative lead to a good ground.

3. Probe all resistances in the circuit with the positive meter lead.

4. Operate the circuit in all modes and observe the voltage readings.

DIRECT MEASUREMENT OF VOLTAGE DROPS

1. Set the voltmeter switch to the 20 volt position.

2. Connect the voltmeter negative lead to the ground side of the resistance load to be measured.

3. Connect the positive lead to the positive side of the resistance or load to be measured.

4. Read the voltage drop directly on the 20 volt scale.

Too high a voltage indicates too high a resistance. If, for example, a blower motor runs too slowly, you can determine if there is too high a resistance in the resistor pack. By taking voltage drop readings in all parts of the circuit, you can isolate the problem. Too low a voltage drop indicates too low a resistance. If, for example, a blower motor runs too fast in the MED and/or LOW position, the problem can be isolated in the resistor pack by taking voltage drop readings in all parts of the circuit to locate a possibly shorted resistor. The maximum allowable voltage drop under load is critical, especially if there is more than one high resistance problem in a circuit because all voltage drops are cumulative. A small drop is normal due to the resistance of the conductors.

HIGH RESISTANCE TESTING

1. Set the voltmeter selector switch to the 4 volt position.

2. Connect the voltmeter positive lead to the positive post of the battery.

3. Turn on the headlights and heater blower to provide a load.

4. Probe various points in the circuit with the negative voltmeter lead.

5. Read the voltage drop on the 4 volt scale. Some average maximum allowable voltage drops are:

FUSE PANEL – 7 volts
IGNITION SWITCH – 5 volts
HEADLIGHT SWITCH – 7 volts
IGNITION COIL (+) – 5 volts
ANY OTHER LOAD – 1.3 volts

NOTE: *Voltage drops are all measured while a load is operating; without current flow, there will be no voltage drop.*

Ohmmeter

The ohmmeter is designed to read resistance (ohms) in a circuit or component. Although there are several different styles of ohmmeters, all will usually have a selector switch which permits the measurement of different ranges of resistance (usually the selector switch allows the multiplication of the meter reading by 10, 100, 1000, and 10,000). A calibration knob allows the meter to be set at zero for accurate measurement. Since all ohmmeters are powered by an internal battery (usually 9 volts), the ohmmeter can be used as a self-powered test light. When the ohmmeter is connected, current from the ohmmeter flows through the circuit or component being tested. Since the ohmmeter's internal resistance and voltage are known values, the amount of current flow through the meter depends on the resistance of the circuit or component being tested.

The ohmmeter can be used to perform continuity test for opens or shorts (either by observation of the meter needle or as a self-powered test light), and to read actual resistance in a circuit. It should be noted that the ohmmeter is used to check the resistance of a component or wire while there is no voltage applied to the circuit. Current flow from an outside voltage source (such as the vehicle battery) can damage the ohmmeter, so the circuit or component should be isolated from the vehicle electrical system before any testing is done. Since the ohmmeter uses its own voltage source, either lead can be connected to any test point.

NOTE: *When checking diodes or other solid state components, the ohmmeter leads can only be connected one way in order to measure current flow in a single direction. Make sure the positive (+) and negative (-) terminal connections are as described in the test procedures to verify the one-way diode operation.*

In using the meter for making continuity checks, do not be concerned with the actual resistance readings. Zero resistance, or any resistance readings, indicate continuity in the circuit. Infinite resistance indicates an open in the circuit. A high resistance reading where there should be none indicates a problem in the circuit. Checks for short circuits are made in the same manner as checks for open circuits except that the circuit must be isolated from both power and normal ground. Infinite resistance indicates no continuity to ground, while zero resistance indicates a dead short to ground.

RESISTANCE MEASUREMENT

The batteries in an ohmmeter will weaken with age and temperature, so the ohmmeter must be calibrated or "zeroed" before taking measurements. To zero the meter, place the selector switch in its lowest range and touch the two ohmmeter leads together. Turn the calibration knob until the meter needle is exactly on zero.

NOTE: *All analog (needle) type ohmmeters*

must be zeroed before use, but some digital ohmmeter models are automatically calibrated when the switch is turned on. Self-calibrating digital ohmmeters do not have an adjusting knob, but its a good idea to check for a zero readout before use by touching the leads together. All computer controlled systems require the use of a digital ohmmeter with at least 10 meagohms impedance for testing. Before any test procedures are attempted, make sure the ohmmeter used is compatible with the electrical system or damage to the on-board computer could result.

To measure resistance, first isolate the circuit from the vehicle power source by disconnecting the battery cables or the harness connector. Make sure the key is OFF when disconnecting any components or the battery. Where necessary, also isolate at least one side of the circuit to be checked to avoid reading parallel resistances. Parallel circuit resistances will always give a lower reading than the actual resistance of either of the branches. When measuring the resistance of parallel circuits, the total resistance will always be lower than the smallest resistance in the circuit. Connect the meter leads to both sides of the circuit (wire or component) and read the actual measured ohms on the meter scale. Make sure the selector switch is set to the proper ohm scale for the circuit being tested to avoid misreading the ohmmeter test value.

CAUTION: *Never use an ohmmeter with power applied to the circuit. Like the self-powered test light, the ohmmeter is designed to operate on its own power supply. The normal 12 volt automotive electrical system current could damage the meter.*

Ammeters

An ammeter measures the amount of current flowing through a circuit in units called amperes or amps. Amperes are units of electron flow which indicate how fast the electrons are flowing through the circuit. Since Ohms Law dictates that current flow in a circuit is equal to the circuit voltage divided by the total circuit resistance, increasing voltage also increases the current level (amps). Likewise, any decrease in resistance will increase the amount of amps in a circuit. At normal operating voltage, most circuits have a characteristic amount of amperes, called "current draw" which can be measured using an ammeter. By referring to a specified current draw rating, measuring the amperes, and comparing the two values, one can determine what is happening within the circuit to aid in diagnosis. An open circuit, for example, will not allow any current to flow so the ammeter reading will be zero. More current flows

through a heavily loaded circuit or when the charging system is operating.

An ammeter is always connected in series with the circuit being tested. All of the current that normally flows through the circuit must also flow through the ammeter; if there is any other path for the current to follow, the ammeter reading will not be accurate. The ammeter itself has very little resistance to current flow and therefore will not affect the circuit, but it will measure current draw only when the circuit is closed and electricity is flowing. Excessive current draw can blow fuses and drain the battery, while a reduced current draw can cause motors to run slowly, lights to dim and other components to not operate properly. The ammeter can help diagnose these conditions by locating the cause of the high or low reading.

Multimeters

Different combinations of test meters can be built into a single unit designed for specific tests. Some of the more common combination test devices are known as Volt/Amp testers, Tach/Dwell meters, or Digital Multimeters. The Volt/Amp tester is used for charging system, starting system or battery tests and consists of a voltmeter, an ammeter and a variable resistance carbon pile. The voltmeter will usually have at least two ranges for use with 6, 12 and 24 volt systems. The ammeter also has more than one range for testing various levels of battery loads and starter current draw and the carbon pile can be adjusted to offer different amounts of resistance. The Volt/Amp tester has heavy leads to carry large amounts of current and many later models have an inductive ammeter pickup that clamps around the wire to simplify test connections. On some models, the ammeter also has a zero-center scale to allow testing of charging and starting systems without switching leads or polarity. A digital multimeter is a voltmeter, ammeter and ohmmeter combined in an instrument which gives a digital readout. These are often used when testing solid state circuits because of their high input impedance (usually 10 megohms or more).

The tach/dwell meter combines a tachometer and a dwell (cam angle) meter and is a specialized kind of voltmeter. The tachometer scale is marked to show engine speed in rpm and the dwell scale is marked to show degrees of distributor shaft rotation. In most electronic ignition systems, dwell is determined by the control unit, but the dwell meter can also be used to check the duty cycle (operation) of some electronic engine control systems. Some tach/dwell meters are powered by an internal battery, while others take their power from the car battery in use. The battery powered testers usually require calibration much like an ohmmeter before testing.

Special Test Equipment

A variety of diagnostic tools are available to help troubleshoot and repair computerized engine control systems. The most sophisticated of these devices are the console type engine analyzers that usually occupy a garage service bay, but there are several types of aftermarket electronic testers available that will allow quick circuit tests of the engine control system by plugging directly into a special connector located in the engine compartment or under the dashboard. Several tool and equipment manufacturers offer simple, hand held testers that measure various circuit voltage levels on command to check all system components for proper operation. Although these testers usually cost about $300-500, consider that the average computer control unit (or ECM) can cost just as much and the money saved by not replacing perfectly good sensors or components in an attempt to correct a problem could justify the purchase price of a special diagnostic tester the first time it's used.

These computerized testers can allow quick and easy test measurements while the engine is operating or while the car is being driven. In addition, the on-board computer memory can be read to access any stored trouble codes; in effect allowing the computer to tell you where it hurts and aid trouble diagnosis by pinpointing exactly which circuit or component is malfunctioning. In the same manner, repairs can be tested to make sure the problem has been corrected. The biggest advantage these special testers have is their relatively easy hookups that minimize or eliminate the chances of making the wrong connections and getting false voltage readings or damaging the computer accidentally.

NOTE: *It should be remembered that these testers check voltage levels in circuits; they don't detect mechanical problems or failed components if the circuit voltage falls within the preprogrammed limits stored in the tester PROM unit. Also, most of the hand held testers are designed to work only on one or two systems made by a specific manufacturer.*

A variety of aftermarket testers are available to help diagnose different computerized control systems. Owatonna Tool Company (OTC), for example, markets a device called the OTC Monitor which plugs directly into the assembly line diagnostic link (ALDL). The OTC tester makes diagnosis a simple matter of pressing the correct buttons and, by changing the internal PROM or inserting a different diagnosis cartridge, it will work on any model from full size to subcompact, over a wide range of years. An adapter is supplied with the tester to allow connection to all types of ALDL links, regardless of the number of pin terminals used. By inserting an updated PROM into the OTC tester, it can be easily updated to diagnose any new modifications of computerized control systems.

Wiring Harnesses

The average automobile contains about ½ mile of wiring, with hundreds of individual connections. To protect the many wires from damage and to keep them from becoming a confusing tangle, they are organized into bundles, enclosed in plastic or taped together and called wire harnesses. Different wiring harnesses serve different parts of the vehicle. Individual wires are color coded to help trace them through a harness where sections are hidden from view.

A loose or corroded connection or a replacement wire that is too small for the circuit will add extra resistance and an additional voltage drop to the circuit. A ten percent voltage drop can result in slow or erratic motor operation, for example, even though the circuit is complete. Automotive wiring or circuit conductors can be in any one of three forms:

1. Single strand wire
2. Multistrand wire
3. Printed circuitry

Single strand wire has a solid metal core and is usually used inside such components as alternators, motors, relays and other devices. Multistrand wire has a core made of many small strands of wire twisted together into a single conductor. Most of the wiring in an automotive electrical system is made up of multistrand wire, either as a single conductor or grouped together in a harness. All wiring is color coded on the insulator, either as a solid color or as a colored wire with an identification stripe. A printed circuit is a thin film of copper or other conductor that is printed on an insulator backing. Occasionally, a printed circuit is sandwiched between two sheets of plastic for more protection and flexibility. A complete printed circuit, consisting of conductors, insulating material and connectors for lamps or other components is called a printed circuit board. Printed circuitry is used in place of individual wires or harnesses in places where space is limited, such as behind instrument panels.

Wire Gauge

Since computer controlled automotive electrical systems are very sensitive to changes in resistance, the selection of properly sized wires is critical when systems are repaired. The wire gauge number is an expression of the cross section area of the conductor. The most common system for expressing wire size is the American Wire Gauge (AWG) system.

Wire cross section area is measured in circular mils. A mil is $\frac{1}{1000}''$ (0.001"); a circular mil is the area of a circle one mil in diameter. For example, a conductor $\frac{1}{4}''$ in diameter is 0.250 in. or 250 mils. The circular mil cross section area of the wire is 250 squared (250^2) or 62,500 circular mils. Imported car models usually use metric wire gauge designations, which is simply the cross section area of the conductor in square millimeters (mm^2).

Gauge numbers are assigned to conductors of various cross section areas. As gauge number increases, area decreases and the conductor becomes smaller. A 5 gauge conductor is smaller than a 1 gauge conductor and a 10 gauge is smaller than a 5 gauge. As the cross section area of a conductor decreases, resistance increases and so does the gauge number. A conductor with a higher gauge number will carry less current than a conductor with a lower gauge number.

NOTE: *Gauge wire size refers to the size of the conductor, not the size of the complete wire. It is possible to have two wires of the same gauge with different diameters because one may have thicker insulation than the other.*

12 volt automotive electrical systems generally use 10, 12, 14, 16 and 18 gauge wire. Main power distribution circuits and larger accessories usually use 10 and 12 gauge wire. Battery cables are usually 4 or 6 gauge, although 1 and 2 gauge wires are occasionally used. Wire length must also be considered when making repairs to a circuit. As conductor length increases, so does resistance. An 18 gauge wire, for example, can carry a 10 amp load for 10 feet without excessive voltage drop; however if a 15 foot wire is required for the same 10 amp load, it must be a 16 gauge wire.

An electrical schematic shows the electrical current paths when a circuit is operating properly. It is essential to understand how a circuit works before trying to figure out why it doesn't. Schematics break the entire electrical system down into individual circuits and show only one particular circuit. In a schematic, no attempt is made to represent wiring and components as they physically appear on the vehicle; switches and other components are shown as simply as possible. Face views of harness connectors show the cavity or terminal locations in all multi-pin connectors to help locate test points.

If you need to backprobe a connector while it is on the component, the order of the terminals must be mentally reversed. The wire color code can help in this situation, as well as a keyway, lock tab or other reference mark.

NOTE: *Wiring diagrams are not included in this book. As trucks have become more complex and available with longer option lists, wiring diagrams have grown in size and complexity. It has become almost impossible to provide a readable reproduction of a wiring diagram in a book this size. Information on ordering wiring diagrams from the vehicle manufacturer can be found in the owner's manual.*

WIRING REPAIR

Soldering is a quick, efficient method of joining metals permanently. Everyone who has the occasion to make wiring repairs should know how to solder. Electrical connections that are soldered are far less likely to come apart and will conduct electricity much better than connections that are only "pig-tailed" together. The most popular (and preferred) method of soldering is with an electrical soldering gun. Soldering irons are available in many sizes and wattage ratings. Irons with higher wattage ratings deliver higher temperatures and recover lost heat faster. A small soldering iron rated for no more than 50 watts is recommended, especially on electrical systems where excess heat can damage the components being soldered.

There are three ingredients necessary for successful soldering; proper flux, good solder and sufficient heat. A soldering flux is necessary to clean the metal of tarnish, prepare it for soldering and to enable the solder to spread into tiny crevices. When soldering, always use a resin flux or resin core solder which is non-corrosive and will not attract moisture once the job is finished. Other types of flux (acid core) will leave a residue that will attract moisture and cause the wires to corrode. Tin is a unique metal with a low melting point. In a molten state, it dissolves and alloys easily with many metals. Solder is made by mixing tin with lead. The most common proportions are 40/60, 50/50 and 60/40, with the percentage of tin listed first. Low priced solders usually contain less tin, making them very difficult for a beginner to use because more heat is required to melt the solder. A common solder is 40/60 which is well suited for all-around general use, but 60/40 melts easier, has more tin for a better joint and is preferred for electrical work.

Soldering Techniques

Successful soldering requires that the metals to be joined be heated to a temperature that will melt the solder — usually 360-460°F (182-238°C). Contrary to popular belief, the purpose of the soldering iron is not to melt the solder itself, but to heat the parts being soldered to a temperature high enough to melt the solder when it is touched to the work. Melting flux-cored solder on the soldering iron will usually destroy the effectiveness of the flux.

NOTE: *Soldering tips are made of copper for good heat conductivity, but must be "tinned" regularly for quick transference of heat to the project and to prevent the solder from sticking to the iron. To "tin" the iron, simply heat it and touch the flux-cored solder to the tip; the solder will flow over the hot tip. Wipe the excess off with a clean rag, but be careful as the iron will be hot.*

After some use, the tip may become pitted. If so, simply dress the tip smooth with a smooth file and "tin" the tip again. An old saying holds that "metals well cleaned are half soldered." Flux-cored solder will remove oxides but rust, bits of insulation and oil or grease must be removed with a wire brush or emery cloth. For maximum strength in soldered parts, the joint must start off clean and tight. Weak joints will result in gaps too wide for the solder to bridge.

If a separate soldering flux is used, it should be brushed or swabbed on only those areas that are to be soldered. Most solders contain a core of flux and separate fluxing is unnecessary. Hold the work to be soldered firmly. It is best to solder on a wooden board, because a metal vise will only rob the piece to be soldered of heat and make it difficult to melt the solder. Hold the soldering tip with the broadest face against the work to be soldered. Apply solder under the tip close to the work, using enough solder to give a heavy film between the iron and the piece being soldered, while moving slowly and making sure the solder melts properly. Keep the work level or the solder will run to the lowest part and favor the thicker parts, because these require more heat to melt the solder. If the soldering tip overheats (the solder coating on the face of the tip burns up), it should be retinned. Once the soldering is completed, let the soldered joint stand until cool. Tape and seal all soldered wire splices after the repair has cooled.

Wire Harness and Connectors

The on-board computer (ECM) wire harness electrically connects the control unit to the various solenoids, switches and sensors used by the control system. Most connectors in the engine compartment or otherwise exposed to the elements are protected against moisture and dirt which could create oxidation and deposits on the terminals. This protection is important because of the very low voltage and current levels used by the computer and sensors. All connectors have a lock which secures the male and female terminals together, with a secondary lock holding the seal and terminal into the connec-

tor. Both terminal locks must be released when disconnecting ECM connectors.

These special connectors are weather-proof and all repairs require the use of a special terminal and the tool required to service it. This tool is used to remove the pin and sleeve terminals. If removal is attempted with an ordinary pick, there is a good chance that the terminal will be bent or deformed. Unlike standard blade type terminals, these terminals cannot be straightened once they are bent. Make certain that the connectors are properly seated and all of the sealing rings in place when connecting leads. On some models, a hinge-type flap proides a backup or secondary locking feature for the terminals. Most secondary locks are used to improve the connector reliability by retaining the terminals if the small terminal lock tangs are not positioned properly.

Molded-on connectors require complete replacement of the connection. This means splicing a new connector assembly into the harness. All splices in on-board computer systems should be soldered to insure proper contact. Use care when probing the connections or replacing terminals in them as it is possible to short between opposite terminals. If this happens to the wrong terminal pair, it is possible to damage certain components. Always use jumper wires between connectors for circuit checking and never probe through weatherproof seals.

Open circuits are often difficult to locate by sight because corrosion or terminal misalignment are hidden by the connectors. Merely wiggling a connector on a sensor or in the wiring harness may correct the open circuit condition. This should always be considered when an open circuit or a failed sensor is indicated. Intermittent problems may also be caused by oxidized or loose connections. When using a circuit tester for diagnosis, always probe connections from the wire side. Be careful not to damage sealed connectors with test probes.

All wiring harnesses should be replaced with identical parts, using the same gauge wire and connectors. When signal wires are spliced into a harness, use wire with high temperature insulation only. With the low voltage and current levels found in the system, it is important that the best possible connection at all wire splices be made by soldering the splices together. It is seldom necessary to replace a complete harness. If replacement is necessary, pay close attention to insure proper harness routing. Secure the harness with suitable plastic wire clamps to prevent vibrations from causing the harness to wear in spots or contact any hot components.

NOTE: *Weatherproof connectors cannot be replaced with standard connectors. Instruc-*

tions are provided with replacement connector and terminal packages. Some wire harnesses have mounting indicators (usually pieces of colored tape) to mark where the harness is to be secured.

In making wiring repairs, it's important that you always replace damaged wires with wires that are the same gauge as the wire being replaced. The heavier the wire, the smaller the gauge number. Wires are color-coded to aid in identification and whenever possible the same color coded wire should be used for replacement. A wire stripping and crimping tool is necessary to install solderless terminal connectors. Test all crimps by pulling on the wires; it should not be possible to pull the wires out of a good crimp.

Wires which are open, exposed or otherwise damaged are repaired by simple splicing. Where possible, if the wiring harness is accessible and the damaged place in the wire can be located, it is best to open the harness and check for all possible damage. In an inaccessible harness, the wire must be bypassed with a new insert, usually taped to the outside of the old harness.

When replacing fusible links, be sure to use fusible link wire, NOT ordinary automotive wire. Make sure the fusible segment is of the same gauge and construction as the one being replaced and double the stripped end when crimping the terminal connector for a good contact. The melted (open) fusible link segment of the wiring harness should be cut off as close to the harness as possible, then a new segment spliced in as described. In the case of a damaged fusible link that feeds two harness wires, the harness connections should be replaced with two fusible link wires so that each circuit will have its own separate protection.

NOTE: *Most of the problems caused in the wiring harness are due to bad ground connections. Always check all vehicle ground connections for corrosion or looseness before performing any power feed checks to eliminate the chance of a bad ground affecting the circuit.*

Repairing Hard Shell Connectors

Unlike molded connectors, the terminal contacts in hard shell connectors can be replaced. Weatherproof hard-shell connectors with the leads molded into the shell have non-replaceable terminal ends. Replacement usually involves the use of a special terminal removal tool that depress the locking tangs (barbs) on the connector terminal and allow the connector to be removed from the rear of the shell. The connector shell should be replaced if it shows any evidence of burning, melting, cracks, or breaks.

Replace individual terminals that are burnt, corroded, distorted or loose.

NOTE: *The insulation crimp must be tight to prevent the insulation from sliding back on the wire when the wire is pulled. The insulation must be visibly compressed under the crimp tabs, and the ends of the crimp should be turned in for a firm grip on the insulation.*

The wire crimp must be made with all wire strands inside the crimp. The terminal must be fully compressed on the wire strands with the ends of the crimp tabs turned in to make a firm grip on the wire. Check all connections with an ohmmeter to insure a good contact. There should be no measurable resistance between the wire and the terminal when connected.

Mechanical Test Equipment

Vacuum Gauge

Most gauges are graduated in inches of mercury (in.Hg), although a device called a manometer reads vacuum in inches of water (in. H_2O). The normal vacuum reading usually varies between 18 and 22 in.Hg at sea level. To test engine vacuum, the vacuum gauge must be connected to a source of manifold vacuum. Many engines have a plug in the intake manifold which can be removed and replaced with an adapter fitting. Connect the vacuum gauge to the fitting with a suitable rubber hose or, if no manifold plug is available, connect the vacuum gauge to any device using manifold vacuum, such as EGR valves, etc. The vacuum gauge can be used to determine if enough vacuum is reaching a component to allow its actuation.

Hand Vacuum Pump

Small, hand-held vacuum pumps come in a variety of designs. Most have a built-in vacuum gauge and allow the component to be tested without removing it from the vehicle. Operate the pump lever or plunger to apply the correct amount of vacuum required for the test specified in the diagnosis routines. The level of vacuum in inches of Mercury (in.Hg) is indicated on the pump gauge. For some testing, an additional vacuum gauge may be necessary.

Intake manifold vacuum is used to operate various systems and devices on late model vehicles. To correctly diagnose and solve problems in vacuum control systems, a vacuum source is necessary for testing. In some cases, vacuum can be taken from the intake manifold when the engine is running, but vacuum is normally provided by a hand vacuum pump. These hand vacuum pumps have a built-in vacuum gauge that allow testing while the device is still attached to the component. For some tests, an additional vacuum gauge may be necessary.

HEATING AND AIR CONDITIONING

Non-Air Conditioned Cars

*BLOWER MOTOR REMOVAL AND
INSTALLATION*

1968-72 Models

1. Disconnect the negative battery cable.
2. Disconnect the blower motor wire leads under the hood.
3. Remove any parts mounted on the inside of the right fender apron.
4. Raise the vehicle on a hoist and remove the right front wheel.
5. Remove the fender apron-to-fender attaching bolts and lower the fender apron.
6. Insert a block of wood between the apron and the fender to gain working space.
7. Reach inside the fender apron and remove the blower motor mounting plate attaching screws.
8. Remove the blower motor, wheel and mounting plate from inside the fender as an assembly.
9. Reverse above procedure to install.

1973-78 Models

1. Disconnect the battery ground cable. Disconnect the blower motor lead wire.
2. Remove the mounting screw from the black ground wire location at the upper cowl. Remove both wires from the clip.
3. Remove the right front tire and wheel.
4. In order to get to the blower motor, an ac-

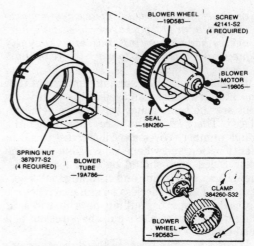

Blower motor removal (1979 shown)

cess hole must be cut out in the right front fender apron. The pattern for this hole has been outlined on the apron by the factory. It appears as a beaded line.

5. A small indentation or drill dimple is present ½″ from the centerline of the bead. Drill a 1″ diameter hole at this drill dimple. Be careful not to damage the heater case by overdrilling.
6. Using aircraft snips, cut along the bear to create the opening. Do not use a saber saw.
7. Remove the blower motor mounting plate screws and disconnect the cooler tube from the motor.
8. Remove the motor and wheel assembly

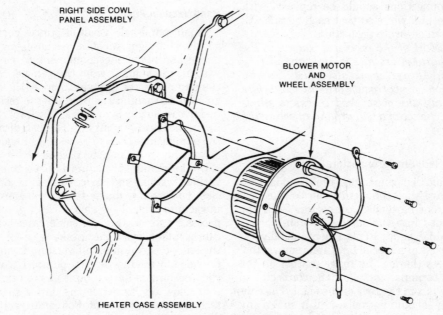

Typical blower motor installation

out of the heater case and out through the access hole.

9. To install, reverse the removal procedure. Apply rope sealer to the motor mounting plate. Obtain a cover plate from your local Ford parts department. Drill 8, ⅛″ holes in the fender apron and install the cover plate.

1979-88

1. Disconnect the battery ground cable.
2. Disconnect the blower motor ground wire and engine ground wire.
3. Disconnect the wiring harness connections.
4. Remove the blower motor cooling tube.
5. Remove the four retaining screws from the mounting plate.
6. Remove the blower motor and wheel assembly. It will be necessary to turn the assembly slightly to the right and follow the contour of the wheel well.
7. Installation is the reverse of removal.

HEATER CORE REMOVAL AND INSTALLATION

Through 1978

The heater core is located in the left side of the case on the engine side of the dash panel.

1. Partially drain cooling system.

CAUTION: *When draining the coolant, keep in mind that cats and dogs are attracted by the ethylene glycol antifreeze, and are quite likely to drink any that is left in an uncovered container or in puddles on the ground. This will prove fatal in sufficient quantity. Always drain the coolant into a sealable container. Coolant should be reused unless it is contaminated or several years old.*

2. Remove heater hoses at core.
3. Remove retaining screws, core cover and seal from plenum.
4. Remove core from plenum.
5. Install in reverse of above, applying a thin coat of silicone to the pads.

1979-88

1. Disconnect the battery ground cable.
2. Drain the coolant from the system.

CAUTION: *When draining the coolant, keep in mind that cats and dogs are attracted by the ethylene glycol antifreeze, and are quite likely to drink any that is left in an uncovered container or in puddles on the ground. This will prove fatal in sufficient quantity. Always drain the coolant into a sealable container. Coolant should be reused unless it is contaminated or several years old.*

3. Disconnect the heater hoses from the heater core tubes. Plug the tubes to prevent leakage.

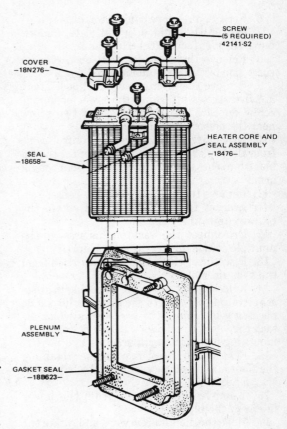

Mark VI Heater Core

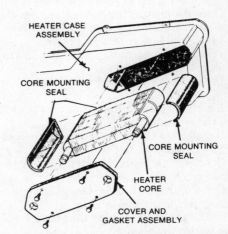

Heater core removal—typical of a non-air conditioned car

4. Disconnect the control system vacuum hose from its source and push the hose and grommet into the passenger compartment.
5. Remove the one bolt located beneath the wiper motor that attaches to the left side of the plenum to the dash. Remove the nut that retains the upper left corner of the heater case.

6. Remove the glove compartment.

7. Loosen the right door sill plate, and remove the right side cowl trim panel.

8. Remove the attaching bolt on the lower right side of the instrument panel.

9. Remove the instrument panel pad. There are five screws attaching the lower edge, one screw on each outboard end, and two screw near the defroster openings.

10. Disengage the temperature control cable from the top of the plenum. Disconnect the cable from the temperature blend door crank arm.

11. Remove the clip attaching the center register bracket to the plenum, and rotate the bracket up to the right.

12. Disconnect the vacuum harness at the multiple connector near the floor duct.

13. Disconnect the white vacuum hose from the vacuum motor.

14. Remove the two screws attaching the passenger's side air duct to the plenum. It may be necessary to remove the two screws which attach the lower panel door vacuum motor to the mounting bracket to gain access.

15. Remove the one plastic fastener retaining the floor air distribution duct to the left end of the plenum, and remove the duct.

16. Remove the two nuts from the lower flange of the plenum.

17. Move the plenum rearward and rotate the top of the plenum down and out from under the instrument panel.

18. Once the plenum is removed, remove the heater core cover and remove the heater core.

19. Install the heater core and cover.

20. Position the plenum under the instrument panel.

21. Install the two on the lower flange of the plenum.

22. Install the air distribution duct at the left end of the plenum.

23. Install the two screws attaching the passenger's side air duct to the plenum.

24. Connect the white vacuum hose at the vacuum motor.

25. Connect the vacuum harness at the multiple connector near the floor duct.

26. Install the clip attaching the center register bracket to the plenum.

27. Disengage the temperature control cable at the top of the plenum and the temperature blend door crank arm.

28. Install the instrument panel pad.

29. Install the attaching bolt on the lower right side of the instrument panel.

30. Install the right side cowl trim panel and door sill plate.

31. Install the glove compartment.

32. Install the one bolt located beneath the wiper motor that attaches to the left side of the plenum to the dash. Install the nut that retains the upper left corner of the heater case.

33. Install and connect the control system vacuum hose.

34. Connect the heater hoses at the heater core tubes.

35. Fill the cooling system.

36. Connect the battery ground cable.

Air Conditioned Cars

CAUTION: *Do not disconnect any air conditioning lines unless you are equipped with the proper tools and gauges and have knowledge of air conditioning systems. Discharging of the system is required before disconnecting the lines. This operation requires special equipment. Failure to follow proper safety precautions may cause personal injury. See Chapter 1 for air conditioning service discharging and charging procedures.*

BLOWER MOTOR REMOVAL AND INSTALLATION

1968 Except Lincoln Models

1. Take off the protective cover from the engine firewall. Disconnect the negative battery cable.

2. Take out the mounting plate-to-evaporator housing attaching screws.

3. Disconnect the motor wires.

4. Lift out the motor assembly.

5. Reverse above procedure to install.

1969-72 Except Lincoln Models

1. Remove the battery.

2. Remove the right front wheel.

3. Remove the vacuum tank bolts and fender apron bolts.

4. Move the fender apron inboard.

5. Remove the blower motor attaching screws and vent hose.

6. Pry upward on the hood hinge and remove the blower.

7. Reverse the above procedure to install.

1968-69 Continental

NOTE: *The blower motor is mounted is the right fender wheel.*

1. Disconnect the negative battery cable. Remove the right front fender splash shield mounting bolts and the shield.

2. Remove the four bolts retaining the blower motor to the housing.

3. Disconnect the electrical leads and remove the blower motor.

4. Install the blower motor in the reverse order of removal.

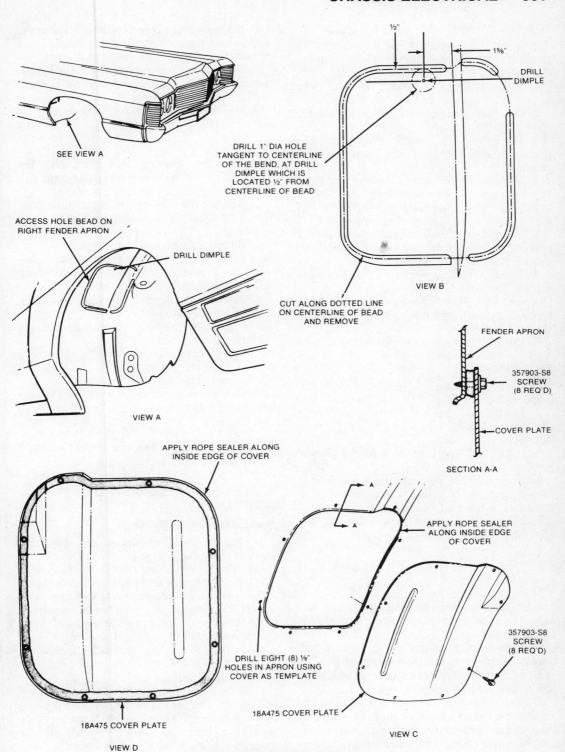

SEE VIEW A

DRILL 1" DIA HOLE
TANGENT TO CENTERLINE
OF THE BEND, AT DRILL
DIMPLE WHICH IS
LOCATED ½" FROM
CENTERLINE OF BEAD

½"

1⅝"

DRILL
DIMPLE

VIEW B

CUT ALONG DOTTED LINE
ON CENTERLINE OF BEAD
AND REMOVE

ACCESS HOLE BEAD ON
RIGHT FENDER APRON

DRILL DIMPLE

VIEW A

FENDER APRON

357903-S8
SCREW
(8 REQ'D)

COVER PLATE

SECTION A-A

APPLY ROPE SEALER ALONG
INSIDE EDGE OF COVER

A

A

APPLY ROPE SEALER
ALONG INSIDE EDGE
OF COVER

357903-S8
SCREW
(8 REQ'D)

DRILL EIGHT (8) ⅛"
HOLES IN APRON USING
COVER AS TEMPLATE

18A475 COVER PLATE

18A475 COVER PLATE

VIEW D

VIEW C

Blower access hole in fender

1970-79 Continental

1. Mark the position of the hood hinges on the hood (for reinstallation location). Remove the hood.

2. Remove the right hood hinge and right fender inner support brace as an assembly.

3. Disconnect the blower motor air cooling tube from the motor.

4. Disconnect the motor lead wire from the harness and the ground wire from the dash panel.

5. Disconnect the rear section of the right front fender panel apron from the fender around the wheel opening and remove the two lower fender to cowl mounting screws.

6. Separate the fender apron from the fender opening so that the apron can be pushed down away from the blower motor.

7. Remove the blower motor mounting plate screws. Move the blower motor forward out of the mounting and remove the assembly through the opening while applying pressure to the fender apron.

8. Install in the reverse order of removal.

1968-69 Mark III

1. Disconnect the negative battery cable. Remove the right side cowl trim panel.

2. Remove the screws that retain the duct to the side cowl panel and sound baffle. Remove the duct.

3. Disconnect the lead wire to the blower motor.

4. Remove the screw from the blower motor mounting plate and rotate the motor and plate clockwise to unlock from the case.

5. Remove the blower motor through the opening in the cowl side of the panel.

6. Install the blower motor in the reverse order of removal.

Mark IV

1. Disconnect the negative battery cable. Remove the love box to gain access to blower motor removal.

2. Remove the recirculation air register and duct assembly from the blower assembly.

3. Remove the screws that attach the blower lower housing to the dash panel.

4. Disconnect the white hose from the outside/recir air door vacuum motor. Remove the vacuum motor from the lower blower housing. Let the motor actuator remain connected to the door crank arm.

5. Disconnect the orange blower motor lead wire from the harness connector and disconnect the black ground wire.

6. Remove the flange screws that retainer the upper and lower blower housings together.

7. Separate the blower housing lower cover and blower motor from the upper housing and remove from behind the instrument panel.

8. Remove the screws that attach the blower motor assembly to the lower housing. Remove the blower motor.

9. Install the blower motor in the reverse order of removal.

Mark V

1. Disconnect the negative battery cable. Remove the instrument panel pad and the glovebox.

2. Remove the side cowl trim panel. Remove the right side instrument panel attachment brackets.

3. Remove the blower housing to firewall attaching nut (in the engine compartment). Remove the blower housing to firewall attaching nut (in the passenger's compartment).

4. Remove the blower housing mounting bracket and cowl top inner screw.

5. Disconnect the white air duct door motor vacuum hose.

6. Disconnect the blower motor wire harness wire and the ground wire.

7. Remove the blower assembly.

8. Install the blower motor in the reverse order of removal.

All 1973-88 Ford, Mercury and Lincoln

The procedure is the same as that outlined for non-air conditioned cars.

HEATER CORE REMOVAL AND INSTALLATION

1968 Except Lincoln Models

1. Drain the cooling system and raise the front of the vehicle.

CAUTION: *When draining the coolant, keep in mind that cats and dogs are attracted by the ethylene glycol antifreeze, and are quite likely to drink any that is left in an uncovered container or in puddles on the ground. This will prove fatal in sufficient quantity. Always drain the coolant into a sealable container. Coolant should be reused unless it is contaminated or several years old.*

2. Remove the right front wheel and tire.

3. To gain access to the core, remove the two upper bolts and the bolts around the wheel well retaining the inner fender apron. Pull the apron down and block it in this position.

4. Disconnect the heater hoses.

5. Remove the water valve retaining screws and position the valve to one side.

6. Remove the core housing-to-dash retaining screws and the core housing from the car.

7. Remove the core from the housing by re-

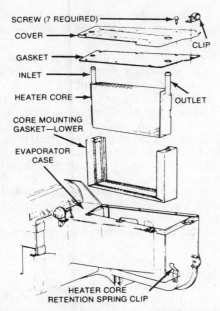

SCREW (7 REQUIRED)
COVER
CLIP
GASKET
INLET
HEATER CORE
OUTLET
CORE MOUNTING GASKET—LOWER
EVAPORATOR CASE
HEATER CORE RETENTION SPRING CLIP

Typical heater core removal—air conditioned cars

moving the retaining screws and separating the housing halves.

8. Reverse the above procedure to install, taking care to seal the housing halves together.

1969-72 Except Lincoln Models

1. Drain the cooling system.

CAUTION: *When draining the coolant, keep in mind that cats and dogs are attracted by the ethylene glycol antifreeze, and are quite likely to drink any that is left in an uncovered container or in puddles on the ground. This will prove fatal in sufficient quantity. Always drain the coolant into a sealable container. Coolant should be reused unless it is contaminated or several years old.*

2. Remove the carburetor air cleaner.

3. Remove the two screws retaining the vacuum manifold to the dash. Disconnect the vacuum hoses as necessary, taking note of their placement, and move the manifold to one side of the heater core cover.

4. Disconnect the heater hoses.

5. Remove the seven attaching screws and the heater core cover.

6. Remove the heater core and pad from the housing.

7. Reverse above procedure to install.

1973-78 Except Lincoln Models

1. Drain the cooling system.

CAUTION: *When draining the coolant, keep in mind that cats and dogs are attracted by the ethylene glycol antifreeze, and are quite*

likely to drink any that is left in an uncovered container or in puddles on the ground. This will prove fatal in sufficient quantity. Always drain the coolant into a sealable container. Coolant should be reused unless it is contaminated or several years old.

2. Disconnect the heater hoses at the heater core tubes.

3. Remove the seven screws which retain the core cover plate to the core housing and lift off the plate.

4. Pull the heater core and mounting gasket up out of the case. Remove the core mounting gasket.

5. Reverse the above procedure to install, taking care to ensure that the core and gasket seat firmly forward of the core retention spring in the case. Fill the cooling system with the recommended mixture of water and antifreeze (coolant).

1968-69 Continental

1. Disconnect the negative battery cable. Drain the cooling system.

CAUTION: *When draining the coolant, keep in mind that cats and dogs are attracted by the ethylene glycol antifreeze, and are quite likely to drink any that is left in an uncovered container or in puddles on the ground. This will prove fatal in sufficient quantity. Always drain the coolant into a sealable container. Coolant should be reused unless it is contaminated or several years old.*

2. Remove the air cleaner assembly. Disconnect the hoses at heater core.

3. Remove the harness clamp from the top of the evaporator/heater case.

4. Remove the temperature blend door actuator.

5. Remove the heater core cover plate screw and the cover plate.

6. Lift the heater core from the housing.

7. Install the heater core in the reverse order of removal.

1970-73 Continental

1. Disconnect the negative battery cable. Drain the cooling system.

CAUTION: *When draining the coolant, keep in mind that cats and dogs are attracted by the ethylene glycol antifreeze, and are quite likely to drink any that is left in an uncovered container or in puddles on the ground. This will prove fatal in sufficient quantity. Always drain the coolant into a sealable container. Coolant should be reused unless it is contaminated or several years old.*

2. Disconnect the vacuum junction valve from the dash panel and move the valve and vacuum hoses out of the way.

3. If equipped with cruise control, remove the servo and bracket from the dash panel and position it out of the way.

4. Disconnect the multiple connector from the blower resistor and remove the harness from the clip retainer on the case.

5. Disconnect the heater hoses from the heater and remove the support clamp from the case. Move the hoses and valve assembly away from the case.

6. Remove the case cover to flange attaching screws and wire harness clip.

7. Remove the cover to back plate attaching nuts. Remove the upper case to dash panel screw.

8. Remove the case to dash stud mounting nuts, one on the inboard mounting flange and the other on the lower flange.

9. Carefully move the heater core assembly forward to clear the mounting studs and lift it up and out of the car.

10. Remove the spring clips from the core tubes on front of the cover assembly.

11. Remove the core end plate mounting screws and remove the plate. Remove the heater core and mounting gasket from the case.

12. Install the heater core in the reverse order of removal.

1974 and Later Continental

1. Disconnect the negative battery cable.

2. Disconnect the heater hose from the heater core.

3. Remove the heater core cover and gasket. it may be necessary to remove the engine vacuum distribution center and electrical harness ground terminal from the firewall for easier access.

4. Lift the heater core and gasket from the housing. Remove the gasket from the core.

5. Install the heater core in the reverse order of removal.

Mark III

1. Disconnect the negative battery cable. Drain the cooling system.

CAUTION: *When draining the coolant, keep in mind that cats and dogs are attracted by the ethylene glycol antifreeze, and are quite likely to drink any that is left in an uncovered container or in puddles on the ground. This will prove fatal in sufficient quantity. Always drain the coolant into a sealable container. Coolant should be reused unless it is contaminated or several years old.*

NOTE: *To gain necessary working room, hood removal may be necessary.*

2. On 1968 and 69 models, disconnect both hydraulic lines at the wiper motor and position them out of the way.

3. Disconnect the heater hoses at the heater core and position the hoses and the heater valve out of the way.

4. Disconnect the vacuum supply hose from the top of the housing. Remove the oil pressure sending unit from the back of the engine.

5. Remove the transmission dipstick tube and dipstick assembly. Place a pan underneath the car to catch any spilled fluid.

6. Disconnect the multiple electrical connector leading to the icing switch.

7. Remove the heater/evaporator housing front cover.

8. Remove the heater core housing cover. Remove the heater core retaining bracket and the heater core.

9. Install the heater core in the reverse order of removal.

Mark IV

1. Disconnect the negative battery cable. Drain the cooling system.

CAUTION: *When draining the coolant, keep in mind that cats and dogs are attracted by the ethylene glycol antifreeze, and are quite likely to drink any that is left in an uncovered container or in puddles on the ground. This will prove fatal in sufficient quantity. Always drain the coolant into a sealable container. Coolant should be reused unless it is contaminated or several years old.*

2. Disconnect the heater hoses from the heater core.

3. Remove the glove box.

4. Remove the heater air outlet register from the plenum assembly by removing the two snap ring retainers.

5. Remove the temperature control cable assembly mounting screw and disconnect the end of the cable from the blend air door crank by removing the spring nut.

6. Remove the blue and red vacuum hoses from the high/low door vacuum motor and the brown hose at the inline tee connector to the temperature bypass door motor.

7. Disconnect the wire connector from the resistor.

8. Remove the mounting screws from around the flange of the plenum case and remove the rear case half of the plenum.

9. Remove the mounting nut from the heater core tube support bracket.

10. Remove the heater core.

11. Install the heater core in the reverse order of removal. To provide a positive seal between the front and rear of the case halves, apply body sealer around the case flanges prior to installation. Be certain that the core mounting gasket is properly installed.

Mark V

1. Disconnect the negative battery cable. Drain the cooling system. Disconnect the heater hoses from the heater core.

CAUTION: *When draining the coolant, keep in mind that cats and dogs are attracted by the ethylene glycol antifreeze, and are quite likely to drink any that is left in an uncovered container or in puddles on the ground. This will prove fatal in sufficient quantity. Always drain the coolant into a sealable container. Coolant should be reused unless it is contaminated or several years old.*

2. Remove the heater core cover mounting screws and the cover plate.

3. Press down on the heater core and tilt it toward the front of the car to release the seal from the housing.

4. Lift the heater core up and out of the housing.

5. Install the heater core in the reverse order of removal. When installing the core, press down and tip the core back so that the notch on the seal aligns with the flange on the evaporator housing. Apply new sealer to the housing on reinstallation.

1979 and Later Ford and Mercury Models
1980 and Later Lincoln Models

1. Disconnect the battery ground cable.
2. Drain the coolant from the system.

CAUTION: *When draining the coolant, keep in mind that cats and dogs are attracted by the ethylene glycol antifreeze, and are quite likely to drink any that is left in an uncovered container or in puddles on the ground. This will prove fatal in sufficient quantity. Always drain the coolant into a sealable container. Coolant should be reused unless it is contaminated or several years old.*

3. Disconnect the heater hoses from the heater core tubes. Plug the tubes to prevent leakage.

4. Disconnect the control system vacuum hose from its source and push the hose and grommet into the passenger compartment.

5. Remove the one bolt located beneath the wiper motor that attaches to the left side of the plenum to the dash. Remove the nut that retains the upper left corner of the heater case.

6. Remove the glove compartment.

7. Loosen the right door sill plate, and remove the right side cowl trim panel.

8. Remove the attaching bolt on the lower right side of the instrument panel.

9. Remove the instrument panel pad. There are five screws attaching the lower edge, one screw on each outboard end, and two screw near the defroster openings.

10. Disengage the temperature control cable from the top of the plenum. Disconnect the cable from the temperature blend door crank arm.

11. Remove the clip attaching the center register bracket to the plenum, and rotate the bracket up to the right.

12. Disconnect the vacuum harness at the multiple connector near the floor duct.

13. Disconnect the white vacuum hose from the vacuum motor.

14. Remove the two screws attaching the passenger's side air duct to the plenum. It may be necessary to remove the two screws which attach the lower panel door vacuum motor to the mounting bracket to gain access.

15. Remove the one plastic fastener retaining the floor air distribution duct to the left end of the plenum, and remove the duct.

16. Remove the two nuts from the lower flange of the plenum.

17. Move the plenum rearward and rotate the top of the plenum down and out from under the instrument panel.

18. Once the plenum is removed, remove the heater core cover and remove the heater core.

19. Install the heater core and cover.

20. Position the plenum under the instrument panel.

21. Install the two on the lower flange of the plenum.

22. Install the air distribution duct at the left end of the plenum.

23. Install the two screws attaching the passenger's side air duct to the plenum.

24. Connect the white vacuum hose at the vacuum motor.

25. Connect the vacuum harness at the multiple connector near the floor duct.

26. Install the clip attaching the center register bracket to the plenum.

27. Disengage the temperature control cable at the top of the plenum and the temperature blend door crank arm.

28. Install the instrument panel pad.

29. Install the attaching bolt on the lower right side of the instrument panel.

30. Install the right side cowl trim panel and door sill plate.

31. Install the glove compartment.

32. Install the one bolt located beneath the wiper motor that attaches to the left side of the plenum to the dash. Install the nut that retains the upper left corner of the heater case.

33. Install and connect the control system vacuum hose.

34. Connect the heater hoses at the heater core tubes.

35. Fill the cooling system.

36. Connect the battery ground cable.

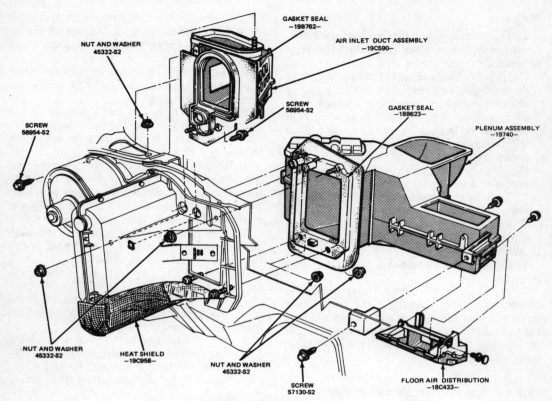

1980 heater case assembly

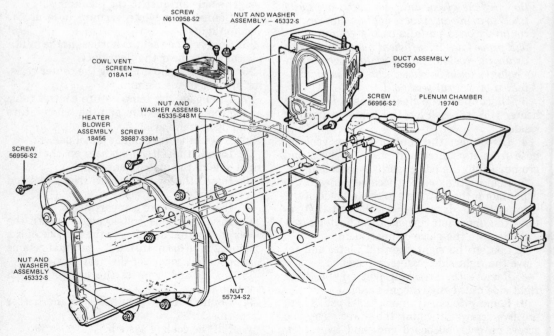

1981–82 heater case assembly

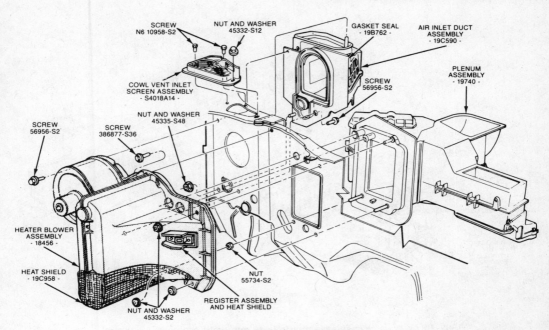

1982—88 heater case assembly

Evaporator

REMOVAL AND INSTALLATION

1968-79

1. Discharge the system. See Chapter 1.

2. Raise and support the front end on jackstands.

3. Remove the right front wheel.

4. On the rearward half of the fender liner is a dimple. Using this dimple as a llocater, drill a 1½" hole.

5. Drain the cooling system and disconnect the heater hoses at the core tubes.

CAUTION: *When draining the coolant, keep in mind that cats and dogs are attracted by the ethylene glycol antifreeze, and are quite*

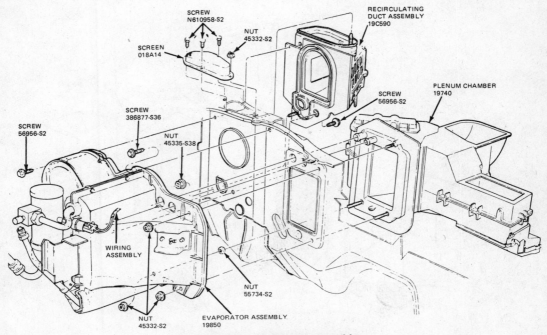

1980—81 evaporator case assembly

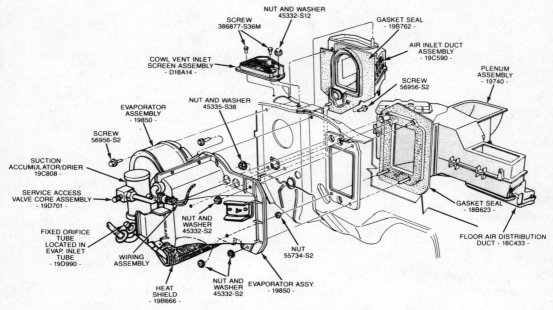

1982–88 evaporator case assembly, except automatic temperature control

likely to drink any that is left in an uncovered container or in puddles on the ground. This will prove fatal in sufficient quantity. Always drain the coolant into a sealable container. Coolant should be reused unless it is contaminated or several years old.

6. Disconnect the refrigerant lines at the suction throttling valve and expansion valve. Cap all openings immediately!.

7. Disconnect the wiring at the blower resistor.

8. From inside the car, remove the nut from the lower flange of the evaporator housing, inboard of the core.

9. In the engine compartment, remove the 2 self-tapping screws located at the top of the evaporator assembly; one on each side of the core.

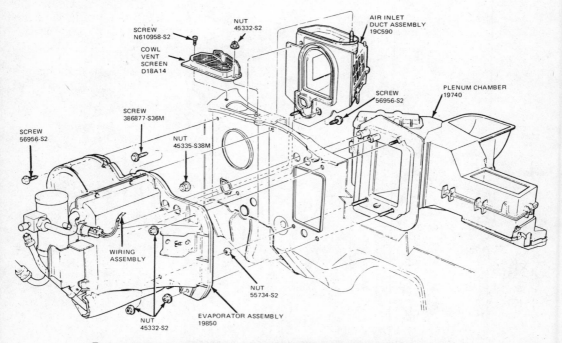

Evaporator case assembly for all models with automatic temperature control

10. Still in the engine compartment, remove 2 nuts from the inboard side of the evaporator. These nuts also retain the plenum.

11. Remove the top nut on the outboard side of the evaporator. This nut also retains the blower.

12. Working through the hole that you drilled in the fender apron, loosen the lower nut on the outboard side and run the nut to the end of the stud, but don't remove it.

13. Back in the passenger compartment, remove the instrument panel pad.

14. Remove the right side cowl trim panel.

15. Remove the 2 fasteners retaining the instrument panel to the body. One fastener is located on the cowl inner panel; the other on the cowl side panel.

16. Pull the instrument panel towards you and remove the air conditioning ducts.

17. Remove the speaker and/or support rod at the instrument cluster.

18. Remove the defroster nozzles.

19. Remove the right side duct.

20. Remove the floor ducts.

21. Remove the center duct.

22. Remove the plenum retaining screws.

23. Remove thew screw retaining the blower assembly support bracket to the inner cowl.

24. Move the plenum and blower towards you to shorten the studs protrusion in the engine compartment.

25. Move the evaporator housing forward and lift it to remove it from the car.

26. Remove the 7 screws retaining the evaporator case halves and separate the halves.

27. Remove the suction throttling valve support clamp.

28. Remove the core from the housing.

29. Assembly and installation is the reverse of removal and disassembly.

Always use new O-rings coated with clean refrigerant oil.

Always use new sealer between the case halves.

When everything is back together, turn on the blower and check for air leaks around the case.

Evacuate, charge and leak test the system. See Chapter 1.

1980-81

1. Discharge the system at the service access port on the underside of the combination valve. See Chapter 1.

2. Remove the instrument panel and lay it on the front seat.

3. Drain the cooling system and disconnect the heater hoses at the core tubes.

CAUTION: *When draining the coolant, keep in mind that cats and dogs are attracted by the ethylene glycol antifreeze, and are quite likely to drink any that is left in an uncovered container or in puddles on the ground. This will prove fatal in sufficient quantity. Always drain the coolant into a sealable container. Coolant should be reused unless it is contaminated or several years old.*

4. Disconnect the refrigerant lines at the combination valve. Use a back-up wrench on the suction throttling valve manifold. Cap all openings immediately!.

5. Disconnect the wiring at the blower resistor. Remove the screw attaching the air inlet duct and blower housing assembly support brace to the cowl top panel.

6. Disconnect the black vacuum supply hose at the check valve, in the engine compartment.

7. In the engine compartment, remove the 2 nuts retaining the evaporator case to the firewall.

8. In the passenger compartment, remove the screw attaching the evaporator case support bracket to the cowl top panel.

9. Remove the nut retaining the left end of the evaporator case to the firewall and the nut retaining the bracket below the evaporator case, to the dash panel.

10. Carefully pull the case away from the firewall and remove the case from the car.

11. Remove the air inlet duct and blower housing from the case.

12. Remove the 5 screws retaining the access cover to the case and lift off the cover.

13. Remove the heater core from the case.

14. Remove the 2 nuts retaining the restrictor door vacuum motor to the mounting bracket.

15. Disengage the vacuum motor arm from the restrictor door.

16. Remove the 11 screws and 6 snap-clips securing the halves of the case and separate the case halves.

17. Lift out the evaporator core, seal and combination valve from the lower case half.

18. Assembly and installation is the reverse of removal and disassembly.

Always use new O-rings coated with clean refrigerant oil.

Be sure that the restrictor is installed in the evaporator inlet line.

Make sure that the core seal fits over the case lower half edge.

Make sure that the temperature blend door and heat/defrost door are properly positioned.

Always use new sealer between the case halves.

Make sure that the drain hose is not kinked.

When everything is back together, turn on the blower and check for air leaks around the case.

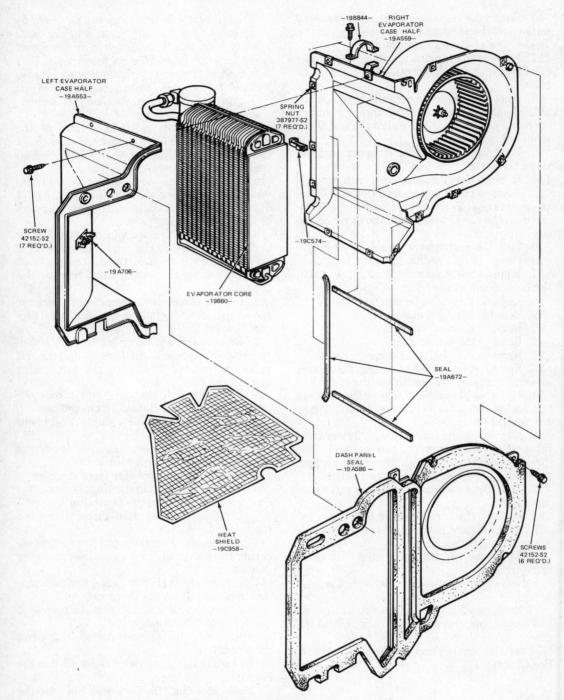

LEFT EVAPORATOR
CASE HALF
−19A553−

SPRING
NUT
387977-S2
(7 REQ'D.)

−19B844−

RIGHT
EVAPORATOR
CASE HALF
−19A559−

SCREW
42152-S2
(7 REQ'D.)

−19A706−

EVAPORATOR CORE
−19860−

−19C574−

SEAL
−19A672−

DASH PANEL
SEAL
−19A586−

HEAT
SHIELD
−19C958−

SCREWS
42152-S2
(6 REQ'D.)

1980 evaporator core installation

Evacuate, charge and leak test the system. See Chapter 1.

1982-84

1. Discharge the system at the service access port located on the suction line. See Chapter 1.

2. Remove the instrument panel and lay it on the front seat.

3. Drain the cooling system and disconnect the heater hoses at the core tubes.

CAUTION: *When draining the coolant, keep in mind that cats and dogs are attracted by the ethylene glycol antifreeze, and are quite*

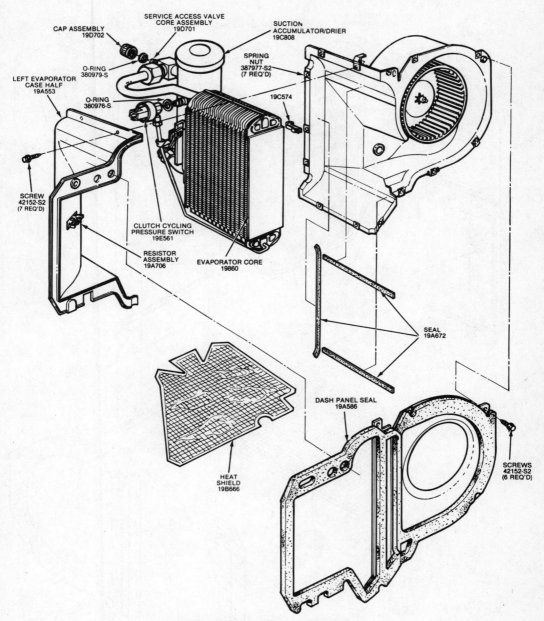

CAP ASSEMBLY
19D702

SERVICE ACCESS VALVE
CORE ASSEMBLY
19D701

SUCTION
ACCUMULATOR/DRIER
19C808

O-RING
380979-S

SPRING
NUT
387977-S2
(7 REQ'D)

LEFT EVAPORATOR
CASE HALF
19A553

O-RING
380976-S

19C574

SCREW
42152-S2
(7 REQ'D)

CLUTCH CYCLING
PRESSURE SWITCH
19E561

RESISTOR
ASSEMBLY
19A706

EVAPORATOR CORE
19860

SEAL
19A672

DASH PANEL SEAL
19A586

HEAT
SHIELD
19B666

SCREWS
42152-S2
(6 REQ'D)

1981–85 evaporator core installation

likely to drink any that is left in an uncovered container or in puddles on the ground. This will prove fatal in sufficient quantity. Always drain the coolant into a sealable container. Coolant should be reused unless it is contaminated or several years old.

4. Disconnect the refrigerant lines using back-up wrenches at each fitting. Cap all openings immediately!.

5. Disconnect the wiring at the blower, and the ATC wiring on cars with electronic auto-

matic temperature control. Remove the screw attaching the air inlet duct and blower housing assembly support brace to the cowl top panel.

6. Disconnect the black vacuum supply hose at the check valve, in the engine compartment, and, on cars with automatic temperature control, the vacuum hoses at the TBL switch, also in the engine compartment.

7. In the engine compartment, remove the 2 nuts retaining the evaporator case to the firewall.

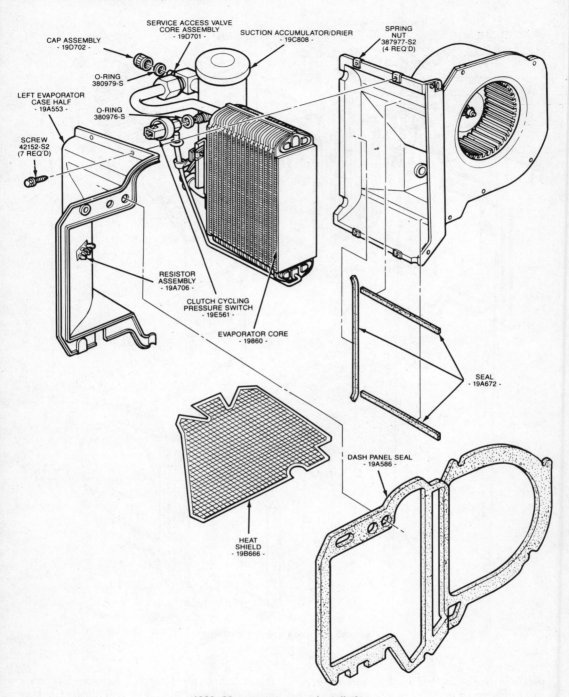

CAP ASSEMBLY
- 19D702 -

SERVICE ACCESS VALVE
CORE ASSEMBLY
- 19D701 -

SUCTION ACCUMULATOR/DRIER
- 19C808 -

SPRING
NUT
387977-S2
(4 REQ'D)

O-RING
380979-S

LEFT EVAPORATOR
CASE HALF
- 19A553 -

O-RING
380976-S

SCREW
42152-S2
(7 REQ'D)

RESISTOR
ASSEMBLY
- 19A706 -

CLUTCH CYCLING
PRESSURE SWITCH
- 19E561 -

EVAPORATOR CORE
- 19860 -

SEAL
- 19A672 -

DASH PANEL SEAL
- 19A586 -

HEAT
SHIELD
- 19B666 -

1986–88 evaporator core installation

8. In the passenger compartment, remove the screw attaching the evaporator case support bracket to the cowl top panel.

9. Remove the screw retaining the bracket below the case, to the firewall.

10. Carefully pull the case away from the firewall and remove the case from the car.

11. Remove the air inlet duct and blower housing from the case.

12. Remove the screws and snap-clips securing the halves of the case and separate the case halves.

13. Lift out the evaporator core and seal from the lower case half.

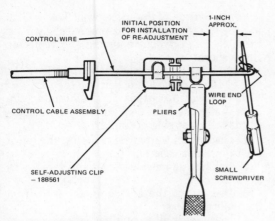

Control cable installation and adjustment

14. Assembly and installation is the reverse of removal and disassembly.

Always use new O-rings coated with clean refrigerant oil.

Make sure that the sore seal fits over the case lower half edge.

Make sure that the temperature blend door and heat/defrost door are properly positioned.

Always use new sealer between the case halves.

Make sure that the drain hose is not kinked.

When everything is back together, turn on the blower and check for air leaks around the case.

Evacuate, charge and leak test the system. See Chapter 1.

1985-88 with Manual Air Conditioning

1. Discharge the air conditioning system. See Chapter 1.

2. Disconnect the suction hose from the accumulator/drier using a spring-lock tool. Capp all openings at once!

3. Disconnect the liquid line at the evaporator using a spring-lock tool. Cap all openings at once!

4. Disconnect the wiring at the de-ice switch on the accumulator/drier.

5. Drain the cooling system.

CAUTION: *When draining the coolant, keep in mind that cats and dogs are attracted by the ethylene glycol antifreeze, and are quite likely to drink any that is left in an uncovered container or in puddles on the ground. This will prove fatal in sufficient quantity. Always drain the coolant into a sealable container. Coolant should be reused unless it is contaminated or several years old.*

6. Disconnect the heater hoses at the core tubes.

7. Remove the 6 screws retaining the right side of the hood seal bracket.

8. Remove the copper hood grounding clip from under the hood seal and fold the seal towards the left side of the car.

9. Disconnect the emission hose at the top of the evaporator case.

10. Position all movable hoses and wires away from the case.

11. Disconnect the blower motor lead from the main harness.

12. Disconnect all wiring harness connectors at the evaporator case.

13. On the passenger's side, fold the carpet back and remove the left, bottom screw that supports the inlet recirculation air duct.

14. In the engine compartment, remove the 3 nuts from the evaporator mounting studs, and the 2 screws from the blower motor.

15. Pull the bottom of the evaporator case assembly away from the firewall to disengage the 2 bottom studs.

16. Move the top of the case away from the firewall, disengaging it from the top stud and maneuver the case up and over the wheel well splash panel.

17. Remove the firewall seal from the case.

18. Remove the case heat shield.

19. Remove the 6 screws attaching the 2 halves of the case and separate the case halves.

20. Remove the core and suction accumualtor/drier.

21. Disconnect the suction accumulator/drier inlet from the evaporator core outlet tube. Cap the openings at once!

22. Remove the screw retaining the accumulator/drier to the core and separate the two.

To install the core and case:

NOTE: *When replacing a core in a system charged by a 6-cylinder aluminum compressor, a measured quatity of 500 viscosity refrigerant oil should be added to the core to ensure that the total oil charge in the system is correct. The amount added should be 3 fluid ounces poured directly into the inlet pipe of the new core with the pipe held vertically so that the oil will circulate in the core.*

23. Attach the accumulator/drier and core.

24. Connect the suction accumulator/drier to the evaporator core outlet tube, using new O-rings coated with clean refrigerant oil.

25. Install the core and suction accumualtor/drier.

26. Apply sealer to the case flange and around the evaporator core tubes.

27. Install the 6 screws attaching the 2 halves of the case.

28. Install the case heat shield.

29. Install the firewall seal on the case.

30. Position the case in the car.

31. Engage the 2 bottom studs, then the top stud.

32. In the engine compartment, install the 3 nuts on the evaporator mounting studs, and the 2 screws at the blower motor. Install all fasteners loosely, then tighten them.

33. Install the left, bottom screw that supports the inlet recirculation air duct.

34. Connect all wiring harness connectors at the evaporator case.

35. Connect the blower motor lead from the main harness.

36. Reposition all movable hoses and wires at the case.

36. Connect the emission hose at the top of the evaporator case.

37. Install the copper hood grounding clip under the hood seal and fold the seal back into position.

38. Install the 6 screws retaining the right side of the hood seal bracket.

39. Connect the heater hoses at the core tubes.

40. Fill the cooling system.

41. Connect the wiring at the de-ice switch on the accumulator/drier.

NOTE: *Whenever the system is opened, a new accumulator/drier must be installed.*

42. Connect the liquid line at the evaporator.

43. Connect the suction hose from the accumulator/drier.

44. Evacuate, charge and leak test the system. See Chapter 1.

1985-88 with Automatic Temperature Control

1. Discharge the air conditioning system. See Chapter 1.

2. Disconnect the suction hose from the accumulator/drier using a spring-lock tool. Cap all openings at once!

3. Disconnect the liquid line at the evaporator using a spring-lock tool. Cap all openings at once!

4. Disconnect the wiring at the clutch cycling switch on the suction accumulator/drier.

5. Drain the cooling system.

CAUTION: *When draining the coolant, keep in mind that cats and dogs are attracted by the ethylene glycol antifreeze, and are quite likely to drink any that is left in an uncovered container or in puddles on the ground. This will prove fatal in sufficient quantity. Always drain the coolant into a sealable container. Coolant should be reused unless it is contaminated or several years old.*

6. Disconnect the heater hoses at the core tubes.

7. Turn the steering wheel full left to position the right side front wheel so that the wheel well splash panel support bracket is accessible.

8. Remove the screw and splash shield from the back portion of the wheel well. This will allow the splash panel to be depressed slightly for extra clearance when removing and replacing the evaporator.

9. Remove the 6 screws retaining the right side of the hood seal bracket.

10. Remove the copper hood grounding clip from under the hood seal and fold the seal towards the right side of the car.

11. Disconnect the emission hose at the top of the evaporator case.

12. Position all movable hoses and wires away from the case.

13. Disconnect the blower motor lead from the main harness.

14. Disconnect all wiring harness connectors at the evaporator case.

15. On the passenger's side, fold the carpet back and remove the left, bottom screw that supports the inlet recirculation air duct.

16. In the passenger compartment, remove the ambient sensor air tube from the evaporator sensor air tube port.

17. In the engine compartment, remove the 3 nuts from the evaporator mounting studs, and the 2 screws from the blower motor.

18. Pull the bottom of the evaporator case assembly away from the firewall to disengage the 2 bottom studs.

19. Move the top of the case away from the firewall, disengaging it from the top stud and maneuver the case up and over the wheel well splash panel.

20. Remove the firewall seal from the case.

21. Remove the case heat shield.

22. Remove the 6 screws attaching the 2 halves of the case and separate the case halves.

23. Remove the core and suction accumualtor/drier.

24. Disconnect the suction accumulator/drier inlet from the evaporator core outlet tube. Cap the openings at once!

25. Remove the screw retaining the accumulator/drier to the core and separate the two.

To install the core and case:

NOTE: *When replacing a core in a system charged by a 6-cylinder aluminum compressor, a measured quatity of 500 viscosity refirgerant oil should be added to the core to ensure that the total oil charge in the system is correct. The amount added should be 3 fluid ounces poured directly into the inlet pipe of the new core with the pipe held vertically so that the oil will circulate in the core.*

26. Attach the accumulator/drier and core.

27. Connect the suction accumulator/drier to the evaporator core outlet tube, using new O-rings coated with clean refrigerant oil.

28. Install the core and suction accumualtor/drier.

29. Apply sealer to the case flange and around the evaporator core tubes.

30. Install the 6 screws attaching the 2 halves of the case.

31. Install the case heat shield.

32. Install the firewall seal on the case.

33. Position the case in the car.

34. Engage the 2 bottom studs, then the top stud.

35. Install the sensor air tube.

36. In the engine compartment, install the 3 nuts on the evaporator mounting studs, and the 2 screws at the blower motor. Install all fasteners loosely, then tighten them.

37. Install the left, bottom screw that supports the inlet recirculation air duct.

38. Connect all wiring harness connectors at the evaporator case.

39. Connect the blower motor lead from the main harness.

40. Reposition all movable hoses and wires at the case.

41. Connect the emission hose at the top of the evaporator case.

42. Install the copper hood grounding clip under the hood seal and fold the seal back into position.

43. Install the 6 screws retaining the right side of the hood seal bracket.

44. Connect the heater hoses at the core tubes.

45. Fill the cooling system.

46. Connect the wiring at the de-ice switch on the accumulator/drier.

47. Install the recirculation air duct assembly screw.

48. Connect the ambient air sensor tube to the evaporator air tube port.

NOTE: *Whenever the system is opened, a new accumulator/drier must be installed.*

47. Connect the liquid line at the evaporator.

48. Connect the suction hose from the accumulator/drier.

49. Evacuate, charge and leak test the system. See Chapter 1.

Control Panel
REMOVAL AND INSTALLATION

1977-79 Without Air Conditioning

1. Disconnect the battery ground.

2. Remove the knobs from the controls.

3. Disconnect the control cables at the operating levers.

4. Remove the 4 control assembly-to-instrument panel screws.

5. Push the control panel forward (towards the engine).

6. Disconnect the wiring from the panel connectors.

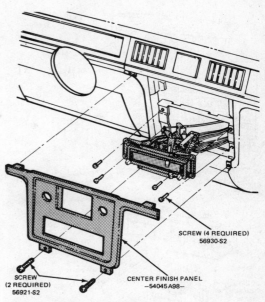

SCREW (4 REQUIRED) 56930-S2

SCREW (2 REQUIRED) 56921-S2

CENTER FINISH PANEL —54045 A98—

1981–88 control panel installation

7. Lower the control panel and remove it.

8. Installation is the reverse of removal. Adjust the cables as necessary.

1977-79 With Air Conditioning

1. Disconnect the battery ground.

2. Remove the control knobs.

3. Remove the 2 lower control assembly attaching screws.

4. Remove the 2 upper attaching screws.

5. Disconnect the temperature control cable at the control head.

6. Disconnect the vacuum harness at the vacuum selector valve.

7. Disconnect the wiring at the blower switch.

8. Push the panel forward and remove it from the instrument panel.

9. Installation is the reverse of removal. Adjust the cables as necessary.

1980-81 with or without Air Conditioning

1. Disconnect the battery ground.

2. Remove the 4 control assembly-to-instrument panel screws.

3. Pull the control panel towards you.

4. Disconnect the wiring from the panel connectors.

5. Disconnect the vacuum harness and the temperature control cable from the control panel.

6. Installation is the reverse of removal. Adjust the cables as necessary. Push on the vacuum harness retaining nut, DO NOT TRY TO SCREW IT ON!

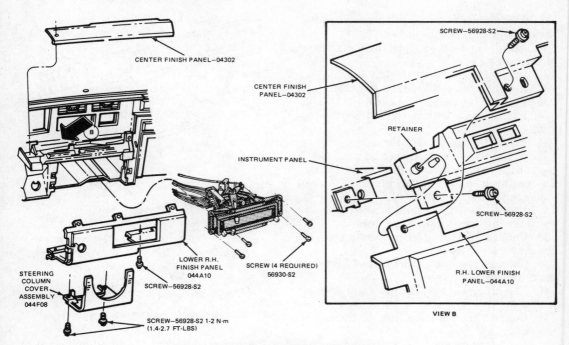

1980 control panel installation

1982-83 with or without Manual Air Conditioning

1. Disconnect the battery ground.

2. Remove the 4 control assembly-to-instrument panel screws.

3. Pull the control panel towards you.

4. Disconnect the wiring from the panel connectors.

5. Disconnect the vacuum harness and the temperature control cable from the control panel.

6. Installation is the reverse of removal. Adjust the cables as necessary. Push on the vacuum harness retaining nut, DO NOT TRY TO SCREW IT ON!

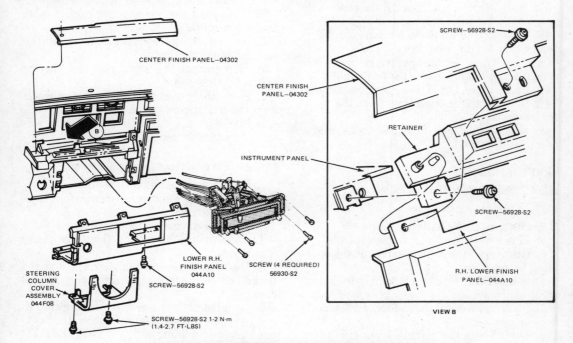

Control panel for 1982–83 automatic temperature control

1982-83 Cars with Automatic Temperature Control

1. Disconnect the battery ground.

2. Remove the radio knobs.

3. Open the ashtray and remove the 2 screws attaching the center finish panel to the instrument panel at the ashtray opening.

4. Open the ashtray and remove the ashtray receptacle.

5. Remove the 4 screws attaching the center finish panel to the instrument panel at the ashtray opening and at the upper edge of the finish panel.

6. Pull the lower edge of the center finish panel away from the instrument panel and disengage the upper tabs of the finish panel from the instrument panel.

7. Remove the 4 screws attaching the control panel to the instrument panel.

8. Pull the control panel towards you about ½". Insert a screwdriver and remove the control panel harness connector locator from the hole in the instrument panel.

9. Pull the control panel from the instrument panel and disconnect the wire connectors from the control panel.

10. Disconnect the vacuum harness and temperature control cable from the control panel. Discard the pushnuts.

11. Installation is the reverse of removal. If the lamp wires become disconnected during the panel removal, put the clips back on the controls before installing the panel.

1984 without Air Conditioning

1. Disconnect the battery ground.

2. Remove the instrument cluster opening finish panel.

3. Remove the 4 screws attaching the control panel to the instrument panel.

4. Pull the control panel out and disconnect the wiring from the control panel.

5. Disconnect the vacuum harness and the temperature control cable from the control panel.

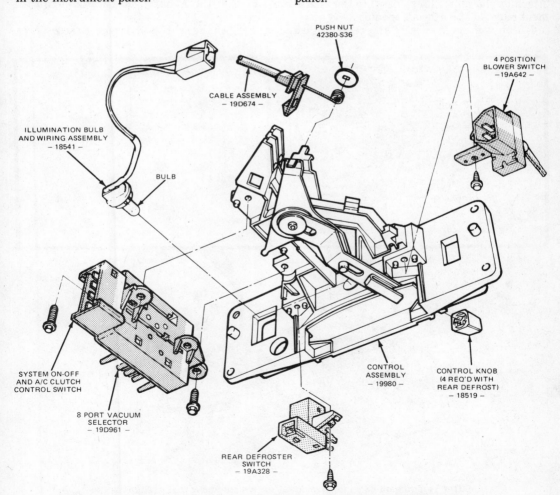

Control panel for all models, except 1982–83 automatic temperature control

6. Installation is the reverse of removal. Remember that the vacuum harness nut is a pushnut. It does not screw on.

1984 with Manual Air Conditioning

1. Disconnect the battery ground.
2. Remove the 4 screws attaching the control panel to the instrument panel.
3. Pull the control panel out and disconnect the wiring from the control panel.
4. Disconnect the vacuum harness and the temperature control cable from the control panel.
5. Installation is the reverse of removal. Remember that the vacuum harness nut is a pushnut. It does not screw on.

1984 with Automatic Temperature Control

1. Disconnect the battery ground.
2. Remove the radio knobs.
3. Open the ashtray and remove the 2 screws attaching the center finish panel to the instrument panel at the ashtray opening.
4. Pull the lower edge of the center finish

panel away from the instrument panel and disengage the upper tabs of the finish panel from the instrument panel.
5. Remove the 4 screws attaching the control panel to the instrument panel.
6. Pull the control panel towards you about ½". Insert a screwdriver and remove the control panel harness connector locator from the hole in the instrument panel.
7. Pull the control panel from the instrument panel and disconnect the wire connectors from the control panel.
8. Disconnect the vacuum harness and temperature control cable from the control panel. Discard the pushnuts.
9. Installation is the reverse of removal. If the lamp wires become disconnected during the panel removal, put the clips back on the controls before installing the panel.

1985-88 All with or without Air Conditioning

1. Disconnect the battery ground cable.
2. Pull the knobs from the radio control shafts.
3. Open the ashtray and remove the 2 screws

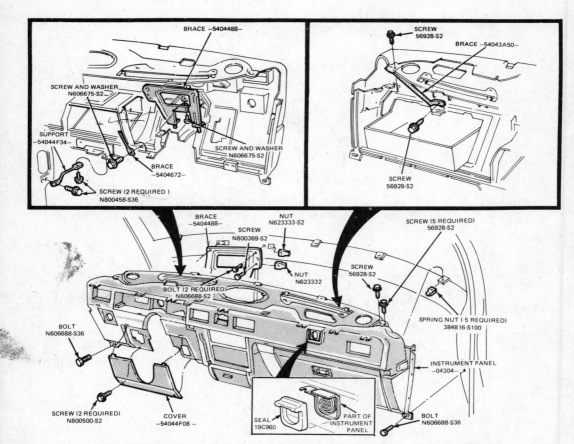

1981–88 instrument panel removal for all except automatic temperature control

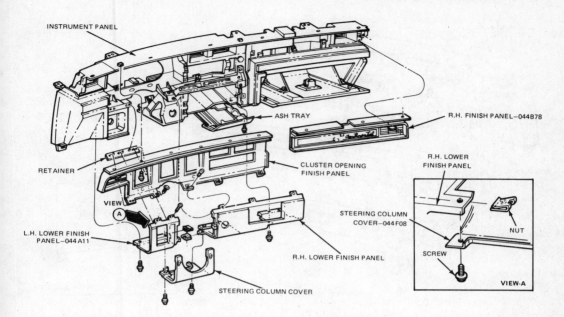

INSTRUMENT PANEL

ASH TRAY

R.H. FINISH PANEL—044B78

RETAINER

CLUSTER OPENING
FINISH PANEL

R.H. LOWER
FINISH PANEL

VIEW
A

STEERING COLUMN
COVER—044F08

NUT

L.H. LOWER FINISH
PANEL—044A11

SCREW

R.H. LOWER FINISH PANEL

VIEW-A

STEERING COLUMN COVER

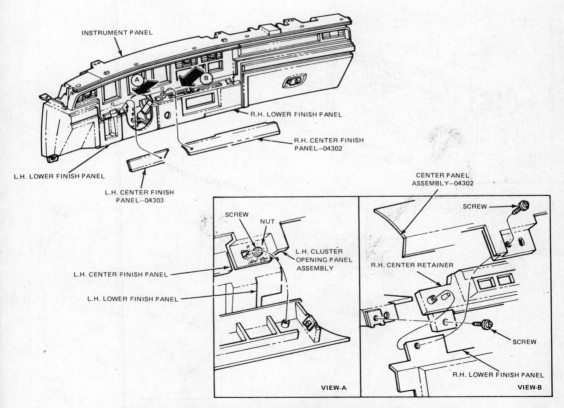

INSTRUMENT PANEL

A   B

R.H. LOWER FINISH PANEL

R.H. CENTER FINISH
PANEL—04302

L.H. LOWER FINISH PANEL

CENTER PANEL
ASSEMBLY—04302

L.H. CENTER FINISH
PANEL—04303

SCREW   NUT

L.H. CLUSTER
OPENING PANEL
ASSEMBLY

L.H. CENTER FINISH PANEL

L.H. LOWER FINISH PANEL

VIEW-A

SCREW

R.H. CENTER RETAINER

SCREW

R.H. LOWER FINISH PANEL

VIEW-B

1982–88 instrument panel removal with automatic temperature control

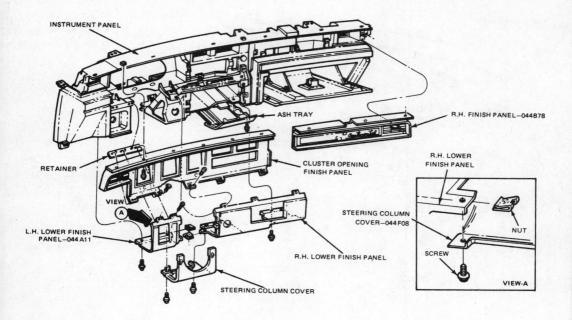

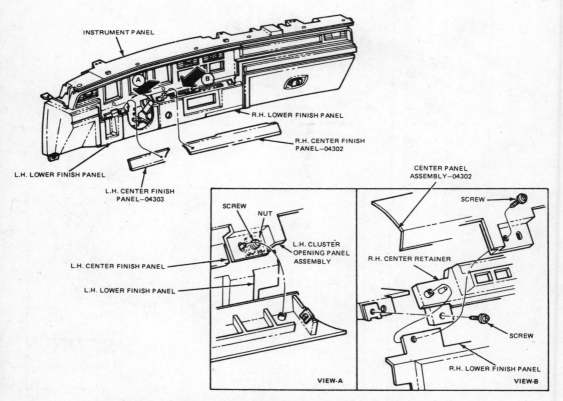

1980 instrument panel disassembly, except automatic temperature control

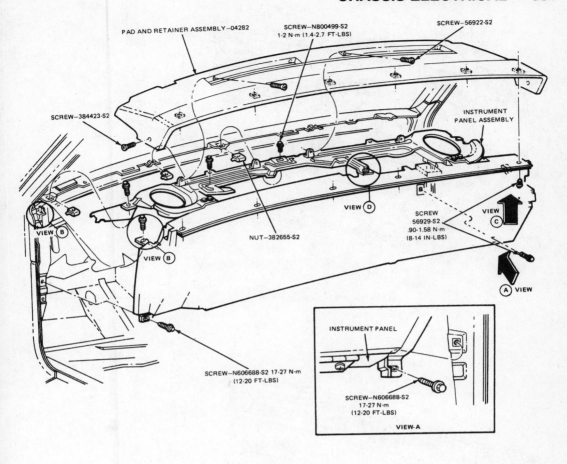

PAD AND RETAINER ASSEMBLY–04282

SCREW–N800499-S2
1-2 N·m (1.4-2.7 FT-LBS)

SCREW–56922-S2

SCREW–384423-S2

INSTRUMENT
PANEL ASSEMBLY

VIEW B

VIEW B

VIEW D

NUT–382655-S2

SCREW
56929-S2
.90-1.58 N·m
(8-14 IN-LBS)

VIEW C

A VIEW

SCREW–N606688-S2 17-27 N·m
(12-20 FT-LBS)

INSTRUMENT PANEL

SCREW–N606688-S2
17-27 N·m
(12-20 FT-LBS)

VIEW-A

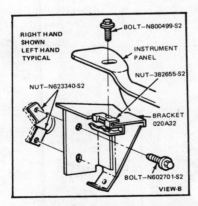

RIGHT HAND
SHOWN
LEFT HAND
TYPICAL

BOLT–N800499-S2

INSTRUMENT
PANEL

NUT–382655-S2

NUT–N623340-S2

BRACKET
020A32

BOLT–N602701-S2

VIEW-B

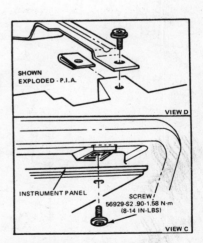

SHOWN
EXPLODED · P.I.A.

VIEW D

INSTRUMENT PANEL

SCREW
56929-S2 .90-1.58 N·m
(8-14 IN-LBS)

VIEW C

1981 instrument panel removal, with automatic temperature control

that attach the center finish panel to the instrument panel.

4. Pull the lower edge of the center finish panel away from the instrument panel and disengage the tabs of the finish panel from the instrument panel.

5. Remove the 4 control panel attaching screws.

6. Carefully pull the control panel away from the instrument panel and disconnect the wires and hoses.

7. Installation is the reverse of removal.

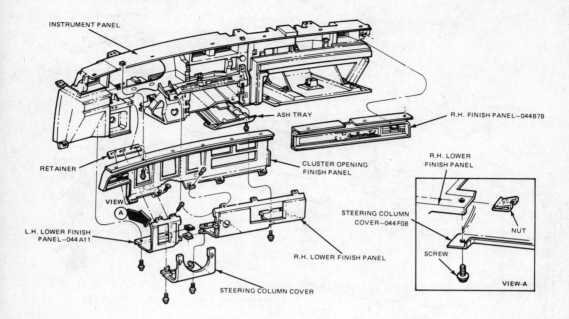

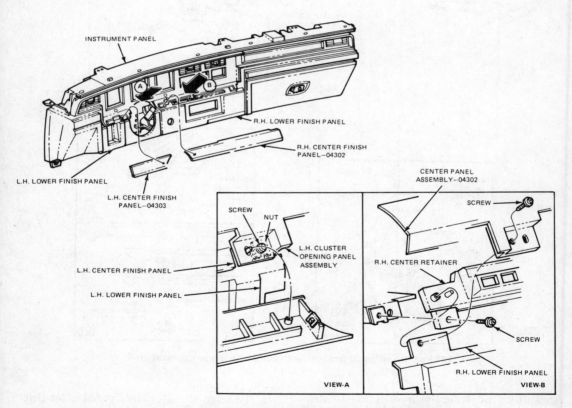

1981 instrument panel disassembly, with automatic temperature control

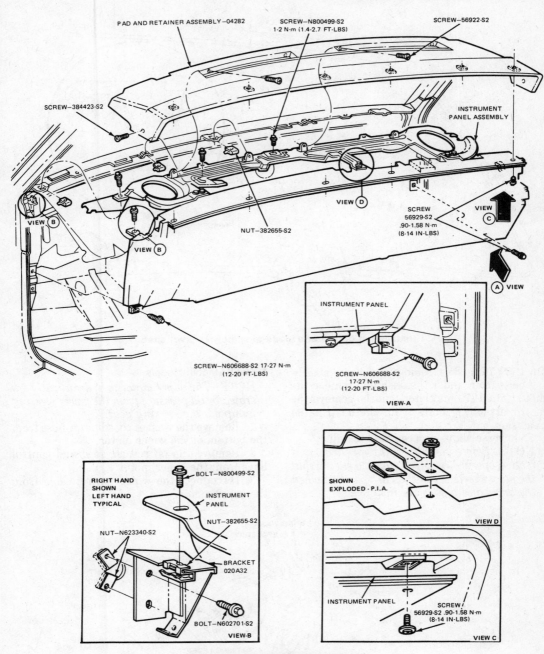

PAD AND RETAINER ASSEMBLY–04282

SCREW–N800499-S2
1-2 N·m (1.4-2.7 FT-LBS)

SCREW–56922-S2

SCREW–384423-S2

INSTRUMENT
PANEL ASSEMBLY

VIEW B

VIEW B

NUT–382655-S2

VIEW D

SCREW
56929-S2
.90-1.58 N·m
(8-14 IN-LBS)

VIEW C

VIEW A

SCREW–N606688-S2 17-27 N·m
(12-20 FT-LBS)

INSTRUMENT PANEL

SCREW–N606688-S2
17-27 N·m
(12-20 FT-LBS)

VIEW-A

RIGHT HAND
SHOWN
LEFT HAND
TYPICAL

BOLT–N800499-S2

INSTRUMENT
PANEL

NUT–382655-S2

NUT–N623340-S2

BRACKET
020A32

BOLT–N602701-S2

VIEW-B

SHOWN
EXPLODED - P.I.A.

VIEW D

INSTRUMENT PANEL

SCREW
56929-S2 .90-1.58 N·m
(8-14 IN-LBS)

VIEW C

1980 instrument panel pad removal

WINDSHIELD WIPERS

Motor

REMOVAL AND INSTALLATION

Ford/Mercury Models

1. Disconnect the negative battery cable.
2. Remove the wiper arms and blade assemblies from the pivots shafts.

3. On 1968-70 models, remove the cowl grille. On 1971-72 and 1977 models, remove the left side cowl grille.
4. Disconnect the wiper links at the wiper output pin by removing the retaining clip.
5. Disconnect the wire leads from the motor.
6. On 1968 models, remove the motor and bracket attaching bolts from the engine side of the firewall and remove the motor from the car.

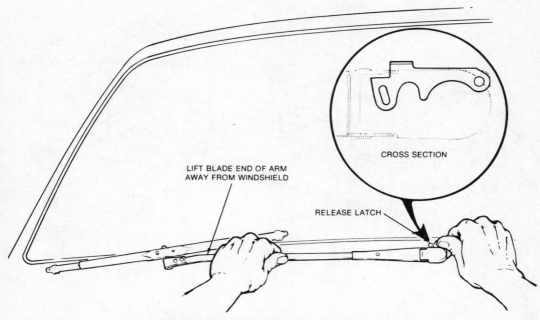

LIFT BLADE END OF ARM
AWAY FROM WINDSHIELD

CROSS SECTION

RELEASE LATCH

Installation of arm and blade assembly to pivot shaft

On 1969-78 models, remove the motor attaching bolts from under the dash and remove the motor. On 1979 and later models, remove the motor attaching bolts from the dash panel extension.

7. Reverse above procedure to install.

NOTE: *Before installing the wiper arms and blades, operate the wiper motor to ensure that the pivot shafts are in the Park position when the arms and blades are installed.*

1968-69 Lincoln Models

NOTE: *The wiper motor is hydraulically operated by oil pressure from the power steering pump via the steering gear.*

1. Remove the washer coordinator hose from the bottom of the wiper motor.

2. Remove the oil return, feed and control lines from the wiper motor.

3. Disconnect the wiper control cable from the wiper motor.

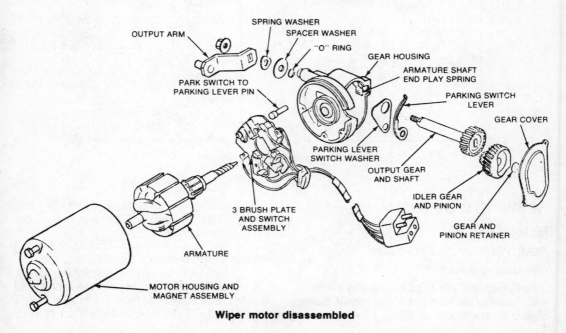

OUTPUT ARM

SPRING WASHER
SPACER WASHER

"O" RING

GEAR HOUSING

ARMATURE SHAFT
END PLAY SPRING

PARKING SWITCH
LEVER

GEAR COVER

PARK SWITCH TO
PARKING LEVER PIN

PARKING LEVER
SWITCH WASHER

OUTPUT GEAR
AND SHAFT

IDLER GEAR
AND PINION

GEAR AND
PINION RETAINER

3 BRUSH PLATE
AND SWITCH
ASSEMBLY

ARMATURE

MOTOR HOUSING AND
MAGNET ASSEMBLY

Wiper motor disassembled

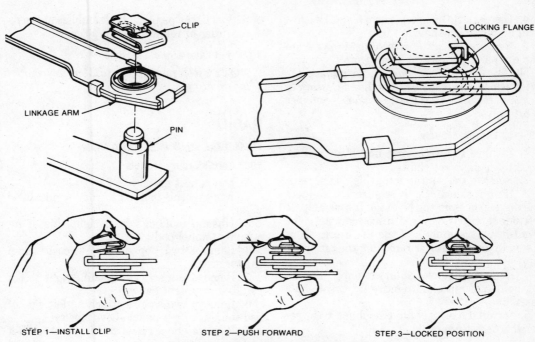

STEP 1—INSTALL CLIP   STEP 2—PUSH FORWARD   STEP 3—LOCKED POSITION

Installation of wiper arm connecting clips

4. Remove the screws holding the wiper motor to the auxiliary drive mounting plate and remove the wiper motor.

5. Install the wiper motor in the reverse order of removal. Refill the power steering system and bleed the lines.

1970 Continental

1. Disconnect the negative battery cable.

2. Remove the wiper arm and blade assemblies from the pivot shafts.

3. Remove the left cowl screen for access.

4. Disconnect the linkage drive arm from the motor output crank pin after removing the retainer clip.

5. Disconnect the two push-on wire connectors from the wiper motor.

6. Remove the wiper motor mounting bolts and the wiper motor.

7. Install the wiper motor in the reverse order of removal.

1970 Mark III

1. Disconnect the negative battery cable.

2. Disconnect the washer hose, remove the cowl top grille retaining bolts and pull the grille out from under the two clips.

3. Disconnect the wiring harness connector plugs from the engine side of the firewall. Push the wiring and wiring grommet through the firewall hole.

4. Remove the motor mounting bolts, when the motor is loose pull the wiper arm and blades

to the left for access to the crank arm and disconnect the drive link from the motor. Remove the motor from the mounting plate.

5. Install the wiper motor in the reverse order of removal.

1971 and Later Lincoln Models

1. Disconnect the negative battery cable.

2. Remove the wiper arm and blade assemblies from the pivot shafts.

3. Remove the left cowl screen for access on models through 1979. On 1980 and later models, remove the motor and linkage cover retaining screws and the cover.

4. Disconnect the linkage drive arm from the output arm crank after removing the retainer clip.

5. Disconnect the wiring harness plugs from the wiper motor. Remove the wiper motor mounting bolts and the wiper motor.

6. Install the wiper motor in the reverse order of removal. Be sure the wiper motor is in the Park position before installation.

Wiper Linkage

REMOVAL AND INSTALLATION

Ford/Mercury Models

1. Disconnect the battery negative cable.

2. Remove the wiper arms and blades from the pivots as an assembly.

3. Remove the cowl grille from the car.

4. Disconnect the linkage arm from the drive arm by removing the clip.

5. Remove the pivot attaching screws from the cowl and remove the pivot from the cowl.

NOTE: *On 1969-72 models, to remove the left wiper transmission, it is first necessary to loosen the attaching screws on the right wiper arm pivot.*

1968-69 Lincoln Models

1. Remove the wiper arm and blade assemblies from the pivot shafts.

2. Remove the ventilation grille and screen.

3. If right side service is required, disconnect the drive arm from the pivot shaft assembly. If left side service is required, disconnect the right hand pivot assembly and the drive arm from the auxiliary drive after removing the retaining clip.

4. Remove the pivot shaft assembly mounting bolts and nuts and remove the pivot shaft assembly.

5. Install the pivot shaft assemblies in the reverse order of removal.

1970 Continental

1. Disconnect the negative battery cable.

2. Remove the wiper arm and blade assemblies from the pivot shafts.

3. Remove the cowl screen for access.

4. Disconnect the left linkage arm from the drive arm after removing the retaining clip. Remove the left side pivot shaft assembly mounting bolts.

5. Disconnect the linkage drive arm from the motor crank pin after removing the retainer clip. Remove the right pivot shaft assembly mounting bolts. Remove the right drive arm and right arm as an assembly.

6. Install the wiper arm pivot shaft assemblies in the reverse order of removal.

1970 Mark III

1. Disconnect the negative battery cable.

2. Disconnect the washer hoses. Remove the cowl top grille retaining screws and slide the grille from under the mounting clips.

3. Remove the wiper arm and blade assemblies from the pivot shafts.

4. To remove the left pivot shaft assembly; remove the pivot shaft retaining bolts and disconnect the left pivot shaft link from the right pivot shaft link pin. Work the left pivot shaft and link assembly out through the cowl opening.

5. To remove the right pivot shaft assembly; remove the pivot shaft retaining bolts and disconnect the linkage from the crank pin after removing the retaining clip. Lift the pivot shaft assembly through the cowl opening.

6. Install the pivot shaft assemblies in the reverse order of removal.

1971 and Later Lincoln Models

NOTE: *Refer to the Ford/Mercury model information.*

RADIO

REMOVAL AND INSTALLATION

1968 Ford/Mercury Models

1. Disconnect battery.

2. Remove the moldings from wind shield pillars.

3. Unsnap moldings from right side of instrument panel pad.

4. Remove two pop off access cover from cluster area.

5. Remove four screws attaching right half of pad to instrument panel.

6. Remove two screws attaching left side of pad to instrument panel above cluster.

7. Remove one screw attaching each end of instrument panel lower pad to upper pad and remove upper pad from vehicle.

8. Pull all knobs from radio control shaft.

9. Remove ten retaining buttons and remove lens and mask from instrument cluster.

10. Remove two screws from blackout cover at right of speedometer and remove cover.

11. Remove four screws attaching radio front plate to instrument cluster.

12. Pull radio out and disconnect leads.

13. Reverse procedure to install radio.

1969-70 Models

1. Remove radio knobs and wiper and washer knobs.

2. Remove lighter and pull off heater switch knobs.

3. Remove ten screws retaining instrument panel trim cover assembly and remove.

4. Remove lower rear radio support bolt.

5. Remove three nuts retaining radio in instrument panel and pull radio half-way out.

6. Disconnect leads and remove radio.

7. Reverse procedure to install radio.

1971-79 Models

NOTE: *For the 1979 all electronic radio, perform Step 6 first.*

1. Disconnect the negative battery cable.

2. Remove the radio knobs and the nuts retaining the radio cover bezel.

3. Remove the bezel and the nut retaining the fader control to the bezel.

4. Remove the upper and lower radio support brackets and bolts.

5. Disconnect all leads from the radio.

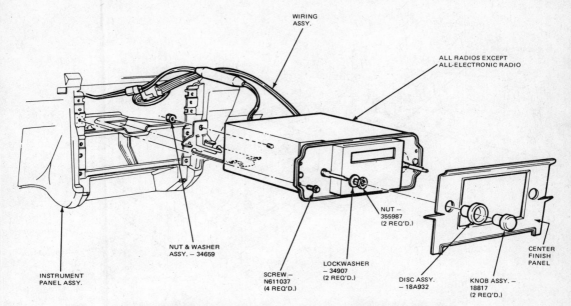

Typical radio installation for all models, except with all-electronic radio

6. Remove the two nuts retaining the radio to the instrument panel and remove the radio.

7. Reverse above procedure to install.

1968-69 Lincoln Except Mark III

1. Disconnect the negative battery cable.

2. Remove the eight screws from the lower housing.

3. Disconnect the speaker leads and the power antenna. If the car is equipped with a foot operated switch for the radio, disconnect the electrical lead. Disconnect the power lead to the radio.

4. Remove the knobs and bezels from the selector shafts.

5. Remove the two nuts and retainers from the selector shafts.

6. Remove the screws holding the radio bracket to the lower reinforcement on the instrument panel.

7. Disconnect additional selector shaft mounting nuts and non-power antenna lead, if equipped.

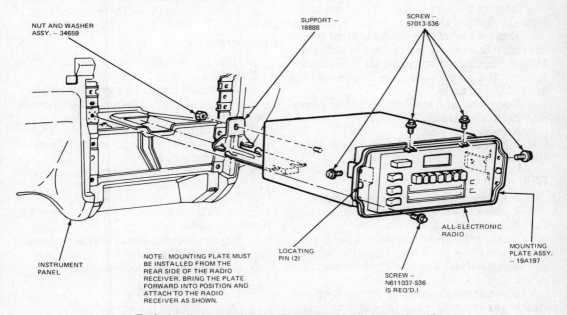

Typical radio installation for all models with all-electronic radio

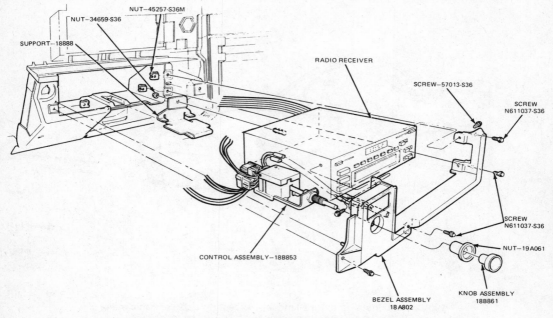

NUT—45257-S36M
NUT—34659-S36
SUPPORT—18888
RADIO RECEIVER
SCREW—57013-S36
SCREW N611037-S36
SCREW N611037-S36
NUT—19A061
CONTROL ASSEMBLY—18B853
KNOB ASSEMBLY 18B861
BEZEL ASSEMBLY 18A802

Typical radio installation for all models with all-electronic radio/tape player

8. Remove the radio.

9. Install the radio in the reverse order of removal.

1968-70 Mark III

1. Disconnect the negative battery cable.

2. Pull the knobs for the selector shafts.

3. Remove the cover plate located below the steering column.

4. Remove the selector shaft nuts that retain the radio trim panel.

5. Remove the six screws and the trim panel from the front of the radio.

6. Remove the selector shaft nuts that retain the radio. Remove the screw that attaches the radio to the instrument panel on the left side. Remove the screw attaching the mounting bracket to the radio.

7. Disconnect the speaker leads, the power lead and the antenna.

8. Remove the radio.

9. Install the radio in the reverse order of removal.

1970 Continental

1. Disconnect the negative battery cable.

2. Remove the map light assembly. Remove the left and right inspection covers.

3. Remove the lower instrument panel pad.

4. Remove the glove box. Open the ashtray and leave it opened. Remove the glove box lamp switch.

5. Reach through the glove box opening and remove the two nuts retaining the radio finish panel to the instrument panel.

6. Remove the radio knobs. Remove the two screws at the top of the finish panel. Disconnect the cigarette lighter and light from the right panel.

7. Reach through the glove box opening and remove the nut from the lower right corner of the center finish panel.

8. Remove the radio support top nut and three mounting screws. Pull the radio out slightly and disconnect the power and speaker leads and the antenna.

9. Install the radio in the reverse order of removal.

1980-85 Models

NOTE: *For the all electronic radio perform Step 6 first.*

1. Disconnect the battery ground cable.

2. Remove the radio knobs and the screws attaching the bezel.

3. Remove the radio plate attaching screws.

4. Pull the radio out to disengage it from the lower rear support bracket.

5. Disconnect the antenna and speaker leads and remove the radio.

6. Remove the radio to mounting plate retaining nuts and washers and remove the mounting plate.

7. Remove the rear upper support retaining nut and remove the support.

8. Reverse the steps to install the radio.

1986-88 Ford and Mercury

1. Disconnect the battery ground.

2. Remove the radio bezel.

3. Remove the radio attaching screws.

4. Pull the radio out to disengage it from the lower mounting bracket.

5. Disconnect the antenna and speaker leads and remove the radio.

6. Installation is the reverse of removal.

1986-88 Lincoln Town Car

1. Disconnect the battery ground.

2. Remove the 3 screws attaching the radio plate to the instrument panel.

3. Pull the radio out until the rear support bracket is clear of the instrument panel.

4. Disconnect the radio power feed 8-way connector and the speaker 8-way shielded connector from the rear of the radio.

5. Unplug the antenna lead.

6. Remove the radio.

7. Installation is the reverse of removal.

INSTRUMENT AND SWITCHES

Instrument Cluster

REMOVAL AND INSTALLATION

1968 Models

1. Disconnect the battery ground cable.

2. Remove right and left windshield mouldings.

3. Pry moulding from right side of instrument panel pad covering the pad retaining screws.

4. Pry off two access covers located above the speedometer leans and on underside of pad.

5. Remove screws retaining instrument panel pad, and remove pad.

6. Remove radio knobs.

7. Remove button clips retaining instrument cluster mask and lens, and remove mask and lens.

8. Disconnect speedometer cable.

9. Remove screws retaining instrument panel lower pad and remove pad.

10. Remove screws from clock retainer and clock and position clock forward.

11. Remove plate under speedometer and two rubber spacers and screws retaining speedometer assembly.

12. Reverse procedure to install.

1969-72 Models

1. Disconnect negative battery cable. Remove upper part of instrument panel by removing screws along lower edge, two screws in each of the defroster registers, and disconnecting the radio speaker.

2. Remove cluster opening finish panels from each side of instrument cluster.

3. Disconnect plugs to printed circuit, radio, heater and air conditioning fan, windshield wipers and washers, and any other electrical connection to cluster.

4. Disconnect heater and air conditioning control cables and speedometer cable.

5. Remove all knobs from instrument panel if required.

6. Remove instrument cluster trim cover.

7. Remove mounting screws and remove cluster.

8. Reverse procedure to install.

1973-79 Models, except Mark V

1. Disconnect negative battery cable.

2. Remove the steering column cover.

3. Disconnect the speedometer cable and the wire plugs to the printed circuit.

4. Remove the cluster trim cover.

5. Remove the screw attaching the transmission selector lever indicator cable to the column.

6. Remove the instrument cluster retaining screws and lift the cluster from the instrument panel.

7. Reverse the above procedure to install, taking care to ensure that the selector pointer is aligned.

1978-79 Mark V

1. Disconnect the negative battery cable.

2. Remove the screws that retain the upper access cover to the instrument panel pad.

3. Remove the screws that retain the lower cluster appliqued cover below the instrument panel.

4. Remove the steering column shroud.

5. Remove the heated rear window control knob.

6. From under the instrument panel, depress the headlight switch lock button and pull the control knob and shaft from the headlight switch.

7. Remove the headlight switch bezel and the wiper/washer control knob and bezel.

8. Remove the cigarette lighter from its socket and remove the screws retaining the cluster front cover.

9. Use a right angle screwdriver (or equivalent) to loosen, evenly in stages, the retainers from along the edges of the finish panel.

10. Remove the cluster front cover.

11. Remove the screw that retains the shift quadrant control cable bracket to the steering column and disconnect the cable while the transmission selector is in the **Park** position.

12. Reach under the instrument panel and disconnect the speedometer cable.

13. Remove the cluster to instrument panel mounting screws and pull the cluster away from the panel.

14. Disconnect the electrical connectors at the rear of the cluster.

15. Install the cluster in the reverse order of removal.

1980-88 Non-Electronic Cluster

1. Disconnect the negative battery cable.

2. Disconnect the speedometer cable (refer to the following section for instructions).

3. Remove the instrument cluster trim cover attaching screws and the lower two steering column cover attaching screws. Remove the trim covers.

4. Remove the lower half of the steering column shroud.

5. Remove the screw attaching the transmission selector indicator bracket to the steering column. Unfasten the cable loop from the retainer on the shift lever. Remove the column bracket.

6. Remove the cluster attaching screws. Disconnect the cluster feed plug and remove the cluster.

7. Reverse the procedure for installation. Be sure to lubricate the speedometer drive head. Adjust the selector indicator if necessary.

1980-88 Electronic Cluster

1. Disconnect negative battery cable.

2. Remove the steering column trim cover and lower instrument panel trim cover. Remove the keyboard trim panel and the trim panel on the left of the column.

3. Remove the instrument cluster trim cover screw and remove the trim panel.

4. Remove the instrument cluster mounting screws and pull the cluster forward. Disconnect the feed plugs and the ground wire from the back of the cluster. Disconnect the speedometer cable (see following section for details).

5. Remove the screw attaching the transmission indicator cable bracket to the steering column. Unfasten the cable loop from the retainer. Remove the bracket.

6. Unfasten the plastic clamp from around the steering column. Remove the cluster.

7. To install the cluster: Apply a small amount of silicone lubricant into the drive hole of the speedometer head.

8. Connect the feed plugs and the ground wire to the cluster. Install the speedometer cable. Attach the instrument cluster to the instrument panel.

9. Install the plastic indicator cable clamp around the steering column and engage the clamp locator pin in the column tube.

10. Place the transmission selector in the **Drive** position. Install the mounting screw into the retainer but do not tighten.

11. Rotate the plastic cable clamp until the indicator flag covers both location dots. Tighten the retainer screw.

12. Move the selector through all positions. Readjust if necessary.

13. The rest of the installation is in the reverse order of removal.

Speedometer Cable Core
REMOVAL AND INSTALLATION

1. Reach up behind the cluster and disconnect the cable by depressing the quick disconnect tab and pulling the cable away.

2. Remove the cable from its casing. If the cable is broken, raise the car and disconnect the cable from the transmission. Pull the cable from the casing.

3. Install the new cable into the casing. Connect the transmission (if disconnected). Engage the cable with the drive head and push it until the tab locks.

Windshield Wiper Switch
REMOVAL AND INSTALLATION

1. Disconnect the battery ground.

2. Remove the steering column cover halves.

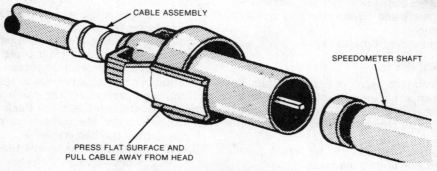

CABLE ASSEMBLY

SPEEDOMETER SHAFT

PRESS FLAT SURFACE AND
PULL CABLE AWAY FROM HEAD

Speedometer cable quick disconnect

3. Remove the 2 wiper switch retaining screws.

4. Disconnect the wiring at the rear of the switch.

5. Installation is the reverse of removal.

Headlight Switch

REMOVAL AND INSTALLATION

All Lincoln and Continental Models

1. Disconnect the battery ground.

2. Insert a thin awl into the slot in the headlamp switch and depress the spring while pulling the knob out.

3. Remove the auto dimmer bezel and the autolamp delay bezel.

4. Remove the steering column lower shroud.

5. Remove the lower left instrument panel trim bezel.

6. Remove the 5 screws retaining the headlamp switch mounting bracket to the instrument panel.

7. Carefully pull the switch and bracket from the instrument panel. Disconnect the wiring.

8. Remove the locknut and screw retaining the switch to the bracket.

9. Installation is the reverse of removal.

All Ford and Mercury Models

1. Disconnect the battery ground.

2. Pull the headlamp switch to the ON position.

3. Reach under the instrument panel and depress the headlamp switch knob and shaft retainer button on the switch. Pull the knob and shaft assembly straight out.

4. Unscrew the locknut.

5. Push the switch inward and out of the panel opening.

6. Disconnect the wiring.

Clock

REMOVAL AND INSTALLATION

1. Disconnect the battery ground.

2. Remove the clock bezel.

3. Remove the 3 retaining screws and pull the clock out carefully. Disconnect the wiring.

4. Installation is the reverse of removal.

LIGHTING

Headlights

REMOVAL AND INSTALLATION

Except Aerodynamic Headlamps

1. Remove the headlight door mounting screws and the headlight door.

2. Remove the three screws that hold the headlight retainer to the adjusting ring, and remove the retainer.

3. Pull the headlight forward and disconnect the wire plug. Remove the headlight.

4. Attach a new headlight to the wiring plug.

5. Install the new light in the housing and replace the retainer ring.

6. Reinstall the headlight door.

Aerodynamic Headlamps

BULB ASSEMBLY

CAUTION: *The halogen bulb contains pressurized gas. If the bulb is dropped or scratched it will shatter. Also, avoid touching the bulb glass with your bare fingers. Grasp the bulb only by its plastic base. Oil from bare skin will cause hot spots on the glass surface and lead to premature burnout. If you do touch the glass, clean it prior to installation.*

1. Make sure that the headlamp switch is OFF.

2. Raise the hood. The bulb protrudes from the rear of the headlamp assembly.

3. Unplug the electrical connector from the bulb.

4. Rotate the bulb retaining ring ⅛ turn counterclockwise and remove it.

5. Pull the bulb straight back out of its socket. Don't rotate it.

6. When installing the bulb, push it into position, turning it slightly right or left to align the grooves in the forward part of the base with the tabs in the socket. When they are aligned, push the bulb firmly into position until the mounting flange on the base contacts the rear face of the socket.

7. Install the locking ring, turning it until a stop is felt.

8. Push the connector onto the bulb until it snaps into position.

HEADLAMP ASSEMBLY

1. Make sure that the headlamp switch is OFF.

2. Raise the hood. The bulb protrudes from the rear of the headlamp assembly.

3. Unplug the electrical connector from the bulb.

4. Remove the 3 nuts and washers from the rear of the headlamp.

5. Push forward on the headlamp at the bulb socket. It may be necessary to loosen the parking lamp and cornering lamp fasteners.

6. Remove the 3 clips which attach the headlamp to the black ring by prying them out from the base with a flat-bladed screwdriver.

7. Installation is the reverse of removal. Make sure that the black rubber shield is securely crimped on the headlamp.

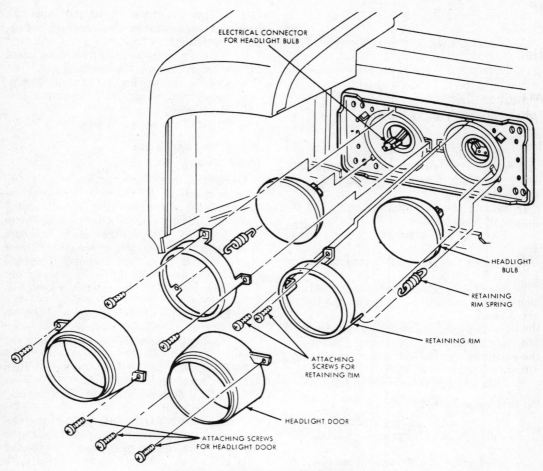

Typical headlight seal beam replacement

Hi-Mount Stop Lamp

REMOVAL AND INSTALLATION

Town Car

1. Remove the trim cao from the front of the lamp.

2. Remove the screw and pull the lamp forward to detach it from the bracket.

3. Locate the wire assembly in the trunk and remove the locator to allow sufficient wire to pull the lamp away from the package tray.

4. From the bottom side of the lamp, remove the bulb and socket by truning it counterclockwise.

5. Installation si the reverse of removal.

Crown Victoria and Grand Marquis, exc. Station Wagon

1. Remove the screw covers from each side of the lamp.

2. Remove the screws from the retainer.

3. Pull the lamp up and forward to detach it from the retainer brackets.

4. On the bottom of the lamp body, pull the wire assembly locator from the lamp body.

5. From the bottom of the lamp, remove the bulb and socket by turning it counterclockwise.

6. Installation is the reverse of removal.

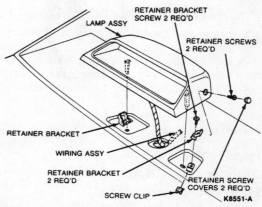

Hi-Mount stoplight for all models, except station wagon

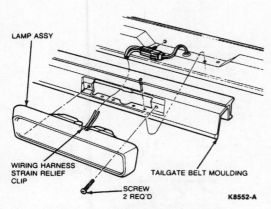

LAMP ASSY

WIRING HARNESS
STRAIN RELIEF
CLIP

TAILGATE BELT MOULDING

SCREW
2 REQ'D

K8552-A

Hi-Mount stoplight for all station wagon models

Station Wagon

1. Remove the 2 screws from the lamp.
2. Pull the lamp rearward and remove it from the tailgate moulding.
3. Disengage the wiring harness strain relief clip by pulling it straight out of the lamp.
4. Remove the bulb and socket by turning it gently while pulling it out of the lamp.
5. Installation is the reverse of removal.

Parking, Side Marker and Rear Lamps

These bulbs are accessed by removing the lamp assembly and turning the bulb socket ½ turn.

In some cases, the bulb socket may be accessed by reaching behind the lamp or sheetmetal, without removing the lamp assembly.

TRAILER WIRING

Wiring the car for towing is fairly easy. There are a number of good wiring kits available and these should be used, rather than trying to design your own. All trailers will need brake lights and turn signals as well as tail lights and side marker lights. Most states require extra marker lights for overwide trailers. Also, most states have recently required back-up lights for trailers, and most trailer manufacturers have been building trailers with back-up lights for several years.

Additionally, some Class I, most Class II and just about all Class III trailers will have electric brakes.

Add to this number an accessories wire, to operate trailer internal equipment or to charge the trailer's battery, and you can have as many as seven wires in the harness.

Determine the equipment on your trailer and buy the wiring kit necessary. The kit will contain all the wires needed, plus a plug adapter set which included the female plug, mounted on the bumper or hitch, and the male plug, wired into, or plugged into the trailer harness.

When installing the kit, follow the manufacturer's instructions. The color coding of the wires is standard throughout the industry.

One point to note, some domestic vehicles, and most imported vehicles, have separate turn signals. On most domestic vehicles, the brake lights and rear turn signals operate with the same bulb. For those vehicles with separate turn signals, you can purchase an isolation unit so that the brake lights won't blink whenever the turn signals are operated, or, you can go to your local electronics supply house and buy four diodes to wire in series with the brake and turn signal bulbs. Diodes will isolate the brake and turn signals. The choice is yours. The isolation units are simple and quick to install, but far more expensive than the diodes. The diodes, however, require more work to install properly, since they require the cutting of each bulb's wire and soldering in place of the diode.

One final point, the best kits are those with a spring loaded cover on the vehicle mounted socket. This cover prevents dirt and moisture from corroding the terminals. Never let the vehicle socket hang loosely. Always mount it securely to the bumper or hitch.

Seat Belt/Starter Interlock

1974-75 Models

All 1974 and some 1975 Ford, Mercury and Lincoln vehicles are equipped with the Federally required starter interlock system. The purpose of this system is to force the wearing of seat belts.

The system includes a warning light and buzzer (as in late 1972 and 1973), weight sensors in the front seats, switches in the outboard front seat belt retractors, and an electronic control module. The center front seat is tied into the warning light and buzzer system, but not into the starter interlock.

The electronic control module requires that the driver and right front passenger first sit down, then pull out their seat belts. If this is not done, the starter will not operate, but the light and buzzer will. The sequence must be followed each time the engine is started unless the driver and passenger have remained seated and buckled. If the seat belts have been pulled out and left buckled, the engine will not start. The switches in the retractors must be cycled for each start. If the belts are released after the start, the light and buzzer will operate.

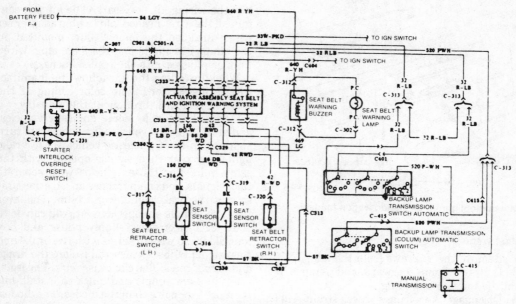

Seat belt/starter interlock system circuit

TROUBLESHOOTING

If the starter will not crank or the warning buzzer will not shut off, perform the following checks:

Problem: Front seat occupant sits on a pre-buckled seat belt.

Solution: Unbuckle the pre-buckled belt, fully retract, extract, and then rebuckle the belt.

Problem: The front seat occupants are buckled, but the start will not crank.

Solution: The unoccupied seat sensor switch stuck closed before the seat was occupied. Reset the unoccupied seat sensor switches by applying and then releasing 50 lbs. or more of weight to the seat directly over the seat sensor switches.

Problem: Starter will not crank with a heavy parcel on the front seat.

Solution: Buckle the seat belt around the parcel somewhere else in the car. Unbuckle the seat belt when the parcel is removed from the front seat.

Problem: Starter will not crank due to starter interlock system component failure.

Solution: An emergency starter interlock override switch is located under the hood on the fender apron. Depress the red push button on the switch and release it. This will allow one

If the system should fail, preventing starting, the interlock by-pass switch under the hood can be used. This switch permits one start without interference from the interlock system. This by-pass switch can also be used for servicing purposes.

complete cycle of the ignition key from Off to Start and back it Off. Do not tape the button down as this will result in the deactivation of the override feature.

DISCONNECTING SEAT BELT/STARTER INTERLOCK

As of October 29, 1974, it is legal to disconnect the seat belt/starter interlock system. however, the warning light portion of the system must be left operational.

1. Apply the parking brake and remove the ignition key.

2. Open the hood and locate the system emergency override switch and connector. Remove the connector.

3. Cut the white wire(s) with the pink dots (#33 circuit) and the red wire(s) with the light blue stripe (#32 circuit).

4. Splice the two (four) wires together and tape the splice. Use a butt connector if available.

NOTE: *Do not cut and splice the other connector wires. If the red/yellow hash wire is spliced to any of the other wires the car will start in gear.*

5. Install the connector back on the override switch. Close the hood.

6. Apply the parking brakes, buckle the seat belt, and turn the key to the **ON** position. If the starter cranks in **ON** or any gear selected, the wrong wires have been cut and spliced. Repeat Steps 3-5.

7. Unbuckle the belt and try to start the car.

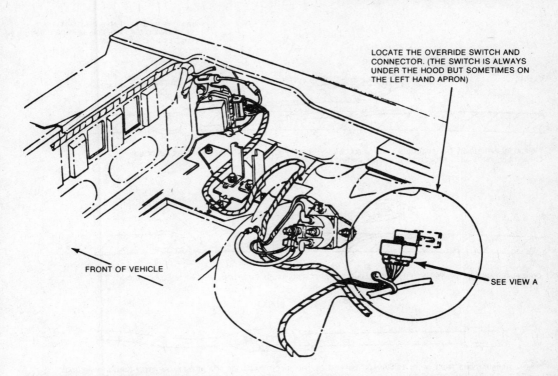

LOCATE THE OVERRIDE SWITCH AND CONNECTOR. (THE SWITCH IS ALWAYS UNDER THE HOOD BUT SOMETIMES ON THE LEFT HAND APRON)

FRONT OF VEHICLE

SEE VIEW A

CAUTION: Set the parking brake and remove the ignition key before any rework is performed. (If the no. 640 circuit is accidentally spliced into the no. 32 or no. 33 circuits, the car will start in gear)

1. Cut the no. 32 and no. 33 circuits
2. On the wiring harness end, splice the no. 32 and no. 33 circuits together. Use a B9A-14487-A butt connector on a 16 to 18 gage wire or a B9A-14487-B connector on a 10 to 14 gage wire
3. Tape the complete splice to water proof the connection
4. Reattach the connector to the override switch to prevent rattling
5. Test the rework by setting the car brakes, buckle up the seat belt and turn the key to on. If the starter cranks in the on position and in any gear the wires have been crossed. (Recheck the rework)
6. The buzzer function can be deleted by removing the buzzer from the connector and taping the connector to the harness to prevent rattling
7. The sequential seat belt warning light feature can be deleted by removing the bulb from its socket. This can only be done on previously sold vehicles. The light cannot be disconnected on a new and unsold car even if the purchaser so requests

NO. 640 CIRCUIT RED/YELLOW HASH

NO. 33 CIRCUIT WHITE/PINK DOT

SPLICE

NO. 32 CIRCUIT RED/LT BLUE STRIPE

NO. 57 CIRCUIT BLACK (T-BIRD, MARK IV, LINCOLN ONLY)

VIEW A

NOTE: If the no. 32 and no. 33 circuit terminals contain two wires, cut and splice all wires from the no. 32 and no. 33 circuits into one butt connector.

Disconnecting the seat belt/starter interlock system

REMOVE EXISTING VINYL TUBE SHIELDING
REINSTALL OVER FUSE LINK BEFORE CRIMPING
FUSE LINK TO WIRE ENDS

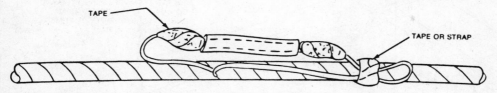

TAPE

TAPE OR STRAP

TYPICAL REPAIR USING THE SPECIAL #17 GA. (9.00″ LONG-YELLOW) FUSE LINK REQUIRED FOR THE AIR/COND.
CIRCUITS (2) #687E and #261A LOCATED IN THE ENGINE COMPARTMENT

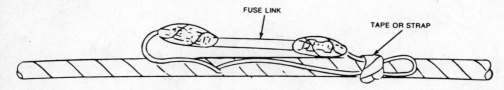

FUSE LINK

TAPE OR STRAP

TYPICAL REPAIR FOR ANY IN-LINE FUSE LINK USING THE SPECIFIED GAUGE FUSE LINK FOR THE SPECIFIC CIRCUIT

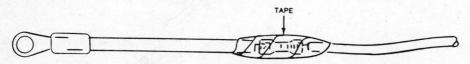

TAPE

TYPICAL REPAIR USING THE EYELET TERMINAL FUSE LINK OF THE SPECIFIED GAUGE FOR ATTACHMENT TO A CIRCUIT WIRE END

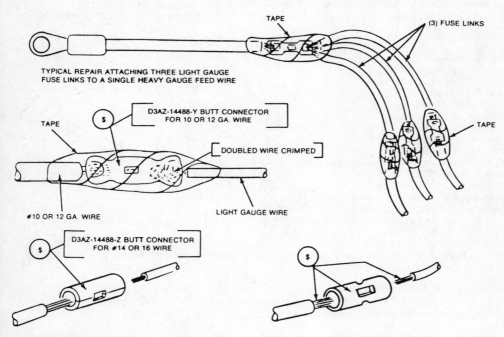

TAPE

(3) FUSE LINKS

TYPICAL REPAIR ATTACHING THREE LIGHT GAUGE
FUSE LINKS TO A SINGLE HEAVY GAUGE FEED WIRE

D3AZ-14488-Y BUTT CONNECTOR
FOR 10 OR 12 GA. WIRE

TAPE

DOUBLED WIRE CRIMPED

TAPE

#10 OR 12 GA. WIRE

LIGHT GAUGE WIRE

D3AZ-14488-Z BUTT CONNECTOR
FOR #14 OR 16 WIRE

FUSIBLE LINK REPAIR PROCEDURE

General fuse link repair procedure

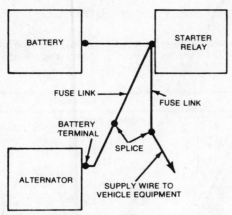

Fuse link location

If the car doesn't start, repeat Steps 3-5. If the car starts, everything is OK.

8. To stop the warning buzzer from operating, remove it from its connector and throw it away. Tape the connector to the wiring harness so that it can't rattle.

CIRCUIT PROTECTION

Fuses, Circuit Breakers and Fusible Links

LOCATION

A fuse link is a short length of insulated wire, integral with the engine compartment wiring harness. It is several wire gauges smaller than the circuit it protects and is located inline directly from the positive terminal of the battery.

When heavy current flows or when a short to ground occurs in the wiring harness, the fuse link burns out and protects the alternator or wiring. Production fuse links are color coded:

   a. 12 gauge: Grey.
   b. 14 gauge: Dark Green.
   c. 16 gauge: Black.
   d. 18 gauge: Brown.
   e. 20 gauge: Dark Blue.

NOTE: *Replacement fuse link color coding may vary from production fuse link color coding.*

Circuit breakers are used on certain electrical components requiring high amperage, such as the headlamp circuit, electrical seats and/or windows to name a few. The advantage of the circuit breaker is its ability to open and close the electrical circuit as the lead demands, rather than the necessity of a part replacement, should the circuit be opened with another protective device in line.

A fuse panel is used to house the numerous fuses protecting the various branches of the electrical system and is normally the most accessible. the mounting of the fuse panel is usually on the left side of the passenger compartment, under the dash, either on the side kick panel or on the firewall to the left of the steering column. Certain models will have the fuse panel exposed while other models will have it covered with a removable trim cover.

Fuses are simply snapped in and out for replacement.

Troubleshooting the Heater

Problem	Cause	Solution
Blower motor will not turn at any speed	• Blown fuse • Loose connection • Defective ground • Faulty switch • Faulty motor • Faulty resistor	• Replace fuse • Inspect and tighten • Clean and tighten • Replace switch • Replace motor • Replace resistor
Blower motor turns at one speed only	• Faulty switch • Faulty resistor	• Replace switch • Replace resistor
Blower motor turns but does not circulate air	• Intake blocked • Fan not secured to the motor shaft	• Clean intake • Tighten security
Heater will not heat	• Coolant does not reach proper temperature • Heater core blocked internally • Heater core air-bound • Blend-air door not in proper position	• Check and replace thermostat if necessary • Flush or replace core if necessary • Purge air from core • Adjust cable
Heater will not defrost	• Control cable adjustment incorrect • Defroster hose damaged	• Adjust control cable • Replace defroster hose

Troubleshooting Basic Turn Signal and Flasher Problems

Most problems in the turn signals or flasher system, can be reduced to defective flashers or bulbs, which are easily replaced. Occasionally, problems in the turn signals are traced to the switch in the steering column, which will require professional service.

F = Front   R = Rear   ● = Lights off   ○ = Lights on

Problem		Solution
Turn signals light, but do not flash		• Replace the flasher
No turn signals light on either side		• Check the fuse. Replace if defective. • Check the flasher by substitution • Check for open circuit, short circuit or poor ground
Both turn signals on one side don't work		• Check for bad bulbs • Check for bad ground in both housings
One turn signal light on one side doesn't work		• Check and/or replace bulb • Check for corrosion in socket. Clean contacts. • Check for poor ground at socket
Turn signal flashes too fast or too slow		• Check any bulb on the side flashing too fast. A heavy-duty bulb is probably installed in place of a regular bulb. • Check the bulb flashing too slow. A standard bulb was probably installed in place of a heavy-duty bulb. • Check for loose connections or corrosion at the bulb socket
Indicator lights don't work in either direction		• Check if the turn signals are working • Check the dash indicator lights • Check the flasher by substitution

One indicator light doesn't light		• On systems with 1 dash indicator: See if the lights work on the same side. Often the filaments have been reversed in systems combining stoplights with taillights and turn signals.
		   Check the flasher by substitution
		• On systems with 2 indicators: Check the bulbs on the same side
		   Check the indicator light bulb
		   Check the flasher by substitution

Troubleshooting Basic Dash Gauge Problems

Problem	Cause	Solution
Coolant Temperature Gauge		
Gauge reads erratically or not at all	• Loose or dirty connections • Defective sending unit • Defective gauge	• Clean/tighten connections • Bi-metal gauge: remove the wire from the sending unit. Ground the wire for an instant. If the gauge registers, replace the sending unit. • Magnetic gauge: disconnect the wire at the sending unit. With ignition ON gauge should register COLD. Ground the wire; gauge should register HOT.
Ammeter Gauge—Turn Headlights ON (do not start engine). Note reaction		
Ammeter shows charge Ammeter shows discharge Ammeter does not move	• Connections reversed on gauge • Ammeter is OK • Loose connections or faulty wiring • Defective gauge	• Reinstall connections • Nothing • Check/correct wiring • Replace gauge
Oil Pressure Gauge		
Gauge does not register or is inaccurate	• On mechanical gauge, Bourdon tube may be bent or kinked • Low oil pressure • Defective gauge • Defective wiring • Defective sending unit	• Check tube for kinks or bends preventing oil from reaching the gauge • Remove sending unit. Idle the engine briefly. If no oil flows from sending unit hole, problem is in engine. • Remove the wire from the sending unit and ground it for an instant with the ignition ON. A good gauge will go to the top of the scale. • Check the wiring to the gauge. If it's OK and the gauge doesn't register when grounded, replace the gauge. • If the wiring is OK and the gauge functions when grounded, replace the sending unit
All Gauges		
All gauges do not operate All gauges read low or erratically All gauges pegged	• Blown fuse • Defective instrument regulator • Defective or dirty instrument voltage regulator • Loss of ground between instrument voltage regulator and car • Defective instrument regulator	• Replace fuse • Replace instrument voltage regulator • Clean contacts or replace • Check ground • Replace regulator
Warning Lights		
Light(s) do not come on when ignition is ON, but engine is not started Light comes on with engine running	• Defective bulb • Defective wire • Defective sending unit • Problem in individual system • Defective sending unit	• Replace bulb • Check wire from light to sending unit • Disconnect the wire from the sending unit and ground it. Replace the sending unit if the light comes on with the ignition ON. • Check system • Check sending unit (see above)

Troubleshooting Basic Lighting Problems

Problem	Cause	Solution
Lights		
One or more lights don't work, but others do	· Defective bulb(s) · Blown fuse(s) · Dirty fuse clips or light sockets · Poor ground circuit	· Replace bulb(s) · Replace fuse(s) · Clean connections · Run ground wire from light socket housing to car frame
Lights burn out quickly	· Incorrect voltage regulator setting or defective regulator · Poor battery/alternator connections	· Replace voltage regulator · Check battery/alternator connections
Lights go dim	· Low/discharged battery · Alternator not charging · Corroded sockets or connections · Low voltage output	· Check battery · Check drive belt tension; repair or replace alternator · Clean bulb and socket contacts and connections · Replace voltage regulator
Lights flicker	· Loose connection · Poor ground · Circuit breaker operating (short circuit)	· Tighten all connections · Run ground wire from light housing to car frame · Check connections and look for bare wires
Lights "flare"—Some flare is normal on acceleration—if excessive, see "Lights Burn Out Quickly"	· High voltage setting	· Replace voltage regulator
Lights glare—approaching drivers are blinded	· Lights adjusted too high · Rear springs or shocks sagging · Rear tires soft	· Have headlights aimed · Check rear springs/shocks · Check/correct rear tire pressure
Turn Signals		
Turn signals don't work in either direction	· Blown fuse · Defective flasher · Loose connection	· Replace fuse · Replace flasher · Check/tighten all connections
Right (or left) turn signal only won't work	· Bulb burned out · Right (or left) indicator bulb burned out · Short circuit	· Replace bulb · Check/replace indicator bulb · Check/repair wiring
Flasher rate too slow or too fast	· Incorrect wattage bulb · Incorrect flasher	· Flasher bulb · Replace flasher (use a variable load flasher if you pull a trailer)
Indicator lights do not flash (burn steadily)	· Burned out bulb · Defective flasher	· Replace bulb · Replace flasher
Indicator lights do not light at all	· Burned out indicator bulb · Defective flasher	· Replace indicator bulb · Replace flasher

Troubleshooting Basic Windshield Wiper Problems

Problem	Cause	Solution
Electric Wipers		
Wipers do not operate— Wiper motor heats up or hums	• Internal motor defect • Bent or damaged linkage • Arms improperly installed on linking pivots	• Replace motor • Repair or replace linkage • Position linkage in park and reinstall wiper arms
Wipers do not operate— No current to motor	• Fuse or circuit breaker blown • Loose, open or broken wiring • Defective switch • Defective or corroded terminals • No ground circuit for motor or switch	• Replace fuse or circuit breaker • Repair wiring and connections • Replace switch • Replace or clean terminals • Repair ground circuits
Wipers do not operate— Motor runs	• Linkage disconnected or broken	• Connect wiper linkage or replace broken linkage
Vacuum Wipers		
Wipers do not operate	• Control switch or cable inoperative • Loss of engine vacuum to wiper motor (broken hoses, low engine vacuum, defective vacuum/fuel pump) • Linkage broken or disconnected • Defective wiper motor	• Repair or replace switch or cable • Check vacuum lines, engine vacuum and fuel pump • Repair linkage • Replace wiper motor
Wipers stop on engine acceleration	• Leaking vacuum hoses • Dry windshield • Oversize wiper blades • Defective vacuum/fuel pump	• Repair or replace hoses • Wet windshield with washers • Replace with proper size wiper blades • Replace pump

Drive Train

7

UNDERSTANDING THE MANUAL TRANSMISSION AND CLUTCH

Because of the way an internal combustion engine breathes, it can produce torque, or twisting force, only within a narrow speed range. Most modern, overhead valve engines must turn at about 2,500 rpm to produce their peak torque. By 4,500 rpm they are producing so little torque that continued increases in engine speed produce no power increases.

The torque peak on overhead camshaft engines is, generally, much higher, but much narrower.

The manual transmission and clutch are employed to vary the relationship between engine speed and the speed of the wheels so that adequate engine power can be produced under all circumstances. The clutch allows engine torque to be applied to the transmission input shaft gradually, due to mechanical slippage. The car can, consequently, be started smoothly from a full stop.

The transmission changes the ratio between the rotating speeds of the engine and the wheels by the use of gears. 4-speed or 5-speed transmissions are most common. The lower gears allow full engine power to be applied to the rear wheels during acceleration at low speeds.

The transmission contains a mainshaft which passes all the way through the transmission, from the clutch to the driveshaft. This shaft is separated at one point, so that front and rear portions can turn at different speeds.

Power is transmitted by a countershaft in the lower gears and reverse. The gears of the countershaft mesh with gears on the mainshaft, allowing power to be carried from one to the other. All the countershaft gears are integral with that shaft, while several of the mainshaft gears can either rotate independently of the shaft or

be locked to it. Shifting from one gear to the next causes one of the gears to be freed from rotating with the shaft and locks another to it. Gears are locked and unlocked by internal dog clutches which slide between the center of the gear and the shaft. The forward gears usually employ synchronizers; friction members which smoothly bring gear and shaft to the same speed before the toothed dog clutches are engaged.

MANUAL TRANSMISSION

A Ford 3.03 3-speed manual transmission is standard equipment on 1968-71 models. All forward gears are fully synchronized, helical-cut and in constant mesh. A column mounted shifter is used with this transmission. On 1972 and later models, the 3-speed manual transmission is no longer available.

A Ford 4-speed manual transmission is available as an option on 1968 models using the 390 and 428 V8 engines, and on 1969 models equipped with the 429 V8. This heavy duty unit is also synchronized in all forward gears. On 1970 and later models, the 4-speed transmission is no longer available. This transmission used a floor mounted shifter.

MANUAL TRANSMISSION LINKAGE ADJUSTMENT

3-Speed

1. Place the gearshift lever in the Neutral position.

2. Loosen the two gearshift adjustment nuts on the shift linkage.

3. Insert a $\frac{3}{16}''$ alignment tool through the 1st and Reverse lever, the 2nd and 3rd gear shift lever, and the two holes in the lower casing. An alignment tool can be fabricated from $\frac{3}{16}''$ rod bent to an **L** shape. The extension that

Troubleshooting the Manual Transmission

Problem	Cause	Solution
Transmission shifts hard	• Clutch adjustment incorrect • Clutch linkage or cable binding • Shift rail binding	• Adjust clutch • Lubricate or repair as necessary • Check for mispositioned selector arm roll pin, loose cover bolts, worn shift rail bores, worn shift rail, distorted oil seal, or extension housing not aligned with case. Repair as necessary.
	• Internal bind in transmission caused by shift forks, selector plates, or synchronizer assemblies	• Remove, dissemble and inspect transmission. Replace worn or damaged components as necessary.
	• Clutch housing misalignment	• Check runout at rear face of clutch housing
	• Incorrect lubricant • Block rings and/or cone seats worn	• Drain and refill transmission • Blocking ring to gear clutch tooth face clearance must be 0.030 inch or greater. If clearance is correct it may still be necessary to inspect blocking rings and cone seats for excessive wear. Repair as necessary.
Gear clash when shifting from one gear to another	• Clutch adjustment incorrect • Clutch linkage or cable binding • Clutch housing misalignment	• Adjust clutch • Lubricate or repair as necessary • Check runout at rear of clutch housing
	• Lubricant level low or incorrect lubricant	• Drain and refill transmission and check for lubricant leaks if level was low. Repair as necessary.
	• Gearshift components, or synchronizer assemblies worn or damaged	• Remove, disassemble and inspect transmission. Replace worn or damaged components as necessary.
Transmission noisy	• Lubricant level low or incorrect lubricant	• Drain and refill transmission. If lubricant level was low, check for leaks and repair as necessary.
	• Clutch housing-to-engine, or transmission-to-clutch housing bolts loose	• Check and correct bolt torque as necessary
	• Dirt, chips, foreign material in transmission	• Drain, flush, and refill transmission
	• Gearshift mechanism, transmission gears, or bearing components worn or damaged	• Remove, disassemble and inspect transmission. Replace worn or damaged components as necessary.
	• Clutch housing misalignment	• Check runout at rear face of clutch housing
Jumps out of gear	• Clutch housing misalignment	• Check runout at rear face of clutch housing
	• Gearshift lever loose	• Check lever for worn fork. Tighten loose attaching bolts.
	• Offset lever nylon insert worn or lever attaching nut loose	• Remove gearshift lever and check for loose offset lever nut or worn insert. Repair or replace as necessary.
	• Gearshift mechanism, shift forks, selector plates, interlock plate, selector arm, shift rail, detent plugs, springs or shift cover worn or damaged	• Remove, disassemble and inspect transmission cover assembly. Replace worn or damaged components as necessary.
	• Clutch shaft or roller bearings worn or damaged	• Replace clutch shaft or roller bearings as necessary

Troubleshooting the Manual Transmission (cont.)

Problem	Cause	Solution
Jumps out of gear (cont.)	• Gear teeth worn or tapered, synchronizer assemblies worn or damaged, excessive end play caused by worn thrust washers or output shaft gears • Pilot bushing worn	• Remove, disassemble, and inspect transmission. Replace worn or damaged components as necessary. • Replace pilot bushing
Will not shift into one gear	• Gearshift selector plates, interlock plate, or selector arm, worn, damaged, or incorrectly assembled • Shift rail detent plunger worn, spring broken, or plug loose • Gearshift lever worn or damaged • Synchronizer sleeves or hubs, damaged or worn	• Remove, disassemble, and inspect transmission cover assembly. Repair or replace components as necessary. • Tighten plug or replace worn or damaged components as necessary • Replace gearshift lever • Remove, disassemble and inspect transmission. Replace worn or damaged components.
Locked in one gear—cannot be shifted out	• Shift rail(s) worn or broken, shifter fork bent, setscrew loose, center detent plug missing or worn • Broken gear teeth on countershaft gear, clutch shaft, or reverse idler gear Gearshift lever broken or worn, shift mechanism in cover incorrectly assembled or broken, worn damaged gear train components	• Inspect and replace worn or damaged parts • Inspect and replace damaged part • Disassemble transmission. Replace damaged parts or assemble correctly.
Transfer case difficult to shift or will not shift into desired range	• Vehicle speed too great to permit shifting • If vehicle was operated for extended period in 4H mode on dry paved surface, driveline torque load may cause difficult shifting • Transfer case external shift linkage binding • Insufficient or incorrect lubricant • Internal components binding, worn, or damaged	• Stop vehicle and shift into desired range. Or reduce speed to 3–4 km/h (2–3 mph) before attempting to shift. • Stop vehicle, shift transmission to neutral, shift transfer case to 2H mode and operate vehicle in 2H on dry paved surfaces • Lubricate or repair or replace linkage, or tighten loose components as necessary • Drain and refill to edge of fill hole with SAE 85W-90 gear lubricant only • Disassemble unit and replace worn or damaged components as necessary
Transfer case noisy in all drive modes	• Insufficient or incorrect lubricant	• Drain and refill to edge of fill hole with SAE 85W-90 gear lubricant only. Check for leaks and repair if necessary. Note: If unit is still noisy after drain and refill, disassembly and inspection may be required to locate source of noise.
Noisy in—or jumps out of four wheel drive low range	• Transfer case not completely engaged in 4L position • Shift linkage loose or binding • Shift fork cracked, inserts worn, or fork is binding on shift rail	• Stop vehicle, shift transfer case in Neutral, then shift back into 4L position • Tighten, lubricate, or repair linkage as necessary • Disassemble unit and repair as necessary
Lubricant leaking from output shaft seals or from vent	• Transfer case overfilled • Vent closed or restricted	• Drain to correct level • Clear or replace vent if necessary

Troubleshooting the Manual Transmission(cont.)

Problem	Cause	Solution
Lubricant leaking from output shaft seals or from vent (cont.)	• Output shaft seals damaged or installed incorrectly	• Replace seals. Be sure seal lip faces interior of case when installed. Also be sure yoke seal surfaces are not scored or nicked. Remove scores, nicks with fine sandpaper or replace yoke(s) if necessary.
Abnormal tire wear	• Extended operation on dry hard surface (paved) roads in 4H range	• Operate in 2H on hard surface (paved) roads

is to be inserted into the levers should be 1″ in length from the elbow.

4. Manipulate the levers so that the alignment tool will move freely through the alignment holes.

5. Tighten the two gearshift rod adjustment nuts.

6. Remove the tool and check linkage operation.

4-Speed

1. Place the gearshift lever in Neutral position, then raise car on a hoist.

2. Insert a ¼″ rod into the alignment holes of the shift levers.

3. If the holes are not in exact alignment, check for bent connecting rods or loose lever locknuts at the rod ends. Make replacements or repairs, then adjust as follows.

4. Loosen the three rod-to-lever retaining locknuts and move the levers until the ¼″ gauge rod will enter the alignment holes. Be sure that the transmission shift levers are in Neutral, and the Reverse shifter lever is in the Neutral detent.

5. Install shift rods and torque locknuts to 18-23 ft. lbs.

6. Remove the ¼″ gauge rod.

7. Operate the shift levers to assure correct shifting.

8. Lower the car and road test.

Neutral Safety And Back-up Light switch

REMOVAL AND INSTALLATION

The switch is located on the steering column tube under the instrument panel. To remove

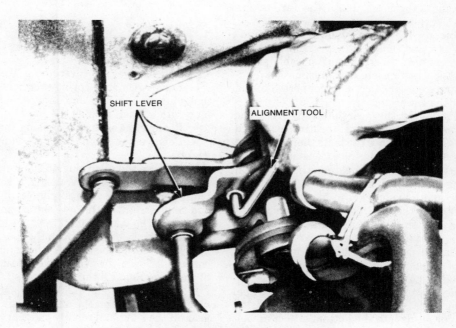

Column-mounted gearshift linkage adjustment

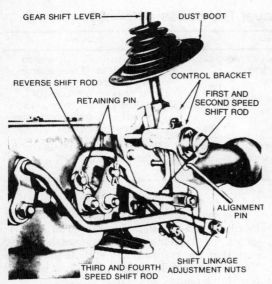

GEAR SHIFT LEVER   DUST BOOT

REVERSE SHIFT ROD

RETAINING PIN

CONTROL BRACKET

FIRST AND SECOND SPEED SHIFT ROD

ALIGNMENT PIN

THIRD AND FOURTH SPEED SHIFT ROD

SHIFT LINKAGE ADJUSTMENT NUTS

Floor-mounted gearshift linkage adjustment

the switch, disconnect the wiring and remove the 2 mounting screws.

If adjustment is needed, loosen the mounting screws, place the selector in Reverse and move the switch so that the actuator depresses the switch plunger.

Transmission
REMOVAL AND INSTALLATION

1. On floor shift models, remove the boot retainer and shift lever. Raise the car, taking proper safety precautions.

2. Disconnect the driveshaft at the rear universal joint and remove the driveshaft.

3. Disconnect the speedometer cable at the transmission extension. On transmission regulated spark equipped cars, disconnect the lead wire at the connector.

4. Disconnect the gearshift rods from the transmission shift levers. If the car is equipped with a 4-speed, remove the bolts that secure the shift control bracket to the extension housing.

5. Remove the bolt holding the extension housing to the rear support, and remove the muffler inlet pipe bracket-to-housing bolt.

6. Remove the two rear support bracket insulator nuts from the underside of the crossmember. Remove the crossmember.

7. Place a jack (equipped with a protective piece of wood) under the rear of the engine oil pan. Raise the engine slightly.

8. Remove the transmission-to-flywheel housing bolts. On clutch removal only, install two guide studs into the bottom attaching bolt holes.

NOTE: *On 8-429 engines, the upper left hand transmission attaching bolt is a seal bolt. Carefully note its position so that it may be reinstalled in its original position.*

9. Slide the transmission back and out of the car.

10. Start the transmission extension housing up and over the rear support. After moving the transmission back just far enough for the pilot shaft to clear the clutch housing, move it upward into position onto the transmission guide studs.

11. Slide the transmission forward and into place against the flywheel housing.

12. Remove the guide studs and torque the transmission to flywheel bolts to 37-42 ft. lbs.

13. Position the crossmember to the frame and install the attaching bolts. Slowly lower the engine onto the crossmember.

14. Install the insulator-to-crossmember nuts. Torque the nuts to 30-50 ft. lbs.

15. Connect the gear shaft rods and the speedometer cable. On cars with transmission regulated spark, connect the lead wires at the plug connector. On floor shift models, install the shift lever and boot.

16. Connect the driveshaft.

17. Refill the transmission to the proper level.

OVERHAUL
Ford 3.03 3-Speed

The Ford 3.03 is a fully synchronized 3-speed transmission. All gears except reverse are in constant mesh. Forward speed gear changes are accomplished with synchronizer sleeves.

DISASSEMBLY

1. Drain the lubricant by removing the lower extension housing bolt.

2. Remove the case cover and gasket.

3. Remove the long spring that holds the detent plug in the case and remove the detent plug with a small magnet.

4. Remove the extension housing and gasket.

5. Remove the front bearing retainer and gasket.

6. Remove the filler plug on the right side of the transmission case. Working through the plug opening, drive the roll pin out of the case and countershaft with a ¼" (6mm) punch.

7. Hold the countershaft gear with a hook. Install dummy shaft and push the countershaft out of the rear of the case. As the countershaft comes out, lower the gear cluster to the bottom of the case. Remove the countershaft.

8. Remove the snapring that holds the speedometer drive gear on the output shaft. Slip the gear off the shaft and remove the gear lock ball.

9. Remove the snapring that holds the out-

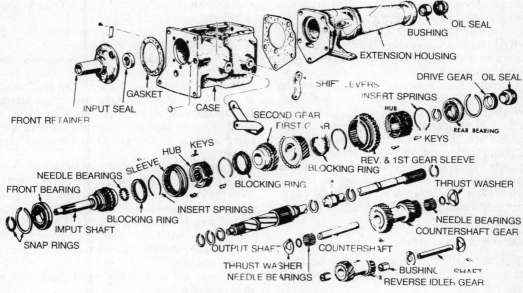

3.03 3-speed exploded view

put shaft bearing. Using a special bearing puller, remove the output shaft bearing.

10. Place both shift levers in the neutral (center) position.

11. Remove the set screw that holds the 1st/reverse shift fork to the shift rail. Slip the 1st/reverse shift rail out through the rear of the case.

12. Move the 1st/reverse synchronizer forward as far as possible. Rotate the 1st/reverse shift fork upwards and lift it out of the case.

13. Place the 2nd/3rd shift fork in the 2nd position. Remove the set screw. Rotate the shift rail 90°.

14. Lift the interlock plug out of the case with a magnet.

15. Remove the expansion plug from the 2nd/3rd shift rail by lightly tapping the end of the rail. Remove the 2nd/3rd shift rail.

16. Remove the 2nd/3rd shift rail detent plug and spring from detent bore.

17. Remove the input gear and shaft from the case.

18. Rotate the 2nd/3rd shift fork upwards and remove from case.

19. Using caution, lift the output shaft assembly out through top of case.

20. Lift the reverse idler gear and thrust washers out of case. Remove the countershaft gear, thrust washer and dummy shaft from case.

21. Remove the snapring from the front of the output shaft. Slip the synchronizer and 2nd gear off shaft.

22. Remove the 2nd snawhile from output

shaft and remove the thrust washer, 1st gear and blocking ring.

23. Remove the 3rd snaring from the output shaft. The 1st/reverse synchronizer hub is a press fit on the output shaft. Remove the synchronizer hub with an arbor press.

WARNING: *Do not attempt to remove or install the synchronizer hub by prying or hammering.*

Shift Levers & Seals

1. Remove shift levers from the shafts. Slip the levers out of case. Discard shaft sealing O-rings.

2. Lubricate and install new O-rings on shift shafts.

3. Install the shift shafts in the case and secure shift levers.

Input Shaft Bearings

1. Remove the snaring securing the input shaft bearing. Using an arbor press, remove the bearing.

2. Press the input shaft bearing onto shaft using correct tool.

Synchronizers

1. Scribe alignment marks on synchronizer hubs before disassembly. Remove each synchronizer hub from the synchronizer sleeves.

2. Separate the inserts and insert springs from the hubs.

CAUTION: *Do not mix parts from the separate synchronizer assemblies.*

3. Install the insert spring in the hub of the

1st/reverse synchronizer. Be sure that the spring covers all the insert grooves. Start the hub on the sleeve making certain that the scribed marks are properly aligned. Place the 3 inserts in the hub, small ends on the inside. Slide the sleeve and reverse gear onto hub.

4. Install 1 insert spring into a groove on the 2nd/3rd synchronizer hub. Be sure that all 3 insert slots are covered. Align the scribed marks on the hub and sleeve and start the hub into the sleeve. Position the 3 inserts on the top of the retaining spring and push the assembly together. Install the remaining retainer spring so that the spring ends cover the same slots as the 1st spring. Do not stagger the springs. Place a synchronizer blocking ring on the ends of the synchronizer sleeve.

Countershaft Gear Bearings

1. Remove the dummy shaft, needle bearings and bearing retainers from the countershaft gear.

2. Coat the bore in each end of the countershaft gear with grease.

3. Hold the dummy shaft in the gear and install the needle bearings in the case.

4. Place the countershaft gear, dummy shaft, and needle bearings in the case.

5. Place the case in a vertical position. Align the gear bore and the thrust washers with the bores in the case and install the countershaft.

6. Place the case in a horizontal position. Check the countershaft gear end play with a feeler gauge. Clearance should be between 0.004-0.018″ (0.10-0.45mm). If clearance does not come within specifications, replace the thrust washers.

7. Install the dummy shaft in the countershaft gear and leave the gear at the bottom of the transmission case.

ASSEMBLY

1. Cover the reverse idler gear thrust surfaces in the case with a thin film of lubricant, and install the 2 thrust washers in the case.

2. Install the reverse idler gear and shaft in the case. Align the case bore and thrust washers with gear bore and install the reverse idler shaft.

3. Measure the reverse idler gear end play with a feeler gauge. Clearance should be between 0.004-0.018″ (0.10-0.45mm). If end play is not within specifications, replace the thrust washers. If clearance is correct, leave the reverse idler gear in case.

4. Lubricate the output shaft splines and machined surfaces with transmission oil.

5. The 1st/reverse synchronizer hub is a press fit on the output shaft. Hub must be installed in an arbor press. Install the synchronizer hub with the teeth end of the gear facing towards the rear of the shaft.

CAUTION: *Do not attempt to install the 1st/reverse synchronizer with a hammer.*

6. Place the blocking ring on the tapered surface of the 1st gear.

7. Slide the 1st gear on the output shaft with the blocking ring toward the rear of the shaft. Rotate the gear as necessary to engage the 3 notches in the blocking ring with the synchronizer inserts. Install the thrust washer and snapring.

8. Slide the blocking ring onto the tapered surface of the 2nd gear. Slide the 2nd gear with blocking ring and the 2nd/3rd synchronizer on the mainshaft. Be sure that the tapered surface of 2nd gear is facing the front of the shaft and that the notches in the blocking ring engage the synchronizer inserts. Install the snapring and secure assembly.

9. Cover the core of the input shaft with a thin coat of grease.

WARNING: *A thick film of grease will plug lubricant holes and cause damage to bearings.*

10. Install bearings. Install the input shaft through the front of the case and insert snapring in the bearing groove.

11. Install the output shaft assembly in the case. Position the 2nd/3rd shift fork on the 2nd/3rd synchronizer.

12. Place a detent plug spring and a plug in the case. Place the 2nd/3rd synchronizer in the 2nd gear position (toward the rear of the case). Align the fork and install the 2nd/3rd shift rail. It will be necessary to depress the detent plug to install the shift rail in the bore. Move the rail forward until the detent plug enters the forward notch (2nd gear).

13. Secure the fork to the shift rail with a set screw and place the synchronizer in neutral.

14. Install the interlock plug in the case.

15. Place the 1st/reverse synchronizer in the 1st gear position (towards the front of the case). Place the shift fork in the groove of the synchronizer. Rotate the fork into position and install the shift rail. Move the shift rail inward until the center notch (neutral) is aligned with the detent bore. Secure shift fork with set screw.

16. Install a new shift rail expansion plug in the front of the case.

17. Hold the input shaft and blocking ring in position and move the output shaft forward to seat the pilot in the roller bearings on the input gear.

18. Tap the input gear bearing into place while holding the output shaft. Install the front bearing retainer and gasket. Torque attaching bolts to 35 ft. lbs.

19. Install the large snapring on the rear bearing. Place the bearing on the output shaft with the snapring end toward the rear of the shaft. Press the bearing into place using a special tool. Secure the bearing to the shaft with the snapring.

20. Hold the speedometer drive gear lock ball in the detent and slide the speedometer drive gear into position. Secure with snapring.

21. Place the transmission in the vertical position. Working with a screwdriver through the drain hole in the bottom of the case, align the bore of the countershaft gear and the thrust washer with the bore in the case.

22. Working from the rear of the case, push the dummy shaft out of the countershaft gear with the countershaft. Align the roll pin hole in the countershaft with the matching hole in the case. Drive the shaft into place and install the roll pin.

23. Position the new extension housing gasket on the case with sealer. Install the extension housing and torque to 50 ft. lbs.

24. Place the transmission in gear and pour gear oil over entire gear train while rotating the input shaft.

25. Install the remaining detent plug and long spring in case.

26. Position the cover gasket on the case with sealer and install the cover. Torque the cover bolts to 15 ft. lbs.

27. Check the operation of the transmission in all gear positions.

Ford 4-Speed Overdrive

The Ford 4-speed overdrive transmission is fully synchronized in all forward gears. The 4-speed shift control is serviced as a unit and should not be disassembled. The lubricant capacity is 4.5 pints.

Unit Disassembly

1. Remove retaining clips and flat washers from the shift rods at the levers.

2. Remove shift linkage control bracket attaching screws and remove shift linkage and control brackets.

3. Remove cover attaching screws. Then lift cover and gasket from the case. Remove the long spring that holds the detent plug in the case. Remove the plug with a magnet.

4. Remove extension housing attaching screws. Then, remove extension housing and gasket.

5. Remove input shaft bearing retainer attaching screws. Then, slide retainer from the input shaft.

6. Working a dummy shaft in from the front of the case, drive the countershaft out the rear of the case. Let the countergear assembly lie in

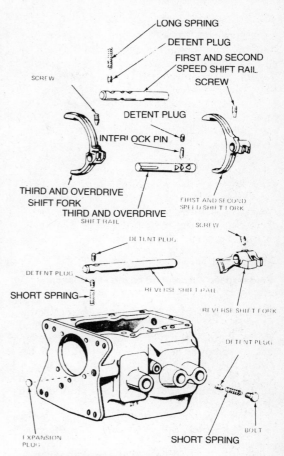

Ford 4-speed shift rails and forks

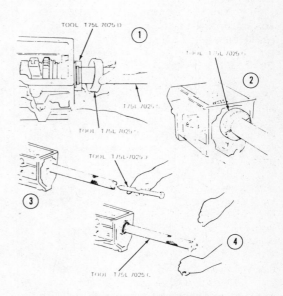

Ford 4-speed output shaft bearing removal

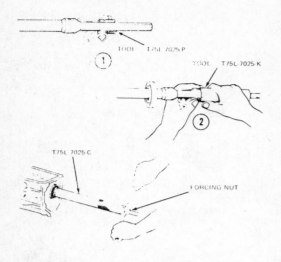

Ford 4-speed output shaft bearing installation

the bottom of the case. Remove the set screw from the 1st/2nd shift fork. Slide the 1st/2nd shift rail out of the rear of the case. Use a magnet to remove the interlock detent from between the 1st/2nd and 3rd/4th shift rails.

7. Locate 1st/2nd speed gear shift lever in neutral. Locate 3rd/4th speed gear shift lever in 3rd speed position.

NOTE: *On overdrive transmissions, locate 3rd/4th speed gear shift lever in the 4th speed position.*

8. Remove the lockbolt that holds the 3rd/4th speed shift rail detent spring and plug in

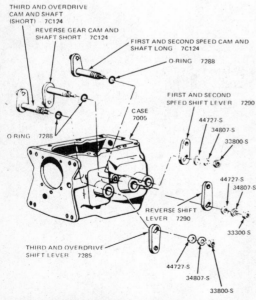

Ford 4-speed shift lever components

the left side of the case. Remove spring and plug with a magnet.

9. Remove the detent mechanism set screw from top of case. Then, remove the detent spring and plug with a small magnet.

10. Remove attaching screw from the 3rd/4th speed shift fork. Tap lightly on the inner end of the shift rail to remove the expansion plug from front of case. Then, withdraw the 3rd/4th speed shift rail from the front. Do not lose the interlock pin from rail.

11. Remove attaching screw from the 1st and 2nd speed shift fork. Slide the 1st/2nd shift rail from the rear of case.

12. Remove the interlock and detent plugs from the top of the case with a magnet.

13. Remove the snapring or disengage retainer that holds the speedometer drive gear to the output shaft, then remove speedometer gear drive ball.

14. Remove the snapring used to hold the output shaft bearing to the shaft. Pull out the output shaft bearing.

15. Remove the input shaft bearing snaprings. Use a press to remove the input shaft bearing. Remove the input shaft and blocking ring from the front of the case.

16. Move output shaft to the right side of the case. Then, maneuver the forks to permit lifting them from the case.

17. Support the thrust washer and 1st speed gear to prevent sliding from the shaft, then lift output shaft from the case.

18. Remove reverse gear shift fork attaching screw. Rotate the reverse shift rail 90°, then, slide the shift rail out the rear of the case. Lift out the reverse shift fork.

19. Remove the reverse detent plug and spring from the case with a magnet.

20. Using a dummy shaft, remove the reverse idler shaft from the case.

21. Lift reverse idler gear and thrust washers from the case. Be careful not to drop the bearing rollers or the dummy shaft from the gear.

22. Lift the countergear, thrust washers, rollers and dummy shaft assembly from the case.

23. Remove the next snapring from the front of the output shaft. Then, slide the 3rd/4th synchronizer blocking ring and the 3rd speed gear from the shaft.

24. Remove the next snapring and the 2nd speed gear thrust washer from the shaft. Slide the 2nd speed gear and the blocking ring from the shaft.

25. Remove the snapring, then slide the 1st/2nd synchronizer, blocking ring and the 1st speed gear from the shaft.

26. Remove the thrust washer from rear of the shaft.

Cam & Shaft Seals

1. Remove attaching nut and washers from each shift lever, then remove the 3 levers.

2. Remove the 3 cams and shafts from inside the case.

3. Replace the old O-rings with new ones that have been well lubricated.

4. Slide each cam and shaft into its respective bore in the transmission.

5. Install the levers and secure them with their respective washers and nuts.

Synchronizers

1. Push the synchronizer hub from each synchronizer sleeve.

2. Separate the inserts and springs from the hubs. Do not mix parts of the 1st/2nd with parts of 3rd/4th synchronizers.

3. To assemble, position the hub in the sleeve. Be sure the alignment marks are properly indexed.

4. Place the 3 inserts into place on the hub. Install the insert springs so that the irregular surface (hump) is seated in one of the inserts. Do not stagger the springs.

Countershaft Gear

1. Dismantle the countershaft gear assembly.

2. Assemble the gear by coating each end of the countershaft gear bore with grease.

3. Install dummy shaft in the gear. Then install 21 bearing rollers and a retainer washer in each end of the gear.

Reverse Idler Gear

1. Dismantle reverse idler gear.

2. Assemble reverse idler gear by coating the bore in each end of reverse idler gear with grease.

3. Hold the dummy shaft in the gear and install the 22 bearing rollers and the retainer washer into each end of the gear.

4. Install the reverse idler sliding gear on the splines of the reverse idler gear. Be sure the shift fork groove is toward the front.

Input Shaft Seal

1. Remove the seal from the input shaft bearing retainer.

2. Coat the sealing surface of a new seal with lubricant, then press the new seal into the input shaft bearing retainer.

Unit Assembly

1. Grease the countershaft gear thrust surfaces in the case. Then, position a thrust washer at each end of the case.

2. Position the countershaft gear, dummy shaft, and roller bearings in the case.

3. Align the gear bore and thrust washers with the bores in the case. Install the countershaft.

4. With the case in a horizontal position, countershaft gear endplay should be from 0.004-0.018″ (0.10-0.45mm). Use thrust washers to obtain play within these limits.

5. After establishing correct endplay, place the dummy shaft in the countershaft gear and allow the gear assembly to remain on the bottom of the case.

6. Grease the reverse idler gear thrust surfaces in the case, and position the 2 thrust washers.

7. Position the reverse idler gear, sliding gear, dummy, etc., in place. Make sure that the shift fork groove in the sliding gear is toward the front.

8. Align the gear bore and thrust washers with the case bores and install the reverse idler shaft.

9. Reverse idler gear endplay should be 0.004-0.018″ (0.10-0.45mm). Use selective thrust washers to obtain play within these limits.

10. Position reverse gear shift rail detent spring and detent plug in the case. Hold the reverse shift fork in place on the reverse idler sliding gear and install the shift rail from the rear of the case. Lock the fork to the rail with the Allen head set screws.

11. Install the 1st/2nd synchronizer onto the output shaft. The 1st and reverse synchronizer hub are a press fit and should be installed with gear teeth facing the rear of the shaft.

NOTE: *On overdrive transmissions, 1st and reverse synchronizer hub is a slip fit.*

12. Place the blocking ring on 2nd gear. Slide 2nd speed gear onto the front of the shaft with the synchronizer coned surface toward the rear.

13. Install the 2nd speed gear thrust washer and snapring.

14. Slide the 4th gear onto the shaft with the synchronizer coned surface front.

15. Place a blocking ring on the 4th gear.

16. Slide the 3rd/4th speed gear synchronizer onto the shaft. Be sure that the inserts in the synchronizer engage the notches in the blocking ring. Install the snapring onto the front of the output shaft.

17. Put the blocking ring on the 1st gear.

18. Slide the 1st gear onto the rear of the output shaft. Be sure that the inserts engage the notches in the blocking ring and that the shift fork groove is toward the rear.

19. Install heavy thrust washer onto the rear of the output shaft.

20. Lower the output shaft assembly into the case.

21. Position the 1st/2nd speed shift fork and the 3rd/4th speed shift fork in place on their respective gears. Rotate them into place.

22. Place a spring and detent plug in the detent bore. Place the reverse shift rail into neutral position.

23. Coat the 3rd/4th speed shift rail interlock pin (tapered ends) with grease, then position it in the shift rail.

24. Align the 3rd/4th speed shift fork with the shift rail bores and slide the shift rail into place. Be sure that the 3 detents are facing the outside of the case. Place the front synchronizer into 4th speed position and install the set screw into the 3rd/4th speed shift fork. Move the synchronizer to neutral position. Install the 3rd/4th speed shift rail detent plug, spring and bolt into the left side of the transmission case. Place the detent plug (tapered ends) in the detent bore.

25. Align 1st/2nd speed shift fork with the case bores and slide the shift rail into place. Lock the fork with the set screw.

26. Coat the input gear bore with a small amount of grease. Then install the 15 bearing rollers.

27. Put the blocking ring in the 3rd/4th synchronizer. Place the input shaft gear in the case. Be sure that the output shaft pilot enters the roller bearing of the input shaft gear.

28. With a new gasket on the input bearing retainer, dip attaching bolts in sealer, install bolts and torque to 30-36 ft. lbs.

29. Press on the output shaft bearing, then install the snapring to hold the bearing.

30. Position the speedometer gear drive ball in the output shaft and slide the speedometer drive gear into place. Secure gear with snapring.

31. Align the countershaft gear bore and thrust washers with the bore in the case. Install the countershaft.

32. With a new gasket in place, install and secure the extension housing. Dip the extension housing screws in sealer, then torque screws to 42-50 ft. lbs.

33. Install the filler plug and the drain plug.

34. Pour E.P. gear oil over the entire gear train while rotating the input shaft.

35. Place each shift fork in all positions to make sure they function properly. Install the remaining detent plug in the case, followed by the spring.

36. With a new cover gasket in place, install the cover. Dip attaching screws in sealer, then torque screws to 14-19 ft. lbs.

37. Coat the 3rd/4th speed shift rail plug bore with sealer. Install a new plug.

38. Secure each shift rod to its respective lever with a spring washer, flat washer and retaining pin.

39. Position the shift linkage control bracket to the extension housing. Install and torque the attaching screws to 12-15 ft. lbs.

TRANSMISSION LOCK ROD ADJUSTMENT

Models with floor or console mounted shifters are manual transmissions incorporate a transmission lock rod which prevents the shifter from being moved from the Reverse position when the ignition lock is in the **OFF** position. The lock rod connects the shift tube in the steering column to the transmission reverse lever. The lock rod cannot be properly adjusted until the manual linkage adjustment is correct.

1. With the transmission selector lever in the Neutral position, loosen the lock rod adjustment nut on the transmission Reverse lever.

2. Insert a 0.180″ diameter rod (no. 15 drill bit) in the gauge pin hole located in the six o'clock position on the steering column socket casting, directly below the ignition lock.

3. Manipulate the pin until the casting will not move with the pin inserted.

CLUTCH

The purpose of the clutch is to disconnect and connect engine power from the transmission. A car at rest requires a lot of engine torque to get all that weight moving. An internal combustion engine does not develop a high starting torque (unlike steam engines), so it must be allowed to operate without any load until it builds up enough torque to move the car. Torque increases with engine rpm. The clutch allows the engine to build up torque by physically disconnecting the engine from the transmission, relieving the engine of any load or resistance. The transfer of engine power to the transmission (the load) must be smooth and gradual; if it weren't, drive line components would wear out or break quickly. This gradual power transfer is made possible by gradually releasing the clutch pedal. The clutch disc and pressure plate are the connecting link between the engine and transmission. When the clutch pedal is released, the disc and plate contact each other (clutch engagement), physically joining the engine and transmission. When the pedal is pushed in, the disc and plate separate (the clutch is disengaged), disconnecting the engine from the transmission.

The clutch assembly consists of the flywheel, the clutch disc, the clutch pressure plate, the throwout bearing and fork, the actuating linkage and the pedal. The flywheel and clutch pressure plate (driving members) are connected to the engine crankshaft and rotate with it. The clutch disc is located between the flywheel and pressure plate, and splined to the transmission shaft. A driving member is one that is attached to the engine and transfers engine power to a driven member (clutch disc) on the transmission shaft. A driving member (pressure plate) rotates (drives) a driven member (clutch disc) on contact and, in so doing, turns the transmission shaft. There is a circular diaphragm spring within the pressure plate cover (transmission side). In a relaxed state (when the clutch pedal is fully released), this spring is convex; that is, it is dished outward toward the transmission. Pushing in the clutch pedal actuates an attached linkage rod. Connected to the other end of this rod is the throwout bearing fork. The throwout bearing is attached to the fork. When the clutch pedal is depressed, the clutch linkage pushes the fork and bearing forward to contact the diaphragm spring of the pressure plate. The outer edges of the spring are secured to the pressure plate and are pivoted on rings so that when the center of the spring is compressed by the throwout bearing, the outer edges bow outward and, by so doing, pull the pressure plate in the same direction — away from the clutch disc. This action separates the disc from the plate, disengaging the clutch and allowing the transmission to be shifted into another gear. A coil type clutch return spring attached to the clutch pedal arm permits full release of the pedal. Releasing the pedal pulls the throwout bearing away from the diaphragm spring resulting in a reversal of spring position. As bearing pressure is gradually released from the spring center, the outer edges of the spring bow outward, pushing the pressure plate into closer contact with the clutch disc. As the disc and plate move closer together, friction between the two increases and slippage is reduced until, when full spring pressure is applied (by fully releasing the pedal), The speed of the disc and plate are the same. This stops all slipping, creating a direct connection between the plate and disc which results in the transfer of power from the engine to the transmission. The clutch disc is now rotating with the pressure plate at engine speed and, because it is splined to the transmission shaft, the shaft now turns at the same engine speed. Understanding clutch operation can be rather difficult at first; if you're still confused after reading this, consider the following analogy. The action of the diaphragm spring can be compared to that of an oil can bottom. The bottom of an oil can is shaped very much like the clutch diaphragm spring and pushing in on the can bot-

Troubleshooting Basic Clutch Problems

Problem	Cause
Excessive clutch noise	Throwout bearing noises are more audible at the lower end of pedal travel. The usual causes are: • Riding the clutch • Too little pedal free-play • Lack of bearing lubrication A bad clutch shaft pilot bearing will make a high pitched squeal, when the clutch is disengaged and the transmission is in gear or within the first 2″ of pedal travel. The bearing must be replaced. Noise from the clutch linkage is a clicking or snapping that can be heard or felt as the pedal is moved completely up or down. This usually requires lubrication. Transmitted engine noises are amplified by the clutch housing and heard in the passenger compartment. They are usually the result of insufficient pedal free-play and can be changed by manipulating the clutch pedal.
Clutch slips (the car does not move as it should when the clutch is engaged)	This is usually most noticeable when pulling away from a standing start. A severe test is to start the engine, apply the brakes, shift into high gear and SLOWLY release the clutch pedal. A healthy clutch will stall the engine. If it slips it may be due to: • A worn pressure plate or clutch plate • Oil soaked clutch plate • Insufficient pedal free-play
Clutch drags or fails to release	The clutch disc and some transmission gears spin briefly after clutch disengagement. Under normal conditions in average temperatures, 3 seconds is maximum spin-time. Failure to release properly can be caused by: • Too light transmission lubricant or low lubricant level • Improperly adjusted clutch linkage
Low clutch life	Low clutch life is usually a result of poor driving habits or heavy duty use. Riding the clutch, pulling heavy loads, holding the car on a grade with the clutch instead of the brakes and rapid clutch engagement all contribute to low clutch life.

tom and then releasing it produces a similar effect. As mentioned earlier, the clutch pedal return spring permits full release of the pedal and reduces linkage slack due to wear. As the linkage wears, clutch free-pedal travel will increase and free-travel will decrease as the clutch wears. Free-travel is actually throwout bearing lash.

The diaphragm spring type clutches used are available in two different designs: flat diaphragm springs or bent spring. The bent fingers are bent back to create a centrifugal boost ensuring quick re-engagement at higher engine speeds. This design enables pressure plate load to increase as the clutch disc wears and makes low pedal effort possible even with a heavy duty clutch. The throwout bearing used with the bent finger design is 1¼" long and is shorter than the bearing used with the flat finger design. These bearings are not interchangeable. If the longer bearing is used with the bent finger clutch, free-pedal travel will not exist. This results in clutch slippage and rapid wear.

The transmission varies the gear ratio between the engine and rear wheels. It can be shifted to change engine speed as driving conditions and loads change. The transmission allows disengaging and reversing power from the engine to the wheels.

CLUTCH PEDAL FREE TRAVEL ADJUSTMENT

1. Disconnect the clutch return spring from the release lever.

2. Loosen the release lever adjusting nut and locknut, 2 or 3 turns.

3. Move the clutch release lever rearward until the throwout bearing can be felt to lightly contact the pressure plate fingers.

4. Adjust the rod length until the rod seats in the pocket in the release lever.

5. Insert a feeler gauge of specified thickness between the adjusting nut and swivel sleeve. Tighten the nut against the feeler gauge. Correct feeler gauge thicknesses are, 1968: 0.206"; 1969: 0.0194".

6. Tighten the locknut against the adjusting nut, being careful not to disturb the adjustment.

7. Connect the clutch return spring.

8. Make a final check with the engine running at 3,000 rpm, and transmission in Neutral. Under this condition, centrifugal weights on release fingers may reduce the clearance. Readjust, if necessary, to obtain at least ½" free-play while maintaining the 3,000 rpm to prevent fingers contacting release bearing. This is important.

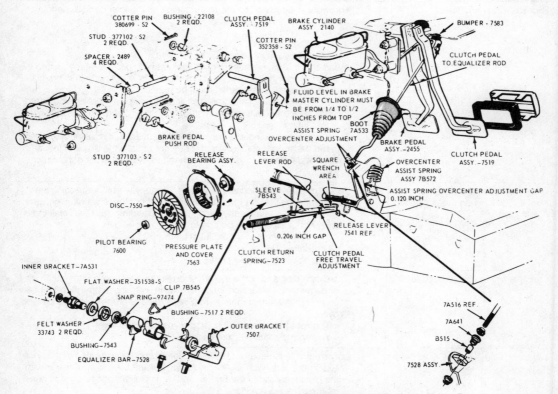

Clutch pedal and linkage adjustment—1968

Clutch Disc

REMOVAL AND INSTALLATION

CAUTION: *The clutch driven disc contains asbestos, which has been determined to be a cancer causing agent. Never clean clutch surfaces with compressed air! Avoid inhaling any dust from any clutch surface! When cleaning clutch surfaces, use a commercially available brake cleaning fluid.*

1. Remove the transmission.

2. Mark the cover and flywheel to facilitate reassembly in the same position. Loosen the six pressure plate cover attaching bolts evenly to release the spring pressure.

3. Remove the six attaching bolts while holding the pressure plate cover. Remove the pressure plate and clutch disc.

WARNING: *Do not depress the clutch pedal while the transmission is removed.*

4. Before installing the clutch, clean the flywheel surface. Inspect the flywheel and pressure plate for wear, scoring, or burn marks (blue color). Light scoring and wear may be cleaned up with emery paper; heavy wear may require refacing of the flywheel or replacement of the damaged parts.

5. Attach the clutch disc and pressure plate assembly to the flywheel. The three dowel pins on the flywheel, if so equipped, must be properly aligned. Damaged pins must be replaced. Avoid touching the clutch plate surface. Tighten the bolts finger tight.

Engine	Disc Diameter (in.)
240 Six	9.5
302 V8	10.0
240, 302 Heavy-Duty	11.0
351, 390, 400 V8	11.0
429 V8	11.5

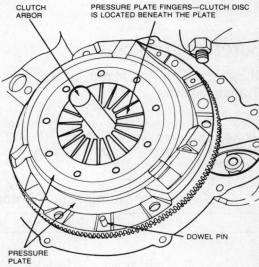

Typical clutch disc alignment

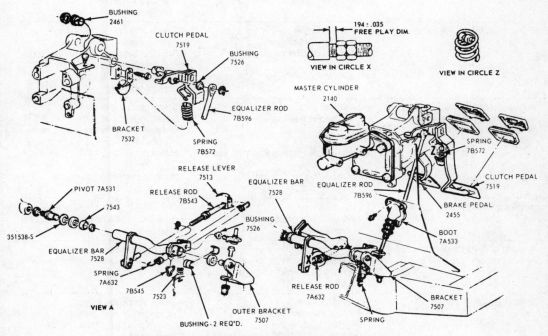

Clutch pedal and linkage adjustments—1969–71

6. Align the clutch disc with the pilot bushing. Torque cover bolts to 12-14 ft. lbs.

7. Lightly lubricate the release lever fulcrum ends.

8. Install the release lever in the flywheel housing and install the dust shield.

9. Apply very little lubricant on the release bearing retainer journal. Fill the groove in release bearing hub with grease. Clean all excess grease from the inside bore of the hub to prevent clutch disc contamination. Attach the release bearing and hub on the release lever.

10. Install the transmission.

AUTOMATIC TRANSMISSION

Understanding Automatic Transmissions

The automatic transmission allows engine torque and power to be transmitted to the rear wheels within a narrow range of engine operating speeds. The transmission will allow the engine to turn fast enough to produce plenty of power and torque at very low speeds, while keeping it at a sensible rpm at high vehicle speeds. The transmission performs this job entirely without driver assistance. The transmission uses a light fluid as the medium for the transmission of power. This fluid also works in the operation of various hydraulic control circuits and as a lubricant. Because the transmission fluid performs all of these three functions, trouble within the unit can easily travel from one part to another. For this reason, and because of the complexity and unusual operating principles of the transmission, a very sound understanding of the basic principles of operation will simplify troubleshooting.

THE TORQUE CONVERTER

The torque converter replaces the conventional clutch. It has three functions:

1. It allows the engine to idle with the vehicle at a standstill, even with the transmission in gear.

2. It allows the transmission to shift from

Troubleshooting Basic Automatic Transmission Problems

Problem	Cause	Solution
Fluid leakage	• Defective pan gasket	• Replace gasket or tighten pan bolts
	• Loose filler tube	• Tighten tube nut
	• Loose extension housing to transmission case	• Tighten bolts
	• Converter housing area leakage	• Have transmission checked professionally
Fluid flows out the oil filler tube	• High fluid level	• Check and correct fluid level
	• Breather vent clogged	• Open breather vent
	• Clogged oil filter or screen	• Replace filter or clean screen (change fluid also)
	• Internal fluid leakage	• Have transmission checked professionally
Transmission overheats (this is usually accompanied by a strong burned odor to the fluid)	• Low fluid level	• Check and correct fluid level
	• Fluid cooler lines clogged	• Drain and refill transmission. If this doesn't cure the problem, have cooler lines cleared or replaced.
	• Heavy pulling or hauling with insufficient cooling	• Install a transmission oil cooler
	• Faulty oil pump, internal slippage	• Have transmission checked professionally
Buzzing or whining noise	• Low fluid level	• Check and correct fluid level
	• Defective torque converter, scored gears	• Have transmission checked professionally
No forward or reverse gears or slippage in one or more gears	• Low fluid level	• Check and correct fluid level
	• Defective vacuum or linkage controls, internal clutch or band failure	• Have unit checked professionally
Delayed or erratic shift	• Low fluid level	• Check and correct fluid level
	• Broken vacuum lines	• Repair or replace lines
	• Internal malfunction	• Have transmission checked professionally

Lockup Torque Converter Service Diagnosis

Problem	Cause	Solution

No lockup	• Faulty oil pump
	• Sticking governor valve
	• Valve body malfunction
	  (a) Stuck switch valve
	  (b) Stuck lockup valve
	  (c) Stuck fail-safe valve
	• Failed locking clutch
	• Leaking turbine hub seal
	• Faulty input shaft or seal ring
		• Replace oil pump
		• Repair or replace as necessary
		• Repair or replace valve body or its internal components as necessary
		
		• Replace torque converter
		• Replace torque converter
		• Repair or replace as necessary

Will not unlock	• Sticking governor valve
	• Valve body malfunction
	  (a) Stuck switch valve
	  (b) Stuck lockup valve
	  (c) Stuck fail-safe valve
		• Repair or replace as necessary
		• Repair or replace valve body or its internal components as necessary

Stays locked up at too low a speed in direct	• Sticking governor valve
	• Valve body malfunction
	  (a) Stuck switch valve
	  (b) Stuck lockup valve
	  (c) Stuck fail-safe valve
		• Repair or replace as necessary
		• Repair or replace valve body or its internal components as necessary

Locks up or drags in low or second	• Faulty oil pump
	• Valve body malfunction
	  (a) Stuck switch valve
	  (b) Stuck fail-safe valve
		• Replace oil pump
		• Repair or replace valve body or its internal components as necessary

Sluggish or stalls in reverse	• Faulty oil pump
	• Plugged cooler, cooler lines or fittings
	• Valve body malfunction
	  (a) Stuck switch valve
	  (b) Faulty input shaft or seal ring
		• Replace oil pump as necessary
		• Flush or replace cooler and flush lines and fittings
		• Repair or replace valve body or its internal components as necessary

Loud chatter during lockup engagement (cold)	• Faulty torque converter • Failed locking clutch • Leaking turbine hub seal	• Replace torque converter • Replace torque converter • Replace torque converter
Vibration or shudder during lockup engagement	• Faulty oil pump • Valve body malfunction • Faulty torque converter • Engine needs tune-up	• Repair or replace oil pump as necessary • Repair or replace valve body or its internal components as necessary • Replace torque converter • Tune engine
Vibration after lockup engagement	• Faulty torque converter • Exhaust system strikes underbody • Engine needs tune-up • Throttle linkage misadjusted	• Replace torque converter • Align exhaust system • Tune engine • Adjust throttle linkage
Vibration when revved in neutral Overheating: oil blows out of dip stick tube or pump seal	• Torque converter out of balance • Plugged cooler, cooler lines or fittings • Stuck switch valve	• Replace torque converter • Flush or replace cooler and flush lines and fittings • Repair switch valve in valve body or replace valve body
Shudder after lockup engagement	• Faulty oil pump • Plugged cooler, cooler lines or fittings • Valve body malfunction • Faulty torque converter • Fail locking clutch • Exhaust system strikes underbody • Engine needs tune-up • Throttle linkage misadjusted	• Replace oil pump • Flush or replace cooler and flush lines and fittings • Repair or replace valve body or its internal components as necessary • Replace torque converter • Replace torque converter • Align exhaust system • Tune engine • Adjust throttle linkage

range to range smoothly, without requiring that the driver close the throttle during the shift.

3. It multiplies engine torque to an increasing extent as vehicle speed drops and throttle opening is increased. This has the effect of making the transmission more responsive and reduces the amount of shifting required.

The torque converter is a metal case which is shaped like a sphere that has been flattened on opposite sides. It is bolted to the rear end of the engine's crankshaft. Generally, the entire metal case rotates at engine speed and servesas the engine's flywheel.

The case contains three sets of blades. One set is attached directly to the case. This set forms the torus or pump. Another set is directly connected to the output shaft, and forms the turbine. The third set is mounted on a hub which, in turn, is mounted on a stationary shaft through a one-way clutch. This third set is known as the stator.

A pump, which is driven by the covnerter hub at engine speed, keeps the torque converter full of transmission fluid at all times. Fluid flows continuously through the unit to provide cooling.

Under low speed acceleration, the torque converter functions as follows:

The torus is turning faster than the turbine. It picks up fluid at the center of the converter and, through centrifugal force, slings it outward. Since the outer edge of the converter moves faster than the portions at the center, the fluid picks up speed.

The fluid then enters the outer edge of the turbine blades. It then travels back toward the

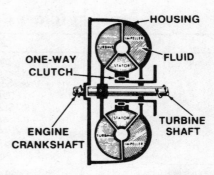

The torque converter housing is roated by the engine's crankshaft, and turns the impeller. The impeller spins the turbine, which gives motion to the turbine shaft, driving the gears

center of the converter case along the turbine blades. In impinging upon the turbine blades, the fluid loses the energy picked up in the torus.

If the fluid were now to immediately be returned directly into the torus, both halves of the converter would have to turn at approximately the same speed at all times, and torque input and output would both be the same.

In flowing through the torus and turbine, the fluid picks up two types of flow, or flow in two spearate directions. It flows through the turbine blades, and it spins with the engine. The stator, whose blades are stationary when the vehicle is being accelerated at low speeds, converts one type of flow into another. Instead of allowing the fluid to flow straight back into the torus, the stator's curved blades turn the fluid almost 90 degrees toward the direction of rotation of the engine. Thus the fluid does not flow as fast toward the torus, but is already spinning

Transmission Fluid Indications

The appearance and odor of the transmission fluid can give valuable clues to the overall condition of the transmission. Always note the appearance of the fluid when you check the fluid level or change the fluid. Rub a small amount of fluid between your fingers to feel for grit and smell the fluid on the dipstick.

If the fluid appears:	It indicates:
Clear and red colored	• Normal operation
Discolored (extremely dark red or brownish) or smells burned	• Band or clutch pack failure, usually caused by an overheated transmission. Hauling very heavy loads with insufficient power or failure to change the fluid, often result in overheating. Do not confuse this appearance with newer fluids that have a darker red color and a strong odor (though not a burned odor).
Foamy or aerated (light in color and full of bubbles)	• The level is too high (gear train is churning oil) • An internal air leak (air is mixing with the fluid). Have the transmission checked professionally.
Solid residue in the fluid	• Defective bands, clutch pack or bearings. Bits of band material or metal abrasives are clinging to the dipstick. Have the transmission checked professionally.
Varnish coating on the dipstick	• The transmission fluid is overheating

when the torus picks it up. This has the effect of allowing the torus to turn much faster than the turbine. This difference in speed may be compared to the difference in speed between the smaller and larger gears in any gear train. The result is that engine power output is higher, and engine torque is multiplied.

As the speed of the turbine increases, the fluid spins faster and faster in the direction of engine rotation. As a result, the ability of the stator to redirect the fluid flow is reduced. Under cruising conditions, the stator is eventually forced to rotate on its one-way clutch in the direction of engine rotation. Under these conditions, the torque converter begins to behave almost like a solid shaft, with the torus and turbine speeds being almost equal.

THE PLANETARY GEARBOX

The ability of the torque converter to multiply engine torque is limited. Also, the unit tends to be more efficient when the turine is rotating at relatively high speeds. Therefore, a planetary gearbox is used to carry the power output of the turbine to the driveshaft.

Planetary gears function very similarly to conventional transmission gears. However, their construction is different in that three elements make up one gear system, and, in that all three elements are different from one another. The three elements are: an outer gear that is shaped like a hoop, with teeth cut into the inner surface; a sun gear, mounted on a shaft and located at the very center of the outer gear; and a set of three planet gears, held by pins in a ring-like planet carrier, meshing with both the sun gear and the outer gear. Either the outer gear or the sun gear may be held stationary, providing more than one possible torque multiplication factor for each set of gears. Also, if all three gears are forced to rotate at the same speed, the gearset forms, in effect, a solid shaft.

Most modern automatics use the planetary gears to provide either a single reduction ratio of about 1.8:1, or two reduction gears: a low of about 2.5:1, and an intermediate of about 1.5:1. Bands and clutches are used to hold various portions of the gearsets to the transmission case or to the shaft on which they are mounted. Shifting is accomplished, then, by changing the portion of each planetary gearset which is held to the tranmission case or to the shaft.

THE SERVOS AND ACCUMULATORS

The servos are hydraulic pistons and cylinders. They resemble the hydraulic actuators used on many familiar machines, such as bulldozers. Hydraulic fluid enters the cylinder, under pressure, and forces the piston to move to engage the band or clutches.

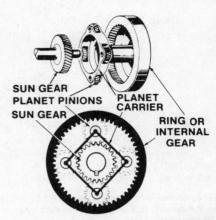

Planetary gears are similar to manual transmission gears but are composed of three parts

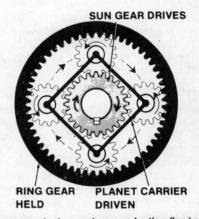

Planetary gears in the maximum reduction (low) range. The ring gear is held and a lower gear ration is obtained

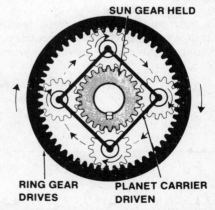

Planetary gears in the minimum reduction (drive) range. The ring gear is allowed to revolve, providing a higher gear ratio

The accumulators are used to cushion the engagement of the servos. The transmission fluid must pass through the accumulator on the way to the servo. The accumulator housing contains

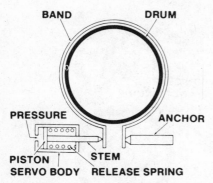

BAND DRUM

PRESSURE ANCHOR

PISTON STEM
SERVO BODY RELEASE SPRING

Servos, operated by pressure, are used to apply or release the bands, to either hold the ring gear or allow it to rotate

a thin piston which is sprung away from the discharge passage of the accumulator. When fluid passes through the accumulator on the way to the servo, it must move the piston against spring pressure, and this action smooths out the action of the servo.

THE HYDRAULIC CONTROL SYSTEM

The hydraulic pressure used to operate the servos comes from the main transmission oil pump. This fluid is channeled to the various servos through the shift valves. There is generally a manual shift valve which is operated by the tranmission selector lever and an automatic shift valvee for each automatic upshift the transmission provides: i.e., 2-speed automatics have a low/high shift valve, while 3-speeds have a 1-2 valve, and a 2-3 vavle.

There are two pressures which effect the operation of these valves. One is the governor pressure which is affected by vehicle speed. The other is the modulator pressure which is affected by intake manifold vacuum or throttle position. Governor pressure rises with an increase

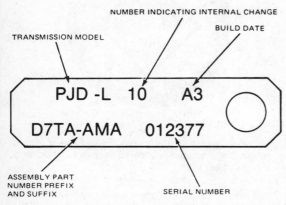

NUMBER INDICATING INTERNAL CHANGE

BUILD DATE

TRANSMISSION MODEL

PJD -L 10 A3

D7TA-AMA 012377

ASSEMBLY PART
NUMBER PREFIX
AND SUFFIX

SERIAL NUMBER

TAG LOCATED UNDER LOWER FRONT
INTERMEDIATE SERVO COVER BOLT

Typical automatic transmission identification tag

in vehicle speed, and modulator pressure rises as the throttle is opened wider. By responding to these two pressures, the shift valves cause the upshift points to be delayed with increased throttle opening to make the best use of the engine's power output.

Most transmissions also make use of an auxiliary circuit for downshifting. This circuit may be actuated by the throttle linkage or the vacuum line which actuates the modulator, or by a cable or solenoid. It applies pressure to a special downshift surface on the shift valve or valves.

The transmission modulator also governs the line pressure, used to actuate the servos. In this way, the clutches and bands will be actuated with a force matching the torque output of the engine.

Pan Removal and Fluid Draining

When filling a completely dry (no fluid) transmission and converter, install five quarts of transmission fluid (see fluid recommendations) and then start the engine. Shift the selector lever through all gear positions briefly and set at Park position. Check the fluid level and add enough fluid to raise the level to between the marks on the dipstick. Do not overfill the transmission.

The procedure for a partial drain and refill of the transmission fluid is a follows:

C4

1. Raise the car on a hoist or jack stands.
2. Place a drain pan under the transmission pan.
   NOTE: *On some models of the C4 transmission, the fluid is drained by disconnecting the filler tube from the transmission fluid pan.*
3. Loosen the pan attaching bolts to allow the fluid to drain.
4. When the fluid has stopped draining to level of the pan flange, remove the mounting bolts starting at the rear and along both sides of the pan, allowing the pan to drop and drain gradually.
5. When all the transmission fluid has drained, remove the pan and the fluid filter and clean them.
   CAUTION: *When removing the filter on C4 transmission, be careful not to lose the throttle pressure limit valve and spring when separating the filter from the valve body. If the valve and spring drop out — the valve is installed, large end first; the spring fits over the valve shaft.*
6. After completing the transmission repairs of adjustments, install the fluid filter screen, a

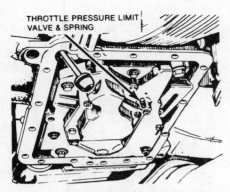

C4 throttle limit valve and spring. They are held in place by the transmission oil filter. The valve is installed with the large end towards the valve body, the spring fits over the valve stem

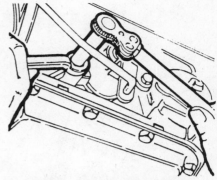

C4 and C5 intermediate band adjustment

new pan gasket, and the pan on the transmission. Tighten the pan attaching bolts on to 12-16 ft. lbs.

7. Install three quarts of transmission fluid (see fluid recommendations) through the filler tube. If the filler tube was removed to drain the transmission, install the filler tube using a new O-ring.

8. Start and run the engine for a few minutes at low idle speed and then at the fast idle speed (about 1,200 rpm) until the normal operating temperature is reached. Do not race the engine.

9. Move the selector lever through all gear positions and place it at the Park position. Check the fluid level, and add fluid until the level is between the **add** and **full** marks on the dipstick. Do not overfill the transmission.

C6, FMX, CW and AOD

1. Raise the car and support on jackstands.
2. Place a drain pan under the transmission.
3. Loosen the pan attaching bolts and drain the fluid from the transmission.
4. When the fluid has drained to the level of the pan flange, remove the remaining pan bolts working from the rear and both sides of the pan to allow it to drop and drain slowly.
5. When all of the fluid has drained, remove the pan and clean it thoroughly. discard the pan gasket.
6. Place a new gasket on the pan, and install the pan on the transmission. Tighten the attaching bolts to 12-16 ft. lbs.
7. Add three quarts of fluid to the transmission through the filler tube.
8. Lower the vehicle. Start the engine and move the gear selector through shift pattern. Allow the engine to reach normal operating temperature.
9. Check the transmission fluid. Add fluid, if necessary, to maintain correct level.

BAND ADJUSTMENT

C4 Intermediate Band

1. Clean all the dirt from the adjusting screw and remove and discard the locknut.
2. Install a new locknut on the adjusting screw using a torque wrench, tighten the adjusting screw to 10 ft. lbs.
3. Back off the adjusting screw exactly 1¾ turns.
4. Hold the adjusting screw steady and tighten the locknut to the proper torque.

C4 Low-Reverse Band

1. Clean all dirt from around the band adjusting screw, and remove and discard the locknut.
2. Install a new locknut of the adjusting screw. Using a torque wrench, tighten the adjusting screw to 10 ft. lbs.
3. Back off the adjusting screw exactly three full turns.
4. Hold the adjusting screw steady and tighten the locknut to the proper torque.

C6 Intermediate Band Adjustment

1. Raise the car on a hoist or place it on jack stands.

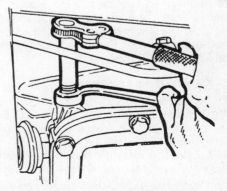

C4, and C5 low-reverse band adjustment

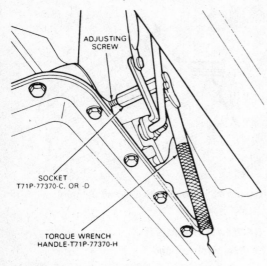

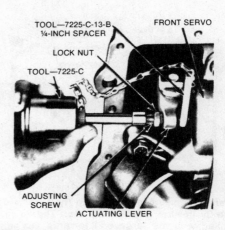

FMX front band adjustment

Adjusting the C6 intermediate band

2. Clean the threads of the intermediate band adjusting screw.

3. Loosen the adjusting screw locknut.

4. Tighten the adjusting screw to 10 ft. lbs. and back the screw off exactly 1½ turns. Tighten the adjusting screw locknut.

FMX, CW Front Band Adjustment

1. Drain the transmission fluid and remove the oil pan, fluid filter screen, and clip.

2. Clean the pan and filter screen and remove the old gasket.

3. Loosen the front servo adjusting screw locknut.

4. Pull back the actuating rod and insert a ¼" spacer bar between the adjusting screw and the servo piston stem. Tighten the adjusting screw to 10 in. lbs. torque. Remove the spacer bar and tighten the adjusting screw an additional ¾ turn. Hold the adjusting screw fast and tighten the locknut securely (20-25 ft. lbs.).

5. Install the transmission fluid filter screen and clip. Install the pan with a new pan gasket.

6. Refill the transmission to the mark on the dipstick. Start the engine, run for a few minutes, shift the selector lever through all positions, and place it in Park. Recheck the fluid level and add fluid if necessary.

FMX, CW Rear Band Adjustments

On certain cars with a console floor shift, the entire console shift lever and linkage will have to be removed to gain access to the rear band external adjusting screw.

1. Locate the external rear ban adjusting screw on transmission case, clean all dirt from the threads, and coat the threads with light oil.

NOTE: *The adjusting screw is located on the*

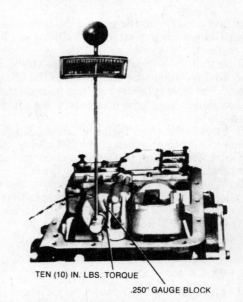

CW front band adjustment

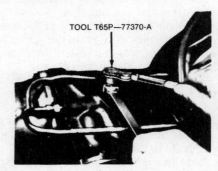

FMX, CW rear band adjustment

upper right side of the transmission case. Access is often through a hole in the front floor to the right of center under the carpet.

2. Loosen the locknut on the rear band external adjusting screw.

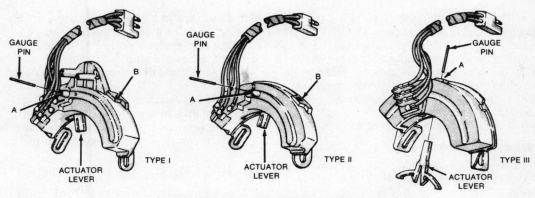

GAUGE PIN

GAUGE PIN

GAUGE PIN

B

A

TYPE I

A

B

TYPE II

A

TYPE III

ACTUATOR LEVER

ACTUATOR LEVER

ACTUATOR LEVER

Neutral start switch adjustment—column shift

3. Using a torque wrench tighten the adjusting screw to 10 ft. lbs. torque. If the adjusting screw is tighten than 10 ft. lbs. torque, loosen the adjusting screw and retighten to the proper torque.

4. Back off the adjusting screw exactly 1½ turns. Hold the adjusting screw steady while tightening the locknut to the proper torque (35-40 ft. lbs.).

NEUTRAL START SWITCH ADJUSTMENT

1968-71 Column Shift

1. With manual linkage properly adjusted, try to engage starter in each position on quadrant. Starter should engage only in Neutral or Park position.

2. Place shift lever in Neutral detent.

3. Disconnect start switch wires at plug connector. Disconnect vacuum hoses, if any. Remove screws securing neutral start switch to steering column and remove switch. Remove actuator lever along with Type III switches.

4. With switch wires facing up, move actuator lever fully to the left and insert gauge pin (No. 43 drill) into gauge pin hole at point A. See accompanying figure. On Type III switch, be sure gauge pin is inserted a full ½″.

5. With pin in place, move actuator lever to right until positive stop is engaged.

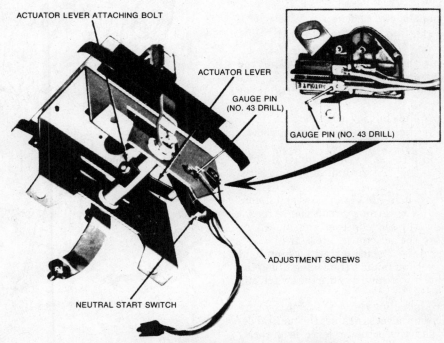

ACTUATOR LEVER ATTACHING BOLT

ACTUATOR LEVER

GAUGE PIN (NO. 43 DRILL)

GAUGE PIN (NO. 43 DRILL)

ADJUSTMENT SCREWS

NEUTRAL START SWITCH

Neutral start switch adjustment—console shift

6. On Type I and type II switches, remove gauge pin and insert it at point **B**. ON Type III switches, remove gauge pin, align two holes in switch at point **A** and reinstall gauge pin.

7. Reinstall switch on steering column. Be sure shift lever is engaged in Neutral detent.

8. Connect switch wires and vacuum hoses and remove gauge pin.

9. Check starter engagement as in Step 1.

1972 and Later Column Shift

1972 and later models which are equipped with a column mounted shift lever are not equipped with neutral start switch. Instead, an ignition lock cylinder-to-shift lever interlock prevents these models from being started in any gear other than Park and Neutral.

1968-71 Console Shift

1. With manual linkage properly adjusted, try to engage starter at each position on quadrant. Starter should engage only in Neutral or Park positions.

2. Remove shift handle from shift lever, and console from vehicle.

3. Loosen switch attaching screws, and move shift lever back and forward until gauge pin (no. 43 drill) can be inserted fully.

4. Place shift lever firmly against Neutral detent stop and slide switch back and forward until switch lever contacts shift lever.

5. Tighten switch attaching screws, and check starter engagement as in Step 1.

6. Reinstall console and shift linkage.

1972-79 Floor Mounted Shifters

1. Place the shift lever in NEUTRAL.

2. Raise and support the car on jackstands.

3. Remove the nut that secures the shift rod to the transmission manual lever. Make sure that the rod is free on the selector lever grommet.

4. Remove the shift lever handle.

5. Remove the shift lever selector housing.

6. Disconnect the dial light.

7. Disconnect the back-up/neutral start switch wires and selector indicator light wires at the instrument panel.

On cars with an FMX transmission, disconnect the seatbelt warning circuit connector.

8. Remove the selector lever housing.

9. Remove the selector pointer shield.

10. Remove the 2 neutral start/back-up light switch screws and remove the switch. Push the harness plug inward and remove the switch and harness.

11. Before installing the new switch, be sure that the selector lever is against the neutral detent stop and the actuator lever is properly aligned in the neutral position.

12. Position the harness and switch in the housing. Install the two screws loosely.

13. Put the selector lever in PARK and hold it against the forward stop.

14. Move the switch to the end of its rearward travel.

15. Hold the switch in this position and tighten the two attaching screws.

16. The remainder of installation is the reverse of removal. Check the operation of the switch.

1981-84 Floor Mounted Shifter

1. Raise and support the front end on jackstands.

2. Remove the downshift linkage rod from the transmission downshift lever.

3. Apply penetrating oil to the downshift lever shaft and nut. Remove the transmission downshift outer lever retaining nut and lever.

4. Remove the 2 switch attaching screws.

5. Unplug the connector and remove the switch.

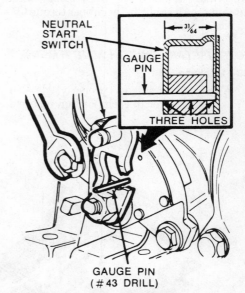

NEUTRAL START SWITCH

GAUGE PIN

$\frac{31}{64}$

THREE HOLES

GAUGE PIN (# 43 DRILL)

C4 neutral start switch adjustment

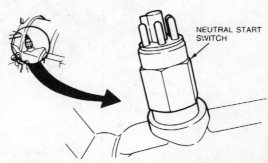

NEUTRAL START SWITCH

Neutral start switch used on the C3, AOD and A4LD

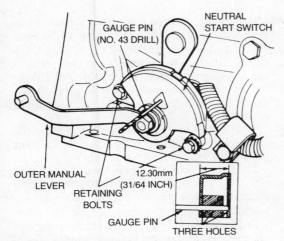

C6 neutral start switch adjustment

6. Position the new switch on the transmission and install the bolts loosely.

7. Place the transmission lever in NEUTRAL, rotate the switch until the hole in the switch aligns with the depression in the case and insert a No. 43 drill bit through the hole and into the depression. Make sure the drill bit is fully inserted. Tighten the switch bolts to 60 in. lbs. Remove the gauge pin.

8. The remainder of installation is the reverse of removal. Torque the shaft nut to 20 ft. lbs.

1985-88 AOD w/Floor Shift

1. Place the selector lever in the MANUAL LOW position.

2. Diasconnect the battery ground.

3. Raise and support the car on jackstands.

4. Disconnect the switch harness by pushing the harness straight up off the switch with a long screwdriver underneath the rubber plug section.

5. Using special tool socket T74P-77247-A, or equivalent, on a ratchet extension at least 9½″ (241mm) long, unscrew the switch. Once the tool is on the switch, reach around the rear of the transmission over the extension housing.

6. Installation is the reverse of removal. Use a new O-ring. Torque the switch to 11 ft. lbs.

LINKAGE ADJUSTMENT

Selector Indicator

1. With engine off, loosen clamp at shift lever so shift rod is free to slide.

2. Position selector lever in D1 position (large green dot) on dual range transmissions. On select shift transmission (P R N D 2 1) position lever in D position tightly against the D stop.

3. Shift lever at transmission into D1 detent position on dual range transmission or into D position on select shift transmissions.

NOTE: *D1 position is second from rear on*

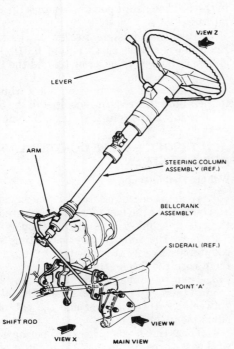

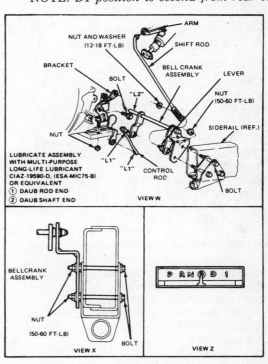

AOD shift control linkage on carbureted engines

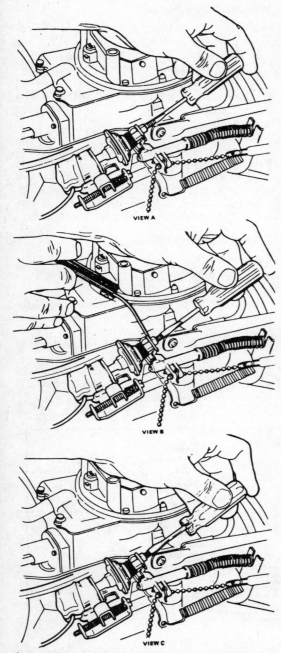

VIEW A

VIEW B

VIEW C

Automatic overdrive throttle linkage adjustment

all dual-range transmissions. D position is third from rear on all column shift select shift transmissions and 1968 console shift select shift transmissions. D position is fourth from rear on 1969-72 console shift select shift transmissions.

LOCK ROD ADJUSTMENT

All 1970-71 models equipped with a floor or console mounted selector lever incorporate a

transmission lock rod to prevent the transmission selector from being moved out of the Park position when the ignition lock is in the Off position. The lock rod connects the shift tube in the steering column to the transmission manual lever. The lock rod cannot be properly adjusted until the manual linkage adjustment is correct.

1. With the transmission selector lever in the Drive position, loosen the lock rod adjustment nut on the transmission manual lever.

2. Insert a 0.180″ diameter rod (No. 15 drill bit) in the gauge pin hole in the steering column socket casting, it is located at the 6 o'clock position directly below the ignition lock.

3. Manipulate the pin so that the casting will not move when the pin is fully inserted.

4. Torque the lock rod adjustment nut to 10-20 ft. lbs.

5. Remove the pin and check the linkage operation.

DOWNSHIFT (THROTTLE) LINKAGE ADJUSTMENT

All Models Except Automatic Overdrive

1. With the engine off, disconnect the throttle and downshift return springs, if equipped.

2. Hold the carburetor throttle lever in the wide open position against the stop.

3. Hold the transmission downshift linkage in the full downshift position against the internal stop.

4. Turn the adjustment screw on the carburetor downshift lever to obtain 0.010-0.080″ clearance between the screw tip and the throttle shaft lever tab.

5. Release the transmission and carburetor to their normal free positions. Install the throttle and downshift return springs, if removed.

AOD THROTTLE VALVE CONTROL LINKAGE ADJUSTMENT

Without Fuel Injection

1. With the engine off, remove the air cleaner and make sure the fast idle cam is released; the throttle lever must be at the idle stop.

2. Turn the linkage lever adjusting screw counterclockwise until the end of the screw is flush with the face of the lever.

3. Turn the linkage lever adjustment screw in until there is a maximum clearance of 0.005″ between the throttle lever and the end of the adjustment screw.

4. Turn the linkage lever adjusting screw clockwise three full turns. A minimum of one turn is permissible if the screw travel is limited.

5. If it is not possible to turn the adjusting screw at least one full turn, or if the initial gap

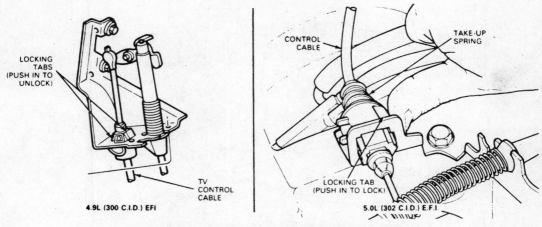

LOCKING TABS (PUSH IN TO UNLOCK)

TV CONTROL CABLE

4.9L (300 C.I.D.) EFI

CONTROL CABLE

TAKE-UP SPRING

LOCKING TAB (PUSH IN TO LOCK)

5.0L (302 C.I.D.) E.F.I

AOD throttle valve linkage control cable locking tab installation

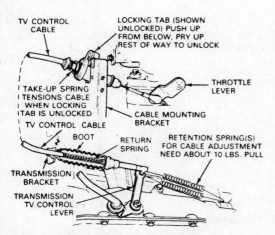

TV CONTROL CABLE

LOCKING TAB (SHOWN UNLOCKED) PUSH UP FROM BELOW, PRY UP REST OF WAY TO UNLOCK

THROTTLE LEVER

TAKE-UP SPRING TENSIONS CABLE WHEN LOCKING TAB IS UNLOCKED

CABLE MOUNTING BRACKET

TV CONTROL CABLE BOOT

RETURN SPRING

RETENTION SPRING(S) FOR CABLE ADJUSTMENT NEED ABOUT 10 LBS. PULL

TRANSMISSION BRACKET

TRANSMISSION TV CONTROL LEVER

Throttle valve control cable adjustment

of 0.005″ could not be obtained, perform the linkage adjustment of the transmission.

ALTERNATE AOD THROTTLE VALVE LINKAGE ADJUSTMENT

Without Fuel Injection

If unable to adjust the throttle valve control linkage at the carburetor, as described above, proceed as follows:

1. At the transmission, loosen the 8mm bolt on the throttle valve (TV) control rod sliding trunnion block. Make sure the trunnion block slides freely on the control rod.

2. Push up on the lower end of the TV control rod to insure that the carburetor linkage lever is held against the throttle lever. When the pressure is released, the control rod must stay in position.

3. Force the TV control lever on the transmission against its internal stop. While main-

taining pressure tighten the trunnion block bolt. Make sure the throttle lever is at the idle stop.

AOD IDLE SPEED ADJUSTMENT

Without Idle Speed Control

Whenever it is necessary to adjust the idle speed by more than 50 rpm either above or below the factory specifications, the adjustment screw on the linkage lever at the carburetor should also be adjusted to the following specifications:

Idle Speed Change (rpm)	Adjustment Screw Turns
50–100 increase	1½ turns out
50–100 decrease	1½ turns in
100–150 increase	2½ turns out
100–150 decrease	2½ turns in

After making any idle speed adjustments, make sure the linkage lever and throttle lever are in contact with the throttle lever at its idle stop and verify that the shift lever is in N (neutral).

With Idle Speed Control

NOTE: *When the engine is shut Off, the ISC (idle speed control) plunger automatically extends and moves the throttle lever to fast idle in preparation for the next time the engine is started. The TV linkage cannot be correctly adjusted in this position. The ISC plunger will retract only if the following procedure is performed in exact sequence.*

1. Locate the Self Test Connector and Self Test Input Test Connector usually on the right

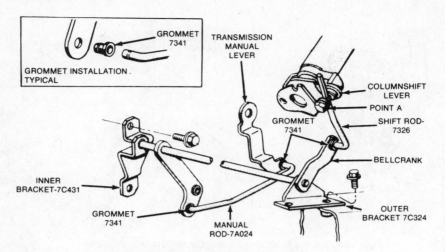

Manual linkage—1968 C6 column shift

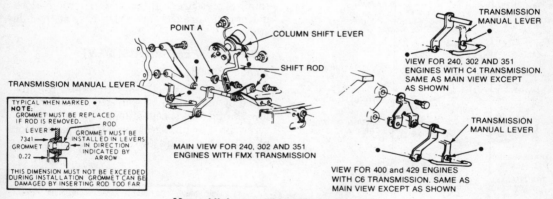

Manual linkage—1969–76 column shift

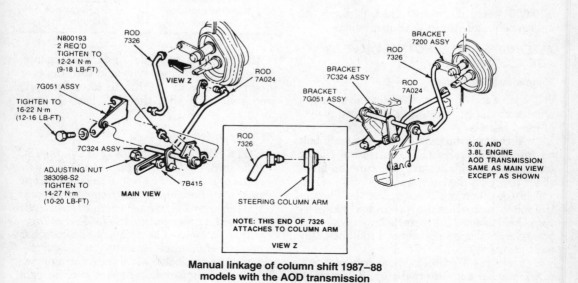

Manual linkage of column shift 1987–88 models with the AOD transmission

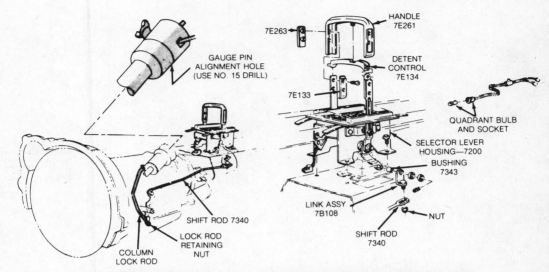

Manual linkage—1970–71 console shift with lock rod shown, 1968–69 similar

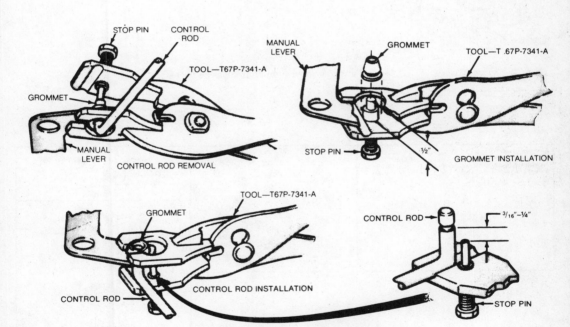

Removing or installing shift linkage grommets

side (passenger side) fender wall. The two connectors are located next to each other.

2. Connect a jumper wire between the STI Connector and the Signal Return Ground on the Self Test Connector.

3. Turn the ignition key to the Run position. Do not start the engine. The ISC plunger will retract. Wait about ten seconds until the plunger is fully retracted. Shut off the key.

4. Adjust linkage as required with the plunger fully retracted.

Transmission

REMOVAL AND INSTALLATION

C4

1. Raise and safely support the vehicle.

2. place the drain pan under the transmission fluid pan. Remove the fluid filler tube from the pan and drain the transmission fluid. On some models it may be necessary to loosen the pan attaching bolts and allow the fluid to drain. Start loosening the bolts at the rear of the pan

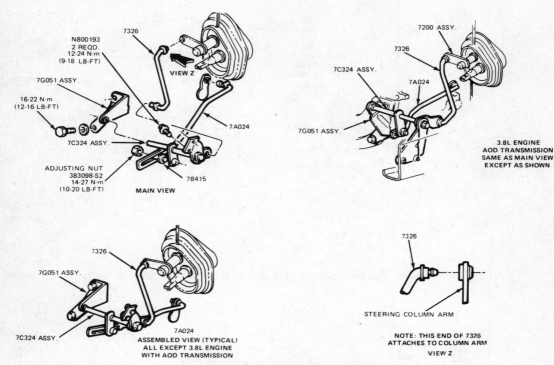

Manual linkage on column shift 1984–86 models

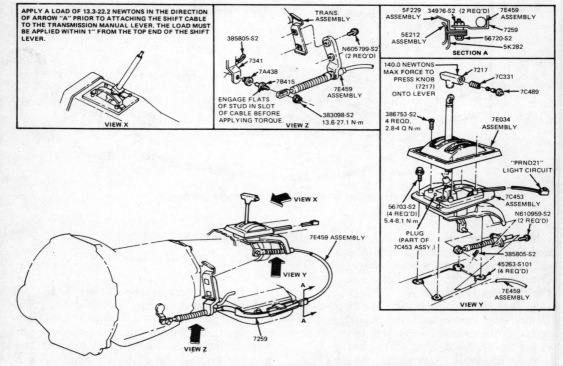

Manual linkage on floor shift 1981 models with the 8-255 engine

and work toward the front. Finally remove all of the pan attaching bolts except two at the front, to allow the fluid to further drain. After the fluid has drained, install two bolts on the rear side of the pan to temporarily hold it in place.

3. Remove the converter drain plug access cover from the lower end of the converter housing.

4. Remove the converter-to-flywheel attaching nuts. Place a wrench on the crankshaft pulley attaching bolt to turn the converter to gain access to the nuts.

5. With the wrench on the crankshaft pulley attaching bolt, turn the converter to gain access to the converter drain plug. Then, remove the plug. Place a drain pan under the converter to catch the fluid. After the fluid has been drained from the converter, reinstall the plug.

6. Remove the driveshaft and install the extension housing seal replacer tool in the extension housing.

7. Remove the vacuum line hose from the transmission vacuum unit. Disconnect the vacuum line from the retaining clip. Disconnect the transmission regulated spark (T.R.S.) switch wire at the transmission, if so equipped.

8. Remove the engine support to crossmember bolts or nuts.

9. Remove the speedometer cable from the extension housing.

10. Disconnect the oil cooler lines from the transmission case.

11. Disconnect the selector rod or cable at the transmission manual lever. Disconnect the downshift rod at the transmission downshift lever.

12. On console and floor shift vehicles, disconnect the column lock rod at the transmission, if so equipped.

13. Disconnect the starter cable. Remove the starter attaching bolts and remove the starter from the converter housing.

14. Remove the bolt that secures the transmission fluid filler tube to the cylinder head and lift the fluid fitter tube from the case.

15. Position the transmission jack to support the transmission and secure the transmission to the jack with a safety chain.

16. Remove the crossmember attaching bolts and lower the crossmember.

17. Remove the five converter housing-to-engine attaching bolts. Lower the transmission and remove it from under the vehicle.

18. Torque the converter drain plug to 20-30 ft. lbs.

19. Position the converter to the transmission making sure the converter drive flats are fully engaged in the pump gear.

20. With the converter properly installed, place the transmission on the jack. Secure the transmission to the jack with a safety chain.

21. Rotate the converter so that the studs and drain plug are in alignment with their holes in the flywheel.

22. With the transmission mounted on a transmission jack, move the converter and transmission assembly forward into position, using care not to damage the flywheel and the converter pilot. The converter must rest squarely against the flywheel. This indicates that the converter pilot is not binding in the engine crankshaft.

23. Install the five converter housing-to-engine attaching bolts. Torque the bolts to 23-28 ft. lbs. Remove the safety chain from the transmission.

24. Position the crossmember and install the attaching bolts. Torque the bolts to 40-50 ft. lbs.

25. Lower the transmission and install the engine support to crossmember bolts or nuts. Torque the bolts or nuts to 30-40 ft. lbs.

26. Install the flywheel to the converter attaching nuts. Torque the nuts to 23-28 ft. lbs.

27. Remove the transmission jack. Install the fluid filler tube in the transmission case or pan. Secure the tube to the cylinder head with the attaching bolt. Install the vacuum hose on the transmission vacuum unit. Install the vacuum line retaining clip. Connect the transmission regulated spark (T.R.S.) switch wires to the switch, if so equipped.

28. Connect the fluid cooling lines to the transmission case.

29. Connect the downshift rod to the downshift lever.

30. Connect the selector rod or cable to the transmission manual lever. Connect the column lock rod on console and floor shift vehicles, if so equipped.

31. Connect the speedometer cable to the extension housing.

32. Install the converter housing cover and torque the attaching bolts to 12-16 ft. lbs.

33. Install the starter and torque the attaching bolts to 25-30 ft. lbs. Connect the starter cable.

34. Install the driveshaft. Torque the companion flange U-bolts attaching nuts to 25-30 ft. lbs.

35. Lower the vehicle. Fill the transmission to the proper level with fluid. Adjust the manual and downshift linkage as required.

C6

1. Working from the engine compartment, remove the two bolts retaining the fan shroud to the radiator.

2. Raise and safely support the vehicle.

3. Place the drain pan under the transmission fluid pan. Starting at the rear of the pan and working toward the front, loosen the attaching bolts and allow the fluid to drain. Finally remove all of the pan attaching bolts except two at the front, to allow the fluid to further drain. After the fluid has drained, install two bolts on the rear side of the pan to temporarily hold it in place.

4. Remove the converter drain plug access cover and adapter plate bolts from the lower end of the converter housing.

5. Remove the converter-to-flywheel attaching nuts.

6. Disconnect the driveshaft from the rear axle and slide the shaft rearward from the transmission. Install the seal installation tool in the extension housing to prevent fluid leakage.

7. Disconnect the speedometer cable from the extension housing.

8. Disconnect the downshift rod from the transmission downshift lever.

9. Disconnect the shift cable form the manual lever at the transmission.

10. Remove the two bolts that secure the shift cable bracket to the converter housing and position the cable and bracket out of the way.

11. Remove the starter motor attaching bolts and position the starter out of the way.

12. Disconnect the rubber hose from the vacuum diaphragm at the rear of the transmission. Remove the vacuum tube from the retaining clip at the transmission. Disconnect the transmission regulated spark (T.R.S.) switch wire at the transmission, if so equipped.

13. Disconnect the muffler inlet pipe at the exhaust manifolds and allow the pipe to hang.

14. Remove the crossmember to frame side support bolts and nuts. Remove the nuts securing the rear engine supports to the crossmember. Position a jack under the transmission and raise it slightly. Remove the bolts securing the rear engine support to the extension housing and remove the crossmember and rear supports from the vehicle.

15. Loosen the parking brake adjusting nut at the equalizer and remove the cable from the idler hook attaching to the floor pan.

16. Lower the transmission, then disconnect the oil cooler lines from the transmission case.

17. Secure the transmission to the jack with a chain.

18. Remove the six bolts that attach the converter housing to the cylinder block.

19. Remove the bolt that secures the transmission filler tube to the cylinder block. Lift the filler tube and dipstick from the transmission.

20. Move the transmission away from the cylinder block.

21. Carefully lower the transmission and remove it from under the vehicle.

22. Remove the converter and mount the transmission in a holding fixture.

23. Torque the converter drain plug to 14-28 ft. lbs.

24. Position the converter to the transmission making sure the converter drive flats are fully engaged in the pump gear.

25. With the converter properly installed, place the transmission on the jack. Secure the transmission to the jack with the safety chain.

26. Rotate the converter so that the studs and drain plug are in alignment with their holes in the flywheel.

27. With the transmission mounted on a transmission jack, move the converter and transmission assembly forward into position using care not to damage the flywheel and converter pilot. The converter must rest squarely against the flywheel. This indicates that the converter pilot is not binding in the engine crankshaft.

28. Install a new O-ring on the lower end of the transmission filler tube. Insert the tube in the transmission case and secure the tube to the engine with the attaching bolts.

29. Install the converter housing-to-engine attaching bolts. Torque the bolts to 40-50 ft. lbs. Remove the safety chain from the transmission.

30. Connect the oil cooler lines to the transmission case.

31. Raise the transmission.

32. Position the parking brake cable in the idler hook and tighten the adjusting nut at the equalizer.

33. Place the rear engine supports on the crossmember and position the crossmember on the frame side supports.

34. Secure the engine rear supports to the extension housing with the attaching bolts. Torque the bolts and nuts to 35-40 ft. lbs.

35. Remove the transmission jack from under the vehicle and install the crossmember-to-frame side support bolts and nuts. Torque the bolts to 35-40 ft. lbs.

36. Install and torque the engine rear support-to-crossmember attaching nuts.

37. Connect the muffler inlet pipe to the exhaust manifolds.

38. Connect the vacuum line to the vacuum diaphragm making sure that the metal tube is secured in the retaining clip. Connect the transmission regulated spark (T.R.S.) switch wire to the switch, if so equipped.

39. Position the starter motor to the converter housing and secure it with the attaching bolts.

40. Install the torque converter-to-flywheel

attaching nuts and torque them to 20-30 ft. lbs.

41. Position the shift cable bracket to the converter housing and install the two attaching bolts.

42. Connect the shift cable to the manual lever at the transmission.

43. Connect the downshift rod to the lever on the transmission.

44. Connect the speedometer cable to the extension housing.

45. Install the driveshaft.

46. Install the converter drain plug access cover and adapter plate bolts. Torque the bolts to 12-16 ft. lbs.

47. Adjust the manual and downshift linkage as required.

48. Lower the vehicle.

49. Working from the engine compartment, position the fan shroud to the radiator and secure with the two attaching bolts.

50. Fill the transmission to the proper level with Dexron®II ATF.

51. Check the transmission, converter assembly and oil cooler lines for leaks.

FMX and CW

1. Position the vehicle in the work area, but do not raise at this time.

2. Remove the two upper bolts and lockwashers which attach the converter housing to the engine.

3. Raise and safely support the vehicle.

4. Place the drain pan under the transmission fluid pan. Starting at the rear of the pan and working toward the front, loosen the attaching bolts and allow the fluid to drain. Finally remove all of the pan attaching bolts except two at the front, to allow the fluid to further drain. With fluid drained, install two bolts on the rear side of the pan to temporarily hold it in place.

5. Remove the converter drain plug access cover from the lower end of the converter housing.

6. Remove the converter-to-flywheel attaching nuts. Place a wrench on the crankshaft pulley attaching bolt to turn the converter to gain access to the nuts.

7. With the wrench on the crankshaft pulley attaching bolt, turn the converter to gain access to the converter drain plug, and remove the plug. Place a drain pan under the converter to catch the fluid. After the fluid has been drained, reinstall the plug.

8. Disconnect the driveshaft from the rear companion flange (marking it to assure correct assembly). Slide the shaft rearward from the transmission. Position a seal installation tool in the extension housing to prevent fluid leakage.

9. Disconnect the vacuum hoses from the vacuum diaphragm unit and the tube from the extension housing clip.

10. Install the converter housing front plate to hold the converter in place when the transmission is removed. Under no conditions should the converter be left attached to the engine when the transmission is removed. This could damage the input shaft, converter and pump.

11. Disconnect the starter cables from the starter and remove the starter.

12. Disconnect the oil cooler lines from the transmission.

13. Disconnect the downshift linkage from the transmission.

14. Disconnect the selector rod or cable from the transmission manual lever.

15. Disconnect the speedometer cable from the extension housing. Disconnect the exhaust inlet pipes at the exhaust manifolds.

16. Support the transmission on a transmission jack. Secure the transmission to the jack with safety chain. Remove the two engine rear support to transmission bolts. Remove the two crossmember to frame side rail attaching bolts and nuts. Raise the transmission slightly to take the weight off the crossmember. Remove the rear support to crossmember bolt and nut and remove the crossmember.

17. Lower the transmission slightly and disconnect the fluid filter tube.

18. Remove the remaining converter housing to engine attaching bolts. Move the transmission and converter assembly to the rear and down to remove it.

19. Torque the converter drain plug to 15-28 ft. lbs.

20. If the converter has been removed from the converter housing, carefully position the converter to the transmission making sure the converter drive flats are fully engaged in the pump gear.

21. With the converter properly installed, place the transmission on the jack. Secure the transmission to the jack with safety chain.

22. Rotate the converter until the studs and drain plug are in alignment with their holes in the flywheel.

23. With the transmission mounted on a transmission jack, move the converter and transmission assembly forward into position, using care not to damage the flywheel and converter pilot. The converter must rest squarely against the flywheel. This indicates that the converter pilot is not binding in the engine crankshaft.

24. Install the lower converter housing-to-engine bolts. Torque bolts to 40-50 ft. lbs. Remove the safety chain from the transmission.

25. Connect the fluid filler tube.

26. Install the crossmember.

27. Lower the transmission until the extension housing rests on the crossmember, and then install the rear support-to-crossmember bolts. Connect the exhaust inlet pipes at the exhaust manifolds.

28. Install the converter attaching nuts. Install the access plates.

29. Connect the oil cooler inlet and outlet lines to the transmission case.

30. Coat the front universal joint yoke seal and spline with C1AZ-19590-B lubricant (or equivalent), and install the driveshaft. Be sure that the driveshaft markings match those of the companion flange for correct balance.

31. Connect the speedometer cable at the transmission.

32. Connect the manual selector rod or cable to the transmission manual lever.

33. Connect the downshift linkage at the transmission downshift lever.

34. Install the starter motor and connect the starter cables.

35. Connect the vacuum hoes to the vacuum diaphragm unit and the tube to its clip.

36. Lower the transmission and install the upper two converter housing-to-engine bolts. Torque bolts to 40-50 ft. lbs.

37. Lower the vehicle and fill the transmission with type F fluid.

38. Check the transmission, converter assembly, and fluid cooler lines for fluid leaks. Adjust the manual and downshift linkages.

Automatic Overdrive (AOD)

1. Raise and safely support the vehicle.

2. Place the drain pan under the transmission fluid pan. Starting at the rear of the pan and working toward the front, loosen the attaching bolts and allow the fluid to drain. Finally removal all of the pan attaching bolts except two at the front, to allow the fluid to further drain. With fluid drained, install two bolts on the rear side of the pan to temporarily hold it in place.

3. Remove the converter drain plug access cover from the lower end of the converter housing.

4. Remove the converter-to-flywheel attaching nuts. place a wrench on the crankshaft pulley attaching bolt to turn the converter to gain access to the nuts.

5. Place a drain pan under the converter to catch the fluid. With the wrench on the crankshaft pulley attaching bolts, turn the converter to gain access to the converter drain plug and remove the plug. After the fluid has been drained, reinstall the plug.

6. Disconnect the driveshaft from the rear axle and slide shaft rearward from the trans-

mission. Install a seal installation tool in the extension housing to prevent fluid leakage.

7. Disconnect the cable from the terminal on the starter motor. Remove the three attaching bolts and remove the starter motor. Disconnect the neutral start switch wires at the plug connector.

8. Remove the rear mount-to-crossmember attaching bolts and the two crossmember-to-frame attaching bolts.

9. Remove the two engine rear support-to-extension housing attaching bolts.

10. Disconnect the TV linkage rod from the transmission TV lever. Disconnect the manual rod from the transmission manual lever at the transmission.

11. Remove the two bolts securing the bellcrank bracket to the converter housing.

12. Raise the transmission with a transmission jack to provide clearance to remove the crossmember. Remove the rear mount from the crossmember and remove the crossmember from the side supports.

13. Lower the transmission to gain access to the oil cooler lines.

14. Disconnect each oil line from the fittings on the transmission.

15. Disconnect the speedometer cable from the extension housing.

16. Remove the bolt that secures the transmission fluid filler tube to the cylinder block. Lift the filler tube and the dipstick from the transmission.

17. Secure the transmission to the jack with the chain.

18. Remove the converter housing-to-cylinder block attaching bolts.

19. Carefully move the transmission and converter assembly away from the engine and, at the same time, lower the jack to clear the underside of the vehicle.

20. Remove the converter and mount the transmission in a holding fixture.

21. Tighten the converter drain plug to 20-28 ft. lbs.

22. Position the converter on the transmission, making sure the converter drive flats are fully engaged in the pump gear by rotating the converter.

23. With the converter properly installed, place the transmission on the jack. Secure the transmission to the jack with a chain.

24. Rotate the converter until the studs and drain plug are in alignment with the holes in the flywheel.

WARNING: *Lube the pilot bushing.*

25. Align the yellow balancing marks on converter and flywheel for Continental.

26. move the converter and transmission assembly forward into position, using care not to

damage the flywheel and the converter pilot. The converter must rest squarely against the flywheel. This indicates that the converter pilot is not binding in the engine crankshaft.

27. Install and tighten the converter housing-to-engine attaching bolts to 40-50 ft. lbs. make sure that the vacuum tube retaining clips are properly positioned.

28. Remove the safety chain from around the transmission.

29. Install a new O-ring on the lower end of the transmission filler tube. Insert the tube in the transmission case and secure the tube to the engine with the attaching bolts.

30. Connect the speedometer cable to the extension housing.

31. Connect the oil cooler lines to the right side of the transmission case.

32. Position the crossmember on the side supports. Position the rear mount on the crossmember and install the attaching bolt and nut.

33. Secure the engine rear support to the extension housing and tighten the bolts to 35-40 ft. lbs.

34. Lower the transmission and remove the jack.

35. Secure the crossmember to the side supports with the attaching bolts and tighten them to 35-40 ft. lbs.

36. Position the bellcrank to the converter housing and install the two attaching bolts.

37. Connect the TV linkage rod to the transmission TV lever. Connect the manual linkage rod to the manual lever at the transmission.

38. Secure the converter-to-flywheel attaching nuts and tighten them to 20-30 ft. lbs.

39. Install the converter housing access cover and secure it with the attaching bolts.

40. Secure the starter motor in place with the attaching bolts. Connect the cable to the terminal on the starter. Connect the neutral start switch wires at the plug connector.

41. Connect the driveshaft to the rear axle.

42. Adjust the shift linkage as required.

43. Adjust throttle linkage.

44. Lower the vehicle.

45. Fill the transmission to the correct level with Dexron®II. Start the engine and shift the transmission to all ranges, then recheck the fluid level.

DRIVELINE

Driveshaft and U-Joints

The driveshaft is the means by which the power from the engine and transmission (in the front of the car) is transferred to the differential and rear axles, and finally to the rear wheels.

The driveshaft assembly incorporates two universal joints, one at each end, and a slip yoke at the front end of the assembly, which fits into the back of the transmission.

All driveshafts are balanced when installed in a car. It is therefore imperative that before applying undercoating to the chassis, the driveshaft and universal joint assembly be completely covered to prevent the accidental application of undercoating to the surfaces, and the subsequent loss of balance.

DRIVESHAFT REMOVAL

The procedure for removing the driveshaft assembly, complete with universal joint and slip yoke, is as follows:

1. Mark the relationship of the rear dirveshaft yoke and the drive pinion flange of the axle. If the original yellow alignment marks are visible, there is not need for new marks. The purpose of this marking is to facilitate installation of the assembly in its exact original position, thereby maintaining proper balance.

2. Remove the four bolts or U-clamps which hold the rear universal joint to the pinion flange. Wrap tape around the loose bearing caps in order to prevent them from falling off the spider.

3. Pull the driveshaft toward the rear of the vehicle until the slip yoke clears the transmission housing and the seal. Plug the hole at the rear of the transmission housing or place a container under the opening to catch any fluid which might leak.

UNIVERSAL JOINT OVERHAUL

Single Cardan Joint

1. Position the driveshaft assembly in a sturdy vise.

2. Remove the snaprings which retain the bearings in the slip yoke (front only) and in the driveshaft (front and rear).

3. Using a large vise or an arbor press and a socket smaller than the bearing cap on one side and a socket larger than the bearing cap on the other side, drive one of the bearings in toward the center of the universal joint, which will force the opposite bearing out.

4. As each bearing is forced far enough out of the universal joint assembly that it is accessible, grip it with a pair of pliers, and pull it from the driveshaft yoke. Drive the spider in the opposite direction in order to make the opposite bearing accessible, and pull it free with a pair of pliers. Use this procedure to remove all bearings from both universal joints.

5. After removing the bearings, lift the spider from the yoke.

6. Thoroughly clean all dirt and foreign matter from the yokes on both ends of the driveshaft.

WARNING: *When installing new bearings in the yokes, it is advisable to use an arbor press. However, if this tool is not available,* *the bearings should be driven into position with extreme car, as a heavy jolt on the needle bearings can easily damage or misalign them, greatly shortening their lift and hampering their efficiency.*

7. Start a new bearing into the yoke at the rear of the driveshaft.

8. Position a new spider in the rear yoke and

Troubleshooting Basic Driveshaft and Rear Axle Problems

When abnormal vibrations or noises are detected in the driveshaft area, this chart can be used to help diagnose possible causes. Remember that other components such as wheels, tires, rear axle and suspension can also produce similar conditions.

BASIC DRIVESHAFT PROBLEMS

Problem	Cause	Solution
Shudder as car accelerates from stop or low speed	• Loose U-joint • Defective center bearing	• Replace U-joint • Replace center bearing
Loud clunk in driveshaft when shifting gears	• Worn U-joints	• Replace U-joints
Roughness or vibration at any speed	• Out-of-balance, bent or dented driveshaft • Worn U-joints • U-joint clamp bolts loose	• Balance or replace driveshaft • Replace U-joints • Tighten U-joint clamp bolts
Squeaking noise at low speeds	• Lack of U-joint lubrication	• Lubricate U-joint; if problem persists, replace U-joint
Knock or clicking noise	• U-joint or driveshaft hitting frame tunnel • Worn CV joint	• Correct overloaded condition • Replace CV joint

BASIC REAR AXLE PROBLEMS

First, determine when the noise is most noticeable.

Drive Noise: Produced under vehicle acceleration.

Coast Noise: Produced while the car coasts with a closed throttle.

Float Noise: Occurs while maintaining constant car speed (just enough to keep speed constant) on a level road.

Road Noise

Brick or rough surfaced concrete roads produce noises that seem to come from the rear axle. Road noise is usually identical in Drive or Coast and driving on a different type of road will tell whether the road is the problem.

Tire Noise

Tire noises are often mistaken for rear axle problems. Snow treads or unevenly worn tires produce vibrations seeming to originate elsewhere. **Temporarily** inflating the tires to 40 lbs will significantly alter tire noise, but will have no effect on rear axle noises (which normally cease below about 30 mph).

Engine/Transmission Noise

Determine at what speed the noise is most pronounced, then stop the car in a quiet place. With the transmission in Neutral, run the engine through speeds corresponding to road speeds where the noise was noticed. Noises produced with the car standing still are coming from the engine or transmission.

Front Wheel Bearings

While holding the car speed steady, lightly apply the footbrake; this will often decease bearing noise, as some of the load is taken from the bearing.

Rear Axle Noises

Eliminating other possible sources can narrow the cause to the rear axle, which normally produces noise from worn gears or bearings. Gear noises tend to peak in a narrow speed range, while bearing noises will usually vary in pitch with engine speeds.

NOISE DIAGNOSIS

The Noise Is	Most Probably Produced By
• Identical under Drive or Coast	• Road surface, tires or front wheel bearings
• Different depending on road surface	• Road surface or tires
• Lower as the car speed is lowered	• Tires
• Similar with car standing or moving	• Engine or transmission
• A vibration	• Unbalanced tires, rear wheel bearing, unbalanced driveshaft or worn U-joint
• A knock or click about every 2 tire revolutions	• Rear wheel bearing
• Most pronounced on turns	• Damaged differential gears
• A steady low-pitched whirring or scraping, starting at low speeds	• Damaged or worn pinion bearing
• A chattering vibration on turns	• Wrong differential lubricant or worn clutch plates (limited slip rear axle)
• Noticed only in Drive, Coast or Float conditions	• Worn ring gear and/or pinion gear

press the new bearing ¼″ (6mm) below the outer surface of the yoke.

9. With the bearing in position, install a new snapring.

10. Start a new bearing into the opposite side of the yoke.

11. Press the bearing until the opposite bearing, which you have just installed, contacts the inner surface of the snapring.

12. Install a new snapring on the second bearing. It may be necessary to grind the surface of this second snapring.

13. Reposition the driveshaft in the vise, so that the front universal joint is accessible.

14. Install the new bearings, new spider, and new snaprings in the same manner as you did for the rear universal joint.

15. Position the slip yoke on the spider. Install new bearings, nylon thrust bearings, and snaprings.

16. Check both reassembled joints for freedom of movement. If misalignment of any part is causing a bind, a sharp rap on the side of the yoke with a brass hammer should seat the bear-

ing needle and provide the desired freedom of movement. Care should be exercised to firmly support the shaft end during this operation, as well as to prevent blows to the bearings them-

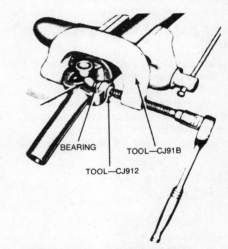

Removing the universal joint bearing

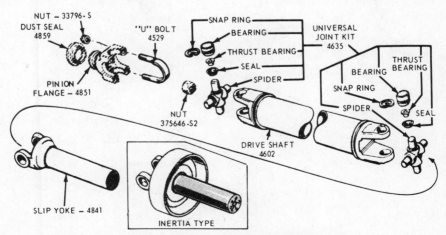

Driveshaft and U-joints disassembled

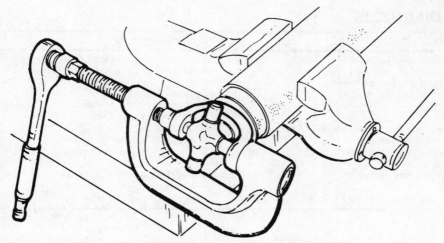

Installing universal joint bearing

selves. Under no circumstances should the driveshaft be installed in a car if there is any binding in the universal joints.

DOUBLE CARDAN JOINT REPLACEMENT (REAR)

1. Working at the rear axle end of the shaft, mark the position of the spiders, the center yoke, and the centering socket yoke as related to the companion flange. The spiders must be assembled with the bosses in their original position to provide proper clearances.

2. Using a large vise or an arbor press and a socket smaller than the bearing cap on one side and a socket larger than the bearing cap on the other side, drive one of the bearings in toward the center of the universal joint, which will force the opposite bearing out.

3. Remove the driveshaft from the vise.

4. Tighten the bearing in the vise and tap on the yoke to free the bearing from the center yoke. Do not tap on the driveshaft tube.

5. Reposition the sockets on the yoke and force the opposite bearing outward and remove it.

6. Position the sockets on one of the remain-

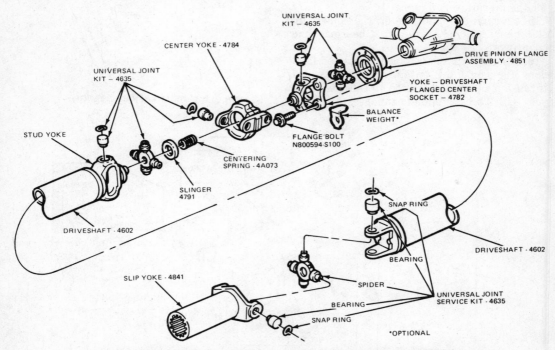

Exploded view of the driveshaft and U-joints with a double cardan U-joint

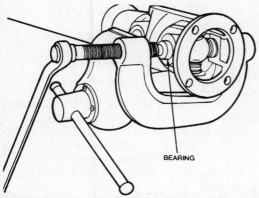

Pressing the bearing from the double cardan center yoke

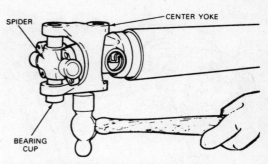

Removing the bearing from the center yoke

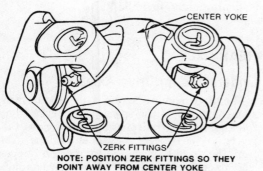

NOTE: POSITION ZERK FITTINGS SO THEY POINT AWAY FROM CENTER YOKE AS SHOWN

Grease fiting locations on the double cardan joint

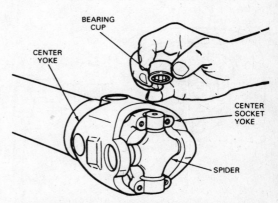

Removing the bearing cup from the center yoke

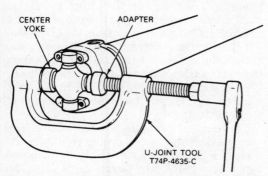

Partially pressing the bearing from the center yoke of the double cardan joint

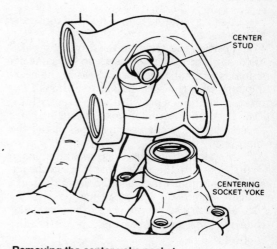

Removing the center yoke socket

ing bearings and force it outward approximately ⅜" (9.5mm).

7. Grip the bearing in the vise and tap on the weld yoke to free the bearing from the center yoke. Do not tap on the driveshaft tube.

8. Reposition the sockets on the yoke to press out the remaining bearing.

9. Remove the spider from the center yoke.

10. Remove the bearings from the driveshaft yoke as outlined above and remove the spider from the yoke.

11. Insert a suitable tool into the centering ball socket located in the companion flange and pry out the rubber seal. Remove the retainer, three piece ball seat, washer and spring from the ball socket.

12. Inspect the centering ball socket assembly for worn or damaged parts. If any damage is evident replace the entire assembly.

13. Insert the spring, washer, three piece ball seat and retainer into the ball socket.

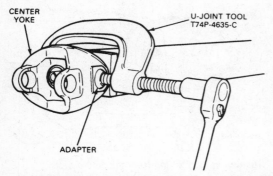

Removing the bearing from the rear of the center yoke

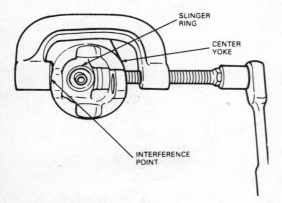

Center yoke interference point

14. Using a suitable tool, install the centering ball socket seal.

15. Position the spider in the driveshaft yoke. Make sure the spider bosses are in the same position as originally installed. Press in the bearing cups with the sockets and vise. Install the internal snaprings provided in the repair kit.

16. Position the center yoke over the spider ends and press in the bearing cups. Install the snaprings.

17. Install the spider in the companion flange yoke. Make sure the spider bosses are in the position as originally installed. Press on the bearing cups and install the snaprings.

18. Position the center yoke over the spider ends and press on the bearing cups. Install the snaprings.

DRIVESHAFT INSTALLATION

1. Carefully inspect the rubber seal on the output shaft and the seal in end of the transmission extension housing. Replace them if they are damaged.

2. Examine the lugs on the axle pinion flange and replace the flange if the lugs are shaved or distorted.

3. Coat the yoke spline with special purpose lubricant. The Ford part number for this lubricant if B8A-19589-A.

4. Remove the plug from the rear of the transmission housing.

5. Insert the yoke into the transmission housing and onto the transmission output shaft. Make sure that the yoke assembly does not bottom on the output shaft with excessive force.

6. Locate the marks which you made on the rear driveshaft yoke and the pinion flange prior to removal of the driveshaft assembly. Install the driveshaft assembly with the marks properly aligned.

7. Install the U-bolts and nuts or bolts which attach the universal joint to the pinion flange. Torque the U-bolts nuts to 8-15 ft. lbs. Flange bolts are tighten to 70-95 ft. lbs.

REAR AXLE

Understanding Drive Axles

The drive axle is a special type of transmission that reduces the speed of the drive from the engine and transmission and divides the power to the wheels. Power enters the axle from the driveshaft via the companion flange. The flange is mounted on the drive pinion shaft. The drive pinion shaft and gear which carry the power into the differential turn at engine speed. The gear on the end of the pinion shaft drives a large ring gear the axis of rotation of which is 90 degrees away from the of the pinion. The pinion and gear reduce the gear ratio of the axle, and change the direction of rotation to turn the axle shafts which drive both wheels. The axle gear ratio is found by dividing the number of pinion gear teeth into the number of ring gear teeth.

The ring gear drives the differential case. The case provides the two mounting points for the ends of a pinion shaft on which are mounted two pinion gears. The pinion gears drive the two side gears, one of which is located on the inner end of each axle shaft.

By driving the axle shafts through the arrangement, the differential allows the outer drive wheel to turn faster than the inner drive wheel in a turn.

The main drive pinion and the side bearings, which bear the weight of the differential case, are shimmed to provide proper bearing preload, and to position the pinion and ring gears properly.

WARNING: *The proper adjustment of the relationship of the ring and pinion gears is critical. It should be attempted only by those with extensive equipment and/or experience.*

Limited-slip differentials include clutches which tend to link each axle shaft to the differential case. Clutches may be engaged either by spring action or by pressure produced by the torque on the axles during a turn. During turning on a dry pavement, the effects of the clutches are overcome, and each wheel turns at the required speed. When slippage occurs at either wheel, however, the clutches will transmit some of the power to the wheel which has the greater amount of traction. Because of the presence of clutches, limited-slip units require a special lubricant.

Determining Axle Ratio

The drive axle is said to have a certain axle ratio. This number (usually a whole number and a decimal fraction) is actually a comparison of the number of gear teeth on the ring gear and the pinion gear. For example, a 4.11 rear means that theoretically, there are 4.11 teeth on the ring gear and one tooth on the pinion gear or, put another way, the driveshaft must turn 4.11 times to turn the wheels once. Actually, on a 4.11 rear, there might be 37 teeth on the ring gear and 9 teeth on the pinion gear. By dividing the number of teeth on the pinion gear into the number of teeth on the ring gear, the numerical axle ratio (4.11) is obtained. This also provides a good method of ascertaining exactly what axle ratio one is dealing with.

Another method of determining gear ratio is to jack up and support the car so that both rear wheels are off the ground. Make a chalk mark on the rear wheel and the driveshaft. Put the transmission in neutral. Turn the rear wheel one complete turn and count the number of turns that the driveshaft makes. The number of turns that the driveshaft makes in one complete revolution of the rear wheel is an approximation of the rear axle ratio.

Differential Overhaul

A differential overhaul is a complex, highly technical, and time consuming operation, which requires a great many tools, extensive knowledge of the unit and the way it works, and a high degree of mechanical experience and ability. It is highly advisable that the amateur mechanic not attempt any work on the differential unit.

Improved Traction Differentials

Ford calls their improved traction differential Traction-Lok®. In this assembly, a multiple-disc clutch is employed to control differential action. Repair procedures are the same as for conventional axles (within the scope of this book).

Pinion Oil Seal

REMOVAL AND INSTALLATION

NOTE: *Special tools are needed for this job.*

1. Raise and support the vehicle and remove the rear wheels and brake drums, or calipers.
2. Mark the driveshaft and yoke for reassembly and disconnect the driveshaft from the rear yoke.
3. With a socket on the pinion nut and an inch lb. torque wrench, rotate the drive pinion several revolutions. Check and record the torque required to turn the drive pinion.
4. Remove the pinion nut. Use a flange holding tool to hold the flange while removing the pinion nut. Discard the pinion nut.
5. Mark the yoke and the drive pinion shaft for reassembly reference.
6. Remove the rear yoke with a puller.
7. Inspect the seal surface of the yoke and replace it with a new one if the seal surface is pitted, grooved, or otherwise damaged.
8. Remove the pinion oil seal using tools 1175-AC and T50T-100A.
9. Before installing the new seal, coat the lip of the seal with rear axle lubricant.
10. Install the seal, driving it into place with a seal driver.

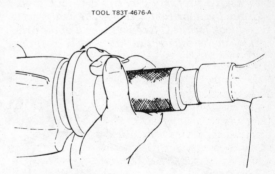

TOOL T83T-4676-A

Pinion seal installation

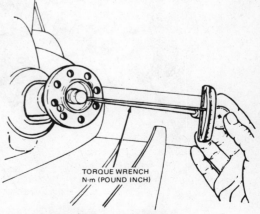

TORQUE WRENCH
N·m (POUND INCH)

Measuring pinion bearing preload

11. Install the yoke on the pinion shaft. Align the marks made on the pinion shaft and yoke during disassembly.

12. Install a new pinion nut. Tighten the nut until endplay is removed from the pinion bearing. Do not overtighten.

13. Check the torque required to turn the drive pinion. The pinion must be turned several revolutions to obtain an accurate reading.

14. Tighten the pinion nut to obtain the torque reading observed during disassembly (Step 3) plus 5 in. lbs. Tighten the nut minutely each time, to avoid overtightening. Do not loosen and then retighten the nut. Pinion preload should be 8-14 in. lbs.

NOTE: *If the desired torque is exceeded a new collapsible pinion spacer sleeve must be installed and the pinion gear preload reset.*

15. Install the driveshaft, aligning the index marks made during disassembly. Install the rear brake drums, or calipers, and wheels.

Axle Shaft and Bearing

NOTE: *Both integral and removable carrier type axles are used. The axle type and ratio are stamped on a plate attached to a rear housing cover bolt. Axle types also indicate whether the axle shafts are retained by C-locks. To properly identify a C-lock axle, drain the lubricant, remove the rear cover and look for the C-lock on the end of the axle shaft in the differential side gear bore. If the axle has no cover (solid housing) it is not a C-lock. If the second letter of the axle model code is F, it is a Traction-Lok axle. Always refer to the axle tag code and ratio when ordering parts.*

REMOVAL AND INSTALLATION

NOTE: *Bearings must be pressed on and off the shaft with an arbor press. Unless you have access to one, it is inadvisable to attempt any repair work on the axle shaft bearing assemblies.*

Flange Type

1. Remove the wheel, tire, and brake drum. With the disc brakes, remove the caliper, retainer, nuts and rotor. New anchor plate bolts will be needed for reassembly.

2. Remove the nuts holding the retainer plate in the backing plate, or axle shaft retainer bolts from the housing. Disconnect the brake line with drum brakes.

3. Remove the retainer and install nuts, finger-tight, to prevent the brake backing plate from being dislodged.

4. Pull out the axle shaft and bearing assembly, using a slide hammer.

On models with a tapered roller bearing, the tapered cup will normally remain in the axle housing when the shaft is removed. The cup must be removed from the housing to prevent seal damage when the shaft is reinstalled. The

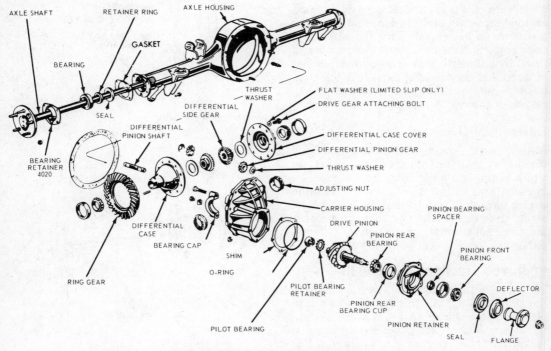

Removable carrier axle assembly

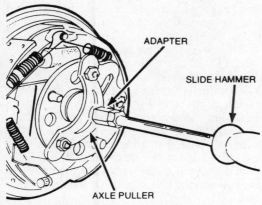

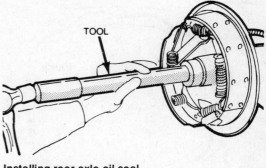

Installing rear axle oil seal

Typical axle shaft removal

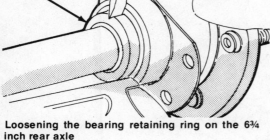

Loosening the bearing retaining ring on the 6¾ inch rear axle

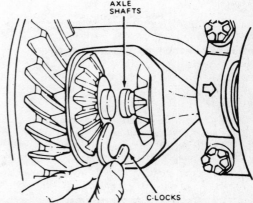

Removal and installation of the C-locks on a 7½ inch rear axle

cup can be removed with a slide hammer and an expanding puller.

WARNING: *If end-play is found to be excessive, the bearing should be replaced. Shimming the bearing is not recommended as this ignores end-play of the bearing itself and could result in improper bearing seating.*

5. Using a chisel, nick the bearing retainer in 3 or 4 places. The retainer does not have to be cut, but merely collapsed sufficiently to allow the bearing retainer to be slid from the shaft.

6. Press off the bearing and install the new one by pressing it into position. With tapered bearings, place the lubricated seal and bearing on the axle shaft (cup rib ring facing the flange). make sure that the seal is the correct length.

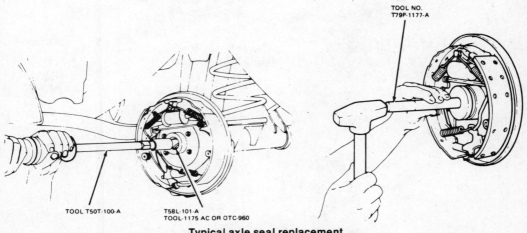

Typical axle seal replacement

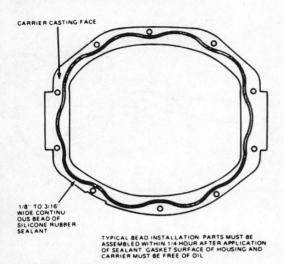

CARRIER CASTING FACE

1/8" TO 3/16"
WIDE CONTINUOUS BEAD OF SILICONE RUBBER SEALANT

TYPICAL BEAD INSTALLATION PARTS MUST BE ASSEMBLED WITHIN 1/4 HOUR AFTER APPLICATION OF SEALANT GASKET SURFACE OF HOUSING AND CARRIER MUST BE FREE OF OIL

Installing sealer on rear axle housing cover

Disc brake seal rims are black, drum brake seal rims are grey. Press the bearing and seal onto the shaft.

7. Press on the new retainer.

NOTE: *Do not attempt to press the bearing and the retainer on at the same time.*

8. On ball bearing models, to replace the seal: remove the seal from the housing with an expanding cone type puller and a slide hammer. the seal must be replaced whenever the shaft is removed. Wipe a small amount of sealer onto the outer edge of the new seal before installation; do not put sealer on the sealing lip. Press the seal into the housing with a seal installation tool.

9. Assemble the shaft and bearing in the housing, being sure that the bearing is seated properly in the housing. On ball bearing models, be careful not to damage the seal with the

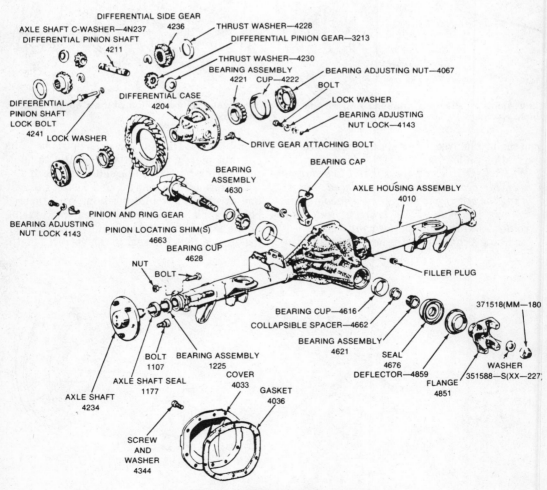

Integral carrier type rear axle assembly

shaft. With tapered bearings, first install the tapered cup on the bearing, and lubricate the outer diameter of the cup and the seal with axle lube. Then install the shaft and bearing assembly into the housing.

10. Install the retainer, drum or rotor and caliper, wheel and tire. Bleed the brakes.

C-Lock Type

1. Jack up and support the rear of the car.
2. Remove the wheels and tires from the brake drums.
3. Place a drain pan under the housing and drain the lubricant by loosening the housing cover.
4. Remove the locks securing the brake drums to the axle shaft flanges and remove the drums.
5. Remove the housing cover and gasket, if used.
6. Position jackstands under the rear frame member and lower the axle housing. This is done to give easy access to the inside of the differential.
7. Working through the opening in the differential case, remove the side gear pinion shaft lockbolt and the side gear pinion shaft.
8. Push the axle shafts inward and remove the C-locks from the inner end of the axle shafts. Temporarily replace the shaft and lockbolt to retain the differential gears in position.
9. Remove the axle shafts with a slide hammer. Be sure the seal is not damaged by the splines on the axle shaft.
10. Remove the bearing and oil seal from the housing. Both the seal and bearing can be removed with a slide hammer. Two types of bearings are used on some axles, one requiring a press fit and the other a loose fit. A loose fitting bearing does not necessarily indicate excessive wear.
11. Inspect the axle shaft housing and axle shafts for burrs or other irregularities. Replace any worn or damaged parts. A light yellow color on the bearing journal of the axle shaft is normal, and does not require replacement of the axle shaft. Slight pitting and wear is also normal.
12. Lightly coat the wheel bearing rollers with axle lubricant. Install the bearings in the axle housing until the bearing seats firmly against the shoulder.
13. Wipe all lubricant from the oil seal bore, before installing the seal.
14. Inspect the original seals for wear. If necessary, these may be replace with new seals, which are prepacked with lubricant and do not require soaking.
15. Install the oil seal.

CAUTION: *Installation of the seal without the proper tool can cause distortion and seal leakage. Seals may be colored coded for side identification. Do not interchange seals form side to side, if they are coded.*

16. Remove the lockbolt and pinion shaft. Carefully slide the axle shafts into place. Be careful that you do not damage the seal with the splined end of the axle shaft. Engage the splined end of the shaft with the differential side gears.
17. Install the axle shaft C-locks on the inner end of the axle shafts and seat the C-locks in the counterbore of the differential side gears.
18. Rotate the differential pinion gears until the differential pinion shaft can be installed. Install the differential pinion shaft lockbolt. Tighten to 15-22 ft. lbs.
19. Install the brake drum on the axle shaft flange.
20. Install the wheel and tire on the brake drum and tighten the attaching nuts.
21. Clean the gasket surface of the rear housing and install a new cover gasket and the housing cover. Some models do not use a paper gasket. On these models, apply a bead of silicone sealer on the gasket surface. The bead should run inside the bolt holes.
22. Raise the rear axle so that it is in the running position. Add the amount of specified lubricant to bring the lubricant level to ½″ (12.7mm) below the filler hole.

AXLE SHAFT SEAL REPLACEMENT

1. Remove the axle shaft from the rear axle assembly, following the procedures previously discussed.
2. Using a two-fingered seal puller (slide hammer), remove the seal from the axle housing.
3. Thoroughly clean the recess in the rear axle housing from which the seal was removed.
4. Position a new seal on the housing and drive it into place with a seal installation tool. If this tool is not available, a wood block may be substituted.

NOTE: *Although the right and left end seals are identical, there are many different types of seals which have been used on rear axle assembles. It is advisable to have one of the old seals with you when you are purchasing new ones.*

5. When the seal is properly installed, install the axle shaft.

Axle Housing
REMOVAL AND INSTALLATION

1. Raise the vehicle and support it on jackstands placed under the frame.

2. Remove the rear wheels.

3. Place an indexing mark on the rear yoke and driveshaft, and disconnect the shaft.

4. Disconnect the shock absorbers from the axle tubes. Disconnect the stabilizer bar at the axle bracket, on vehicles so equipped.

5. Disconnect the brake hose from the tee fitting on the axle housing. Disconnect the brake lines at the clips on the housing. Disconnect the vent tube at the axle.

6. Disconnect the parking brake cable at the frame mounting.

7. Support the rear axle with a jack.

8. Disconnect the lower control arms at the axle and swing them down out of the way.

9. Disconnect the upper control arms at the axle and swing them up out of the way.

10. Lower the axle slightly, remove the coil springs and insulators.

11. Lower the axle housing.

To install:

12. Raise the axle into position and connect the lower arms. Don't tighten the bolts yet.

13. Lower the axle slightly and install the coil springs and insulators.

14. Raise the axle and connect the upper control arms. Don't tighten the bolts yet.

15. Connect the parking brake cable at the frame mounting.

16. Connect the brake hose at the tee fitting on the axle housing.

17. Connect the vent tube at the axle. Apply thread locking compound to the threads.

18. Connect the stabilizer bar at the axle bracket, on vehicles so equipped.

19. Connect the shock absorbers from the axle tubes.

20. Connect the driveshaft.

21. Install the rear wheels.

22. Lower the vehicle.

23. Once the car is back on its wheels, observe the following torques:

Removeable carrier axles:

- Lower control arm bolts — 90 ft. lbs.
- Lower shock absorber nuts — 85 ft. lbs.
- Upper control arm bolts — 120 ft. lbs.

Integral carrier axles:

- Lower arm bolts — 100 ft. lbs.
- Lower shock absorber nuts — 55 ft. lbs.
- Upper arm bolts — 100 ft. lbs.

WARNING: *Bleed and adjust the brakes accordingly.*

Suspension and Steering

FRONT SUSPENSION

Each front wheel rotates on a spindle. The spindle's upper and lower ends attach to the upper and lower ball joints which mount to an upper and lower arm respectively. Through 1978 the upper arm pivots on a bushing and shaft assembly bolted to the frame. The lower arm pivots on a No. 2 crossmember bolt. The coil spring is seated between the lower arm and the top of the spring housing on the underside of the upper arm. A shock absorber is bolted to the lower arm at the bottom and the top of the spring housing. For 1979, the front suspension was redesigned. The arm and strut assembly has been replaced by a new lower A-arm. The upper ball

Troubleshooting Basic Steering and Suspension Problems

Problem	Cause	Solution
Hard steering (steering wheel is hard to turn)	• Low or uneven tire pressure • Loose power steering pump drive belt • Low or incorrect power steering fluid • Incorrect front end alignment • Defective power steering pump • Bent or poorly lubricated front end parts	• Inflate tires to correct pressure • Adjust belt • Add fluid as necessary • Have front end alignment checked/adjusted • Check pump • Lubricate and/or replace defective parts
Loose steering (too much play in the steering wheel)	• Loose wheel bearings • Loose or worn steering linkage • Faulty shocks • Worn ball joints	• Adjust wheel bearings • Replace worn parts • Replace shocks • Replace ball joints
Car veers or wanders (car pulls to one side with hands off the steering wheel)	• Incorrect tire pressure • Improper front end alignment • Loose wheel bearings • Loose or bent front end components • Faulty shocks	• Inflate tires to correct pressure • Have front end alignment checked/adjusted • Adjust wheel bearings • Replace worn components • Replace shocks
Wheel oscillation or vibration transmitted through steering wheel	• Improper tire pressures • Tires out of balance • Loose wheel bearings • Improper front end alignment • Worn or bent front end components	• Inflate tires to correct pressure • Have tires balanced • Adjust wheel bearings • Have front end alignment checked/adjusted • Replace worn parts
Uneven tire wear	• Incorrect tire pressure • Front end out of alignment • Tires out of balance	• Inflate tires to correct pressure • Have front end alignment checked/adjusted • Have tires balanced

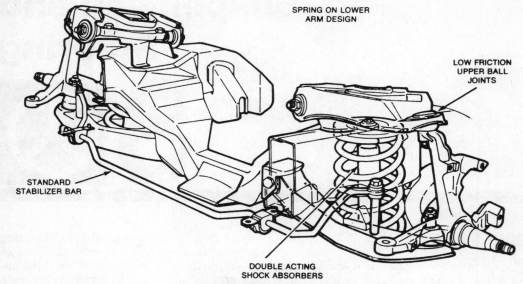

SPRING ON LOWER
ARM DESIGN

LOW FRICTION
UPPER BALL
JOINTS

STANDARD
STABILIZER BAR

DOUBLE ACTING
SHOCK ABSORBERS

Front suspension from 1977

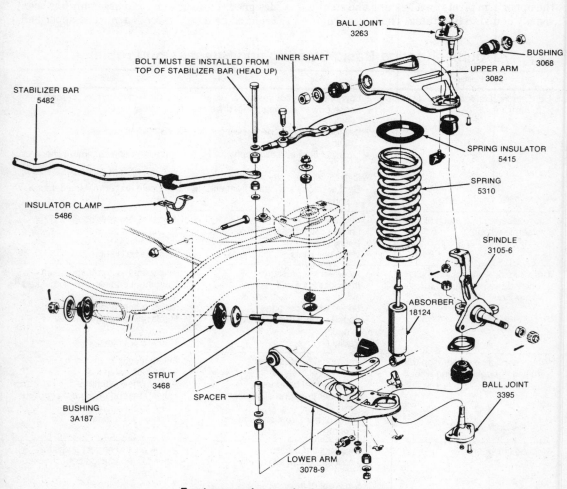

BALL JOINT
3263

BOLT MUST BE INSTALLED FROM
TOP OF STABILIZER BAR (HEAD UP)

INNER SHAFT

BUSHING
3068

UPPER ARM
3082

STABILIZER BAR
5482

SPRING INSULATOR
5415

SPRING
5310

INSULATOR CLAMP
5486

SPINDLE
3105-6

ABSORBER
18124

STRUT
3468

SPACER

BALL JOINT
3395

BUSHING
3A187

LOWER ARM
3078-9

Front suspension—spring between "A" arms

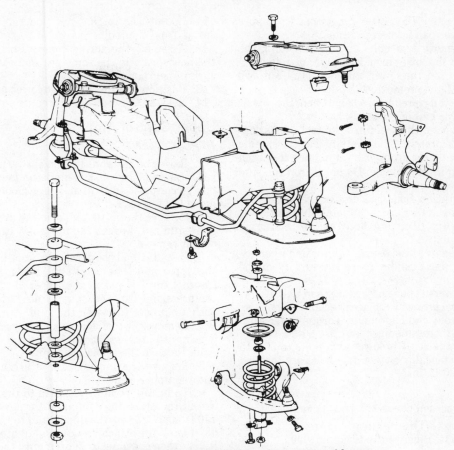

Front suspension—spring between lower arm and frame

joint incorporates a new low friction design, and the lower ball joint has a built-in wear indicator. A front stabilizer bar is standard.

Front Shock Absorber

REPLACEMENT

1. Remove the nut, washer, and bushing from the upper end of the shock absorber.

2. Raise the vehicle on a hoist and install jackstands under the frame rails.

3. Remove the two bolts securing the shock absorber to the lower arm and remove the shock absorber.

4. Inspect the shock absorber for leaks. Extend and compress the unit several times to check the damping action and remove any trapped air. Replace in pairs if necessary.

5. Install a new bushing and washer on the top of the shock absorber and position the unit inside the front spring. Install the two lower attaching bolts and torque them to 8-15 ft. lbs.

6. Remove the safety stands and lower the vehicle.

7. Place a new bushing and washer on the shock absorber top stud and install the attaching nut. Torque to 22-30 ft. lbs.

Coil Spring and Lower Control Arm

REMOVAL AND INSTALLATION

Spring between A-Arms

1. Raise car and support with stands placed back of lower arms.

2. If equipped with drum type brakes, remove the wheel and brake drum as an assembly. Remove the brake backing plate attaching bolts and remove the backing plate from the spindle. Wire the assembly back out of the way.

3. If equipped with disc brakes, remove the wheel from the hub. Remove two bolts and washers which hold the caliper and brake hose bracket to the spindle. Remove the caliper from the rotor and wire it back out of the way. Then, remove the hub and rotor from the spindle.

4. Disconnect lower end of the shock absorber and push it up to the retracted position.

5. Disconnect stabilizer bar link from the lower arm.

6. Remove the cotter pins from the upper and lower ball joint stud nuts.

7. Remove two bolts and nuts holding the strut to the lower arm. (through 1978 only).

8. Loosen the lower ball joint stud nut two turns. Do not remove this nut.

9. Install spreader tool between the upper and lower ball joints studs.

10. Expand the tool until the tool exerts considerable pressure on the studs. Tap the spindle near the lower stud with a hammer to loosen the stud in the spindle. Do not loosen the stud with tool pressure only.

11. Position floor jack under the lower arm and remove the lower ball joint stud nut.

12. Lower floor jack and remove the spring and insulator.

13. Remove the A-arm-to-crossmember attaching parts, and remove the arm from the car.

14. Reverse above procedure to install. If lower control arm was replaced because of damage, check front end alignment. Torque lower arm-to-No. 2 crossmember nut to 60-90 ft. lbs. Torque the strut-to-lower arm bolts to 80-115 ft. lbs. The caliper-to-spindle bolts are torqued to 90-120 ft. lbs.

Spring between Lower Arm and Frame

1. Raise the car and support it with jackstands. Remove the tire and wheel.

2. Disconnect the stabilizer bar link from the lower arm.

3. Remove the lower shock absorber attaching bolts.

4. Remove the shock absorber upper nut and remove the shock.

5. Remove the steering center link from the pitman arm.

6. Install a spring compressor tool. Insert the securing pin through the upper ball nut and the compression rod. This pin can only be inserted one way. With the upper ball nut secured, turn the upper plate so it walks up the coil and contacts the upper spring seat. Back the nut off ½ turn.

7. Install the lower ball nut and the thrust washer on the compression rod and tighten the forcing nut until the spring is free in the seat.

8. Remove the two lower control arm pivot bolts.

9. Disengage the arm from the frame and remove the spring assembly.

10. If a new spring is being installed, mark the position of the upper and lower plates on the old spring. Also, measure the length of the spring and the amount of curvature in order to simplify the compressing and installation of the new spring.

11. Loosen the forcing nut and remove the spring from the tool.

12. Assemble the spring compressor tool on the new spring in the same position as the old spring was removed.

13. Position the spring in the lower arm.

14. Reverse the removal procedure to install.

Upper Control Arm
REPLACEMENT

1. Raise the car and support the frame with jack stands placed just behind the lower arm pivot (rear pivot on 1979 and later models). Remove the wheel.

2. Remove the cotter pin from the upper ball joint stud nut. Loosen the nut a few turns but do not remove.

3. Install a ball joint removal tool between the upper and lower ball joint studs. Expand the tool until it places the upper stud under compression. Tap the spindle near the stud with a hammer to loosen the stud.

4. Remove the tool. Raise the lower arm with a jack until pressure is relieved from the upper stud. Remove the upper stud nut.

5. Remove the upper shaft attaching bolts and the upper arm.

6. To install, position the arm to the frame, install the attaching nuts, and torque to 120-140 ft. lbs. Connect the upper stud to the spindle. Install the attaching nut, and tighten to 75 ft. lbs., then continue to tighten until the cotter pin holes align. Install a new cotter pin. Install the wheel, adjust the wheel bearings, and lower the car. Caster, camber, and toe must be adjusted after installation.

Lower Ball Joint
INSPECTION
Through 1978

1. Raise the vehicle by placing a floor jack under the lower arm or, raise the vehicle on a hoist and place a jackstand under the lower arm and lower the vehicle onto it to remove the preload from the lower ball joint.

2. have an assistant grasp the top and bottom of the wheel and apply alternate in and out pressure to the top and bottom of the wheel.

3. Radial play of ¼" is acceptable measured at the inside of the wheel adjacent to the lower arm.

NOTE: *This radial play is multiplied at the outer circumference of the tire and should be measured only at the inside of the wheel.*

1979 and Later

1979 lower ball joints have built-in wear indicators. The checking surface is the round boss

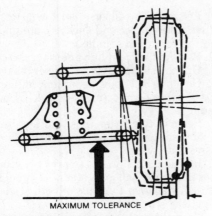

Measuring lower ball joint redial play

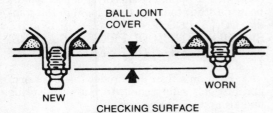

Lower ball joint wear indicator

into which the grease fitting is threaded. If the ball joint is not worn, the checking surface should project outside the cover. If the joint is worn out, the checking surface will be flush with the cover. Do not jack the vehicle up to perform this check.

REPLACEMENT

NOTE: *Ford Motor Company recommends replacement of control arm and ball joint as an assembly, rather than replacement of the ball joint only. However, aftermarket replacement parts are available.*

1. Raise the vehicle on a hoist and allow the front wheels to fall to their full down position.
2. Drill a ⅛" hole completely through each ball joint attaching rivet.
3. Us a ⅜" drill in the pilot hole to drill off the head of the rivet.
4. Drive the rivets from the lower arm.
5. Place a jack under the lower arm and lower the vehicle about 6".
6. Remove the lower ball joint stud cotter pin and attaching nut.
7. Using a suitable tool, loosen the ball joint from the spindle and remove the ball joint from the lower arm.
8. Clean all metal burrs from the lower arm and install the new ball joint, using the service parts nuts and bolts to attach the ball joint to the lower arm. Do not attempt to rivet the ball joint against once it has been removed.
9. Check front end alignment.

Upper Ball Joint
INSPECTION

1. Raise the vehicle by placing a floor jack under the lower arm. Do not allow the lower arm to hang freely with the vehicle on a hoist or bumper jack.

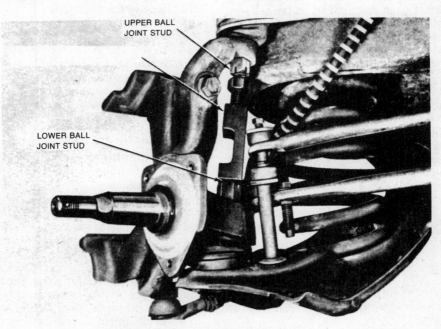

Loosening lower ball joint stud

2. Have an assistant grasp the top and bottom of the tire and move the wheel in and out.

3. As the wheel is being moved, observe the upper control arm where the spindle attaches to it. Any movement between the upper part of the spindle and the upper ball joint indicates a bad ball joint which must be replaced.

NOTE: *During this check, the lower ball joint will be unloaded and may move; this is normal and not an indication of a bad ball joint. Also, do not mistake a loose wheel bearing for a defective ball joint.*

REPLACEMENT

NOTE: *Ford Motor Company recommends replacement of control arm and ball joint as an assembly, rather than replacement of the ball joint only. However, aftermarket replacement parts are available.*

1. Raise the vehicle on a hoist and allow the front wheels to fall to their full down position.

2. Drill a 1/8" hole completely through each ball joint attaching rivet.

3. Using a large chisel, cut off the head of each rivet and drive them from the upper arm.

4. Place a jack under the lower arm and lower the vehicle about 6".

5. Remove the cotter pin and attaching nut from the ball joint stud.

6. Using a suitable tool, loosen the ball joint stud from the spindle and remove the ball joint from the upper arm.

7. Clean all metal burrs from the upper arm and install the new ball joint, using the service part nuts and bolts to attach the ball joint to the upper arm. Do not attempt to rivet the ball joint again once it has been removed.

8. Check front end alignment.

Sway (Stabilizer) Bar
REMOVAL AND INSTALLATION

1. Raise the front end and place support under both front wheels. A pair of drive-on ramps is ideal for this purpose.

2. Disconnect the stabilizer bar from each link, or disconnect the links at the control arms.

3. Remove the stabilizer bar brackets and remove the bar.

4. Installation is the reverse of removal. Torque the link-to-control arm nuts and/or link-to-bar nuts to 18 ft. lbs. and the bar bracket screws to 20 ft. lbs.

Spindle
REMOVAL AND INSTALLATION

1. Raise and support the front end on jackstands.

2. Remove the front wheels.

3. Remove the caliper-to-anchor plate bolts and wire the caliper and anchor plate up away from the rotor and spindle.

4. Remove the front hub and rotor assembly.

5. Unbolt and remove the caliper shield.

6. Using a ball joint separator, disconnect the spindle connecting rod link from the spindle.

7. Remove the cotter pins and loosen both ball joint stud nuts a few turns each, but don't remove them yet.

8. Position a ball joint remover between the upper and lower ball joint studs. The tool must seat firmly against the ends of both studs; not against the stud nuts.

9. Turn the tool with a wrench until the tool places the studs under considerable tension, and, with a hammer, sharply hit the spindle near the studs to break them loose in the spindle. DON'T LOOSEN THE STUDS IN THE SPINDLE WITH TOOL PRESSURE ALONE! DON'T HIT THE BOOT SEAL WITH THE HAMMER!

10. Position a floor jack under the lower arm and install a safety chain through the spring and around the lower arm.

11. Remove the upper and lower ball stud nuts, lower the jack and remove the spindle.

12. Position the spindle on the lower ball stud and install the nut. Torque the nut to 75-90 ft. lbs. and install a new cotter pin.

13. Raise the lower arm and guide the upper ball stud into the spindle. Install the stud nut and torque it to 105-120 ft. lbs. Install a new cotter pin.

14. Remove the floor jack.

15. Connect the spindle connecting rod to the spindle and install a new nut. Torque the nut to 43-47 ft. lbs. and install a new cotter pin.

16. Install the caliper splash shield and torque the fasteners to 15 ft. lbs.

17. Install the hub and rotor.

18. Install the caliper anchor plate on the spindle. Torque the bolts to 90-120 ft. lbs.

19. Install the wheels.

Wheel Alignment

NOTE: *The procedure for checking and adjusting front wheel alignment requires specialized equipment and professional skills. The following descriptions and adjustment procedures are for general reference only.*

Front wheel alignment is the position of the front wheels relative to each other and to the vehicle. It is determined, and must be maintained to provide safe, accurate steering with minimum tire wear. Many factors are involved in wheel alignment and adjustment are provided to return those that might change due to

Wheel Alignment Specifications—Ford–Mercury

Year	Model	Caster Range (deg)	Caster Pref Setting (deg)	Camber Range (deg)	Camber Pref Setting (deg)	Toe-in (in.)	Steering Axis Inclin. (deg)	Wheel Pivot Ratio (deg) Inner Wheel	Wheel Pivot Ratio (deg) Outer Wheel
1968–69	All	0 to 2P	1P	1/4N to 1 1/4P	3/4P	1/8 to 1/4	7 3/4	20	18 1/8
1970–71	All	0 to 2P	1P	1/4N to 1 1/4P	1/2P	1/16 to 5/16	7 3/4	20	19 4/25
1972	All	1N to 3P	1P	1/2N to 1 1/2P	1/2P	1/16 to 7/16	7 3/4	20	19 4/25
1973	All	0 to 4P	2P	1N to 1P	0	1/16 to 7/16	7 3/4	20	18 3/4
1974	All	0 to 4P	2P	①	②	3/16	9 1/2	20	18 3/4
1975	All	0 to 4P	2P	③	②	3/16	9 1/2	20	18 3/4
1976–77	All	1 1/4P to 2 3/4P	2P	④	②	3/16	9 1/2	20	18 3/4
1978	All	1 1/4P to 2 3/4P	2P	④	②	1/16 to 5/16	9.44	20	18.69
1979	All	2 1/4P to 3 3/4P	3P	1/4N to 1 1/4P	1/2P	1/16 to 5/16	11.20	20	18
1980–88	All	2 1/4P to 3 3/4P	3P	1/4N to 1 1/4P	1/2P	1/16 to 3/16	10.87	20	18.51

① Left wheel—0 to 1P
  Right wheel—1/4N to 3/4P
② Left wheel—1/2P
  Right wheel—1/4P
③ Left wheel—3/4N to 1 1/4P
  Right wheel—3/4N to 1 1/4P

N Negative   P Positive
④ Left wheel—1/4N to 1 1/4P
  Right wheel—1/2N to 1P

Wheel Alignment Specifications—Lincoln

Year	Model	Caster Range (deg)	Caster Pref Setting (deg)	Camber Range (deg)	Camber Pref Setting (deg)	Toe-in (in.)	Steering Axis Inclin. (deg)	Wheel Pivot Ratio (deg) Inner Wheel	Wheel Pivot Ratio (deg) Outer Wheel
1968–70	Continental	2 1/2N to 1/2N	1 1/2N	1/4P to 1 1/2P	3/4P	0 to 1/4	7	20	17 3/4
1968–70	Mark III	0 to 2P	1	1/4N to 1 1/4P	1/2P	1/16 to 5/16	7 3/4	20	18 1/16
1971	Continental	2 1/2N to 1/2N	1 1/2N	1/4P to 1 1/2P	3/4P	0 to 1/4	7	20	17 3/4
	Mark III	0–2P	1	1/4N to 1 1/4P	1/2P	1/16 to 5/16	7 3/4	20	18 1/16
'72	Continental	1/2N to 2 1/2P	1 1/2P	1/2N to 1 1/2P	1/2P	0 to 1/4	7 3/4	20	18 7/16
'72–'74	Mark IV	0 to 2P	1P	1/4N to 1 1/4P	1/2P	1/16 to 5/16	7 3/4	20	17 3/4
'73–'74	Continental	1/2N to 2 1/2P	1P	1/4N to 1 1/4P	1/2P	0 to 1/4	9 1/2	20	17 3/4 ①
'75–'77	Mark IV, V	1/4P–2 3/4P	2P	②	③	1/16–5/16	7 3/4	20	18.09
'78–'79	Mark V	3 1/4P–4 3/4P	4P	②	③	1/16–5/16	9 1/2	20	18.09
'75–'79	Continental	1 1/4P–2 3/4P	2P	②	③	0–1/4	9 1/2	20	18.16
1980–88				Use Ford/Mercury Specs					

N Negative   P Positive
① 18 1/2° in 1974
② Left: 1/4N to 1 1/4P; Right: 1/2N to 1P
③ Left—1/2P; Right—1/4P

normal wear to their original value. The factors which determine wheel alignment are dependent on one another; therefore, when one of the factors is adjusted the others must be adjusted to compensate.

Descriptions of these and their affects on the car are provided below.

NOTE: *Do not attempt to check and adjust the front wheel alignment without first making a thorough inspection of the front suspension components.*

CAMBER

Camber angle is the number of degrees that the centerline of the wheel in inclined from the vertical. Camber reduces loading of the outer wheel bearing and improves the tire contact patch while cornering.

CASTER

Caster angle is the number of degrees that a line drawn through the steering knuckle pivots is inclined from the vertical, toward the front or rear of the car. Caster improves directional stability and decreases susceptibility to crosswinds or road surface deviations.

TOE-IN

Toe-in is the difference of the distance between the centers of the front and rear of the front wheels. It is most commonly measured in inches, but is occasionally referred to as an angle between the wheels. Toe-in is necessary to compensate for the tendency of the wheels to deflect rearward while in motion. due to this tendency, the wheels of a vehicle, with properly adjusted toe-in, are traveling straight forward when the vehicle itself is traveling straight forward, resulting in directional stability and minimum tire wear.

Steering wheel spoke misalignment is often an indication of incorrect front end alignment. Care should be exercised when aligning the front end to maintain steering wheel spoke position. When adjusting the tie rod ends, adjust each an equal amount (in the opposite direction) to increase or decrease toe-in. If, following toe-in adjustment, further adjustments are necessary to center the steering wheel spokes,

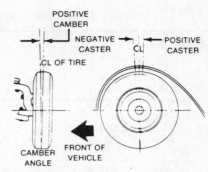

Caster and camber angles

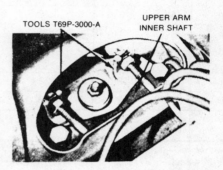

Caster and Camber adjusting tool installed

adjust the tie rod ends an equal amount in the same direction.

ADJUSTMENT PROCEDURES

Install Ford tool T65P-3000D (through 1978) or TP79P-3000A (from 1979), or its equivalent, on the frame rail, position the hooks around the upper control arm pivot shaft, and tighten the adjusting nuts slightly. Loosen the pivot shaft retaining bolts to permit adjustment.

To adjust caster, loosen or tighten either the front and rear adjusting nut. After adjusting caster, adjust the camber by loosening or tightening both nuts an equal amount. Tighten the shaft retaining bolts to specifications, remove the tool, and recheck the adjustments.

Adjust toe-in by loosening the clamp bolts, and turning the adjuster sleeves at the outer ends of the tie rod. Turn the sleeves an equal amount in the opposite direction, to maintain steering wheel spoke alignment.

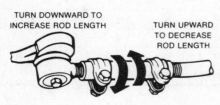

Tie-rod (toe-in) adjustments

REAR SUSPENSION

Coil Link Suspension

Large, low-rate coil springs are mounted between rear axle pads and frame supports. Parallel lower arms extend forward of the spring seats to rubber frame anchor to accommodate driving and braking forces. A third link is mounted between the axle and the frame to control torque reaction forces from the rear wheels.

Lateral (side sway) motion of the rear axle is controlled by a rubber bushed rear track bar, linked laterally between the axle and frame.

Four Link Suspension

The coil springs are mounted between the top of the axle and the frame pads, providing room for vertical placement of the shock absorbers in front of the axle. Two lower arms mount to axle forward of the outer ends, while the two shorter upper arms mount near the top center of the axle, with an included angle of 90 degrees.

Coil Springs

REMOVAL AND INSTALLATION

1. Place car on a hoist and lift under rear axle housing. Place jack stands under frame side rails.
2. Disconnect track bar at the rear axle housing bracket, (through 1978).
3. Disconnect rear shock absorbers from the rear axle housing brackets.
4. Disconnect hose from axle housing vent. Disconnect the rear of the front-to-rear brake tube from the rear brake hose at the No. 1 crossmember bracket. Remove the brake hose-to-bracket clip.
5. Lower hoist with axle housing until coil springs are released.
6. Remove spring lower retainer with bolt, nut, washer and insulator.
7. Remove spring with large rubber insulator pads from car.
8. Install in reverse of above. Bleed the brakes as outlined in Chapter 9.

Rear Shock Absorber

REPLACEMENT

1. Raise the rear of the vehicle. Install jackstands beneath the axle.
2. Remove the shock absorber attaching nut, washer, and insulator from the stud at the top side of the spring upper seat. compress the shock absorber sufficiently to clear the spring seat hole and remove the inner insulator and washer from the upper attaching stud.
3. Remove the locknut and disconnect the shock absorber lower stud at the mounting bracket on the axle housing.
4. Remove the shock absorber from the vehicle and check for leakage. If the shock absorber is in good condition, compress and expand the unit several times to expel any trapped air prior to reinstallation.
5. Position the inner washer and insulator on the upper attaching stud. Place the shock absorber in such a position that the upper attaching stud enters the hole in the spring upper seat. While maintaining the shock absorber in this position, install the outer insulator, washer, and new nut on the stud from the top side of the spring upper seat. Torque the attaching nut to 14-26 ft. lbs.

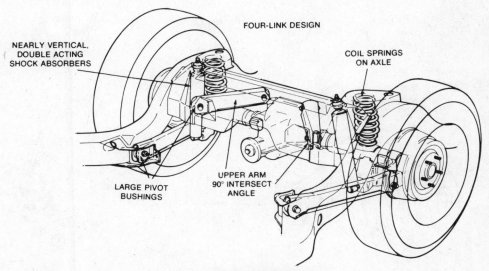

FOUR-LINK DESIGN

NEARLY VERTICAL, DOUBLE ACTING SHOCK ABSORBERS

COIL SPRINGS ON AXLE

LARGE PIVOT BUSHINGS

UPPER ARM 90° INTERSECT ANGLE

Four link rear suspension

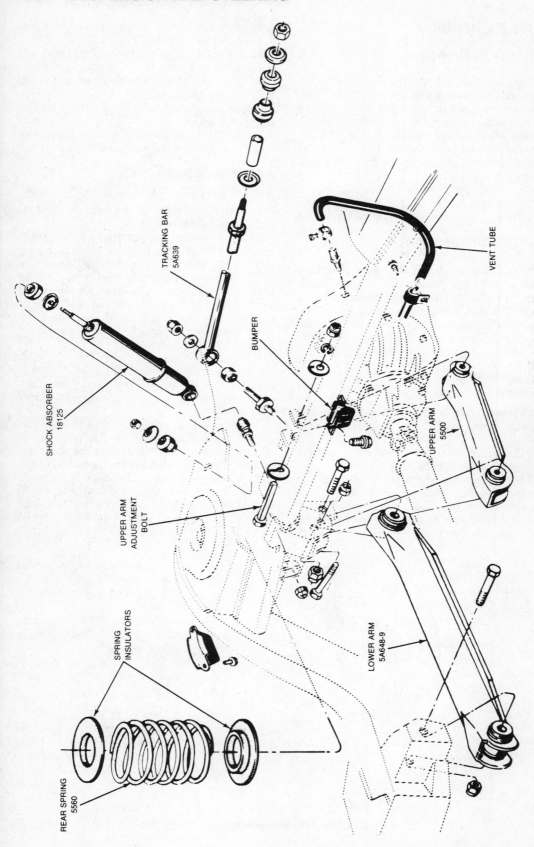

TRACKING BAR
5A639

VENT TUBE

SHOCK ABSORBER
18125

BUMPER

UPPER ARM
5500

UPPER ARM
ADJUSTMENT
BOLT

LOWER ARM
5A648-9

SPRING
INSULATORS

REAR SPRING
5560

Coil link rear suspension

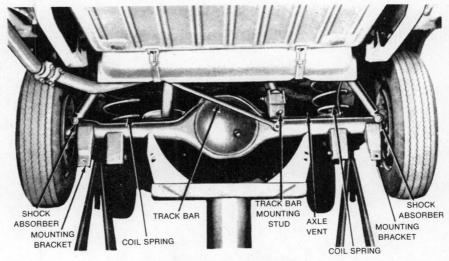

Removing the rear coil spring

6. Extend the shock absorber. Locate the lower stud in the mounting bracket hole on the axle housing. Install and torque the locknut to 50-85 ft. lbs.

7. Remove the jack stands and lower the car. Road test the car.

Sway (Stabilizer) Bar

REMOVAL AND INSTALLATION

1. Raise and support the rear end on jackstands under the axle housing.

2. Remove the stabilizer bar-to-rear link nuts and bolts on both sides.

3. Remove the mounting bracket-to-U-bolt nuts and remove the stabilizer bar.

4. Installation is the reverse of removal. The color-coded end of the bar goes on the left side. Torque the all fasteners to 20 ft. lbs. on 1977-78 models; 25 ft. lbs. on 1979 and later models.

AIR SUSPENSION

CAUTION: *Do not remove an air spring under any circumstances when there is pressure in the air spring. Do not remove any components supporting an air spring without either exhausting the air or providing support for the air spring.*

Components

SUSPENSION FASTENERS

Suspension fasteners are important attaching parts in that they could affect performance of vital components and systems and/or could result in major service expense. They must be replaced with fasteners of the same part number, or with an equivalent part, if replacement becomes necessary. Do not use a replacement part of less quality or substitute design. Torque values must be used, as specified, during assembly to assure proper retention of parts. New fasteners must be used whenever old fasteners are loosened or removed and when new component parts are installed.

AIR SPRING SUSPENSION

• Air compressor (less dryer), regenerative dryer, O-ring mounting bracket and the isolator mounts are all serviced as separate components.

• Height sensors and modules are replaceable.

• Air springs are replaceable as assemblies (including the solenoid valve).

• Air spring solenoid valves and external O-rings are replaceable.

• Air lines are replaceable, however quick connect unions and bulk tubing are available to mend a damaged air line.

• Collet and O-rings of the quick connect type fittings are replaceable.

FRONT SUSPENSION

• Gas filled shock absorber struts must be replaced as assemblies. They are not servicable. Replace only the damaged shock absorber strut. It is not necessary to replace in matched pairs.

• Strut upper mounts may be replaced individually.

• Air springs are replaced as assemblies. It is not necessary to replace in pairs.

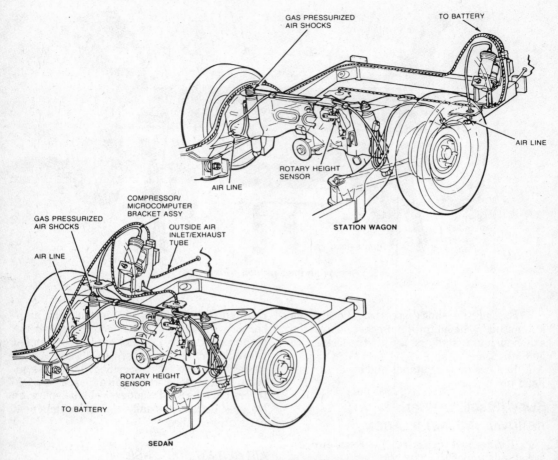

Automatic leveling rear suspension

• The lower control arm is replaceable as an assembly with the ball joint and bushings included.

• The spindle is replaceable.

• The stabilizer bar is replaceable with stabilizer bar-to-body insulators included.

• The stabilizer bar-to-body bushing is replaceable.

REAR SUSPENSION

The following rear suspension components may be replaced individually:

• Gas filled shock absorbers must be replaced as assemblies. They are not serviceable. Replace only the damaged shock absorber. It is not necessary to replace in matched pairs.

• Air springs are replaced as assemblies. It is not necessary to replace in pairs.

• Lower control arms, including both end bushings, are replaceable as assemblies. (Must be replaced in pairs).

• Upper control arms, including body end bushing, are replaceable as assemblies. (Must be replaced in pairs).

• Stabilizer bar is replaceable with stabilizer bar-to-axle insulator included.

• Stabilizer bar-to-body bushings are replaceable.

JACKING AND SUPPORTING

CAUTION: *The electrical power supply to the air suspension system must be shut off prior to hoisting, jacking or towing an air suspension vehicle. This can be accomplished by disconnecting the battery or turning off the power switch located in the trunk on the LH side. Failure to do so may result in unexpected inflation or deflation of the air springs which may result in shifting of the vehicle during these operations.*

Raise the front of the vehicle at the No. 2 crossmember until the tires are above the floor. Support the vehicle body with jackstands at each front corner and then lower the floor jack so that the front suspension is in full rebound. Repeat this procedure for the rear suspension, except raise the body at the rear jacking location.

Air Spring System

CAUTION: *Power to the air system must be shut-off by turning the air suspension switch (in luggage compartment) Off or by disconnecting the battery when servicing any air suspension components.*

• Do not attempt to install or inflate any air spring that has become unfolded.

• Any spring which has unfolded must be refolded, prior to being installed in a vehicle.

• Do not attempt to inflate any air spring which has been collapsed while uninflated from the rebound hanging position to the jounce stop.

• After inflating an air spring in hanging position, it must be inspected for proper shape.

• Failure to follow the above procedures may result in a sudden failure of the air spring or suspension system.

Air Spring Solenoid

The air spring solenoid valve has a two stage solenoid pressure relief fitting similar to a radiator cap. A clip is first removed, and rotation of the solenoid out of the spring will release air from the assembly before the solenoid can be removed.

1. Turn the air suspension switch Off.

2. Raise the vehicle. Remove wheel and tire assembly.

3. Disconnect the electrical connector and then disconnect the air line.

4. Remove the solenoid clip. Rotate the solenoid counterclockwise to the first stop.

5. Pull the solenoid straight out slowly to the second stop to bleed air from the system.

CAUTION: *Do not fully release solenoid until air is completely bled from the air spring.*

6. After the air is fully bled from the system, rotate the solenoid counterclockwise to the third stop, and remove the solenoid from the air spring assembly.

7. Check the solenoid O-ring for abrasion or cuts. Replace O-ring as required. Lightly grease the O-ring area of solenoid with silicone dielectric compound WA-10, D7AZ-19A331-A or equivalent.

8. Insert the solenoid into the air spring end cap and rotate clockwise to the third stop, push into the second stop, then rotate clockwise to the first stop.

9. Install solenoid clip. Connect the air line and the electrical connector.

10. Refill the air spring(s). Install the wheel and tire assembly.

Air Spring Fill

1. Turn On the air suspension switch. Diagnostic pigtail is to be ungrounded.

2. Connect a battery charger to reduce battery drain.

3. Cycle the ignition from the Off to Run position, hold in the Run position for a minimum of five seconds, then return to the Off position. Driver's door is open with all other doors shut.

4. Change the diagnostic pigtail from an ungrounded state to a grounded state by attaching a lead from the diagnostic pigtail to vehicle ground. The pigtail must remain grounded during the spring fill sequence.

5. While applying the brakes, turn the ignition switch to the Run position. (The door must be open. Do not start the vehicle). The warning lamps will blink continuously once every two seconds to indicate the spring pump sequence has been entered.

6. To fill a rear spring(s), close and open the door twice. After a 6 second delay, the front spring will be filled for 60 seconds.

7. To fill a front spring(s), close and open the door twice. After a 6 second delay, the front spring will be filled for 60 seconds.

8. To fill rear and front spring, fill the rear spring first (step 6). When the rear fill has finished, close and open the door once to initiate the front spring fill.

9. Terminate the air spring fill by turning the ignition switch to Off, actuating the brake, or ungrounding the diagnostic pigtail. The diagnostic pigtail must be ungrounded at the end of the spring fill.

10. Lower vehicle and start engine. Allow the vehicle to level with doors closed.

Air Spring — Front or Rear

1. Turn the air suspension switch Off.

2. Raise and support the vehicle. Suspension must be at full rebound.

3. Remove tire and wheel assembly.

4. Remove the air spring solenoid.

5. Remove the spring to lower arm fasteners. Remove the clip for front spring and/or remove bolts for rear spring.

6. Push down on the spring clip on the collar of the air spring and rotate collar counterclockwise to release the spring from the body spring seat. Remove the air spring.

7. Install the air spring solenoid. Correctly position the solenoid. For LH installation (front or rear spring), the notch on the collar is to be in line with the centerline of the solenoid. For RH installation (front or rear), the flat on the collar is to be in line with the centerline of the solenoid.

8. Install the air spring into the body spring seat, taking care to keep the solenoid air and electrical connections clean and free of damage. Rotate the air spring collar until the spring clip snaps into place. Be sure that the air spring col-

lar is retained by the three rolled tabs on the body spring seat.

9. Attach and secure the lower arm to spring attachment with suspension at full rebound and supported by the shock absorbers.

CAUTION: *The air springs may be damaged is suspension is allowed to compress before spring is inflated.*

10. Replace the tire and wheel assembly.

11. Lower the vehicle until the tire and wheel assembly are 1-3″ (25-75mm) above floor. Refill the air spring(s).

Air Compressor and Dryer Assembly

1. Turn the air suspension switch Off.

2. Disconnect the electrical connector located on the compressor.

3. Remove the air line protector cap form the dryer by releasing the two latching pins located on the bottom of the cap 180° apart.

4. Disconnect the four air lines from dryer.

5. Remove the three screws retaining the air compressor to mounting bracket.

6. Position the air compressor and dryer assembly to the mounting bracket and install the three mounting screws.

7. Connect the four air lines into the dryer.

8. Connect the electrical connection. Install the air line protector cap onto the dryer.

9. Turn the air suspension switch On.

Dryer, Air compression

1. Turn the air suspension switch Off.

2. Remove the air line protector cap from the dryer by releasing the two latching pins located on the bottom of the cap 180° apart.

3. Disconnect the four air lines from the dryer.

4. Remove the dryer retainer clip and screw.

5. Remove from the head assembly.

6. Check to ensure the old O-ring is not in the head assembly.

7. Check the dryer end to ensure new O-ring is in proper position.

8. Insert the dryer into the head assembly and install the retainer clip and screw.

9. Connect the four air liens into the dryer.

10. Install the air line protector cap onto the dryer.

11. Turn the air suspension switch On.

Mounting Bracket, Air Compressor

1. Turn the air suspension switch Off.

2. Remove the air compressor and dryer assembly.

3. Raise and support the vehicle on jackstands.

4. Remove the left front tire and wheel assembly.

5. Remove the left front inner fender liner.

6. Remove the three bolts attaching the mounting bracket to body side apron.

7. Position the mounting bracket to the body side apron with the two locating tabs.

8. Secure the three bolts attaching the bracket to the body side apron.

9. Install the left front inner fender liner.

10. Install the tire and wheel assembly.

11. Lower the vehicle.

12. Install compressor and dryer assembly. Turn the air suspension switch On.

Front Height Sensors

1. Turn the air suspension switch Off.

2. Disconnect the sensor electrical connector. The front sensor connectors are located in the engine compartment behind the shock towers.

3. Push the front sensor connector through the access hole in the rear of the shock tower.

4. Raise and support the vehicle on jackstands. Suspension must be at full rebound.

5. Disconnect the bottom and then the top end of the sensor from the attaching studs.

6. Disconnect the sensor wire harness from the plastic clips on the shock tower and remove sensor.

7. Connect the top and then the bottom end of the sensor to the attaching studs. Route the sensor electrical connector as required to connect to the vehicle wire harness.

8. Lower the vehicle. Connect the sensor connector. Turn the air suspension switch On.

Rear Height Sensor

1. Turn the air suspension switch Off.

2. Disconnect the electrical connector located in the luggage compartment in front of the forward trim panel. Also pull the luggage compartment carpet back for access to the sensor sealing grommet located on the floor pan.

3. Raise and support the vehicle on jackstands. Suspension must be at full rebound.

4. Disconnect the bottom and then the top end of the sensor from the attaching studs.

5. Push upwards on the sealing grommet to unseat and then push sensor through the floor pan hole into the luggage compartment.

6. Lower the vehicle.

7. Connect the sensor connector and then push sensor through the floor pan hole being sure to seat the sealing grommet. Replace the luggage compartment carpet.

8. Raise and support the vehicle on jackstands.

9. Connect the top and then the bottom end of the sensor. Lower the vehicle.

10. Turn the air suspension switch On.

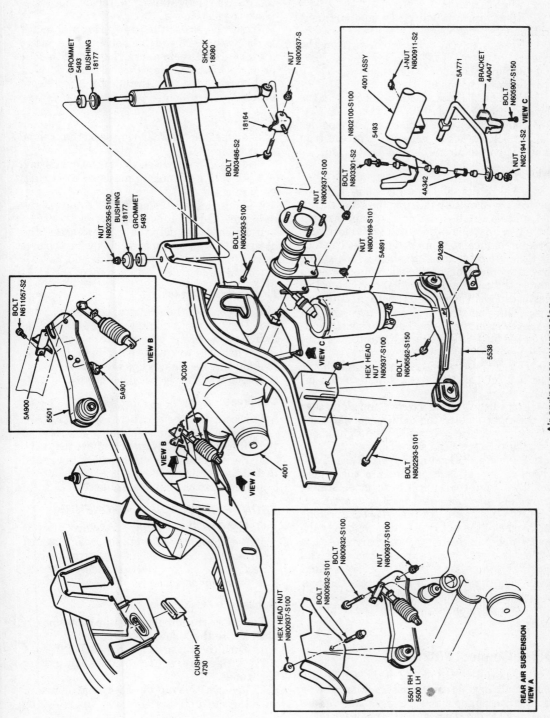

GROMMET 5493
BUSHING 18177
SHOCK 18080
NUT N800937-S

NUT N802356-S100
BUSHING 18177
GROMMET 5493

18164
BOLT N803486-S2

J-NUT N800911-S2
4001 ASSY
5A771
BRACKET 4A047
BOLT N605907-S150
VIEW C
BOLT N802100-S100
5493
BOLT N803301-S2
NUT N621941-S2
4A342
NUT N622041-S

BOLT N800293-S100
NUT N800937-S100
BOLT N800169-S101
NUT N800937-S100
5A891
2A280

BOLT N611057-S2
VIEW B
5A900
5501
5A901

3C034

VIEW B
VIEW A
4001

HEX HEAD NUT N800937-S100
BOLT N606562-S150
5538

BOLT N802293-S101

CUSHION 4730

BOLT N800932-S101
BOLT N800932-S100
NUT N800937-S100

HEX HEAD NUT N800937-S100
5501 RH
5500 LH
REAR AIR SUSPENSION
VIEW A

Air spring rear suspension

Control Module

1. Turn the air suspension switch Off. Ignition switch is also to be Off.
2. Remove the left luggage compartment trim panel.
3. Disconnect the wire harness from the module.
4. Remove the three attaching nuts.
5. Remove the module.
6. Position the module and secure it with the three attaching nuts.
7. Connect the wire harness to the module.
8. Attach the left luggage compartment trim panel. Turn the air suspension switch On.

Nylon Air Line

If a leak is detected in an air line, it can be serviced by carefully cutting the line with a sharp knife to ensure a good, clean, straight cut. Then, install a service fitting. If more tube is required, it can be obtained in bulk. The four air lines are color coded to show which spring they are connecting, but do not require orientation at the air compressor dryer. A protective plastic cap and convoluted tube protect the air lines from the dryer rearward over the left shock tower in the engine compartment. Routing of the lines after exiting the protective tube follows:

- Left Front/Grey: Down and through the rear wall of the left shock tower to the air spring solenoid.
- Right Front/Black: To cowl and along cowl on the right side of the vehicle, forward and down through the rear wall of the right shock tower to the air spring solenoid.
- Left Rear/Green, Right Rear/Tan: Through the left side apron into the fender well, through the left upper dash panel (sealing grommet) into the passenger compartment, down the dash panel to the left rocker, along the rocker to the left rear fender well, over the fender well into the luggage compartment. The left air line goes down through the floor pan (sealing grommet) in front of the left rear shock tower. The right air line goes across the rear seat support and then down through the floor pan (sealing grommet) in front of the right rear shock tower.

Quick Connect Fittings

If a leak is detected in any of the eight quick connect fittings, it can be serviced using a repair kit containing a new O-ring, collet, release ring, and O-ring removal tool. The outer housing of the fitting cannot be serviced.

To remove the collet and O-ring, insert a scrap piece of air line, grasp the air line firmly (do not use pliers) and pull straight out (DO NOT use the release button). A force of 30-50 lbs. is required to remove the collet. After the retainer is removed, use the repair tool to remove the old O-ring.

To service, insert the new O-ring and seat it in the bottom of the fitting housing. The, insert the new collet, being sure the end with four prongs is inserted. Press the collet into position with finger pressure. Install the new release button.

O-ring Seals

The areas that have O-ring seals that can be serviced are:

- air compressor head to dryer: One O-ring.
- Air spring solenoid to end cap: Two O-rings each solenoid.
- Quick connect fitting: Four O-rings at the dryer, one O-ring at each spring.

If air leaks are detected in these areas, the components can be removed, following the procedures outlined in this Section, and new O-rings can be installed.

Air Suspension Switch

1. Disconnect the electrical connector.
2. Depress the retaining clips that retain the switch to the brace, and remove switch.
3. Push the switch into position in the brace, making sure retaining clips are fully seated.
4. Connect the electrical connector.

Compressor Relay

1. Disconnect the electrical connector.
2. Remove the screw retaining the relay to the left front shock tower and remove the relay.
3. Position the relay on the shock tower and install the retaining screw.
4. Connect the electrical connector.

FRONT SUSPENSION COMPONENTS

CAUTION: *Power to the air system must be shut-off by turning the air suspension switch (in luggage compartment) Off or by disconnecting the battery when servicing any suspension components.*

Stabilizer Bar Link Insulators

To replace the link insulator on each stabilizer link, use the following procedure:

1. Turn the air suspension switch Off.
2. Raise the vehicle and support on jackstands.
3. Remove the nut, washer, and insulator from the end of the stabilizer bar link attaching bolt.
4. Remove the bolt and the remaining washers, insulator and spacer.
5. Install the stabilizer bar link insulators by reversing the removal procedure.

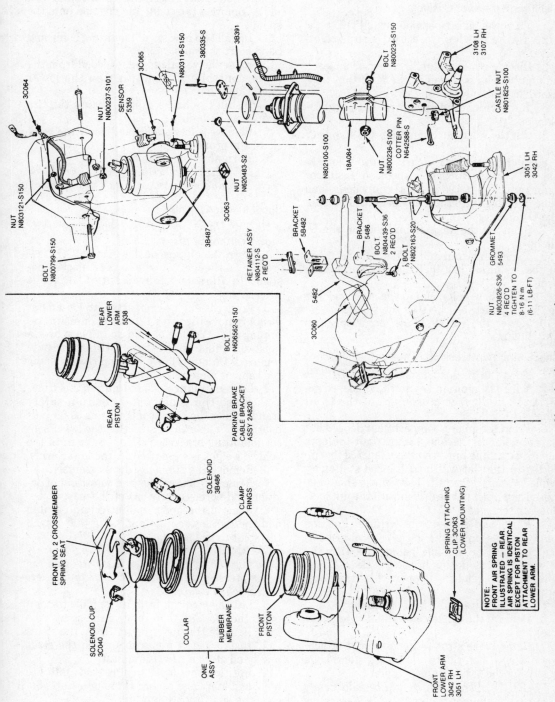

3B391

3C065

380335-S

N803116-S150

3C064

NUT
N800237-S101

SENSOR
5359

NUT
N803121-S150

BOLT
N800799-S150

3B487

3C063

NUT
N620483-S2

BOLT
N800234-S150

3108 LH
3107 RH

CASTLE NUT
N801825-S100

COTTER PIN
N64258B-S

N802100-S100

18A084

NUT
N800236-S100

N802163-S20

3051 LH
3042 RH

GROMMET
5493

BOLT
N804439-S36
2 REQ D

BOLT
N804112-S
2 REQ D

BRACKET
5B482

BRACKET
5486

5482

3C060

RETAINER ASSY

NUT
N803826-S36
4 REQ D
TIGHTEN TO
8-16 N·m
(6-11 LB-FT)

Air spring front suspension

REAR
LOWER
ARM
5538

BOLT
N606562-S150

REAR
PISTON

PARKING BRAKE
CABLE BRACKET
ASSY 2A820

SOLENOID
3B486

CLAMP
RINGS

FRONT NO 2 CROSSMEMBER
SPRING SEAT

SOLENOID CUP
3C040

ONE
ASSY

COLLAR

RUBBER
MEMBRANE

FRONT
PISTON

SPRING ATTACHING
CLIP 3C063
(LOWER MOUNTING)

FRONT
LOWER ARM
3042 RH
3051 LH

NOTE:
FRONT AIR SPRING
ILLUSTRATED — REAR
AIR SPRING IS IDENTICAL
EXCEPT FOR PISTON
ATTACHMENT TO REAR
LOWER ARM.

6. Tighten the attaching nut.

7. Lower the vehicle. Turn air suspension system On.

Stabilizer Bar and/or Bushing

1. Turn the air suspension switch Off.

2. Raise the vehicle and support on jackstands.

3. Disconnect the stabilizer bar from each link and bushing U-clamps. Remove the stabilizer bar assembly.

4. Remove the adapter brackets and U-clamps.

5. Cut the worn bushings from the stabilizer bar.

6. Coat the necessary parts of the stabilizer bar with Ford Rubber Suspension Insulator Lubricant. E25Y-19553-A or equivalent, and slide bushings onto the stabilizer bar. Reinstall the U-clamps.

7. Reinstall the adapter brackets on the U-clamps.

8. Using a new nut and bolt, secure each end of the stabilizer bar to the lower suspension arm.

9. Using new bolts, clamp the stabilizer bar to the attaching brackets on the side rail.

10. Lower the vehicle. Turn air suspension switch On.

Shock Strut Replacement

1. Turn the air suspension switch Off.

2. Turn the ignition key to the unlocked position to allow free movement of the front wheels.

3. From the engine compartment, loosen but do not remove the one 16mm strut-to-upper mount attaching nut. A suitable tapered tool inserted in the slot will hold the rod stationary while loosening the nut. The vehicle should be raised and must not be driven with the nut loosened or removed.

4. Raise and support the vehicle. Position safety stands under the lower control arms as far outboard as possible being sure that the lower sensor mounting bracket is clear. Lower until vehicle weight is supported by the lower arms.

5. Remove tire and wheel assembly.

6. Remove the brake caliper and wire out of the way.

7. Remove the strut-to-upper mount attaching nut and then the two lower nuts and bolts attaching the strut to the spindle.

WARNING: *The strut should be held firmly during the removal of the last bolt since the gas pressure will cause the strut to fully extend when removed.*

8. Lift the strut up from the spindle to compress the rod and then remove the strut.

9. Prime the new strut by extending and compressing the strut rod five times.

10. Place the strut rod through the upper mount, hand start and secure a new 16mm nut.

11. Compress the strut, and position onto the spindle.

12. Install two new lower mounting bolts, and hand start the nuts.

13. Raise the vehicle to remove load from the lower control arms, and tighten the lower mounting nuts.

14. Install the brake caliper, install the tire and wheel assembly.

15. Remove safety stands and lower the vehicle to the ground.

16. Turn air suspension switch On.

NOTE: *Front wheel alignment should be checked and adjusted, if out of specification.*

Upper Mount Assembly

NOTE: *Upper mounts are one piece units and cannot be disassembled.*

1. Turn the air suspension system Off.

2. Turn the ignition key to the unlocked position to allow free movement of the front wheels.

3. From the engine compartment, loosen but do not remove the three 12mm upper mount retaining nuts. Vehicle should be in place over a hoist and must not be driven with these nuts removed. Do not remove the pop rivet holding the camber plate in position.

4. Loosen 16mm strut rod nut at this time.

5. Raise the vehicle and position safety stands under the lower control arms as far outboard as possible being sure that the lower sensor mounting bracket is clear. Lower until the vehicle weight is supported by the lower arms.

6. Remove the tire and wheel assembly.

7. Remove brake caliper and rotate out of position and wire securely out of the way.

8. Remove the upper mount retaining nuts and the two lower nuts and bolts that attach the strut to the spindle.

WARNING: *The strut should be held firmly during the removal of the last bolt since the gas pressure will cause the strut to fully extend when removed.*

9. Lift the strut up from the spindle to compress the rod, and then remove the strut.

10. Remove the upper mount from the strut.

11. Install a new upper mount on the strut and hand start a new 16mm nut.

12. Position the upper mount studs into the body and start and secure three new nuts. Secure the strut rod 16mm nut.

13. Compress the strut and position onto the spindle.

14. Install two new lower mounting bolts, and hand start nuts.

15. Raise the vehicle to remove load from the lower control arms and tighten the lower mounting nuts to 126-179 ft. lbs.

16. Install the brake caliper. Install the tire and wheel assembly.

17. Remove safety stands and lower vehicle to the ground.

18. Turn air suspension switch On.

19. Front wheel alignment should be checked and adjusted if out of specification.

Spindle Assembly

1. Turn the air suspension switch Off.

2. Raise and support the vehicle on jackstands.

3. Remove the wheel and tire assembly.

4. Remove the brake caliper, rotor and dust shield.

5. Remove the stabilizer link from the lower arm assembly.

6. Remove the tie rod end from the spindle.

7. Remove the cotter pin from the ball joint stud nut, and loosen the nut one or two turns. CAUTION: *DO NOT remove the nut from the ball joint stud at this time.*

8. Tap the spindle boss smartly to relieve stud pressure.

9. Place a floor jack under the lower arm, compress the air spring and remove the stud nut.

10. Remove the two bolts and nuts attaching the spindle to the shock strut. Compress the shock strut until working clearance is obtained.

11. Remove the spindle assembly.

12. Place the spindle on the ball joint stud, and install the new stud nut. DO NOT tighten at this time.

13. Lower the shock strut until the attaching holes are in line with the holes in the spindle. Install two new bolts and nuts.

14. Tighten ball joint stud nut and install cotter pin.

15. Lower the floor jack from under the suspension arm, and remove jack.

16. Tighten the shock strut to spindle attaching nuts.

17. Install stabilizer bar link and tighten attaching nut.

18. Attach the tie rod end, and tighten the retaining nut.

18. Attach the tie rod end, and tighten the retaining nut.

19. Install the disc brake dust shield, rotor, and caliper.

20. Install the wheel and tire assembly.

21. Remove the safety stands, and lower the vehicle.

22. Turn air suspension switch On.

23. Front wheel alignment should be checked and adjusted if out of specification.

Suspension Control Arm

1. Turn the air suspension switch Off.

2. Raise the vehicle and support on jackstands, so the control arms hang free (full rebound).

3. Remove the wheel and tire assembly.

4. Disconnect the tie rod assembly from the steering spindle.

5. Remove the steering gear bolts, if necessary, and position the gear so that the suspension arm bolt may be removed.

6. Disconnect the stabilizer bar link from the lower arm.

7. Disconnect the lower end of the height sensor from the lower control arm sensor mounting stud. Remove the sensor mounting stud and unscrew from lower arm, noting the position of stud on the lower arm bracket.

8. Remove the cotter pin from the ball joint stud nut, and loosen the ball joint nut one or two turns. DO NOT remove the nut at this time. Tap the spindle boss smartly to relieve stud pressure.

9. Vent the air spring(s) to atmospheric pressure. Then, reinstall the solenoid.

10. Remove the air spring to lower arm fastener clip.

11. Remove the ball joint nut, and raise the entire strut and spindle assembly (strut, rotor, caliper and spindle). Wire it out of the way to obtain working room.

12. Remove the suspension arm to crossmember nuts and bolts. and remove the arm from the spindle.

13. Position the arm into the crossmember and install new arm to crossmember bolts and nuts. DO NOT tighten at this time.

14. Remove the wire from the strut and spindle assembly and attach to the ball joint stud. Install a new ball joint stud nut. DO NOT tighten at this time.

15. Position the air spring in the arm and install a new fastener.

16. Attach the sensor mounting stud and screw to lower arm in the same position as original arm location. Connect the lower end of sensor to the lower arm mounting stud.

17. With a suitable jack, raise the suspension arm to curb height.

18. With the jack still in place, tighten the lower arm to crossmember attaching nut to 150-180 ft. lbs.

19. Tighten ball joint stud nut to 100-120 ft. lbs., and install a new cotter pin. Remove jack.

20. Install the steering gear to crossmember bolts and nuts (if removed). Hold the bolts, and tighten nuts to 90-100 ft. lbs.

21. Position the tie rod assembly into the steering spindle, and install the retaining nut.

Tighten the nut to 35 ft. lbs., and continue tightening the nut to align the next castellation with cotter pin hole in the stud. Install a new cotter pin.

22. Connect the stabilizer bar link to the lower suspension arm, and tighten the attaching nut to 9-12 ft. lbs.

23. Install the wheel and tire assembly, and lower the vehicle but DO NOT allow tires to touch the ground.

24. Turn the air suspension switch On.

25. Refill the air spring(s).

26. Front wheel alignment should be checked and adjusted if out of specification.

REAR SUSPENSION

Shock Absorber

CAUTION: *Power to the air system must be shut-off by turning the air suspension switch (in luggage compartment) Off or by disconnecting the battery when servicing any suspension components.*

1. Turn the air suspension switch Off.

2. Open the luggage compartment and remove inside trim panels to gain access to the upper shock stud.

3. Loosen but do not remove the shock rod attaching nut.

4. Raise the vehicle and position two safety stands under the rear axle. Lower the vehicle until weight is supported by the rear axle.

5. Remove the upper attaching nut, washer and insulator and then remove the lower shock protective cover (right shock only) and lower shock absorber cross bolt and nut from the lower shock brackets.

6. From under the vehicle, compress the shock absorber to clear it from the hold in the upper shock tower.

CAUTION: *Shock absorbers will extend unassisted. Do not apply heat or flame to the shock absorber tube during removal.*

7. Remove the shock absorber.

8. Prime the new shock absorber by extending and compressing shock absorber five times.

9. Place the inner washer and insulator on the upper attaching stud. Position stud through shock tower mounting hole and position an insulator, washer on stud from the luggage compartment. Hand start the attaching nut and then secure.

10. Place the shock absorber's lower mounting eye between the ears of the lower shock mounting bracket, compressing shock as required. Insert the bolt, (bolt head must seat on the inboard side of the shock bracket), through the shock bracket and the shock absorber mounting eye. Hand start and then secure the original attaching nut.

11. Install the protective cover, to the right shock absorber. This is done by inserting the bolt point and nut into the cover's open end, sliding the cover over the shock bracket, and snapping the closed end of the cover over the bolt head. Properly installed, the cover will completely conceal the bolt point, nut, and bolt head. The rounded or closed end of the cover should be pointing inboard.

12. Raise the vehicle and remove safety stands from under axle, then lower the vehicle.

13. Reinstall the inside trim panels.

14. Turn air suspension switch On.

Lower Control Arm

NOTE: *If one arm requires replacement, replace the other arm also.*

1. Turn the air suspension switch Off.

2. Raise and support the vehicle so that the suspension will be at full rebound.

3. Remove tire and wheel assembly.

4. Vent air spring(s) to atmospheric pressure. Then, reinstall the solenoid.

5. Remove the two air spring-to-lower arm bolts and remove the air spring from the lower arm.

6. Remove the frame-to-arm and the axle-to-arm bolts and remove the arm from the vehicle.

7. Position the lower arm assembly into the front arm brackets, and insert a new, arm-to-frame pivot bolt and nut with nut facing outwards. DO NOT tighten at this time.

8. Position the rear bushing in the axle bracket and install a new arm-to-axle pivot bolt and nut with nut facing outwards. DO NOT tighten at this time.

9. Install two new air spring-to-arm bolts. DO NOT tighten at this time.

10. Using a suitable jack, raise the axle to curb height. Tighten the lower arm front bolt, the rear pivot bolt, and the air spring-to-arm bolt being sure that the air spring piston is flat on the lower arm. Remove the jack.

11. Replace tire and wheel assembly.

12. Lower the vehicle.

13. Turn the air suspension switch On.

14. Refill the air spring(s).

Upper Control Arm and Axle Bushing

NOTE: *If one arm requires replacement, replace the other arm also.*

1. Turn the air suspension switch Off.

2. Raise and support the vehicle so that the suspension will be at full rebound.

3. On the right side detach rear height sensor from side arm. Note position of the sensor adjustment bracket on the upper arm.

4. Remove the upper arm-to-axle pivot bolt and nut.

5. Remove the upper arm-to-frame pivot bolt and nut. Remove upper arm from vehicle.

If upper arm axle bushing is to be replaced, use Tool T78P-5638-A or equivalent and the following procedure:

6. Place the upper arm axle bushing remover tool in position and remove the bushing assembly.

7. Using the installer tool, install the bushing assembly into the bushing ear of the rear axle.

8. Place the upper arm into the bracket of body side rail. Insert a new upper arm-to-frame pivot bolt and nut (nut facing outboard). DO NOT tighten at this time.

9. Align the upper arm-to-axle pivot hole with the hole in the axle bushing. If required, raise the axle using a suitable jack to align. Install a new pivot bolt and nut (nut inboard). DO NOT tighten at this time.

10. On the right side, attach rear height sensor to the arm. Set the adjustment bracket to the same position as on the replaced arm and tighten nut.

11. Using a suitable jack, raise the axle to curb height, and tighten the front upper arm bolt, and the rear upper arm bolt.

12. Remove the jackstands supporting the axle.

13. Lower the vehicle.

14. Turn the air suspension switch On.

Stabilizer Bar Link Insulators

1. Turn the air suspension switch Off.

2. Raise and support the vehicle on jackstands.

3. Remove the nut, washer and insulator from the end of the stabilizer bar link attaching bolt.

4. Remove the bolt and the remaining spacer, washer and insulators.

5. Install the stabilizer bar link insulators by reversing the removal procedure. A new bolt and nut must be used.

6. Tighten the attaching nut.

7. Lower the vehicle.

8. Turn the air suspension switch On.

Stabilizer Bar Bushings

1. Turn the air suspension switch Off.

2. Raise and support the vehicle on jackstands.

3. Disconnect the stabilizer bar from each link and bushing U-clamp. Remove the stabilizer bar assembly.

4. Remove the U-clamps.

5. Cut the worn bushings from the stabilizer bar.

6. Coat the necessary parts of the stabilizer bar with Ford Rubber Suspension Insulator Lubricant E25Y-19553-A or equivalent and slide new bushings onto the stabilizer bar. Reinstall U-clamps.

7. Using new bolts and nuts, attach stabilizer bar to the axle. Do not tighten bolts at this time.

8. Using new bolts and nuts, attach the link end of the stabilizer bar to the body. Tighten the link attaching nut and then the axle attaching bolts.

9. Lower the vehicle.

10. Turn the air suspension switch On.

STEERING

The steering gear on all models with manual steering is the worm and recirculating ball type. A sector shaft is straddle-mounted in the cover above the gear and a housing mounted roller bearing below the gear.

All full size models with power steering use the integral type power steering gear. On this type of steering, hydraulic assist is provided directly to the steering gear, eliminating all hoses and hardware which was previously mounted under the chassis. the most common type of steering gear used with integral power steering

Troubleshooting the Ignition Switch

Problem	Cause	Solution
Ignition switch electrically inoperative	• Loose or defective switch connector • Feed wire open (fusible link) • Defective ignition switch	• Tighten or replace connector • Repair or replace • Replace ignition switch
Engine will not crank	• Ignition switch not adjusted properly	• Adjust switch
Ignition switch wil not actuate mechanically	• Defective ignition switch • Defective lock sector • Defective remote rod	• Replace switch • Replace lock sector • Replace remote rod
Ignition switch cannot be adjusted correctly	• Remote rod deformed	• Repair, straighten or replace

Troubleshooting the Steering Column

Problem	Cause	Solution
Will not lock	• Lockbolt spring broken or defective	• Replace lock bolt spring
High effort (required to turn ignition key and lock cylinder)	• Lock cylinder defective	• Replace lock cylinder
	• Ignition switch defective	• Replace ignition switch
	• Rack preload spring broken or deformed	• Replace preload spring
	• Burr on lock sector, lock rack, housing, support or remote rod coupling	• Remove burr
	• Bent sector shaft	• Replace shaft
	• Defective lock rack	• Replace lock rack
	• Remote rod bent, deformed	• Replace rod
	• Ignition switch mounting bracket bent	• Straighten or replace
	• Distorted coupling slot in lock rack (tilt column)	• Replace lock rack
Will stick in "start"	• Remote rod deformed	• Straighten or replace
	• Ignition switch mounting bracket bent	• Straighten or replace
Key cannot be removed in "off-lock"	• Ignition switch is not adjusted correctly	• Adjust switch
	• Defective lock cylinder	• Replace lock cylinder
Lock cylinder can be removed without depressing retainer	• Lock cylinder with defective retainer	• Replace lock cylinder
	• Burr over retainer slot in housing cover or on cylinder retainer	• Remove burr
High effort on lock cylinder between "off" and "off-lock"	• Distorted lock rack	• Replace lock rack
	• Burr on tang of shift gate (automatic column)	• Remove burr
	• Gearshift linkage not adjusted	• Adjust linkage
Noise in column	• One click when in "off-lock" position and the steering wheel is moved (all except automatic column)	• Normal—lock bolt is seating
	• Coupling bolts not tightened	• Tighten pinch bolts
	• Lack of grease on bearings or bearing surfaces	• Lubricate with chassis grease
	• Upper shaft bearing worn or broken	• Replace bearing assembly
	• Lower shaft bearing worn or broken	• Replace bearing. Check shaft and replace if scored.
	• Column not correctly aligned	• Align column
	• Coupling pulled apart	• Replace coupling
	• Broken coupling lower joint	• Repair or replace joint and align column
	• Steering shaft snap ring not seated	• Replace ring. Check for proper seating in groove.
	• Shroud loose on shift bowl. Housing loose on jacket—will be noticed with ignition in "off-lock" and when torque is applied to steering wheel.	• Position shroud over lugs on shift bowl. Tighten mounting screws.
High steering shaft effort	• Column misaligned	• Align column
	• Defective upper or lower bearing	• Replace as required
	• Tight steering shaft universal joint	• Repair or replace
	• Flash on I.D. of shift tube at plastic joint (tilt column only)	• Replace shift tube
	• Upper or lower bearing seized	• Replace bearings
Lash in mounted column assembly	• Column mounting bracket bolts loose	• Tighten bolts
	• Broken weld nuts on column jacket	• Replace column jacket
	• Column capsule bracket sheared	• Replace bracket assembly

Troubleshooting the Steering Column (cont.)

Problem	Cause	Solution
Lash in mounted column assembly (cont.)	• Column bracket to column jacket mounting bolts loose	• Tighten to specified torque
	• Loose lock shoes in housing (tilt column only)	• Replace shoes
	• Loose pivot pins (tilt column only)	• Replace pivot pins and support
	• Loose lock shoe pin (tilt column only)	• Replace pin and housing
	• Loose support screws (tilt column only)	• Tighten screws
Housing loose (tilt column only)	• Excessive clearance between holes in support or housing and pivot pin diameters	• Replace pivot pins and support
	• Housing support-screws loose	• Tighten screws
Steering wheel loose—every other tilt position (tilt column only)	• Loose fit between lock shoe and lock shoe pivot pin	• Replace lock shoes and pivot pin
Steering column not locking in any tilt position (tilt column only)	• Lock shoe seized on pivot pin	• Replace lock shoes and pin
	• Lock shoe grooves have burrs or are filled with foreign material	• Clean or replace lock shoes
	• Lock shoe springs weak or broken	• Replace springs
Noise when tilting column (tilt column only)	• Upper tilt bumpers worn	• Replace tilt bumper
	• Tilt spring rubbing in housing	• Lubricate with chassis grease
One click when in "off-lock" position and the steering wheel is moved	• Seating of lock bolt	• None. Click is normal characteristic sound produced by lock bolt as it seats.
High shift effort (automatic and tilt column only)	• Column not correctly aligned	• Align column
	• Lower bearing not aligned correctly	• Assemble correctly
	• Lack of grease on seal or lower bearing areas	• Lubricate with chassis grease
Improper transmission shifting—automatic and tilt column only	• Sheared shift tube joint	• Replace shift tube
	• Improper transmission gearshift linkage adjustment	• Adjust linkage
	• Loose lower shift lever	• Replace shift tube

is the Ford torsion bar model. The torsion bar type power steering unit includes a worm and one-piece rack piston, which is meshed with the gear teeth on the steering sector shaft.

The steering linkage consists of a steering (pitman) arm, a pitman arm-to-idler arm rod, and idler arm, and tie rods.

Steering Wheel

REMOVAL AND INSTALLATION

1. Disconnect the negative battery cable.
2. Remove the horn ring or hub cap by pushing it down and rotating it counterclockwise. Remove the retaining screws (from underside of steering wheel) and the crash pad. On 1969-70 models with speed control, the switch bezels must be pried up with a thin knife blade and the center trim plate removed to gain access to the crash pad retaining screw. On later models with speed control, the switches simply snap into plastic retainers inside the crash pad. Disconnect the horn and speed control wires.

3. Remove the steering wheel nut. Install a steering wheel puller on the end of the shaft and remove the wheel.

WARNING: *The use of a knock-off type steer-*

TOOL T67L-3000-A

Steering wheel removal

Troubleshooting the Turn Signal Switch

Problem	Cause	Solution
Turn signal will not cancel	• Loose switch mounting screws • Switch or anchor bosses broken • Broken, missing or out of position detent, or cancelling spring	• Tighten screws • Replace switch • Reposition springs or replace switch as required
Turn signal difficult to operate	• Turn signal lever loose • Switch yoke broken or distorted • Loose or misplaced springs • Foreign parts and/or materials in switch • Switch mounted loosely	• Tighten mounting screws • Replace switch • Reposition springs or replace switch • Remove foreign parts and/or material • Tighten mounting screws
Turn signal will not indicate lane change	• Broken lane change pressure pad or spring hanger • Broken, missing or misplaced lane change spring • Jammed wires	• Replace switch • Replace or reposition as required • Loosen mounting screws, reposition wires and retighten screws
Turn signal will not stay in turn position	• Foreign material or loose parts impeding movement of switch yoke • Defective switch	• Remove material and/or parts • Replace switch
Hazard switch cannot be pulled out	• Foreign material between hazard support cancelling leg and yoke	• Remove foreign material. No foreign material impeding function of hazard switch—replace turn signal switch.
No turn signal lights	• Inoperative turn signal flasher • Defective or blown fuse • Loose chassis to column harness connector • Disconnect column to chassis connector. Connect new switch to chassis and operate switch by hand. If vehicle lights now operate normally, signal switch is inoperative • If vehicle lights do not operate, check chassis wiring for opens, grounds, etc.	• Replace turn signal flasher • Replace fuse • Connect securely • Replace signal switch • Repair chassis wiring as required
Instrument panel turn indicator lights on but not flashing	• Burned out or damaged front or rear turn signal bulb • If vehicle lights do not operate, check light sockets for high resistance connections, the chassis wiring for opens, grounds, etc. • Inoperative flasher • Loose chassis to column harness connection • Inoperative turn signal switch • To determine if turn signal switch is defective, substitute new switch into circuit and operate switch by hand. If the vehicle's lights operate normally, signal switch is inoperative.	• Replace bulb • Repair chassis wiring as required • Replace flasher • Connect securely • Replace turn signal switch • Replace turn signal switch
Stop light not on when turn indicated	• Loose column to chassis connection • Disconnect column to chassis connector. Connect new switch into system without removing old.	• Connect securely • Replace signal switch

Troubleshooting the Turn Signal Switch (cont.)

Problem	Cause	Solution
Stop light not on when turn indicated (cont.)	Operate switch by hand. If brake lights work with switch in the turn position, signal switch is defective.	
	• If brake lights do not work, check connector to stop light sockets for grounds, opens, etc.	• Repair connector to stop light circuits using service manual as guide
Turn indicator panel lights not flashing	• Burned out bulbs • High resistance to ground at bulb socket	• Replace bulbs • Replace socket
	• Opens, ground in wiring harness from front turn signal bulb socket to indicator lights	• Locate and repair as required
Turn signal lights flash very slowly	• High resistance ground at light sockets	• Repair high resistance grounds at light sockets
	• Incorrect capacity turn signal flasher or bulb	• Replace turn signal flasher or bulb
	• If flashing rate is still extremely slow, check chassis wiring harness from the connector to light sockets for high resistance	• Locate and repair as required
	• Loose chassis to column harness connection	• Connect securely
	• Disconnect column to chassis connector. Connect new switch into system without removing old. Operate switch by hand. If flashing occurs at normal rate, the signal switch is defective.	• Replace turn signal switch
Hazard signal lights will not flash—turn signal functions normally	• Blow fuse • Inoperative hazard warning flasher	• Replace fuse • Replace hazard warning flasher in fuse panel
	• Loose chassis-to-column harness connection	• Conect securely
	• Disconnect column to chassis connector. Connect new switch into system without removing old. Depress the hazard warning lights. If they now work normally, turn signal switch is defective.	• Replace turn signal switch
	• If lights do not flash, check wiring harness "K" lead for open between hazard flasher and connector. If open, fuse block is defective	• Repair or replace brown wire or connector as required

ing wheel puller or the use of a hammer on the steering shaft will damage the column bearing and, on collapsible columns, the column itself may be damaged.

4. Lubricate the steering shaft bushing with white grease. Transfer all serviceable parts to the new steering wheel.

5. With the front wheels pointing in a straight-ahead direction, and with the alignment marks on steering wheel and the steering shaft lined up, install the steering wheel and locknut.

6. Connect the horn and speed control wires and install the horn ring or hub cap. Install the crash pad and retaining screw.

7. Connect the negative battery cable.

Turn Signal Switch
REPLACEMENT
Through 1978

1. Disconnect the negative battery cable.

2. Remove the steering wheel as previously outline in the "Steering Wheel Removal and Installation" section.

Troubleshooting the Manual Steering Gear

Problem	Cause	Solution
Hard or erratic steering	• Incorrect tire pressure	• Inflate tires to recommended pressures
	• Insufficient or incorrect lubrication	• Lubricate as required (refer to Maintenance Section)
	• Suspension, or steering linkage parts damaged or misaligned	• Repair or replace parts as necessary
	• Improper front wheel alignment	• Adjust incorrect wheel alignment angles
	• Incorrect steering gear adjustment	• Adjust steering gear
	• Sagging springs	• Replace springs
Play or looseness in steering	• Steering wheel loose	• Inspect shaft spines and repair as necessary. Tighten attaching nut and stake in place.
	• Steering linkage or attaching parts loose or worn	• Tighten, adjust, or replace faulty components
	• Pitman arm loose	• Inspect shaft splines and repair as necessary. Tighten attaching nut and stake in place
	• Steering gear attaching bolts loose	• Tighten bolts
	• Loose or worn wheel bearings	• Adjust or replace bearings
	• Steering gear adjustment incorrect or parts badly worn	• Adjust gear or replace defective parts
Wheel shimmy or tramp	• Improper tire pressure	• Inflate tires to recommended pressures
	• Wheels, tires, or brake rotors out-of-balance or out-of-round	• Inspect and replace or balance parts
	• Inoperative, worn, or loose shock absorbers or mounting parts	• Repair or replace shocks or mountings
	• Loose or worn steering or suspension parts	• Tighten or replace as necessary
	• Loose or worn wheel bearings	• Adjust or replace bearings
	• Incorrect steering gear adjustments	• Adjust steering gear
	• Incorrect front wheel alignment	• Correct front wheel alignment
Tire wear	• Improper tire pressure	• Inflate tires to recommended pressures
	• Failure to rotate tires	• Rotate tires
	• Brakes grabbing	• Adjust or repair brakes
	• Incorrect front wheel alignment	• Align incorrect angles
	• Broken or damaged steering and suspension parts	• Repair or replace defective parts
	• Wheel runout	• Replace faulty wheel
	• Excessive speed on turns	• Make driver aware of conditions
Vehicle leads to one side	• Improper tire pressures	• Inflate tires to recommended pressures
	• Front tires with uneven tread depth, wear pattern, or different cord design (i.e., one bias ply and one belted or radial tire on front wheels)	• Install tires of same cord construction and reasonably even tread depth, design, and wear pattern
	• Incorrect front wheel alignment	• Align incorrect angles
	• Brakes dragging	• Adjust or repair brakes
	• Pulling due to uneven tire construction	• Replace faulty tire

3. Unscrew the turn signal lever from the side of the column. Remove the emergency flasher retainer and knob, if so equipped.

4. Locate and remove the finish cover on the steering column and disconnect the wiring connector plugs.

5. On all 1968 and all models with a tilt steering column it is necessary to separate the wires from the connector plug in order to remove the switch and wires. First note the location and color code of each wire, prior to removal, with the wire terminal removal tool. Remove

Troubleshooting the Power Steering Gear

Problem	Cause	Solution
Hissing noise in steering gear	• There is some noise in all power steering systems. One of the most common is a hissing sound most evident at standstill parking. There is no relationship between this noise and performance of the steering. Hiss may be expected when steering wheel is at end of travel or when slowly turning at standstill.	• Slight hiss is normal and in no way affects steering. Do not replace valve unless hiss is extremely objectionable. A replacement valve will also exhibit slight noise and is not always a cure. Investigate clearance around flexible coupling rivets. Be sure steering shaft and gear are aligned so flexible coupling rotates in a flat plane and is not distorted as shaft rotates. Any metal-to-metal contacts through flexible coupling will transmit valve hiss into passenger compartment through the steering column.
Rattle or chuckle noise in steering gear	• Gear loose on frame • Steering linkage looseness • Pressure hose touching other parts of car • Loose pitman shaft over center adjustment **NOTE:** A slight rattle may occur on turns because of increased clearance off the "high point." This is normal and clearance must not be reduced below specified limits to eliminate this slight rattle. • Loose pitman arm	• Check gear-to-frame mounting screws. Tighten screws to 88 N·m (65 foot pounds) torque. • Check linkage pivot points for wear. Replace if necessary. • Adjust hose position. Do not bend tubing by hand. • Adjust to specifications • Tighten pitman arm nut to specifications
Squawk noise in steering gear when turning or recovering from a turn	• Damper O-ring on valve spool cut	• Replace damper O-ring
Poor return of steering wheel to center	• Tires not properly inflated • Lack of lubrication in linkage and ball joints • Lower coupling flange rubbing against steering gear adjuster plug • Steering gear to column misalignment • Improper front wheel alignment • Steering linkage binding • Ball joints binding • Steering wheel rubbing against housing • Tight or frozen steering shaft bearings • Sticking or plugged valve spool • Steering gear adjustments over specifications • Kink in return hose	• Inflate to specified pressure • Lube linkage and ball joints • Loosen pinch bolt and assemble properly • Align steering column • Check and adjust as necessary • Replace pivots • Replace ball joints • Align housing • Replace bearings • Remove and clean or replace valve • Check adjustment with gear out of car. Adjust as required. • Replace hose
Car leads to one side or the other (keep in mind road condition and wind. Test car in both directions on flat road)	• Front end misaligned • Unbalanced steering gear valve **NOTE:** If this is cause, steering effort will be very light in direction of lead and normal or heavier in opposite direction	• Adjust to specifications • Replace valve

Troubleshooting the Power Steering Gear (cont.)

Problem	Cause	Solution
Momentary increase in effort when turning wheel fast to right or left	• Low oil level • Pump belt slipping • High internal leakage	• Add power steering fluid as required • Tighten or replace belt • Check pump pressure. (See pressure test)
Steering wheel surges or jerks when turning with engine running especially during parking	• Low oil level • Loose pump belt • Steering linkage hitting engine oil pan at full turn • Insufficient pump pressure • Pump flow control valve sticking	• Fill as required • Adjust tension to specification • Correct clearance • Check pump pressure. (See pressure test). Replace relief valve if defective. • Inspect for varnish or damage, replace if necessary
Excessive wheel kickback or loose steering	• Air in system • Steering gear loose on frame • Steering linkage joints worn enough to be loose • Worn poppet valve • Loose thrust bearing preload adjustment • Excessive overcenter lash	• Add oil to pump reservoir and bleed by operating steering. Check hose connectors for proper torque and adjust as required. • Tighten attaching screws to specified torque • Replace loose pivots • Replace poppet valve • Adjust to specification with gear out of vehicle • Adjust to specification with gear out of car
Hard steering or lack of assist	• Loose pump belt • Low oil level **NOTE:** Low oil level will also result in excessive pump noise • Steering gear to column misalignment • Lower coupling flange rubbing against steering gear adjuster plug • Tires not properly inflated	• Adjust belt tension to specification • Fill to proper level. If excessively low, check all lines and joints for evidence of external leakage. Tighten loose connectors. • Align steering column • Loosen pinch bolt and assemble properly • Inflate to recommended pressure
Foamy milky power steering fluid, low fluid level and possible low pressure	• Air in the fluid, and loss of fluid due to internal pump leakage causing overflow	• Check for leak and correct. Bleed system. Extremely cold temperatures will cause system aeriation should the oil level be low. If oil level is correct and pump still foams, remove pump from vehicle and separate reservoir from housing. Check welsh plug and housing for cracks. If plug is loose or housing is cracked, replace housing.
Low pressure due to steering pump	• Flow control valve stuck or inoperative • Pressure plate not flat against cam ring	• Remove burrs or dirt or replace. Flush system. • Correct
Low pressure due to steering gear	• Pressure loss in cylinder due to worn piston ring or badly worn housing bore • Leakage at valve rings, valve body-to-worm seal	• Remove gear from car for disassembly and inspection of ring and housing bore • Remove gear from car for disassembly and replace seals

Troubleshooting the Power Steering Pump

Problem	Cause	Solution
Chirp noise in steering pump	• Loose belt	• Adjust belt tension to specification
Belt squeal (particularly noticeable at full wheel travel and stand still parking)	• Loose belt	• Adjust belt tension to specification
Growl noise in steering pump	• Excessive back pressure in hoses or steering gear caused by restriction	• Locate restriction and correct. Replace part if necessary.
Growl noise in steering pump (particularly noticeable at stand still parking)	• Scored pressure plates, thrust plate or rotor • Extreme wear of cam ring	• Replace parts and flush system • Replace parts
Groan noise in steering pump	• Low oil level • Air in the oil. Poor pressure hose connection.	• Fill reservoir to proper level • Tighten connector to specified torque. Bleed system by operating steering from right to left—full turn.
Rattle noise in steering pump	• Vanes not installed properly • Vanes sticking in rotor slots	• Install properly • Free up by removing burrs, varnish, or dirt
Swish noise in steering pump	• Defective flow control valve	• Replace part
Whine noise in steering pump	• Pump shaft bearing scored	• Replace housing and shaft. Flush system.
Hard steering or lack of assist	• Loose pump belt • Low oil level in reservoir **NOTE:** Low oil level will also result in excessive pump noise • Steering gear to column misalignment • Lower coupling flange rubbing against steering gear adjuster plug • Tires not properly inflated	• Adjust belt tension to specification • Fill to proper level. If excessively low, check all lines and joints for evidence of external leakage. Tighten loose connectors. • Align steering column • Loosen pinch bolt and assemble properly • Inflate to recommended pressure
Foaming milky power steering fluid, low fluid level and possible low pressure	• Air in the fluid, and loss of fluid due to internal pump leakage causing overflow	• Check for leaks and correct. Bleed system. Extremely cold temperatures will cause system aeration should the oil level be low. If oil level is correct and pump still foams, remove pump from vehicle and separate reservoir from body. Check welsh plug and body for cracks. If plug is loose or body is cracked, replace body.
Low pump pressure	• Flow control valve stuck or inoperative • Pressure plate not flat against cam ring	• Remove burrs or dirt or replace. Flush system. • Correct
Momentary increase in effort when turning wheel fast to right or left	• Low oil level in pump • Pump belt slipping • High internal leakage	• Add power steering fluid as required • Tighten or replace belt • Check pump pressure. (See pressure test)
Steering wheel surges or jerks when turning with engine running especially during parking	• Low oil level • Loose pump belt • Steering linkage hitting engine oil pan at full turn • Insufficient pump pressure	• Fill as required • Adjust tension to specification • Correct clearance • Check pump pressure. (See pressure test). Replace flow control valve if defective.

Troubleshooting the Power Steering Pump (cont.)

Problem	Cause	Solution
Steering wheel surges or jerks when turning with engine running especially during parking (cont.)	• Sticking flow control valve	• Inspect for varnish or damage, replace if necessary
Excessive wheel kickback or loose steering	• Air in system	• Add oil to pump reservoir and bleed by operating steering. Check hose connectors for proper torque and adjust as required.
Low pump pressure	• Extreme wear of cam ring • Scored pressure plate, thrust plate, or rotor • Vanes not installed properly • Vanes sticking in rotor slots • Cracked or broken thrust or pressure plate	• Replace parts. Flush system. • Replace parts. Flush system. • Install properly • Freeup by removing burrs, varnish, or dirt • Replace part

the plastic cover from the wiring harness. Attach a piece of heavy cord to the switch wires to pull them down through the column during installation.

6. Remove the retaining clips and screws from the turn signal switch and lift the switch and wire assembly from the top of the column.

7. Tape the ends of the new switch wires together and transfer the pull cord to these wires.

8. Pull the wires down through the column with the cord and attach the new switch to the column hub.

9. If the switch wires were separated from the connector plug, press the wires into their proper location. Connect the wiring connector plugs and install the finish cover on the column.

10. Install the turn signal lever. Install the

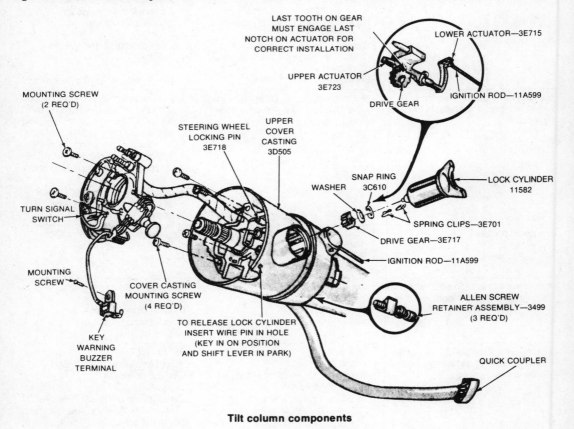

Tilt column components

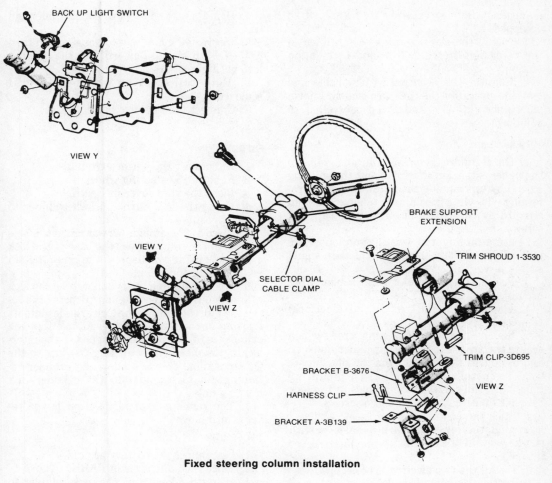

BACK UP LIGHT SWITCH

VIEW Y

VIEW Y

VIEW Z

SELECTOR DIAL
CABLE CLAMP

VIEW Z

BRAKE SUPPORT
EXTENSION

TRIM SHROUD 1-3530

TRIM CLIP-3D695

BRACKET B-3676

HARNESS CLIP

BRACKET A-3B139

Fixed steering column installation

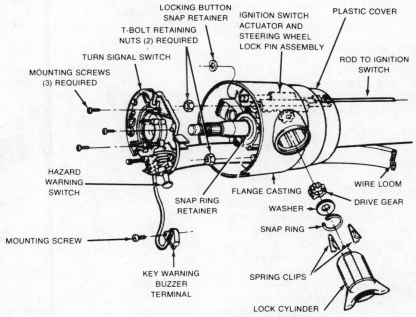

LOCKING BUTTON
SNAP RETAINER

T-BOLT RETAINING
NUTS (2) REQUIRED

TURN SIGNAL SWITCH

MOUNTING SCREWS
(3) REQUIRED

IGNITION SWITCH
ACTUATOR AND
STEERING WHEEL
LOCK PIN ASSEMBLY

PLASTIC COVER

ROD TO IGNITION
SWITCH

HAZARD
WARNING
SWITCH

SNAP RING
RETAINER

FLANGE CASTING

WIRE LOOM

DRIVE GEAR

WASHER

SNAP RING

MOUNTING SCREW

KEY WARNING
BUZZER
TERMINAL

SPRING CLIPS

LOCK CYLINDER

Fixed steering column components

emergency flasher retainer and knob, if so equipped.

11. Install the steering wheel as outlined in the Steering Wheel Removal and Installation section.

12. Connect the negative battery cable and test the operation of the turn signals, horn, emergency flashers, and speed control, if so equipped.

1979 and Later

1. On standard steering columns, remove the upper extension shroud (below the steering wheel) by unsnapping the shroud from the retaining clip. On tilt columns, remove the trim shroud by removing the five self-tapping screws.

2. use a pulling and twisting motion, while pulling straight out, to remove the turn signal switch lever.

3. Peel back the piece of foam rubber from around the switch.

4. Disconnect the two switch electrical connectors.

5. Remove the two self-tapping screws which secure the switch to the lock cylinder housing, and disengage the switch from the housing.

6. To install, align the switch mounting holes with the corresponding holes in the lock cylinder housing. Install the two screws.

7. Stick the foam back into place.

8. Align the key on the turn signal lever with the keyway in the switch and push the lever into place.

9. Install the two electrical connectors.

10. Install the trim shrouds.

Ignition Lock Cylinder

REMOVAL AND INSTALLATION

1968-69

1. Insert key and turn to Acc. position.

2. With stiff wire in hole, depress lock pin and rotate cylinder counterclockwise, then pull out cylinder.

1970-76

1. disconnect the negative battery cable.

2. On cars with a fixed steering column, remove the steering wheel trim pad and the steering wheel. Insert a stiff wire into the hold located in the lock cylinder housing. On cars with a tilt steering wheel, this hole is located on the outside of the steering column near the emergency flasher button and it is not necessary to remove the steering wheel.

3. Place the gear shift lever in Reverse on cars with manual transmission and in Park on cars with automatic transmission, and turn the ignition key to the ON position.

4. Depress wire and remove lock cylinder and wire.

5. Insert new cylinder into housing and turn to the OFF position. This will lock the cylinder into position.

6. Reinstall steering wheel and pad if removed.

7. Connect the negative battery cable.

1977-79

FIXED COLUMN

1. Disconnect the battery ground.

2. Remove the steering wheel.

3. Place the shift lever in PARK.

4. Using the key, turn the lock cylinder to the ON position.

5. Place a ⅛″ diameter wire or pin in the hole located in the column near the base of the lock cylinder housing and depress the retaining pin while pulling the cylinder out.

6. When installing the cylinder, turn the lock cylinder to the ON position and depress the retaining pin, then insert the lock cylinder into its housing in the flange casting. Assure that the cylinder is fully seated and aligned in the interlocking washer before turning the key to the OFF position. This will allow the cylinder retaining pin to extend into the cylinder cast housing hole.

7. The remainder of installation is the reverse of removal.

TILT COLUMN

1. Disconnect the battery ground.

2. Place the shift lever in PARK.

4. Using the key, turn the lock cylinder to the ON position.

5. Place a ⅛″ diameter wire or pin in the hole

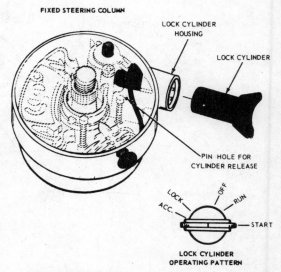

FIXED STEERING COLUMN

LOCK CYLINDER HOUSING

LOCK CYLINDER

PIN HOLE FOR CYLINDER RELEASE

LOCK
ACC.
OFF
RUN
START

LOCK CYLINDER OPERATING PATTERN

Lock cylinder replacement

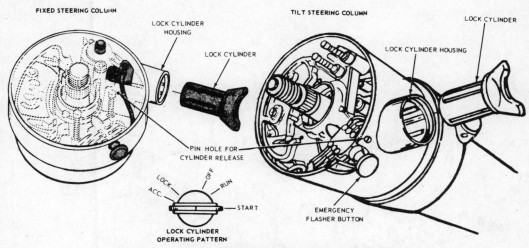

FIXED STEERING COLUMN

LOCK CYLINDER HOUSING

LOCK CYLINDER

PIN HOLE FOR CYLINDER RELEASE

TILT STEERING COLUMN

LOCK CYLINDER HOUSING

LOCK CYLINDER

EMERGENCY FLASHER BUTTON

LOCK
OFF
ACC.
RUN
START

LOCK CYLINDER OPERATING PATTERN

Lock cylinder replacement on locking type column

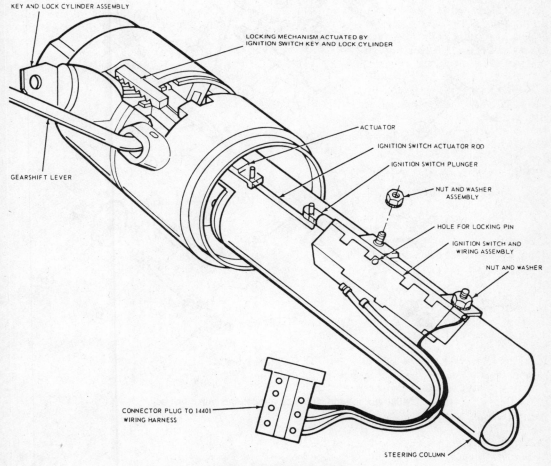

KEY AND LOCK CYLINDER ASSEMBLY

LOCKING MECHANISM ACTUATED BY IGNITION SWITCH KEY AND LOCK CYLINDER

ACTUATOR

IGNITION SWITCH ACTUATOR ROD

IGNITION SWITCH PLUNGER

NUT AND WASHER ASSEMBLY

HOLE FOR LOCKING PIN

IGNITION SWITCH AND WIRING ASSEMBLY

NUT AND WASHER

GEARSHIFT LEVER

CONNECTOR PLUG TO 14401 WIRING HARNESS

STEERING COLUMN

Ignition switch assembly

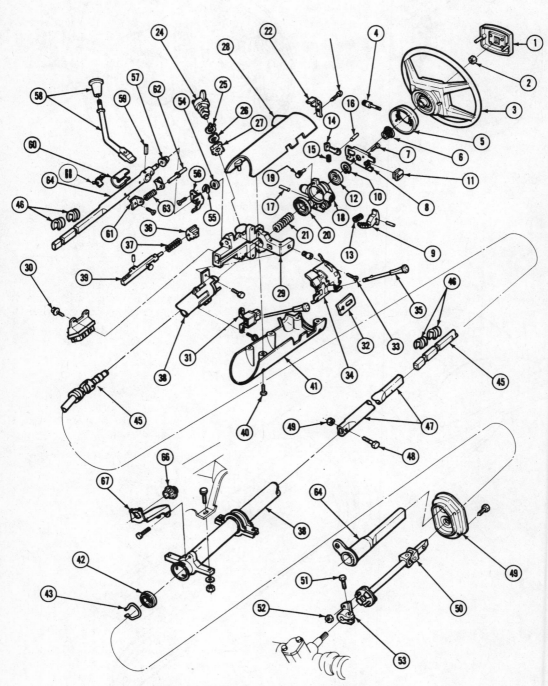

1980–81 column shift steering column with tilt wheel

located on the column near hazard flasher button and depress the retaining pin while pulling the cylinder out.

6. When installing the cylinder, turn the lock cylinder to the ON position and depress the retaining pin, then insert the lock cylinder into its housing in the flange casting. Assure that the cylinder is fully seated and aligned in the interlocking washer before turning the key to the OFF position. This will allow the cylinder retaining pin to extend into the cylinder cast housing hole.

7. The remainder of installation is the reverse of removal.

1980-88

1. Disconnect the battery ground.

2. On tilt columns, remove the upper extension shroud by unsnapping the shroud from the retaining clip at the 9 o'clock position.

3. Remove the trim shroud halves.

4. Unplug the wire connector at the key warning switch.

5. Place the shift lever in PARK and turn the key to RUN.

6. Place a ⅛" wire pin in the hole in the casting surrounding the lock cylinder and depress

the retaining pin while pulling out on the cylinder.

7. When installing the cylinder, turn the lock cylinder to the RUN position and depress the retaining pin, then insert the lock cylinder into its housing in the flange casting. Assure that the cylinder is fully seated and aligned in the interlocking washer before turning the key to the OFF position. This will allow the cylinder retaining pin to extend into the cylinder cast housing hole.

8. The remainder of installation is the reverse of removal.

REMOVAL AND INSTALLATION NON-FUNCTIONING LOCK CYLINDER

1968-79

FIXED COLUMN

1. Disconnect the battery ground.

2. Remove the steering wheel.

3. Remove the turn signal lever.

4. Remove the steering column trim shrouds.

5. Remove the instrument cluster.

6. Remove the ignition switch and secure it in the LOCK position as described earlier in this Chapter.

1. Emblem assy.
2. Nut ⅝-18 hex.
3. Wheel assy.—strng.
4. Handle & shank assy. tilt strng. wheel lever
5. Extension—strng. col. shroud
6. Spring—strng. col. upper bearing
7. Screw
8. Plate strng. col. clip retainer
9. Lever strng. col. link
10. Ring ¾ retaining type
11. Clip—strng. col. shroud
12. Bearing assy.—strng. col. upper
13. Pin 4mm × 25.6 straight round end
14. Release lever
15. Spring—strng. col. release lever
16. Pin—4mm × 5.75
17. Pivot pin
18. Flange casting
19. Bumpers
20. Bearing assy.—strng. col. upper
21. Position spring
22. Cover—strng. col. lock actuator
23. Screw 8-18 × .62 pan head tapping
24. Lock cyl. (body)
25. Ring 24 × 1.07 retainer type
26. Bearing
27. Gear—strng. col. lock
28. Shroud—upper
29. Housing—strng. col. lock cyl.
30. Bolt (break off head) (2 req'd.)
31. Wash/wipe switch & screws (body)
32. Foam cover—turn signal & w/w switch
33. Screw no. 8—18 × .62 pan head tap (2 req'd.)
34. Turn signal switch

35. Handle & shank assy.—turn sig. switch
36. Pawl—strng. col. lock
37. Spring—strng. col. lock
38. Tube assy. col. outer
39. Actuator assy.—strng. col. lock
40. Screw no. 8-18 × 1.50 pan head tap (5 req'd.)
41. Shroud—strng. col. lower
42. Bearing assy.—strng. gear shaft lower
43. Ring—strng. gear shaft lower bearing retainer
44. Boot assy.—strng. col.
45. Shaft—strng. col. upper
46. Anti-rattle clips
47. Shaft—strng. gear lower
48. Bolt ⁷⁄₁₆-14 × 1.50 hex
49. Nut ⁷⁄₁₆-14 hex lock
50. Shaft assy.—strng. col. lower
51. ⅜-24 × 1.22
52. Nut ⅜-16 hex lock
53. Flange—strng. shaft lower
54. Ring—⁵⁄₁₆ retainer
55. Washer—8.23 flat
56. Insert—trans. control selector position
57. Bearing—trans. gear shift lever socket
58. Lever assy.—trans. control selector
59. Pin 5mm spring coiled
60. Cover—trans. control selector lever opening
61. Screw 4mm—0.7 × 12.7 type "D" oval (2 req'd.)
62. Plunger—trans. control selector lever
63. Spring—trans. control selector lever return
64. Tube assy.—trans. control selector
66. Bushing—trans. gear shift shaft
67. Brkt.—trans. gear shift support
68. Spacer clip

1980–81 column shift steering column with tilt wheel

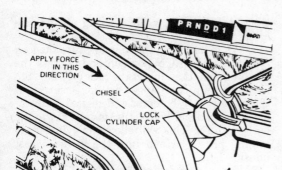

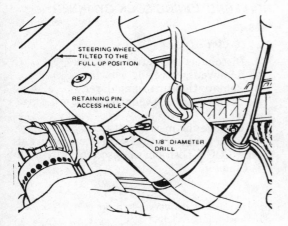

Breaking the cap away from the lock cylinder

Drilling out the lock cylinder retaining pin

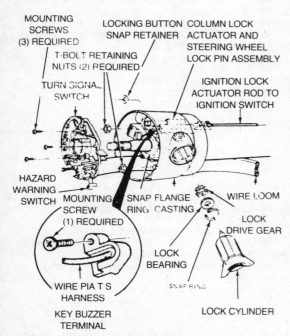

Non-tilting column mechanism

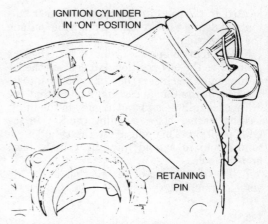

Lock retaining pin access slot on non-tilt columns

7. Remove the turn signal switch.

8. Remove the upper bearing snapring and T-bolt retaining nuts that secure the flange casting to the outer tube.

9. Remove the entire flange casting assembly, the upper shaft bearing, the lock cylinder assembly, the ignition switch actuator and the ignition switch actuator rod by pulling the assembly over the end of the steering column shaft. Replace this entire assembly, retaining the ignition switch actuator rod.

10. Installation is the reverse of removal.

TILT COLUMN

1. Disconnect the battery ground.

2. Remove the steering column shrouds.

3. Using masking tape, tape the gap between the steering wheel hub and the cover casting. Cover the entire circumference of the casting. Cover the seat and floor area with a drop-cloth.

4. Pull out the hazard switch and tape it in a downward position.

5. The lock cylinder retaining pin is located on the outside of the steering column cover casting adjacent to the hazard flasher button.

6. Tilt the steering column to the full up position and prepunch the lock cylinder retaining pin with a sharp punch.

7. Using a ⅛″ drill bit, mounted in a right angle drive drill adapter, drill out the retaining pin, going no deeper than ½″ (12.7mm).

8. Tilt the column to the full down position. Place a chisel at the base of the ignition lock cylinder cap and using a hammer break away the cap from the lock cylinder.

9. Using a ⅜″ drill bit, drill down the center of the ignition lock cylinder key slot about 1¾″ (44mm), until the lock cylinder breaks loose from the steering column cover casting.

10. Remove the lock cylinder and the drill shavings.

11. Remove the steering wheel.

12. Remove the turn signal lever.

13. Remove the turn signal switch attaching screws.

14. Remove the key buzzer attaching screw.

15. Remove the turn signal switch up and over the end of the column, but don't disconnect the wiring.

16. Remove the 4 attaching screws from the cover casting and lift the casting over the end of the steering shaft, allowing the turn signal switch to pass through the casting. The removal of the casting cover will expose the upper actuator. Remove the upper actuator.

17. Remove the drive gear, snapring and washer from the cover casting along with the upper actuator.

18. Clean all components and replace any that appear damaged or worn.

19. Installation is the reverse of removal.

1980-88

1. Disconnect the battery ground.

2. Remove the steering wheel.

3. On tilt columns, remove the upper extension shroud by unsnapping the shroud from the retaining clip at the 9 o'clock position.

4. Remove the steering column trim shrouds.

5. Disconnect the wiring at the key warning switch.

6. Using a ⅛" drill bit, mounted in a right angle drive drill adapter, drill out the retaining pin, going no deeper than ½" (12.7mm).

7. Tilt the column to the full down position. Place a chisel at the base of the ignition lock cylinder cap and using a hammer break away the cap from the lock cylinder.

8. Using a ⅜" drill bit, drill down the center of the ignition lock cylinder key slot about 1¾" (44mm), until the lock cylinder breaks loose from the steering column cover casting.

9. Remove the lock cylinder and the drill shavings from the housing.

10. Remove the upper bearing snapring washer and steering column lock gear.

11. Carefully inspect the steering column housing for signs of damage from the previous operation. If any damage is apparent, the components should be replaced.

12. Installation is the reverse of removal.

Ignition Switch

REMOVAL AND INSTALLATION

1968-69

1. Remove cylinder as above.

2. Unscrew the bezel from the ignition switch and remove switch from panel.

3. Remove insulated plug from rear of switch.

4. Install in reverse of above.

1970 through 1978

1. Disconnect the negative battery cable.

2. Remove the shrouding from the steering column, and detach and lower the steering column from the brake support bracket.

3. Disconnect the switch wiring at the multiple plug.

4. Remove the two nuts that retain the switch to the steering column.

5. On vehicles with column mounted gearshift lever, detach the switch plunger from the switch actuator rod and remove the switch. On vehicles with console mounted gearshift lever, remove the pin connecting the plunger to the actuator and remove the switch.

6. To reinstall the switch, place both the lock mechanism at the top of the column and the switch itself in lock position for correct adjustment. To hold the column in the lock position, place the automatic shift lever in PARK or manual shift lever in Reverse, and turn to LOCK and remove the key. New switches are helf in lock by plastic shipping pins. To pin existing switches, pull the switch plunger out as far as it will go and push it back into the first detent. Insert a ³⁄₃₂" diameter wire in the locking hole in the top of the switch.

7. Connect the switch plunger to the switch actuator rod.

8. Position the switch on the column and install the attaching nut. Do not tighten them.

9. Move the switch up and down to locate mid-position of rod lash, and then tighten the nuts.

10. Remove the locking pin or wire.

11. Attach the steering column to the brake support bracket and install the shrouding.

1979-81

1. Disconnect the battery ground.

2. On tilt columns, remove the upper extension shroud by unsnapping the shroud from the retaining clip at the 9 o'clock position.

3. Remove the trim shroud halves.

4. Disconnect the switch wiring.

5. Drill out the break-off head bolts attaching the switch to the lock cylinder with a ⅛" drill bit.

6. Remove the remainder of the bolts with a screw extractor.

7. Disengage the switch from the actuator pin.

To install:

8. Slide the switch carrier to the switch lock position. Insert a ⁷⁄₁₆" drill bit shank through the switch housing and into the carrier, there-

by, preventing any movement. New replacement switch already have a pin installed for this purpose.

9. Turn the key to the LOCK position and remove the key.

10. Position the switch on the actuator pin.

11. Install new break-off bolts and hand tighten them.

12. Push the switch towards the steering wheel, parallel with the column, to remove any slack between the bolts and the switch slots.

13. While holding the switch in this position, tighten the bolts until the heads break off.

14. Remove the drill bit or packaging pin.

15. Connect the wiring.

16. The remainder of installation is the reverse of removal.

1982-88

1. Disconnect the battery ground.

2. On tilt columns, remove the upper extension shroud by unsnapping the shroud from the retaining clip at the 9 o'clock position.

3. Remove the trim shroud halves.

4. Disconnect the switch wiring.

5. On 1982-85 cars, drill out the break-off head bolts attaching the switch to the lock cylinder with a ⅛″ drill bit. Remove the remainder of the bolts with a screw extractor.

6. On 1986-88 cars, remove the bolts securing the switch to the lock cylinder housing.

7. Disengage the switch from the actuator pin.

To install:

8. Slide the switch carrier to the ON RUN position. New replacement switches will be in this position.

9. Turn the key to the ON RUN position.

10. Position the switch on the actuator pin.

11. On 1982-85 cars, install new break-off bolts and hand tighten them.

On 1986-88 cars, install the bolts and tighten them to 50-60 in. lbs.

12. Push the switch towards the steering wheel, parallel with the column, to remove any slack between the bolts and the switch slots.

13. While holding the switch in this position, tighten the bolts until the heads break off.

14. Remove the drill bit or packaging pin.

15. Connect the wiring.

16. The remainder of installation is the reverse of removal.

Steering Column

REMOVAL AND INSTALLATION

1968-79

1. Disconnect the battery ground.

2. Remove the steering wheel.

3. Remove the instrument cluster trim cover.

4. Remove the steering column trim shrouds.

5. Disconnect the selector cable from the column.

6. Remove the instrument cluster.

7. Disconnect all wiring and vacuum hoses at the column.

8. Disconnect the transmission shift cable at the column.

9. Disengage the dust boot at the base of the column.

10. Remove the 2 flexible coupling-to-steering input shaft flange nuts. Disengage the safety strap and bolt from the flexible coupling.

11. Through the opening in the instrument panel, remove the 2 upper collar attaching bolts on the brake pedal support bracket.

12. From under the instrument panel, remove the 2 bolts that attach the lower collar to the brake support bracket.

13. When installing the column, install all fasteners finger tight until the column is in place, then, torque the fasteners to 35 ft. lbs.

Torque the flexible coupling fasteners to 35 ft. lbs. Make sure that the safety strap is properly positioned to prevent metal-to-metal contact after torquing the nuts. The flexible coupling must not be distorted when tightening the nuts. Pry the steering shaft up or down to provide a ± ⅛″ (3mm) coupling insulator flatness.

The remainder of installation is the reverse of removal. Adjust all linkages as necessary.

1980-88

1. Disconnect the battery ground.

2. Unbolt the flexible coupling from the steering input shaft.

3. Disengage the safety strap and bolt from the flexible coupling.

4. Disconnect the transmission shift rod from the control selector lever.

NOTE: *Column type automatic transmission linkage use oil impregnated plastic grommets to connect the rods and levers. Whenever a grommet type connection is changed, the grommets should be replaced.*

5. Remove the steering wheel.

6. Remove the steering column trim shrouds.

7. Remove the steering column cover.

8. Remove the hood release lever.

9. Disconnect all electrical and vacuum connections at the column.

10. Loosen the 4 nuts securing the column to the brake pedal support bracket, allowing the column to be lowered enough to access the selector lever cable and cable. Don't lower the col-

umn too far or damage to the lever and/or cable will occur!

11. Reach between the column and instrument panel and gently lift off the selector cable from the pin on the lever.

12. Remove the cable clamp from the steering column tube.

13. Remove the 4 dust boot-to-dash panel screws.

14. Remove the 4 nuts attaching the column to the brake pedal support.

15. Lower the column to clear the 4 mounting bolts and pull the column out.

To install:

16. Position the column in the car.

17. Install the column collar-to-brake pedal support nuts loosely.

18. Install the selector cable clamp loosely.

19. Attach the cable to the lever pin.

20. Tighten the 4 column-to-brake pedal support nuts to 35 ft. lbs.

21. Move the shift selector to the DRIVE position, against the drive stop. Rotate the selector bracket clockwise or counterclockwise until the selector pointer in the cluster centers on the letter **D**. Tighten the bracket nut.

22. Connect the electrical and vacuum connectors.

23. Install the safety strap and bolt on the flange on the steering input flange.

24. Install the 2 nuts connecting the steering shaft to the flexible coupling. Tighten the nuts to 35 ft. lbs. The safety strap must be properly positioned to avoid metal-to-metal contact. The flexible coupling must not be distorted when the nuts are tightened. Pry the shaft up or down to allow a $\pm$ 1/8″ (3mm) insulator flatness.

25. Connect the shift rod to the shift lever on the lower end of the steering column. Make sure the grommet is replaced.

26. The remainder of installation is the reverse of removal. Adjust the shift linkage.

Pitman Arm

REMOVAL AND INSTALLATION

1. Raise and support the front end on jackstands.

2. Remove the cotter pin and nut securing the center link to the Pitman arm.

3. Using a tie rod end separator, disconnect the center link from the Pitman arm.

4. Matchmark the Pitman arm and steering gear.

5. Remove the nut securing the Pitman arm to the steering gear shaft.

6. Using a puller, remove the Pitman arm from the gear shaft.

7. Position the wheels in the straight ahead position.

8. Align the matchmarks on the Pitman arm and gear. Some cars will have blind teeth on both the gear shaft and Pitman arm for alignment. Position the Pitman arm on the gear shaft and install the lockwasher and nut. Torque the nut to 236-250 ft. lbs.

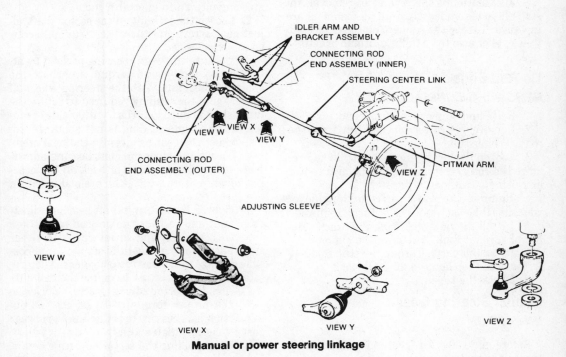

Manual or power steering linkage

9. Connect the center link and Pitman arm. Torque the nut to 45 ft. lbs. and install a new cotter pin. Always tighten the nut to align the cotter pin hole.

Idler Arm

REMOVAL AND INSTALLATION

1. Raise and support the front end on jackstands.

2. Remove the cotter pin, nut and washer attaching the center link to the idler arm.

3. Unbolt the idler arm and bracket from the frame.

4. Installation is the reverse of removal. Install all fasteners loosely until all fasteners are installed. Torque the idler arm bracket-to-frame bolts to 50 ft. lbs.; the idler arm-to-center link nut to 70 ft. lbs.

Center Link

REMOVAL AND INSTALLATION

1. Raise and support the front end on jackstands.

2. Remove the cotter pins and nuts attaching the inner connecting rod ends to the center link.

3. Using a tie rod end separator, disconnect the inner rod ends from the center link.

4. Remove the cotter pin and nut attaching the idler arm to the center link.

5. Remove the cotter pin and nut attaching the Pitman arm to the center link.

6. Installation is the reverse of removal. Install all fasteners loosely until all fasteners are installed. Torque the connecting rod ends to 45 ft. lbs.; idler arm to 70 ft. lbs.; Pitman arm to 45 ft. lbs.

Tie Rod Ends

REMOVAL AND INSTALLATION

1. Raise and support the front end.

2. Remove the cotter pin and nut from the rod end ball stud.

3. Loosen the sleeve and clamp bolts and remove the rod end from the spindle arm center link using a ball joint separator.

4. Remove the rod end from the sleeve, counting the exact number of turns required.

5. Install the new end using the exact number of turns it took to remove the old one.

6. Install all parts. Torque the stud to 40-43 ft. lbs. and the clamp to 20-22 ft. lbs.

7. Check the toe-in.

Manual Steering Gear

INSPECTION

Before any steering gear adjustments are made, it is recommended that the front end of the car be raised and a thorough inspection be made for stiffness or lost motion in the steering gear, steering linkage, and front suspension. Worn or damaged parts should be replaced, since a satisfactory adjustment of the steering gear cannot be obtained if bent or badly worn parts exist.

It is also very important that the steering gear be properly aligned in the car. Misalignment of the gear places a stress on the steering worm shaft, therefore a proper adjustment is impossible. To align the steering gear, loosen the mounting bolts to permit the gear to align itself. Check the steering gear mounting seat and if there is a gap at any of the mounting bolts, proper alignment may be obtained by placing shims where excessive gap appears. Tighten the steering gear bolts. Alignment of the gear in the car is very important and should be done carefully so that a satisfactory, trouble-free gear adjustment may be obtained.

STEERING WORM AND SECTOR GEAR ADJUSTMENT

The ball nut assembly and the sector gear must be adjusted properly to maintain a minimum amount of steering shaft end-play and a minimum amount of backlash between the sector gear and the ball nut. There are only two adjustments that may be done on this steering gear and they should be done as given below:

1. Disconnect the pitman arm from the steering pitman-to-idler arm rod.

2. Loosen the locknut on the sector shaft adjustment screw and turn the adjusting screw counterclockwise.

3. Measure the worm bearing preload by attaching an inch-pound torque wrench to the steering wheel nut. With the steering wheel off center, note the reading required to rotate the input shaft about 1½ turns to either side of center. If the torque reading is not about 4-5 in. lbs., adjust the gear as given in the next step.

4. Loosen the steering shaft bearing adjustment locknut and tighten or back off the bearing adjusting screw until the preload is within the specified limits.

5. Tighten the steering shaft bearing adjuster locknut and recheck the preload torque.

6. Turn the steering wheel slowly to either stop. Turn gently against the stop to avoid possible damage to the ball return guides. Then rotate the wheel 2¾ turns to center the ball nut.

7. Turn the sector adjusting screw clockwise until the proper torque (9-10 in. lbs.) is obtained that is necessary to rotate the worm gear past its center (high spot).

8. While holding the sector adjusting screw, tighten the sector screw adjusting locknut to

32-40 ft. lbs. and recheck the backlash adjustment.

9. Connect the pitman arm to the steering arm-to-idler.

REMOVAL AND INSTALLATION

1. Remove the bolt(s) that retains the flex coupling to the steering shaft.

2. Remove the nut and lock washer that secures the Pitman arm to the sector shaft. Using a puller, remove the Pitman arm from the sector shaft. Do not hammer on the end of the puller as this can damage the steering gear.

3. On vehicles with standard transmissions it may be necessary to disconnect the clutch linkage to obtain clearance. On 8-cylinder models, it may be necessary to lower the exhaust system.

4. Remove the bolts that attach the steering gear to the side rail. Remove the gear.

5. Position the steering gear and flex coupling on the steering shaft. Install steering gear-to-side rail bolts and torque to 50-65 ft. lbs.

6. Install the clutch linkage if disconnected. Reposition the exhaust system if it was lowered.

7. Place the Pitman arm on the sector shaft and install the attaching nut and lock washer. Torque the nut to 150-225 ft. lbs.

8. Install the flex coupling attaching nut(s) and torque to 18-23 ft. lbs.

Power Steering Gear
ADJUSTMENTS

Ford Integral System

MESH LOAD

During the vehicle breaking-in period, some factory adjustments may change. These changes will not necessarily affect operation of the steering gear assembly, and need not be adjusted unless there is excessive lash or other malfunctioning. Adjust the total overcenter position load to eliminate excessive lash between the sector and rack teeth as follows:

1. Disconnect the Pitman arm from the sector shaft.

2. Disconnect the fluid return line at the reservoir and cap the reservoir return line pipe.

3. Place the end of the return line in a clean container and turn the steering wheel from left to right to discharge the fluid from the gear.

4. Turn the steering wheel to 45° from the left stop.

5. Using an in. lbs. torque wrench on the steering wheel nut, determine the torque required to rotate the shaft slowly approximately ⅛ turn from the 45° position.

6. Turn the steering wheel back to center,

and determine the torque required to rotate the shaft back and forth across the center position. Loosen the nut, and turn the adjuster screw until the reading is 11 to 12 in. lbs. greater than the torque measured at 45° from the stop. Tighten the nut while holding the screw in place.

7. Recheck the readings and replace the Pitman arm and steering wheel hub cover.

8. Connect the fluid return line to the reservoir and fill the reservoir. Do not pry against the reservoir to obtain proper belt load. Pressure may deform the reservoir causing it to leak.

9. Recheck belt tension and adjust, if necessary. Torque the bolts and nut to 30-40 ft. lbs.

VALVE SPOOL CENTERING CHECK

1. Install a 0-2,000 psi (0-13,790 kpa) pressure gauge in the pressure line between the power steering pump outlet port and the integral steering gear inlet port. Be sure the valve on the gauge is fully open.

2. Check the fluid level and add fluid, if necessary.

3. Start the engine and turn the steering wheel from stop-to-stop to bring the steering lubricant to normal operating temperature. Turn off the engine and recheck fluid level. Add fluid, if necessary.

4. With the engine running at approximately 1,000 rpm and the steering wheel centered, attach an in. lbs. torque wrench to the steering wheel nut. Apply sufficient torque in each direction to get a gauge reading of 250 psi (1,723.75 kpa).

5. The reading should be the same in both directions at 250 psi (1,723.75 kpa). If the difference between the readings exceeds 4 in. lbs., remove the steering gear and install a thicker or thinner valve centering shim in the housing. Use as many shims as necessary, but do not allow thickness of the shim pack to exceed 0.030″ (0.762mm). The piston must be able to bottom on the valve housing face. No clearance is allowed in this area.

6. Test for clearance between the piston end and valve housing face as follows:

   a. Hold the valve assembly so the piston is up and try to turn the input shaft to the right.

   b. If there is no clearance, the input shaft will not turn. If there is clearance, the piston and worm will rotate together.

   c. If two or more shims must be used to center the spool valve, and a restriction or interference condition is experienced when turning the piston to its stop on the valve housing, replace the shaft and control assembly. If steering effort is heavy to the left, increase shim thickness. If steering effort is light to the left, decrease shim thickness.

7. When performing the valve spool centering check outside the vehicle, use the procedures described above except take torque and pressure readings at the right and left stops instead of at either side of center.

STEERING GEAR REMOVAL AND INSTALLATION

Ford Integral System

1. Tag the pressure and return lines for future identification.

2. Disconnect the pressure and return lines from the steering gear. Plug the lines and ports in the gear to prevent entry of dirt.

3. Remove the bolts that secure the flexible coupling to the steering gear and column.

4. Raise the vehicle and remove the sector shaft attaching nut.

5. Remove the Pitman arm from the sector shaft with Tool T64P-3590-F. Remove the tool from the Pitman arm. Do not damage the seals.

6. On vehicles with standard transmissions, remove the clutch release lever retracting spring to provide clearance for removing the steering gear.

7. Support the steering gear. Remove the steering gear attaching bolts.

8. Remove the clamp bolt that holds the flexible coupling to the steering gear. Work the gear free of the flex coupling and remove.

9. If the flex coupling did not come off with the gear, lift it off the shaft.

10. Slide the flex coupling into place on the steering shaft assembly. Turn the steering wheel so the spokes are in the normal position.

11. Center the steering gear input shaft.

12. Slide the steering gear input shaft into the flex coupling and into place on the frame side rail. Install the attaching bolts and torque to 35-40 ft. lbs.

13. Be sure the wheels are in the straight ahead position. Then install the Pitman arm on the sector shaft. Install and tighten the sector shaft and attaching bolts. Torque the bolts to 55-70 ft. lbs.

14. Move the flex coupling into place on the input and steering column shaft. Install the attaching bolts and torque to 18-22 ft. lbs.

15. Connect the pressure and the return lines to the steering gear. Tighten lines.

16. Disconnect the coil wire.

17. Fill the reservoir. Turn on the ignition and turn the steering wheel from stop-to-stop to distribute the fluid.

18. Recheck the fluid level and add fluid, if necessary.

19. Install the coil wire. Start the engine and

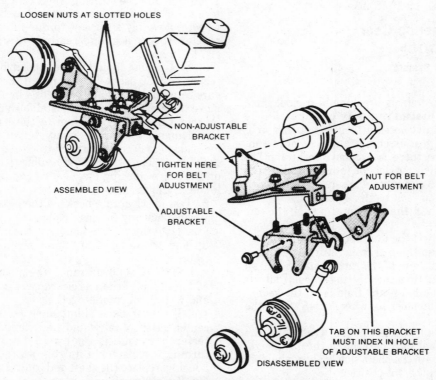

LOOSEN NUTS AT SLOTTED HOLES

NON-ADJUSTABLE BRACKET

ASSEMBLED VIEW

TIGHTEN HERE FOR BELT ADJUSTMENT

ADJUSTABLE BRACKET

NUT FOR BELT ADJUSTMENT

TAB ON THIS BRACKET MUST INDEX IN HOLE OF ADJUSTABLE BRACKET

DISASSEMBLED VIEW

Power steering pump installation (typical)

turn the steering wheel from left to right. Inspect for fluid leaks.

Power Steering Pump

REMOVAL AND INSTALLATION

1. Drain the fluid from the pump reservoir by disconnecting the fluid return hose at the pump. Disconnect the pressure hose from the pump.

2. Remove the mounting bolts from the front of the pump. On 1968-77 8-cylinder engines, there is a nut on the rear of the pump that must be removed. After removal, move the pump inward to loosen the belt tension and remove the belt from the pulley. Remove the pump from the car.

3. To install the pump, position on mounting bracket and loosely install the mounting bolts and nuts. Put the drive belt over the pulley and move the pump outward against the belt until the proper belt tension is obtained. Do not pry against the pump body. Measure the belt tension with a belt tension gauge for the proper adjustment. Only in cases where a belt tension gauge is not available should the belt deflection method be used.

4. Tighten the mounting bolts and nuts.

Brakes

BASIC OPERATING PRINCIPLES

Hydraulic systems are used to actuate the brakes of all automobiles. The system transports the power required to force the frictional surfaces of the braking system together from the pedal to the individual brake units at each wheel. A hydraulic system is used for two reasons.

First, fluid under pressure can be carried to all parts of an automobile by small pipes and flexible hoses without taking up a significant amount of room or posing routing problems.

Second, a great mechanical advantage can be given to the brake pedal end of the system, and the foot pressure required to actuate the brakes can be reduced by making the surface area of the master cylinder pistons smaller than that of any of the pistons in the wheel cylinders or calipers.

The master cylinder consists of a fluid reservoir and a double cylinder and piston assembly. Double type master cylinders are designed to separate the front and rear braking systems hydraulically in case of a leak.

Steel lines carry the brake fluid to a point on the vehicle's frame near each of the vehicle's wheels. The fluid is then carried to the calipers and wheel cylinders by flexible tubes in order to allow for suspension and steering movements.

In drum brake systems, each wheel cylinder contains two pistons, one at either end, which push outward in opposite directions.

In disc brake systems, the cylinders are part of the calipers. One cylinder in each caliper is used to force the brake pads against the disc.

All pistons employ some type of seal, usually made of rubber, to minimize fluid leakage. A rubber dust boot seals the outer end of the cylinder against dust and dirt. The boot fits around the outer end of the piston on disc brake calipers, and around the brake actuating rod on wheel cylinders.

The hydraulic system operates as follows: When at rest, the entire system, from the piston(s) in the master cylinder to those in the wheel cylinders or calipers, is full of brake fluid. Upon application of the brake pedal, fluid trapped in front of the master cylinder piston(s) is forced through the lines to the wheel cylinders. Here, it forces the pistons outward, in the case of drum brakes, and inward toward the disc, in the case of disc brakes. The motion of the pistons is opposed by return springs mounted outside the cylinders in drum brakes, and by spring seals, in disc brakes.

Upon release of the brake pedal, a spring located inside the master cylinder immediately returns the master cylinder pistons to the normal position. The pistons contain check valves and the master cylinder has compensating ports drilled in it. These are uncovered as the pistons reach their normal position. The piston check valves allow fluid to flow toward the wheel cylinders or calipers as the pistons withdraw. Then, as the return springs force the brake pads or shoes into the released position, the excess fluid reservoir through the compensating ports. It is during the time the pedal is in the released position that any fluid that has leaked out of the system will be replaced through the compensating ports.

Dual circuit master cylinders employ two pistons, located one behind the other, in the same cylinder. The primary piston is actuated directly by mechanical linkage from the brake pedal through the power booster. The secondary piston is actuated by fluid trapped between the two pistons. If a leak develops in front of the secondary piston, it moves forward until it bottoms against the front of the master cylinder, and the fluid trapped between the pistons will operate the rear brakes. If the rear brakes develop a leak, the primary piston will move forward until direct contact with the secondary piston takes place, and it will force the second-

Troubleshooting the Brake System

Problem	Cause	Solution
Low brake pedal (excessive pedal travel required for braking action.)	• Excessive clearance between rear linings and drums caused by inoperative automatic adjusters	• Make 10 to 15 alternate forward and reverse brake stops to adjust brakes. If brake pedal does not come up, repair or replace adjuster parts as necessary.
	• Worn rear brakelining	• Inspect and replace lining if worn beyond minimum thickness specification
	• Bent, distorted brakeshoes, front or rear	• Replace brakeshoes in axle sets
	• Air in hydraulic system	• Remove air from system. Refer to Brake Bleeding.
Low brake pedal (pedal may go to floor with steady pressure applied.)	• Fluid leak in hydraulic system	• Fill master cylinder to fill line; have helper apply brakes and check calipers, wheel cylinders, differential valve tubes, hoses and fittings for leaks. Repair or replace as necessary.
	• Air in hydraulic system	• Remove air from system. Refer to Brake Bleeding.
	• Incorrect or non-recommended brake fluid (fluid evaporates at below normal temp).	• Flush hydraulic system with clean brake fluid. Refill with correct-type fluid.
	• Master cylinder piston seals worn, or master cylinder bore is scored, worn or corroded	• Repair or replace master cylinder
Low brake pedal (pedal goes to floor on first application—o.k. on subsequent applications.)	• Disc brake pads sticking on abutment surfaces of anchor plate. Caused by a build-up of dirt, rust, or corrosion on abutment surfaces	• Clean abutment surfaces
Fading brake pedal (pedal height decreases with steady pressure applied.)	• Fluid leak in hydraulic system	• Fill master cylinder reservoirs to fill mark, have helper apply brakes, check calipers, wheel cylinders, differential valve, tubes, hoses, and fittings for fluid leaks. Repair or replace parts as necessary.
	• Master cylinder piston seals worn, or master cylinder bore is scored, worn or corroded	• Repair or replace master cylinder
Decreasing brake pedal travel (pedal travel required for braking action decreases and may be accompanied by a hard pedal.)	• Caliper or wheel cylinder pistons sticking or seized	• Repair or replace the calipers, or wheel cylinders
	• Master cylinder compensator ports blocked (preventing fluid return to reservoirs) or pistons sticking or seized in master cylinder bore	• Repair or replace the master cylinder
	• Power brake unit binding internally	• Test unit according to the following procedure: (a) Shift transmission into neutral and start engine (b) Increase engine speed to 1500 rpm, close throttle and fully depress brake pedal (c) Slow release brake pedal and stop engine (d) Have helper remove vacuum check valve and hose from power unit. Observe for backward movement of brake pedal. (e) If the pedal moves backward, the power unit has an internal bind—replace power unit

Troubleshooting the Brake System (cont.)

Problem	Cause	Solution
Spongy brake pedal (pedal has abnormally soft, springy, spongy feel when depressed.)	• Air in hydraulic system • Brakeshoes bent or distorted • Brakelining not yet seated with drums and rotors • Rear drum brakes not properly adjusted	• Remove air from system. Refer to Brake Bleeding. • Replace brakeshoes • Burnish brakes • Adjust brakes
Hard brake pedal (excessive pedal pressure required to stop vehicle. May be accompanied by brake fade.)	• Loose or leaking power brake unit vacuum hose • Incorrect or poor quality brakelining • Bent, broken, distorted brakeshoes • Calipers binding or dragging on mounting pins. Rear brakeshoes dragging on support plate. • Caliper, wheel cylinder, or master cylinder pistons sticking or seized • Power brake unit vacuum check valve malfunction • Power brake unit has internal bind • Master cylinder compensator ports (at bottom of reservoirs) blocked by dirt, scale, rust, or have small burrs (blocked ports prevent fluid return to reservoirs). • Brake hoses, tubes, fittings clogged or restricted • Brake fluid contaminated with improper fluids (motor oil, transmission fluid, causing rubber components to swell and stick in bores • Low engine vacuum	• Tighten connections or replace leaking hose • Replace with lining in axle sets • Replace brakeshoes • Replace mounting pins and bushings. Clean rust or burrs from rear brake support plate ledges and lubricate ledges with molydisulfide grease. **NOTE:** If ledges are deeply grooved or scored, do not attempt to sand or grind them smooth—replace support plate. • Repair or replace parts as necessary • Test valve according to the following procedure: (a) Start engine, increase engine speed to 1500 rpm, close throttle and immediately stop engine (b) Wait at least 90 seconds then depress brake pedal (c) If brakes are not vacuum assisted for 2 or more applications, check valve is faulty • Test unit according to the following procedure: (a) With engine stopped, apply brakes several times to exhaust all vacuum in system (b) Shift transmission into neutral, depress brake pedal and start engine (c) If pedal height decreases with foot pressure and less pressure is required to hold pedal in applied position, power unit vacuum system is operating normally. Test power unit. If power unit exhibits a bind condition, replace the power unit. • Repair or replace master cylinder **CAUTION:** Do not attempt to clean blocked ports with wire, pencils, or similar implements. Use compressed air only. • Use compressed air to check or unclog parts. Replace any damaged parts. • Replace all rubber components, combination valve and hoses. Flush entire brake system with DOT 3 brake fluid or equivalent. • Adjust or repair engine

Troubleshooting the Brake System (cont.)

Problem	Cause	Solution
Grabbing brakes (severe reaction to brake pedal pressure.)	• Brakelining(s) contaminated by grease or brake fluid	• Determine and correct cause of contamination and replace brakeshoes in axle sets
	• Parking brake cables incorrectly adjusted or seized	• Adjust cables. Replace seized cables.
	• Incorrect brakelining or lining loose on brakeshoes	• Replace brakeshoes in axle sets
	• Caliper anchor plate bolts loose	• Tighten bolts
	• Rear brakeshoes binding on support plate ledges	• Clean and lubricate ledges. Replace support plate(s) if ledges are deeply grooved. Do not attempt to smooth ledges by grinding.
	• Incorrect or missing power brake reaction disc	• Install correct disc
	• Rear brake support plates loose	• Tighten mounting bolts
Dragging brakes (slow or incomplete release of brakes)	• Brake pedal binding at pivot	• Loosen and lubricate
	• Power brake unit has internal bind	• Inspect for internal bind. Replace unit if internal bind exists.
	• Parking brake cables incorrrectly adjusted or seized	• Adjust cables. Replace seized cables.
	• Rear brakeshoe return springs weak or broken	• Replace return springs. Replace brakeshoe if necessary in axle sets.
	• Automatic adjusters malfunctioning	• Repair or replace adjuster parts as required
	• Caliper, wheel cylinder or master cylinder pistons sticking or seized	• Repair or replace parts as necessary
	• Master cylinder compensating ports blocked (fluid does not return to reservoirs).	• Use compressed air to clear ports. Do not use wire, pencils, or similar objects to open blocked ports.
Vehicle moves to one side when brakes are applied	• Incorrect front tire pressure	• Inflate to recommended cold (reduced load) inflation pressure
	• Worn or damaged wheel bearings	• Replace worn or damaged bearings
	• Brakelining on one side contaminated	• Determine and correct cause of contamination and replace brakelining in axle sets
	• Brakeshoes on one side bent, distorted, or lining loose on shoe	• Replace brakeshoes in axle sets
	• Support plate bent or loose on one side	• Tighten or replace support plate
	• Brakelining not yet seated with drums or rotors	• Burnish brakelining
	• Caliper anchor plate loose on one side	• Tighten anchor plate bolts
	• Caliper piston sticking or seized	• Repair or replace caliper
	• Brakelinings water soaked	• Drive vehicle with brakes lightly applied to dry linings
	• Loose suspension component attaching or mounting bolts	• Tighten suspension bolts. Replace worn suspension components.
	• Brake combination valve failure	• Replace combination valve
Chatter or shudder when brakes are applied (pedal pulsation and roughness may also occur.)	• Brakeshoes distorted, bent, contaminated, or worn	• Replace brakeshoes in axle sets
	• Caliper anchor plate or support plate loose	• Tighten mounting bolts
	• Excessive thickness variation of rotor(s)	• Refinish or replace rotors in axle sets
Noisy brakes (squealing, clicking, scraping sound when brakes are applied.)	• Bent, broken, distorted brakeshoes	• Replace brakeshoes in axle sets
	• Excessive rust on outer edge of rotor braking surface	• Remove rust

Troubleshooting the Brake System (cont.)

Problem	Cause	Solution
Noisy brakes (squealing, clicking, scraping sound when brakes are applied.) (cont.)	• Brakelining worn out—shoes contacting drum of rotor	• Replace brakeshoes and lining in axle sets. Refinish or replace drums or rotors.
	• Broken or loose holdown or return springs	• Replace parts as necessary
	• Rough or dry drum brake support plate ledges	• Lubricate support plate ledges
	• Cracked, grooved, or scored rotor(s) or drum(s)	• Replace rotor(s) or drum(s). Replace brakeshoes and lining in axle sets if necessary.
	• Incorrect brakelining and/or shoes (front or rear).	• Install specified shoe and lining assemblies
Pulsating brake pedal	• Out of round drums or excessive lateral runout in disc brake rotor(s)	• Refinish or replace drums, re-index rotors or replace

ary piston to actuate the front brakes. In either case, the brake pedal moves farther when the brakes are applied, and less braking power is available.

All dual circuit systems use a switch to warn the driver when only half of the brake system is operational. This switch is located in a valve body which is mounted on the firewall or the frame below the master cylinder. A hydraulic piston receives pressure from both circuits, each circuit's pressure being applied to one end of the piston. When the pressures are in balance, the piston remains stationary. When one circuit has a leak, however, the greater pressure in that circuit during application of the brakes will push the piston to one side, closing the switch and activating the brake warning light.

In disc brake systems, this valve body also contains a metering valve and, in some cases, a proportioning valve. The metering valve keeps pressure from traveling to the disc brakes on the front wheels until the brake shoes on the rear wheels have contacted the drums, ensuring that the front brakes will never be used alone. The proportioning valve controls the pressure to the rear brakes to lessen the chance of rear wheel lock-up during very hard braking.

Warning lights may be tested by depressing the brake pedal and holding it while opening one of the wheel cylinder bleeder screws. If this does not cause the light to go on, substitute a new lamp, make continuity checks, and, finally, replace the switch as necessary.

The hydraulic system may be checked for leaks by applying pressure to the pedal gradually and steadily. If the pedal sinks very slowly to the floor, the system has a leak. This is not to be confused with a springy or spongy feel due to the compression of air within the lines. If the system leaks, there will be a gradual change in

the position of the pedal with a constant pressure.

Check for leaks along all lines and at wheel cylinders. If no external leaks are apparent, the problem is inside the master cylinder.

Disc Brakes
BASIC OPERATING PRINCIPLES

Instead of the traditional expanding brakes that press outward against a circular drum, disc brake systems utilize a disc (rotor) with brake pads positioned on either side of it. Braking effect is achieved in a manner similar to the way you would squeeze a spinning phonograph record between your fingers. The disc (rotor) is a casting with cooling fins between the two braking surfaces. This enables air to circulate between the braking surfaces making them less sensitive to heat buildup and more resistant to fade. Dirt and water do not affect braking action since contaminants are thrown off by the centrifugal action of the rotor or scraped off the by the pads. Also, the equal clamping action of the two brake pads tends to ensure uniform, straight line stops. Disc brakes are inherently self-adjusting.

There are three general types of disc brake:
1. A fixed caliper.
2. A floating caliper.
3. A sliding caliper.

The fixed caliper design uses two pistons mounted on either side of the rotor (in each side of the caliper). The caliper is mounted rigidly and does not move.

The sliding and floating designs are quite similar. In fact, these two types are often lumped together. In both designs, the pad on the inside of the rotor is moved into contact with the rotor by hydraulic force. The caliper, which is not held in a fixed position, moves slightly,

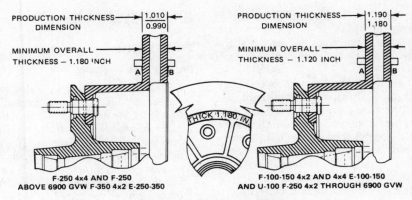

PRODUCTION THICKNESS —— 1.010
DIMENSION   0.990

MINIMUM OVERALL ——
THICKNESS — 1.180 INCH   A   B

PRODUCTION THICKNESS —— 1.190
DIMENSION   1.180

MINIMUM OVERALL ——
THICKNESS — 1.120 INCH   A   B

THICK 1.180 IN

F-250 4x4 AND F-250
ABOVE 6900 GVW F-350 4x2 E-250-350

F-100-150 4x2 AND 4x4 E-100-150
AND U-100 F-250 4x2 THROUGH 6900 GVW

Disc brake rotor service limits

bringing the outside pad into contact with the rotor. There are various methods of attaching floating calipers. Some pivot at the bottom or top, and some slide on mounting bolts. In any event, the end result is the same.

All the cars covered in this book employ the sliding caliper design.

Drum Brakes
BASIC OPERATING PRINCIPLES

Drum brakes employ two brake shoes mounted on a stationary backing plate. These shoes are positioned inside a circular drum which rotates with the wheel assembly. The shoes are held in place by springs. This allows them to slide toward the drums (when they are applied) while keeping the linings and drums in alignment. The shoes are actuated by a wheel cylinder which is mounted at the top of the backing plate. When the brakes are applied, hydraulic pressure forces the wheel cylinder's actuating links outward. Since these links bear directly against the top of the brake shoes, the tops of the shoes are then forced against the inner side of the drum. This action forces the bottoms of the two shoes to contact the brake drum by rotating the entire assembly slightly (known as servo action). When pressure within the wheel cylinder is relaxed, return springs pull the shoes back away from the drum.

Most modern drum brakes are designed to self-adjust themselves during application when the vehicle is moving in reverse. This motion causes both shoes to rotate very slightly with the drum, rocking an adjusting lever, thereby causing rotation of the adjusting screw.

Power Boosters

Power brakes operate just as non-power brake systems except in the actuation of the master cylinder pistons. A vacuum diaphragm is located on the front of the master cylinder and assists the driver in applying the brakes, reducing both the effort and travel he must put into moving the brake pedal.

The vacuum diaphragm housing is connected to the intake manifold by a vacuum hose. A check valve is placed at the point where the hose enters the diaphragm housing, so that during periods of low manifold vacuum brake assist vacuum will not be lost.

Depressing the brake pedal closes off the vacuum source and allows atmospheric pressure to enter on one side of the diaphragm. This causes the master cylinder pistons to move and apply the brakes. When the brake pedal is released, vacuum is applied to both sides of the diaphragm, and return springs return the diaphragm and master cylinder pistons to the released position. If the vacuum fails, the brake pedal rod will butt against the end of the master cylinder actuating rod, and direct mechanical application will occur as the pedal is depressed.

The hydraulic and mechanical problems that apply to conventional brake systems also apply to power brakes, and should be checked for if the tests below do not reveal the problem.

Test for a system vacuum leak as described below:

1. Operate the engine at idle without touching the brake pedal for at least one minute.

2. Turn off the engine, and wait one minute.

3. Test for the presence of assist vacuum by depressing the brake pedal and releasing it several times. Light application will produce less and less pedal travel, if vacuum was present. If there is no vacuum, air is leaking into the system somewhere.

Test for system operation as follows:

1. Pump the brake pedal (with engine off) until the supply vacuum is entirely gone.

2. Put a light, steady pressure on the pedal.

3. Start the engine, and operate it at idle. If the system is operating, the brake pedal should

fall toward the floor if constant pressure is maintained on the pedal.

Power brake systems may be tested for hydraulic leaks just as ordinary systems are tested.

Most full-sized models have been equipped with power brakes. On all drum brake equipped car, as well as those equipped with a disc front/drum rear brake configuration, the power assist has been supplied by a manifold vacuum-operated servo, located between the master cylinder and the firewall. All models equipped with the 4 wheel disc brake system utilize a hydraulically-operated servo, also located between the master cylinder firewall. This system, known as the hydro-boost system, is connected to the power steering pump via hydraulic hoses, using steering pump fluid pressure to supply and circulate the fluid (type ATF) to the servo.

Hydro-Boost

The hydro-boost unit contains a spool valve with an open center which controls the strength of pump pressure when braking occurs. A lever assembly controls the valve's position. A boost piston provides the force necessary to operate the conventional master cylinder on the front of the booster.

A reserve of at least two assisted brake applications is supplied by a spring-loaded accumulator, which retains power steering fluid under pressure.

The brakes can be operated without assist, once the reserve is depleted.

BRAKE SYSTEMS

Adjustment

Drum Brakes

NOTE: *Drum brakes installed in Fords are self-adjusting. All that is normally required to adjust the brakes is to apply them moderately heard several times while carefully backing the car in Reverse. However, if this action proves unsatisfactory, or if it proves necessary to readjust the brakes after replacing the linings or removing the drum, the following procedure may be used.*

1. Raise the car and support it with safety stands.

2. Remove the rubber plug from the adjusting slot on the backing plate.

3. Insert a brake adjusting spoon into the slot and engage the lowest possible tooth on the starwheel. Move the end of the brake spoon downward to move the starwheel upward and expand the adjusting screw. Repeat this operation until the brakes lock the wheel.

4. Insert a small prybar or piece of firm wire (coat-hand wire) into the adjusting slot and push the automatic adjuster lever out and free of the starwheel on the adjusting screw.

5. Holding the adjusting lever out of the way, engage the topmost tooth possible on the starwheel with a brake adjusting spoon. Move the end of the adjusting spoon upward to move the adjusting screw starwheel downward and contract the adjusting screw. Back off the ad-

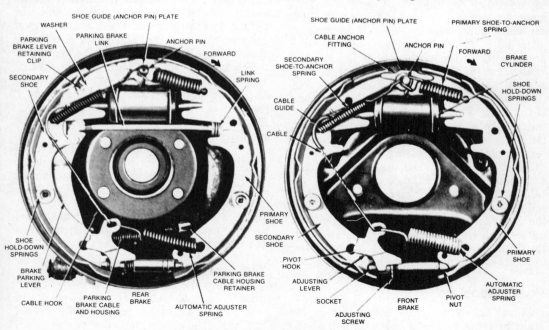

Self-adjusting drum brake assemblies

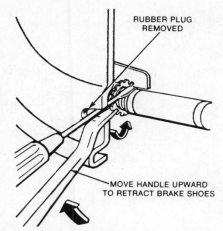

Backing off brake adjustment

justing screw starwheel until the wheel spins freely with the minimum of drag. Keep track of the number of turns the starwheel is backed off.

6. Repeat this operation for the other side. When backing off the brakes on the other side, the adjusting lever must be backed off the same number of turns to prevent side-to-side brake pull.

7. Repeat this operation on the other set of brakes (front or rear).

8. When all four brakes are adjusted, make several stops, while backing the car, to equalize all of the wheels.

9. Road test the car.

Parking Brake

WITH REAR DRUM BRAKES

The parking brake should be adjusted for proper operation every 12 months or 12,000 miles and adjusted whenever there is slack in the cables. A cable with too much slack will not hold a vehicle on an incline which presents a serious safety hazard. Usually, a rear brake adjustment will restore parking brake efficiency, but if the cables appear loose or stretched when the parking brake is released, adjust as necessary.

The procedure for adjusting the parking brake on all pedal actuated systems is as follows:

1. Fully release the parking brake.

2. Depress the parking brake pedal one notch from its normal released position. On vacuum release brakes, the first notch is approximately 2″ (51mm) of travel.

3. Taking proper safety precautions, raise the car and place the transmission in Neutral.

4. Loosen the equalizer locknut and turn the adjusting nut forward against the equalizer until moderate drag is felt when turning the rear wheels. Tighten the locknut.

5. Release the parking brake, making sure that the brake shoes return to the fully released position.

6. Lower the car and apply the parking brake. Under normal conditions, the third notch will hold the car if the brake is adjusted properly.

WITH REAR DISC BRAKES

1. Fully release the parking brake.

2. Place the transmission in Neutral. If it is necessary to raise the car to reach the adjusting nut and observe the parking brake levers, use an axle hoist or a floor jack positioned beneath the differential. This is necessary so that the rear axle remains at the curb attitude, not stretching the parking brake cables.

CAUTION: *If you are raising the rear of the car only, block the front wheels.*

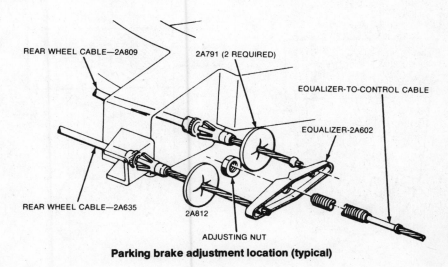

Parking brake adjustment location (typical)

3. Locate the adjusting nut beneath the car on the driver's side. While observing the parking brake actuating levers on the rear calipers, tighten the adjusting nut until the levers just begin to move. Then, loosen the nut sufficiently for the levers to fully return to the stop position. The levers are in the stop position when a ¼" (6mm) pin can be inserted past the side of the lever into the holes in the cast iron housing.

4. Check the operation of the parking brake. Make sure the actuating levers return to the stop position by attempting to pull them rearward. If the lever moves rearward, the cable adjustment is too tight, which will cause a dragging rear brake and consequent brake overheating and fade.

Brake Light Switch

REMOVAL AND INSTALLATION

1968-79

1. Unplug the wiring harness at the switch.
2. Remove the hairpin clip from the stud and slide the switch and washers off of the pedal.
3. Installation is the reverse of removal.

1980-88

1. Raise the locking tab and unplug the wiring harness at the switch.
2. Remove the hairpin clip from the stud and slide the switch up and down, remove the switch and washers off of the pedal.

NOTE: *It is not necessary to remove the pushrod from the stud.*

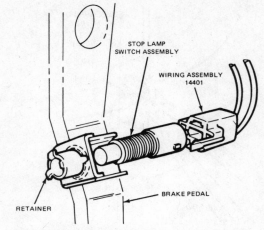

1979 brake light switch

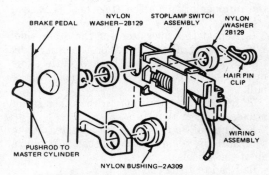

1980–83 brake light switch w/non-power brakes

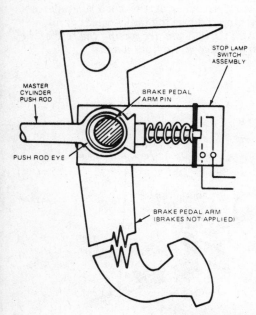

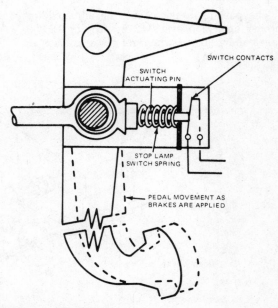

1981–88 brake light switch w/power brakes

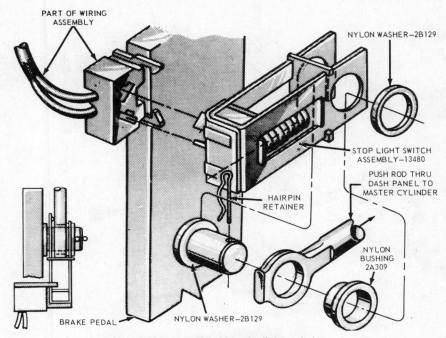

1975–78 and 1980 brake light switch

3. Installation is the reverse of removal. Position the U-shaped side nearest the pedal and directly over/under the pin. Slide the switch up and down trapping the pushrod and bushing between the switch sideplates.

HYDRAULIC SYSTEM

Master Cylinder
REMOVAL AND INSTALLATION
Non-Power Brakes

1. Working under the dash, disconnect the master cylinder pushrod from the brake pedal. The pushrod cannot be removed from the master cylinder.

2. Disconnect the stoplight switch wires and remove the switch from the brake pedal, using care not to damage the switch.

3. Disconnect the brake lines from the master cylinder.

4. Remove the attaching screws from the firewall and remove the master cylinder from the car.

5. Reinstall in reverse of above order, leaving the brake line fitting loose at the master cylinder.

6. Fill the master cylinder, and with the brake lines loose, slowly bleed the air from the master cylinder using the foot pedal.

Power Brakes
EXCEPT WITH ANTI-LOCK BRAKING SYSTEM

1. Disconnect the brake lines from the master cylinder.

2. Remove the two nuts and lockwashers which attach the master cylinder to the brake booster.

3. Remove the master cylinder from the booster.

4. Reverse the above procedure to reinstall.

5. Fill master cylinder and bleed entire brake system.

MASTER CYLINDER OVERHAUL
Except with Anti-Lock Braking System

1. Remove the cylinder from the car and drain the brake fluid.

2. Mount the cylinder in a vise so that the outlets are up then remove the seal from the hub.

3. Remove the stopscrew from the bottom of the front reservoir.

4. Remove the snapring from the front of the bore and remove the rear piston assembly.

5. Remove the front piston assembly using compressed air. Cover the bore opening with a cloth to prevent damage to the piston.

6. Clean metal parts in brake fluid and discard the rubber parts.

7. Inspect the bore for damage or wear, and check the pistons for damage and proper clearance in the bore.

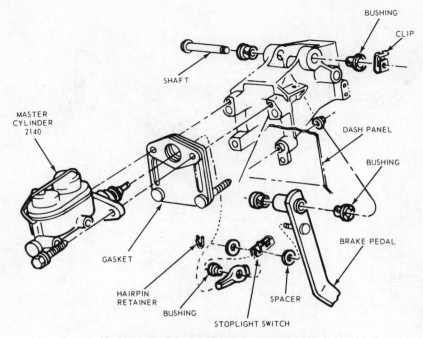

BUSHING

CLIP

SHAFT

MASTER
CYLINDER
2140

DASH PANEL

BUSHING

BRAKE PEDAL

GASKET

HAIRPIN
RETAINER

BUSHING

SPACER

STOPLIGHT SWITCH

Master cylinder installation—manual brakes

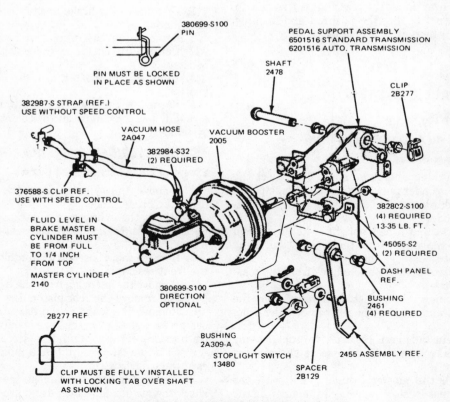

380699-S100
PIN

PIN MUST BE LOCKED
IN PLACE AS SHOWN

PEDAL SUPPORT ASSEMBLY
6501516 STANDARD TRANSMISSION
6201516 AUTO. TRANSMISSION

SHAFT
2478

CLIP
2B277

382987-S STRAP (REF.)
USE WITHOUT SPEED CONTROL

VACUUM HOSE
2A047

VACUUM BOOSTER
2005

382984-S32
(2) REQUIRED

376588-S CLIP REF.
USE WITH SPEED CONTROL

3828C2-S100
(4) REQUIRED
13-35 LB. FT.

FLUID LEVEL IN
BRAKE MASTER
CYLINDER MUST
BE FROM FULL
TO 1/4 INCH
FROM TOP

45055-S2
(2) REQUIRED

MASTER CYLINDER
2140

DASH PANEL
REF.

380699-S100
DIRECTION
OPTIONAL

BUSHING
2461
(4) REQUIRED

2B277 REF

BUSHING
2A309-A

STOPLIGHT SWITCH
13480

SPACER
2B129

2455 ASSEMBLY REF.

CLIP MUST BE FULLY INSTALLED
WITH LOCKING TAB OVER SHAFT
AS SHOWN

Master cylinder installation—power brakes

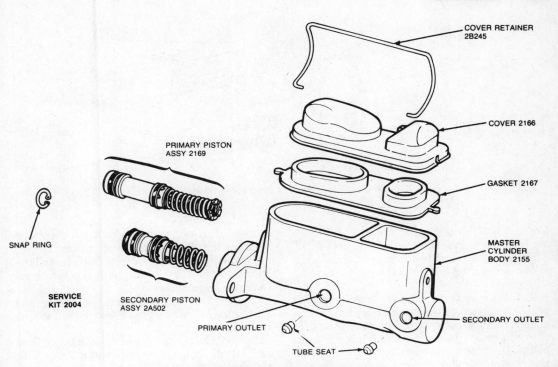

Exploded view of the 1981–86 master cylinder

COVER RETAINER 2B245

COVER 2166

GASKET 2167

MASTER CYLINDER BODY 2155

SECONDARY OUTLET

PRIMARY PISTON ASSY 2169

SNAP RING

SERVICE KIT 2004

SECONDARY PISTON ASSY 2A502

PRIMARY OUTLET

TUBE SEAT

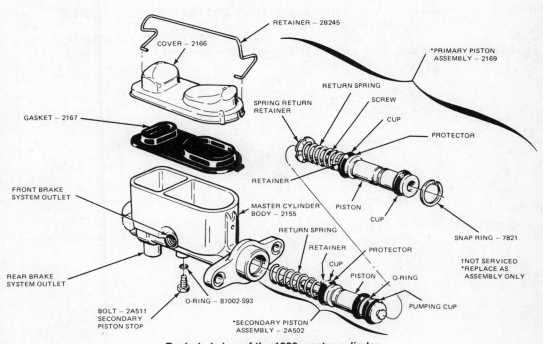

Exploded view of the 1980 master cylinder

RETAINER – 2B245

COVER – 2166

GASKET – 2167

FRONT BRAKE SYSTEM OUTLET

MASTER CYLINDER BODY – 2155

REAR BRAKE SYSTEM OUTLET

BOLT – 2A511 SECONDARY PISTON STOP

O-RING – 87002-S93

*SECONDARY PISTON ASSEMBLY – 2A502

*PRIMARY PISTON ASSEMBLY – 2169

RETURN SPRING

SPRING RETURN RETAINER

SCREW

CUP

PROTECTOR

RETAINER

PISTON

CUP

SNAP RING – 7821

†NOT SERVICED
*REPLACE AS ASSEMBLY ONLY

RETURN SPRING

RETAINER

CUP

PROTECTOR

PISTON

O-RING

PUMPING CUP

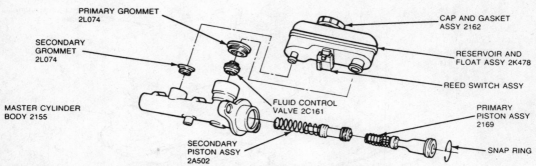

Exploded business view of the 1987 master cylinder

CAUTION: *Late models are equipped with aluminum master cylinders. DO NOT HONE! If the bore is pitted or scored deeply, the master cylinder assembly must be replaced.*

8. If the bore is only slightly scored or pitted it may be honed. Always use hones that are in good condition and completely clean the cylinder with brake fluid when the honing is completed. If any evidence of contamination exist in the master cylinder, the entire hydraulic system should be flushed and refilled with clean brake fluid. Blow out the passages with compressed air.

NOTE: *The rebuilding kit may contain secondary and primary piston assemblies instead of just rubber seals. In this case, seal installation is not required.*

9. Install new secondary seals in the two grooves in the flat end of the front piston. The lips of the seals will be facing away from each other.

10. Install a new primary seal and the seal protector on the opposite end of the front piston with the lips of the seal facing outward.

11. Coat the seals with brake fluid. Install the spring on the front piston with the spring retainer in the primary seal.

12. Insert the piston assembly, spring end first, into the bore and use a wooden rod to seat it.

13. Coat the rear piston seals with brake fluid and install them into the piston grooves with the lips facing the spring end.

14. Assemble the spring onto the piston and install the assembly into the bore spring first. Install the snapring.

15. Hold the piston train at the bottom of the bore and install the stopscrew. Install a new seal on the hub. Bench-bleed the cylinder or install and bleed the cylinder on the car.

Bleeding the Hydraulic System

See the **4 Wheel Anti-Lock Section** if your vehicle is equipped with that system.

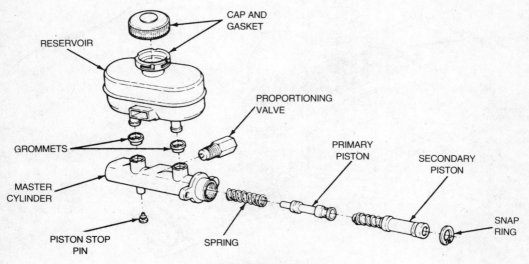

1988 master cylinder

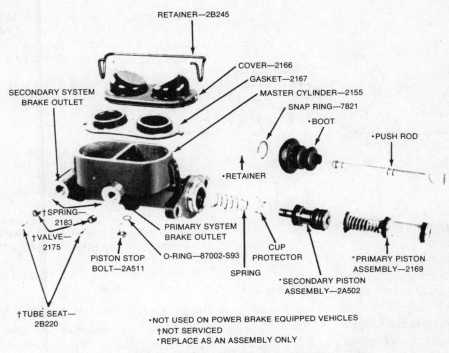

RETAINER—2B245

COVER—2166

GASKET—2167

MASTER CYLINDER—2155

SNAP RING—7821

SECONDARY SYSTEM
BRAKE OUTLET

•BOOT

•PUSH ROD

•RETAINER

•SPRING—
2183

•VALVE—
2175

PRIMARY SYSTEM
BRAKE OUTLET

PISTON STOP
BOLT—2A511

O-RING—87002-S93

CUP
PROTECTOR

SPRING

•PRIMARY PISTON
ASSEMBLY—2169

•SECONDARY PISTON
ASSEMBLY—2A502

†TUBE SEAT—
2B220

•NOT USED ON POWER BRAKE EQUIPPED VEHICLES
†NOT SERVICED
•REPLACE AS AN ASSEMBLY ONLY

Master cylinder disassembled—drum brakes

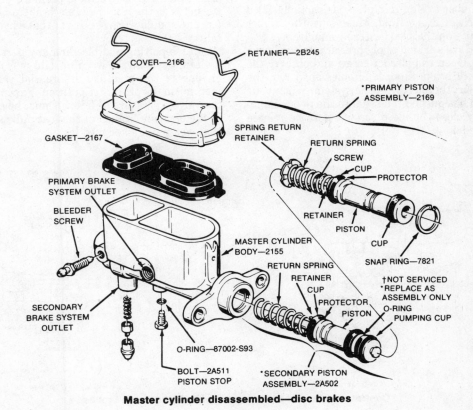

RETAINER—2B245

COVER—2166

•PRIMARY PISTON
ASSEMBLY—2169

SPRING RETURN
RETAINER

RETURN SPRING

SCREW

CUP

PROTECTOR

GASKET—2167

PRIMARY BRAKE
SYSTEM OUTLET

BLEEDER
SCREW

RETAINER

PISTON

CUP

SNAP RING—7821

MASTER CYLINDER
BODY—2155

RETURN SPRING

RETAINER

CUP

PROTECTOR

PISTON

†NOT SERVICED
•REPLACE AS
ASSEMBLY ONLY

O-RING
PUMPING CUP

SECONDARY
BRAKE SYSTEM
OUTLET

O-RING—87002-S93

BOLT—2A511
PISTON STOP

•SECONDARY PISTON
ASSEMBLY—2A502

Master cylinder disassembled—disc brakes

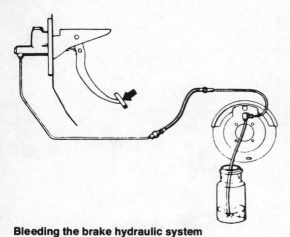

Bleeding the brake hydraulic system

NOTE: *Since the front and rear hydraulic systems are independent of each other, if it is known that only one system has air in it, only that system has to be bled.*

Wheel Cylinders and Calipers

1. Fill the master cylinder with brake fluid.
2. Install a ⅜″ box-end wrench to the bleeder screw on the right rear wheel.
3. Push a piece of small diameter rubber tubing over the bleeder screw until it is flush against the wrench. Submerge the other end of the rubber tubing in a glass jar partially filled with clean brake fluid. Make sure the rubber tube fits on the bleeder screw snugly.
4. Have a friend apply pressure to the brake pedal. Open the bleeder screw and observe the bottle of brake fluid. If bubbles appear in the glass jar; there is air in the system. When your friend has pushed the pedal to the floor, immediately close the bleed screw before he release the pedal.

5. Repeat this procedure until no bubbles appear in the jar. Refill the master cylinder right front and left front wheels, in that order. Periodically refill the master cylinder so it does not run dry.
6. Center the pressure differential warning valve as outlined in the Pressure Differential Warning Valve section.

Master Cylinder

1. Fill the master cylinder reservoirs.
2. Place absorbent rags under the fluid lines at the master cylinder.
3. Have an assistant depress and hold the brake pedal.
4. With the pedal held down, slowly crack open the hydraulic line fitting, allowing the air to escape. Close the fitting and have the pedal released.
5. Repeat Steps 3 and 4 for each fitting until all the air is released.

Pressure Differential Warning Valve

Since the introduction of dual master cylinders to the hydraulic brake system, a pressure differential warning signal has been added. This signal consists of a warning light on the dashboard activated by a differential pressure switch located below the master cylinder. The signal indicates a hydraulic pressure differential between the front and rear brakes of 80-150 psi, and should warn the driver that a hydraulic failure has occurred.

After repairing and bleeding any part of the hydraulic system the warning light may remain on due to the pressure differential valve remaining in the off-center position. To centralize the valve a pressure difference must be created in the opposite branch of the hydraulic system that was repaired or bled last.

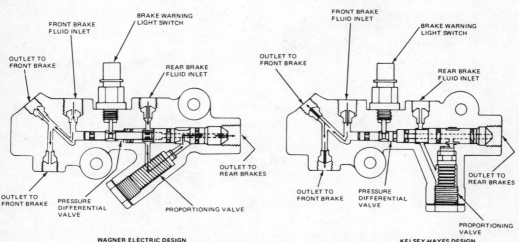

Control valve assembly on models with 4-wheel disc brakes

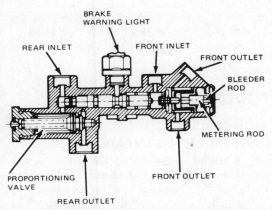

1980–82 3-way aluminum control valve assembly (contains metering, pressure differential and proportioning valves)

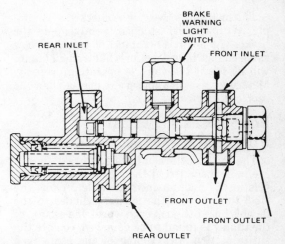

1980–87 2-way aluminum control valve assembly (contains the pressure differential and proportioning valves)

NOTE: *Front wheel balancing of cars equipped with disc brakes may also cause a pressure differential in the front branch of the system.*

VALVE CENTERING PROCEDURE

1. Turn the ignition to either the **ACC** or **ON** position.

2. Check the fluid level in the master cylinder reservoirs. Fill to within ¼" (6mm) of the top if necessary.

3. Depress the brake pedal firmly. The valve will centralize itself causing the brake warning light to go out.

4. Turn the ignition off.

5. Prior to driving the vehicle, check the operation of the brakes and obtain a firm pedal.

Proportioning Valve

On vehicles equipped with front disc and rear drum brakes, a proportioning valve is an important part of the system. It is installed in the hydraulic line to the rear brakes. Its function is to maintain the correct proportion between line pressures to the front and rear brakes. No attempt at adjustment of this valve should be made, as adjustment is preset and tampering will result in uneven braking action.

To assure correct installation when replacing the valve, the outlet to the rear brakes is stamped with the letter **R**.

Metering Valve

On vehicles through 1980 equipped with front disc brakes, a metering valve is used. This valve is installed in the hydraulic line to the front brakes, and functions to delay pressure buildup to the front brakes on application. Its purpose is to reduce front brake pressure until rear brake pressure builds up adequately to overcome the rear brake shoe return springs. In

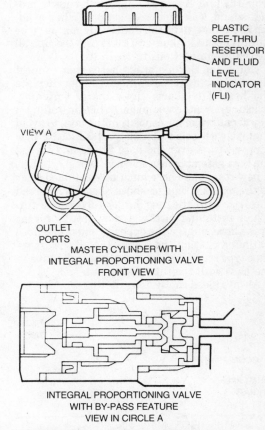

MASTER CYLINDER WITH INTEGRAL PROPORTIONING VALVE FRONT VIEW

INTEGRAL PROPORTIONING VALVE WITH BY-PASS FEATURE VIEW IN CIRCLE A

1987–88 integral pressure differential valve

this way disc brake pad lift is extended because it prevents the front disc brakes from carrying all or most of the braking load at low operating line pressures.

The metering valve can be checked very simply. With the car stopped, gently apply the brakes. At about 1″ (25mm) of travel, a very small change in pedal effort (like a small bump) will be felt if the valve is operating properly. Metering valves are not serviceable and must be replaced if defective.

Brake Hoses and Lines
HYDRAULIC BRAKE LINE CHECK

The hydraulic brake lines and brake linings are to be inspected at the recommended intervals in the maintenance schedule. Follow the steel tubing from the master cylinder to the flexible hose fitting at each wheel. If a section of the tubing is found to be damaged, replace the entire section with tubing of the same type (steel, not copper), size, shape, and length. When installing a new section of brake tubing, flush clean brake fluid or denatured alcohol through to remove any dirt or foreign material from the line. Be sure to flare both ends to provide sound, leak-proof connections. When bending the tubing to fit the underbody contours, be careful not to kink or crack the line. Torque all hydraulic connections to 10-15 lbs.

Check the flexible brake hoses that connect the steel tubing to each wheel cylinder. Replace the hose if it shows any signs of softening, cracking, or other damage. When installing a new front brake hose, position the hose to avoid contact with other chassis parts. Place a new copper gasket over the hose fitting and thread the hose assembly into the front wheel cylinder. A new rear brake hose must be positioned clear of the exhaust pipe or shock absorber. Thread the hose into the rear brake tube connector. When installing either a new front or rear brake hose, engage the opposite end of the hose to the bracket on the frame. Install the horseshoe type retaining clip and connect the tube to the hose with the tube fitting nut.

Always bleed the system after hose or line replacement. Before bleeding, make sure that the master cylinder is topped up with high temperature, extra heavy duty fluid of at least SAE 70R3 quality.

POWER ASSIST SYSTEMS

Vacuum Booster
REMOVAL AND INSTALLATION

1. Working inside the car below the instrument panel, disconnect the booster valve operating rod from the brake pedal assembly.
2. Open the hood and disconnect the wires from the stop light switch at the brake master cylinder.
3. Disconnect the brake line at the master cylinder outlet fitting.
4. Disconnect the manifold vacuum hose from the booster unit.
5. Remove the four bracket-to-dash panel attaching bolts.
6. Remove the booster and bracket assembly from the dash panel, sliding the valve operating rod out from the engine side of the dash panel.
7. Mount the booster and bracket assembly to the dash panel by sliding the valve operating rod in through the hole in the dash panel, and installing the attaching bolts.
8. Connect the manifold vacuum hose to the booster.
9. Connect the brake line to the master cylinder outlet fitting.
10. Connect the stop light switch wires.
11. Working inside the car below the instrument panel, install the rubber boot on the valve operating rod at the passenger side of the dash panel.
12. Connect the valve operating rod to the brake pedal with the bushings, eccentric shoulder bolt, and nut.

Hydro-Boost Hydraulic Booster
REMOVAL AND INSTALLATION

The hydro-boost assembly contains a valve which controls pump pressure while braking, a lever to control the position of the valve and a boost piston to provide the force to operate a conventional master cylinder attached to the front of the booster. The hydro-boost also has a reserve system, designed to store sufficient pressurized fluid to provide at least 2 brake applications in the event of insufficient fluid flow from the power steering pump. The brakes can also be applied unassisted if the reserve system is depleted.

Before removing the hydro-boost, discharge

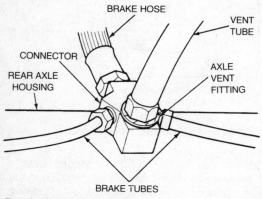

BRAKE HOSE

VENT TUBE

CONNECTOR

REAR AXLE HOUSING

AXLE VENT FITTING

BRAKE TUBES

Rear brake tube connector

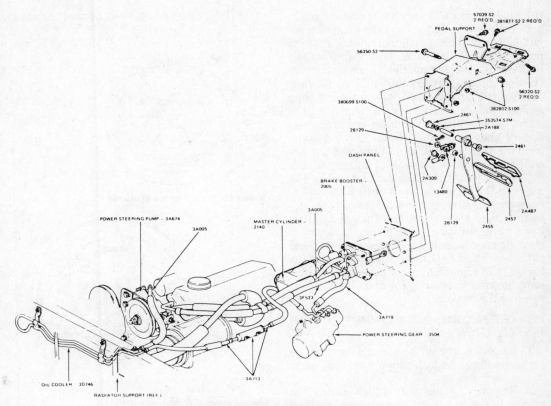

Hydro-Boost assembly and related parts

the accumulator by making several brake applications until a hard pedal is felt.

1. Working from inside the vehicle, below the instrument panel, disconnect the pushrod from the brake pedal. Disconnect the stoplight switch wires at the connector. Remove the hairpin retainer. Slide the stoplight switch off the brake pedal far enough for the switch outer hole to clear the pin. Remove the switch from the pin. Slide the pushrod, nylon washers and bushing off the brake pedal pin.

2. Open the hood and remove the nuts attaching the master cylinder to the hydro-boost. Remove the master cylinder. Secure it to one side without disturbing the hydraulic lines.

3. Disconnect the pressure, steering gear and return lines from the booster. Plug the lines to prevent the entry of dirt.

4. Remove the nuts attaching the hydro-boost. Remove the booster from the firewall, sliding the pushrod link out of the engine side of the firewall.

5. Install the hydro-boost on the firewall and install the attaching nuts.

6. Install the master cylinder on the booster.

7. Connect the pressure, steering gear and return lines to the booster.

8. Working below the instrument panel, install the nylon washer, booster pushrod and bushing on the brake pedal pin. Install the switch so that it straddles the pushrod with the switch slot on the pedal pin and the switch outer hole just clearing the pin. Slide the switch completely onto the pin and install the nylon washer. Attach these parts with the hairpin retainer. Connect the stoplight switch wires and install the wires in the retaining clip.

9. Remove the coil wire so that the engine will not start. Fill the power steering pump and engage the starter. Apply the brakes with a pumping action. Do not turn the steering wheel until air has been bled from the booster.

10. Check the fluid level and add as required. Start the engine and apply the brakes, checking for leaks. Cycle the steering wheel.

11. If a whine type noise is heard, suspect fluid aeration.

FRONT DRUM BRAKES

Drum brakes on all Fords employ single anchor, internal-expanding, and self-adjusting brake assemblies. The automatic adjuster continuously maintains correct operating clearance between the linings and the drums by adjusting the brake in small increments in direct proportion to lining wear. When applying the brakes while backing up, the linings tend to follow the rotating drum counterclockwise, thus forcing the upper end of the primary shoe against the anchor pin. simultaneously, the wheel cylinder pushes the upper end of the secondary shoe and cable guide outward, away from the anchor pin. This movement of the secondary shoe causes the cable to pull the adjusting lever upward and against the end of the tooth on the adjusting screw starwheel. As lining wear increases, the upward travel of the adjusting lever also increases. When the linings have worn sufficiently to allow the lever to move upward far enough, it passes over the end of the tooth and engages it. Upon release of the brakes, the adjusting spring pulls the adjuster lever downward, turning the starwheel and expanding the brakes.

BRAKE REMOVAL, INSPECTION, INSTALLATION

1. Raise the rear of the car and support the car with safety stands. Make sure that the parking brake is not on.
2. Remove the lug nuts which attach the wheels to the axle shaft and remove the tires and wheels from the car. Using a pair of pliers, remove the tinnerman nuts from the wheel studs. Pull the brake drum off the axle shaft. If the brakes are adjusted too tightly to remove the drum, see Step 3. If you can remove the drum, see Step 4.
3. If the brakes are too tight to remove the drum, get under the car (make sure that your have jack stands under the car to support it) and remove the rubber plug from the bottom of the brake backing plate. shine a flashlight into the slot in the plate. You will see the top of the adjusting screw starwheel and the adjusting le-

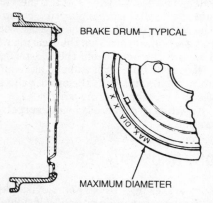

BRAKE DRUM—TYPICAL

MAXIMUM DIAMETER

The maximum inside diameter is stamped on each brake drum

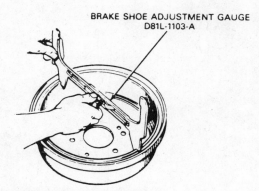

BRAKE SHOE ADJUSTMENT GAUGE
D81L-1103-A

Measuring drum inside diameter

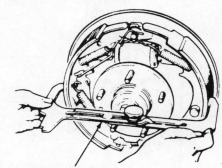

BRAKE SHOE ADJUSTMENT GAUGE
D81L-1103-A

Measuring brake shoe installation

ver for the automatic brake adjusting mechanism. To back off on the adjusting screw, you must first insert a small thin prybar or a piece of firm wire (coathanger wire) into the adjusting slot and push the adjusting lever away from the adjusting screw. Then, insert a brake adjusting spoon into the slot and engage the top of the starwheel. Lift up on the bottom of the adjusting spoon to force the adjusting screw starwheel downward. Repeat this operation until the brake drum is free of the brake shoes and can be pulled off.

4. Clean the brake shoes and the inside of the brake drum. There must be at least 1/16 in. of brake lining above the heads of the brake shoe attaching rivets. The lining should not be cracked or contaminated with grease or brake fluid. If there is grease or brake fluid on the lining, it must be replaced and the source of the leak must be found and corrected. Brake fluid on the lining means leaking wheel cylinders. Grease on the brake lining means a leaking axle seal. If the lining is slightly glazed but otherwise in good condition, it can be cleaned up with medium sandpaper. Lift up the bottom of the wheel cylinder boots and inspect the ends of the wheel cylinders. A small amount of fluid in the end of the cylinders should be considered normal. If fluid runs out of the cylinder when the

boots are lifted, however, the wheel cylinder must be rebuilt or replaced. Examine the inside of the brake drum; it should have a smooth, dull finish. If excessive brake shoe wear caused grooves to wear in the drum it must be machined or replaced. If the inside of the drum is slightly glazed, but otherwise good, it can be cleaned up with medium sandpaper.

5. If no repairs are required, install the drum and wheel. If the brake adjustment was changed to remove the drum, adjust the brakes until the drum will just fit over the brakes. After the wheel is installed it will be necessary to complete the adjustment. See Brake Adjustment in this chapter.

Brake Shoes

REMOVAL AND INSTALLATION

NOTE: *If you are not thoroughly familiar with the procedures involved in brake replacement, disassemble and assemble only one side at a time, leaving the other wheel intact as a reference.*

1. Remove the brake drum. See the inspection procedure.

2. Place the hollow end of a brake spring service tool (available at auto parts stores) on the brake shoe anchor pin and twist it to disengage one of the brake retracting springs. Repeat this operation to remove the other spring.

CAUTION: *Be careful the springs do not slip off the tool during removal, as they could cause personal injury.*

3. Reach behind the brake backing plate and place a finger on the end of one of the brake holddown spring mounting pins. Using a pair of pliers, grasp the washer on the top of the holddown spring which corresponds to the pin that you are holding. Push down on the pliers and turn them 90° to align the slot in the washer with the head on the spring mounting pin. Remove the spring and washer and repeat this operation on the holddown spring on the other brake shoe.

4. Place the top of a prybar on the top of the brake adjusting screw and move the brake adjusting lever. When there is enough slack in the automatic adjuster cable, disconnect the loop on the top of the cable from the anchor. Grasp the top of each brake shoe and move it outward to disengage it from the wheel cylinder and parking brake link. When the brake shoes are clear, lift them from the backing plate. Twist the shoes slightly and the automatic adjuster assembly will disassemble itself.

5. Grasp the end of the brake cable spring with a pair of pliers and, using the brake lever as a fulcrum, pull the end of the spring away

from the lever. Disengage the cable from the brake lever.

The brake shoes are installed as follows:

6. The brake cable must be connected to the secondary brake shoe before the shoe is installed on the backing plate. to do this, first transfer the parking brake lever from the old secondary shoe to the new one. This is accomplished by spreading the bottom of the horseshoe clip and disengaging the lever. Position the lever on the new secondary shoe and install the spring washer and the horseshoe clip. Grasp the metal tip of the parking brake cable with a pair of pliers. Position a pair of side cutter pliers on the end of the cable coil spring, and using the pliers as a fulcrum, pull the coil spring back with the side cutters. Position the cable in the parking brake lever.

7. Apply a light coating of high-temperature grease to the brake shoe contact points on the backing plate. Position the primary brake shoe on the front of the backing plate and install the holddown spring and washer over the mounting pin. Install the secondary shoe on the rear of the backing plate.

8. Install the parking brake link between the notch in the primary brake shoe and the notch in the parking brake lever.

9. Install the automatic adjuster cable loop end on the anchor pin. Make sure that the crimped side of the loop faces the backing plate.

10. Install the return spring in the primary brake shoe and, using the tapered end of a brake spring service tool, slide the top of the spring onto the anchor pin.

Be careful to make sure that the spring does not slip off the tool during installation, as it could cause injury.

11. Install the automatic adjuster cable guide in the secondary brake shoe, making sure that the flared hole in the cable guide is inside the hole in the brake shoe. Fit the cable into the groove in the top of the cable guide.

12. Install the secondary shoe return spring through the hole in the cable guide and the brake shoe. Using the brake spring tool, slide the top of the spring onto the anchor pin.

13. Clean the threads on the adjusting screw and apply a light coating of high temperature grease to the threads. Screw the adjuster closed, then open it ½ turn.

14. Install the adjusting screw between the brake shoes with the starwheel nearest to the secondary shoe. Make sure that the starwheel is in a position that is accessible from the adjusting slot in the backing plate.

15. Install the short hooked end of the automatic adjuster spring in the proper hole in the primary brake shoe.

16. Connect the hooked end of the automatic

adjuster cable and the free end of the automatic adjuster spring in the slot in the top of the automatic adjuster lever.

17. Pull the automatic adjuster lever (the lever will pull the cable and spring with it) downward and to the left and engage the pivot hook of the lever in the hole in the secondary brake shoe.

18. Check the entire brake assembly to make sure that everything is installed properly. Make sure that the shoes engage the wheel cylinder properly and are flush on the anchor pin. Make sure that the automatic adjuster cable is flush on the anchor pin and in the slot on the back of the cable guide. Make sure that the adjusting lever rests on the adjusting screw starwheel. Pull upward on the adjusting cable until the adjusting lever is free of the starwheel, then release the cable. the adjusting lever should snap back into place on the adjusting screw starwheel and turn the wheel one tooth.

19. Expand the brake adjusting screw until the brake drum will just fit over the brake shoes.

20. Install the wheel and drum and adjust the brakes.

Wheel Cylinder

REMOVAL AND INSTALLATION

1. Remove the brake shoes.

2. Loosen the brake line on the rear of the cylinder but do not pull the line away from the cylinder or it may bend.

3. Remove the bolts and lockwashers which attach the wheel cylinder to the backing plate and remove the cylinder.

4. Position the new wheel cylinder on the backing plate and install the cylinder attaching bolts and lockwashers.

5. Attach the metal brake line.

6. Install the brakes.

OVERHAUL

Since the travel of the pistons in the wheel cylinder changes when new brake shoes are installed, it is possible for previously good wheel cylinders to start leaking after new brakes are installed. Therefore, to save yourself the expense of having to replace new brakes which become saturated with brake fluid and the aggravation of having to take everything apart again, it is strongly recommended that wheel cylinders be rebuilt every time new brake shoes are installed. This is especially true on high mileage cars.

1. Remove the brakes.

2. Place a bucket or old newspaper under the brake backing plate to catch the brake fluid that will run out of the wheel cylinder.

3. Remove the boots from the ends of the wheel cylinders.

4. Push one piston toward the center of the cylinder to force the opposite piston and cup out of the other end of the cylinder. Reach in the open end of the cylinder and push the spring, cup, and piston out of the cylinder.

5. Remove the bleeder screw from the rear of the cylinder on the back of the backing plate.

6. Inspect the inside of the wheel cylinder. If it is scored in any way, the cylinder must be honed with a wheel cylinder hone or fine emery paper, and finished with crocus cloth if emery paper is used. If the inside of the cylinder is excessively worn, the cylinder will have to be replaced, as only 0.003 in. of material can be removed from the cylinder walls. When honing or cleaning the wheel cylinders, keep a small amount of brake fluid in the cylinder to serve as a lubricant.

7. Clean any foreign matter from the pistons. The side of the pistons must be smooth for the wheel cylinders to operate properly.

8. Clean the cylinder bore with alcohol and a lint-free rag. Pull the rag through the bore several times to remove all foreign matter and dry the cylinder.

9. Install the bleeder screw and the return spring in the cylinder.

10. Coat new cylinder cups with new brake fluid and install them in the cylinder. make sure that they are square in the bore or they will leak.

11. Install the pistons in the cylinder after coating them with new brake fluid.

12. Coat the insides of the boots with new

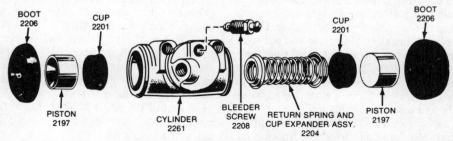

Drum brake wheel cylinder disassembled

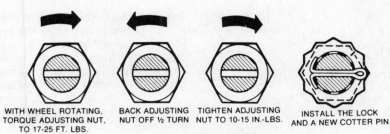

WITH WHEEL ROTATING, TORQUE ADJUSTING NUT, TO 17-25 FT. LBS.

BACK ADJUSTING NUT OFF ½ TURN

TIGHTEN ADJUSTING NUT TO 10-15 IN.-LBS.

INSTALL THE LOCK AND A NEW COTTER PIN

Front wheel bearing adjustment

brake fluid and install them in the cylinder. Install the brakes.

Front Wheel Bearings

ADJUSTMENT

The front wheels each rotate on a set of opposed, tapered roller bearings as shown in the accompanying illustration. The grease retainer at the inside of the hub prevents lubricant from leaking into the brake drum.

Adjustment of the wheel bearings is accomplished as follows: Lift the car so that the wheel and tire are clear of the ground, then remove the grease cap and remove excess grease from the end of the spindle. Remove the cotter pin and nut lock shown in the illustration.

NOTE: *In order to prevent the brake pads from stopping the hub and rotor from seating properly, rock the rotor in and out to push the brake pads back into their bores.*

Rotate the wheel hub, and drum assembly while tightening the adjusting nut to 17-25 ft. lbs. in order to seat the bearings. Back off the adjusting nut one half turn, then retighten the adjusting nut to 10-15 in. lbs. (inch-pound). Locate the nut lock on the adjusting nut so that the castellations on the lock are lined up with

the cotter pin hole in the spindle. Install a new cotter pin, bending the ends of the cotter pin around the castellated flange of the nut lock. Check the front wheel for proper rotation, then install the grease cap. If the wheel still does not rotate properly, inspect and clean or replace the wheel bearings and cups.

REMOVAL, REPACKING AND INSTALLATION

The procedure for cleaning, replacing and adjusting front wheel bearings on vehicles equipped with self-adjusting drum brakes is as follows:

1. Taking proper safety precautions, raise the car until the wheel and tire clear the floor. Install jackstands under the lower control arms.

2. Remove the wheel cover. Remove the grease cap from the hub. then remove the cotter pin, nut lock, adjusting nut, and flat washer from the spindle. Remove the outer bearing cone and roller assembly.

3. Pull the wheel, hub and drum assembly off the spindle. When encountering a brake drum which will not come off, disengage the adjusting lever from the adjusting screw by inserting a narrow pry bar through the adjusting

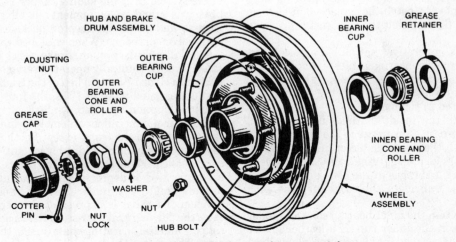

HUB AND BRAKE DRUM ASSEMBLY

INNER BEARING CUP

GREASE RETAINER

ADJUSTING NUT

OUTER BEARING CUP

OUTER BEARING CONE AND ROLLER

GREASE CAP

WASHER

NUT

COTTER PIN

NUT LOCK

HUB BOLT

INNER BEARING CONE AND ROLLER

WHEEL ASSEMBLY

Front hub, wheel bearings and grease retainer

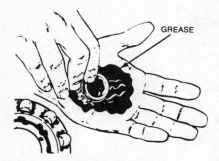

GREASE

Packing the front wheel bearings

hole in the carrier plate. While the lever is disengaged, back off the adjusting screw with a brake adjusting tool. The self-adjusting mechanism will not function properly if the adjusting screw if burred, chipped, or otherwise damaged in the process, so exercise extreme care.

4. Remove the grease retainer and the inner bearing cone and roller assembly from the hub.

5. Clean all grease off from the inner and outer bearing cups with solvent. Inspect the cups for pits, scratches, or excessive wear. If the cups are damaged, remove them with a drift.

6. Clean the inner and outer cone and roller assemblies with solvent and shaft them dry. If the cone and roller assemblies show excessive wear of damage, replace them with the bearing cups as a unit.

7. If the new grease retainer is of leather, soak it in light engine oil for 30 minutes, prior to installation. Wipe any excess from the metal portion of the retainer. Clean the spindle and the inside of the hub with solvent to thoroughly remove all old grease.

8. Covering the spindle with a clean cloth, brush all loose dirt and dust from the brake assembly. Remove the cloth carefully so as to not get dirt on the spindle.

9. If the inner and/or outer bearing cups were removed, install the replacement cups on the hub. Be sure that the cups seat properly in the hub.

10. It is imperative that all old grease be removed from the bearings and surrounding surfaces before repacking. The new lithium-based grease is not compatible with the sodium base grease used in the past.

11. Pack the inside of the hub with wheel bearing grease. Add grease to the hub until it is flush with the inside diameter of both bearing cups. Work as much grease as possible between the rollers and cages in the cone and roller assemblies. Lubricate the cone surfaces with grease.

12. Position the inner bearing cone and roller assembly in the inner cup. If a leather grease retainer has soaked for 30 minutes, wipe all excess from the metal portion of the retainer and install. Other grease retainers require a light film of grease on the lips before installation. Using a wooden block to evenly distribute the blow of a hammer, install the retainer. Make sure that the retainer is properly seated.

13. Install the wheel, hub, and drum assembly on the wheel spindle. To prevent damage to the grease retainer and spindle threads, keep the hub centered on the spindle.

14. Install the outer bearing cone and roller assembly and the flat washer on the spindle. Install the adjusting nut.

15. Adjust the wheel bearings by tightening the adjusting nut to 17-25 ft. lbs. with the wheel rotating to seat the bearing. Then back off the adjusting nut ½ turn. Retighten the adjusting nut to 10-15 in. lbs. Install the locknut so that the castellations are aligned with the cotter pin hole. Install the cotter pin. Bend the ends of the cotter pin around the castellations of the locknut to prevent interference with the radio static collector in the grease cap. Install the grease cap.

16. Remove the adjusting hole cover from the carrier plate and, from the carrier plate side, turn the adjusting screw starwheel upward with a brake adjusting tool. Expand the brake shoes until a slight drag is felt with the drum rotating. Replace the adjusting hole cover.

17. Install the wheel cover.

FRONT DISC BRAKES

Front disc brakes have been available as an option on full size models since the mid 1960s. From 1968 to 1972 floating caliper front disc brakes were available on all models. Starting in 1973, sliding caliper front discs were made standard equipment with vacuum power assist.

Beginning in 1976 models, a 4-wheel disc brake system utilizing sliding caliper rear disc brakes is standard equipment on all station wagons and police interceptor packages, and optional on all sedans. When equipped with the 4-wheel disc brake system, brake assist is provided by a hydraulically operated servo system known as Hydro-Boost, in lieu of the traditional vacuum assisted type. In 1979, the four wheel disc brake option was discontinued.

The rear sliding caliper assembly is similar to the one used on the front, except for the parking brake mechanism and a bigger anti-rattle spring. The parking brake lever on the caliper is cable operated by depressing (or releasing), the parking brake pedal under the dash panel.

When the pedal is depressed, the cable rotates the parking brake lever (on the back of the caliper) and the operating shaft (inside the caliper). Three steel balls, which are located in

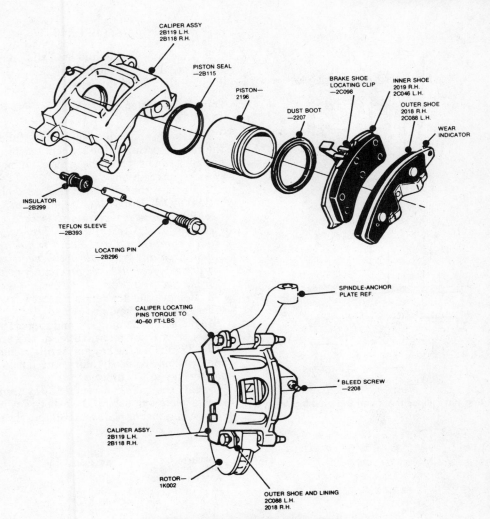

Typical front disc brakes from 1979

pockets on the opposing heads of the shaft and thrust screw, roll between ramps formed in the pockets. The motion of the balls forces the thrust screw away from the shaft which, in turn, forces the piston and pad assembly against the disc to create braking action.

Brake Pads

REPLACEMENT

Floating Caliper Front Disc Brakes

1. Raise the vehicle on a hoist and remove the front wheels.

2. Remove the lockwires from the two mounting bolts and lift the caliper away from the disc.

3. Remove the retaining clips with a pry bar and slide the outboard pad and retaining pins out of the caliper. Remove the inboard pad.

4. Slide the new inboard pad into the caliper

so that the tabs are between the retaining clips and anchor plate and the backing plate lies flush against the piston.

5. Insert the inboard pad retaining pins into the outboard pad and position them in the caliper.

NOTE: *Stabilizer, insulator, pad clips, and pins should always be replaced when the disc pads are replaced.*

6. Hold the retaining pins in place (one at a time) with a short drift pin or dowel and install the retaining clips.

7. Slide the caliper assembly over the disc and align the mounting bolt holes.

8. Install the lower bolt finger-tight. Install the upper bolt and torque to specification. Torque the lower bolt to specification. Safety-wire both bolts.

CAUTION: *Do not deviate from this procedure. The alignment of the anchor plate de-*

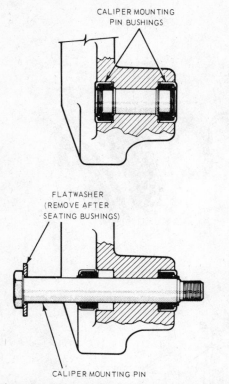

CALIPER MOUNTING
PIN BUSHINGS

FLATWASHER
(REMOVE AFTER
SEATING BUSHINGS)

CALIPER MOUNTING PIN

Floating pin caliper mounting pin bushing installation

pends on the proper sequence of bolt installation.

9. Check the brake fluid level and pump and brake pedal to seat the lining against the disc. Replace the wheels and road-test the car.

Ford Single Piston Sliding Caliper Disc Brakes 1973-79 Models

1. Remove approximately ⅔ of the fluid from the rear reservoir of the tandem master cylinder. Raise and support the vehicle, taking proper safety precautions.

2. Remove the wheel and tire assembly.

CAUTION: *Brake shoes contain asbestos, which has been determined to be a cancer causing agent. Never clean the brake surfaces with compressed air! Avoid inhaling any dust from any brake surface! When cleaning brake surfaces, use a commercially available brake cleaning fluid.*

3. Remove the key retaining screw from the caliper retaining key.

4. Slide the retaining key and support spring either inward or outward from the anchor plate. To remove the key and spring, a hammer and drift may be used, taking care not to damage the key in the process.

5. Lift the caliper assembly away from the anchor plate by pushing the caliper downward against the anchor plate and rotating the upper

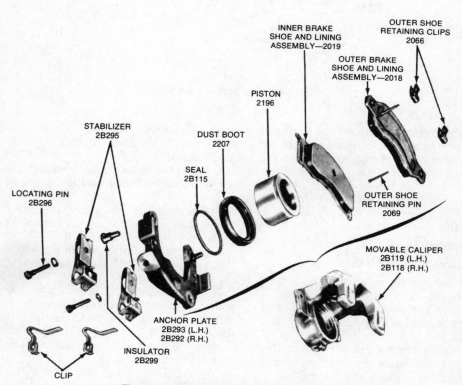

INNER BRAKE
SHOE AND LINING
ASSEMBLY—2019

OUTER SHOE
RETAINING CLIPS
2066

OUTER BRAKE
SHOE AND LINING
ASSEMBLY—2018

PISTON
2196

STABILIZER
2B295

DUST BOOT
2207

SEAL
2B115

OUTER SHOE
RETAINING PIN
2069

LOCATING PIN
2B296

MOVABLE CALIPER
2B119 (L.H.)
2B118 (R.H.)

ANCHOR PLATE
2B293 (L.H.)
2B292 (R.H.)

INSULATOR
2B299

CLIP

Floating caliper disc brake caliper disassembled

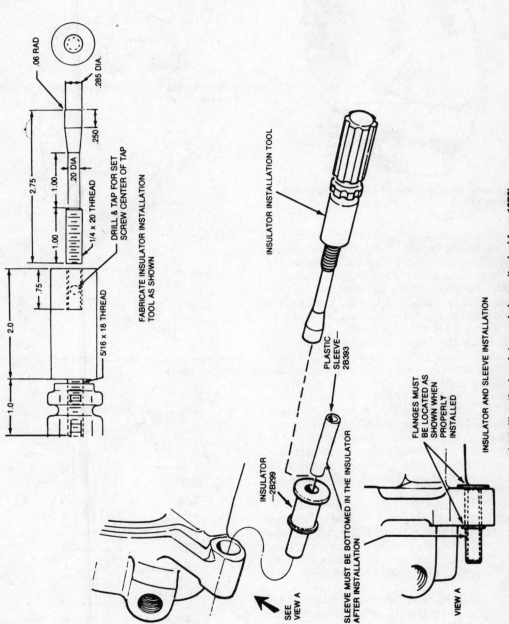

.06 RAD

.285 DIA.

.250

.20 DIA

1.00

1.00

2.75

1/4 x 20 THREAD

DRILL & TAP FOR SET
SCREW CENTER OF TAP

FABRICATE INSULATOR INSTALLATION
TOOL AS SHOWN

.75

2.0

5/16 x 18 THREAD

1.0

INSULATOR INSTALLATION TOOL

PLASTIC
SLEEVE—
2B393

INSULATOR
—2B299

SEE
VIEW A

SLEEVE MUST BE BOTTOMED IN THE INSULATOR
AFTER INSTALLATION

FLANGES MUST
BE LOCATED AS
SHOWN WHEN
PROPERLY
INSTALLED

INSULATOR AND SLEEVE INSTALLATION

VIEW A

Installing the insulator and sleeve (typical from 1979)

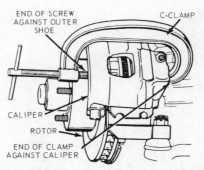

Bottoming the caliper piston on light duty sliding calipers through 1985

Removing sliding caliper support spring and retaining key

end upward out of the anchor plate. Be careful not to stretch or twist the flexible brake hose.

6. Remove the inner shoe and lining assembly from the anchor plate. The inner shoe anti-rattle clip may become displaced at this time and should be repositioned on the anchor plate. Lightly tap on the outer shoe and lining assembly to free it from the caliper.

7. Clean the caliper, anchor plate, and disc assemblies, and inspect them for brake fluid leakage, excessive wear or signs of damage. Replace the pads if either of them are worn to within $\frac{1}{32}''$ (0.8mm) of the rivet heads.

8. To install new pads, use a 4" (101mm) C-clamp and a block of wood $1\frac{3}{4}''$ x 1" and approximately $\frac{3}{4}''$ thick (44mm x 25mm x 19mm) to seat the caliper hydraulic piston in its bore. this must be done in order to provide clearance for the caliper to fit over the rotor when new linings are installed.

9. At this point, the anti-rattle clip should be in its place on the lower inner brake shoe support of the anchor plate with the pigtail of the clip toward the inside of the anchor plate. Position the inner brake shoe and lining assembly on the anchor plate with the pad toward the disc.

10. Install the outer brake shoe with the lower flange ends against the caliper leg abutments and the brake shoe upper flanges over the shoulders on the caliper legs. The shoe is installed correctly when its flanges fit snugly against the machined surfaces of the shoulders.

11. Remove the C-clamps used to seat the caliper piston in its bore. The piston will remain seated.

12. Position the caliper housing lower V-

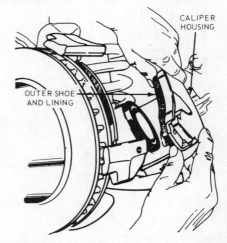

Removing the outer shoe on light duty sliding calipers through 1985

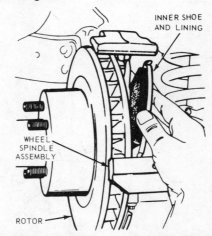

Removing the inner shoe on light duty sliding calipers through 1985

groove on the anchor place lower abutment surface.

13. Pivot the caliper housing upward toward the disc until the outer edge of the piston dust boot is about $\frac{1}{4}''$ (6mm) from the upper edge of the inboard pad.

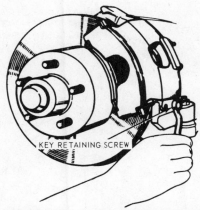

Removing the key retaining screw on light duty sliding calipers through 1985

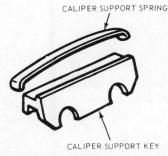

Caliper support spring and key used on light duty sliding calipers through 1985

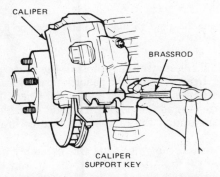

Removing the caliper support spring and key on light duty sliding calipers through 1985

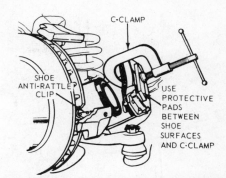

Installing the anti-rattle clip and outer shoe on light duty sliding calipers through 1985

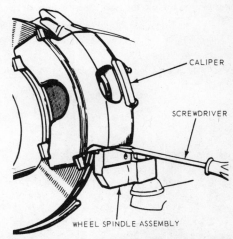

Installing the light duty sliding caliper, through 1985

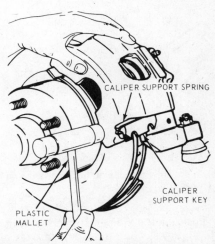

Installing the light duty sliding caliper support spring and key, through 1985

14. In order to prevent pinching of the dust boot between the piston and the inboard pad during installation of the caliper, place a clean piece of thin cardboard between the inboard pad and the lower half of the piston dust boot.

15. Rotate the caliper housing toward the disc until a slight resistance is felt. At this point, pull the cardboard downward toward the disc centerline while rotating the caliper over the disc. Then remove the cardboard and complete the rotation of the caliper down over the disc.

16. Slide the caliper up against the upper abutment surfaces of the anchor plate and center the caliper over the lower anchor plate abutment.

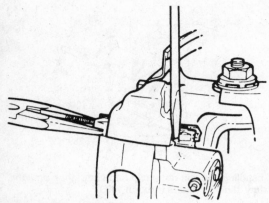

Compressing the pin tabs on 1986–88 light duty calipers

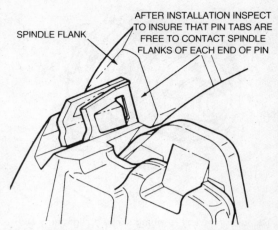

SPINDLE FLANK

AFTER INSTALLATION INSPECT TO INSURE THAT PIN TABS ARE FREE TO CONTACT SPINDLE FLANKS OF EACH END OF PIN

The caliper pin correctly installed on 1986–88 light duty calipers

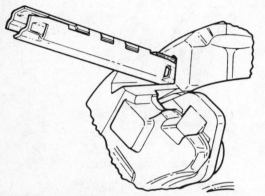

Caliper pin installation on 1986–88 light duty calipers

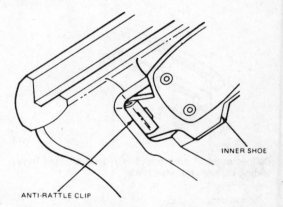

INNER SHOE

ANTI-RATTLE CLIP

Installing the inner shoe and anti-rattle clip on light duty calipers

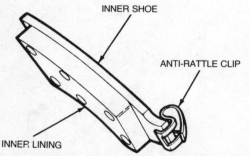

INNER SHOE

ANTI-RATTLE CLIP

INNER LINING

Installing the anti-rattle clip on the inner shoe on light duty calipers

17. Position the caliper support spring and key in the key slot and slide them into the opening between the lower end of the caliper and the lower anchor plate abutment until the key semicircular slot is centered over the retaining screw threaded hole in the anchor plate.

18. Install the key retaining screw and torque to 12-16 ft. lbs.

19. Check the fluid level in the master cylinder and fill as necessary. Install the reservoir cover. Depress the brake pedal several times to properly seat the caliper and pads. Check for leakage around the caliper and pads. Check for leakage around the caliper and flexible brake hose.

20. Install the wheel and tire assembly and torque the nuts to 70-115 ft. lbs. Install the wheel cover.

21. Lower the car. Make sure that you obtain a firm brake pedal and then road test the car for proper brake operation.

1980-88 Ford Single Piston Sliding Caliper Disc Brakes

1. Remove the master cylinder cap, and check the fluid level in the primary (large) reservoir. Remove brake fluid until the reservoir is half full. Discard this fluid.

2. Raise and safely support the vehicle. Remove the wheel and tire assembly from the hub. Be careful to avoid damage to or interference

with the caliper splash shield or bleeder screw fitting.

CAUTION: *Brake shoes contain asbestos, which has been determined to be a cancer causing agent. Never clean the brake surfaces with compressed air! Avoid inhaling any dust from any brake surface! When cleaning brake surfaces, use a commercially available brake cleaning fluid.*

3. Remove the caliper locating pins.

4. Lift the caliper assembly from the integral spindle/anchor plate and rotor.

5. Remove the inner shoe and lining assembly. Inspect both rotor braking surfaces. Minor scoring or building of lining material does not require machining or replacement of the rotor.

6. Suspend the caliper inside the fender housing with a wire hooked through the outer leg hole of the caliper. Be careful not to damage the caliper or stretch the brake hose.

7. Remove and discard the plastic sleeves that are located inside the caliper locating pin insulators. These parts must not be reused.

8. Remove and discard the caliper locating insulator. These parts must not be reused.

9. Use a 4″ (101mm) C-clamp and a block of wood 2¾″ x 1″ and approximately ¾″ thick (70mm x 25mm x 19mm) to seat the caliper hydraulic piston in its bore. This must be done to provide clearance for the caliper assembly to fit over the rotor when installed. Remove the C-clamp from the caliper (the caliper piston will remain seated in its bore).

10. Install new locating pin insulators and plastic sleeves in the caliper housing. Do not use a sharp edge tool to insert the insulators in the caliper housing. Check to see if both insulator flanges straddle the housing holes and if the plastic sleeves are bottomed in the insulators as well as slipped under the upper lip.

11. Install the correct inner shoe and lining assembly in the caliper piston. All vehicles have a separate anti-rattle clip and insulator that must be installed to the inner shoe and lining prior to their assembly to the caliper. The inner shoes are marked LH or RH and must be installed in the proper caliper. Also, care should be taken not to bend the anti-rattle clips too far in the piston or distortion and rattles can result.

12. Install the correct outer brake shoe and lining assembly (RH/LH), making sure that the clip and/or buttons located on the shoe are properly seated. The outer shoe can be identified as right hand or left hand by the war indicator which must always be installed toward the front of the vehicle or by a LH or RH mark. Refill the master cylinder.

13. Install the wheel and tire assembly, and tighten the wheel attaching nuts to 80-105 ft. lbs.

14. Pump the brake pedal prior to moving the vehicle to position the brake linings.

15. Road test the vehicle.

Caliper
REMOVAL, OVERHAUL, AND INSTALLATION
Floating Caliper

1. Raise the vehicle on a hoist and remove the front wheels.

2. Disconnect and plug the brake line.

3. Remove the lockwires from the two caliper mounting bolts and remove the bolt. Lift the caliper off the disc.

4. Remove and discard the locating pin insulators. Replace all rubber parts at reassembly.

5. Remove the retaining clips with a screw-

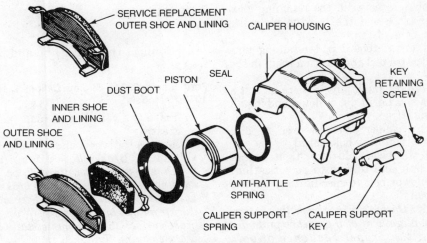

Light duty sliding caliper

driver and slide the outboard pad and retaining pins out of the caliper. Remove the inboard pad. Loosen the bleed screw and drain the brake fluid.

6. Remove the two small bolts and caliper stabilizers.

7. Remove the inboard pad retaining clips and bolts.

8. Clean and inspect all parts, and reinstall on the anchor plate. Do not tighten the stabilizer bolts at this time.

9. Remove the piston by applying compressed air to the fluid inlet hole. use care to prevent the piston from popping out of control.

CAUTION: *Do not attempt to catch the piston with the hand. Use folded towels to cushion it.*

10. Remove the piston boot. Inspect the piston for scoring, pitting or corrosion. The piston must be replaced if there is any visible damage or wear.

11. Remove the piston seal from the cylinder bore. Do not use any metal tools for this operation.

12. Clean the caliper with fresh brake fluid. Inspect the cylinder bore for damage or ear. Light defects can be removed by rotating crocus cloth around the bore. (do not use any other type of abrasive).

13. Lubricate all new rubber pars in brake fluid. Install the piston seal in the cylinder groove. Install the boot into its piston groove.

14. Install the piston, open end out, into the bore while working the boot around the outside of the piston. Make sure that the boot lip is seated in the piston groove.

15. Slide the anchor plate assembly onto the caliper housing and reinstall the locating pins. Tighten the pins to specification. Tighten the stabilizer anchor plate bolts.

16. Slide the inboard pad into the caliper so that the tabs are between the retaining clips and anchor plate and the backing plate lies flush against the piston.

17. Insert the outboard pad retaining pins into the outboard pad and position them in the caliper.

18. Hold the retaining pins in place (one at a time) with a short drift pin or dowel and install the retaining clips.

19. Slide the caliper assembly over the disc and align the mounting bolt holes.

20. Install the lower bolt finger-tight. Install the upper bolt and torque to specification. Torque the lower bolt to specification. Safety-wire both bolts.

CAUTION: *Do not deviate from this procedure. The alignment of the anchor plate depends on the proper sequence of bolt installation.*

Removing piston using compressed air

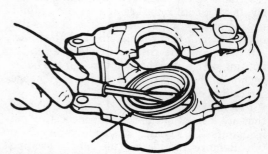

Removing the dust seal

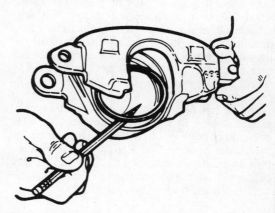

Removing the O-ring

21. Connect the brake line and bleed the brakes.

Ford Single Piston Sliding Caliper Disc Brakes 1973-79 Models

1. Raise the vehicle and place jackstands underneath.

2. Remove the wheel and tire assembly.

CAUTION: *Brake shoes contain asbestos, which has been determined to be a cancer causing agent. Never clean the brake surfaces with compressed air! Avoid inhaling any dust from any brake surface! When cleaning brake surfaces, use a commercially available brake cleaning fluid.*

3. Disconnect the flexible brake hose from

the caliper. To disconnect the hose, loosen the tube fitting which connects the end of the hose to the brake tube at its bracket on the frame. Remove the horseshoe clip from the hose and bracket, disengage the hose, and plug the end. Then unscrew the entire hose assembly from the caliper.

4. Remove the key retaining screw from the caliper retaining key.

5. Slide the retaining key and support spring either inward or outward from the anchor plate. To remove the key and spring, a hammer and drift may be used, taking care not to damage the key in the process.

6. Lift the caliper assembly away from the anchor plate by pushing the caliper downward against the anchor plate and rotating the upper end upward out of the anchor plate.

7. Remove the piston by applying compressed air to the fluid inlet port with a rubber tipped nozzle. Place a towel or thick cloth over the piston before applying air pressure to prevent damage to the piston. If the piston is seized in the bore and cannot be forced from the caliper, lightly tap around the outside of the caliper while applying air pressure.

CAUTION: *Do not attempt to catch the piston with your hand. Cushion with a shop towel.*

8. Remove the dust boot from the caliper assembly.

9. Remove the piston seal from the cylinder and discard it.

10. Clean all metal parts with isopropyl alcohol or a suitable non-petroleum solvent and dry them with compressed air. Be sure there is not foreign material in the bore or component parts. Inspect the piston and bore for excessive wear or damage. Replace the piston if it is pitted, scored, or if the chrome plating is wearing off.

11. Lubricate all new rubber parts in brake fluid. Install the piston seal in the cylinder groove, being careful not to twist it. Install the dust boot by setting the flange squarely in the outer groove of the bore.

12. Coat the piston with brake fluid and install it in the bore. Work the dust boot around the outside of the piston, making sure that the boot lip is seated in the piston groove.

13. Install the caliper as outlined in Steps 12-18 in the sliding caliper Shoe and Lining Replacement procedure.

14. Thread the flexible brake hose and gasket onto the caliper fitting. Torque the fitting to 12-20 ft. lbs. Place the upper end of the flexible brake hose in its bracket and install the horseshoe clip. Remove the plug from the brake tube and connect the tube to the hose. Torque the tube fitting nut to 10-15 ft. lbs.

15. Bleed the brake system as outlined in the Brake Bleeding section.

16. Check the fluid level in the master cylinder and fill as necessary. Install the reservoir cover. Depress the brake pedal several times to properly seat the caliper and shoes. Check for leakage around the caliper and the flexible brake hose.

17. Install the wheel and tire assembly and torque the nuts to 70-115 ft. lbs. Install the wheel cover.

18. Lower the car. Make sure that you obtain a firm brake pedal and then road test the car for proper brake operation.

Ford Single Piston Sliding Caliper Disc Brakes 1980 and Later

CAUTION: *Brake shoes contain asbestos, which has been determined to be a cancer causing agent. Never clean the brake surfaces with compressed air! Avoid inhaling any dust from any brake surface! When cleaning brake surfaces, use a commercially available brake cleaning fluid.*

1. Remove the caliper assembly from the vehicle as outlined in Pad Replacement. Disconnect the brake hose. Place a cloth over the piston before applying air pressure to prevent damage to the piston.

2. Apply air pressure to the fluid port in the caliper with a rubber tipped nozzle to remove the piston. On Continental and Mark VII models, use layers of shop towels to cushion possible impact of the phenolic piston against the caliper iron when piston comes out of the piston bore. Do not use a screwdriver or similar tool to pry piston out of the bore, damage to the phenolic piston may result. If the piston is seized and cannot be forced from the caliper, tap lightly around the piston while applying air pressure. Use care because the piston can develop considerable force from pressure buildup.

3. Remove the dust boot from the caliper assembly.

4. Remove the rubber piston seal from the cylinder, and discard it.

5. Clean all metal parts and phenolic piston with isopropyl alcohol. Then, clean out and dry the grooves and passageways with compressed air. Make suer the caliper bore and component parts are thoroughly clean.

6. Check the cylinder bore and piston for damage or excessive wear. Replace the piston if it is pitted, scored, corroded, or the plating is worn off. Do not replace phenolic piston cosmetic surface irregularities or small chips between the piston boot groove and shoe face.

7. Apply a film of clean brake fluid to the new caliper piston seal, and install it in the cylinder

bore. Be sure the seal does not become twisted but is firmly seated in the groove.

8. Install a new dust boot by seating the flange squarely in the outer groove of the caliper bore.

9. Coat the piston with brake fluid, and install the piston in the cylinder bore. Be sure to use a wood block or other flat stock when installing the piston back into the piston bore. Never apply C-clamp directly to a phenolic piston, and be sure pistons are not cocked. Spread the dust boot over the piston as it is installed. Seat the dust boot in the piston groove.

10. Install the caliper over the rotor as outlined.

Brake Disc (Rotor)

REMOVAL AND INSTALLATION

With Floating Caliper

1. Raise the front of the car and support it with jack stands.

NOTE: *In order to remove the rotor, the caliper and anchor plate must be removed from the car.*

2. Remove the front wheels.

3. Loosen, but do not remove, the upper anchor plate attaching bolt with a ¾″ socket.

4. Using a ⅝″ socket, remove the lower anchor plate attaching bolt.

NOTE: *When the caliper is removed from the car it must be wired out of the way of the rotor. Also, the brake pads will fall out of the caliper if they are not held in place when the caliper is removed. You will have to insert a small piece of wood or a folded piece of heavy cardboard between the shoes to hold them in place. Have a piece of wire and a piece of wood handy before you start the next step.*

5. Hold the caliper in place and remove the upper anchor plate attaching bolt.

6. Slide the caliper and anchor plate assembly off the rotor, inserting the block of wood between the brake pads as they become visible above the rotor.

7. When the anchor plate is clear of the rotor, wire it out of the way.

8. Remove the dust cap from the rotor hub by either prying it off with a screwdriver or pulling it off with a pair of channel-lock pliers.

9. Remove the cotter pin and nut lock from the spindle.

10. Loosen the bearing adjusting nut until it is at the end of the spindle.

11. Grasp the rotor with a rag and pull it outward, push it inward.

12. Remove the adjusting nut and the outer bearing.

13. Remove the rotor from the spindle.

14. Pack the inside of the rotor hub with a

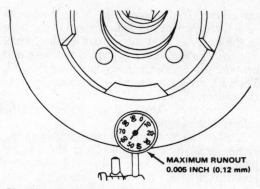

MAXIMUM RUNOUT
0.005 INCH (0.12 mm)

Checking the rotor lateral runout

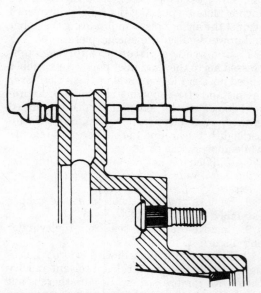

Measuring the rotor thickness with a micrometer

moderate amount of grease, between the bearing cups. Do not overload the hub with grease.

15. Apply a small amount of grease to the spindle.

16. Coat the lip of a new grease seal with a small amount of grease and position it on the rotor.

17. Position the rotor on the spindle.

18. Install the outer bearing and washer on the spindle, inside the rotor hub.

19. Install the bearing adjusting nut and tighten it to 17-25 inch lbs. while spinning the rotor. This will seat the bearing.

20. Back off the adjusting nut one half turn.

21. Tighten the adjusting nut to 10-15 in. lbs.

22. Install the nut lock on the adjusting nut so two of the slots align with the holes in the spindle.

23. Install a new cotter pin and bend the ends back so that they will not interfere with the dust cap.

24. Install the dust cap.

25. Install the front tires.

With Sliding Caliper

1. Raise and safely support the vehicle. Remove the wheel.

CAUTION: *Brake shoes contain asbestos, which has been determined to be a cancer causing agent. Never clean the brake surfaces with compressed air! Avoid inhaling any dust from any brake surface! When cleaning brake surfaces, use a commercially available brake cleaning fluid.*

2. Remove the caliper. Slide the caliper assembly away from the disc and suspend it with a wire loop. It is not necessary to disconnect the brake line.

3. Remove the grease cap from the hub. Remove the cotter pin, nut lock, adjusting nut, and flat washer from the spindle.

4. Remove the outer wheel bearing cone and roller assembly from the hub.

5. Remove the hut and disc assembly from the spindle.

INSTALLATION

WARNING: *If a new disc is being installed, remove the protective coating with carburetor degreaser. If the original disc is being installed, make sure that the grease in the hub is clean and adequate, that the inner bearing and grease retainer are lubricated and in good condition, and that the disc breaking surfaces are clean.*

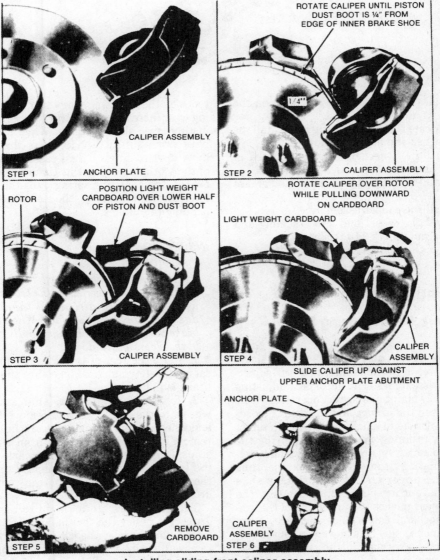

Installing sliding front caliper assembly

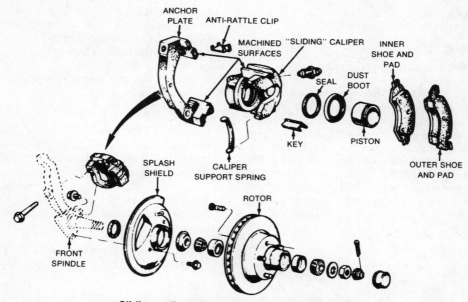

Sliding caliper front disc brake disassembled

1. Install the hub and disc assembly on the spindle.

2. Lubricate the outer bearing and install the thrust washer and adjusting nut.

3. Adjust the wheel bearing as outlined in the Wheel Bearing Adjustment section.

4. Install the nut lock, cotter pin, and grease cap.

5. Install the caliper assembly.

6. Install the wheel and tire assembly and torque the nuts to 75-110 ft. lbs.

7. Lower the vehicle and road test it.

REAR DRUM BRAKES

Duo-Servo Self-Adjusting Drum Brakes

Drum brakes on all Ford cars employ single anchor, internally expanding, and self-adjusting brake assemblies. The automatic adjusting continuously maintains correct operating clearance between the linings and the drums by adjusting the brake in small increments in direct proportion to lining wear. When applying the brakes while backing up, the linings tend to follow the rotating drum counterclockwise, thus forcing the upper end of the primary shoe against the anchor pin. Simultaneously, the wheel cylinder pushes the upper end of the secondary shoe and cable guide outward, away from the anchor pin. This movement of the secondary shoe causes the cable to pull the adjusting lever upward and against the end of the

tooth on the adjusting screw star wheel. As lining wear increases, the upward travel of the adjusting lever also increases. When the linings have worn sufficiently to allow the lever to move upward far enough, it passes over the end of the tooth and engages it. Upon release of the brakes, the adjusting spring pulls the adjuster level downward, turning the star wheel and expanding the brakes.

INSPECTION

CAUTION: *Brake shoes contain asbestos, which has been determined to be a cancer causing agent. Never clean the brake surfaces with compressed air! Avoid inhaling any dust from any brake surface! When cleaning brake surfaces, use a commercially available brake cleaning fluid.*

1. Raise the rear of the car and support the car with safety stands. Make sure the parking brake is not on.

2. Remove the lug nuts that attach the wheels to the axle shaft and remove the tires and wheels from the car. Using a pair of pliers, remove the Tinnerman nuts from the wheel studs. Pull the brake drum of the axle shaft. If the brakes are adjusted too tightly to remove the drum, see Step 3. If you can remove the drum, see Step 4.

3. If the brakes are too tight to remove the drum, get under the car (make sure you have safety stands under the car to support it) and remove the rubber plug from the bottom of the brake backing plate. Shine a flashlight into the

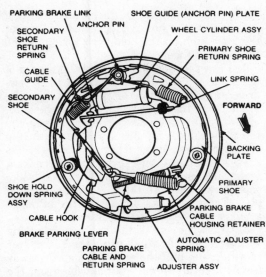

9 inch drum brake

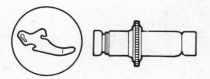

E-250-350 REAR; F-250,F-350

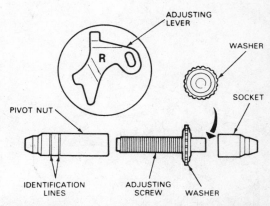

Adjusting screw and lever for self-adjusting brakes

slot in the plate. You will see the top of the adjusting screw star wheel and the adjusting lever for the automatic brake adjusting mechanism. To back off on the adjusting screw, you must first inert a small, thin screwdriver or a piece of firm wire (coat hanger wire) into the adjusting slot and push the adjusting lever away from the adjusting screw. Then, insert a brake adjusting spoon into the slot and engage the top of the star wheel. Lift up on the bottom of the adjusting spoon to force the adjusting screw star wheel downward. Repeat this operation until

the brake drum is free of the brake shoes and can be pulled off.

4. Clean the brake shoes and the inside of the brake drum. There must be at least $\frac{1}{16}''$ (1.6mm) of brake lining above the heads of the brake shoe attaching rivets. The lining should not be cracked or contaminated with grease or brake fluid. If there is grease or brake fluid on the lining it must be replaced and the source of the leak must be found and corrected. Brake fluid on the lining means leaking wheel cylinders. Grease on the brake lining means a leaking grease retainer (front wheels) or axle seal (rear brakes). If the lining is slightly glazed but otherwise in good condition, it can be cleaned up with medium sandpaper. Lift up the bottom of the wheel cylinder boots and inspect the ends of the wheel cylinders. A small amount of fluid in the end of the cylinder should be considered normal. If fluid runs out of the cylinder when the boots are lifted, however, the wheel cylinder must be rebuilt or replaced. Examine the inside of the brake drum; it should have a smooth, dull finish. If excessive brake shoe wear caused grooves to wear in the drum it must be machined or replaced. If the inside of the drum is slightly glazed, but otherwise good, it can be cleaned up with medium sandpaper.

5. If no repairs are required, install the drum and wheel. If the brake adjustment was changed to remove the drum, adjust the brakes until the drum will just fit over the brakes. After the wheel is installed it will be necessary to complete the adjustment. See Brake Adjustment later in this chapter.

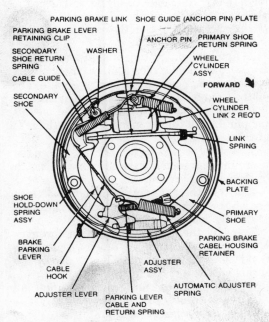

10 inch drum brake

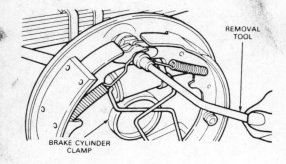

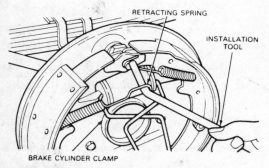

Brake spring replacement

Brake Shoes

REMOVAL

CAUTION: *Brake shoes contain asbestos, which has been determined to be a cancer causing agent. Never clean the brake surfaces with compressed air! Avoid inhaling any dust from any brake surface! When cleaning brake surfaces, use a commercially available brake cleaning fluid.*

WARNING: *If you are not thoroughly familiar with the procedures involved in brake replacement, only disassembly and assemble one side at a time, leaving the other wheel intact as a reference.*

1. Remove the brake drum. See the inspection procedure.

2. Place the hollow end of the brake spring service tool (available at auto parts stores) on the brake shoe anchor pin and twist it to disengage one of the brake retracting springs. Repeat this operation to remove the other spring.

CAUTION: *Be careful that the springs do not slip off the tool during removal, as they could cause personal injury.*

3. Reach behind the brake backing plate and place a finger on the end of one of the brake holddown spring mounting pins. Using a pair of pliers, grasp the washer on the top of the holddown spring that corresponds to the pin that you are holding. Push down on the pliers and turn them 90 degrees to align the slot in the washer with the head on the spring mounting pin. Remove the spring and washer and repeat this operation on the holddown spring on the other brake shoe.

4. Place the tip of a screwdriver on the top of the brake adjusting screw and move the screwdriver upward to lift up on the brake adjusting lever. When there is enough slack in the automatic adjuster cable, disconnect the loop on the top of the cable from the anchor. Grasp the top of each brake shoe and move it outward to disengage it from the wheel cylinder (and parking brake link on rear wheels). When the brake shoes are clear, lift them from the backing plate. Twist the shoes slightly and the automatic adjuster assembly will disassemble itself.

5. Grasp the end of the brake cable spring with a pair of pliers and, using the brake lever as a fulcrum, pull the end of the spring away from the lever. Disengage the cable from the brake lever.

INSTALLATION

1. The brake cable must be connected to the secondary brake shoe before the shoe is installed on the backing plate. To do this, first transfer the parking brake lever from the old secondary shoe to the new one. This is accomplished by spreading the bottom of the horseshoe clip and disengaging the lever. Position the lever on the new secondary shoe and install the spring washer and the horseshoe clip. Close the bottom of the clip after installing it. Grasp the metal tip of the parking brake cable with a pair of pliers. Position a pair of side cutter pliers on the end of the cable coil spring, and using the plier as a fulcrum, pull the coil spring back with the side cutters. Position the cable in the parking brake lever.

2. Apply a light coating of high temperature grease to the brake shoe contact points on the backing plate. Position the primary brake shoe on the front of the backing plate and install the holddown spring and washer over the mounting pin. Install the secondary shoe on the rear of the backing plate.

3. Install the parking brake link between the notch in the primary brake shoe and the notch in the parking brake lever.

4. Install the automatic adjuster cable loop end on the anchor pin. Make sure the crimped side of the loop faces the backing plate.

5. Install the return spring in the primary brake shoe and, using the tapered end of the brake spring service tool, slide the top of the spring onto the anchor pin.

CAUTION: *Be careful to make sure that the spring does not slip off the tool during installation, as it could cause injury.*

6. Install the automatic adjuster cable guide

in the secondary brake shoe, making sure the flared hole in the cable guide is inside the hole in the brake shoe. Fit the cable into the groove in the top of the cable guide.

7. Install the secondary shoe return spring through the hole in the cable guide and the brake shoe. Using the brake spring tool, slide the top of the spring onto the anchor pin.

8. Clean the threads on the adjusting screw and apply a light coating of high temperature grease to the threads. Screw the adjuster closed, then open it ½ turn.

9. Install the adjusting screw between the brake shoes with the star wheel nearest to the secondary shoe. Make sure the star wheel is in a position that is accessible from the adjusting slot in the backing plate.

10. Install the short hooked end of the automatic adjuster spring in the proper hole in the primary brake shoe.

11. Connect the hooked end of the automatic adjuster cable and the free end of the automatic adjuster spring in the slot in the top of the automatic adjuster lever.

12. Pull the automatic adjuster lever (the lever will pull the cable and spring with it) downward and to the left and engage the pivot hook of the lever in the hole in the secondary brake shoe.

13. Check the entire brake assembly to make sure that everything is installed properly. Make sure that the shoes engage the wheel cylinder properly and are flush on the anchor pin. Make sure that the automatic adjuster cable is flush on the anchor pin and in the slot on the back of the cable guide. Make sure that the adjusting lever rests on the adjusting screw star wheel. Pull upward on the adjusting cable until the adjusting lever is free of the star wheel, then release the cable. The adjusting lever should snap back into place on the adjusting screw star wheel and turn the wheel one tooth.

14. Expand the brake adjusting screw until the brake drum will just fit over the brake shoes.

15. Install the wheel and drum and adjust the brakes.

Wheel Cylinders

REPLACEMENT

1. Remove the brake shoes.

2. On rear brakes, loosen the brake line on the rear of the cylinder but do not pull the line away from the cylinder or it may bend.

3. On front brakes, disconnect the metal brake line from the rubber brake hose where they join in the wheel well. Pull off the horseshoe clip that attaches the rubber brake hose to the underbody of the car. Loosen the hose at the cylinder, then turn the whole brake hose to remove it from the wheel cylinder.

4. Remove the bolts and lockwashers that attach the wheel cylinder to the backing plate and remove the cylinder.

5. Position the new wheel cylinder on the backing plate and install the cylinder attaching bolts and lockwashers.

6. Attach the metal brake line or rubber hose by reversing the procedure given in Steps 2 or 3.

7. Install the brakes.

OVERHAUL

Since the travel of the pistons in the wheel cylinder changes when new brakes shoes are installed, it is possible for previously good wheel cylinders to start leaking after new brakes are installed, Therefore, to save yourself the expense of having to replace new brakes that become saturated with brake fluid and the aggravation of having to take everything apart again, it is strongly recommended that wheel cylinders be rebuilt every time new brake shoes are installed. This is especially true on high mileage cars.

1. Remove the brakes.

CAUTION: *Brake shoes contain asbestos, which has been determined to be a cancer causing agent. Never clean the brake surfaces with compressed air! Avoid inhaling any dust from any brake surface! When cleaning brake surfaces, use a commercially available brake cleaning fluid.*

2. Place a bucket or old newspapers under

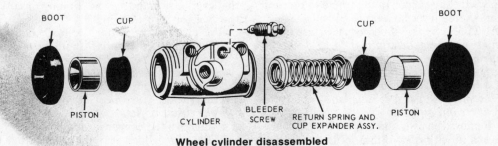

Wheel cylinder disassembled

the brake backing plate to catch the brake fluid that will run out of the wheel cylinder.

3. Remove the boots from the ends of the wheel cylinders.

4. Push one piston toward the center of the cylinder to force the opposite piston and cup out of the other end of the cylinder. Reach in the open end of the cylinder and push the spring cup, and piston out of the cylinder.

5. Remove the bleeder screw from the rear of the cylinder, on the back of the backing plate.

6. Inspect the inside of the wheel cylinder. If it is scored in any way, the cylinder must be honed with a wheel cylinder hone or fine emery paper, and finished with crocus cloth if emery paper is used. If the inside of the cylinder is excessively worn, the cylinder will have to be replaced, as only 0.003″ (0.0762mm) of material can be removed from the cylinder walls. When honing or cleaning the wheel cylinders, keep a small amount of brake fluid in the cylinder to serve as a lubricant.

7. Clean any foreign matter from the pistons. The sides of the pistons must be smooth for the wheel cylinders to operate properly.

8. Clean the cylinder bore with alcohol and a lint-free rag. Pull the rag through the bore several times to remove all foreign matter and dry the cylinder.

9. Install the bleeder screw and the return spring in the cylinder.

10. Coat new cylinder cups with new brake fluid and install them in the cylinder. Make sure that they are square in the bore or they will leak.

11. Install the pistons in the cylinder after coating them with new brake fluid.

12. Coat the insides of the boots with new brake fluid and install them on the cylinder. Install the brakes.

REAR DISC BRAKES

Disc Brake Pads

REMOVAL AND INSTALLATION

1. Remove the caliper. In this case, however, it is not necessary to disconnect the brake line. Simply wire the caliper to the frame to prevent the brake line from breaking.

CAUTION: *Brake shoes contain asbestos, which has been determined to be a cancer causing agent. Never clean the brake surfaces with compressed air! Avoid inhaling any dust from any brake surface! When cleaning brake surfaces, use a commercially available brake cleaning fluid.*

2. Remove the pads and inspect them. If they are worn to within ⅛″ (3mm) of the shoe sur-

TOOL—T75P-2588-B

Bottoming the caliper piston

face, they must be replace. Do not replace pads on just one side of the car. Uneven braking will result.

3. To install new pads, remove the disc and install the caliper without the pads. Use only the key to retain the caliper.

4. Seat the special tool firmly against the piston by holding the shaft and rotating the tool handle.

5. Loosen the handle ¼ turn. Hold the handle and rotate the tool shaft clockwise until the caliper piston bottoms in the bore. It will continue to turn after it bottoms.

6. Rotate the handle until the piston is firmly seated.

7. Remove the caliper and install the disc.

8. Place the new inner brake pad on the anchor plate. Place the new outer pad in the caliper.

9. Reinstall the caliper according to the directions given earlier.

Caliper

REMOVAL AND INSTALLATION

1. Raise the vehicle, and install safety stands. Block both front wheels if a jack is used.

2. Remove the wheel and tire assembly from the axle. Use care to avoid damage or interference with the splash shield.

3. Disconnect the parking brake cable from the lever. Use care to avoid kinking or cutting the cable or return spring.

CAUTION: *Brake shoes contain asbestos, which has been determined to be a cancer causing agent. Never clean the brake surfaces with compressed air! Avoid inhaling any dust from any brake surface! When cleaning brake surfaces, use a commercially available brake cleaning fluid.*

4. Remove the caliper locating pins.

5. Lift the caliper assembly away from the

anchor plate by pushing the caliper upward toward the anchor plate, and then rotate the lower end of the anchor plate.

6. If insufficient clearance between the caliper and shoe and lining assemblies prevents removal of the caliper, it is necessary to loosen the caliper end retainer ½ turn, maximum, to allow the piston to be forced back into its bore. To loosen the end retainer, remove the parking brake lever, then mark or scribe the end retainer and caliper housing to be sure that the end retainer is not loosened more than ½ turn. Force the piston back in its bore, then remove the caliper.

CAUTION: *If the retainer must be loosened more than ½ turn, the seal between the thrust screw and the housing may be broken, and brake fluid may leak into the parking brake mechanism chamber. In this case, the end retainer must be removed, and the internal parts cleaned and lubricated; refer to Caliper Overhaul.*

7. Remove the outer shoe and lining assembly from the anchor plate. mark shoe for identification if it is to be reinstalled.

8. Remove the two rotor retainer nuts and the rotor from the axle shaft.

9. Remove the inner brake shoe and lining assembly from the anchor plate. Mark shoe for identification if it is to be reinstalled.

10. Remove anti-rattle clip from anchor plate.

11. Remove the flexible hose from the caliper

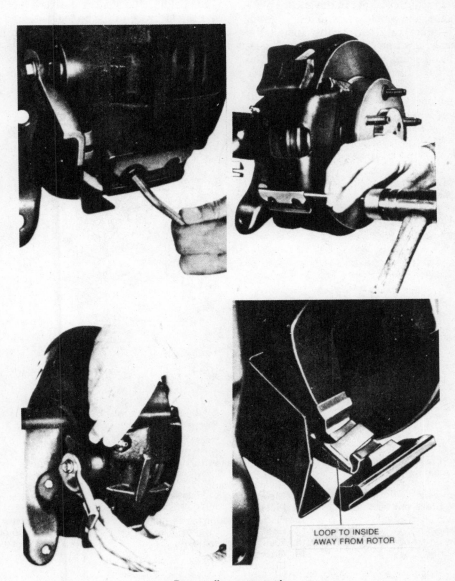

LOOP TO INSIDE
AWAY FROM ROTOR

Rear caliper removal

by removing the hollow retaining bolt that connects the hose fitting to the caliper.

12. Clean the caliper, anchor plate, and rotor assemblies and inspect for signs of brake fluid leakage, excessive wear, or damage. The caliper must be inspected for leakage both in the piston boot area and at the operating shaft seal area. Lightly sand or wire brush any rust or corrosion from the caliper and anchor plate sliding surfaces as well as the outer and inner brake shoe abutment surfaces. Inspect the brake shoes for wear. If either lining is worn to within ⅛″ (3mm) of the shoe surface, both shoe and lining assemblies must be replaced using the shoe and lining removal procedures.

13. If the end retainer has been loosened only ½ turn, reinstall the caliper in the anchor plate without shoe and lining assemblies. Tighten the end retainer to 75-96 ft. lbs. Install the parking brake lever on its keyed spline. The lever arm must point down and rearward. The parking brake cable will then pass freely under

the axle. Tighten the retainer screw to 16-22 ft. lbs. The parking brake lever must rotate freely after tightening the retainer screw. Remove the caliper from the anchor plate.

14. If new shoe and lining assemblies are to be installed, the piston must be screwed back into the caliper bore, using Tool T75P-2588-B or equivalent to provide installation clearance. This tool requires a slight modification for use on Continental rear disc brakes. This modification will not prevent using the tool on prior year applications. New tools purchased from the Special Service Tool catalog under the T75P-2588-B number will already be modified. Remove the rotor, and install the caliper, less shoe and lining assemblies, in the anchor plate. While holding the shaft, rotate the tool handle counterclockwise until the tool is seated firmly against the piston. Now, loosen the handle about ¼ turn. While holding the handle, rotate the tool shaft clockwise until the piston is fully bottomed in its bore; the piston will continue to

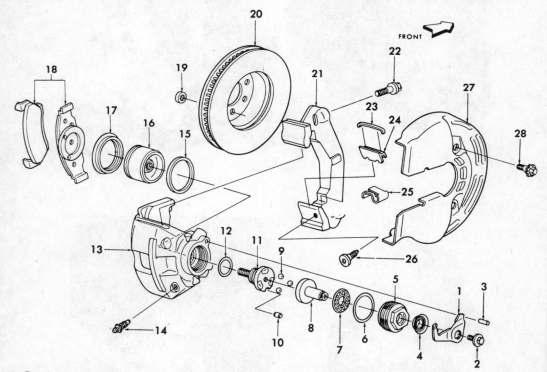

1. Parking brake actuating lever	11. Parking brake thrust screw	21. Anchor plate
2. Lever retaining bolt	12. Seal	22. Retaining bolt
3. Pin	13. Caliper housing	23. Caliper support spring
4. Retainer seal	14. Bleeder screw	24. Caliper retaining key
5. Parking brake end retainer	15. Piston seal	25. Anti-rattle clip
6. Seal	16. Piston and adjuster assembly	26. Retaining screw
7. Thrust bearing	17. Boot	27. Anti-splash shield
8. Parking brake operating shaft	18. Brake pad assemblies	28. Retaining bolt
9. Ball bearing	19. Grommet	
10. Pin	20. Disc rotor	

Rear sliding caliper assembly

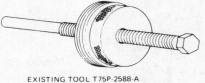

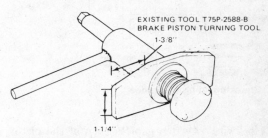

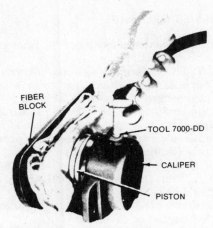

Removing the piston from the caliper

turn even after it becomes bottomed. When there is not further inward movement of the piston and the tool handle is rotated until there is a firm seating force, the piston is bottomed. Remove the tool and the caliper from the anchor plate.

15. Lubricate anchor plate sliding ways with lithium or silicone grease. Use only specified grease because a lower temperature type of lubricant may melt and contaminate the brake pads. Use care to prevent any lubricant from getting on the braking surface.

16. Install the anti-rattle clip on the lower rail of the anchor plate.

17. Install inner brake shoe and lining assembly on the anchor plate with the lining toward the rotor.

18. Be sure shoes are installed in their original positions as marked for identification before removal.

19. Install rotor and two retainer nuts.

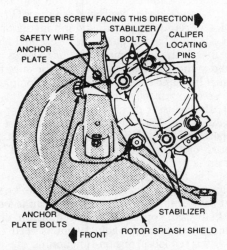

Floating caliper installed—rear view

EXISTING TOOL T75P-2588-A
DISC BRAKE PISTON REMOVER
(DOES NOT REQUIRE MODIFICATION)

EXISTING TOOL T75P-2588-B
BRAKE PISTON TURNING TOOL

MODIFY TOOL BY REMOVING
METAL AS INDICATED BY
DOTTED LINES

Special tools needed for servicing the rear disc brake caliper

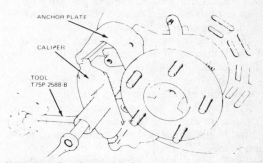

Adjusting the piston depth

20. Install the correct hand outer brake shoe and lining assembly on the anchor plate with the lining toward the rotor and wear indicator toward the upper portion of the brake.

21. Install the flexible hose by placing a new washer on each side of the fitting outlet and inserting the attaching bolt through the washers and fitting. Tighten to 20-30 ft. lbs.

22. Position the upper tab of the caliper housing on the anchor plate upper abutment surface.

23. Rotate the caliper housing until it is completely over the rotor. Use care so that the piston dust boot is not damaged.

24. Piston Position Adjustment: Pull the caliper outboard until the inner shoe and lining is firmly seated against the rotor, and measure the clearance between the outer shoe and caliper. The clearance must be $1/32$-$3/32$" (0.8-2.4mm). If it is not, remove the caliper, then readjust the piston to obtain required gap. Follow the procedure given in Step 13, and rotate the shaft counterclockwise to narrow gap and

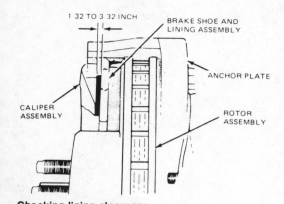

1 32 TO 3 32 INCH

BRAKE SHOE AND LINING ASSEMBLY

ANCHOR PLATE

CALIPER ASSEMBLY

ROTOR ASSEMBLY

Checking lining clearance

clockwise to widen gap (¼ turn of the piston move it approximately ⅟₁₆" [1.6mm]).

WARNING: *A clearance greater than ³⁄₃₂" (2.4mm) may allow the adjuster to be pulled out of the piston when the service brake is applied. This will cause the parking brake mechanism to fail to adjust. It is then necessary to replace the piston/adjuster assembly following the procedures under Overhaul.*

25. Lubricate locating pins and inside of insulator with silicone grease.

26. Add one drop of Loctite® E0AC-19554-A or equivalent to locating pin threads.

27. Install the locating pins through caliper insulators and into the anchor plate; the pins must be hand inserted and hand started. Tighten to 29-37 ft. lbs.

28. Connect the parking brake cable to the lever on the caliper.

29. Bleed the brake system. Replace rubber bleed screw cap after bleeding.

30. Fill the master cylinder as required to within ⅛" (3mm) of the top of the reservoir.

31. Caliper Adjustment: With the engine running, pump the service brake lightly (approximately 14 lbs. pedal effort) about 40 times. Allow at least one second between pedal applications. As an alternative, with the engine Off, pump the service brake lightly (approximately 87 lbs. pedal effort) about 30 times. Now check the parking brake for excessive travel or very light effort. In either case, repeat pumping the service brake, or if necessary, check the parking brake cable for proper tension. The caliper levers must return to the Off position when the parking brake is released.

32. Install the wheel and tire assembly. Tighten the wheel lug nuts. Install the wheel cover. Remove the safety stands, and lower the vehicle.

33. Be sure a firm brake pedal application is obtained, and then road test for proper brake operation, including parking brakes.

CALIPER OVERHAUL

1. Remove the caliper assembly from the vehicle as outlined.

CAUTION: *Brake shoes contain asbestos, which has been determined to be a cancer causing agent. Never clean the brake surfaces with compressed air! Avoid inhaling any dust from any brake surface! When cleaning brake surfaces, use a commercially available brake cleaning fluid.*

2. Remove the caliper and retainer.

3. Lift out the operating shaft, thrust bearing, and balls.

4. Remove the thrust screw anti-rotation pin with a magnet or tweezers.

NOTE: *Some anti-rotation pins may be difficult to remove with a magnet or tweezers. In that case, use the following procedure.*

a. Adjust the piston out from the caliper bore using the modified piston adjusting tool. The piston should protrude from the housing at least 1" (25mm).

b. Push the piston back into the caliper housing with the adjusting tool. With the tool in position on the caliper, hold the tool shaft in place, and rotate the handle counterclockwise until the thrust screw clears the anti-rotation pin. Remove the thrust screw and the anti-rotation pin.

5. Remove the thrust screw by rotating it counterclockwise with a ¼" allen wrench.

6. Remove the piston adjuster assembly by installing Tool T75P-2588-A or equivalent through the back of the caliper housing and pushing the piston out.

WARNING: *Use care not to damage the polished surface in the thrust screw bore, and do not press or attempt to move the adjuster can. It is a press fit in the piston!*

7. Remove and discard the piston seal, boot, thrust screw C-ring seal, end retainer O-ring seal, end retainer lip seal, and pin insulators.

8. Clean all metal parts with isopropyl alcohol. use clean, dry, compressed air to clean out and dry the grooves and passages. Be sure the caliper bore and component parts are completely free of any foreign material.

9. Inspect the caliper bores for damage or excessive wear. The thrust screw bore must be smooth and free of pits. If the piston is pitted, scored, or the chrome plating is worn off, replace the piston/adjuster assembly.

10. The adjuster can must be bottomed in the piston to be properly seated and provide consistent brake function. If the adjuster can is loose in the piston, appears high in the piston, or is damaged, or if brake adjustment is regularly too tight, too loose, or non-functioning, replace the piston/adjuster assembly.

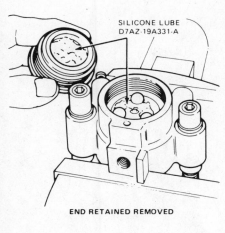

END RETAINED REMOVED

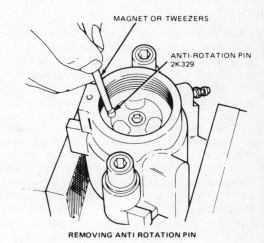

REMOVING ANTI ROTATION PIN

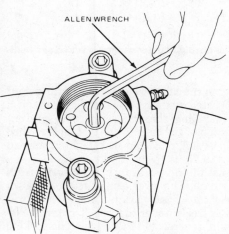

REMOVING THRUST SCREW

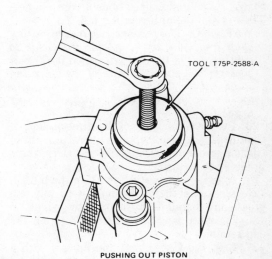

PUSHING OUT PISTON

Servicing the caliper assembly

WARNING: *Do not attempt to service the adjuster at any time. When service is necessary replace the piston/adjuster assembly.*

11. Check adjuster operation by first assembling the thrust screw into the piston/adjuster assembly, pulling the two pieces apart by hand approximately ¼" (6mm), and then releasing them. When pulling on the two pieces, the brass drive ring must remain stationary, causing the nut to rotate. When releasing the two parts, the nut must remain stationary, and the drive ring must rotate. If the action of the components does not follow this pattern, replace the piston/adjuster assembly.

12. Inspect ball pockets, threads, grooves, and bearing surfaces of the thrust screw and operating shaft for wear, pitting, or brinelling. Inspect balls and anti-rotation pin for wear, brinelling, or pitting. Replace operating shaft, balls, thrust screw, and anti-rotation pin if any of these parts are worn or damaged. A polished appear-

ance on the ball paths is acceptable if there is no sign of wear into the surface.

13. Inspect the thrust bearing for corrosion, pitting, or wear. Replace if necessary.

14. Inspect the bearing surface of the end plug for wear or brinelling. Replace if necessary. A polished appearance on the bearing surface is acceptable if there is no sign of wear into the surface.

15. Inspect the lever for damage. Replace if necessary.

16. Lightly sand or wire brush any rust or corrosion from the caliper housing insulator bores.

17. Apply a coat of clean brake fluid to the new caliper piston seal, and install it in the cylinder bore. Be sure that the seal is not twisted and that it is seated fully in the groove.

18. Install a new dust boot by seating the flange squarely in the outer groove of the caliper bore.

19. Coat the piston/adjuster assembly with clean brake fluid, and install it in the cylinder bore. Spread the dust boot over the piston, like it is installed. Seat the dust boot in the piston groove.

20. Install the caliper in a vise and fill the piston/adjuster assembly with clean brake fluid to the bottom edge of the thrust screw bore.

21. Coat a new thrust screw O-ring seal with clean brake fluid, and install it in the groove in the thrust screw.

22. Install the thrust screw by turning it into the piston/adjuster assembly with a ¼" allen wrench until the top surface of the thrust screw is flush with the bottom of the threaded bore. Use care to avoid cutting the O-ring seal. Index the thrust screw, so that the notches on the thrust screw and caliper housing are aligned. Then install the anti-rotation pin.

WARNING: *The thrust screw and operating shaft are not interchangeable from side to side because of the ramp direction in the ball pockets. The pocket surface of the operating shaft and the thrust screw are stamped with the proper letter (R or L), indicating part usage.*

23. Place a ball in each of the three pockets of the thrust screw, and apply a liberal amount of silicone grease on all components in the parking brake mechanism.

24. Install the operating shaft on the balls.

25. Coat the thrust bearing with silicone grease and install it on the operating shaft.

26. Install a new lip seal and O-ring on the end retainer.

27. Coat the O-ring seal and lip seal with a light film of silicone grease, and install the end

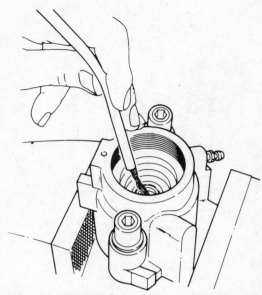

Filling the piston/adjuster assembly with clean fluid

retainer in the caliper. Hold the operating shaft firmly seated against the internal mechanism while installing the end retainer to prevent mislocation of the balls. If the lip seal is pushed out of position, reset the seal. Tighten the end retainer to 75-95 ft. lbs.

28. Install the parking brake lever on its keyed spline. The lever arm must point down and rearward. The parking brake cable will then pass freely under the axle. Tighten the lever retaining screw to 16-22 ft. lbs. The parking brake lever must rotate freely after tightening.

29. Arrange the caliper in a vise and bottom the piston with modified Tool T75P-2588-B.

30. Install new pin insulators in the caliper housing. Check to see if both insulator flanges straddle the housing holes.

31. Install the caliper on the vehicle.

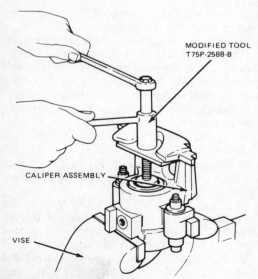

MODIFIED TOOL
T75P-2588-B

CALIPER ASSEMBLY

VISE

Bottoming the piston in the caliper

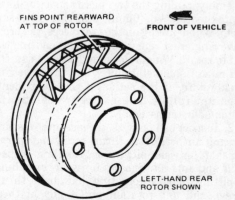

FINS POINT REARWARD
AT TOP OF ROTOR

FRONT OF VEHICLE

LEFT-HAND REAR
ROTOR SHOWN

1982 Continental rear rotor

Brake Discs

REMOVAL AND INSTALLATION

1. Raise the car and support it. Remove the wheels.

CAUTION: *Brake shoes contain asbestos, which has been determined to be a cancer causing agent. Never clean the brake surfaces with compressed air! Avoid inhaling any dust from any brake surface! When cleaning brake surfaces, use a commercially available brake cleaning fluid.*

2. Remove the caliper, as outlined earlier.

3. Remove the retaining bolts and remove the disc from the axle.

4. Inspect the disc for excessive rust, scoring or pitting. A certain amount of rust on the edge of the disc is normal. Refer to the specifications chart and measure the thickness of the disc, using a micrometer. If the disc is below specifications, replace it.

5. Reinstall the discs, keeping in mind that the two sides are not interchangeable. The words **left** and **right** are cast into the inner surface of the raised section of the disc. Proper reinstallation of the discs is important, since the cooling vanes cast into the disc must face opposite forward rotation.

6. Reinstall the caliper.

7. Install the wheels and lower the car.

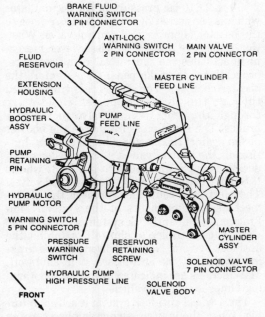

Anti-skid hydraulic cylinder/booster unit

4-WHEEL ANTI-LOCK BRAKE SYSTEM

The 4-Wheel Anti-Lock brake system is a compact integral power brake system that uses brake fluid for both brake function and hydraulic boost.

Individual front wheel brake circuits and a combined rear wheel brake circuit are used. Major components of the system are:

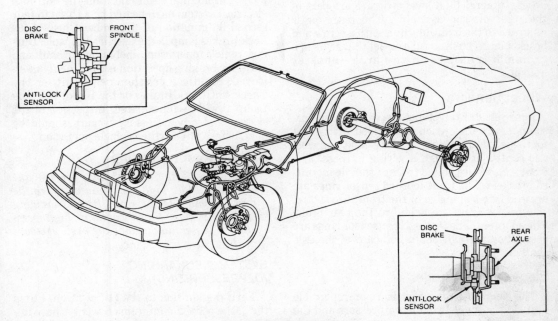

Anti-skid brake system

Master Cylinder and Hydraulic Booster

The master cylinder and brake booster are mounted in the conventional manner. The booster control valve is located in a parallel bore above the master cylinder centerline and is operated by a lever mechanism connected to the brake pedal pushrod.

Electric Pump and Accumulator

A high pressure electric pump runs for short periods at frequent intervals to charge the hydraulic accumulator. The accumulator is a gas filled pressure chamber that is part of the pump and motor assembly. The pump, motor and accumulator are mounted to the master cylinder/booster assembly.

Valve Body Assembly

The valve body contains three pairs of solenoid valves, one pair for each front wheel and the third pair for both the rear wheels combined. The paired solenoid valves are inlet/outlet valves with the inlet valve normally open and the outlet valve normally closed. The valve body is bolted to the inboard side of the master cylinder/booster assembly.

Reservoir and Fluid Level Warning Switches

A translucent plastic reservoir having two main chambers is connected to the pump assembly and master cylinder by two low pressure hoses. Integral fluid level switches are part of the reservoir cap assembly. The reservoir is mounted to the hydraulic unit with a screw and bracket and a push-in tube outlet that seats in a grommet mounted in the brake booster housing.

Wheel Sensors

Four variable reluctance electronic sensor assemblies are used, each is provided with a 104 tooth ring. Each sensor is connected to an electric controller through a wiring harness. The front sensors are bolted to front spindle mounted brackets. The front toothed sensor rings are pressed into the inside of the front disc rotors. The rear sensors are bolted to the rear brake axle adapters. The toothed rear sensor rings are pressed on the axle shafts, inboard of the axle shaft flange.

Electronic Controller

The electronic controller is a non-repairable unit consisting of two microprocessors and the necessary circuitry for operation. The controller monitors system operation during normal driving as well as during anti-lock (panic) braking. Under wheel locking conditions signals are triggered from the controller that open and close solenoid valves resulting in moderate pulsations in the brake pedal and equal anti-locking control to all four wheels.

System Operation

The hydraulic pump maintains between 2,030 to 2,610 psi pressure in the accumulator which is connected by a high pressure hose to the booster chamber and control valve. When the brakes are applied, a scissor/lever mechanism activates the control valve and pressure, proportional to brake pedal travel, enters the booster chamber. The pressure is transmitted through the normally open solenoid valve through the proportioning valve to the rear brakes. The same pressure moves the booster piston against the master cylinder piston, shutting off the central valves in the master cylinder. This applies pressure to the front wheels through the two normally open solenoid valves. The electronic controller monitor the electromechanical components of the system. Malfunction of the anti-lock system will cause the electronic controller to shut off or inhibit the anti-lock system. Normal power assisted braking remains if the anti-lock system shuts off. Malfunctions are indicated by one or two warning lamps inside the vehicle.

The 4-wheel anti-lock system is self-monitoring. When the ignition switch is placed in the Run position, the electronic controller will preform a preliminary self check on the anti-lock electrical system as indicated by a three to four second illumination of the amber Check Anti-Lock Brakes lamp in the overhead console. During vehicle operation, including normal and anti-lock braking operation is continually monitored. Should a problem occur, either the Check Anti-Lock Brakes or the Brake Warning Lamp(s) will be illuminated. Inspection of the system and any necessary repairs should be done before any further vehicle operation.

Brake System Bleeding

CAUTION: *The 4-Wheel Anti-Lock brake system is under high accumulator hydraulic pressure most of the time. Before servicing any component which contains high pressure, it is mandatory that the high pressure in the system be discharged.*

SYSTEM DISCHARGING (DEPRESSURIZING)

Turn the ignition to the Off position. Pump the brake pedal a minimum of twenty times until an increase in pedal force is clearly felt.

FRONT BRAKE BLEEDING

The front brakes can be bled in the conventional manner, with or without the accumulator being charged. Refer to the previous brake bleeding section at the beginning of this Chapter for instructions.

REAR BRAKE BLEEDING

A fully charged accumulator is required for successful rear brake system bleeding. Once accumulator pressure is applied to the system, the rear brakes can be bled by opening the rear caliper bleeder screw while holding the brake pedal in the applied position with the ignition switch in the Run position. Repeat the procedure until an air free flow of brake fluid comes from the bleeder screw. Close the bleeder screw. Close the bleeder screw. Add fluid to the master cylinder reservoir until required level is reached.

CAUTION: *Care must be used when opening the bleeder screws. The fluid is under high pressure and could cause injury if splashed into eyes, etc.*

Hydraulic Reservoir
CHECKING FLUID LEVEL AND REFILLING

1. With the ignition switch On, pump the brake pedal until the hydraulic pump motor starts.
2. Wait until the pump shuts off and check the brake fluid level in the reservoir. If the level is below the MAX fill line, add fluid until the line is reached.

WARNING: *Do not overfill! The level may be over the MAX line depending upon the accumulator charge. Perform the above procedure before adding or removing brake fluid.*

Component Removal and Installation
HYDRAULIC CYLINDER/BOOSTER UNIT ASSEMBLY

CAUTION: *Depressurize the system before working on the system. To depressurize the system, turn the ignition OFF and pump the brake pedal at least 20 times, until an obvious increase in pedal pressure is felt.*

1. Disconnect the negative battery cable.
2. Disconnect the electrical connectors from the fluid reservoir cap, main valve, solenoid valve body, pressure warning switch, hydraulic pump motor and the ground connector from the master cylinder. Label them for installation identification.
3. Disconnect the brake lines from the solenoid valve body and plug them to prevent fluid loss.
4. Disconnect the booster pushrod from the

brake pedal by first disconnecting the spotlight switch wires at the connector on the brake pedal. Then, remove the hairpin connector at the stoplight switch and slide the switch off the pedal pin until the large end of the switch (outer hole) is off of the pin. Remove the switch using a twisting motion. Remove the unit's four retaining nuts at the firewall.
5. Remove the booster from the engine compartment.
6. Install in the reverse order. Bleed the brake system.

HYDRAULIC ACCUMULATOR

CAUTION: *Depressurize the system before working on the system.*

1. Disconnect the negative battery cable. Disconnect the electrical connector at the hydraulic pump motor.
2. Use a 8mm hex wrench, loosen and unscrew the accumulator. Do not allow any dirt to enter the open port.
3. Loosen and remove the accumulator mounting block, if necessary.
4. Install in the reverse order using new O-ring seals.
5. Turn the ignition switch to the On position. Check that the Check Anti-Lock Brakes lamp goes out after a maximum of one minute. Fill the reservoir as necessary.

HYDRAULIC PUMP MOTOR

CAUTION: *Depressurize the system before working on the system.*

1. Disconnect the negative battery cable.
2. Disconnect the electrical connections at the hydraulic pump motor and pressure warning switch.
3. Use a 8mm hex wrench and remove the accumulator, make sure not dirt falls into the open port.
4. Remove the suction line between the reservoir and the pump at the reservoir by twisting the hose and pulling. Plug the hose to prevent fluid loss. Install a plugged piece of large vacuum hose on the reservoir nipple to prevent fluid loss.
5. Remove the banjo bolt (hollow hex headed bolt) connecting the high pressure hose to the booster housing, at the housing. Be sure to catch and save the sealing O-rings, one on each side of the banjo bolt head.
6. Remove the allen headed bolt attaching the pump and motor assembly to the extension housing which is located directly under the accumulator. A long extension and universal swivel socket will help reach the bolt.
7. Move the pump assembly toward the engine and remove the retainer pin on the inboard

side of the extension housing. Remove the pump and motor assembly.

8. Installation is in the reverse order of removal. Tighten the allen head bolt to 60-84 in. lbs. Tighten the banjo bolt to 12-15 ft. lbs. after installing new O-rings (if necessary). Install a new O-ring on the accumulator and tighten to 30-40 ft. lbs.

9. Turn the ignition switch to On. Check that the Check Anti-Lock Brakes lamp goes out after a maximum of one minute. Check the brake level in the reservoir, add fluid if necessary.

RESERVOIR ASSEMBLY

CAUTION: *Depressurize the system before working on the system.*

1. Disconnect the negative battery cable.

2. Remove the electrical connectors from the reservoir cap. Unlock and remove the cap.

3. Empty the reservoir of as much fluid as possible using a large rubber syringe or suction gun.

4. Remove the line between the pump and reservoir, from the reservoir by twisting and pulling the hose from the reservoir fitting.

5. Remove the return line between the reservoir and master cylinder at the reservoir in the same manner as Step 4.

6. Remove the allen head reservoir mounting screw.

7. Pry the reservoir from the booster housing carefully. Be sure the short sleeve and O-ring are removed from the booster housing.

8. Install the reservoir mounting bracket in its guide on the bottom of the reservoir. Check to be sure that the short sleeve and O-ring are in position at the bottom of the reservoir. Wet the mounting grommet with brake fluid.

9. Insert the reservoir into the grommet as far as it will go on the booster housing, make sure the short sleeve and O-ring are in place. The reservoir should be held vertical to the booster during installation.

10. The rest of the installation is in the reverse order of removal.

11. Fill the reservoir to the correct level with a charged accumulator.

ELECTRONIC CONTROLLER

The controller is located in the luggage compartment in front of the forward trim panel.

1. Disconnect the 35 pin connector from the controller.

2. Remove the three retaining screws holding the controller to the seat back brace and remove the controller.

3. Install in the reverse order.

PRESSURE SWITCH

CAUTION: *Depressurize the system before working on the system.*

1. Disconnect the negative battery cable.

2. Disconnect the valve body seven pin connector. Failure to disconnect the connector can result in damage to the connector if struck by removal tool.

3. Remove the pressure switch with special socket T85P-20215-B or equivalent.

4. Inspect the mounting O-ring, replace if necessary. Install the switch in the reverse order of removal. Tighten to 15-25 ft. lbs.

FRONT WHEEL SENSOR

1. Disconnect the harness connector on the inside of the engine compartment for either the right or left sensor.

2. Raise and support the front side of the vehicle to be worked on. Remove wheel, caliper and disc rotor assemblies.

3. Disengage the wire grommet at the shock tower and draw the sensor cable carefully through the grommet mounting hole. Remove the harness from the mounting brackets.

4. Loosen the 5mm set screw that hold the sensor to the mounting bracket. Remove the sensor through the hole in the disc brake splash shield.

5. Clean the sensor face, if reusing the original sensor. Install in the reverse order of removal. Install a new paper spacer on the sensor mounting flange before installation.

REAR WHEEL SENSOR

1. Disconnect the sensor connector for the side requiring service. The connector is located on the inside of the luggage compartment behind the forward trim panel.

2. Lift the carpet and push the sensor wire mounting grommet through the mounting hole.

3. Raise and support the rear of the vehicle. Remove the wire harness from the retaining brackets and C-clip. Pull rearward on the clip to disengage.

4. Remove the wheel, caliper and rotor assemblies.

5. Remove the sensor mounting bolt. Slip the grommet out of the splash shield and pull the sensor wire through the hole.

6. Install in the reverse order. If the original sensor is to be used clean the sensor face. Install a new paper spacer on the sensor mounting flange before installation.

FRONT WHEEL SENSOR RING

NOTE: *Toothed sensor ring replacement requires the use of an arbor press. An automo-*

tive machine shop or well equipped garage should be able to handle the job.

1. Remove the rotor assembly.

2. Position the rotor face up on the arbor press bed.

3. Using the proper adapters, press each stud down until they contact the sensor ring.

4. Position an approximate adapter on the top of all five studs and press the studs and sensor ring from the rotor.

5. Install the studs into the rotor using the press. Install the sensor ring with the press until the ring bottoms in position.

6. Install the rotor in the reverse order of removal.

REAR WHEEL SENSOR RING

1. Remove the rear axle shaft. Install the necessary adapter between the axle shaft flange and sensor ring.

2. Position the axle in an arbor press and remove the sensor ring.

3. Press the sensor ring into position until a gap of 47mm between the sensor ring and face of the axle flange is obtained.

4. Reinstall the axle shaft and removed components.

PARKING BRAKE

Brake Cables

CAUTION: *Brake shoes contain asbestos, which has been determined to be a cancer causing agent. Never clean the brake surfaces with compressed air! Avoid inhaling any dust from any brake surface! When cleaning brake surfaces, use a commercially available brake cleaning fluid.*

REMOVAL AND INSTALLATION

1968-79

FRONT CABLE

1. Raise and support the rear end on jackstands.

2. Remove the adjusting nut at the equalizer and remove the equalizer from the cable.

3. Remove the clip that holds the cable to the frame or body bracket.

4. Remove the screws that retain the front fender apron to the frame seal and remove the seal.

5. Attach a length of wire to the control cable.

6. Remove the hairpin clip retaining the cable assembly to the control.

7. Disconnect the cable from the control assembly.

8. Pull the cable up through the opening in the dash panel and remove the cable from the length of wire.

9. Installation is the reverse of removal. Adjust the parking brake.

INTERMEDIATE CABLE

1. Raise and support the rear end on jackstands.

2. Remove the equalizer adjusting nut.

3. Remove the cable end from the equalizer.

4. Unhook the cable from the multiplier lever and remove it.

5. Installation is the reverse of removal. Adjust the parking brake.

REAR CABLE

1. Raise and support the rear end on jackstands.

2. Remove the equalizer adjusting nut and remove the equalizer.

3. Disconnect the cable ball ends from the adjuster.

4. Remove the cable from the retainer hooks.

5. Remove the hairpin clip retaining the cable housing to the side rail bracket.

6. Remove the brake drums.

7. Remove the brake shoes and disconnect the cable end from the self-adjusting lever.

8. Compress the pronged retainers and remove the cable assembly from the backing plate.

9. Installation is the reverse of removal. Adjust the parking brake.

1980-88

FRONT CABLE

1. Raise and support the rear end on jackstands.

2. Remove the adjusting nut at the equalizer and remove the equalizer from the cable.

3. Remove the clip that holds the cable to the frame or body bracket.

4. Remove the clip that retains the cable to the parking brake control, inside the car.

5. Disconnect the cable from the control assembly.

NOTE: *Some cars have cables with snap-in fittings. On these cables, compress the tangs and remove them from the mounting surface.*

8. Pull the cable up through the opening in the dash panel.

9. Installation is the reverse of removal. Adjust the parking brake.

INTERMEDIATE CABLE

1. Raise and support the rear end on jackstands.

2. Remove the cable adjusting nut.

3. Disconnect the intermediate cable ends from the left rear and the transverse cables.

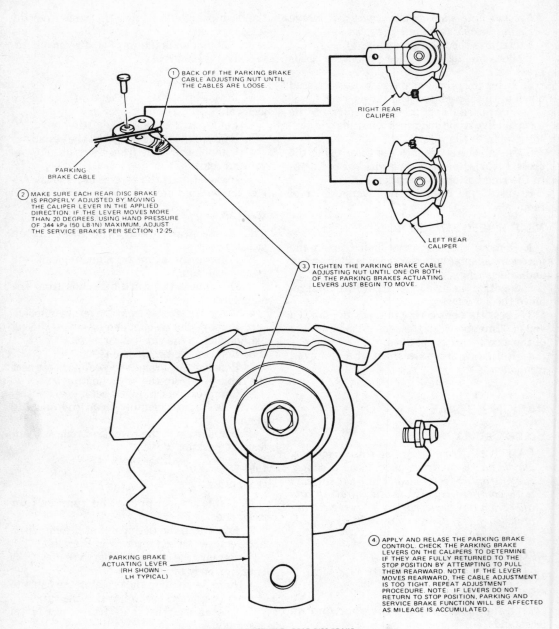

① BACK OFF THE PARKING BRAKE
CABLE ADJUSTING NUT UNTIL
THE CABLES ARE LOOSE.

RIGHT REAR
CALIPER

PARKING
BRAKE CABLE

② MAKE SURE EACH REAR DISC BRAKE
IS PROPERLY ADJUSTED BY MOVING
THE CALIPER LEVER IN THE APPLIED
DIRECTION. IF THE LEVER MOVES MORE
THAN 20 DEGREES, USING HAND PRESSURE
OF 344 kPa (50 LB·IN) MAXIMUM, ADJUST
THE SERVICE BRAKES PER SECTION 12-25.

LEFT REAR
CALIPER

③ TIGHTEN THE PARKING BRAKE CABLE
ADJUSTING NUT UNTIL ONE OR BOTH
OF THE PARKING BRAKES ACTUATING
LEVERS JUST BEGIN TO MOVE.

④ APPLY AND RELASE THE PARKING BRAKE
CONTROL. CHECK THE PARKING BRAKE
LEVERS ON THE CALIPERS TO DETERMINE
IF THEY ARE FULLY RETURNED TO THE
STOP POSITION BY ATTEMPTING TO PULL
THEM REARWARD. NOTE : IF THE LEVER
MOVES REARWARD, THE CABLE ADJUSTMENT
IS TOO TIGHT. REPEAT ADJUSTMENT
PROCEDURE. NOTE : IF LEVERS DO NOT
RETURN TO STOP POSITION, PARKING AND
SERVICE BRAKE FUNCTION WILL BE AFFECTED
AS MILEAGE IS ACCUMULATED.

PARKING BRAKE
ACTUATING LEVER
(RH SHOWN —
LH TYPICAL)

PARKING BRAKE ADJUSTMENT · REAR DISC BRAKE

Parking brake adjustment on models with rear disc brakes

4. Remove the cotter pin, washer and spring from the pin protruding from the equalizer assembly, and remove the lever.

NOTE: *The intermediate cable cannot be separated from the lever.*

5. Installation is the reverse of removal. Adjust the parking brake.

TRANSVERSE CABLE

1. Raise and support the rear end on jackstands.

2. Remove the adjusting nut.

3. Remove the transverse cable ends from the right rear and intermediate cables.

4. Remove the hairpin clips or conduit brackets and remove the cable.

5. Installation is the reverse of removal. Adjust the parking brake.

REAR CABLES

1. Raise and support the rear end on jackstands.

Brake Specifications Ford/Mercury

All measurements given are (in.) unless noted

Year	Model	Lug Nut Torque (ft. lb.)	Master Cylinder Bore	Brake Disc		Brake Drum			Minimum Lining Thickness	
				Minimum Thickness	Maximum Run-Out	Diameter	Max Machine O/S	Max Wear Limit	Front	Rear
1968–71	All	70–115	1.000	.875	.0007	11.03	11.090	11.090	$2/32$	$2/32$
1972–75	All	70–115	1.000	1.180	.0007	11.03	11.090	11.090	$2/32$	$2/32$
1976–78	All	70–115	1.000	1.120 (front) .895 (rear)	.003 .003	11.03	11.090	11.090	$1/8$	$3/32$
1979–88	All	80–105	1.000	.972	.003	11.030	11.090	11.090	$1/8$	$2/32$

NOTE: *Minimum lining thickness is as recommended by the manufacturer. Because of variations in state inspection regulations, the minimum allowable thickness may be different than recommended by the manufacturer.*

2. Remove the equalizer adjusting nut and remove the equalizer.

3. Disconnect the rear cables from the right and left rear cable connectors.

4. Remove the cable from the retainer hooks.

5. Remove the hairpin clip retaining the cable housing to the side rail bracket.

6. On cars with rear drum brakes:

a. Remove the brake drums.

b. Remove the brake shoes and disconnect the cable end from the self-adjusting lever.

c. Compress the pronged retainers and remove the cable assembly from the backing plate.

7. On cars with rear disc brakes, remove the clevis pin securing the cable to the caliper actuating arm.

8. Installation is the reverse of removal. Adjust the parking brake.

CABLE ADJUSTMENT

All Cars with Rear Drums Brakes

1. Fully release the parking brake.

2. If an axle-type hoist is available, place the transmission in Neutral and raise the vehicle. If the hoist is not available, block the front wheels, place a floor jack beneath the axle housing (following the instructions in Chapter 1), place transmission in Neutral, and raise the back of the car. It is important in all cases to raise the car by the rear axle so that the suspension does not become off-loaded thereby stretching the brake cables and giving a faulty adjustment.

NOTE: *Install jack stands beneath the frame when using a floor jack.*

3. Tighten the equalizer nut against the cable equalizer sufficiently to cause rear wheel brake drag when the wheel is turned by hand. Then, loosen the adjusting nut until the rear brakes just may be tuned freely. There should be no brake drag when the cable is properly adjusted. Tighten the locknut, if so equipped, to 7-10 ft. lbs.

4. Remove the jack stands, if used, and lower the car. Check the operation of the parking brake.

Models with Rear Disc Brakes

1. Fully release the parking brake.

2. Place the transmission in Neutral. If it is necessary to raise the car to reach the adjusting nut and observe the parking brake levers, use an axle hoist or a floor jack positioned beneath the differential. this is necessary so that the rear axle remains at the curb attitude, not stretching the parking brake cables.

CAUTION: *If you are raising the rear of the car only, block the front wheels.*

3. Locate the adjusting nut beneath the car on the driver's side. While observing the parking brake actuating levers on the rear calipers, tighten the adjusting nut until the levers just begin to move. Then, loosen the nut sufficiently for the levers to fully return to the stop position.

4. check the operation of the parking brake. make sure that the actuating levers return to the stop position by attempting to pull them rearward. If the lever moves rearward, the cable adjustment is too tight, which will cause a dragging rear brake and consequent brake overheating and fade.

Body

10

EXTERIOR

Doors

REMOVAL AND INSTALLATION

1. Remove the door trim panel.
2. Remove the watershield, and, if a new door is being installed, save all the moulding clips and mouldings.
3. Remove the wiring harness, actuator and speakers.
4. If a new door is being installed, remove all window and lock components.
5. Support the door and unbolt the hinges from the door.
6. Installation is the reverse of removal. New holes may have to be drilled in a replacement door for the trim. Align the door and tighten the hinge bolts securely.

ADJUSTMENT

Door alignment is obtained by loosening the hinge-to-door bolts and moving the door as required to obtain a proper fit. Similarly, the latch striker must be loosed and repositioned for proper engagement with the latch.

Door Lock Cylinder

REMOVAL AND INSTALLATION

NOTE: *The key code is stamped on the driver's door lock cylinder to aid in replacing lost keys. Remember, if you replace a door lock cylinder you'll have to replace your ignition lock cylinder as well.*

1. Remove the trim panel and watershield.
2. Disconnect the lock control-to-door lock cylinder rod from the lock cylinder arm.

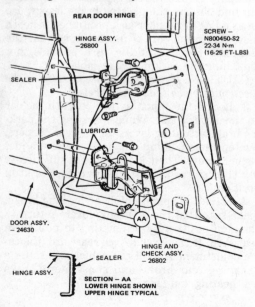

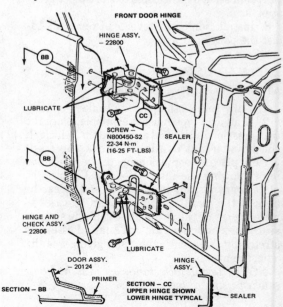

1968–80 door hinge adjustments

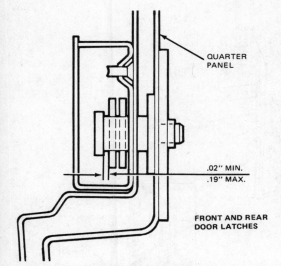

1968–80 door lock striker adjustments

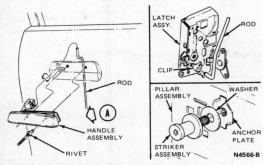

1968–80 door latch striker installation

3. Remove the door lock cylinder retainer and slide the cylinder from the door. If a new lock cylinder is being installed transfer the arm to the new cylinder.

4. Installation is the reverse of removal.

Power Door Locks

REMOVAL AND INSTALLATION

Actuator Motor

1. Remove the door trim panel and watershield.

2. Disconnect the actuator motor link from the door latch.

3. Remove the pop rivet attaching the actuator motor to the door.

4. Disconnect the wiring at the connector.

5. Remove the actuator motor.

6. Installation is the reverse of removal. Be careful to avoid twisting the actuator's boot. Make sure that the actuator is tight against the inner panel when installing the pop rivet.

Hood

REMOVAL AND INSTALLATION

1. Open and support the hood.

2. Matchmark the hood-to-hinge positions.

3. Have an assistant support the hood while you remove the hinge-to-hood bolts.

4. You and your assistant can remove the hood.

5. Installation is the reverse of removal.

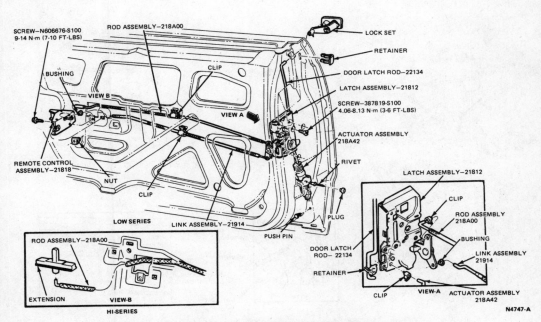

1968–80 power door lock assembly on 2-door Ford and Mercury

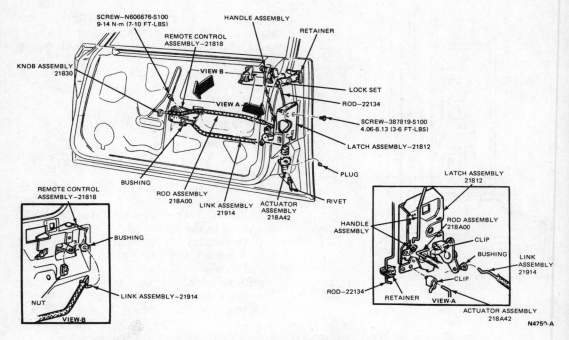

1968—80 power door lock assembly on the front door of 4-door Lincoln and Mark VI

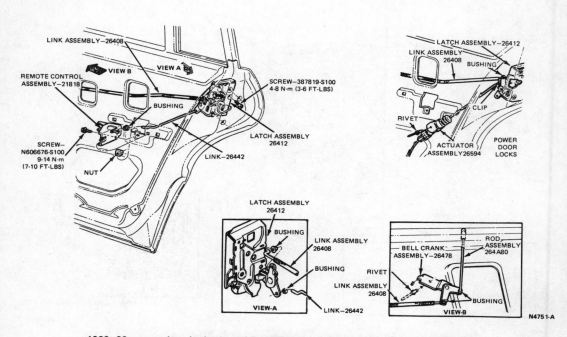

1968—80 power door lock assembly on the rear door of 4-door Ford and Mercury

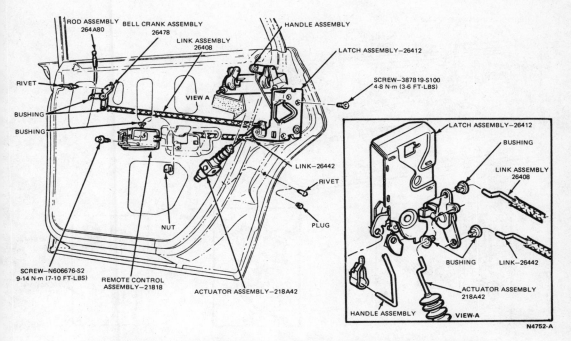

1968—80 power door lock assembly on the rear door of 4-door Lincoln and Mark VI

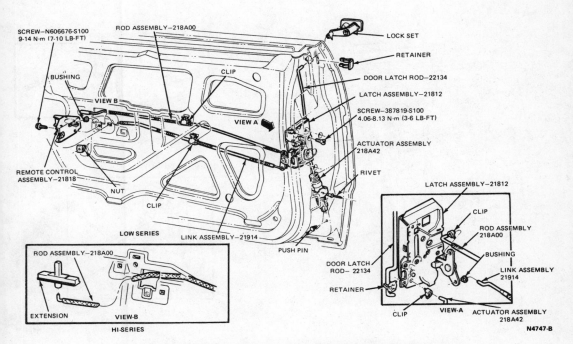

1981—88 power door lock assembly on 2-door Ford and Mercury

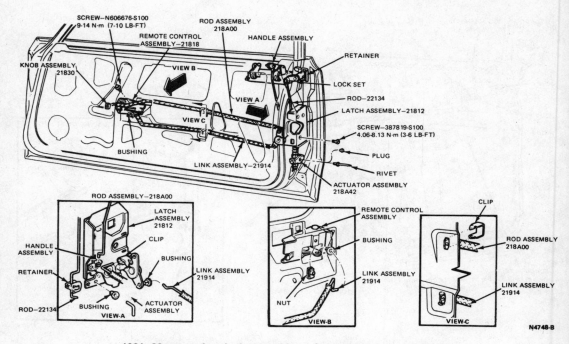

SCREW—N606676-S100
9-14 N·m (7-10 LB-FT)

KNOB ASSEMBLY
21830

REMOTE CONTROL
ASSEMBLY—21818

VIEW B

ROD ASSEMBLY
218A00

HANDLE ASSEMBLY

VIEW A

VIEW C

BUSHING

LINK ASSEMBLY—21914

RETAINER

LOCK SET

ROD—22134

LATCH ASSEMBLY—21812

SCREW—387819-S100
4.06-8.13 N·m (3-6 LB-FT)

PLUG

RIVET

ACTUATOR ASSEMBLY
218A42

ROD ASSEMBLY—218A00

LATCH
ASSEMBLY
21812

CLIP

HANDLE
ASSEMBLY

BUSHING

LINK ASSEMBLY
21914

RETAINER

ROD—22134

BUSHING

ACTUATOR
ASSEMBLY

VIEW-A

REMOTE CONTROL
ASSEMBLY

BUSHING

LINK ASSEMBLY
21914

NUT

VIEW-B

CLIP

ROD ASSEMBLY
218A00

LINK ASSEMBLY
21914

VIEW-C

N4748-B

1981—88 power door lock assembly on 2-door Lincoln and Mark VI

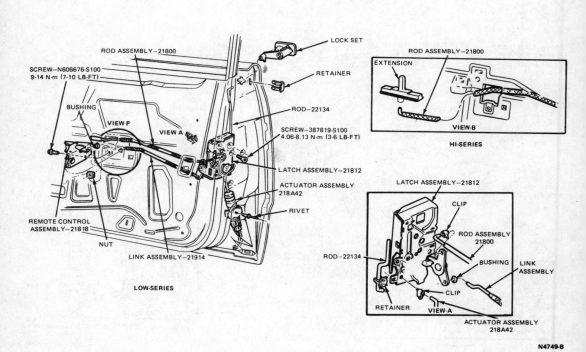

ROD ASSEMBLY—21800

SCREW—N606676-S100
9-14 N·m (7-10 LB-FT)

BUSHING

VIEW P

VIEW A

REMOTE CONTROL
ASSEMBLY—21818

NUT

LINK ASSEMBLY—21914

LOW-SERIES

LOCK SET

RETAINER

ROD—22134

SCREW—387819-S100
4.06-8.13 N·m (3-6 LB-FT)

LATCH ASSEMBLY—21812

ACTUATOR ASSEMBLY
218A42

RIVET

ROD ASSEMBLY—21800

EXTENSION

VIEW-B

HI-SERIES

LATCH ASSEMBLY—21812

CLIP

ROD ASSEMBLY
21800

BUSHING

LINK
ASSEMBLY

ROD—22134

CLIP

RETAINER

VIEW-A

ACTUATOR ASSEMBLY
218A42

N4749-B

1981—88 power door lock assembly on the front door of 4-door Ford and Mercury

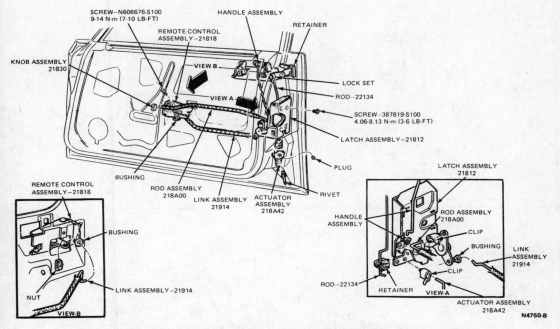

1981–88 power door lock assembly on the front door of 4-door Lincoln and Mark VI

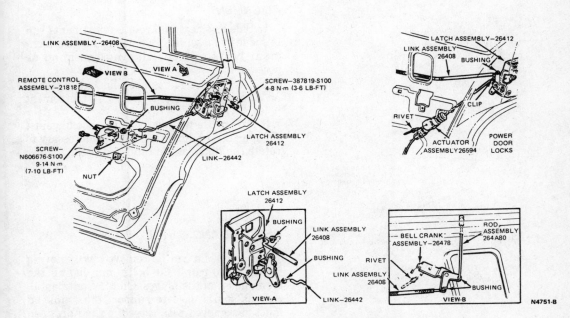

1981–88 power door lock assembly on the rear door of 4-door Ford and Mercury

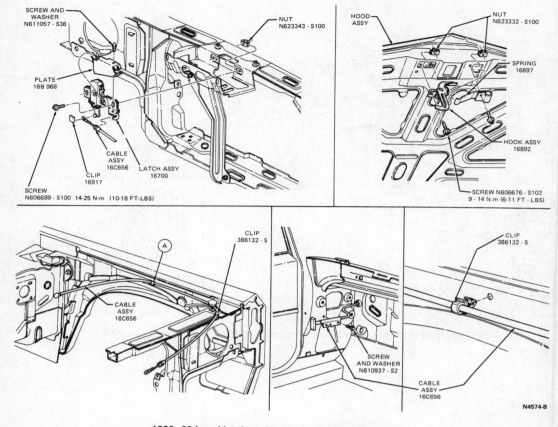

1968–80 hood latch and cable for Ford and Mercury

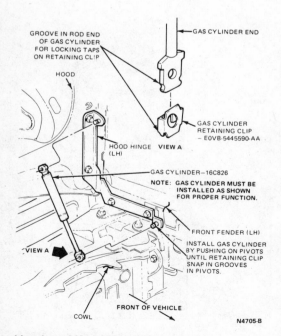

Lincoln and Mark VI hood hinges

ALIGNMENT

1. Side-to-side and fore-aft adjustments can be made by loosening the hood-to-hinge attachment bolts and positioning the hood as necessary.

2. Hood vertical fit can be adjusted by raising or lowering the hinge-to-fender reinforcement bolts.

3. To ensure a snug fit of the hood against the rear hood bumpers, it may be necessary to rotate the hinge around the 3 attaching bolts.

Trunk Lid
REMOVAL AND INSTALLATION

The trunk lid can be removed by removing the hinge-to-trunk lid bolts and sliding the trunk lid off of the hinges. On the Continental, the gas struts used to support the trunk lid must be removed with the lid in the fully open position.

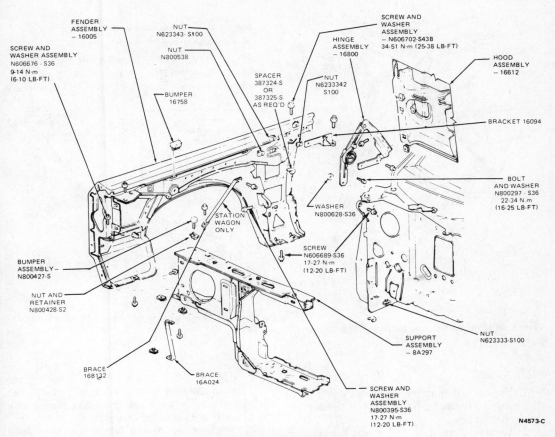

SCREW AND
WASHER ASSEMBLY
N606676 · S36
9-14 N·m
(6-10 LB-FT)

FENDER
ASSEMBLY
– 16005

NUT
N623343· S100

NUT
N800538

BUMPER
16758

SPACER
387324-S
OR
387325-S
AS REQ'D

HINGE
ASSEMBLY
– 16800

NUT
N6233342
S100

SCREW AND
WASHER
ASSEMBLY
– N606702-S43B
34-51 N·m (25-38 LB-FT)

HOOD
ASSEMBLY
– 16612

BRACKET 16094

BOLT
AND WASHER
N800297 · S36
22-34 N·m
(16-25 LB-FT)

WASHER
N800628-S36

SCREW
N606689-S36
17-27 N·m
(12-20 LB-FT)

STATION
WAGON
ONLY

BUMPER
ASSEMBLY–
N800427-S

NUT AND
RETAINER
N800428-S2

BRACE
16B132

BRACE
16A024

SUPPORT
ASSEMBLY
– 8A297

NUT
N623333-S100

SCREW AND
WASHER
ASSEMBLY
N800395-S36
17-27 N·m
(12-20 LB-FT)

N4573-C

Ford/Mercury hood hinges

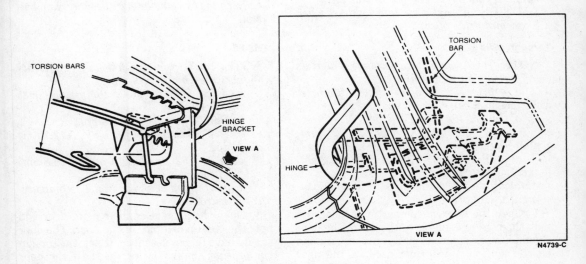

TORSION BARS

HINGE
BRACKET

VIEW A

TORSION
BAR

HINGE

VIEW A

N4739-C

1981–88 trunk lid hinge torsion bar

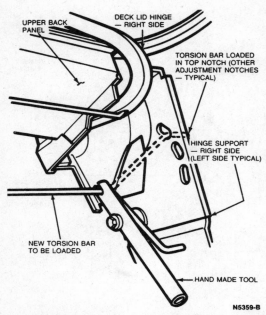

Trunk lid hinge torsion bar loading and adjustment

N5359-B

TOOL FABRICATION
LOCALLY OBTAIN THE FOLLOWING MATERIALS:

- WATER PIPE OR STEEL PIPE · 1/2 INCH x 10 INCH
- 381813-S2 5/16-18 x 1-3/4 INCH HEX HEAD WASHER BOLT · 1 REQ'D
- 55736-S2 · 5/16- x 1/2 INCH HEX HEAD NUT 1 REQ'D
- STEEL FLATWASHER · 1-5/8 INCH O.D. x 1/4 INCH I.D. x 1/8 INCH REQ'D

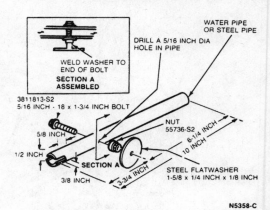

N5358-C

Trunk lid hinge torsion bar loading and adjustment tool

ALIGNMENT

1. Fore-aft fit may be adjusted by loosening the hinge to trunk lid bolts and positioning the lid as necessary.

2. Vertical fit can be adjusted by adding or deleting shims located between the the hinges and trunk lid.

TRUNK LID TORSION BAR LOADING ADJUSTMENT

NOTE: *Lincoln does not use torsion bars for support, rather, it uses gas struts.*
CAUTION: *Always wear safety glasses when performing this operation!*

Through 1984

NOTE: *You'll need the following materials to fabricate an adjusting tool:*
a. 4 feet (122cm) of ¼" (6mm) diameter flexible steel cable.
b. One ¼" (6mm) cable clamp.
c. A 2" (52mm) length of ½" (12.7mm) steel pipe.
d. A 6" (152mm) length of ⅝" (15.8mm) rubber heater hose.
Assemble the tool as shown in the accompanying illustration.

1. Open the luggage compartment door and note the pop-up distance of the door. The door should have finger clearance. If not, the torsion bar tension should be increased. If the door pops open with more than necessary force, the torsion bar tension should be decreased.

CAUTION: *The torsion bar is under great tension! Be very careful when adjusting it as it can spring out of control with considerable force if not handled properly!*

2. Support the trunk lid in the fully open position.

3. Using the homemade tool, pull one end of the torsion bar towards you and place it in a different hole to increase or decrease tension, then, move the other end of the bar to the corresponding hole.
WARNING: *At no time should the difference between the torsion bar ends be more than one slot.*

1985-88

NOTE: *You'll need the following materials to fabricate an adjusting tool:*
a. 4 feet (122cm) of ¼" (6mm) diameter flexible steel cable.
b. One ¼" (6mm) cable clamp.
c. A 2" (52mm) length of ½" (12.7mm) steel pipe.
d. A 6" (152mm) length of ⅝" (15.8mm) rubber heater hose.
Assemble the tool as shown in the accompanying illustration.

1. Open the luggage compartment door and note the pop-up distance of the door. The door should have finger clearance. If not, the torsion bar tension should be increased. If the door pops open with more than necessary force, the torsion bar tension should be decreased.

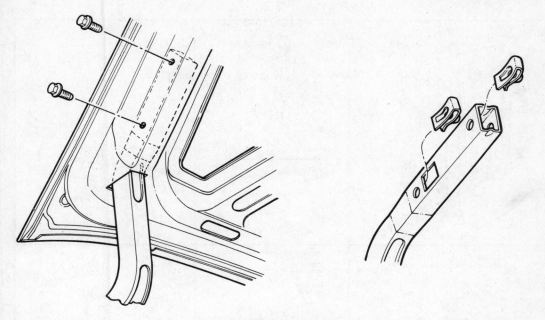

1968–80 trunk lid hinge installation

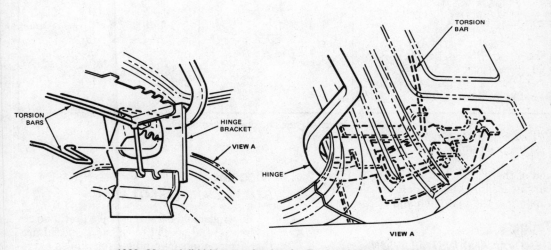

1968–80 trunk lid hinge torsion bar for Ford and Mercury models

CAUTION: *The torsion bar is under great tension! Be very careful when adjusting it as it can spring out of control with considerable force if not handled properly!*

2. Support the trunk lid in the fully open position.

3. Position the homemade tool on one end of the torsion bar. With an assistant, place a long, flat bladed bar over the top of the torsion bar as shown in the accompanying illustration. Pull one end of the torsion bar towards you with the homemade tool, with the assistant holding the flat bladed bar, guide the torsion bar down along the rear edge of the support into the lower groove of the hinge support so the torsion bar can be locked in the lowest outboard adjustment notch.

4. Using the homemade tool, pull the torsion bar towards you and work the bar up the hinge support to the second notch and release it. If further adjustment is necessary, proceed to the next step.

5. Using a ⅜″ drive with a ½″ deep-well socket and 6″ extension, position the socket over the

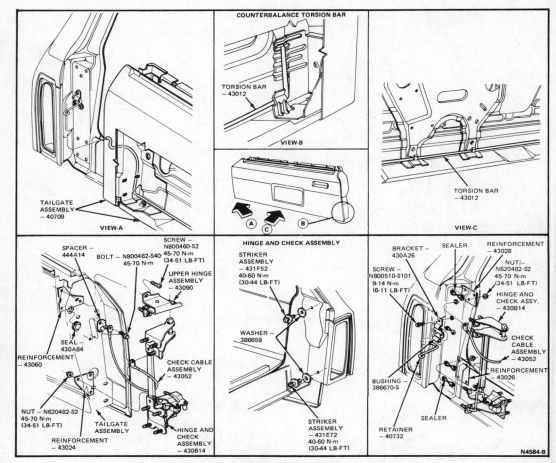

1981—88 tailgate hinge and check assembly

end of the torsion bar and lift it to unlock the bar. Reposition the torsion bar up the hinge support to the top notch and release it.

Tailgate
REMOVAL AND INSTALLATION

1. Open the tailgate in the drop-down position.
2. Remove the tailgate trim panel.
3. Remove the torsion bar retaining bracket. CAUTION: *Be careful! The torison bar is under tension!*
4. Remove the left quarter trim panel.
5. Latch the upper tailgate latch by hand.
6. Raise the tailgate glass to the full up position and support it there.
7. Mark the location of the hinge on the tailgate and remove the nuts retaining the hinge to the tailgate.
8. Unlatch the upper latch and remove the tailgate.
9. Installation is the reverse of removal.

Windshield
REMOVAL AND INSTALLATION

The windshield is retained by a urethane adhesive. Several special tools and a special urethane compound are required for windshield replacement. Replacement bonding must meet Federal Motor Vehicle Safety standards. For these reasons, bonded windshield replacement should be left to a professional shop.

Rear Window Glass
REMOVAL AND INSTALLATION

The rear window glass is retained by a urethane adhesive. Several special tools and a special urethane compound are required for windshield replacement. Replacement bonding must meet Federal Motor Vehicle Safety standards. For these reasons, bonded windshield replacement should be left to a professional shop.

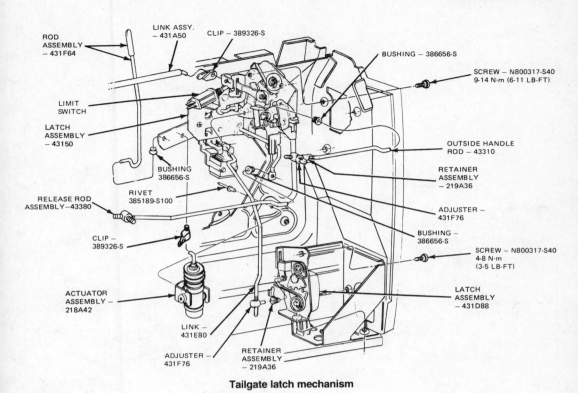

ROD ASSEMBLY — 431F64

LINK ASSY. — 431A50

CLIP — 389326-S

BUSHING — 386656-S

SCREW — N800317-S40 9-14 N·m (6-11 LB-FT)

LIMIT SWITCH

LATCH ASSEMBLY — 43150

BUSHING 386656-S

RIVET 385189-S100

RELEASE ROD ASSEMBLY—43380

CLIP — 389326-S

ACTUATOR ASSEMBLY — 218A42

LINK — 431E80

ADJUSTER — 431F76

RETAINER ASSEMBLY — 219A36

OUTSIDE HANDLE ROD — 43310

RETAINER ASSEMBLY — 219A36

ADJUSTER — 431F76

BUSHING — 386656-S

SCREW — N800317-S40 4-8 N·m (3-5 LB-FT)

LATCH ASSEMBLY — 431D88

Tailgate latch mechanism

Front Bumpers

REMOVAL AND INSTALLATION

1980-88 Ford and Mercury
1980 Lincoln and Mark VI
1968-79 All Models

1. Remove the 6 bolts or nuts attaching the reinforcement to the isolators.

WARNING: *Never use heat to loosen the nuts!*

2. Remove the bumper from the car.

3. Installation is the reverse of removal. Tighten the nuts to 40 ft. lbs.

4. Check the bumper installation clearance specifications in the accompanying illustrations.

1987-88 Lincoln Town Car

1. Remove the center air deflector from the reinforcement.

2. Remove the 6 nuts attaching the bumper to the isolators.

WARNING: *Never use heat to loosen the nuts!*

3. Installation is the reverse of removal. Tighten the nuts to 40 ft. lbs.

4. Check the bumper installation clearance specifications in the accompanying illustrations.

1984-86 Lincoln Town Car
1983 Lincoln and Mark VI

1. Remove the 2 grille actuator bracket-to-bumper reinformcement bolts.

2. Remove the lower sight shield-to-bumper attachment.

3. Remove the center air deflector-to-reinforment attachment.

4. Remove the 6 bolts attaching the bumper to the isolators.

WARNING: *Never use heat to loosen the nuts!*

5. Installation is the reverse of removal. Tighten the bolts to 55 ft. lbs.

6. Check the bumper installation clearance specifications in the accompanying illustrations.

1981-82 Lincoln and Mark VI

1. Remove the 2 grille actuator bracket-to-bumper reinformcement bolts.

2. Remove the center air deflector-to-reinforment attachment.

3. Remove the 6 bolts attaching the bumper to the isolators.

WARNING: *Never use heat to loosen the nuts!*

4. Installation is the reverse of removal. Tighten the bolts to 55 ft. lbs.

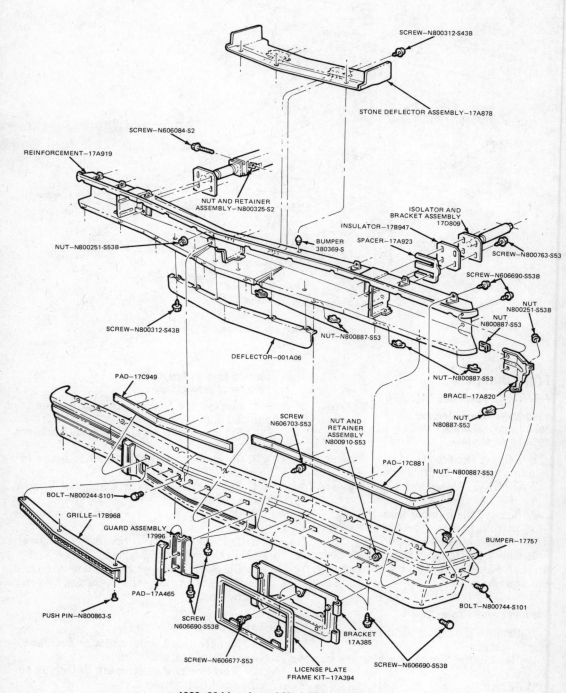

SCREW—N800312-S43B

STONE DEFLECTOR ASSEMBLY—17A878

SCREW—N606084-S2

REINFORCEMENT—17A919

NUT AND RETAINER ASSEMBLY—N800325-S2

ISOLATOR AND BRACKET ASSEMBLY 17D809

INSULATOR—17B947

SPACER—17A923

NUT—N800251-S53B

BUMPER 380369-S

SCREW—N800763-S53

SCREW—N606690-S53B

NUT N800251-S53B

NUT N800887-S53

SCREW—N800312-S43B

NUT—N800887-S53

DEFLECTOR—001A06

NUT—N800887-S53

BRACE—17A820

NUT N80887-S53

PAD—17C949

SCREW N606703-S53

NUT AND RETAINER ASSEMBLY N800910-S53

PAD—17C881

NUT—N800887-S53

BOLT—N800244-S101

GRILLE—17B968

GUARD ASSEMBLY 17996

BUMPER—17757

PAD—17A465

PUSH PIN—N800863-S

SCREW N606690-S53B

BRACKET 17A385

BOLT—N800744-S101

SCREW—N606677-S53

LICENSE PLATE FRAME KIT—17A394

SCREW—N606690-S53B

1968—80 Lincoln and Mark VI front bumper

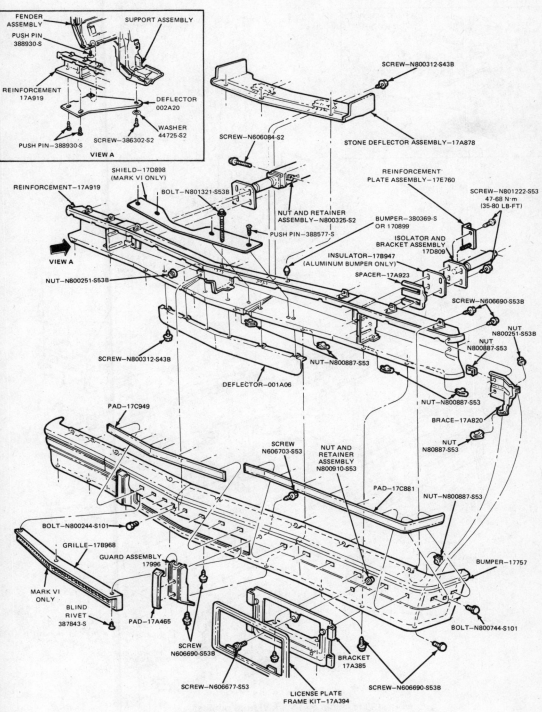

VIEW A

FENDER ASSEMBLY
PUSH PIN 388930-S
SUPPORT ASSEMBLY
REINFORCEMENT 17A919
DEFLECTOR 002A20
WASHER 44725-S2
PUSH PIN—388930-S
SCREW—386302-S2
VIEW A

SCREW—N800312-S43B
SCREW—N606084-S2
STONE DEFLECTOR ASSEMBLY—17A878
REINFORCEMENT PLATE ASSEMBLY—17E760
SCREW—N801222-S53 47-68 N·m (35-80 LB-FT)
REINFORCEMENT—17A919
SHIELD—17D898 (MARK VI ONLY)
BOLT—N801321-S53B
NUT AND RETAINER ASSEMBLY—N800325-S2
BUMPER—380369-S OR 170899
ISOLATOR AND BRACKET ASSEMBLY 17D809
PUSH PIN—388577-S
INSULATOR—17B947 (ALUMINUM BUMPER ONLY)
SPACER—17A923
SCREW—N606690-S53B
NUT—N800251-S53B
NUT N800251-S53B
NUT N800887-S53
SCREW—N800312-S43B
DEFLECTOR—001A06
NUT—N800887-S53
NUT—N800887-S53
BRACE—17A820
NUT N80887-S53
PAD—17C949
SCREW N606703-S53
NUT AND RETAINER ASSEMBLY N800910-S53
PAD—17C881
NUT—N800887-S53
BOLT—N800244-S101
GRILLE—17B968
GUARD ASSEMBLY 17996
BUMPER—17757
MARK VI ONLY
BLIND RIVET 387843-S
PAD—17A465
SCREW N606690-S53B
BRACKET 17A385
BOLT—N800744-S101
SCREW—N606677-S53
LICENSE PLATE FRAME KIT—17A394
SCREW—N606690-S53B

1981–82 Lincoln and Mark VI front bumper

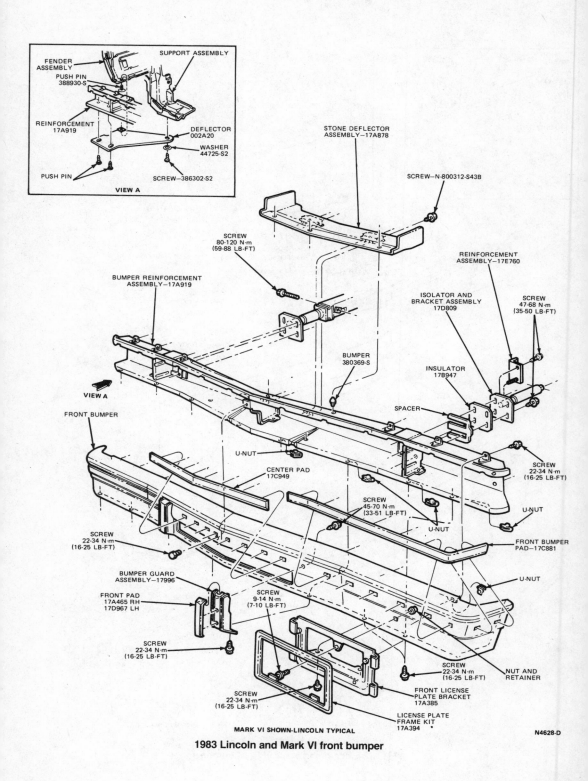

VIEW A

FENDER ASSEMBLY

SUPPORT ASSEMBLY

PUSH PIN 388930-S

REINFORCEMENT 17A919

DEFLECTOR 002A20

WASHER 44725-S2

PUSH PIN

SCREW—386302-S2

STONE DEFLECTOR ASSEMBLY—17A878

SCREW—N-800312-S43B

SCREW 80-120 N·m (59-88 LB-FT)

REINFORCEMENT ASSEMBLY—17E760

BUMPER REINFORCEMENT ASSEMBLY—17A919

ISOLATOR AND BRACKET ASSEMBLY 17D809

SCREW 47-68 N·m (35-50 LB-FT)

BUMPER 380369-S

INSULATOR 17B947

VIEW A

SPACER

FRONT BUMPER

U-NUT

CENTER PAD 17C949

SCREW 22-34 N·m (16-25 LB-FT)

SCREW 45-70 N·m (33-51 LB-FT)

U-NUT

U-NUT

FRONT BUMPER PAD—17C881

SCREW 22-34 N·m (16-25 LB-FT)

BUMPER GUARD ASSEMBLY—17996

U-NUT

FRONT PAD 17A465 RH 17D967 LH

SCREW 9-14 N·m (7-10 LB-FT)

SCREW 22-34 N·m (16-25 LB-FT)

SCREW 22-34 N·m (16-25 LB-FT)

NUT AND RETAINER

SCREW 22-34 N·m (16-25 LB-FT)

FRONT LICENSE PLATE BRACKET 17A385

LICENSE PLATE FRAME KIT 17A394

MARK VI SHOWN-LINCOLN TYPICAL

N4628-D

1983 Lincoln and Mark VI front bumper

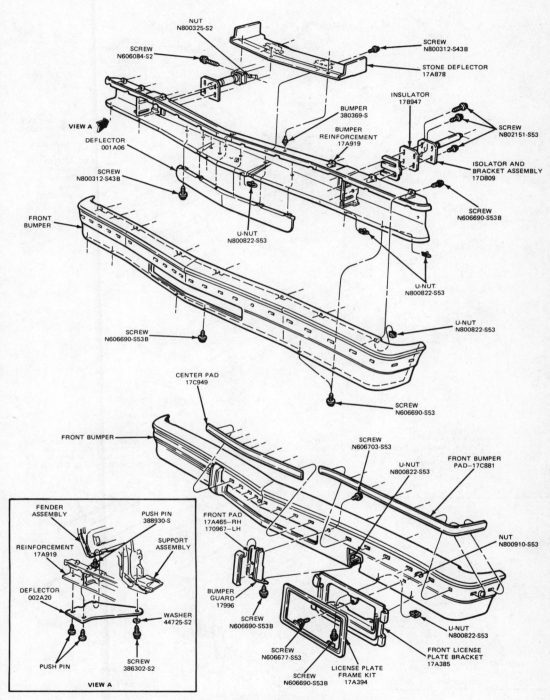

NUT
N800325-S2

SCREW
N606084-S2

SCREW
N800312-S43B

STONE DEFLECTOR
17A878

VIEW A

BUMPER
380369-S

INSULATOR
17B947

DEFLECTOR
001A06

BUMPER
REINFORCEMENT
17A919

SCREW
N802151-S53

ISOLATOR AND
BRACKET ASSEMBLY
17D809

SCREW
N800312-S43B

SCREW
N606690-S53B

FRONT
BUMPER

U-NUT
N800822-S53

U-NUT
N800822-S53

SCREW
N606690-S53B

U-NUT
N800822-S53

CENTER PAD
17C949

SCREW
N606690-S53

FRONT BUMPER

SCREW
N606703-S53

U-NUT
N800822-S53

FRONT BUMPER
PAD—17C881

FRONT PAD
17A465—RH
170967—LH

NUT
N800910-S53

BUMPER
GUARD
17996

SCREW
N606690-S53B

U-NUT
N800822-S53

SCREW
N606677-S53

FRONT LICENSE
PLATE BRACKET
17A385

SCREW
N606690-S53B

LICENSE PLATE
FRAME KIT
17A394

FENDER
ASSEMBLY

PUSH PIN
388930-S

REINFORCEMENT
17A919

SUPPORT
ASSEMBLY

DEFLECTOR
002A20

WASHER
44725-S2

PUSH PIN

SCREW
386302-S2

VIEW A

1984 Lincoln Town Car front bumper

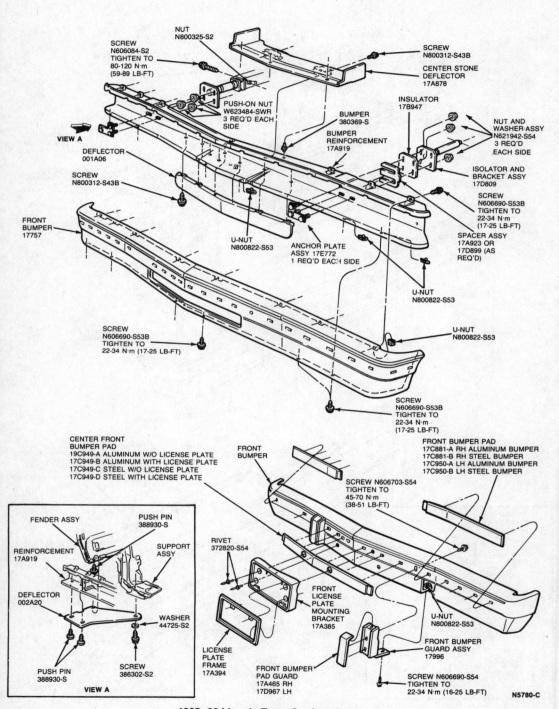

SCREW
N606084-S2
TIGHTEN TO
80-120 N·m
(59-89 LB-FT)

NUT
N800325-S2

SCREW
N800312-S43B

CENTER STONE
DEFLECTOR
17A878

PUSH-ON NUT
W623484-SWR
3 REQ'D EACH
SIDE

BUMPER
380369-S

INSULATOR
17B947

NUT AND
WASHER ASSY
N621942-S54
3 REQ'D
EACH SIDE

VIEW A

BUMPER
REINFORCEMENT
17A919

ISOLATOR AND
BRACKET ASSY
17D809

DEFLECTOR
001A06

SCREW
N800312-S43B

SCREW
N606690-S53B
TIGHTEN TO
22-34 N·m
(17-25 LB-FT)

FRONT
BUMPER
17757

U-NUT
N800822-S53

ANCHOR PLATE
ASSY 17E772
1 REQ'D EACH SIDE

SPACER ASSY
17A923 OR
17D899 (AS
REQ'D)

U-NUT
N800822-S53

SCREW
N606690-S53B
TIGHTEN TO
22-34 N·m (17-25 LB-FT)

U-NUT
N800822-S53

SCREW
N606690-S53B
TIGHTEN TO
22-34 N·m
(17-25 LB-FT)

CENTER FRONT
BUMPER PAD
19C949-A ALUMINUM W/O LICENSE PLATE
17C949-B ALUMINUM WITH LICENSE PLATE
17C949-C STEEL W/O LICENSE PLATE
17C949-D STEEL WITH LICENSE PLATE

FRONT
BUMPER

SCREW N606703-S54
TIGHTEN TO
45-70 N·m
(38-51 LB-FT)

FRONT BUMPER PAD
17C881-A RH ALUMINUM BUMPER
17C881-B RH STEEL BUMPER
17C950-A LH ALUMINUM BUMPER
17C950-B LH STEEL BUMPER

FENDER ASSY

PUSH PIN
388930-S

SUPPORT
ASSY

RIVET
372820-S54

REINFORCEMENT
17A919

FRONT
LICENSE
PLATE
MOUNTING
BRACKET
17A385

DEFLECTOR
002A20

WASHER
44725-S2

FRONT BUMPER
GUARD ASSY
17996

U-NUT
N800822-S53

PUSH PIN
388930-S

SCREW
386302-S2

LICENSE
PLATE
FRAME
17A394

FRONT BUMPER
PAD GUARD
17A465 RH
17D967 LH

SCREW N606690-S54
TIGHTEN TO
22-34 N·m (16-25 LB-FT)

VIEW A

N5780-C

1985–86 Lincoln Town Car front bumper

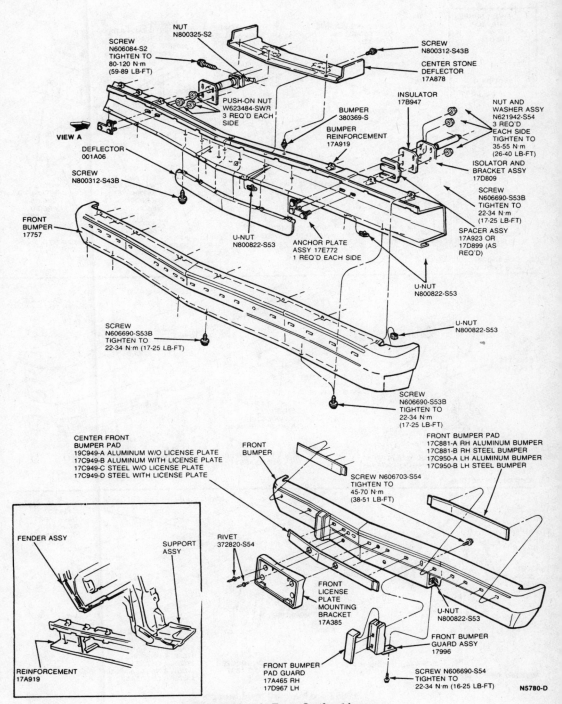

SCREW
N606084-S2
TIGHTEN TO
80-120 N·m
(59-89 LB-FT)

NUT
N800325-S2

SCREW
N800312-S43B

CENTER STONE
DEFLECTOR
17A878

PUSH-ON NUT
W623484-SWR
3 REQ'D EACH
SIDE

VIEW A

BUMPER
380369-S

BUMPER
REINFORCEMENT
17A919

INSULATOR
17B947

NUT AND
WASHER ASSY
N621942-S54
3 REQ'D
EACH SIDE
TIGHTEN TO
35-55 N·m
(26-40 LB-FT)

DEFLECTOR
001A06

SCREW
N800312-S43B

FRONT
BUMPER
17757

U-NUT
N800822-S53

ANCHOR PLATE
ASSY 17E772
1 REQ'D EACH SIDE

ISOLATOR AND
BRACKET ASSY
17D809

SCREW
N606690-S53B
TIGHTEN TO
22-34 N·m
(17-25 LB-FT)

SPACER ASSY
17A923 OR
17D899 (AS
REQ'D)

U-NUT
N800822-S53

SCREW
N606690-S53B
TIGHTEN TO
22-34 N·m (17-25 LB-FT)

U-NUT
N800822-S53

SCREW
N606690-S53B
TIGHTEN TO
22-34 N·m
(17-25 LB-FT)

CENTER FRONT
BUMPER PAD
19C949-A ALUMINUM W/O LICENSE PLATE
17C949-B ALUMINUM WITH LICENSE PLATE
17C949-C STEEL W/O LICENSE PLATE
17C949-D STEEL WITH LICENSE PLATE

FRONT
BUMPER

FRONT BUMPER PAD
17C881-A RH ALUMINUM BUMPER
17C881-B RH STEEL BUMPER
17C950-A LH ALUMINUM BUMPER
17C950-B LH STEEL BUMPER

SCREW N606703-S54
TIGHTEN TO
45-70 N·m
(38-51 LB-FT)

FENDER ASSY

SUPPORT
ASSY

RIVET
372820-S54

FRONT
LICENSE
PLATE
MOUNTING
BRACKET
17A385

U-NUT
N800822-S53

FRONT BUMPER
GUARD ASSY
17996

REINFORCEMENT
17A919

FRONT BUMPER
PAD GUARD
17A465 RH
17D967 LH

SCREW N606690-S54
TIGHTEN TO
22-34 N·m (16-25 LB-FT)

N5780-D

1987–88 Lincoln Town Car front bumper

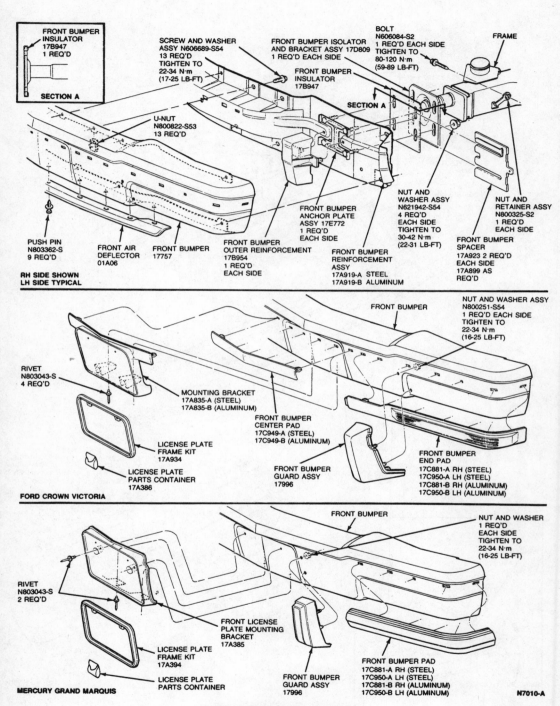

FRONT BUMPER
INSULATOR
17B947
1 REQ'D

SECTION A

SCREW AND WASHER
ASSY N606689-S54
13 REQ'D
TIGHTEN TO
22-34 N·m
(17-25 LB-FT)

FRONT BUMPER ISOLATOR
AND BRACKET ASSY 17D809
1 REQ'D EACH SIDE

FRONT BUMPER
INSULATOR
17B947

BOLT
N606084-S2
1 REQ'D EACH SIDE
TIGHTEN TO
80-120 N·m
(59-89 LB-FT)

FRAME

SECTION A

U-NUT
N800822-S53
13 REQ'D

PUSH PIN
N803362-S
9 REQ'D

FRONT AIR
DEFLECTOR
01A06

FRONT BUMPER
17757

FRONT BUMPER
OUTER REINFORCEMENT
17B954
1 REQ'D
EACH SIDE

FRONT BUMPER
ANCHOR PLATE
ASSY 17E772
1 REQ'D
EACH SIDE

FRONT BUMPER
REINFORCEMENT
ASSY
17A919-A STEEL
17A919-B ALUMINUM

NUT AND
WASHER ASSY
N621942-S54
4 REQ'D
EACH SIDE
TIGHTEN TO
30-42 N·m
(22-31 LB-FT)

NUT AND
RETAINER ASSY
N800325-S2
1 REQ'D
EACH SIDE

FRONT BUMPER
SPACER
17A923 2 REQ'D
EACH SIDE
17A899 AS
REQ'D

RH SIDE SHOWN
LH SIDE TYPICAL

RIVET
N803043-S
4 REQ'D

MOUNTING BRACKET
17A835-A (STEEL)
17A835-B (ALUMINUM)

FRONT BUMPER
CENTER PAD
17C949-A (STEEL)
17C949-B (ALUMINUM)

FRONT BUMPER

NUT AND WASHER ASSY
N800251-S54
1 REQ'D EACH SIDE
TIGHTEN TO
22-34 N·m
(16-25 LB-FT)

LICENSE PLATE
FRAME KIT
17A934

LICENSE PLATE
PARTS CONTAINER
17A386

FRONT BUMPER
GUARD ASSY
17996

FRONT BUMPER
END PAD
17C881-A RH (STEEL)
17C950-A LH (STEEL)
17C881-B RH (ALUMINUM)
17C950-B LH (ALUMINUM)

FORD CROWN VICTORIA

RIVET
N803043-S
2 REQ'D

FRONT BUMPER

NUT AND WASHER
1 REQ'D
EACH SIDE
TIGHTEN TO
22-34 N·m
(16-25 LB-FT)

FRONT LICENSE
PLATE MOUNTING
BRACKET
17A385

LICENSE PLATE
FRAME KIT
17A394

LICENSE PLATE
PARTS CONTAINER

FRONT BUMPER
GUARD ASSY
17996

FRONT BUMPER PAD
17C881-A RH (STEEL)
17C950-A LH (STEEL)
17C881-B RH (ALUMINUM)
17C950-B LH (ALUMINUM)

MERCURY GRAND MARQUIS

N7010-A

1988 Ford/Mercury front bumper

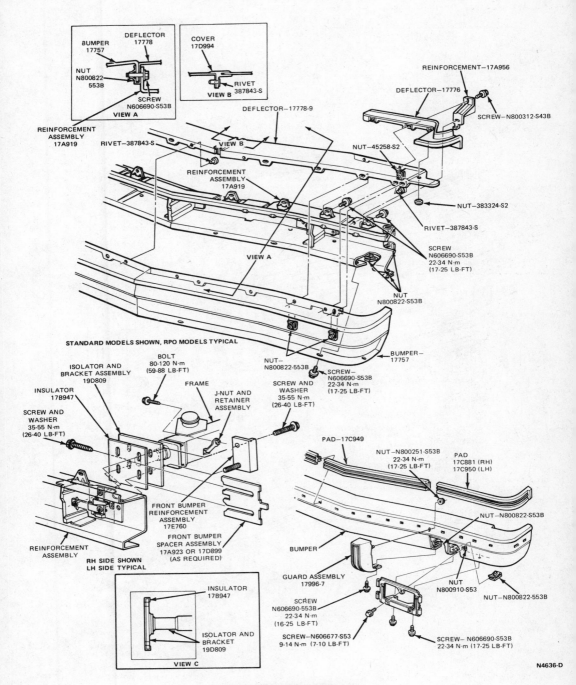

BUMPER 17757
DEFLECTOR 17778
NUT N800822 553B
SCREW N606690-S53B
VIEW A

COVER 17D994
RIVET 387843-S
VIEW B

REINFORCEMENT ASSEMBLY 17A919

REINFORCEMENT—17A956
DEFLECTOR—17776
SCREW—N800312-S43B

DEFLECTOR—17778-9
VIEW B
NUT—45258-S2

RIVET—387843-S
REINFORCEMENT ASSEMBLY 17A919

NUT—383324-S2
RIVET—387843-S

VIEW A

SCREW N606690-S53B 22-34 N·m (17-25 LB-FT)

NUT N800822-S53B

STANDARD MODELS SHOWN, RPO MODELS TYPICAL

BUMPER— 17757

NUT— N800822-553B

SCREW— N606690-S53B 22-34 N·m (17-25 LB-FT)

BOLT 80-120 N·m (59-88 LB-FT)
ISOLATOR AND BRACKET ASSEMBLY 19D809
INSULATOR 17B947
FRAME
J-NUT AND RETAINER ASSEMBLY
SCREW AND WASHER 35-55 N·m (26-40 LB-FT)

SCREW AND WASHER 35-55 N·m (26-40 LB-FT)

FRONT BUMPER REINFORCEMENT ASSEMBLY 17E760
FRONT BUMPER SPACER ASSEMBLY 17A923 OR 17D899 (AS REQUIRED)

REINFORCEMENT ASSEMBLY
RH SIDE SHOWN LH SIDE TYPICAL

PAD—17C949
NUT—N800251-S53B 22-34 N·m (17-25 LB-FT)
PAD 17C881 (RH) 17C950 (LH)

NUT—N800822-S53B

BUMPER

NUT N800910-S53
NUT—N800822-553B

GUARD ASSEMBLY 17996-7
SCREW N606690-553B 22-34 N·m (16-25 LB-FT)
SCREW—N606677-S53 9-14 N·m (7-10 LB-FT)
SCREW— N606690-S53B 22-34 N·m (17-25 LB-FT)

INSULATOR 17B947
ISOLATOR AND BRACKET 19D809
VIEW C

N4636-D

1985–87 Ford front bumper

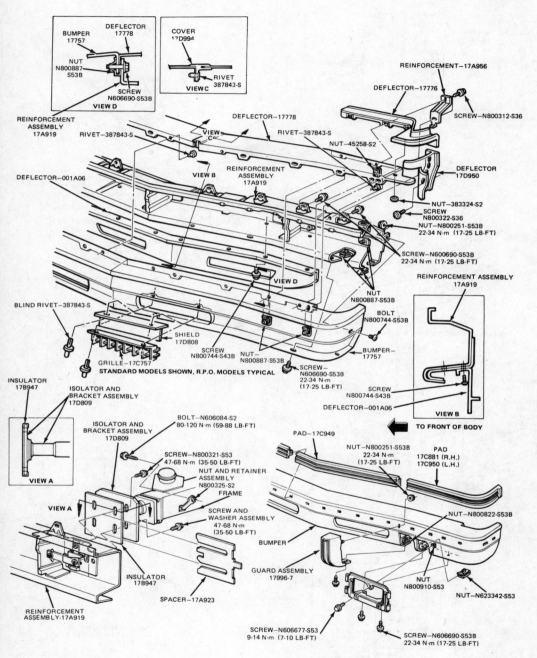

BUMPER 17757
DEFLECTOR 17778
NUT N800887 S53B
SCREW N606690-S53B
VIEW D

COVER 17D994
RIVET 387843-S
VIEW C

REINFORCEMENT—17A956
DEFLECTOR—17776
SCREW—N800312-S36

REINFORCEMENT ASSEMBLY 17A919
RIVET—387843-S
VIEW C
DEFLECTOR—17778
RIVET—387843-S
NUT—45258-S2

DEFLECTOR 17D950

DEFLECTOR—001A06
VIEW B
REINFORCEMENT ASSEMBLY 17A919

NUT—383324-S2
SCREW N800322-S36
NUT—N800251-S53B
22-34 N·m (17-25 LB-FT)

SCREW—N600690-S53B
22-34 N·m (17-25 LB-FT)

REINFORCEMENT ASSEMBLY 17A919

VIEW D
NUT N800887-S53B

BLIND RIVET—387843-S

BOLT N800744-S53B

SHIELD 17D808
SCREW N800744-S43B
NUT— N800887-S53B
SCREW— N606690-S53B
22-34 N·m (17-25 LB-FT)

BUMPER— 17757

SCREW N800744-S43B
DEFLECTOR—001A06
VIEW B
TO FRONT OF BODY

GRILLE—17C757
STANDARD MODELS SHOWN, R.P.O. MODELS TYPICAL

INSULATOR 17B947
ISOLATOR AND BRACKET ASSEMBLY 17D809

VIEW A

ISOLATOR AND BRACKET ASSEMBLY 17D809
BOLT—N606084-S2 80-120 N·m (59-88 LB-FT)
SCREW—N800321-S53 47-68 N·m (35-50 LB-FT)
NUT AND RETAINER ASSEMBLY N800325-S2
FRAME
SCREW AND WASHER ASSEMBLY 47-68 N·m (35-50 LB-FT)

PAD—17C949
NUT—N800251-S53B 22-34 N·m (17-25 LB-FT)
PAD 17C881 (R.H.) 17C950 (L.H.)

NUT—N800822-S53B

VIEW A
INSULATOR 17B947
SPACER—17A923

BUMPER
GUARD ASSEMBLY 17996-7
NUT N800910-S53
NUT—N623342-S53

REINFORCEMENT ASSEMBLY-17A919

SCREW-N606677-S53 9-14 N·m (7-10 LB-FT)
SCREW-N606690-S53B 22-34 N·m (17-25 LB-FT)

1981–82 Ford front bumper

N4636-B

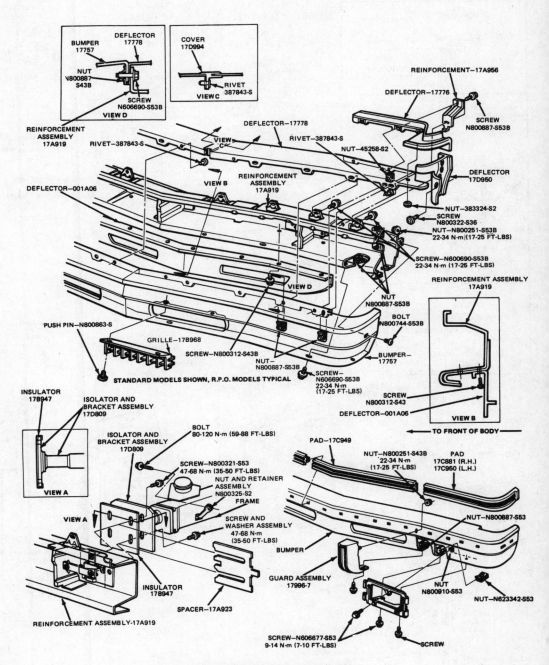

BUMPER 17757
DEFLECTOR 17778
NUT N800887 S43B
SCREW N606690-S53B
VIEW D

COVER 17D994
RIVET 387843-S
VIEW C

REINFORCEMENT ASSEMBLY 17A919

REINFORCEMENT–17A956
DEFLECTOR–17776
SCREW N800887-S53B

DEFLECTOR–17778
VIEW C
RIVET–387843-S
RIVET–387843-S
NUT–45258-S2
DEFLECTOR 17D950

DEFLECTOR–001A06
VIEW B
REINFORCEMENT ASSEMBLY 17A919

NUT–383324-S2
SCREW N800322-S36
NUT–N800251-S53B 22-34 N·m (17-25 FT-LBS)

SCREW–N600690-S53B 22-34 N·m (17-25 FT-LBS)

VIEW D

NUT N800887-S53B

REINFORCEMENT ASSEMBLY 17A919

BOLT N800744-S53B

PUSH PIN–N800863-S

GRILLE–17B968

SCREW–N800312-S43B

NUT– N800887-S53B

SCREW– N606690-S53B 22-34 N·m (17-25 FT-LBS)

BUMPER– 17757

SCREW N800312-S43

DEFLECTOR–001A06
VIEW B

TO FRONT OF BODY

STANDARD MODELS SHOWN, R.P.O. MODELS TYPICAL

INSULATOR 17B947

ISOLATOR AND BRACKET ASSEMBLY 17D809

ISOLATOR AND BRACKET ASSEMBLY 17D809

BOLT 80-120 N·m (59-88 FT-LBS)

SCREW–N800321-S53 47-68 N·m (35-50 FT-LBS)

NUT AND RETAINER ASSEMBLY N800325-S2 FRAME

VIEW A

SCREW AND WASHER ASSEMBLY 47-68 N·m (35-50 FT-LBS)

PAD–17C949
NUT–N800251-S43B 22-34 N·m (17-25 FT-LBS)
PAD 17C881 (R.H.) 17C950 (L.H.)

NUT–N800887-S53

VIEW A

INSULATOR 17B947

SPACER–17A923

BUMPER

GUARD ASSEMBLY 17996-7

NUT N800910-S53

NUT–N623342-S53

REINFORCEMENT ASSEMBLY–17A919

SCREW–N606677-S53 9-14 N·m (7-10 FT-LBS)

SCREW

1968–80 Ford/Mercury front bumper

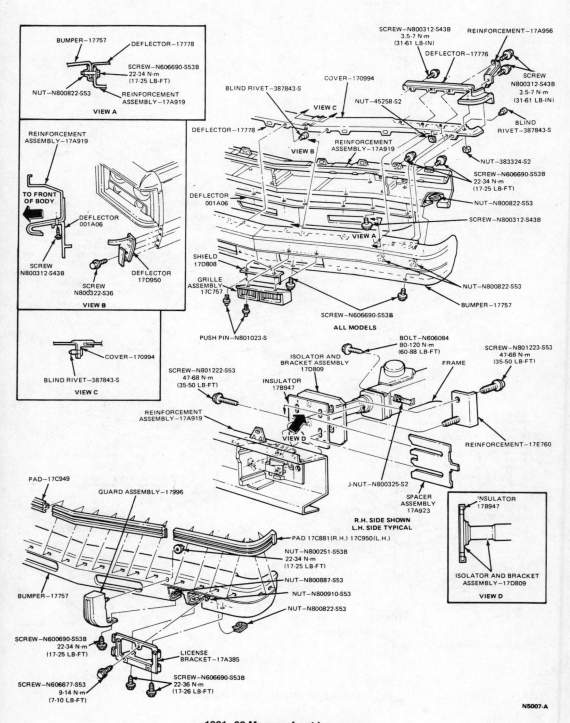

1981–82 Mercury front bumper

N5007-A

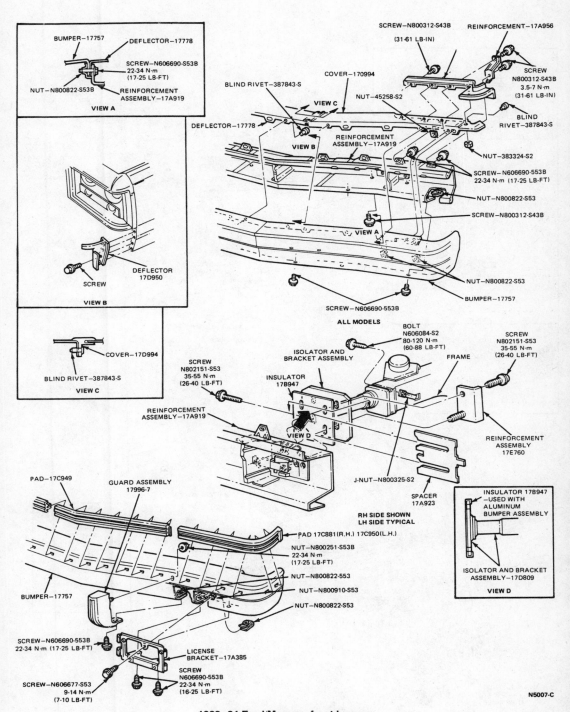

VIEW A

BUMPER—17757
DEFLECTOR—17778
SCREW—N606690-S53B
22-34 N·m
(17-25 LB-FT)
NUT—N800822-S53B
REINFORCEMENT
ASSEMBLY—17A919

VIEW B

DEFLECTOR
17D950
SCREW

VIEW C

COVER—17D994
BLIND RIVET—387843-S

SCREW—N800312-S43B
(31-61 LB-IN)
REINFORCEMENT—17A956
SCREW
N800312-S43B
3.5-7 N·m
(31-61 LB-IN)
BLIND
RIVET—387843-S
NUT—383324-S2
SCREW—N606690-553B
22-34 N·m (17-25 LB-FT)
NUT—N800822-S53
SCREW—N800312-S43B

COVER—170994
BLIND RIVET—387843-S
VIEW C
NUT—45258-S2
DEFLECTOR—17778
REINFORCEMENT
ASSEMBLY—17A919
VIEW B

VIEW A
NUT—N800822-S53
BUMPER—17757
SCREW—N606690-553B

ALL MODELS

BOLT
N606084-S2
80-120 N·m
(60-88 LB-FT)
ISOLATOR AND
BRACKET ASSEMBLY
FRAME
SCREW
N802151-S53
35-55 N·m
(26-40 LB-FT)
SCREW
N802151-S53
35-55 N·m
(26-40 LB-FT)
INSULATOR
17B947
REINFORCEMENT
ASSEMBLY—17A919
VIEW D
J-NUT—N800325-S2
SPACER
17A923
REINFORCEMENT
ASSEMBLY
17E760

**RH SIDE SHOWN
LH SIDE TYPICAL**

PAD—17C949
GUARD ASSEMBLY
17996-7
PAD 17C881(R.H.) 17C950(L.H.)
NUT—N800251-S53B
22-34 N·m
(17-25 LB-FT)
NUT—N800822-553
NUT—N800910-S53
NUT—N800822-S53
BUMPER—17757
SCREW—N606690-553B
22-34 N·m (17-25 LB-FT)
LICENSE
BRACKET—17A385
SCREW
N606690-553B
22-34 N·m
(16-25 LB-FT)
SCREW—N606677-S53
9-14 N·m
(7-10 LB-FT)

INSULATOR 17B947
—USED WITH
ALUMINUM
BUMPER ASSEMBLY
ISOLATOR AND BRACKET
ASSEMBLY—17D809
VIEW D

N5007-C

1983–84 Ford/Mercury front bumper

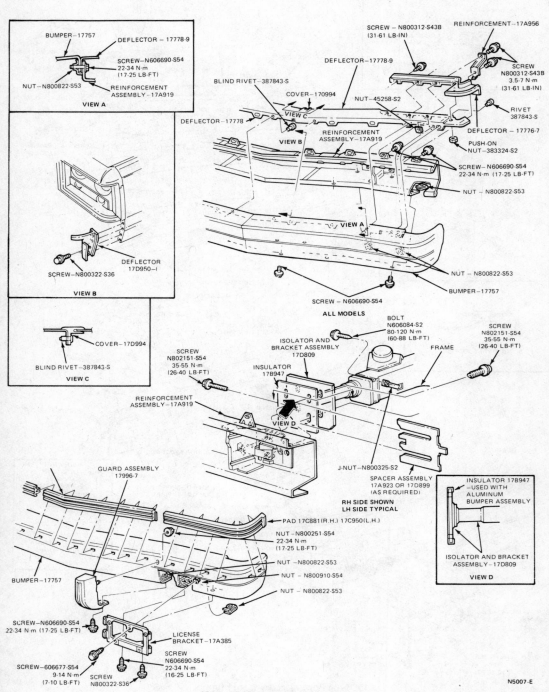

BUMPER—17757

DEFLECTOR — 17778-9

SCREW—N606690-S54
22-34 N·m
(17-25 LB-FT)

NUT—N800822-S53

REINFORCEMENT
ASSEMBLY—17A919

VIEW A

SCREW — N800312-S43B
(31-61 LB-IN)

REINFORCEMENT—17A956

DEFLECTOR—17778-9

SCREW
N800312-S43B
3.5-7 N·m
(31-61 LB-IN)

BLIND RIVET—387843-S

COVER—170994

NUT—45258-S2

RIVET
387843-S

DEFLECTOR—17778

VIEW C

VIEW B

REINFORCEMENT
ASSEMBLY—17A919

DEFLECTOR — 17776-7

PUSH-ON
NUT—383324-S2

SCREW—N606690-S54
22-34 N·m (17-25 LB-FT)

NUT — N800822-S53

VIEW A

SCREW—N800322-S36

DEFLECTOR
17D950-I

VIEW B

NUT — N800822-S53

BUMPER—17757

SCREW — N606690-S54

ALL MODELS

COVER—17D994

BLIND RIVET—387843-S

VIEW C

SCREW
N802151-S54
35-55 N·m
(26-40 LB-FT)

REINFORCEMENT
ASSEMBLY—17A919

INSULATOR
17B947

BOLT
N606084-S2
80-120 N·m
(60-88 LB-FT)

ISOLATOR AND
BRACKET ASSEMBLY
17D809

FRAME

SCREW
N802151-S54
35-55 N·m
(26-40 LB-FT)

VIEW D

J-NUT—N800325-S2

SPACER ASSEMBLY
17A923 OR 17D899
(AS REQUIRED)

**RH SIDE SHOWN
LH SIDE TYPICAL**

GUARD ASSEMBLY
17996-7

PAD 17C881(R.H.) 17C950(L.H.)

NUT—N800251-S54
22-34 N·m
(17-25 LB-FT)

NUT —N800822-S53

NUT — N800910-S54

NUT — N800822-S53

INSULATOR 17B947
—USED WITH
ALUMINUM
BUMPER ASSEMBLY

BUMPER—17757

SCREW—N606690-S54
22-34 N·m (17-25 LB-FT)

LICENSE
BRACKET—17A385

ISOLATOR AND BRACKET
ASSEMBLY—17D809

VIEW D

SCREW—606677-S54
9-14 N·m
(7-10 LB-FT)

SCREW
N800322-S36

SCREW
N606690-S54
22-34 N·m
(16-25 LB-FT)

N5007-E

1985—87 Mercury front bumper

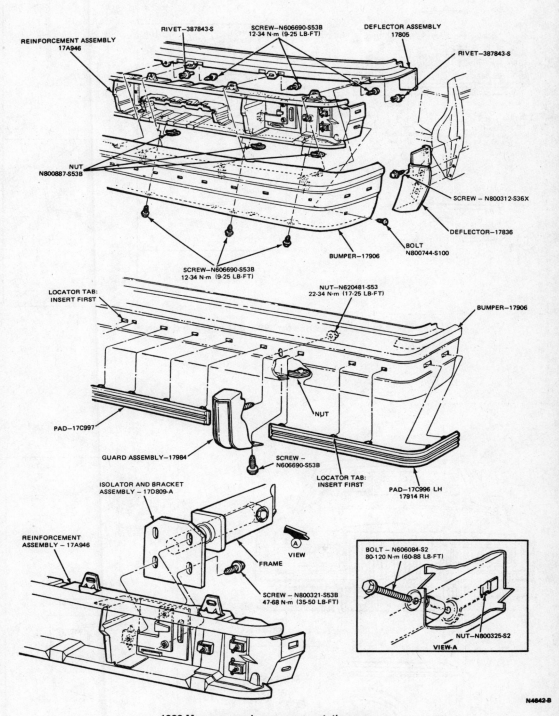

REINFORCEMENT ASSEMBLY
17A946

RIVET—387843-S

SCREW—N606690-S53B
12-34 N·m (9-25 LB-FT)

DEFLECTOR ASSEMBLY
17805

RIVET—387843-S

NUT
N800887-S53B

SCREW — N800312-S36X

DEFLECTOR—17836

BOLT
N800744-S100

BUMPER—17906

SCREW—N606690-S53B
12-34 N·m (9-25 LB-FT)

LOCATOR TAB:
INSERT FIRST

NUT—N620481-S53
22-34 N·m (17-25 LB-FT)

BUMPER—17906

PAD—17C997

GUARD ASSEMBLY—17984

SCREW —
N606690-S53B

NUT

LOCATOR TAB:
INSERT FIRST

PAD—17C996 LH
17914 RH

ISOLATOR AND BRACKET
ASSEMBLY — 17D809-A

REINFORCEMENT
ASSEMBLY — 17A946

VIEW

FRAME

SCREW — N800321-S53B
47-68 N·m (35-50 LB-FT)

BOLT — N606084-S2
80-120 N·m (60-88 LB-FT)

NUT—N800325-S2

VIEW-A

N4642-B

1988 Mercury rear bumper, exc. station wagon

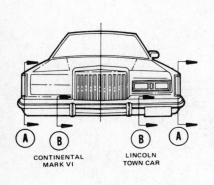

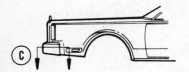

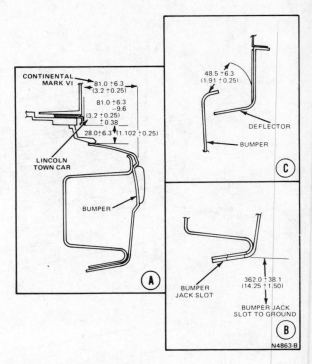

CONTINENTAL
MARK VI

81.0 ⁺6.3
(3.2 ⁺0.25)

81.0 ⁺6.3
−9.6
(3.2 ⁺0.25)
⁺0.38

28.0⁺6.3 (1.102 ⁺0.25)

LINCOLN
TOWN CAR

BUMPER

48.5 ⁺6.3
(1.91 ⁺0.25)

DEFLECTOR

BUMPER

C

BUMPER
JACK SLOT

362.0 ⁺38.1
(14.25 ⁺1.50)

BUMPER JACK
SLOT TO GROUND

A

B

N4863-B

Front bumper clearance for 1981–82 Lincoln and Mark VI

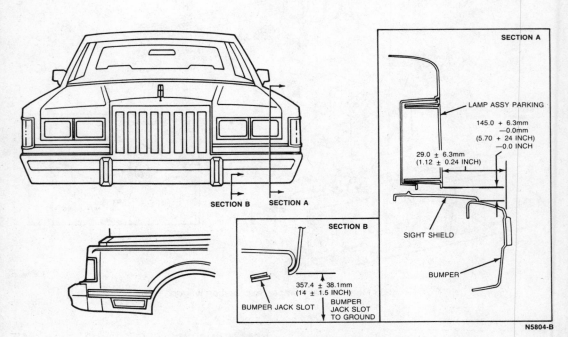

SECTION A

LAMP ASSY PARKING

145.0 + 6.3mm
−0.0mm
(5.70 + 24 INCH)
−0.0 INCH

29.0 ± 6.3mm
(1.12 ± 0.24 INCH)

SIGHT SHIELD

BUMPER

SECTION B   SECTION A

SECTION B

357.4 ± 38.1mm
(14 ± 1.5 INCH)

BUMPER JACK SLOT

BUMPER
JACK SLOT
TO GROUND

N5804-B

Front bumper clearance for 1986–88 Lincoln Town Car

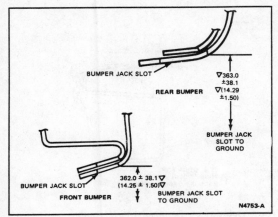

BUMPER JACK SLOT

REAR BUMPER

▽363.0
±38.1
▽(14.29
±1.50)

BUMPER JACK
SLOT TO
GROUND

BUMPER JACK SLOT

FRONT BUMPER

362.0 ± 38.1 ▽
(14.25 ± 1.50)▽

BUMPER JACK SLOT
TO GROUND

N4753-A

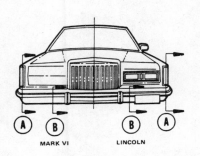

Ⓐ Ⓑ   Ⓑ Ⓐ

MARK VI   LINCOLN

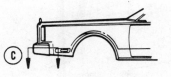

Ⓒ

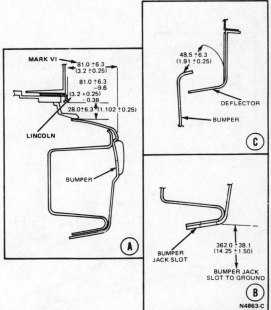

MARK VI

81.0 ⁺6.3
(3.2 ±0.25)

81.0 ⁺6.3
−9.6
(3.2 +0.25)
− 0.38

28.0⁺6.3 (1.102 ±0.25)

LINCOLN

BUMPER

Ⓐ

48.5 ⁺6.3
(1.91 ⁺0.25)

DEFLECTOR

BUMPER

Ⓒ

BUMPER
JACK SLOT

362.0 ⁺38.1
(14.25 ⁺1.50)

BUMPER JACK
SLOT TO GROUND

Ⓑ

N4863-C

Front bumper clearance for 1982–85 Lincoln and Mark VI

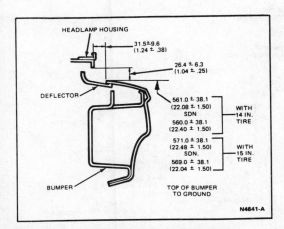

HEADLAMP HOUSING

31.5±9.6
(1.24 ± .38)

26.4 ± 6.3
(1.04 ± .25)

DEFLECTOR

561.0 ± 38.1
(22.08 ± 1.50)
SDN.
560.0 ± 38.1
(22.40 ± 1.50)

WITH
14 IN.
TIRE

571.0 ± 38.1
(22.48 ± 1.50)
SDN.
569.0 ± 38.1
(22.04 ± 1.50)

WITH
15 IN.
TIRE

BUMPER

TOP OF BUMPER
TO GROUND

N4641-A

Front bumper clearance for 1968–80 Mercury

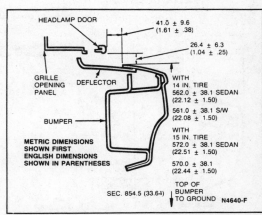

HEADLAMP DOOR

41.0 ± 9.6
(1.61 ± .38)

26.4 ± 6.3
(1.04 ± .25)

GRILLE
OPENING
PANEL

DEFLECTOR

WITH
14 IN. TIRE
562.0 ± 38.1 SEDAN
(22.12 ± 1.50)
561.0 ± 38.1 S/W
(22.08 ± 1.50)

BUMPER

WITH
15 IN. TIRE
572.0 ± 38.1 SEDAN
(22.51 ± 1.50)

METRIC DIMENSIONS
SHOWN FIRST
ENGLISH DIMENSIONS
SHOWN IN PARENTHESES

570.0 ± 38.1
(22.44 ± 1.50)

SEC. 854.5 (33.64)

TOP OF
BUMPER
TO GROUND   N4640-F

**Front bumper clearance for 1984–87 Ford Crown
Victoria High Series**

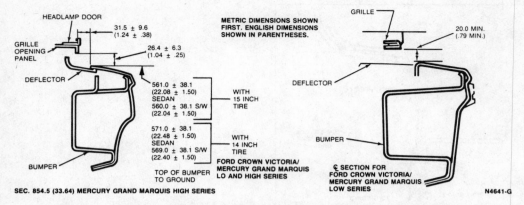

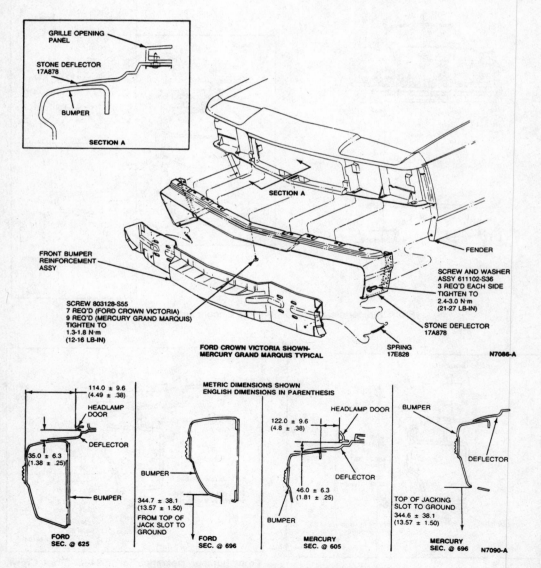

Front bumper clearance for 1984–87 Ford Crown Victoria Low Series/Grand Marquis

Front bumper clearance for 1988 Ford/Mercury

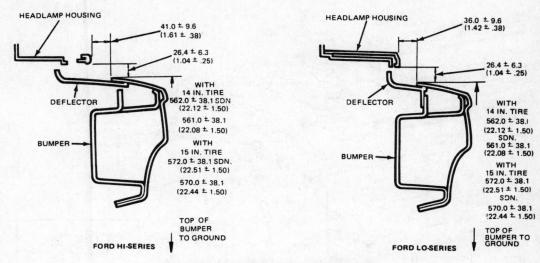

Front bumper clearance for 1968—80 Ford

5. Check the bumper installation clearance specifications in the accompanying illustrations.

Rear Bumpers

REMOVAL AND INSTALLATION

1980-88 Ford and Mercury
1980 Lincoln and Mark VI
1968-79 All Models

1. Remove the 6 bolts/nuts attaching the reinforcement to the isolator.

WARNING: *Never use heat to loosen the nuts!*

2. Remove the bumper from the car.

3. Installation is the reverse of removal. Tighten the nuts to 50 ft. lbs.

4. Check the bumper installation clearance specifications in the accompanying illustrations.

1986-88 Lincoln Town Car

1. Remove the lower stone deflector-to-bumper attachment springs.

2. Remove the isolator-to-bumper nuts.

WARNING: *Never use heat to loosen the nuts!*

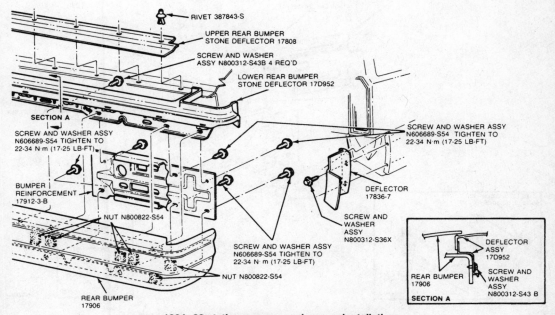

1984—88 station wagon rear bumper installation

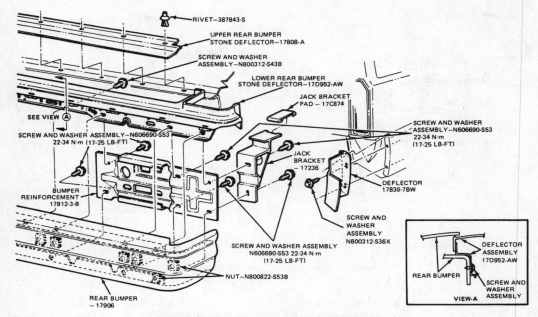

1968–83 station wagon rear bumper installation

3. Disconnect the license plate light wiring.

4. Remove the bumper.

5. Installation is the reverse of removal. Tighten the nuts to 40 ft. lbs.

6. Check the bumper installation clearance specifications in the accompanying illustrations.

1984-85 Lincoln Town Car
1981-83 Lincoln and Mark VI

1. Remove the 6 bolts/nuts attaching the reinforcement to the isolator.

WARNING: *Never use heat to loosen the nuts!*

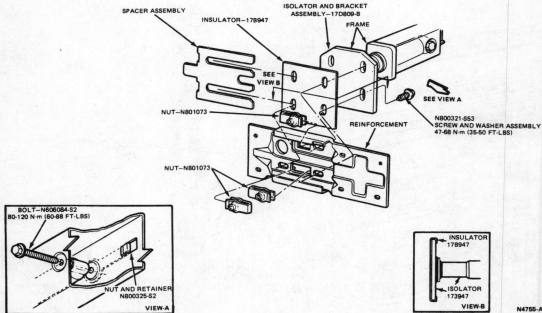

1968–88 Ford/Mercury rear bumper isolator and bracket

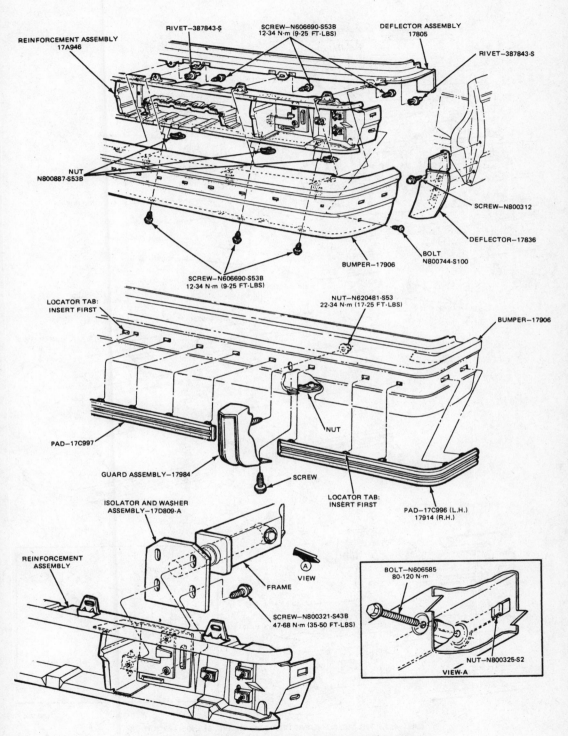

REINFORCEMENT ASSEMBLY
17A946

RIVET—387843-S

SCREW—N606690-S53B
12-34 N·m (9-25 FT-LBS)

DEFLECTOR ASSEMBLY
17805

RIVET—387843-S

NUT
N800887-S53B

SCREW—N800312

DEFLECTOR—17836

BOLT
N800744-S100

BUMPER—17906

SCREW—N606690-S53B
12-34 N·m (9-25 FT-LBS)

LOCATOR TAB:
INSERT FIRST

NUT—N620481-S53
22-34 N·m (17-25 FT-LBS)

BUMPER—17906

PAD—17C997

NUT

GUARD ASSEMBLY—17984

SCREW

LOCATOR TAB:
INSERT FIRST

PAD—17C996 (L.H.)
17914 (R.H.)

ISOLATOR AND WASHER
ASSEMBLY—17D809-A

FRAME

VIEW A

BOLT—N606585
80-120 N·m

REINFORCEMENT
ASSEMBLY

SCREW—N800321-S43B
47-68 N·m (35-50 FT-LBS)

NUT—N800325-S2

VIEW-A

1968—80 Ford/Mercury rear bumper, except station wagon

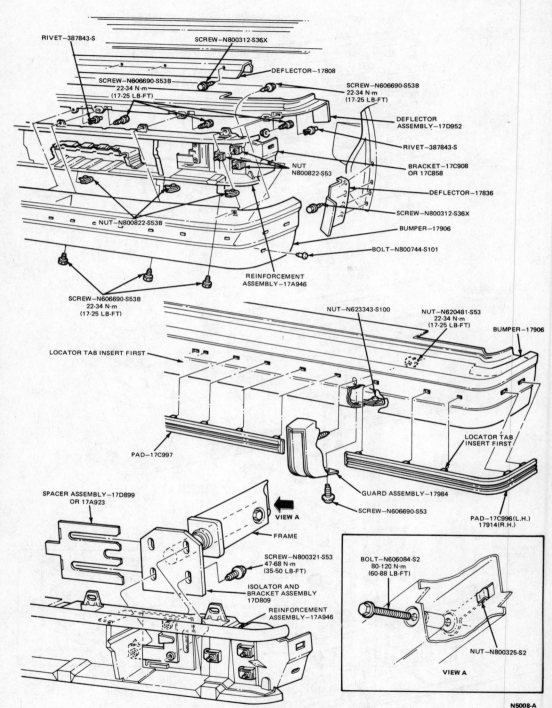

1981–83 Ford/Mercury rear bumper, except station wagon

N5008-A

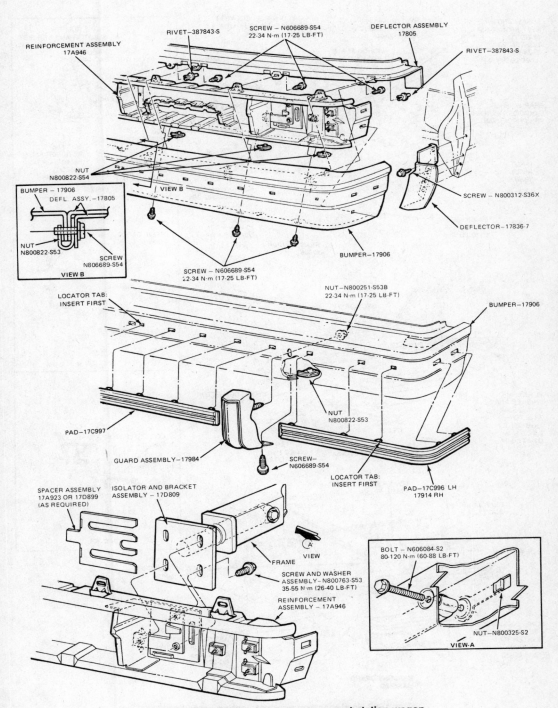

REINFORCEMENT ASSEMBLY 17A946

RIVET—387843-S

SCREW — N606689-S54
22-34 N·m (17-25 LB-FT)

DEFLECTOR ASSEMBLY 17805

RIVET—387843-S

SCREW — N800312-S36X

DEFLECTOR—17836-7

VIEW B

NUT N800822-S54

VIEW B

BUMPER — 17906
DEFL. ASSY.—17805

NUT N800822-S53

SCREW N806689-S54

BUMPER—17906

SCREW — N606689-S54
22-34 N·m (17-25 LB-FT)

NUT—N800251-S53B
22-34 N·m (17-25 LB-FT)

BUMPER—17906

LOCATOR TAB: INSERT FIRST

NUT N800822-S53

PAD—17C997

GUARD ASSEMBLY—17984

SCREW— N606689-S54

LOCATOR TAB: INSERT FIRST

PAD—17C996 LH 17914 RH

SPACER ASSEMBLY 17A923 OR 17D899 (AS REQUIRED)

ISOLATOR AND BRACKET ASSEMBLY – 17D809

VIEW

FRAME

SCREW AND WASHER ASSEMBLY—N800763-S53 35-55 N·m (26-40 LB-FT)

REINFORCEMENT ASSEMBLY – 17A946

BOLT — N606084-S2 80-120 N·m (60-88 LB-FT)

NUT—N800325-S2

VIEW-A

1984–87 Ford/Mercury rear bumper, except station wagon

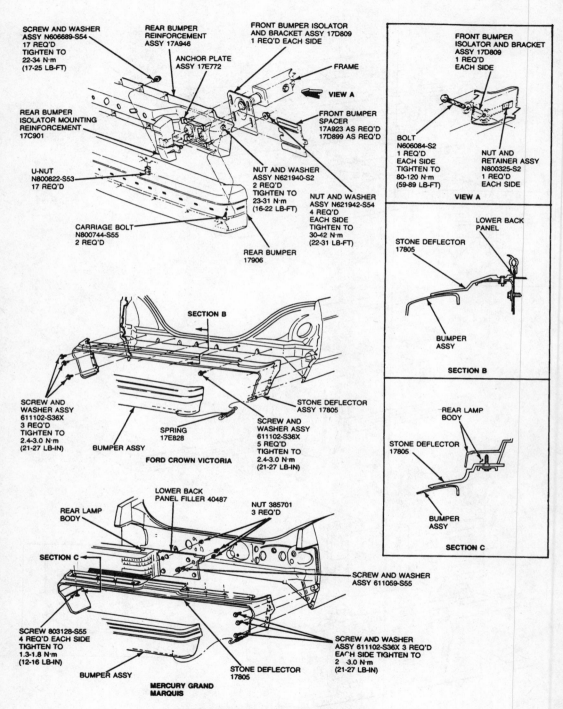

SCREW AND WASHER
ASSY N606689-S54
17 REQ'D
TIGHTEN TO
22-34 N·m
(17-25 LB-FT)

REAR BUMPER
REINFORCEMENT
ASSY 17A946

FRONT BUMPER ISOLATOR
AND BRACKET ASSY 17D809
1 REQ'D EACH SIDE

ANCHOR PLATE
ASSY 17E772

FRAME

VIEW A

REAR BUMPER
ISOLATOR MOUNTING
REINFORCEMENT
17C901

FRONT BUMPER
SPACER
17A923 AS REQ'D
17D899 AS REQ'D

U-NUT
N800822-S53
17 REQ'D

NUT AND WASHER
ASSY N621940-S2
2 REQ'D
TIGHTEN TO
23-31 N·m
(16-22 LB-FT)

NUT AND WASHER
ASSY N621942-S54
4 REQ'D
EACH SIDE
TIGHTEN TO
30-42 N·m
(22-31 LB-FT)

CARRIAGE BOLT
N800744-S55
2 REQ'D

REAR BUMPER
17906

FRONT BUMPER
ISOLATOR AND BRACKET
ASSY 17D809
1 REQ'D
EACH SIDE

BOLT
N606084-S2
1 REQ'D
EACH SIDE
TIGHTEN TO
80-120 N·m
(59-89 LB-FT)

NUT AND
RETAINER ASSY
N800325-S2
1 REQ'D
EACH SIDE

VIEW A

SECTION B

SCREW AND
WASHER ASSY
611102-S36X
3 REQ'D
TIGHTEN TO
2.4-3.0 N·m
(21-27 LB-IN)

BUMPER ASSY

SPRING
17E828

STONE DEFLECTOR
ASSY 17805

SCREW AND
WASHER ASSY
611102-S36X
5 REQ'D
TIGHTEN TO
2.4-3.0 N·m
(21-27 LB-IN)

FORD CROWN VICTORIA

LOWER BACK
PANEL

STONE DEFLECTOR
17805

BUMPER
ASSY

SECTION B

LOWER BACK
PANEL FILLER 40487

NUT 385701
3 REQ'D

REAR LAMP
BODY

SECTION C

SCREW AND WASHER
ASSY 611059-S55

SCREW 803128-S55
4 REQ'D EACH SIDE
TIGHTEN TO
1.3-1.8 N·m
(12-16 LB-IN)

BUMPER ASSY

STONE DEFLECTOR
17805

SCREW AND WASHER
ASSY 611102-S36X 3 REQ'D
EACH SIDE TIGHTEN TO
2 3.0 N·m
(21-27 LB-IN)

MERCURY GRAND
MARQUIS

REAR LAMP
BODY

STONE DEFLECTOR
17805

BUMPER
ASSY

SECTION C

1988 Ford rear bumper, exc. station wagon

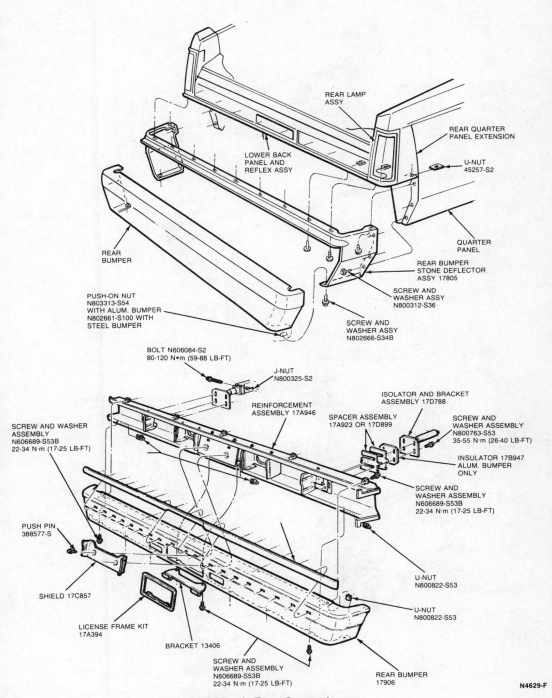

REAR LAMP
ASSY

REAR QUARTER
PANEL EXTENSION

U-NUT
45257-S2

LOWER BACK
PANEL AND
REFLEX ASSY

QUARTER
PANEL

REAR
BUMPER

REAR BUMPER
STONE DEFLECTOR
ASSY 17805

SCREW AND
WASHER ASSY
N800312-S36

PUSH-ON NUT
N803313-S54
WITH ALUM. BUMPER
N802661-S100 WITH
STEEL BUMPER

SCREW AND
WASHER ASSY
N802666-S34B

BOLT N606084-S2
80-120 N·m (59-88 LB-FT)

J-NUT
N800325-S2

ISOLATOR AND BRACKET
ASSEMBLY 17D788

REINFORCEMENT
ASSEMBLY 17A946

SPACER ASSEMBLY
17A923 OR 17D899

SCREW AND
WASHER ASSEMBLY
N800763-S53
35-55 N·m (26-40 LB-FT)

SCREW AND WASHER
ASSEMBLY
N606689-S53B
22-34 N·m (17-25 LB-FT)

INSULATOR 17B947
ALUM. BUMPER
ONLY

SCREW AND
WASHER ASSEMBLY
N606689-S53B
22-34 N·m (17-25 LB-FT)

PUSH PIN
388577-S

U-NUT
N800822-S53

SHIELD 17C857

U-NUT
N800822-S53

LICENSE FRAME KIT
17A394

BRACKET 13406

SCREW AND
WASHER ASSEMBLY
N606689-S53B
22-34 N·m (17-25 LB-FT)

REAR BUMPER
17906

1985 Lincoln Town Car rear bumper

N4629-F

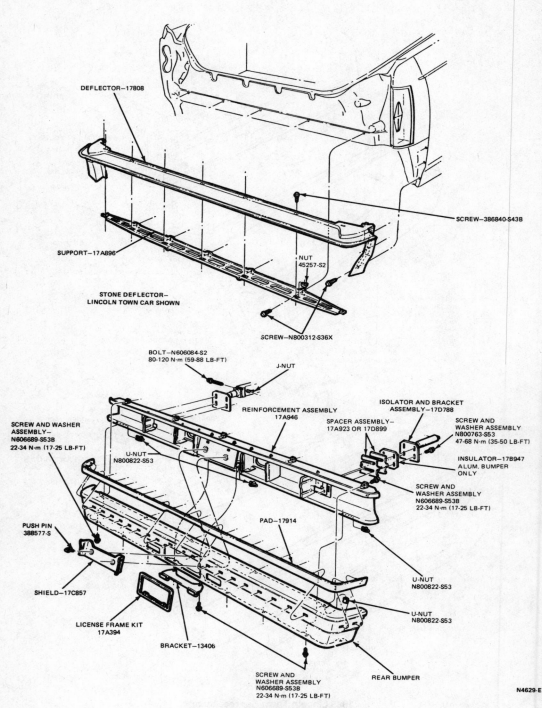

DEFLECTOR—17808

SCREW—386840-S43B

SUPPORT—17A896

NUT
45257-S2

STONE DEFLECTOR—
LINCOLN TOWN CAR SHOWN

SCREW—N800312-S36X

BOLT—N606084-S2
80-120 N·m (59-88 LB-FT)

J-NUT

REINFORCEMENT ASSEMBLY
17A946

ISOLATOR AND BRACKET
ASSEMBLY—17D788

SCREW AND WASHER
ASSEMBLY—
N606689-S53B
22-34 N·m (17-25 LB-FT)

SPACER ASSEMBLY—
17A923 OR 17D899

SCREW AND
WASHER ASSEMBLY
N800763-S53
47-68 N·m (35-50 LB-FT)

U-NUT
N800822-S53

INSULATOR—17B947
ALUM. BUMPER
ONLY

PUSH PIN
388577-S

SCREW AND
WASHER ASSEMBLY
N606689-S53B
22-34 N·m (17-25 LB-FT)

PAD—17914

SHIELD—17C857

U-NUT
N800822-S53

LICENSE FRAME KIT
17A394

U-NUT
N800822-S53

BRACKET—13406

SCREW AND
WASHER ASSEMBLY
N606689-S53B
22-34 N·m (17-25 LB-FT)

REAR BUMPER

N4629-E

1984 Lincoln Town Car rear bumper

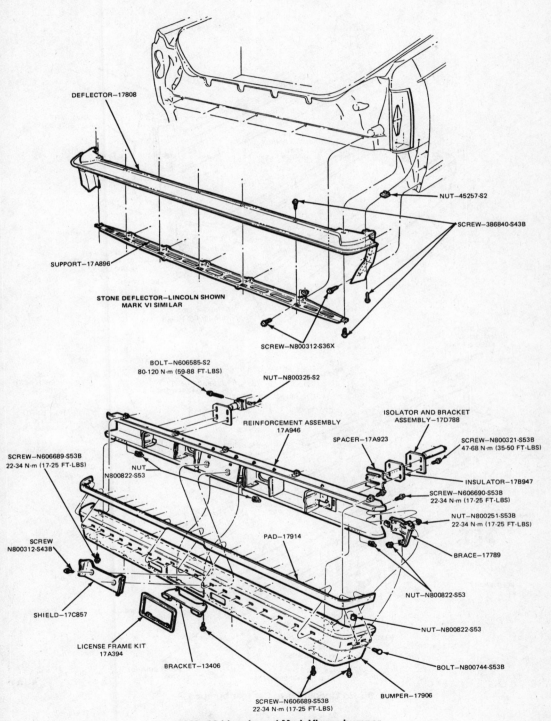

DEFLECTOR—17808

NUT—45257-S2

SCREW—386840-S43B

SUPPORT—17A896

**STONE DEFLECTOR—LINCOLN SHOWN
MARK VI SIMILAR**

SCREW—N800312-S36X

BOLT—N606585-S2
80-120 N·m (59-88 FT-LBS)

NUT—N800325-S2

REINFORCEMENT ASSEMBLY
17A946

ISOLATOR AND BRACKET
ASSEMBLY—17D788

SPACER—17A923

SCREW—N800321-S53B
47-68 N·m (35-50 FT-LBS)

SCREW—N606689-S53B
22-34 N·m (17-25 FT-LBS)

NUT
N800822-S53

INSULATOR—17B947

SCREW—N606690-S53B
22-34 N·m (17-25 FT-LBS)

NUT—N800251-S53B
22-34 N·m (17-25 FT-LBS)

SCREW
N800312-S43B

PAD—17914

BRACE—17789

NUT—N800822-S53

SHIELD—17C857

LICENSE FRAME KIT
17A394

NUT—N800822-S53

BRACKET—13406

BOLT—N800744-S53B

SCREW—N606689-S53B
22-34 N·m (17-25 FT-LBS)

BUMPER—17906

1968–83 Lincoln and Mark VI rear bumper

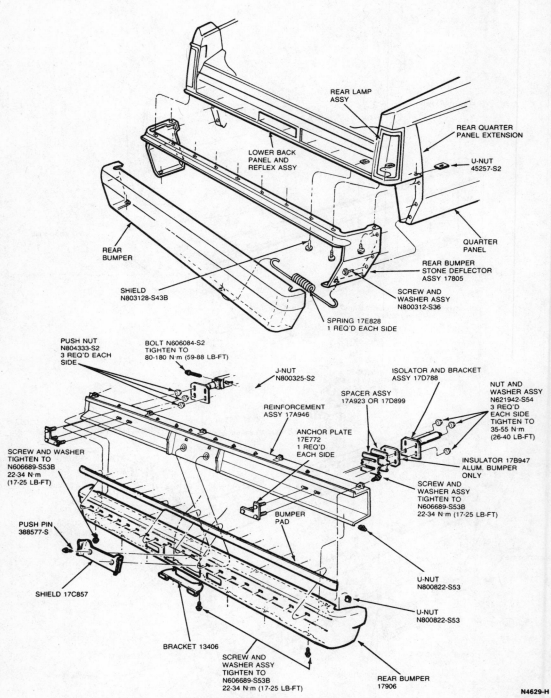

REAR LAMP
ASSY

REAR QUARTER
PANEL EXTENSION

LOWER BACK
PANEL AND
REFLEX ASSY

U-NUT
45257-S2

QUARTER
PANEL

REAR
BUMPER

REAR BUMPER
STONE DEFLECTOR
ASSY 17805

SHIELD
N803128-S43B

SCREW AND
WASHER ASSY
N800312-S36

SPRING 17E828
1 REQ'D EACH SIDE

PUSH NUT
N804333-S2
3 REQ'D EACH
SIDE

BOLT N606084-S2
TIGHTEN TO
80-180 N·m (59-88 LB-FT)

J-NUT
N800325-S2

ISOLATOR AND BRACKET
ASSY 17D788

NUT AND
WASHER ASSY
N621942-S54
3 REQ'D
EACH SIDE
TIGHTEN TO
35-55 N·m
(26-40 LB-FT)

REINFORCEMENT
ASSY 17A946

SPACER ASSY
17A923 OR 17D899

ANCHOR PLATE
17E772
1 REQ'D
EACH SIDE

SCREW AND WASHER
TIGHTEN TO
N606689-S53B
22-34 N·m
(17-25 LB-FT)

INSULATOR 17B947
ALUM. BUMPER
ONLY

SCREW AND
WASHER ASSY
TIGHTEN TO
N606689-S53B
22-34 N·m (17-25 LB-FT)

PUSH PIN
388577-S

BUMPER
PAD

U-NUT
N800822-S53

SHIELD 17C857

U-NUT
N800822-S53

BRACKET 13406

SCREW AND
WASHER ASSY
TIGHTEN TO
N606689-S53B
22-34 N·m (17-25 LB-FT)

REAR BUMPER
17906

N4629-H

1986—88 Lincoln Town Car rear bumper

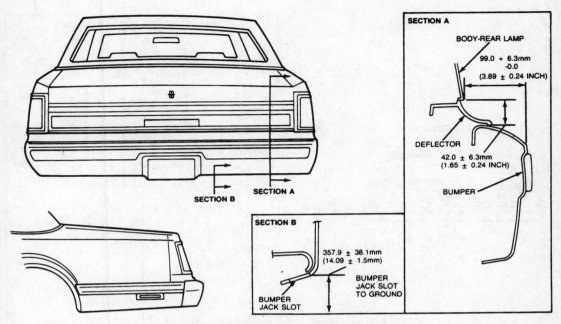

SECTION A

BODY-REAR LAMP

99.0 + 6.3mm
       -0.0
(3.89 ± 0.24 INCH)

DEFLECTOR

42.0 ± 6.3mm
(1.65 ± 0.24 INCH)

BUMPER

SECTION B

SECTION A

SECTION B

357.9 ± 38.1mm
(14.09 ± 1.5mm)

BUMPER
JACK SLOT
TO GROUND

BUMPER
JACK SLOT

1987–88 Lincoln Town Car rear bumper clearance

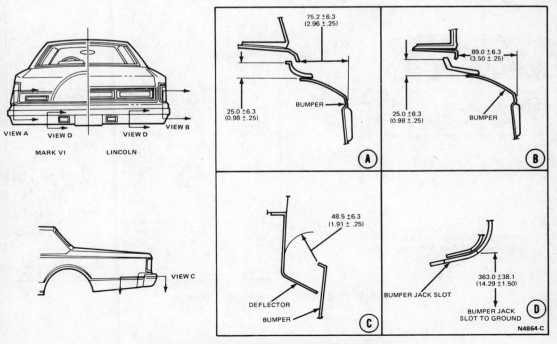

VIEW A   VIEW B
VIEW D   VIEW D

MARK VI   LINCOLN

VIEW C

75.2 ±6.3
(2.96 ±.25)

25.0 ±6.3
(0.98 ±.25)

BUMPER

Ⓐ

89.0 ±6.3
(3.50 ±.25)

25.0 ±6.3
(0.98 ±.25)

BUMPER

Ⓑ

48.5 ±6.3
(1.91 ±.25)

DEFLECTOR

BUMPER

Ⓒ

BUMPER JACK SLOT

363.0 ±38.1
(14.29 ±1.50)

BUMPER JACK
SLOT TO GROUND

Ⓓ

N4864-C

1968–83 Lincoln and Mark VI rear bumper clearance

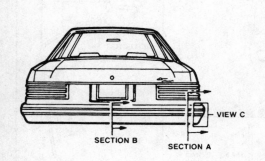

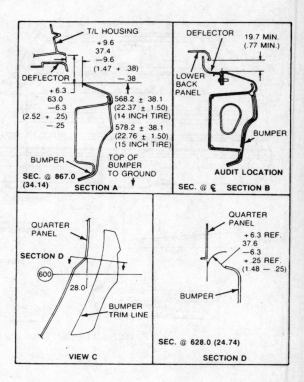

T/L HOUSING

+9.6
37.4
—9.6
(1.47 + .38)
— .38

DEFLECTOR

+6.3
63.0
—6.3
(2.52 + .25)
— .25

568.2 ± 38.1
(22.37 ± 1.50)
(14 INCH TIRE)

578.2 ± 38.1
(22.76 ± 1.50)
(15 INCH TIRE)

BUMPER

TOP OF
BUMPER
TO GROUND

SEC. @ 867.0
(34.14)   **SECTION A**

DEFLECTOR   19.7 MIN.
(.77 MIN.)

LOWER
BACK
PANEL

BUMPER

AUDIT LOCATION

SEC. @ ₵   **SECTION B**

QUARTER
PANEL

SECTION D

(600)

28.0

BUMPER
TRIM LINE

VIEW C

QUARTER
PANEL

+6.3 REF.
37.6
—6.3
+ .25 REF.
(1.48 — .25)

BUMPER

SEC. @ 628.0 (24.74)

SECTION D

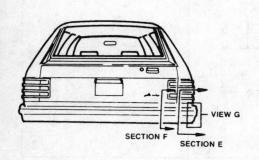

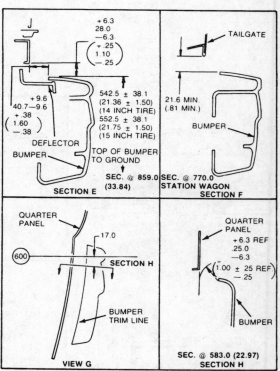

+6.3
28.0
—6.3
+ .25
1.10
— .25

542.5 ± 38.1
(21.36 ± 1.50)
(14 INCH TIRE)
552.5 ± 38.1
(21.75 ± 1.50)
(15 INCH TIRE)

+9.6
40.7—9.6
+ .38
(1.60   )
— .38

DEFLECTOR

BUMPER

TOP OF BUMPER
TO GROUND

SEC. @ 859.0
(33.84)

SECTION E

TAILGATE

21.6 MIN.
(.81 MIN.)

BUMPER

SEC. @ 770.0
**STATION WAGON
SECTION F**

QUARTER
PANEL

17.0

(600)   **SECTION H**

BUMPER
TRIM LINE

VIEW G

QUARTER
PANEL
+6.3 REF
.25.0
—6.3
(1.00 ± 25 REF.)
— .25

BUMPER

SEC. @ 583.0 (22.97)
SECTION H

METRIC DIMENSIONS SHOWN FIRST.
ENGLISH DIMENSIONS IN PARENTHESES

1981—88 Ford/Mercury rear bumper clearance

1968–80 Ford rear bumper clearance

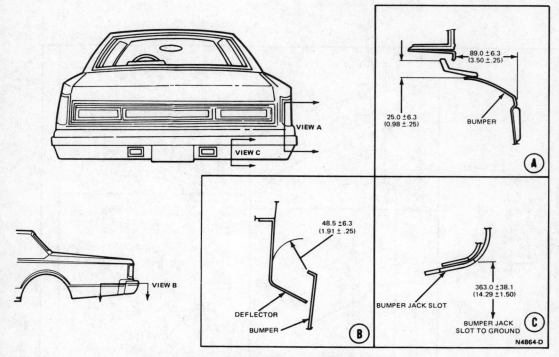

1984–86 Lincoln Town Car rear bumper clearance

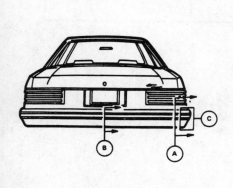

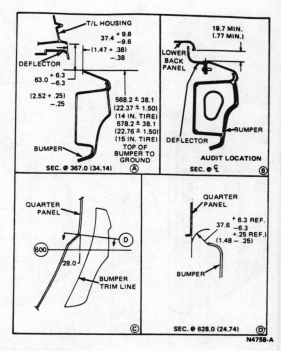

N4758-A

1968–80 Mercury rear bumper clearance

2. Disconnect all wiring from the bumper.

3. Remove the bumper from the car.

4. Installation is the reverse of removal. Tighten the nuts to 50 ft. lbs.

5. Check the bumper installation clearance specifications in the accompanying illustrations.

Grille
REMOVAL AND INSTALLATION
1968-82 Ford and Mercury
1986-87 Ford

The grille is attached with 7 screws removed through the front of the grille.

1983-85 Ford and Mercury
1986-87 Mercury

The grille is attached with 6 screws removed through the front of the grille.

1988 Ford

The grille is attached with 4 screws and locking tabs, removed through the front of the grille.

1988 Mercury

The grille is attached with 6 locking tabs. To remove the grille, depress the locking tabs with a flat-bladed screwdriver and pull the tabs from the retainers.

1968-85 Lincoln and Continental

1. Open the hood and remove the 2 bolts which secure the grille actuating brackets to the front bumper reinforcement.

2. Remove the 6 bolts or nuts - 2 on each side and 2 at the top - that secure the grille to the grille opening panel.

3. Installation is the reverse of removal.

1986-88 Lincoln Town Car

Remove the 6 nuts that fasten the grille to the grille opening panel, accessed through the front of the grille.

Outside Rearview Mirrors
REMOVAL AND INSTALLATION
Left Side Manual Remote Control Through 1986
LINCOLN AND CONTINENTAL

1. Remove the large nut retaining the control lever in the trim panel armrest.

2. Remove the door trim panel.

3. Remove the wiring and support straps the retain the cable inside the door.

4. On cars with a heated mirror, disconnect the wiring.

5. Remove the 2 locknuts that retain the mirror to the door.

6. Carefully remove the mirror and cable.

7. Installation is the reverse of removal.

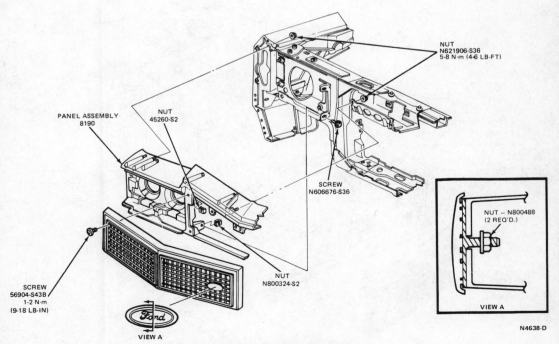

1983 Ford grille; Mercury similar

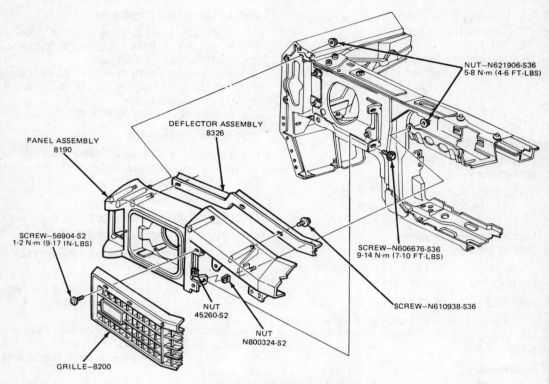

NUT—N621906-S36
5-8 N·m (4-6 FT-LBS)

DEFLECTOR ASSEMBLY
8326

PANEL ASSEMBLY
8190

SCREW-56904-S2
1-2 N·m (9-17 IN-LBS)

SCREW—N606676-S36
9-14 N·m (7-10 FT-LBS)

NUT
45260-S2

NUT
N800324-S2

SCREW—N610938-S36

GRILLE—8200

1968–82 Ford Low Series grille

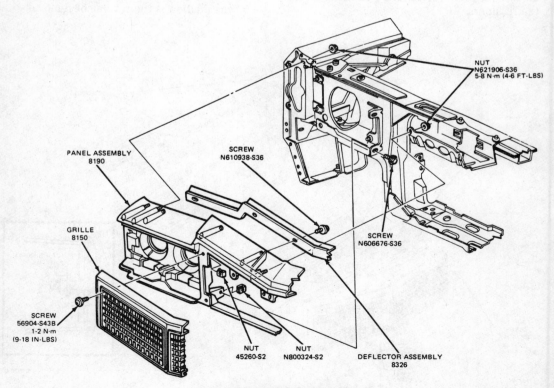

NUT
N621906-S36
5-8 N·m (4-6 FT-LBS)

PANEL ASSEMBLY
8190

SCREW
N610938-S36

GRILLE
8150

SCREW
N606676-S36

SCREW
56904-S43B
1-2 N·m
(9-18 IN-LBS)

NUT
45260-S2

NUT
N800324-S2

DEFLECTOR ASSEMBLY
8326

1968–82 Ford High Series grille

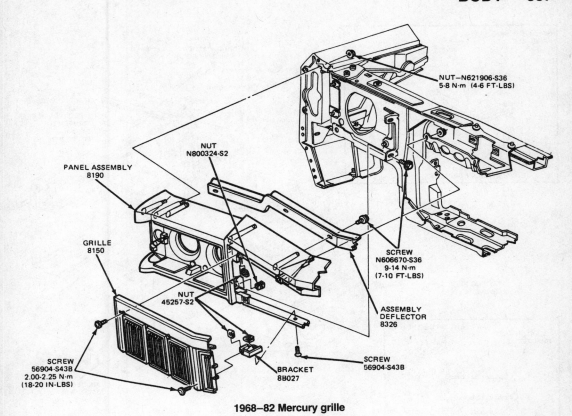

NUT—N621906-S36
5-8 N·m (4-6 FT-LBS)

NUT
N800324-S2

PANEL ASSEMBLY
8190

GRILLE
8150

NUT
45257-S2

SCREW
N606670-S36
9-14 N·m
(7-10 FT-LBS)

ASSEMBLY
DEFLECTOR
8326

SCREW
56904-S43B
2.00-2.25 N·m
(18-20 IN-LBS)

BRACKET
8B027

SCREW
56904-S43B

1968–82 Mercury grille

NUT
N621906-S36
2 REQ'D EACH SIDE
TIGHTEN TO
5-8 N·m
(45-70 LB-IN)

NUT
N621906-S36
TIGHTEN TO
5-8 N·m
(45-70 LB-IN)

PANEL ASSY
8190

RADIATOR
GRILLE 8200

NUT
N804250-S2

SCREW
N606676-S36
2 REQ'D
TIGHTEN TO
9-14 N·m
(7-11 LB-FT)

NUT
N800324-S2

SCREW
56904-S100
7 REQ'D
TIGHTEN TO
1-2 N·m
(9-17 LB-IN)

STRAP
95874

VIEW A

DEFLECTOR ASSY
8A211 RH
8A261 LH

PUSH PIN
801023-S

DEFLECTOR
ASSY
8A211 RH
8A261 LH

ISOLATOR AND
BRACKET ASSY

STRAP
95874

VIEW A

N5781-D

1984–87 Crown Victoria grille; Mercury similar

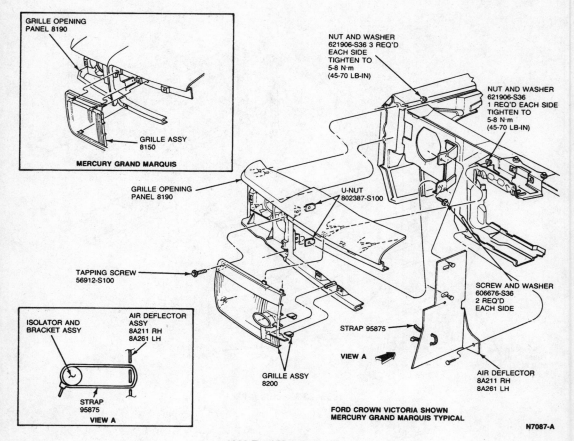

GRILLE OPENING
PANEL 8190

GRILLE ASSY
8150

MERCURY GRAND MARQUIS

GRILLE OPENING
PANEL 8190

NUT AND WASHER
621906-S36 3 REQ'D
EACH SIDE
TIGHTEN TO
5-8 N·m
(45-70 LB-IN)

NUT AND WASHER
621906-S36
1 REQ'D EACH SIDE
TIGHTEN TO
5-8 N·m
(45-70 LB-IN)

U-NUT
802387-S100

TAPPING SCREW
56912-S100

SCREW AND WASHER
606676-S36
2 REQ'D
EACH SIDE

STRAP 95875

VIEW A

ISOLATOR AND
BRACKET ASSY

AIR DEFLECTOR
ASSY
8A211 RH
8A261 LH

STRAP
95875

VIEW A

GRILLE ASSY
8200

AIR DEFLECTOR
8A211 RH
8A261 LH

**FORD CROWN VICTORIA SHOWN
MERCURY GRAND MARQUIS TYPICAL**

N7087-A

1988 Ford/Mercury grille

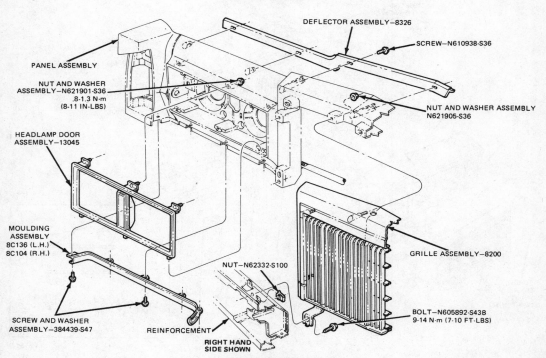

DEFLECTOR ASSEMBLY—8326

SCREW—N610938-S36

PANEL ASSEMBLY

NUT AND WASHER
ASSEMBLY—N621901-S36
.8-1.3 N·m
(8-11 IN-LBS)

NUT AND WASHER ASSEMBLY
N621905-S36

HEADLAMP DOOR
ASSEMBLY—13045

MOULDING
ASSEMBLY
8C136 (L.H.)
8C104 (R.H.)

GRILLE ASSEMBLY—8200

NUT—N62332-S100

SCREW AND WASHER
ASSEMBLY—384439-S47

REINFORCEMENT

RIGHT HAND
SIDE SHOWN

BOLT—N605892-S43B
9-14 N·m (7-10 FT-LBS)

1968—80 Lincoln grille

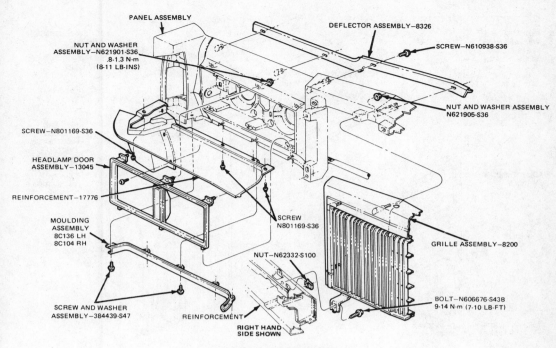

PANEL ASSEMBLY

NUT AND WASHER
ASSEMBLY—N621901-S36
.8-1.3 N·m
(8-11 LB-INS)

DEFLECTOR ASSEMBLY—8326

SCREW—N610938-S36

SCREW—N801169-S36

NUT AND WASHER ASSEMBLY
N621905-S36

HEADLAMP DOOR
ASSEMBLY—13045

REINFORCEMENT—17776

SCREW
N801169-S36

MOULDING
ASSEMBLY
8C136 LH
8C104 RH

GRILLE ASSEMBLY—8200

NUT—N62332-S100

SCREW AND WASHER
ASSEMBLY—384439-S47

REINFORCEMENT

BOLT—N606676-S43B
9-14 N·m (7-10 LB-FT)

RIGHT HAND
SIDE SHOWN

Grille for the 1981 Lincoln

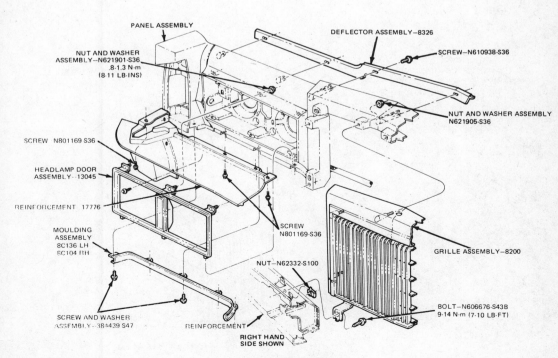

PANEL ASSEMBLY

NUT AND WASHER
ASSEMBLY—N621901-S36
.8-1.3 N·m
(8-11 LB-INS)

DEFLECTOR ASSEMBLY—8326

SCREW—N610938-S36

NUT AND WASHER ASSEMBLY
N621905-S36

SCREW N801169 S36

HEADLAMP DOOR
ASSEMBLY—13045

REINFORCEMENT 17776

SCREW
N801169-S36

MOULDING
ASSEMBLY
8C136 LH
8C104 RH

GRILLE ASSEMBLY—8200

NUT—N62332-S100

SCREW AND WASHER
ASSEMBLY—384439 S47

REINFORCEMENT

BOLT—N606676-S43B
9-14 N·m (7-10 LB-FT)

RIGHT HAND
SIDE SHOWN

1982 Town Car grille

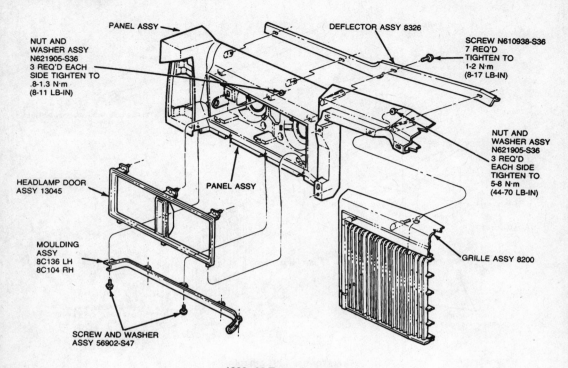

NUT AND
WASHER ASSY
N621905-S36
3 REQ'D EACH
SIDE TIGHTEN TO
.8-1.3 N·m
(8-11 LB-IN)

PANEL ASSY

DEFLECTOR ASSY 8326

SCREW N610938-S36
7 REQ'D
TIGHTEN TO
1-2 N·m
(8-17 LB-IN)

NUT AND
WASHER ASSY
N621905-S36
3 REQ'D
EACH SIDE
TIGHTEN TO
5-8 N·m
(44-70 LB-IN)

HEADLAMP DOOR
ASSY 13045

PANEL ASSY

MOULDING
ASSY
8C136 LH
8C104 RH

GRILLE ASSY 8200

SCREW AND WASHER
ASSY 56902-S47

1983–88 Town Car grille

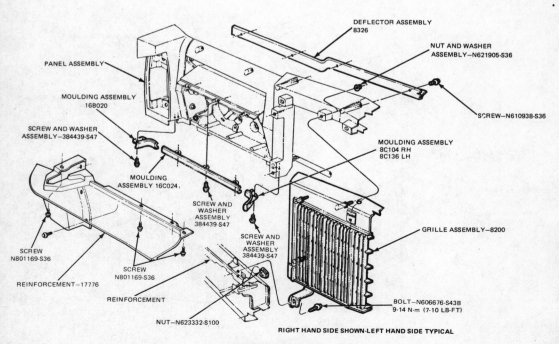

DEFLECTOR ASSEMBLY
8326

NUT AND WASHER
ASSEMBLY—N621905-S36

PANEL ASSEMBLY

MOULDING ASSEMBLY
16B020

SCREW—N610938-S36

SCREW AND WASHER
ASSEMBLY—384439-S47

MOULDING ASSEMBLY
8C104 RH
8C136 LH

MOULDING
ASSEMBLY 16C024

SCREW AND
WASHER
ASSEMBLY
384439-S47

GRILLE ASSEMBLY—8200

SCREW
N801169-S36

SCREW AND
WASHER
ASSEMBLY
384439-S47

REINFORCEMENT—17776

SCREW
N801169-S36

REINFORCEMENT

BOLT—N606676-S43B
9-14 N·m (7-10 LB-FT)

NUT—N623332-S100

RIGHT HAND SIDE SHOWN-LEFT HAND SIDE TYPICAL

1984 Mark VI grille

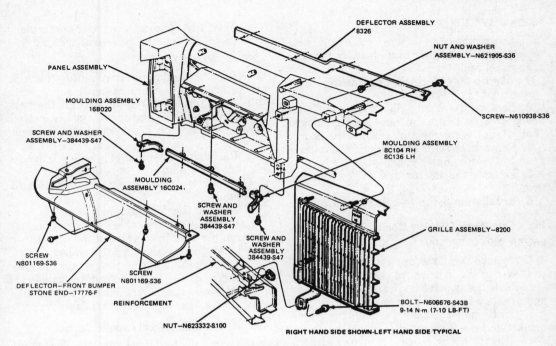

DEFLECTOR ASSEMBLY
8326

NUT AND WASHER
ASSEMBLY—N621905-S36

PANEL ASSEMBLY

MOULDING ASSEMBLY
16B020

SCREW—N610938-S36

SCREW AND WASHER
ASSEMBLY—384439-S47

MOULDING ASSEMBLY
8C104 RH
8C136 LH

MOULDING
ASSEMBLY 16C024

SCREW AND
WASHER
ASSEMBLY
384439-S47

GRILLE ASSEMBLY—8200

SCREW AND
WASHER
ASSEMBLY
384439-S47

SCREW
N801169-S36

SCREW
N801169-S36

DEFLECTOR—FRONT BUMPER
STONE END—17776-F

REINFORCEMENT

BOLT—N606676-S43B
9-14 N·m (7-10 LB-FT)

NUT—N623332-S100

RIGHT HAND SIDE SHOWN-LEFT HAND SIDE TYPICAL

1983 Mark VI grille

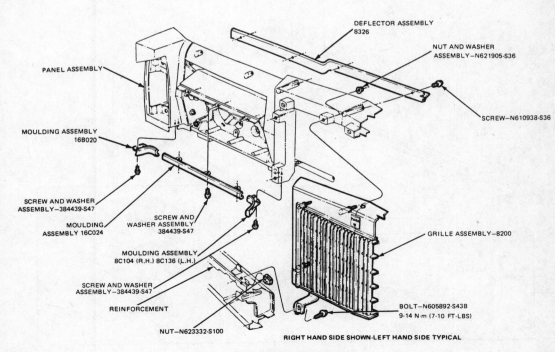

DEFLECTOR ASSEMBLY
8326

NUT AND WASHER
ASSEMBLY—N621905-S36

PANEL ASSEMBLY

SCREW—N610938-S36

MOULDING ASSEMBLY
16B020

SCREW AND WASHER
ASSEMBLY—384439-S47

MOULDING
ASSEMBLY 16C024

SCREW AND
WASHER ASSEMBLY
384439-S47

GRILLE ASSEMBLY—8200

MOULDING ASSEMBLY
8C104 (R.H.) 8C136 (L.H.)

SCREW AND WASHER
ASSEMBLY—384439-S47

REINFORCEMENT

BOLT—N605892-S43B
9-14 N·m (7-10 FT-LBS)

NUT—N623332-S100

RIGHT HAND SIDE SHOWN-LEFT HAND SIDE TYPICAL

1968–82 Mark VI grille

FORD AND MERCURY

1. Loosen the bezel setscrew (standard trim) or retaining nut (deluxe trim) to allow for door trim panel removal.

2. Remove the door trim panel and watershield.

3. Remove the 2 ring clips (with vent windows) or 4 ring clips (without vent windows) that retain the mirror cables inside the door.

4. Remove the screws that retain the mirror head to the door outer panel.

5. Remove the mirror and cable from the door.

6. Installation is the reverse of removal.

Right Side Manual Remote Control Through 1986

LINCOLN AND CONTINENTAL

1. Remove the large nut retaining the control lever in the instrument panel.

2. Push the control lever through the hole and unscrew the control lever retainer.

3. Gently pull the cable through the chime bracket and the 2 wiring clips.

4. Remove the door trim panel and watershield.

5. Remove the door and hinge pillar grommets.

6. Push out the wiring clips retaining the cable to the door reinforcement.

7. Remove the 2 nuts that retain the mirror head assembly to the door outer panel.

8. Carefully remove the mirror and cable.

9. Installation is the reverse of removal.

FORD AND MERCURY

1. Remove the large nut retaining the control lever in the instrument panel.

2. Push the control lever through the hole and disconnect the 3 plastic cable guides located along the lower back side of the instrument panel.

3. Push out the A-pillar plug and pull the cable through the hole.

4. Remove the door trim panel and watershield.

5. Remove the door grommet.

6. Carefully pull the cable and rubber plug(s) through the hole in the face of the door inner panel and through the support strap.

7. Remove the 2 screws that retain the mirror head assembly to the door outer panel.

8. Carefully remove the mirror and cable.

9. Installation is the reverse of removal.

1987-88 Left Side Manual Remote Control

1. Loosen the bezel setscrew (standard trim) or retaining nut (deluxe trim) to allow for door trim panel removal.

2. Remove the door trim panel and watershield.

3. Remove the 2 ring clips (with vent windows) or 4 ring clips (without vent windows) that retain the mirror cables inside the door.

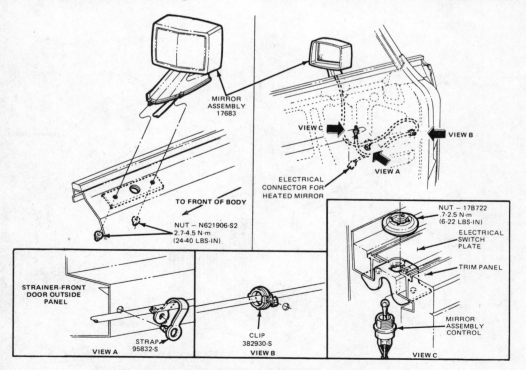

Remote control mirror for the Lincoln and Mark VI; right side is similar

4. Remove the screws that retain the mirror head to the door outer panel.

5. Remove the mirror and cable from the door.

6. Installation is the reverse of removal.

1987-88 Right Side Manual Remote Control

1. Remove the large nut retaining the control lever in the instrument panel.

2. Push the control lever through the hole

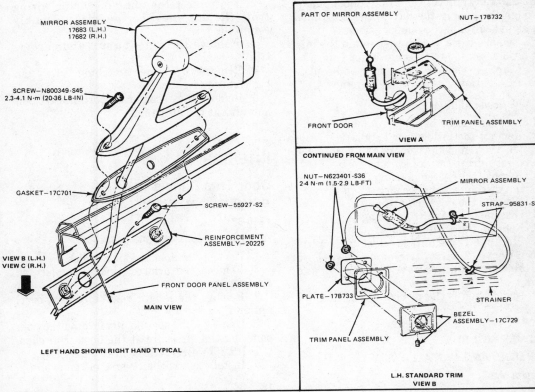

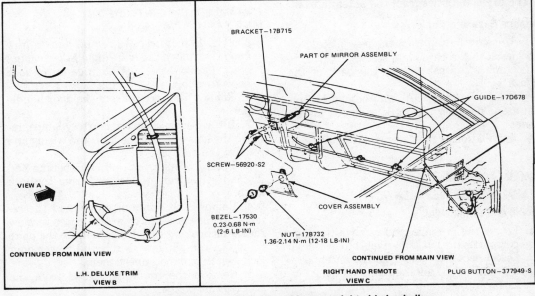

Remote control mirror for the Ford/Mercury; right side is similar

and disconnect the 3 plastic cable guides located along the lower back side of the instrument panel.

3. Push out the A-pillar plug and pull the cable through the hole.

4. Remove the door trim panel and watershield.

5. Remove the door grommet.

6. Carefully pull the cable and rubber plug(s) through the hole in the face of the door inner panel and through the support strap.

7. Remove the 2 screws that retain the mirror head assembly to the door outer panel.

8. Carefully remove the mirror and cable.

9. Installation is the reverse of removal.

1984-88 Power Mirrors

1. Disconnect the battery ground.

2. Remove the inside door handle.

3. On the left door, remove the bezel from the power mirror control switch.

4. Remove the switch housing from the armrest and disconnect the wiring.

5. Remove the door trim panel.

6. Disconnect the mirror wiring.

7. Remove the wiring guides.

8. Remove the 2 mirror retaining nuts (Town Car) or 2 mirror retaining screws (Ford and Mercury) and remove the mirror and wiring.

9. Installation is the reverse of removal.

Manual Antenna
REMOVAL AND INSTALLATION

Antenna Mast

The mast unscrews from the antenna base.

Antenna Base and Cable

1. Unsnap the cap from the base plate.

2. Remove the base plate screws.

3. Unplug the cable from the back of the radio.

4. Guide the cable out from behind the instrument panel while pulling it out of the fender.

5. Installation is the reverse of removal.

Power Antenna
REMOVAL AND INSTALLATION

Lincoln and Continental

1. Lower the antenna and remove the luggage compartment left trim panel.

2. Disconnect the cable from the antenna.

3. Disconnect the antenna motor wiring.

4. Remove the antenna trim nut.

5. Remove the screw from the antenna

mounting bracket located at the bottom of the motor.

6. Lift the antenna from the car.

Ford and Mercury

1. From inside the engine compartment, disconnect the antenna lead from the antenna, near the right plastic fender apron.

2. Disconnect the antenna motor wiring from the antenna overlay wire assembly connector.

3. Remove the antenna nut and chrome trim.

4. Remove the fender attaching bolts from the right fender.

5. Remove the antenna support bracket bolt and lift out the antenna.

INTERIOR

Door Trim Panels
REMOVAL AND INSTALLATION

1968-88

FORD AND MERCURY WITH STANDARD TRIM

1. Remove the inside door handles.

2. Remove the armrest and disconnect all electrical connectors.

3. Remove the mirror remote control bezel nut and bezel.

4. Using a wood spatula, pry around the trim panel putting pressure at the door trim clips. NEVER PRY BETWEEN THE CLIPS!

5. Installation is the reverse of removal.

1968-84

FORD AND MERCURY WITH DELUXE TRIM
LINCOLN AND CONTINENTAL

NOTE: *Disconnect the remote rod-to-lock knob assembly prior to lifting off the housing plate, to avoid possible damage to the lock knob assembly.*

1. Remove the screws from the door handle cup.

2. If the car has armrest courtesy lamps, remove the lens, remove the bulb and wiring and remove the pull cup.

3. Reach through the pull cup opening and disconnect the remote lock rod from the lock knob.

4. Remove the retaining screw and the remote mirror bezel nut from the power window regulator housing switch plate. Raise the plate to expose the window switch and power door lock switch and disconnect them.

5. Remove the retaining screws from the arm rest assembly.

6. Using a wood spatula, pry around the trim

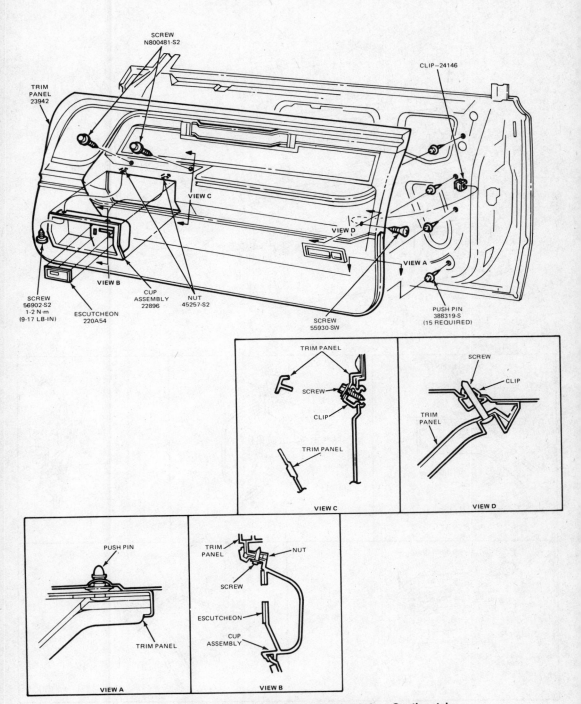

Front door trim panel for the Low Series 2-door Continental

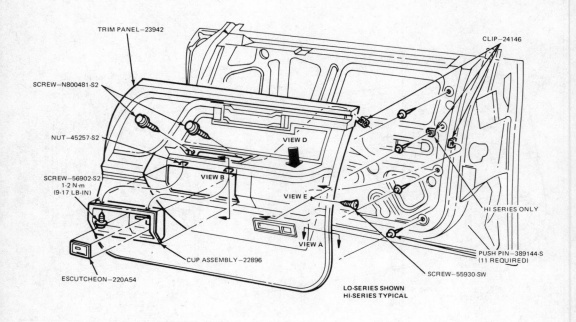

TRIM PANEL—23942

CLIP—24146

SCREW—N800481-S2

NUT—45257-S2

SCREW—56902-S2
1-2 N·m
(9-17 LB-IN)

VIEW D

VIEW B

VIEW E

VIEW A

HI SERIES ONLY

CUP ASSEMBLY—22896

ESCUTCHEON—220A54

PUSH PIN—389144-S
(11 REQUIRED)

SCREW—55930-SW

LO-SERIES SHOWN
HI-SERIES TYPICAL

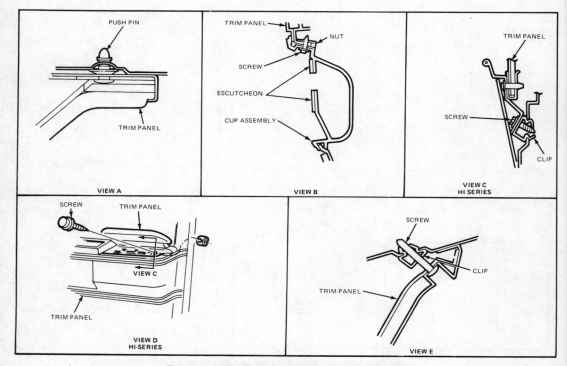

PUSH PIN

TRIM PANEL

VIEW A

TRIM PANEL

NUT

SCREW

ESCUTCHEON

CUP ASSEMBLY

VIEW B

TRIM PANEL

SCREW

CLIP

**VIEW C
HI SERIES**

SCREW

TRIM PANEL

VIEW C

TRIM PANEL

**VIEW D
HI-SERIES**

SCREW

CLIP

TRIM PANEL

VIEW E

Front door trim panel for the 4-door Continental

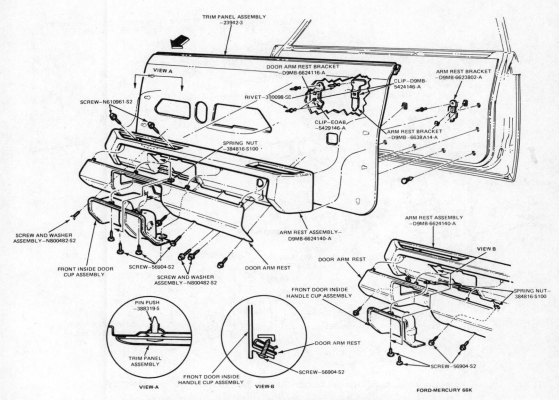

Front door trim panel for the 4-door High Series 1968–80 Ford/Mercury

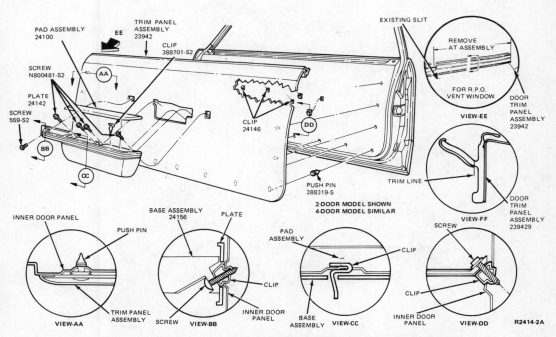

Front door trim panel for the 4-door Standard Series 1968–80 Ford/Mercury

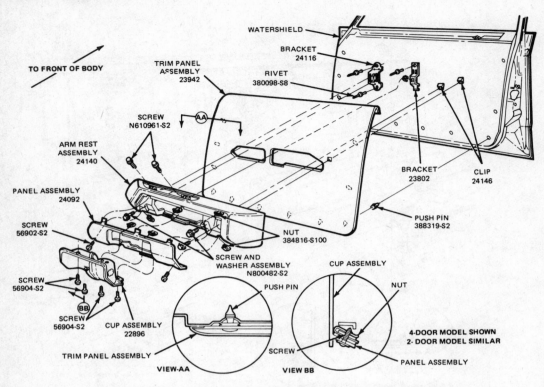

Front door trim panel for the 4-door Custom Series 1968—80 Ford/Mercury

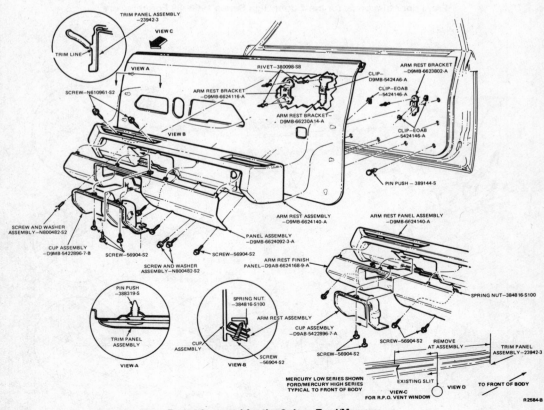

Door trim panel for the 2-door Ford/Mercury

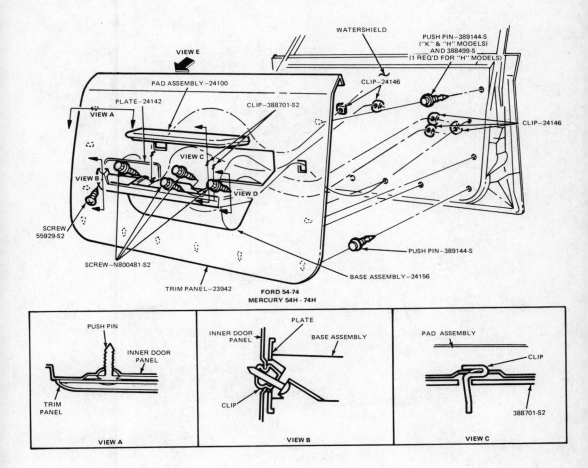

VIEW E

WATERSHIELD

PUSH PIN—389144-S
("K" & "H" MODELS)
AND 388499-S
(1 REQ'D FOR "H" MODELS)

PAD ASSEMBLY—24100

CLIP—24146

PLATE—24142

CLIP—388701-S2

VIEW A

CLIP—24146

VIEW C

VIEW B

VIEW D

SCREW
55929-S2

PUSH PIN—389144-S

SCREW—N800481-S2

BASE ASSEMBLY—24156

TRIM PANEL—23942

FORD 54-74
MERCURY 54H - 74H

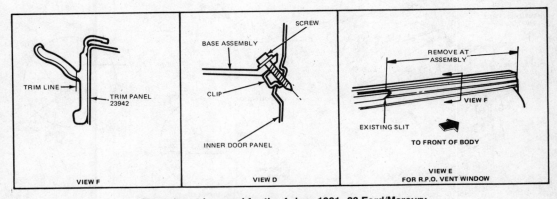

PUSH PIN

INNER DOOR
PANEL

TRIM
PANEL

VIEW A

INNER DOOR
PANEL

PLATE

BASE ASSEMBLY

CLIP

VIEW B

PAD ASSEMBLY

CLIP

388701-S2

VIEW C

TRIM LINE

TRIM PANEL
23942

VIEW F

BASE ASSEMBLY

SCREW

CLIP

INNER DOOR PANEL

VIEW D

REMOVE AT
ASSEMBLY

VIEW F

EXISTING SLIT

TO FRONT OF BODY

VIEW E
FOR R.P.O. VENT WINDOW

Front door trim panel for the 4-door 1981—88 Ford/Mercury

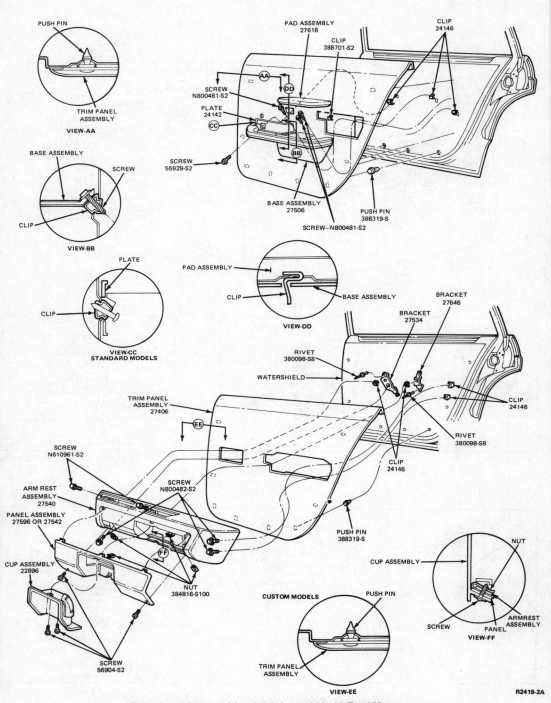

Rear door trim panel for the 4-door 1968–80 Ford/Mercury

PUSH PIN

TRIM PANEL
ASSEMBLY

VIEW-AA

BASE ASSEMBLY

SCREW

CLIP

VIEW-BB

PLATE

CLIP

**VIEW-CC
STANDARD MODELS**

PAD ASSEMBLY
27618

CLIP
388701-S2

CLIP
24146

SCREW
N800481-S2

PLATE
24142

SCREW
55929-S2

BASE ASSEMBLY
27506

PUSH PIN
388319-S

SCREW–N800481-S2

PAD ASSEMBLY

CLIP

BASE ASSEMBLY

VIEW-DD

BRACKET
27646

BRACKET
27534

RIVET
380098-S8

WATERSHIELD

TRIM PANEL
ASSEMBLY
27406

CLIP
24146

RIVET
380098-S8

CLIP
24146

SCREW
N610961-S2

ARM REST
ASSEMBLY
27540

PANEL ASSEMBLY
27596 OR 27542

SCREW
N800482-S2

CUP ASSEMBLY
22896

NUT
384816-S100

PUSH PIN
388319-S

SCREW
56904-S2

CUSTOM MODELS

PUSH PIN

TRIM PANEL
ASSEMBLY

VIEW-EE

NUT

CUP ASSEMBLY

ARMREST
ASSEMBLY

SCREW

PANEL

VIEW-FF

R2419-2A

panel putting pressure at the door trim clips. NEVER PRY BETWEEN THE CLIPS!

7. Disconnect the speaker wiring and lift off the panel.

8. Installation is the reverse of removal.

1985-86

LINCOLN TOWN CAR
FORD AND MERCURY WITH DELUXE TRIM

1. Remove the screws from the door handle cup.

2. If the car has armrest courtesy lamps, remove the lens, remove the bulb and wiring and remove the pull cup.

3. Reach through the pull cup opening and disconnect the remote lock rod from the lock knob.

4. Remove the retaining screw and the remote mirror bezel nut from the power window regulator housing switch plate. Raise the plate to expose the window switch and power door lock switch and disconnect them.

5. Remove the retaining screws from the arm rest finish panel, except on the Town Car.
On the Town Car, remove the armrest assembly screws and remove the armrest.

6. Using a wood spatula, pry around the trim panel putting pressure at the door trim clips. NEVER PRY BETWEEN THE CLIPS!

7. Disconnect the speaker wiring and lift off the panel.

8. Installation is the reverse of removal.

1987-88

LINCOLN TOWN CAR
FORD AND MERCURY WITH DELUXE TRIM

1. Remove the screws from the door handle cup.

2. If the car has armrest courtesy lamps, remove the lens, remove the bulb and wiring and remove the pull cup.

3. Reach through the pull cup opening and disconnect the remote lock rod from the lock knob.

4. On the Town Car, using a putty knife, or similar tool, carefully pry the window switch bezel from the armrest.

5. Remove the retaining screw and the remote mirror bezel nut from the power window regulator housing switch plate. Raise the plate to expose the window switch and power door lock switch and disconnect them.

6. On the Ford and Mercury, remove the retaining screws from the arm rest finish panel, remove the armrest assembly screws and remove the armrest.

7. Using a wood spatula, pry around the trim panel putting pressure at the door trim clips. NEVER PRY BETWEEN THE CLIPS!

8. Disconnect the speaker wiring and lift off the panel.

9. Installation is the reverse of removal.

Manual Door Glass
REMOVAL AND INSTALLATION
Through 1988

1. Remove the door trim panel and watershield. On 2-door models, loosen the glass belt stabilizers.

2. Raise the glass sufficiently to access the 3 glass bracket rivets and support it in that position.

3. Drill out the rivets with a ¼" drill bit.

4. Remove the glass.

5. Installation is the reverse of removal. Replace the rivets with ¼-20 bolts, nuts and lockwashers.

Door Glass Regulator
REMOVAL AND INSTALLATION
Through 1988

1. Remove the door trim panel and watershield. On 2-door models, loosen the glass belt stabilizers.

2. Raise the glass sufficiently to access the 3 glass bracket rivets and support it in that position.

3. Drill out the rivets with a ¼" drill bit.

4. Disengage the regulator slide arm from the glass C-channel and remove the regulator from the door.

5. Installation is the reverse of removal. Replace the rivets with ¼-20 bolts, nuts and lockwashers.

Front Door Electric Window Motor
REMOVAL AND INSTALLATION
Ford and Mercury Through 1988

1. Raise the window to the full up position.

2. Disconnect the battery ground.

3. Remove the door trim panel and watershield.

4. Disconnect the power window motor wiring.

5. Using the accompanying illustration, drill 3, ½" holes in the door to expose the motor attaching bolts.

6. Remove the bolts.

7. Push the motor outward to disengage the motor and drive assembly from the regulator gear.

8. Remove the motor from the door.

9. Install the new motor and torque the bolts to 50-85 in. lbs. The new motor kit will have plugs to fill the drilled holes.

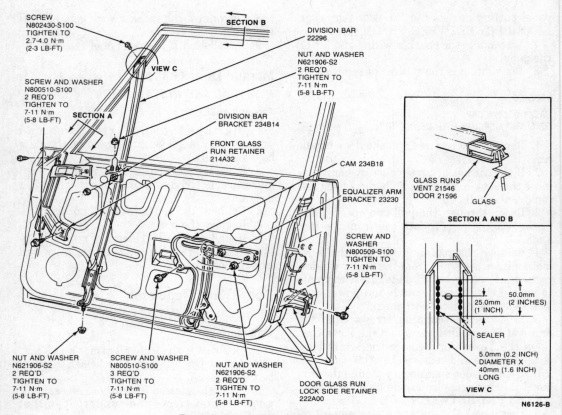

SCREW
N802430-S100
TIGHTEN TO
2.7-4.0 N·m
(2-3 LB-FT)

VIEW C

SECTION B

DIVISION BAR
22296

NUT AND WASHER
N621906-S2
2 REQ'D TIGHTEN TO
7-11 N·m
(5-8 LB-FT)

SCREW AND WASHER
N800510-S100
2 REQ'D
TIGHTEN TO
7-11 N·m
(5-8 LB-FT)

SECTION A

DIVISION BAR
BRACKET 234B14

FRONT GLASS
RUN RETAINER
214A32

CAM 234B18

EQUALIZER ARM
BRACKET 23230

SCREW AND
WASHER
N800509-S100
TIGHTEN TO
7-11 N·m
(5-8 LB-FT)

GLASS RUNS
VENT 21546
DOOR 21596

GLASS

SECTION A AND B

50.0mm
(2 INCHES)

25.0mm
(1 INCH)

SEALER

5.0mm (0.2 INCH)
DIAMETER X
40mm (1.6 INCH)
LONG

VIEW C

NUT AND WASHER
N621906-S2
2 REQ'D
TIGHTEN TO
7-11 N·m
(5-8 LB-FT)

SCREW AND WASHER
N800510-S100
3 REQ'D
TIGHTEN TO
7-11 N·m
(5-8 LB-FT)

NUT AND WASHER
N621906-S2
2 REQ'D
TIGHTEN TO
7-11 N·m
(5-8 LB-FT)

DOOR GLASS RUN
LOCK SIDE RETAINER
222A00

N6126-B

Front door vent and window adjustments

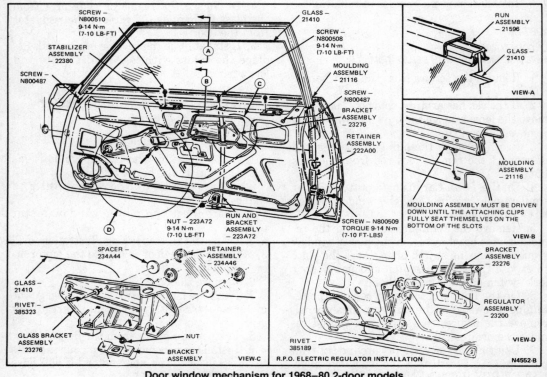

SCREW –
N800510
9-14 N·m
(7-10 LB-FT)

GLASS –
21410

SCREW –
N800508
9-14 N·m
(7-10 LB-FT)

STABILIZER
ASSEMBLY –
22380

MOULDING
ASSEMBLY
– 21116

SCREW –
N800487

SCREW –
N800487

BRACKET
ASSEMBLY
– 23276

RETAINER
ASSEMBLY
– 222A00

NUT – 223A72
9-14 N·m
(7-10 LB-FT)

RUN AND
BRACKET
ASSEMBLY
– 223A72

SCREW – N800509
TORQUE 9-14 N·m
(7-10 FT-LBS)

RUN
ASSEMBLY
– 21596

GLASS –
21410

VIEW-A

MOULDING
ASSEMBLY
– 21116

MOULDING ASSEMBLY MUST BE DRIVEN
DOWN UNTIL THE ATTACHING CLIPS
FULLY SEAT THEMSELVES ON THE
BOTTOM OF THE SLOTS

VIEW-B

SPACER –
234A44

RETAINER
ASSEMBLY
– 234A46

GLASS –
21410

RIVET –
385323

GLASS BRACKET
ASSEMBLY – 23276

NUT

BRACKET
ASSEMBLY

VIEW-C

BRACKET
ASSEMBLY
– 23276

REGULATOR
ASSEMBLY
– 23200

RIVET –
385189

VIEW-D

R.P.O. ELECTRIC REGULATOR INSTALLATION

N4552-B

Door window mechanism for 1968–80 2-door models

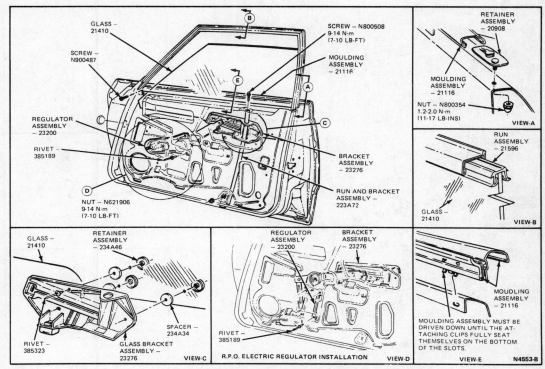

Front door window mechanism for 4-door models

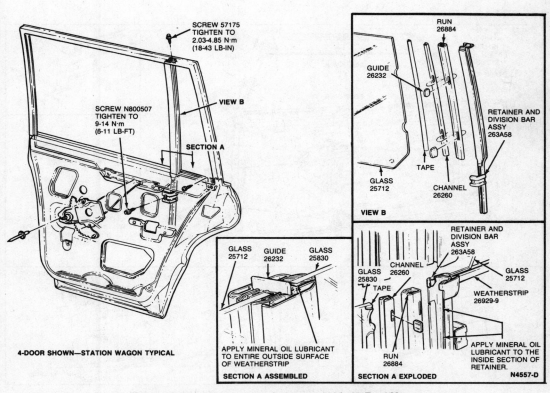

Division bar/stationary rear window on 1980–87 Ford/Mercury

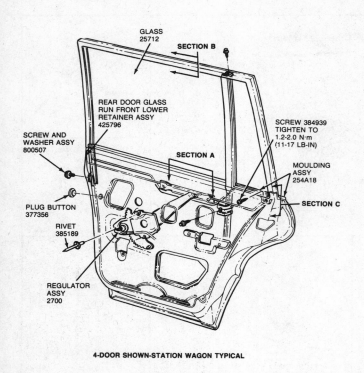

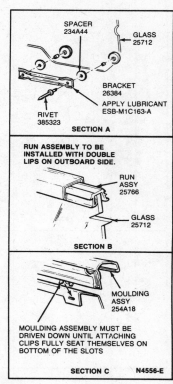

GLASS
25712

SECTION B

REAR DOOR GLASS
RUN FRONT LOWER
RETAINER ASSY
425796

SCREW 384939
TIGHTEN TO
1.2-2.0 N·m
(11-17 LB-IN)

SECTION A

SCREW AND
WASHER ASSY
800507

MOULDING
ASSY
254A18

SECTION C

PLUG BUTTON
377356

RIVET
385189

REGULATOR
ASSY
2700

4-DOOR SHOWN-STATION WAGON TYPICAL

SPACER
234A44

GLASS
25712

BRACKET
26384

APPLY LUBRICANT
ESB-M1C163-A

RIVET
385323

SECTION A

RUN ASSEMBLY TO BE
INSTALLED WITH DOUBLE
LIPS ON OUTBOARD SIDE.

RUN
ASSY
25766

GLASS
25712

SECTION B

MOULDING
ASSY
254A18

MOULDING ASSEMBLY MUST BE
DRIVEN DOWN UNTIL ATTACHING
CLIPS FULLY SEAT THEMSELVES ON
BOTTOM OF THE SLOTS

SECTION C   N4556-E

Rear window mechanism on 1980–87 Ford/Mercury

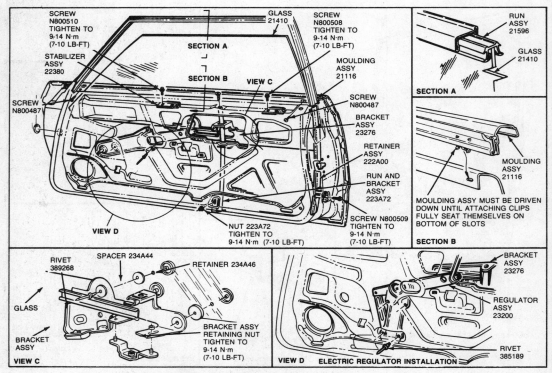

SCREW
N800510
TIGHTEN TO
9-14 N·m
(7-10 LB-FT)

GLASS
21410

SCREW
N800508
TIGHTEN TO
9-14 N·m
(7-10 LB-FT)

SECTION A

STABILIZER
ASSY
22380

SECTION B   VIEW C

MOULDING
ASSY
21116

SCREW
N800487

SCREW
N800487

BRACKET
ASSY
23276

RETAINER
ASSY
222A00

RUN AND
BRACKET
ASSY
223A72

VIEW D

NUT 223A72
TIGHTEN TO
9-14 N·m (7-10 LB-FT)

SCREW N800509
TIGHTEN TO
9-14 N·m
(7-10 LB-FT)

RUN
ASSY
21596

GLASS
21410

SECTION A

MOULDING
ASSY
21116

MOULDING ASSY MUST BE DRIVEN
DOWN UNTIL ATTACHING CLIPS
FULLY SEAT THEMSELVES ON
BOTTOM OF SLOTS

SECTION B

RIVET
389268

SPACER 234A44

RETAINER 234A46

GLASS

BRACKET
ASSY

BRACKET ASSY
RETAINING NUT
TIGHTEN TO
9-14 N·m
(7-10 LB-FT)

VIEW C

BRACKET
ASSY
23276

REGULATOR
ASSY
23200

RIVET
385189

VIEW D   ELECTRIC REGULATOR INSTALLATION

Door window mechanism for 1981–88 2-door models

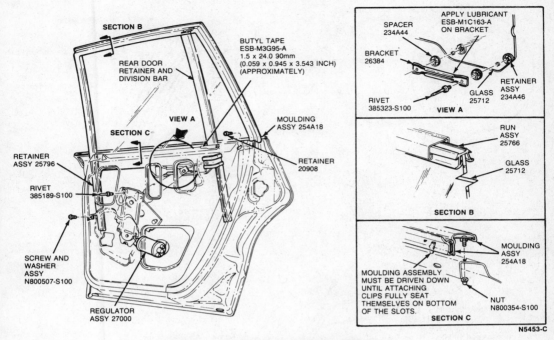

Rear door window mechanism on the Town Car

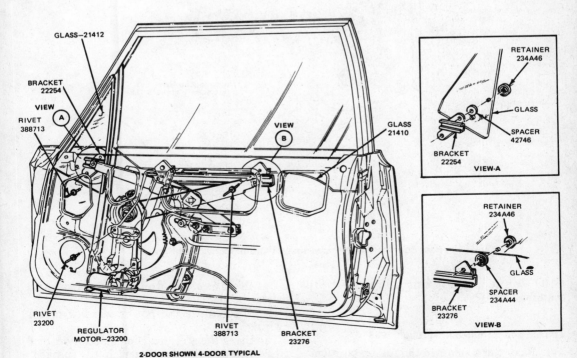

2-DOOR SHOWN 4-DOOR TYPICAL

Front door window power regulator on the Continental and Mark VI

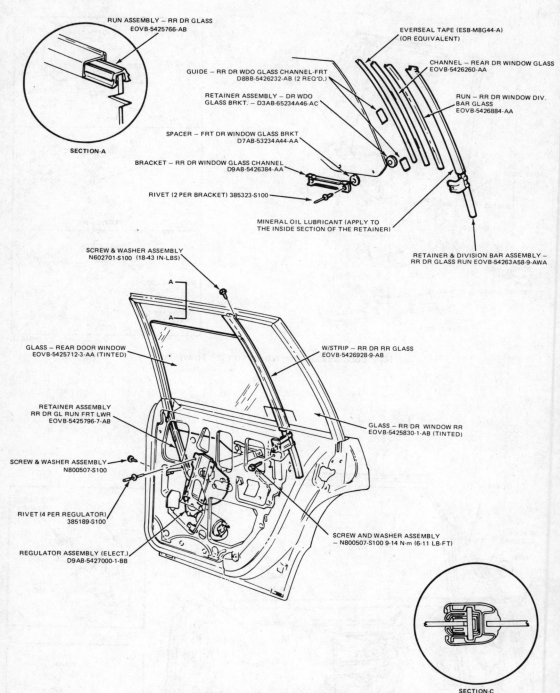

RUN ASSEMBLY — RR DR GLASS
EOVB-5425766-AB

EVERSEAL TAPE (ESB-M8G44-A)
(OR EQUIVALENT)

CHANNEL — REAR DR WINDOW GLASS
EOVB-5426260-AA

GUIDE — RR DR WDO GLASS CHANNEL-FRT
D8BB-5426232-AB (2 REQ'D.)

RUN — RR DR WINDOW DIV.
BAR GLASS
EOVB-5426884-AA

RETAINER ASSEMBLY — DR WDO
GLASS BRKT. — D3AB-65234A46-AC

SPACER — FRT DR WINDOW GLASS BRKT
D7AB-53234A44-AA

BRACKET — RR DR WINDOW GLASS CHANNEL
D9AB-5426384-AA

RIVET (2 PER BRACKET) 385323-S100

MINERAL OIL LUBRICANT (APPLY TO
THE INSIDE SECTION OF THE RETAINER)

RETAINER & DIVISION BAR ASSEMBLY —
RR DR GLASS RUN EOVB-54263A58-9-AWA

SECTION-A

SCREW & WASHER ASSEMBLY
N602701-S100 (18-43 IN-LBS)

A

A

GLASS — REAR DOOR WINDOW
EOVB-5425712-3-AA (TINTED)

W/STRIP — RR DR RR GLASS
EOVB-5426928-9-AB

RETAINER ASSEMBLY
RR DR GL RUN FRT LWR
EOVB-5425796-7-AB

GLASS — RR DR WINDOW RR
EOVB-5425830-1-AB (TINTED)

SCREW & WASHER ASSEMBLY
N800507-S100

RIVET (4 PER REGULATOR)
385189-S100

SCREW AND WASHER ASSEMBLY
— N800507-S100 9-14 N·m (6-11 LB-FT)

REGULATOR ASSEMBLY (ELECT.)
D9AB-5427000-1-BB

SECTION-C

Rear door window mechanism on the Continental and Mark VI

10. Connect the wiring and install the watershield.

Lincoln and Continental Through 1988

1. Raise the window to the full up position.
2. Disconnect the battery ground.

3. Remove the door trim panel and watershield.

4. Disconnect the power window motor wiring.

5. Using the accompanying illustration, drill a ¾" hole at point **A**, adjacent to the speaker.

6. At the upper motor mount screw head, the

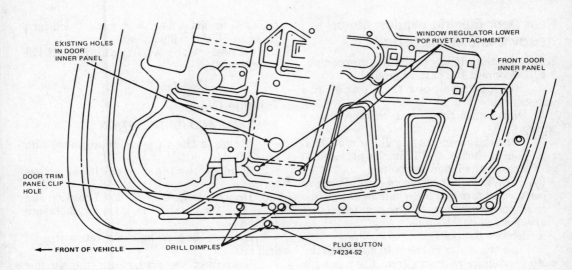

EXISTING HOLES
IN DOOR
INNER PANEL

WINDOW REGULATOR LOWER
POP RIVET ATTACHMENT

FRONT DOOR
INNER PANEL

DOOR TRIM
PANEL CLIP
HOLE

← FRONT OF VEHICLE →   DRILL DIMPLES   PLUG BUTTON
                                                      74234-S2

FRONT DOOR RIGHT HAND SIDE SHOWN—
LEFT HAND SIDE TYPICAL

1980–87 front door power window motor removal

sheet metal can be removed by grinding out the inner panel sufficiently to clear the screw head.

CAUTION: *Prior to removing the mounting bolts, make sure that the regulator arm is in a fixed position to prevent the counterbalance arm from suddenly unwinding!*

7. Remove the bolts.

8. Push the motor outward to disengage the motor and drive assembly from the regulator gear.

9. Remove the motor from the door.

10. Install the new motor and torque the bolts to 50-85 in. lbs. The new motor kit will have plugs to fill the drilled holes.

11. Connect the wiring and install the watershield.

← FRONT OF VEHICLE →

WINDOW REGULATOR
LOWER POP RIVET
ATTACHMENT

EXISTING HOLE IN DOOR
INNER PANEL

REAR DOOR
INNER PANEL

EXISTING DRILL DIMPLES IN DOOR INNER PANEL
FOR 1/2" DIA. DRILLED ACCESS HOLES FOR MOTOR
REMOVAL. TEMPLATE IS NOT REQUIRED.

NOTE:
MODEL 54 REAR DOOR RIGHT HAND SIDE
SHOWN LEFT HAND SIDE TYPICAL MODEL
74 TYPICAL.

1980–87 rear door power window motor removal

Rear Door Electric Window Motor
REMOVAL AND INSTALLATION

1. Raise the window to the full up position.
2. Disconnect the battery ground.
3. Remove the door trim panel and watershield.
4. Disconnect the power window motor wiring.
5. Using the accompanying illustration, drill a ¾" hole at each of the 3 dimples provided to gain acces to the mounting bolts.

CAUTION: *Prior to removing the mounting bolts, make sure that the regulator arm is in a fixed position to prevent the counterbalance arm from suddenly unwinding!*

6. Remove the bolts.
7. Push the motor outward to disengage the motor and drive assembly from the regulator gear.
8. Remove the motor from the door.
9. Install the new motor and torque the bolts

to 50-85 in. lbs. The new motor kit will have plugs to fill the drilled holes.

10. Connect the wiring and install the watershield.

Tailgate Glass
REMOVAL AND INSTALLATION

1. Remove the tailgate trim panel and watershield.
2. Remove the inner panel lower access cover.
3. Drop the tailgate to the down position and raise the glass until the glass brackets are accessible.
4. Drill out the glass bracket rivets with a ¼" drill bit.
5. Disconnect the wiring from the window glass defroster grid.
6. Slide the glass from the door.
7. Installation is the reverse of removal. Use

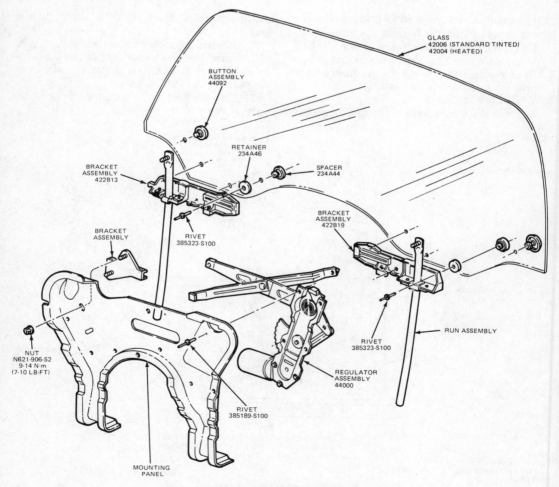

Tailgate window glass regulator

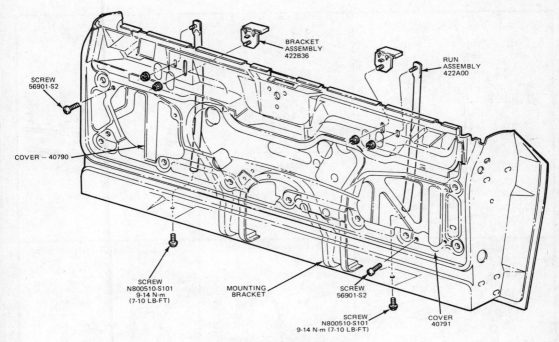

SCREW
56901-S2

BRACKET
ASSEMBLY
422B36

RUN
ASSEMBLY
422A00

COVER – 40790

SCREW
N800510-S101
9-14 N·m
(7-10 LB-FT)

MOUNTING
BRACKET

SCREW
56901-S2

SCREW
N800510-S101
9-14 N·m (7-10 LB-FT)

COVER
40791

Tailgate window glass run

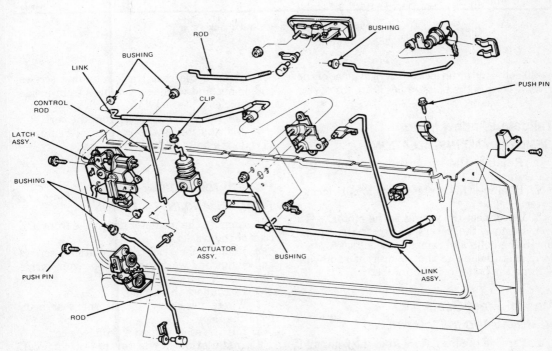

ROD

BUSHING

PUSH PIN

LINK

BUSHING

CONTROL
ROD

CLIP

LATCH
ASSY.

BUSHING

PUSH PIN

ROD

ACTUATOR
ASSY.

BUSHING

LINK
ASSY.

1968–80 tailgate window motor

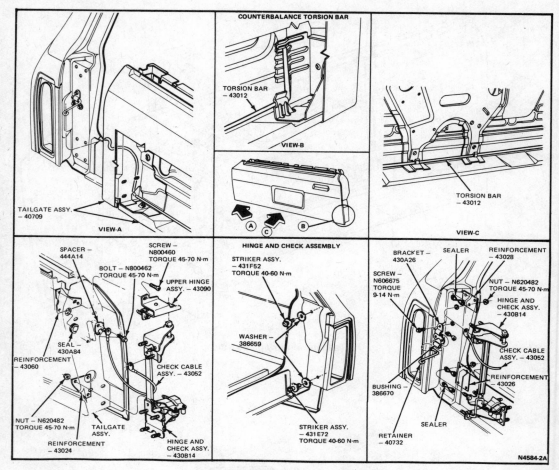

1968–80 tailgate hinge and check

¼-20 bolts, nuts and lockwashers in place of the rivets. Torque the bolts to 36-60 in. lbs.

Tailgate Window Motor

REMOVAL AND INSTALLATION

1. Remove the tailgate trim panel and watershield.
2. Remove the inner panel lower access cover.
3. Disconnect the wiring at the motor.
4. Remove the covers to access the motor mounting bolts and remove the bolts.
5. Installation is the reverse of removal. Torque the bolts to 50-85 in. lbs.

Manual Front Seats

REMOVAL AND INSTALLATION

1. Remove the insulators from the front and rear of the tracks.

2. Remove the seat track retaining screws and/or nut and washer assemblies from inside the vehicle.
3. Lift the seat and track from the car.
4. Installation is the reverse of removal. Torque the bolts to 20 ft. lbs.

Power Front Seats

REMOVAL AND INSTALLATION

1. Remove the insulators from the front and rear of the tracks.
2. Remove the seat track retaining screws and/or nut and washer assemblies from inside the vehicle.
3. Disconnect the wiring.
4. Where necessary, unbolt the seat belts from the floor.
5. Lift the seat and track from the car.
6. Installation is the reverse of removal. Torque the bolts to 20 ft. lbs.

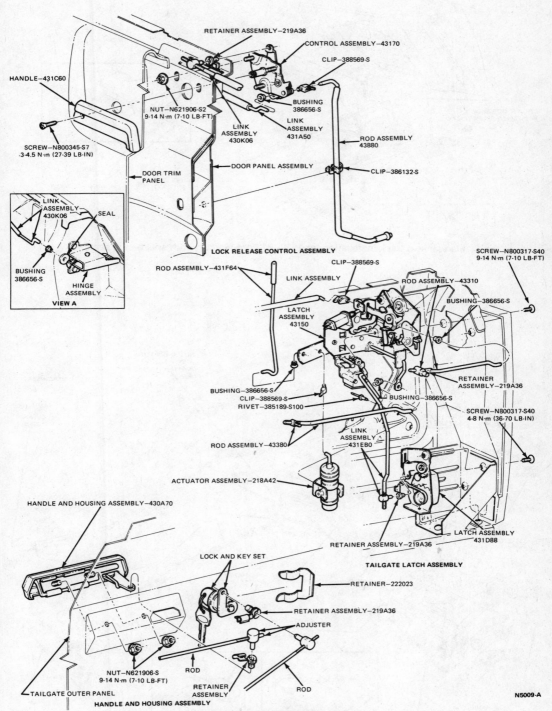

RETAINER ASSEMBLY—219A36

CONTROL ASSEMBLY—43170

CLIP—388569-S

HANDLE—431C60

NUT—N621906-S2
9-14 N·m (7-10 LB-FT)

BUSHING
386656-S

SCREW—N800345-S7
.3-4.5 N·m (27-39 LB-IN)

LINK
ASSEMBLY
430K06

LINK
ASSEMBLY
431A50

ROD ASSEMBLY
43880

DOOR TRIM
PANEL

DOOR PANEL ASSEMBLY

CLIP—386132-S

LINK
ASSEMBLY
430K06

SEAL

BUSHING
386656-S

HINGE
ASSEMBLY

VIEW A

LOCK RELEASE CONTROL ASSEMBLY

SCREW—N800317-S40
9-14 N·m (7-10 LB-FT)

ROD ASSEMBLY—431F64

CLIP—388569-S

LINK ASSEMBLY

ROD ASSEMBLY—43310

BUSHING—386656-S

LATCH
ASSEMBLY
43150

BUSHING—386656-S
CLIP—388569-S
RIVET—385189-S100

BUSHING—386656-S

RETAINER
ASSEMBLY—219A36

SCREW—N800317-S40
4-8 N·m (36-70 LB-IN)

LINK
ASSEMBLY
431EB0

ROD ASSEMBLY—43380

ACTUATOR ASSEMBLY—218A42

LATCH ASSEMBLY
431D88

RETAINER ASSEMBLY—219A36

TAILGATE LATCH ASSEMBLY

HANDLE AND HOUSING ASSEMBLY—430A70

LOCK AND KEY SET

RETAINER—222023

RETAINER ASSEMBLY—219A36

ADJUSTER

NUT—N621906-S
9-14 N·m (7-10 LB-FT)

ROD

RETAINER
ASSEMBLY

ROD

TAILGATE OUTER PANEL

HANDLE AND HOUSING ASSEMBLY

N5009-A

1981–88 tailgate window motor

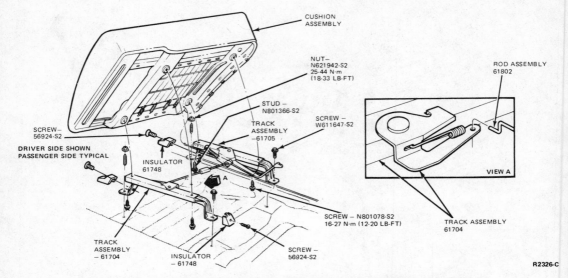

CUSHION
ASSEMBLY

NUT –
N621942-S2
25-44 N·m
(18-33 LB-FT)

STUD –
N801366-S2

SCREW –
W611647-S2

TRACK
ASSEMBLY
–61705

SCREW–
56924-S2

DRIVER SIDE SHOWN
PASSENGER SIDE TYPICAL

INSULATOR
61748

TRACK
ASSEMBLY
– 61704

INSULATOR
– 61748

SCREW –
56924-S2

SCREW – N801078-S2
16-27 N·m (12-20 LB-FT)

ROD ASSEMBLY
61802

VIEW A

TRACK ASSEMBLY
61704

R2326-C

Manual seat track installation for 1980–81 Ford/Mercury with split bench seats

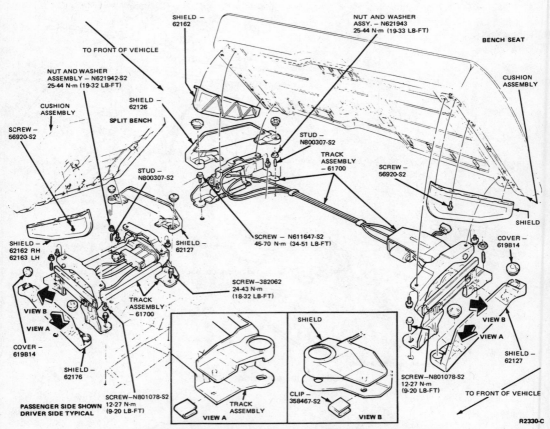

SHIELD –
62162

NUT AND WASHER
ASSY. – N621943
25-44 N·m (19-33 LB-FT)

BENCH SEAT

TO FRONT OF VEHICLE

CUSHION
ASSEMBLY

NUT AND WASHER
ASSEMBLY – N621942-S2
25-44 N·m (19-32 LB-FT)

CUSHION
ASSEMBLY

SHIELD –
62126

SPLIT BENCH

SCREW –
56920-S2

STUD –
N800307-S2

STUD –
N800307-S2

TRACK
ASSEMBLY
– 61700

SCREW –
56920-S2

SHIELD –
62127

SHIELD

SHIELD –
62162 RH
62163 LH

SCREW – N611647-S2
45-70 N·m (34-51 LB-FT)

VIEW B

COVER –
619B14

VIEW A

TRACK
ASSEMBLY
– 61700

SCREW–382062
24-43 N·m
(18-32 LB-FT)

SHIELD –
62127

COVER –
619B14

VIEW B

VIEW A

SHIELD –
62162

SHIELD

CLIP –
358467-S2

VIEW B

SHIELD –
62176

SCREW–N801078-S2
12-27 N·m
(9-20 LB-FT)

PASSENGER SIDE SHOWN
DRIVER SIDE TYPICAL

TRACK
ASSEMBLY

VIEW A

SCREW–N801078-S2
12-27 N·m
(9-20 LB-FT)

TO FRONT OF VEHICLE

R2330-C

Front seat track assembly for Ford/Mercury with rack and pinion drive

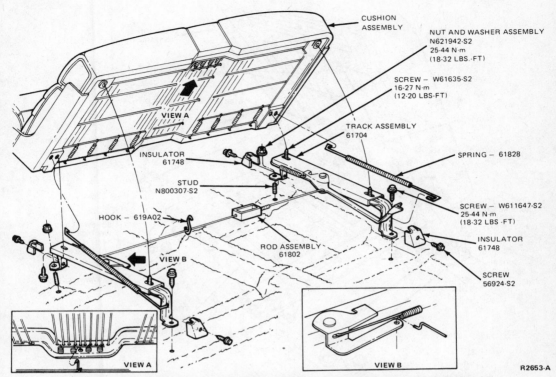

CUSHION
ASSEMBLY

NUT AND WASHER ASSEMBLY
N621942-S2
25-44 N·m
(18-32 LBS.-FT)

SCREW – W61635-S2
16-27 N·m
(12-20 LBS-FT)

VIEW A

TRACK ASSEMBLY
61704

SPRING – 61828

INSULATOR
61748

STUD
N800307-S2

SCREW – W611647-S2
25-44 N·m
(18-32 LBS -FT)

HOOK – 619A02

INSULATOR
61748

VIEW B

ROD ASSEMBLY
61802

SCREW
56924-S2

VIEW A

VIEW B

R2653-A

Manual seat track installation on the flight bench seat on 1980–81 Lincoln and Mark VI

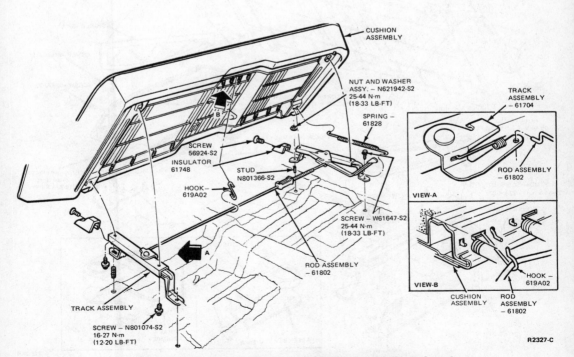

CUSHION
ASSEMBLY

NUT AND WASHER
ASSY. – N621942-S2
25-44 N·m
(18-33 LB-FT)

TRACK
ASSEMBLY
– 61704

SPRING –
61828

SCREW
56924-S2

INSULATOR
61748

STUD
N801366-S2

HOOK–
619A02

ROD ASSEMBLY
– 61802

VIEW-A

SCREW – W61647-S2
25-44 N·m
(18-33 LB-FT)

ROD ASSEMBLY
– 61802

VIEW-B

HOOK–
619A02

TRACK ASSEMBLY

CUSHION
ASSEMBLY

ROD
ASSEMBLY
– 61802

SCREW – N801074-S2
16-27 N·m
(12-20 LB-FT)

R2327-C

Manual seat track installation for Ford/Mercury with full bench seats

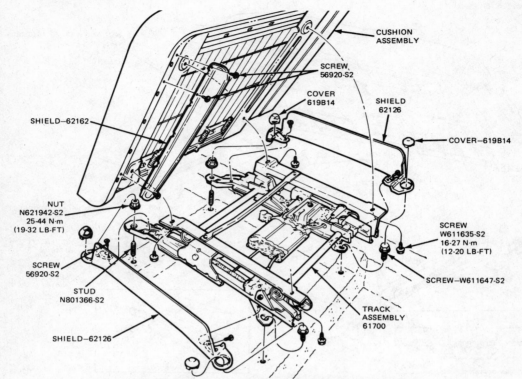

Front split bench seat track on Lincoln with 6-way power seats

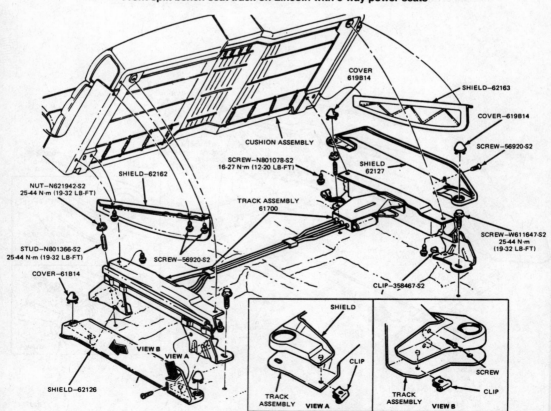

Front seat track assembly for Lincoln with rack and pinion drive

R2856-A

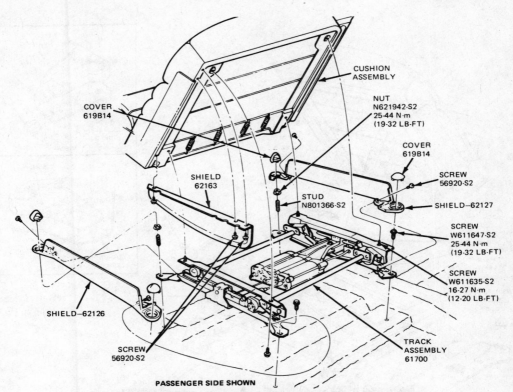

**COVER
619B14**

**CUSHION
ASSEMBLY**

**NUT
N621942-S2
25-44 N·m
(19-32 LB-FT)**

**COVER
619B14**

**SCREW
56920-S2**

SHIELD—62127

**SHIELD
62163**

**STUD
N801366-S2**

**SCREW
W611647-S2
25-44 N·m
(19-32 LB-FT)**

**SCREW
W611635-S2
16-27 N·m
(12-20 LB-FT)**

SHIELD—62126

**SCREW
56920-S2**

**TRACK
ASSEMBLY
61700**

PASSENGER SIDE SHOWN

Front split bench seat track on Ford/Mercury with 6-way power seats

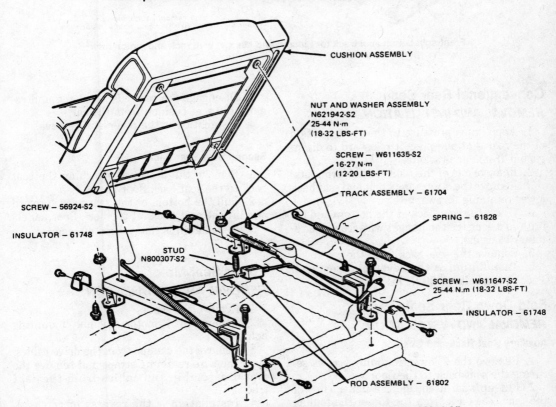

CUSHION ASSEMBLY

**NUT AND WASHER ASSEMBLY
N621942-S2
25-44 N·m
(18-32 LBS-FT)**

**SCREW - W611635-S2
16-27 N·m
(12-20 LBS-FT)**

TRACK ASSEMBLY - 61704

SCREW - 56924-S2

SPRING - 61828

INSULATOR - 61748

**STUD
N800307-S2**

**SCREW - W611647-S2
25-44 N.m (18-32 LBS-FT)**

INSULATOR - 61748

ROD ASSEMBLY - 61802

Manual seat track installation with split bench seat on Lincoln and Mark VI

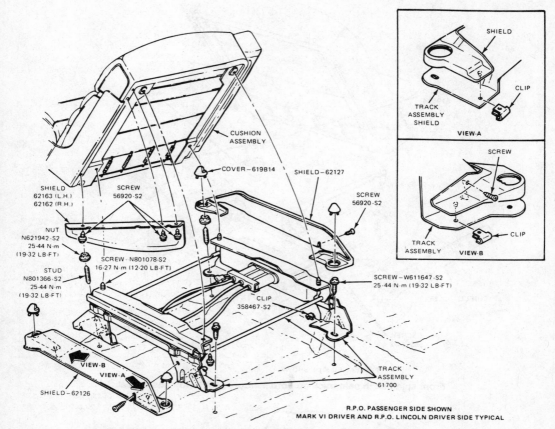

SHIELD

TRACK
ASSEMBLY
SHIELD

CLIP

VIEW-A

SCREW

TRACK
ASSEMBLY

CLIP

VIEW-B

CUSHION
ASSEMBLY

COVER – 619B14

SHIELD – 62127

SCREW
56920-S2

SHIELD
62163 (L.H.)
62162 (R.H.)

SCREW
56920-S2

NUT
N621942-S2
25-44 N·m
(19-32 LB-FT)

SCREW – N801078-S2
16-27 N·m (12-20 LB-FT)

STUD
N801366-S2
25-44 N·m
(19-32 LB-FT)

SCREW – W611647-S2
25-44 N·m (19-32 LB-FT)

CLIP
358467-S2

VIEW-B

VIEW-A

SHIELD – 62126

TRACK
ASSEMBLY
61700

R.P.O. PASSENGER SIDE SHOWN
MARK VI DRIVER AND R.P.O. LINCOLN DRIVER SIDE TYPICAL

Front split bench seat track for Lincoln and Mark VI with rack and pinion drive

Conventional Rear Seats

REMOVAL AND INSTALLATION

1. Apply knee pressure to the lower portion of the rear seat and push it rearward to disengage it from the brackets.
2. Remove one of the rear quarter armrests.
3. Remove the outer safety belt and seat back lower retaining screws.
4. Grasp the seat back at the bottom and lift it up to disengage the hanger wire from the retainer brackets.
5. Remove the seat back from the car.
6. Installation is the reverse of removal. Torque the bolts to 30 ft. lbs.

Fold-Down Rear Seats

REMOVAL AND INSTALLATION

Auxiliary Seat Back and Cushion

1. Remove the 2 lower retaining screws securing the seat back to the floor.
2. Lift up and disengage the upper clips of the rear seat back from the top of the folding floor.

3. Disengage the seat cushion latch and remove the seat cushion from the car.
4. Installation is the reverse of removal.

Second Seat Seat Back

1. Remove the 3 screws attaching the seat back to the seat back floor panel.
2. Pull the bottom of the seat back forward and lift the seat back off the back floor panel.
3. Installation is the reverse of removal.

Power Seat Motor

REMOVAL AND INSTALLATION

1. Remove the seats.
2. Remove the 3 motor assembly mounting bolts.
3. Remove the clamps from the drive cables, open the wire retaining straps and remove the motor assembly and cables from the seat tracks.
4. Installation is the reverse of removal. Torque the bolts to 20 ft. lbs.

How to Remove Stains from Fabric Interior

For rest results, spots and stains should be removed as soon as possible. Never use gasoline, lacquer thinner, acetone, nail polish remover or bleach. Use a 3' x 3" piece of cheesecloth. Squeeze most of the liquid from the fabric and wipe the stained fabric from the outside of the stain toward the center with a lifting motion. Turn the cheesecloth as soon as one side becomes soiled. When using water to remove a stain, be sure to wash the entire section after the spot has been removed to avoid water stains. Encrusted spots can be broken up with a dull knife and vacuumed before removing the stain.

Type of Stain	How to Remove It
Surface spots	Brush the spots out with a small hand brush or use a commercial preparation such as K2R to lift the stain.
Mildew	Clean around the mildew with warm suds. Rinse in cold water and soak the mildew area in a solution of 1 part table salt and 2 parts water. Wash with upholstery cleaner.
Water stains	Water stains in fabric materials can be removed with a solution made from 1 cup of table salt dissolved in 1 quart of water. Vigorously scrub the solution into the stain and rinse with clear water. Water stains in nylon or other synthetic fabrics should be removed with a commercial type spot remover.
Chewing gum, tar, crayons, shoe polish (greasy stains)	Do not use a cleaner that will soften gum or tar. Harden the deposit with an ice cube and scrape away as much as possible with a dull knife. Moisten the remainder with cleaning fluid and scrub clean.
Ice cream, candy	Most candy has a sugar base and can be removed with a cloth wrung out in warm water. Oily candy, after cleaning with warm water, should be cleaned with upholstery cleaner. Rinse with warm water and clean the remainder with cleaning fluid.
Wine, alcohol, egg, milk, soft drink (non-greasy stains)	Do not use soap. Scrub the stain with a cloth wrung out in warm water. Remove the remainder with cleaning fluid.
Grease, oil, lipstick, butter and related stains	Use a spot remover to avoid leaving a ring. Work from the outisde of the stain to the center and dry with a clean cloth when the spot is gone.
Headliners (cloth)	Mix a solution of warm water and foam upholstery cleaner to give thick suds. Use only foam—liquid may streak or spot. Clean the entire headliner in one operation using a circular motion with a natural sponge.
Headliner (vinyl)	Use a vinyl cleaner with a sponge and wipe clean with a dry cloth.
Seats and door panels	Mix 1 pint upholstery cleaner in 1 gallon of water. Do not soak the fabric around the buttons.
Leather or vinyl fabric	Use a multi-purpose cleaner full strength and a stiff brush. Let stand 2 minutes and scrub thoroughly. Wipe with a clean, soft rag.
Nylon or synthetic fabrics	For normal stains, use the same procedures you would for washing cloth upholstery. If the fabric is extremely dirty, use a multi-purpose cleaner full strength with a stiff scrub brush. Scrub thoroughly in all directions and wipe with a cotton towel or soft rag.

Mechanic's Data

General Conversion Table

Multiply By	To Convert	To	
LENGTH			
2.54	Inches	Centimeters	.3937
25.4	Inches	Millimeters	.03937
30.48	Feet	Centimeters	.0328
.304	Feet	Meters	3.28
.914	Yards	Meters	1.094
1.609	Miles	Kilometers	.621
VOLUME			
.473	Pints	Liters	2.11
.946	Quarts	Liters	1.06
3.785	Gallons	Liters	.264
.016	Cubic inches	Liters	61.02
16.39	Cubic inches	Cubic cms.	.061
28.3	Cubic feet	Liters	.0353
MASS (Weight)			
28.35	Ounces	Grams	.035
.4536	Pounds	Kilograms	2.20
—	To obtain	From	Multiply by

Multiply By	To Convert	To	
AREA			
.645	Square inches	Square cms.	.155
.836	Square yds.	Square meters	1.196
FORCE			
4.448	Pounds	Newtons	.225
.138	Ft./lbs.	Kilogram/meters	7.23
1.36	Ft./lbs.	Newton-meters	.737
.112	In./lbs.	Newton-meters	8.844
PRESSURE			
.068	Psi	Atmospheres	14.7
6.89	Psi	Kilopascals	.145
OTHER			
1.104	Horsepower (DIN)	Horsepower (SAE)	.9861
.746	Horsepower (SAE)	Kilowatts (KW)	1.34
1.60	Mph	Km/h	.625
.425	Mpg	Km/1	2.35
—	To obtain	From	Multiply by

Tap Drill Sizes

National Coarse or U.S.S.

Screw & Tap Size	Threads Per Inch	Use Drill Number
No. 5	40	39
No. 6	32	36
No. 8	32	29
No. 10	24	25
No. 12	24	17
$1/4$	20	8
$5/16$	18	F
$3/8$	16	$5/16$
$7/16$	14	U
$1/2$	13	$27/64$
$9/16$	12	$31/64$
$5/8$	11	$17/32$
$3/4$	10	$21/32$
$7/8$	9	$49/64$

National Coarse or U.S.S.

Screw & Tap Size	Threads Per Inch	Use Drill Number
1	8	$7/8$
$1 1/8$	7	$63/64$
$1 1/4$	7	$1 7/64$
$1 1/2$	6	$1 11/32$

National Fine or S.A.E.

Screw & Tap Size	Threads Per Inch	Use Drill Number
No. 5	44	37
No. 6	40	33
No. 8	36	29
No. 10	32	21

National Fine or S.A.E.

Screw & Tap Size	Threads Per Inch	Use Drill Number
No. 12	28	15
$1/4$	28	3
$6/16$	24	1
$3/8$	24	Q
$7/16$	20	W
$1/2$	20	$29/64$
$9/16$	18	$33/64$
$5/8$	18	$37/64$
$3/4$	16	$11/16$
$7/8$	14	$13/16$
$1 1/8$	12	$1 3/64$
$1 1/4$	12	$1 11/64$
$1 1/2$	12	$1 27/64$

Drill Sizes In Decimal Equivalents

Inch	Decimal	Wire/Letter	mm
1/64	.0156		.39
	.0157		.4
	.0160	78	
	.0165		.42
	.0173		.44
	.0177		.45
	.0180	77	
	.0181		.46
	.0189		.48
	.0197		.5
	.0200	76	
	.0210	75	
	.0217		.55
	.0225	74	
	.0236		.6
	.0240	73	
	.0250	72	
	.0256		.65
	.0260	71	
	.0276		.7
	.0280	70	
	.0292	69	
	.0295		.75
	.0310	68	
1/32	.0312		.79
	.0315		.8
	.0320	67	
	.0330	66	
	.0335		.85
	.0350	65	
	.0354		.9
	.0360	64	
	.0370	63	
	.0374		.95
	.0380	62	
	.0390	61	
	.0394		1.0
	.0400	60	
	.0410	59	
	.0413		1.05
	.0420	58	
	.0430	57	
	.0433		1.1
	.0453		1.15
	.0465	56	
3/64	.0469		1.19
	.0472		1.2
	.0492		1.25
	.0512		1.3
	.0520	55	
	.0531		1.35
	.0550	54	
	.0551		1.4
	.0571		1.45
	.0591		1.5
	.0595	53	
	.0610		1.55
1/16	.0625		1.59
	.0630		1.6
	.0635	52	
	.0650		1.65
	.0669		1.7
	.0670	51	
	.0689		1.75
	.0700	50	
	.0709		1.8
	.0728		1.85
	.0730	49	
	.0748		1.9
	.0760	48	
	.0768		1.95
5/64	.0781		1.98
	.0785	47	
	.0787		2.0
	.0807		2.05
	.0810	46	
	.0820	45	
	.0827		2.1
	.0846		2.15
	.0860	44	
	.0866		2.2
	.0886		2.25
	.0890	43	
	.0906		2.3
	.0925		2.35
	.0935	42	
3/32	.0938		2.38
	.0945		2.4
	.0960	41	
	.0965		2.45
	.0980	40	
	.0981		2.5
	.0995	39	
	.1015	38	
	.1024		2.6
	.1040	37	
	.1063		2.7
	.1065	36	
	.1083		2.75
7/64	.1094		2.77
	.1100	35	
	.1102		2.8
	.1110	34	
	.1130	33	
	.1142		2.9
	.1160	32	
	.1181		3.0
	.1200	31	
	.1220		3.1
1/8	.1250		3.17
	.1260		3.2
	.1280		3.25
	.1285	30	
	.1299		3.3
	.1339		3.4
	.1360	29	
	.1378		3.5
	.1405	28	
9/64	.1406		3.57
	.1417		3.6
	.1440	27	
	.1457		3.7
	.1470	26	
	.1476		3.75
	.1495	25	
	.1496		3.8
	.1520	24	
	.1535		3.9
	.1540	23	
5/32	.1562		3.96
	.1570	22	
	.1575		4.0
	.1590	21	
	.1610	20	
	.1614		4.1
	.1654		4.2
	.1660	19	
	.1673		4.25
	.1693		4.3
	.1695	18	
11/64	.1719		4.36
	.1730	17	
	.1732		4.4
	.1770	16	
	.1772		4.5
	.1800	15	
	.1811		4.6
	.1820	14	
	.1850	13	
	.1850		4.7
	.1870		4.75
3/16	.1875		4.76
	.1890		4.8
	.1890	12	
	.1910	11	
	.1929		4.9
	.1935	10	
	.1960	9	
	.1969		5.0
	.1990	8	
	.2008		5.1
	.2010	7	
13/64	.2031		5.16
	.2040	6	
	.2047		5.2
	.2055	5	
	.2067		5.25
	.2087		5.3
	.2090	4	
	.2126		5.4
	.2130	3	
	.2165		5.5
7/32	.2188		5.55
	.2205		5.6
	.2210	2	
	.2244		5.7
	.2264		5.75
	.2280	1	
	.2283		5.8
	.2323		5.9
	.2340	A	
15/64	.2344		5.95
	.2362		6.0
	.2380	B	
	.2402		6.1
	.2420	C	
	.2441		6.2
	.2460	D	
	.2461		6.25
	.2480		6.3
1/4	.2500	E	6.35
	.2520		6.
	.2559		6.5
	.2570	F	
	.2598		6.6
	.2610	G	
	.2638		6.7
17/64	.2656		6.74
	.2657		6.75
	.2660	H	
	.2677		6.8
	.2717		6.9
	.2720	I	
	.2756		7.0
	.2770	J	
	.2795		7.1
	.2810	K	
9/32	.2812		7.14
	.2835		7.2
	.2854		7.25
	.2874		7.3
	.2900	L	
	.2913		7.4
	.2950	M	
	.2953		7.5
19/64	.2969		7.54
	.2992		7.6
	.3020	N	
	.3031		7.7
	.3051		7.75
	.3071		7.8
	.3110		7.9
5/16	.3125		7.93
	.3150		8.0
	.3160	O	
	.3189		8.1
	.3228		8.2
	.3230	P	
	.3248		8.25
	.3268		8.3
21/64	.3281		8.33
	.3307		8.4
	.3320	Q	
	.3346		8.5
	.3386		8.6
	.3390	R	
	.3425		8.7
11/32	.3438		8.73
	.3445		8.75
	.3465		8.8
	.3480	S	
	.3504		8.9
	.3543		9.0
	.3580	T	
	.3583		9.1
23/64	.3594		9.12
	.3622		9.2
	.3642		9.25
	.3661		9.3
	.3680	U	
	.3701		9.4
	.3740		9.5
3/8	.3750		9.52
	.3770	V	
	.3780		9.6
	.3819		9.7
	.3839		9.75
	.3858		9.8
	.3860	W	
	.3898		9.9
25/64	.3906		9.92
	.3937		10.0
	.3970	X	
	.4040	Y	
13/32	.4062		10.31
	.4130	Z	
	.4134		10.5
27/64	.4219		10.71
	.4331		11.0
7/16	.4375		11.11
	.4528		11.5
29/64	.4531		11.51
15/32	.4688		11.90
	.4724		12.0
31/64	.4844		12.30
	.4921		12.5
1/2	.5000		12.70
	.5118		13.0
33/64	.5156		13.09
17/32	.5312		13.49
	.5315		13.5
35/64	.5469		13.89
	.5512		14.0
9/16	.5625		14.28
	.5709		14.5
37/64	.5781		14.68
	.5906		15.0
19/32	.5938		15.08
39/64	.6094		15.47
	.6102		15.5
5/8	.6250		15.87
	.6299		16.0
41/64	.6406		16.27
	.6496		16.5
21/32	.6562		16.66
	.6693		17.0
43/64	.6719		17.06
11/16	.6875		17.46
	.6890		17.5
45/64	.7031		17.85
	.7087		18.0
23/32	.7188		18.25
	.7283		18.5
47/64	.7344		18.65
	.7480		19.0
3/4	.7500		19.05
49/64	.7656		19.44
	.7677		19.5
25/32	.7812		19.84
	.7874		20.0
51/64	.7969		20.24
	.8071		20.5
13/16	.8125		20.63
	.8268		21.0
53/64	.8281		21.03
27/32	.8438		21.43
	.8465		21.5
55/64	.8594		21.82
	.8661		22.0
7/8	.8750		22.22
	.8858		22.5
57/64	.8906		22.62
	.9055		23.0
29/32	.9062		23.01
59/64	.9219		23.41
	.9252		23.5
15/16	.9375		23.81
	.9449		24.0
61/64	.9531		24.2
	.9646		24.5
31/32	.9688		24.6
	.9843		25.0
63/64	.9844		25.0
1	1.0000		25.4

AIR/FUEL RATIO: The ratio of air to gasoline by weight in the fuel mixture drawn into the engine.

AIR INJECTION: One method of reducing harmful exhaust emissions by injecting air into each of the exhaust ports of an engine. The fresh air entering the hot exhaust manifold causes any remaining fuel to be burned before it can exit the tailpipe.

ALTERNATOR: A device used for converting mechanical energy into electrical energy.

AMMETER: An instrument, calibrated in amperes, used to measure the flow of an electrical current in a circuit. Ammeters are always connected in series with the circuit being tested.

AMPERE: The rate of flow of electrical current present when one volt of electrical pressure is applied against one ohm of electrical resistance.

ANALOG COMPUTER: Any microprocessor that uses similar (analogous) electrical signals to make its calculations.

ARMATURE: A laminated, soft iron core wrapped by a wire that converts electrical energy to mechanical energy as in a motor or relay. When rotated in a magnetic field, it changes mechanical energy into electrical energy as in a generator.

ATMOSPHERIC PRESSURE: The pressure on the Earth's surface caused by the weight of the air in the atmosphere. At sea level, this pressure is 14.7 psi at 32°F (101 kPa at 0°C).

ATOMIZATION: The breaking down of a liquid into a fine mist that can be suspended in air.

AXIAL PLAY: Movement parallel to a shaft or bearing bore.

BACKFIRE: The sudden combustion of gases in the intake or exhaust system that results in a loud explosion.

BACKLASH: The clearance or play between two parts, such as meshed gears.

BACKPRESSURE: Restrictions in the exhaust system that slow the exit of exhaust gases from the combustion chamber.

BAKELITE: A heat resistant, plastic insulator material commonly used in printed circuit boards and transistorized components.

BALL BEARING: A bearing made up of hardened inner and outer races between which hardened steel ball roll.

BALLAST RESISTOR: A resistor in the primary ignition circuit that lowers voltage after the engine is started to reduce wear on ignition components.

BEARING: A friction reducing, supportive device usually located between a stationary part and a moving part.

BIMETAL TEMPERATURE SENSOR: Any sensor or switch made of two dissimilar types of metal that bend when heated or cooled due to the different expansion rates of the alloys. These types of sensors usually function as an on/off switch.

BLOWBY: Combustion gases, composed of water vapor and unburned fuel, that leak past the piston rings into the crankcase during normal engine operation. These gases are removed by the PCV system to prevent the build-up of harmful acids in the crankcase.

BRAKE PAD: A brake shoe and lining assembly used with disc brakes.

BRAKE SHOE: The backing for the brake lining. The term is, however, usually applied to the assembly of the brake backing and lining.

BUSHING: A liner, usually removable, for a bearing; an anti-friction liner used in place of a bearing.

BYPASS: System used to bypass ballast resistor during engine cranking to increase voltage supplied to the coil.

CALIPER: A hydraulically activated device in a disc brake system, which is mounted straddling the brake rotor (disc). The caliper contains at least one piston and two brake pads. Hydraulic pressure on the piston(s) forces the pads against the rotor.

CAMSHAFT: A shaft in the engine on which are the lobes (cams) which operate the valves. The camshaft is driven by the crankshaft, via a belt, chain or gears, at one half the crankshaft speed.

CAPACITOR: A device which stores an electrical charge.

CARBON MONOXIDE (CO): a colorless, odorless gas given off as a normal byproduct of combustion. It is poisonous and extremely dangerous in confined areas, building up slowly to toxic levels without warning if adequate ventilation is not available.

CARBURETOR: A device, usually mounted on the intake manifold of an engine, which mixes the air and fuel in the proper proportion to allow even combustion.

CATALYTIC CONVERTER: A device installed in the exhaust system, like a muffler, that converts harmful byproducts of combustion into carbon dioxide and water vapor by means of a heat-producing chemical reaction.

CENTRIFUGAL ADVANCE: A mechanical method of advancing the spark timing by using flyweights in the distributor that react to centrifugal force generated by the distributor shaft rotation.

CHECK VALVE: Any one-way valve installed to permit the flow of air, fuel or vacuum in one direction only.

CHOKE: A device, usually a moveable valve, placed in the intake path of a carburetor to restrict the flow of air.

CIRCUIT: Any unbroken path through which an electrical current can flow. Also used to describe fuel flow in some instances.

CIRCUIT BREAKER: A switch which protects an electrical circuit from overload by opening the circuit when the current flow exceeds a predetermined level. Some circuit breakers must be reset manually, while other reset automatically

COIL (IGNITION): A transformer in the ignition circuit which steps of the voltage provided to the spark plugs.

COMBINATION MANIFOLD: An assembly which includes both the intake and exhaust manifolds in one casting.

COMBINATION VALVE: A device used in some fuel systems that routes fuel vapors to a charcoal storage canister instead of venting them into the atmosphere. The valve relieves fuel tank pressure and allows fresh air into the tank as fuel level drops to prevent a vapor lock situation.

COMPRESSION RATIO: The comparison of the total volume of the cylinder and combustion chamber with the piston at BDC and the piston at TDC.

CONDENSER: 1. An electrical device which acts to store an electrical charge, preventing voltage surges.
2. A radiator-like device in the air conditioning system in which refrigerant gas condenses into a liquid, giving off heat.

CONDUCTOR: Any material through which an electrical current can be transmitted easily.

CONTINUITY: Continuous or complete circuit. Can be checked with an ohmmeter.

COUNTERSHAFT: An intermediate shaft which is rotated by a mainshaft and transmits, in turn, that rotation to a working part.

CRANKCASE: The lower part of an engine in which the crankshaft and related parts operate.

CRANKSHAFT: The main driving shaft of an engine which receives reciprocating motion from the pistons and converts it to rotary motion.

CYLINDER: In an engine, the round hole in the engine block in which the piston(s) ride.

CYLINDER BLOCK: The main structural member of an engine in which is found the cylinders, crankshaft and other principal parts.

CYLINDER HEAD: The detachable portion of the engine, fastened, usually, to the top of the cylinder block, containing all or most of the combustion chambers. On overhead valve engines, it contains the valves and their operating parts. On overhead cam engines, it contains the camshaft as well.

DEAD CENTER: The extreme top or bottom of the piston stroke.

DETONATION: An unwanted explosion of the air fuel mixture in the combustion chamber caused by excess heat and compression, advanced timing, or an overly lean mixture. Also referred to as "ping".

DIAPHRAGM: A thin, flexible wall separating two cavities, such as in a vacuum advance unit.

DIESELING: A condition in which hot spots in the combustion chamber cause the engine to run on after the key is turned off.

DIFFERENTIAL: A geared assembly which allows the transmission of motion between drive axles, giving one axle the ability to turn faster than the other.

DIODE: An electrical device that will allow current to flow in one direction only.

DISC BRAKE: A hydraulic braking assembly consisting of a brake disc, or rotor, mounted on an axle, and a caliper assembly containing, usually two brake pads which are activated by hydraulic pressure. The pads are forced against the sides of the disc, creating friction which slows the vehicle.

DISTRIBUTOR: A mechanically driven device on an engine which is responsible for electrically firing the spark plug at a predetermined point of the piston stroke.

DOWEL PIN: A pin, inserted in mating holes in two different parts allowing those parts to maintain a fixed relationship.

DRUM BRAKE: A braking system which consists of two brake shoes and one or two wheel cylinders, mounted on a fixed backing plate, and a brake drum, mounted on an axle, which revolves around the assembly. Hydraulic action applied to the wheel cylinders forces the shoes outward against the drum, creating friction and slowing the vehicle.

DWELL: The rate, measured in degrees of shaft rotation, at which an electrical circuit cycles on and off.

ELECTRONIC CONTROL UNIT (ECU): Ignition module, module, amplifier or igniter. See Module for definition.

ELECTRONIC IGNITION: A system in which the timing and firing of the spark plugs is controlled by an electronic control unit, usually called a module. These systems have not points or condenser.

ENDPLAY: The measured amount of axial movement in a shaft.

ENGINE: A device that converts heat into mechanical energy.

EXHAUST MANIFOLD: A set of cast passages or pipes which conduct exhaust gases from the engine.

FEELER GAUGE: A blade, usually metal, of precisely predetermined thickness, used to measure the clearance between two parts. These blades usually are available in sets of assorted thicknesses.

F-Head: An engine configuration in which the intake valves are in the cylinder head, while the camshaft and exhaust valves are located in the cylinder block. The camshaft operates the intake valves via lifters and pushrods, while it operates the exhaust valves directly.

FIRING ORDER: The order in which combustion occurs in the cylinders of an engine. Also the order in which spark is distributed to the plugs by the distributor.

FLATHEAD: An engine configuration in which the camshaft and all the valves are located in the cylinder block.

FLOODING: The presence of too much fuel in the intake manifold and combustion chamber which prevents the air/fuel mixture from firing, thereby causing a no-start situation.

FLYWHEEL: A disc shaped part bolted to the rear end of the crankshaft. Around the outer perimeter is affixed the ring gear. The starter drive engages the ring gear, turning the flywheel, which rotates the crankshaft, imparting the initial starting motion to the engine.

FOOT POUND (ft.lb. or sometimes, ft. lbs.): The amount of energy or work needed to raise an item weighing one pound, a distance of one foot.

FUSE: A protective device in a circuit which prevents circuit overload by breaking the circuit when a specific amperage is present. The device is constructed around a strip or wire of a lower amperage rating than the circuit it is designed to protect. When an amperage higher than that stamped on the fuse is present in the circuit, the strip or wire melts, opening the circuit.

GEAR RATIO: The ratio between the number of teeth on meshing gears.

GENERATOR: A device which converts mechanical energy into electrical energy.

HEAT RANGE: The measure of a spark plug's ability to dissipate heat from its firing end. The higher the heat range, the hotter the plug fires.

HUB: The center part of a wheel or gear.

HYDROCARBON (HC): Any chemical compound made up of hydrogen and carbon. A major pollutant formed by the engine as a byproduct of combustion.

HYDROMETER: An instrument used to measure the specific gravity of a solution.

INCH POUND (in.lb. or sometimes, in. lbs.): One twelfth of a foot pound.

INDUCTION: A means of transferring electrical energy in the form of a magnetic field. Principle used in the ignition coil to increase voltage.

INJECTION PUMP: A device, usually mechanically operated, which meters and delivers fuel under pressure to the fuel injector.

INJECTOR: A device which receives metered fuel under relatively low pressure and is activated to inject the fuel into the engine under relatively high pressure at a predetermined time.

INPUT SHAFT: The shaft to which torque is applied, usually carrying the driving gear or gears.

INTAKE MANIFOLD: A casting of passages or pipes used to conduct air or a fuel/air mixture to the cylinders.

JOURNAL: The bearing surface within which a shaft operates.

KEY: A small block usually fitted in a notch between a shaft and a hub to prevent slippage of the two parts.

MANIFOLD: A casting of passages or set of pipes which connect the cylinders to an inlet or outlet source.

MANIFOLD VACUUM: Low pressure in an engine intake manifold formed just below the throttle plates. Manifold vacuum is highest at idle and drops under acceleration.

MASTER CYLINDER: The primary fluid pressurizing device in a hydraulic system. In automotive use, it is found in brake and hydraulic clutch systems and is pedal activated, either directly or, in a power brake system, through the power booster.

MODULE: Electronic control unit, amplifier or igniter of solid state or integrated design which controls the current flow in the ignition primary circuit based on input from the pickup coil. When the module opens the primary circuit, the high secondary voltage is induced in the coil.

NEEDLE BEARING: A bearing which consists of a number (usually a large number) of long, thin rollers.

OHM: (Ω) The unit used to measure the resistance of conductor to electrical flow. One ohm is the amount of resistance that limits current flow to one ampere in a circuit with one volt of pressure.

OHMMETER: An instrument used for measuring the resistance, in ohms, in an electrical circuit.

OUTPUT SHAFT: The shaft which transmits torque from a device, such as a transmission.

OVERDRIVE: A gear assembly which produces more shaft revolutions than that transmitted to it.

OVERHEAD CAMSHAFT (OHC): An engine configuration in which the camshaft is mounted on top of the cylinder head and operates the valve either directly or by means of rocker arms.

OVERHEAD VALVE (OHV): An engine configuration in which all of the valves are located in the cylinder head and the camshaft is located in the cylinder block. The camshaft operates the valves via lifters and pushrods.

OXIDES OF NITROGEN (NOx): Chemical compounds of nitrogen produced as a byproduct of combustion. They combine with hydrocarbons to produce smog.

OXYGEN SENSOR: Used with the feedback system to sense the presence of oxygen in the exhaust gas and signal the computer which can reference the voltage signal to an air/fuel ratio.

PINION: The smaller of two meshing gears.

PISTON RING: An open ended ring which fits into a groove on the outer diameter of the piston. Its chief function is to form a seal between the piston and cylinder wall. Most automotive pistons have three rings: two for compression sealing; one for oil sealing.

PRELOAD: A predetermined load placed on a bearing during assembly or by adjustment.

PRIMARY CIRCUIT: Is the low voltage side of the ignition system which consists of the ignition switch, ballast resistor or resistance wire, bypass, coil, electronic control unit and pick-up coil as well as the connecting wires and harnesses.

PRESS FIT: The mating of two parts under pressure, due to the inner diameter of one being smaller than the outer diameter of the other, or vice versa; an interference fit.

RACE: The surface on the inner or outer ring of a bearing on which the balls, needles or rollers move.

REGULATOR: A device which maintains the amperage and/or voltage levels of a circuit at predetermined values.

RELAY: A switch which automatically opens and/or closes a circuit.

RESISTANCE: The opposition to the flow of current through a circuit or electrical device, and is measured in ohms. Resistance is equal to the voltage divided by the amperage.

RESISTOR: A device, usually made of wire, which offers a preset amount of resistance in an electrical circuit.

RING GEAR: The name given to a ring-shaped gear attached to a differential case, or affixed to a flywheel or as part a planetary gear set.

ROLLER BEARING: A bearing made up of hardened inner and outer races between which hardened steel rollers move.

ROTOR: 1. The disc-shaped part of a disc brake assembly, upon which the brake pads bear; also called, brake disc.
2. The device mounted atop the distributor shaft, which passes current to the distributor cap tower contacts.

SECONDARY CIRCUIT: The high voltage side of the ignition system, usually above 20,000 volts. The secondary includes the ignition coil, coil wire, distributor cap and rotor, spark plug wires and spark plugs.

SENDING UNIT: A mechanical, electrical, hydraulic or electromagnetic device which transmits information to a gauge.

SENSOR: Any device designed to measure engine operating conditions or ambient pressures and temperatures. Usually electronic in nature and designed to send a voltage signal to an on-board computer, some sensors may operate as a simple on/off switch or they may provide a variable voltage signal (like a potentiometer) as conditions or measured parameters change.

SHIM: Spacers of precise, predetermined thickness used between parts to establish a proper working relationship.

SLAVE CYLINDER: In automotive use, a device in the hydraulic clutch system which is activated by hydraulic force, disengaging the clutch.

SOLENOID: A coil used to produce a magnetic field, the effect of which is produce work.

SPARK PLUG: A device screwed into the combustion chamber of a spark ignition engine. The basic construction is a conductive core inside of a ceramic insulator, mounted in an outer conductive base. An electrical charge from the spark plug wire travels along the conductive core and jumps a preset air gap to a grounding point or points at the end of the conductive base. The resultant spark ignites the fuel/air mixture in the combustion chamber.

SPLINES: Ridges machined or cast onto the outer diameter of a shaft or inner diameter of a bore to enable parts to mate without rotation.

TACHOMETER: A device used to measure the rotary speed of an engine, shaft, gear, etc., usually in rotations per minute.

THERMOSTAT: A valve, located in the cooling system of an engine, which is closed when cold and opens gradually in response to engine heating, controlling the temperature of the coolant and rate of coolant flow.

TOP DEAD CENTER (TDC): The point at which the piston reaches the top of its travel on the compression stroke.

TORQUE: The twisting force applied to an object.

TORQUE CONVERTER: A turbine used to transmit power from a driving member to a driven member via hydraulic action, providing changes in drive ratio and torque. In automotive use, it links the driveplate at the rear of the engine to the automatic transmission.

TRANSDUCER: A device used to change a force into an electrical signal.

TRANSISTOR: A semi-conductor component which can be actuated by a small voltage to perform an electrical switching function.

TUNE-UP: A regular maintenance function, usually associated with the replacement and adjustment of parts and components in the electrical and fuel systems of a vehicle for the purpose of attaining optimum performance.

TURBOCHARGER: An exhaust driven pump which compresses intake air and forces it into the combustion chambers at higher than atmospheric pressures. The increased air pressure allows more fuel to be burned and results in increased horsepower being produced.

VACUUM ADVANCE: A device which advances the ignition timing in response to increased engine vacuum.

VACUUM GAUGE: An instrument used to measure the presence of vacuum in a chamber.

VALVE: A device which control the pressure, direction of flow or rate of flow of a liquid or gas.

VALVE CLEARANCE: The measured gap between the end of the valve stem and the rocker arm, cam lobe or follower that activates the valve.

VISCOSITY: The rating of a liquid's internal resistance to flow.

VOLTMETER: An instrument used for measuring electrical force in units called volts. Voltmeters are always connected parallel with the circuit being tested.

WHEEL CYLINDER: Found in the automotive drum brake assembly, it is a device, actuated by hydraulic pressure, which, through internal pistons, pushes the brake shoes outward against the drums.

ABBREVIATIONS AND SYMBOLS

A: Ampere

AC: Alternating current

A/C: Air conditioning

A-h: Ampere hour

AT: Automatic transmission

ATDC: After top dead center

μA: Microampere

bbl: Barrel

BDC: Bottom dead center

bhp: Brake horsepower

BTDC: Before top dead center

BTU: British thermal unit

C: Celsius (Centigrade)

CCA: Cold cranking amps

cd: Candela

cm^2: Square centimeter

cm^3, cc: Cubic centimeter

CO: Carbon monoxide

CO_2: Carbon dioxide

cu.in., in^3: Cubic inch

CV: Constant velocity

Cyl.: Cylinder

DC: Direct current

ECM: Electronic control module

EFE: Early fuel evaporation

EFI: Electronic fuel injection

EGR: Exhaust gas recirculation

Exh.: Exhaust

F: Fahrenheit

F: Farad

pF: Picofarad

μF: Microfarad

FI: Fuel injection

ft.lb., ft. lb., ft. lbs.: foot pound(s)

gal: Gallon

g: Gram

HC: Hydrocarbon

HEI: High energy ignition

HO: High output

hp: Horsepower

Hyd.: Hydraulic

Hz: Hertz

ID: Inside diameter

in.lb.; in. lb.; in. lbs: inch pound(s)

Int.: Intake

K: Kelvin

kg: Kilogram

kHz: Kilohertz

km: Kilometer

km/h: Kilometers per hour

kΩ: Kilohm

kPa: Kilopascal

kV: Kilovolt

kW: Kilowatt

l: Liter

l/s: Liters per second

m: Meter

mA: Milliampere

mg: Milligram

mHz: Megahertz

mm: Millimeter

mm^2: Square millimeter

m^3: Cubic meter

MΩ: Megohm

m/s: Meters per second

MT: Manual transmission

mV: Millivolt

μm: Micrometer

N: Newton

N-m: Newton meter

NOx: Nitrous oxide

OD: Outside diameter

OHC: Over head camshaft

OHV: Over head valve

Ω: Ohm

PCV: Positive crankcase ventilation

psi: Pounds per square inch

pts: Pints

qts: Quarts

rpm: Rotations per minute

rps: Rotations per second

R-12: A refrigerant gas (Freon)

SAE: Society of Automotive Engineers

SO$_2$: Sulfur dioxide

T: Ton

t: Megagram

TBI: Throttle Body Injection

TPS: Throttle Position Sensor

V: 1. Volt; 2. Venturi

μV: Microvolt

W: Watt

∞: Infinity

<: Less than

>: Greater than

Index

A

Abbreviations and Symbols, 626
Air cleaner, 9
Air conditioning
  Blower, 360
  Charging, 43
  Compressor, 162
  Condenser, 170
  Control panel, 375
  Discharging, 42
  Evacuating, 42
  Evaportor, 367
  Gauge sets, 38
  General service, 34
  Inspection, 40
  Leak testing, 43
  Preventive maintenance, 38
  Safety precautions, 38
  Sight glass check, 40
  System tests, 41
  Troubleshooting, 36, 42
Air pump, 229
Alternator
  Alternator precautions, 116
  Operation, 115
  Removal and installation, 118
  Troubleshooting, 116
Alignment, wheel, 454
Antenna, 594
Antifreeze, 46
Automatic transmission
  Adjustments, 421
  Application chart, 6
  Back-up light switch, 405
  Fluid change, 420
  Linkage adjustments, 425
  Neutral safety switch, 423
  Operation, 416
  Pan removal, 420
  Removal and installation, 429
  Troubleshooting, 416

B

Back-up light switch
  Automatic transmission, 423
  Manual transmission, 405
Ball joints, 450 ff
Battery
  Cables & clamps, 26
  Fluid level and maintenance, 25
  Jump starting, 63
  Removal and installation, 129
Belts, 27–33
Brakes
  Anti-lock brakes, 535
  Bleeding, 502
  Brake light switch, 498
  Front disc brakes
    Caliper, 519

Description, 512
Operating principals, 494
Pads, 513
Rotor (Disc), 522
Rear disc brakes
  Caliper, 528
  Pads, 528
  Rotor (disc), 535
Front drum brakes
  Adjustment, 496
  Drum, 508
  Operating Principals, 495
  Shoes, 509
  Wheel cylinder, 510
Rear drum brakes
  Adjustment, 496
  Drum, 526
  Operating principals, 495, 524
  Shoes, 526
  Wheel cylinder, 527
Fluid level, 46
Hoses and lines, 506
Master cylinder, 499
Operation, 490
Parking brake
  Adjustment, 497
  Removal and installation, 539
Power booster
  Operating principals, 495
  Removal and installation, 506
Proportioning valve, 504
Specifications, 541
Troubleshooting, 491
Breaker points, 81
Bumpers, 553–585

C

Calipers
  Overhaul, 519ff, 528ff
  Removal and installation, 519, 528
Camber, 454
Camshaft and bearings, 194
Capacities Chart, 65
Carburetor
  Adjustments, 105, 311–332
  Overhaul, 306
  Removal and Installation, 301
  Specifications, 302
Caster, 454
Catalytic converter, 109, 215
Center link/Connecting rod/Drag link, 486
Charging system, 115
Chassis electrical system
  Circuit protection, 397
  Heater and air conditioning, 358
  Instrument panel, 389
  Lighting, 391
  Windshield wipers, 383
Chassis lubrication, 58
Choke, 299

Circuit breakers, 397
Clock, 391
Clutch
    Adjustment, 414
    Operation, 412
    Removal and installation, 415
    Troubleshooting, 413
Coil (ignition), 113
Combination manifold, 161
Compression testing, 137
Compressor, 162
Condenser
    Air conditioning, 170
    Ignition, 82
Connecting rods and bearings, 203
Control arm
    Lower, 449
    Upper, 450
Cooling system, 44
Crankcase filler cap, 25
Crankcase ventilation valve, 22
Crankshaft, 205
Crankshaft damper, 187
Cylinder head, 172
Cylinders, 202

D

Disc brakes, 519, 528
Distributor
    Breaker points, 81
    Condenser, 82
    Removal and installation, 113
Door glass, 601
Door locks, 542
Doors, 542
Door trim panel, 594
Drive axle
    Axle shaft, 442
    Axle shaft bearing, 442
    Fluid recommendations, 52
    Identification, 9
    Lubricant level, 52
    Operation, 440
    Pinion oil seal, 441
    Ratios, 441
    Removal and installation, 445
    Troubleshooting, 436
Driveshaft, 435
Drum brakes, 508, 526
Dwell angle, 84

E

EGR valve, 247
Electrical
    Chassis
        Battery, 25
        Bulbs, 391–393
        Circuit breakers, 397
        Fuses, 397
        Fusible links, 396

Heater and air conditioning, 358
    Jump starting, 63
    Spark plug wires, 80
Engine
    Alternator, 115
    Coil, 113
    Distributor, 113
    Electronic engine controls, 219
    Ignition module, 113
    Starter, 124
Electronic Ignition, 85
Emission controls
    Air pump, 229
    Applications chart, 217
    Catalytic Converter, 256
    Dual Diaphragm Distributor, 239
    Evaporative canister, 225
    Exhaust Gas Recirculation (EGR) system, 247
    Improved combustion system, 237
    Maintenance warning light, 257
    Oxygen (O_2) sensor, 258
    PCV valve, 223
    Ported vacuum switch, 240
    Thermostatically controlled air cleaner, 237
    Transmission controlled spark system, 246
Engine
    Application chart, 6
    Camshaft, 194
    Combination manifold, 161
    Compression testing, 137
    Connecting rods and bearings, 203
    Crankshaft, 205
    Crankshaft damper, 187
    Cylinder head, 172
    Cylinders, 202
    Design, 129
    Electronic controls, 219
    Exhaust manifold, 161
    Fluids and lubricants, 47
    Flywheel, 209
    Front (timing) cover, 188
    Front seal, 188, 194
    Identification, 5
    Intake manifold, 154
    Main bearings, 209
    Oil pan, 182
    Oil pump, 186
    Overhaul, 130
    Piston pin, 197
    Pistons, 197
    Rear main seal, 210
    Removal and installation, 139ff
    Rings, 200
    Rocker arms, 151
    Rocker cover, 149
    Rocker shafts and studs, 150, 152
    Spark plug wires, 80
    Specifications, 140
    Thermostat, 153
    Timing chain and gears, 189, 192, 193
    Troubleshooting, 131
    Valve guides, 181
    Valve lifters, 182

Engine (*continued*)
 Valves, 179
 Valve seats, 181
 Valve springs, 180
 Valve timing, 181
 Water pump, 170
Evaporative canister, 25
Evaporator, 367
Exhaust Manifold, 161
Exhaust pipe, 241
Exhaust system, 213

F

Fan, 169
Filters
 Air, 9
 Crankcase, 22
 Fuel, 21
 Oil, 48
Firing orders, 81
Fluids and lubricants
 Automatic transmission, 49
 Battery, 25
 Chassis greasing, 58
 Coolant, 44
 Drive axle, 52
 Engine oil, 47
 Fuel, 47
 Manual transmission, 49
 Master cylinder, 46
 Power steering pump, 46
 Steering gear, 47
Flywheel and ring gear, 209
Front bumper, 553
Front brakes, 508, 519
Front suspension
 Ball joints, 450ff
 Description, 449
 Lower control arm, 449
 Shock absorbers, 449
 Spindles, 452
 Springs, 449
 Stabilizer bar, 452
 Troubleshooting, 447
 Upper control arm, 450
 Wheel alignment, 452
Front wheel bearings, 52, 511
Fuel injection
 Air bypass valve, 342
 Fuel body, 333, 343
 Fuel pressure regulator, 345
 Fuel pump, 294
 Fuel supply manifold, 346
 Injectors, 345
 Operation, 332, 339
 Quick-connect fittings, 297
 Relieving fuel system pressure, 342
 Throttle body, 342
 Throttle position sensor, 347
Fuel filter, 21
Fuel pump, 291

Fuel system
 Carbureted, 299
 Fuel injection, 332, 339
 General system components, 291
 Troubleshooting, 291, 339
Fuel tank, 298
Fuses and circuit breakers, 397
Fusible links, 396

G

Gearshift linkage adjustment
 Automatic, 426
 Manual, 402
Glossary, 620
Grille, 585

H

Headlights, 391
Heater
 Blower, 358, 360
 Control panel, 375
 Core, 359, 362
Heat riser, 22
Hi-mount stop lamp, 392
Hood, 543
Hoses
 Brake, 506
 Coolant, 34, 35
 Fuel, 297
How to Use This Book, 1

I

Identification
 Axle, 9
 Engine, 6, 8
 Model, 5
 Serial number, 5
 Transmission, 6, 8
 Vehicle, 5
Idle speed and mixture adjustment, 105ff
Ignition
 Coil, 113
 Electronic, 85
 Lock cylinder, 478
 Module, 113
 Switch, 483
 Timing, 100
Injectors, fuel, 345
Instrument cluster, 389
Instrument panel
 Cluster, 389
 Radio, 386
 Speedometer cable, 390
Intake manifold, 154

J

Jacking points, 62
Jump starting, 63

L

Lighting
   Headlights, 391
   Signal and marker lights, 393
Lubrication
   Automatic transmission, 49
   Chassis, 58
   Differential, 52
   Engine, 47
   Manual transmission, 49

M

Main bearings, 209
Maintenance intervals, 67
Maintenance warning light, 257
Manifolds
   Combination, 161
   Intake, 154
   Exhaust, 161
Manual steering gear
   Adjustments, 486
   Removal and installation, 487
   Troubleshooting, 472
Manual transmission
   Application chart, 6
   Linkage adjustment, 402
   Operation, 402
   Overhaul, 406
   Removal and installation, 406
   Troubleshooting, 403
Marker lights, 393
Master cylinder, 499
Mechanic's data, 618
Mirrors, 585
Model identification, 5
Module (ignition), 113
Muffler, 213

N

Neutral safety switch, 423

O

Oil and fuel recommendations, 47
Oil and filter change (engine), 48
Oil level check
   Differential, 52
   Engine, 48
   Transmission, 49
Oil pan, 182
Oil pump, 186
Outside vehicle maintenance, 58
Oxygen (O₂) sensor, 258

P

Parking brake, 497, 539
Piston pin, 197
Pistons, 197
Pitman arm, 485
PCV valve, 22

Points, 81
Power brake booster, 506
Power steering gear
   Adjustments, 487
   Removal and installation, 488
   Troubleshooting, 473
Power steering pump, 489
Preventive Maintenance Charts, 67
Pushing 58

R

Radiator, 168
Radiator cap, 45
Radio, 386
Rear axle
   Axle shaft, 442
   Fluid recommendations, 52
   Identification, 9
   Lubricant level, 52
   Operation, 440
   Pinion oil seal, 441
   Ratios, 441
   Removal and installation, 445
Rear brakes, 526, 528
Rear bumper, 571
Rear main oil seal, 210
Rear suspension
   Shock absorbers, 455
   Springs, 455
   Sway bar, 457
Regulator
   Operation, 118
   Removal and installation, 119
   Testing and adjustment, 119
Rings, 200
Rocker arms or shaft, 150–152
Rotor (Brake disc), 522, 535
Routine maintenance, 9

S

Safety notice, 4
Seat belts, 393
Seats, 610
Serial number location, 5
Shock absorbers, 449, 455
Solenoid, 129
Spark plugs, 69
Spark plug wires, 80
Special tools, 2
Specifications Charts
   Brakes, 541
   Capacities, 65
   Carburetor, 302ff
   Crankshaft and connecting rod, 146
   General engine, 140
   Piston and ring, 145
   Preventive Maintenance, 67
   Torque, 144
   Tune-up, 75
   Valves, 142
   Wheel alignment, 453

Speedometer cable, 390
Spindles, 452, 455
Springs, 449
Stabilizer bar, 452, 457
Stain removal, 617
Starter
   Drive replacement, 127
   Operation, 121
   Overhaul, 124
   Removal and installation, 124
   Solenoid or relay replacement, 129
   Troubleshooting, 123
Steering column, 484
Steering gear
   Manual, 486
   Power, 487
Steering linkage
   Center link/Connecting rod/Drag link, 486
   Idler arm, 486
   Pitman arm, 485
   Tie rod ends, 486
Steering lock, 478
Steering wheel, 469
Stirupped threads, 136
Switches
   Back-up light, 405
   Headlight, 391
   Ignition switch, 483
   Windshield wiper, 390

T

Tailgate, 552
Thermostat, 153
Throttle body, 342
Tie rod ends, 486
Timing (ignition), 100
Timing chain and gears, 189, 192, 193
Timing gear cover, 188
Tires
   Description, 54
   Rotation, 57
   Troubleshooting, 55
   Wear problems, 57
Toe-in, 454
Tools, 2
Torque specifications, 144
Towing, 58
Trailer towing, 62
Transmission
   Automatic, 416
   Manual, 402
Troubleshooting Charts
   Air conditioning, 116
   Automatic transmission, 416
   Brakes, 491
   Charging system, 116
   Clutch, 413
   Cooling system, 134
   Drive belts, 135
   Driveshaft, 436
   Engine mechanical, 131

Engine performance, 71
   Fuel system, 291, 339
   Gauges, 399
   Heater, 397
   Ignition switch, 467
   Ignition system, 88ff
   Lights, 400
   Lockup torque converter, 417
   Manual steering gear, 472
   Manual transmission, 403
   Power steering gear, 473
   Power steering pump, 475
   Rear axle, 436
   Starting system, 123
   Steering and suspension, 447
   Steering column, 468
   Tires, 55
   Transmission fluid indications, 418
   Turn signals and flashers, 398
   Turn signal switch, 470
   Wheels, 55
   Windshield wipers, 401
Tune-up
   Condenser, 82
   Distributor, 113
   Dwell angle, 84
   Idle speed, 105ff
   Ignition timing, 100
   Points, 81
   Procedures, 69
   Spark plugs and wires, 69
   Specifications, 75
   Troubleshooting, 71
Turn signal switch, 471

U

U-joints, 435
Understanding the manual transmission, 402
Upper control arm, 450

V

Vacuum diagrams, 257–290
Valve guides, 181
Valve lash adjustment, 104
Valve seats, 181
Valve service, 179
Valve specifications, 142
Valve springs, 180
Valve timing, 181
Vehicle identification, 5, 8

W

Water pump, 170
Wheel alignment
   Adjustment, 452
   Specifications, 453

Wheel bearings, 52
Wheel cylinders, 527
Window glass, 552, 608
Window regulator, 601
Windshield, 552

Windshield wipers
    Blade, 28
    Linkage, 385
    Motor, 383
    Windshield wiper switch, 390